The Law of Corporations and Other Business Organizations

THIRD EDITION

The West Legal Studies Series

Your options keep growing with West Legal Studies

Each year our list continues to offer you more options for every area of the law to meet your course or on-the-job reference requirements. We now have over 140 titles from which to choose in the following areas:

Administrative Law	Family Law
Alternative Dispute Resolution	Federal Taxation
Bankruptcy	Intellectual Property
Business Organizations/Corporations	Introduction to Law
Civil Litigation and Procedure	Introduction to Paralegalism
CLA Exam Preparation	Law Office Management
Client Accounting	Law Office Procedures
Computer in the Law Office	Legal Research, Writing, and Analysis
Constitutional Law	Legal Terminology
Contract Law	Paralegal Employment
Criminal Law and Procedure	Real Estate Law
Document Preparation	Reference Materials
Environmental Law	Torts and Personal Injury Law
Ethics	Will, Trusts, and Estate Administration

You will find unparalleled, practical support

Each text is augmented by instructor and student supplements to ensure the best learning experience possible. We also offer custom publishing and other benefits such as West's Student Achievement Award. In addition, our sales representatives are ready to provide you with dependable service.

We want to hear from you

Our best contributions for improving the quality of our books and instructional materials is feedback from the people who use them. If you have a question, concern, or observation about any of our materials, or you have a product proposal or manuscript, we want to hear from you. Please contact your local representative or write us at the following address:

West Legal Studies, 3 Columbia Circle, P.O. Box 15015, Albany, NY 12212-5015

For additional information point your browser at

www.westlegalstudies.com

The Law of Corporations and Other Business Organizations

◆

THIRD EDITION

Angela Schneeman

WEST

★

THOMSON LEARNING ™

Australia   Canada   Mexico   Singapore   Spain   United Kingdom   United States

WEST

THOMSON LEARNING

WEST LEGAL STUDIES

The Law of Corporations and Other Business Organizations 3E
Angela Schneeman

Business Unit Director:
Susan L. Simpfenderfer

Executive Editor:
Marlene McHugh Pratt

Senior Acquisitions Editor:
Joan M. Gill

Developmental Editor:
Rhonda Dearborn

Editorial Assistant:
Lisa Flatley

Executive Production Manager:
Wendy A. Troeger

Production Manager:
Carolyn Miller

Production Editor:
Betty L. Dickson

Technology Manager:
James Considine

Executive Marketing Manager:
Donna J. Lewis

Channel Manager:
Nigar Hale

Cover Designer:
Harry Voigt Graphic Design

Cover Image:
Super Stock

For permission to use material from this text or product, contact us by
Tel   (800) 730-2214
Fax (800) 730-2215
www.thomsonrights.com

Library of Congress Cataloging-in-Publication Data
Schneeman, Angela.
  The law of corporations and other business organizations / Angela Schneeman.—3rd ed.
      p. cm.
  Rev. ed. of: The law of corporations, partnerships, and sole proprietorships. 2nd ed. c1997.
    Includes index.
    ISBN 0-7668-3198-1
      1. Business enterprises—Law and legislation—United States. 2. Corporation law—United States. I. Schneeman, Angela. Law of corporations, partnerships, and sole proprietorships. II. Title.
  KF1355.Z9 S36 2001
  346.73′066—dc21   2001046687

NOTICE TO THE READER

DEDICATION

To my parents, Al and Anna Lutterman

CONTENTS

Preface xvii
About the Author xxi
Table of Cases xxiii

CHAPTER 1
Sole Proprietorships 1

Introduction 1
§ 1.1 Sole Proprietorship Defined 1
§ 1.2 Sole Proprietorships in the United States 2
§ 1.3 Advantages of Doing Business as a Sole Proprietor 3
Full Management Authority 3
Minimal Formalities and Regulatory and Reporting Requirements 3
Low Cost of Organization 4
Income Tax Benefits 4
§ 1.4 Disadvantages of Doing Business as a Sole Proprietor 5
Unlimited Liability 5
Lack of Business Continuity 6
No Diversity in Management 7
Difficulty in Transferring Proprietary Interest 7
Limited Ability to Raise Capital 7
§ 1.5 Formation and Operation of the Sole Proprietorship 7
Using an Assumed Name, Trade Name, or Fictitious Name 8
Hiring Employees and Using Tax Identification Numbers 9
Sales Tax Permits 12
Licensing 12
Registering Intellectual Property 12
§ 1.6 The Paralegal's Role in Sole Proprietorship Matters 12
Corporate Paralegal Profile 13
§ 1.7 Resources 14
United States Small Business Administration 14

State and Local Government Offices 15
State Statutes 15
Secretaries of State 17
U.S. Patent and Trademark Office 17
Internet Resources 17

CHAPTER 2
Partnerships 20

Introduction 20
§ 2.1 An Introduction to Partnerships 21
Partnership Defined 21
Registered Limited Liability Partnership 23
Joint Ventures 24
Partnerships in the United States 24
Law Governing Partnerships 24
The Partnership as a Separate Entity 27
§ 2.2 The Relationship Between Partners and Others 29
Partners as Agents 29
Acts Requiring Unanimous Consent of the Partners 29
Statement of Partnership Authority 33
Statement of Denial 34
Liability of Partners 34
Limited Liability Partnerships 34
§ 2.3 The Relationship Among Partners and Between Partners and the Partnership 35
Partners' Rights in Partnership Assets 35
Partnership Property 36
Partners' Rights in Dealing with Each Other 37
Partners' Duties in Dealing with Each Other 40

§ 2.4   Advantages of Doing Business as a
         General Partnership 41
         Participation and Flexibility in
         Management 41
         Minimal Formalities and Regulatory
         and Reporting Requirements 42
         Low Cost of Organization 43
         Income Tax Benefits 43
         Diversified Capital Resources 43
         Limited Personal Liability 43
§ 2.5   Disadvantages of Doing Business as a
         Partnership 44
         Unlimited Liability 44
         Loosely Structured Management 44
         Lack of Business Continuity 45
         Difficulty in Transferring Partnership
         Interest 45
         Limited Ability to Raise Capital 45
         Legal and Organizational
         Expenses 45
         Tax Disadvantages 46
§ 2.6   Organization and Management of a
         General Partnership 46
         Management and Control 47
         Oral Partnership Agreements 48
         Partnership Agreements 48
         The Limited Liability Partnership
         Election 56
§ 2.7   Financial Structure of a
         Partnership 57
         Partnership Capital 57
         Profits and Losses 59
§ 2.8   Dissolution, Dissociation, Winding
         Up, and Termination of the
         Partnership 60
         Dissociation, Dissolution, and
         Winding Up 60
         Events Causing Partner's
         Dissociation 60
         Wrongful Dissociation 61
         Effect of Partner's Dissociation 62
         Statement of Dissociation 62
         Events Causing Dissolution and
         Winding Up of Partnership
         Business 62
         Dissolution Agreement 64
         Notice to Third Parties 65

         Winding Up 65
         Distribution of Assets 65
§ 2.9   The Paralegal's Role in Partnership
         Matters 66
         Corporate Paralegal Profile 68
§ 2.10   Resources 70
         State Statutes 70
         Legal Form Books 70
         Secretary of State or Other
         Appropriate State Authority 70
         State and Local Government
         Offices 72
         Internet Resources 73

CHAPTER 3
Limited Partnerships 78

         Introduction 78
§ 3.1   An Introduction to Limited
         Partnerships 79
         Limited Partnership Defined 79
         Limited Partnerships in the United
         States 79
         Law Governing Limited
         Partnerships 81
         The Limited Partnership as a
         Separate Entity 81
§ 3.2   Partners' Rights and
         Responsibilities 82
         General Partners' Rights and
         Responsibilities 82
         Limited Partners' Rights and
         Responsibilities 83
         The Relationship between General
         Partners and Limited Partners 84
§ 3.3   Advantages of Doing Business as a
         Limited Partnership 86
         Limited Liability for Limited
         Partners 87
         Income Tax Benefits 88
         Transferability of Partnership
         Interest 89
         Business Continuity 89
         Diversified Capital Resources 89
§ 3.4   Disadvantages of Doing Business as a
         Limited Partnership 90

Unlimited Liability 90
Prohibition on Control of
    Business 90
Formalities and Regulatory and
    Reporting Requirements 90
Legal and Organizational
    Expenses 91

§ 3.5   Organization and Management of a
    Limited Partnership 92
Management and Control 92
Limited Partnership Certificate 92
Limited Liability Limited
    Partnership Election 93
Amendment to Limited Partnership
    Certificate 94
Records Required by Statute 94
Limited Partnership Agreement 96

§ 3.6   Changes in Partnership 102
Admission of New General
    Partners 102
Admission of New Limited
    Partners 102
Withdrawal of General Partners 103
Withdrawal of Limited Partners 103

§ 3.7   Financial Structure of a Limited
    Partnership 103
Partnership Capital
    Contributions 103
Limited Partnership Profits and
    Losses 104
Limited Partnership Income and
    Disbursements 104

§ 3.8   Derivative Actions 105

§ 3.9   Dissolution, Winding Up, and
    Termination of the Limited
    Partnership 106
Dissolution versus
    Winding Up 106
Causes of Dissolution 106
Cancellation of Certificate of Limited
    Partnership 107
Winding Up 107
Settlement and Distribution of
    Assets 107

§ 3.10   The Paralegal's Role in Limited
    Partnership Matters 108
Corporate Paralegal Profile 110

§ 3.11   Resources 111
State Statutes 111
Legal Form Books 112
Secretary of State or Other
    Appropriate State Authority 112
Government Tax Offices 112
Internet Resources 113

CHAPTER 4
Limited Liability Companies 117

§ 4.1   An Introduction to Limited Liability
    Companies 117
Limited Liability Company
    Defined 118
Limited Liability Company
    Characteristics 118
Professional Limited Liability
    Companies 123

§ 4.2   Limited Liability Companies in the
    United States 124

§ 4.3   Law Governing Limited Liability
    Companies 125
State Law and the Uniform Limited
    Liability Company Act 125
Securities Laws 125

§ 4.4   Limited Liability Company Rights and
    Powers 126

§ 4.5   Members' Rights and
    Responsibilities 127
Members Rights 127
Members as Agents 128

§ 4.6   Organization and Management of a
    Limited Liability Company 128
Organizers of the Limited Liability
    Company 129
Articles of Organization 129
Management and Control of the
    Limited Liability Company 133
Member-Managed Limited Liability
    Companies 133
Manager-Managed Limited Liability
    Companies 134
Matters Requiring Consent of All
    Members 134
The Operating Agreement 135

Annual Reporting Requirements 136

§ 4.7   Financial Structure of a Limited
         Liability Company 137
         Member Contributions 137
         Member Reimbursement 137
         Distributions to Members 137

§ 4.8   Dissolution of the Limited Liability
         Company 138
         Member's Dissociation 138
         Dissolution of the Limited Liability
           Company 139
         Winding Up the Limited Liability
           Company 140
         Distribution of Assets 140
         Articles of Termination 140

§ 4.9   Advantages of Doing Business as a
         Limited Liability Company 140
         Limited Liability for All Owners 142
         Unrestrictive Ownership 142
         Ability to Raise Capital for the
           Business 142
         Beneficial Tax Treatment 142
         Flexibility of Management 144

§ 4.10   Disadvantages of Doing Business as a
         Limited Liability Company 145
         Limited Transferability of
           Ownership 145
         Possibility of Piercing the Limited
           Liability Company Veil 145
         Lack of Uniformity in State
           Laws 145
         Limited Liability Company
           Formalities and Reporting
           Requirements 146

§ 4.11   Transacting Business as a Foreign
         Limited Liability Company 146
         Transacting Business as a Foreign
           Limited Liability Company 147
         Application for a Certificate of
           Authority 148
         Name Registration 149

§ 4.12   The Paralegal's Role 152
         Drafting Limited Liability
           Documentation 152
         Corporate Paralegal Profile 153
         Limited Liability Company
           Research 153

§ 4.13   Resources 154
         State Statutes 154
         State Authorities 157
         Internal Revenue Code 157
         Articles, Form Books, and
           Treatises 158
         Internet Resources 158

CHAPTER 5
Corporations 162

Introduction 162

§ 5.1   An Introduction to
         Corporations 162
         Corporation Defined 163
         The Corporation as a Separate
           Legal Entity 163
         Piercing the Corporate Veil 163
         Law Governing Corporations 165

§ 5.2   Corporations in the United
         States 170

§ 5.3   Corporate Rights and Powers 170

§ 5.4   Advantages of Doing Business as a
         Corporation 172
         Limited Liability 173
         Employee Benefit Plans 173
         Choice of Tax Year 173
         Business Continuity 174
         Ability to Raise Capital 174
         Centralized Management 174
         Transferability of Ownership 174

§ 5.5   Disadvantages of Doing Business as
         a Corporation 175
         Corporate Formalities and Reporting
           Requirements 175
         Taxation 176

§ 5.6   Types and Classifications of
         Corporations 176
         Business Corporations 176
         Professional Corporations 177
         Nonprofit Corporations 177
         S Corporations 178
         Statutory Close Corporations 181
         Parents and Subsidiaries 183

§ 5.7   The Paralegal's Role in Corporate
            Law Matters 183
            Corporate Paralegal Profile 184
§ 5.8   Resources 187
            State Statutes 187
            Federal Statutes 189
            Legal Encyclopedias 189
            Forms and Form Books 189
            Secretary of State or Other State
                Corporation Agency 190
            Internet Resources 190

CHAPTER 6
Formation of the Corporation 194

            Introduction 194
§ 6.1   Preincorporation Matters 194
            Deciding on the Corporate
                Structure 195
            Choosing a Domicile 195
            Promoters 197
            Preincorporation Agreements 200
            Stock Subscriptions 201
            Gathering Client Information to
                Incorporate 203
§ 6.2   Incorporators 204
§ 6.3   Articles of Incorporation 205
            Mandatory Provisions 205
            Optional Provisions 209
            Execution 214
            Filing 214
            Effective Time and Date 215
§ 6.4   Organizational Meetings 216
            Organizational Meeting
                Requirements 217
            Purpose of Organizational
                Meeting 218
            Incorporators' Resolutions 218
            Board of Directors' Resolutions 218
            Shareholder Resolutions 225
            Unanimous Writings versus
                Minutes 226
§ 6.5   Bylaws 228
            Office of the Corporation 228
            Shareholder Meetings 228
            Number and Term of Directors 229

            Meetings of the Board of
                Directors 230
            Removal and Resignation of
                Directors 231
            Director Compensation 231
            Director Liability 231
            Officers 231
            Stock Certificates 232
            Dividends 233
            Fiscal Year 233
            Corporate Seal 233
            Corporate Records 233
            Amendment of Bylaws 233
            Signatures on Bylaws 233
§ 6.6   Formation of Special Types of
                Corporations 233
            Statutory Close Corporations 233
            Professional Corporations 234
            Nonprofit Corporations 234
§ 6.7   The Paralegal's Role in Corporate
                Formation 234
            Corporate Paralegal Profile 237
§ 6.8   Resources 239
            State Statutes 239
            Secretary of State 240
            Form Books 240
            Incorporation Services 240
            Internet Resources 240

CHAPTER 7
The Corporate Organization 244

            Introduction 244
§ 7.1   Authority and Duties of
                Directors 245
            Directors' Authority 245
            Directors' Duties 247
§ 7.2   Personal Liability of Directors 253
            Business Judgment Rule 253
            Imposition of Personal Liability on
                Directors 254
§ 7.3   Compensation and Indemnification of
                Directors 255
            Compensation of Directors 256
            Indemnification 256

§ 7.4   Election and Term of Directors 259
         Election of Directors 259
         Number and Qualifications of
            Directors 260
         Term of Directors 260

§ 7.5   Board of Directors Meetings and
            Resolutions 262
         Board of Directors Meetings 262
         Annual Meetings of the Board of
            Directors 263
         Notice of Meetings 264
         Quorum 264
         Minutes 265
         Board Actions Without Meeting 265
         Corporate Minute Books 269

§ 7.6   Corporate Officers 269
         Titles and Duties of Officers 270
         Personal Liability of Officers 272
         Election and Term of Office 272

§ 7.7   Shareholders' Rights and
            Responsibilities 272
         Shareholders' Preemptive Rights 273
         Shareholders' Right to Inspect
            Corporate Records 274
         Personal Liability of
            Shareholders 276

§ 7.8   Shareholder Meetings 276
         Requirements for Annual
            Meetings 277
         Requirements for Special
            Meetings 278
         Location 278
         Notice 278
         Proxies 282
         Quorum 283
         Voting at Shareholder Meetings 283
         Election of Directors 285
         Other Acts Requiring Shareholder
            Approval 285
         Minutes of Shareholder
            Meetings 285
         Unanimous Consents of
            Shareholders 286

§ 7.9   Restrictions on Transfer of Shares of
            Corporate Stock 286
         Shareholder Agreements Restricting
            Stock Transfers 288

         Considerations in Drafting
            Shareholder Agreements 290
         Other Restrictions on Share
            Transfers 290

§ 7.10   Shareholder Actions 291
         Individual Actions 291
         Representative Actions 291
         Derivative Actions 292

§ 7.11   The Paralegal's Role in Corporate
            Organizational Matters 293
         Corporate Paralegal Profile 294

§ 7.12   Resources 297
         Internet Resources 297

CHAPTER 8
The Corporate Financial Structure 302

         Introduction 302

§ 8.1   Capitalization of the
            Corporation 303

§ 8.2   Equity Financing 304
         Authorized and Issued Stock 305
         Common Stock 308
         Preferred Stock 309

§ 8.3   Par Value 311
         Trend Toward Eliminating Par
            Value 312
         Consideration for Par Value
            Stock 312
         Accounting for Par Value Stock 313

§ 8.4   Consideration for Shares of
            Stock 313

§ 8.5   Issuance of Stock 315
         Stock Certificates 315
         Lost or Destroyed Stock
            Certificates 317
         Fractional Shares and Scrip 317

§ 8.6   Redemption of Equity Shares 317

§ 8.7   Dividends 319
         Availability of Funds for
            Dividends 319
         Types of Dividends 319
         Declaration of Dividends 320
         Right to Receive Dividends 322

§ 8.8   Stock Splits 323

§ 8.9   Debt Financing 324
            Authority for Debt Financing 324
            Bank Loans 325
            Bonds 325

§ 8.10   The Paralegal's Role in Corporate
            Financial Matters 326
            Corporate Paralegal Profile 327

§ 8.11   Resources 328
            State Statutes 329
            Forms and Form Books 329
            Internet Resources 329

CHAPTER 9
Publicly Held Corporations and Securities Regulations 332

            Introduction 332
§ 9.1   The Publicly Held Corporation 333
§ 9.2   Securities and Securities Markets 335
            Definition of Securities 335
            Markets 336
§ 9.3   The Securities and Exchange
            Commission 339
§ 9.4   Federal Regulation of Securities
            Offerings Under the Securities Act
            of 1933 340
            Securities Registration 341
            Prospectus Requirements 347
            EDGAR 350
§ 9.5   Exemptions from the Registration
            Requirements of the Securities Act
            of 1933 350
            Exempted Securities 350
            Exemptions for Limited Offerings and
            Offerings of Limited Dollar
            Amounts 351
            Intrastate Offering Exemptions 354
§ 9.6   Antifraud Provisions of the
            Securities Act 354
            Section 11 355
            Section 12 356
            Section 17 356
§ 9.7   Federal Regulations Imposed on
            Publicly Held Corporations
            Under the Securities Exchange
            Act of 1934 357

            Registration Under the Exchange
            Act 358
            Periodic Reporting
            Requirements 359
            Liability for Short-Swing
            Profits 362
            Proxy Regulations 364
            Antifraud Provisions Under the
            Exchange Act 365
§ 9.8   State Securities Regulation—Blue
            Sky Laws 373
§ 9.9   State Regulation of Stock
            Offerings 374
            Registration by Filing 374
            Registration by Coordination 374
            Registration by Qualification 375
            Exemptions 375
§ 9.10   State Securities Regulation—Antifraud
            Provisions 375
§ 9.11   The Paralegal's Role 376
            Initial Public Offerings 376
            Corporate Paralegal Profile 377
            Periodic Reporting
            Requirements 378
§ 9.12   Resources 378
            Federal Law 378
            Federal Securities Forms and
            Information 379
            Blue Sky Laws 379
            Internet Resources 379

CHAPTER 10
Mergers, Acquisitions, and Other Changes to the Corporate Structure 384

            Introduction 384
§ 10.1   Statutory Mergers and Share
            Exchanges 385
            Mergers 387
            Share Exchanges 391
            Consolidations 392
            State and Federal Laws Affecting
            Statutory Mergers and Share
            Exchanges 393

Significant Federal Antitrust Law
Provisions Affecting Mergers and
Acquisitions 394

§ 10.2   Statutory Merger and Share Exchange
Procedures 396
Negotiations and Letter of
Intent 396
Plan of Merger 397
Plan of Exchange 402
Due Diligence and Preclosing
Matters 409
Closing the Statutory Merger or Share
Exchange Transaction 413
Postclosing Matters 414

§ 10.3   Asset and Stock Acquisitions 414
Asset Acquisitions 415
Stock Acquisitions 415
Hostile Takeovers 416
De Facto Mergers 416
State and Federal Laws Affecting
Asset and Stock Acquisitions 417

§ 10.4   Asset and Stock Acquisition
Procedures 417
Negotiations and Letter of
Intent 418
Asset Purchase Agreement 418
Stock Purchase Agreement 420
Due Diligence and Preclosing
Matters 420
Closing the Asset or Stock Acquisition
Transaction 421
Postclosing Matters 422

§ 10.5   Amendments to Articles of
Incorporation 422
Approval of the Articles of
Amendment 423
Articles of Amendment 424
Restated Articles of
Incorporation 426

§ 10.6   Reorganizations 427
Type A Transactions 427
Type B Transactions 427
Type C Transactions 427
Type D Transactions 427
Type E Transactions 427
Type F Transactions 427
Type G Transactions 428

§ 10.7   The Paralegal's Role in Mergers and
Acquisitions 428
Corporate Paralegal Profile 429
Letter of Intent 430
Agreement 430
Federal Antitrust Law
Compliance 430
Supplementary Documents 430
Review and Production of
Documents 430
Plan and Articles of Merger or Share
Exchange 431
Corporate Resolutions 431
Stock and Asset Transfer
Documents 431
Assignments of Contracts 431
Closing 432
Post Closing 432

§ 10.8   Resources 432
State Statutes 432
Federal Antitrust Law 433
Secretary of State 433
Forms and Form Books 433
Internet Resources 433

CHAPTER 11
Qualification of a Foreign Corporation 438

Introduction 438

§ 11.1   Determining When Foreign
Corporation Qualification is
Necessary 439
State Long-Arm Statutes and
Jurisdiction over Foreign
Corporations 439
Statutory Requirements for
Qualification of Foreign
Corporations 440
Consequences of Not Qualifying as a
Foreign Corporation 441

§ 11.2   Rights, Privileges, and Responsibilities
of a Foreign Corporation 446

§ 11.3   Qualification Requirements 447
Application for Certificate of
Authority 447

Foreign Name Requirements 448
Registered Agent and Registered
    Office 450

§ 11.4   Amending the Certificate of
             Authority 451

§ 11.5   Maintaining the Good Standing of the
             Foreign Corporation 451

§ 11.6   Withdrawing from Doing Business as
             a Foreign Corporation 453

§ 11.7   Registration of a Corporate
             Name 455

§ 11.8   The Paralegal's Role 455
         Corporate Paralegal Profile 455

§ 11.9   Resources 458
         State Statutes 458
         Secretaries of State 458
         Corporation Service Companies 458
         Internet Resources 458

CHAPTER 12
Corporate Dissolution 462

Introduction 462

§ 12.1   Voluntary Dissolution 463
         Board of Director and Shareholder
             Approval of Dissolution 463
         Articles of Dissolution and Notice of
             Intent to Dissolve 467
         Winding Up and Liquidation 472
         Tax Considerations 481
         Revocation of Dissolution 481

§ 12.2   Involuntary Dissolution 483
         Administrative Dissolution 483
         Judicial Dissolutions 485

§ 12.3   The Paralegal's Role in Dissolving
             Corporations 486
         Corporate Paralegal Profile 487

§ 12.4   Resources 488
         State Statutes 488
         Legal Form Books 488
         Secretary of State or Other
             Appropriate State Authority 488
         Corporation Service Companies 488
         Local and Federal Tax Offices 489
         Internet Resources 489

CHAPTER 13
Employee Benefit Plans 492

Introduction 492

§ 13.1   Qualified Plans 493

§ 13.2   Laws Governing Qualified Plans 493
         Employee Retirement Income Security
             Act of 1974 (ERISA) 493
         Internal Revenue Code 494

§ 13.3   Elements of a Qualified Plan 495
         The Sponsor 495
         The Plan 495
         The Plan Administrator 495
         The Plan Participants 496

§ 13.4   ERISA and IRC Requirements
             Common to All Types of
             Qualified Plans 496
         Plan Must Be Established for the
             Exclusive Benefit of
             Employees 497
         Minimum Coverage and Participation
             Requirements 497
         Exemptions from the Provisions
             of ERISA 498

§ 13.5   Qualified Pension Plans 498
         Contributions 499
         The Trust 499
         Benefits 499
         Distributions 500
         Defined Benefit Plans 501
         Defined Contribution Plans 503
         Integrated Plans 507
         Self-Employed Plans 507
         Individual Retirement Accounts 508

§ 13.6   Nonqualified Pension Plans 508

§ 13.7   Employee Welfare Benefit Plans 509
         Welfare Benefits 509
         Funding 509
         Voluntary Employee Benefit
             Association (VEBA) 510

§ 13.8   Qualified Plan Adoption and IRS
             Approval 510

§ 13.9   Annual Reporting Requirements and
             Disclosure Requirements 510
         Form 5500 512
         Summary Annual Reports 512

§ 13.10   The Paralegal's Role in Working with
                Qualified Plans 512
                Corporate Paralegal Profile 514
§ 13.11   Resources 515
                Federal Law 515
                Secondary Materials 515
                Federal Agencies 515
                Internet Resources 515

CHAPTER 14
Employment Agreements 519

                Introduction 519
§ 14.1   Special Considerations for the
                Employer 520
§ 14.2   Special Considerations for the
                Employee 521
§ 14.3   Drafting the Employment
                Agreement 521
                Term of the Agreement 523
                Description of Duties 523
                Covenant Not to Compete 524
                Inventions and Patents 528
                Trade Secrets 528
                Compensation 531
                Employee Benefits 531
                Termination of Employment 531
                Arbitration of Disputes 532
                Vacations 532
                Assignability of Contract 532
                Amendment or Renewal of
                    Agreement 533
                Date and Signatures 533
§ 14.4   Sample Employment Agreement 533
§ 14.5   The Paralegal's Role in Drafting
                Employment Agreements 533
                Corporate Paralegal Profile 539
§ 14.6   Resources 540
                Internet Resources 540

APPENDIX A
Secretary of State Directory A1

APPENDIX B
**On-line Resources for the
Corporate Paralegal A5**

APPENDIX C
Ethics for Corporate Paralegals A8

APPENDIX D
Workplace Scenario Data A17

APPENDIX E
Uniform Partnership Act A19

APPENDIX F
Uniform Partnership Act (1997) A31

APPENDIX G
**Uniform Limited Partnership Act (1976)
With 1985 Amendments A52**

APPENDIX H
**Uniform Limited Liability
Company Act A73**

APPENDIX I
**Excerpts from the Model Business
Corporation Act A101**

APPENDIX J
Forms A154

Glossary G1

Index I1

PREFACE

This book is an in-depth introduction to the law of business organizations for paralegal students. Although the main focus of the text is corporations, chapters on sole proprietorships, partnerships, limited partnerships, and the limited liability entities are also included. This text includes an overview of the law and theory behind the law, as well as practical information that the paralegal can use on the job.

Relying on my own experience as a corporate paralegal, and input from several other paralegals, I have included practical information that paralegals need to succeed on the job—without sacrificing content concerning the law. Paralegals need to know the law, but they also need to know how to get things done. Each chapter of this text includes a discussion of the law, as well as a section entitled *The Paralegal's Role,* which focuses on procedures and includes several valuable resources.

Because most law concerning corporations is based on state law and can vary among the states, this text focuses on the Model Business Corporation Act, which is the basis for most of the state business corporation acts in the country. Discussions in the partnership and limited liability company chapters focus on the pertinent uniform laws. State charts are included where practical, as well as cites for state statutes and URLs for state statutes that are on-line. In addition, examples, sample documents, sample paragraphs, and practical advice are included for the paralegal student, providing information and resources the corporate paralegal can use on the job. This is the text students will want to take from the classroom to the office.

TEXT ORGANIZATION

Each chapter begins with a discussion of the law and ends with procedural information specifically for paralegals. A typical chapter of this text includes:

◆ An in-depth discussion of the law, with a general focus on the pertinent model and uniform acts and how the law may differ among the states.

◆ Current charts and statistics pertinent to the subject.

◆ Edited cases illustrating some of the more important points made in the chapter.

◆ Sample documents and document paragraphs.

◆ *The Paralegal's Role* section with a general discussion of the paralegal's role in working with the particular subject of the chapter, checklists, and a profile of a paralegal who works in that area of law.

◆ Resources (including on-line resources).

◆ Chapter Summary.

◆ Review Questions.

◆ Practical Problems.

◆ Workplace Scenario.

NEW TO THE THIRD EDITION

Previous editions of this text have been published under the title *The Law of Corporations, Partnerships, and Sole Proprietorships.* The title of this edition has been changed to more accurately reflect the contents. This edition includes more information on several other forms of business organizations, especially limited liability companies, limited liability partnerships and limited liability limited partnerships.

This text has been updated to reflect changes in the Model Business Corporation Act and trends and developments in the law of business organizations over the past several years. Charts and statistics are included with the most recent data available on the types of business organizations being formed in the United States.

Other new features include:

Expanded Resource Section Each chapter now includes an expanded Resource section for further information and forms pertinent to the chapter subject. Internet resources are included, as well as a reference to the on-line companion Web page to this text.

Online Resource This text will be kept up to date through the use of a companion Web page, which is linked through West Legal Studies' Web page located at **www.westlegalstudies.com**. The companion page to this text will include downloadable forms, links to several sites for further information (including state corporate statutes), career information for corporate paralegals, and updates to the text itself.

Corporate Paralegal Profiles Within The Paralegal's Role section of each chapter is a one to two page profile of a corporate paralegal. The paralegals profiled work in a variety of settings and have varied responsibilities. The profiles focus on the paralegal's work environment, employer, and the responsibilities of his or her position. These profiles will give the students an idea of how the knowledge they gain through their business organizations courses can be put to use after graduation.

Ethics Information and Resources Ethical considerations are dispersed throughout this text within the discussion of the paralegal's role. For example, the chapter on Publicly Held Corporations includes an *Ethical Consideration* discussion of the importance of client confidentiality when working with publicly held corporations. Appendix C to this text also includes the codes of ethics of NALA and NFPA, as well as several resources for researching questions of legal ethics.

Additional charts, graphs, and forms To make the text more useful, and more appealing to the eye, several charts, graphs, checklists, and forms have been added.

Practical Problems Practical problems have been added to the end of each chapter to require the student to locate the pertinent laws and procedures in their home state and answer questions. For example, at the end of the chapter on incorporating businesses, students will be asked to locate the pertinent state law for their home state and to report on what is required for articles of incorporation (or other incorporating document) in that state. In addition, they will need to research the procedures for filing incorporation documents in their home state.

Workplace Scenario Each chapter ends with a *Workplace Scenario* that asks the students to read a continuing story involving fictional clients, a supervising attorney, and a paralegal. Students are to play the role of the paralegal in the story and complete an assignment based on the information given in the scenario, information from appendix D to the text, and the information they have learned from the chapter. Throughout the text, students will be asked to file a certificate of assumed name, prepare partnership documents, and incorporate a business for the fictional clients (among other things). These exercises will familiarize students with the pertinent laws and procedures in their home states, as well as the type of assignments frequently given to paralegals.

ANCILLARY MATERIALS

- ◆ The *Instructor's Manual with Test Bank* is available both in print and online at **www.westlegalstudies.com** in the Instructor's Lounge under Resource. Written by the author of the text, the *Instructor's Manual* contains outlines, suggested approaches, case briefs of the cases in the text, additional review questions and exercises, a test bank, and transparency masters.

- ◆ **Computerized Test Bank:** The Test Bank found in the *Instructor's Manual* is also available in a computerized format on CD-ROM. The platforms supported include Windows™ 3.1 and 95, Windows™ NT, and Macintosh. Features include:
  — Multiple methods of question selection.
  — Multiple outputs—print, ASCII, and RTF.
  — Graphic support (black and white).
  — Random questioning output.
  — Special character support.

- ◆ **Web Page:** Come visit our Web page at **www.westlegalstudies.com**, where you will find valuable information specific to this book such as hot links and sample materials to download, as well as other West Legal Studies products.

- ◆ **WESTLAW®**: West's online computerized legal research system offers students hands-on experience with a system commonly used in law offices. Qualified adopters can receive ten free hours of WESTLAW®. WESTLAW® can be accessed with Macintosh and IBM PC and compatibles. A modem is required.

- ◆ **Strategies and Tips for Paralegal Educators**, a pamphlet by Anita Tebbe of Johnson County Community College, provides teaching strategies specifically designed for paralegal educators. A copy of this pamphlet is available to each adopter. Quantities for distribution to adjunct instructors are available for purchase at a minimal price. A coupon in the pamphlet provides ordering information.

- ◆ **Survival Guide for Paralegal Students**, a pamphlet by Kathleen Mercer Reed and Bradene Moore covers practical and basic information to help students make the most their paralegal courses. Topics covered include choosing courses of study and notetaking skills.

◆ **West's Paralegal Video Library:** West Legal Studies is pleased to offer the following videos at no charge to qualified adopters:
— *The Drama of the Law II:* Paralegal Issues Video ISBN 0-314-07088-5
— *I Never Said I Was a Lawyer:* Paralegal Ethics Video ISBN 0-314-08049-X
— *The Making of a Case* Video ISBN 0-314-07300-0
— Mock Trial Video—*Anatomy of a Trial: A Contracts Case* ISBN 0-314-07343-4

ACKNOWLEDGMENTS

I would like to express my gratitude to several people for the assistance they have given me on this project, especially Rhonda Dearborn, Developmental Editor, Lisa Flatley, Editorial Assistant, and Betty Dickson, Production Editor.

My thanks also go to Chris Brock and Sharon Green at Graphics West for their hard work and attention to detail.

I would like to acknowledge the contributions of Daniel Oran, author of *Dictionary of the Law,* and William Statsky, author of *West's Legal Thesaurus/Dictionary,* for providing many of the glossary definitions throughout this text.

I would also like to thank my family, friends, and co-workers for their advice and encouragement. A very special thanks to my husband, Greg, and our children, Alex and Katherine, for their patience and support.

Lastly, I acknowledge the contributions of the following reviewers, whose suggestions and insights have helped me enormously:

Eli Bortman
Suffolk University, MA

Paul D. Guymon
William Rainey Harper College, IL

Louise P. Hoover
Rockford Business College, IL

Richard Hacker
University of Alaska Southeast

Steve Maple
University of Indianapolis, IN

Kathryn Myers
St. Mary of the Woods College, IN

Randi Ray
Des Moines Area Community College, IA

Jeff Rubel
University of Cincinnati-Clermont, OH

Alex Yarbrough
VA College at Birmingham, VA

Laurel A. Vietzen
Elgin Community College, IL

Angela Schneeman

Please note the Internet resources are of a time sensitive nature and URL addresses may often change or be deleted.

Contact us at westlegalstudies@delmar.com.

ABOUT THE AUTHOR

Angela Schneeman is a freelance paralegal who specializes in the corporate area of law. She has been a paralegal since she received her legal assistant certificate from the University of Minnesota in 1984. She also earned her Bachelor of Science Degree in Business and Legal Studies from the University of Minnesota. Angela has worked as a paralegal for law firms, the legal department of a publicly held corporation, and a major accounting firm. She currently offers her services to attorneys in Minneapolis, St. Paul, and White Bear Lake, Minnesota.

TABLE OF CASES

Addy v. Myers, 143–44

Beckman v. Cox Broadcasting Corporation, 526–27
Biondi v. Beekman, 258–59
BT-I v. Equitable Life Assurance Society, 85–86

Carpenter v. United States, 367–69
Celotex Corporation v. Pickett, 392–93
Commonwealth of Pennsylvania, Department of Revenue for the Bureau of Accounts Settlement v. McKelvey, 87–88
Cubic Corporation v. Marty, 528–30

Dreyfuss v. Dreyfuss, 22–23

Electric Railway Securities Co. v. Hendricks, 444–45

First National Bank and Trust Company of Williston v. Scherr, 31–32

Hunter v. Fort Worth Capital Corporation, 480–81

Jacobson v. Buffalo Rock Shooters Supply, 167–69

Lakota Girl Scout Council v. Havey Fund-Raising Management, 166–67

Merrill Lynch v. Livingston, 363–64
Mo. ex rel. National Supermarkets v. Sweeny, 478–79
Moneywatch Companies v. Wilbers, 199–200

Republic Acceptance Corporation v. Bennett, 442–44

State ex rel. Pillsbury v. Honeywell, Inc., 274–76

Thomas v. Colvin, 8–9

Weatherby v. Weatherby Lumber Company, 250–51
Welch v. Fuhrman, 215–16

CHAPTER 1

Sole Proprietorships

CHAPTER OUTLINE

§ 1.1   Sole Proprietorship Defined

§ 1.2   Sole Proprietorships in the United States

§ 1.3   Advantages of Doing Business as a Sole Proprietor

§ 1.4   Disadvantages of Doing Business as a Sole Proprietor

§ 1.5   Formation and Operation of the Sole Proprietorship

§ 1.6   The Paralegal's Role in Sole Proprietorship Matters

§ 1.7   Resources

INTRODUCTION

Before we begin our in-depth discussion of corporations in this text, we will investigate the characteristics of some simpler forms of business organizations and determine how those business organizations compare to corporations.

This chapter focuses on **sole proprietorships,** the most prevalent form of business in the United States. We begin by defining the term *sole proprietorship* and taking a look at the role of sole proprietorships in the United States. We then consider the advantages and disadvantages of doing business as a sole proprietorship, in contrast to the other types of business organizations. Next we focus on what it takes to form and operate a sole proprietorship, the role of paralegals working with sole proprietorships, and the resources that are available to paralegals whose work involves sole proprietorships.

§ 1.1   SOLE PROPRIETORSHIP DEFINED

The sole proprietorship is the simplest type of business organization. A **sole proprietor** is the sole owner of all of the assets of the business and is solely liable for all the debts and obligations of the business.

◆ ───

sole proprietorship   An unincorporated business owned by one person.

sole proprietor   The owner of a sole proprietorship.

Unlike a corporation, the business of the sole proprietor is not considered a separate entity. Rather, it is considered an extension of the individual. The sole proprietor is personally responsible for all legal debts and obligations of the business and is entitled to all of the profits of the business.

The sole proprietor may delegate decisions and management of the business to agents, but all authority to make decisions must come directly from the sole proprietor, who is responsible for all business-related acts of employees.

§ 1.2 SOLE PROPRIETORSHIPS IN THE UNITED STATES

The small business owned by a sole proprietor is the most common form of business in the United States. Although sole proprietorships make up the majority of business enterprises in this country, they account for a much smaller portion of gross business receipts than corporations do. For example, income tax returns for 1997 indicated that there were over 17 million sole proprietorships in the United States and only 4.7 million corporations. However, those 4.7 million corporations showed business receipts of over $15.89 trillion, while the sole proprietorships accounted for receipts of only $870 billion (see Figure 1-1).[1]

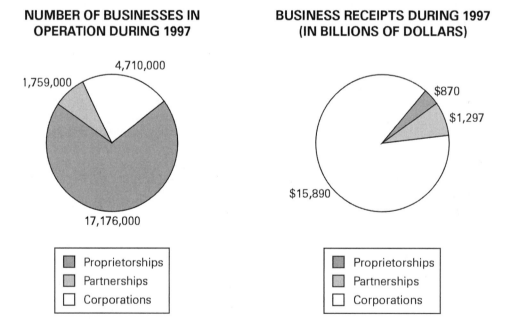

NUMBER OF BUSINESSES IN OPERATION DURING 1997

4,710,000
1,759,000
17,176,000

- ▨ Proprietorships
- ▨ Partnerships
- ▢ Corporations

BUSINESS RECEIPTS DURING 1997 (IN BILLIONS OF DOLLARS)

$870
$1,297
$15,890

- ▨ Proprietorships
- ▨ Partnerships
- ▢ Corporations

FIGURE 1-1 Comparison of Business Types and Receipts. From *The Statistical Abstract of the United States (2000).*

§ 1.3 ADVANTAGES OF DOING BUSINESS AS A SOLE PROPRIETOR

The small business person can find several advantages in doing business as a sole proprietor. This section focuses on some of the more important advantages of operating as a sole proprietorship, in contrast to operating as a corporation or limited liability company, including the sole proprietor's full management authority of the business, the minimal formalities and reporting requirements associated with sole proprietorships, the low cost of organizing sole proprietorships, and the income tax benefits offered by sole proprietorships.

Full Management Authority

The sole proprietor has the advantage of having full authority to manage the business in any way he or she sees fit, without having to obtain permission from a partner or a board of directors. Because the sole proprietor is not required to document decisions or obtain permission from others, the sole proprietorship is not subject to the bureaucracy and delays in the decision-making process that are often associated with other types of business organizations.

Any number of employees or agents may be hired by a sole proprietor, and any authority the sole proprietor chooses may be delegated. However, as the only owner of the business, the sole proprietor is always in command. If the sole owner of a business chooses to grant an ownership interest in the business to an employee in exchange for the employee's services, the business is no longer a sole proprietorship, but rather a partnership.

Minimal Formalities and Regulatory and Reporting Requirements

Sole proprietorships are not created or governed by statute, so there are very few formalities that must be followed by a sole proprietor. A sole proprietor must, however, comply with licensing and taxation regulations that are imposed on all forms of businesses. A sole proprietor must be aware of and obtain any necessary licenses, sales tax permits, and tax identification numbers before commencing business. Also, if the business is transacted under a name other than the sole proprietor's personal name, the state where the business is transacted will probably require that an application for **certificate of assumed name, trade name, or fictitious name** be filed. Assumed names, trade names, and fictitious names are discussed in § 1.5 of this chapter.

There are no qualification requirements for transacting business in a foreign state as a sole proprietorship. Unlike a corporation, a sole proprietor may transact

---

certificate of assumed name, trade name, or fictitious name A certificate issued by the proper state authority to an individual or an entity that grants the right to use an assumed or fictitious name for the transaction of business in that state.

business in a neighboring state without having to qualify and pay a fee to the appropriate state authority. The sole proprietor must, however, be sure to comply with any licensing and taxation requirements peculiar to that foreign state.

Low Cost of Organization

Formalities and regulatory requirements for beginning and operating a sole proprietorship are minimal. As a result, the costs for starting and maintaining a sole proprietorship are relatively low. There are no minimum capital restrictions and few, if any, state filing fees. Some possible startup expenses include attorneys' fees for legal advice, license fees, and filing and publishing fees for a certificate of assumed name, trade name, or fictitious name.

Income Tax Benefits

The income of the sole proprietorship is reported on a schedule to the sole proprietor's individual income tax return. The profit or loss of the business is added to the sole proprietor's other income, if any, and taxed at the individual rate of the taxpayer. This can be particularly advantageous for new businesses, which often incur a loss in the first year or so. If a sole proprietorship experiences a net loss during a particular year, the sole proprietor can use that loss to offset other income.

Dividends ◆

Sole Proprietors in the Digital Economy

Sole proprietors have always been a driving force in our economy and in our culture. According to a report published by the United States Small Business Administration, an estimated 21 million Americans were engaged in some entrepreneurial activity—either full- or part-time, in the late 1990s. In addition, from 1994 to 1998 about 11.1 million new jobs were added to the United States economy. Sole proprietorships and businesses with four or fewer employees generated over 60 percent of the new jobs for that period.* Large companies have continued to downsize, while sole proprietorships and small businesses continue to generate more income and jobs for our economy.

In years past, the term *sole proprietor* would often bring to mind the man or woman who owned and operated the local corner store or barbershop. In the twenty-first century, sole proprietors have taken on a new identity, being more likely to run a computer or technology-based business from a home office.

And, of course, people have the option of operating numerous types of businesses from home offices, including consulting businesses, retail businesses, travel agencies, bookkeeping, and billing services, to name just a few. For several reasons, entrepreneurs are finding it more feasible to own and operate their own businesses today. The most important reason, obviously, is the advent of the Internet.

According to a 1999 report by the Commerce Department, more than 100 million people worldwide use the Internet for their research, e-mail communication, and certain business transactions. The Internet has a vast array of tools to offer the sole proprietor and a wealth of information on almost every topic imaginable. Thus, a sole proprietor can research nearly every facet of his or her business without the assistance of staff or the time and expense associated with pre-Internet research. There are Web pages designed specifically for entrepreneurs just beginning a business and for those seeking assistance with everything from operating franchises and exploring small business opportunities to preparing a business plan.

Through their own Web pages and banner advertising, sole proprietors can reach millions of people with information about their products and services. The consumer Internet commerce market is estimated at $59 billion in the year 2001.[†] Business-to-business Internet commerce is estimated at $177 billion.[‡]

Maybe most importantly for the sole proprietor, the Internet offers plentiful networking and communication opportunities. Internet e-mail provides an efficient way to communicate not only with potential customers and suppliers, but also with peers. A common complaint of those who have left the traditional workforce and begun their own businesses is a feeling of isolation that comes from working at a home office or business. Listservs and chat rooms offer numerous opportunities for the sole proprietor to locate and communicate with others in similar situations. In addition to providing an excellent means for sole proprietors to share professional information, the Internet makes it possible for them to feel connected to the rest of the business world.

---

[*] U.S. Small Business Administration Office of Advocacy, *The Facts about Small Business 1999* **http://www.sba.gov/advo** (1999).

[†] *Computer Industry Report,* Internet Commerce: where is the money? Who are the players? (January 1, 1998).

[‡] *Computer Industry Report,* Internet Commerce: where is the money? Who are the players? (January 1, 1998).

Another income tax benefit to the sole proprietor is that there is no double taxation, which is often a drawback to corporate ownership. *Double taxation* refers to a situation whereby the income of the business is taxed twice: income taxes are paid once at the corporate level and again as the income flows through to the individual shareholders in the form of a salary or dividend.

§ 1.4 DISADVANTAGES OF DOING BUSINESS AS A SOLE PROPRIETOR

Along with the advantages of doing business as a sole proprietor, there are several disadvantages. Operating as a sole proprietorship can significantly restrict the growth of the business under many circumstances. Many sole proprietors eventually incorporate to achieve their business's full growth potential.

The disadvantages discussed in this section include the unlimited liability of the sole proprietor, the sole proprietorship's lack of business continuity, and the fact that there is no diversity in the management of a sole proprietorship. Next, we examine the difficulty in transferring the proprietary interest of a sole proprietorship and the limitations on raising capital for a sole proprietorship. All of these disadvantages must be weighed against potential advantages before a sound business decision can be made as to the best business format (see Figure 1-2).

Unlimited Liability

One of the most significant disadvantages of doing business as a sole proprietor is the unlimited liability faced by the owner of the business. The owner is solely responsible for all debts and obligations of the business, as well as any torts committed personally by the sole proprietor or by employees acting within the scope of their employment, without any protection of the sole proprietor's personal assets.

Advantages	Disadvantages
◆ Full management authority	◆ Unlimited liability
◆ Minimal formalities	◆ Lack of business continuity
◆ Ease of formation	◆ No diversity in management
◆ Low cost of organization	◆ Difficulty in transferring proprietary interest
◆ No double taxation	◆ Restricted ability to raise capital

FIGURE 1-2   Advantages and Disadvantages to Doing Business as a Sole
Proprietorship

Creditors may look to both the business and personal assets of the sole proprietor
to satisfy their claims.

For example, suppose that a sole proprietor owns a messenger service and has a
college student working for him during the summer as a driver. If the student hits a
pedestrian and seriously injures her, the sole proprietor would be responsible for
the damages sustained by the injured pedestrian. If the sole proprietor does not
have adequate insurance, the injured pedestrian could bring a suit against him personally. The sole proprietor would be personally responsible for any damages
awarded to the injured pedestrian and might even be forced to sell personal assets
to compensate the injured pedestrian.

Insurance can help to prevent a personal catastrophe to the sole proprietor, but
insurance is not available to cover every potential type of liability. Individuals who
operate businesses that have a high, uninsurable liability risk will almost always do
best to incorporate or form a limited liability company.

Lack of Business Continuity

Because the sole proprietorship is in many ways merely an extension of the individual, when the individual owner dies or ceases to do business, the business itself
often terminates. Although the sole proprietor may have employed several employees or agents, the agency relationship terminates upon the death of the sole proprietor. In most states, the sole proprietor may direct the personal representative of
the estate to oversee the continuance of the business until the estate has been settled and the business is passed to the **heirs**. However, if the business was dependent
upon the sole proprietor for its management, it may be difficult to maintain the
business. The decision as to whether to continue the business may be left to an heir
who has little or no interest in it. If all of the assets of the business are transferred
to another individual and the business is kept intact, another sole proprietorship is
formed.

---

heir A person who inherits property; a person who has a right to inherit property; or a
person who has a right to inherit property only if another person dies without leaving
a valid, complete will. [pronounce: air]

No Diversity in Management

Although it may be very appealing to an individual starting a new business to be able to make all the business decisions, there are many instances in which diversity in management can be advantageous. The sole proprietor does not have the experience and expertise of other partners, directors, or shareholders to rely on.

Difficulty in Transferring Proprietary Interest

When it comes time to sell the business, transferring the full interest of a sole proprietor may be difficult. Because the business is linked closely with the identity of the owner, the business may be worth much less when broken down by tangible assets. The sole proprietor may be the key to the success of the business. If no buyer is available for the business, the sole proprietor may have to take a loss by selling off the assets of the business.

The sale of a sole proprietorship also may be expensive. Unlike the shareholder of a publicly traded corporation, who can sell shares of stock on an exchange for a broker's fee, selling a sole proprietorship can be a difficult, time-consuming, and expensive ordeal. Many sales require extensive appraisals of the assets of the business. It may be difficult to place a fair dollar value on several assets of the business, including the **goodwill** and name of the business.

Limited Ability to Raise Capital

A wealthy entrepreneur starting a second or third business may not have a problem with lack of capital to start a sole proprietorship. However, to most individuals a barrier is created by the limitations of their own financial wealth. The funds they are able to borrow based on their personal assets and their business plan may not be sufficient to fund the type of business they desire to run.

§ 1.5 FORMATION AND OPERATION OF THE SOLE PROPRIETORSHIP

Very few formalities must be followed for an individual to commence business as a sole proprietorship. Because a sole proprietorship is not considered to be a separate entity, but rather an extension of the individual owner, one need do nothing to "form" the sole proprietorship. The formalities that must be followed are not unique to sole proprietorships, but are required of all types of business organizations. These may include filing a certificate of assumed name, trade name, or fictitious name, applying for tax identification numbers, sales tax permits, and licenses, and registering any pertinent trademarks, copyrights, or patents.

◆ ───

goodwill   The reputation and patronage of a company. The monetary worth of a company's *goodwill* is roughly what a company would sell for over the value of its physical property, money owed to it, and other assets.

Using an Assumed Name, Trade Name, or Fictitious Name

Most states allow a sole proprietor to transact business under a name other than his or her own name, provided that the purpose for doing so is not a fraudulent design or the intent to injure others.[2] The statutes of most states set forth certain requirements that must be followed before an individual may transact business under an **assumed name, trade name**, or **fictitious name,** as it may variously be called.

As indicated in *Thomas v. Colvin*, the following case, operating under a fictitious or assumed name does not change the nature of the sole proprietorship, nor does it limit the liability of the sole proprietor in any way.

CASE

Johnnie E. THOMAS, Appellee,
v.
Bennie J. COLVIN, and R. A. Coker,
d/b/a Sherwood Motors, Appellants.

No. 50209.
Court of Appeals of Oklahoma, Division No. 1.
Jan. 16, 1979.
Rehearing Denied Feb. 27, 1979.
Appeal from the District Court of Oklahoma County;
William S. Myers, judge.

AFFIRMED.
REYNOLDS, Judge:

Does an individual who does business as a sole proprietor under one or several names remain one person, personally liable for all his obligations?

Jury returned verdict in **conversion** action against defendant-appellant, R. A. Coker, d/b/a Sherwood Motors, for $1,625 actual damages and $17,500 punitive. Defendant appeals, contending that trial court erred in overruling his **demurrer** to plaintiff's evidence.

Plaintiff's action was premised on defendant's wrongful repossession of plaintiff's automobile. The car had been purchased from defendant on a credit plan, and the resulting security agreement and promissory note were assigned to B.F.T.C. Finance Corporation, of which Coker is president. Evidence established that Coker called Bennie Colvin in Oklahoma City and hired him to repossess the car. This was done even though plaintiff was not in default on the note.

Defendant argues that trial court erred since evidence failed to establish that Colvin was the agent of "R. A. Coker, d/b/a Sherwood Motors."

---

assumed name Alias that may be used to transact business. Usually requires filing or notification at the state or local level. Same as fictitious name.

trade name The name of a business. It will usually be legally protected in the area where the company operates and for the types of products in which it deals.

fictitious name Alias that may be used to transact business. Usually requires filing or notification at the state or local level. Same as assumed name.

conversion Any act that deprives an owner of property without that owner's permission and without just cause. For example, it is conversion to refuse to return a borrowed book.

demurrer A legal pleading that says, in effect, "even if, for the sake of argument, the facts presented by the other side are correct, those facts do not give the other side a legal argument that can possibly stand up in court." The demurrer has been replaced in many courts by a motion to dismiss.

Defendant treats this **nomenclature** as a separate entity arguing that since Coker was not acting on behalf of Sherwood Motors when he hired Colvin and directed him to convert plaintiff's car, he is not liable. Coker argues that since he was not sued "individually" he is not responsible for any individual actions apart from the operation of Sherwood Motors. Plaintiff argues correctly that even though Colvin may not have been the agent of "Sherwood Motors" in repossessing the car, Coker's participation in the commission of this tort as an individual and as agent of B.F.T.C. makes him liable. ...

Defendant treats this case as if the use of the "d/b/a" designation limited the capacity in which he could be liable. No authority is cited to support this contention that a separate entity is created by this nomenclature. The Oklahoma Supreme Court decided in *National Surety Co. v. Oklahoma Presbyterian College for Girls*, 38 Okl. 429, 132 P. 652 (1913), that naming a sole proprietor defendant under his trade name was the same as naming the defendant individually.

This same result has been reached elsewhere. In *Duval v. Midwest Auto City, Inc.*, 425 F.Supp. 1381 (D.Neb.1977), the court noted:

The designation "d/b/a" means "doing business as" but is merely descriptive of the person or corporation who does business under some other name. Doing business under another name does not create an entity distinct from the person operating the business. The individual who does business as a sole proprietor under one or several names remains one person, personally liable for all his obligations.

... R. A. Coker was before the trial court as a defendant individually liable for his actions whether performed on behalf of B.F.T.C. Finance Corporation or as operator of his other business.

Plaintiff presented sufficient evidence to support a finding that defendant participated in the commission of a tort in Oklahoma. There being no absence of proof, trial court properly overruled defendant's demurrer....

AFFIRMED.
ROMANG, P. J., and BOX, J., concur.

Typically, if the proposed name is available and otherwise complies with state statutes, an application for certificate of assumed name, trade name, or fictitious name, or similar document, is filed with the secretary of state of the state in which the sole proprietor intends to do business. State statutes often require publication of a notice of intent to transact business under an assumed name. The intent of these statutes is to protect the public by giving notice or information as to the persons with whom they deal and to afford protection against fraud and deceit.[3]

The appropriate state statutes should be carefully reviewed to ascertain the state requirements for assumed names, trade names, or fictitious names, and the secretary of state or other appropriate state official should be contacted. Often the secretary of state's office will provide its own forms to be completed to apply for a certificate of assumed name. Figure 1-3 on page 10 shows a fictitious or assumed name certificate that may be used by a sole proprietor.

Hiring Employees and Using Tax Identification Numbers

If a sole proprietor will be hiring employees, a federal employer identification number (EIN) must be obtained. This number is obtained by completing and filing an

nomenclature Designation, title, or name of something.

Application for Employer Identification Number (Form SS-4), (see Figure 1-4 on page 11). The application and a complete set of instructions can be obtained by contacting your local IRS office or calling the IRS at 1-800-829-1040. Form SS-4 can also be downloaded from the IRS Web page at **http://www.irs.gov**.

Some states require employers to have a state tax identification number separate from the federal tax identification number. The appropriate state authority should be contacted to ensure that the sole proprietor is in compliance with all requirements for tax identification numbers.

The sole proprietor must also be aware of and comply with all requirements concerning state and federal withholding and unemployment taxes.

[From 13B Am. Jur. Legal Forms 2d *Name* § 182:15 (Rev 1996)]

§ 182:15. APPLICATION—CONDUCT OF BUSINESS UNDER FICTITIOUS OR ASSUMED NAME—GENERAL FORM

APPLICATION

To: _____ [Secretary of State of _____ (state) or other public official] _____ [address]

Pursuant to _____ [cite statute], relating to the conduct of business under _____ [a fictitious or an assumed] name, the undersigned _____ [person or persons or partnership or corporation] who _____ [is or are], or will be, carrying on business in _____ [state] under _____ [a fictitious or an assumed] name, hereby present(s) for filing the following application in the office of _____ [the Secretary of State or other public official]:

1. The _____ [fictitious or assumed] name under which the business is, or will be, carried on is: _____.

2. The real name and address of each person owning or interested in the business is: _____.

3. The nature of the business is: _____.

4. The business will be conducted at _____ [address], City of _____, County of _____, State of _____, _____ [ZIP].

If applicable, add:

5. The name of the agent through whom the business is, or will be, carried on is _____, whose address is _____, City of _____, County of _____, State of _____, _____ [ZIP].

Dated: _____.

[Signature(s)]

FIGURE 1-3 Sample Application for Conduct of Business Under Fictitious or Assumed Name Form. Reprinted with permission from *American Jurisprudence Legal Forms 2d*. © 2000 West Group.

Form **SS-4**	**Application for Employer Identification Number**	EIN
(Rev. April 2000)	(For use by employers, corporations, partnerships, trusts, estates, churches, government agencies, certain individuals, and others. See instructions.)	
Department of the Treasury Internal Revenue Service	▶ Keep a copy for your records.	OMB No. 1545-0003

Please type or print clearly.

1 Name of applicant (legal name) (see instructions)

2 Trade name of business (if different from name on line 1) | 3 Executor, trustee, "care of" name

4a Mailing address (street address) (room, apt., or suite no.) | 5a Business address (if different from address on lines 4a and 4b)

4b City, state, and ZIP code | 5b City, state, and ZIP code

6 County and state where principal business is located

7 Name of principal officer, general partner, grantor, owner, or trustor- SSN or ITIN may be required (see instructions) ▶

8a Type of entity (Check only one box.) (see instructions)
Caution: If applicant is a limited liability company, see the instructions for line 8a.

☐ Sole proprietor (SSN) _____   ☐ Estate (SSN of decedent) _____
☐ Partnership   ☐ Personal service corp.   ☐ Plan administrator (SSN) _____
☐ REMIC   ☐ National Guard   ☐ Other corporation (specify) ▶ _____
☐ State/local government   ☐ Farmers' cooperative   ☐ Trust
☐ Church or church-controlled organization   ☐ Federal government/military
☐ Other nonprofit organization (specify) ▶ _____ (enter GEN if applicable) _____
☐ Other (specify) ▶

8b If a corporation, name the state or foreign country (if applicable) where incorporated | State _____ | Foreign country _____

9 Reason for applying (Check only one box.) (see instructions)   ☐ Banking purpose (specify purpose) ▶ _____
☐ Started new business (specify type) ▶_____   ☐ Changed type of organization (specify new type) ▶ _____
☐ Purchased going business
☐ Hired employees (Check the box and see line 12.)   ☐ Created a trust (specify type) ▶ _____
☐ Created a pension plan (specify type) ▶   ☐ Other (specify) ▶

10 Date business started or acquired (month, day, year) (see instructions) | 11 Closing month of accounting year (see instructions)

12 First date wages or annuities were paid or will be paid (month, day, year). **Note:** If applicant is a withholding agent, enter date income will first be paid to nonresident alien. (month, day, year) . . . . ▶

13 Highest number of employees expected in the next 12 months. **Note:** If the applicant does not expect to have any employees during the period, enter -0-. (see instructions) . . . . . ▶	Nonagricultural	Agricultural	Household

14 Principal activity (see instructions) ▶

15 Is the principal business activity manufacturing? . . . . ☐ Yes ☐ No
If "Yes," principal product and raw material used ▶

16 To whom are most of the products or services sold? Please check one box.   ☐ Business (wholesale)
☐ Public (retail)   ☐ Other (specify) ▶   ☐ N/A

17a Has the applicant ever applied for an employer identification number for this or any other business? . . . . ☐ Yes ☐ No
Note: If "Yes," please complete lines 17b and 17c.

17b If you checked "Yes" on line 17a, give applicant's legal name and trade name shown on prior application, if different from line 1 or 2 above.
Legal name ▶   Trade name ▶

17c Approximate date when and city and state where the application was filed. Enter previous employer identification number if known.
Approximate date when filed (mo., day, year) | City and state where filed | Previous EIN

Under penalties of perjury, I declare that I have examined this application, and to the best of my knowledge and belief, it is true, correct, and complete. | Business telephone number (include area code) ( )
| Fax telephone number (include area code) ( )

Name and title (Please type or print clearly.) ▶

Signature ▶   Date ▶

Note: Do not write below this line. For official use only.

Please leave blank ▶ | Geo. | Ind. | Class | Size | Reason for applying

For Privacy Act and Paperwork Reduction Act Notice, see page 4.   Cat. No. 16055N   Form **SS-4** (Rev. 4-2000)

FIGURE 1-4 Application for Employer Identification Number

Sales Tax Permits

Most states require businesses to obtain a sales tax permit before sales are made. Again, the appropriate state authority must be contacted to ensure that the proper procedures are followed.

Licensing

Many types of businesses are required to obtain licenses of one form or another. The proper city and state authorities must be contacted to ascertain whether a license is required for the type of business that the sole proprietor proposes to commence.

Registering Intellectual Property

Often when a sole proprietor forms a new business, the business may involve **intellectual property**, including inventions, the use of words and symbols that represent the business or product, and creative material prepared by the sole proprietor. The registration of **patents, trademarks,** or **copyrights** will protect the sole proprietor's exclusive rights and make it illegal for anyone else to use this material.

§ 1.6 THE PARALEGAL'S ROLE IN SOLE PROPRIETORSHIP MATTERS

The involvement of paralegals in working with attorneys who advise sole proprietors varies greatly, depending on the circumstances and the client. If the client is an experienced businessperson who perhaps has started a business before, he or she may need little legal assistance from the attorney and the paralegal. Legal services may be confined to legal advice given by the attorney to the sole proprietor. An

intellectual property 1. A copyright, patent trademark, trade secret, or similar intangible right in an original tangible or perceivable work. 2. The works themselves in (no. 1). 3. The right to obtain a copyright, patent, etc., for the works in no. 1.

patent An exclusive right granted by the federal government to a person for a limited number of years (usually 20) for the manufacture and sale of something that person has discovered or invented.

trademark A distinctive mark, brand name, motto, or symbol used by a company to identify or advertise the products it makes or sells. *Trademarks* (and *service marks*) can be federally registered and protected against use by other companies if the marks meet certain criteria. A federally registered mark bears the symbol ®.

copyright The right to control the copying, distributing, performing, displaying, and adapting of works (including paintings, music, books and movies). The right belongs to the creator, or to persons employing the creator, or to persons who buy the right from the creator. The right is created, regulated, and limited by the federal Copyright Act of 1976 and by the Constitution. The symbol for copyright is ©. The legal life (*duration*) of a copyright is the author's life plus 50 years, or 75 years from publication date, or 100 years from creation, depending on the circumstances.

experienced businessperson may decide to personally handle all formalities connected with the sole proprietorship.

Other clients, however, because of inexperience or lack of time, may decide to ask more assistance of the attorney and the paralegal. The attorney may meet with the client to give legal advice as requested, and then ask the paralegal to directly assist the client by seeing that all of the necessary formalities are complied with.

The paralegal may prepare for the client, or assist the client in preparing, all necessary documents, including tax identification number applications and an application for a certificate of assumed name. For this reason, it is important for paralegals to be familiar with state and local requirements and procedures that must be followed to form and operate a sole proprietorship.

Following is a checklist that may be used to ensure that the client is given all the necessary information and assistance to begin his or her own sole proprietorship.

CHECKLIST FOR STARTING A SOLE PROPRIETORSHIP

- ☐ Contact proper state and federal agencies to request information regarding taxation, unemployment insurance, workers compensation insurance, etc. (The law firm may keep extra state and federal information and forms on hand for clients.)
- ☐ Complete and file necessary applications for employer identification numbers—both federal and state if necessary.
- ☐ File application for certificate of assumed name, trade name, or fictitious name with secretary of state or other appropriate state agency if necessary.
- ☐ Publish notice of transacting business under assumed name in local newspaper if necessary.
- ☐ Secure necessary business licenses and permits—state and local.
- ☐ Obtain sales tax permits if necessary.
- ☐ Ascertain whether the sole proprietor has any intellectual property rights that must be protected through application for a patent, trademark, or copyright.

Corporate Paralegal Profile
Donna G. Frye, PLS

In an age when everyone is cost conscious, not only do I save the attorneys time and money, but I also save the client time and money, thereby retaining client loyalty.

Name Donna G. Frye, PLS

Location Elgin, South Carolina

Title Corporate Paralegal

Specialty Corporate Law

Education Associate Degree, Midlands Technical College

Experience 13 years (21 years total legal experience)

Donna Frye works for a law firm that often assists sole proprietors. Donna began her legal career as a legal secretary in 1980 and was promoted to a legal assistant position in 1987. She is currently a corporate paralegal with Turner, Padget, Graham & Laney, P.A., a 58-attorney law firm in South Carolina that employs 21 paralegals.

Although Donna works primarily in the corporate area of law, she has also had the opportunity to assist attorneys in providing services to sole proprietors. Donna has found that the needs of sole proprietors can vary greatly from individual to individual. For example, whereas some sole proprietors use their social security numbers for tax identification purposes, sole proprietors who have employees are required to obtain federal employer identification numbers. For those sole proprietors, Donna prepares a Form SS-4, Application for Employer Identification Number, specifically noting that the individual's business is conducted as a sole proprietorship. She then files the SS-4 with the IRS for processing. The IRS issues a Federal Identification Number for use by the sole proprietor in the operation of the sole proprietor's business.

Donna has also helped to meet other needs of sole proprietors, including drafting leases for business properties and drafting agreements for office-sharing opportunities, shared work interests, and other business arrangements. She has assisted as well with preparing employment agreements for employees and independent contractors working with the sole proprietor.

Donna's responsibilities in the corporate area of law include all aspects of the formation of new corporations and limited liability companies. She prepares and files official state and federal documents, bylaws, stock certificates, and shareholder agreements. In addition, Donna is responsible for corporate maintenance, including the preparation of minutes and other corporate documents.

Like many corporate paralegals who work in law firms, Donna's work is not exclusively in the corporate area and related fields. She is also given assignments pertaining to commercial/residential real estate and estate planning and probate.

Donna handles files from start to finish, including drafting and creating documents, telephone communications with clients and other contacts, and accomplishing as many tasks as possible to allow the attorneys time to concentrate on matters which only they, as attorneys, can handle.

What Donna enjoys most about her position is the flexibility and the opportunity to grow. Often, drafting documents requires multiple levels of legal research, which keeps her educated and up to date on laws directly affecting the attorneys' area of practice. What she doesn't like is spending the majority of her day behind a desk and computer screen—*it can be very tiring!*

Donna's advice to new paralegals?

Work and gain experience in several types of law before deciding on one in particular. In addition to corporate, real estate, and estate/probate law, there are many other areas of law available, including, but not limited to, plaintiff and defendant litigation, bankruptcy, foreclosures, collections, and criminal law. Experience in multiple types of law will equip you with a well-rounded education and starting base in the legal field, especially since so many areas of the law are closely related. Knowledge of one type of law can actually increase your knowledge in other areas, enhancing your marketability and reliability. If the attorney cannot rely on the paralegal, the paralegal is not doing his or her job!

For more information on careers for corporate paralegals, see the *Careers* feature on the companion Web page to this text at **www.westlegalstudies.com**.

§ 1.7 RESOURCES

Many resources are available to the paralegal who is working with a sole proprietorship. Much of this information is published by the government and is free for the asking. Some of the most valuable resources include United States Small Business Administration publications, publications and information available from state and local government offices, state statutes, and the secretary of state's office.

United States Small Business Administration

The United States Small Business Administration (SBA) has offices in nearly every major city in the country. The local SBA office can often provide a wide variety of free information on federal requirements for forming and operating small businesses, including sole proprietorships. The SBA's "Starting a Business" Web page can be found at **http://www.sba.gov/starting**. The United States Business Advisor site can be found at **http://www.business.gov/busadv**.

State and Local Government Offices

Licensing and taxation requirements vary by state and locality, and it is important that the appropriate authorities be contacted to obtain information relating to all state and local licensing and taxation matters, including unemployment insurance, withholding for employee income taxation, and sales tax permits and licenses. Again, the information obtainable from your local SBA office can help direct you to the appropriate offices that must be contacted. Many state and local agencies have helpful Web pages.

State Statutes

The appropriate state statutes must be consulted for information regarding use of assumed names, trade names, or fictitious names, if applicable, as well as for any requirements or regulations related to sole proprietorships (see Figure 1-5).

State	Statute Citation
Arizona	Ariz. Rev. Stat. Ann. §§ 44-1236, 44-1460
Arkansas	Ark. Code Ann. § 4-27-404
California	Cal. Bus. & Prof. Code § 17910 *et seq.*
Colorado	Colo. Rev. Stat. § 7-71-101
Connecticut	Conn. Gen. Stat. Ann. § 35-1
Delaware	Del. Code Ann. tit. 6 § 3101
District of Columbia	D.C. Code Ann. § 47-2855.2
Florida	Fla. Stat. Ann. § 865.09
Georgia	Ga. Code Ann. §§ 10-1-490, 10-1-493
Idaho	Idaho Code § 53-504
Illinois	805 ILCS 5/4.15
Indiana	Ind. Code Ann. §§ 23-15-1-1, 23-15-1-3
Iowa	Iowa Code Ann. § 547.1
Kentucky	Ky. Rev. Stat. Ann. § 365.015
Louisiana	La. Rev. Stat. Ann. §§ 51:281, 51:283
Maine	Me. Rev. Stat. Ann. tit.13-A § 307
Maryland	Md. Corps. & Assns. § 1-406

FIGURE 1-5 List of State Statutes Concerning Assumed, Fictitious, or Trade Names

State	*Statute Citation*
Massachusetts	Mass. Ann. Laws ch. 110, §§ 4; 5
Michigan	Mich. Comp. Laws Ann. § 445.1
Minnesota	Minn. Stat. §§ 333.01–333.06
Missouri	Mo. Rev. Stat. §§ 417.200, 417.210
Montana	Mont. Code Ann. § 30-13-201 *et seq.*
Nebraska	Neb. Rev. Stat. § 87-208 *et seq.*
Nevada	Nev. Rev. Stat. § 602.010 *et seq.*
New Hampshire	N.H. Rev. Stat. Ann. § 349:1 *et seq.*
New Jersey	N.J. Rev. Stat. § 14A:2-2.1
New York	N.Y. Gen. Bus. Law §§ 130, 133
North Carolina	N.C. Gen. Stat. §§ 66–68
North Dakota	N.D. Stat. Ann. § 47-25-01 *et seq.*
Ohio	Ohio Rev. Code Ann. §§ 1329.01–1329.06
Oklahoma	Okla. Stat. Ann. tit. 18 § 1140
Oregon	Or. Rev. Stat. § 648.005 *et seq.*
Pennsylvania	54 Pa. Cons. Stat. § 301 *et seq.*
Rhode Island	R.I. Gen. Laws § 6-1-1
South Dakota	S.D. Codified Laws Ann. § 37-11 *et seq.*
Tennessee	Tenn. Code Ann. § 48-14-101(d)
Texas	Tex. Bus. & Com. § 36.10 *et seq.*
Utah	Utah Code Ann. § 4-2-5 *et seq.*
Vermont	Vt. Stat. Ann. tit. 11 § 1621
Virginia	Va. Code Ann. § 59.1-69 *et seq.*
Washington	Wash. Rev. Code § 19.80.001 *et seq.*
West Virginia	W. Va. Code § 47-8-2 *et seq.*
Wisconsin	Wis. Stat. § 134.17
Wyoming	Wyo. Stat §§ 40-2-101 to 40-2-109

FIGURE 1-5 (*continued*)

ETHICAL CONSIDERATION

Does your supervising attorney need to review *all* of the work you do for a sole proprietor? When is it okay to release a corporate client's financial information? Is it okay to discuss a corporation's legal problems with *anyone* from the corporation who calls? Is it okay to give legal advice to partnership clients on routine matters? These are all questions of ethics, the type of ethical dilemmas often faced by paralegals who work with sole proprietorships, corporations, and all types of business organizations, whether they work for the business organization's legal department or for a law firm that represents business organizations.

Every day paralegals must make important ethical decisions. Their decisions can affect not only their employers and clients, but also the public. In addition to costing the paralegal his or her job, unethical behavior may cause the paralegal's supervising attorney to be disciplined—possibly even disbarred. In some instances, a civil lawsuit or even criminal prosecution may result.

The rules of ethics applicable to attorneys generally apply to the paralegals who work for them as well. In addition, the National Association of Legal Assistants (NALA), and the National Federation of Paralegal Associations (NFPA) have both established codes of ethics for their members. The rules of ethics as they apply to paralegals who work for corporations and other business organizations will be discussed briefly throughout this text. The NALA and NFPA codes of ethics, as well as Internet resources for researching legal ethics, are included as appendix C to this text.

Secretaries of State

The secretary of state or other appropriate state authority should be contacted for procedural information regarding filing of an application for use of assumed or fictitious name, if applicable. The appropriate secretary of state's office may also be able to advise you on the procedures for registering a trademark at the state level. See Appendix A of this text for a directory of secretaries of state.

U.S. Patent and Trademark Office

The U.S. Patent and Trademark Office provides information concerning the registration of trademarks and patents at the federal level. The Patent and Trademark Office may be contacted by calling (800) 786-9199, or by visiting their Web page at **www.uspto.gov**.

 Internet Resources www.

A number of Web pages are useful to sole proprietors and those advising and assisting sole proprietors. Some have been described in this chapter. Following is a more comprehensive list.

Business Plans	**www.bplans.com**
Business Resource Center	**www.morebusiness.com/**
Internal Revenue Service	**www.irs.gov**
National Association for the Self-Employed	**www.nase.org/**
Small Business Administration	**www.sbaonline.sba.gov/**

State Statutes	
American Law Source Online	**www.lawsource.com/also**
Findlaw	**www.findlaw.com**
Legal Information Institute	**www.law.cornell.edu/states/listing.html**
U.S. Patent and Trademark Office	**www.uspto.gov**

An alphabetical list of Internet Resources for the Corporate Paralegal is included as appendix B to this text.

Web Page

For links to several of the previously listed sites, as well as downloadable state forms for applying for a certificate of assumed name, trade name, or fictitious name, log on to **www.westlegalstudies.com**, and click through to the book link for this text.

SUMMARY

- ◆ The sole proprietorship is the simplest, most common form of business ownership in the United States.
- ◆ The sole proprietor is the sole owner of all assets of the sole proprietorship. He or she is personally responsible for all debts and liabilities of the business.
- ◆ Sole proprietors may hire employees to act on their behalf, but they retain full authority and responsibility.
- ◆ Sole proprietorships may conduct their business under assumed names, trade names, or fictitious names by filing the appropriate documentation with state authorities.
- ◆ Some of the advantages to conducting business as a sole proprietorship include (1) the full management authority possessed by the sole proprietor, (2) the minimal formalities and regulatory reporting requirements to form and maintain a sole proprietorship, (3) the low cost of organization, and (4) income tax benefits.
- ◆ Some of the disadvantages to conducting business as a sole proprietorship include (1) the sole proprietor's unlimited liability for debts and obligations of the business, (2) the lack of business continuity, (3) the lack of diversity in management, (4) the difficulty in transferring the proprietary interest of the sole proprietorship, and (5) the sole proprietor's limited ability to raise capital.

REVIEW QUESTIONS

1. What form of business ownership is the most prevalent in the United States? What form of business entity generates the most income?

2. Explain why doing business as a sole proprietor instead of as a corporation can be an income tax advantage to some individuals.

3. Suppose that the Johnson Grocery Store is a sole proprietorship owned by Jill Johnson. If her store manager, Ben, in the ordinary course of business, orders too many tomatoes, can Jill Johnson refuse the order? Why or why not?

4. Explain why an individual with limited financial resources might choose to incorporate rather than form and operate a sole proprietorship.

5. Jim is contemplating going into business for himself as a general contractor specializing in apartment complexes. For what reasons may Jim choose to operate as a sole proprietorship? What factors may cause him to consider incorporating?

PRACTICAL PROBLEMS

1. What are the requirements for filing a certificate of assumed name in your state? Find the pertinent statutes in your state, or contact your secretary of state's office or other appropriate state office to answer the following questions.
   a. What is the document called in your state?
   b. What is the filing fee for filing the certificate of assumed name in your state?
   c. How long does the assumed name, or fictitious name, remain active?
   d. What is the procedure for filing the certificate of assumed name?

2. Is a state tax identification number required for sole proprietors who hire employees in your state?
   a. What are the procedures for requesting such a number?
   b. Who must be contacted?
   c. What forms must be completed?

WORKPLACE SCENARIO

Assume that you are a paralegal for a small, general practice law firm. You and Belinda Benson, one of the attorneys you work for, have just come out of a meeting with a new client, Bradley Harris. Mr. Harris has just started up a computer repair business, and he has come to your law firm seeking advice as to any formalities he must comply with to operate his business within the law. Mr. Harris operates out of his home under the name of Cutting Edge Computer Repair. He has one employee, who works as his secretary/assistant.

Using the Client Information Sheet provided in appendix D-1 to this text, prepare the necessary documents for Mr. Harris. You may create your own form using the sample forms in this chapter, or you may obtain the appropriate state-specific form from the appropriate state and federal offices.

Several of these forms are available for downloading on the companion Web page to this text, or the secretary of state Web pages. Form SS-4 is available for downloading on the Internal Revenue Service Web page.

Your documents should be prepared with cover letters to the appropriate state and federal authorities, making mention of the appropriate filing fee (if required). The necessary documents may include

1. Application for Certificate of Assumed Name (or similar document as required in your state).

2. Application for federal employer identification number.

3. Application for state employer identification number (if required in your state).

END NOTES

1. U.S. Census Bureau, *The Statistical Abstract of the United States (2000)*, 854.

2. 57 Am. Jur. 2d *Name* § 64 (1988).

3. *Id.* § 66.

CHAPTER 2
Partnerships

CHAPTER OUTLINE

§ 2.1   An Introduction to Partnerships

§ 2.2   The Relationship between Partners and Others

§ 2.3   The Relationship among Partners and between Partners and
        the Partnership

§ 2.4   Advantages of Doing Business as a General Partnership

§ 2.5   Disadvantages of Doing Business as a Partnership

§ 2.6   Organization and Management of a General Partnership

§ 2.7   Financial Structure of a Partnership

§ 2.8   Dissolution, Dissociation, Winding Up, and Termination of
        the Partnership

§ 2.9   The Paralegal's Role in Partnership Matters

§ 2.10 Resources

INTRODUCTION

Although partnerships are not as prevalent as sole proprietorships or corporations, they are a common form of business organization. Partnerships necessarily involve two or more people and are naturally somewhat more complex than sole proprietorships. However, for many of the reasons discussed in this chapter, the formation of a partnership is often a viable alternative to incorporating.

In this chapter, we define the term *partnership* and take a look at the legal relationships between partners and others and among the partners. We then investigate the specific advantages and disadvantages of doing business as a partnership. Next we examine the organization and management of the partnership, including the partnership agreement. We then focus on the financial structure of a partnership and the dissolution, dissociation, winding up, and termination of the partnership. This chapter concludes with a discussion of the role of the paralegal working with partnerships and the resources available to assist in that area.

§ 2.1 AN INTRODUCTION TO PARTNERSHIPS

The **partnership** is a unique type of business organization that creates a unique relationship among its members. In this section, we define *partnership*, take a look at two deviations from the general partnership—the limited liability partnership and the joint venture—discuss the role of partnerships in the United States, and review the law that governs partnerships. We conclude with a look at the interpretation of partnership law with regard to the aggregate and entity theories of partnerships.

Partnership Defined

A *partnership* is an "association of two or more persons to carry on as co-owners of a business for profit."[1] The essential elements of the partnership definition are "association of two or more persons," "carry on," "co-owners," "business," and "for profit."

The "association of two or more persons" element differentiates the partnership from the sole proprietorship. The word "persons," as used in this definition, includes "individuals, partnerships, corporations, and other associations."[2] Generally, any individual or entity with the capacity to enter into a contract can be a partner.

The "carry on" element implies that the partners must actively carry on the partnership business together, in addition to possessing co-ownership of the business or of property.

The "co-ownership" element refers to ownership of the business of the partnership and requires that the business be a single business entity owned by more than one person. Co-ownership also means that the partners have a right to participate in the management of the partnership and to share in the profits (and losses) of the partnership.

The "business" element of the definition includes "every trade, occupation, or profession."[3]

The "for profit" element refers to the intention of the partnership. Obviously, not every partnership earns a profit, but earning a profit must be an objective of the partnership. Nonprofit organizations may not be partnerships.

Although a partnership can be formed informally, without a written agreement, it cannot exist without all the partnership elements just discussed. In *Dreyfuss v. Dreyfuss,* the case on page 22, the court found that, contrary to the son's assertions, no oral partnership agreement existed between father and son because there was no joint proprietary interest. In other words, there was no intent to carry on a business co-owned by the partners.

A **general partnership** differs from a limited partnership in that all partners to a general partnership are considered **general partners**. In contrast, a combination

---

partnership An association of two or more persons to carry on as co-owners a business for profit.

general partnership A typical partnership in which all partners are general partners.

general partner Synonymous with *partner.* A partner in a general partnership, or limited partnership, who typically has unlimited personal liability for the debts and liabilities of the partnership.

CASE

District Court of Appeal of Florida,
Third District
Kenneth R. DREYFUSS, Appellant,
v.
Jacques F. DREYFUSS and Brickell Earth
Station, Inc., Appellees.

No. 96-1381.
Nov. 19, 1997.

...Appellant, Kenneth R. Dreyfuss ("Kenneth"), appeals the final judgment entered in favor of the appellees, Jacques F. Dreyfuss ("Jacques") and Brickell Earth Station, Inc. ("BESI"), in a breach of contract action. We affirm finding there is competent, substantial evidence in support of the trial court's conclusion that no contract was formed.

The facts of this case sadly involve a dispute between a father and son. Appellant Kenneth initiated this action in 1992, claiming entitlement to one-half of the gross revenues of his father's business. The case eventually went to trial on a third amended complaint which alleged breach of an oral partnership agreement that was formed during a conversation between Kenneth and his father, Jacques.

At trial, the facts revealed that Kenneth incorporated BESI for Jacques in 1981. BESI's sole shareholder, officer, and director is Jacques, who formed the company to obtain cable television contracts with condominium associations. Kenneth, who was employed in a private law firm, performed BESI's legal work, and drafted some of the company's first service contracts. Although Kenneth was terminated by the law firm in July of 1982, he continued to provide legal services to BESI.

In September of 1982, the Cricket Club Condominium approved a service contract that was negotiated by Jacques. Jacques invited Kenneth to attend a sales presentation at the Cricket Club, to give Kenneth some experience and to lift his spirits from his recent termination by the law firm. After the presentation, Jacques and Kenneth had a "car conversation" which Kenneth claims created an oral partnership agreement.

According to Kenneth, during this "car conversation" Jacques offered to pay Kenneth a percentage of BESI's potential future revenues. In return, Kenneth would give up his right to hourly compensation for his legal services, forgive any existing debt for services rendered, and join Jacques as a salesman. Although Kenneth could not remember if any terms regarding profits and losses were discussed during the conversation, he claims he relied on the alleged agreement between 1982 and 1986 in working to obtain six cable contracts for BESI.

According to Jacques, there was never an agreement to form a partnership to share equally in BESI's profits. The conversation was merely an attempt to help his son who had just lost a job by suggesting that Kenneth join the family business. Jacques asserted that instead of profits, Kenneth was paid a share of gross revenues for the time he spent obtaining cable contracts, and for his legal services. Additionally, Jacques testified that he first learned about his son's claim for a partner's share of the gross revenues only after he read the third amended complaint, filed eleven years after the "car conversation." Based on this evidence, the trial court found that there was no meeting of the minds to support a binding partnership contract.

It is a fundamental principle of appellate review that findings made by a lower court are presumed correct and will not be disturbed on appeal unless these findings are totally unsupported by competent, substantial evidence. ... Here, there is competent, substantial evidence to support the trial court's finding that there was no meeting of the minds on the essential elements necessary to form a contractual partnership. ... The record clearly reflects that Kenneth failed to sustain his burden of proving the existence of a binding contract. ...

Specifically, Kenneth failed to identify such essential terms as the parties to the contract, or the contract's duration. Indefiniteness regarding the duration of an agreement can be fatal to its enforceability as a binding contract. ... In order to be binding, a contract must also be definite and certain as to the parties' obligations to one another. ...However, Kenneth failed to define the parties' corresponding rights and duties. Kenneth could not even recall the financial specifics of the alleged partnership: whether the partnership profits would be gross or net; split equally; stated as revenue, profit or income.

There was no discussion concerning the duration of the alleged oral agreements. Kenneth asserts that his agreement was for at least as long as the term of the six underlying service contracts. However, three of these did not even exist until two to three years after the car conversation.

A partnership is only established when both parties contribute to the capital or labor of the business, have a mutuality of interest in both profits and losses, and agree to share in the assets and liabilities of the business. ... To establish a partnership, there must be a "community of interest in performance of a common purpose, joint control or right of control, joint propriety of interest in subject matter, right to share in the profits, and duty to share in any losses which may be sustained." ... These requirements are strictly construed and the absence of even one is fatal to the finding of a partnership. Here the record does not show a joint proprietary interest because Kenneth and his father never

agreed to work exclusively together in obtaining cable contracts. In fact, in mid-1983, Kenneth represented one of BESI's competitors, Telesat, without the knowledge of Jacques. Interestingly, Kenneth did not share with Jacques or BESI the resulting commission profits. Further, Kenneth did not share in any of the losses of his alleged partnership. Additionally, Kenneth failed to report the income he received from BESI as partnership income and never received a partnership K-1 for his income tax returns. More importantly, there was never any discussion concerning the distribution of partnership gains, losses, payment of business loans, payment of overhead costs, how to dissolve the partnership or the distribution of assets. ...

There is clearly competent, substantial evidence in the record to support the trial court's conclusion that there was no meeting of the minds on the elements essential to a contractual partnership. Thus, it is the duty of this court to affirm the order below. ... Accordingly, we affirm the final judgment entered in favor of the appellees in all respects.

Affirmed.

---

of both general partners and limited partners comprise a **limited partnership**. General partners typically have unlimited personal liability for the debts and liabilities of a partnership, whereas limited partners risk no more than their investment. Limited partnerships and limited liability limited partnerships are discussed in Chapter 3 of this text.

Registered Limited Liability Partnership

Since the mid-1990s statutes of most states have provided for the formation of **limited liability partnerships (LLPs)**. These entities are very similar to general partnerships with one important distinction. Under most circumstances, partners of a general partnership are personally liable for the debts and obligations of the partnership—partners of an LLP are not. LLPs are generally provided for as an

---

limited partnership A partnership formed by general partners (who run the business and have liability for all partnership debts) and limited partners (who partly or fully finance the business, take no part in running it, and have no liability for partnership debts beyond the money they put in or promise to put in).

limited liability partnership A partnership in which the partners have less than full liability for the actions of other partners, but full liability for their own actions.

election under the partnership act adopted by each state. This means that they cannot be formed unless a special election is made under the state statutes of the pertinent state. Typically, an LLP must be registered with the secretary of state to be formed. We will return to the subject of LLPs throughout this chapter.

Joint Ventures

Joint ventures and partnerships are very similar, but not identical. They are governed by the same basic legal principles. A joint venture that meets the definition of a partnership may, for certain purposes, be considered a partnership when determining its rights and obligations. The primary difference is that a joint venture is narrower in scope and purpose, and is usually formed for a single transaction or isolated enterprise, whereas a partnership is formed to operate an ongoing concern.

Partnerships in the United States

Partnerships in the United States are fewer in number and earn less than either sole proprietorships or corporations. During 1997, there were approximately 1.75 million partnerships in the United States, with business receipts totaling $1.3 trillion. During the same period, there were over 4.7 million corporations and 17.18 million sole proprietorships, with business receipts of approximately $15.9 trillion and $870 billion, respectively.[4] The number of partners in these partnerships ranged from two partners to several hundred partners.

United States partnerships are formed for a variety of business purposes. During 1997, there were 974,000 partnerships in existence in the finance, insurance, and real estate category, which is by far the largest category of existing partnerships in the United States. The services category ranked second, with 311,000 partnerships, and the wholesale and retail trade category ranked third, with 292,000 partnerships.[5] (See Figure 2-1.)

Law Governing Partnerships

Prior to 1914 partnerships were governed by state statues that codified **common law** and **civil law**. In 1914 the **Commission on Uniform State Laws** approved

---

joint venture Sometimes referred to as a joint adventure; the relationship created when two or more persons combine jointly in a business enterprise with the understanding that they will share in the profits or losses and that each will have a voice in its management. Although a joint venture is a form of partnership, it customarily involves a single business project rather than an ongoing business relationship.

common law 1. Judge-made law (based on ancient customs, mores, usages, and principles handed down through the ages) in the absence of controlling statutory or other enacted law. 2. All the statutory and case law of England and the American colonies before the American Revolution.

civil law 1. Law that originated from ancient Rome rather than from the common law or from canon law. 2. The law governing private rights and remedies as opposed to criminal law, military law, international law, natural law, etc.

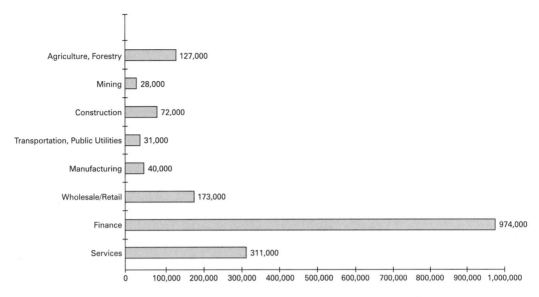

FIGURE 2-1   Number of Partnerships by Industry. From *The Statistical Abstract of the United States (2000)*.

Dividends

Agency and Business Organizations

Partners are considered agents of the partnership and agents of each other—but what exactly does this mean? What is an *agent,* and what authority does he or she have?

The law of agency deals with the principal-agent relationship. In this fiduciary relationship, the agent has the legal authority to act on behalf of the principal. Corporations and other business entities may act as either principal or agent. A basic understanding of the agency relationship is important in all facets of the law of business organizations.

Creating the Agency Relationship

An agency relationship is created by agreement of the principal and agent. The principal agrees to let the agent act on his or her behalf with regard to certain actions, and the agent agrees to act on behalf of the principal, under the principal's control. This agreement may be express or implied.

Express agreements include formal powers of attorney, written contracts, and verbal agreements. When a homeowner, for example, contracts with a realtor to sell his or her home on agreed terms and conditions, the homeowner becomes the principal and the realtor becomes an agent granted **express authority** (in this case by written agreement) to act on the principal's behalf. The homeowner maintains control over the realtor. He or she must approve any contract presented by the realtor for the purchase of the home, and the realtor may not sell the home without the homeowner's consent.

commission on uniform state laws   An organization that, along with the American Law Institute, proposes various Model Acts and Uniform Acts for adoption by the states.

express authority   Authority delegated to an agent by words that expressly, plainly, and directly authorize him or her to perform a delegated act.

In contrast to express authority, **implied authority** needs neither a written contract nor a verbal agreement. An example would be an office manager, whose responsibility for the day-to-day management of an office *implies* the authority to purchase routine office supplies. Thus, the manager's authority to order paper for the photocopier is implied by the manager's title, rather than a specific agreement pertaining to the photocopier paper.

Agent Authority

An agent's authority is his or her power to act on behalf of the principal for the principal's benefit. This means that the authority for the action must come from the principal, not the agent. In addition to being express or implied, the authority may be actual or apparent.

Actual authority is the authority that is actually granted to the agent, whether express or implied. A car salesman has actual authority to sell cars off the car lot for a price within a specified range.

Apparent authority is that authority which a third party may reasonably assume the agent possesses—in other words, authority that the agent *apparently* possesses. Apparent authority includes authority that the principal knowingly permits the agent to exercise as well as authority the agent represents as holding. A corporation's president has apparent authority to enter the corporation into contracts.

Duties of Principals and Agents

Agents owe a duty of loyalty, honesty, and fair dealings in all matters concerning the agency and the agent's representation of the principal's interests. The agent must act in good faith and in the best interests of the principal. The agent cannot act in his or her own best interests to the detriment of the principal.

The agent's exact duties to the principal depend, in part, on the agreement between the principal and agent and the scope of the authority conferred upon the agent. The agent is under a duty to act only as authorized by the principal and may be personally liable for losses or damages incurred by actions taken not within the scope of the agency agreement.

Liability for Acts by the Agent

In general, the principal is responsible for all authorized actions taken by the agent on his or her behalf. In addition, the principal is liable to third parties for unauthorized acts of his or her agent when those acts are done for the principal in the course of the agent's regular duties that fall within the actual or apparent scope of the agency.

When an agent commits a tort (such as negligence or battery) or otherwise causes a third party to incur harm or damages as a result of the agent's actions, either the agent or the principal may be liable to the third party depending on the circumstances. Generally, a principal will be liable for torts committed by an agent if that agent was acting within the scope of the agency agreement. The principal will generally not be responsible for torts committed by an agent who is an independent contractor, since this type of agent is expected to use his or her own judgment and is not under the control of the principal even when acting on behalf of the principal.

All types of business organizations act through their agents. Sole proprietors hire employees who act as their agents. Partners are agents of one another and of the partnership. Corporations are entities that must, by necessity, act through their agents. Officers, directors, and corporate employees may all serve as agents of a corporation.

---

implied authority Actual power given by a principal to his or her agent, which necessarily follows from the express authority that is given; authority that is necessary, usual, and proper to accomplish the main authority that is expressly conferred.

actual authority In the law of agency, the right and power to act that a principal (often an employer) intentionally gives to an agent (often an employee) or at least allows the agent to believe has been given. This includes both express and implied authority.

apparent authority Authority an agent appears to have, judged by the words or actions of the person who gave the authority or by the agent's own words or actions. You may be liable for the actions of a person who has apparent authority to act for you.

the *Uniform Partnership Act (UPA),* which was designed to codify existing statutory and common law,[6] and recommended it for adoption by all state legislatures. The American Bar Association approved the UPA in 1915. It was adopted by nearly every state in the country.

In 1987 work began on revising the UPA. In 1994 a revised version was approved by the American Bar Association House of Delegates. This newer version is commonly referred to as the *Revised Uniform Partnership Act (RUPA).*

Again, in 1996 and 1997, major changes came about in partnership law. The RUPA was amended to include provisions for the election of limited liability partnerships. These amendments were largely reactive changes—an attempt to codify and provide a uniform model for changes that had already been made by several states. By 1996 over 40 states had already adopted limited liability provisions in their general partnership acts.

Adoption of a uniform law by the Commission on Uniform State Laws does not constitute the passing of a law. Rather, uniform laws are laws that are recommended for adoption by each state in the country. State legislatures *may* adopt uniform laws in whole or in part, or they may choose not adopt them at all. As of 2000, every state in the country except Louisiana has adopted the UPA or the RUPA, and most states have added provisions for limited liability partnerships to their version of the act. For that reason, our focus in this chapter is on the UPA and the RUPA as amended in 1997. It is always important to consult the state statutes for specific information on partnerships in the state in which you are working. A list of state statues and their origin is included in Section 2.10 of this chapter.

Partnerships are governed mainly by the provisions of the UPA or the RUPA, as modified by the state of domicile, but also by the partnership agreement and common law. The partnership agreement is often considered to be the law of the partnership. Partnerships are governed by the provisions of the partnership agreement so long as those provisions are permissible under the state's partnership law. The UPA or RUPA, as modified by the state of domicile, governs on all issues for which the partnership agreement is silent. Because the partnership agreement is a form of contract, partnerships are subject to contract law. Figure 2-2 summarizes the history of partnership law in the United States.

The Partnership as a Separate Entity

Whereas the sole proprietor's business is considered an extension of the individual, and the corporation is considered to be a separate entity, the exact nature of the partnership is not so readily defined. There are arguments to support both the **aggregate theory**, which suggests that a partnership is the totality of persons engaged in a business, rather than an entity in itself, and the **entity theory**. Under

---

aggregate theory   Theory regarding partnerships suggesting that a partnership is the totality of the partners rather than a separate entity.

entity theory   Theory that suggests that a partnership is an entity separate from its partners, much like a corporation.

Prior to 1914	Partnerships were governed by state statutes based on common law and civil law.
1914	The Commission on Uniform State Laws approved the Uniform Partnership Act and recommended it for adoption by all state legislatures.
1915	The American Bar Association approved the Uniform Partnership Act.
1994	The Revised Uniform Partnership Act was approved by the American Bar Association.
By 1996	Over 40 states had adopted limited liability provisions in their general partnership acts.
1996 and 1997	Revisions were made to the Revised Uniform Partnership Act to add provisions for the election of limited liability partnerships.
2001	Every state except Louisiana has adopted the Uniform Partnership Act or the Revised Uniform Partnership Act.

FIGURE 2-2   History of Partnership Law in the United States

common law the partnership was not considered to be a separate entity, but rather an extension of its partners.

The UPA recognized a partnership as a separate entity for certain purposes. For example, there are specific provisions in the UPA for property ownership and transfer in the name of the partnership, and for the continuance of the partnership after the assignment of a partner's interest. Also, under the UPA partners are charged with a **fiduciary** duty to the partnership itself, in addition to their fiduciary duty to each other. Partnerships are also considered legal entities for purposes of taxation, attachment, licensing, garnishment, liability for tortious injury to third parties, and enforcement of judgments against partnership property.[7]

The aggregate theory applies in many sections of the UPA relating to substantive liabilities and duties of the partners. Most importantly, the act provides that partners are jointly and severally liable on certain obligations.

Unlike its predecessor, the RUPA specifically states that, "[a] partnership is an entity distinct from its partners."[8] This appears to be the modern view, as noted in several recent court cases.

It is important to note that both the UPA and the RUPA serve only as models for the states that have adopted them. State statutes and common law are the final authority on whether a partnership is considered a separate entity or an aggregate of its partners in a particular state.

fiduciary   1. A person who manages money or property for another person and in whom that other person has a right to place great trust. 2. A relationship like that in definition (no. 1). 3. Any relationship between persons in which one person acts for another in a position of trust; for example, lawyer and client or parent and child.

§ 2.2 THE RELATIONSHIP BETWEEN PARTNERS AND OTHERS

Whether the partnership is viewed as an aggregate of its partners or as a separate entity, it must act through its partners when dealing with outside parties. This section examines the unique legal relationship partners have with regard to others when acting on behalf of the partnership and the other partners. First we look at how partners act as agents for the partnership and the statement of authority or denial that may be filed to give notice of each partner's authority (or lack of it) to act on behalf of the partnership. Then we discuss the personal liability of partners.

With a few exceptions, each partner may act on behalf of the partnership when dealing with others concerning partnership business, having actual authority to bind the partnership to contractual relationships with third parties. That authority may be express, stemming from the partnership agreement, or it may be implied, based on the nature of the partnership relationship. In addition, partners have apparent authority to bind the partnership in a contractual relationship so long as the partner *appears* to be acting as an agent of the partnership in accordance with the usual business of the partnership.

Partners as Agents

Partnership law has always considered partners to be agents of the other partners and of the partnership. Acts of any one partner are binding on the partnership so long as the partner's act is apparently undertaken for the purpose of carrying on the ordinary course of the partnership business or businesses of the kind carried on by the partnership. For example, a partner of a partnership formed to own and operate an automobile dealership has apparent authority to enter into contracts to purchase cars from manufacturers and to sell them to customers.

The act of one partner is usually sufficient to bind the partnership, even if that partner is not acting in good faith. The signature of one partner is sufficient to execute any instrument in the name of the partnership, so long as the instrument is executed for the apparent purpose of carrying on, in the usual way, the business of the partnership. Outsiders dealing with a partnership may reasonably assume that a partner has the authority to enter the partnership into a contractual agreement that appears to be in line with the usual business of the partnership.

Acts Requiring Unanimous Consent of the Partners

Certain acts, specifically those that are not within the normal course of business, require unanimous consent of the partners. Ideally, the partnership agreement will outline the types of transactions that require the unanimous consent of the partners. For example, if one partner of a partnership formed to own and operate a bicycle shop were to sell its entire inventory of bicycles to a competitor, the action would require the unanimous consent of all partners. If one partner sold the inventory without the knowledge of the other partners, the sale would not be binding on the partnership.

State statutes set forth important exceptions to the rule that acts of any partner are binding on the partnership. Under the UPA the following acts are not binding on the partnership unless all partners have approved the act:

1. Acts undertaken with a third party who has knowledge that the act is not authorized.[9]
2. Acts not apparently for the carrying on of the business of the partnership in the usual way.[10]
3. Acts to assign the partnership property in trust for creditors or the assignee's promise to pay the debts of the partnership.[11]
4. Acts to dispose of the goodwill of the business.[12]
5. Acts that would make it impossible to carry on the ordinary business of a partnership.[13]
6. Acts to confess a judgment on behalf of the partnership.[14]
7. Acts submitting a partnership claim or liability to arbitration or reference.[15]
8. Acts admitting new partners to the partnership.[16]

There is some room for discretion in determining which acts of the partnership require the consent of all partners, and at times such decisions are made in the courts. The RUPA leaves even more room for discretion, as it relies more heavily on the partnership agreement that is signed by all partners. The partnership agreement will usually set forth exactly what issues must be agreed on by all partners.

Under the RUPA the following actions must have the unanimous consent of all partners to be binding on the partnership:

1. Acts undertaken with a third party who has knowledge, or has received notification, that the act is not authorized.[17]
2. Acts apparently not undertaken for the purpose of carrying on in the ordinary course of the partnership business.[18]

Amending the partnership agreement and adopting limited liability partnership status usually requires unanimous consent of the partners also, unless otherwise specified in the partnership agreement.

Often, when a partnership enters into an agreement with an outside party, the agreement will include provisions indicating certain limitations on the authority of the individual partners. Such an agreement may also provide that the outside party will be notified by the partnership of any changes or additional restrictions placed on the authority of individual partners. An agreement entered into by one partner exceeding such authority will not be binding on the partnership. For example, suppose the agreement of a partnership formed to own and operate a chain of electronics stores limits the spending authority of each partner to $250,000 unless he or she has the approval of all partners, and that all of the partnership's distributors have been given notice of the limitation. A contract between one partner and a distributor to purchase $350,000 worth of computers for the partnership would not be binding on the partnership if the distributor had prior knowledge of the partner's lack of authority.

In *First National Bank and Trust Company of Williston v. Scherr,* the following case, the court found that a partnership and one of its partners were not liable for an unsecured note executed by one partner on behalf of the partnership because the lender was given notice that the signature of two partners was required to bind the partnership to such an obligation.

CASE

Supreme Court of North Dakota.
FIRST NATIONAL BANK AND
TRUST COMPANY OF WILLISTON,
Plaintiff and Appellant,

v.

Albinus SCHERR, individually and
d/b/a Scherr & Scherr, a general partnership,
Defendants and Appellees.

Civ. No. 900091.
March 19, 1991.

... The First National Bank & Trust Company of Williston appealed from a judgment that Albinus Scherr, a partner, and Scherr and Scherr, the partnership, were not liable on a $65,000 note to the Bank signed for the partnership by only one partner, Pius Scherr, contrary to a restriction in the partnership agreement known to the Bank. We affirm.

Pius Scherr and Albinus Scherr started a general partnership to construct and invest in buildings. On September 15, 1981, this new partnership, Scherr and Scherr, opened a checking account at the Bank. The Partnership Checking Account Signature Card, signed by each of the partners, authorized the Bank to accept ... checks, endorsements, notes, ... mortgages or any other instruments for the deposit or withdrawal of funds, for borrowing money and pledging or mortgaging assets of the partnership as security for the payment thereof and for the transaction of any other business with it, when signed by any _____ of the undersigned.

A separate box adjacent to the partners' signatures on the signature card had in it printed instructions, "Number of Signatures Required," and was filled in with a typed "1." This signature card was kept in the checking account files, not the loan files, of the Bank.

Later a written partnership agreement was completed. It was dated, signed, and acknowledged by Pius on October 1, 1981, and by Albinus on December 21, 1981, when a copy was delivered to the Bank. This agreement included a clause restricting the authority of a single partner to engage in certain transactions for the partnership:

> ... Without the written consent of the other partner, neither partner shall on behalf of the partnership borrow or lend money, or make, deliver or accept any commercial paper, or execute any mortgage, security agreement, bond or lease, or purchase or contract to purchase, or sell or contract to sell any property for or of the partnership. ...

The signed copy of the partnership agreement was completed and delivered to the Bank at its request, and was kept in the Bank's loan file for the partnership.

Beginning in November 1981 and continuing into 1984, Scherr and Scherr borrowed large sums from the Bank to acquire property and to construct various buildings in Williston. One venture was construction of a building leased to a Famous Recipe Chicken fast-food franchisee. This project began with a mortgage, signed by both Pius and Albinus, to the Bank on April 29, 1983, for a construction advance of $100,000. Later, Pius alone signed the four notes to the Bank drawing on this short-term loan: ... This loan was soon converted to a $100,000 note secured by a long-term mortgage to the Bank, both dated October 26, 1983, and both signed by Pius and Albinus.

The next day, October 27, Pius Scherr alone signed another short-term partnership note to the

Bank for $65,000. This note was filled in to say, "THE PURPOSE OF THIS LOAN IS: Final construction on Famous Recipe Chicken." The Bank repeatedly renewed this note through May 1985. Each renewal note was signed for the partnership by Pius alone.

The Scherrs defaulted on their Famous Recipe Chicken obligations to the Bank. The Bank foreclosed the $100,000 mortgage, and then sued the Scherrs to collect the $65,000 note. The trial court entered summary judgment for the Bank against Pius, Albinus, and the partnership for the balance due on the $65,000 note and interest. Pius, Albinus, and the partnership appealed. We affirmed the summary judgment against Pius but reversed the summary judgment against Albinus and the partnership. ...

After trial on remand, the trial court determined that Pius was not authorized to sign the unsecured, $65,000 note for the partnership because the Bank "had written knowledge" about the specific restriction on his authority in the partnership agreement and because the Bank "thereafter established a course of conduct of business with the partnership consistent with those restrictions." ...

We recognized that statutes regulate the authority of a partner to act for the partnership. North Dakota has adopted the Uniform Partnership Act, as have nearly all states. ... NDCC 45-06-01 (part) says:

1. Every partner is an agent of the partnership for the purpose of its business, and the act of every partner, including the execution in the partnership name of any instrument, for apparently carrying on in the usual way the business of the partnership ... binds the partnership, unless the partner so acting has in fact no authority to act for the partnership in the particular matter, and the person with whom he is dealing has knowledge of the fact that he has no such authority.

* * *

4. No act of a partner in contravention of a restriction on authority shall bind the partnership to persons having knowledge of the restriction.

... A partner, as an agent of the partnership, normally binds the partnership by executing any instrument that carries on the business of the partnership in the usual way. NDCC 45-06-01(1). But, as with any agent, that is not so if the partner's authority is restricted, and if the restriction is known to the person with whom the partner deals. ...

Many decisions by other courts have ruled that a person cannot recover from a second partner or the partnership for additional transactions with an acting partner after that person had notice of a later restriction on the acting partner's authority. ... These precedents demonstrate that knowledge of a restriction on, or revocation of, an individual partner's authority controls over a preexisting arrangement with a creditor.

In this case, Pius had initial authority to act individually for the partnership in borrowing money from the Bank through the signature card authorization. Afterward, the partnership agreement restricted that authority. When a third person has "previously extended credit" to the principal through the agent "in reliance upon a manifestation from the principal of continuing authority in the agent," that authority can be restricted or revoked by notice to the third person. Restatement (Second) of Agency s 136(2)(a) (1958). ... The question in this case is whether delivery of the written partnership agreement to the Bank was effective notice that Pius's individual authorization had been restricted. The trial court found as a matter of fact that effective notice of restriction had been given.

Under agency principles and the Uniform Partnership Act, the trial court's factual determinations that Pius acted in contravention of a restriction on his authority as a partner, known to the Bank, controls this case. ...

We conclude that the trial court's finding, that the Bank was bound by its knowledge of the restriction in the written partnership agreement delivered to the Bank after the signature card, was not clearly erroneous.

We affirm.

Any one partner can generally transfer partnership property to third parties by an instrument of transfer executed in the partnership name. However, under the RUPA, transfers contrary to a certified copy of a filed statement of partnership authority recorded in the office for recording transfers of that real estate are not binding on the partnership.[19]

Statement of Partnership Authority

The RUPA provides that partners have the option of filing a **statement of authority** with the secretary of state or other appropriate state official. The statement of authority gives public notice of the authority granted or denied certain partners. Pursuant to § 303 of the RUPA the statement of authority must include

- The name of the partnership.
- The street address of its chief executive office and of one office in this state, if there is one.
- The names and mailing addresses of all of the partners or of an agent appointed and maintained by the partnership.
- The names of the partners authorized to execute an instrument transferring real property held in the name of the partnership.

In addition, the statement of authority may set forth the authority, or limitations on the authority, of some or all of the partners to enter into other transactions on behalf of the partnership and any other matter.

A statement of authority that is in full force and effect supplements the authority of a partner to enter into transactions on behalf of the partnership as follows:[20]

1. Except for real estate transfers, a grant of authority in the statement of authority is conclusive in favor of a person who gives value without knowledge to the contrary, so long as and to the extent that a limitation on that authority is not then contained in another filed statement.
2. A grant of authority to transfer real estate held in the name of the partnership contained in a certified copy of a filed statement of partnership authority recorded in the office for recording transfers of that real estate is conclusive in favor of a person who gives value without knowledge to the contrary.

In general, outside parties may rely on the authority granted by a valid statement of authority as binding on the partnership. However, persons transacting business with the partnership are not deemed to know of a limitation on the authority of a partner merely because the limitation is contained in the filed statement.

---

statement of authority A statement filed for public record by the partners of a partnership to expand or limit the agency authority of a partner, to deny the authority or status of a partner or to give notice of certain events such as the dissociation of a partner or the dissolution of the partnership.

Although the filing of a statement of authority is optional, partnerships that routinely transact business such as buying and selling real estate may be required to file a statement by those who wish to transact business with the partnership.

Statement of Denial

In addition to the statement of authority a **statement of denial** may also be filed at the state level on behalf of the partnership. A statement of denial can be filed by a partner or other interested party to contradict the information included in a statement of authority. For example, a withdrawing partner may file a denial of his or her status as a partner.

Liability of Partners

In states that follow the RUPA in this regard, partners have **joint and several** liability for all obligations of the partnership unless otherwise agreed by the claimant or provided by law.[21] This means that any claimant or creditor of the partnership can sue the partners either individually or together, and any partner can be held liable for the entire amount of the damages or obligation.

The partnership's creditors or claimants can look to the individual partners for payment after the partnership's assets have been exhausted. If the debts of a partnership exceed its assets, the creditors of the partnership can collect from the personal assets of all or any one of the partners until their claim has been satisfied. If only one partner has substantial personal assets, that partner can be held responsible for the entire obligation of the partnership, even if the obligation arose from the wrongdoing of another partner. Joint and several liability for the partners of all partnership obligations is one of the biggest drawbacks to forming a partnership.

Partners are not personally liable for the obligations of the partnership in all instances. For example, newer partners are generally not personally liable for obligations arising from action taken prior to their admission to the partnership. In addition, the new limited liability partnership provisions of the RUPA, and the partnership law of most states, provide a new means to limit the personal liability of partners.

Limited Liability Partnerships

A partnership obligation that is incurred while a partnership is operating under an election to be a limited liability partnership is solely the liability of the partnership. The partners have no personal liability for such obligations, and they cannot be required to make additional contributions to the partnership solely to cover

---

statement of denial A statement filed for public record by a partner or other interested party to contradict the information included in a statement of authority.

joint and several Both together and individually. For example, a liability or debt is joint and several if the creditor may sue the debtors either together as a group (with the result that the debtors would have to split the loss) or individually (with the result that one debtor might have to pay the whole thing).

partnership obligations. If the partnership was formed as a general partnership and later elects to become a limited liability partnership, partners will be personally liable for any obligations incurred prior to the partnership's election. The advantages offered to partners by the new limited liability provisions in partnership law are causing many partnerships to elect limited liability partnership status—something that was unavailable prior to the mid-1990s.

§ 2.3 THE RELATIONSHIP AMONG PARTNERS AND BETWEEN PARTNERS AND THE PARTNERSHIP

Partners have a unique relationship both among themselves and with the partnership. This section examines the rights of partners with regard to the partnership property and the rights and duties partners owe to each other and to the partnership.

Partners' Rights in Partnership Assets

Under the UPA each partner was considered a co-owner with the other partners of specific partnership property. Partnership property was held in a **tenancy in partnership**. Each partner had an equal right to possess specific partnership property for partnership purposes, but had no right to possess such property for any other purpose without the consent of the other partners.[22] The RUPA treats partnerships as separate entities. It does not recognize the concept of tenancy in partnership. Rather, the partnership property is considered to be owned by the partnership itself, as an entity separate from the partners. The RUPA states specifically that a partner "is not a co-owner of partnership property and has no interest in partnership property which can be transferred, either voluntarily or involuntarily."[23] This restriction on transfers refers only to the partnership property itself, not to each partner's right to receive income or profits and losses from the partnership property.

Because partnership property is owned by the partnership rather than the individual partners, in states that follow the RUPA, partners cannot transfer their rights to the partnership property. They can, however, transfer their rights to receive income, or profits and losses from the partnership. For example, assume that Andy, Barbara, and Chet are partners in a partnership that owns a $300,000 rental property. Pursuant to the partnership agreement, each partner is entitled to receive $1,000 in rent from the partnership each month. Under the RUPA Barbara could transfer her right to receive $1,000 to her sister to cover a debt. She could not, however, transfer any right to co-own the building itself. She could not transfer a one-third interest in the building to repay a $100,000 debt.

A partner's right in specific partnership property is not assignable except in connection with the assignment of rights of all the partners in the same property, nor is

---

tenancy in partnership Form of ownership provided for under the Uniform Partnership Act whereby all partners are co-owners with the other partners. Each partner has an equal right to possess the property for partnership purposes, but has no right to possess the property for any other purpose without the consent of the other partners.

the right in specific partnership property subject to attachment or execution, except on a claim against the partnership. For example, if Barbara defaulted on the loan to her sister, her sister would have no legal right to the partnership's rental property. She could not force the partnership to sell the property to collect what she is entitled to from Barbara. The rental property could not be assigned or sold to Barbara's sister unless Andy and Chet agreed that it would be in their best interests to sell or assign the rights of the entire partnership in the rental property to her.

Not all states have adopted this view of partnership property. As always, it is important that the pertinent state statutes be consulted.

Partnership Property

Typically, all real or personal property that is initially contributed to the partnership by the partners, all subsequent contributions, and all property acquired with the funds of the partnership is considered partnership property and not property of the individual partners. Accurate partnership records must be kept so that there is no question as to which property is considered partnership property and which property is the personal property of a partner.

Acquisitions of significant partnership property should be approved by unanimous written consent of the partners to alleviate any possible problems in the future. Following is § 204 of the RUPA, which discusses when property is partnership property:

§ 204. WHEN PROPERTY IS PARTNERSHIP PROPERTY

    (a) Property is partnership property if acquired in the name of:
        (1) the partnership; or
        (2) one or more partners with an indication in the instrument transferring title to the property of the person's capacity as a partner or of the existence of a partnership but without an indication of the name of the partnership.
    (b) Property is acquired in the name of the partnership by a transfer to:
        (1) the partnership in its name; or
        (2) one or more partners in their capacity as partners in the partnership, if the name of the partnership is indicated in the instrument transferring title to the property.
    (c) Property is presumed to be partnership property if purchased with partnership assets, even if not acquired in the name of the partnership or of one or more partners with an indication in the instrument transferring title to the property of the person's capacity as a partner of the existence of a partnership.
    (d) Property acquired in the name of one or more of the partners, without an indication in the instrument transferring title to the property of the person's capacity as a partner or of the existence of a partnership and without use of partnership assets, is presumed to be separate property, even if used for partnership purposes.

Figure 2-3 summarizes the characteristics of partnership property under the UPA and the RUPA.

Characteristics under the UPA	*Characteristics under the RUPA*
◆ Each partner is considered a co-owner with the other partners of specific partnership property.	◆ Partnership property is owned by the partnership itself.
◆ Property is held in a tenancy in partnership.	◆ Partners are not considered co-owners of the property.
◆ Each partner has equal right to possess specific partnership property for partnership purposes, but no right to possess for any other purpose without consent of other partners.	◆ Individual partners have no interest in the partnership property itself that can be transferred, either voluntarily or involuntarily.

FIGURE 2-3 Partnership Property

Partners' Rights in Dealing with Each Other

Many rights are granted to partners by state statute. These rights vary by state, and many can be waived or expanded on in the partnership agreement. Some cannot be waived—not even by agreement. To avoid any potential conflicts, the partnership agreement should be carefully drafted to address any desired deviations from the applicable statutes regarding the partners' rights in dealing with each other. Following is a list of typical rights granted to partners by state statute. But, remember, these rights vary by state, and many of them can be modified by the partnership agreement.

1. The right to have a separate account that reflects the partners' contributions, share of the gains, and share of the losses in the partnership assets.
2. The right to an equal share of the partnership profits.
3. The right to be repaid contributions and share equally in the surplus remaining after partnership liabilities are satisfied.
4. The right to reimbursement for certain money spent by the partner on behalf of the partnership.
5. The right of each partner to share equally in the management and conduct of the business.
6. The right of access to the books and records of the partnership.
7. The right to reasonable compensation for services rendered in winding up the partnership affairs.
8. The right to have one's partnership interest purchased by remaining partners after a permissible dissociation from the partnership.

Partners' Rights to a Separate Account Under the RUPA each partner is deemed to have a separate account in an amount equal to the partner's contributions and share of the partnership profits, less the partner's distributions received and the partner's share of partnership losses.[24] This is generally the manner for accounting for each partner's interest in the partnership in states following either the RUPA or the UPA, although more details or a different method can be set forth in the partnership agreement.

Partners' Rights to an Equal Share of Partnership Profits   Under the RUPA each partner is entitled to an equal share of the partnership's profits and is chargeable a proportionate share of the losses. This rule is substantially the same as the rule established under the UPA. It is important to note, however, that this is a right that can be—and often is—revised in a partnership agreement. To offer the partnership maximum flexibility, it is common for partners to make contributions to the partnership in unequal amounts. In that event, profits and losses are usually not shared equally among all partners, but rather in proportion to their contributions. Any arrangements which suit the partners with regard to sharing the profits and losses of the partnership can be made in the partnership agreement.

Partners' Rights to Reimbursement   Certain partners may be called on to spend their own money on behalf of the partnership. In almost every instance the partner has the right to be reimbursed for these expenditures. Most of these expenditures are considered to be loans to the partnership made by the partner and must be repaid with interest, which accrues from the date of payment or advance. The default rules under the RUPA and the UPA provide for reimbursement when partners put forth their own money for payments made (1) in the ordinary course of business of the partnership or for the preservation of its business or property, or (2) as an advance to the partnership beyond the amount of the partner's agreed contribution.[25] Details regarding repayment of loans made to the partnership by a partner generally are set forth in the partnership agreement, but both the RUPA and the UPA make it clear that repayment must be made with interest.

Partners' Rights to Participate in Management   Each partner is granted by statute the right to participate in the management of the partnership. However, because full management participation by every partner is often not practical or desirable, the partnership agreement may appoint a managing partner or a managing partnership committee. Note that the right to participate in the management of the partnership must be specifically waived by any partner giving up that right.

Partners' Rights to Access to Books and Records   Unless otherwise specified in the partnership agreement, the partnership must keep its books and records, if any, at its principal place of business or chief executive office, and these books and records must be available to each partner and his or her agents and attorneys, within reason.

Partners' Rights to Wind up Partnership Business   Both the UPA and the RUPA provide that partners who have not caused a wrongful dissolution or dissociation of the partnership have the right to **wind up** the partnership business. Any partner may also petition for a court-supervised winding up if he or she feels it necessary.

Whereas partners are typically not entitled to receive payment for their services rendered to the partnership, when a partnership dissolves, any partner who is charged with the duty of winding up the affairs of the partnership is entitled to receive fair compensation for this service.

Figure 2-4 lists the rights of partners under the UPA and the RUPA. Note that some rights can be altered in the partnership agreement, and others cannot.

Under the UPA	*Under the RUPA*
◆ The right of access to the books and records of the partnership.	◆ The right of access to the books and records of the partnership.
◆ The right to a formal account as to partnership affairs (under certain circumstances).	◆ The right to dissociate from the partnership upon giving proper notice.
◆ The right to co-own specific partnership property as a tenant in partnership.	
Unless Altered in the Partnership Agreement	*Unless Altered in the Partnership Agreement*
◆ The right to be repaid contributions made to the partnership, after the liabilities of the partnership have been paid.	◆ The right to have a separate account reflecting the partners' contributions, share of the gains, and share of the losses in partnership assets.
◆ The right to an equal share of the partnership profits.	◆ The right to an equal share of the partnership profits.
◆ The right to reimbursement for certain money spent by the partner on behalf of the partnership.	◆ The right to reimbursement for certain money spent by the partner on behalf of the partnership.
◆ The right to share equally in the management and conduct of the business.	◆ The right to share equally in the management and conduct of the business.
◆ The right to repayment of loans made to the partnership, with interest.	◆ The right to repayment of loans made to the partnership, with interest.
◆ The right to reasonable compensation for services rendered in winding up the partnership affairs.	◆ The right to reasonable compensation for services rendered in winding up the partnership affairs.

FIGURE 2-4   Rights of Partners

wind up   Finish current business, settle accounts and turn property into cash in order to end a corporation or a partnership and split up the assets.

Unless Altered in the Partnership Agreement	Unless Altered in the Partnership Agreement
◆ The right to wind up the affairs of the partnership on dissolution.	◆ The right to wind up the affairs of the partnership on dissolution.
◆ The right to be repaid contributions made to the partnership, after the liabilities of the partnership have been paid.	◆ The right to have the partner's interest purchased by remaining partners after a permissible dissociation from the partnership.

FIGURE 2-4 (*continued*)

Partners' Duties in Dealing with Each Other

Partners' duties are also prescribed by statute. Although many of the prescribed duties cannot be amended by the partnership agreement, they can be clarified by it. Following is a list of duties typically required by statute or by partnership agreement:

1. The duty of partners to contribute toward losses sustained by the firm according to each partner's share in the profits.
2. The duty of partners to work for the partnership without remuneration.
3. The duty of partners to submit to a vote of the majority of the partners when differences arise among the partners as to any ordinary matters connected with the partnership affairs.
4. The duty of partners to provide information concerning the partnership to the other partners.
5. The fiduciary duty to all partners and the partnership.

Partners' Duties to Contribute to Partnership Losses Unless the partnership agreement specifically states otherwise, each partner has the duty to contribute equally to any losses and liabilities incurred by the partnership.

Partners' Duties to Work without Remuneration Partners are not entitled to remuneration for services performed for the partnership, except for reasonable compensation for services rendered in winding up the partnership business. This stipulation can, of course, be revised in the partnership agreement in the event that the participation of the partners is unequal. Often one partner contributes only capital or other resources to the partnership whereas another may devote his or her full-time services to the business. In such an event the partnership agreement could be worded so that the working partner receives compensation from the partnership business.

Partners' Duties to Submit to a Vote of the Majority Unless the partnership agreement states otherwise, the vote of the majority of the partners will be the deciding factor in resolving a disagreement among the partners.

Partners' Duties to Render Information   For partners to protect their rights in the partnership, it is important that they be kept informed of all important matters concerning the partnership business. Both the UPA and the RUPA provide that each partner has a duty to the other partners to provide true and full information in all things concerning the partnership so as to enable the partners to exercise their rights and duties under the partnership agreement or state statute.

Partners' Fiduciary Duties to Partnership and Other Partners   Under the UPA and common law, partners have always owed a fiduciary duty to each other. Courts have held that partners owe one another the duty of the finest loyalty. Many forms of conduct permissible in a workaday world for those acting at arm's length are forbidden to those bound by fiduciary ties. "Not honesty alone, but the punctilio of an honor the most sensitive is then the standard of behavior."[26] For example, suppose one partner of a real estate management partnership receives an offer for the partnership to manage a high rise apartment building. That partner has a duty to present the offer to the other partners for their consideration and cannot accept the offer personally to become the sole manager of the high rise. To do so would be a breach of the partner's fiduciary duty.

Section 404 of the RUPA states specifically that the fiduciary duty partners owe to the partnership and other partners includes the duty of loyalty and the duty of care. In general, a *duty of loyalty* means that partners must be loyal to the partnership and other partners and not engage in outside activities that compete with or are detrimental to the partnership. A *duty of care* means that partners must not behave in a manner that is considered negligent or reckless and must not engage in intentional misconduct or knowingly commit a violation of the law when conducting partnership business.

These duties may be further defined or expanded on in the partnership agreement, but they cannot be diminished or eliminated.

§ 2.4 ADVANTAGES OF DOING BUSINESS AS A GENERAL PARTNERSHIP

In many respects, the advantages of doing business as a partnership are similar to the advantages offered by the sole proprietorship, yet partnerships offer some unique advantages as well. In this section, we discuss some of those unique advantages, including the flexibility of the management of the partnership, the minimal formalities and regulatory and reporting requirements, and the low cost of organizing a partnership. We also examine the unique income tax benefits available to partners and the expanded base from which capital may be raised for the partnership This section concludes with a look at the advantages offered by limited liability partnerships

Participation and Flexibility in Management

Unless one or more partners waive their rights, every partner has equal power and authority to manage the partnership affairs. Partners of smaller partnerships may find this appealing if the partners have varied backgrounds and areas of expertise and all wish to actively participate. All partners are allowed to act freely on behalf of the partnership, with few restrictions.

Larger partnerships, on the other hand, are allowed the flexibility of putting the management of the partnership into the hands of the best individual or group of individuals for the job.

Minimal Formalities and Regulatory and Reporting Requirements

Although partnerships are governed by statute, the required statutory formalities are few. A concise written partnership agreement is a good investment in almost any circumstance. However, it is not required, and a partnership may be formed by a verbal agreement between two or more people and can be implied by behavior.

State statutes vary with regard to partnership filing requirements and other formalities, and the pertinent state statutes must always be reviewed and complied with. Most states do not require partnership registration with the secretary of state or other state official before commencing business. However, a certificate of assumed name or other similar document is usually required when the partnership is going to transact business under an assumed name, trade name, or fictitious name. If the partnership name consists of the names of the partners, it usually is not considered a fictitious name that must be recorded in compliance with a statute requiring registration of fictitious partnership names. However, some state statutes provide that the name of a partner followed by "& Co." or "Co." may require the filing of an application for certificate for assumed name, trade name, or fictitious name, or other similar document.[27]

A number of states require the registration of every partnership with the appropriate state official, regardless of whether the partnership is using a fictitious name. Typically, a certificate setting forth the name of the partnership, its principal place of business, and the names of all partners is filed with the secretary of state or the county clerk of the county in which the partnership's principal place of business is located.

A partnership, especially a limited liability partnership, transacting business in any state other than its state of domicile may be required to register with the secretary of state of the foreign state as a foreign partnership. Again, a thorough review of the pertinent statutes must be made to ensure that all statutory requirements with regard to fictitious name filings, partnership registrations, and qualification of foreign partnerships are complied with.

Although it is an option rather than a requirement, a partnership in a state that follows the RUPA closely may find it advantageous to file a statement of partnership authority with the secretary of state or other designated state authority that specifies which partners are authorized to execute real estate transfer documents, and which contains other information concerning the authority of individual partners to act on behalf of the partnership.

Any business carried on by a partnership that requires licensing must be licensed by the partnership or by the individual partners. Typically, no special licensing requirements are imposed on a partnership because it is a partnership; rather, the licensing requirements are imposed because of the nature of the business transacted by the partnership.

Partnerships are required to file a United States Partnership Return of Income, which reports the income and distributions of the partnership. A tax return also may be required at the state level.

Low Cost of Organization

There are no minimum capital requirements for starting a partnership, and the startup costs, including any required state filing fees, tend to be lower than those for corporations.

Income Tax Benefits

The partners of a general partnership are taxed in much the same way as sole proprietors. The net income or loss of the partnership is passed through to the partners, according to the partnership agreement or statute. The partnership is required to file a Partnership Return (Form 1065) annually with the Internal Revenue Service, but no income tax is owed by the partnership itself. Rather, the partnership's return indicates the income earned by the partnership and allocated to the individual partners. The individual partners must report their partnership income on a Schedule K-1 filed with their personal tax returns and pay income tax based on their personal income tax rates. The principal tax benefit to the partners over doing business as a corporation is that a corporation is subject to a first tax on its income, and then a second tax is paid by the shareholders when corporate after-tax income is distributed to them. A partnership, on the other hand, is not taxable as a separate entity, so that only a single tax is paid by the partners on income derived from the partnership.

Also, because the income of the partnership flows through to the individual partners, if the partnership experiences a net loss, each partner's share of that loss may be written off on the partner's individual income tax return, offsetting any other income. The partnership allocation of profits and losses must, however, comply with the substantial economic effect requirements of the Internal Revenue Service.

Diversified Capital Resources

Although partnerships are generally restricted to the personal capital of the partners and the capital that they are able to borrow based on their personal wealth, the partnership does have an advantage over a sole proprietorship, in that there is a broader base from which to obtain capital. Simply put, more than one person is contributing to the business; therefore, more is potentially available.

Limited Personal Liability

The limitations on personal liability offered to partners of limited liability partnerships gives those partners a distinct advantage over partners of other general partnerships and over sole proprietors. Partners of a limited liability partnership can experience all of the advantages of doing business as a partnership, without risking their personal wealth and assets.

§ 2.5   DISADVANTAGES OF DOING BUSINESS AS A PARTNERSHIP

Some of the same partnership characteristics that present advantages to the partners in certain circumstances, can be considered disadvantages under other circumstances. This section discusses the disadvantages of doing business as a partnership. We start with the partnership characteristic that is often considered to be the most significant disadvantage—the unlimited liability exposure of the partners. Next, we look at the loosely structured management of the partnership, the partnership's lack of business continuity, and the difficulty in transferring a proprietary interest in a partnership. We also investigate the possible hardships in raising capital for a partnership and the possibly substantial legal and organizational expenses. This section concludes with an examination of the potential income tax disadvantages to partners.

Unlimited Liability

One of the strongest arguments against doing business as a general partnership is the unlimited liability characteristic of the partnership. Partners in a partnership that is not a registered limited liability partnership are personally liable for the debts, obligations, and torts committed by or on behalf of the partnership. This disadvantage is compounded by the fact that all partners are liable for the acts of any one partner who is acting on behalf of the partnership. Wealthy partners may be at a disadvantage when the liabilities of the partnership exceed the partnership assets and creditors turn to the individual partners for payment.

In addition to electing limited liability partnership status, there are ways to reduce the probability that the partners will have to personally cover the debts and liabilities of the partnership. The partnership may, for instance, purchase insurance to cover many potential liabilities, and third parties may agree in their contracts with the partnership to limit their recovery to partnership assets. However, not all liabilities are insurable, and lenders may not work with a partnership without the personal guarantees of the partners.

Loosely Structured Management

Although the loosely structured management of a partnership may be an advantage under certain circumstances, it may also work as a definite disadvantage to other partnerships. The number and personalities of the partners can greatly affect the success, or failure, of the loosely structured management prescribed for partnerships by statute. Because the majority rules, in the event of disagreement regarding management decisions, a stalemate can result if the partnership consists of an even number of partners. This, in turn, can lead to the partnership's inability to act. The fact that each partner can act on behalf of the partnership can also cause problems when partners disagree on fundamental issues.

A carefully constructed partnership agreement that delegates the authority to make management decisions can alleviate some of these problems when there is disagreement among the partners, but the partnership agreement cannot account for all possible contingencies.

Lack of Business Continuity

Under the UPA, unless otherwise specified in the partnership agreement or other written agreement among the partners, the partnership dissolves whenever one partner ceases to be a partner, for whatever reason. This can be a definite disadvantage for a going concern, as the dissolution may be untimely and costly to the remaining partners.

Upon the death of a partner, the deceased partner's right to specific partnership property will pass to the remaining partners, who have the right to possess the property for partnership purposes. However, the deceased partner's financial interests in the partnership pass to the deceased partner's heirs. Unless addressed in a carefully worded agreement, the remaining partners often have to liquidate the partnership assets to distribute the deceased partner's interest to his or her heirs.

Under the RUPA, it is much easier for the partnership to continue after the death or withdrawal of one partner. However, if the partnership is a **partnership at will**, the partnership may be dissolved whenever one of the partners decides to withdraw and dissolve the partnership.

Difficulty in Transferring Partnership Interest

Unlike corporate shareholders, who may generally sell their shares of stock without restriction, a partner's entire right to the partnership is not freely transferable. Although a partner may sell or assign his or her rights to receive profits and losses from the partnership business, the right to specific partnership property may not be sold or assigned unless sold or assigned by all partners. In addition, a partner's right to participate in the management of the partnership is not assignable. Therefore, a partner's share of the partnership may not simply be sold to another individual who will become a partner.

Limited Ability to Raise Capital

Unlike a corporation, a partnership may not sell shares of stock to raise capital to run its business. The capital of the partnership usually consists of contributions from the partners and any loans obtained based on the partners' personal wealth and the partnership assets. This can be a great deterrent to businesses that have substantial initial capital requirements.

Legal and Organizational Expenses

Although the legal and organizational expenses involved in forming and operating a partnership are usually less than those involved in forming and operating a corporation, these costs can still be substantial. In addition to any necessary state filing fees for the partnership certificate and a certificate of assumed or fictitious name, there are typically significant legal fees associated with the drafting of the partnership

partnership at will   Partnership formed for an indefinite period of time, without a designated date for termination.

agreement. Because of the diverse nature of partnerships, a good partnership agreement will usually require significant and specific drafting, and the initial legal fees can be considerable.

Tax Disadvantages

Again, as with the sole proprietorship, partnership income flows through to the partners, to be taxed at each partner's personal income tax rate. If the partnership is earning a substantial income, partners with other income who are already in a high income tax bracket may be at a disadvantage.

In addition, the individual partners are responsible for the income tax on their share of the profits of the partnership, even if those profits are retained in the partnership business and not distributed to the partners. Under this scenario, it is possible that partners will be required to pay more in income tax than they received from the partnership in a given year.

Figure 2-5 lists the advantages and disadvantages of doing business as a partnership.

Advantages	Disadvantages
◆ All partners are entitled to manage the partnership. ◆ Maximum flexibility in management. ◆ Minimal formalities and regulatory and reporting requirements. ◆ Low cost of organization. ◆ No double taxation. ◆ Diversified pool of capital resources. ◆ Partners of limited liability partnership may limit their personal liability.	◆ Under most circumstances partners may be held personally responsible for the debts and obligations of the partnership. ◆ Lack of business continuity. ◆ Difficulty in transferring interest in partnership. ◆ Limited ability to raise capital for the partnership business. ◆ Significant legal and organizational expenses. ◆ Partnership taxation may not be beneficial for all partners under all circumstances.

FIGURE 2-5   Advantages and Disadvantages of Doing Business as a Partnership

§ 2.6 ORGANIZATION AND MANAGEMENT OF A GENERAL PARTNERSHIP

The organization and management of partnerships can vary significantly depending on the partners of the partnership and other circumstances. The parameters of the organization and management are defined by the statutes of the state of domicile and by the partnership agreement.

This section focuses on the agreement among the partners, beginning with a look at the management and control of the partnership and a brief discussion of oral partnership agreements. It then discusses the essential elements of the partnership agreement, and includes specific examples of partnership agreement provisions.

Management and Control

Although all partners have equal rights to manage the partnership, this is not always a practical or desirable method of management, and these rights may be altered in the agreement among the partners. Often, especially with larger partnerships, the partners will delegate the management of the partnership to one or more partners. This delegation of the right to manage must be granted by all partners, and no partner can be denied the right to manage the partnership unless that right is waived.

When one partner is delegated to see to the management of the partnership, that partner is usually referred to as the *managing partner*. Management also may be delegated to a management committee, a senior or voting partner, or one or more other partners named in the partnership agreement.

Often, the partners each agree to be responsible for a different area of partnership management. For example, one partner may be in charge of the partnership accounting, while another takes care of public relations and promotion. Regardless of the style of management decided upon by the partners, it is highly desirable that the management duties of each partner be fully described in the partnership agreement.

The general rule regarding a dispute in the internal management affairs of the partnership is that the decision is made by a majority of the partners.[28] There are, however, many exceptions to that rule. For example, acts taken outside of the ordinary course of business of the partnership require the unanimous consent of all partners, as do acts not in accordance with the partnership agreement and acts amending the partnership agreement. Acts not in accordance with the partnership agreement and amendments to the partnership agreement also require the unanimous consent of all partners.

Another circumstance in which the majority does not rule is when the partnership agreement provides an alternate method for resolving disputes among the partners. For instance, the managing partner or partners may be given authority to make the final decision in the event of a disagreement among the partners. The partnership agreement may also prescribe arbitration for certain disagreements among the partners.

References to a majority of the partners generally do not take into account the disproportionate percentages of interest that the partners may hold. The partnership agreement may contain provisions fixing a different method for determining what is the majority of the partners, such as the contributors of a majority of the partnership capital.

Managing partners and other partners who are often required to spend a significant amount of their time managing the business and assets of the partnership are usually compensated by way of a salary and paid expenses by the partnership. This salary is over and above any profits to which the managing partner is entitled pursuant to the other terms of the partnership agreement. Any salaries paid to partners for their management of the partnership should be specifically designated as such on the books and records of the partnership.

Oral Partnership Agreements

Although the partnership agreement is fundamental to the partnership, the agreement may be oral, or a partnership may exist with no express agreement between the parties whatsoever, so long as all the elements of a partnership are present. Although an oral partnership agreement may be legal and binding, it is inadvisable, because it is difficult to prove the terms of an oral partnership agreement—or even that a partnership exists—when there is no written agreement.

Certain types of oral partnership agreements may be prohibited by law. For instance, under the **Statute of Frauds**, it is impossible to form an oral agreement for a period longer than one year.

Although it is possible to have a binding oral partnership agreement, attorneys almost always advise their clients to put their agreement into a formal, written contract to avoid future disputes.

Partnership Agreements

The partnership agreement, or *partnership articles,* as that document is sometimes referred to, is the contract entered into by all partners setting forth the agreed-upon terms of the partnership. The partnership agreement is considered the "law of the partnership" and will be enforced as such, unless any of the terms of the partnership agreement are contrary to law. The partnership agreement is a contract among the partners and thus is subject to contract law.

Following is a discussion of some of the various matters that should be contained in a partnership agreement. The sample paragraphs used here are only a small representation of the types of clauses that may be included in a partnership agreement. See § 2.9 of this text for a checklist of items to be considered when drafting a partnership agreement, and appendix J-1 for a partnership agreement form.

Names and Addresses of Partners   The full name and address of each partner should be included in the first section of the partnership agreement.

Name of Partnership   This section of the partnership agreement should set forth the full name of the partnership. The name of the partnership may, but need not, include any or all of the names of the partners, or it may be a totally fictitious name. If a fictitious name is used, a certificate of assumed or fictitious name may be required.[29] If a limited liability partnership is being formed, the words "Limited Liability Partnership" or the abbreviation "LLP" may be a required part of the name.

Purpose of Partnership   A specific purpose may be set forth in this agreement section, or a general purpose, such as the one shown in the following example, may be

---

statute of frauds   Any of various state laws, modeled after an old English law, that require many types of contracts (such as contracts for the sale of real estate or of goods over a certain dollar amount, contracts to guarantee another's debt, and certain long-term contracts) to be signed and in writing to be enforceable in court.

stated. This section may also set limitations on business activities and on partners' competitive business activities.

EXAMPLE: Partnership Purpose

The partnership shall have a general business purpose and may exercise all powers now or hereafter conferred by the laws of the State of _____ to partnerships.

Address of Principal Place of Doing Business In addition to setting forth the address of the principal place of business of the partnership, this section may also contain a provision designating the governing law under which the terms of the partnership agreement must be applied and construed.

Term of Partnership Agreement This section of the partnership agreement may designate a date upon which the partnership will terminate, such as in the following example, or it may designate a condition upon which such termination shall occur. For instance, if a partnership is formed for the development and sale of several specific pieces of real estate, the partnership agreement may designate that the partnership will terminate when all of the designated real estate has been sold.

A partnership that is formed without designating a date for termination of the partnership, or without stating a condition under which the partnership will terminate, is a *partnership at will*. This type of partnership continues as long as the parties give their mutual consent. The partnership at will may be terminated when agreed to by the partners, or upon the withdrawal of any one partner.

When a partnership for a fixed term or particular undertaking is continued after the termination of such term or particular undertaking without any express agreement, the partnership continues as if it were a partnership at will.

EXAMPLE: Duration of Partnership

The partnership shall exist for a term of _____ years, commencing on _____, and terminating on _____, unless terminated sooner by mutual consent of the partners or by operation of this agreement.

Contribution of Partners This section should be drafted with care, because it may be crucial to the division of the profits and losses of the partnership and the distribution of assets upon the partnership's termination. This section may include the amount of contribution made by each partner, the date the contribution is made to the partnership, the form of contribution, and valuation of contributions other than cash. In addition, provisions for any interest to be paid on contributions, adjustments in contributions required from each partner, and provisions for loans to the partnership by the partners may be included in this section.

EXAMPLE: Contribution to Partnership Capital—Parties and Shares

The capital of the partnership shall be $_____, which shall consist of the estimated value of the combined real and personal assets contributed to the business as of _____, ___. _____ shall contribute ___ % of this value, and _____ shall contribute ___ % of this value. Partners shall share in the profits and losses of the business in the above proportions.[30]

Additional Contribution Requirements This section should set forth the procedure for establishing the necessity of additional capital contributions, the amount of those contributions required from each partner, the notification requirements for additional contribution, and the redistribution of partnership interest for nonproportional contributions.

Assets of Partnership This section should identify the assets of the partnership, including a valuation of the assets, the manner for handling the control of assets and accountability therefore, and the distribution of assets. Following is an example of a paragraph that may be used with an attached schedule, which may be updated from time to time.

EXAMPLE: Description of Assets by Attached List

All property, both personal and real, specifically set forth in Exhibit ___ attached to this agreement and made a part of it, is deemed by the partners to be partnership property and shall be and constitute the assets of the partnership as of the date of this agreement. The items of partnership property set forth in the attached Exhibit ___ are set forth by way of specification and not by way of limitation, and may be added to subsequently at the discretion of the partners.[31]

EXAMPLE: Distribution of Assets in Proportion to Investment

On the termination or reorganization of the partnership, the assets of the partnership shall be used to discharge all outstanding indebtedness of the partnership, and the balance of the assets shall be distributed among the partners in proportion to their respective interests in the partnership.[32]

Goodwill Evaluation to Be Considered on Distribution of Assets The goodwill of a partnership may be considered a sizable asset to a continuing business. However, it may be no asset at all to a partnership that is terminating. This section should set forth the conditions under which the goodwill of the partnership will be considered as a part of the evaluation of the assets of the partnership, and set forth the formula to be used in that evaluation of goodwill when applicable.

Liability This section may restate and amend many of the provisions for partner liability found in the statutes. It may also be used to address more specific conditions regarding liability among the partners. It should address the partners' liability to one another, the partners' liability to third parties, and the liability of the partnership. If the partnership will be electing limited liability partnership status, a statement to that effect should be included.

Distribution of Profits and Losses This is another crucial section of the partnership agreement, which should address all matters regarding distribution of the profits and losses of the partnership, including how the division of profits and losses is to be made. In this section, the partners may also specifically guarantee profits to any one partner and set forth how salaries may be an element of profits for distribution. The partners may also set forth a schedule for distribution, establish reserve funds for partnership expenses prior to distribution, and set limitations on distribution of profits or liability for losses by one partner and distributions made to the partnership.

Following are examples of paragraphs that may be used when equal distribution among all partners is desired or when proportional distribution is desired, respectively:

EXAMPLE: Equal Distribution of Profits and Losses

Each partner shall be entitled to an equal share of the net profits of the business. All losses occurring in the course of business shall be borne equally unless the losses are due to the willful neglect or default, and not the mere mistake or error, of any of the partners, in which case the loss so incurred shall be borne solely by the partner or partners whose neglect or default caused the loss. Distribution of profits shall be made on the ___ day of _____ each year.

EXAMPLE: Proportionate Distribution of Profits and Losses

_____ has contributed $_____ to the capital of the partnership, which is equal to ___ % of the partnership interest, and _____ has contributed $_____ to the capital of the partnership, which is equal to ___ % of the partnership interest. Each partner shall be entitled to a share of the partnership net profits or shall be assessed for the partner's share of the partnership losses in direct proportion to the partner's partnership interest.[33]

Indemnity Provisions This section should set forth the partners' agreement for indemnification of their obligations on behalf of the partnership.

EXAMPLE: Indemnity by Partnership—Obligation of Existing Partners

Each partner shall be indemnified by the partnership on all obligations incurred by that partner in the normal course of conducting partnership business. The partners are limited by the provisions of Section _____ of this agreement in the scope of obligations they shall incur on behalf of the partnership.[34]

Duties of Partners This section should set forth the duties of the partners in as much detail as practical, and address the specific responsibilities of each partner and the approximate amount of time required of each partner.

EXAMPLE: Duties of Partners—Division of Duties

The duties of the partners shall be divided to provide for the economical and timely conduct of the partnership business. _____ shall manage the office, fiscal, customer relations, and sales portions of the partnership. _____ shall manage the purchasing, designing, manufacturing, and shipping portions. Each partner shall have sole responsibility for the personnel policies and internal operating procedures within those areas of responsibility assigned to the partner. Partners shall consult with each other in establishing and determining overall business policies that will affect the partnership business.[35]

Powers of Partners and Limitations Thereon   This section of the partnership agreement should set forth the powers of the partners and any limitations on those powers. It should also address the scope of partnership business, partnership employee policies, contractual rights and limitations, and patents and trade secrets.

Compensation and Benefits for Partners   This section may address any compensation and benefits that will be given to the partners in any form, including salaries, drawing accounts, vacations, holidays, retirement, and other benefits.

EXAMPLE: Salary—In General

In consideration for the services performed on behalf of the partnership, _____ shall receive a salary of $_____ per month, and _____ shall receive a salary of $_____ per month. These salaries shall be considered an expense of the partnership, and shall be payable whether or not the partnership earns a profit. These salaries shall not affect any other distributions payable to _____ and _____ under this agreement.

EXAMPLE: Drawing Account—In General

Each partner shall be authorized to draw $_____ per week from the funds of the partnership to meet that partner's personal expenses. Any draw shall be chargeable against that partner's share of partnership net profits, and the total amount of draw taken by each partner during the fiscal year shall be deducted from his share of the net profits prior to distribution of net profits.[36]

Provisions for Expenses of Partners and Partnership   This section should address all matters concerning the expenses of the partners and the partnership. It should designate a depository for the partnership funds, name the party responsible for controlling income and distribution, designate the authorized signatures on checks and drafts, and authorize partners to negotiate loans. In addition, it should set forth a method and time for disbursing payments on indebtedness and set limitations on indebtedness of partners.

Management and Control of Business   This section should set forth all partnership policies for the management and control of the business. It should appoint any desired managing partner or committee and should specify the management rights and duties of each partner, to the extent practical.

The partnership agreement should also specify a designated time for partnership meetings to discuss various management matters concerning the partnership business. This section may specify who will keep the books and records of the partnership and what types of books and records should be kept.

EXAMPLE: Management and Control—In General

Each partner shall have an equal role in the management and conduct of the partnership business. All decisions affecting the policy and management of the partnership, including compensation of partners and personnel policies, may be made on behalf of the partnership by any active partner. In the event of a disagreement among the partners, a decision by the majority of them shall be binding on the partnership. All partners shall be authorized to sign checks and to make, deliver, accept, or endorse any commercial paper in connection with the business and affairs of the partnership.

The partners shall conduct a _____ [weekly] meeting at the principal office of the partnership to discuss matters of general interest to the partnership. A vote of partners representing ___% of the partnership interest shall be necessary to implement any policy or procedure introduced at a partnership meeting, except for any change in this partnership agreement, which shall require a unanimous vote.[37]

EXAMPLE: Management and Control—Consent of Both Partners Required

Each partner has an equal voice in the management of the partnership business. Either partner has the right to make decisions relating to the day-to-day operations of the partnership in the normal course of its business, provided that the consent of both partners is required to do any of the following:

1. Borrow or lend money on behalf of the partnership, other than purchases made on credit in the normal course of business or the partnership not exceeding $_____ each, or make, execute, deliver, or endorse any negotiable instrument for the partnership, or agree for the partnership to indemnify or hold harmless any other person, firm, or corporation;
2. Assign, sell, transfer, pledge, or encumber any assets of the partnership;
3. Assign, transfer or pledge any debts due the partnership or release any debts due, except on payment in full;
4. Compromise any claim due to the partnership or submit to arbitration or litigation of any dispute or controversy involving the partnership;
5. Lease or purchase any property for the partnership except for purchases in the normal course of the partnership's business, or purchases out of the normal course of business not exceeding $_____ each;
6. Assign the partnership's property in trust for creditors or on the assignee's promise to pay the debt to the partnership;
7. Dispose of the goodwill of the partnership;
8. Confess a judgment against the partnership; or
9. Commit any other act which would make it difficult or impossible to carry on the ordinary business of the partnership.[38]

Partnership Accounting   This section should set forth all accounting methods and policies of the partnership, including the accounting period and fiscal year of the partnership, the frequency and types of reports to be completed, details regarding the books of accounts, audit provisions, and provision for examination of books.

Changes in Partners One restriction that is an essential characteristic of the partnership relation is that no person can become a member of a partnership without the consent of all of the partners, unless there is a contrary provision in the partnership agreement. This very important section of the partnership agreement should set forth the partners' wishes regarding the admission of new partners, if allowed, acceptance requirements, and provisions for the redistribution of assets. This section should also address all matters concerning withdrawing partners, including the necessity of the consent of the other partners, notice requirements, valuation of the withdrawing partner's share of the partnership, the option of the remaining partners to purchase the interest, and the assignment of the withdrawing partner's interest to a third party. It should describe the conditions for expulsion of a partner, notice requirements, and all other matters concerning the expulsion of a partner.

The partnership's policy regarding a retiring partner should also be addressed in this section, including the reorganization of partnership rights and duties.

EXAMPLE: New Partner—In General

The admission of new partners to the partnership is authorized by this agreement, and shall be accomplished by the approval of partners holding at least ___ % of the partnership interest.

A supplemental agreement shall be created prior to admission of a new partner to the partnership. This supplemental agreement shall provide, as a minimum (1) the contributions to partnership capital required of the new partner, (2) the new partner's percentage interest in the partnership, (3) any special offices or duties the new partner shall have in the partnership, and (4) the adjusted percentage of interests in the partnership of all existing partners based on the new partner's contribution.

All partners, including the new partner, shall execute the supplemental agreement, which shall become effective on the date signed by the last partner. The supplemental agreement shall then be attached to this agreement as an appendix.[39]

EXAMPLE: Withdrawing Partner—Option of Remaining Partners to Purchase Interest

---

Any partner desiring to withdraw from the partnership prior to termination or dissolution of the partnership shall be allowed to do so only with the consent of the remaining partners. Prior to granting or denying approval of a partner's request to withdraw, the remaining partners shall have the option to purchase a proportionate share of the partner's interest in the partnership. On their election to exercise the option, the withdrawing partner shall immediately be paid the appraised value of the partner's share, and the remaining partners' interests shall be proportionately increased.

If any of the remaining partners approve of the withdrawal of the partner, but do not desire to purchase a portion of the partner's share, the other remaining partners may purchase the additional segment and thereby obtain a larger proportionate share in the partnership.[40]

EXAMPLE: Retirement of Partner—In General

In the event any partner shall desire to retire from the partnership, the partner shall give ___ months' notice in writing to the other partners. The continuing partners shall pay to the retiring partner at the termination of the ___ months' notice the value of the interest of the retiring partner in the partnership. The value shall be determined by a closing of the books and a rendition of the appropriate profit and loss, trial balance, and balance sheet statements. All disputes arising from such determination shall be resolved as provided in Article Twenty.[41]

Death of Partner The section dealing with the death of any partner should address all aspects of the purchase of the deceased partner's interest, including the valuation of the deceased partner's share, the dissolution of the partnership, and any desired provision for the estate of the deceased to act as a partner.

EXAMPLE: Termination of Partnership on Death of Partner—at Conclusion of Fiscal Year

The partnership shall terminate at the close of the current partnership fiscal year on the death of any partner during that fiscal year. The estate of the deceased partner shall be paid the full share to which the deceased partner shall be entitled, at the time of distribution of partnership assets, ____ days after winding up the partnership business.[42]

EXAMPLE: Partnership to Continue after Death of Partner—Estate to Continue as Partner

In the event of the death of one partner, the legal representative of the deceased partner shall remain as a partner in the firm, except that the exercise of this right on the part of the representative of the deceased partner shall not continue for a period in excess of ___ months, even though under the terms of this agreement a greater period of time is provided before the termination of this agreement. The original rights of the partners shall accrue to their heirs, executors, or assigns.[43]

Sale or Purchase of Partnership Interest In this section of the partnership agreement, the partners may set forth all desired provisions regarding the potential sale or purchase of the partnership interest, including conditions for right of first refusal in remaining partners, limitations on purchase of interest, terms of sale, and the reorganization of the partnership.

EXAMPLE: Sale of Interest—Other Partner Given First Refusal

Neither partner shall, during the partner's lifetime, sell, assign, encumber, transfer, or otherwise dispose of all or any part of the partner's interest in the partnership without complying with the following procedure:

If one of the partners wishes to dispose of that partner's interest voluntarily, the partner shall first offer in writing to sell the partner's interest to the other partner at the price determined in accordance with the provisions of Section ___. If the other partner wishes to purchase the partnership interest, that partner shall notify the offering partner of the partner's decision in writing within _____ days after receipt of the offer and shall pay for the partnership interest in any case within _____ days after giving notice of the partner's acceptance. In the event the offer to sell has not been accepted within such _____-day period, the offering partner shall have the right to take legal steps to dissolve the partnership.[44]

Arbitration of Differences   The partners may provide in their partnership agreement that certain differences between the partners will be settled by arbitration, upon the terms and conditions set forth in the agreement.

Termination of Partnership   The partnership agreement should set forth all matters concerning the termination of the partnership, including the set date of termination, if there is one, events requiring termination, and procedures for terminating the partnership.

Dissolution and Winding Up   This section of the partnership agreement sets forth all of the agreed-upon terms of the partnership for dissolving and winding up the partnership. It should include provisions for an individual or committee who will be responsible for winding up the partnership business, and compensation for that individual or committee.

EXAMPLE: Dissolution—By Unanimous Agreement of Partners

The partnership shall not be dissolved prior to the termination date set forth in Section ___ of this agreement, except by the unanimous consent of all partners to this agreement at least _____ days prior to the intended date of dissolution.

The unanimous consent shall be obtained at a duly constituted business meeting of the partnership, and the proceedings of the meeting shall be properly and accurately recorded.[45]

EXAMPLE: Winding Up—Appointment of Committee

In the event of the dissolution of the partnership, a management committee shall be selected, with the approval of partners owning ___ % of the partnership interest, to consist of ___ partners, who shall have the right to wind up the partnership business and dispose of or liquidate the partnership's assets. In the event of liquidation, the committee members are appointed as liquidating partners.

Members of the committee shall each be entitled to receive $_____ per month as compensation for services during the duration of the committee.[46]

Date of Agreement and Signature of Partners   The partnership agreement must be dated and signed by all partners.

The Limited Liability Partnership Election

Limited liability partnerships are managed and operated in much the same way as other general partnerships. In addition, though, certain formalities must be followed to maintain the limited liability status. These formalities vary by state, and are set forth in the pertinent statutes.

In most states, a partnership becomes a limited liability partnership by filing a *statement of qualification*. The decision to become a limited liability partnership must be approved by a vote of the partners necessary to amend the partnership agreement.

Statement of Qualification   The limited liability provisions to the RUPA provide that the statement of qualification, shown in Figure 2-6 on page 58, must include:

1. The name of the partnership. The name of the partnership must include the words "Registered Limited Liability Partnership," "Limited Liability Partnership," "RLLP," "LLP," "R.L.L.P.," or "L.L.P."

2. The street address of the partnership's chief executive office and, if different, the street address of an office in the state of domicile (if any).

3. For partnerships that do not have an office in the state, the statement of qualification must include the name and street address of the partnership's agent for service of process.

4. A statement that the partnership elects to be a limited liability partnership.

5. A deferred effective date, if any.[47]

Annual Report   In addition to the statement of qualification, limited liability partnerships may be required to file an *annual report* with the secretary of state. The information that must be included in the annual report is minimal, usually consisting merely of the name and address of the limited liability partnership, the current street address of the partnership's chief executive officer, and the name and address of the partnership's agent for process of service (if one has been appointed). Failure to file the annual report of a limited liability partnership may cause the partnership to lose its limited liability status in some states.

§ 2.7 FINANCIAL STRUCTURE OF A PARTNERSHIP

Partnerships have a unique financial structure that can often be tailored to suit the needs of the partners. This section discusses the capital of the partnership and the allocation and distribution of profits and losses.

Partnership Capital

The partnership capital, which includes all the assets of the partnership, consists of contributions from the partners and the undistributed income earned by the partnership.

Capital Contributions   There are no minimum capital requirements for partnerships under the UPA or the RUPA. The partnership capital is usually contributed by the partners, and it may be in the form of cash, real or personal property, or the personal expertise or services rendered by a partner. The partnership agreement should state the required capital contribution of each partner and the form of that contribution. In addition to the initial capital contribution, the partnership agreement

---

Minnesota Secretary of State
LIMITED LIABILITY PARTNERSHIP
STATEMENT OF QUALIFICATION
CHAPTER 323A

PLEASE TYPE OR PRINT IN BLACK INK.

Please read the instructions on the reverse side before completing. Fee: $135

1. List the Partnership name:

_____

_____

_____

2. Address of the partnership's chief executive officer:

_____

_____

Complete Street Address or Rural Route and Rural Route Box Number, City, State, ZIP.

(Please note: PO Box is unacceptable)

3. List office of partnership in Minnesota, if different from item 2:

_____

_____

_____

Complete Street Address or Rural Route and Rural Route Box Number, City, State, ZIP.

(Please note: PO Box is unacceptable)

4. This partnership elects to be a limited liability partnership.

5. The effective date of this filing if different from the date of filing, is _____.

6. I certify that I am a partner authorized to sign this document on behalf of this partnership and I further certify that by signing this document I am subject to the penalties of perjury as set forth in Minnesota Statutes, section 5.15 as if I had signed this document under oath. **Note that this statement must be signed/executed by at least two (2) partners.**

_____   _____

Signature of a partner   Signature of a partner

_____

Print name and daytime telephone number

10980529 Rev. 11/98

FIGURE 2-6 Sample Limited Liability Partnership Statement of Qualification Form from the State of Minnesota

may require each partner to contribute additional capital to the partnership as needed for the continuance of the partnership business.

Generally, no withdrawal of capital from the partnership is permitted until the partnership is dissolved. If this is not desirable, the appropriate provisions should be made in the partnership agreement for the withdrawal of capital prior to dissolution of the partnership.

Partner Loans and Advances   In addition to the capital contribution, partners may provide capital to the partnership in the form of a loan or an advance, which may be repaid with interest on terms provided for in the partnership agreement, or on terms agreed to by the loaning partner and the remaining partners.

Partners' Right to Accounting   Under the UPA, every partner is entitled to a formal accounting as to the partnership affairs. This right may be exercised whenever a partner is wrongfully excluded from the partnership business or possession of its property by the co-partners; whenever such rights exist under the partnership agreement or other agreement; whenever appropriate because of the fiduciary nature of each partner to the partnership; or whenever other circumstances render it just and reasonable.[48]

The statutory language concerning the partners' rights to a formal account is quite broad, so these rights should be more clearly defined in the partnership agreement.

While the RUPA is silent on the right of a partner to a formal accounting, it does provide for broad rights of inspection of the books and records of the partnership by the partners, their agents, and their attorneys.

Partnership Records   Unless otherwise provided for in the partnership agreement, the partnership books must be kept at the partnership's executive office and are subject to inspection by any partner at any time. The duty to keep the books of the partnership usually falls to the managing partner or another partner, as appointed in the partnership agreement or by oral agreement between the partners.

Profits and Losses

Another of the more important characteristics of a partnership is a sharing of the profits and losses among the partners. Under the UPA and the RUPA the partners share the profits and losses of the partnership equally, regardless of each partner's capital contribution to the partnership. The partners may, however, set their own formula for sharing in the profits and losses of the partnership, which may be based on several factors, including (1) the amount of the initial capital contribution by each partner, (2) additional capital contributions, and (3) services rendered on behalf of the partnership by each partner. If partners' contributions to the partnership are unequal, their shares of the profits and losses may be unequal as well.

The Internal Revenue Service (IRS) generally recognizes a profit and loss allocation that is agreed to by all partners, so long as it has "substantial economic effect." If the IRS determines that the profit and loss allocation set forth in the partnership agreement has no economic effect, but has been drafted merely as a means to avoid paying income taxes, the IRS will allocate profits and losses pursuant to each partner's ownership interest in the partnership.

In any event, if it is not desirable for all partners to share all profits and all losses equally, it is crucial that this matter be addressed in the written partnership agreement.

§ 2.8 DISSOLUTION, DISSOCIATION, WINDING UP, AND TERMINATION OF THE PARTNERSHIP

The dissolution of a partnership is more of a process than an event. This section first examines the definition of the terms *dissociation, dissolution,* and *winding up* of a partnership. Next, it discusses the events that cause partnership dissociation and the effects of partnership dissociation, the events causing dissolution and the effects of partnership dissolution, the continuation of a partnership after dissolution, wrongful dissociation of a partnership, and the use of a dissolution agreement. This section concludes with a look at giving notice to third parties of a partnership dissolution, winding up the partnership, and distributing partnership assets.

Dissociation, Dissolution, and Winding Up

The term **dissociation** is a term new to the RUPA. It is distinctly different from **dissolution**. Under the UPA, whenever one partner ceased being a partner for any reason, the partnership was considered to be dissolved. Under the RUPA, one or more partners may be dissociated from a partnership without causing its dissolution. As used in the RUPA, the term *dissociation* denotes the change in the relationship caused by a partner's ceasing to be associated in the carrying on of the business.

The term *dissolution* refers to the commencement of the winding up process. Upon dissolution, the partnership relationship terminates with respect to all future transactions and the authority of all partners to act on behalf of the partnership and on behalf of each other terminates, except to the extent necessary for the winding up of the partnership. The partnership will cease to exist upon completion of the winding-up process—the disposition of all liabilities and assets of the partnership.

Events Causing Partner's Dissociation

A partner's dissociation can be caused by agreement, by statute, or wrongfully. The RUPA sets forth the following acts that can cause a partner's dissociation:[49]

1. The partner giving notice to the partnership of his or her express will to withdraw as a partner on some specific date.
2. The occurrence of an event agreed to in the partnership agreement as causing the partner's dissociation.

◆──

dissociation The event that occurs when a partner withdraws or otherwise ceases to be associated in the carrying on of the partnership business.

dissolution The termination of a corporation, partnership or other business entity's existence.

3. The partner's expulsion pursuant to the partnership agreement.
4. The partner's expulsion by the unanimous vote of the other partners if
   a. it is unlawful to carry on the partnership business with that partner.
   b. the partner transfers all or substantially all of his or her transferable interest in the partnership.
   c. the partner is a corporation that has filed a certificate of dissolution, had its charter revoked, or its right to conduct business suspended.
   d. the partner is a partnership that has been dissolved and its business is being wound up.
5. Judicial determination, based on an application by the partnership or another partner because
   a. the partner engaged in wrongful conduct that adversely and materially affected the partnership.
   b. the appointment of a trustee, receiver, or liquidator of the partner's property.
6. The partner's death.
7. Appointment of a guardian or general conservator for the partner.
8. A judicial determination that the partner has otherwise become incapable of performing the partner's duties under the partnership agreement.
9. If the partner is a trust, distribution of the trust's entire transferable interest in the partnership.
10. If the partner is an estate, distribution of the estate's entire transferable interest in the partnership.
11. Termination of a partner who is not an individual, corporation, trust, or estate.

Wrongful Dissociation

Under the RUPA partners always have the power to dissociate from the partnership, although, under some circumstances, the dissociation may be considered a wrongful dissociation. A partner's dissociation will be considered wrongful if it is contrary to the partnership agreement. The partner's dissociation will also be considered wrongful if the dissociation occurs prior to the expiration of any set term for the partnership or prior to the completion of any preestablished task, and if one of the following events occurs:

♦ The partner withdraws of his or her express will, unless the withdrawal follows within 90 days the dissociation of another party.
♦ The partner is expelled from the partnership by the court.
♦ The partner is dissociated by becoming a debtor in bankruptcy.
♦ The partner is a trust or estate that becomes willfully dissolved or terminated.

A partner who is wrongfully dissociated from a partnership is liable to the partnership and the other partners for damages caused by the wrongful dissociation.

Effect of Partner's Dissociation

Generally, upon a partner's dissociation, the partner's rights to participate in the management and conduct of the partnership business terminate. The dissociated partner will no longer be able to act on behalf of the partnership except to wind up the affairs of a dissolving partnership. Likewise, the dissociated partner will not be liable for any obligations incurred by the partnership after his or her dissociation. The partner's duty of loyalty and duty of care continue only with regard to matters arising and events occurring before the partner's dissociation, unless the partner participates in the winding up of the partnership's business.

The effect a partner's dissociation will have upon the partner and upon the partnership depends on whether the dissociation causes the dissolution and winding up of the partnership and whether the partner's dissociation was wrongful.

Effect of Partner's Dissociation When Partnership Continues   In most instances, a dissociating partner has the right to have his or her interest in the partnershipÿpurchased for a *buyout price* as set forth in the partnership agreement or by statute. The RUPA defines the buyout price of a dissociated partner's interest as "the amount that would have been distributable to the dissociating partner if, on the date of dissociation, the assets of the partnership were sold at a price equal to the greater of the liquidation value or the value based on a sale of the entire business as a going concern without the dissociated partner and the partnership were wound up as of that date."[50]

In the case of a wrongful dissociation, the damages caused by that dissociation can be used to offset the buyout price paid to the dissociated partner.

The buyout of a dissociated partner is a new concept under the RUPA. Previously, whenever a partner dissociated, the partnership would be dissolved.

In the event of the death of a partner, the deceased partner is considered to be dissociated, and the partner's transferable interest in the partnership will pass to his or her estate. The remaining partners or the partnership typically will then buy out that interest from the estate and continue the partnership business.

Statement of Dissociation

In states where the RUPA has been adopted, either the dissociated partner or the partnership may file with the appropriate state authority a *statement of dissociation* stating the name of the partnership and that the partner is dissociated from the partnership. The statement of dissociation is a public notice of the dissociated partner's limitation of authority and liability with regard to partnership matters.

Events Causing Dissolution and Winding Up of Partnership Business

Exactly what precipitates the dissolution and winding up of a partnership will be dictated by state statute. Pursuant to § 31 of the UPA, the following acts cause dissolution:

- The expiration of the term or completion of a particular undertaking specified in the partnership agreement.
- The express will of any partner when no definite term or particular undertaking is specified.
- The express will of all the partners who have not assigned their interests in the partnership.
- The expulsion of any partner from the business pursuant to the partnership agreement.
- The express will of any partner at any time if contrary to the agreement when circumstances do not permit a dissolution under any other statutory provision.
- Any event that makes it unlawful for the business of the partnership to be carried on.
- The death of any partner.
- The bankruptcy of any partner or the partnership.
- The order of a court.

Regardless of this provision, it is not uncommon for partnerships governed under the UPA to continue to operate after the withdrawal of one or more partners. Technically, under the UPA, the partnership is dissolved and a new partnership is formed every time there is a change in the partners.

In states that have adopted the RUPA, only the following events cause a dissolution and winding up of the partnership business:

1. In a partnership at will, the partnership's receiving notice from a partner of that partner's express will to withdraw as a partner.
2. In a partnership for a definite term or particular undertaking,
   a. the expiration of a 90-day period after a partner's dissociation by death or otherwise or through wrongful dissociation, unless a majority of the remaining partners agree to continue the partnership.
   b. the express will of all of the partners to wind up the partnership business.
   c. the expiration of the term or the completion of the undertaking.
3. An event agreed to in the partnership agreement as being sufficient to cause the winding up of the partnership business.
4. An event that makes it unlawful for the partnership business to be continued.
5. A judicial determination based on an application by a partner that one of the following conditions prevails:
   a. the economic purpose of the partnership is likely to be unreasonably frustrated.
   b. another partner has engaged in conduct that makes it not reasonably practicable to carry on the business in partnership with that partner.
   c. it is not reasonably practicable to carry on the partnership business in conformity with the partnership agreement.
6. A judicial determination based on an application by a transferee of a partner's transferable interest that the term for the partnership has expired or the

undertaking has been completed, or at any time if the partnership was a partnership at will at the time of transfer.

Most of the foregoing provisions can be amended by the partnership agreement. For example, the partnership agreement can provide that the partnership will continue after the dissociation of one or more partners.

When it is the desire of the partners to plan for the continuation of the partnership after the death of one or more of the partners, life insurance on the life of each partner is often purchased by the partnership or by the partners to fund the buyout of a deceased partner.

Figure 2-7 lists the causes of dissolution as set forth by the UPA and the RUPA.

Under the UPA	*Under the RUPA*
◆ Expiration of the term established for the partnership pursuant to the partnership agreement.	◆ Any partner giving notice to partnership of his or her withdrawal (in a partnership at will).
◆ Completion of undertaking by partnership formed for specific undertaking.	◆ Expiration of 90-day period after death or wrongful dissociation of a partner (unless a majority of remaining partners agree to continue partnership).
◆ Express will of all partners.	◆ Express will of all partners to wind up business.
◆ Expulsion of any partner pursuant to partnership agreement.	◆ Expiration of term of partnership for definite term.
◆ Express will of a partner that is contrary to the partnership agreement when the circumstances do not permit a dissolution under any other provision.	◆ Completion of task of partnership formed for particular task.
◆ The happening of any event that makes it unlawful to carry on the partnership.	◆ Any event resulting in winding up of partnership business pursuant to partnership agreement.
◆ The death of any partner.	◆ Happening of event that makes it unlawful to continue partnership.
◆ The bankruptcy of any partner or the partnership.	◆ Judicial determination.
◆ By decree of a court upon application by or for a partner.	

FIGURE 2-7   Causes of Partnership Dissolution

Dissolution Agreement

A written dissolution agreement among the partners of a dissolving partnership can help alleviate any disputes as to the method and timing of the dissolution, as well as any disputes that may arise subsequent to the winding up of the partnership due to unforeseen circumstances. In the dissolution agreement, the partners who have the right to wind up the partnership generally appoint a liquidating partner or partners and delegate the authority to liquidate the partnership and settle the partnership affairs.

Notice to Third Parties

Notice of the partnership dissolution or withdrawal of a partner must be given to parties who have previously dealt with the partnership. Creditors who are not given notice and do not know of the dissolution are entitled to hold former partners liable for obligations incurred by continuing partners after dissolution.

The RUPA provides for an optional filing of a statement of dissolution by any partner of a dissolving partnership who has not wrongfully dissociated. The statement of dissolution cancels any statement of partnership authority that may have been filed on behalf of the partnership.

Winding Up

Winding up is the process by which the accounts of the partnership are settled and the assets are liquidated in order to make distribution of the net assets of the partnership to the partners and dissolve the partnership. This may include the performance of existing contracts, the collection of debts or claims due to the partnership, and the payment of the partnership debts.

Distribution of Assets

The partnership agreement will typically set forth guidelines for the distribution of assets on dissolution of the partnership—including the proportionate share of assets to be received and losses to be covered by each partner. Unless otherwise specified in the partnership agreement, the rules for distribution of the partnership assets are set by statute. In general terms, the partnership assets will be liquidated and used to pay debts and obligations of the partnership, and the surplus will be distributed to the partners. If there are not enough partnership assets to pay the creditors of the partnership, the partners must contribute a sufficient amount.

In states that follow the UPA with regard to the rules for distribution of assets on dissolution, the assets of the partnership are used to pay the liabilities of the partnership in the order set forth as follows.

1. Those owing to creditors other than partners.
2. Those owing to partners other than for capital and profits.
3. Those owing to partners in respect of capital.
4. Those owing to partners in respect of profits.

The assets of the partnership include the partnership property as well as any contributions required by statute or partnership agreement for the payment of all liabilities of the partnership. Partners are entitled to receive their distribution in cash.

The partners must contribute to the assets of the partnership to the extent necessary to pay the liabilities of the partnership. The partners will all contribute equally unless otherwise provided for in the partnership agreement.

The procedures for distributing partnership assets on winding up the partnership are very similar in states that follow the RUPA. Again, the procedures for liquidating and distributing the assets may be set forth in the partnership agreement so long as the partnership agreement does not violate the statutes.

One difference in the RUPA is that, unlike the UPA, it does not give preference to creditors who are not partners. Therefore, the assets of the partnership must be first applied to discharge the partnership obligations to creditors, including partners who are creditors.

Also, the RUPA provides that each partner is entitled to a settlement of all partnership accounts upon winding up. In settling the accounts of the partnership, the partnership property is first used to pay the creditors of the partnership. If the partnership property is insufficient to cover all of the partnership liabilities, then the partners are required to make contributions to cover the liabilities. If there is a surplus of assets after all creditors are paid, the surplus is paid to the partners.

Each partner is entitled to receive a share of the assets as determined by the partnership agreement. If the partnership agreement is silent on distribution of assets upon winding up, each partner is entitled to a share in the same proportion as the proportion of profits and losses that he or she is entitled to receive either under the partnership agreement, or under law.

Both the UPA and the RUPA provide that if any, but not all, of the partners are insolvent, or otherwise unable or unwilling to contribute to the payment of the liabilities, the liabilities of the partnership must be paid by the remaining partners in the same proportion as their share of the profits of the partnership. Any partner, or the legal representative of any partner, who is required to pay in excess of his or her fair share of the liabilities to settle the affairs of the partnership has the right to enforce the contributions of the other partners pursuant to statute and the partnership agreement, to the extent of the amount paid in excess of his or her share of the liability.

The exact method of distribution should be set forth clearly in the partnership agreement. Generally, the partners are entitled to a distribution of the assets in the same percentage as their contribution of capital to the partnership, with adjustments made for subsequent contributions in the form of capital contributions and services rendered on behalf of the partnership. If partners' contributions to the partnership are unequal, their shares of the profits and losses may be unequal as well, so long as the appropriate provision is made in the partnership agreement.

Figure 2-8 lists the UPA and RUPA requirements as to distribution of partnership assets upon dissolution.

§ 2.9 THE PARALEGAL'S ROLE IN PARTNERSHIP MATTERS

As with sole proprietorships, the bulk of legal services performed for persons forming and operating a partnership is usually in the form of legal advice given by the attorney. The paralegal, however, may be instrumental in drafting the partnership

UPA	*RUPA*
◆ Partnership assets must be liquidated and used to pay all outstanding debts and obligations of the partnership. Nonpartnership creditors are given priority over those partners who are creditors of the partnership.	◆ Partnership assets must be liquidated and used to pay all outstanding debts and obligations of the partnership. Partners who are creditors of the partnership are treated the same as nonpartnership creditors.
◆ Debts and obligations owing to partners other than for capital and profits are paid.	◆ Partners are entitled to a separate accounting of the partnership assets. Any gain or loss due to the liquidation of assets of the partnership is credited to a separate account for each partner, either equally or pursuant to the partnership agreement.
◆ Capital owing to partners is paid to partners.	◆ Any partner with a negative balance in his or her account must pay in an amount equal to the negative balance.
◆ Profits owing to partners are paid to partners.	◆ Any partner with a positive balance in his or her account is entitled to receive an amount equal to the balance.
◆ If necessary and unless otherwise established in the partnership agreement, partners must contribute equally to pay the liabilities of the partnership, including capital owing to partners.	

FIGURE 2-8 Distribution of Partnership Assets upon Dissolution Under the UPA and the RUPA

agreement and performing research regarding the requirements for forming, operating, and dissolving a partnership, as well as research regarding partnership disputes. Most law firms have partnership agreement forms integrated into their word processing systems. The paralegal is often responsible for the revising and drafting required to make each agreement fit the unique circumstances of each new partnership.

Form books commonly found in law libraries may help with the drafting of unique language, as will samples of previous work done by the paralegal or others in the law firm.

The following is a checklist of items that should be considered when drafting a partnership agreement.

PARTNERSHIP AGREEMENT CHECKLIST

☐ Names and addresses of partners.
☐ Name of partnership.

Corporate Paralegal Profile
Gail M. Pell, CLA

What keeps my job interesting is the extreme variety of projects that I am given.

Name Gail M. Pell, CLA

Location Rancho Cordova, California

Title Legal Assistant

Specialty Corporate

Education Associate of Applied Science Degree in Legal Assisting from MTI Western Business College; Bachelor of Science in Business Management from the University of Phoenix; first year student at Lincoln Law School of Sacramento

Experience 7 years

Gail Pell is a legal assistant for Catholic Healthcare West, a California nonprofit public benefit corporation. Catholic Healthcare West employs 18 in-house attorneys and 10 paralegals in its legal department, which is spread through five separate locations in California and Arizona. Gail reports to the regional general counsel for the Northern California division and also to the senior vice-president of Legal Services/General Counsel for Catholic Healthcare West.

Gail's experience with partnerships includes forming both general and limited partnerships, and assisting with their contracting, management, and profit-and-loss arrangements. In addition, Gail drafts partnership agreements, buy-sell agreements, and related documents. She is also responsible for maintaining corporate records, drafting corporate documents, and assisting with incorporations and dissolutions. Her position involves contract negotiations and drafting and revising complex legal documents.

Gail really enjoys the independence her position offers. Typically, her supervising attorney will give her a verbal outline of how a project is supposed to work, then Gail sees the project through to completion. She has worked on many interesting and exciting projects, and particularly enjoys negotiations. She gets the task of relaying legal positions on issues and finding ways to make compromises. She has worked on million-dollar deals and finds it interesting to watch clients negotiate deals of all sizes.

Gail is a member of both NALA and NFPA, as well as the Sacramento Association of Legal Assistants. She has offered her paralegal services pro bono to the Sacramento County Family Law Clinic.

Gail's advice to new paralegals?

Paralegals must be brilliant at writing correspondence and preparing documents, ferreting out details, being streetwise, and being flexible to the attorney's priorities. Be an overachiever! You really do have to make a conscious choice about the path that your career will take, and it is solely up to you.

For more information on careers for corporate paralegals, log on to the companion Web page to this text at **www.westlegalstudies.com.**

☐ Purpose of partnership.

☐ Limited liability status.

☐ Address of principal place of doing business.

☐ Term of partnership agreement.

☐ Partner contributions.

☐ Requirements for additional contributions.

☐ Partnership assets.

☐ Goodwill evaluation on distribution of assets.

☐ Partners' and partnership liability.

- ☐ Distribution of profits and losses.
- ☐ Partner indemnification.
- ☐ Partners' duties.
- ☐ Partners' powers and limitations thereon.
- ☐ Partner compensation and benefits.
- ☐ Partner and partnership expenses.
- ☐ Management and control of business.
- ☐ Life insurance on lives of partners.
- ☐ Accounting procedures and record keeping.
- ☐ Changes in partners.
- ☐ Death of partner.
- ☐ Sale or purchase of partnership interest.
- ☐ Arbitration of differences among partners.
- ☐ Partnership termination.
- ☐ Dissolution and winding up.
- ☐ Date of agreement.
- ☐ Signatures of all partners.

The paralegal may also be asked to help with the other formalities associated with forming and operating a partnership, including research regarding filing requirements for partnerships, the actual filing of the partnership certificate, filing and publishing a certificate of assumed or fictitious name, and applying for tax identification numbers.

ETHICAL CONSIDERATION

If you are a paralegal who works with partnerships, you may become familiar with your clients' personal and financial affairs. It is not uncommon for paralegals to assist in preparing financial documents for the partnership, as well as employment agreements and other agreements, the nature of which must be kept strictly confidential.

The rules of ethics that apply to attorneys and to paralegals provide that, with certain exceptions, attorneys and paralegals have an ethical duty to keep all information learned from clients confidential. The client-lawyer relationship is based on loyalty and requires that the lawyer, and any paralegals involved, maintain confidentiality of information relating to the representation. The confidential relationship between the client and attorney encourages the client to communicate fully and frankly with the attorney, even with regard to matters that may be damaging or embarrassing to the client.

Most law firms have strict policies regarding the divulgence of client information to the press or any outsider. Typically, all requests for information regarding a client should be directed to an attorney who is responsible for the client's affairs, and no one else will be permitted to pass on any information regarding a client without permission, even information that may seem quite inconsequential.

As a paralegal, it will be important for you to help ensure client confidentiality by meeting with clients in a private location where you cannot be overheard by others who may be meeting in the office, and avoiding unnecessary office conversation and gossip concerning a client. Never discuss a client with your friends or family.

It is also important to keep client files and written information in a secure location in the office. Drafts of sensitive documents should be shredded when practical.

There are several exceptions to the rules of confidentiality. For example, confidential client information may be released when requested by the client or when ordered by a court. If you are in doubt as to whether to divulge any information that may be considered confidential, always be sure to ask your supervising attorney or an experienced paralegal first.

For more information concerning the rules of ethics and the duty of confidentiality, see appendix C to this text.

§ 2.10 RESOURCES

The paralegal has many resources available for researching statutory requirements for partnerships and drafting partnership agreements. State statutes provide the statutory requirements for partnerships, and legal form books provide many possible clauses for partnership agreements. For state and local formalities concerning partnerships, the secretary of state and other state and local government offices should be contacted.

State Statutes

Figure 2-9 lists the statutory citations of the UPA or RUPA as adopted by each state.

Legal Form Books

Legal form books such as *Am. Jur. Forms 2d.*, *Nichols Cyclopedia of Legal Forms Annotated, Rabkin & Johnson Current Legal Forms,* and *West's Legal Forms Second Edition* are good sources for general information and for obtaining sample paragraphs for drafting partnership agreements and other documents related to the formation and operation of partnerships.

Secretary of State or Other Appropriate State Authority

The secretary of state or other appropriate state authority must be contacted to determine what the requirements are for partnership registration with the state, and to determine what the procedures are for complying with that requirement. (See appendix A for a secretary of state directory.)

The secretary of state should also be consulted for procedural information regarding filing of an application for a certificate of assumed name, trade name, or fictitious name, and filing a statement of qualification for a limited liability partnership election, if applicable.

State	*Code*	*Version of Uniform Act Adopted*
Alabama	Ala. Code §§ 10-8A–101 *et seq.*	RUPA
Alaska	Alaska Stat. § 32.05.010 *et seq.*	UPA
Arizona	Arizona Rev. Stat. Ann. 29-1001 *et seq.*	RUPA
Arkansas	Ark. Code Ann. § 4-46-101 *et seq.*	RUPA
California	Cal. Corp. Code 16100 to 16962	RUPA
Colorado	Colo. Rev. Stat. § 7-64-101 *et seq.*	RUPA
Connecticut	Conn. Gen. Stat. 34-300 *et seq.*	RUPA
Delaware	Del. Code Ann. tit. 6 § 15-101 *et seq.*	RUPA
District of Columbia	D.C. Code Ann. 41-151.1 *et seq.*	RUPA
Florida	Fla. Stat. ch. 620.81001 *et seq.*	RUPA
Georgia	Ga. Code Ann. § 14-8-1 *et seq.*	UPA
Hawaii	Haw. Rev. Stat. § 425-101 *et seq.*	RUPA
Idaho	Idaho Code § 53-3-101 *et seq.*	RUPA
Illinois	805 ILCS 205/1 *et seq.*	UPA
Indiana	Ind. Code § 23-4-1-1 *et seq.*	UPA
Iowa	Iowa Code 486A.101 *et seq.*	RUPA
Kansas	Kan. Stat. Ann. § 56a-101 *et seq.*	RUPA
Kentucky	Ky. Rev. Stat. Ann. § 362.150 *et seq.*	UPA
Louisiana	La. Rev. Stat. Ann. § 9:3401 *et seq.*	Not an adaptation of either the UPA or the RUPA
Maine	Me. Rev. Stat. Ann. tit. 31, § 281 *et seq.*	UPA
Maryland	Md. Code Ann., Corps. & Ass'ns 9A-101 *et seq.*	RUPA
Massachusetts	Mass. Gen. L. ch. 108A, § 1 *et seq.*	UPA
Michigan	Mich. Comp. Laws § 449.1 *et seq.*	UPA
Minnesota	Minn. Stat. § 323.01 *et seq.*	RUPA
Mississippi	Miss. Code Ann. § 79-12-1 *et seq.*	UPA
Missouri	Mo. Rev. Stat. § 358.010 *et seq.*	UPA
Montana	Mont. Rev. Stat. § 35-10-101 *et seq.*	RUPA
Nebraska	Neb. Rev. Stat. § 67-401 *et seq.*	RUPA

FIGURE 2-9   Uniform Partnership Acts Adopted by State as of 2001

State	Code	Version of Uniform Act Adopted
Nevada	Nev. Rev. Stat. § 87.010 *et seq.*	UPA
New Hampshire	N.H. Rev. Stat. Ann. § 304-A:1 *et seq.*	UPA
New Jersey	N.J. Rev. Stat. § 42:1-1 *et seq.*	UPA
New Mexico	N.M. Stat. Ann. § 54-1-47 *et seq.*	RUPA
New York	N.Y. Partnership Law § 1 *et seq.*	UPA
North Carolina	N.C. Gen. Stat. § 59-31 *et seq.*	UPA
North Dakota	N.D. Cent. Code § 45-13-01 *et seq.*	RUPA
Ohio	Ohio Rev. Code Ann. § 1775.01 *et seq.*	UPA
Oklahoma	Okla. Stat. tit. 54 § 1-100 *et seq.*	RUPA
Oregon	Or. Rev. Stat. § 67.005 *et seq.*	RUPA
Pennsylvania	15 Pa. Cons. Stat. Ann. § 8301 *et seq.*	UPA
Rhode Island	Gen. Laws 1956, § 8301 *et seq.*	UPA
South Carolina	S.C. Code Ann. § 33-41-10 *et seq.*	UPA
South Dakota	S.D. Codified Laws Ann. § 48-1-1 *et seq.*	UPA
Tennessee	Tenn. Code Ann. § 61-1-101 *et seq.*	UPA
Texas	Tex. Rev. Civ. Stat. Ann. art. 6132b-1 *et seq.*	RUPA
Utah	Utah Code Ann. § 48-1-1 *et seq.*	UPA
Vermont	Vt. Stat. Ann. tit. 11 § 3201 *et seq.*	RUPA
Virginia	Va. Code Ann. § 50-73.79	RUPA
Washington	Wash. Rev. Code § 25.05.005 *et seq.*	RUPA
West Virginia	W. Va. Code § 47B-1-1 *et seq.*	RUPA
Wisconsin	Wis. Stat. § 178.01 *et seq.*	UPA
Wyoming	Wyo. Stat. § 17-21-101 *et seq.*	RUPA

FIGURE 2-9 (*continued*)

State and Local Government Offices

Because the formalities for operating a partnership vary by state, it is important that the appropriate state authority be contacted to obtain information relating to all state taxation matters, including unemployment insurance, withholding for employee income taxation, sales tax permits, and licenses.

Internet Resources   www.

Following is a list of some Web pages that may be useful when assisting partnerships:

For state statutes concerning limited partnerships

American Law Source Online	**www.lawsource.com/also**
Findlaw.com	**www.findlaw.com/11stategov/**
Legal Information Institute	**www.law.cornell.edu/states/listing.html**

For partnership forms

All About Forms.Com	**www.allaboutforms.com/**
Findlaw.com (Legal Forms)	**www.findlaw.com**
The 'Lectric Law Library's Business and General Forms	**www.lectlaw.com/formb.htm**

For links to state government forms

Findlaw.com State Corporation and Business Forms	**www.findlaw.com/11stategov/indexcorp.html**

For links to the secretary of state offices

Corporate Housekeeper	**www.danvi.vi/link2.html**
National Association of Secretaries of State	**www.nass.org**

For the Uniform Partnership Act and RUPA

National Conference of Commissioners on Uniform State Law	**www.law.upenn.edu/bll/ulc/ulc_frame.htm**

For partnership taxation information

Internal Revenue Service	**www.irs.gov**

For general information about partnership law

Legal Information Institute	**www.law.cornell.edu/topics/partnership.html**

An alphabetical list of internet resources for the corporate paralegal is included as appendix B to this text.

Web Page

For updates and links to several of the previously listed sites, as well as download-able state forms for filing a statement of intent to become a limited liability partner-ship, log on to **www.westlegalstudies.com** and click through to the book link for this text.

SUMMARY

- A partnership is an association of two or more persons to carry on as co-owners a business for profit.
- All the partners of a general partnership are general partners.
- Limited partnerships have as partners both limited partners and general partners.
- Partnerships in most states may elect to become limited liability partnerships to limit the personal liability of all partners.
- Partnerships are not as numerous and do not earn as much income in the United States as either corporations or sole proprietorships.
- Most states have adopted a version of either the Uniform Partnership Act (UPA) or the Revised Uniform Partnership Act (RUPA).
- The partnership is considered a separate entity for most purposes and an aggregate of its partners for other purposes.
- Each partner typically has the right to act on behalf of the partnership when dealing with others concerning partnership business.
- Unless otherwise agreed to in the partnership agreement, each partner has an equal right to manage the partnership business.
- Unless otherwise agreed to in the partnership agreement, each partner has the right to receive an equal share of the profits and pay an equal share of the losses of the partnership.
- Certain acts outside the ordinary course of business require the unanimous consent of all partners. Acts requiring the unanimous consent of partners may be prescribed by statute or by the partnership agreement.
- Partners may file a statement of authority with the proper state authority to give public notice of the authority granted or denied certain partners.
- In states that follow the UPA, partnership property is held in tenancy of partnership.
- In states that follow the RUPA, partnership property is owned by the partnership itself.
- Partners owe a fiduciary duty to each other and to the partnership. That duty may be expanded on and detailed in the partnership agreement, but the fiduciary duty of partners cannot be diminished under the partnership agreement.
- The partnership agreement is considered the law of the partnership for most purposes. The terms of the partnership agreement govern the partnership unless they are contrary to the laws of the state.
- Under the UPA, the withdrawal of any partner causes a dissolution of the partnership.
- Under the RUPA, partners may be dissociated from the partnership without dissolving the partnership.

◆ Winding up is the process by which the accounts of the partnership are settled and the assets are liquidated in order to make final distributions to the partners and dissolve the partnership.

◆ In general, the liabilities of the partnership must be paid before final distributions can be made to the partners of a dissolving partnership.

REVIEW QUESTIONS

1. What five elements are necessary to form a partnership?

2. In what ways are partnerships similar to sole proprietorships? In what ways do they differ from sole proprietorships?

3. Suppose that John, Megan, and Alex form a partnership to operate a restaurant pursuant to the RUPA. John decides to buy hamburger buns from the Fresh Bread Bakery. He enters into a contract with the owner of the Fresh Bread Bakery, on behalf of the partnership, for the delivery of 500 hamburger buns each week, for the price of $70 per week. If Megan and Alex disagree with this decision because they prefer another baker, is the partnership still liable for this contract? Must the Fresh Bread Bakery be paid out of the partnership funds?

4. Suppose again that John, Megan and Alex form a partnership, and John has contributed 50 percent of the capital, Megan has contributed 30 percent of the capital, and Alex has contributed 20 percent of the capital. Who has the right to manage the partnership under the RUPA, assuming the partnership agreement has no contrary provisions? How will decisions be made in the event of a disagreement?

5. Is it possible for two individuals to form a partnership with an oral agreement to operate a construction business for three years? Why or why not?

6. Kara, Tim, and Anna have formed a partnership to purchase and renovate old homes. Kara and Tim have contributed the bulk of the capital for the corporation and Anna's main contribution has been her services. All partners agree that either Kara or Tim should have the authority to sign documents transferring real estate on behalf of the partnership and that Anna should not have that authority. If the partnership is formed in a state that follows the RUPA, what steps must they take to give notice to those dealing with their partnership of their agreement with regard to the authority to transfer real estate?

7. Janet is a partner in a 10-partner partnership located in a state that follows the RUPA. If Janet decides to withdraw from the partnership before its duration lapses, what are the possible outcomes to the partnership and the remaining partners? What if the partnership is located in a state that follows the UPA?

PRACTICAL PROBLEMS

1. Locate and cite the partnership act in your state to answer the following questions.

   a. Is your state's partnership act based on the UPA or the RUPA?

   b. When was your state's current act adopted?

   c. Is it possible to form a limited liability partnership in your state? If yes, what is the statute section that provides for the formation of limited liability partnerships?

2. Do the statutes of your state provide for the filing of a statement of authority? Where is that document filed?

3. What are the basic steps for dissolving a partnership under the statutes of your state?

WORKPLACE SCENARIO

Assume that you and the attorney you work for have just met with your new client, Bradley Harris, from chapter 1 of this text. Instead of operating as a sole proprietor, Mr. Harris has entered into a partnership with a former colleague of his, whose name is Cynthia Lund. They have decided to elect limited liability partnership status for their partnership, which is called Cutting Edge Partners. The main office address for Cutting Edge Partners is Mr. Harris's home address.

Using the above information and the information provided in appendices D-1 and D-2 to this text, prepare for filing in your state a statement of qualification, or similarly titled document. You may create your own form that conforms to the statutes of your state, or you can download a form from the appropriate state office. Some statement of qualification forms for specific states are also available for downloading on the companion Web page to this text at **www.westlegalstudies.com.**

If the limited liability partnership entity is not available in your state, assume for purposes of this assignment that your state has elected the pertinent sections of the RUPA.

In addition to the statement of qualification, prepare a cover letter filing the form with the appropriate state authority, along with any required filing fee.

END NOTES

1. Uniform Partnership Act (1914) § 6.
2. Uniform Partnership Act (1914) § 2.
3. Uniform Partnership Act (1914) § 3.
4. *The Statistical Abstract of the United States (2000)* § 854.
5. *The Statistical Abstract of the United States (2000)* § 856.
6. 59A AM. JUR. 2d Partnership § 26 (1987).
7. *Id.* § 7.
8. Revised Uniform Partnership Act (1997) § 201.
9. Uniform Partnership Act (1914) § 9(1).
10. *Id.* § 9(2).
11. *Id.* § 9(3)(a).
12. *Id.* § 9(3)(b).
13. *Id.* § 9(3)(c).
14. *Id.* § 9(3)(d).
15. *Id.* § 9(3)(e).
16. *Id.* § 18(e).
17. Revised Uniform Partnership Act (1997) § 301(1).
18. *Id.* § 302(2).
19. *Id.* § 303(d)(2).
20. *Id.* § 303(d).
21. *Id.* § 306(a).
22. Uniform Partnership Act (1914) § 25(2)(a).
23. Revised Uniform Partnership Act (1997) § 501.
24. *Id.* § 401(a).
25. Uniform Partnership Act § 18(b), Revised Uniform Partnership Act (1997) § 401(c).
26. *Meinhard v. Salmon, et al.,* 164 NE 545 (NY Ct. App. 1928).
27. See § 1.5 of this text.
28. Revised Uniform Partnership Act § 401(j), Uniform Partnership Act § 18(h).
29. See § 1.5 of this text.
30. 14 AM. JUR. Legal Forms 2d (Rev 2000) § 194:103. Reprinted with permission from *American Jurisprudence Legal Forms 2d.* © 2000 West Group.
31. *Id.* § 194:136.
32. *Id.* § 194:148.
33. *Id.* § 194:244.
34. *Id.* § 194:186.
35. *Id.* § 194: 190.
36. *Id.* § 194:273.
37. *Id.* § 194:307.
38. *Id.* § 194:310.
39. *Id.* § 194:359.
40. *Id.* § 194:376.

41. *Id.* § 194:18.

42. *Id.* § 194:406.

43. *Id.* § 194:18.

44. *Id.* § 194:454.

45. *Id.* § 194:481.

46. *Id.* § 194:500.

47. Revised Uniform Partnership Act (1997) § 1001.

48. Uniform Partnership Act (1914) § 22.

49. Revised Uniform Partnership Act (1997) § 801.

50. *Id.* § 701(b).

CHAPTER 3

Limited Partnerships

CHAPTER OUTLINE

§ 3.1   An Introduction to Limited Partnerships

§ 3.2   Partners' Rights and Responsibilities

§ 3.3   Advantages of Doing Business as a Limited Partnership

§ 3.4   Disadvantages of Doing Business as a Limited Partnership

§ 3.5   Organization and Management of a Limited Partnership

§ 3.6   Changes in Partnership

§ 3.7   Financial Structure of a Limited Partnership

§ 3.8   Derivative Actions

§ 3.9   Dissolution, Winding Up, and Termination of the Limited Partnership

§ 3.10   The Paralegal's Role in Limited Partnership Matters

§ 3.11   Resources

INTRODUCTION

Limited partnerships are a special type of partnership that offers certain partners limited liability. This business organization shares many of the characteristics of general partnerships, with a few important differences. Those differences are highlighted in this chapter.

First, we define the characteristics of a limited partnership and look at a special type of limited partnership—the limited liability limited partnership. We then discuss the rights and responsibilities of the general and limited partners and the advantages and disadvantages of doing business as a limited partnership. The examination of limited partnerships then continues with a look at the organization and management of a limited partnership, including the contents of a limited partnership agreement. Next, we briefly investigate the financial structure of a limited partnership. This chapter concludes with a discussion of derivative actions, dissolution of a limited partnership, the role of paralegals who work with limited partnerships, and resources available to aid the paralegal.

§ 3.1   AN INTRODUCTION TO LIMITED PARTNERSHIPS

This section begins by defining the terms *limited partnership* and *limited liability limited partnership*. Next, it discusses the role of limited partnerships in the United States and the laws governing limited partnerships. Finally, it examines the separate entity nature of limited partnerships.

Limited Partnership Defined

A **limited partnership** is a partnership created by statute with one or more **general partners** and one or more **limited partners**. The status of the general partners in a limited partnership is very similar to that of the partners in general partnerships, and they have many of the same rights, duties, and obligations. Limited partners, on the other hand, are in many ways more like investors than partners, as their risk is limited to the amount of their contribution to the limited partnership, and they are not entitled to manage the business of the partnership.

As with a general partnership, a partner may be a "natural person, partnership, limited partnership (domestic or foreign), trust, estate, association, or corporation."[1]

Limited Liability Limited Partnerships   Some jurisdictions have adopted statutes providing for the formation of **limited liability limited partnerships (LLLPs)**. This new type of limited partnership provides for the limitation of the liability of general partners in much the same way that the liability of general partners of limited liability partnerships (LLPs) is limited. The amount of protection offered to the general partners of LLLPs varies by state. Limited liability limited partnerships are discussed throughout this chapter where pertinent.

Limited Partnerships in the United States

The popularity of limited partnerships in the United States has been attributed mainly to the unique tax advantages they offer. Because the limited partnership is

◆ ───

limited partnership   A partnership formed by general partners (who run the business and have liability for all partnership debts) and limited partners (who partly or fully take no part in running it, and have no liability for partnership debts beyond the money they put in or promise to put in).

general partner   A member of a general or limited partnership who shares in the profits and losses of the partnership and may participate fully in the management of the partnership. General partners are usually personally liable for the debts and obligations of the partnership.

limited partner   A partner who invests in a limited partnership, but does not assume personal liability for the debts and obligations of the partnership. Limited partners may not participate in the management of the limited partnership.

limited liability limited partnership   A type of limited partnership permissible in some states in which the general partners have less than full liability for the actions of other general partners.

usually not taxed as a separate entity, that business form offers the opportunity to pass profits and losses directly to the limited partners (within certain limitations). For that reason, and because limited partners are not personally liable for the debts and obligations of the partnership, the limited partnership has become a favored vehicle for investments in this country, particularly in the area of real estate.[2]

With the increasing availability of new types of business organizations that offer both limited liability and partnership taxation treatment, we may see a decrease in the number of new limited partnerships formed in the future. Two such entities are the limited liability partnership and the limited liability company. Limited liability companies are discussed in Chapter 4 of this text.

Dividends ———————————————————————◆

Family Limited Partnerships

Family limited partnerships are a type of limited partnership that is becoming increasingly popular in the United States. Family limited partnerships are popular because attorneys and estate planners recognize the value of these entities in protecting family assets while decreasing income and estate tax liability.

A family limited partnership is just what the name implies—a limited partnership owned and operated by a family. Most often, the family limited partnership is established by individuals who are concerned about protecting their assets and transferring them to their children with the least amount of income and estate tax liability. Typically, the parents will establish the limited partnership as both general and limited partners. They will often fund the family limited partnership with assets of a family business or family investments. The parents then gift their children with interests in the limited partnership as limited partners. As general partners, the parents retain the exclusive right to manage the limited partnership.

Assets held in a family limited partnership can be protected from the claims of creditors and others. A partner's interest in a limited partnership is considered to be personal property. The partnership property is owned by the family limited partnership, not by the individual partners. Creditors who have a judgment against a limited partner may seize cash or assets distributed out of the partnership to limited partners. However, creditors may not take family limited partnership property to fulfill an obligation to them unless the partnership is

dissolved. Typically, the dissolution of the family limited partnership requires the unanimous consent of all partners.

The family limited partnership allows parents the flexibility to manage the business by retaining control as general partners, while gradually transferring the responsibilities and ownership to their children. In addition, parents who are general partners of the family limited partnership can give their children the benefit of owning a piece of the business, while still ensuring that their interests will not be transferred to others outside the family—at least not until after their deaths. The family limited partnership can be established to provide that new limited partners can only be admitted with the unanimous consent of all partners.

The family limited partnership can be used to reduce the amount of estate taxes paid, when transferring wealth from one generation to the next. Parents who are general partners and holders of the majority interest as limited partners, can take advantage of the annual gift tax exclusion that allows them to gift up to $20,000 per child annually, tax free. By gifting shares in the limited partnership equal to the annual gift tax exclusion to each child each year, parents can reduce the size of their estates on their deaths, while gradually transferring the limited partnership to their children.

The value of the gift of limited partnership interests may be discounted for purposes of gift and estate taxes because they are not transferable. In addition, the interest may be discounted due to the fact that limited partners are not in control of the business—as limited partners they are prohibited from participating in the management of the partnership.

The Internal Revenue Service (IRS) is beginning to scrutinize discounted gifts (and all other transactions concerning family limited partnerships) closely. The IRS may dispute the amount of dis-counts under certain circumstances. Also, if the IRS determines that the formation of the family limited partnership is an illusory transaction with the sole purpose of avoiding estate taxes, it may seek to ignore the effect of the family limited partnership and the partnership agreement for purposes of determining tax liability.

Law Governing Limited Partnerships

The first uniform law concerning limited partnerships in the United States was the Uniform Limited Partnership Act of 1916 (ULPA), which was adopted by the vast majority of the states. In 1976, the Revised Uniform Limited Partnership Act was introduced. In 1985 substantial changes were made to that Act. Over the years, most states have adopted the Revised Uniform Limited Partnership Act with 1985 amendments (RULPA).[3] Several states, however, have recently amended, or are in the process of amending, their limited liability partnership acts to provide for limited liability limited partnerships. As of the end of 2000, the National Conference of Commissioners on Uniform State Law was working on major revisions to the RULPA, although no changes had been approved by the Commission or the American Bar Association at that time. The new revised act is being drafted to meet the needs of business owners that are not currently being met by limited liability partnerships and limited liability companies. Section 3.11 of this chapter includes a list of the state limited partnership statutes. (See appendix G of this text for the RULPA with the 1985 revisions.)

Throughout this chapter, references to the ULPA are to the original act as approved in 1916. References to the RULPA are to the Revised Act with the 1985 amendments thereto, unless otherwise indicated. Uniform laws are not always adopted verbatim, and it is very important, when researching limited partnerships, that the proper state's statutes be consulted, as even seemingly minor variations can be important.

The Limited Partnership as a Separate Entity

A limited partnership is usually treated as a separate entity. When dealing with matters such as real estate ownership and the capacity to sue, the limited partnership is considered a separate entity. For other purposes, however, the limited partnership is still considered an aggregate of the individual partners. Under common law, no partnership was ever considered a separate entity, and some states still subscribe to the common law approach when dealing with limited partnerships.[4] The limited partnership is generally not considered a separate entity for income tax purposes.

Figure 3-1 on page 82 provides a comparison of the principal features of general versus limited partnerships.

General Partnerships	*Limited Partnerships*
◆ All partners are general partners.	◆ The limited partnership must have at least one general partner and may have any number of limited partners.
◆ All partners are personally liable for the debts and obligations of the partnership.	◆ The general partners are personally responsible for the debts and obligations of the limited partnership. Limited partners risk only their investment in the limited partnership.
◆ Unless otherwise provided in the partnership agreement, all partners have an equal right to manage the partnership business.	◆ Limited partners may not participate in the control and management of the limited partnership or they will lose their limited liability status.
◆ The partners may elect to become a limited liability partnership in many states to limit the liability of all partners.	◆ The partners may elect to become a limited liability limited partnership in many states to limit the liability of all partners.
◆ In most instances, a general partnership may be formed without filing any documentation at the state level.	◆ State statutes provide for the formation of limited partnerships. A limited partnership certificate must be filed at the state level before the entity exists.
◆ The partnership is considered an entity separate from its partners for most purposes.	◆ The limited partnership is considered an entity separate from its partners for most purposes.

FIGURE 3-1   Limited Partnerships v. General Partnerships

§ 3.2 PARTNERS' RIGHTS AND RESPONSIBILITIES

Limited partnerships consist of more than one type of partner, and those partners are subject to different statutory rights and responsibilities. This section examines the rights and responsibilities unique to general partners and those unique to limited partners. The section concludes with a discussion of the relationship between general partners and limited partners.

General Partners' Rights and Responsibilities

Except as otherwise provided by statute and the limited partnership agreement, the rights and responsibilities of a general partner in a limited partnership are the same as the rights and responsibilities of those of a partner in a general partnership. Unlike limited partners, general partners are personally responsible for the liabilities of the limited partnership.

If a limited partnership opts to become a limited liability limited partnership, the general partners will not be liable for the obligations of the partnership under most circumstances. The statutes of most states that have adopted provisions permitting the formation of limited liability limited partnerships simply state that the limited liability provisions of the Uniform Partnership Act (as adopted by that state) apply to both general and limited partners of a limited liability limited partnership. The limited liability limited partnership does not protect any partner from personal liability arising from his or her own misconduct or wrongdoing.

Limited Partners' Rights and Responsibilities

The limited partner is often seen as more of an investor than an actual partner to the partnership. The limited partner has few of the rights granted to partners in a general partnership, and correspondingly few of the responsibilities. One of the most important characteristics of limited partners is that they have limited liability. The risk of a limited partner is limited to the amount of that partner's investment in the limited partnership.

The interest of a limited partner in a partnership is considered to be personal property, even if the partnership assets include or consist solely of land. The limited partner holds no title to the assets of the partnership, but has only his or her interest in the partnership.[5]

Unlike the partners in a general partnership, limited partners have no right to participate in the management of the partnership, and may actually be in danger of losing their limited liability status if they do participate in the control of the partnership business. In that event, the limited partner may be held personally liable for the debts and obligations of the limited partnership. Under the RULPA, a limited partner who participates in control of the business is liable only to persons who transact business with the limited partnership reasonably believing, based upon the limited partner's conduct, that the limited partner is a general partner.[6]

Exactly what constitutes "taking part in control" of the business has been the subject of many a court case and is still subject to debate. However, under the RULPA, some guidance is given by way of a list of "safe harbor" activities. The RULPA states:

A limited partner does not participate in the control of the business ... solely by doing one or more of the following:

(1) being a contractor for or an agent or employee of the limited partnership or of a general partner or being an officer, director, or shareholder of a general partner that is a corporation;

(2) consulting with and advising a general partner with respect to the business of the limited partnership;

(3) acting as surety for the limited partnership or guaranteeing or assuming one or more specific obligations of the limited partnership;

(4) taking any action required or permitted by law to bring or pursue a derivative action in the right of the limited partnership;

(5) requesting or attending a meeting of partners;

(6) proposing, approving, or disapproving, by voting or otherwise, one or more of the following matters:

(i) the dissolution and winding up of the limited partnership;

    (ii)   the sale, exchange, lease, mortgage, pledge, or other transfer of all or substantially all of the assets of the limited partnership;

    (iii) the incurrence of indebtedness by the limited partnership other than in the ordinary course of its business;

    (iv) a change in the nature of the business;

    (v) the admission or removal of a general partner;

    (vi) the admission or removal of a limited partner;

    (vii) a transaction involving an actual or potential conflict of interest between a general partner and the limited partnership or the limited partners;

    (viii) an amendment to the partnership agreement or certificate of limited partnership; or

    (ix) matters related to the business of the limited partnership not otherwise enumerated in this subsection (b), which the partnership agreement states in writing may be subject to the approval or disapproval of limited partners;

(7) winding up the limited partnership … or

(8) exercising any right or power permitted to limited partners under this Act and not specifically enumerated in this subsection (b).[7]

The RULPA further states that the possession or exercise of any powers not included in the preceding list does not necessarily constitute participation of the limited partner in the partnership business.

    Although limited partners have no right to manage the business of the partnership, they are granted certain rights by statute, including the statutory right to information regarding the partnership business. Limited partners are generally entitled to inspect the limited partnership records at any reasonable time.[8]

The Relationship between General Partners and Limited Partners

Because limited partners are prohibited from participating in the control of the business, the relationship between general partners and limited partners differs significantly from the relationship among partners in a general partnership. General partners owe a fiduciary duty to limited partners, and the sole general partner of a limited partnership owes to limited partners an even greater duty than that normally imposed on partners, especially when the general partner holds a majority interest.[9] The duty of a general partner, acting in complete control, has been compared both to the fiduciary duty of a trustee to the beneficiaries of a trust, and to the fiduciary relationship of a corporate director to a shareholder.

    One person may be both a general partner and a limited partner in the same partnership. In that event, the partner will have all of the rights and responsibilities of a general partner. However, his or her contribution to the partnership as a limited partner will be protected in the same manner as the contribution of any other limited partner.

    In *BT-I v. Equitable Life Assurance Society,* the case on page 85, the court found that the general partner breached its fiduciary duty to the limited partner and acted

CASE

BT-I, Plaintiff and Appellant,

v.

**EQUITABLE LIFE ASSURANCE
SOCIETY OF the UNITED STATES,
Defendant and Respondent.**

No. G020711.
Court of Appeal, Fourth District, Division 3, California.
Oct. 29, 1999.

BEDSWORTH, J.

This is an appeal by a limited partner who was squeezed out of the partnership when the general partner purchased and foreclosed a **deed of trust** on the partnership's sole asset, an office building.

BT-I, the limited partner, brought this action against The Equitable Life Assurance Society of the United States (Equitable), the general partner, alleging breach of fiduciary duty, breach of contract (three causes of action) and breach of the covenant of good faith and fair dealing. The trial judge ... found the partnership agreement authorized Equitable's conduct and relieved it of any duty to BT-I... .

BT-I argues the limited partnership agreement could not **abrogate** Equitable's fiduciary duty not to engage in self-dealing. ... We agree... and reverse.

* * *

In 1985, BT-I (a California general partnership) entered into a general partnership with Equitable named Brin-Mar I, to develop and operate a commercial office building and retail complex in Orange County ... . Banque Paribas provided a $62.5 million loan secured by a trust deed on the project.

In 1991, BT-I and Equitable canceled their 1985 general partnership and entered into the present limited partnership, Brin-Mar I, L.P., with Equitable the general partner and BT-I the limited partner. Equitable had a 70 percent interest and BT-I had a 30 percent interest... .

Equitable put up $6 million in additional capital and received in return sole title to the retail complex along with extensive powers giving it the sole right to manage and control the partnership and its assets. It is one of these many powers that is at the crux of this appeal.

Paragraph 5.1(c) of the limited partnership agreement gave Equitable broad powers to refinance and restructure the partnership debt ...

As the due date of the Paribas loans approached, Equitable no longer wanted BT-I as a partner and maneuvered to oust it. Equitable learned the bank was interested in selling the loans at a steep discount, notified BT-I that the bank was soliciting bids, and suggested an offer of $35 million would succeed. Unknown to BT-I or other bidders, the bank had already agreed to sell the loans to Equitable if it matched the high bid, and further agreed not to deal directly with BT-I. BT-I alleged Equitable's proffer of the opportunity was a charade, since neither the partnership nor BT-I had the necessary funds.

Equitable bought the loans on August 21, 1995 for $38.5 million. On September 1, 1995, the day after the loans were due, Equitable demanded full payment of approximately $65 million within 10 days. On the 11th day, no payment having been received, Equitable recorded notices of default.

In October 1995, Equitable offered to sell the loan to the partnership at its own cost. The offer was not accepted. BT-I asked Equitable to attempt to refinance the project, but the general partner refused. It made no attempt to sell the building, nor did it consider filing for bankruptcy protection. BT-I's own attempts to locate a new lender came to naught, because Equitable refused to provide partnership balance sheets and other financial information when requested, and refused to give BT-I access to the partnership books and records. A foreclosure sale was scheduled for March 1996.

deed of trust A document, similar to a mortgage, by which a person transfers the legal ownership of land to independent trustees to be held until a debt on the land is paid off.

abrogate To abolish, annul, or repeal a former law, rule, or custom.

Three days before the sale, BT-I made a $39 million cash offer for the project but Equitable turned it down, both as lender and on behalf of the partnership. Equitable then acquired the building at the foreclosure sale.

BT-I claimed $5 million in damages for: (1) the loss of its equity in the project; (2) the post-foreclosure loss of appreciation as the building increased in value when market conditions improved; and (3) being forced to recognize a taxable gain in 1995 because Equitable bought the loans, when otherwise it would have been postponed to 1996 or later if a third party acquired the debt and foreclosed.

BT-I contends the partnership agreement did not expressly authorize Equitable's purchase and foreclosure of partnership debt, and we should not interpret it to allow such conduct because the fiduciary duties of loyalty and good faith cannot be waived. We agree.

Partnership is a fiduciary relationship, and partners are held to the standards and duties of a trustee in their dealings with each other. "Partners are trustees for each other, and in all proceedings connected with the conduct of the partnership every partner is bound to act in the highest good faith to his copartner and may not obtain any advantage over him in the partnership affairs by the slightest misrepresentation, concealment, threat or adverse pressure of any kind." ... Moreover, this duty extends to all aspects of the relationship and all transactions between the partners. "Each [partner] occupie[s] the position of a trustee to the other with regard to all the partnership transactions, including the transactions contemplated by the firm and constituting the object or purpose for which the partnership was formed."

In general, under the California Revised Limited Partnership Act (Corp. Code, § 15611, *et. seq.*), partners may determine by agreement many aspects of their relationship. (Corp. Code, § 15618.) But there are limitations. A general partner of a limited partnership is subject to the same restrictions, and has the same liabilities to the partnership and other partners, as in a general partnership (Corp. Code, § 15643). One of these is the duty to account to the partnership for any benefit, and hold as trustee for it any profits, "derived ... without the consent of the other partners from any transaction connected with the ... conduct ... of the partnership ... ."

While there are no California cases dealing with the acquisition of partnership debt by a general partner, we agree with recent out-of-state decisions holding such conduct is a breach of fiduciary duty. ...A general partner who acquires a partnership obligation cannot foreclose on partnership assets. ...

The question then becomes whether the fiduciary duty not to purchase partnership debt and foreclose out one's partner can be contracted away in the partnership agreement. We hold it cannot. ...

We agree with several recent decisions holding a limited partnership agreement cannot relieve the general partner of its fiduciary duties in matters fundamentally related to the partnership business. ... Exactly where the line resides between those matters upon which partners may and may not reduce or eliminate their fiduciary duties is a question we need not decide, because Equitable's transgression is beyond all doubt on the wrong side of the line. ...

The judgment is reversed. Appellant is entitled to its costs on appeal.

---

in a self-serving manner when it purchased an outstanding loan of the limited partnership and then foreclosed on it—forcing the limited partner out of the partnership.

§ 3.3 ADVANTAGES OF DOING BUSINESS AS A LIMITED PARTNERSHIP

Limited partnerships have several unique advantages to offer both general and limited partners. In this section, we look at some of the more important advantages of doing business as a limited partnership, including the limited liability available to limited partners, potential income tax benefits, the relative transferability of partnership interests and continuity of business as compared to general partnerships, and the availability of diversified capital resources.

Limited Liability for Limited Partners

One of the best features of a limited partnership is the limited liability offered to its limited partners. Limited partners can invest money without becoming liable for the debts of the firm as long as they do not participate in the control of the business or hold themselves out to be general partners.

In *Commonwealth of Pennsylvania, Department of Revenue for the Bureau of Accounts Settlement v. McKelvey,* a schoolteacher who invested in a bicycle business protected his personal liability by acting as a limited partner. When the business failed to pay its taxes, the court determined that a tax lien could not be placed on the property of the limited partner, and that the partner could not be held personally responsible for taxes owed by the limited partnership.

CASE

**SUPREME COURT OF PENNSYLVANIA.
COMMONWEALTH OF PENNSYLVANIA,
DEPARTMENT OF REVENUE
FOR THE BUREAU OF ACCOUNTS
SETTLEMENT, APPELLEE,
V.
PATRICK J. MCKELVEY, PETER BRADLEY
T/A DIFFERENT SPOKES.
APPEAL OF PETER BRADLEY T/A
DIFFERENT SPOKES.**

NO. 81 E.D. APPEAL 1990.
ARGUED JAN. 15, 1991.
DECIDED MARCH 7, 1991.

OPINION OF THE COURT
LARSEN, Justice.

The issues raised by this appeal are whether appellant, Peter Bradley, received actual notice of a tax assessment against the business in which he was a limited partner, and whether appellant, as a limited partner, was liable for a partnership debt under the Uniform Limited Partnership Act.

Appellant is a school teacher who was requested by Patrick McKelvey to provide the financial backing for a retail bicycle business. The two men entered into a limited partnership agreement, and appellant provided an $18,000.00 loan to the

business. As a limited partner, appellant took no part in the operation or management of the bicycle shop. McKelvey, as general partner, handled all of the purchases, sales and financial aspects of the business. Identifying himself as the partnership's "principal" partner (we interpret this as meaning the partnership's general partner), McKelvey filed an application for sales, use and hotel occupancy license with the Department of Revenue of the Commonwealth of Pennsylvania, and designated appellant as a limited partner in the business, which was known as "Different Spokes."

On October 10, 1985, appellee, Commonwealth of Pennsylvania, Department of Revenue for the Bureau of Accounts Settlement, mailed a notice of Sales and Use tax assessment to the business address of Different Spokes for a series of tax periods beginning July 1, 1983, and ending June 30, 1985, in the amount of $17,636.86. The total assessment amounted to $27,974.21 with penalties and interest. No challenge was made to this assessment nor was the assessment paid.

In April of 1986, appellee issued liens in the amount of $27,974.21 against the business and its general and limited partners. Appellant, who had not been individually notified of the assessment by the appellee, did not discover the lien that had been filed against properties he owned until he was conducting a title search several months thereafter during a routine application for a mortgage. Appellant promptly filed a Petition to Strike Tax Lien in the Court of Common Pleas of Delaware County. That court determined that its jurisdiction was limited to the question of whether or not appellant had received notice of the assessment. The common pleas court then held that notice to the partnership constituted notice to the appellant, and thus, that the appellant had received notice of the assessment. Accordingly, appellant's petition to strike tax lien was denied.

Appellant filed an appeal to Commonwealth Court which affirmed, holding that the notice of tax assessment sent to the limited partnership was "sufficient to support the lien entered against [appellant] as a limited partner." ... We granted appellant's petition for allowance of appeal, and we now reverse.

The trial court erred in holding that notice to a partnership constitutes notice to a limited partner. The trial court also erred in holding by implication that the personal assets of a limited partner can be liened to satisfy the debt of a limited partnership.

As a matter of law, notice to a limited partnership can never constitute notice to a limited partner. A limited partner has no role in the exercise,

control or management of the limited partnership business. Limited partners, by statutory definition, do not take part in the control or management of partnership business.

Section 521 of the Uniform Limited Partnership Act which was in effect at the time of the events giving rise to this litigation provided as follows:

A limited partner shall not become liable as a general partner unless, in addition to the exercise of his rights and powers as a limited partner, he takes part in the control of the business. 59 Pa.C.S.A. § 521 (now repealed).

Appellant was a limited partner and did not take part in the control or management of Different Spokes; accordingly, the notice received by the partnership of the tax assessment did not constitute actual notice to appellant. ...

Finally, it is the law of this Commonwealth that a limited partner is not liable for the obligations of the limited partnership. ... Thus, assuming proper notice to appellant, his liability would be limited.

Accordingly, we reverse the decision of the Commonwealth Court, and we remand to the Court of Common Pleas of Delaware County for the entry of an order granting appellant's petition to strike tax lien.

In states that allow the formation of limited liability limited partnerships, the personal liability of all partners, including general partners, may be limited. Neither the general partners nor the limited partners may be held personally responsible for the debts and obligations of the limited partnership in excess of their contributions to the limited liability limited partnership.

The limitations on personal liability offered to all partners of limited liability limited partnerships gives partners a distinct advantage over partners of other limited liability partnerships and over general partnerships and sole proprietors. Partners of a limited liability limited partnership can experience all of the advantages of doing business as a limited partnership, without risking their personal wealth and assets.

Income Tax Benefits

A limited partnership is usually not treated as a separate tax entity for federal income tax purposes. Therefore, limited partnerships can offer attractive tax advantages to both general and limited partners. The ability of the limited partnership to pass tax profits and losses directly to the limited partners, without the limited partners risking anything more than their investment, can be a significant advantage over the corporate and general partnership tax structures. There are, however, limits to the amount of loss partners can claim on their income tax returns. All partners are subject to limits established by the Internal Revenue Service on losses that can be claimed, based on the amount of the partners' investment in the partnership and the amount for which the partner is actually considered at risk. In addition, limited partners especially may be subject to limits on the losses they may claim under rules that apply to income derived from passive activities. Although limited partnerships generally are not subject to federal income taxation, they are subject to state income taxation in many states.

Transferability of Partnership Interest

Although a partner's interest in a limited partnership is not as easily transferred as a corporate interest, the limited partner's interest is generally assignable with fewer restrictions than those imposed on the partners of a general partnership. The assignment of a limited partner's interest in a limited partnership does not cause a dissolution of the limited partnership. In some situations, the entire interest of the limited partner may be assigned, with the assignee becoming a substitute partner. An assignment that has the effect of admitting new limited partners to the limited partnership must be permissible under the limited partnership agreement, or it must be approved by the unanimous consent of all partners.

General partners also have certain rights to assign their interests in the limited partnership. A general partner may have all of the same rights of assignability as a limited partner, although certain assignments may be considered an event of withdrawal. In any event, the limited partnership offers much more flexibility with regard to the transfer of partnership interests than the general partnership.

Business Continuity

The limited partnership does not enjoy the continuity of business to the same extent as does a corporation, but it is not always necessary for a limited partnership to dissolve upon the death, retirement, or withdrawal of a partner.

The limited partnership will not necessarily dissolve upon the withdrawal of a general partner if at the time (1) there is at least one other general partner, (2) the written provisions of the partnership agreement permit the business of the limited partnership to be carried on by the remaining general partner, and (3) that partner does so. In any event, the limited partnership need not be dissolved and is not required to be wound up by reason of any event of withdrawal if, "within 90 days after the withdrawal, all partners agree in writing to continue the business of the limited partnership and to the appointment of one or more additional general partners if necessary or desired."[10]

Diversified Capital Resources

In addition to the capital resources that are typically available to the general partnership, the limited partnership has the ability to raise initial capital by attracting passive investors. The limited partnership may raise additional capital when required by adding new limited partners.

§ 3.4 DISADVANTAGES OF DOING BUSINESS AS A LIMITED PARTNERSHIP

Although there are several advantages to doing business as a limited partnership, this type of entity also has some serious disadvantages. This section explains the disadvantages associated with operating as a limited partnership due to the unlimited liability of the general partners, the prohibition on control of the business by limited partners, the formalities and regulatory and reporting requirements, and the associated legal and organizational expenses.

Unlimited Liability

Because limited partners put at risk only their investment in the limited partnership, a limited partnership cannot exist without at least one general partner who has unlimited liability for the debts and obligations of the limited partnership. As discussed in previous chapters, there are ways to decrease the impact of unlimited personal liability, and in states where limited liability limited partnerships can be formed, personal liability of both general and limited partners can be avoided. However, where personal liability of the general partners cannot be eliminated, it is a serious drawback to doing business as a limited partnership.

Prohibition on Control of Business

Although every partner is entitled to an equal share of the management of a general partnership, limited partners must relinquish all control over partnership matters in order to maintain their status and enjoy limited liability. Limited partners must place their full trust in the general partners for the successful management and control of the business.

Formalities and Regulatory and Reporting Requirements

The limited partnership is a creature of statute and, as such, must be "created" by documentation filed with the proper state authority. A **limited partnership certificate** must be executed, and filed, before the limited partnership's existence begins. Therefore, many more formalities are associated with the creation of a limited partnership than with a sole proprietorship or a general partnership. Limited partnerships are also subject to many of the same reporting requirements as corporations.

---

limited partnership certificate Document required for filing at the state level to form a limited partnership.

Limited partnerships may be required to register or qualify to do business as a foreign limited partnership in any state, other than their state of domicile, in which they propose to transact business. The registration or qualification requirements are set by the statutes of the state where the foreign limited partnership is proposing to transact business, and are often the same or similar to the requirements for foreign corporations transacting business in that state.[11] These requirements vary greatly from state to state, so the appropriate statutes must be consulted whenever a limited partnership is considering transacting business in a state other than its state of domicile.

In addition, limited partnerships are required to file annual tax returns to report any income or loss, and they are required to distribute annual schedules to each partner to report their distributive share of the limited partnership's income or loss.

Legal and Organizational Expenses

Compared with the sole proprietorship or general partnership, the legal and organizational expenses of a limited partnership can be quite substantial. In addition to the capital required for the ordinary expenses incurred in operating the limited partnership business, the founders of a limited partnership will usually incur significant legal fees for preparation of a limited partnership agreement and certificate, filing fees for the certificate of limited partnership, and possibly for filing a certificate of assumed name.

Figure 3-2 provides a comparison of the advantages and disadvantages of doing business as a limited partnership

Advantages	*Disadvantages*
♦ *Limited Liability for Limited Partners* Limited partners have no personal liability for the debts and obligations of the limited partnership.	♦ *General Partners Do Not Usually Have Limited Liability* Unless an election is made to become a limited liability limited partnership, every limited partnership must have at least one general partner who is personally liable for the debts and obligations of the limited partnership.
♦ *Limited Liability for All Partners of Limited Liability Limited Partnerships* General and limited partners of a limited liability limited partnership have no personal liability for the debts and obligations of the limited liability limited partnership.	♦ *Limited Partnerships May Be Subject to State Income Taxation*
♦ *Income Tax Benefits* Limited partnerships are not subject to federal income taxation. Income "flows through" to the partners.	♦ *Prohibition on Control of Business* Limited partners cannot be involved in the management of the limited partnership.

FIGURE 3-2   Advantages and Disadvantages of Doing Business as a Limited Partnership

Advantages	Disadvantages
• *Transferability of Partnership Interest* Compared with general partnerships, limited partners have much more freedom to transfer their interests in the limited partnership.	• *Formalities and Regulatory and Reporting Requirements* Limited partnerships cannot exist until the proper documentation is filed at the state level. In addition, limited partnerships may be subject to various reporting requirements that are not imposed on sole proprietorships and general partnerships.
• *Business Continuity* In contrast to the general partnership or sole proprietorship, the limited partnership offers much more continuity of business.	• *Legal and Organizational Expense* The legal and organizational expenses associated with forming and maintaining a limited partnership are typically considerably greater than those associated with partnerships and sole proprietorships.
• *Diversified Capital Resources* Unlike sole proprietorships and general partnerships, limited partnerships have the ability to attract passive investors who accept no personal liability.	

FIGURE 3-2 (*continued*)

§ 3.5 ORGANIZATION AND MANAGEMENT OF A LIMITED PARTNERSHIP

The organization and management of a limited partnership are unlike that of any other type of entity. This section discusses the management and control of the limited partnership by the general partners, the preparation and filing of the limited partnership certificate, and the contents of the limited partnership agreement.

Management and Control

The management and control of a limited partnership are similar to that of a general partnership, with one important distinction: only the general partners of the limited partnership have control of the partnership business.

Limited Partnership Certificate

The document that is filed with the secretary of state or other appropriate state authority to form the limited partnership is called the limited partnership certificate. This document may include the entire agreement between the partners, but more commonly it contains the minimum amount of information required by state statute, with the full agreement of the partners contained in a limited partnership agreement or in other documents that are not filed for public record.

Under the RULPA, many of the provisions concerning the management of the limited partnership may be included in the limited partnership agreement or records kept by the limited partnership. They need not be made public in the limited partnership certificate. In states that have adopted the RULPA, the certificate of limited partnership must include the following:

1. The name of the limited partnership.
2. The office address and the name and address of the agent for service of process.
3. The name and business address of each general partner.
4. The latest date upon which the limited partnership is to dissolve.
5. Any other matters the general partners desire to include in the certificate.[12]

The limited partnership certificate in Figure 3-3 is an example of a limited partnership certificate that could be filed in a state following the RULPA.

In states following the RULPA, the limited partnership certificate must be signed by the general partner(s) of the limited partnership. The limited partnership certificate must be filed with the appropriate state authority along with the required filing fee to be effective. In addition, any other filing requirements set forth in the state statutes must be complied with.

LIMITED PARTNERSHIP CERTIFICATE

1. The name of the limited partnership is _____.

2. The office address of the principal place of business of the limited partnership is: _____.

3. The name and office address of the agent for service of process are:

_____

_____.

4. The name and business address of each general partner are as follows:

Name   Address

_____   _____

_____   _____

_____   _____

5. The latest date upon which the limited partnership is to dissolve is

_____, ____.

Signed this ___ day of _____, ____.

GENERAL PARTNERS:

_____

FIGURE 3-3 Limited Partnership Certificate

Limited Liability Limited Partnership Election

In states that provide for the formation of limited liability limited partnerships, that entity is usually formed when a limited partnership that complies with all other requirements affecting limited partnerships files an additional election to become a limited liability limited partnership with the secretary of state or other state authority. The election to become a limited liability limited partnership must contain a statement that the election has been approved pursuant to the provisions of the limited partnership agreement. If the approval of limited liability limited partnership status is not addressed in the limited partnership agreement, the election must be approved as required by statute. Figure 3-4 on page 95 is a sample of a form that may be filed in the State of Arizona to convert a limited partnership to a limited liability limited partnership. Again, this election is not provided for by the laws of all states.

Amendment to Limited Partnership Certificate

The RULPA sets forth events that necessitate the filing of an amendment to the limited partnership certificate and the requirements for the certificate of amendment itself.[13] In general, when any significant information that is included in the limited partnership certificate changes or when an error in the information on the limited partnership certificate is detected, an amendment must be filed. Under most circumstances, amendments to the limited partnership certificate must be approved and executed by all partners.

Records Required by Statute

Partly because so little information is required to be filed for the limited partnership certificate, state statutes typically require that certain records and documents be maintained for the inspection of limited partners. The following records are usually required to be kept at a designated partnership office.

1. A current list of the names and business addresses of all partners. This list must identify the general partners, in alphabetical order, and separately list, in alphabetical order, the limited partners.
2. A copy of the certificate of limited partnership and all certificates of amendment thereto, together with executed copies of any powers of attorney pursuant to which any certificate has been executed.
3. Copies of the limited partnership's federal, state, and local income tax returns and reports, if any, for the three most recent years.
4. Copies of any effective written partnership agreements.
5. Copies of any financial statements of the limited partnership for the three most recent years.[14]

The following information must be set forth in documents kept at the partnership office, unless it is contained in the limited partnership agreement:

1. The amount of cash and a description and statement of the agreed value of any other property or services contributed by each partner and which each partner has agreed to contribute.

Betsey Bayless
Secretary of State
Limited Partnership Division
1700 West Washington 7th Fl
Phoenix, Arizona 85007
Fee: $3.00

STATEMENT OF QUALIFICATION FOR CONVERSION
OF LIMITED PARTNERSHIP OR LIMITED LIABILITY PARTNERSHIP
TO A LIMITED LIABILITY LIMITED PARTNERSHIP
A.R.S. 29-308

The filing of a Statement of Conversion Qualification automatically cancels any existing Limited or Limited Liability Partnerships.

1. _____

 Name of the Limited Partnership   Name of the Limited Liability Partnership

2. _____

 Name of LLLP

3. _____

 Street address of the **chief** executive office of the partnership (if the chief executive office is not located in Arizona, please provide the street address of an office in this state)

 _____

 Name of the Service of Process Agent

 _____

 Arizona Address of the Service of Process Agent (Post Office Box Numbers not acceptable)

In the event that the above named designated agent for service of process resigns and a new agent for service of process has not been filed with the Secretary of State, or if the above named agent for service of process cannot be found or served with reasonable diligence, then the Secretary of State's office is appointed the agent for service of process.

4. Statement of Status:

_____

Signature of at least two partners:

_____   _____

Signature   Print Name

_____   _____

Signature   Print Name

FIGURE 3-4 Sample Statement of Qualification for Conversion of Limited Partnership or Limited Liability Partnership to a Limited Liability Limited Partnership Form from the State of Arizona

2. The times at which, or events on the happening of which, any additional contributions agreed to be made by each partner are to be made.

3. Any rights of partners to receive, or of a general partner to make, distributions, which include a return of all or any part of the partner's contribution.

4. Any events upon the happening of which the limited partnership is to be dissolved and its affairs wound up.[15]

These records must be kept and are subject to inspection and copying at the reasonable request and at the expense of any partner during ordinary business hours.

Limited Partnership Agreement

The limited partnership agreement should encompass the entire agreement among all partners. This document usually goes into much more detail than the limited partnership certificate, because it is not a document of public record, and because it is more easily amended than the limited partnership certificate.

Following is a discussion of some of the various matters that should be contained in a limited partnership agreement. The examples used in the following sections are only a small representation of the type of paragraphs and clauses that may be included in a limited partnership agreement. See appendix J-2 of this text for a limited partnership agreement form.

Name of Limited Partnership   The full name of the limited partnership should be set forth in this section. Special consideration must be given to the name of a limited partnership, for several reasons. First, the name chosen for the limited partnership must be available. A call to the appropriate state authority will usually verify the availability of a proposed name. (See appendix A of this text for a secretary of state directory.)

Second, state statutes may require that the name of the limited partnership contain the words "limited partnership" or other specific language. Finally, the name of the limited partnership may not contain the name of a limited partner unless it is also the name of a general partner or the corporate name of a corporate general partner, or the business of the limited partnership was carried on under that name before the admission of that limited partner. The appropriate state statutes must be consulted to be certain that all requirements regarding the name of the limited partnership are complied with.

State statutes also have special requirements for the names of limited liability limited partnerships. If the limited partnership is opting to be a limited liability limited partnership, its name must comply with any such statutory requirements.

Names and Addresses of Partners and Designation of Partnership Status   This section of the partnership agreement should contain the names and addresses of all partners and, most importantly, the designation as to which partners are general partners, which partners are limited partners, and which partners (if any) are both.

Purpose of Partnership   There are few statutory restrictions on the nature of business that may be carried on by a limited partnership. The RULPA provides that a limited partnership may carry on any business that can be transacted by a general partnership.[16] However, the statutes of some states may prohibit certain regulated industries, such as insurance or banking, from transacting business as a limited partnership.

This section of the limited partnership agreement should set forth the purpose of the limited partnership, without being restrictively specific.

EXAMPLE: Partnership Purpose—Generally

This limited partnership is formed for the purpose of _____ and all lawful purposes and activities incidental to that purpose. This purpose shall not be construed as limiting or restricting in any manner the limited partnership from conducting any other purposes or powers authorized under the laws of the State of _____ concerning limited partnerships.

Principal Place of Business   This section should set forth the address of the partnership's principal place of business. This is important because certain documents are required by law to be kept at the principal place of business of the limited partnership.

Duration of Limited Partnership Agreement   This section should set forth the intended duration of the limited partnership, as well as certain conditions that may cause the termination of the partnership.

EXAMPLE: Duration of Partnership—Termination on Notice from a Partner

The limited partnership shall commence on _____, and shall continue until terminated by ___ months' notice in writing from a partner desiring to withdraw from the partnership and requesting the partnership's termination. Outstanding partnership business shall be consummated and obligations discharged during the period between receipt of notice and the effective date of termination contained in this agreement.[17]

Contributions of Both General and Limited Partners   This very important section of the agreement should set forth the partners' agreement regarding all contributions to the limited partnership, including the form of each contribution, any interest to be paid on contributions, any adjustment provisions for contributions, any additional contribution requirements, and the time when contributions are to be returned to limited partners. This section should also set forth any rights of partners to demand property in lieu of cash for a return of contribution.

EXAMPLE: Capital Contribution of General Partner

General partner shall contribute $_____ to the original capital of the partnership. The contribution of general partner shall be made on or before _____ [date]. If general partner does not make ____ [his or her] entire contribution to the capital of the partnership on or before that date, this agreement shall be void. Any contributions to the capital of the partnership made at that time shall be returned to the partners who have made the contributions.[18]

EXAMPLE: Capital Contributions of Limited Partners

The capital contributions of limited partners shall be as follows:

Name	Amount
_____	$_____
_____	$_____
_____	$_____

Receipt of the capital contribution from each limited partner as specified above is acknowledged by the partnership. No limited partner has agreed to contribute any additional cash or property as capital for use of the partnership.[19]

Assets of Limited Partnership All information regarding the assets of the limited partnership should be included in this section, including identification, valuation, control, and distribution of assets, and accountability therefor.

EXAMPLE: Distribution of Assets—Return of Contribution Plus Increment on Dissolution

The contribution of each limited partner, increased by any gains and not withdrawn or decreased by losses, is to be returned on the termination of the partnership in accordance with the terms of Section ___, or on any earlier dissolution of the partnership if caused by the death, retirement, or insanity of a general partner, provided, however, that at any such time all liabilities of the partnership, except liabilities to general partners and to limited partners on account of their contributions, shall have been paid, and that there shall then remain property of the partnership sufficient to make such return.[20]

EXAMPLE: Distribution of Assets—Proration if Assets Insufficient

If the property remaining following the payment of all liabilities of the partnership is not sufficient to repay in full all the partners' (general and limited) contributions adjusted to reflect accumulated gains or losses, then each of the partners shall receive such proportion of the remaining property as his, her, or their respective contribution, as adjusted, shall bear to the aggregate of all such adjusted partnership contributions that have not been repaid. In such event limited partners shall not have any further claim against the partners for the return of the balance of their contributions or credited gains.[21]

Liability This section of the agreement should contain all provisions regarding the liability of general and limited partners to one another and to third parties. If the limited partnership is to be a limited liability limited partnership, the partnership agreement should include a statement concerning the limitation of the liability of all partners.

EXAMPLE: Liability to Third Party—Limitation of Liability

Notwithstanding any other provision contained in this agreement, except to have a limited partner's capital account charged for losses to be borne by the limited partner as provided in this agreement, no limited partner shall have any personal responsibility whatever for or on account of any losses or liabilities of the partnership. To the extent that losses and liabilities of the partnership exceed its assets, the losses shall be borne solely by the general partners.[22]

EXAMPLE: Limited Liability of Limited Liability Limited Partnership

Any obligation of the limited partnership incurred while the limited partnership is a limited liability limited partnership, whether arising in contract, tort, or otherwise, is solely the obligation of the limited partnership. No partner, general or limited, is personally liable, directly or indirectly, by way of contribution or otherwise, for such partnership obligation.

Distribution of Profits and Losses to General and Limited Partners   This section should set forth the terms and conditions for distributions from the partnership, including restrictions on distributions and distributions made to various classes of partners.

EXAMPLE: Profit and Loss Sharing by Limited Partners

The limited partners shall receive the following shares of the net profits of the partnership:

Name	Share
_____	_____
_____	_____
_____	_____

Each limited partner shall bear a share of the losses of the partnership equal to the share of the profits to which the partner is entitled. The share of the losses of each limited partner shall be charged against the partner's contribution to the capital of the partnership.

No limited partner shall at any time become liable to any obligations or losses of the partnership beyond the amount of the partner's respective capital contribution.[23]

Indemnity   This section should set forth the partners' agreement for indemnification of their expenses on behalf of the partnership.

Duties of General Partners   This section should set forth the duties of each general partner in as much detail as practical.

EXAMPLE: Duties of General Partners

The general partners shall at all times during the continuance of this partnership diligently and exclusively devote themselves to the business of the partnership to the utmost of their skills and abilities, and on a full-time basis.

The general partners shall not engage, either directly or indirectly, in any business similar to the business of the partnership at any time during the term of this agreement without obtaining the written approval of all other parties.

Duties of Limited Partners This section should set forth the duties of any limited partners who are employees of the limited partnership. This section should be carefully drafted so that no misunderstanding arises regarding the inability of limited partners to control the partnership business.

Limited Partners' Rights of Substitution This section should address all of the desired rights of partners to substitution, including the right to admit additional limited partners and priorities of certain limited partners over others.

> ### EXAMPLE: Powers of Partners—Assignment of Limited Partner's Interest
>
> A limited partner's interests shall be assignable in whole or in part. All limited partners shall have the right to confer upon the assignee of their interests or a part thereof the rights of a substituted limited partner as provided by the [Uniform Limited Partnership Act or Revised Uniform Limited Partnership Act] of the State of _____ [cite appropriate statute].[24]

Compensation and Benefits for Partners This section should set forth all matters concerning the compensation of and benefits for general partners, including salaries, retirement benefits, health and other insurance, etc.

> ### EXAMPLE: Salary—General Partner
>
> General partner shall be entitled to a monthly salary of $_____ for the services rendered by general partner. The salary shall commence on _____ [date], and be payable on the ___ day of each subsequent month. The salary shall be treated as an expense of the operation of the partnership business and shall be payable whether or not the partnership shall operate at a profit. [25]

Management and Control of Business by General Partners This section should set forth the management and control policies of the limited partnership.

> ### EXAMPLE: Limited Partners' Participation in Conduct of Business
>
> No limited partner shall have any right to be active in the conduct of the partnership's business, or have power to bind the partnership in any contract, agreement, promise, or undertaking.[26]

Limited Partners' Rights in Review of Business Policies This section should set forth the limited partnership's policy with regard to the limited partners' rights to review the business policies of the partnership.

Policies of Business Any policies that the partners desire to set forth in a written agreement may be set forth in this section of the limited partnership agreement.

Accounting Practices and Procedures This section should set forth all accounting methods, practices, and policies of the partnership, including the accounting period and fiscal year of the partnership, the frequency and types of reports to be completed, details regarding the books of accounts, audit provisions, and provisions for examination of books.

Changes in General or Limited Partners by Withdrawal, Expulsion, Retirement, or Death In this very important section of the limited partnership agreement, the partners may set forth their desires regarding the admission of new general and limited partners, their acceptance requirements, and the redistribution of assets. This section should also address all matters concerning withdrawing partners, including the necessity of the consent of the other partners, notice requirements, valuation of the withdrawing partner's share of the partnership, the option of the remaining partners to purchase the interest, and the assignment of the withdrawing partner's interest to a third party. Partners may also want to include conditions for expulsion of a partner, notice requirements, and all other matters concerning the expulsion of a partner.

The partnership's policy regarding a retiring partner should likewise be addressed in this section, including the reorganization of partnership rights and duties.

EXAMPLE: New Limited Partner

Amendments to the certificate of limited partnership of the partnership for the purpose of substituting a limited partner will be validly made if signed only by the general partners and by the person to be substituted and by the assigning limited partner. If any one or all general partners resign or are expelled or otherwise cease to be a general partner under the provision of this agreement, and pursuant to this agreement a new general partner or partners are elected, the amendment to the certificate to make the change will be validly made if signed only by the remaining general partner and the new general partner or by the new general partners.[27]

EXAMPLE: Expulsion of Partner by Vote of Limited Partners

Upon the vote of limited partners holding a majority in interest of the partnership, a general partner may be expelled as a general partner of the partnership and a new general partner may be elected by the same vote.[28]

Sale or Purchase of Limited Partnership Interest This section of the limited partnership agreement should set forth the partners' desires with regard to the sale of new limited partners' interests, either to replace a withdrawing limited partner or to add new limited partners to raise additional capital for the partnership. It may also contain provisions for the purchase of a withdrawing limited partner's interest by the limited partnership.

Termination of Limited Partnership This section should set forth the desired provisions regarding termination of the limited partnership.

Dissolution and Winding Up   This section should set forth the desired provisions regarding the dissolution and winding up of the limited partnership, including the settlement and distribution of partnership assets.

EXAMPLE: *Winding Up—Distribution of Assets*

On the dissolution or termination of the partnership, after the liabilities shall have been paid, payment shall be made to the partners in the following order: (1) to the limited partners the sums to which they are entitled by way of interest on their capital contributions and their share of profits; (2) to the limited partners the amount of their capital contributions; (3) to the general partners such sums as may be due, if any other than for capital and profits; (4) to the general partners the amount they are entitled to receive as interest on their capital contributions and as profits; and (5) to the general partners for their capital contributions.[29]

Date of Agreement and Signatures   The limited partnership agreement should be dated and signed by all partners, both general and limited.

§ 3.6 CHANGES IN PARTNERSHIP

Many types of changes in the limited partnership affect the continuance of the limited partnership. This section examines the effects of common changes on the limited partnership, including the admission of new general partners, the admission of new limited partners, and the withdrawal of both general and limited partners.

Admission of New General Partners

The requirements for admitting new general partners vary from state to state. Typically, in states following the RULPA, general partners may be admitted with the written consent of all partners, or by another means set forth in the limited partnership agreement.

Admission of New Limited Partners

In states following the RULPA, an additional limited partner may be admitted in compliance with the provisions of the limited partnership agreement. If such an event is not provided for in the limited partnership agreement, an additional limited partner may be admitted by the written consent of all partners.[30] Amendment of the limited partnership certificate is not necessary because the names of the limited partners do not have to be set forth in the limited partnership certificate. The assignee of a limited partner's interest in a limited partnership may become a limited partner to the extent that the assignor gives the assignee that right, or if all other partners consent.

Withdrawal of General Partners

As with the general partnership, the death or withdrawal of a general partner generally causes the dissolution of a limited partnership. However, there are many exceptions to this rule.[31]

A general partner may withdraw from a limited partnership at any time by giving written notice to the other partners. However, if a general partner withdraws from the partnership in violation of the terms of the limited partnership agreement, the limited partnership may recover damages from the withdrawing partner for breach of the partnership agreement, and those damages may be used to offset any distribution to which the withdrawing general partner is otherwise entitled.

Withdrawal of Limited Partners

The limited partnership is not dissolved upon the death or withdrawal of a limited partner. In the event of the death of a limited partner, the executor, representative, or administrator of the deceased limited partner's estate succeeds to all of the decedent's rights for the purpose of settling the estate.

A limited partner may generally withdraw at the time specified in the partnership agreement or in another agreement entered into by the partners. Unless otherwise indicated in the limited partnership agreement, a limited partner may generally withdraw at any time with six months' notice to each general partner.[32]

The withdrawing partner is entitled to receive the distribution as set forth in the limited partnership agreement. Pursuant to the RULPA, if the amount of distribution is not provided for in the limited partnership agreement, the withdrawing partner is entitled to receive the fair value of his or her interest in the limited partnership based upon his or her right to share in distributions from the limited partnership.[33]

The distribution to which each partner is entitled under the partnership agreement will be in cash, unless otherwise indicated in the partnership agreement.

§ 3.7 FINANCIAL STRUCTURE OF A LIMITED PARTNERSHIP

The financial structure of a limited partnership is typically more complex than that of either a sole proprietorship or a general partnership. This section focuses on the capital of the limited partnership, the withdrawal of contributions from the limited partnership, and limited partnership profits and losses.

Partnership Capital Contributions

A basic concept of the limited partnership is that a limited partner must "make a stated contribution to the partnership, and place it at risk."[34] The limited partners' contribution may be in the form of cash, property, or services. In addition, the RULPA specifically states that the contribution may be in the form of a "promissory note or other obligation to contribute cash or property or perform services."[35] Any promise made by a limited partner to contribute to the limited partnership must be in writing to be enforceable.

Limited Partnership Profits and Losses

The profits and losses of the limited partnership derived from the contributions and efforts of the partners are shared among the partners pursuant to the partnership agreement or certificate. The RULPA provides that the profits and losses of a limited partnership shall be allocated among the partners in the manner provided in writing in the partnership agreement. If the partnership agreement does not specify a manner for allocating profits and losses, they shall be allocated on the basis of the value, as stated in the partnership records, of the contributions made by each partner to the extent they have been received by the partnership and have not been returned.[36]

Limited Partnership Income and Disbursements

The income of the limited partnership is reinvested in the limited partnership or disbursed to the limited partners and general partners as specified in the limited partnership agreement. The agreement may provide for mandatory payment of income to the limited partners, or it may give very broad discretion to the general partners. However, there are certain statutory restrictions on the withdrawal of contributions. Under the RULPA, distributions to partners are forbidden to the extent that, after giving effect to the distribution, all liabilities, other than those to partners on account of their interests, exceed the fair value of the partnership assets. This law prohibits the limited partnership from making distributions to the partners in priority of outside creditors. The limited partnership may not distribute all of its assets to its partners if there is not enough to meet its liabilities. For example, if the limited partnership had assets of $10,000 and liabilities of $6,000, Distributions to the partners may not be made in excess of $4,000.

The partners will owe income tax on the amount allocated to them, whether or not that amount was actually distributed to them or reinvested in the limited partnership. Often, the limited partnership agreement will be drafted to provided that all partners will receive an annual distribution from the limited partnership that is at least equal to their income tax liability generated by allocations to them from the limited partnership. This minimum distribution will ensure that partners will have the ability to meet their limited partnership income tax liability each year. As discussed previously in this chapter, if a loss from the limited partnership is allocated to the partners, they may use that loss to offset other income and reduce their personal income tax liability.

Income Tax Reporting   The limited partnership's income is reported to the Internal Revenue Service on a Form 1065 Partnership Return in the same manner that a general partnership's income is reported. The limited partnership is not subject to income taxation at the federal level. Rather, the general and limited partners pay income tax on their allocation of the limited partnership's income, as reported on the Schedule K-1 filed with their personal income tax returns. A sample of Schedule K-1 is shown in Figure 3-5.

CORRECTED (if checked)	PUBLICLY TRADED PARTNERSHIP (if checked)		
PARTNERSHIP'S name, street address, city, state, and ZIP code.	**1** Taxable income (loss) from passive activities	OMB No. 1545-1626 2000 Schedule K-1 (Form 1065-B)	**Partner's Share of Income (Loss) From an Electing Large Partnership**
	2 Taxable income (loss) from other activities		
PARTNERSHIP'S Employer I.D. number / PARTNER'S identifying number	**3** Net capital gain (loss) from passive activities	**4** Net capital gain (loss) from other activities	**Copy B For Partner**
PARTNER'S name	**5** Net passive AMT adjustment	**6** Net other AMT adjustment	See the separate **Partner's Instructions for Schedule K-1 (Form 1065-B).**
Street address (including apt. no.)	**7** General credits	**8** Low-income housing credit	This is important tax information and is being furnished to the Internal Revenue Service. If you are required to file a return, a negligence penalty or other sanction may be imposed on you if this income is taxable and the IRS determines that it has not been reported.
City, state, and ZIP code	**9** Other		
Partner's share of liabilities:			
a Nonrecourse . . . . $ --------------- **b** Qualified nonrecourse financing . . . . $ --------------- **c** Other . . . . $ --------------- Tax shelter registration number			
Schedule K-1 (Form 1065-B)	(Keep for your records.)		Department of the Treasury - Internal Revenue Service

FIGURE 3-5   Sample Schedule K-1 to Form 1065 Partnership Return

§ 3.8   DERIVATIVE ACTIONS

A **derivative action** is an action brought by a limited partner in the right of a limited partnership to recover a judgment in its favor. The RULPA expressly grants limited partners the right to bring an action on behalf of the limited partnership if the general partners with authority have refused to bring an action or if an effort to cause those general partners to bring the action is not likely to succeed.[37] A derivative action may be needed when the general partner to the partnership has a conflict of interest that would prevent or discourage the general partner from bringing an action on behalf of the limited partnership.

Derivative actions are not accepted or permitted in all states. A few jurisdictions apply a strict interpretation of the original ULPA, holding that only a general partner may maintain an action on behalf of the partnership, leaving the limited partner to pursue redress of any wrong through dissolution or individual action against the wrongdoer.[38]

The plaintiff to a derivative suit must be a partner at the time the action is brought and must have been a partner at the time of the transaction of which the plaintiff complains, or the plaintiff's status as a partner "must have devolved upon

◆

derivative action   A lawsuit by a stockholder of a corporation against another person (usually an officer of the company) to enforce claims the stockholder thinks the corporation has against that person.

him by operation of law or pursuant to the terms of the partnership agreement from a person who was a partner at the time of the transaction."[39]

§ 3.9 DISSOLUTION, WINDING UP, AND TERMINATION OF THE LIMITED PARTNERSHIP

The process of terminating a limited partnership involves several steps. This section investigates the termination process, including the distinction between limited partnership dissolution and winding up, the causes of dissolution, cancellation of the limited partnership certificate, winding up the affairs of the limited partnership, and settlement and distribution of the assets of the limited partnership.

Dissolution Versus Winding Up

As with the general partnership, once a limited partnership has been dissolved, the partnership does not terminate until the affairs of the limited partnership have been wound up.

Causes of Dissolution

In states following the RULPA, a limited partnership is dissolved, and its affairs must be wound up, when the first of the following events occurs:

1. The time period specified in the certificate expires.
2. Specific events specified in writing in the certificate occur.
3. All the partners consent in writing to dissolve the partnership.
4. An event of withdrawal of a general partner occurs.
5. A decree of judicial dissolution is entered.[40]

An *event of withdrawal,* as that term is used in the RULPA, refers to:

1. The general partner's voluntary withdrawal.
2. Assignment of the general partner's interest.
3. Removal of the general partner in accordance with the partnership agreement.
4. Certain transactions of the general partner's insolvency (unless otherwise provided in the certificate of limited partnership).
5. In the case of a general partner who is an individual, the partner's death or an adjudication that the partner is incompetent to manage his or her person or estate.
6. In the case of a general partner acting as such by virtue of being the trustee of a trust, the termination of the trust.
7. In the case of a general partner that is a separate partnership, its dissolution and the commencement of its winding up.
8. In the case of a general partner that is a corporation, the filing of a certificate of its dissolution (or the equivalent) or the revocation of its charter.

9. In the case of an estate, the distribution by the fiduciary of the estate's entire interest in the partnership.[41]

An event of withdrawal does not cause dissolution if there is at least one other general partner and the certificate of limited partnership allows continuation under the circumstances, or if, within ninety days after such an event, all partners agree in writing to continue the business. If all partners agree to continue the business, they may appoint one or more additional general partners if necessary or desirable.

State statutes usually provide that a limited partner may apply for a court decree to dissolve a limited partnership whenever it is not reasonably practicable to carry on the business of the limited partnership in conformity with the partnership agreement.

Cancellation of Certificate of Limited Partnership

Because a limited partnership is created by the certificate of limited partnership that is filed with the secretary of state or other state authority, the certificate of limited partnership must be canceled before the limited partnership is terminated. The certificate of limited partnership is canceled upon the dissolution of the limited partnership and the commencement of its winding up, or at any other time that there are no limited partners. The certificate is canceled by means of a certificate of cancellation, which is filed with the secretary of state and must contain:

1. The name of the limited partnership.
2. The date of filing of the certificate of limited partnership.
3. The reason for filing the certificate of cancellation.
4. The effective date of cancellation, if not effective upon filing the certificate.
5. Any other information determined by the general partners filing the certificate.[42]

The certificate must be signed by all general partners.

Figure 3-6 on page 108 is a sample of a form that may be filed in the State of Florida to cancel a limited partnership agreement.

Winding Up

Under the RULPA, "the general partners who have not wrongfully dissolved a limited partnership or, if none, the limited partners, may wind up the limited partnership's affairs."[43] Any partner or any partner's legal representative or assignee may also make application to an appropriate court to wind up the limited partnership's affairs.

Settlement and Distribution of Assets

State statutes provide the means for distributing the assets upon the dissolution of the limited partnership. In most states, assets of a dissolving limited partnership are paid out until they are exhausted in the following order:

CERTIFICATE OF CANCELLATION
FOR

_____

(Insert name currently on file with Florida Dept. of State)

Pursuant to the provisions of section 620.113, Florida Statutes, this Florida limited partnership, whose certificate was filed with the Florida Department of State on _____, hereby submits this certificate of cancellation.

FIRST: Reason for cancellation: (State why partnership is submitting cancellation)

SECOND: This certificate of cancellation shall be effective at the time of its filing with the Florida Department of State.

THIRD: Signatures of all general partners:

_____

_____

_____

FIGURE 3-6   Sample Certificate of Cancellation from the State of Florida

1. To the creditors, including any partners who are creditors, to satisfy liabilities of the limited partnership (other than liabilities for distributions to partners).
2. To partners to satisfy any distributions due to them under the partnership agreement.
3. To partners as a return of their contributions.
4. To partners as a return of their partnership interest in the same proportions in which the partners share distributions.

Partners (except partners who are creditors of the limited partnership) will not receive a distribution from the partnership unless the limited partnership's assets are sufficient to pay all creditors.

§ 3.10 THE PARALEGAL'S ROLE IN LIMITED PARTNERSHIP MATTERS

The role of the paralegal in working with limited partnerships is very similar to that in working with general partnerships, with a few additions. Paralegals are often responsible for drafting and filing limited partnership documents, for researching limited partnership law, and for assisting limited partnership clients to comply with other formalities for forming and operating their businesses. The paralegal may be asked to help draft the limited partnership agreement, usually with the aid of office forms and examples of previously drafted limited partnership agreements. Following is a checklist of items to be considered when drafting a limited partnership agreement.

LIMITED PARTNERSHIP AGREEMENT CHECKLIST

- ☐ Name and address of each limited partner and each general partner and a designation of partnership status.
- ☐ Name of the limited partnership.
- ☐ Purpose of the limited partnership.
- ☐ Address of principal place of business of the limited partnership.
- ☐ Duration of limited partnership agreement.
- ☐ Contributions of both general partners and limited partners.
- ☐ Limited partnership assets.
- ☐ Liability of general partners and limited partners to each other and third parties.
- ☐ Distribution of profits and losses to general and limited partners.
- ☐ Indemnification of partners.
- ☐ Duties of general partners.
- ☐ Duties of limited partners.
- ☐ Limited partners' rights of substitution.
- ☐ Limitation on powers.
- ☐ General partner compensation.
- ☐ Partnership expenses.
- ☐ Management and control of business by general partners.
- ☐ Limited partners' rights in review of business policies.
- ☐ Business policies.
- ☐ Accounting practices and procedures.
- ☐ Changes in general or limited partners by withdrawal, expulsion, retirement, or death.
- ☐ Sale or purchase of limited partnership interest.
- ☐ Arbitration provisions.
- ☐ Termination of limited partnership.
- ☐ Dissolution and winding up.
- ☐ Date of agreement.
- ☐ Signatures of all general and limited partners.

The paralegal may also be responsible for filing the limited partnership certificate pursuant to state statutes. If there are any publication or county recording requirements for the limited partnership certificate, it will often be the paralegal's responsibility to see that those requirements are complied with as well.

Corporate Paralegal Profile
Patricia E. Rodgers

I thoroughly enjoy working with clients and the challenge of always learning about new law-related topics.

Name Patricia E. Rodgers

Location East Hartford, Connecticut

Title Corporate Paralegal

Specialty Corporate

Education Associate Degree from Bryant College

Experience 22 Years

Patricia Rodgers is a corporate paralegal who has worked extensively with limited partnerships. Limited partnership law is one of her specialties at Murtha Cullina LLP, a large law firm with offices in Hartford and New Haven, Connecticut, and Boston and Woburn, Massachusetts. Murtha Cullina employs 116 attorneys and 22 paralegals.

Murtha Cullina LLP acts as counsel to a large New York real estate syndicate that has formed hundreds of limited partnerships in Connecticut. Patricia has been responsible for assisting with all aspects of the formation of the limited partnerships, as well as issuing voting rights and financing opinions, and restructuring the entities.

In addition to limited partnerships, Patricia works with entities of all types, including corporations, limited liability companies, and limited liability partnerships. Her responsibilities include the formation and dissolution of business entities, mergers and acquisitions, annual letters to auditors, corporate financings, qualifications of foreign entities, formation of nonstock corporations, and preparation of state and federal tax forms. She reports to the chairman of Murtha Cullina's Corporate Department.

Patricia enjoys working with clients and the challenge of learning about new law-related topics.

One of Patricia's favorite areas is mergers and acquisitions, which sometimes involves travel and long hard days of work (including weekends and all-nighters). To Patricia, the satisfaction and rewards associated with the successful completion of a transaction make all the hard work worthwhile.

Although Patricia enjoys a challenge, she admits that working for several different attorneys and clients can sometimes be frustrating. She doesn't enjoy being torn in 10 different directions at the same time. She finds it difficult to plan her day because too often one of the lawyers or a client will have a need that requires her immediate attention.

Patricia has used her corporate expertise to provide some pro bono services to the National Kidney Foundation of Connecticut and the Connecticut Self Advocates for Mental Health, Inc. She assisted them with issues involving their charter documents. Patricia was recognized by both organizations for her outstanding service.

Patricia was one of the founders of the Central Connecticut Association of Legal Assistants in 1982, and she has been very active since its incorporation. She has served as vice president, chair of the Constitution and Bylaws Committee, Public Relations Chair, Connecticut Alliance Chair, Legislative Committee Chair, and NFPA Primary Representative. She has been a member of the Central Connecticut Paralegal Association's NFPA National Affairs Committee for approximately 18 years.

Patricia's advice to new paralegals?

Work hard; be open to suggestions; do not turn down work if at all possible; try to be pleasant at all times; do not be afraid to admit that you have made a mistake; and most of all—be a team player.

The paralegal must be well acquainted with the state statutory requirements for limited partnerships, as well as the procedural requirements at the state level. In addition, the paralegal must be aware of any requirements for qualifying the limited partnership as a foreign limited partnership in other states in which the limited partnership intends to transact business.

If the limited partnership elects limited liability limited partnership status, the paralegal must be aware of the requirements for such an election and see that all formalities are complied with. Failure to do so could cause the limited partnership to lose its limited liability status.

§ 3.11 RESOURCES

Numerous resources are available to the paralegal working with limited partnerships. This section lists some of the more important resources, including state statutes, legal form books, and information available from the office of the secretary of state, state and local government offices, and the Internal Revenue Service.

State Statutes

It is always important to be familiar with the state statutes of the limited partnership's state of domicile. Here is a list of the statutory citations of the limited partnership acts that have been adopted in each state.

Ala. Code § 10-9B-101 *et seq.*
Alaska Stat. § 32.11.010 *et seq.*
Ariz. Rev. Stat. Ann. § 29-301 *et seq.*
Ark. Code Ann. § 4-43-101 *et seq.*
Cal. Corp. Code § 15611 *et seq.*
Colo. Rev. Stat. § 7-62-101 *et seq.*
Conn. Gen. Stat. § 34-9 *et seq.*
Del. Code Ann. tit. 6, § 17-101 *et seq.*
D.C. Code Ann. § 41-401 *et seq.*
Fla. Stat. Ann. § 620.101 *et seq.*
Ga. Code Ann. § 14-9-100 *et seq.*
Haw. Rev. Stat. § 425D-101 *et seq.*
Idaho Code § 53-201 *et seq.*
805ILCS 210/100 *et seq.*
Ind. Code § 23-16-1-1 *et seq.*
Iowa Code § 487.101 *et seq.*
Kan. Stat. Ann. § 56-1a101 *et seq.*
Ky. Rev. Stat. Ann. § 362.401 *et seq.*
La. Rev. Stat. Ann. § 9:3401 *et seq.*[44]
Me. Rev. Stat. Ann. tit. 31, § 401 *et seq.*
Md. Corps. & Ass'ns § 10-101 *et seq.*
Mass. Gen. L. ch. 109, § 1 *et seq.*
Mich. Comp. Laws § 449.1101 *et seq.*
Minn. Stat. § 322A.01 *et seq.*
Miss. Code Ann. § 79-14-101 *et seq.*
Mo. Rev. Stat. § 359.011 *et seq.*
Mont. Code Ann. § 35-12-501 *et seq.*
Neb. Rev. Stat. § 67-233 *et seq.*

Nev. Rev. Stat. § 88.010 *et seq.*
N.H. Rev. Stat. Ann. § 304-B:1 *et seq.*
N.J. Ann. Stat. § 42:2A-1 *et seq.*
N.M. Ann. Stat. § 54-2-1 *et seq.*
N.Y. Partnership Law § 121-101 *et seq.*
N.C. Gen. Stat. § 59-101 *et seq.*
N.D. Cent. Code § 45-10.1-01 *et seq.*
Ohio Rev. Code Ann. § 1782.01 *et seq.*
Okla. Stat. Ann. tit. 54, § 301 *et seq.*
Or. Rev. Stat. § 70.005 *et seq.*
15 Pa. Cons. Stat. Ann. § 8501 *et seq.*
R.I. Gen. Laws § 7-13-1 *et seq.*
S.C. Code Ann. § 33-42-10 *et seq.*
S.D. Codified Laws Ann. § 48-7-101 *et seq.*
Tenn. Code Ann. § 61-2-101 *et seq.*
Tex. Rev. Civ. Stat. Ann. art. 6132a-1
Utah Code Ann. § 48-2a-101 *et seq.*
Vt. Stat. Ann. tit. 11, § 3401 *et seq.*
Va. Code Ann. § 50-73.1 *et seq.*
Wash. Rev. Code § 25.10.010 *et seq.*
W. Va. Code § 47-9-1 *et seq.*
Wis. Stat. § 179.01 *et seq.*
Wyo. Stat. § 17-14-201 *et seq.*

Legal Form Books

Because a limited partnership is formed only by the filing of a certificate of limited partnership, the drafting of a suitable certificate and the limited partnership agreement are vital. As well as limited partnership certificates and agreements previously drafted by the law firm and those provided by the secretary of state's office, legal form books can be an excellent resource for finding appropriate forms and optional language to use in limited partnership documents.[45] State-specific continuing legal education (CLE) materials are also an excellent resource for forms and information to assist with drafting limited partnership documents.

Secretary of State or Other Appropriate State Authority

The secretary of state or other appropriate state authority often must be contacted to inquire as to the proper filing procedures and fees. The appropriate state office will also have forms, guidelines, and other useful information available. See appendix A of this text for a secretary of state directory.

Government Tax Offices

As when working with a general partnership, it is important that the appropriate state offices be contacted regarding state income taxation matters. It is also advisable to contact the local Internal Revenue Service office to request information regarding the income tax filing requirements for limited partnerships.

Internet Resources

Following is a list of some Web pages that may be useful when assisting limited partnerships:

For state statutes concerning limited partnerships

American Law Source Online	**www.lawsource.com/also**
Findlaw.com	**www.findlaw.com/11stategov/**
Legal Information Institute	**www.law.cornell.edu/states/listing.html**

For limited partnership forms

All About Forms.Com	**www.allaboutforms.com/**
Findlaw.com (Legal Forms)	**www.findlaw.com**
The 'Lectric Law Library's Business and General Forms	**www.lectlaw.com/formb.htm**

For links to state government forms

Findlaw.com State Corporation and Business Forms	**www.findlaw.com/11stategov/indexcorp.html**

For links to the secretary of state offices

Corporate Housekeeper	**www.danvi.vi/link2.html**
National Association of Secretaries of State	**www.nass.org**

For the Uniform Limited Partnership Act

National Conference of Commissioners on Uniform State Law	**www.law.upenn.edu/bll/ulc/ulc_frame.htm**

For information on limited partnership taxation

Internal Revenue Service	**www.irs.gov**

For general information about limited partnership law

Legal Information Institute	**www.law.cornell.edu/topics/partnership.html**

An alphabetical list of Internet Resources for the Corporate Paralegal is included as appendix B to this text.

Web Page

For updates and links to several of the previously listed sites, as well as download-able state limited partnership certificate forms, log on to **www.westlegalstudies.com**, and click through to the book link for this text.

SUMMARY

- A limited partnership is a special type of partnership that offers limited liability to certain of its partners (limited partners).
- Limited partnerships must have at least one general partner.
- Any individual or entity may be a general partner or limited partner of a limited partnership.
- An individual or entity may be both a general and limited partner of a limited partnership.
- General partners in limited partnerships, other than limited liability limited partnerships, have personal liability for the debts and obligations of the limited partnership.
- The statutes of some states provide for the formation of a limited liability limited partnership—a new form of limited partnership that allows for limited personal liability of all partners, including general partners.
- Most states have adopted a version of the Revised Uniform Limited Partnership Act for their own Limited Partnership Act.
- Limited partnerships are treated as separate entities for most purposes

REVIEW QUESTIONS

1. Is a limited partnership treated as a separate entity for all purposes? If not, give an example of an instance in which a limited partnership is treated under the aggregate theory.

2. Why is the fiduciary duty between the general partner and limited partners even greater than the fiduciary duty between partners in a general partnership?

3. Suppose that Beth Henderson is a limited partner of the ABC Limited Partnership, a limited partnership formed for the purpose of purchasing and developing real estate. Beth wanted to be a limited partner because she has considerable personal assets that she wants to protect. Soon after the formation of the limited partnership, Beth becomes concerned about its management by the general partners. She starts attending the general partners' meetings and participating in all major decisions concerning

the limited partnership. However, the partnership becomes insolvent anyway. Creditors are left with thousands of dollars' worth of unpaid bills. The limited partnership and the general partners have no substantial cash or other assets. Might creditors prevail in a lawsuit against Beth Henderson to recover their losses? Why or why not?

4. Brian, Jeanne, and William have formed OakRidge Limited Partnership, a limited partnership for shopping center development and management. William is the general partner and Brian and Jeanne are limited partners. The limited partnership is about to enter into an agreement to purchase a new shopping center; however, the bank that is lending them the money wants personal guarantees from each partner. If the limited partnership is governed by the laws of a state that follows the Revised

Uniform Limited Partnership Act, would Brian and Jeanne be able to guarantee the obligation of the OakRidge Limited Partnership without risking their limited liability status?

5. Suppose that Jake, Bryan, and Jill decide to form a limited partnership for the purpose of owning and operating a liquor store. They are all concerned about their personal liability, so they decide that they will all be limited partners. Would this be possible? Why or why not? What if Jill agreed to be both a general partner and a limited partner?

6. Why might a limited partnership want to put only the minimum required information in the limited partnership certificate and go into more detail in the limited partnership agreement or other documents?

7. What is one advantage the limited partnership has over the general partnership with regard to raising capital for the business?

8. Who may initiate a derivative action?

PRACTICAL PROBLEMS

1. Locate and cite the limited partnership act in your state to answer the following questions.
   a. When was your state's current act adopted?
   b. What is the name of the document that must be filed in your state to form a limited partnership?
   c. What must be included in that document?
   d. Where is that document filed?

2. Are there provisions in your state for forming a limited liability limited partnership? If so, what are the requirements for forming such an entity?

WORKPLACE SCENARIO

Assume the same set of facts as in the Workplace Scenario from Chapter 2 of this text, except now Bradley Harris and Cynthia Lund want to form a limited partnership. Bradley Harris will be the general partner. Cynthia Lund will be the limited partner.

Using the above information and the information provided in appendices D-1 and D-2 to this text, prepare a limited partnership certificate in your state. You may create your own form that conforms to the statutes of your state, or you can download a form from the appropriate state office. Some limited partnership certificate forms are available for downloading on the companion Web page to this text at **www.westlegalstudies.com.**

Also prepare a cover letter to the appropriate state authority filing the limited partnership certificate and enclosing the appropriate filing fee.

END NOTES

1. Revised Uniform Limited Partnership Act § 101(11).
2. 59A AM. JUR. 2d *Partnership* § 1240 (1987).
3. Louisiana is governed by statutes based on common law.
4. 59A AM. JUR. 2d *Partnership* § 1246 (1987).
5. *Id.* § 1345.
6. Revised Uniform Limited Partnership Act § 303(a).
7. *Id.* § 303(b).
8. *Id.* § 105; Uniform Limited Partnership Act § 10.
9. 59A AM. JUR. 2d *Partnership* § 1333 (1987).
10. Revised Uniform Limited Partnership Act § 801.
11. See chapter 12 of this text.
12. Revised Uniform Limited Partnership Act § 201.
13. *Id.* § 202.
14. *Id.* § 105.

15. *Id.*

16. *Id.* § 106.

17. 14A AM. JUR. Legal Forms 2d *Partnership* § 194:681 (Rev. 2000).

18. *Id.* § 194:681.

19. *Id.*

20. *Id.* § 194:692.

21. *Id.* § 194:693.

22. *Id.* § 194:698.

23. *Id.* § 194:724.

24. *Id.* § 194:708.

25. *Id.* § 194:664.

26. *Id.* § 194:738.

27. *Id.* § 194:742.

28. *Id.* § 194:746.

29. *Id.* § 194:762.

30. Revised Uniform Limited Partnership Act § 704.

31. See § 3.9(b) for more information on causes of dissolution.

32. Uniform Limited Partnership Act § 16; Revised Uniform Limited Partnership Act § 603.

33. Revised Uniform Limited Partnership Act § 604.

34. 59A AM. JUR. 2d *Partnership* § 1354 (1987).

35. Revised Uniform Limited Partnership Act § 501.

36. Revised Uniform Limited Partnership Act § 503.

37. *Id.* § 1001.

38. 59A AM. JUR. 2d *Partnership* § 1395 (1987).

39. Revised Uniform Limited Partnership Act § 1002.

40. Revised Uniform Limited Partnership Act § 801.

41. *Id.* § 402.

42. Uniform Limited Partnership Act § 24; Revised Uniform Limited Partnership Act § 203.

43. Revised Uniform Limited Partnership Act § 803.

44. Louisiana limited partnerships are governed by state statutes based on common law.

45. See § 2.10(b) of this text for a list of selected form books.

CHAPTER 4

Limited Liability Companies

CHAPTER OUTLINE

§ 4.1   An Introduction to Limited Liability Companies

§ 4.2   Limited Liability Companies in the United States

§ 4.3   Law Governing Limited Liability Companies

§ 4.4   Limited Liability Company Rights and Powers

§ 4.5   Members' Rights and Responsibilities

§ 4.6   Organization and Management of a Limited Liability Company

§ 4.7   Financial Structure of a Limited Liability Company

§ 4.8   Dissolution of the Limited Liability Company

§ 4.9   Advantages of Doing Business as a Limited Liability Company

§ 4.10 Disadvantages of Doing Business as a Limited Liability Company

§ 4.11 Transacting Business as a Foreign Limited Liability Company

§ 4.12 The Paralegal's Role

§ 4.13 Resources

§ 4.1   AN INTRODUCTION TO LIMITED LIABILITY COMPANIES

One of the newest and fastest growing types of business entities in the United States is the **limited liability company.** The limited liability company (LLC) is a type of non-corporate entity that is something of a cross between a partnership and a corporation. It offers many of the benefits of both a partnership and a corporation.

---

limited liability company   A cross between a partnership and a corporation owned by members who may manage the company directly or delegate to officers or managers who are similar to a corporation's directors. Governing documents are usually publicly-filed articles of organization and a private operating agreement. Members are not usually liable for company debts, and company income and losses are usually divided among and taxed to the members individually according to share.

In this chapter, we define the term *limited liability company,* look at their unique characteristics, and examine the history and status of limited liability companies in the United States. Our discussion then turns to the law governing limited liability companies and the rights and powers limited liability companies possess. Next, we focus on members' rights and responsibilities, the organization and management of the limited liability company, its financial structure, and the dissolution of the limited liability company. After a discussion of the advantages and disadvantages of doing business as a limited liability company, especially as compared with other types of business entities, this chapter concludes with a look at the foreign limited liability company and the role of the paralegal working with limited liability companies.

Limited Liability Company Defined

The limited liability company has many of the characteristics of a corporation, including limited liability for all owners or members; yet it also has many similarities to partnerships, and it is usually taxed as a partnership. State statutes dictate the exact requirements for the formation and operation of limited liability companies.

Limited Liability Company Characteristics

The limited liability company is an unincorporated entity based on the concept of freedom of contract. It is a legal entity distinct from its owners. The owners of a limited liability company are generally referred to as its **members**.

The characteristics of any limited liability company will depend on its members' objectives and the statutes of the state in which it is formed. However, most limited liability companies have common characteristics, including limited liability, flexible management, continuity of life, restricted transferability of interest, unrestricted ownership, certain formalities for formation, and partnership taxation status.

Limited Liability   Like a corporation, the owners of a limited liability company typically have no personal liability for the debts and obligations of the limited liability company.

Management   Management of the limited liability company is very flexible. All members of the limited liability company are granted the right to manage its business unless otherwise provided for in the limited liability company's **articles of organization.**

---

member   An owner of a limited liability company.

articles of organization   Document required to be filed with the proper state authority to form a limited liability company.

Dividends ————————————————————————————————————◆

Choices, Choices, Choices ...

Never before have there been more types of business entities to choose from in the United States. In the not too distant past, an individual or group of individuals wishing to begin business could choose from operating as a sole proprietor, partnership, limited partnership, or corporation. The recent addition of several more new types of business entities has made the selection more appealing, but also more confusing. Organizers of business enterprises in most states may now add to their list of options S corporations, limited liability companies, limited liability partnerships, and a vast array of other business entities that are unique to one or a few states.

Each of these new business entities was designed to fill a void, or a need in the business community.

For example, the limited liability company was designed for those individuals who wanted both the tax status of a partnership and the limited liability of a corporation.

It is important to know the major characteristics of each type of existing business entity, and to keep abreast of new developments in the future. The chart in Figure 4-1 on pages 120 and 121 sets forth some characteristics of the most popular types of business entities. It is important to keep in mind that some of these factors may vary by state, and the statutes of the entities' state of organization is the final authority for defining the business enterprise.

State statutes typically permit the owners of a limited liability company to allocate the management authority among its members in any manner they choose. They may decide to be managed by one individual, by committee, or by the majority of the owners. Most limited liability companies appoint a **board of managers,** similar to a corporation's board of directors. A written agreement among the members, referred to as an **operating agreement,** sets forth the details concerning the management of the limited liability company.

Decisions of a limited liability company are usually made by the members holding a majority of the limited liability company interest, unless otherwise provided for in the operating agreement or by statute.

Continuity of Life   The statutes of most states provide that a limited liability company may be designed for continuity. Unless the articles of organization provide that the limited liability company will be a term company that will dissolve on a certain future date or event, the limited liability company will be an **entity at will,** meaning that it exists indefinitely, until the members dissolve it. The statutes of some states, however, provide that a limited liability company has a limited duration (such as 30 years).[1]

◆ ———

board of managers   Group of individuals elected by the members of a limited liability company to manage the limited liability company. Similar to a corporation's board of directors.

operating agreement   Document that governs the limited liability company. Similar to a corporation's bylaws.

entity at will   Entity that may be dissolved at the wish of one or more members or owners.

	Formation	Management	Restrictions on Ownership	Limited Personal Liability	Taxation	Duration
Sole Proprietorship	No formalities required.	Sole proprietor has sole management responsibility; may delegate to employees and agents.	Only one owner	None	Sole proprietor reports income on personal return; pays tax accordingly.	At will of sole proprietor. Business ends with sole proprietor's death or withdrawal.
Partnership	No formalities required. Written partnership agreement is recommended.	All partners have equal right to manage partnership unless otherwise agreed to in partnership agreement.	Two or more owners	None	Income allocated among partners who pay tax at personal rate. Informational return filed on behalf of partnership.	Indefinite. May dissolve on death or withdrawal of partner unless otherwise agreed to in partnership agreement.
Limited Liability Partnership	Statement of qualification must be filed at state level.	All partners have equal right to manage partnership unless otherwise agreed to in partnership agreement.	Two or more owners	Yes, for all partners	Income allocated among partners who pay tax at personal rate. Informational return filed on behalf of partnership.	Indefinite. May dissolve on death or withdrawal of partner unless otherwise agreed to in partnership agreement.
Limited Partnership	Articles of limited partnership (or similarly named document) must be filed at state level.	All general partners have equal right to manage partnership unless otherwise agreed to in partnership agreement. Limited partners may not participate in management of limited partnership.	Two or more owners	Yes, for limited partners only	Income allocated among partners who pay tax at personal rate. Informational return filed on behalf of partnership.	Indefinite. May dissolve on death or withdrawal of general partner unless otherwise agreed to in partnership agreement.
Limited Liability Limited Partnership	Articles of limited partnership and statement of qualification must be filed at state level.	All general partners have equal right to manage partnership unless otherwise agreed to in partnership agreement. Limited partners may not participate in management of limited partnership.	Two or more owners	Yes, for all partners	Income allocated among partners who pay tax at personal rate. Informational return filed on behalf of partnership.	Indefinite. May dissolve on death or withdrawal of general partner unless otherwise agreed to in partnership agreement.

FIGURE 4-1   Business Organizations and Their Characteristics

	Formation	Management	Restrictions on Ownership	Limited Personal Liability	Taxation	Duration
Limited Liability Company	Articles of organization must be filed at state level.	All members have right to participate in management of business unless otherwise agreed to in articles of organization or operating agreement. Management is often delegated to board of managers.	Minimum of two owners in a few states. No maximum number of owners.	Yes, for all owners/members	Income allocated among members/owners who pay tax at personal rate. Informational return filed on behalf of limited liability company.	Perpetual in most states
S Corporation	Articles of incorporation must be filed at state level; Election to become S Corporation must be filed with Internal Revenue Service.	Shareholders elect board of directors to oversee management.	Minimum of one; maximum of 75. Shareholders must all be individuals, estates, or exempt organizations or trusts that meet certain prerequisites.	Yes, for all owners/shareholders	Income allocated among shareholders who pay tax at personal rate. Informational return filed on behalf of S Corporation.	Perpetual
C Corporation	Articles of incorporation must be filed at state level.	Shareholders elect board of directors to oversee management.	No, or few restrictions	Yes, for all owners/shareholders	Corporation responsible for tax on corporate income. Shareholders responsible for income tax on income and dividends received.	Perpetual

FIGURE 4-1   (*continued*)

The death or dissociation of one or more of the members of a limited liability company does not necessarily cause the dissolution of the limited liability company. The statutes of some states provide that the members of a limited liability company must give six months' notice of their intent to dissociate from the company.

Transferability of Interest State statutes typically place restrictions on the transfer of the ownership interest of the members of limited liability companies. Many of these restrictions may be modified by the company's operating agreement.

Members of a limited liability company are not considered to be co-owners of the company's property. That property is owned by the limited liability company itself. A member may usually transfer or assign his or her right to receive distributions to another person. This transfer does not necessarily make the new owner of the right to receive distributions a member of the limited liability company. The transferee of a member's financial rights to a limited liability company does not have the same rights to participate in the management and operation of the limited liability company that members do. A person may become a member of a limited liability company only if he or she is substituted, or admitted, to the limited liability company as provided by the company's articles of organization.

Ownership There are very few restrictions on the number or type of owners who may own limited liability companies. Initially, the statutes of many states required limited liability companies to have at least two members. Most states now permit single-owner limited liability companies.

Formalities of Organization The limited liability company is formed in much the same way that the business corporation is formed. Articles of organization are filed with the secretary of state or other appropriate state authority. In addition, a limited liability company may be subject to annual reporting requirements imposed by the state in which it was organized.

Taxation One of the most important benefits to forming a limited liability company is the partnership taxation status, which is preferable to corporation taxation for most members. Prior to 1997, limited liability companies were taxed as partnerships only if they met certain tests prescribed by the Internal Revenue Service. If the limited liability company had too many characteristics of a corporation, it was taxed as a corporation. Specifically, the Internal Revenue Service considered the following characteristics:

1. Continuity of life.
2. Centralization of management.
3. Limited liability.
4. Free transferability of interests.

If a limited liability company possessed three or more of the foregoing *corporation* characteristics, it was considered a corporation for federal income taxation purposes.

This rule meant that organizers of limited liability companies had to carefully design the entity to get the income tax results they wanted, and the statutes of several states were designed specifically so that limited liability companies formed in those states would meet the test to be taxed as a limited liability company. For example, many limited liability companies were formed for a maximum of 30 years, with restrictions placed on the transfer of company interests. The statutes of many states required those conditions.

All of this changed in 1997 when the Internal Revenue Service adopted *Check the Box* regulations[2] that made it much simpler for a limited liability company to be taxed as a partnership—which is usually the desired outcome. Now, when the members of a limited liability company file an income tax return for the company, the limited liability company is classified, by default, as a partnership. If the members prefer, they can simply check the box on an election form and elect to be taxed as a corporation. Single-member limited liability companies are disregarded as entities separate from their owners unless the sole member elects to be taxed as a corporation.

A few states consider limited liability companies to be corporations for state income tax purposes and have imposed a corporate tax on limited liability companies.[3] Figure 4-2 lists the particular characteristics of a limited liability company.

- ◆ Unincorporated entity
- ◆ Legal entity distinct from its members
- ◆ Limited personal liability for members
- ◆ Flexible management
- ◆ Restricted transferability of interest
- ◆ Partnership taxation status
- ◆ Few ownership restrictions
- ◆ Formed by filing articles of organization at state level

FIGURE 4-2   Limited Liability Company Characteristics

Professional Limited Liability Companies

The limited liability company acts of most states provide for the formation of professional limited liability companies by doctors, lawyers, and other professionals. The requirements for professional limited liability companies are generally very similar to those of regular limited liability companies with a few distinctions. Following are some of the typical requirements unique to professional limited liability companies:

- ◆ Professionals are generally personally liable for any acts of malpractice by them.
- ◆ Membership in professional limited liability companies may be restricted to licensed professionals.
- ◆ The name of the company must include the words professional limited liability company or the initials PLLC.

§ 4.2 LIMITED LIABILITY COMPANIES IN THE UNITED STATES

Limited liability companies are one of the newest forms of business entities in the United States and the first new entity to be introduced in several decades. While similar entities have existed in other countries for several years, the first state legislation adopting limited liability companies was not passed in this country until 1977. This first state, Wyoming, was followed by Florida in 1982. These statutes did not receive much national attention until a 1988 IRS Revenue Ruling[4] classified a Wyoming limited liability company as a partnership for federal tax purposes—a decided advantage for many business owners. The new Check the Box rules adopted by the Internal Revenue Service in 1997 make the limited liability company even more appealing. At this time, every state in the country and the District of Columbia has adopted legislation approving the limited liability company. In 1998, 470,657 limited liability companies filed partnership tax returns in the United States.[5] Figure 4-3 shows a chart of the growth of limited liability companies in the United States since 1993.

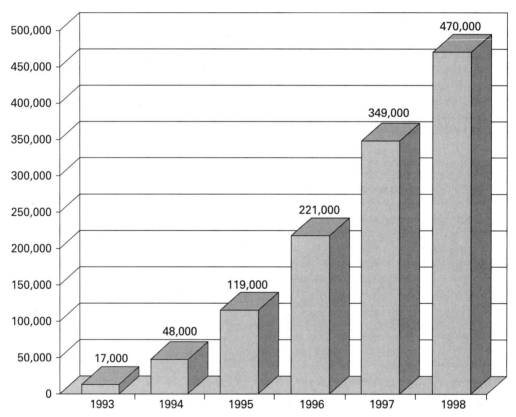

Number of limited liability companies filing partnership returns in the United States. From the Internal Revenue Service *SOI Bulletin, Fall 2000.*

FIGURE 4-3 Growth of Limited Liability Companies in the United States

§ 4.3 LAW GOVERNING LIMITED LIABILITY COMPANIES

Limited liability companies are governed by the statutes of the state in which they are formed. Many of the state statutory acts resemble the **Uniform Limited Liability Company Act.** In addition, limited liability companies may be subject to the Securities Act of 1933 and the Securities Exchange Act of 1934.

State Law and the Uniform Limited Liability Company Act

In the early 1990s state legislatures adopted limited liability company acts rapidly, and the statutes were very diverse. The differences between state acts created difficulties for limited liability companies that transact business in more than one state. To compound that problem, little case law existed because of the relative newness of the limited liability company.

In 1994, the National Conference of the Commissions of Uniform State Law adopted the Uniform Limited Liability Company Act, which was amended in 1995. Its main purpose was to give state legislatures some uniform guidelines for drafting state legislation. The Uniform Act encompasses many of the provisions that have already been adopted by individual states, but it allows for maximum flexibility. Because it is impossible to discuss the laws of each state individually in one chapter, this chapter will focus on the provisions of the Uniform Limited Liability Company Act. (The Uniform Limited Liability Company Act is included in this text as appendix H.) It is important to remember, however, that the limited liability company act of your state may vary significantly, and state law must always be consulted. Figure 4-11 in the Resources section of this chapter includes a list of state limited liability company statutes as of late 2000.

Securities Laws

Most limited liability companies have a small number of members who all participate in the company's business to a certain extent. Compliance with state and federal securities acts, which are designed primarily to protect inactive investors in larger corporations and other entities, is of little concern to such companies.

However, the applicability of state and federal securities laws to some limited liability company interests is still an open question in many respects. If a member's interest is determined to be an **investment contract** under the Securities Exchange Act, then the interest is considered a **security** subject to state and federal securities laws. For purposes of determining the existence of an investment contract as defined

---

uniform limited liability company act Uniform Act adopted by the National Conference of the Commissions of Uniform State Laws in 1994 and amended in 1995 to give states guidance when drafting limited liability company statutes.

investment contract Under federal law, any agreement that involves an investment of money pooled with others' money to gain profits solely from the efforts of others.

security A share of stock, a bond, a note, or one of many different kinds of documents showing a share in a company or a debt owed by a company or a government. ... The

in federal securities law, the investment must have the following three elements: It must be (1) an investment (2) in a common enterprise (3) with an expectation of profits to be derived solely from the efforts of others.

A membership interest in a limited liability company will include these first two elements. It is the third element that requires an expectation of profits *to be derived solely from the efforts of others* that will determine whether a member's interest is considered a security. In a limited liability company where all members play an active role in the operation of the business, the limited liability company may *not* be considered a security. Whereas, the interest of a member in a limited liability company with very centralized management may be considered a security.

In several court cases in the late 1990s the courts held that membership interests in wireless cable limited liability companies were considered investment contracts. In one case, it was determined that the limited liability company interests sold were securities because (1) they were sold by the defendant to over 700 individual investors in 43 states, (2) members were required to purchase at least two $5000 "units," and (3) the defendant "exercised near-total control" over the management of the limited liability company.[6]

Some states have attempted to answer the question by passing laws that include interests in limited liability companies in their list of securities subject to regulation. However, not all states have taken this step, and even those that have list exceptions to the rule. For example, an interest in a small limited liability company in which all members actively participate is almost never considered a security. An interest in a limited liability company that *is* determined to be a security is subject to both federal securities laws and state blue sky laws, which are discussed in Chapter 9 of this text.

§ 4.4   LIMITED LIABILITY COMPANY RIGHTS AND POWERS

Much like a partnership or corporation, the limited liability company is granted certain powers by statute and by its articles of organization. In states that follow § 112 of the Uniform Limited Liability Company Act, limited liability companies have the same powers as individuals to do all things necessary or convenient to carry on business, including the powers to:

♦ Sue and be sued, and defend in the name of the limited liability company.

♦ Purchase, receive, lease, or otherwise acquire and own real or personal property.

♦ Sell, convey, mortgage, grant a security interest in, lease, exchange, or otherwise encumber or dispose of all or any parts of its property.

♦ Purchase, receive, or otherwise acquire and own shares or other interest in any other entity.

♦ Sell, mortgage, grant a security interest in, or otherwise dispose of and deal in and with shares or other interest of any other entity.

♦ ───

U.S. Supreme Court has defined a security as any investment in a common enterprise from which the investor is "led to expect profits solely from the efforts of a promoter or a third party."

- Make contracts and other obligations, which may be convertible into or include the option to purchase other securities of the limited liability company.
- Secure any of its obligations by a mortgage on, or a security interest in, any of its property, franchises, or income.
- Lend money, invest and reinvest funds, and receive and hold real and personal property as security for repayment.
- Be a promoter, partner, member, associate, or manager of any partnership, joint venture, trust, or other entity.
- Conduct its business, locate offices, and exercise the powers granted by the Act within or without this state.
- Elect managers and appoint officers, employees, and agents of the limited liability company, define their duties, fix their compensation, and lend them money and credit.
- Pay pensions and establish pension plans, pension trusts, profit sharing plans, and any other type of employee benefit plan for any or all of its current or former members, managers, officers, employees, and agents.
- Make charitable donations.
- Make payments or donations, or perform any other act, not inconsistent with law, that furthers the business of the limited liability company.

Many state statutes are similar to the Uniform Limited Liability Company Act. Others simply state that a limited liability company *has all powers necessary to transact business in that state.*

§ 4.5 MEMBERS' RIGHTS AND RESPONSIBILITIES

The owners of a limited liability company are referred to as members. The role of members is similar to that of partners of a general partnership, and, in some instances, the shareholders of a corporation. There are few restrictions on the membership of a limited liability company. Members may include corporations, trusts, and other entities, as well as individuals. Some states require that more than one member must form the company, but most statutes now provide for single-member limited liability companies. There are generally no restrictions on the maximum number of members.

Members Rights

The Uniform Limited Liability Company Act and state statutes grant several different rights to members of the limited liability company. These rights vary by state, and many of the rights may be amended in the limited liability company's articles of organization or operating agreement. Following is a list of rights typically granted to members of limited liability companies:

- Each member has an equal right to manage the limited liability company or to appoint managers to manage the company.

- Members have the right to be reimbursed for liabilities they incur in the ordinary course of the business of the company or for the preservation of its business or property.
- Each member has the right to receive an equal share of any distribution made by the limited liability company before its dissolution and winding up.
- Members have the right to access the records of the limited liability company at the company's principal office or other reasonable location specified in the operating agreement.
- Members have the right to certain information concerning the company's business or affairs.
- Members have the right to receive a copy of the company's written operating agreement.
- Members have the right to maintain an action against a limited liability company or other member to enforce the operating agreement and other rights.
- Members have the right to dissociate from a limited liability company and have their shares purchased by the limited liability company.
- Members generally have the right to wind up the business of the limited liability company.

The vast majority of member rights will be provided for in the limited liability company's operating agreement.

Members as Agents

If a limited liability company has no designated manager, its members are considered to be agents of the limited liability company, in much the same way as partners may act on behalf of a partnership. Each member has the authority to bind the limited liability company in actions that are apparently aimed at carrying on the ordinary course of the company's business, or business of the kind that is carried on by the limited liability company. The act of a member that is not apparently aimed at carrying on the ordinary course of the company's business does not bind the company unless such act is authorized by the other members. The authority of members to act on behalf of the limited liability company is a matter that can be amended in the operating agreement of the limited liability company, and also by the statutes of the limited liability company's state of organization.

§ 4.6 ORGANIZATION AND MANAGEMENT OF A LIMITED LIABILITY COMPANY

A limited liability company is formed when the articles of organization are filed with the secretary of state or other appropriate state authority. The limited liability company is then *given its life* by the proper state authority. A limited liability company generally can be formed for any lawful business purpose. State statutes may restrict the formation of not-for-profit limited liability companies or limited liability companies formed for providing services by professionals such as doctors or lawyers.

Organizers of the Limited Liability Company

Although the Uniform Limited Liability Act provides that any one or more persons may form a limited liability company, in some states two or more persons are required to form a limited liability company. State statutes must be checked carefully on this point.

Articles of Organization

The articles of organization must contain the information prescribed by the statutes in the state in which the limited liability company is formed. Typically, the articles of organization will include:

- The name of the limited liability company.
- The address of the initial designated office.
- The name and address of the initial agent for service of process.
- The name and address of each organizer.
- The duration of the existence of the limited liability company or a statement that the limited liability company will exist perpetually.
- The name and address of the limited liability company's initial managers if the limited liability company is to be managed by managers.
- Information concerning the members' liability for any debts, obligations, and liabilities of the limited liability company.

Name of the Limited Liability Company   There are two types of requirements set by state statute with regard to the name of a limited liability company, as set forth in its articles of organization:

1. The name must contain language specifying that the entity is a limited liability company.
2. The name must be available for use in the state in question.

The name of a limited liability company must include certain words or abbreviations required by state statute. For example, the names of limited liability companies in states following the Uniform Limited Liability Company Act must include the words *limited liability company* or *limited company* or the abbreviation *L.L.C.* or *LC. Limited* may also be abbreviated as *Ltd.*, and *company* may be abbreviated as *Co.*

The name of a limited liability company must be distinguishable upon the records of the secretary of state from the names of other limited liability companies, corporations, partnerships, and limited partnerships. State statutes set forth the exact standards to which the names of limited liability companies must adhere.

A paralegal who is responsible for filing articles of organization must first determine that the name the limited liability company organizers wish to use is available for use in the state of organization. To do this, the secretary of state's office, or other appropriate office must be contacted. Typically, the office of the secretary of state will grant a preliminary approval of a name over the telephone, but not guarantee the availability until the articles of organization are filed or until the name is formally reserved pursuant to state statutes. In some states, name availability may be checked on the secretary of state's Web page. See appendix A of this text for a directory of state secretary of state offices. Tips for drafting articles of organization are given in Figure 4-4.

- ◆ Always begin by checking state statutes for requirements.
- ◆ Make sure the name being used for the limited liability company is available and that it conforms to state requirements.
- ◆ Do not use a post office box for the address of the agent for service of process.
- ◆ Be sure the articles are signed by the proper individual or individuals.
- ◆ Information not *required* to be included in the articles of organization by state statute may be included in the operating agreement, which is not filed for public record.

FIGURE 4-4 Tips for Drafting Articles of Organization

Not only must the name set forth in the articles of organization include words that indicate the entity is a limited liability company, but the company must be sure that the full name with such an indication is used in all correspondence, stationery, checks, and other materials that the company uses to conduct its business. It is important that the company establishes itself as a limited liability company with those with whom the company transacts business. In fact, if the company does not use those specific words in its name when it transacts business, and individuals doing business with the limited liability company are deceived into thinking they are dealing with a partnership, the members of the limited liability company may be held personally accountable for any debts or obligations to such individuals who were so deceived. Figure 4-5 lists tips for checking name availability.

- ◆ The name you are checking should be in compliance with state statute as to format (it must contain the words *Limited Liability Company* or similar words or abbreviations).
- ◆ Before you place a call to the secretary of state or other state authority, have one or two alternate names ready to check.
- ◆ Most states will allow you to call for a preliminary check of name availability or check availability online (see secretary of state directory at appendix A of this text).
- ◆ Telephone lines to the secretary of state offices are notoriously busy—be patient.
- ◆ If articles of organization will not be filed very shortly after name availability is checked, the name should be reserved with the secretary of state.
- ◆ Clients should be advised *not* to use their new name until (1) articles of organization have been accepted for filing, or (2) the name has been reserved.

FIGURE 4-5 Tips for Checking Limited Liability Company Name Availability

Address of the Limited Liability Company's Initial Office The articles of organization must set forth the complete address of the limited liability company's initial office.

Registered Agent for Service of Process Within the articles of organization, a limited liability company must designate the name and address of an agent who is located within the state of organization and who is authorized to accept service of process on behalf of the limited liability company. The address set forth in this section may not be a post office box. It must be a physical location where service of process may be made in person.

Names and Addresses of the Organizers of the Limited Liability Company The full names and addresses of the organizers of the limited liability company, who may or may not be the original members, must be set forth in the articles of organization.

Duration of the Limited Liability Company Prior to the *Check the Box* regulations adopted by the Internal Revenue Service, the statutes of most states required limited liability companies to have a limited duration. Most states have now amended their statutes to permit perpetual existence for limited liability companies. The articles of organization must state the duration of the limited liability company in compliance with state statutes.

Names and Addresses of the Managers of the Limited Liability Company If the limited liability company is formed as a manager-managed limited liability company, the names and addresses of the initial manager or managers must be set forth in the articles of organization.

Information Concerning Personal Liability of the Limited Liability Company's Members Pursuant to the Uniform Limited Liability Company Act, no member or manager of the limited liability company is personally liable for the debts, obligations, or liabilities of the limited liability company. If, however, the organizers of a limited liability company feel that it is in the best interests of the company for certain managers or members to be held personally liable for certain types of debts, obligations, or liabilities of the company, they can so provide by setting forth those exceptions in the articles of organization. No member or manager can be held personally liable for any debts, obligations, or liabilities of a limited liability company unless he or she agrees to be held personally liable in a written agreement with the company.

Statutory Requirements Several other requirements for articles of organization are set by state statutes. Some of the more common requirements for inclusion in the articles of organization are:

◆ Powers of the limited liability company.
◆ Terms and conditions for new members.

- Rights of members to continue business after death or withdrawal of one or more members.
- Rights of members to withdraw.
- Rights of members upon dissolution.

Figure 4-6 shows a sample of a form for articles of organization for a limited liability company.

ARTICLES OF ORGANIZATION
OF

_____ , LLC

Limited Liability Company Act § _____
State of _____

ARTICLE ONE
NAME OF COMPANY

The name of the Company is _____.

ARTICLE TWO
DESIGNATED OFFICE

The address of the initial designated office of the Company is:

_____
_____.

ARTICLE THREE
AGENT FOR SERVICE OF PROCESS

The name and street address of the registered agent to receive service of process for the Company is:

_____
_____.

ARTICLE FOUR
ORGANIZERS

The name and street address of the organizers of the Company are:

_____
_____.

FIGURE 4-6 Sample Articles of Organization

ARTICLE FIVE
PERPETUAL EXISTENCE

The Company shall not be a term company, but shall exist perpetually, until properly dissolved under the laws of the state of _____.

ARTICLE SIX
COMPANY MANAGERS

The Company shall be manager-managed, as that term is defined in § ____ of the _____ Statutes. The initial managers of the Company shall be:

_____

_____

_____

In witness, these Articles of Organization have been subscribed by the undersigned organizer, who affirms the foregoing as true under the penalties of perjury, this _____ [date].

_____
Signature, name, and address of organizer

FIGURE 4-6   (*continued*)

Management and Control of the Limited Liability Company

The management of a limited liability company is generally very flexible. Most details concerning the operation and management of the limited liability company may be set forth in the operating agreement. The limited liability company may be either member-managed, or manager-managed.

Member-Managed Limited Liability Companies

In a **member-managed limited liability company**, each member has equal rights in the management of the limited liability company's business. Each member has the right to act on behalf of the limited liability company with regard to most matters. Decisions relating to the business of the company are made by a majority of the members.

Except as otherwise provided by statute or the limited liability company's operating agreement, any matter relating to the business of the company may be decided by a majority of the members.

◆ ——————————————————————————————————————

member-managed limited liability company   A limited liability company in which the members have elected to share the managing of the company's affairs.

Much like partners in a general partnership, members of a member-managed limited liability company owe a fiduciary duty to one another. In states that follow the Uniform Limited Liability Company Act in this regard, the members owe each other a duty of loyalty and a duty of care, as prescribed by statute.

Manager-Managed Limited Liability Companies

The organizers of a limited liability company may decide to elect a board of managers to manage the business of the company. In that event, the limited liability company is referred to as a **manager-managed limited liability company**. Such managers are typically named in the company's articles of organization, which must be amended if the managers change. If the limited liability company is manager-managed, the managers are agents of the limited liability company and other members are not considered to be agents. Non-managers lack the authority to act on behalf of the limited liability company in most instances. The acts of a limited liability company manager generally bind the limited liability company unless:

1. The manager has no authority to act for the company in that particular matter and the individual with whom the manager was dealing knew or had notice that the manager lacked authority.

2. The act of the manager was not apparently aimed at carrying on the ordinary course of the company's business or the business of the kind carried on by the company, and the members of the limited liability company did not authorize such act.

Because managers are given the authority to act on behalf of the other members of the limited liability company, they owe a fiduciary duty to the other members. In states that follow the Uniform Limited Liability Company Act, managers owe the members the duty of loyalty and the duty of care prescribed in that Act.

Matters Requiring Consent of All Members

Certain matters provided for in state statutes or the limited liability company's articles of organization or organization agreement require the consent of all members. Actions that often require unanimous consent of the members include:

◆ Amendment of the limited liability company's operating agreement.

◆ Approval of acts or transactions by certain members or managers that would otherwise violate the duty of loyalty.

◆ Amendments to the articles of organization.

◆ The compromise of an obligation to make a contribution.

---

manager-managed limited liability company A limited liability company in which the members have agreed to have the company's affairs managed by one or more managers.

- The compromise, as among members, of an obligation of a member to make a contribution or return money or other property paid or distributed in violation of state statute.
- The making of interim distributions.
- The admission of a new member.
- The use of the company's property to redeem an interest subject to a charging order.
- Dissolution of the company.
- A waiver of the right to have the company's business wound up and the company terminated.
- The merger of the limited liability company with another entity.
- The sale, lease, exchange, or other disposal of all, or substantially all, of the company's property with or without goodwill.

The above matters require the consent of all members, regardless of whether the limited liability company is member managed or manager managed.

When the act of a limited liability company requires the consent of all members, the act may be approved at a meeting of the members or by a written consent signed by all members.

The Operating Agreement

Operating agreements set forth the agreement of the members of the limited liability company concerning the management and operation of the company. Because the operating agreement is not filed for public record, information that may be contained in either the articles of organization or the operating agreement is often contained in the operating agreement. The items that can be included in an operating agreement are numerous and will vary depending on the pertinent state statutes and the particular circumstances. Following is a sample checklist including items that often are included in an operating agreement.

OPERATING AGREEMENT CHECKLIST

- ☐ Formation and Term.
- ☐ Nature of Business.
- ☐ Accounting and Records.
- ☐ Names and Addresses of Members.
- ☐ Rights and Duties of Members.
- ☐ Meetings of Members.
- ☐ Managing Members.
- ☐ Contributions and Capital Accounts.
- ☐ Allocations and Distributions.
- ☐ Taxes.
- ☐ Disposition of Membership Interests.

☐ Dissociation of a Member.

☐ Additional and Substitute Members.

☐ Dissolution and Winding Up.

☐ Amendment.

☐ Miscellaneous Provisions.

See appendix J-3 for a sample Limited Liability Company Operating Agreement.

Most state statutes allow for maximum flexibility concerning the contents of the operating agreement. The Uniform Limited Liability Company Act sets forth certain restrictions concerning the contents of the operating agreement with regard to the rights and duties of its members. Section 103(b) of the Act provides:

(b) The operating agreement may not:

(1) unreasonably restrict a right to information or access to records under Section 408;

(2) eliminate the duty of loyalty under Section 409(b) or 603(b)(3), but the agreement may:

(i) identify specific types or categories of activities that do not violate the duty of loyalty, if not manifestly unreasonable; and

(ii) specify the number or percentage of members or disinterested managers that may authorize or ratify, after full disclosure of all material facts, a specific act or transaction that otherwise would violate the duty of loyalty;

(3) unreasonably reduce the duty of care under Section 409(c) or 603(b)(3);

(4) eliminate the obligation of good faith and fair dealing under Section 409(d), but the operating agreement may determine the standards by which the performance of the obligation is to be measured, if the standards are not manifestly unreasonable;

(5) vary the right to expel a member in an event specified in Section 601(5);

(6) vary the requirement to wind up the limited liability company's business in a case specified in Section 801(3); or

(7) restrict rights of a person, other than a manager, a member, or a transferee of a member's distributional interest, under this [Act].

Annual Reporting Requirements

Like corporations, limited liability companies in most states are subject to annual reporting requirements with the secretary of state or other appropriate state authority. The statutes of the limited liability company's state of organization must be checked carefully to be sure that all annual reporting requirements are complied with. Typically, annual reports must be filed that contain such information as:

◆ Name of the limited liability company.

◆ State or country where limited liability company is organized.

◆ Name and address of agent within state for service of process.

◆ Address of the limited liability company's principal office.

◆ Names and addresses of any managers.

In some states, failure to file the annual report can cause the limited liability company to be dissolved by the state—usually after several notices from the state.

§ 4.7 FINANCIAL STRUCTURE OF A LIMITED LIABILITY COMPANY

The financial structure of a limited liability company resembles that of a partnership in many ways. Financing generally comes from member contributions. Members who spend money on behalf of the limited liability company are entitled to reimbursement for expenditures they make on behalf of the company, and members are entitled to receive distributions pursuant to statute and the limited liability company's operating agreement.

Member Contributions

The initial assets of the limited liability company typically consist of the contributions of members. Limited liability company members will be required to make certain contributions to the company as provided for in the company's operating agreement, articles of organization, and agreements of the members. Unless otherwise prohibited by statute or by the limited liability company's articles of organization or operating agreement, the contributions of members may be in the form of cash or tangible or intangible property, including services. For example, if a limited liability company formed for the purposes of developing a piece of property is in need of the services of a general contractor, the members of the company may decide to grant membership to a general contractor in return for his or her services. Other new members may be required to make cash contributions.

Member Reimbursement

From time to time, certain members who are involved in the operation of the limited liability company may make expenditures on behalf of the company. These members are entitled to reimbursement of certain expenses made by them on behalf of the limited liability company, as provided by state statute and the company's operating agreement.

Distributions to Members

Details concerning distributions made to members of the limited liability company should be set forth in the operating agreement of the company. Unless otherwise provided for in the operating agreement or articles of operating agreement, any distributions made by the limited liability company must be made pursuant to state statute. Most state statutes provide that any distributions must be made to the members in equal shares. This, however, can be amended in the operating agreement of the organization. Members who contribute more to the company are usually entitled to receive larger distributions.

Member interests are sometimes sold to raise funds for the limited liability company. Certificates may be issued to evidence the interest owned by the members. Although such interests are similar in many respects to the shares of stock that are issued by corporations, the term *stock* is usually used exclusively for corporations.

Distributions may be prohibited by statute under certain circumstances, such as when the limited liability company would not be able to pay its debts when they are due in the ordinary course of business.

The members of most limited liability companies report their income in the same manner as partners of a general partnership. The income of the limited liability company is reported on the same form, the Form 1065 Partnership Return. As with partnerships, the income or loss of the limited liability company is allocated among the members, who include their distributive allocation of the income or loss on their personal income tax returns.

§ 4.8 DISSOLUTION OF THE LIMITED LIABILITY COMPANY

The dissolution of a limited liability company may be prompted either by the end of its planned and stated duration, or by some other event that triggers a dissolution. Like most partnerships, one or more members may be dissociated from the limited liability company without causing a dissolution of the company.

Member's Dissociation

In states that follow the Uniform Limited Liability Company Act[7] in this regard, dissociation may be caused by several events, including a member's withdrawal (with written notice), death, bankruptcy, or appointment of a guardian for the member. Members may also become dissociated from the limited liability company upon the occurrence of an event agreed to in the operating agreement to cause the dissociation of a member, upon the transfer of all of a member's interest in the limited liability company, or by unanimous vote of the other members under certain circumstances, such as when it is unlawful to carry on the company's business with the member.

Wrongful Dissociation A member's dissociation may be wrongful, as in instances where the dissociation is in breach of an express provision of the operating agreement; or, under certain circumstances, when the dissociation is before the expiration of the term of a company that has a definite term. If a member wrongfully dissociates from a limited liability company, he or she may be liable to the company and the remaining members for damages caused by his or her wrongful dissociation.

Effect of Dissociation of a Member Upon a member's dissociation from a limited liability company:

 ◆ The member loses all right to participate in the management of the company's business.

♦ The member's duty of loyalty and duty of care continue only with regard to events occurring before the dissociation, unless the member participates in winding up the company's business.

Purchase of the Dissociated Member's Interest State statutes and the limited liability company's operating agreement typically will provide specific terms and conditions for the purchase of a dissociating member's interest in the limited liability company. Members who dissociate from a limited liability company at-will are usually entitled to have their interest purchased shortly after their dissociation.

When the member's dissociation results in the dissolution of the limited liability company, the dissociating member is generally entitled to a final distribution when the business of the company is wound up.

Dissolution of the Limited Liability Company

The events that cause the dissolution of a limited liability company are provided for by the limited liability company's articles of organization, operating agreement, and by state statute. In states that follow the Uniform Limited Liability Company Act,[8] the following events cause a dissolution and winding up of the limited liability company business:

1. An event specified in the operating agreement
2. Consent of the members, as specified in the operating agreement
3. An event that makes it unlawful for the business to continue, if such illegality is not cured within ninety days after notice is given to the company of the event
4. Entry of a judicial decree, upon the application by a member, that:
   (i) the economic purpose of the company is likely to be unreasonably frustrated;
   (ii) another member has engaged in conduct relating to the company's business that makes it not reasonably practicable to carry on the company's business with that member;
   (iii) it is not otherwise reasonably practicable to carry on the company's business in conformity with the articles of organization and the operating agreement;
   (iv) the company failed to purchase the petitioner's distributional interest as required by statute;
   (v) actions of the managers or members in control of the company are, or have been, illegal, oppressive, fraudulent, or unfairly prejudicial to the petitioner
5. A judicial determination, based on application by a transferee of a member's interest, that it is equitable to wind up the company's business:
   (i) after the expiration of a specified term; or
   (ii) at any time, if the company is a company at will.

After the limited liability company has been dissolved, it continues only for the purpose of winding up its business.

Winding Up the Limited Liability Company

After a decision has been made to dissolve a limited liability company, its business must be wound up. Any member, except a member who has wrongfully dissociated from the limited liability company, may participate in winding up its business. Judicial supervision of the winding up may be ordered upon the application of any member of the company for good cause.

Distribution of Assets

The rules for distribution of the assets of the limited liability company may be set by the articles of organization, or the company's operating agreement. However, state statutes may have provisions regarding distribution of the limited liability company's assets that may not be superseded. These rules may provide that the property of the limited liability company must first be used to pay the debts and obligations of the limited liability company, before the members receive distributions.

Articles of Termination

Because the articles of organization are filed with the secretary of state or other state authority to give notice of the company's existence, notice of the company's dissolution must also be filed at the state level. In states that follow the Uniform Limited Liability Company Act,[9] this involves filing **articles of termination** or articles of dissolution with the secretary of state.

Articles of termination would typically include the following information:

1. The name of the company.
2. The date of the company's dissolution.
3. A statement that the company's business has been wound up and the legal existence of the company has been terminated.

The existence of the limited liability company is terminated when the articles of termination are filed, or on a later date specified in the document. Figure 4-7 on page 141 is a sample articles of dissolution form that may be filed in the state of Florida.

§ 4.9 ADVANTAGES OF DOING BUSINESS AS A LIMITED LIABILITY COMPANY

There can be several advantages to doing business as a limited liability company. Some of the most important reasons include the limited liability offered to owners of the company, the beneficial tax treatment received by the owners, and the flexible management structure available to the limited liability company.

articles of termination Document filed with proper state authority to dissolve a limited liability company. Same as articles of dissolution.

ARTICLES OF DISSOLUTION
FOR
A FLORIDA LIMITED LIABILITY COMPANY

1. The name of the limited liability company is _____

_____.

2. The effective date of the limited liability company's dissolution is _____.

3. A description of the occurrence that resulted in the limited liability company's dissolution pursuant to section 508.441, Florida Statutes, (copy of 608.441 on back of cover letter).

_____

_____

_____

_____

4. **CHECK ONE:**

☐ All debts, obligations, and liabilities of the limited liability company have been paid or discharged.

–OR–

☐ Adequate provision has been made for the debts, obligations, and liabilities pursuant to s. 608.4421.

5. All remaining property and assets have been distributed among its members in accordance with their respective rights and interests.

6. **CHECK ONE:**

☐ There are no suits pending against the company in any court.

–OR–

☐ Adequate provision has been made for the satisfaction of any judgment, order, or decree which may be entered against it in any pending suit.

Signatures of the members having the same percentage of membership interests necessary to approve the dissolution:

Signature   Typed or Printed name

_____   _____

_____   _____

_____   _____

_____   _____

_____   _____

Filing Fee: $25.00

FIGURE 4-7 Articles for Dissolution Form for Florida Limited Liability Company

Limited Liability for All Owners

The fact that the owners of the limited liability company are not subject to personal liability for the debts and obligations of the company is probably the most significant advantage to doing business as a limited liability company instead of as a limited partnership, general partnership, or sole proprietorship. Whereas sole proprietors and general partners may be held personally liable for the debts and other obligations of their business, owners of a limited liability company may not. The owners of a limited liability company generally have the same protection from personal liability that is granted to shareholders of a corporation.

Although members of a limited liability company, especially a start-up company, may find it necessary to give personal guarantees to secure financing for their business, members of a limited liability company cannot be held personally liable for the company's debts and obligations merely because of their status in the company.

In *Addy v. Myers,* the case which follows in this chapter, two members of a limited liability company borrowed funds from a bank on behalf of the company and gave personal guarantees. When the business of the limited liability company failed and the bank loans became due, the two members who gave personal guarantees for the funds were found to be responsible for the loans. Because the members of a limited liability company are not personally liable for the debts of the company, the court determined that members who did not give personal guarantees for the loans could not be held responsible.

Unrestrictive Ownership

S Corporations, which are discussed in Chapter 5 of this text, are very similar to limited liability companies in many respects and offer many of the same benefits. However, there are several statutory restrictions on the ownership of S Corporations. For example, S Corporations may have no more than 75 shareholders and these shareholders must be natural persons, estates, or exempt organizations or trusts that meet certain requirements. Partnerships and other corporations may not be shareholders. There are fewer restrictions placed on ownership of limited liability companies.

Ability to Raise Capital for the Business

Membership interests in the limited liability company offer maximum flexibility to investors. In general, the details of the membership interests sold in the limited liability company are up to the company's members. Unlike S Corporations, investors in a limited liability company may include corporate or foreign investors.

Beneficial Tax Treatment

By default, the owners of a limited liability company will be taxed as a partnership by the Internal Revenue Service. Or, in the case of a single-owner limited liability company, the entity is disregarded for federal income tax purposes and the owner

CASE

Supreme Court of North Dakota.
Boyd ADDY and Tom Hutchens, dba the M.A.H.D. Group, L.L.C., Plaintiffs and Appellants,
v.
Guy MYERS, Defendant, and
Nancy Myers, individually and as part of M.A.H.D., L.L.C., Defendants and Appellees.
No. 990387.
Aug. 31, 2000.

VANDE WALLE, Chief Justice.

Boyd Addy and Tom Hutchens appealed from a judgment dismissing their action against Guy and Nancy Myers. ...

I

In June 1995, the M.A.H.D. Group was formed ... to establish a restaurant in Bismarck named Ed Foo Yungs. ... Each of the named owners of the M.A.H.D. Group contributed $32,500 and owned 25% of the company.

Although they were not all formally named in the M.A.H.D. Group organizational papers, the company informally consisted of four families: Guy and Nancy Myers, Boyd and Deb Addy, Tom and Kathy Hutchens, and Lance and Lori Doerr.

Ed Foo Yungs opened in February 1996 and in a short time began experiencing financial difficulties. The minutes of a May 15, 1996 meeting for the M.A.H.D. Group state "[i]t was agreed that a $30,000.00 line of credit be set up at BNC National Bank." According to Boyd Addy and Tom Hutchens, they personally signed for what they described as a $15,000 line of credit for Ed Foo Yungs in May 1996 and for another $15,000 line of credit in July 1996. Boyd Addy and Tom Hutchens testified they loaned the $30,000 to the M.A.H.D. Group and it was to repay BNC National Bank with proceeds from the business.

In November 1996, Ed Foo Yungs was still experiencing financial difficulties. On November 7, 1996, Boyd Addy, Tom Hutchens, Lance and Lori Doerr, and Guy and Nancy Myers attended a company meeting at the Myers' home. According to

Nancy Myers, she was told Ed Foo Yungs needed another $15,000 line of credit, the money would be borrowed by the M.A.H.D. Group, and it would repay the loan. ... On November 8, 1996, Boyd Addy and Tom Hutchens personally signed for the $15,000 line of credit.

Ed Foo Yungs continued to experience financial difficulties, and the minutes of a February 13, 1997 meeting state the owners decided to close the business on February 16, 1997. The minutes of a March 26, 1997 meeting state "[i]t was agreed that the $45,000.00 due BNC National would be assumed equally by the Addys, Myers and Hutchens, to be assumed by the 15th of April." Boyd Addy testified Nancy Myers objected at that meeting to paying $15,000. Guy and Nancy Myers subsequently retained an attorney, who wrote a letter to Lori Doerr requesting the minutes of the March 26 meeting be revised to reflect the Myers had not agreed to assume any personal liability for the $15,000.

Boyd Addy and Tom Hutchens sued Guy and Nancy Myers. The trial court granted summary judgment for Guy Myers, concluding he was not personally obligated for the $15,000 loan because he was not listed as a capital contributer, an owner, a manager, a governor, or an officer of the company. After a bench trial, the court decided Nancy Myers had not guaranteed repayment of the $15,000 loan because there was no written guaranty signed by her. The court decided the $15,000 loan signed for by Boyd Addy and Tom Hutchens in November 1996 was for the M.A.H.D. Group; however, the company's articles of organization specifically stated its members were not liable for its debt, obligation, or liability and Nancy Myers did not intend to assume any personal liability for the $15,000 loan. ...

The M.A.H.D. Group was established as a limited liability company under N.D.C.C. ch. 10-32, which was enacted in 1993 N.D. ... A limited liability company combines the flow-through income tax advantages and capital structure of a partnership with the limited liability and governance structure of a corporation. ... Limited liability companies are taxed like partnerships, but are like corporations in that members have limited liability like corporate shareholders. ... A limited liability company is a separate business entity and its owners or members are not exposed to personal liability for the entity's debts unless there are personal guarantees. ... Owners or members of a limited liability company can participate in management of the company without becoming personally liable for the entity's debt.

Although a majority of members and owners of the M.A.H.D. Group could take action on its behalf to render it liable for its debt, ... there is a difference between the company itself being liable for its debt and individual owners of the company being personally liable for its debt. Under N.D.C.C. s 10-32-29 and the articles of organization of the M.A.H.D. Group, owners and members of the limited liability company generally are not, merely because of that status, personally liable for a judgment, decree or order of a court, or in any other manner for a debt, obligation or liability of the company. ...

To the extent the additional $15,000 loan constituted debt for the company, the owners or members of the company are not, merely because of that status, personally liable for the company debt under N.D.C.C. s 10-32-29 and the company's articles of organization. ...

The trial court found Nancy Myers did not intend or agree to assume any personal liability for the debt. ... Although there is some evidence Nancy Myers believed she might be personally liable for one fourth of the $15,000 loan, her belief was apparently based on her erroneous assumption that owners were personally liable for the debt of a limited liability company. Nancy Myers' mistaken belief does not constitute an agreement to be personally liable for any part of the $15,000 loan. On this record, we are not left with a definite and firm conviction the trial court made a mistake in finding Nancy Myers did not intend or agree to assume any personal liability for the loan. We therefore conclude the trial court's finding is not clearly erroneous under N.D.R.Civ.P. 52(a).

We affirm the judgment.

---

is taxed in the same manner as a sole proprietor. This gives the limited liability company a decided tax advantage over the corporation. When a limited liability company is treated like a partnership for federal income tax purposes, the income earned by the limited liability company *flows through* to the owners of the company and is added to their personal income. The limited liability company's income is taxed once, at the income tax rate of the individual owners. Corporate income, on the other hand, may be subject to double taxation—once at the corporate level when the income is received by the corporation, and once at the shareholder level when dividends are received.

Flexibility of Management

In comparison with other forms of business, there are generally few statutory restrictions placed on the management of a limited liability company. Unlike the limited partnership, for example, all members of the limited liability company are free to contribute to the management of the company without the threat of losing their limited liability status. In addition, limited liability companies are not subject to the requirements for holding shareholder meetings to which corporations must adhere.

§ 4.10 DISADVANTAGES OF DOING BUSINESS AS A LIMITED LIABILITY COMPANY

The advantages to doing business as a limited liability company must be weighed against the potential disadvantages. One disadvantage is the limitation on transferring the ownership interest of a limited liability company. Other disadvantages include the uncertainties associated with piercing the veil of the limited liability company, the lack of uniformity in limited liability law among the states, and the formalities and reporting requirements associated with limited liability companies.

Limited Transferability of Ownership

There may be several restrictions placed on the transfer of ownership of a limited liability company. As discussed previously in this chapter, a member of a limited liability company may not merely transfer his or her interest to another individual who will become the new member. While a member may transfer his or her financial rights to a limited liability company, the transferee may only become a new member of the limited liability company pursuant to the provisions of state statutes and the company's operating agreement.

Possibility of Piercing the Limited Liability Company Veil

A limited liability company does not protect the members from personal liability in every instance. Under certain circumstances, such as when the members of a limited liability company have used the company to defraud creditors or investors, members may be found personally liable for the debts and obligations of the limited liability company. Disregarding the limited liability entity and looking to the members personally is referred to as *piercing the limited liability company veil.*

Rules for piercing the corporate veil of a corporation and holding shareholders personally liable for certain debts and obligations of the corporation are widely accepted and established by case law. Under the statutes and case law of several states, it has been established that the conditions and circumstances under which the corporate veil may be pierced also apply to limited liability companies. Piercing the corporate veil is discussed further in Chapter 5.

Lack of Uniformity in State Laws

Although the whole intent of the Uniform Limited Liability Company Act was to bring uniformity to state law, as of early 2001, only seven states had adopted the Act. Thus, there is little uniformity in statutory law between states with regard to limited liability companies. To further complicate matters, there is little case law concerning limited liability companies published to date. These two factors make it very difficult for limited liability companies that transact business in several states.

Limited Liability Company Formalities and Reporting Requirements

Compared to sole proprietorships and partnerships, there are several formalities that must be followed to form and operate a limited liability company. The limited liability company must be *formed* by filing articles of organization with the appropriate state authority, and annual registration with the state's secretary of state is usually required. Also, a limited liability company must qualify to do business in any state other than its state of domicile.

Figure 4-8 lists the advantages and disadvantages of doing business as a limited liability company.

Advantages	Disadvantages
• Limited liability for all owners	• Limited transferability of ownership
• Unrestrictive ownership	• Possibility of piercing the LLC veil
• Ability to raise capital for business	• Lack of uniformity in state LLC law
• Beneficial tax treatment	• Formalities and reporting requirements
• Flexibility of management	

FIGURE 4-8   Advantages and Disadvantages of Doing Business as a Limited Liability Company

§ 4.11 TRANSACTING BUSINESS AS A FOREIGN LIMITED LIABILITY COMPANY

In every state in which a limited liability company transacts business, other than its state of organization, it is considered a **foreign limited liability company**. A foreign limited liability company must be granted a **certificate of authority to transact business as a foreign limited liability company** (or similar document) before it begins transacting business in any state other than its state of organization.

As with corporations, a foreign limited liability company subjects itself to the jurisdiction of the courts of each state in which it transacts business. For that reason, foreign limited liability companies must comply with state statutes that pertain to the transaction of business in the foreign state, and they must comply with statutory formalities regarding foreign limited liability companies.

When the owners of a limited liability company organize their business or expand it, a decision must be made as to what its legal obligations are with regard to

foreign limited liability company   A limited liability company that is transacting business in any state other than the state of its organization.

certificate of authority to transact business as a foreign limited liability company   Certificate issued by the secretary of state, or other appropriate state official, to a foreign limited liability company to allow it to transact business in that state.

states with which the company comes in contact, other than the company's state of organization. First, it must be determined whether the limited liability company is actually *transacting business* within the foreign state, as defined by the statutes of the foreign state. If the limited liability company is in fact transacting business in the foreign state, or if it plans to in the future, the limited liability company must obtain a certificate of authority from the secretary of state of the foreign state and appoint an agent for service of process who is located within the foreign state. If it is determined that the limited liability company is not actually *transacting business* within the foreign state, the limited liability company will not need to apply for a certificate of authority, but the organizers of the company may decide that it would be beneficial to register the name of the limited liability company within that state.

The statutes of each state in which the limited liability company wishes to transact business must be carefully reviewed before the company begins transacting business in that state.

Transacting Business as a Foreign Limited Liability Company

At times, there is no question whether a limited liability company is transacting business in another state; for instance, if the expansion of a limited liability company into another state involves the construction of a factory in that state and hiring employees from that state to work in the factory. In other instances, however, such as when a salesperson occasionally crosses state borders to make a sale, the question requires a closer look at state statutes.

The statutes of most states address the matter either by giving a general definition of what constitutes transacting business in their state or by providing a list of activities that *do not* constitute the transaction of business. The Uniform Limited Liability Company Act addresses the question by providing such a list in § 1003, which follows:

SECTION 1003. ACTIVITIES NOT CONSTITUTING TRANSACTING BUSINESS.

(a) Activities of a foreign limited liability company that do not constitute transacting business within the meaning of this [article] include:

    (1) maintaining, defending, or settling an action or proceeding;

    (2) holding meetings of its members or managers or carrying on any other activity concerning its internal affairs;

    (3) maintaining bank accounts;

    (4) maintaining offices or agencies for the transfer, exchange, and registration of the foreign company's own securities or maintaining trustees or depositories with respect to those securities;

    (5) selling through independent contractors;

    (6) soliciting or obtaining orders, whether by mail or through employees or agents or otherwise, if the orders require acceptance outside this State before they become contracts;

    (7) creating or acquiring indebtedness, mortgages, or security interests in real or personal property;

(8) securing or collecting debts or enforcing mortgages or other security interests in property securing the debts, and holding, protecting, and maintaining property so acquired;

(9) conducting an isolated transaction that is completed within 30 days and is not one in the course of similar transactions of a like manner; and

(10) transacting business in interstate commerce.

(b) For purposes of this [article], the ownership in this State of income-producing real property or tangible personal property, other than property excluded under subsection (a), constitutes transacting business in this State.

(c) This section does not apply in determining the contacts or activities that may subject a foreign limited liability company to service of process, taxation, or regulation under any other law of this State.

There can be several negative consequences to the limited liability company that transacts business in another state without first receiving a certificate of authority. Probably the most significant consequence is the lack of access to the courts in that state. For example, if a limited liability company must seek a court action to enforce a contract in a neighboring state, the unauthorized company will be unable to enforce that contract in the courts of the neighboring state.

Application for a Certificate of Authority

Before a limited liability company begins transacting business in a foreign state, it must obtain a certificate of authority from the secretary of state or other appropriate state official in the foreign state. The certificate of authority is obtained by completing an Application for Certificate of Authority to Transact Business as a Foreign Limited Liability Company, and filing it with the appropriate state authority. The application must be completed pursuant to the statutes of the foreign state and further requirements prescribed by the secretary of state. The application typically includes the following information:

- Name of the limited liability company.
- State where the limited liability company is organized.
- Address of the principal office of the limited liability company.
- Address of the initial designated office within the foreign state.
- Name and street address of the limited liability company's agent for service of process within the foreign state.
- Duration of the limited liability company.
- Name and address of the limited liability company's managers if the company is manager managed.
- Statement regarding any personal liability assumed by any managers or members of the limited liability company.

One requirement that is uniform in all states is that any limited liability company that wishes to transact business in a foreign state must designate, in its application for certificate of authority, an agent within that state to accept service of process on its behalf. This ensures that if there is ever a cause of action against a limited liability company that arises within the foreign state, service of process may be made upon that limited liability company by service on its agent within the state.

The secretary of state may have additional requirements, such as the filing of a copy of the company's articles of organization or a certificate of existence from the limited liability company's state of organization.

Figure 4-9 is a sample application for certificate of authority by a limited liability company for the State of Texas.

CHECKLIST FOR FILING APPLICATION FOR CERTIFICATE OF AUTHORITY TO TRANSACT BUSINESS AS A FOREIGN LIMITED LIABILITY COMPANY

☐ Complete Application for Certificate of Authority in format prescribed by state authority of foreign state (the secretary of state may require that the application be completed on a form furnished by their office).

☐ Be sure that the application includes a *street address within the foreign state* where service of process may be made on an agent of the LLC.

☐ Be sure the application is signed by an authorized individual.

☐ Include the appropriate filing fee.

☐ Include copy of the articles of organization if required by the foreign state.

☐ Include certificate of existence or similar document if required by the foreign state.

Name Registration

One important factor for the organizers of a limited liability company to consider is its name, and its name availability in other states. If a limited liability company plans to expand its business into several states in the future, the organizers must make sure that its name will be available for use in each state. For example, suppose a limited liability company is organized under the laws of Iowa as Peterson Engineering Limited Liability Company. The organizers plan to build their business on the reputation of its founders and expand it into the entire Midwest region. If their state-by-state expansion begins in three years, they may have a problem if the name *Peterson Engineering Limited Liability Company* is not available for use in any of the surrounding states.

One way around this problem is foreign name registration. In states that follow the Uniform Limited Liability Company Act in this regard, a foreign limited liability company may register its name in a foreign state, provided that name meets with the state's requirements. Names of foreign limited liability companies are typically registered for a one-year period. A registered name will be reserved for future use for the limited liability company if the limited liability company decides to transact business in that state in the future.

Office of the Secretary of State
Corporations Section
P.O. Box 13697
Austin, Texas 78711-3697

APPLICATION FOR CERTIFICATE OF AUTHORITY
BY A LIMITED LIABILITY COMPANY

Pursuant to the provisions of article 7.05 of the Texas Limited Liability Company Act, the undersigned limited liability company hereby applies for a certificate of authority to transact business in Texas:

1.   The name of the limited liability company is _____

2.   (A) If the name of the limited liability company does not contain the words, "Limited Liability Company" or "Limited Company," or the abbreviations "L.L.C.," "LLC," "LC," or "L.C.," then the name of the foreign limited liability company with the words or abbreviation which it elects to add thereto for use in Texas is

_____

(B) If the name is not available in Texas, then set forth the name under which the foreign limited liability company will qualify and transact business in Texas.

_____

3.   The federal tax identification number is _____

4.   The date of its organization is _____ and the period

of duration is _____ (State term of years or other duration authorized in its home jurisdiction.)

5.   The address of its principal office in the state or country under the laws of which it is

organized is _____

(If the company does not maintain its principal office in the jurisdiction of organization, provide the address of its registered office address in such jurisdiction.)

6.   The street address of its proposed registered office in Texas is (a P.O. Box or lock box

is not sufficient)_____

_____and

the name of its proposed registered agent in Texas at such address is

_____

FIGURE 4-9   Application for a Certificate of Authority by a Limited Liability Company Form for Texas

7.   The purpose or purposes of the company which it proposes to pursue in the transaction of business in Texas are:

_____

_____

8.   It is authorized to pursue such purpose or purposes in the state or country under the laws of which it is organized.

9.   (Complete either A or B below.)

(A) The names and respective addresses of its managers are:

NAME   ADDRESS

_____   _____

_____   _____

_____   _____

or

(B) The company is member-managed. The names and addresses of its managing members are:

NAME   ADDRESS

_____   _____

_____   _____

_____   _____

10.   The application is accompanied by a certificate issued by the secretary of state or other authorized officer of the jurisdiction of organization evidencing the existence of the limited liability company.

Date:_____   _____
                                                    Name of Company

                                        By _____
                                                    An Authorized Manager or Member

Form No. 304
Revised 8/99

FIGURE 4-9   (*continued*)

§ 4.12 THE PARALEGAL'S ROLE

Paralegals can perform a variety of functions to assist with the formation, maintenance, and dissolution of limited liability companies. Many of the services to be performed on behalf of a limited liability company will be procedural in nature and can easily be performed by an experienced paralegal with the proper resources. Most of the functions performed by paralegals will involve drafting appropriate legal documentation and performing research.

Drafting Limited Liability Documentation

Paralegals, with the use of current forms and form books, may be responsible for drafting virtually all documents associated with the limited liability company. These documents may include the articles of organization, operating agreement, applications for certificates of authority to transact business as a foreign limited liability company, and others.

The paralegal may be responsible for attending an initial client meeting to collect information concerning the formation of a limited liability company. With the use of a customized checklist, the paralegal can collect all of the information required to prepare drafts of the organization documents. The paralegal may also become the client contact to assist with future needs of the limited liability company client.

Figure 4-10 provides a checklist for drafting articles of organization.

The following items must be considered for inclusion in the articles of organization for a limited liability company:

☐ Name of the limited liability company; it must contain the words "limited liability company," "LLC," or "L.L.C."

☐ The address of the principal place of business within the state.

☐ The purpose of the limited liability company.

☐ The name of the limited liability company's registered agent and the address of its registered office (not a P.O. box).

☐ The names and business addresses of the initial manager or managers, if any.

☐ The names and addresses of the initial members of the limited liability company.

☐ The duration of the limited liability company.

☐ The names and addresses of all organizers, who need not be members of the limited liability company.

☐ The effective date of the limited liability company.

☐ Any other provisions required by the statutes of the state or organization or desired by the members of the limited liability company.

FIGURE 4-10 Checklist for Drafting Articles of Organization

Corporate Paralegal Profile
Linda M. Racette

Because I work in-house, I wear many hats. I have learned about corporate law, intellectual property law, real property law, and securities issues.

Name Linda M. Racette

Location Manchester, New Hampshire

Title Legal Assistant

Specialty Corporate Law

Education Associate of Science Degree in Computer Science; Certificate in Paralegal Studies; Bachelor of Science Degree in Business Studies

Experience 4½ years

Linda M. Racette is the only paralegal employed by Rock of Ages Corporation, a company that owns granite quarries in the United States and Canada, and manufacturing plants and retail offices in the United States.

As a legal assistant to the vice president and general counsel of Rock of Ages, Linda's duties are numerous and varied. She is responsible for record-keeping for Rock of Ages Corporation and its several subsidiaries. From time to time, her work involves forming new business entities, including limited liability companies, in connection with the acquisition of new businesses. In addition, she drafts corporate resolutions, limited liability company resolutions, and correspondence. Linda helps prepare for the annual meeting of the corporation and manages a large trademark portfolio. She also works on securities filings and mergers and acquisitions.

Linda enjoys the diversity of her position. Each day brings a new experience. Because she works in-house, she has had the opportunity to learn about corporate law, limited liability company law, intellectual property law, real property law, and securities

law. At times, she has the opportunity to travel to other states to assist with closings.

On the down side, because she is in a rather small office, Linda is responsible for some secretarial duties. At times, she is asked to make travel arrangements for her supervisor, transcribe documents, and answer the telephone.

Linda has been very active in her local and national paralegal associations. She is vice president to the board of directors for the Paralegal Association of New Hampshire, and a member of the National Federation of Paralegal Associations and the National Paralegal Association.

She has also contributed her time to work pro bono. Recently, she completed a project for New Hampshire Legal Assistance for the "DOVE" program. The DOVE program handles domestic violence cases in conjunction with several shelters. The project involved creating a database in Word that paralegals could use to input data and generate reports for each center.

Linda's advice for new paralegals?

Do not try to learn everything all at once—take it one day at a time. If possible, intern if you can. Call the bar association in your area and ask if you can assist with a pro bono project. Don't get discouraged if things don't go exactly as planned. Don't be afraid to ask questions. If you make a mistake, correct it and move on. Life is too short. Don't be afraid to try something new. The attorney will appreciate your willingness to try and to learn. Above all, keep your sense of humor with you at all times. You will need it.

For more information on careers for corporate paralegals, see the Corporate Careers features on the companion Web page to this text at **www.westlegalstudies.com.**

Limited Liability Company Research

Because limited liability company law is relatively new, and because it varies so much between states, there may be a great need for legal research in this area. Most research will include state statutes, case law, the Internal Revenue Code and Revenue Rulings, and Securities Acts.

§ 4.13 RESOURCES

The main resources paralegals will use when working with limited liability companies are the state statutes, state authorities, the Internal Revenue Code, and form books and treatises.

State Statutes

The main source for answering questions concerning limited liability companies is the statutes of the state of organization. State statutes will include all basic information regarding the formation, operation, and dissolution of a limited liability company within that state. In addition, state statutes also contain information required by foreign limited liability companies doing business within that state. See Figure 4-11 for a list of state limited liability company statutes.

State	Act
Alabama	Alabama Limited Liability Company Act, Ala. Code §§ 10-12-1 through 10-12-61*
Alaska	Alaska Limited Liability Company Act, Alaska Stat. §§ 10.50.010 through 10.50.995
Arizona	Arizona Limited Liability Company Act, Ariz. Rev. Stat. §§ 29-601 through 29-857
Arkansas	Arkansas Small Business Entity Tax Pass Through Act, Ark. Code Ann. §§ 4-32-101 through 4-32-1316 (Michie 1996)
California	California Beverly-Killea Limited Liability Company Act, Cal. Corp. Code §§ 17000 through 17705
Colorado	Colorado Limited Liability Company Act, Colo. Rev. Stat. §§ 7-80-101 through 7-80-1006
Connecticut	Connecticut Limited Liability Company Act, Conn. Gen. Stat. Ann. §§ 34-100 through 34-242
Delaware	Delaware Limited Liability Company Act, Del. Code Ann. tit. 6 §§ 18-101 through 18-1109
District of Columbia	D.C. Code Ann. §§ 29-1301 to -1375
Florida	Florida Limited Liability Company Act, Fla. Stat. ch. 608.401 through 608.514

FIGURE 4-11 State Limited Liability Company Statutes

State	Act
Georgia	Georgia Limited Liability Company Act, Ga. Code Ann. §§ 14-11-100 through 14-11-1109
Hawaii	Hawaii Uniform Limited Liability Company Act, Haw. Rev. Stat. §§ 428-101 through 428-1302*
Idaho	Idaho Limited Liability Company Act, Idaho Code §§ 53-601 through 53-672
Illinois	Illinois Limited Liability Company Act, 805 ILCS 180/1-1 through 180/60-1
Indiana	Indiana Business Flexibility Act, Ind. Code §§ 23-18-1-1 through 23-18-13-1
Iowa	Iowa Limited Liability Company Act, Iowa Code §§ 490A.100 through 490A.1601
Kansas	Kansas Limited Liability Company Act, Kan. Stat. Ann. §§ 17-7601 through 17-7652
Kentucky	Kentucky Limited Liability Company Act, Ky. Rev. Stat. Ann. §§ 275.001 through 275.455
Louisiana	Louisiana Limited Liability Company Law, La. Rev. Stat. Ann. §§ 12:1301 through: 1369
Maine	Maine Limited Liability Company Act, Me. Rev. Stat. Ann. tit. 31, §§ 601 through 762
Maryland	Maryland Limited Liability Company Act, Md. Code Ann., Corps. & Ass'ns §§ 4A-101 through 4A-1103
Massachusetts	Massachusetts Limited Liability Company Act, Mass. Gen. Laws ch. 156C, §§ 1 through 68
Michigan	Michigan Limited Liability Company Act, Mich. Comp. Laws §§ 450.4101 through 450.5200
Minnesota	Minnesota Limited Liability Company Act, Minn. Stat. Ann. §§ 322B.01 through 322B.960
Mississippi	Mississippi Limited Liability Company Act, Miss. Code Ann. §§ 79-29-101 through 79-29-1204
Missouri	Missouri Limited Liability Company Act, Mo. Rev. Stat. § 347.010 *et seq.*
Montana	Montana Limited Liability Company Act, Mont. Code Ann. §§ 35-8-101 through 35-8-130*
Nebraska	Nebraska Limited Liability Company Act, Neb. Rev. Stat. §§ 21-2601 through 21-2653

FIGURE 4-11 (*continued*)

State	Act
Nevada	Nevada Limited Liability Company Act, Nev. Rev. Stat. §§ 86.010 through 86.571
New Hampshire	New Hampshire Limited Liability Company Act, N.H. Rev. Stat. Ann. §§ 304-C:1 through 304-D:20
New Jersey	New Jersey Limited Liability Company Act, N.J. Stat. Ann. §§ 42:2B-1 through 42:2B-70
New Mexico	New Mexico Limited Liability Company Act, N.M. Stat. Ann. §§ 53-19-1 through 53-19-74
New York	New York Limited Liability Company Act, N.Y. Limited Liability Company Law §§ 101 through 1403
North Carolina	North Carolina Limited Liability Company Act, N.C. Gen. Stat. §§ 57C-1-101 through 57C-10-07
North Dakota	North Dakota Limited Liability Act, N.D. Cent. Code §§ 10-32-01 through 10-32-155
Ohio	Ohio Limited Liability Company Act, Ohio Rev. Code Ann. §§ 1705.01 through 1705.58
Oklahoma	Oklahoma Limited Liability Company Act, Okla. Stat. Ann. tit. 18 §§ 2000 through 2060
Oregon	Oregon Limited Liability Company Act, Or. Rev. Stat. §§ 63.001 through 63.990
Pennsylvania	Pennsylvania Limited Liability Company Law, 15 Pa. Cons. Stat. §§ 8901 through 8998
Rhode Island	Rhode Island Limited Liability Company Act, R.I. Gen. Laws §§ 7-16-1 through 7-16-75
South Carolina	South Carolina Uniform Limited Liability Company Act of 1996, S.C. Code Ann. §§ 33-44-101 through 33-44-1409*
South Dakota	South Dakota Limited Liability Company Act, S.D. Codified Laws §§ 47-34-1 through 47-34-59*
Tennessee	Tennessee Limited Liability Company Act, Tenn. Code Ann. §§ 48-201-101 through 48-248-606
Texas	Texas Limited Liability Company Act, Tex. Rev. Civ. Stat. Ann. 1528n §§ 1.01 through 11.07
Utah	Utah Limited Liability Company Act, Utah Code Ann. §§ 48-2b-101 through 48-2b-158
Vermont	Vermont Limited Liability Company Act, Vt. Stat. Ann. tit. 11, §§ 3001 through 3162*

FIGURE 4-11 (*continued*)

State	Act
Virginia	Virginia Limited Liability Company Act, Va. Code Ann. §§ 13.1-1000 through 13.1-1121
Washington	Washington Limited Liability Company Act, Wash. Rev. Code §§ 25.15.005 through 25.15.902
West Virginia	West Virginia Limited Liability Company Act, W. Va. Code §§ 31-1A-1 through 31-1A-69*
Wisconsin	Wisconsin Limited Liability Company Act, Wis. Stat. §§ 183.0102 through 183.1305
Wyoming	Wyoming Limited Liability Company Act, Wyo. Stat. Ann. §§ 17-15-101 through 17-15-144

* State adoption of the Uniform Limited Liability Company Act.

FIGURE 4-11 (*continued*)

State Authorities

At times, the quickest way to find an answer concerning requirements for forming or operating a limited liability company (especially procedural questions regarding state filings) may be to contact the office of the secretary of state or other appropriate state official. The office of the secretary of state will often provide the following forms to use for filing in their office:

◆ Articles of organization.

◆ Reservation of name.

◆ Annual reports.

◆ Name registration.

◆ Application for certificate of authority to transact business as a foreign liability company.

In addition, the office of the secretary of state will often provide filing fee schedules and instructions for filing procedures. A directory of secretary of state offices is included as appendix A.

Internal Revenue Code

Questions concerning the taxation of a limited liability company may be answered by researching the Internal Revenue Code (IRC), Treasury Regulations, and Revenue Rulings and Procedures. Information on the taxation of limited liability companies can also be found on the Internal Revenue's Web page at **www.irs.gov**.

Articles, Form Books, and Treatises

In recent years, numerous law review and periodical articles, as well as texts and treatises, have been written on the topic of limited liability companies. These books are a good source for general information, forms, and state-by-state treatment of limited liability companies.

 Internet Resources **WWW.**

Several of the resources mentioned in this section, including the statutes of several states, and Internal Revenue Service information, are available on-line.

Following is a list of some Web pages that may be useful to paralegals who are working with limited liability companies:

For state statutes

American Law Source Online	**www.lawsource.com/also**
Findlaw.com	**www.findlaw.com/11stategov/**
Legal Information Institute	**www.law.cornell.edu/states/listing.html**

For information on federal taxation of limited liability companies

Internal Revenue Service	**www.irs.gov**

For limited liability company forms

All About Forms.Com	**www.allaboutforms.com/**
Findlaw.com (Legal Forms)	**www.findlaw.com**
The 'Lectric Law Library's Business and General Forms	**www.lectlaw.com/formb.htm**

For links to state government forms

Findlaw.com State Corporation and Business Forms	**ww.findlaw.com/11stategov/indexcorp.html**

For links to the secretary of state offices

Corporate Housekeeper	**www.danvi.vi/link2.html**
National Association of Secretaries of State	**www.nass.org**

For the Uniform Limited Liability Company Act

National Conference of Commissioners on Uniform State Law	**www.nccusl.org/nccusl/default.asp**

Information on the Limited Liability Company

Limited Liability Companies Reporter	**www.llc-reporter.com/**

An alphabetical list of Internet Resources for the Corporate Paralegal is included as appendix B to this text.

Web Page

For updates and links to several of the previously listed sites, as well as download-able state limited liability company forms, log on to **www.westlegalstudies.com**, and click through to the book link for this text.

SUMMARY

- ♦ The limited liability company is a type of business entity that has some character-istics of partnerships and some of corporations.
- ♦ All states in the United States and the District of Columbia now have statutes providing for limited liability companies.
- ♦ The owners of a limited liability company are referred to as its members.
- ♦ The members of a limited liability company typically have no personal liability for the debts and obligations of the limited liability company.
- ♦ A limited liability company may be member managed or manager managed.
- ♦ The limited liability company is formed when articles of organization or some similar document is filed with the appropriate state authority.
- ♦ The limited liability company is one of the fastest growing types of business entities in the United States.
- ♦ Limited liability companies are taxed as partnerships unless the members elect corporation taxation.
- ♦ Most states allow limited liability companies to be formed by one member.
- ♦ Single-member limited liability companies are disregarded as separate entities for federal income tax purposes. The income of the single-member limited liability company is allocated to the sole owner.
- ♦ Members of a member-managed limited liability company act as agents for the limited liability company.
- ♦ The managers of a manager-managed limited liability company act as its agents—the members who are not managers do not.
- ♦ The provisions of the limited liability company's operating agreement govern the limited liability company, so long as those provisions are not contrary to the pertinent state statutes.

REVIEW QUESTIONS

1. In what ways are limited liability companies dif-ferent from general partnerships?
2. If Sandy owes Mike $5,000 that she is unable to repay, can she assign to him her rights as a limited liability company member to receive payments as set forth in the company's operat-ing agreement? Can Sandy assign her entire rights in the limited liability to Mike, making

him a new member with the right to manage the business?

3. Katherine is a member of a member-managed limited liability company that designs software called K & A Software Ltd. Liability Company. Can she enter the company into a contract for the design of new educational software for a local college? What if the K & A Software Ltd. Liability Company is manager-managed?

4. Are the members of a limited liability company always protected from personal liability for the debts and obligations of the company? What are some circumstances under which members of a limited liability company may be personally liable for the company's debts and obligations?

5. Suppose that you are forming a limited liability company that will own and operate auto dealerships. Your company will only operate one dealership in Missouri to start with, but you want to expand into Illinois, Texas, and Arizona. What steps might you take during the organization process to plan for your future expansion?

6. If you are a family practice physician going into business with three other doctors, what options are available in your state for transacting business? Why might a limited liability partnership be an attractive alternative?

PRACTICAL PROBLEMS

1. Locate the limited liability company act from your state to answer the following questions:
   a. What is the cite for your state's limited liability company act?
   b. When was your state's act adopted?
   c. May limited liability companies in your state be formed by one individual?
   d. May limited liability companies in your state have a perpetual existence? If not, what is the maximum duration for a limited liability company in your state?

2. Locate the pertinent section of your state's limited liability company act, or contact the appropriate state office to answer the following questions:
   a. What is the title of the document for forming limited liability companies in your state?
   b. Where is this document filed?
   c. What is the filing fee for filing the document to organize a limited liability company?
   d. Are there any additional documents that must be filed with the organization document in your state? If so, what are they?

WORKPLACE SCENARIO

Assume that our fictional clients, Bradley Harris and Cynthia Lund, want to form a limited liability company in your state for their business, Cutting Edge Computer Repair. Bradley and Cynthia will each invest an equal amount in the limited liability company, which will be member managed.

Using the information provided in appendices D-1 and D-2 to this text, prepare for filing articles of organization for a limited liability company in your state. You may create your own form that conforms to the statutes of your state, or you can download and complete a form from the appropriate state office. Some articles of organization forms are available for downloading on the companion Web page to this text at **www.westlegalstudies.com**. If your state requires the filing of any other documentation to form a limited liability company, prepare that documentation also.

Then prepare a cover letter to the appropriate state authority filing the articles of organization and enclosing the appropriate filing fee and any other documentation required by the secretary of state.

END NOTES

1. Arkansas, North Carolina, North Dakota, West Virginia, and the District of Columbia do not permit perpetual duration of limited liability companies. Utah permits a maximum duration of 99 years.

2. Treas. Reg. § 301.7701-3 (1997).

3. Florida and Texas treat the limited liability company as a corporation for income tax purposes.

4. Rev. Rul. 88-76.

5. Zemple, Alan, Partnership Returns, 1998, Internal Revenue Service *Statistics of Income Bulletin, Fall 2000.*

6. *SEC v. Parkersburg Wireless,* 991 F.Supp. 6 (D.C. 1997).

7. Uniform Limited Liability Company Act § 601.

8. Uniform Limited Liability Company Act § 801.

9. Uniform Limited Liability Company Act § 805.

CHAPTER 5

Corporations

CHAPTER OUTLINE

§ 5.1   An Introduction to Corporations

§ 5.2   Corporations in the United States

§ 5.3   Corporate Rights and Powers

§ 5.4   Advantages of Doing Business as a Corporation

§ 5.5   Disadvantages of Doing Business as a Corporation

§ 5.6   Types and Classifications of Corporations

§ 5.7   The Paralegal's Role in Corporate Law Matters

§ 5.8   Resources

INTRODUCTION

The corporation is one of the most complex forms of business organizations. There are many types of corporations, most of which are subjects of entire texts of their own. This chapter and the rest of this book focus on the *business corporation,* which is the predominant form of corporation. First we look at the unique characteristics of business corporations, and discuss the role of business corporations in the United States. Next, we examine the rights and powers of a corporation and consider both the advantages and disadvantages of doing business as a business corporation in contrast to other types of business organizations. This chapter concludes with a discussion of other types and classifications of corporations, a look at the role of the paralegal working in the corporate law area, and the resources available to assist paralegals working in the corporate law area.

§ 5.1   AN INTRODUCTION TO CORPORATIONS

This section defines the term *corporation* and looks at some of the characteristics common to business corporations, including the fact that corporations are considered to be separate entities for most purposes. Next it defines and discusses "piercing the corporate veil" and examines the law governing corporations.

Corporation Defined

An early Supreme Court decision defined the corporation as "an artificial being, invisible, intangible, and existing only in contemplation of law."[1] This definition has been used frequently over the years. Another definition that is popular in the courts defines the corporation as a "creature of the law, with an identity or personality separate and distinct from that of its owners, and which, by necessity, must act through its agents."[2] Whatever the exact definition, the corporation possesses four characteristics that distinguish it from other types of business organizations:

1. The corporation is an artificial entity created by law.
2. The corporation is an entity separate from its owners or managers.
3. The corporation has certain rights and powers, which it exercises through its agents.
4. The corporation has the capacity to exist perpetually.

The Corporation as a Separate Legal Entity

In contrast to the sole proprietorship and general partnership, which are extensions of the individual owner or owners, the corporation is considered "an entity distinct from its individual members or stockholders, who, as natural persons, are merged in the corporate identity, and remains unchanged and unaffected in its identity by changes in its individual membership."[3] In many respects, corporations are treated as artificial persons under law, unless the law provides otherwise. As an artificial person, a corporation is subject to many of the same rights and obligations under law as a natural person. The courts have found on several occasions that "[w]hile all statutes which speak of persons cannot be construed to include artificial persons—that is, corporations—the term 'person' may unquestionably include a corporation."[4] It is the intent behind the statute that must be considered.

Because the corporation is a separate entity, the corporation itself is liable for any debts and obligations it incurs. The shareholders, directors, and officers of a corporation are generally not personally liable for the debts and obligations of the corporation merely by virtue of their interest in the corporation.

Piercing the Corporate Veil

Although the shareholders of a corporation are generally free from personal liability for the corporation's obligations, there are certain circumstances under which the corporate entity may be disregarded and shareholders may be considered personally liable for its debts and obligations. This is referred to as *piercing the corporate veil*. If a court finds the circumstances warrant, corporate directors and officers may be held personally liable for certain obligations.

When a corporation is formed or operated to commit fraud or other illegal activity, or to defend a crime, the corporate veil may be pierced and any shareholder, director, or officer who is responsible for the wrongdoing may be held personally accountable.

Dividends ————————————————————————————— ◆

Pro Bono Work in the Law Firm and Corporate Legal Department

Access to the legal system for all Americans is a goal that members of the legal community aspire to. Attorneys and paralegals work toward this goal by providing their services *pro bono*. The term pro bono publico means "for the public good." Free legal work done by lawyers and paralegals to help society is referred to as pro bono work.

Most pro bono work is in the form of legal services provided to the poor who may not otherwise have access to the legal system. Attorneys may represent the poor to obtain divorces, to collect child support, to defend themselves in criminal matters, or in numerous other types of legal matters. Paralegals may work with attorneys as part of the legal team to provide pro bono services to those in need. They may also act independently to provide their services pro bono, provided their services do not constitute the unauthorized practice of law.

Attorneys and paralegals who specialize in corporate law may find pro bono work an opportunity to expand their expertise. Many legal clinics and other types of agencies that serve the poor offer free training to attorneys and paralegals who are willing to offer a certain number of hours of their time. For those who prefer to limit their work to their area of expertise, nonprofit organizations of all types are often in need of legal services.

It is not uncommon for attorneys who specialize in corporate law to offer pro bono services to nonprofit and charitable organizations. They may serve as counsel for, or serve on the board of directors of, nonprofit corporations, community groups, environmental groups, or similar organizations.

Corporate paralegals may team with attorneys to provide pro bono services by assisting with incorporations and annual reporting requirements, and by preparing all types of legal documents for a favorite charitable organization or community nonprofit corporation.

Providing pro bono services may be an ethical duty. The rules of ethics of most states provide that attorneys have an ethical duty to provide pro bono services to persons of limited means and organizations that address the needs of persons of limited means. The rules of ethics of the paralegal associations have similar provisions. Many paralegals who provide pro bono services indicate that it is one of the most rewarding experiences of their careers.

The national and state bar associations and paralegal associations are excellent resources for advice on providing pro bono services and finding pro bono opportunities. Most state and local paralegal associations have committees that work to match paralegal volunteers with pro bono opportunities.

Courts are reluctant to pierce the corporate veil, but may do so when the corporation is used to avoid a clear legislative purpose,[5] or when it is necessary to preserve, protect, and enforce the rights of others or to prevent an injustice.[6]

The corporate veil of a small or closely held corporation may also be pierced when the corporation is found to be an alter ego of an individual and if such attribution of liability is in the interest of securing a just determination of the action.[7] Courts have found that the "corporate entity may be disregarded where there is such unity of interest and ownership that the separate personalities of the corporation and the individual no longer exist and where, if the acts are treated as those of the corporation alone, an inequitable result will follow."[8]

Keeping in mind that courts will usually seek to pierce the corporate veil only to prevent inequity, injustice, or fraud, other factors are taken into consideration. The corporation is closely scrutinized to determine if it is actually being operated as a corporation and to determine if statutory formalities for incorporating and operating the corporation have been followed. The following factors are often taken into consideration in support of piercing the corporate veil:

1. Improper or incomplete incorporation.
2. Commingling of corporate and shareholder funds.
3. Failure to follow statutory formalities.
4. Failure to hold regular shareholders' and directors' meetings.
5. Failure of shareholders to represent themselves as agents of a corporation, rather than individuals, when dealing with outside parties.
6. Undercapitalization.

To provide an equitable settlement of the corporation's debts and to preserve the rights of certain creditors, the corporate veil may be pierced and the corporate existence ignored by a bankruptcy court under the Federal Bankruptcy Act. The Internal Revenue Service also may seek to pierce the corporate veil when the corporate entity is used solely for the purpose of income tax evasion.

The fact that it is possible for the corporate veil to be pierced under certain circumstances makes it imperative that all corporate formalities be followed by the corporation and that those formalities be properly documented. The cases that follow in this chapter both involve plaintiffs seeking to pierce the corporate veil of the defendant corporation and recover losses from the shareholder of the corporation. In *Lakota Girl Scout Council v. Havey Fund-Raising Management*, the corporate defendant was found to be merely an alter ego of its owner, and the corporate veil was pierced. In the *Jacobson v. Buffalo Rock Shooters Supply*, the court found that the corporation was basically formed and operated as a corporation and the fact that it missed one annual meeting was not sufficient showing of failure to observe corporate formalities. In that case, the corporate veil was not pierced, and the shareholder of the corporation was not found to be personally liable for amounts owed by the corporation.

Law Governing Corporations

As a separate entity, the corporation must be in compliance with all laws concerning it. The sources of most laws to which corporations are subject are state statutes, common law, case law, and federal statutes.

State Statutes Corporations are created by and generally governed by the statutes of the state of **domicile** (the state in which the corporation is incorporated). A corporation that is qualified to do business in a foreign state, however, subjects itself to the statutes of that state for certain purposes.

---

domicile A person's permanent home, legal home, or main residence. The words "abode," "citizenship," "habitancy," and "residence" sometimes mean the same as *domicile* and sometimes not. A *corporate domicile* is the corporation's legal home (usually where its headquarters is located); an elected domicile is the place the persons who make a contract specify as their legal homes in the contract.

CASE

LAKOTA GIRL SCOUT COUNCIL
v.
HAVEY FUND-RAISING MANAGEMENT

Eighth Circuit
519 F.2d 634 (8th Cir. 1975)
June 27, 1975
Webster, Circuit Judge

Havey Fund-Raising Management, Inc., and Francis P. Havey appeal from a jury verdict and a judgment awarding damages against them for breach of a contract to provide fund-raising services to the plaintiff, Lakota Girl Scout Council, Inc. They do not challenge the jury's finding that the contract was breached, but contend instead that (1) the District Court lacked personal jurisdiction over Francis P. Havey, founder and chief executive officer of Havey Fund-Raising Management, Inc.; (2) there was insufficient evidence to find Francis P. Havey liable as the alter ego of the corporation, the entity with which plaintiff Lakota Girl Scout Council, Inc., had contracted; and (3) the court erroneously allowed the jury to consider lost profits as a measure of damages and improperly admitted opinion evidence in support thereof. We affirm the judgment of the District Court.

In 1968, the Lakota Girl Scout Council decided to hold a fund-raising drive, the proceeds of which would be used to develop year-around facilities at its 175-acre campsite near Dayton, Iowa. Four professional fund-raising firms, including Havey Fund-Raising, Inc. were considered to coordinate the campaign. Havey Fund-Raising conducted a survey and informed the Council that it was feasible to raise $325,000-$350,000 for the project. The Council thereupon set its goal at $345,000 and selected Havey Fund-Raising, Inc. to assist it.

On October 1, 1968, the parties executed a contract: Havey Fund-Raising was to provide professional assistance to help the Council reach its goal in return for a fee of $28,000; the Havey firm did not guarantee that any money would in fact be raised. When Havey Fund-Raising failed to perform in accordance with the contract and the campaign fell far short of its goal, the Council instituted this action, seeking various enumerated damages.

In the course of discovery, the Council determined to its satisfaction that Havey Fund-Raising, Inc. was the alter ego of Francis P. Havey and accordingly sought to join Havey as a party defendant. The District Court allowed Havey to be joined, pursuant to Fed.R.Civ.P. 20, and later denied Havey's motion to quash service for want of **in personam** jurisdiction.

The case was tried and submitted to a jury, which awarded the Council $35,000 in damages and, in response to a **special interrogatory**, found the corporation to be Havey's alter ego. The District Court entered judgment against both defendants for $35,000, "piercing the corporate veil" of Havey Fund-Raising, Inc. on the basis of the jury's answer to the special interrogatory. ...

[T]he propriety of the District Court's assertion of jurisdiction in the instant case ultimately depends upon the propriety of its decision to pierce the corporate veil of Havey Fund-Raising, Inc.

Evidence was introduced at trial showing that (1) Francis P. Havey is and has always been the sole shareholder of Havey Fund-Raising, Inc.; (2) Havey was the firm's sole incorporator and his capital contribution was $550.00; (3) Havey, and no one else, gave loans to and borrowed money from the corporation; (4) Havey and his wife

---

in personam   Against the person. In personam jurisdiction is the power that a court has over the defendant himself or herself as distinguished from the more limited power a court has over his or her interest in property (quasi in rem) or over the property itself (in rem).

special interrogatories   Written questions asked by a judge to a jury to see if the jury's answers conflict with the jury's verdict.

owned the building where the company was headquartered and received rental payments from the company; (5) the company purchased a Lincoln automobile for Havey's business use which Havey also used for incidental personal business. In short, the evidence was overwhelming that Havey dominated and controlled the business and treated it as his own.

Judge Hanson submitted a special interrogatory to the jury on this subject in which he stated that a corporation's existence is presumed to be separate, but can be disregarded if (1) the corporation is undercapitalized, (2) without separate books, (3) its finances are not kept separate from individual finances, individual obligations are paid by the corporation, (4) the corporation is used to promote fraud or illegality, (5) corporate formalities are not followed or (6) the corporation is merely a sham. In response, the jury found the corporation to be the alter ego of Francis P. Havey.

Judge Hanson's interrogatory properly enumerates the factors that may be considered in determining if a corporation is merely the alter ego of its dominating shareholder. ...There was ample evidence from which the jurors could find that the corporation was Havey's alter ego; their finding is supported by substantial evidence and the determination of the trial judge to hold Havey liable by piercing the veil was not an abuse of his equity power... .

CASE

Steven Daniel Jacobson et al., Minor Children of Pamela Ellsworth, Deceased, by William Boyle, Guardian and Next Friend, Petitioners,

v.

Buffalo Rock Shooters Supply, Inc., et al., Respondents-Appellees (Raymond Bruce Scamen, Adm'r of the Estate of Ronea Scamen, Petitioner-Appellant).

No. 3-95-0683, Appellate Court of Illinois, Third District.
April 11, 1996.
Rehearing Denied May 9, 1996.

Justice McCUSKEY delivered the opinion of the court:

Pamela Ellsworth and Ronea Scamen were both killed in an explosion while employed by Buffalo Rock Shooters Supply, Inc. (Buffalo Rock). The plaintiffs, Steven Daniel Jacobson and Christopher Michael Boyle, the minor children of Pamela Ellsworth, deceased, by their guardian and next friend, William Boyle, filed a complaint seeking to pierce Buffalo Rock's corporate veil and collect a judgment of $251,750 from the corporation's shareholders. The plaintiff, Raymond Bruce Scamen, administrator of the estate of Ronea Scamen, filed an almost identical complaint, also seeking to collect a $251,750 judgment.

Buffalo Rock's shareholders were Ellsbeth S. Fullmer, Roger W. Fullmer and Patricia Ann Smith. Roger and Patricia Ann were killed in the same explosion. As a consequence, in both actions, the plaintiffs sought recovery from Ellsbeth, individually and as administrator of Roger's estate and Evelyn Muffler, as administrator of Patricia Ann's estate. The trial court consolidated the complaints. Subsequently, the trial court entered an order which granted a motion to dismiss Roger's and Patricia Ann's estates as defendants and granted judgment in favor of Ellsbeth.

On appeal, the plaintiffs argue: (1) the trial court erred when it granted the estates' motion to dismiss; and (2) the trial court should have pierced the corporate veil and enforced the judgments against the shareholders of Buffalo Rock.

Following our careful review of the record, we find the evidence does not support piercing the corporate veil and imposing liability on Buffalo Rock's shareholders. As a result, we affirm because we conclude the trial court's ruling was not against the manifest weight of the evidence.

FACTS

Buffalo Rock was incorporated on August 11, 1987. Roger and Ellsbeth, husband and wife, each received 40 shares in the corporation. Ellsbeth's daughter, Patricia Ann, received 20 shares. The shareholders paid a total of $1,000 for these shares. Buffalo Rock was in the business of operating a shooting range. It also sold guns and related equipment and manufactured and sold ammunition. Prior to incorporation, Ellsbeth ran the business for 17 years as a sole proprietorship. The assets of the business were sold by Ellsbeth to the corporation. ...

On October 7, 1988, the explosion occurred. Roger, Patricia Ann, Pamela Ellsworth and Ronea Scamen were all working that day and were killed. Buffalo Rock's assets were destroyed in the explosion. Buffalo Rock had a general liability insurance policy. However, the policy provided no coverage for the explosion. Moreover, Buffalo Rock had no workers' compensation insurance coverage and was not self-insured for workers' compensation liability.

Subsequently, a $251,750 workers' compensation award was entered against Buffalo Rock on behalf of Ellsworth's children. A $251,750 award was also entered on behalf of Scamen's estate. On August 26, 1992, the circuit court of La Salle County entered judgment against Buffalo Rock on the basis of each award.

On October 8, 1992, the plaintiffs filed their complaints seeking to pierce the corporate veil and collect the judgments from Ellsbeth and the estates of Roger and Patricia Ann. Both complaints stated that Buffalo Rock was undercapitalized because it failed to either purchase and maintain workers' compensation insurance or have sufficient assets to be a self-insurer.

Patricia Ann's estate filed a motion to dismiss the complaints, arguing that they were not timely filed under the Probate Act of 1975 ... . The causes were submitted to the trial court on stipulated evidence. On August 15, 1995, an order was entered which granted the motion to dismiss as to both estates and granted judgment in favor of Ellsbeth. The plaintiffs filed timely notices of appeal.

PIERCING THE CORPORATE VEIL

The plaintiffs argue that the trial court should have pierced Buffalo Rock's corporate veil and found its shareholders liable for the judgment against Buffalo Rock. ...

A corporation is a legal entity which exists separate and distinct from its shareholders, directors and officers. ... Accordingly, the shareholders, directors and officers are not, as a general rule, liable for the corporation's obligations. ... For a court to pierce the corporate veil and find liability on the part of the shareholders for the corporation's obligations, two principal requirements must be met: (1) a unity of interest and ownership that causes the separate personalities of the corporation and the individual to no longer exist; and (2) the presence of circumstances under which adherence to the fiction of a separate corporate existence would sanction a fraud, promote injustice or promote inequitable consequences. ...

Courts are reluctant to pierce the corporate veil. ...Accordingly, a party seeking to pierce the corporate veil has the burden to make a substantial showing that the corporation is really a dummy or sham for another dominating entity. ...

Courts look at numerous factors in determining whether to pierce the corporate veil. ... These factors include: inadequate capitalization; failure to issue stock; failure to observe corporate formalities; nonpayment of dividends; insolvency of the debtor corporation; on functioning of the other officers or directors; absence of corporate records; commingling of funds; diversion of assets from the corporation by or to a shareholder; failure to maintain arm's length relationships among related entities; and whether the corporation is a mere facade for the operation of the dominant shareholders. ...

The plaintiffs claim the corporate veil should be pierced because: (1) Buffalo Rock did not observe corporate formalities and did not pay dividends; (2) the corporation paid the mortgage on real estate owned only by Ellsbeth; (3) two businesses owned by Roger operated out of the same building; and (4) the corporation failed to maintain workers' compensation insurance and had no liquid assets available to pay claims against it.

We cannot agree with the plaintiffs that Buffalo Rock did not observe corporate formalities. Buffalo Rock completed all of the required documents necessary to its formation. Additionally, Buffalo Rock issued shares of stock and filed the appropriate corporate tax returns. We find that Buffalo Rock merely failed to hold an annual meeting in August 1988. We hold that merely missing one annual meeting is not a sufficient showing of failure to observe corporate formalities. ...

The remaining facts relied on by the plaintiffs are Buffalo Rock's failure to have workers' compensation insurance and lack of liquid assets to pay its debts. The plaintiffs assert these facts as proof that Buffalo Rock was not adequately capitalized. Again, we disagree with the plaintiffs.

It is well settled that undercapitalization of a corporation is a significant factor in piercing the corporate veil. ...

Here, in the instant case, the undisputed evidence shows that Buffalo Rock had substantial assets, including inventory and equipment. ... we conclude that Buffalo Rock was adequately capitalized. The fact that Buffalo Rock's assets were destroyed in the explosion does not change our analysis.

Finally, we conclude that Buffalo Rock's failure to obtain workers' compensation insurance is not an adequate basis for piercing the corporate veil. It is very unfortunate that Buffalo Rock did not have workers' compensation insurance to cover the tragic death of its employees. However, the failure of a corporation to obtain workers' compensation insurance is not a sufficient basis to pierce the corporate veil and find a shareholder personally liable. ...

CONCLUSION

The record supports the trial court's finding that Buffalo Rock was a separate entity and was not the alter ego of its shareholders. ... Therefore, we conclude the plaintiffs failed to make the substantial showing necessary to pierce Buffalo Rock's corporate veil and impose individual liability on the shareholders. As a result, we find the trial court's ruling was not against the manifest weight of the evidence.

For the reasons indicated, we affirm the judgment of the circuit court of La Salle County.

Affirmed.
SLATER and LYTTON, JJ., concur.

The statutes of every state in the country are derived, at least in part, from the Model Business Corporation Act (MBCA), first published in 1950, or the 1984 Revised Model Business Corporation Act. These acts were drafted by the American Bar Association Section of Corporation, Banking and Business Law, and the 1984 Revised Model Business Corporation Act continues to be revised through the date of this publication. In this text, all references to the "Model Business Corporation Act" are to the 1984 Revised Model Business Corporation Act, as amended through 2000. (See appendix I for the 1984 Revised Model Business Corporation Act, as amended.)

Unlike the Uniform Partnership and Limited Partnership Acts, the model corporation acts are just *model* acts, not *uniform* acts. The model acts serve only as an aid to the state legislatures in drafting their own statutes, and corporate laws still vary significantly from state to state. The laws of the state of Delaware, which is often referred to as the "incorporation state," also often serve as a model to the legislatures of other states.

Common Law and Case Law Corporations are created and governed by statute. Therefore, common and case law play a less significant role in governing corporations. However, the number of corporate issues decided in court illustrates that case law is relevant in interpreting the law governing corporations and in ruling on matters not covered by the statutes. Because Delaware has such a disproportionately high number of domestic corporations, much of today's corporate law has been derived from the decisions of the courts of Delaware.

Federal Statutes   Federal law also governs certain aspects of a corporation. For instance, securities matters of publicly held corporations are subject to federal statutes and regulations, as well as the statutes of the state of incorporation. The Securities Exchange Act of 1934 and the Securities Act of 1933 are the major federal laws governing corporations that sell shares of stock or other securities publicly. Corporations are also subject to federal legislation in other areas, including bankruptcy, intellectual property, antitrust, interstate commerce, and taxation.

§ 5.2   CORPORATIONS IN THE UNITED STATES

This text focuses on the law of corporations; therefore, a full analysis of the influence of United States corporations on our society is beyond its scope. However, it is important to recognize the magnitude of the role that corporations play in the United States economy and in each of our lives. During 1997, United States corporations reported nearly $16 trillion in business receipts compared to $1.3 trillion for partnerships and $870 billion for sole proprietorships.[9]

Most of us are dependent on a corporation for our livelihoods, be it a small, family-owned corporation or a multimillion-dollar corporate conglomerate. We also cannot overlook the great influence that corporate marketing has over the consumer purchases we make and the prices we pay for those goods. The most recent figures available indicate that corporations report over $188 billion per year in advertising expenses.[10]

Figure 5-1 provides a chart of corporate net worth in the United States, 1980–1997.

§ 5.3   CORPORATE RIGHTS AND POWERS

As a separate entity, the corporation enjoys certain rights and powers separate from those of its shareholders, directors, or officers. Corporations, as artificial persons, are entitled to many of the same rights as natural persons, including many of the same constitutional rights. There are, however, many exceptions to this rule. For instance, the Fourteenth Amendment to the Constitution, which guarantees liberty, and the Fifth Amendment, which protects persons from self-incrimination, apply to natural persons only. Additionally, corporations are generally not considered to be "citizens" as that word is used in the federal constitution.

Many powers are granted to corporations by state statute, and may be limited or enhanced by the corporation's **articles of incorporation**. The following

♦ ──

articles of incorporation   The document used to set up a corporation. Articles of incorporation contain the most basic rules of the corporation and control other corporate rules such as the bylaws.

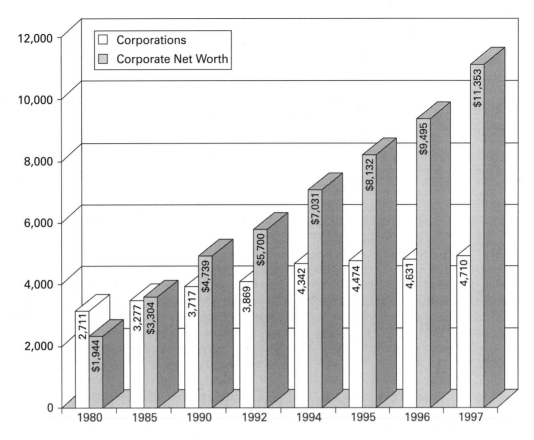

Number of corporate income tax returns filed, and the net worth reported by those corporations. Corporations in thousands (2,000 = 2,000,000 corporations). Net worth in billions of dollars ($1,944 = $1,944,000,000,000).

FIGURE 5-1   Corporations and Corporate Net Worth in the United States. From *The Statistical Abstract of the United States (2000)*.

section from the MBCA enumerates the powers granted to corporations under that Act:

3.02 GENERAL POWERS

Unless its articles of incorporation provide otherwise, every corporation has perpetual duration and succession in its corporate name and has the same powers as an individual to do all things necessary or convenient to carry out its business and affairs, including without limitation power:

(1) to sue and be sued, complain and defend in its corporate name;

(2) to have a corporate seal, which may be altered at will, and to use it, or a facsimile of it, by impressing or affixing it or in any other manner reproducing it;

(3) to make and amend bylaws, not inconsistent with its articles of incorporation or with the laws of this state, for managing the business and regulating the affairs of the corporation;

(4) to purchase, receive, lease, or otherwise acquire, and own, hold, improve, use, and otherwise deal with, real or personal property, or any legal or equitable interest in property, wherever located;

(5) to sell, convey, mortgage, pledge, lease, exchange, and otherwise dispose of all or any part of its property;

(6) to purchase, receive, subscribe for, or otherwise acquire; own, hold, vote, use, sell, mortgage, lend, pledge, or otherwise dispose of; and deal in and with shares or other interests in, or obligations of, any other entity;

(7) to make contracts and guarantees, incur liabilities, borrow money, issue its notes, bonds, and other obligations (which may be convertible into or include the option to purchase other securities of the corporation), and secure any of its obligations by mortgage or pledge of any of its property, franchises, or income;

(8) to lend money, invest and reinvest its funds, and receive and hold real and personal property as security for repayment;

(9) to be a promoter, partner, member, associate, or manager of any partnership, joint venture, trust or other entity;

(10) to conduct its business, locate offices, and exercise the powers granted by this Act within or without this state;

(11) to elect directors and appoint officers, employees, and agents of the corporation, define their duties, fix their compensation, and lend them money and credit;

(12) to pay pensions and establish pension plans, pension trusts, profit sharing plans, share bonus plans, share option plans, and benefit or incentive plans for any or all of its current or former directors, officers, employees, and agents;

(13) to make donations for the public welfare or for charitable, scientific, or educational purposes;

(14) to transact any lawful business that will aid governmental policy;

(15) to make payments or donations, or do any other act, not inconsistent with law, that furthers the business and affairs of the corporation.

§ 5.4 ADVANTAGES OF DOING BUSINESS AS A CORPORATION

The advantages of doing business as a corporation are both numerous and unique. Most of the advantages stem from the separate entity characteristic of the corporation. This section discusses the corporation's advantages over limited liability companies, partnerships, and sole proprietorships. The advantages we focus on include the limited liability available to the officers, directors, and shareholders of the corporation, the benefits of employee benefit plans for corporations, the continuity of the business of a corporation, and the increased opportunities to raise capital for corporations. We also examine the benefits of the centralized management structure of a corporation and the relative ease with which corporate ownership can be transferred.

Limited Liability

Probably the most prevalent reason for forming a corporation is the limited liability that the corporate structure offers to its shareholders, directors, and officers. Theoretically, the corporation is responsible for its own debts and obligations, leaving the shareholders, directors, and officers free from personal liability.

This can be a benefit to an individual or group of individuals wanting to start a business in several ways. Most obviously, the founders of the corporation put at risk only their initial investment in the corporation and protect their personal assets. Also, the ability to raise capital to start and operate the business is increased, because potential investors may own a piece of the corporation and put at risk no more than their investment to purchase shares of stock.

The limited liability benefit of incorporating does have its boundaries, however. As discussed previously in § 5.1, the corporate veil may be pierced under certain circumstances, leaving the individual shareholders exposed to personal liability for the corporation's debts and obligations. Also, as a practical matter, shareholders of a new or small corporation are often required to give their personal guarantees to obtain financing on behalf of the corporation. If the corporation has few assets in its own name, banks and other lenders often refuse financing to the corporation without the personal guarantee of individual shareholders who have an adequate net worth to secure the corporation's loan.

Employee Benefit Plans

The owners of a corporation may be in a position to take advantage of several employee benefit plans that can be used both to compensate employees and to reduce the income tax liability of the corporation. These benefits may be in the form of contributions to qualified pension and profit-sharing plans, group-term life insurance, medical care insurance, medical reimbursement plans, and other employee benefits. Many of these benefits constitute tax-deferred, or nontaxable income to the employee/shareholders of the corporation and can be used as a means to pass tax-free income through to the shareholders of the corporation, while giving the added bonus of a tax deduction to the corporation.

In recent years the Internal Revenue Service (IRS) has put several restrictions on plans that are designed for the benefit of highly compensated key employees/shareholders and discriminate against lesser-paid employees. Many types of employee benefit plans must be qualified under provisions of the Internal Revenue Code to ensure the full deduction to the corporation. Qualified retirement plans are discussed in Chapter 13.

Choice of Tax Year

With the exception of S corporations, corporations may freely choose their fiscal tax year, which may be different from the calendar year. The corporation can choose the tax year that is most advantageous to its business and that best fits its natural business cycle.

Business Continuity

Another important advantage of doing business as a corporation is that the corporation has the ability to exist perpetually. Unlike the sole proprietorship or partnership, the corporation does not dissolve upon the death or withdrawal of any of its shareholders, officers, or directors. Shares of stock may be sold, given, or bequeathed to others without affecting the continuity of the corporation or its business.

Ability to Raise Capital

Compared to sole proprietorships or partnerships, the corporation has an increased potential for raising capital. Investors may be enticed by the tax benefits and limited liability offered by corporations. The flexible nature of the corporate capital structure allows corporations to appeal to a wide variety of investors with varying needs; for example, the corporation may sell shares of stock of different classes. The financial structure of a corporation is discussed in Chapter 8 of this text. Securities are discussed in Chapter 9.

Centralized Management

Although the shareholders of a corporation have the right to vote for directors of the corporation, they generally do not have an automatic right to participate directly in the management of the business, as general partners do. Shareholders participate in management of the corporation through their votes for the directors of the corporation. The directors, in turn, are given the right to elect the officers of the corporation—the individuals they feel are the best people to operate the day-to-day business of the corporation. The officers are given the authority to operate the business as they see fit, with little interference from the board of directors or shareholders. Shareholder or director approval, or both, must be given to certain extraordinary actions taken by the officers on behalf of the corporation, however.

In small, closely held corporations, the shareholders often elect themselves to be the directors and officers of the corporation. In effect, the small corporation is often run by the owners of the corporation. In contrast, directors and officers of larger corporations may own little or no stock in the corporation they work for. Corporate management and the roles of the officers, shareholders, and directors are discussed in more detail in Chapter 7 of this text.

Transferability of Ownership

In contrast to the sole proprietorship, limited liability company, and partnership, the ownership interest of a corporation is easily transferred. Barring a prohibitive agreement among the shareholders, or restrictions in the corporation's articles of incorporation or bylaws, shares of stock may be bought and sold freely. Because a shareholder's interest in the corporation is represented by stock certificates, the transfer of unrestricted stock may be as simple as an endorsement by the shareholder, on the back of the certificate, to the purchaser or transferee of the stock.

In many situations, however, restrictions are placed on the transfer of shares of closely held corporations, either by statute, the articles of incorporation, bylaws, or in an agreement between the shareholders. These agreements often give the corporation or existing shareholders the first option to purchase the shares of a shareholder who would like to sell stock in the corporation. An agreement of the shareholders may also provide for purchase of shares of a deceased shareholder by the corporation or the other shareholders. Unless addressed in a written agreement, a deceased shareholder's shares of stock are passed on to his or her heirs, just like any other asset. Shareholder agreements restricting the transfer of stock are discussed in more detail in Chapter 7 of this text.

§ 5.5 DISADVANTAGES OF DOING BUSINESS AS A CORPORATION

The many advantages of doing business as a corporation must be weighed against the disadvantages before a determination can be made as to whether to incorporate. Figure 5-2 summarizes both sides of the question. In this section we explore some of the disadvantages of doing business as a corporation, including the formalities and reporting requirements that must be followed by corporations, and the income taxation disadvantages.

Advantages	*Disadvantages*
◆ Limited liability for shareholders ◆ Business continuity ◆ Ability to raise capital ◆ Centralized management ◆ Transferability of ownership	◆ Corporate formalities and reporting requirements ◆ Double taxation ◆ Legal expenses

FIGURE 5-2 Advantages and Disadvantages of Doing Business as a Corporation

Corporate Formalities and Reporting Requirements

The corporation is the most complex type of business entity, and there are numerous formalities and reporting requirements associated with its formation and maintenance.

First, because the corporation is a creature of statute, it does not exist until formed by the proper documentation filed with the designated state authority in accordance with state law. Articles of incorporation must be filed, and all other statutory requirements for incorporating must be complied with before the corporate existence begins. Corporate formation is discussed in detail in Chapter 6 of this text. Also, unlike sole proprietorships and most partnerships, for a corporation to transact business in any state other than its state of domicile, it must qualify with the proper state authority in the foreign state.

Once the corporation is formed, several ongoing statutory requirements must also be complied with. Annual meetings of the shareholders and directors may be required, and annual reports often are required by the state of domicile. In addition, corporations may be subject to securities regulations that include securities registration and annual and quarterly reporting.

The corporation, as a separate entity, must file a separate corporate income tax return and pay income tax each year to the Internal Revenue Service, its state of domicile, and states in which it transacts business.

All of the foregoing requirements can be time-consuming and costly. However, as mentioned previously in this chapter, it is important that a corporation comply with all corporate formalities to ensure that there is no cause for the corporate veil to be pierced.

Taxation

Although the corporate structure can offer advantages under certain circumstances, in other instances the tax disadvantages may be enough reason to choose another form of business organization.

Double Taxation   The most serious corporate tax drawback is double taxation of the corporate income. Unlike sole proprietorships, partnerships, limited liability companies, and S corporations, most corporations are taxed as entities separate from their shareholders, and must pay income tax on their earnings. In addition, the shareholders of the corporation must pay income tax on income or dividends received from the corporation. The income of the corporation is, in effect, taxed twice.

Taxes Peculiar to Corporations   In addition to income tax, corporations may be subject to special state taxes, including incorporation taxes and franchise taxes. Corporations are also subject to fees and taxes in any foreign states in which they transact business.

§ 5.6   TYPES AND CLASSIFICATIONS OF CORPORATIONS

There are many types and classifications of corporations, stemming from their financial structure, ownership, and purpose. This section deals only with the more common types and classifications of corporations, to give a general understanding of their nature and purpose, including business corporations, professional corporations, nonprofit corporations, S corporations, statutory close corporations, and parent and subsidiary corporations.

Business Corporations

Business corporations, which include large, publicly held corporations and smaller, closely held corporations, are by far the most common type of corporation in this country. This is the type of corporation that this text focuses on, unless otherwise indicated. As discussed previously in this chapter, business corporations may be formed for the purpose of engaging in any lawful business, unless a more limited purpose is desired.

Professional Corporations

Under common law, professionals were allowed to practice only as individuals or partners. Most states have now adopted statutes providing for the formation of *professional corporations,* or *professional service corporations,* as they are sometimes called. These corporations are treated in much the same way as a business corporation, with a few important distinctions.

Typically, state statutes provide that the professional corporation is subject to all the provisions of that state's business corporation act, except to the extent that it is inconsistent with the professional corporation act of that state. Many professional corporation acts are based on the Model Professional Corporation Act, which provides that professional corporations may be formed "only for the purpose of rendering professional services and services ancillary thereto within a single profession."[11] An exception to the single profession rule permits one or more professions to be combined to the extent permitted by the licensing laws of the state of domicile.

Some state statutes enumerate the types of professions that may be incorporated under the professional corporation statutes. These lists typically include many of the following professions: physicians and surgeons, chiropractors, podiatrists, engineers, electrologists, physical therapists, psychologists, certified public accountants and public accountants, dentists, veterinarians, optometrists, attorneys, and licensed acupuncturists. Often the statutes provide that professional corporations may be formed for the performance of any type of service which may be rendered only pursuant to a license issued by law.

Many types of professionals have the option as to whether to incorporate as a professional corporation or a business corporation. Given a choice, it is usually advantageous to incorporate under the business corporation laws of the state in question, as the professional corporation laws are generally more restrictive.

The enactment of professional corporation acts has allowed professionals to realize many of the tax and other benefits normally associated with corporations that were not previously available to them as partners or sole proprietors. Of special interest to professionals is the limited liability benefit associated with the corporate structure. Although licensed professionals remain personally liable for their own acts and omissions, professionals practicing in a group may incorporate to provide protection against personal liability for the acts and omissions of their associates, or for torts committed by them.

In addition to the restricted corporate purpose, several other restrictions also apply to professional corporations. For instance, stock ownership of professional corporations typically has statutory restrictions placed upon it. The stock of a professional corporation usually may be owned only by licensed professionals, or partnerships consisting only of partners who are licensed professionals.

Nonprofit Corporations

Another common type of corporation is the *nonprofit corporation,* or *not-for-profit corporation* as it is sometimes referred to, which is formed only for certain nonprofit purposes. Many nonprofit corporations are formed for charitable, civic, educational, and religious purposes. However, nonprofit corporations may be formed for several different reasons.

Nonprofit corporations are generally governed under the nonprofit corporation statutes of the state of domicile. Many states' nonprofit corporation acts were based on the Model Nonprofit Corporation Act (1964).

Incorporating as a nonprofit corporation does not insure exemption from federal income taxation. To qualify for federal tax exemption, the nonprofit corporation must meet the requirements of the Internal Revenue Code (IRC) and obtain approval from the Internal Revenue Service. IRC § 501(c)(3) lists specifically the purposes that may qualify a nonprofit corporation for tax-exempt status. The articles of incorporation of a nonprofit corporation should specifically indicate that the corporation has, as its purpose, one of the purposes listed under IRC § 501(c)(3).

S Corporations

The Internal Revenue Service recognizes a special category of corporations, referred to as *S corporations,* for federal income tax purposes. This category is made up of eligible small business corporations that file elections to be treated as S corporations. All shareholders of the corporation must agree to the election. There is usually no distinction between S corporations and other types of corporations at the state level.

Unlike other business corporations, the income of S corporations is not taxed at the corporate level, but is passed through to the corporation's shareholders, much like income is passed through to the partners of a partnership or members of a limited liability company. S corporation status is often elected by smaller, closely held corporations that are formed with the expectation of incurring a net loss for the first few years. The loss of the corporation is passed on to the shareholders of the corporation, who may use it to offset their other income.

The pass-through taxation of S corporations has made this type of corporation one of the most popular types of business entities in the United States. During 1997, S corporations accounted for more than half of all the corporate income tax returns. Further, the Internal Revenue Service has predicted that the percentage of S corporation returns will increase at an annual average rate of 4.16 percent between 1999 and 2005.[12]

Figure 5-3 provides a comparison of the number of corporate income tax returns filed between 1980 and 1997, showing all corporations and S corporations.

Pursuant to § 1361 of the Internal Revenue Code, S corporations must make an election to be treated as such by filing a Form 2553 (shown in Figure 5-4 on page 180), and they must meet the following eligibility requirements:

1. The corporation must be a domestic corporation.
2. The corporation must have no more than 75 shareholders.
3. The corporation's shareholders must all be individuals, estates, or exempt organizations or trusts that meet certain prerequisites.
4. Nonresident aliens may not be shareholders.
5. The corporation cannot issue more than one class of stock.

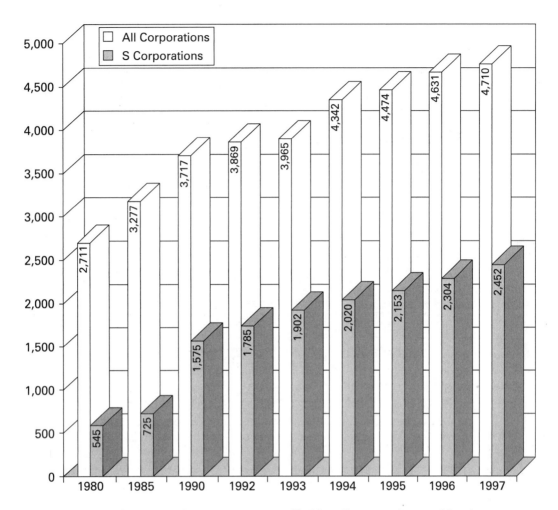

Number of corporate income tax returns filed for all corporations and for those filing as S corporations. Corporations in thousands (2,000 = 2,000,000 corporations). From the *Statistical Abstract of the United States (2000)* § 862.

FIGURE 5-3   S Corporations in the United States. From *The Statistical Abstract of the United States (2000)*.

6. The corporation may not be a bank or thrift institution that uses a reserve method of accounting for bad debts under Internal Revenue Code § 585.

7. The corporation may not be an insurance company taxable under Subchapter L of the Internal Revenue Code.

8. The corporation may not have elected to come under IRC § 936 concerning the Puerto Rico and possession tax credits.

9. The corporation may not be a domestic international sales corporation (DISC) or former DISC under the Internal Revenue Code.

Form **2553**
(Rev. January 2001)

Department of the Treasury
Internal Revenue Service

Election by a Small Business Corporation
(Under section 1362 of the Internal Revenue Code)
▶ See Parts II and III on back and the separate instructions.
▶ **The corporation may either send or fax this form to the IRS. See page 1 of the instructions.**

OMB No. 1545-0146

Notes: **1.** *This election to be an S corporation can be accepted only if all the tests are met under Who May Elect on page 1 of the instructions; all signatures in Parts I and III are originals (no photocopies); and the exact name and address of the corporation and other required form information are provided.*

2. *Do not file Form 1120S, U.S. Income Tax Return for an S Corporation, for any tax year before the year the election takes effect.*

3. *If the corporation was in existence before the effective date of this election, see Taxes an S Corporation May Owe on page 1 of the instructions.*

Part I	Election Information		
Please Type or Print	Name of corporation (see instructions)	**A**	Employer identification number
	Number, street, and room or suite no. (If a P.O. box, see instructions.)	**B**	Date incorporated
	City or town, state, and ZIP code	**C**	State of incorporation

D Election is to be effective for tax year beginning (month, day, year) . . . . ▶ ___/___/___

E Name and title of officer or legal representative who the IRS may call for more information

F Telephone number of officer or legal representative
(   )

G If the corporation changed its name or address after applying for the EIN shown in **A** above, check this box . . . . ▶ ☐

H If this election takes effect for the first tax year the corporation exists, enter month, day, and year of the **earliest** of the following: (1) date the corporation first had shareholders, (2) date the corporation first had assets, or (3) date the corporation began doing business . . . . ▶ ___/___/___

I Selected tax year: Annual return will be filed for tax year ending (month and day) ▶ _____

If the tax year ends on any date other than December 31, except for an automatic 52-53-week tax year ending with reference to the month of December, you **must** complete Part II on the back. If the date you enter is the ending date of an automatic 52-53-week tax year, write "52-53-week year" to the right of the date. See Temporary Regulations section 1.441-2T(e)(3).

J Name and address of each shareholder; shareholder's spouse having a community property interest in the corporation's stock; and each tenant in common, joint tenant, and tenant by the entirety. (A husband and wife (and their estates) are counted as one shareholder in determining the number of shareholders without regard to the manner in which the stock is owned.)	K Shareholders' Consent Statement. Under penalties of perjury, we declare that we consent to the election of the above-named corporation to be an S corporation under section 1362(a) and that we have examined this consent statement, including accompanying schedules and statements, and to the best of our knowledge and belief, it is true, correct, and complete. We understand our consent is binding and may not be withdrawn after the corporation has made a valid election. (Shareholders sign and date below.)		L Stock owned		M Social security number or employer identification number (see instructions)	N Shareholder's tax year ends (month and day)
	Signature	Date	Number of shares	Dates acquired		

Under penalties of perjury, I declare that I have examined this election, including accompanying schedules and statements, and to the best of my knowledge and belief, it is true, correct, and complete.

Signature of officer ▶ _____   Title ▶ _____   Date ▶ _____

For Paperwork Reduction Act Notice, see page 4 of the instructions.   Cat. No. 18629R   Form **2553** (Rev. 1-2001)

FIGURE 5-4 IRS Form 2553 Election by a Small Business Corporation to be an S Corporation.

S corporation status may be revoked only if shareholders holding a majority of the shares of stock of the corporation consent to the revocation. If the corporation ceases to meet these requirements, and all other requirements set forth in the Internal Revenue Code, the business may lose its S corporation status.

All S corporations have a calendar year as their tax year, unless a special election proving acceptable business purposes for a different year is filed with, and approved by, the Internal Revenue Service.

Statutory Close Corporations

Corporations with stock that is not publicly traded, including family-owned corporations and corporations with relatively few stockholders are often referred to as **closely held corporations** or **close corporations**. These smaller corporations are generally governed by the Business Corporation Acts of their states of domicile. The provisions of the state's Business Corporation Act will apply to the close corporation or closely held corporation unless the statutes specifically indicate otherwise.

Because the needs and realities of the smaller corporations are often different from those of their larger counterparts, some states have adopted special statutes for closely held corporations. In many states, corporations that fit the state's definition of a *closely held corporation* may elect to become statutory close corporations and be governed by the special close corporation acts adopted by that state. Small corporations usually have a choice as to whether or not they wish to elect to become statutory close corporations. If they do not elect to become a statutory close corporation, they are treated under the Business Corporation Act like any other corporation in the state.

A **statutory close corporation** is generally considered to be a corporation having no more than 50 shareholders (or some other number specified by statute) that has elected to be treated as a statutory close corporation. Statutes applying to statutory close corporations take into consideration the nature of these smaller corporations, which are often operated in a manner similar to partnerships. Courts have recognized that a statutory close corporation often "has a small number of stockholders, there is no ready market for its stock, and all or a substantial majority of the stockholders participate in the management, direction and operations of the corporation."[13]

Statutory close corporations are usually governed by specific statute provisions within the business corporation act of the state of domicile, or in a separate act similar to the Close Corporation Supplement to the MBCA, which states, "The ... Business Corporation Act applies to statutory close corporations to the extent

---

closely held corporation   Refers to stock or a company that is owned by a family or another company.

close corporation   A corporation with total ownership in a few hands.

statutory close corporation   A closely held corporation having no more than 50 shareholders that has elected to be treated as a statutory close corporation under the relevant statutes of its state of domicile.

not inconsistent with the provisions of this Supplement."[14] Pursuant to the Close Corporation Supplement, a statutory close corporation must include a statement in its articles of incorporation specifically stating that it is a close corporation.[15] Any corporation electing to become a statutory close corporation after its incorporation typically must have the approval of at least two-thirds of the corporation's shareholders. In addition, the stock certificates representing shares of stock of statutory close corporations must contain specific language on their face to indicate to the shareholder that the corporation is a statutory close corporation and that the rights of a shareholder of a statutory close corporation may differ from those of other corporations. State statute provisions may vary from the requirements in the MBCA's Close Corporation Supplement. However, all state statutes have some type of provisions regarding the notification of an election to become a statutory close corporation.

Typically, statutory close corporations are allowed to place certain restrictions on the transfer of shares of the corporation. There may be provisions within the articles of incorporation or another, separate document that provide for such transfer restrictions. The Close Corporation Supplement provides that shares of a close corporation may not be transferred, except as permitted by the articles of incorporation or without first giving the corporation the right of first refusal pursuant to the Close Corporation Supplement, except as follows:

1. A transfer may be made to the corporation or to any other holder of the same class or series of shares.[16]

2. A transfer may be made to members of the shareholder's immediate family.[17]

3. A transfer may be made if it has been approved in writing by all of the holders of the corporation's shares having general voting rights.[18]

4. A transfer may be made to an executor or administrator, upon the death of a shareholder, or to a trustee or receiver as the result of a bankruptcy, insolvency, dissolution, or similar proceeding brought by or against a shareholder.[19]

5. A transfer may be made by a merger or share exchange or an exchange of existing shares for other shares of a different class or series in the corporation.[20]

6. A transfer may be made by a pledge as collateral for a loan that does not grant the pledgee any voting rights possessed by the pledgor.[21]

7. A transfer may be made after termination of the corporation's status as a statutory close corporation.[22]

Statutory close corporations are generally allowed to operate without all of the statutory formalities imposed on other types of corporations. Recognizing that the shareholders and directors of small corporations are often the same individuals, statutory close corporations are usually permitted to operate without a board of directors, leaving the management and operation to the shareholders.

Another formality that may be waived for statutory close corporations is the necessity of having bylaws. Under § 22 of the MBCA's Close Corporation Supplement, "A statutory close corporation need not adopt bylaws if provisions required by law to be contained in bylaws are contained in either the articles of incorporation or a shareholder agreement authorized by section 20."

In the broadest sense, § 25 of the Close Corporation Supplement grants the close corporation the right to transact business without complying with all of the usual corporate formalities imposed on other types of corporations. Section 25 reads as follows:

> The failure of a statutory close corporation to observe the usual corporate formalities or requirements relating to the exercise of its corporate powers or management of its business and affairs is not a ground for imposing personal liability on the shareholders for liabilities of the corporation.

Parents and Subsidiaries

The parent and subsidiary classifications given to corporations refer to a relationship between corporations, depending on the ownership and control of the corporations. A **parent corporation** is a corporation that owns stock in a **subsidiary corporation** which is sufficient to control the subsidiary corporation.

The terms **sister corporations** and **affiliate** corporations are both used to refer to corporations that are owned or controlled by the same owners. For example, two subsidiary corporations that are owned by the same parent corporation may be referred to as *sister corporations,* or *affiliated corporations.*

§ 5.7 THE PARALEGAL'S ROLE IN CORPORATE LAW MATTERS

In the fast-growing paralegal field, the number of paralegals employed in the corporate area of law is second only to the number working in litigation.[23] In addition to paralegals employed in the corporate law departments of law firms, approximately 20 percent of all paralegals work for corporations, typically in their legal departments.

Short of giving legal advice to corporate clients, corporate paralegals are allowed to assist with almost all areas and aspects of corporate law. Typically the paralegal's duties will be dominated by document drafting and research.

The duties performed by paralegals who specialize in corporate law often include:

1. Drafting corporate documents.
2. Reviewing and updating corporate minute books.

---

parent corporation A corporation that fully controls or owns another company.

subsidiary corporation A corporation that is owned by another corporation (the parent corporation).

sister corporations Two (or more) companies with the same or mostly the same owners.

affiliate A person or company with an inside business connection to another company. Under bankruptcy, securities, and other laws, if one company owns more than a certain amount of another company's voting stock, or if the companies are under common control, they are affiliates.

Corporate Paralegal Profile
Sherryl D. Bryant

I enjoy working independently—initiating and completing various projects, including domestic and international corporate law research.

Name Sherryl D. Bryant

Location Columbia, South Carolina

Title Senior Legal Assistant

Specialty Corporate Law

Education Associate Degree, Columbia Junior College Professional Center for Paralegal Studies

Experience 3 years

Sherryl Bryant is a paralegal whose work includes several different aspects of corporate law. She is a Senior Legal Assistant with the Mynd Corporation, a subsidiary of Computer Sciences Corporation (CSC). CSC is one of the world's leading technology service providers. The Mynd Corporation, which provides insurance and financial services, employs nine attorneys and two legal assistants. Sherryl reports directly to CSC corporate headquarters in El Sugundo, California.

Sherryl is the legal department's primary contact person for the Mynd Corporation's subsidiaries, which operate throughout the United States and in 23 foreign countries. She works with the in-house counsel and local counsel in various countries to assist in registering and forming various types of corporate entities worldwide. She is also responsible for maintaining corporate minute books and scheduling and attending the board of directors' meetings.

Sherryl enjoys nearly everything about her position. She finds it both challenging and rewarding and reports that it gives her a sense that she is really making a difference. One of the most interesting projects she has worked on was a corporate name change. Sherryl was responsible for researching the requirements and gathering and completing the various documents needed to effect the global name change for the company and its 30+ subsidiaries, branch offices and joint ventures, both domestic and international. Sherryl had the chance to interact with in-house counsel, local counsel, and members of the various subsidiaries to keep them abreast of the project from start to finish.

Sherryl is a voting member of the Palmetto Paralegal Association, a paralegal association with over 200 members, based in Columbia, South Carolina.

Sherryl's advice to new paralegals?

Find an area of law that most interests you. Pay close attention to your supervising attorney as he or she explains what needs to be done and never be afraid to ask questions. Communication is definitely the key to a good start and a good working relationship between the attorney and the paralegal. Always read and try to understand what you are reading. Enjoy what you do and you will always come out on top.

For more information on careers for corporate paralegals, see the Corporate Careers features on the companion Web page to this text at **www.westlegalstudies.com.**

3. Drafting corporate minutes and resolutions.
4. Incorporating and dissolving corporations.
5. Preparing foreign qualification documents.
6. Assisting with mergers and acquisitions.
7. Assisting with securities rules and regulation compliance.
8. Researching state securities laws (blue sky laws).
9. Drafting all types of corporate agreements and contracts.

The duties performed by paralegals who work in a corporate legal department can include all of the above. In addition, the corporate legal department paralegal may be responsible for:

1. Subsidiary maintenance, including preparing all documents for incorporating and dissolving subsidiaries, and preparing corporate resolutions.
2. Shareholder relations, including drafting correspondence to shareholders to answer questions concerning stock transfers and other matters concerning their interests in the corporation.
3. Board of director communications.
4. Coordinating stock transfers and notices to shareholders with the transfer agent.
5. Acting as liaison between the corporation, in-house counsel, and outside counsel.
6. Confirming proper service of legal process and opening files for new lawsuits brought against the corporation.

The paralegal working in the corporate law area often specializes in one or more areas within that field, including incorporation and organization of business corporations or nonprofit corporations, corporate mergers and acquisitions, securities law, or qualified retirement plans. Specific duties in each of these areas are discussed in the pertinent chapters of this text.

ETHICAL CONSIDERATION

Both corporate paralegals who work for law firms and those who work in corporate legal departments often take on a tremendous amount of responsibility. Experienced paralegals can be given very important tasks to complete with very little supervision.

As an important member of the legal services team, it is important for paralegals to assume as much responsibility as they are competent to handle and feel comfortable with. However, it is also important for all paralegals to be aware of the limitations imposed on them by the rules prohibiting the **unauthorized practice of law**.

As set forth in Rule 5.3 of the Model Rules of Professional Conduct and similar rules in each state, attorneys are responsible for the conduct of their non-attorney employees, and they may be held accountable for the unethical actions of their employees. Licensed attorneys must responsibly supervise the actions of any employees or agents to assure that they are not engaging in the unauthorized practice of law or

---

unauthorized practice of law   Nonlawyers doing things that only lawyers are permitted to do. Who and what fits into this definition is constantly changing and the subject of dispute. If, however, a clear case comes up (for example, a nonlawyer pretending to be a lawyer and setting up a law office), the practice may be prohibited and the person punished under the state's criminal laws.

they will be in violation of the pertinent rules or statutes concerning the unauthorized practice of law.

Paralegals who work for corporations must be aware of their legal and ethical boundaries. A corporation may not designate a non-attorney to represent it in matters of a legal nature. Again, if you work under the direct supervision of attorneys in a legal department, you probably need not be too concerned. However, if you find you are working on legal matters with very little or no attorney supervision, you must consider the possibility that the work you are performing could be considered the unauthorized practice of law.

5.5 Unauthorized Practice of Law. A lawyer shall not:

(a) practice law in a jurisdiction where doing so violates the regulation of the legal profession in that jurisdiction; or

(b) assist a person who is not a member of the bar in the performance of activity that constitutes the unauthorized practice of law.

Defining exactly what constitutes the *practice of law* can be problematic. The term has been defined differently by state statutes and by the courts. The practice of law generally includes the following activities:

1. Setting fees for legal work.
2. Giving legal advice.
3. Preparing or signing legal documents.
4. Representing another before a court or other tribunal.

Following are suggestions for avoiding the unauthorized practice of law:

- Always disclose your status as a paralegal.
- Get the approval and signature of your supervising attorney for any legal documents and any correspondence prepared by you that may express a legal opinion.
- Communicate important issues concerning each case or legal matter with your supervising attorney concerning matters on which you are working.
- Never give legal advice.
- Never agree to represent a client on behalf of an attorney.
- Never represent a client at a deposition, in a court of law, or before an administrative board (unless specifically authorized by the court's rules or agency regulation).
- Make sure that any letterhead or business cards with your name on them indicate that you are a paralegal.

See appendix C to this text for the rules concerning the unauthorized practice of law adopted by the National Federation of Paralegal Associations and the

National Association of Legal Assistants in their Codes of Ethics, as well as several resources for researching the unauthorized practice of law and other legal ethics issues.

§ 5.8 RESOURCES

Many resources are available to assist the paralegal working in the corporate law area. In addition to the statutes that the paralegal must be familiar with, there are several sources that may provide useful information, including legal encyclopedias, form books, CLE materials, and state agencies.

State Statutes

The primary source of information on business corporations is the business corporation act (or similar act) in the statutes of the corporation's state of domicile. Information regarding special types of corporations can be found in the pertinent state's close corporation act or supplement, its professional corporation act, and its nonprofit corporation act, any or all of which may be part of the state's business corporation act. Figure 5-5 is a list of state business corporation statutes, many of which can be found on-line.

Alabama	Alabama Business Corporation Act; Ala. Code § 10-2B-1.01 *et seq.*
Alaska	Alaska Corporations Code; Alaska Stat. § 10.06.005 *et seq.*
Arizona	Arizona Revised Statutes; Ariz. Rev. Stat. Ann. § 10-120 *et seq.*
Arkansas	Arkansas Business Corporation Act; Ark. Code Ann. § 4-27-101 *et seq.*
California	California Corporations Code § 100 *et seq.*
Colorado	Colorado Business Corporation Act; Colo. Rev. Stat. § 7-101-101 *et seq.*
Connecticut	Connecticut Business Corporation Act; Conn. Gen. Stat. § 33-600 *et seq.*
Delaware	Delaware Corporation Law; Del. Code Ann. tit. 8 § 101 *et seq.*
District of Columbia	District of Columbia Business Corporation Act; D.C. Code Ann. § 29-301 *et seq.*
Florida	Florida Business Corporation Act; Fla. Stat. Ann. § 607.0101 *et seq.*
Georgia	Georgia Business Corporation Code; Ga. Code Ann. § 14-2-101 *et seq.*
Hawaii	Hawaii Business Corporation Act; Haw. Rev. Stat. ch. 415
Idaho	Idaho Business Corporation Act; Idaho Code § 30-1-101 *et seq.*
Illinois	Business Corporation Act of 1983; 805 ILCS 5/1.01 *et seq.*

FIGURE 5-5 State Business Corporation Acts

Indiana	Indiana Business Corporation Law; Ind. Code § 23-1-17-1 *et seq.*
Iowa	Iowa Business Corporation Act; Iowa Code Ann. § 490.101 *et seq.*
Kansas	Kansas General Corporation Code § 17-6001 *et seq.*
Kentucky	Kentucky Business Corporation Act; Ky. Rev. Stat. Ann. 271B.1-010 *et seq.*
Louisiana	Louisiana Business Corporation Law; La. Rev. Stat. Ann. § 12.1 *et seq.*
Maine	Maine Business Corporation Act; Me. Rev. Stat. Ann. tit. 13-A § 101 *et seq.*
Maryland	Maryland Corporations and Associations 1-101 *et seq.*
Massachusetts	General Laws of Massachusetts; Corporations, Chapter 155
Michigan	Michigan Business Corporation Act; Mich. Comp. Laws Ann. § 450.1101 *et seq.*
Minnesota	Minnesota Business Corporation Act; Minn. Stat. Ann. § 302A.001 *et seq.*
Mississippi	Mississippi Business Corporation Act; Miss. Code Ann. § 79-4-1.0l *et seq.*
Missouri	General and Business Corporation Law of Missouri; Mo. Rev. Stat. § 351.010 *et seq.*
Montana	Montana Business Corporation Act; Mont. Code Ann. § 35-1-112 *et seq.*
Nebraska	Business Corporation Act; Neb. Rev. Stat. § 21-2001 *et seq.*
Nevada	Private Corporations, Business Corporation Act; Nev. Rev. Stat. § 78.010 *et seq.*
New Hampshire	New Hampshire Business Corporation Act; N.H. Rev. Stat. Ann. § 293-A:1.01 *et seq.*
New Jersey	New Jersey Business Corporation Act; N.J. Stat. Ann. § 14A:1-1 *et seq.*
New Mexico	Business Corporation Act; N.M. Stat. Ann. § 53-11-1 *et seq.*
New York	Business Corporation Law; N.Y. Bus. Corp. § 101 *et seq.*
North Carolina	North Carolina Business Corporation Act; N.C. Gen. Stat. § 55-1-01 *et seq.*
North Dakota	North Dakota Business Corporation Act; N.D. Cent. Code § 10-19.1-01 *et seq.*
Ohio	General Corporation Law; Ohio Rev. Code Ann. § 1701.01 *et seq.*
Oklahoma	Oklahoma General Corporation Act; Okla. Stat. tit. 18 § 1001 *et seq.*
Oregon	Oregon Business Corporation Act; Or. Rev. Stat. § 60.001 *et seq.*
Pennsylvania	Business Corporation Law of 1988; Pa. Stat. 15 Pa.C.S.A. § 1101 *et seq.*
Rhode Island	Rhode Island Business Corporation Act; R.I. Gen. Laws § 7-1.1-1 *et seq.*
South Carolina	South Carolina Business Corporation Act of 1988; S.C. Code Ann. § 33-1-101 *et seq.*

FIGURE 5-5 (*continued*)

South Dakota	Business Corporations; S.D. Codified Laws Ann. § 47-2-1 *et seq.*
Tennessee	Tennessee Business Corporation Act; Tenn. Code Ann. § 48-11-101 *et seq.*
Texas	Texas Business Corporation Act; Tex. Bus. Corp. Act Art. 1.01 *et seq.*
Utah	Utah Revised Business Corporation Act; Utah Code Ann. § 16-10a-101 *et seq.*
Vermont	Vermont Business Corporation Act; Vt. Stat. Ann. tit. 11A § 1.01 *et seq.*
Virginia	Virginia Stock Corporation Act; Va. Code Ann. § 13.1-601 *et seq.*
Washington	Washington Business Corporation Act; Wash. Rev. Code § 23B.01.010 *et seq.*
West Virginia	West Virginia Corporation Act; W. Va. Code § 31-1-1 *et seq.*
Wisconsin	Wisconsin Business Corporation Law; Wis. Stat. 180.0101 *et seq.*
Wyoming	Wyoming Business Corporation Act; Wyo. Stat. § 17-16-101 *et seq.*

FIGURE 5-5   (*continued*)

Federal Statutes

Although state law is the primary source of law for corporations, corporations are also subject to special federal statutes and regulations in specific areas, such as interstate commerce, income taxation, bankruptcy, intellectual property, and securities. The paralegal should be aware of the corporation's business focus and alert for possible applications of such federal statutes.

Legal Encyclopedias

Legal encyclopedias, such as *American Jurisprudence 2d* and *Corpus Juris Secundum*, can be a good place to begin research regarding a specific topic concerning corporations that you are unfamiliar with. These references can give you a good background on the topic and refer you to pertinent case law.

Forms and Form Books

For drafting corporate documents, most law firms and corporate law departments have systems and forms to follow. Standard forms and previously drafted documents can be invaluable resources and save the paralegal from having to reinvent the wheel every time a corporate document is to be drafted. However, it is crucial that these resources not be used without careful consideration. All pertinent information must be gathered and appropriately adapted whenever it might be used in newly drafted corporate documents.

Numerous form books are available in the public law libraries and in most in-house law libraries. These may include state-specific form books as well as more generic form books. Some of the more popular form books are *Am. Jur. Forms 2d.,*

Nichols Cyclopedia of Legal Forms Annotated, Rabkin & Johnson Current Legal Forms, and *West's Legal Forms Second Edition.*

Secretary of State or Other State Corporation Agency

For procedural information regarding incorporations and annual reporting, contact the secretary of state of the business's state of domicile. (See appendix A for a secretary of state directory.)

 Internet Resources www.

There is a wealth of information concerning corporations and corporate law to be found on the Internet. All of the following types of information can be found by researching the Internet:

- ◆ State corporate statutes.
- ◆ Federal statutes concerning corporations.
- ◆ Case law concerning corporations.
- ◆ General information and treatises concerning issues in corporate law.
- ◆ Information concerning filing corporate documents.
- ◆ Financial and other information on publicly held corporations.
- ◆ Annual reports and other pertinent documents filed with the Securities Exchange Commission.
- ◆ Forms for forming corporations and transacting business as a corporation.
- ◆ Discussions concerning corporate law.
- ◆ Association information, including listservs and on-line discussions for corporate paralegals.

Following are just a few of the important Web pages for researching corporations and corporate law:

For researching specific corporations

Business.com—Pure Business Information	**www.business.com/**
Corporate Information	**www.corporateinformation.com/**
Hoover's Online— The Business Network	**www.hoovers.com/**

For state and federal law

American Law Source Online	**www.lawsource.com/also/**

For state statutes

American Law Source Online	**www.lawsource.com/also/**
Findlaw.com	**www.findlaw.com/11stategov/**

| Legal Information Institute | **www.law.cornell.edu/states/listing.html** |

For information on federal taxation of corporations

| Internal Revenue Service | **www.irs.gov** |

For links to the secretary of state offices

| Corporate Housekeeper | **www.danvi.vi/link2.html** |
| National Association of Secretaries of State | **www.nass.org** |

For articles and general information on corporate law

Legal Information Institute	**www.law.cornell.edu/topics/corporations.html**
The 'Lectric Law Library's Business Lounge	**www.lectlaw.com/bus.html**
Law Journal Extra!	**www.ljx.com/practice/corporate/index.html**

An alphabetical list of Internet Resources for the Corporate Paralegal is included as appendix B to this text.

Web Page

For updates and links to several of the previously listed sites, log on to **www. westlegalstudies.com**, and click through to the book link for this text.

SUMMARY

- Corporations are considered entities separate from their owners.
- Under certain circumstances, the corporate entity may be disregarded (piercing the corporate veil) when the court finds it necessary to prevent inequity, injustice, or fraud.
- Corporations are governed predominantly by state statute.
- As a separate entity, the corporation enjoys certain rights and powers that are typically prescribed by state statute.
- Shareholders of a corporation are usually not personally responsible for the debts and obligations of a corporation.
- There are several types of corporations, including business corporations, professional corporations, nonprofit corporations, and S corporations.
- S corporations are one of the most common types of corporations.
- Most small business corporations can file an election with the Internal Revenue Service to become an S corporation and receive *pass-through* taxation status.

REVIEW QUESTIONS

1. What are four characteristics of a corporation that distinguish it from the sole proprietorship and the partnership?

2. If a corporation defaults on its debts, may the creditors typically look to the shareholders for payment? Under what circumstances might the shareholders become personally liable for the debts of the corporation?

3. Suppose that John's Appliance, Inc., is a corporation formed by John Miller. John Miller is the only owner and employee of John's Appliance, Inc., an appliance repair service business. John Miller has formed the corporation to shelter his personal assets. He has put title to the repair truck (which he often uses for his own personal enjoyment), all of his equipment and tools, and his workshop in his own name, although he leases these items back to the corporation. What are some of the potential problems with this arrangement? What can John Miller do to decrease the risk that the corporate veil of John's Appliances could be pierced in the event of a lawsuit?

4. Dave Breen and Sue Martin would like to start a business involving themselves and D&S Equipment, Inc., a corporation that holds certain of their assets. Could they form a regular business corporation with Dave Breen, Sue Martin, and D&S Equipment, Inc., being the shareholders? Could they form an S corporation?

5. Who elects the directors of a corporation? Who elects the officers? Could an individual be a shareholder, director, and officer all at the same time?

6. Could a group of attorneys and physicians form a professional corporation? Why or why not?

7. Are all corporations incorporated as nonprofit corporations automatically exempt from paying income tax?

8. Explain the general differences between a regular business corporation and an S corporation.

9. What are some of the practical differences between regular business corporations and statutory close corporations?

10. Suppose that Mike and Sandy want to start a business to market a new food product they have invented. Limited liability is important to them because of the potential product liability problems associated with manufacturing and selling food products. Initially, Mike and Sandy will be the only investors, and they may not see a profit in their business for a few years. What types of business organizations are available to Mike and Sandy? What type of organization would you suggest? Why?

PRACTICAL PROBLEMS

1. Locate the business corporation act for your state. What is the name of the act?

2. Cite the acts, or portions of acts, in your state for forming the following types of corporations:
   a. Business corporation
   b. Statutory close corporation
   c. Nonprofit corporation
   d. Professional corporation

   There may not be provisions for all of the preceding types of corporations in your state.

WORKPLACE SCENARIO

Assume you are a paralegal working for a corporate law firm. New clients, Bradley Harris and Cynthia Lund, have just finished an initial meeting with your supervising attorney. Your supervising attorney, Belinda Benson, has briefed you on their situation.

Bradley Harris and Cynthia Lund have just incorporated a business called Cutting Edge Computer Repair, Inc. After consulting with Belinda, they feel it would be in their best interests to be taxed as an S corporation. Belinda has asked you to prepare the necessary Form 2553 to elect S corporation status for their signatures.

Using the above information, and the information in appendix D-3 to this text, prepare a Form 2553 for Cutting Edge Computer Repair, Inc. This form may be downloaded from the Internal Revenue Service's Web page at **www.gov**. In addition, prepare the necessary cover letter to file the form.

END NOTES

1. Trustees of Dartmouth College v. Woodward, 17 U.S. (4 Wheat.) 518 (1819); 18 AM. JUR. 2d *Corporations* § 1 (1985).
2. 18 AM. JUR. 2d *Corporations* § 1 (1985).
3. *Id.* § 42.
4. United States v. Union Supply Co., 215 U.S. 50 (1909); 18 AM. JUR. 2d *Corporations* § 65 (1985).
5. 18 AM. JUR. 2d *Corporations* § 43 (1985).
6. *Id.* § 44.
7. *Id.* § 45.
8. Flynt Distrib. Co. v. Harvey, 734 F.2d 1389 (9th Cir. 1984); 18 AM. JUR. 2d *Corporations* § 45 (1985).
9. U.S. Census Bureau, *The Statistical Abstract of the United States: 2000,* no. 854.
10. *Id.* no. 862.
11. Model Professional Corporation Act § 3.
12. Hamilton, Amy, "S Corporations 'Most Popular Corporate Entity Choice.' IRS Finds," *Tax Notes Today,* July 6, 2000.
13. 18 AM. JUR. 2d *Corporations* § 36 (1985).
14. Statutory Close Corporation Supplement § 2(a).
15. *Id.* § 3(a).
16. *Id.* § 11(b)(1).
17. *Id.* § 11(b)(2).
18. *Id.* § 11(b)(3).
19. *Id.* § 11(b)(4).
20. *Id.* § 11(b)(5).
21. *Id.* § 11(b)(6).
22. *Id.* § 11(b)(7).
23. According to the *1999 Paralegal Compensation and Benefits Report* by the National Federation of Paralegal Associations, 8.7% of the respondents specialized in corporate law and 18.1% specialized in litigation.

CHAPTER 6

Formation of the Corporation

CHAPTER OUTLINE

§ 6.1   Preincorporation Matters

§ 6.2   Incorporators

§ 6.3   Articles of Incorporation

§ 6.4   Organizational Meetings

§ 6.5   Bylaws

§ 6.6   Formation of Special Types of Corporations

§ 6.7   The Paralegal's Role in Corporate Formation

§ 6.8   Resources

INTRODUCTION

The corporation is an entity that cannot exist unless it has been properly incorporated. Articles or a certificate of incorporation must be filed with the secretary of state or other appropriate state official, who will give the corporation its life and its right to transact business. This chapter discusses the formation of the corporation, from preincorporation matters through the organizational meeting following incorporation. Special attention is given to preincorporation concerns, the incorporator, the articles of incorporation, organizational meeting, bylaws, and the formation of special types of corporations. This chapter concludes with a look at the role of the paralegal in corporation formations and the resources available to assist paralegals in that area.

§ 6.1 PREINCORPORATION MATTERS

The life of the corporation does not begin until the proper documentation is filed with the appropriate state authorities. Therefore, some actions concerning the incorporation must be taken before the corporation actually exists. In this section, we examine the preincorporation matters that are often dealt with by the incorporators of a business corporation, including the decision to incorporate and the choice of a domicile for the corporation. We also discuss the actual promoters of the corporation, preincorporation agreements, and stock subscription agreements. The section concludes with a look at the important task of gathering client information prior to incorporating a business.

Deciding on the Corporate Structure

When an attorney meets with clients to advise them concerning the formation of a business organization or the expansion of an ongoing business, one of the first issues they must decide on is the proper format for the business. The attorney and client will consider the advantages and disadvantages of each type of available business organization, as discussed in previous chapters. Then, considering the income tax implications, capital requirements, applicable statutory requirements, and desired management structure, and weighing the importance of limited liability, transferability of ownership, ease of forming and dissolving the business entity, and business continuity, a decision will be made as to whether to incorporate.

This chapter investigates the process of forming a business corporation, assuming that the corporation is being created based on an informed consideration of all possibilities.

Choosing a Domicile

The state in which a corporation's articles or certificate of incorporation are filed is considered the corporation's home state or the *state of domicile*. Although it may seem obvious that incorporators should incorporate their businesses in the state in which they live and intend to operate, this is not necessarily true, and should not be taken for granted. Persons forming a corporation usually have their choice of the domicile or state in which they wish to incorporate, and their actual home state may not be the most advantageous for the business. The nature of the state's corporate law is usually the primary consideration, although there are several others. Following is a list of factors to be considered when choosing a state of domicile:

1. Does the law of the state being considered allow the corporation to be operated in the manner desired?
2. What costs are associated with incorporating in the state being considered?
3. What is the state's judicial policy toward corporations?
4. Is the proposed corporate name available in the state being considered?
5. May shareholder meetings be held out of state?
6. What is the statutory treatment of shareholder and director liability?
7. Must any corporate records be kept in the proposed state?
8. What are the annual reporting requirements in the proposed state (tax and informational)?

In addition to the foregoing factors, the incorporators must be aware of the foreign corporation requirements in states other than the state of domicile. The corporation will be required to qualify to do business as a foreign corporation in any state, other than the state of domicile, in which it transacts business. Each state's statutes set requirements for qualifying as a foreign corporation. These

Dividends

Why Incorporate in Delaware?

Over 393,000 businesses have chosen to incorporate in the state of Delaware. Why is the second smallest state in the country the state of domicile for nearly half of the corporations listed on the New York Stock Exchange? For years Delaware has attracted corporations by adopting corporate laws that are among the most liberal in the country. In addition, the Delaware Department of State, Division of Corporations, is one of the most user-friendly in the country.

The state of Delaware places a high priority on attracting corporations. The Delaware Corporate Law Council of the Delaware State Bar Association works closely with the legislature to keep their state laws among the most attractive in the country. Some of the laws that Delaware has passed to attract corporations include the following features:

- Maximum protection against hostile takeovers.
- Limited personal liability of directors and shareholders.
- No minimum capital requirements.
- No corporate state income tax for corporations that do not conduct business in the state.
- Anonymous ownership of a corporation, if desired.
- Written consents and conference calls are permitted in lieu of directors' meetings.
- Mergers and acquisitions can be completed with a minimum of red tape.
- Directors may determine what part of consideration received for stock is capital.
- Corporations may purchase shares of their own stock and hold, sell, or transfer those shares.
- No limitations are set on the amount of stock held by the corporation, either inside or outside the state.

Furthermore, the judicial system of Delaware has proven that it can handle an incredible volume of corporate law cases quickly, efficiently, and consistently.

In addition to offering attractive corporate laws and an efficient judicial system, the Delaware Department of State, Division of Corporations, has been set up to handle an enormous number of incorporations in an easy and efficient manner. Some of the special features offered by the Delaware Division of Corporations include the following:

- The division will provide the names and addresses of over fifty professional registered agents that may be retained to act as the corporation's representative in Delaware.
- Most documents filed with the division need not be notarized or witnessed.
- Professional registered agents in Delaware are allowed direct access to the division's corporate databases.
- Corporate names may be reserved by telephone.
- Name availability can be checked by telephone free of charge.
- Corporate documents may be filed on the same day they are received by the division.
- The certificate of incorporation and other forms required to incorporate are provided free of charge by the division, upon request.
- Many documents can be submitted to the division by facsimile transmission.

Incorporation can be big business, and Delaware has reaped substantial revenues as a result of that business. Currently, many other states are competing with Delaware to attract more incorporations. It remains to be seen what effect the stiff competition will have on the state of Delaware, and on corporate law in the United States.

requirements should be researched carefully before deciding where to incorporate. Qualification of foreign corporations is discussed in Chapter 11.

Historically, many incorporators have chosen to incorporate in the state of Delaware, which is known for its liberal corporate laws and favorable judicial treatment of corporations. In recent years, however, many states have revised their corporate laws to conform more closely to the current Model Business Corporation Act (MBCA), and the advantages to incorporating in Delaware have diminished somewhat. One clear advantage to incorporating in Delaware remains, however, in that compared to most other states, the corporate law of Delaware has been interpreted extensively by that state's courts. Attorneys and incorporators find much more certainty in incorporating in Delaware where there are few questions concerning the court's interpretation of the state's corporate law that have not been answered. Figure 6-1 on page 198 lists the number of United States 1998 incorporations by state.

Promoters

The formation of some, but not all, corporations involves one or more individuals acting in the role of a **promoter**. A *promoter* is generally considered to be "one who actively assists in creating, projecting, and organizing a corporation."[1] The promoter of a corporation will often bring interested parties together, obtain subscriptions for stock of the proposed corporation, and see to the actual formation of the corporation.

Any transactions made by the promoter on behalf of the corporation before the actual incorporation are considered to be **preincorporation transactions**. The corporation does not legally exist until its articles of incorporation are properly filed. Therefore, any preincorporation transactions must be ratified by the corporation after it is formed if they are to be valid. Promoters may be liable for contracts entered into on behalf of the future corporation until the contracts are ratified by the corporation, unless the contracts specifically state that the promoter is acting only on behalf of the future corporation and assumes no personal liability. In *Moneywatch Companies v. Wilbers*, which appears on page 199, the appellant was held personally responsible for breach of a commercial lease entered into by him on behalf of a future corporation. The court held that promoters are released from personal liability under terms of contract only where contract provides that performance is to be the obligation of the corporation, the corporation is ultimately formed, and corporation formally adopts the contract.

Corporations are not required to have a promoter prior to their formation, and most corporations are formed without anyone assuming that role. If the formation of a corporation does involve a promoter, he or she will often be responsible for obtaining subscriptions for stock of the proposed corporation.

---

promoter   A person who forms a corporation.

preincorporation transaction   Actions taken by promoters or incorporators prior to the actual formation of the corporation.

State	Number of Incorporations	State	Number of Incorporations
Alabama	7,559	Montana	2,812
Alaska	995	Nebraska	3,348
Arizona	11,499	Nevada	27,571
Arkansas	6,029	New Hampshire	2,346
California	46,935	New Jersey	29,282
Colorado	14,392	New Mexico	2,763
Connecticut	2,617	New York	72,568
Delaware	48,074	North Carolina	17,762
District of Columbia	1,353	North Dakota	762
Florida	108,355	Ohio	17,134
Georgia	28,916	Oklahoma	7,349
Hawaii	3,792	Oregon	8,393
Idaho	2,322	Pennsylvania	18,852
Illinois	35,319	Rhode Island	2,334
Indiana	11,996	South Carolina	7,524
Iowa	4,173	South Dakota	1,515
Kansas	4,780	Tennessee	6,463
Kentucky	7,867	Texas	38,829
Louisiana	9,196	Utah	6,864
Maine	2,669	Vermont	1,217
Maryland	16,714	Virginia	17,808
Massachusetts	11,798	Washington	12,179
Michigan	28,983	West Virginia	1,908
Minnesota	12,481	Wisconsin	7,049
Mississippi	5,003	Wyoming	1,897
Missouri	9,579		
Total Incorporations			759,925

Source: The Dun & Bradstreet Corporation, Economic Analysis Department, Dun & Bradstreet Corporation Web page, www.dnb.com.

FIGURE 6-1   1998 Incorporations by State

CASE

Court of Appeals of Ohio,
Twelfth District, Butler County.

MONEYWATCH COMPANIES, Appellee,

v.

WILBERS, Appellant.

No. CA95-03-055.
Decided Aug. 28, 1995.

POWELL, Judge.

Defendant-appellant, Jeffrey Wilbers, appeals a decision of the Butler County Court of Common Pleas in favor of plaintiff-appellee, Moneywatch Companies, in a breach of contract action.

In December 1992, appellant entered into negotiations with appellee, through its property manager, Rebecca Reed, for the lease of commercial property space in the Kitty Hawk Center located in Middletown, Ohio. During the negotiations, appellant indicated that he intended to create a corporation and needed the space for a golfing business he wanted to open. Reed testified that although appellant told her that he would be forming a corporation, she advised appellant that he would have to remain personally liable on the lease even if a corporation was subsequently created. Appellant testified that he never intended to assume personal liability on the lease and that appellee never advised him that he would have to be personally liable under the lease. At appellee's request, appellant submitted a personal financial statement and business plan.

On December 23, 1992, a lease agreement was signed naming appellee as landlord and "Jeff Wilbers, dba Golfing Adventures" as tenant. The lease agreement provided that rent would not be due until March 1, 1993. On January 11, 1993, articles of incorporation for "J & J Adventures, Inc." were signed by "Jeff Wilbers, Incorporator." On February 3, 1993, a trade name registration

was signed for "Golfing Adventures" to be used by J & J Adventures, Incorporated. ...

Appellant notified appellee of the incorporation of J & J Adventures, Inc. and asked that the name of the tenant on the lease be changed from "Jeff Wilbers, dba Golfing Adventures" to "J & J Adventures, Inc., dba Golfing Adventures." In a letter dated March 1, 1993, from appellee to appellant, appellee informed appellant that the name of the tenant on the lease would be so changed and that "[t]his name change shall be deemed a part of the entire Lease Agreement." Reed testified that appellant did not request a release of personal liability under the lease at this time. Appellant testified that he did not seek release of personal liability because he never thought he was personally liable under the lease. ...

At some time during 1993, the corporation defaulted and vacated the premises. Appellee brought a breach of contract action against appellant in his personal capacity. After a bench trial, the trial court entered judgment in favor of appellee and ordered appellant to pay appellee the sum of $13,922.67 plus interest and costs. ...

In his sole assignment of error, appellant contends that he is not personally liable under the lease agreement because a **novation** was accomplished by the substitution of "J & J Adventures, Inc., dba Golfing Adventures," a corporate party, for "Jeff Wilbers, dba Golfing Adventures," an individual party. ...

In this case, the substitution of tenant names on the lease does not constitute a novation because there was no discharge of appellant from his original obligations under the lease. ...

Appellant also contends that he is not personally liable under the lease agreement because he executed the lease as a corporate promoter on behalf of a future corporation. Corporate promoters are "those who participate in bringing about

---

novation The substitution by agreement of a new contract for an old one, with all the rights under the old one ended. The new contract is often the same as the old one, except that one or more of the parties is different.

the organization of an incorporated company, and in getting it in condition for transacting the business for which it is organized." ... A promoter is not personally liable on a contract made prior to incorporation which is made "in the name and solely on the credit of the future corporation." ...

Further, a corporation does not assume a contract made on its behalf by the mere act of incorporation. ...

In addressing the issue of promoter liability on contracts executed on behalf of a corporation to be formed in the future, the Ohio Supreme Court recently stated:

> It is axiomatic that the promoters of a corporation are at least initially liable on any contracts they execute in furtherance of the corporate entity prior to its formation. The promoters are released from liability only where the contract provides that performance is to be the obligation of the corporation, the corporation is ultimately formed, and the corporation then formally adopts the contract. ...

In this case, appellant can be deemed a promoter because he participated in bringing about the organization of the corporation and in getting it ready for business. However, the original lease was not made "in the name and solely on the credit of the future corporation." ... To the contrary, the lease was executed by appellant, individually, on his own credit, as evidenced by the submission of appellant's personal financial statement during the negotiation and execution of the lease.

Promoters are released from personal liability under the terms of a contract only where the contract provides that performance is to be the obligation of the corporation, the corporation is ultimately formed and the corporation formally adopts the contract. ... In this case, the lease agreement does not provide that the corporation will be exclusively liable under its terms even though the corporation is now listed as tenant. In fact, appellant's individual signature remains on the lease agreement. ... In addition, there is no evidence that the corporation, once formed, formally adopted the lease agreement as executed by appellant. In the absence of the necessary steps which must be taken to ensure that appellant is not personally liable and the corporation is solely liable under the lease, appellant is liable under the lease.

...After thoroughly reviewing the record, we find competent, credible evidence to support the trial court's decision to hold appellant personally liable under the lease. We will not substitute our judgment for that of the trial court. ...

Accordingly, appellant's sole assignment of error is overruled.

Judgment affirmed.
WILLIAM W. YOUNG, P.J., and
KOEHLER, J., concur.

Preincorporation Agreements

Under certain circumstances, the founders of a corporation may find it beneficial to enter into a formal **preincorporation agreement** to set forth their understanding and agreement concerning the formation of a new corporation. Because the incorporation process can usually be completed within a few days at most, a formal preincorporation agreement is generally not necessary. However, under any of the following circumstances, a formal preincorporation agreement may be desirable:[2]

1. When a considerable amount of time will lapse between the decision to incorporate and the actual incorporation.

preincorporation agreement Agreement entered into between parties setting forth their intentions with regard to the formation of a corporation.

2. When extensive financial contributions in advance of incorporation are required.

3. When it is desirable to bind participants to make future financial contributions that may be essential to the business venture.

4. When one or more participants are being induced to participate in the venture by promises of employment or other business advantage.

5. When it is necessary to protect a trade or business secret.

A preincorporation agreement should, in general, include the agreement of the future corporation's shareholders regarding the terms for formation of the corporation. The preincorporation agreement should address such matters as the content of the articles of incorporation and bylaws, the state of incorporation, the identity and initial term of the first board of directors, and the identity of the statutory agent of the corporation, if one is to be appointed. The preincorporation agreement may also include the subscription agreement of the future shareholders of the corporation who are entering into the preincorporation agreement.

Stock Subscriptions

A *stock subscription* is an agreement to purchase a stated number of shares of a corporation or a future corporation at a stated price. Often a promoter helps obtain preincorporation stock subscriptions to finance the corporation. Once the corporation is actually formed, the subscription agreement is ratified by the corporation and then executed as shares of stock are issued to the subscribers pursuant to the agreements.

Stock subscription agreements may be used at any time during the life of the corporation to add new shareholders to the corporation, or to document the purchase of additional shares by existing shareholders. Following is a checklist of matters to be considered when drafting a stock subscription agreement:[3]

◆ Name and address of each subscriber.

◆ Name of corporation to be formed.

◆ Other identification of corporation, in the event the proposed name is not available.

◆ Class and number of shares subscribed.

◆ Statement of consideration for subscription.

◆ Conditions on subscription, if any.

◆ Date on or before which subscription is to be executed by issuance of stock and payment of subscription price.

◆ If stock is to be paid for other than in cash, description and value of property to be exchanged.

---

stock subscription agreement   Agreement to purchase a specific number of shares of a corporation.

- ◆ Identification of subscriber as incorporator or promoter, in appropriate case.
- ◆ Date of subscription agreement.
- ◆ Special provisions regarding stock subscribed to, such as redemption of preferred stock.

Figure 6-2 shows an example of a stock subscription agreement form to be used by incorporators.

Subscription—By Incorporators
[From 6 AM. JUR. Legal Forms Corp. § 74:83 (1995)]

SUBSCRIPTION AGREEMENT

The undersigned, as incorporators of the corporation to be known as _____ _____ [corporate name], in accordance with the agreement to incorporate, dated and executed by them this date, and in consideration of the mutual subscriptions hereby made, do agree among themselves, each with the others, and with the corporation, to subscribe to and purchase from the corporation, at _____ [par or book] value, the class and number of shares of the corporation set forth opposite their respective signatures below. Each of the undersigned hereby subscribes for the kind and number of shares set opposite his or her name, and his or her obligation hereunder shall not be dependent upon performance by any of the other signatories.

The respective subscription prices shall be due and paid after the formation and organization of the corporation substantially in accordance with the agreement to incorporate, and on issuance to and receipt by the corporation of a stock permit from _____ [the Secretary of State, or the Corporation Commission, or as the case may be] of the State of _____.

In the event that such stock permit is not received by the corporation on or before _____, ___, or such later date as may hereafter be agreed upon by all the subscribers below signed, then this agreement and the obligations of the respective subscribers shall be null and void and of no further force and effect.

In witness whereof the subscribers have executed this subscription at _____ [place of execution] this ____ day of _____, ___.

Subscribers' Signatures	Class of Shares	Number of Shares
_____	_____	_____
_____	_____	_____
_____	_____	_____
_____	_____	_____

FIGURE 6-2   Sample Stock Subscription Agreement Form. Reprinted with permission from *American Jurisprudence Legal Forms 2d*. © 2000 West Group.

Gathering Client Information to Incorporate

Once the decision has been made to incorporate, the attorney or paralegal must gather the necessary information from the client to begin the incorporation process. This can be done at an initial meeting between the client, attorney, and the paralegal. Collecting this information is extremely important for two reasons. First, the information is necessary to correctly prepare the initial incorporation documents and subsequent documents that may be prepared on behalf of the corporate client. Second, the collection of this information may lead to discussions that cause the client or clients to consider and discuss facets of the business that have not previously been contemplated. Following is a list of information that typically must be obtained from the client to begin the incorporation process:[4]

- Is the corporation the appropriate business organization? Has the client considered:
  - A partnership?
  - A limited partnership?
  - A limited liability company?
- What is the proposed corporate name?
  - What is the client's first choice?
  - What are possible alternatives?
- What business is to be conducted?
  - What is the corporation's primary business?
  - Is the corporation to be authorized to conduct other businesses?
  - Are any limits to be placed on the business the corporation is to be allowed to conduct, if state law allows corporations to engage in any lawful business?
  - Should specific business purposes be set out in the articles of incorporation, if not required by state law?
- Will the corporation's business be conducted in the state of incorporation?
- Will the corporation's business be conducted in other states?
  - Through offices or branches in the other states?
  - By making sales through independent contractors?
  - By soliciting orders by mail or through employees, agents, or otherwise, if such orders must be accepted outside the state before becoming binding contracts?
  - Through sales made wholly in interstate commerce?
  - As isolated, nonrepetitive business only?
- How much total capital is needed to begin business?
- How much of the capital do the founders plan to contribute?
  - What amount is to be treated as equity?
  - What amount will be loaned and on what terms?
- Is any public financing planned?
  - Through sale of stock?
  - By debt financing?

— If debt financing is planned, what interest would the corporation be willing to pay and what loan period is contemplated?

— Are the investors' equity interests to be protected against dilution?

◆ Do the founders want corporate income taxed directly to stockholders (i.e., should election to be treated as an S corporation be made if the corporation is eligible)?

— What are the tax brackets of the stockholders?

— What is the projected income of the corporation?

— Does the corporation need to accumulate capital?

◆ Who is to have control of the corporation?

— If public financing is not needed, but there is to be more than one stockholder, is each founder to have a veto over corporate actions, or will one of the founders or a group of founders have effective control of the corporation?

— If public financing is needed, is effective control, to the extent possible, to be kept in the hands of the founders?

◆ How many initial directors of the corporation are planned and what are their names?

◆ What officers will the corporation have?

— Who are they?

— What are the proposed salaries for each officer, including bonuses?

— What is the term of office?

— Will the corporation have power to remove officers without cause, or only for cause?

◆ Where is the principal office to be located?

◆ Where is the annual meeting of stockholders to be held?

◆ What will the corporation's fiscal year be?

§ 6.2 INCORPORATORS

The *incorporator* is the individual who actually signs the articles or certificate of incorporation to form the corporation. The role played by the incorporator is usually very minor, and the involvement of the incorporator typically ceases after the articles or certificate of incorporation are filed or after the organizational meeting electing the first board of directors is held. At times, the attorney for the corporate client will serve as the incorporator so that the attorney can sign and file the articles of incorporation on behalf of the client.

Qualifications for incorporators are usually set forth in the statutes of the state of domicile. The MBCA states only that "One or more persons may act as the incorporator or incorporators of a corporation by delivering articles of incorporation to the secretary of state for filing."[5] *Persons,* as defined by the MBCA, means individuals and entities, including other profit or not-for-profit corporations, whether foreign or domestic, as well as business trusts, estates, partnerships, trusts, unincorporated associations, and governments. State statutes with more restrictive provisions may require that the incorporators be natural persons.[6]

§ 6.3 ARTICLES OF INCORPORATION

The document that is actually filed with the secretary of state or other appropriate state authority to form the corporation is typically called the *articles of incorporation,* although in some states that document may be referred to as the *certificate of incorporation* or **charter**. For ease in discussion, we refer to the incorporation document as the "articles of incorporation" throughout the rest of this chapter. The articles of incorporation contain essential information regarding the corporation and must comply with statutory requirements of the state of domicile.

The articles of incorporation must be filed with the secretary of state or other designated state official in order to be valid. For ease in discussion, here we refer to every state official responsible for accepting the articles of incorporation for filing as the secretary of state. The secretary of state's office typically supplies forms for articles of incorporation that may be used in that state. In a few states, articles of incorporation must be filed on the secretary of state's form. Most states will mail the forms on request, several offer the forms on-line for downloading. Statutes regarding the articles of incorporation vary from state to state. However, most states have provisions similar to the MBCA, which is discussed later in this chapter.

This section examines the mandatory articles of incorporation provisions required by most state statutes, the articles of incorporation provisions that are usually considered optional, and the statutory provisions that apply to all corporations unless contrary provision is made in the articles of incorporation.

Mandatory Provisions

The mandatory provisions for articles of incorporation vary from state to state and depend upon the type of corporation to be formed. Under the MBCA, the only four provisions that are required to be set forth are:

1. A corporate name for the corporation that satisfies all statutory requirements.[7]
2. The number of shares the corporation is authorized to issue.[8]
3. The street address of the corporation's initial registered office and the name of its initial registered agent at that office.[9]
4. The name and address of each incorporator.[10]

Name The name chosen by the corporation must comply with the statutes of the state of domicile. Basically, there are three aspects of name availability that the incorporators must comply with. First, the name must include at least one of a number of specific words that may be required by statute, and must not contain

---

charter An organization's basic starting document (for example, a corporation's articles of incorporation).

any prohibited words. Second, the name of the corporation must not be the same as, or deceptively similar to, the name of another corporation or entity of record in the office of the secretary of state of the state of domicile. Third, most state statutes require that the name of the corporation not mislead as to the purpose of the corporation.

Most state statutory requirements provide that the name of the corporation must contain a word or words indicating that the corporation is a corporate entity, as opposed to a partnership or other type of business entity. The names of corporations domiciled in states following the MBCA must include the word *corporation, incorporated, company,* or *limited,* or the abbreviation *corp., inc., co.,* or *ltd.,* or words or abbreviations of like import in another language.

The proposed name of the corporation must not be already in use in the state of domicile. The name must also not be deceptively similar to the name of another corporation incorporated in the state or qualified to do business in the state. For example, *Acme Hardware Company* would be considered deceptively similar to the name *Acme Hardware Corporation.*

There are several remedies that may be available if the first choice of a corporate name is not available. At times, the corporation already using the similar name may consent to the use of the name if the two corporate names are not *identical.* At other times, the incorporators may use a variation of the name to distinguish it from the similar name. For example, *Acme Hardware Company of St. Paul,* may be permissible if *Acme Hardware of Chicago* is already in use. The secretary of state's office will make the final determination as to the permissibility of the name.

A corporate name may be considered misleading if it includes language stating or implying that the corporation is organized for a purpose other than its actual purpose. For example, a corporation with the name of Main Street Bank may be considered misleading if it is a corporation that is not a bank and therefore subject to the regulations imposed on banks. Corporate names that include words such as *bank, insurance,* or *trust* may be considered misleading if those words are not indicative of the purpose of the corporation.

The secretary of state or other appropriate state official of most states will check the apparent availability of a proposed corporation name over the telephone. Name availability may be checked via the secretary of state's Web page in some states. See appendix A of this text for a secretary of state directory.

Figure 6-3 gives a brief list of requirements for corporate names.

REQUIREMENTS FOR CORPORATE NAMES

- The name must include the word *Corporation, Incorporated,* or a similar word permitted by state statute indicating that the entity is a corporation.
- The name must not be the same as, or deceptively similar to, the name of another corporation incorporated or qualified to do business in the state.
- The name of the corporation must not be misleading.

FIGURE 6-3 Typical Requirements for Corporate Names

Authorized Stock The articles of incorporation must set forth the number of shares of each class of stock that the corporation is authorized to issue in accordance with the statutes of the state of domicile. When there is only one class of stock, that class is typically referred to as **common stock**.

State statutes may require additional information regarding the corporation's authorized stock, such as the par value of the stock and the rights and preferences of all classes of stock. Capitalization of the corporation is discussed in further detail in Chapter 8 of this text. The following examples show articles of incorporation paragraphs setting forth the number of shares of stock of the corporation.

EXAMPLE: Authorized Stock

The corporation is authorized to issue _____ shares (_____) of common stock of the corporation.[11]

EXAMPLE: Capitalization

The total number of shares of all classes of stock which the corporation shall have authority to issue is _____ divided into _____ [number] shares of common stock at _____ dollars ($_____) par value each and _____ [number] shares of preferred stock, at _____ dollars ($_____) par value each. _____ [State designations and powers, preferences, and rights, and the qualifications, limitations, or restrictions of the classes of stock.]

This corporation will not commence business until it has received for the issuance of its shares consideration of the value of _____ dollars ($_____), consisting of money, labor done, or property actually received, which sum is not less than _____ dollars ($_____).

This Article can be amended only by the vote or written consent of the holders of _____ percent (_____%) of the outstanding shares.[12]

Registered Office and Registered Agent This section of the articles of incorporation must set forth the corporation's **registered office** and its **registered agent,** or statutory agent, as it is sometimes referred to (if one is required and appointed).

---

common stock Shares in a corporation that depend for their value on the value of the company. These shares usually have voting rights (which other types of company stock may lack). Usually, they earn a dividend (profit) only after all other types of the company's obligations and stocks have been paid.

registered office Office designated by the corporation as the office where process may be served. The secretary of state or other appropriate state authority must be informed as to the location of the registered office. Corporations are generally required to maintain a registered office in each state in which the corporation is qualified to transact business.

registered agent Individual appointed by a corporation to receive service of process on behalf of the corporation and perform such other duties as may be necessary. Registered agents may be required in the corporation's state of domicile and in each state in which the corporation is qualified to transact business.

Under the MBCA, each corporation must appoint and maintain both a registered office and a registered agent. The registered office of the corporation may be the same as any of the corporation's places of business within the state of domicile. The registered agent required by the MBCA may be an individual resident of the state of domicile whose business office is identical with the registered office, or a domestic corporation or qualified foreign corporation with a business office identical to the registered office of the corporation. This requirement is typical of most states, although there are some deviations regarding it. For example, not all states require the appointment of a registered agent.

Following is an example of an articles of incorporation paragraph in which the registered office and registered agent of the corporation are appointed.

EXAMPLE: Registered Office and Registered Agent

The street address of the corporation's initial registered office and the name of its initial registered agent at that office are as follows:

Registered Office: _____

_____

Registered Agent: _____.[13]

Name and Address of Incorporators The name and address of each incorporator must be set forth in the articles of incorporation. The incorporators also must sign the articles of incorporation in the method prescribed by state statute. Figure 6-4 illustrates a form that may be used for articles of incorporation in states that follow the MBCA. Figure 6-5 on page 210 is a sample certificate of incorporation form to incorporate a business in Delaware.

[In compliance with minimum requirements of the
Revised Model Business Corporation Act]

ARTICLES OF INCORPORATION

The undersigned, acting as Incorporator(s) of a corporation under the
_____ Business Corporation Act, adopt(s) the following Articles of Incorporation for such corporation:

I. NAME

The name of this corporation is _____.

II. AUTHORIZED STOCK

The number of shares that the corporation is authorized to issue is _____ shares, all of one class.

FIGURE 6-4   Sample Articles of Incorporation to be Used in States Following the Model Business Corporation Act

III. INITIAL REGISTERED OFFICE AND AGENT

The name and address of the initial registered agent and office of this corporation are as follows:

_____

_____.

IV. INCORPORATOR(S)

The name(s) and address(es) of the Incorporator(s) signing these Articles of Incorporation [is] [are]:

Name   Address

_____   _____

_____   _____

_____   _____

IN WITNESS WHEREOF, the undersigned Incorporator(s) has/have executed these Articles of Incorporation this ____ day of _____, ____.

_____

Incorporator

_____

Incorporator

STATE OF _____

COUNTY OF _____

BEFORE ME, the undersigned authority, personally appeared _____ and _____, to me known to be the persons who executed the foregoing Articles of Incorporation, and [he] [she] [they] acknowledged to and before me that [he] [she] [they] executed such instrument.

IN WITNESS WHEREOF, I have hereunto set my hand and seal this ____ day of _____, ____.

_____

(Notarial Seal)   Notary Public, State of _____

My Commission Expires:

FIGURE 6-4 (*continued*)

Optional Provisions

The articles of incorporation may contain any information that the incorporators choose to include regarding the management and administration of the corporate affairs. The MBCA states that the articles of incorporation may set forth:

1. The names and addresses of the individuals who are to serve as the initial directors.[14]

STATE OF DELAWARE
CERTIFICATE OF INCORPORATION
A STOCK CORPORATION

◆ **First:** The name of this Corporation is _____

_____

◆ **Second:** Its registered office in the State of Delaware is to be located at _____
_____ Street, in the City of _____ County of
_____ Zip Code _____. The registered agent in charge thereof is

_____

_____

◆ **Third:** The purpose of the corporation is to engage in any lawful act or activity
for which corporations may be organized under the General Corporation Law of
Delaware.

◆ **Fourth:** The amount of the total authorized capital stock of this corporation is
_____ Dollars ($_____) divided into _____ shares of _____
_____ Dollars ($_____) each.

◆ **Fifth:** The name and mailing address of the incorporator are as follows:
Name _____
Mailing Address _____
_____ Zip Code _____

I, The Undersigned, for the purpose of forming a corporation under the laws of the
State of Delaware, do make, file and record this Certificate, and do certify that the
facts herein stated are true, and I have accordingly hereunto set my hand this
_____ day of _____, A.D. 20___.

BY: _____
(Incorporator)

NAME: _____
(Type or Print)

FIGURE 6-5 State of Delaware Certificate of Incorporation Form

2. The purpose or purposes for which the corporation is organized.[15]

3. Provisions regarding the management of the business and regulation of the affairs of the corporation.[16]

4. Provisions defining, limiting, and regulating the powers of the corporation, its board of directors, and shareholders.[17]

5. Provisions setting a par value for authorized shares or classes of shares.[18]

6. Provisions imposing personal liability on shareholders for the debts of the corporation to a specified extent and upon specified conditions.[19]

7. Any provision that is required or permitted by statute to be set forth in the bylaws.[20]

8. Provisions eliminating or limiting the liability of directors of the corporation or its shareholders for money damages for any action taken, or any failure to take any action, as a director, except under certain circumstances.[21]

9. Provisions permitting or requiring indemnification of directors for liability to any person arising from their actions taken (or not taken) as directors.[22]

Initial Board of Directors In the past, most statutes have required that the initial board of directors be appointed in the articles of incorporation. The MBCA, and several state statutes that are following suit, now give incorporators the option of including this information. However, the directors are often appointed in the articles of incorporation to relieve the incorporators of any further responsibility.

Purpose The purpose of the corporation is often set forth in the articles of incorporation, and the statutes of most states require it. The purpose of the corporation must be a lawful purpose in compliance with state statutes. The purpose clause in the articles serves to notify both the public and its own shareholders of the corporation's general business purposes. Courts have found that "the corporate purpose stated in the articles of incorporation serves to inform the public of the nature of the organization, thus benefiting those with whom it deals, and serves to inform its members of the scope and range of its proper activities and to assure them that they will not be involved in remote and uncontemplated lines of activity."[23]

State statutes may require at least one specific purpose, or merely a vague statement that the purpose of the corporation is "any lawful business." Section 3.01 of the MBCA, which follows, is typical of the purpose provisions under many state statutes.

§ 3.01 PURPOSES

(a) Every corporation incorporated under this Act has the purpose of engaging in any lawful business unless a more limited purpose is set forth in the articles of incorporation.

(b) A corporation engaging in a business that is subject to regulation under another statute of this state may incorporate under this Act only if permitted by, and subject to all limitations of, the other statute.

Following is an example of a purpose paragraph that is often used in states that follow the MBCA.

EXAMPLE: Purpose

The purpose of this corporation is to engage in any lawful business or activities permitted under the laws of the United States and the State of _____.

Certain regulated businesses, such as banking and insurance businesses, as well as special types of corporations, such as professional service corporations or nonprofit corporations, may be required to incorporate under different statutes.

Management of Corporation The MBCA states that the articles of incorporation may include any lawful provision regarding the management of the business and regulation of the affairs of the corporation. The incorporators may be as specific as they wish in this regard. However, because the articles of incorporation may be amended only with shareholder approval, and because an amendment requires an additional filing at the state level, specific information regarding management of the corporation is usually included in the corporation's **bylaws**.

Powers of Corporation The powers of the corporation, the directors, and the shareholders of the corporation are typically prescribed by statute, unless amended by the articles of incorporation. Any desired limitations on the statutory powers granted to the corporation, or the directors or shareholders of the corporation, must be made in the articles of incorporation within the scope of the state statutes.

Par Value of Shares of Stock and Classes of Stock The **par value** of the shares of stock may be included in the articles of incorporation, if desired. Under the MBCA, this information is not mandatory. However, the statutes of many states require that the par value of each class of authorized stock be set forth in the articles. Par value is discussed further in Chapter 8.

Imposition of Personal Shareholder Liability Shareholders are not normally responsible for any debts or obligations of the corporation. If the incorporators feel that it is desirable that the shareholders assume personal liability to a certain extent, provision must be made in the corporation's articles of incorporation.

Provisions That May Be Required or Permitted in Bylaws There are many matters that the incorporators may choose to include in either the articles or the bylaws of the corporation. Incorporators should choose the inclusions to the articles carefully, because amendments to the articles usually involve shareholder approval and an additional filing with the secretary of state.

Limitation on Board of Director Liability In states that have followed the MBCA in this regard, the incorporators may draft the articles of incorporation to limit the liability of directors of the corporation for actions arising based on their actions or inactions on behalf of the corporation, except in the event of wrongful financial

bylaws Rules or regulations adopted by an organization such as a corporation, club, or town.

par value The nominal value assigned to shares of stock, which is imprinted upon the face of the stock certificate as a dollar value. Most state statutes do not require corporations to assign a par value to their shares of stock.

benefit to the director, intentional infliction of harm, a violation of the director's duty of care, or an intentional violation of criminal law. Director liability is discussed further in Chapter 7.

Indemnification of Directors   The statutes of most states provide for **indemnification** of directors who are involved in lawsuits because of their actions on behalf of the corporation, so long as the director acted in good faith and believed his or her conduct was in the best interests of the corporation. Provisions for the indemnification of directors are often included in the articles, and it is often the case that statutory provisions for director indemnification may be amended only in the articles.

Statutory Provisions That May Be Amended Only in the Articles of Incorporation   The statutes of most states contain several provisions that govern the internal affairs of corporations, unless the corporation has provisions in its articles of incorporation to the contrary. Depending on the format of the statutes, a specific list of these provisions may be provided, or these provisions may be found under the section of the act relating to the subject matter. Following is a list of some of the provisions that are most often set by statute but that may be amended in the articles of incorporation:

1. A corporation has perpetual existence.[24]
2. The board of directors has the power to adopt, amend, or repeal the bylaws.
3. The affirmative vote of a majority of directors present is required for an action of the board.
4. A written action by the board, taken without a meeting, must be signed by all directors.[25]
5. The affirmative vote of the holders of a majority of the voting power of the shares present and entitled to vote at a duly held meeting is required for an action of the shareholders, except where state statutes require the affirmative vote of a majority of the voting power of all shares entitled to vote.
6. Shareholders do not have a right to cumulate their votes for directors.[26] (Cumulative voting is discussed in Chapter 7.)
7. The shareholders may remove one or more directors with or without cause.[27] (Removal of directors is discussed in Chapter 7.)
8. All shares of the corporation are of one class with identical rights.[28] (Share classes are discussed in Chapter 8.)
9. Shareholders have no preemptive rights to acquire unissued shares.[29] (Preemptive rights are discussed in Chapter 7.)

◆ ───

indemnification   The act of compensating or promising to compensate a person who has suffered a loss or may suffer a future loss.

Execution

The articles of incorporation must be properly executed by the incorporators, in accordance with state statutory provisions, to be valid. Many state statutes require that the signature or signatures on the articles of incorporation be witnessed, acknowledged, or notarized.

Filing

The articles of incorporation and the appropriate filing fee must be filed with the secretary of state within the state of domicile. Statutes regarding filing requirements should be reviewed carefully, and the appropriate state authority should be contacted, to ensure that all filing procedures are complied with. Failure to comply with filing requirements could seriously delay incorporation.

Publication The statutes of a few states in the country have publication laws requiring that the articles of incorporation, or a notice of incorporation, be published in a legal newspaper in accordance with statutory provisions.[30] It is important that the statutes be consulted to assure that this requirement is complied with, if necessary.

County Filing Often, state statutes require that the articles of incorporation or a copy thereof be filed with the county recorder or other county official of the county in which the registered office of the corporation is located.[31] Again, the state statutes must be consulted to determine if county recording is necessary.

Figure 6-6 provides a list of reasons frequently given by state authorities for rejecting articles of incorporation for filing.

- ◆ Corporate name chosen is unavailable or otherwise unacceptable.
- ◆ Inclusion of a provision giving authority to the board of directors to change the authorized number of directors, where such provision is contrary to state statute.
- ◆ Improper execution and/or acknowledgment of the articles of incorporation.
- ◆ Failure to name a street address for the registered office and/or registered agent of the corporation for service of process. P.O. boxes are *not* acceptable in most jurisdictions.
- ◆ Nonpayment of fees and taxes as required by state and local law.
- ◆ Failure to state the specific number of authorized directors (where required by statute).
- ◆ Failure to state the total number of authorized shares.
- ◆ Failure to state the aggregate par value of all shares of stock having a par value (where required by statute).
- ◆ Failure to state the par value, preferences, privileges and restrictions, and number of shares of each class of authorized stock (where required by statute).

FIGURE 6-6   Reasons Frequently Given by State Authorities for Rejecting Articles of Incorporation for Filing

Effective Time and Date

The effective time and date of the articles of incorporation are important because they are, in effect, the time and date for the commencement of the corporate entity. Again, this matter is addressed by state statute. Most state statutes provide that the articles of incorporation are effective when filed with the secretary of state or at a different time specified in the articles of incorporation. Most statutes that allow a later effective date and time to be specified limit that time to ninety days.

In *Welch v. Fuhrman*, the defendant builders were sued for breach of contract. They were found personally liable for the contract they had entered into, partly because the corporation they formed did not come into existence until two weeks after the contract was signed.

CASE

WELCH
v.
FUHRMAN

496 So. 2d 484 (La. Ct. App. 1986)
Louisiana Court of Appeals
October 15, 1986
Savoie, Judge

Defendant, Robert Fuhrman, appeals from the judgment of the trial court finding him individually liable for breach of building contract.

On August 10, 1982 plaintiffs, Leroy J. Welch and Glynda H. Welch, entered into an oral contract with Capital Builders and Distributors, represented by Leroy Joslin, Sr. for the construction of an addition to their home. At the time of this contract, Capital Builders and Distributors was owned and operated by defendants Robert Fuhrman and Joseph A. Kunstler and Richard Hurt. Mr. Joslin presented plaintiffs with a floor plan and a pier plan drawing of the proposed addition, along with a cost breakdown of work to be performed. The agreed price for the job was $21,979.63. Plaintiffs paid $4,000.00 as a down-payment and financed the balance due of $17,979.63, which was paid upon substantial completion.

After final payment was made, plaintiffs noticed that the job was not fully completed and that numerous faults and defects existed. As a result, plaintiffs secured an estimate of $6,750.09 to complete the job and make the necessary repairs. In addition, defendants had failed to pay an electrical sub-contractor which resulted in a lien in the amount of $1,149.50 being filed against the property by Marshall Electrical, Inc.

Plaintiffs then instituted the present action to recover the sums expended to complete the job along with attorney's fees. Named as defendants were Robert Fuhrman and Joseph A. Kunstler, d/b/a Capital Builders of Louisiana. Defendant Fuhrman answered, filing a general denial, and claimed that any contract plaintiffs entered into was with Capital Builders of Louisiana, Inc., a separate legal entity. It was later determined at trial that the actual name of the corporation was Capital Builders and Distributors, Inc., and that the charter for this corporation had not been issued until August 24, 1982. Listed as directors of this corporation were Robert Fuhrman, Joseph Kunstler and Richard Hurt.

Following trial on the merits, judgment was rendered against defendants Fuhrman and Kunstler individually as well as against the organization known as Capital Builders of Louisiana. In addition to the amounts prayed for, plaintiffs were awarded $500.00 for attorney's fees. From this judgment defendant Fuhrman appeals alleging the following **assignments of error:**

1. The trial court erred in finding the defendant-appellant, Robert Fuhrman, individually, liable for the damages awarded to the plaintiff-appellees.

2. Error was committed in awarding attorney's fees to the plaintiff.

3. Error was committed in not finding that the entity Capital Builders and Distributors, Inc.

was and is a corporation existing under the laws of Louisiana.

ASSIGNMENTS OF ERROR
NOS. 1 & 3

By these assignments of error defendant contends that the trial court erred in determining that he, individually, and not the corporation, was liable to plaintiffs. In his reasons for judgment, the trial judge stated:

Defendants contend that Capital Builders of Louisiana is the only proper party to the suit. The plaintiffs point out that the articles of incorporation were filed with the Secretary of State's office on August 24, 1982, although they were drafted and executed on July 12, 1982.

The sole issue before the Court, as to the defendants, is whether defendants are liable under the contract, or was the corporate entity legally constituted at the time the contract was confected.

This Court is of the opinion that the plaintiffs were of the opinion that Capital Builders of Louisiana was an organization owned by Robert Fuhrman and Joseph A. Kunstler and were doing business with them and not a corporate entity. ...

This Court must conclude that the plaintiffs are entitled to judgment against Robert Fuhrman and Joseph A. Kunstler, individually and against the organization known as Capital Builders of Louisiana.

We agree with the findings of the trial court. [La. Rev. Stat. Ann. §] 12:25(C) provides as follows:

Upon the issuance of the certificate of incorporation, the corporation shall be duly incorporated, and the corporate existence shall begin, as of the time when the articles were filed with the secretary of state, except that, if the articles were so filed within five days (exclusive of legal holidays) after acknowledgment thereof or execution thereof as an authentic act the corporation shall be duly incorporated, and the corporate existence shall begin, as of the time of such acknowledgment or execution.

The record clearly indicates that the articles of incorporation, although executed on July 12, 1982, were not filed with the Secretary of State's office until August 24, 1982. Accordingly, the corporate existence did not begin until that date, some fourteen days after entering into the contract with plaintiffs. As such, plaintiffs' contract was not with Capital Builders and Distributors, Inc. but rather was with the organization known as Capital Builders and Distributors which was owned and operated by Robert Fuhrman and Joseph Kunstler.

Additionally, we note that the record is void of any evidence that plaintiffs were put on notice that they were dealing with a corporation. ...

For the above and foregoing reasons, the judgment of the trial court awarding attorney's fees is hereby reversed. In all other respects, the judgment of the trial court is affirmed. All costs of this appeal are to be paid by defendant-appellant, Robert Fuhrman.

AFFIRMED IN PART, REVERSED IN PART.

§ 6.4 ORGANIZATIONAL MEETINGS

After the articles of incorporation have been filed, the organizational meeting of the corporation is usually held. The requirements for this organizational meeting and the organizational actions that must be taken vary greatly from state to state. Depending on the statutes of the state of domicile, the incorporators or a majority

---

assignment of error Alleged errors of the trial court specified by an appellant in seeking a reversal, vacation, or modification of the trial court's judgment.

of the directors named in the articles of incorporation may be required to call the organizational meeting and give notice to the directors and/or shareholders of the corporation.

This section examines the various requirements for organizational meetings, the purpose of organizational meetings, and the resolutions typically passed by incorporators, directors, and shareholders at organizational meetings. The section concludes with a discussion of the use of unanimous written consents in lieu of organizational meetings.

Organizational Meeting Requirements

The statutes of most states require that an organizational meeting of the corporation be held shortly after its incorporation to adopt bylaws, elect directors, and take care of other details necessary to the operation of the corporation. As a practical matter, the organizational meeting is usually attended by the incorporators, the initial board of directors, and the shareholders, which often total only a very few people. Under certain circumstances, a unanimous written consent in lieu of an organizational meeting may be used to approve the necessary resolutions. Unanimous written consents are discussed in § 6.6 of this chapter.

Requirements for the organizational meeting under the MBCA are set forth in § 2.05:

§ 2.05 ORGANIZATION OF CORPORATION

(a) After incorporation:
   (1) if initial directors are named in the articles of incorporation, the initial directors shall hold an organizational meeting, at the call of a majority of the directors, to complete the organization of the corporation by appointing officers, adopting bylaws, and carrying on any other business brought before the meeting;
   (2) if initial directors are not named in the articles, the incorporator or incorporators shall hold an organizational meeting at the call of a majority of the incorporators:
      (i) to elect directors and complete the organization of the corporation; or
      (ii) to elect a board of directors who shall complete the organization of the corporation.
(b) Action required or permitted by this Act to be taken by incorporators at an organizational meeting may be taken without a meeting if the action taken is evidenced by one or more written consents describing the action taken and signed by each incorporator.
(c) An organizational meeting may be held in or out of this state.

In any event, the statutes of the state of domicile should be consulted regarding the organizational meeting to determine the following:

1. Who is responsible for giving notice of the organizational meeting?
2. Who is entitled to receive notice of and attend the organizational meeting?

3. What are the notice requirements?

4. What actions must be taken by the incorporators, directors, and shareholders at the organizational meeting?

5. May a written resolution signed by all interested parties be substituted for an actual organizational meeting?

Purpose of Organizational Meeting

The purpose of the organizational meeting is to organize the corporation. This usually includes electing directors (when not appointed in the articles of incorporation), executing subscriptions for shares of the corporation, and any other steps necessary to give the corporation the capacity to transact business.

Incorporators' Resolutions

When the first board of directors is not named in the articles of incorporation, the incorporators may hold the organizational meeting.

Election of Board of Directors Typically, the first and only order of business at an organizational meeting held by incorporators is to elect the first board of directors. Following is an example of a resolution that might be made by the incorporators at the organizational meeting to elect the first board of directors.

EXAMPLE: *Election of First Board of Directors*

RESOLVED, by the incorporators, that the following individuals, having been duly nominated, are hereby elected as the first board of directors of this corporation, to serve until the first annual meeting of the shareholders, or until their successors are elected and qualified:

_____

_____

_____.

Adoption of Bylaws In some jurisdictions, the incorporators may adopt the bylaws of the corporation at the organizational meeting. Figure 6-7 is an example of a form of minutes of an organizational meeting of the incorporators.

Board of Directors' Resolutions

The items discussed in this section are often considered for action by the board of directors at the organizational meeting or the first meeting of the board of directors. Depending on state statute, some of these actions may also require shareholder approval. Figure 6-8 on page 220 shows a sample of a form of minutes of the first board of directors' meeting, which includes the items discussed in the rest of this section.

MINUTES OF ORGANIZATIONAL
MEETING OF INCORPORATORS

The organizational meeting of _____ [name of corporation], a corporation duly incorporated under the laws of the State of _____, was held on _____ [date], at _____ [address] pursuant to the attached waiver of notice.

The following incorporators were present: _____
_____.

On motion duly made, seconded and carried, _____ [name] was chosen chairperson of the meeting and _____ [name] was chosen as secretary.

The chairperson reported that the articles of incorporation had been filed with the Secretary of State of the State of _____ on _____ [date]. The Secretary was directed to file a copy of the articles of incorporation and the certificate of incorporation in the corporate minute book.

On motion duly made, seconded, and carried, the following resolutions were adopted:

RESOLVED, that the number of initial directors of the corporation shall be _____.

FURTHER RESOLVED, that the following individuals shall serve as the initial directors of the corporation, to serve in accordance with the bylaws of the corporation until the first annual meeting of the shareholders and until their successors are elected and shall have qualified:

_____
_____
_____.

FURTHER RESOLVED, that the Board of Directors is hereby authorized to issue the capital stock of this corporation to the full extent authorized by the Articles of Incorporation in such amounts and for such consideration as from time to time shall be determined by the Board of Directors and as may be permitted by law, provided, however, that par value stock shall not be issued for less than par.

There being no further or other business to come before the meeting, on motion duly made, seconded, and carried, the meeting was adjourned.

_____
Chairman

_____
Secretary

FIGURE 6-7   Minutes of Organizational Meeting of Incorporators

MINUTES OF THE FIRST MEETING OF THE BOARD OF DIRECTORS

Minutes of meeting of _____
[corporation]

Pursuant to _____ [notice or call and waiver of notice], the first board of directors of _____ [corporation] assembled and held its first meeting at _____ [address], City of _____, State of _____, at ___ o'clock ___.M., on _____, ____.

The following, being all of the directors of the corporation, were present at the meeting:

_____   _____

_____   _____

_____ [Name] called the meeting to order. On motion duly made and seconded, she was appointed temporary chairman, and _____ [name] was appointed temporary secretary.

The election of officers was thereupon declared to be in order. The following individuals were elected to the offices set forth opposite their names:

_____   President

_____   Vice President

_____   Secretary and Treasurer.

_____ [Name] took the chair and presided at the meeting.

The chairman then announced that the _____ [articles or certificate] of incorporation had been filed with the _____ [Secretary of State or other appropriate official] on _____, ____. The secretary was instructed to cause a copy of the _____ [articles or certificate] of incorporation to be inserted in the front of the minute book of this corporation.

The secretary presented a form of bylaws for the regulation of the affairs of the corporation, which were read, section by section.

On motion duly made, seconded, and carried, it was

Resolved, that the bylaws submitted at and read to this meeting be, and the same hereby are, adopted as and for the bylaws of this corporation, and that the secretary be, and he hereby is, instructed to certify the bylaws, and cause the same to be inserted in the minute book of this corporation, and to certify a copy of the bylaws, which shall be kept at the principal office of this corporation and open to inspection by the stockholders at all reasonable times during office hours.

On motion duly made, seconded, and carried, it was

Resolved, that the seal, an impression of which is herewith affixed, be adopted as the corporate seal of the corporation.

[Corporate Seal]

FIGURE 6-8 Minutes of First Meeting of Board of Directors

The secretary was authorized and directed to procure the proper corporate books.

On motion duly made, seconded, and carried, it was

Resolved, that _____ [bank] of the City of _____, State of _____, be, and it hereby is, selected as a depository for the monies, funds, and credit of this corporation and that _____, _____, and _____ be, and they are, authorized and empowered to draw checks (including checks payable to their own order or to bearer) on the above depository, against the account of this corporation with the depository, and to endorse in the name of this corporation and receive payment of all checks, drafts, and commercial papers payable to this corporation either as payee or endorsee.

Further resolved, that the authority hereby conferred above shall remain in full force and effect until it shall have been revoked and until a formal written notice of such revocation shall have been given to and received by _____ [bank] of the City of _____, State of _____.

Further resolved, that the certification of the secretary of this corporation as to the election and appointment of persons so authorized to sign such checks and as to the signatures of such persons shall be binding on this corporation;

Further resolved, that the secretary of this corporation be, and he hereby is, authorized and directed to deliver to _____ [bank] of the City of _____, State of _____, a copy of these resolutions properly certified by him.

On motion duly made, seconded, and carried, it was

Resolved, that the principal office of the corporation for the transaction of its business be, and it hereby is, fixed at _____ [address], City of _____, State of _____.

On motion duly made, seconded, and carried, the following preambles and resolutions were unanimously adopted:

Whereas, this corporation is authorized, in its _____ [articles or certificate] of incorporation, to issue ____ [number] shares of its capital stock without nominal or par value; and

Whereas, this corporation has received stock subscriptions for a total of ____ shares of its authorized stock, and consideration for those shares of stock, in an amount deemed sufficient by the board of directors, has been received, the following number of authorized shares of stock are to be issued to the following individuals:

Shareholder	Number of Shares
_____	_____
_____	_____
_____	_____
_____	_____

FIGURE 6-8 (*continued*)

> A copy of the certificate of stock proposed to be issued by the corporation was considered, and
>
> On motion, duly made, seconded, and carried, it was
>
> Resolved, that the above certificate be substantially in the following form: _____ [set out certificate of stock in full].
>
> There being no further business, the meeting was adjourned.
>
> [Signature of secretary]

FIGURE 6-8   *(continued)*

Approval and Acceptance of Articles of Incorporation   Often, as a formality, the incorporators will present to the board of directors a copy of the articles of incorporation, and report on its filing at the organizational meeting. This action should be noted by a resolution in the minutes of the meeting of the board of directors. Following is an example of a resolution that may be made by the board of directors to approve the articles of incorporation.

EXAMPLE: *Acceptance of Articles of Incorporation*

RESOLVED, that the articles of incorporation of the corporation, a copy of which is presented by the incorporator, are hereby ratified and approved. The secretary of the corporation is directed to file the articles in the corporate minute book of the corporation, along with the certificate of incorporation issued by the secretary of state, providing evidence of the filing and acceptance of the articles.

Acceptance of Stock Subscriptions   Although the MBCA does not require any paid-in capital before the commencement of business, the statutes of some states require that a certain proportion of the stock be subscribed for, or even paid in, before the commencement of corporate business. Other states may require subscription for, or payment for, a specified amount of stock as a condition precedent to corporate existence.

In any event, it is important that the statutory requirements regarding the subscription and payment for stock of the corporation be complied with at the organizational meeting. This typically involves the acceptance of subscriptions and the issuance of stock of the corporation in accordance with the subscription agreements. The names of the shareholders, number and class of shares received by the shareholders, and the consideration received by the corporation from each shareholder should be noted. A statement regarding the paid-in capital of the corporation, in accordance with state statute, should be agreed on and noted in the minutes of the meeting. Following is an example of a resolution that could be passed by the board of directors regarding the issuance of stock of the corporation.

EXAMPLE: *Issuance of Stock*

RESOLVED, that the subscriptions for the shares of the corporation dated
_____, and filed in the corporate minute book of the corporation are hereby
accepted and the amount and fair value of the consideration recited therein
are hereby approved. The corporation has received the consideration recited,
and the officers of the corporation are hereby authorized to issue to each such
subscriber, a certificate or certificates for the shares therein subscribed as
follows:

Subscriber	Number of Shares	Consideration Received
_____	_____	_____
_____	_____	_____
_____	_____	_____

The corporation, having received the minimum consideration for the
issuance of the shares of the corporation fixed in the articles of incorporation, is
duly organized and ready to commence business.

Ratification of Acts of Incorporator(s) It is usually prudent, even if not required,
for the directors of the corporation to approve and ratify the acts of the incorporator or incorporators taken on behalf of the corporation, even if those acts consisted
only of filing the articles of incorporation.

Election of Officers The directors of the corporation will elect the officers of the
corporation, which may include a chairman of the board, chief executive officer,
president, vice president or vice president(s), chief financial officer or treasurer, secretary, and any other or different officers as may be desired by the board of directors and in accordance with the statutes of the corporation's state of domicile and
the corporation's bylaws. Following is an example of a resolution that could be
passed by the directors to elect the officers of the corporation.

EXAMPLE: *Election of Officers*

RESOLVED, that the following persons are hereby elected as officers of the
corporation to assume the duties and responsibilities fixed by the Bylaws, and to
serve until their respective successors are chosen and qualify:

Chief Executive Officer: _____
President: _____
Vice President: _____
Secretary: _____
Treasurer: _____
Assistant Secretary: _____

Adoption of Bylaws The bylaws of the corporation, which are typically prepared
in advance of the organizational meeting and reviewed by all directors, should be
approved at the organizational meeting by the appropriate individuals in accordance
with state statute. Often, the bylaws are adopted by the corporation's directors and

ratified by its shareholders. Following is an example of a resolution that could be passed by the board of directors to adopt the bylaws of the corporation.

EXAMPLE: Adoption of Bylaws

That the proposed bylaws, a copy of which is filed in the corporate minute book of the corporation, are hereby adopted by the board of directors as the by-laws of the corporation, and the secretary of the corporation is hereby authorized to sign said bylaws on behalf of the corporation.

Approval of Accounting Methods The board of directors should agree upon the general accounting methods to be used by the corporation, including the fiscal year of the corporation, if a fiscal year other than the calendar year is an option.

Authorization of Appropriate Securities Filings If the corporation will be subject to any securities filings, the board of directors is generally responsible for those filings. Any potential filings should be discussed during the organizational meeting, and a resolution should be passed authorizing certain officers of the corporation to prepare and file the necessary documentation.

Approval of Form of Stock Certificate The board of directors will often approve a form of stock certificate to be used by the corporation, including any necessary restrictive legends. Following is an example of a resolution that could be passed by the board of directors to approve a form of stock certificate for use by the corporation.

EXAMPLE: Approval of Form of Stock Certificates

RESOLVED, that the form of stock certificate attached hereto as Exhibit ___ be and hereby is adopted and approved.

Adoption of Corporate Seal If a corporate seal is required by state statute, or if a seal is desired, the seal should be approved at the organizational meeting. If no corporate seal is to be used by the corporation, that should be so agreed upon and noted.

Banking Resolutions The directors of the corporation should agree on and establish a corporate bank account or bank accounts, and the terms of the bank account(s) should be determined, including the type of account(s) to be opened, where such account(s) should be opened, and who the authorized signatories on the bank account will be. Following is an example of a resolution that could be passed by the board of directors regarding the designation of a bank for corporate accounts.

EXAMPLE: Banking Resolution

RESOLVED, that the standard form of resolution of _____ Bank, with respect to checking accounts at said bank, is hereby adopted, and a copy thereof is ordered to be filed with the minutes of this meeting. The proper offi-cers are hereby authorized and directed to file the necessary papers with said bank, including the signature authorization card, with respect to said checking account.

Approval of S Corporation Election   The directors should discuss the advisability of electing to be treated as an S corporation for federal income tax purposes. If it is decided that the corporation will elect to become an S corporation, a resolution must be completed and must be approved by the directors and all shareholders. Fol-lowing is an example of a resolution that could be passed by the board of directors to approve the election of S corporation status for the corporation.

EXAMPLE: S Corporation Election

RESOLVED, that the corporation shall elect to be taxed as an S Corporation in accordance with Section 1372 of the Internal Revenue Code of 1954, as amended. The officers of the corporation are hereby authorized and directed to do all acts and to execute and file all papers, documents, and instruments necessary to cause the corporation to make such election.

Adoption of Employee Benefit Plans   Any employee benefit plans to be adopted by the corporation may be approved by the board of directors at the organizational meeting or the first meeting of the board of directors. These plans may include medical insurance plans, medical expense reimbursement plans, life insurance plans, qualified retirement plans, or any other employee benefit plans.

Shareholder Resolutions

The shareholders may be required by statute to be a part of the organizational meet-ing or to hold a different meeting referred to as the *first meeting of shareholders*. This meeting is often a part of, or held immediately following, the organizational meeting or the first meeting of the board of directors. The items discussed in this section are often considered for action by the shareholders of the corporation at their first meeting.

Election of Directors   The directors of the corporation must be elected pursuant to the statutes of the state of domicile. The statutes may permit this to be done by the incorporators if not done in the articles of incorporation, or the first board of directors may be elected or ratified by the shareholders of the corporation at the organizational meeting. Following is an example of a resolution that could be used by the shareholders of the corporation to elect the first board of directors.

EXAMPLE: Election of First Board of Directors

RESOLVED, that the following individuals, having been duly nominated, are hereby elected as the first board of directors of this corporation, to serve until the next annual meeting of the shareholders, or until their successors are elected and qualified:

    _____

    _____

    _____

    _____.

Approval of S Corporation Election For a corporation to become an S corporation, the shareholders of the corporation must unanimously approve the adoption of S corporation status and the proper documents must be signed by all shareholders.

Approval of Bylaws In most states, the directors of the corporation are granted the authority to adopt the bylaws of the corporation. However, this adoption of bylaws may be ratified by the shareholders of the corporation.

Unanimous Writings versus Minutes

Traditionally, formal organizational meetings were required by statutes in most every state. However, two changes in corporate law in recent years have made the formal organizational meeting unnecessary in certain instances.

First, the required minimum number of directors has gone from three to one in almost every state in the country. Previously, an organizational meeting of the directors was considered necessary to have a "meeting of the minds." This is obviously not necessary when there is only one director, who may also be the only shareholder of the corporation.

Second, modern corporate law typically provides for the use of unanimous writings in lieu of meetings. Unanimous writings do away with the necessity of having to give notice of and attend a formal meeting every time an action of the board of directors or shareholders is called for. Especially when the individual directors or shareholders live far apart, the use of unanimous writings can be invaluable.

In unanimous writings, the directors, or shareholders, as the case may be, waive their statutory right to notice and attendance at a meeting and agree to set forth the agreed-upon resolutions in the form of a written consent, often referred to as a *unanimous writing*. Under most circumstances, the unanimous writing must be signed and dated by all individuals entitled to notice and attendance at a meeting of the directors or shareholders. If permissible under state statute, the articles of incorporation may provide that directors' resolutions may be made by a written consent signed by the number of directors required to pass the resolution at a meeting. Under those circumstances, the signature of *all* directors may not be required. State statutes must be consulted and followed carefully if a unanimous writing is used. Figure 6-9 is a sample form of a unanimous writing in lieu of an organizational meeting.

CONSENT TO ACTION TAKEN IN LIEU OF
ORGANIZATIONAL MEETING
of

_____

The undersigned, being all of the incorporators, shareholders, and directors of the corporation, hereby consent to and ratify the actions taken to organize the corporation as hereafter stated:

The Certificate of Incorporation filed on _____, ____, with the Secretary of State of this state is hereby approved and it shall be inserted in the record book of the corporation.

The persons whose names appear below are hereby duly appointed directors of the corporation to serve for a period of one year and until their successors are appointed or elected and shall qualify:

The persons whose names appear below are hereby duly appointed officers of the corporation to serve for a period of one year and until their successors are appointed or elected and shall qualify:

President:

Vice President:

Secretary:

Treasurer:

Bylaws, regulating the conduct of the business and affairs of the corporation, as prepared by _____, counsel for the corporation, are hereby adopted and inserted in the record book.

The corporation shall have no seal.

The directors are hereby authorized to issue the unsubscribed capital stock of the corporation at such times and in such amounts as they shall determine, and to accept in payment therefor cash, labor done, personal property, real property or leases therefor, or such other property as the board may deem necessary for the business of the corporation.

The treasurer is hereby duly authorized to open a bank account with _____, located at _____, and is authorized to execute a resolution for that purpose on the printed form of said bank.

The president is hereby duly authorized to designate the principal office of the corporation in this state as the office for service of process on the corporation, and to designate such further agents for service of process within or without this state as is in the best interests of the corporation. The president is hereby further authorized to execute any and all certificates or documents to implement the above.

Dated _____

_____

_____

_____

FIGURE 6-9   Sample Unanimous Writing in Lieu of Organizational Meeting

§ 6.5 BYLAWS

Bylaws are considered the "rules and guidelines for the internal government and control of a corporation."[32] The bylaws, which are typically adopted by the board of directors, prescribe the rights and duties of the shareholders, directors, and officers with regard to the management and governance of the corporation. They are considered to be a contract between the members of a corporation and between the corporation and its members.[33]

Some state statutes specifically address the information to be contained in the bylaws. The MBCA merely states that the "bylaws of a corporation may contain any provision for managing the business and regulating the affairs of the corporation that is not inconsistent with law or the articles of incorporation."[34]

The following paragraphs discuss and show examples of some of the more common matters addressed in corporate bylaws. See appendix I-4 for a sample bylaws form.

Office of the Corporation

The bylaws typically set forth the principal office of the corporation and any other significant offices to be used by the corporation.

EXAMPLE: Principal Corporate Office

The principal office of the corporation shall be located at _____, City of _____, County of _____, State of _____. The board of directors may establish and maintain branch or subordinate offices at any other locations they deem appropriate within the State of _____.

Shareholder Meetings

Requirements for shareholder meetings are sometimes specifically set by state statute. However, details regarding the shareholder meetings are typically left to the corporation. The bylaws often set the time, place, and notice requirements for the annual meetings and the requirements for calling and holding special meetings of the shareholders. In addition, the bylaws should address the question of who is entitled to receive notice of shareholder meetings.

EXAMPLE: Annual Meetings of Shareholders

The annual meeting of the stockholders shall be held on the ___ [ordinal number] day in the month of _____ in each year, beginning with the year _____, at _____ o'clock ___.M., for the purpose of electing directors and for the transaction of such other business as may come before the meeting. If the day fixed for the annual meeting shall be a legal holiday in the State of _____, such meeting shall be held on the next succeeding business day. If the election of directors is not held on the day designated herein for any annual meeting of the shareholders, or at any adjournment thereof, the board of directors shall cause the election to be held at a special meeting of the stockholders as soon thereafter as is convenient.[35]

EXAMPLE: Special Meetings of Shareholders

Special meetings of the stockholders, for any purpose or purposes, unless otherwise prescribed by statute, may be called by the president or by the board of directors, and shall be called by the president at the request of the holders of not less than ____ [number] of all the outstanding shares of the corporation entitled to vote at the meeting.[36]

EXAMPLE: Place of Shareholder Meetings

The board of directors may designate any place within [if desired, add: or without] the State of _____, as the place of meeting for any annual meeting or for any special meeting called by the board of directors. A waiver of notice signed by all stockholders entitled to vote at a meeting may designate any place, either within or without the State of _____, as the place for the holding of such meeting. If no designation is made, or if a special meeting is otherwise called, the place of meeting shall be the principal office of the corporation in the City of _____, _____ [state].[37]

EXAMPLE: Notice of Shareholder Meetings

Written or printed notice stating the place, day, and hour of the meeting and, in case of a special meeting, the purpose or purposes for which the meeting is called, shall be delivered not less than ____ nor more than ____ days before the date of the meeting, either personally or by mail, by or at the direction of the president, or the secretary, or the officer or persons calling the meeting, to each shareholder of record entitled to vote at such meeting. If mailed, such notice shall be deemed to be delivered when deposited in the United States mail, addressed to the shareholder at his or her address as it appears on the stock transfer books of the corporation, with postage thereon prepaid. [If appropriate, add: Notice of each meeting shall also be mailed to holders of stock not entitled to vote, as herein provided, but lack of such notice shall not affect the legality of any meeting otherwise properly called and noticed.][38]

Number and Term of Directors

The bylaws often include information on the directors of the corporation, including the number of directors required, the term of office, and the qualifications of the directors.

For more flexibility, the bylaws may indicate that the number of directors will be established from time to time by the shareholders. Then, if the number of directors is increased or decreased, the action may be approved at the shareholder meeting electing the new board of directors, and it will not be necessary to amend the bylaws.

EXAMPLE: Number, Tenure, and Qualifications of Directors

The number of directors of the corporation shall be established by the shareholders of the corporation from time to time. Directors shall be elected at the annual meeting of shareholders, and the term of office of each director shall be until the next annual meeting of shareholders and the election and qualification of his or her successor. Directors need not be residents of the State of _____, and need not be shareholders of the corporation.

Meetings of the Board of Directors

The bylaws should contain information regarding the annual and special meetings of the directors, such as the time and place of the meetings, who may call the meetings, and notice requirements. The bylaws should also set a quorum of directors who may take action at a meeting.

If permitted by statute, the bylaws may also provide that meetings of the board of directors of the corporation may be transacted via telephone, or that meetings may be waived and replaced by a unanimous written consent of the directors in lieu of meeting.

EXAMPLE: Regular Meetings of Board of Directors

A regular meeting of the board of directors shall be held without notice other than this bylaw immediately after and at the same place as the annual meeting of stockholders. The board of directors may provide, by resolution, the time and place for holding additional regular meetings without other notice than such resolution. Additional regular meetings shall be held at the principal office of the corporation in the absence of any designation in the resolution.[39]

EXAMPLE: Special Meetings of Board of Directors

Special meetings of the board of directors may be called by or at the request of the president or any two directors, and shall be held at the principal office of the corporation or at such other place as the directors may determine.[40]

EXAMPLE: Notice of Board of Directors' Meetings

Notice of any special meeting shall be given at least _____ [48 hours or as the case may be] before the time fixed for the meeting, by written notice delivered personally or mailed to each director at his or her business address, or by telegram. If mailed, such notice shall be deemed to be delivered when deposited in the United States mail so addressed, with postage thereon prepaid, not less than _____ days prior to the commencement of the above-stated notice period. If notice is given by telegram, such notice shall be deemed to be delivered when the telegram is delivered to the telegraph company. Any director may waive notice of any meeting. The attendance of a director at a meeting shall constitute a waiver of notice of such meeting, except where a director attends a meeting for the express purpose of objecting to the transaction of any business because the meeting is not lawfully called or convened. Neither the business to be transacted at, nor the purpose of, any regular or special meeting of the board of directors need be specified in the notice or waiver of notice of such meeting.[41]

EXAMPLE: Quorum

A majority of the number of directors fixed by these bylaws shall constitute a quorum for the transaction of business at any meeting of the board of directors, but if less than such majority is present at a meeting, a majority of the directors present may adjourn the meeting from time to time without further notice.[42]

EXAMPLE: Board Decisions

The act of the majority of the directors present at a meeting at which a quorum is present shall be the act of the board of directors _____ [except that vote of not less than _____ (fraction) of all the members of the board shall be required for the amendment of or addition to these bylaws or as the case may be].[43]

Removal and Resignation of Directors

The bylaws should set forth the procedures for removing directors from the board, including who may remove the directors, for what cause directors may be removed, how resignations of directors are to be tendered, and how vacancies on the board of directors are to be handled.

Director Compensation

The compensation of the directors or the means for determining the directors' compensation should be set forth in the bylaws. The bylaws should also address the directors' expense reimbursement and the indemnification of directors.

Director Liability

The liability of the directors may be limited or expanded in the bylaws of the corporation, within the limits imposed by statute.

Officers

The bylaws of the corporation should name the titles of the officers that the corporation will have, define the powers and duties of each officer, and set forth the compensation for each officer, or the means for determining that compensation.

EXAMPLE: Number of Officers

The officers of the corporation shall include a chief executive officer, president, one or more vice presidents, a secretary, and a chief financial officer, each of whom shall be elected by the board of directors. Such other officers and assistant officers as may be deemed necessary may be elected or appointed by the board of directors. Any two or more offices may be held by the same person, except the offices of president and secretary.

EXAMPLE: Election and Term of Office

The officers of the corporation to be elected by the board of directors shall be elected annually at the first meeting of the board of directors held after each annual meeting of the stockholders. If the election of officers is not held at such meeting, such election shall be held as soon thereafter as is convenient. Each officer shall hold office until his or her successor has been duly elected and qualified or until his or her death or until he or she resigns or is removed in the manner hereinafter provided.[44]

EXAMPLE: Removal of Officers

Any officer elected by the board of directors may be removed by the board of directors whenever the board determines it is in the best interests of the corporation. Such removal shall be without prejudice to the contract rights, if any, of the removed officer.

EXAMPLE: Vacancies

A vacancy in any office because of death, resignation, removal, disqualification, or otherwise may be filled by the board of directors for the unexpired portion of the term.[45]

EXAMPLE: Powers and Duties of Officers

The powers and duties of the officers of the corporation shall be as provided by the board of directors. In the absence of a directive from the board of directors, the officers shall have the powers and duties customarily and usually held by like officer of corporations similar in organization and business purposes to this corporation.

Stock Certificates

The bylaws should approve a form of stock certificate for the corporation for each class or type of stock to be used, including the required signatures on each stock certificate. The bylaws should also provide the means for transfer of stock and replacement of lost, stolen, or destroyed certificates. If there is any restriction on the transfer of shares, this restriction should be set forth in the bylaws, as well as on each stock certificate.

EXAMPLE: Certificates for Shares

Certificates representing shares of the corporation shall be in such form as shall be determined by the board of directors. Such certificates shall be signed by the president or a vice-president and by the secretary or an assistant secretary. All certificates for shares shall be consecutively numbered or otherwise identified. The name and address of the person to whom the shares represented thereby are issued, with the number of shares and date of issue, shall be entered on the stock transfer books of the corporation. All certificates surrendered to the corporation for transfer shall be canceled and no new certificate shall be issued until the former certificate for a like number of shares shall have been surrendered and canceled, except that in case of a lost, destroyed, or mutilated certificate a new one may be issued therefor on such terms and indemnity to the corporation as the board of directors may prescribe.[46]

Dividends

The bylaws may provide the method for determining the dividends to be paid on the stock of the corporation, and the timing and method for payment of those dividends.

Fiscal Year

The fiscal year of the corporation should be set forth in the bylaws of the corporation.

Corporate Seal

If the corporation plans to use a corporate seal, the seal should be described or reproduced in the bylaws. If the corporation does not plan to use a corporate seal, a statement to that effect should be included.

Corporate Records

A statement should be made regarding the corporate records that are to be kept, their location, and the inspection rights of the officers, directors, and shareholders. Corporate records may include the stock certificate book, the stock transfer ledger, the minute book, and records of accounts.

Amendment of Bylaws

Procedures for amending the bylaws of the corporation, congruent with state statutes, should be set forth in the bylaws.

Signatures on Bylaws

The bylaws of the corporation are typically dated and signed by the secretary of the corporation in accordance with statute.

§ 6.6 FORMATION OF SPECIAL TYPES OF CORPORATIONS

Corporations other than business corporations are often subject to statutory incorporation requirements that differ from those prescribed for business corporations. In this section, we look at the special statutory provisions for incorporating statutory close corporations, professional corporations, and nonprofit corporations.

Statutory Close Corporations

The statutes of states that provide for statutory close corporations usually have different or additional requirements for such an entity's articles of incorporation. If a corporation is to be incorporated as a statutory close corporation, it typically must so state in its articles of incorporation.

Under the Close Corporation Supplement to the MBCA , the articles of incorporation must include a statement that the corporation is a statutory close corporation. Other provisions unique to close corporations may be required as well, and the appropriate close corporation statutes must be consulted.

Special attention must also be paid to the stock certificates and bylaws of a statutory close corporation. Close corporations are typically required to include a statement on each stock certificate indicating that the corporation is a statutory close corporation and including any pertinent restrictions on transfer of the stock of the corporation.

Bylaws may be optional for close corporations. Many of the provisions included in the bylaws of other types of corporations are included in the articles of a close corporation or in resolutions by the shareholders or directors, if the corporation has directors.

Professional Corporations

The professional corporation must be incorporated in accordance with the professional corporation act or the professional corporation supplement to the business corporation act of the state of domicile. The requirements for forming a professional corporation are generally very similar to the requirements for forming a business corporation, with the exception of the restrictions on the officers, directors, and shareholders that were discussed in Chapter 5. The name of a professional corporation often must indicate that it is a professional corporation rather than a business corporation. Figure 6-10 is a form that may be used to incorporate a professional corporation in the State of Texas.

Nonprofit Corporations

Incorporation requirements for nonprofit corporations are also set by state statute, usually a state nonprofit corporation act. Requirements will vary, although they typically resemble the business corporation incorporation requirements at least in part. Typically, requirements for the articles of incorporation of a nonprofit corporation differ from those for a business corporation, but the articles must be filed in much the same way.

§ 6.7 THE PARALEGAL'S ROLE IN CORPORATE FORMATION

The paralegal can handle almost all aspects of the incorporation process under the direction of an attorney. Given correct and complete information, the paralegal can prepare all incorporation documents, including the articles of incorporation, bylaws, and first minutes or unanimous writings of the board of directors and shareholders. The specific tasks that can be performed by the paralegal are numerous and include the following:

1. Attend initial attorney/client meeting to collect information required to complete incorporation process.

Form 203
(revised 9/00)

Return in Duplicate to:
Secretary of State
P.O. Box 13697
Austin, TX 78711-3697
FAX: 512/463-5709

Filing Fee: $300

Articles of Incorporation
Pursuant to Article
1528e
Texas Professional
Corporation Act

This space reserved for office use.

Article 1 – Corporate Name

The corporation formed is a professional corporation. The name of the corporation is as set forth below:

The name must contain one of the words of incorporation required for business corporations or an abbreviation thereof, or the phrase "Professional Corporation" or the initials "P.C." The name must not be the same as, deceptively similar to or similar to that of an existing corporate, limited liability company, or limited partnership name on file with the secretary of state. A preliminary check for "name availability" is recommended.

Article 2 – Registered Agent and Registered Office (Select and complete either A or B and complete C)

☐ A. The initial registered agent is a corporation (cannot be corporation named above) by the name of:

OR

☐ B. The initial registered agent is an individual resident of the state whose name is set forth below:

First Name	M.I.	Last Name	Suffix

C. The business address of the registered agent and the registered office address is:

Street Address	City		Zip Code
		TX	

Article 3 – Directors

The number of directors constituting the initial board of directors and the names and addresses of the person or persons who are to serve as directors until the first annual meeting of shareholders or until their successors are elected and qualified are set forth below:

Director 1: First Name	M.I.	Last Name		Suffix
Street Address	City	State	Zip Code	
Director 2: First Name	M.I	Last Name		Suffix
Street Address	City	State	Zip Code	
Director 3: First Name	M.I	Last Name		Suffix
Street Address	City	State	Zip Code	

FIGURE 6-10 Articles of Incorporation Form for Texas Professional Corporation

Article 4 – Authorized Shares

☐ A. The total number of shares the corporation has authority to issue is
and the par value of the authorized shares is $

OR (You must select and complete <u>either</u> option A or option B, <u>do not select both</u>.)

☐ B: The total number of shares the corporation is authorized to issue is
and the shares shall have no par value.

If the shares are to be divided into classes, you must set forth the designation of each class, the number of shares of each class, the par value (or statement of no par value), and the preferences, limitations, and relative rights of each class in the space provided for supplemental information on this form.

Article 5 – Initial Capitalization

The corporation will not commence business until it has received for the issuance of its shares consideration of the value of one thousand dollars ($1,000).

Article 6 – Duration

The period of duration is perpetual.

Article 7 – Purpose

The purpose for which the corporation is organized is for the rendition of the professional service set forth below (only one specific type of professional service is permitted) and services ancillary to the rendition thereto.

Supplemental Provisions/Information

Text Area

Incorporator

The name and address of the incorporator is set forth below.

Name

Street Address	City	State	Zip Code

Execution

The undersigned incorporator signs these articles of incorporation subject to the penalty imposed by article 10.02, Texas Business Corporation Act, for the submission of a false or fraudulent document.

Signature of incorporator

FIGURE 6-10 (*continued*)

2. Check name availability and prepare and file application for name reservation, if desired.

3. Prepare and file articles of incorporation.

4. Check for compliance with any publication or county recording requirements.

5. Draft corporate documents, including:
   a. Bylaws
   b. Notices of organizational meetings
   c. Minutes or unanimous writings in lieu of organizational meeting or first meeting of directors and shareholders
   d. Stock subscription agreements
   e. Stock certificates
   f. Banking resolutions

6. Assist client with obtaining any required licenses to operate business.

7. Order corporate minute book, seal, and stock certificates.

8. Organize corporate minute book.

9. Prepare stock certificates and stock ledger.

10. Follow up with client concerning corporate formalities and procedures to be followed.

Corporate Paralegal Profile
Beckie K. Mills, RP

I truly enjoy the contact I have with our clients. It is a wonderful opportunity to network with the people you need to obtain information from and complete your job in the most efficient way possible.

Name Beckie K. Mills, RP

Location Elkhart, Indiana

Title Paralegal

Specialty Corporate and Securities Law

Education Bachelors Degree in Business Administration from Ferris State University; Associates Degree in Legal Assisting from Ferris State University

Experience 13 years

Beckie Mills is a paralegal with Baker & Daniels law firm in Elkhart, Indiana. Beckie works in the smallest of Baker & Daniels six offices, which employ a total of approximately 300 attorneys and 40 paralegals. She specializes in corporate and securities law, and reports to a senior partner of the Elkhart office.

Because Beckie works in the smallest of the Baker & Daniels offices, she has a variety of responsibilities, including business incorporations, corporate maintenance, and securities matters. Beckie's incorporating responsibilities include drafting articles of incorporation, bylaws, initial minutes, and stock certificates. She also maintains the corporate minute books and prepares annual reports for about 30 corporations. Her work in the securities area includes reviewing 10-Q, 10-K, 8-K, 13-G and 13-D filings, and preparing these documents for electronic filing with the Securities and Exchange Commission. In addition, Beckie is the marketing coordinator for the Elkhart office of Baker & Daniels.

Beckie is also involved, from time to time, in corporate transaction work. She has been involved in many merger and acquisition transactions on both the buyer and seller sides, and has been responsible for due diligence, as well as preparing and organizing all of the documents necessary to successfully complete the closing in a timely manner. Beckie reports that it is very rewarding once the closing is complete and both parties are satisfied. However, it is usually a very long road to that end.

Beckie enjoys the law firm atmosphere, especially the contact she has with clients. She finds that meeting with clients is a wonderful opportunity to network with the people you serve and to obtain the information needed to complete your job in the most efficient way possible.

Although Beckie acknowledges the importance of timekeeping in a law firm environment, like many paralegals who work in law firms, she reports that her least favorite task is preparing timesheets and keeping track of her time.

Beckie has made contributions to the paralegal profession through her participation in the Michiana Paralegal Association, an association with over 100 members from the northwestern portion of Indiana and the southwestern portion of Michigan. She is currently serving her second term as vice president. She is also the chairperson of the Seminars Committee.

Beckie's advice to new paralegals?

I believe the mistake that I have seen new paralegals make the most often is not feeling comfortable enough with the attorney they work for to ask enough questions when they receive a project. Some of this is lack of experience—not knowing what questions to ask—however, most of the time it appears that they are intimidated by the attorney. It is my belief that the attorneys will respect you more if you simply ask the questions at the beginning of the project rather than attempting to do the project without all of the pertinent information. It is also important that you have a paralegal mentor either in the law firm or corporation you work for or in your local paralegal association. My final piece of advice is that you must be organized, organized, organized!

For more information on careers for corporate paralegals, see the Corporate Careers features on the companion Web page to this text at **www.westlegalstudies.com.**

Initial Client Meeting   The corporate paralegal will often attend the initial attorney/client meeting. The paralegal may take notes using a customized checklist to collect the information discussed in § 6.1 of this chapter. The paralegal is often introduced as the contact person to answer procedural questions the client may have during the incorporation process.

Reserve Corporate Name   If it is determined that the corporate name must be reserved, the paralegal will often assume that responsibility. The paralegal must be familiar with the state procedures for reserving corporate names. It is very important that the corporate name be reserved promptly, as the client may be taking actions (such as ordering letterhead and supplies) on the assumption that the corporate name will be available.

Prepare Articles of Incorporation and Other Incorporation Documents   The paralegal will often assume responsibility for preparing the initial draft of the articles of incorporation and other incorporation documents for the attorney's review and approval, using the information learned during the initial client meeting and form books or standard forms that are used by the office.

Filing Articles of Incorporation   The paralegal is often responsible for filing the articles of incorporation and any other required documents with the secretary of state. Each state has its own unique filing requirements, and it is imperative that the paralegal be familiar with those requirements. Figure 6-11 provides a sample checklist of all tasks that must be completed in the incorporation process.

This is just a sample list. The exact steps to be taken, and the order in which they will be taken, will depend on the jurisdiction and other circumstances.

- ☐ Select corporate name.
- ☐ Check name availability and reserve name if necessary.
- ☐ Prepare articles of incorporation.
- ☐ Prepare designation of registered agent (in jurisdictions where required).
- ☐ File articles of incorporation and any other accompanying documents required in jurisdiction.
- ☐ Record articles of incorporation (in jurisdictions where required).
- ☐ Provide for publication of notice of incorporation (in jurisdictions where required).
- ☐ Prepare bylaws.
- ☐ Order corporate minute book and other supplies needed, including corporate seal and stock certificates.
- ☐ Prepare stock subscriptions and stock certificates.
- ☐ Prepare minutes of organizational meeting, or unanimous written resolution in lieu of organizational meeting.
- ☐ Prepare S corporation election (if desired).
- ☐ Prepare any required employment agreements or shareholder agreements.
- ☐ Prepare applications for certificates of authority to transact business as a foreign corporation.
- ☐ Calendar any dates that will be important to corporation.

FIGURE 6-11   Incorporation Checklist

§ 6.8 RESOURCES

The resources that the paralegal will find useful when working on the formation of a corporation include the state statutes, information from the secretary of state, legal form books, Internet resources, and incorporation services.

State Statutes

As discussed in this chapter, incorporation requirements for business corporations are found in the business corporation act of the statutes of the corporation's state of domicile.

Secretary of State

The articles or certificate of incorporation must be filed with the secretary of state or other appropriate state official. The secretary of state's office must be contacted to ascertain the appropriate forms to use, current filing fees, and specific instructions for filing articles of incorporation and other incorporation documents. Most secretary of state offices have Web pages that include the appropriate forms for downloading, current schedules of filing fees, and detailed filing instructions.

Some states are beginning to accept articles of incorporation and other corporate documents via facsimile or e-mail, with payment made by credit card or by means of a pre-established account with the secretary of state. This service is not available in all states, however. Most states offer the option of downloading the proper forms from the secretary of state's Web page. These downloaded forms can be completed and either mailed or delivered to the appropriate office for filing. (See appendix A for a secretary of state directory.)

Form Books

In addition to the forms typically found within law firms or corporate law departments, numerous forms and form books are available to assist with the drafting of incorporation documents, including those mentioned in Chapter 5. Web pages offering free forms to download may also be helpful in preparing incorporation documents. However, when using generic forms for incorporating, it is important to use state-specific forms, when available, or to make allowances for specific state requirements when using other forms.

Incorporation Services

There are several businesses that assist attorneys and lay persons with the formation of corporations. These services usually have the ability to incorporate businesses in any state in the country within a very short time period. These services may be useful to paralegals who need to form a corporation in a distant state quickly. For the names of services in your location, you can consult your telephone directory, search the Internet, or ask for referrals from attorneys and other paralegals.

 Internet Resources www.

There are several on-line resources to assist paralegals with the incorporation process. Some of these resources include general information on the incorporation process, on-line corporate statutes, and secretary of state Web pages.

Following is a list of some Web pages that may be useful to paralegals who are assisting with the incorporation process:

For links to state incorporation forms

Findlaw.com State Corporation   **www.findlaw.com/11stategov/indexcorp.html**
  and Business Forms

For links to the secretary of state offices

Corporate Housekeeper	**www.danvi.vi/link2.html**
National Association of Secretaries of State	**www.nass.org**

An alphabetical list of Internet Resources for the Corporate Paralegal is included as appendix B to this text.

Web Page

For updates and links to several of the previously listed sites, as well as download-able state incorporation forms, log on to **www.westlegalstudies.com**, and click through to the book link for this text.

SUMMARY

- Corporations do not exist until they are properly incorporated pursuant to state statute.

- The corporation's state of domicile is the state where the corporation is incorporated.

- At times, corporations may have a *promoter*, an individual who organizes, promotes, and forms the corporation.

- When the incorporation is complex and may take a considerable amount of time, the initial shareholders may enter into a preincorporation agreement to formal-ize their understanding about the formation of the corporation.

- A stock subscription is an agreement to purchase shares of stock of a corporation at an agreed-upon price.

- The incorporator is the individual who actually signs the incorporation docu-ments. The incorporator may not have an active role in the corporation after it is formed. At times, the corporation's attorney acts as incorporator.

- The document filed at the state level to form the corporation is usually referred to as the articles of incorporation or certificate of incorporation.

- Requirements for the articles of incorporation are established by state statute, but usually require the document to include (at a minimum) the corporation's name, number of authorized shares, street address of a registered office, and name and address of each incorporator.

- An organizational meeting of the initial shareholders and directors is often held immediately following the incorporation of the company.

- The initial board of directors is either named in the articles of incorporation or elected by the shareholders at the organizational meeting.

- The bylaws are considered the rules and guidelines for the internal control of the corporation. Most corporations are required to have bylaws.

◆ Shareholders and directors take actions by passing resolutions at meetings pursuant to the corporation's bylaws and state statute.

◆ Under some circumstances, the shareholders and directors may take action by means of a unanimous written consent or a consent signed by the number of shareholders or directors required to take the action.

REVIEW QUESTIONS

1. Under what circumstances are corporations bound to contracts made by the promoter prior to incorporation?

2. Can two individuals from New York form a Florida corporation?

3. If two residents of Texas file articles of incorporation in New York and transact the majority of their business in Florida, what is their state of domicile?

4. In addition to filing articles of incorporation, what incorporation formalities are imposed by some states before the incorporation process is complete?

5. Can the incorporator also be a director of a corporation?

6. What required provisions must be included in the articles of incorporation in a state following the Model Business Corporation Act?

7. Why is it advisable to gather more information from the client than the minimum required for the incorporation documents?

8. Why might it be preferable to put information in the bylaws, as opposed to the articles of incorporation, when the statute provides that the information could be in either document?

9. Would the name "Johnson Brothers Furniture Store" be a valid corporate name in a state following the Model Business Corporation Act? Why or why not?

10. When must the incorporator(s) attend the organizational meeting?

PRACTICAL PROBLEMS

1. Find the pertinent incorporation statute in your state to answer the following questions:
   a. What is the name of the document filed to form a corporation in your state?
   b. What is the minimum information required for that document?

2. What is the name of the state agency in your state that accepts incorporation documents for filing?

3. What are the basic procedures for filing incorporation documents in your state? What documents must be filed? How can that filing be accomplished? What is the filing fee for incorporation documents?

WORKPLACE SCENARIO

Assume, once again, that you are a paralegal for a corporate law firm. Our fictional clients, Bradley Harris and Cynthia Lund, have just met with your supervising attorney, Belinda Benson. Belinda has advised them to have their business, Cutting Edge Computer Repair, incorporated. Using the information in appendix D-3, prepare articles of incorporation and any other document required for filing with the appropriate state office in your state to form a corporation. Also prepare a cover letter with accompanying filing fee. Note that for the workplace scenario in Chapter 5 this incorporation had already taken place.

END NOTES

1. 18 AM. JUR. 2d *Corporations* § 98 (1985).
2. *Id.* § 99.
3. *Id.* § 100.
4. *Id.* § 162.
5. Revised Model Business Corporation Act § 2.01.
6. Alaska, Hawaii, Maryland, Minnesota, Missouri, New York, North Dakota, South Dakota, and Vermont have statutory provisions requiring that the incorporator or incorporators be natural persons.
7. Revised Model Business Corporation Act § 2.02(a)(1).
8. *Id.* § 2.02(a)(2).
9. *Id.* § 2.02(a)(3).
10. *Id.* § 2.02(a)(4).
11. Minimum required information under Revised Model Business Corporation Act § 2.02(a)(2).
12. 6 AM. JUR. Legal Forms 2d *Corporations* § 74:991 (Rev. 1995).
13. Minimum Required information under Revised Model Business Corporation Act § 2.02(a)(3).
14. Revised Model Business Corporation Act § 2.02(b)(1).
15. *Id.* § 2.02(b)(2)(i).
16. *Id.* § 2.02(b)(2)(ii).
17. *Id.* § 2.02(b)(2)(iii).
18. *Id.* § 2.02(b)(2)(iv).
19. *Id.* § 2.02(b)(2)(v).
20. *Id.* § 2.02(b)(3).
21. *Id.* § 2.02(b)(4).
22. *Id.* § 2.02(b)(5).
23. 18A AM. JUR. 2d *Corporations* § 204 (1985).
24. Revised Model Business Corporation Act § 2.02 Official Comment (1999).
25. *Id.* § 8.21(a).
26. *Id.* § 7.28(b).
27. *Id.* § 8.08(a).
28. *Id.* § 6.01.
29. *Id.* § 6.30.
30. Georgia and Pennsylvania have publication requirements for incorporating in those states.
31. Alabama, Illinois, Kentucky, Louisiana, New York, and West Virginia all have requirements for filing the articles of incorporation or a copy thereof at the county or local level.
32. 18A AM. JUR. 2d *Corporations* § 310 (1985).
33. *Id.* § 313.
34. Revised Model Business Corporation Act § 2.06.
35. 6 AM. JUR. Legal Forms 2d *Corporations* § 74:991 (1995).
36. *Id.* Reprinted with permission from *American Jurisprudence Legal Forms 2d.* © 2000 West Group.
37. *Id.* Reprinted with permission from *American Jurisprudence Legal Forms 2d.* © 2000 West Group.
38. *Id.* Reprinted with permission from *American Jurisprudence Legal Forms 2d.* © 2000 West Group.
39. *Id.* Reprinted with permission from *American Jurisprudence Legal Forms 2d.* © 2000 West Group.
40. *Id.* Reprinted with permission from *American Jurisprudence Legal Forms 2d.* © 2000 West Group.
41. *Id.* Reprinted with permission from *American Jurisprudence Legal Forms 2d.* © 2000 West Group.
42. *Id.* Reprinted with permission from *American Jurisprudence Legal Forms 2d.* © 2000 West Group.
43. *Id.* Reprinted with permission from *American Jurisprudence Legal Forms 2d.* © 2000 West Group.
44. *Id.* Reprinted with permission from *American Jurisprudence Legal Forms 2d.* © 2000 West Group.
45. *Id.* Reprinted with permission from *American Jurisprudence Legal Forms 2d.* © 2000 West Group.
46. *Id.* Reprinted with permission from *American Jurisprudence Legal Forms 2d.* © 2000 West Group.

CHAPTER 7

The Corporate Organization

CHAPTER OUTLINE

§ 7.1   Authority and Duties of Directors

§ 7.2   Personal Liability of Directors

§ 7.3   Compensation and Indemnification of Directors

§ 7.4   Election and Term of Directors

§ 7.5   Board of Directors Meetings and Resolutions

§ 7.6   Corporate Officers

§ 7.7   Shareholders' Rights and Responsibilities

§ 7.8   Shareholder Meetings

§ 7.9   Restrictions on Transfer of Shares of Corporate Stock

§ 7.10   Shareholder Actions

§ 7.11   The Paralegal's Role in Corporate Organizational Matters

§ 7.12   Resources

INTRODUCTION

A corporate entity must act through its agents, the most visible agents being its officers and directors. The officers, directors, and shareholders may play very different roles, but each functions as an integral part of the operation of the business corporation. This chapter discusses the role of each type of member of the corporation, beginning with the authority, duties, liabilities, and compensation of the directors of the corporation. It examines how they are elected and how they act through directors' meetings. Next we investigate the officers, who are elected by the directors of the corporation, and follow with a study of the rights and responsibilities of the shareholders of the corporation, and how they participate in the corporate affairs through shareholder meetings. We then take a brief look at the restrictions that may be placed on the transfer of shares of corporate stock. This chapter concludes with a discussion of the paralegal's role in corporate organizational matters and the resources available to assist paralegals working in that area.

§ 7.1 AUTHORITY AND DUTIES OF DIRECTORS

Directors are given the statutory authority to make most decisions regarding the operation of the corporation, and it may appear that they have a free rein to operate the corporation as they see fit. However, it is important to remember that, although directors have full authority in most matters, they are elected by the shareholders of the corporation. The director who does not serve what the shareholders feel to be their best interests could be voted out of office at the next election, or even removed before his or her term expires. In this section we will look at both the authority and the duties of corporate directors.

Directors' Authority

It has been said that the "corporate board of directors, exercising their reasonable and good faith business judgment, possess the paramount right to corporate control and management."[1] The corporation, in effect, acts through its directors. Most corporations are required to have a board of directors.

Directors have statutory authority to act for the corporation. Corporate control is granted to the board of directors except as may otherwise be provided in the corporation's articles of incorporation. Section 8.01(b) of the Model Business Corporation Act (MBCA) represents the common statutory grant of authority to a corporation's board of directors:

> (b) All corporate powers shall be exercised by or under the authority of, and the business and affairs of the corporation managed under the direction of, its board of directors, subject to any limitation set forth in the articles of incorporation or in an agreement authorized under section 7.32.

In addition to granting the board of directors the authority to manage the business and affairs of the corporation, the MBCA, like most state business corporation acts, grants the board of directors the authority to delegate the management of the business and affairs of the corporation.

Delegation of Authority to Officers Directors generally are given the authority to appoint officers and to delegate certain authority to them. Under the MBCA, the business affairs of the corporation may be managed "under the direction of" the board of directors. This recognizes the fact that the directors of the corporation, alone, are often not the appropriate individuals to run the day-to-day business of the corporation. Directors are frequently employed outside the corporation, or have other interests that make demands on their time. Some individuals serve on the boards of several corporations.

There is a difference between the delegation of authority and power and the delegation of responsibility. It is generally accepted that, although the board of directors may delegate authority to corporate officers, the board must continue to exercise general supervision over their activities. The directors of a corporation may not delegate to others those duties that lie at the "heart of the management of the corporation."[2] Directors are generally responsible for the acts of the officers whom they appoint.

The powers delegated to the officers of the corporation may be very broad, or they may be set forth very specifically in the articles or bylaws of the corporation, or by director resolution. The extent to which the officers are directed and limited in their authority by the board of directors will depend on the statutes of the corporation's state of domicile and the governing instruments of the corporation.

Delegation of Authority to Committees Directors also commonly delegate authority to one or more committees that are comprised of members of the board of directors. With the complexities of managing a modern business, groups such as executive committees, nominating committees, finance committees, public affairs committees, audit committees, and litigation committees are often appointed to oversee specific areas of concern.

The authority of directors to appoint committees may come from the statutes of the corporation's state of domicile, or the articles or bylaws of the corporation. Under the MBCA, the board of directors is granted the authority to create committees, unless the articles of incorporation or bylaws of the corporation provide otherwise. The creation of the committee and the appointment of its members must be approved by a majority of the board of directors, unless a larger number is required for a **quorum** under the articles of incorporation or bylaws of the corporation.

The only authority that a committee has to act on behalf of the corporation is the authority delegated to it by the board of directors, or as authorized in the articles of incorporation or bylaws of the corporation. Restrictions on the authority of the committee and the powers that may be delegated to it are often found in the state statutes. Additional restrictions may be imposed by the articles or bylaws of the corporation. The MBCA specifically states that a committee may not do any of the following:

1. Authorize dividends or distributions to the shareholders of the corporation.[3]
2. Approve or propose to shareholders action that the MBCA requires to be approved by shareholders.[4]
3. Fill vacancies on the board of directors or on any of its committees.[5]
4. Amend the articles of incorporation.[6]
5. Adopt, amend, or repeal bylaws.[7]
6. Approve a plan of merger that does not require shareholder approval.[8]
7. Authorize or approve reacquisition of shares, except according to a formula or method prescribed by the board of directors.[9]
8. Authorize or approve the issuance, sale, or contract for sale of shares, or determine the designation and relative rights, preferences, and limitations of a class or series of shares, except that the board of directors may authorize a

---

quorum The number of persons who must be present to make the votes and other actions of a group (such as a board) valid. This number is often a majority (over half) of the whole group, but is sometimes much less or much more.

committee (or a senior executive officer of the corporation) to do so within limits specifically prescribed by the board of directors.[10]

Limitations on Directors' Authority The state statutes generally grant full authority to the board of directors to manage the business and affairs of the corporation. However, that authority may be limited in the articles of incorporation of the corporation. In addition, certain corporate acts, not considered to be within the ordinary business and administration of the corporation, may require approval of the shareholders of the corporation. This restriction on the directors' actions may be either a statutory restriction or a restriction in the corporation's articles of incorporation.

Following is a list of actions that often require shareholder approval:

1. Amendment and restatement of the articles of incorporation.
2. Enactment, amendment, or repeal of bylaws.
3. Issuance of stock of the corporation.
4. Dissolution of the corporation.
5. Calling of shareholder meetings.
6. Approval of merger and consolidation plans.
7. Sale of corporate assets other than in the regular course of business.

Directors' Duties

The duties of a director to the corporation are several and complex. Directors' duties often are based on common law that has been upheld by numerous court cases, as well as specific statutes dealing with the duty of directors to the corporation.

In general, directors owe the following types of duties to the corporation and its shareholders:

1. A director's fiduciary duty to the corporation and its shareholders.
2. A director's duty of care to the corporation and its shareholders.
3. A director's duty of loyalty to the corporation and its shareholders.

Fiduciary Duty One duty owed to a corporation and its shareholders by the directors has been compared to a fiduciary duty. It is probably more accurate to refer to the relationship as a quasi-fiduciary relationship—one that has several but not all of the elements of an actual fiduciary relationship.

The duty of the director to the corporation and its shareholders resembles a fiduciary duty in that the entire management of corporate affairs is often entrusted to the directors of the corporation, who are responsible for acting in the best interests of the corporation and the shareholders.

In numerous court cases, courts have defined the directors' "quasi-fiduciary" relationship to the corporation and its shareholders as follows:

> They are required to act in the utmost good faith, and in accepting the office, they impliedly undertake to give to the enterprise the benefit of their care

and best judgment and to exercise the powers conferred solely in the interest of the corporation or the stockholders as a body or corporate entity, and not for their own personal interests.[11]

A director who acts contrary to the best interests of the corporation for his or her own personal gain is breaching his or her fiduciary duty to the corporation. Shareholders have the expectation of sharing in the profits of the corporation, and when a director is personally benefited at the expense of the corporation, the director breaches his or her duty to the shareholders of the corporation by depriving them of the full potential profit from the corporation.[12]

Dividends ◆

White-Collar Criminals: Trading in Cuff Links for Hand Cuffs

Not all thieves wear ski masks and carry guns. Each year, white-collar criminals steal millions of dollars from United States citizens and businesses. White-collar crime includes various nonviolent crimes such as theft, fraud, insider trading, embezzlement, bribery, racketeering, and other forms of theft that involve the violation of trust.

Because of the nature of white-collar crime, statistics are hard to come by. Even the Federal Bureau of Investigation admits that there are no accurate tallies of the number of white-collar crimes committed each year in the United States. However, one recent report of the Association of Certified Fraud Examiners estimated that white-collar workers now misappropriate more than $400 billion per year from their organizations. They calculate this amount equals approximately 6% of the annual revenue of the employing organizations.* See Figure 7-1 for approximate statistics on who commits white-collar crime.

There is little public tolerance for white-collar crime. Responses to a recent survey by the National White Collar Crime Center[†] indicate that violations by those in positions of authority or public trust are treated as more serious offenses than if they were committed by ordinary citizens. According to the survey results, "The public tends to believe that those committing fraud are not likely to be apprehended and if they are, they are not likely to receive the punishment they 'deserve'."

Due in large part to the substantial losses and public outrage caused by white-collar crime, more and more federal resources are being allocated to combating the problem. Increasing emphasis is

being placed on the criminal prosecution of corporate executives and of corporations. Corporations, as separate entities, can be charged with crimes. See Figure 7-2 for a breakdown of who is responsible for losses and the magnitude of those losses.

While losses due to white-collar crime are of great concern to corporate executives, so is the increasing federal prosecution of white-collar crime, and possible criminal liability for corporate executives. White-collar crime can be doubly dangerous for the corporation and its executives. Not only can corporate executives face personal prosecution for crimes committed by the corporation, but the corporation can also be liable for crimes committed by its executives.

Corporate executives who commit white-collar crimes such as insider trading or fraud may face severe penalties, including fines and imprisonment. Corporations that are implicated in white-collar crime face federal sentencing guidelines that provide for corporate fines of up to $500 million under certain circumstances. The 1990s saw several fines and settlements in excess of $100 million stemming from criminal charges against corporations. For example, Archer Daniels Midland was assessed a fine in excess of $100 million for price fixing in 1992. In addition, two of its top executives were sentenced to more than two years in prison for their part in the conspiracy. In 1996, Daiwa Bank received a record fine of $340 million for fraud.

Although corporate attorneys are generally not too concerned with criminal law, they are becoming increasingly aware of the criminal liability risks faced by their corporate clients. Many are assisting their

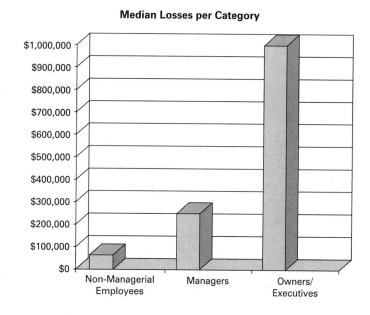

FIGURE 7-1 Who Commits White Collar Crime? (Fraud and Abuse). From the FBI Web page, quoting a report of the Association of Fraud Examiners, **http://trac.syr.edu/tracfbi/ findings/ geoData/fbiwhitecollar.html.**

FIGURE 7-2 Who is Responsible for Losses?

corporate clients in taking a proactive stance to prevent criminal liability by enacting corporate compliance programs. Under the U.S. Federal Sentencing Guidelines issued in 1991, consideration is given to corporations that have implemented an effective corporate compliance program.

The seven elements of an effective corporate compliance program are:

1. Compliance standards and procedures reasonably capable of reducing the prospect of misconduct by corporate executives and employees must be instituted.

2. Specific high-level personnel must be assigned to oversee the compliance.

3. Due care must be given in the delegation of authority.

4. Standards and procedures must be effectively communicated to all employees.

5. Reasonable compliance measures, such as monitoring, auditing and reporting systems, must be implemented.

6. There must be consistent enforcement through corrective actions.

7. All reasonable and appropriate steps must be taken to respond after an offense has been detected.[‡]

Corporate compliance plans are designed to deter and detect activity that may be grounds for both criminal and civil liability. In addition, if the corporation is found guilty of criminal wrongdoing, the fine imposed on the corporation may be reduced if an effective compliance program is in place.

---

[*] Association of Certified Fraud Examiners, *News & Facts*, **http://www.cfenet.com/newsandfacts... dfacts/fraudstatistics/index.shtml** (October 2000).

[†] Preliminary Survey Results of survey by National White Collar Crime Center, **www.nw3c.org/ monograph.htm** (October 2000).

[‡] Basari, Carole, Self-Policing Compliance Workshop: "Best Practices" to Detect and Prevent Fraud, *Practising Law Institute Corporate Law and Practice Handbook Series* (May 2000).

In *Weatherby v. Weatherby Lumber Company,* the court found that the defendant, who was an officer and director of the defendant corporation, breached his fiduciary duty to his brother and sister, who were also shareholders of the corporation, by purchasing their stock in the corporation without disclosing to them that negotiations for the sale of the corporation were underway.

CASE

Ermal WEATHERBY and
Chloe Weatherby Johnson,
Plaintiffs, Respondents and Cross-Appellants,
v.
WEATHERBY LUMBER COMPANY, Inc.,
and William Weatherby,
Defendants, Appellants and
Cross-Respondents.

No. 10439.
Supreme Court of Idaho.
Jan. 6, 1972.

McQUADE, Chief Justice.

The defendant, William Weatherby, originally entered into the lumber business in 1943 with his father. He and his father continued in business until 1946, at which time his father died. The business at that time was worth approximately $1,500 and the father and son each had ½ interest. The defendant son continued in the lumber business, and in 1953, the defendant incorporated the Weatherby Lumber Company and issued 177 shares to himself and 140 shares to Sarah Weatherby, his mother. This evidently was to represent the share of the business owned by the deceased father.

The plaintiffs, Ermal Weatherby and Chloe Weatherby Johnson and the defendant William Weatherby are brothers and sister. The case involves three corporations—the Weatherby Lumber Company, the Weatherby Planing Company, and the Weatherby Logging Company, all of which were incorporated in the early 1950's. Indirectly, another corporation called Weatherby Ranches, Inc., is involved.

Defendant William Weatherby was the majority stockholder of the lumber company and the sole stockholder of the planing, logging and ranch companies. Defendant Weatherby owned 55.8% of the lumber company and the plaintiffs each owned 22.1%, having inherited the stock from their mother. Defendant William Weatherby was the manager and director of each of the corporations involved. ... Neither Ermal nor Chloe took an active part in the management of the corporation.

Defendant William Weatherby purchased the stock of the plaintiffs (his brother and sister) in the lumber company. However, defendant William failed to disclose to his brother or his brother's attorney-agent or his sister, who was not represented by counsel, that a possible sale of that corporation was being negotiated. William was negotiating a package sale of the three lumber related corporations. ...

During the negotiations for the sale of stock William made no disclosure to either his brother Ermal or Ermal's attorney-agent regarding the possible sale of the assets of the lumber company.

Defendant William sold the Weatherby Planing Company and the Weatherby Lumber Company in which his brother and sister had an interest to the Boise Cascade Corporation. The result was one lump sale's proceeds amount without allocation of the proceeds among the various corporations ...

The trial court held that the defendant breached his fiduciary duty to disclose the pending sale negotiation at the time he purchased the plaintiffs' stock. To determine the value of the stock the trial court used the book value method. The trial court determined that each of the plaintiffs was entitled to $28,258.51 or 22.1% of the sale proceeds of $127,866.00 it allocated to the lumber company. Because Ermal had been paid $15,490.00 for his shares, the trial court awarded judgment in his favor in the amount of $12,768.51. Chloe received $25,000.00 for her interest from William and she was therefore awarded $3,258.57.

The defendant has assigned error to the trial court finding that a fiduciary relation existed between he and his brother. The defendant's appeal is not from that portion of the judgment regarding his sister. ...

I.

We will deal initially with the defendants' appeal. Defendants have first assigned error to the trial court's finding that a confidential or fiduciary relationship existed between the plaintiff, Ermal Weatherby, and the defendant William Weatherby. A pertinent statute is I.C. § 30-142 which states that:

> 'Officers and directors shall be deemed to stand in a fiduciary relation to the corporation, and shall discharge the duties of their respective positions in good faith, and with that diligence, care and skill which ordinarily prudent men would exercise under similar circumstances in like positions.'

... In Idaho a director has a fiduciary responsibility to both the corporation and to shareholders. Failure of defendant William to disclose the negotiations for the sale and liquidation of the assets of the lumber corporation was a breach of his fiduciary responsibility to the other stockholders. The case of Fox v. Cosgriff, under facts similar to the case at bar, stated that:

> '(I)t was the duty of appellants, and particularly Thamm, as director and cashier, to disclose the fact that the bank was being liquidated, or in the course of negotiations looking to its liquidation which, if consummated, would result in enhancing the value of the stock.'

Appellants next assign error to the trial court's finding that there was a duty of disclosure of the information concerning negotiations for a sale which had not been finalized. The fact that negotiations with Boise Cascade had not been finalized is immaterial to the issue of failure to disclose. The duty to disclose was breached when William Weatherby purchased the shares of stock from his brother and sister without disclosing the negotiations for sale, the culmination of which would result in enhancing the value of the stock. The duty was breached at that point; it was immaterial whether or not the sale was finalized.

The next point relates to appellants' allegation that a fiduciary duty to disclose is suspended when a minority shareholder employs counsel. Persons dealing with an agent of a disclosed principal must act toward the agent the same as though the principal himself were personally involved. A third person is liable to the principal for any alleged wrongs practiced upon the agent, including misrepresentations or breach of any duty imposed by law. The fact that an agent is acting on behalf of a disclosed principal does not affect any rights, liabilities, or duties as between the principal and the purchaser. ...

The trial court's holding that defendant William Weatherby bears liability for breach of fiduciary duty is affirmed on appeal.

McFADDEN, J., and SCOGGIN and LODGE, DJJ., concur.

Duty of Care Directors must use "due care" and be diligent in the management and administration of the affairs of the corporation and in the use or preservation of its property.[13] The exact measure of the degree of care that must be exercised is difficult to define, although one test often used is the *ordinarily prudent person test,* which means acting with the diligence and care that would be exercised by an ordinarily prudent person in like circumstances. The director's duty of care can be measured, in part, by the time and attention he or she devotes to the affairs of the corporation and the skill and judgment he or she uses in business decisions. The following list indicates typical actions of directors who would generally be considered to be acting in the manner of a prudent person:[14]

1. Attend board meetings and committee meetings on a regular basis.

2. Read, understand, and act on (when necessary) information received between the meetings of the board of directors, including minutes of past meetings, proposed agendas, proposals, and financial statements.

3. Participate in discussions of the board of directors.

4. Make independent inquiries when needed.

5. Make objections when warranted.

6. Review stockholder reports.

The MBCA, which defines the general standards for directors, indicates that the directors must discharge their duties:

(1) In good faith.[15]

(2) In a manner [they] reasonably believe to be in the best interests of the corporation.[16]

(3) With the care that a person in a like position would reasonably believe appropriate under similar circumstances.[17]

Duty of Loyalty   Numerous times courts have found that a director "must remain loyal to the corporation, acting at all times in the best interests of the corporation and its shareholders and unhampered by any personal pecuniary gain."[18] Directors must at all times act in a manner that serves the best interest of the corporation, as opposed to a director's other interests or the director's personal interests. Directors who are also directors of related corporations or have interests in related businesses may find themselves in a position of a potential conflict of interest from time to time. Directors should abstain from participating in corporate decisions that might give even the appearance of a conflict of interest. Statutes modeled after the MBCA with regard to director conflicts of interest require that directors disclose the existence and nature of potential conflicting interests and all known material facts with regard to the decision as to whether to proceed with the proposed transaction.

Reliance upon Information from Others   Directors cannot reasonably be expected to have firsthand knowledge of all business affairs of the corporation for which they are responsible. For that reason, it is assumed that directors are entitled to rely upon information given to them and statements made to them by those who are in immediate charge of the corporation's business. Under § 8.30 of the MBCA, if directors have no knowledge that makes their reliance unwarranted, they are entitled to rely on information, opinions, reports, or statements, including financial statements and other financial data, prepared or presented by:

(1) one or more officers or employees of the corporation whom the director reasonably believes to be reliable and competent in the functions performed or the information, opinions, reports or statements provided;

(2) legal counsel, public accountants, or other persons retained by the corporation as to matters involving skills or expertise the director reasonably believes are matters (i) within the particular person's professional or expert competence or (ii) as to which the particular person merits confidence; or

(3) a committee of the board of directors of which the director is not a member if the director reasonably believes the committee merits confidence.

§ 7.2 PERSONAL LIABILITY OF DIRECTORS

The imposition of personal liability on corporate directors for poor business decisions would be an impractical, if not impossible, task. Directors generally cannot be held personally liable for any damages caused to the corporation as the result of decisions made by them in good faith.

However, there are several instances in which personal liability may be imposed. Under certain conditions, personal liability is imposed on the directors of a corporation by statute, unless the corporation's articles of incorporation provide otherwise. It is, therefore, important that the incorporators of a business be well informed regarding the potential for director liability, and that the incorporation documents be drafted accordingly.

This section discusses application of the business judgment rule to corporate directors. It also considers the risk of personal liability to directors under certain circumstances.

Business Judgment Rule

The courts have recognized for years that the decisions made by directors involve a certain amount of risk, and that even an informed, good faith decision can still result in an unfavorable outcome for the corporation.

Because it would be unfair for officers and directors to be held personally liable for poor outcomes of informed decisions made in good faith, the courts have looked to the **business judgment rule** in deciding such cases. The business judgment rule is a standard of judicial review that provides that officers and directors will not be held personally liable for honest, careful decisions within their corporate powers.

The *business judgment rule*, provides that:

A corporate transaction that involves no self-dealing by, or other personal interest of, the directors who authorized the transaction will not be enjoined or set aside for the directors' failure to satisfy the standards that govern a director's performance of his or her duties, and directors who authorized the transaction will not be held personally liable for resultant damages, unless:

(1) The directors did not exercise due care to ascertain the relevant and available facts before voting to authorize the transaction; or
(2) The directors voted to authorize the transaction even though they did not reasonably believe or could not have reasonably believed the transaction to be for the best interest of the corporation; or

---

business judgment rule   The principle that if persons running a corporation make honest, careful decisions within their corporate powers, no court will interfere with these decisions even if the results are bad.

(3) In some other way, the directors' authorization of the transaction was not in good faith.[19]

Courts have held that the business judgment rule "bars inquiry into actions of corporate directors taken in good faith and in the exercise of honest judgment in the lawful and legitimate furtherance of corporate purposes."[20] However, courts have also made it clear that the rule will not be applied in cases where the good faith or oppressive conduct of the officers and directors is in question.[21]

Imposition of Personal Liability on Directors

As we have discussed, personal liability is generally not imposed on corporate directors for their poor business decisions. However, the amount of litigation involving personal liability of directors in recent years is indicative of the many exceptions to that rule.

Breach of Fiduciary Duty, Duty of Due Care, or Duty of Loyalty   A director who fails in his or her fiduciary duty, duty of due care, or duty of loyalty to the corporation may be subject to the imposition of personal liability for any damages caused to the corporation or the shareholders of the corporation.

Unauthorized Acts   When directors clearly act beyond the scope of their authority, personal liability may be imposed upon them for losses to the corporation caused by their unauthorized acts. Directors acting beyond the scope of their authority may be required to make good any losses caused by their acts out of their personal assets.

Negligence   Directors are personally liable for their negligent acts that involve injury or loss to the corporation or to third parties. Personal liability of the directors for negligent acts is based on the common law rule "which renders every agent liable who violates his authority or neglects his duty to the damage of his principal."[22]

Fraud or Other Illegal Acts   Directors may also be personally liable to the corporation and to third parties for any fraudulent or other **tortious** acts committed by them, or by the corporation with their knowledge. Corporate directors are not personally liable for fraud involving the corporation that they were unaware of, if they should not have reasonably been expected to be aware of it.

Statutory Imposition of Personal Liability   State statutes or the articles of incorporation of a corporation, or both, may specify that the directors of a corporation are personally liable for certain actions. Under the MBCA, directors may be held personally liable for the payment of distributions in violation of state statutes or the articles of incorporation.

---

tortious   Wrongful. A civil (as opposed to a criminal) wrong [tort], other than a breach of contract. For an act to be a tort, there must be: a legal duty owed by one person to another, a breach (breaking) of that duty and harm done as a direct result of the action. Examples of torts are negligence, battery, and libel.

Director liability has been the subject of much debate and many court cases in recent years. There has been a significant increase in the number of lawsuits filed against directors and officers by shareholders. Shareholders reportedly prevail in 80–90 percent of the cases, by obtaining a favorable settlement or judgment.[23] These factors have made officer and director liability a major concern for corporate executives. Figure 7-3 lists some of the actions for which directors may be held personally liable. Many states have amended their state statutes to clarify the state's position on director liability, and many corporations have amended their articles of incorporation, usually to afford their directors the greatest amount of protection available under law. Many of the newer statutes have yet to be tested in court, and the full impact of the new laws regarding directors' liability remains to be seen.

Directors May Be Held Personally Liable For

- Breaches of the director's fiduciary duty, duty of care, or duty of loyalty
- Unauthorized acts (acts clearly beyond the scope of their authority)
- Negligent acts
- Fraud or other illegal acts
- Acts that are controlled by state statute that provide for personal liability by directors

---

FIGURE 7-3 Personal Liability of Directors

State corporate statutes not only impose personal liability on directors under certain circumstances, they provide the means for corporations to limit the personal liability of their directors and to indemnify them for certain litigation-related expenses.

In addition to the business judgment rule, a director's personal liability may be further limited by the corporation's articles of incorporation. Section 2.02 of the Revised Model Business Corporation Act provides that a corporation's articles of incorporation may be drafted to eliminate or limit the liability of its directors *except* liability for:

1. The amount of financial benefit received by a director to which he is not entitled
2. An intentional infliction of harm on the corporation or the shareholders
3. A violation of Section 8.33 (concerning unlawful distributions); and
4. An intentional violation of criminal law.[24]

§ 7.3 COMPENSATION AND INDEMNIFICATION OF DIRECTORS

Directors are often called upon to serve the corporation in several different ways, and they may or may not be directly compensated by the corporation. This section scrutinizes the compensation of directors and their indemnification for expenses incurred on behalf of the corporation.

Compensation of Directors

Directors may or may not receive compensation specifically for their roles as directors in the corporation. Director compensation is usually set by the board of directors, unless the right to set director compensation is limited to the shareholders in the statutes of the state of domicile, or the corporation's articles of incorporation or bylaws.

Indemnification

A director generally has a right to be reimbursed for advances made or expenses incurred by him or her on behalf of the corporation. A director, however, has no right to be reimbursed for expenses incurred by his or her own wrongdoing.

Indemnification refers to the act by which corporations reimburse directors for expenses incurred by them in defending a lawsuit to which they become a party because of their involvement with the corporation. This type of reimbursement is addressed separately by law and usually by the articles and bylaws of the corporation. Typically, the statutes of the state of domicile will set guidelines directing mandatory indemnification under certain circumstances and prohibiting indemnification of the directors under other circumstances.

Mandatory Indemnification Statutes typically prescribe certain conditions under which a director must be indemnified, usually when a director is successful in the defense of any proceeding to which he or she was a party because of his or her directorship of the corporation. Section 8.52 of the MBCA addresses mandatory indemnification as follows:

§ 8.52 MANDATORY INDEMNIFICATION

A corporation shall indemnify a director who was wholly successful, on the merits or otherwise, in the defense of any proceeding to which he was a party because he was a director of the corporation against reasonable expenses incurred by him in connection with the proceeding.

Optional Indemnification Statutes typically address several circumstances under which directors may be indemnified if the articles of incorporation or bylaws of the corporation provide for indemnification under those conditions. Provisions such as these require careful drafting of the articles and bylaws to provide the desired indemnification of directors of the corporation. A corporation normally indemnifies its directors when they conduct themselves in good faith and when they reasonably believed that their actions were in the best interests of the corporation. In the event of criminal proceedings, directors will often be indemnified, pursuant to the corporation's articles of incorporation or bylaws, if the directors had no reasonable cause to believe that their conduct was unlawful. Again, the articles of incorporation or bylaws of the corporation must provide for this type of director indemnification in accordance with statute, if desired.

Following is a sample paragraph that could be included in a corporation's by-laws when it is the desire of the directors and shareholders to indemnify the officers and directors of the corporation to the fullest extent permitted by law.

EXAMPLE: *Indemnification*

The corporation shall hereby indemnify the officers and directors of the corporation and their heirs, executors, and administrators to the full extent permitted by _____ [cite appropriate statute section]. The board of directors and officers of the corporation are hereby authorized to take the necessary and appropriate action to indemnify the officers and directors of the corporation, and their heirs, executors, and administrators to the full extent permitted by the aforesaid statute.

Corporations that do not indemnify their directors in accordance with the corporation's bylaws, may be sued for breach of contract. Such was the case in *Salaman v. National Media Corp.*[25] In that case, tried before a Delaware jury in 1994, a director was forced to defend himself in two federal actions because of his position with the corporation. The corporation amended its bylaws after the fact to provide no indemnification for the director and refused to pay the director's attorneys fees and costs, even though the director was not found to be guilty of any wrongdoing. The jury in that case returned a verdict that awarded the director compensatory damages to cover his costs and attorneys' fees, plus an additional $1,550,000 in **punitive damages**.

Prohibited Indemnification   Statutory provisions such as subsection (d) of § 8.51 of the MBCA make it clear that directors are not to be indemnified for expenses incurred for defense in proceedings involving their own wrongdoing:

(d) Unless ordered by a court under section 8.54(a)(3), a corporation may not indemnify a director:

(1) in connection with a proceeding by or in the right of the corporation, except for reasonable expenses incurred in connection with the proceeding if it is determined that the director has met the relevant standard of conduct under subsection (a); or

(2) in connection with any proceeding with respect to conduct for which he was adjudged liable on the basis that he received a financial benefit to which he was not entitled, whether or not involving action in his official capacity.

In the following case, on page 258, *Biondi v. Beekman,* it was determined that indemnification of the director of an apartment corporation was prohibited because he acted in bad faith and not in the best interests of the corporation.

punitive damages   Extra money given to punish the defendant and to help keep a particular bad act from happening again.

CASE

Court of Appeals of New York.

Nicholas A. BIONDI, Appellant,
v.
BEEKMAN HILL HOUSE APARTMENT CORPORATION, Respondent.

April 11, 2000.

OPINION OF THE COURT

CIPARICK, J.

This appeal brings up for review two issues: (1) whether public policy bars a cooperative apartment corporation from indemnifying one of its directors for punitive damages imposed on the director who, in violation of various civil rights laws, denies a proposed tenant's sublease application on the basis of race and retaliates against a shareholder for opposing the denial; and (2) whether, under the same facts, Business Corporation Law § 721 bars indemnification where the underlying judgment establishes that the director acted in bad faith. We conclude that, in these circumstances, indemnification is prohibited.

Plaintiff, Nicholas Biondi, is the former president of the board of directors of defendant Beekman Hill House Apartment Corporation. In 1995, Simone Demou, a shareholder of Beekman, informed Biondi that she intended to sublease her apartment to Gregory and Shannon Broome, a financially eligible couple. Biondi assured Demou that he would meet with Gregory Broome and that, in keeping with the usual practice, a full board interview would not be required. Nevertheless, after Biondi's meeting with Gregory Broome, Beekman's managing agent advised the Broomes that a full board meeting was necessary. Prior to that meeting, Biondi informed another board member that Gregory Broome was African-American, and told yet another board member that he felt "uneasy" about him. The board unanimously denied the Broomes' application and issued a notice of default against Demou for "objectionable conduct" arising from her accusations of racism against Biondi and the board.

On February 2, 1996, the Broomes filed a lawsuit ... alleging that Beekman and its directors (the Beekman defendants), including Biondi, violated various State and Federal civil rights laws by denying their sublease application based on Gregory Broome's race. ...

After trial, the jury found that the Beekman defendants, including Biondi both personally and in his official capacity, violated the Federal Fair Housing Act (42 USC §§ 1981, 1982) and New York Human Rights Law (Executive Law § 296[5]). The jury awarded the Broomes $230,000 in compensatory damages and $410,000 in punitive damages, $125,000 of which was assessed individually against Biondi. As to Demou, the jury found that Biondi and the Beekman defendants violated her rights under the Federal Fair Housing Act and the New York Human Rights Law, breached their fiduciary duties to her and tortiously interfered with her sublease agreement with the Broomes. The jury awarded Demou a total of $107,000 in compensatory damages and $57,000 in punitive damages, $29,000 of which was assessed individually against Biondi. ...

Following the verdict, the Beekman defendants moved, in part, for a new trial. In denying the motion, the Federal District Court concluded that: (1) the evidence supporting Demou's breach of fiduciary duty claim established that "the Beekman Board members acted in bad faith and with a purpose that was not in the best interests of the cooperative"; and (2) the evidence established that the Beekman defendants acted "willfully or maliciously when they rejected the Broomes' sublet application * * * and retaliated against Demou for trying to oppose the Board's actions" (Broome v. Biondi, 17 F.Supp.2d 211, 220, 228 [S.D.N.Y.]). ...

Biondi subsequently sued Beekman for indemnification under article VII of its by-laws, and Beekman moved to dismiss Biondi's complaint for failure to state a cause of action pursuant to CPLR 3211. Supreme Court denied Beekman's motion. It held that Beekman's by-laws authorized indemnification for directors who act in good faith, and the "mere fact" that the Federal jury found Biondi liable for violating the Broomes' civil rights was not "dispositive" of that issue. It further held that the public policy prohibition against indemnification for punitive damages did not apply because the settlement agreement did not clearly identify Biondi's damages as punitive.

The Appellate Division unanimously reversed and dismissed the complaint. The Court held that Biondi's settlement agreement limited his liability to punitive damages and that indemnification for punitive damages is prohibited by public policy. The Court also held that Business Corporation Law § 721 barred indemnification, where the jury in the underlying action found that Biondi had acted in bad faith toward the Broomes and Demou. We now affirm.

Analysis

Under the facts of this case, Biondi cannot obtain indemnification for the punitive damages imposed for his acts of bad faith against Beekman. ... Indemnification "defeats the purpose of punitive damages, which is to punish and deter others from acting similarly" ... .

So too, Beekman should not bear the burden of indemnifying its director for punitive damages imposed for acts of bad faith.

Biondi's racial discrimination against the Broomes and retaliation against Demou is precisely the type of conduct for which public policy should preclude indemnification. The jury in the Federal action found that Biondi willfully violated the Broomes' and Demou's civil rights, and it imposed personal liability on Biondi. Indeed, the punitive damages assessed against Biondi were greater than those against any other director, confirming that Biondi was singled out for punishment. To allow Biondi now to shift that penalty to Beekman would eviscerate the deterrent effect of punitive damages, and "violate the 'fundamental principle that no one shall be permitted to take advantage of his own wrong' " ... we conclude that neither the Business Corporation Law nor Beekman's by-laws entitle Biondi to indemnification, where the underlying judgment establishes that he acted in bad faith. ...

Accordingly, the order of the Appellate Division should be affirmed, with costs.

Chief Judge KAYE and Judges BELLACOSA, SMITH, LEVINE, WESLEY and ROSENBLATT concur.

Order affirmed, with costs.

§ 7.4   ELECTION AND TERM OF DIRECTORS

The board of directors is chosen by vote of the shareholders of the corporation to serve a definite term. In this section we examine the election of directors and the terms they serve.

Election of Directors

The directors of a corporation are elected by the shareholders to operate and manage the affairs of the corporation. With the possible exception of statutory close corporations, corporations are required to elect a board of directors and to have a board of directors at all times.

If the first board of directors is named in the articles of incorporation, those directors serve only until the first meeting of the shareholders. At that time, the initial directors are either reelected or replaced by a vote of the shareholders, as discussed below under "Term of Directors."

Often, especially in smaller corporations, shareholders elect themselves, or some of themselves, to serve as directors and officers of the corporation. In larger firms, *outside directors* may be elected. These are directors who are neither shareholders nor officers of the corporation. These individuals, who are often directors or officers of other corporations, are usually elected to the board because of their unique expertise and management experience.

Number and Qualifications of Directors

Traditionally, corporations were required by statute to have at least three directors on their boards. Often, those individuals were required to be shareholders of the corporation or residents of the state of the corporation's domicile, or both. With the relaxation of corporate law restrictions and the advent of the one-person corporation, most state statutes now allow the board of directors to consist of one individual, who may or may not be a shareholder of the corporation or a resident of the corporation's state of domicile. Modern corporate law typically allows restrictions on either the number of directors or their qualifications to be made by provisions in the articles of incorporation or bylaws of the corporation.

The MBCA states that the "board of directors must consist of one or more individuals, with the number specified in or fixed in accordance with the articles of incorporation or bylaws."[26] Section 8.02 of the MBCA addresses director qualifications as follows:

§ 8.02 QUALIFICATIONS OF DIRECTORS

The articles of incorporation or bylaws may prescribe qualifications for directors. A director need not be a resident of this state or a shareholder of the corporation unless the articles of incorporation or bylaws so prescribe.

Because the directors typically have the authority to amend the bylaws of the corporation, many state statutes that allow the number of directors to be prescribed by the bylaws of the corporation also place limits on the power of the board of directors to increase or decrease their own number. This may be done by providing that a range in the number of directors be stated in the articles of incorporation of the corporation (which may only be amended with shareholder approval), or by providing that the number of directors may not be increased or decreased by more than a certain amount without shareholder approval.

Special types of corporations may have different statutory requirements for the number and qualifications of directors. As discussed in Chapter 5, certain statutory close corporations are not required to have a board of directors, but may be managed by the shareholders of the corporation instead.

Directors of professional corporations are usually subject to more specific qualifications, such as being license holders of the profession being practiced by the professional corporation.

Term of Directors

Under the MBCA, the term of each director expires at the next annual meeting of the shareholders following their election, when the director's successor is elected and qualifies. Directors may be reelected for any number of terms.

The shareholders may decide to ensure the continuity of management of the corporation by staggering the terms of the directors. The MBCA provides that corporations may stagger their terms by dividing the total number of directors into two or three groups, as nearly equal in number as possible. These groups may be elected for one-, two-, or three-year terms that will expire in different years. At each annual shareholder meeting, directors will be elected or reelected to fill the positions of the directors whose terms are expiring that particular year.

For example, if a board of directors is eventually to consist of nine directors who will each serve for a two-year term, three of the first directors may be elected for an initial three-year term, three may be elected for an initial two-year term, and three may be elected for an initial one-year term. Annual board of director elections in subsequent years will be required only for the reelection or replacement of those directors whose terms are expiring in that particular year.

Resignation   Directors are generally allowed to resign their positions at any time, in accordance with state statute. Courts have found that directors "may resign at any time and for any reason if they act in good faith and without personal gain."[27] Resignation is generally given by written notice delivered to the chairman of the board of directors or to the board itself.

Removal of Directors   The board of directors is elected to serve the best interests of the corporation and, more specifically, the shareholders. It is generally the shareholders' right to remove any director or directors with or without cause by a majority vote at a special shareholder meeting called specifically for that purpose. Corporations that allow cumulative voting may provide that the number of votes required to elect a director, if cast in favor of retaining a director, is sufficient to keep the director in office. Cumulative voting is discussed in § 7.8 of this text.

The statutes of a few states protect the directors of the corporation by providing that they may not be removed without cause unless specific provisions for removal without cause are included in the articles of incorporation or bylaws of the corporation. Requirements and procedures for removing a director of the corporation may be set by the articles of incorporation or the bylaws of the corporation, so long as those provisions fall within the boundaries of the statutes of the state of domicile. The MBCA provides for the removal of directors in § 8.08:

(a) The shareholders may remove one or more directors with or without cause unless the articles of incorporation provide that directors may be removed only for cause.

(b) If a director is elected by a voting group of shareholders, only the shareholders of that voting group may participate in the vote to remove him.

(c) If cumulative voting is authorized, a director may not be removed if the number of votes sufficient to elect him under cumulative voting is voted against his removal. If cumulative voting is not authorized, a director may be removed only if the number of votes cast to remove him exceeds the number of votes cast not to remove him.

(d) A director may be removed by the shareholders only at a meeting called for the purpose of removing him and the meeting notice must state that the purpose, or one of the purposes, of the meeting is removal of the director.

Under certain circumstances, when it is desirable to remove a director who is a shareholder with sufficient voting power to prevent his or her own removal, or in larger, publicly held corporations where it is impractical to call a special meeting of the shareholders for the purpose of removing a director, it may be necessary or desirable to remove a director by court order. Pursuant to § 8.09 of the MBCA, which is followed closely by most states in this regard, shareholders of a corporation holding at least 10 percent of the outstanding shares of any class, or the corporation itself, may initiate a court action to request the removal of a director when it can be shown that the director "engaged in fraudulent or dishonest conduct, or gross abuse of authority or discretion, with respect to the corporation,"[28] or when it can be shown that the removal of the director is "in the best interest of the corporation."[29]

Filling Vacancies on the Board   In some states a vacancy on the board of directors may be filled by a vote of the remaining directors. Statutes of other states provide that a special meeting of the shareholders may be called to elect a director to fill a vacancy on the board. In either event, the replacement director serves until the next annual meeting of the shareholders, or until his or her successor is duly elected and qualified.

§ 7.5   BOARD OF DIRECTORS MEETINGS AND RESOLUTIONS

Most actions of the board of directors are taken through resolutions passed at meetings of the board. This section examines the requirements for board of directors meetings, including requirements for holding annual meetings and for notifying the directors about meetings. It also discusses the requisite quorum for passing a resolution of the board of directors at a board meeting, and the minutes taken to formalize the resolutions of the board of directors. Finally, we focus on the ability of directors to act without a meeting, through the use of unanimous written consents and telephonic meetings.

Board of Directors Meetings

Under common law, a corporation could act only through its directors at regularly held meetings. Early state statutes almost uniformly required annual meetings of the board of directors and dictated the procedures for calling and holding the annual and special board meetings that were necessary for the directors to take action.

The tendency of modern corporate law, however, recognizes the impracticality of mandatory, formal directors' meetings for all board of director actions, and the following three changes to the MBCA have been adopted by most states to make it easier for a board of directors to take action:

1. Annual board of directors meetings are optional.
2. Action may be taken by the board of directors by a unanimous written consent, signed by each director.
3. Telephonic meetings by the board of directors are generally acceptable.

Notice requirements for board meetings have also been relaxed in most states.

Corporations generally address the issue of directors' meetings in the bylaws of the corporation. If an annual meeting is desired, the date for the annual meeting is typically set forth, as well as the place and time for the meeting and the notice requirements.

Depending on the degree to which directors are directly involved in the day-to-day business of a corporation, the board of directors may meet regularly for monthly or even weekly meetings. Other corporations, especially large and publicly held corporations, may limit their board of directors meetings to annual meetings, which typically are held immediately following the annual meeting of the shareholders of the corporation, as prescribed in the bylaws of the corporation.

The directors of the corporation must be aware of and follow all requirements for annual and special meetings, as prescribed by statute, and by the corporation's articles of incorporation and bylaws.

Annual Meetings of the Board of Directors

Annual board of directors meetings are held for several purposes. In almost all instances, an election is held to reelect or replace the current officers, and to ratify the acts of the officers for the past year. In addition, the board of directors reviews important events that have occurred during the past year and acts on those matters requiring attention for the upcoming year.

An agenda for an annual meeting of a board of directors might include several of the following items:

1. Approve the minutes from the last meeting of the board of directors.
2. Approve dividends to be paid to the shareholders of the corporation.
3. Approve the annual report to be filed with the appropriate state authority (if required).
4. Review the financial reports of the corporation.
5. Elect officers of the corporation to serve until the next annual meeting or until their successors are duly elected and qualified.
6. Set the compensation of the officers of the corporation for the succeeding year.
7. Approve bonuses for the officers and directors.
8. Ratify the acts of the officers and directors for the past year.
9. Address any other matters of concern regarding the operation and business of the corporation.

Notice of Meetings

Notice of annual and special meetings of the board of directors must be given in accordance with statute and with the articles of incorporation or bylaws of the corporation. In states that follow the MBCA in this regard, regular meetings of the board of directors may be held without notice, unless the articles or bylaws of the corporation include mandatory provisions. Under the MBCA, "Unless the articles of incorporation or bylaws provide otherwise, regular meetings of the board of directors may be held without notice of the date, time, place, or purpose of the meeting."[30] Specific notice requirements for special meetings are usually included in state statutes, as they are in the MBCA, which provides that at least two days' notice of the date, time, and place of the meeting must be given. It is common for the statutes or the corporation's articles or bylaws to require that the purpose of a special meeting of the board of directors be included in the notice of the meeting.

Typically, notice requirements set forth in the bylaws of the corporation for annual and special meetings of the board of directors include a statement to the effect that the directors of the corporation may waive any required notice and that a director's attendance at any meeting constitutes a waiver of notice for that meeting. It is not considered a waiver of notice for a meeting if a director attends a meeting only to object to the holding of the meeting or the transaction of business at the meeting.

Figure 7-4 shows a form that could be used for a notice of annual meeting of a board of directors.

**NOTICE OF ANNUAL MEETING
OF THE BOARD OF DIRECTORS**

OF THE _____ CORPORATION

You are hereby notified that the 2003 Annual Meeting of the Board of Directors of the _____ Corporation will be held at the registered office of the corporation, at _____ [address], at _____, on _____, 2003, for the purpose of transacting all such business as may properly come before the board.

Dated the ____ day of _____, 2003.

_____
Secretary

FIGURE 7-4 Sample Notice of Annual Meeting of Board of Directors

Quorum

A *quorum* is the minimum number of individuals who must be present or represented at a meeting as a prerequisite to the valid transaction of business. Section 8.24 of the MBCA, which is followed by most states in this regard, sets forth the following quorum and voting requirements for taking action at a meeting of the board of directors:

1. A quorum of the board of directors consists of a majority of the fixed number of directors if the corporation has a fixed board size, or a majority of the number of prescribed directors or the number of officers in office immediately before the meeting begins if the corporation has a variable-range size board.
2. The affirmative vote of a majority of the directors present is the act of the board of directors if a quorum is present when the vote is taken.
3. A director who is present at a meeting of the board of directors when corporate action is taken is deemed to have assented to the action taken unless:
   a. The director objects at the beginning of the meeting (or promptly upon arrival) to holding it or transacting business at the meeting
   b. The director's dissent or abstention from the action taken is entered in the minutes of the meeting; or
   c. The director delivers written notice of dissent or abstention to the presiding officer of the meeting before its adjournment or to the corporation immediately after adjournment of the meeting.

The MBCA provides that the articles of incorporation or the bylaws of the corporation may provide for the following deviations from statutory requirements:

1. The articles or bylaws may require a greater number for the quorum of a meeting.
2. The articles of incorporation may require a lesser number for a quorum of a meeting of the board of directors, so long as the number is no fewer than one-third of the number prescribed by statute.

These requirements for quorum and voting are typical of the laws of many states. However, the quorum and voting requirements vary by state, and the corporation's articles of incorporation and bylaws must always be consulted to see that quorum and voting requirements are complied with in order for an action of the board of directors to be valid.

Minutes

Complete and accurate minutes must be taken at every meeting of the board of directors. These minutes of the board of directors typically are taken and signed by the secretary of the corporation, who then places them in the corporate minute book, along with a copy of the notice of the meeting that was sent to all directors, any waivers of notice received from the directors, and any other documents pertaining to the meeting. Figure 7-5 on page 266 is a form of annual minutes that could be used for an annual meeting of a board of directors.

Board Actions Without Meeting

Modern corporate law recognizes the complexity of assembling a board of directors every time a board resolution is required by allowing for such resolutions to be passed by unanimous written consents and by telephonic meetings.

MINUTES OF THE ANNUAL MEETING
OF THE BOARD OF DIRECTORS

OF THE _____ CORPORATION

The annual meeting of the Board of Directors of the _____ Corporation was held on _____, at the registered office of the corporation at _____.

Present at the meeting were the following persons:

_____

_____

_____

_____

which constitutes all of the members of the Board of Directors.

The Chairman of the Board of the corporation, _____, presided as chairman of the meeting, and _____ acted as its secretary.

The chairman called the meeting to order and stated that a quorum of directors was present for the conduct of business.

The secretary presented and read a waiver of notice to the meeting signed by all directors of the corporation, which was ordered to be made part of the minutes of this meeting.

A discussion was had on the corporation's financial statements, salary increases and bonuses for the officers and directors of the corporation, and dividends to be paid on the outstanding stock of the corporation.

After motions duly made, seconded, and carried, the following resolutions were adopted by the Board of Directors:

RESOLVED, that the financial statements, as presented to the Board of Directors at this meeting, are hereby ratified and approved.

RESOLVED, that due to the profitable nature of the business of the corporation during the past fiscal year, the following officers shall be given a bonus in the following amounts:

_____	$ _____
_____	$ _____
_____	$ _____
_____	$ _____

RESOLVED, that the following persons are hereby elected to the following described offices, to serve in such capacities until their successors are elected at the next annual meeting and qualify:

Chairman of the Board	_____
Chief Executive Officer	_____
President	_____
Vice President	_____

FIGURE 7-5 Sample Minutes of Annual Meeting of Board of Directors

Secretary   _____

Treasurer   _____.

    Each of the above-named officers accepted the office to which he or she was elected.

    RESOLVED, that in consideration of their services to the corporation, the following annual salaries of the officers of the corporation for the fiscal year beginning _____, ____, were approved:

_____	$ _____
_____	$ _____
_____	$ _____
_____	$ _____.

    RESOLVED, that a dividend is hereby declared out of the capital surplus of the corporation to be payable to the stockholders of the corporation in an amount of $_____ per share. Such dividend shall be payable on the ____ day of _____, ____, in cash, to shareholders of record on the ____ day of _____, ____. The treasurer of the corporation is hereby authorized to set aside the sum necessary to pay said dividends.

    There being no further business before the meeting, it was, on motion duly made, seconded, and unanimously carried, adjourned.

                                                       _____

                                                          Secretary

FIGURE 7-5 (*continued*)

Written Consents As discussed in Chapter 6, the unanimous writing of the board of directors has become a very popular means for taking a formal action of the board of directors. The unanimous writing can be very useful to corporations whose board of directors may be spread out over a large geographical distance. Unanimous writings are also a useful means of formalizing the agreement of directors of smaller corporations who may work side by side every day without ever going through the formality of holding a "meeting" of the board of directors.

    Unanimous writings do have some drawbacks, the foremost being that it is generally required that the consent in fact be *unanimous*. If any one director disagrees with the proposed action, a meeting must be held and a vote must be taken.

    A few states provide that, if specifically provided for in the articles of a corporation, the board of directors may take action by a written resolution signed by the number of directors required to take the action if it were voted on at a meeting of the board. Under those circumstances, the signature of *all* directors may not be required.

    The sample in Figure 7-6 on page 268 demonstrates how the same resolutions that are typically passed at an annual meeting of a board of directors can be passed by the unanimous written consent of the directors.

**UNANIMOUS WRITTEN CONSENT
OF THE BOARD OF DIRECTORS**

OF THE _____ CORPORATION

The undersigned persons, being all of the Directors of the _____ Corporation (hereinafter referred to as the "Corporation"), hereby take the following actions by written consent in lieu of an annual meeting of the Board of Directors, pursuant to _____ [cite pertinent statute].

RESOLVED, that due to the profitable nature of the business of the corporation during the past fiscal year, the following officers shall be given a bonus in the following amounts:

_____ $ _____
_____ $ _____
_____ $ _____
_____ $ _____

RESOLVED, that the following persons are hereby elected to the following described offices, to serve in such capacities until their successors are elected at the next annual meeting and qualify:

Chairman of the Board   _____
Chief Executive Officer   _____
President   _____
Vice President   _____
Secretary   _____
Treasurer

RESOLVED, that in consideration of their services to the corporation, the following annual salaries of the officers of the corporation for the fiscal year beginning _____, _____, are hereby approved:

_____ $ _____
_____ $ _____
_____ $ _____
_____ $ _____

RESOLVED, that a dividend is hereby declared out of the capital surplus of the corporation to be payable to the stockholders of the corporation in an amount of $_____ per share. Such dividend shall be payable on the _____ day of _____, _____, in cash, to shareholders of record on the _____ day of _____, _____. The treasurer of the corporation is hereby authorized to set aside the sum necessary to pay said dividends.

Dated: _____.

_____   _____
_____   _____

FIGURE 7-6 Sample Unanimous Written Consent of Board of Directors

Telephonic Meetings   Another modernization of corporate laws, which is found in the MBCA and has been followed by most states, allows regular or special meetings of the board of directors to be conducted through "any means of communication by which all directors participating may simultaneously hear each other during the meeting"[31]—the conference call.

Corporate Minute Books

The minutes or unanimous written consents of both directors' and shareholder meetings are kept in a corporate minute book, along with other important documents regarding the corporation. The contents of the corporate minute book often include the articles or certificate of incorporation, the corporate charter, the corporate bylaws, the minutes of the organizational meeting, all minutes of meetings of the board of directors or shareholders, and all unanimous written consents of the board of directors and shareholders (see Figure 7-7). Corporate minute books are often kept in the office of the corporate attorney, and the task of keeping the corporate minute book in order and up to date often falls to the paralegal.

FIGURE 7-7   Corporate minute books contain the corporation's incorporation documents, meeting minutes, and unanimous writings. (Photo courtesy of Liberty Legal, Houston, Texas.)

§ 7.6 CORPORATE OFFICERS

Officers are in the broadest sense considered to be agents of the corporation.[32] They are individuals elected by the board of directors to oversee the business of the corporation, under the authority of the directors. Officers are usually charged with important managerial functions such as administering and operating the company, recruiting key personnel, and signing checks.[33] An individual may be an officer and a director at the same time; in small corporations, all of the officers are commonly directors of the corporation as well.

This section examines the titles and typical duties of various corporate officers, and the officers' potential for personal liability. The section concludes with a discussion of the election and terms of office of corporate officers.

Titles and Duties of Officers

Generally, the officers of a corporation have the titles, duties, and responsibilities assigned to them under the statutes of the state of domicile, by the articles of incorporation or bylaws of the corporation, or by resolution of the board of directors. Statutes may be very specific regarding the required officers of a corporation, naming the titles and duties that must be assumed by officers of a corporation. More often, however, in modern corporate law the corporation is given much latitude regarding the officers it chooses and the duties assigned to those officers.

The MBCA addresses the required officers of a corporation in § 8.40:

§ 8.40 REQUIRED OFFICERS

(a) A corporation has the officers described in its bylaws or appointed by the board of directors in accordance with the bylaws.

(b) A duly appointed officer may appoint one or more officers or assistant officers if authorized by the bylaws or the board of directors.

(c) The bylaws or the board of directors shall delegate to one of the officers responsibility for preparing minutes of the directors' and shareholders' meetings and for authenticating records of the corporation.

(d) The same individual may simultaneously hold more than one office in a corporation.

The MBCA also gives further latitude to corporations in assigning duties of the officers. In states following the MBCA, officers have the authority to perform the duties set forth in the bylaws, or prescribed by the board of directors, or at the direction of an officer authorized by the board of directors to prescribe the duties of other officers.

Typically, bylaws of the corporation will set forth:

1. The titles of the officers of the corporation.

2. A description of the duties of the officers of the corporation.

3. The method for electing the officers of the corporation.

4. Any special qualifications for the officers of the corporation.

The following subsections list the officers that are often elected to serve a corporation and describe the duties often assigned to those officers, in terms that might be used in corporate articles or bylaws.

Chief Executive Officer   The chief executive officer of the corporation (CEO) shall actively manage the business of the corporation and directly and actively supervise all other officers, agents, and employees. The chief executive officer shall preside over all meetings of the shareholders and the board of directors.

President   The president of the corporation shall preside at all meetings of the board of directors and shareholders, in the absence of the chief executive officer. The president shall perform all duties incident to the office of the president as may from time to time be assigned by the board of directors, and shall perform the duties of the chief executive officer in the chief executive officer's absence.

Chairman of the Board   The chairman of the board, if elected, shall be a member of the board of directors and, if present, shall preside at each meeting of the board of directors. The chairman of the board shall keep in close touch with the administration of the affairs of the corporation, advise and counsel with the chief executive officer, and perform such other duties as may from time to time be assigned by the board of directors.

Vice President   Each vice president shall perform all such duties as from time to time may be assigned by the board of directors, the chief executive officer, or the president. At the request of the chief executive officer, the vice president shall perform the duties of the president, in the president's absence, and when so acting, shall have the powers of and be subject to the restrictions placed upon the president in respect of the performance of such duties.

Chief Financial Officer   The chief financial officer of the corporation shall be the custodian of the funds, securities, and property of the corporation. The chief financial officer shall receive and give receipts for moneys due and payable to the corporation from any source whatsoever, and deposit all such moneys in the name of the corporation in such banks, trust companies, or other depositories as shall be selected. The chief financial officer shall perform all of the duties incident to the office, and such other duties as may be delegated by the board of directors. If required by the board of directors, the chief financial officer shall give a bond for the faithful discharge of duties in such sum and with such surety or sureties as the board of directors shall determine.

Treasurer   The treasurer of the corporation, if one is appointed, shall have such duties as the chief financial officer and the board of directors may delegate. The treasurer shall give bonds for the faithful discharge of his or her duties in such sums and with such sureties as the board of directors shall determine.

Secretary   The secretary shall be responsible for the prompt and correct recording of all proceedings of the board of directors. The secretary shall further supervise the preparation and publication of reports, studies, and other publications of the board of directors, and shall prepare such correspondence and perform such other duties as may be required.

Assistant Secretary   The assistant secretary of the corporation, if one is appointed, shall have such duties as the secretary and the board of directors may delegate. The assistant secretary may sign, with the president or vice president, certificates for authorized shares of the corporation.

Personal Liability of Officers

Under the MBCA, as in most states, officers are generally held to the same standards of conduct as directors of the corporation. Officers not acting in good faith or who breach their fiduciary duty, duty of care, or duty of loyalty, may be subject to personal liability for damages caused to the corporation by them, often in the same manner as directors of the corporation. Some courts have held officers to a higher degree of care than directors, due to their functions in the day-to-day operation of the corporation.[34]

Election and Term of Office

Officers are generally elected by a majority of the board of directors at an annual meeting of the board of directors. Traditionally, officers hold their office for one year and are either reelected or replaced at the annual meeting of the board of directors. In recent years, however, key corporate officers have negotiated contracts with the board of directors that extend well beyond the traditional one-year term.

§ 7.7   SHAREHOLDERS' RIGHTS AND RESPONSIBILITIES

A shareholder, or stockholder, is the owner of one or more shares of the stock of a corporation. The shareholder is, in effect, at least part owner of the corporation itself. The relationship between the shareholder and the corporation is a contractual relationship separate from any other relationship the shareholder may have with the corporation.

There are generally no qualifications that must be met by shareholders of business corporations. A shareholder may be an individual or an entity. There are, however, restrictions on who may be a shareholder of special types of corporations. For example, the shareholders of professional corporations may be required to be licensed professionals; shareholders of S corporations generally must be individuals (and may not be entities). Not-for-profit corporations that do not issue stock may have members instead of shareholders.

This section examines the rights of shareholders, including the shareholder's preemptive right to purchase shares of the corporation and the shareholder's right to inspect the books of the corporation. We also discuss the possibility of shareholders being held personally liable for the debts and obligations of the corporation.

Shareholders' Preemptive Rights

Preemptive rights give shareholders the opportunity to protect their position in the corporation by granting to shareholders the right to purchase newly issued shares of the corporation's stock in an amount proportionate to their current stock ownership.

Shareholders who have preemptive rights are entitled to a fair and reasonable opportunity to purchase a sufficient portion of newly issued shares to preserve their proportionate interest in the corporation. This can be very important in smaller corporations with only a few shareholders. For example, suppose a corporation has four shareholders who each own 200 shares of common stock. If the board of directors decides to raise funds by selling an additional 1,000 shares of the corporation, the existing shareholders could lose their voting influence on all decisions to be made by the shareholders of the corporation. If the existing shareholders have been granted preemptive rights by statute or the corporation's articles of incorporation, they must each be given the opportunity to purchase additional shares at a price not less favorable than the price proposed for sale to those outside the corporation. They must each have the opportunity to purchase shares sufficient to maintain their ownership position in the corporation.

In corporations that have many shareholders, especially publicly held corporations, the average shareholder is not as concerned with his or her proportionate ownership of the corporation. In addition, the number of shareholders in larger corporations would make preemptive rights extremely difficult to execute. For these reasons, shareholders in larger and publicly held corporations are very rarely granted preemptive rights.

Traditionally, shareholders were granted preemptive rights as a matter of law. In recent years, however, the tendency is to grant preemptive rights to shareholders only in corporations that specifically grant that right to shareholders in the articles of incorporation. Statutes vary from state to state, however, and many states still provide that preemptive rights are granted unless waived in the articles of incorporation.

Under the MBCA, shareholders do not have a preemptive right unless, and to the extent, granted in the articles of incorporation. The MBCA provides that if a corporation states that its shareholders are granted preemptive rights in its articles of incorporation, they are deemed to have the preemptive rights described in § 6.30 of the MBCA, which reads, in part, as follows:

> (1) The shareholders of the corporation have a preemptive right, granted on uniform terms and conditions prescribed by the board of directors to provide a fair and reasonable opportunity to exercise the right, to acquire proportional amounts of the corporation's unissued shares upon the decision of the board of directors to issue them.

---

preemptive right The right of some stockholders to have the first opportunity to buy any new stock the company issues.

Special consideration must be given to the statutory treatment of preemptive rights in the corporation's state of domicile, and the incorporation documents must be drafted accordingly.

Shareholders' Right to Inspect Corporate Records

The shareholders are the owners of the corporation. As such, they are entitled to certain rights to inspect the corporate records of the corporation. These rights are usually set forth in the statutes of the state of domicile and may be further elaborated on in either the bylaws or the articles of incorporation of the corporation.

Section 16.02 of the MBCA provides that shareholders are entitled to inspect and copy minutes of meetings, accounting records, and shareholder records. To exercise these rights, the shareholder must give the corporation at least five business days' notice, and the inspection and copying must be done during regular business hours. In addition, the demand for inspection must be made "in good faith for a proper purpose" and the demand must describe the shareholder's purpose for the inspection. Further, the records inspected must be directly connected with the shareholder's purpose.

In *State ex rel. Pillsbury v. Honeywell, Inc.,* the court found that the shareholder's purpose for inspecting corporate records was not a proper purpose, and the shareholder's demand for inspection was denied.

CASE

STATE ex rel. PILLSBURY
v.
HONEYWELL, INC.

Supreme Court of Minnesota
291 Minn. 322, 191 N.W.2d 406,
50 A.L.R.3d 1046 (1971)
October 22, 1971
Kelly, Justice

Petitioner appeals from an order and judgment of the district court denying all relief prayed for in a petition for **writ of mandamus** to compel respondent, Honeywell, Inc., (Honeywell) to produce its original shareholder ledger, current shareholder ledger, and all corporate records dealing with weapons and munitions manufacture. We must affirm.

The issues raised by petitioner are as follows: (1) Whether Minnesota or Delaware law determines the right of a shareholder to inspect respondent's corporate books and records; (2) whether petitioner, who bought shares in respondent corporation for the purpose of changing its policy of manufacturing war munitions, had a proper purpose germane to a shareholder's interest... .

Petitioner attended a meeting on July 3, 1969, of a group involved in what was known as the "Honeywell Project." Participants in the project believed that American involvement in Vietnam was wrong, that a substantial portion of Honeywell's production consisted of munitions used in that war, and that Honeywell should stop this production of munitions. Petitioner had long opposed the Vietnam war, but it was at the July 3rd meeting

writ of mandamus   Court order that directs a public official or government department to do something. It may be sent to the executive branch, the legislative branch, or a lower court.

that he first learned of Honeywell's involvement. He was shocked at the knowledge that Honeywell had a large government contract to produce antipersonnel fragmentation bombs. Upset because of knowledge that such bombs were produced in his own community by a company which he had known and respected, petitioner determined to stop Honeywell's munitions production.

On July 14, 1969, petitioner ordered his fiscal agent to purchase 100 shares of Honeywell. He admits that the sole purpose of the purchase was to give himself a voice in Honeywell's affairs so he could persuade Honeywell to cease producing munitions. Apparently not aware of that purpose, petitioner's agent registered the stock in the name of a Pillsbury family nominee—Quad & Co. Upon discovering the nature of the registration, petitioner bought one share of Honeywell in his own name on August 11, 1969. ...

During 1969, subsequent to the July 3, 1969, meeting and after he had ordered his agent to purchase the 100 shares of Honeywell stock, petitioner inquired into a trust which had been formed for his benefit by his grandmother. The purpose of the inquiry was to discover whether shares of Honeywell were included in the trust. It was then, for the first time, that petitioner discovered that he had a contingent beneficial interest under the terms of the trust in 242 shares of Honeywell.

Prior to the instigation of this suit, petitioner submitted two formal demands to Honeywell requesting that it produce its original shareholder ledger, current shareholder ledger, and all corporate records dealing with weapons and munitions manufacture. Honeywell refused.

On November 24, 1969, a petition was filed for writs of mandamus ordering Honeywell to produce the above mentioned records. In response, Honeywell answered the petition and served a notice of **deposition** on petitioner, who moved that the answer be stricken as procedurally premature and that an order be issued to limit the deposition. After a hearing, the trial court denied the motion, and the deposition was taken on December 15, 1969.

In the deposition petitioner outlined his beliefs concerning the Vietnam war and his purpose for his involvement with Honeywell. He expressed his desire to communicate with other shareholders in the hope of altering Honeywell's board of directors and thereby changing its policy. To this end, he testified, business records are necessary to insure accuracy.

A hearing was held on January 8, 1970, during which Honeywell introduced the deposition, conceded all material facts stated therein, and argued that petitioner was not entitled to any relief as a matter of law. Petitioner asked that alternative writs of mandamus issue for all the relief requested in his petition. On April 8, 1970, the trial court dismissed the petition, holding that the relief requested was for an improper and indefinite purpose. Petitioner contends in this appeal that the dismissal was in error. ...

2. The trial court ordered judgment for Honeywell, ruling that petitioner had not demonstrated a proper purpose germane to his interest as a stockholder. Petitioner contends that a stockholder who disagrees with management has an absolute right to inspect corporate records for purposes of soliciting proxies. He would have this court rule that such solicitation is per se a "proper purpose." Honeywell argues that a "proper purpose" contemplates concern with investment return. We agree with Honeywell. ...

The act of inspecting a corporation's shareholder ledger and business records must be viewed in its proper perspective. In terms of the corporate norm, inspection is merely the act of the concerned owner checking on what is in part his property. In the context of the large firm, inspection can be more akin to a weapon in corporate warfare. ...

Petitioner had utterly no interest in the affairs of Honeywell before he learned of Honeywell's production of fragmentation bombs. Immediately after obtaining this knowledge, he purchased stock in Honeywell for the sole purpose of asserting ownership privileges in an effort to force Honeywell to cease such production. ... But

---

deposition   The process of taking a witness's sworn out-of-court testimony. The questioning is usually done by a lawyer, with the lawyer from the other side given a chance to attend and participate.

for his opposition to Honeywell's policy, petitioner probably would not have bought Honeywell stock, would not be interested in Honeywell's profits and would not desire to communicate with Honeywell's shareholders. His avowed purpose in buying Honeywell stock was to place himself in a position to try to impress his opinions favoring a reordering of priorities upon Honeywell management and its other shareholders. Such a motivation can hardly be deemed a proper purpose germane to his economic interest as a shareholder. ...

We do not mean to imply that a shareholder with a bona fide investment interest could not bring this suit if motivated by concern with the long- or short-term economic effects on Honeywell resulting from the production of war munitions. Similarly, this suit might be appropriate when a shareholder has a bona fide concern about the adverse effects of abstention from profitable war contracts on his investment in Honeywell.

In the instant case, however, the trial court, in effect, has found from all the facts that petitioner was not interested in even the long-term well-being of Honeywell or the enhancement of the value of his shares. His sole purpose was to persuade the company to adopt his social and political concerns, irrespective of any economic benefit to himself or Honeywell. This purpose on the part of one buying into the corporation does not entitle the petitioner to inspect Honeywell's books and records. ...

The order of the trial court denying the writ of mandamus is affirmed.

Personal Liability of Shareholders

One of the greatest advantages of incorporating is that the corporate entity shelters the individual shareholders from personal liability for the corporation's debts and obligations. A shareholder's liability generally consists of no more than the consideration paid for the shareholder's own stock in the corporation.

The two most common exceptions to the rule of nonliability occur when the corporate veil is pierced, or when the individual shareholder grants a personal guarantee for some obligation of the corporation. Both of these occurrences are discussed in Chapter 5.

Although, in most cases, the imposition of personal liability stems from disregard of the corporate entity, at times a shareholder can be held personally liable for the tortious acts of the corporation if it can be proved that the shareholder participated in the commission of the action. Certainly, a shareholder who participates directly in the management of the corporation, such as in a statutory close corporation, is exposed to a higher degree of risk for the imposition of personal liability than that commonly associated with shareholders.

§ 7.8 SHAREHOLDER MEETINGS

Shareholder meetings are often the forum for the most important decisions made regarding the future of the corporation (Figure 7-8). This section discusses the requirements for annual and special meetings, including their location and notice. It also examines the use of proxies for voting at shareholder meetings and the necessity of having a quorum to adopt a shareholder resolution. We then

FIGURE 7-8 Shareholders participate in the management of the corporation through participation in annual shareholder meetings.

focus on the actual voting at shareholder meetings, concentrating on the election of directors and other acts that require shareholder approval. This section concludes with an investigation of the documents that formalize shareholder resolutions, the minutes of shareholder meetings, and the unanimous written consents of shareholders.

Requirements for Annual Meetings

Annual meetings of the shareholders are often required under state statutes, although the statutes generally allow that the time and place for holding the annual meeting may be set in the bylaws of the corporation. Statutory provisions for holding annual meetings require only that a meeting of the shareholders be held annually at a time stated in, or fixed by, the bylaws. Under the MBCA, shareholder meetings may be held at any place indicated in the corporate bylaws within or without the state of domicile. If no place for the meeting is set forth in the bylaws, the meeting will be held at the corporation's principal office.

If a corporation does not hold annual meetings of the shareholders in accordance with its bylaws, shareholders are generally granted the statutory right to move for a court order to compel the corporation to call and hold an annual shareholder meeting. Typically, any shareholder may apply to the appropriate court for an order to compel an annual meeting if an annual meeting was not held within six months after the end of the corporation's fiscal year, within fifteen months after the last annual meeting of the shareholders, or some other time prescribed by statute.

Requirements for Special Meetings

It is sometimes necessary or desirable to hold shareholder meetings between the regularly scheduled annual meetings of a corporation. These meetings are referred to as *special meetings*. Special meetings are held for special and specific purposes. Some of the purposes for holding special meetings include the replacement of directors who have died or resigned before the expiration of their term, the consideration of merger proposals, and other extraordinary events that affect the corporation and require attention prior to the next annual meeting. Business outside the scope of the purpose for which a special meeting is called may not be transacted at a special meeting. Specific requirements as to who may call a special meeting are prescribed by statute and generally may be further specified in the articles of incorporation or bylaws of a corporation. The MBCA provides that a special meeting may be called by the corporation's board of directors, persons holding at least 10 percent of all the votes entitled to be cast on the proposed matter, or persons authorized by the articles of incorporation or bylaws.

Location

Requirements for the location of both annual and special meetings of the shareholders of a corporation are usually outlined in the state's statutes and set forth in further detail in the corporation's bylaws. Modern corporate law tends to be very liberal regarding the location of both annual and special meetings. Requirements in the MBCA for both annual and special meetings dictate only that the meeting "may be held in or out of this state at the place stated in or fixed in accordance with the bylaws."[35] If no provision is made in the bylaws regarding the location of annual and special meetings of the shareholders, the MBCA provides that such meetings must take place at the corporation's principal office.

Notice

The actual notice given of an annual shareholder meeting will vary, depending on the size and circumstances of the corporation. In small, closely held corporations, the notice may be a telephone call to one or two individuals, followed by waivers of notice signed at the actual meeting. Giving notice to shareholders of corporations that may have hundreds of shareholders is a much more complicated matter.

First, there must be a determination as to which individuals are entitled to receive notice of the meeting. A *record date* for determining the shareholders of the corporation is generally fixed by the bylaws of the corporation or by the board of directors. All shareholders of the corporation on the record date are entitled to notice of the annual meeting and are entitled to vote at the meeting. Because any purchasers of stock subsequent to that date, but before the annual meeting, will not be entitled to receive notice of the meeting, the record date must be chosen carefully. The date picked will depend on the number of shareholders and the complexity of sending the notice. State statutes usually place restrictions on the record date as well.

In states following the MBCA, the record date may be fixed by the directors as directed in the bylaws of the corporation. However, the record date cannot be more than seventy days before the annual meeting.

The bylaws of the corporation typically prescribe the exact method for determining the record date. Following is an example of a bylaw paragraph regarding the record date.

EXAMPLE: *Fixing Record Date*

For the purpose of determining those shareholders entitled to notice of or to vote at any meeting of shareholders, or to receive payment of any dividend, or in order to make a determination of shareholders for any other proper purpose, the board of directors may fix, in advance, a date as the record date for the determination of shareholders. Such date shall be not more than _____ days, and for a meeting of shareholders, not less than _____ days, or in the case of a meeting where a merger or consolidation will be considered, not less than _____ days, immediately preceding such meeting.[36]

Once the record date has been set, the corporation must prepare a list of shareholders entitled to notice of the meeting. This task typically falls to the individual who is responsible for overseeing all stock transfers of the corporation. In the case of a small corporation, this may be the corporate secretary who keeps the stock certificate ledger in the corporate minute book. In larger corporations, on the other hand, this may be a significant task that is delegated to an individual or another company referred to as the **transfer agent.** The transfer agent is responsible for overseeing all transfers of stock, including the surrender of old stock certificates and the issuance of new ones, and for maintaining an up-to-date record of all shareholders.

The list of shareholders entitled to receive notice of the annual meeting must be made available to all shareholders for inspection for a period prior to the annual meeting that is usually prescribed by statute. Under the MBCA, the shareholder list must be available for inspection by any shareholder beginning two business days after notice of the meeting is given and continuing through the time of the meeting.

Once a record date has been set and a list of shareholders entitled to receive notice has been compiled, the directors, the corporate secretary, or other officer or individual, who is normally designated by the corporation's bylaws, must be sure that proper notice is given to all shareholders entitled to receive notice in compliance with the statutes of the state of domicile and the articles and bylaws of the corporation.

The notice of the meeting typically includes the date, time, and place of the meeting. If the meeting is a special meeting, a purpose for the meeting is given, as is often required by state statute or corporate bylaws. The statutes of the state of

◆ ————————————————————————————————————

transfer agent A person (or an institution such as a bank) who keeps track of who owns a company's stocks and bonds. Also called a registrar. A transfer agent sometimes also arranges dividend and interest payments.

domicile usually provide guidelines within which the notice of shareholder meetings must be given, and the bylaws of the corporation typically set forth a more precise manner for giving notice.

Section 7.05(a) of the MBCA sets forth the notice requirements for annual shareholder meetings:

> (a) A corporation shall notify shareholders of the date, time, and place of each annual and special shareholders' meeting no fewer than 10 nor more than 60 days before the meeting date. Unless this Act or the articles of incorporation require otherwise, the corporation is required to give notice only to shareholders entitled to vote at the meeting.

Figure 7-9 shows a sample notice of annual shareholder meeting.

**NOTICE OF ANNUAL MEETING
OF THE SHAREHOLDERS**

OF THE _____ CORPORATION

PLEASE TAKE NOTICE that the ___ Annual Meeting of the Shareholders of the _____ Corporation will be held on the _____ day of _____, _____, at ___ P.M., at the office of the corporation at _____, for the purpose of electing directors of the corporation and transacting such other business as may properly come before the meeting.

Dated this _____ day of _____, _____.

_____
Secretary

FIGURE 7-9   Sample Notice of Annual Shareholder Meeting

The secretary of the corporation, or any other individual responsible for mailing the notice of annual meeting, will often prepare an affidavit of mailing to evidence the proper mailing of the notice of the annual meeting in a timely manner. Figure 7-10 is an example of an affidavit of mailing of notice of annual shareholder meeting.

Waiver of Notice   Shareholders may waive notice of a meeting if they so choose. Typically, shareholders may waive notice by delivering to the corporation a signed waiver of notice, or by attending the meeting. In small corporations with only a few shareholders, the shareholders often meet without ever sending any formal notice. The shareholders' attendance at the meeting, as well as their waiver of formal notice, should be noted in the minutes of the meeting. A shareholder's attendance at any meeting is generally considered to constitute a waiver of notice, unless at the beginning of the meeting, the shareholder objects to the holding of the meeting or the transaction of business at the meeting. The waiver of notice in Figure 7-11 is a sample form that could be used at an annual meeting of the shareholders of a small corporation, when notice of the meeting was not mailed.

**AFFIDAVIT OF MAILING OF NOTICE
OF ANNUAL SHAREHOLDERS' MEETING**

OF THE _____ CORPORATION

STATE OF _____)

) SS

COUNTY OF _____)

_____, being first duly sworn on oath, deposes and says:

I am the Secretary of the _____ Corporation and that on the ____ day of _____, ____, I personally deposited in a post-office box in the City of _____, State of _____, each in a postage-paid envelope, one Notice of the Annual Meeting of the Shareholders of the Corporation to each person whose name appears on the annexed list, and to their respective post-office addresses as therein set forth.

_____

Secretary

Subscribed and sworn to before me
this ____ day of _____, ____.

_____

Notary Public

FIGURE 7-10 Sample Affidavit of Mailing Notice

**WAIVER OF NOTICE OF THE ANNUAL MEETING
OF THE SHAREHOLDERS OF THE**

_____ CORPORATION

We, the undersigned being all of the shareholders of the above corporation, hereby agree and consent to the annual meeting of the shareholders held on the ____ day of _____, ____, at ___ P.M., at the office of the corporation at _____, for the purpose of electing directors of the corporation and all such other business as may lawfully come before said meeting and hereby waive all notice of the meeting and any adjournment thereof. Dated this ____ day of _____, ____.

_____

_____

_____

_____

FIGURE 7-11 Sample Waiver of Notice

Proxies

A **proxy** is "an authority given by the holder of the stock who has the right to vote it to another to exercise his voting rights."[37] Shareholders who are unable to attend shareholder meetings may vote through the use of a proxy. The term *proxy* is often used both to define the person who will cast the vote in the place of the shareholder, and the document that transfers the voting power to the person voting in place of the shareholder.

A proxy may be a *general proxy*, which grants the right to vote the shareholder's shares of stock on all matters with limited restrictions, or it may be a *limited proxy*, which is specific to the situation and authorizes the proxy holder to vote the shares on a specific matter in a specific way.

General proxies are often used by shareholders of small corporations when one shareholder will be unavailable to attend shareholder meetings for an extended period. The shareholder of a closely held corporation may grant the power to vote his or her shares to an individual who is trusted to vote as the shareholder would if he or she were attending the meeting. Figure 7-12 is an example of a proxy conveying general authority to the proxy holder.

PROXY

[From 6A Am. Jur. Legal Forms Corporations § 74:1855 (2000)]

I, _____ [name of stockholder], do hereby constitute and appoint _____ [name], attorney and agent for me, and in my name, place, and stead, to vote as my proxy at any stockholders' meetings to be held between the date of this proxy and _____ [date], unless sooner revoked, with full power to cast the number of votes that all my shares of stock in _____ [corporation] should entitle me to cast as if I were then personally present, and authorize _____ [name of proxy] to act for me and in my name and stead as fully as I could act if I were present, giving to _____ [name of proxy]; attorney and agent, full power of substitution and revocation, hereby revoking all previous proxies.

In witness whereof, I have executed this proxy on _____ [date].

_____
[Signature of stockholder]

Witness: _____
[Signature]

FIGURE 7-12   Proxy. Reprinted with permission from *American Jurisprudence Legal Forms 2d*. © 2000 West Group.

---

proxy   A person who acts for another person (usually to vote in place of the other person in a meeting the other cannot attend). A document giving that right.

Larger, publicly held corporations use limited proxies to solicit the vote of shareholders who will not be attending the shareholder meeting. The officers or directors of the corporation send a **proxy statement** to each shareholder along with the notice of a meeting of the shareholders. The proxy statement describes the matters to be voted on at the meeting in an attempt to give shareholders enough information to make an informed decision. The proxy statement is accompanied by a proxy form for the shareholder to complete and return to the corporation. The shareholder indicates his or her voting preferences on the proxy and returns it to the corporation. The proxy may appoint an officer or director of the corporation to vote as indicated on the proxy form, unless prohibited by state statute. Often, the voting at the meetings of large corporations is merely a formality, as the corporation will receive enough proxy votes prior to the meeting to reach a majority voting consensus.

Rules for the solicitation of proxies and their use by publicly held corporations is discussed in Chapter 9.

Quorum

For an action to be taken at a meeting of the shareholders, (1) a quorum must be present, and (2) a sufficient number of shareholders present must vote in favor of the proposed action. Unless the articles of incorporation provide otherwise, a majority of the votes entitled to be cast typically constitutes a quorum. State statutes usually provide that the articles may prescribe a different quorum within certain limitations. For action to be taken at a meeting, a majority of the votes cast must be in favor of the action, unless some other manner for approving an action is prescribed by statute or set forth in the corporation's articles of incorporation.

Voting at Shareholder Meetings

It is generally assumed that each share of stock is entitled to one vote, although corporations with more than one class of stock may include a class of stock that has no voting rights or limited voting rights. Votes are cast by ballot at most formal shareholder meetings, and those ballots, along with the proxies received from shareholders not in attendance, are tallied to determine whether a quorum is present and whether enough votes were received to adopt the proposed resolutions. The ballot used at a shareholder meeting must be in accordance with the provisions of the statutes of the corporation's state of domicile and the corporation's articles and bylaws, and must be in a form that clearly shows the intent of the voting shareholder.

Voting at meetings held by small corporations may be done by a voice vote that is properly noted by the secretary, or other appointed individual, in the minutes of the meeting.

◆ _____

proxy statement   The document sent or given to stockholders when their voting proxies are requested for a corporate decision. The SEC has rules for when the statements must be given out and what must be in them.

Although it is generally not required by statute, **inspectors of election** are often appointed to oversee the election of directors at the shareholder meetings of large corporations. These inspectors are impartial individuals who are sworn to oversee the election of directors. Inspectors must determine the number of outstanding shares of stock, the presence of a quorum, and the validity of all proxies used. It is the inspectors' duty to count all votes, whether by ballot or proxy, to determine the outcome of the election.

Voting Trusts   To gain voting control of a corporation, a group of shareholders with common interests may decide to form a voting trust. A *voting trust* is an agreement among shareholders and a trustee whereby rights to vote the stock are transferred to the trustee, and all other rights incident to the ownership of the stock are retained by the shareholders. State statutes generally recognize voting trusts as valid, and the following three criteria are often used to identify a true voting trust:

1. A grant of voting rights for an indefinite period of time.
2. Acquisition of voting control of the corporation as the common purpose of the shareholders to the trust.
3. Voting rights are separated from the other attributes of stock ownership.

The MBCA allows the formation of voting trusts within the guidelines of § 7.30:

> (a) One or more shareholders may create a voting trust, conferring on a trustee the right to vote or otherwise act for them, by signing an agreement setting out the provisions of the trust (which may include anything consistent with its purpose) and transferring their shares to the trustee. When a voting trust agreement is signed, the trustee shall prepare a list of the names and addresses of all owners of beneficial interest in the trust, together with the number and class of shares each transferred to the trust, and deliver copies of the list and agreement to the corporation's principal office.

Subsections (b) and (c) of § 7.30 further provide that a voting trust may not be valid for a period of more than ten years after its effective date, unless extended by the signing of an extension agreement.

Voting Agreements   Shareholders may also seek to gain voting control of a corporation by means of a voting agreement, which is recognized and regulated in the statutes of most states. A *voting agreement* is an agreement among two or more shareholders that provides for the manner in which they will vote their shares for one or more specific purposes.

---

inspectors of election   Impartial individuals who are often appointed to oversee the election of directors at the shareholder meetings of large corporations.

Election of Directors

The involvement of the shareholder in the corporate affairs is often confined to and dominated by the annual meeting of the shareholders, when the shareholders vote for the directors of the corporation. Annual meetings are held for the purpose of electing directors of the corporation and for any other matters that may require the attention or approval of shareholders.

Straight Voting versus Cumulative Voting   There are two methods of voting for the election of directors: straight voting and cumulative voting. **Cumulative voting** is designed to give the minority shareholder a chance to elect at least one director to the board of directors. Cumulative voting may be required by statute, or it may be permitted by statute if the articles of incorporation require that cumulative voting be permitted.

When straight voting is the method used for electing the directors of the corporation, each share of stock may cast a vote for the number of directors that are to be elected to the board of directors. For example, if the board of directors is to consist of three individuals, a shareholder voting under the straight method, who owns 100 shares in the corporation, could cast 100 votes for Candidate 1, 100 votes for Candidate 2, and 100 votes for Candidate 3. If cumulative voting were used, the shareholder would have the same total number of votes to cast (300), but could choose to vote all 300 shares for Candidate 4 if desired, thereby granting the shareholder a better chance of getting at least one director of his or her choice elected to the board of directors.

Other Acts Requiring Shareholder Approval

In addition to electing the directors of the corporation, shareholders typically vote to ratify acts of the directors taken during the past year, and vote on any other business that might require shareholder approval, such as amendment of the articles of incorporation, issuance of stock, acquisitions and mergers involving the corporation, sale of corporate assets outside the normal course of business, or dissolution of the corporation. See Figure 7-13 on page 286. The state statutes or the articles of incorporation or bylaws of the corporation may set forth other or different actions that also require shareholder approval.

Minutes of Shareholder Meetings

Just as it is important that minutes be taken at every meeting of the board of directors, accurate minutes of shareholder meetings are crucial. Minutes of the shareholder meetings are typically taken and signed by the secretary of the corporation, who then places them in the corporate minute book, along with a copy of

---

cumulative voting   The type of voting in which each person (or each share of stock, in the case of a corporation) has as many votes as there are positions to be filled. Votes can be either concentrated on one or on a few candidates or spread around.

- ◆ Election of directors
- ◆ Amendment of bylaws
- ◆ Amendment of articles of incorporation
- ◆ Issuance of corporate stock
- ◆ Mergers and acquisitions
- ◆ Sale of corporate assets outside the normal course of business
- ◆ Dissolution of the corporation

FIGURE 7-13 Acts That Typically Require Shareholder Approval

the notice of the meeting that was sent to all shareholders, any waivers of notice received from the shareholders, any proxies received, and any other documents pertaining to the meeting. Figure 7-14 is an example of minutes of an annual shareholder meeting.

Unanimous Consents of Shareholders

The MBCA, and the statutes of most states, allow shareholders to take action without a meeting through means of a written consent signed by all shareholders entitled to vote on the action. For small corporations, this written consent or "unanimous writing of the shareholders in lieu of meeting" has become an invaluable tool for approving matters that require shareholder consent, especially matters that require attention between the regularly scheduled shareholder meetings.

In recent years, revisions to the MBCA and many state statutes make it clear that the approved action may be evidenced by more than one document, making it even easier to obtain the consent of a large number of shareholders within a relatively short time period. For example, if there are ten shareholders of a corporation, the corporate secretary can now send out ten identical consents, one to each shareholder, to be signed and returned, instead of having one document that must be circulated to all ten shareholders for signature.

Figure 7-15 on page 288 shows a sample unanimous written consent of the shareholders in lieu of an annual meeting.

§ 7.9 RESTRICTIONS ON TRANSFER OF SHARES OF CORPORATE STOCK

The freedom to transfer corporate stock without restrictions has always been considered a basic shareholder right. However, recognizing the value of limited restrictions on the transfer of stock under certain conditions, the courts have found that "restrictions may be imposed for the mutual convenience and protection of the parties, so long as such restrictions are not unreasonable and do not constitute an impairment of the stockholder's contractual rights."[38]

This section focuses on the restrictions placed on stock transfers by shareholder agreements and considerations in drafting shareholder agreements. The section concludes with a look at other restrictions that may be placed on share transfers.

MINUTES OF
ANNUAL MEETING OF SHAREHOLDERS

OF THE _____ CORPORATION

The annual meeting of the Shareholders of the _____ Corporation was held on _____, at the registered office of the corporation at _____.

_____ presided as chairman of the meeting, and _____ acted as its secretary.

The secretary reported that the notice of meeting of the annual shareholders' meeting was mailed in accordance with state statute and with the articles and bylaws of the corporation, and that the notice of meeting and affidavit of mailing were filed in the corporate minute book of the corporation.

The following shareholders were present in person:

_____

_____

_____

_____.

The following shareholders were present by proxy:

_____

_____.

It was determined that at least ___% of the shareholders were present, and the meeting was called to order.

The reports of the president, secretary, and treasurer were presented to the shareholders, received, and filed in the corporate minute book.

The chairman then called for the election of the directors of the corporation.

Upon motion duly made, seconded, and carried, the following persons were elected to the board of directors, to serve as director of the Corporation until their successors are elected at the next annual meeting and qualify:

_____

_____

_____

_____.

There being no further business before the meeting, it was, on motion duly made, seconded, and unanimously carried, adjourned.

_____
Secretary

FIGURE 7-14 Sample Minutes of Annual Shareholder Meeting

**UNANIMOUS WRITING IN LIEU
OF ANNUAL MEETING OF THE SHAREHOLDERS**

OF THE _____ CORPORATION

The undersigned, being all of the shareholders of _____ (the "Corporation"), hereby adopt the following resolutions in lieu of holding an annual meeting of the shareholders, effective the _____ day of _____, _____.

RESOLVED, that the following persons are hereby elected to the board of directors, to serve as directors of the Corporation until their successors are elected at the next annual meeting and qualify:

_____

_____

_____

_____.

FURTHER RESOLVED, that the acts of the directors on behalf of the corporation for the past fiscal year are hereby ratified, affirmed, and approved.

_____

_____

_____

FIGURE 7-15 Sample Unanimous Writing in Lieu or Annual Shareholder Meeting

Shareholder Agreements Restricting Stock Transfers

The shareholders of a corporation may desire to place certain restrictions on the transfer of shares to protect their status in the corporation and to monitor the inclusion of new shareholders in the corporation. Shareholders of a close corporation may wish to have the option to purchase shares of a withdrawing shareholder before the shares are sold to an outsider. Also, shareholders looking toward the future may desire to insure a market for their stock when they decide to sell. For all these reasons, shareholders of a corporation may agree to place restrictions on the sale of their stock.

Restrictions on the transfer of stock may be placed in the articles of incorporation, in the bylaws of the corporation, or in a separate shareholder agreement, or **buy-sell agreement,** as it may be called. Restrictions on the transfer of stock of statutory close corporations may also be prescribed by the close corporation act or close corporation provisions of the business corporation act of the company's state of domicile.

◆

buy-sell agreement An agreement among partners or owners of a company that if one dies or withdraws from the business, his or her share will be bought by the others or disposed of according to a pre-arranged plan.

Agreements Granting Option to Purchase Stock   Shareholder agreements that give the corporation or shareholders of the corporation the option to purchase shares of any shareholder upon the happening of a specified event are the least restrictive type of agreement. This sort of agreement does not obligate the shareholders to purchase the shares of a selling shareholder, nor does it guarantee a market for a shareholder who desires to sell his or her shares.

Shareholders of statutory close corporations may be granted, by statute, the option of purchasing the shares of selling shareholders before those shares are sold to third parties. Under the Close Corporation Supplement to the MBCA, a shareholder desiring to sell stock in a close corporation who obtains an offer to purchase the shares for cash from an eligible third person must first offer the shares to the corporation, pursuant to statute, upon the same terms as the offer. However, the Close Corporation Supplement provides that this restriction does not apply to transfers within the corporation. More specifically, shareholders are free to sell or transfer their shares to any of the following without restriction:

1. The corporation or to any other holder of the same class or series of shares.
2. Members of the shareholder's immediate family or a trust whose beneficiaries are members of the shareholder's immediate family.
3. An executor or administrator upon the death of a shareholder.
4. A trustee or receiver as the result of a bankruptcy, insolvency, dissolution, or similar proceeding brought by or against a shareholder.

The restrictions also do not apply to transfers of stock that have been approved in writing by all holders of the corporation's shares that have voting rights, or to transfers resulting from a merger or share exchange, a pledge as loan collateral that does not grant voting rights, or the termination of the corporation's status as a statutory close corporation.

The shareholders of corporations that are not subject to statutory restrictions such as those in the Close Corporation Supplement may adopt similar provisions in the articles of incorporation of the corporation, in the corporate bylaws, or in a separate agreement executed by the corporation and all shareholders.

Agreements Mandating the Purchase of Stock   Corporate shareholders may decide it is in their best interests to enter into mandatory stock purchase agreements. This type of agreement among the shareholders obligates the corporation or other shareholders to purchase the shares of a deceased or withdrawing shareholder upon the happening of a particular event, at a pre-established price. This type of agreement guarantees a market for the shares of a shareholder who wishes to withdraw from the corporation, upon certain conditions.

Statutory provisions mandating the transfer of stock in any regard are rare. Although the Close Corporation Supplement to the MBCA contains provisions for the compulsory purchase of shares after the death of a shareholder, it is clearly stated that that particular section of the Supplement applies only to statutory close corporations that elect so to provide in their articles of incorporation.[39] Section 14(a) of the Close Corporation Supplement, if adopted, provides that "the executor or administrator of the estate of a deceased shareholder may require the corporation to purchase or cause to be purchased all (but not less than all) of the decedent's shares or to be dissolved."

Considerations in Drafting Shareholder Agreements

The shareholder agreement, or buy-sell agreement, need not be exclusively for the optional or mandatory purchase for shares. It may be a hybrid of these two types of agreements, giving shareholders the option to purchase shares of a withdrawing shareholder under certain circumstances and mandating purchase under other circumstances.

Events Triggering Agreement The events that trigger a buy-sell agreement will vary, depending on the purpose and intent of the shareholders. Buy-sell agreements may be triggered by any of the following events:

1. Death of a shareholder.
2. Retirement of a shareholder-employee.
3. Disability of a shareholder-employee.
4. Proposed sale by any shareholder to a third party.

Purchase Price The purchase price found in buy-sell agreements that mandate the purchase of stock of a shareholder upon the happening of a specific event is often the most important element in the agreement. The agreement rarely sets a specific price for the stock purchase, but rather specifies a formula for determining the price of the stock. Determining the price of stock of a closely held corporation can be very difficult, because it is impossible to determine a "market value" for stock which, in effect, has no market.

Often the shareholders will agree on a price per share in a supplement to the buy-sell agreement. This supplement is then updated periodically, with the most recent supplement providing the price in effect in the event the agreement is activated. The corporation may use the book value of the stock or the best offer of a third party to determine the price. Other formulas may be used so long as the formula is agreed upon by all shareholders in the buy-sell agreement.

Insurance Funding Shareholders usually recognize that the mandated buyout of a deceased shareholder could impose a severe financial hardship on the corporation, so they seek to cover that loss by purchasing life insurance on the life of major shareholders. The proceeds of the life insurance policy can then be used to purchase the deceased's shares of stock from the estate.

Other Restrictions on Share Transfers

Corporate shareholders may find it necessary or desirable to place restrictions on the transfer of corporate stock for reasons other than monitoring the ownership of the corporation and ensuring a market for the corporation's stock. For example, shareholders of S corporations may have to place restrictions on the transfer of corporate stock to remain in compliance with the S corporation requirements. Large corporations and publicly held corporations may find it necessary to restrict the transfer of corporate shares in order to comply with securities regulations.

In any event, any restriction on the transfer of shares of stock must be considered reasonable and generally must be approved by all shareholders of the corporation. In addition, the specific restriction must be located on the face or reverse of the stock certificate of any affected shares.

§ 7.10 SHAREHOLDER ACTIONS

There are three general types of shareholder lawsuits:

1. Individual shareholder actions.
2. Representative actions.
3. Derivative actions.

The nature of and requirements for each of these types of actions are discussed briefly in this section.

Individual Actions

An individual shareholder who is injured by an action of the corporation may bring suit against the corporation for damages. An individual shareholder may maintain a suit against a corporation in much the same way as any other individual would. Generally, individual actions are brought only when the individual shareholder alleges that the action committed by the corporation is a direct fraud on the individual shareholder and that such wrongs do not affect the other shareholders. However, the same action that causes injury to the individual plaintiff may also affect a substantial number of other shareholders.

Representative Actions

Representative actions are actions in which the parties are "too numerous to be joined, one party or a few being permitted to sue on behalf of all."[40] The representative action is typically brought by a shareholder on behalf of the shareholder and his or her entire class of shareholders against the corporation.

The term *representative action* is sometimes used interchangeably with the term **direct action**. Both terms refer to lawsuits by shareholders in which the claim belongs to the shareholders—not the corporation. Any benefit derived from a

---

representative action A lawsuit brought by one stockholder in a corporation to claim rights or to fix wrongs done to many or all stockholders in the company.

direct action A lawsuit by a stockholder to enforce his or her own rights against a corporation or its officers rather than to enforce the corporation's rights in a derivative action.

representative action belongs to the shareholders. Some typical representative actions include actions against the corporation and its management for fraudulent public statements made affecting the stock price, actions to compel the payment of dividends, and actions to preserve shareholders' voting rights.

Derivative Actions

A shareholder's **derivative action** has been defined as "an action brought by one or more stockholders of a corporation to enforce a corporate right or remedy a wrong to the corporation in cases where the corporation, because it is controlled by the wrongdoers or for other reasons, fails and refuses to take appropriate action for its own protection."[41]

Because the corporation is a separate entity, it is possible that the entity could sustain damages at the expense of its shareholders. Shareholders may prosecute derivative lawsuits on behalf of the corporation to protect their own interests in the corporation, especially if they feel that the directors of the corporation are not acting with the corporation's best interests in mind. The derivative action is distinguished from other types of shareholder lawsuits in that the cause of action belongs to the corporation, not to the individual shareholder or shareholders. Although most derivative actions are against corporate management for waste of corporate assets, self-dealing, or mismanagement, it is also possible for shareholders to maintain derivative actions against unrelated third parties to enforce rights of the corporation. Any benefit derived from a derivative action belongs to the corporation itself and not the shareholders.

The following must generally be present for a stockholder in a corporation to maintain a derivative action:[42]

1. Some action or threatened action of the managing board of directors or trustees of the corporation which is beyond the authority conferred on them by their charter or other source of organization.

2. Such a fraudulent transaction, completed or contemplated by the acting managers, in connection with some other party, or among themselves, or with other shareholders, as will result in serious injury to the corporation, or to the interests of the other shareholders.

3. Action by the board of directors, or a majority of them, in their own interest, destructive of the corporation itself, or of the rights of the other shareholders.

4. Action by the majority of shareholders themselves in oppressively and illegally pursuing a course in the name of the corporation, which is in violation of the rights of the other shareholders, and which can only be restrained by the aid of a court of equity.

◆ ———————————————————————————————————————

derivative action   A lawsuit by a stockholder of a corporation against another person (usually an officer of the company) to enforce claims the stockholder thinks the corporation has against that person.

Many states have enacted legislation in an attempt to alleviate unnecessary litigation. Most state statutes require shareholders to make a good faith attempt to prompt the corporation to take action in its own behalf to prevent or remedy the injustice that the shareholders are seeking to cure, before a derivative action may be commenced. Section 7.42 of the MBCA, which is typical of such statutory provisions, sets forth strict requirements for the commencement of derivative suits:

§ 7.42 DEMAND

No shareholder may commence a derivative proceeding until:

(1) a written demand has been made upon the corporation to take suitable action; and
(2) 90 days have expired from the date the demand was made unless the shareholder has earlier been notified that the demand has been rejected by the corporation or unless irreparable injury to the corporation would result by waiting for the expiration of the 90 day period.

§ 7.11 THE PARALEGAL'S ROLE IN CORPORATE ORGANIZATIONAL MATTERS

Whether the paralegal works in a law firm or in a corporation, the paralegal will often be asked to assist the attorney and the corporate client in complying with statutory requirements for corporate formalities. This can include extensive research to ascertain the rights, duties, and potential for personal liability of the corporation's officers, directors, and shareholders. Statutory research may also be necessary to insure that the formalities for director and shareholder annual and special meetings and elections are being complied with.

Paralegals who work for corporations, especially publicly held corporations, may be very involved in preparing for meetings of the board of directors. They may also be asked to assist with the many tasks that need to be undertaken to hold the annual shareholder meeting. Specifically, the paralegal may be involved in:

◆ Researching statutes and corporate bylaws to determine requirements for annual meeting.
◆ Preparing notices and proxy statements.
◆ Arranging for the mailing of notices of the meeting and proxy materials.
◆ Making physical arrangements for the meeting, including reserving a place for the meeting and making sure all needed equipment and refreshments are available.
◆ Arranging for press coverage.
◆ Coordinating travel arrangements for the directors.

Corporate Paralegal Profile
Mary Beth Riley-Wallis

Interacting with all departments of the company who are considered our "clients" gives me a better understanding of how the company operates and meets its goals.

Name Mary Beth Riley-Wallis

Location Westfield, Massachusetts

Title Corporate Paralegal

Specialty Business and Real Estate

Education Associate Degree in Paralegal Studies from Bay Path College in Massachusetts; Bachelor Degree in Paralegal Studies from Roger William College in Rhode Island

Experience 17 Years

Mary Beth Riley-Wallis is an experienced corporate paralegal with a background in real estate who works for the general counsel of Casual Corner Group, Inc. Casual Corner's legal department employs three attorneys and four paralegals.

In her position, Mary Beth has the opportunity to learn about many different facets of the company. Her primary responsibilities include maintaining corporate records for four corporations and two limited liability companies. This includes drafting minutes, seeing to it that the entities are qualified to do business in the appropriate states, and performing similar tasks associated with corporate maintenance. She also reviews all corporate contracts the company enters into and coordinates discovery and the progress of litigation that Casual Corner may be involved in.

Mary Beth's favorite aspects of her position are the diversity and the handling of several differ-ent types of issues at once. Interacting with all departments of the company gives her an understanding of how the company operates and meets its goals.

She is also responsible for filing virtually every document that passes through the law department, and Mary Beth admits that, at times, figuring how to organize files so that items can easily be retrieved can be a challenge.

Recently, Mary Beth assisted with the launching of Casual Corner's Web page. She was responsible for reviewing all the contracts for software and services associated with the site and assisted in the development of the site's legal content such as the Privacy Policy and Terms of Use.

Mary Beth has also used her Web page knowledge and experience to assist the Central Connecticut Paralegal Association (CCPA). She was the chairperson of the Technology Committee of the CCPA and has assisted in making changes to that organization's Web page.

Mary Beth's advice to new paralegals?

I think the most important thing is to keep an open mind to what is expected of you. ... The key is to be open to learning new things because this gives you diversity. You need to be diverse, organized, flexible, and a team player, and this carries over to any position you hold.

For more information on careers for corporate paralegals, see the Corporate Careers features on the companion Web page to this text at **www. westlegalstudies.com.**

Corporate paralegals who work in law firms are often assigned the task of maintaining and updating the corporate minute books, which the law firm maintains for its corporate clients.

Paralegals may be asked to draft letters to all corporate clients, reminding them of the statutory annual meeting requirements and the annual meeting requirements established by the articles of incorporation or bylaws of the corporation. Paralegals frequently follow up with each client by drafting and sending out notices of annual meetings and preparing minutes for the minute book, or by drafting unanimous writings in lieu of meetings of the board of directors of the corporation and seeing to their execution.

When conducting a thorough review of a corporate minute book, you should answer the following questions:

Incorporation Documents

♦ What is the exact name of the corporation?

♦ What was the corporation's date of incorporation?

♦ What is the corporation's registered office address, and who is the registered agent?

♦ How many shares of each type of stock is the corporation authorized to issue?

♦ Is the corporation in compliance with any statutory incorporation formalities concerning publication of notice of incorporation or filing notice of incorporation at the local level?

♦ Has the corporation received certificates of authority to transact business in any foreign state in which it transacts business?

♦ Does the minute book contain other pertinent incorporation documentation required by the statues of the corporation's state of domicile?

Corporate Bylaws

♦ How many directors are required under the bylaws? Does the corporation currently have the requisite number of directors?

♦ If the fiscal year is set forth in the bylaws of the corporation, is it correct?

♦ Are other procedures for managing the corporation's affairs, as set forth in the bylaws, being complied with?

Corporate Minutes

♦ Are there any missing minutes (for example, minutes not prepared for a certain year or years)?

♦ Are there minutes or unanimous writings of the shareholders electing the current directors of the corporation?

♦ Are there minutes or unanimous writings of the directors electing the current officers of the corporation?

♦ Are there any missing signatures (for example, all elected directors must sign unanimous writings of the board of directors)?

♦ Have resolutions made by the board of directors or shareholders been carried through?

Stock Certificates

♦ Are the certificates, subscription agreements, and ledgers consistent with each other?

♦ Are all stock certificates signed and in place?

- Is there a record of the location of all stock certificates not kept in the minute book?
- If the corporation has a shareholder agreement, do the stock certificates have the appropriate legends concerning restrictions on their transfer?

ETHICAL CONSIDERATION

All attorneys and paralegals owe a duty of loyalty to their clients, including corporate clients. During your paralegal career, you must be aware of any personal interests you may have that conflict with the interests of any clients you work to represent. What if a corporation your law firm represents is suing your spouse's business? In addition, you must be aware of any conflicts between clients you have helped to represent—both currently and in the past. What if the law firm that has just hired you represents a corporation that is suing a client of the firm you just left?

When the interests of a client conflict with the personal interests of an attorney, or with the interests of another client of the attorney, or a past client of the attorney, the attorney has a potential conflict of interest. If the representation of a new client presents a possible conflict of interest, the attorney must turn down the new representation or obtain consent of both parties.

An attorney representing a corporation or other business organization has a duty of loyalty to the organization itself and must act to protect the interests of the organization. The attorney may not represent officers, directors, or others associated with the firm if the interests of the individual conflicts with the interests of the organization.

If an attorney becomes aware of actions being taken by officers, directors, agents, or others that are harmful to the organization the attorney represents, the attorney must act according to prescribed ethical rules to protect the organization.

Paralegals must be aware of and abide by the ethical rules concerning conflicts of interest that apply to attorneys. The paralegal's personal interests must not conflict with those of a client of an attorney the paralegal is assisting. In addition, the paralegal must not be in a position to assist a client who has an interest adverse to a current or former client.

Undisclosed conflicts of interest can have serious consequences for the paralegal, the attorney, and the entire law firm or legal department. You must be sure to keep current with your firm's or department's conflict of interest procedures. Law firms commonly circulate weekly lists of new clients and new matters that the firm is representing. You should carefully review these lists to make sure you have no potential conflict of interest.

Above all, if you have any questions concerning conflicts of interest, consult the rules of your paralegal association and the rules applicable to attorneys in your jurisdiction. Specific rules concerning conflicts of interest are included in the rules of ethics for attorneys in every state, as well as in the Model Rules of Ethics of the National Federation of Paralegal Associations and the National Association of Legal Assistants, which are included in appendix C to this text.

---

§ 7.12 RESOURCES

By far the most important resource in working with corporate organizational matters is the statutes of the state of domicile. The corporate paralegal should be so familiar with state statutes that he or she can quickly locate statutory provisions regarding the organizational formalities that must be complied with by corporations.

Other important resources are the state-specific corporate procedure manuals that are available for every state, and continuing education materials published on a state-by-state basis. Much of this information is available on-line.

Internet Resources www.

Information available on-line to assist with corporate maintenance includes state statutes and corporate forms to be used for preparing minutes and unanimous writings.

For state statutes

American Law Source Online	**www.lawsource.com/also**
Findlaw.com	**www.guide.lp.findlaw.com/11stategov/**
Legal Information Institute	**www.law.cornell.edu/states/listing.html**

For corporate resolution forms

All About Forms.Com	**www.allaboutforms.com/**
Findlaw.com (Legal Forms)	**www.findlaw.com**
The 'Lectric Law Library's Business and General Forms	**www.lectlaw.com/formb.htm**

For articles and general information on corporate law

Legal Information Institute	**www.law.cornell.edu/topics/corporations.html**
The 'Lectric Law Library's Business Lounge	**www.lectlaw.com/bus.html**

An alphabetical list of Internet Resources for the Corporate Paralegal is included as appendix B to this text.

Web Page

For updates and links to several of the previously listed sites, log on to **www. westlegalstudies.com,** and click through to the book link for this text.

SUMMARY

- Corporations act through officers and directors who serve as agents of the corporation.

- State statutes grant the directors the authority to act on behalf of the corporation.

- In most corporations, the shareholders elect directors at annual meetings and the directors elect the officers of the corporation.

- Directors may delegate certain authority to officers, but they are generally responsible for the acts of the officers they appoint.

- Directors may delegate authority to one or more committees that are comprised of members of the board of directors.

- Directors owe a fiduciary duty, a duty of care, and a duty of loyalty to the corporation and its shareholders.

- The business judgment rule provides that directors cannot be held personally liable for the poor outcome of their informed decisions made in good faith.

- Indemnification refers to the act by which corporations reimburse officers and directors for expenses incurred by them in defending lawsuits to which they become a party due to their involvement with the corporation.

- Indemnification may be mandatory in some instances (such as when it is found that the officer or director is guilty of no wrongdoing), and it may be prohibited in some instances (such as when the action arises from the officer or director's personal wrongdoing).

- The number of directors a corporation has may be set by the articles of incorporation, the bylaws, or by corporate resolution (depending on state statute).

- In lieu of holding a meeting, the board of directors and the shareholders may take action by a written resolution signed by all directors or all shareholders.

- The corporate secretary generally maintains a corporate minute book that contains the corporation's articles of incorporation, bylaws, minutes of meetings of both shareholders and directors, stock certificates, and a ledger of all issued shares of stock.

- Preemptive rights give shareholders the opportunity to protect their position in the corporation by giving them priority to purchase newly issued shares of the corporation.

- A corporation's officers may include a chief executive officer, chairman of the board, president, one or more vice presidents, chief executive officer, treasurer, assistant treasurer, secretary, and assistant secretary.

- Some of the most important decisions made on behalf of the corporation are made by the vote of shareholders at annual shareholder meetings.

- Shareholder meetings are typically called by the directors of the corporation. However, if the directors fail to call the meeting within a reasonable time, state statutes and the corporation's bylaws usually provide a means for the shareholders to call an annual meeting.

◆ Special meetings of the shareholders may be called to transact extraordinary business that requires shareholder approval.

◆ Shareholders may grant proxies to others to vote in their place at shareholder meetings.

◆ Cumulative voting grants each shareholder as many votes for each share of stock as there are directors to be elected. Shareholders may cumulate their votes for one director or spread them among the directors to be elected. Cumulative voting rights are designed to give minority shareholders a chance to elect at least one director to the board.

◆ Corporate actions that typically require shareholder approval include: the election of directors, the adoption of amendments to the bylaws or articles of incorporation, the issuance of corporate stock, the approval of mergers and acquisitions, the sale of corporate assets, and the dissolution of the corporation.

◆ Shareholders may enter into agreements to restrict the transfer of corporate stock and to provide a market for their stock in the event of their retirement or death.

◆ Derivative actions are lawsuits brought by shareholders on behalf of the corporation.

◆ Paralegals often assist with preparing minutes of board of directors' and shareholders' meetings, with preparation for annual meetings, and with corporate minute book maintenance.

REVIEW QUESTIONS

1. Where does a committee get its authority? Who is ultimately responsible for the acts of the committee?

2. What are the three types of duties a director owes to the corporation?

3. If a board of directors, exercising due care, makes a poor business decision that results in a substantial financial loss to the corporation, can the shareholders of the corporation look to the directors' personal assets to recover their damages? What if one director withheld information from the other directors and personally benefited from the decision?

4. Albert is on the board of directors of Acme Sailboard Company, Inc. As the result of a contract dispute, Acme Sailboard Company, Inc. and Albert are both named in a lawsuit brought by one of their suppliers. If Albert is found at the trial to be innocent of any wrongdoing, who is responsible for paying his attorney's fees and

legal expenses? What if it is determined at trial that there has been an illegal conversion of funds by Albert that resulted in the lawsuit?

5. Can a corporation incorporated under a state following the MBCA consist of one individual who is an officer, director, and shareholder?

6. Must all corporations have a board of directors?

7. Who typically elects the officers of the corporation?

8. Under the MBCA, what is the minimum number of votes required to pass a resolution of the shareholders if 1,000 shares of the corporation's stock have been issued?

9. If the shareholders of a corporation feel that their stock has lost its value due to the mismanagement and/or misconduct of the corporation's officers and directors, what if any recourse do they have?

10. Who typically benefits when cumulative voting for the directors of a corporation is allowed?

PRACTICAL PROBLEMS

1. How do the statutes in your state address pre-emptive rights for shareholders? Locate the pertinent section in your state's statutes to answer the following questions:
   a. In what section of your state's statutes are preemptive rights addressed?
   b. If a corporation's articles of incorporation are silent on the issue, are the shareholders granted preemptive rights?

2. How do the statutes in your state address cumulative voting rights for the directors of a corporation? Locate the pertinent section in your state's statutes to answer the following questions:
   a. In what section of your state's statues is cumulative voting for directors addressed?
   b. If a corporation's articles of incorporation are silent on the issue, are the shareholders granted cumulative voting rights?

WORKPLACE SCENARIO

Assume that one year has passed since you assisted with the incorporation of our fictitious corporation, Cutting Edge Computer Repair, Inc. It is time for an annual meeting of the shareholders and directors of the corporation. Bradley Harris and Cynthia Lund have met again with Belinda Benson to discuss the progress of the business over the past year and the formalities required for holding annual meetings. Belinda has decided, with her clients, that it will not be necessary to hold a formal meeting. Belinda will instead prepare unanimous writings of the directors and the shareholders of Cutting Edge Computer Repair, Inc. to approve certain transactions that have occurred during the past year and reelect officers and directors.

Using the information in appendix D-3 of this text and the forms and examples throughout this chapter, prepare unanimous writings of the board of directors and shareholders to approve the following resolutions:

Unanimous Written Consent of the Shareholders

1. Reelect the current directors of the corporation.
2. Approve and ratify the acts of the directors for the previous year.

Unanimous Written Consent of the Board of Directors

1. Reelect the current officers of the corporation.
2. Approve salaries of the officers of the corporation for the next year in the amount of $75,000 each.
3. Approve and ratify the acts of the officers for the previous year.

END NOTES

1. 8B AM. JUR. 2d *Corporations* § 1483 (1999).
2. *Chapin v. Benwood Foundation, Inc.,* 402 A2d 1205 (1979).
3. Revised Model Business Corporation Act § 8.25(e)(1).
4. *Id.* § 8.25(e)(2).
5. *Id.* § 8.25(e)(3).
6. *Id.* § 8.25(e)(4).
7. *Id.* § 8.25(e)(5).
8. *Id.* § 8.25(e)(6).
9. *Id.* § 8.25(e)(7).
10. *Id.* § 8.25(e)(8).
11. 18B AM. JUR. 2d *Corporations* § 1689 (1999).
12. *Id.* § 1689.
13. *Id.* § 1695.
14. *Id.* § 1699.
15. Revised Model Business Corporation Act § 8.30(a)(1).

16. *Id.* § 8.330(a)(2).

17. *Id.* § 8.30(b).

18. 18B AM. JUR. 2d *Corporations* § 1711 (1999).

19. *Id.* § 1703.

20. *Auerbach v. Bennett,* 393 NE2d 994 (1979).

21. *Scheuer Family Foundation v. 61 Associates,* 582 NYS2d 662 (1992).

22. 18B AM. JUR. 2d *Corporations* § 1700 (1999).

23. Frisby Fain, Constance, Corporate Director and Officer Liability, *University of Arkansas at Little Rock Law Journal,* Spring 1996.

24. Revised Model Business Corporation Act § 2.02.

25. *Salaman v. National Media Corp.,* 1994 WL 465534 (Del. Super.).

26. Revised Model Business Corporation Act § 8.03.

27. 18B AM. JUR. 2d *Corporations* § 1419 (1999).

28. Revised Model Business Corporation Act § 8.09.

29. *Id.* § 8.09.

30. *Id.* § 8.22(a).

31. *Id.* § 8.20(b).

32. 18B AM. JUR. 2d *Corporations* § 1342 (1999).

33. 2 Fletcher Cyclopedia of Private Corp. § 269 (2000).

34. Frisby Fain, Constance, Corporate Director and Officer Liability, *University of Arkansas at Little Rock Law Journal,* Spring 1996.

35. Revised Model Business Corporation Act § 7.01.

36. 6 AM. JUR. Legal Forms 2d *Corporations* § 74:992 (Rev 1995). Reprinted with permission from *American Jurisprudence Legal Forms 2d.* © 2000 West Group.

37. 18A AM. JUR. 2d *Corporations* § 1342 (1999).

38. *Id.* § 683.

39. Close Corporation Supplement to the Model Business Corporation Act § 14(a).

40. 19 AM. JUR. 2d *Corporations* § 2244 (1985).

41. *Id.* § 2250.

42. *Id.* § 2260.

CHAPTER 8

The Corporate Financial Structure

CHAPTER OUTLINE

§ 8.1   Capitalization of the Corporation

§ 8.2   Equity Financing

§ 8.3   Par Value

§ 8.4   Consideration for Shares of Stock

§ 8.5   Issuance of Stock

§ 8.6   Redemption of Equity Shares

§ 8.7   Dividends

§ 8.8   Stock Splits

§ 8.9   Debt Financing

§ 8.10   The Paralegal's Role in Corporate Financial Matters

§ 8.11   Resources

INTRODUCTION

Three main concerns must be addressed regarding a corporation's financial structure: (1) its ability to raise and maintain the level of capital necessary to operate the business, (2) the distribution of earnings and profits to its shareholders, and (3) the division of its assets upon dissolution. This chapter explores many of the options available to the incorporators or directors of a corporation when deciding which choices will best raise capital for the corporation and distribute profits to the corporation's shareholders, in a manner that is equitable and beneficial to both the corporation and its shareholders. The distribution of assets upon dissolution of a corporation is discussed in Chapter 12.

Paralegals are not responsible for advising corporate clients on the financial structure of their organizations. Nevertheless, a basic understanding of the corporation's financial structure will benefit paralegals, who are often responsible for drafting articles of incorporation, minutes, and other corporate documents that are affected by the manner in which the financial structure of the corporation is designed.

This chapter begins with a general discussion of the capitalization of a corporation. Next, it focuses on equity financing, including par value of stock, the consideration given in exchange for stock of the corporation, and the issuance of stock. The focus then shifts to the redemption of equity shares, dividends, and stock splits. This chapter concludes with an examination of debt financing and a look at the paralegal's role in corporate financial matters.

§ 8.1 CAPITALIZATION OF THE CORPORATION

Before a corporation can begin transacting business, it must have capital with which to work. The *capital* of a corporation is generally considered to be all of the corporation's assets, although the term is sometimes used more narrowly to define only the portion of the corporation's assets that is utilized for operation of the corporation's business.[1] The directors of a corporation typically rely on both equity and debt financing to raise the initial capital for the corporation. Equity financing is a means of raising capital by selling **equity securities**—shares of stock in the corporation that represent an ownership stake. Debt financing is achieved by issuing **debt securities**—notes and any other securities that represent loans to the corporation that must be repaid. Capital generated by the issuance of equity securities is often referred to as *equity capital;* the issuance of debt securities generates *debt capital.* After the corporation begins operating, income generated by the business of the corporation is also a major source of capital.

Corporate management has the duty of determining how much capital, and what type of capital, the corporation requires.

Some of the advantages of issuing equity securities include the fact that the amount invested by shareholders does not have to be repaid, and **dividends** typically need not be paid to shareholders when the corporation is not earning a profit. As opposed to debt financing, the issuance of equity securities maintains a lower debt/equity ratio for the corporation, which increases the corporation's attractiveness to creditors and potential creditors and lowers the risk of insolvency. In addition, the corporation is not required to expend large sums of money on interest payments, as is usually the case with debt financing. One disadvantage of selling equity securities is the fact that the current shareholders' control over the corporation may be diluted.

Although debt capital must be repaid, debt financing offers several advantages to the corporation. Most importantly, the control of the existing shareholders is not diluted by the issuance of debt securities. Also, the issuance of debt securities, as

---

equity securities   Securities that represent an ownership interest in the corporation.

debt securities   Securities that represent loans to the corporation, or other interests that must be repaid.

dividend   A share of profits or property; usually a payment per share of a corporation's stock.

opposed to equity securities, offers certain tax advantages to the corporation, as the payment of interest on debt securities is generally tax-deductible as an expense, whereas dividends paid to equity shareholders are not.

Some of the disadvantages of debt financing include the fact that interest must generally be paid on the securities, whether or not the corporation has any income for a particular period. Also, too high a debt/equity ratio in a corporation may hinder the corporation's ability to obtain short-term loans and may increase the likelihood of insolvency.

The corporation's capital typically consists of a mixture of debt and equity capital, and it is usually a function of the incorporators or the board of directors to determine the best debt/equity mixture and the best sources for the required capital. One significant factor in that decision is the possible impact of the federal Securities Act of 1933, the Securities and Exchange Act of 1934, and the securities acts of the corporation's state of domicile. Public securities offerings are regulated by the Securities and Exchange Commission and are subject to the provisions of the federal and state securities acts. Securities regulations and exemptions are discussed in Chapter 9.

Directors may also be limited, in a very practical sense, by the types of financing available to the corporation. Corporations engaging in high-risk ventures may be forced to rely more heavily on equity financing to raise funds, because debt financing can be difficult to obtain. Lenders are much more willing to finance low-risk ventures. Other available means of raising capital for a corporation include sale and leaseback arrangements and employee stock ownership plans (ESOPs). ESOPs are discussed in Chapter 14.

Not only is adequate capitalization of a corporation crucial to its financial success, it can also be important to protect the personal liability of the shareholders. If a corporation is organized and carries on business without substantial capital and is likely to have insufficient assets available to meet its debts, it is inequitable to allow the shareholders to escape personal liability.[2]

§ 8.2 EQUITY FINANCING

Equity financing involves the issuance of shares of stock of the corporation in exchange for cash or other consideration that will become corporate capital. Equity securities must be authorized in the corporation's articles of incorporation and are usually designated as common or **preferred stock**. The sale of stock is noted in the corporation's books by a debit to the assets column (usually cash) and a credit to the capital account column (or shareholder equity column, as it is sometimes referred to). See Figure 8-1.

The usual method of equity financing is the issuance of common stock in exchange for cash. However, many variations are available. The issuance of equity securities means granting certain rights to the individuals who have given

---

preferred stock   A type of stock that is entitled to certain rights and privileges over other outstanding stock of the corporation.

Balance Sheet	
Assets	*Liabilities*
Cash $10,000	
	Shareholder's Equity
	Common Stock $10,000

FIGURE 8-1 Balance Sheet Depicting Issuance of $10,000 in Common Stock

consideration for those securities. Those rights generally include the shareholder's proportionate right in the corporation with respect to the earnings, assets, and management of the corporation. Unlike debt security holders, the holders of equity securities are not guaranteed a return on their investment in the corporation, and therefore place at risk their entire investment in the equity securities.

The rest of this section focuses on defining authorized and issued stock of a corporation and the two most common types of equity financing—common stock and preferred stock.

Authorized and Issued Stock

When a corporation is formed, the articles of incorporation must set forth the number and type of shares the corporation is authorized to issue and any other information required by statute. These shares are referred to as the **authorized shares**. Following is a sample provision from the articles of incorporation for a corporation that has authorized only one class of stock.

EXAMPLE: Authorized Stock

The authorized stock of the corporation shall consist of 10,000 shares of Class A Common Stock, without par value.

Once consideration has been received for shares of stock and the shares have been delivered to the shareholders, they are considered to be **issued and outstanding shares.** Shares of stock remain issued and outstanding until they are reacquired, redeemed, converted, or canceled.

The board of directors may not issue equity shares in excess of the authorized shares. If the directors deem it appropriate to increase the number of authorized shares, the articles of incorporation must be amended to provide for the

---

authorized shares Total number of shares, provided for in the articles or certificate of incorporation, that the corporation is authorized to issue.

issued and outstanding shares The total shares of stock of a corporation that have been authorized by the corporation's articles or certificate of incorporation and issued to shareholders.

increased number of authorized shares. Such an amendment usually requires shareholder approval.

The articles of incorporation generally must set forth the preferences, limitations, and relative rights of each class of authorized shares before any shares of that class are issued. Although shareholder approval is typically required for amendments to the articles of incorporation concerning the authorized shares of the corporation, the Model Business Corporation Act (MBCA) provides that the board of directors

Dividends ————————————————————————◆

IOLTA

How do the rules of ethics provide for the safekeeping of client funds and the generation of millions of dollars to provide legal services to the poor? By mandating IOLTA (Interest on Lawyers Trust Accounts).

When an attorney receives money or property that belongs to clients or third parties, the attorney must act as a fiduciary for the owner of the money or property. Any funds that belong to the client, or in which the client has an interest, must be held in trust for the client in a specially-designated client trust account. This is done to prevent the danger of losing a client's money when it is commingled with the money of the attorney or the law practice.

Funds that must be held in trust include:

1. Advance payment of legal fees and costs.
2. Client funds that may be used in the event of a settlement of a lawsuit.
3. Personal injury settlement checks.
4. Payments of child support or alimony by a client or for the benefit of a client.
5. Funds for real estate closings.
6. Client funds to pay income taxes.
7. Estate funds held during a probate process.
8. Funds associated with merger or acquisition closings.

In some jurisdictions, all fees received in advance of the work completed must be held in a client trust account.

When client funds entrusted to attorneys are in a small amount to be held for a short period of time, attorneys may be required to hold the money in an IOLTA account. An IOLTA account is a special type of trust account designed for the pooling of the funds of several clients when those funds individually are too small to generate the interest income required for the administrative costs associated with setting up a separate account. Attorneys pool all such funds together by depositing them in an IOLTA account, thus creating a large enough sum to earn interest. Any interest earned on IOLTA accounts is donated to nonprofit organizations that provide for the delivery of legal services to low income individuals. The principal in such accounts remains the property of the individual clients.

All 50 states and the District of Columbia have IOLTA programs. Use of IOLTA accounts under established guidelines is mandatory in most states. These programs generate an estimated $100 million per year in interest, which is used to provide legal services for the indigent and disadvantaged.

The future of the IOLTA account is somewhat uncertain. Some groups have challenged the legality of IOLTA accounts on the grounds that their use is an unconstitutional taking of client's funds. The opponents to IOLTA argue that the funds generated by the client's funds may be used to promote charitable purposes not philosophically supported by the clients. Advocates of personal property rights have argued that the IOLTA accounts violate the constitutional rights of clients to the ownership of the interest earned on their funds—even though there would be no interest generated if not for the IOLTA account.

Questions concerning the constitutionality of IOLTA and its future may be addressed in the courts in the near future.

may be granted the right, in the articles of incorporation, to amend the corporation's articles of incorporation without shareholder approval to set forth the rights, preferences, and limitations of any new class of stock. This right does not apply to any class of stock of which there are issued and outstanding shares. Not all state statutes allow this much power to be vested in the board of directors, and it is important that the proper state statutes be consulted with regard to requirements for authorizing new classes of shares of stock. In addition to the articles of incorporation, rights and preferences granted to certain classes of common stock typically must be set forth on the face of the stock certificates of each class, pursuant to statute.

Statutory Requirements for Authorized Stock   Statutory requirements for the authorized stock of a corporation vary greatly. The MBCA grants corporations the opportunity to creatively structure the authorized stock of the corporation to meet its specific needs and the needs of its shareholders and investors. The MBCA gives corporations the freedom to authorize classes of stock with a number of differing rights and preferences, provided that the number of each class of shares is set forth in the corporation's articles of incorporation, along with a distinguishing designation for each class of stock if more than one class is authorized.

Most states follow the MBCA in requiring that the authorized stock of a corporation include one or more classes of shares that have unlimited voting rights and one or more classes of shares that together are entitled to receive the net assets of the corporation upon dissolution. These two stock characteristics are commonly found in one class of shares, as is required in many states. These widely accepted requirements guarantee that at all times there will be shareholders that have the voting rights necessary to take any required corporate actions, and that the corporation will always have shareholders who are entitled to receive the net assets of the corporation, should the corporation dissolve. It is important to note that shares of stock including these two fundamental rights must at all times be issued, not just authorized.

When drafting the articles of incorporation to specify the initial authorized shares, the immediate and future capital requirements of the corporation must be taken into consideration, as well as the control of the corporation, state and federal securities regulations, the potential market for sale of the stock, and any state taxation or filing fees that may be based on the authorized shares of the corporation. Many states, including Delaware, base an initial incorporation tax on the authorized capital stock of the corporation.

The MBCA no longer uses the term *preferred stock*. However, the Act specifically provides that many of the characteristics commonly found in preferred stock may be found in certain classes of stock, whatever they may be called. For purposes of this discussion, we distinguish between common and preferred stock and discuss the characteristics commonly associated with those types of stock, keeping in mind that those characteristics may be assigned to any class of stock, regardless of what it is labeled.

While it is very common for a corporation to have only one class of common stock with all holders having identical rights and preferences, the corporation's articles of incorporation may be drafted to provide any number of different rights and preferences for different classes of stock. Some of the rights and preferences that may be established by the articles of incorporation include:

◆ Limitations on voting rights for certain classes of stock.

◆ Preference in payment of dividends.

◆ Preference in payment of assets on liquidation.

◆ Rights to redeem stock.

◆ Rights to convert one type of stock to another.

Common Stock

The ownership of almost all corporations is represented, at least in part, by stock referred to as *common stock*. In the event no designation is made in the articles of incorporation, the authorized stock is considered to be common stock if only one class is authorized. Unless otherwise provided in the articles of incorporation, the owners of the corporation's common stock are entitled to a pro rata share of the corporation's profits, and a pro rata share of the corporation's assets on the corporation's dissolution. As discussed in Chapter 7, the holders of the corporation's common stock are entitled to participate in the management of the corporation by voting their shares.

Classes of Common Stock   The articles of incorporation may authorize more than one class of common stock, with different rights and preferences as set forth in the articles of incorporation. Common stock may also be issued in series in some states. In any event, all shares of common stock within the same class and series are entitled to identical rights.

Common stock may be issued in classes to certain groups with common interests to assure their representation on the board of directors. For example, the articles of incorporation may provide that Class A common stock may elect three directors, and Class B common stock may elect two directors to the board.

Voting Rights   Unless otherwise indicated in the articles of incorporation, holders of common stock are entitled to one vote per share of stock owned. Other voting rights may be prescribed in the articles of incorporation, and this is commonly done when there is more than one class of common stock of the corporation.

The initial shareholders of a corporation may, at times, consent to the subsequent issue of nonvoting common stock to new shareholders. The issue of nonvoting stock can be used to raise capital for the corporation without diluting the management power of the existing shareholders. The corporation may, for example, be authorized to issue Class A common stock that is entitled to one vote per share, and Class B common stock that is not entitled to vote. Following is a sample provision for the articles of incorporation that authorizes two classes of stock, one with voting rights and one without voting rights.

EXAMPLE: Authorized Shares

The authorized capital stock of this corporation shall consist of one million shares of Class A Common Stock, without par value, and one million shares of Class B Common Stock, without par value.

Each shareholder of Class A Common Stock shall be entitled to one (1) vote per share.

Shareholders of Class B Nonvoting Common Stock shall have no voting rights except those prescribed by statute for both voting and nonvoting shareholders.

Liquidation Rights Unless otherwise prescribed by the articles of incorporation, the shareholders of the corporation's common stock will be entitled to the net assets of the corporation upon dissolution. Shareholders will divide the net assets in proportion to their share ownership.

Preferred Stock

Preferred stock is "stock which enjoys certain limited rights and privileges (usually dividend and liquidation priorities) over other outstanding stock but which doesn't participate in corporate growth in any significant extent."[3] Preferred stock is distinguished from common stock in that it is entitled to a priority over other stock in the distribution of profits. This preference may include the right to cumulative or noncumulative dividends. The terms of the preferred stock are set forth in the articles of incorporation and on the face of the preferred stock certificate, in accordance with state statute, and the specified terms and provisions serve as a contract between the preferred stockholder and the corporation.

The terms of preferred stock can vary and may be restricted by state statute. Typically, preferred stockholders are granted a dividend preference over the common stockholders in a fixed amount per share or in a certain percentage. Aside from this preference, preferred stockholders may also be granted voting rights, redemption rights, conversion rights, and priority in entitlement to the assets of the corporation on dissolution. Following is a sample provision for the articles of incorporation of a corporation that has authorized common and preferred stock.

EXAMPLE: Authorized Shares

The authorized capital stock of this corporation shall consist of one million shares of Common Stock, without par value, and one million shares of Nonvoting Preferred Stock, without par value.

Each shareholder of Common Stock shall be entitled to one (1) vote per share.

The holders of Preferred Stock will be entitled to receive cumulative dividends on an annual basis of twelve percent (12%) of the stated value of the Preferred Stock prior to the distribution of any dividends to the holders of Common Stock. Holders of Common Stock will be entitled to dividends of ten percent (10%) of the surplus remaining, with the balance of such surplus to be distributed to holders of both classes of stock on a participating basis equally without distinction as to class.

Voting Rights Preferred stock may be issued with voting rights, with limited voting rights, or with no voting rights at all, at the discretion of the board of directors. So long as at least one class of issued stock is granted unlimited voting rights, preferred stock is not required to provide unlimited voting rights. The statutes of some states provide that all shareholders, including shareholders of preferred stock, must be allowed to vote on certain matters affecting shareholder rights.

Redemption Rights Often, when a corporation issues preferred stock, that stock will be issued with provisions that allow the corporation, or the preferred shareholder, the right of redemption at a future date, upon the terms and conditions set forth on the stock certificate or in an agreement between the preferred shareholder and the corporation. Following is a sample articles of incorporation provision providing for the redemption of preferred stock.

> ### *EXAMPLE: Redemption of Preferred Stock*
>
> The preferred stock of the corporation may be redeemed in whole or in part on any date after _____, _____, at the option of the board of directors on not less than _____ days' notice to the preferred stockholders of record. Such stock shall be redeemed by payment in cash of _____ percent (___%) of par value of each share to be redeemed, as well as all accrued unpaid dividends on each such share.

Redemption of equity shares is discussed in more detail in § 8.6 of this chapter.

Conversion of Preferred Stock The preferred stock rights and preferences may include **conversion rights** providing that the issued shares may be converted into common stock at some specific point in time, usually at the shareholder's option. Specific provisions in the articles of incorporation and on the stock certificates, or in a separate agreement between the corporation and the preferred stockholder, should include a conversion rate indicating the number of preferred shares that may be converted into common stock and the number of common shares to be issued in the exchange. In addition, the conversion provisions should include the exact method for the conversion, including the period during which the conversion option may validly be exercised, and any other pertinent information. Following is a sample articles of incorporation provision providing for the conversion of preferred stock.

> ### *EXAMPLE: Right of Conversion*
>
> The holder of any shares of preferred stock of the Corporation may, after the fourth anniversary date of the issuance of such stock, and until such time as may

◆ ──

conversion rights Rights, often granted to preferred shareholders with the issuance of preferred stock, that allow the preferred shareholders to convert their shares of preferred stock into common stock at some specific point in time, usually at the shareholder's option.

be determined by the Board of Directors, elect to convert such shares of preferred stock to shares of common stock of the Corporation. Upon giving the Corporation ninety (90) days' notice by registered mail of such intent and on surrender at the office of the Corporation of the certificates for such preferred shares, duly endorsed to the Corporation, the shareholder shall be entitled to receive one share of common stock for every share of preferred stock so surrendered.

Priority Rights to Assets upon Dissolution   Preferred stockholders may be granted a specific preference over common stockholders with regard to the assets of the corporation upon its dissolution.

Priority Rights to Dividends   Preferred stockholders may be granted a priority over other shareholders to receive dividends from the corporation. The rights granted to preferred stockholders often include dividends in specific amounts, paid on certain dates. The payment of dividends is discussed in § 8.7 of this chapter.

Series of Preferred Shares   Preferred stock may be issued in classes and series to the extent that such issuance is authorized in the corporation's articles of incorporation. A *series* of preferred stock refers to a type of shares within a class of preferred stock. The exact rights and preferences of a series of shares may be set by the board of directors before issuance, without shareholder approval or amendment of the articles of incorporation. This allows the board of directors to act quickly, to take advantage of market conditions, without having to amend the articles of incorporation. All rights and preferences of shares of stock within a series must be identical.

Factors in Deciding Whether to Issue Preferred Stock   The board of directors or incorporators must take several factors into consideration when deciding whether to authorize preferred stock in the corporation's articles of incorporation. Preferred stock may be used to attract investors who are interested in a more conservative investment that offers a steady income in lieu of growth potential. Other factors to be considered by the board of directors or incorporators include the cost of issuing preferred stock, the risk of capital, the flexibility of the payment obligation, and the permanence of the capital represented.[4]

§ 8.3 PAR VALUE

Par value is the nominal value assigned to shares of stock, which amount is imprinted upon the face of the stock certificate as a dollar value. The par value requirement was primarily intended to protect corporate creditors, senior security holders, and other shareholders by setting a benchmark to insure fair contribution from all shareholders. It was also intended to establish the corporation's permanent capital on which creditors could rely.[5] Corporations were not allowed to make distributions out of the "stated capital account"—an account that equaled the total par value of all issued shares.

Because the actual value of all stock fluctuates and because corporations often set a nominal value for the par value of their stock, the par value provided for in articles of incorporation and on the face of stock certificates may have little actual meaning. Requiring corporations to issue stock with a par value has provided little actual benefit to shareholders or creditors. It is widely accepted that "par value and actual value of issued stock are not synonymous, and there is often a wide disparity between them."[6] This section examines the trend toward eliminating par value and the consideration and accounting requirements for par value stock.

Trend Toward Eliminating Par Value

Traditionally, all stock was assigned a par value. However, the trend in modern corporate law is to eliminate the par value requirement. Most states provide that a corporation's authorized stock can be without par value or with no par value. However, if no par value is assigned to the stock of a corporation, the authorities in those states will assign a specific par value to the shares of stock for certain purposes, such as taxation and filing fees. The statutes of states following the MBCA do not require that a par value be assigned to the authorized stock of the corporation. However, if a par value is assigned, it must be set forth in the corporation's articles of incorporation.

EXAMPLE: Articles of Incorporation Clause Concerning Par Value

ONE CLASS OF SHARES—WITHOUT PAR VALUE
    The aggregate amount of the total authorized capital stock of this corporation is _____ shares of common stock without nominal or par value, and which shall be all of the same class. The stock may be issued from time to time without action by the stockholders, for such consideration as may be fixed from time to time by the board of directors, and shares issued in this manner, the full consideration for which has been paid or delivered, shall be deemed full paid stock and the holder of these shares shall not be liable for any further payment on them.[7]

Consideration for Par Value Stock

If a corporation authorizes par value stock, special consideration must be given to the issuance of that stock with regard to the corporation's accounting. Like stock with no par value, par value stock may be issued for any price deemed adequate by the board of directors, with one exception: the consideration received must be at least equal to the par value of the shares issued. For instance, 100 shares of $10 par value common stock could be issued at a price of $5,000 if the board deems it adequate consideration. However, in no event could the board of directors issue the shares of stock for less than $1,000.

Shares issued for less than the par value, which may be the case when consideration is in a form other than cash, are considered **watered stock**, and the

---

watered stock A stock issue that is sold as if fully paid for, but that is not (often because some or all of the shares were given out for less than full price).

shareholder receiving them may be liable to the corporation for the difference between the amount paid and the par value of the shares received. However, the imposition of liability on the shareholders of a corporation for purchase of watered
shares, in the absence of fraud or misrepresentation, is becoming a rare event. The
MBCA provides only that "[a] purchaser from a corporation of its own shares is
not liable to the corporation or its creditors with respect to the shares except to pay
for the consideration for which the shares were authorized to be issued."[8]

Accounting for Par Value Stock

Generally, when a corporation receives consideration for the issuance of par value
stock, the total amount of the par value of the issued stock is considered **stated
capital**. Any amount received in excess of the par value of the shares is considered
capital surplus. Any amount received by the corporation that is considered stated
capital must be maintained by the corporation. The issuance of stock without
par value allows the directors of the corporation greater flexibility in manipulating
the available capital surplus to provide for greater dividends and the redemption of
issued stock.[9] If the authorized stock of a corporation is without par value, directors are frequently allowed to make their own determination as to what part of
the consideration received is stated capital and what part is capital surplus. (See
Figure 8-2 on page 314.)

Because the par value amount typically represents only the *minimum* amount
that shares may be issued for, and because a high par value may tie up the funds of
the corporation, most corporations in states that require par value opt to assign a
very nominal amount of par value. Another reason for the frequent use of a nominal par value is that some state authorities employ the par value of stock as part of a
taxation formula, with corporations being taxed on the par value of authorized or
issued stock of the corporation. Par value may also be a factor in determining state
filing fees.

§ 8.4 CONSIDERATION FOR SHARES OF STOCK

Unless the right is granted to the shareholders under statute or the articles of incorporation, the board of directors is typically responsible for the issuance of stock
for adequate consideration. This really involves two issues. First, the board must
determine a fair value at which the stock should be issued; then they must determine the adequacy of the consideration. Obviously, if the consideration is in the
form of cash, the second part of that task is simple.

The price per share of stock for the initial issue of shares is determined by the
amount of capital required to begin the business, the number of initial investors,

---

stated capital The amount of capital contributed by stockholders. The capital or equity of a corporation as it appears in the balance sheet.

capital surplus Property paid into a corporation by the shareholders in excess of capital stock liability.

Balance Sheet of a Corporation after Issuance of 10,000 Shares of Common Stock, $1.00 par value	
Assets	**Liabilities**
Cash $10,000	
	Shareholder's Equity
	Common Stock
	Stated Capital: $10,000
	Capital Surplus: 0

Balance Sheet of a Corporation after Issuance of 10,000 Shares of Common Stock, $.50 par value	
Assets	**Liabilities**
Cash $10,000	
	Shareholder's Equity
	Common Stock
	Stated Capital: $5,000
	Capital Surplus: 5,000

FIGURE 8-2   Balance Sheets Contrasting Different Treatment of Stated Capital and Capital Surplus

and the number of shares to be issued. For example, if it is determined that a corporation requires $50,000 to begin business, and five initial investors are all willing to invest $10,000, the number and price of the authorized and issued shares will be determined accordingly. The corporation may decide to issue 50,000 shares of common stock at $1.00 per share, or the board may decide to issue 5 shares at $10,000 per share. For ease in transferring stock, it is advisable to put a lower price on the shares of stock. For example, if a shareholder in this example wished to sell half of his or her shares, it would be much easier to transfer 5,000 $1.00 shares than half of a single $10,000 share.

Placing a value on subsequent issues of stock of closely held corporations is a more difficult matter. Obviously, stock cannot be priced too high, or it will not sell. On the other hand, if the stock price is too low, it will dilute the interest of the current stockholders by bringing down the per-share value. Also, shares of stock that are issued within a relatively short time period generally must be sold for the same price. If the shares of stock to be issued are par value stock, the consideration must be at least equal to the par value of the shares issued.

Historically, restrictions were placed on the type of consideration that could be accepted by the board of directors for shares of equity stock. Statutes generally restricted the use of promissory notes, the rendering of future services, and other types of contracts that called for payment or performance at some time in the future. The intent behind this restriction was to ensure that the corporation had enough immediate capital with which to operate its business. Many states still place some restrictions on the form of consideration that may be accepted for the issuance of stock.

The tendency of modern corporate law is to allow any consideration deemed adequate by the board of directors for the payment of shares of stock. Under the MBCA, consideration for shares of stock may be in the form of "any tangible or intangible property or benefit to the corporation."[10] This may include cash, promissory notes, services performed on behalf of the corporation, contracts for services to be performed on behalf of the corporation, or other securities of the corporation. It is typically left to the discretion of the board of directors to determine the adequacy of consideration. Obviously, if the board of directors decides to accept promissory notes, or other contracts for future benefit to the corporation, there must be an adequate mix of cash or other immediate rewards that gives the corporation the needed initial funds. When a corporation receives valid consideration for shares, the shares are issued and considered to be fully paid and nonassessable.

§ 8.5 ISSUANCE OF STOCK

Typically, the first shares of stock of a corporation are issued at the first meeting of the board of directors. This is often done by executing or ratifying **stock subscription agreements** that were received before or immediately after incorporation of the business, with the issuance of stock certificates in exchange for the agreed-upon consideration. The right to issue shares of stock is generally granted to the board of directors. However, the statutes of many states allow the shareholders to reserve that power in the articles of incorporation if desired. If the shareholders of the corporation have preemptive rights, the existing shareholders must be given the opportunity to exercise their rights prior to the issuance of any additional shares of stock.

Shares of issued stock are usually represented by stock certificates, as may be required by state statute, the articles of incorporation or bylaws of the corporation, or both. However, in many instances, stock issued under a valid agreement but without the formal stock certificate has been found to be a valid issue of stock.

Stock Certificates

Although the MBCA prescribes the minimum form and content for stock certificates, it also allows corporations to issue stock without the formality of a stock certificate, so long as the information prescribed for stock certificates is included in a written statement sent to the shareholder within a reasonable time after the issue or

---

stock subscription agreement   Agreement to purchase a specific number of shares of a corporation.

transfer of the shares without a certificate.[11] Section 6.25(b) of the MBCA prescribes the requirements for stock certificates, as follows:

> (b) At a minimum each share certificate must state on its face:
>
> (1) the name of the issuing corporation and that it is organized under the law of this state;
>
> (2) the name of the person to whom issued; and
>
> (3) the number and class of shares and the designation of the series, if any, the certificate represents.

See Figure 8-3.

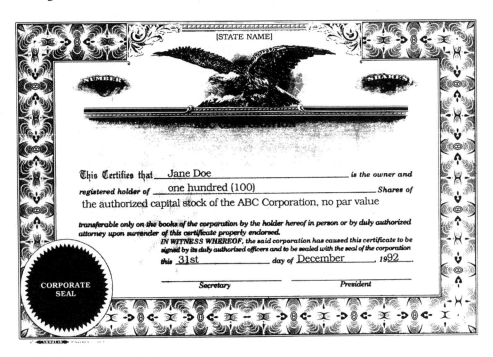

FIGURE 8-3 Sample Common Stock Certificate. (Certificate compliments of A.R. Maul Co., Minneapolis, Minnesota.)

The statutes of most states also require, that the stock certificates contain a summary of the designations, relative rights, preferences, and limitations of the represented class of shares if the corporation has more than one class or series of authorized shares. Alternatively, corporations may provide the pertinent information regarding share classes and series rights and preferences to shareholders upon request, so long as the stock certificate "conspicuously state[s] on its front or back that the corporation will furnish the shareholder this information on request in writing without charge."[12]

Stock certificates must be signed by two officers of the corporation, typically the president or chief executive officer and the secretary or assistant secretary.

Lost or Destroyed Stock Certificates

Lost stock certificates can usually be replaced if the shareholder submits an affidavit affirming that the certificate was lost or destroyed. The new stock certificate is typically issued with an indication that it is a "duplicate" stock certificate.

Fractional Shares and Scrip

At times, because of various stock transactions involving the transfer or issuance of shares of stock, a shareholder may be entitled to own an amount of shares of stock that is represented by a fraction. For instance, the corporation may declare a **stock dividend** of one share for every 10 shares that are issued and outstanding. In that event, a shareholder holding 15 shares would be entitled to receive 1.5 more shares of stock.

A corporation may issue a fractional share, which is entitled to voting and all rights incident to stock ownership, or it may issue a **scrip**. A scrip is an instrument that represents the right to receive a fraction of a share. This instrument is freely transferable, but it does not include voting rights or other rights associated with stock ownership. Scrip is often issued with a provision that it must be combined with other fractional shares of stock and exchanged for a whole share or shares of stock within a prescribed time period. If the exchange is not completed within the time prescribed, the scrip becomes void.

§ 8.6 REDEMPTION OF EQUITY SHARES

Redemption refers to the repurchase by a corporation of its own shares of stock. Often, a corporation's preferred stock will be issued with provisions that allow the corporation the right of redemption at a future date, upon the terms and conditions set forth on the stock certificate or in an agreement between the preferred stockholder and the corporation. This may be of particular interest to corporations when the market interest rate is declining, or when the corporation expects substantial profits in the near future, because redemption of preferred stock allows the corporation to terminate its obligations to pay fixed dividends on the stock. In a close corporation, rights of redemption allow shareholders to withdraw from participation in the corporation without forfeiting their investment. The corporation will buy the stock back from the shareholder.

Redemption may be at the option of the corporation, the shareholder, or a third party. Shares redeemable at the option of the corporation are often referred to as

---

stock dividend Profits of stock ownership (dividends) paid out by a corporation in more stock rather than in money. This additional stock reflects the increased worth of the company.

scrip A piece of paper that is a temporary indication of a right to something valuable. Scrip includes paper money issued for temporary use; partial shares of stock after a stock split; certificates of a deferred stock dividend that can be cashed in later; etc.

callable shares; the option of a shareholder to redeem shares is sometimes referred to as a *put*. The price paid to redeem shares is set in the articles of incorporation or by a formula prescribed in the articles of incorporation.

Treasury shares are shares of stock that were previously issued by the corporation but later reacquired. Reacquired shares may be subject to special accounting treatment, although the MBCA has eliminated any special treatment of treasury shares in recent years, stating merely that "corporation may acquire its own shares and shares so acquired constitute authorized but unissued shares."[13] Several states, however, require that treasury shares be accounted for under a special status as issued but not outstanding shares. Shares that are issued but not outstanding have no voting rights, and they are not counted in any necessary determinations of the number of outstanding shares of the corporation.

EXAMPLE: Resolution of Directors—Authorizing Redemption

Whereas, the board of directors has reviewed the available assets and outstanding liabilities of the corporation and has found that certain outstanding shares may be redeemed in full compliance with the provisions of the _____ [General Corporation Law] of the State of _____; and

Whereas, the board of directors deems it to be in the best interests of the corporation that such shares be called for redemption;

RESOLVED, that _____ [all] of the outstanding _____ [7% cumulative convertible preferred or as the case may be] shares of the corporation are hereby called for redemption pursuant to the provisions of _____ [the _____ (articles or certificate) of incorporation of _____ (corporation)]. The redemption shall take place at the principal executive office of the corporation at _____ [address], _____ [city], _____ County, _____ [state], on _____ [date], at which time and place _____ [all] the holders of _____ [7% cumulative convertible preferred or as the case may be] shares may obtain _____ Dollars ($_____) per share plus accrued dividends, on surrender of their share certificates, duly endorsed.

FURTHER RESOLVED, that from and after _____ [Date], such _____ [7% cumulative convertible preferred or as the case may be] shares shall no longer be deemed outstanding, and no rights shall exist with respect to the shares except the right to receive payment of the redemption price without interest.

FURTHER RESOLVED, that the _____ [secretary] of the corporation is directed to give written notice of this redemption to _____ [each] holder of _____ [7% cumulative convertible preferred or as the case may be] shares in accordance with the provisions of _____ [the _____ (articles or certificate) of incorporation].

FURTHER RESOLVED, that the sum of _____ Dollars ($_____) is hereby appropriated and set aside to fund this redemption.[14]

---

treasury shares   Shares of stock that have been rebought by the corporation that issued them.

§ 8.7   DIVIDENDS

Once the business of the corporation has net earnings, the profits of the corporation are usually distributed to the appropriate shareholders, in an equitable manner, in the form of dividends. A *dividend* is considered to be a payment to the stockholders of a corporation as a return on their investment. Generally, recurring dividends are paid on a more or less regular basis in the ordinary course of business without reducing the stockholders' equity or their position to enjoy future returns from the corporation. These dividends are payable out of the surplus or profits of the corporation, and may be in the form of cash, stock, or other property of the corporation.

This section investigates the availability of funds for dividends and the different types of dividends. It also discusses the declaration of dividends and the shareholders' right to receive dividends after they have been declared.

Availability of Funds for Dividends

It is generally accepted that dividends may be paid only out of the profits of the corporation. This principle has been upheld in courts numerous times, as it has been found that "[g]enerally, the net earnings or surplus of a going corporation constitute the proper fund for the payment of dividends, whether on its common stock or preferred stock, and dividends cannot, as a rule, legally be declared and paid out of the capital of the corporation."[15] Dividends are normally payable out of the surplus or profits of a corporation, and it is usually within the discretion of the corporation's directors to decide whether to reinvest the corporation's profits in the corporation or to distribute the profits to the corporation's shareholders.

Newer and smaller, closely held corporations may opt for the declaration of minimal dividends and keep the profits in the corporation to expand its business and increase the value of its stock. Often, the shareholders of these smaller corporations are also employees of the corporation and receive their share of the earnings of the corporation in the form of salaries.

On the other hand, larger, publicly held corporations may find it necessary to declare and pay dividends consistently at a rate attractive to potential investors who are looking for stock investments with steady income potential. The matter of dividend declaration is consistently addressed in state statutes. Under the MBCA, dividends are prohibited if their payment would cause the corporation to be unable to pay its debts as they become due in the usual course of business, or if the corporation's total assets would be less than the sum of its total liabilities plus the amount that would be needed to satisfy the preferential rights, upon dissolution, of the shareholders whose preferential rights are superior to those receiving the distribution. These tests to determine the availability of funds vary by state.

Types of Dividends

Dividends may be paid in several forms. The most common types consist of cash, stock, or other property.

Cash The vast majority of corporate dividends are cash dividends. In its simplest form, the cash dividend merely divides and distributes the profits of the corporation, in cash, to the shareholders of the corporation pursuant to the terms of the shares of stock that have been issued.

Stock Dividends At times, stock dividends may be distributed in lieu of cash. An issue of stock dividends involves the authorization and issuance of new stock to existing shareholders on a pro rata basis. Because stock dividends make no demands on the funds of a corporation, they are not regulated by statute to the extent that cash dividends are regulated.

So as not to unfairly dilute the shares of one class of stock, shareholders of one class of shares may not be issued shares of another class in a stock dividend, unless the articles of incorporation so provide, or unless, prior to declaration of the stock dividend, no shares of the class to be distributed as a dividend have been issued. Although the corporation issues additional stock, it continues with the same assets and liabilities. The declaration of a stock dividend has the effect of allowing the portion of surplus capital represented by the new stock to be transferred to the permanent capital account of the corporation.

Because the issued shares of the corporation are increased, and all shareholders receive a proportionate amount of shares in the event of a stock dividend, shareholders receiving stock dividends are, in effect, no better off than they were prior to the stock distribution. The stock dividend effectively lowers the price of the issued stock to reflect the value of the corporation.

Other Property On occasion, dividends may be in a form other than cash or the corporation's stock. These dividends might be any property owned by the corporation, including real or personal property, bonds, scrip, or the stock of another corporation.

Declaration of Dividends

The corporation generally has no legal obligation to pay an undeclared dividend to the shareholders. However, once a dividend is declared, it becomes a debt payable to the shareholders, and the shareholders of the corporation have the legal remedies available to creditors to collect the dividend as declared.

Dividend Preferences Dividends that are payable, by virtue of contract, to one class of shareholders in priority over another class of shareholders are often referred to as *preferred* or *preferential* dividends.[16] Preferred stockholders generally have a right to priority over other shareholders in the receipt of dividends. Although corporations typically pay consistent dividends to preferred stockholders at regular intervals, preferred stockholders do not have the right to dividends when there is no corporate profit or surplus earnings to justify the dividends. Courts have found in several instances that a "corporation cannot make a valid contract to pay dividends otherwise than from profits, and an agreement to pay such dividends out of capital is unlawful and void."[17]

Cumulative Dividends   Courts have held in several instances that the "omission of a dividend on either the preferred or the common stock of a corporation for any year, because net earnings which will permit the payment of a dividend are lacking, deprives such stock of all right to a share of profits for that year, unless the contract provides for the cumulation of dividends on such stock."[18] If the preferred shareholders have a cumulative right to the dividends, dividends omitted in one year generally must be paid the next year before dividends are paid on the shares of common stock.

Authority to Declare Dividends   The authority to declare dividends generally rests with the board of directors, with the exception of stock dividends, which may require shareholder approval. Dividends are approved by board of director resolution and declared as a formal act of the corporation. The following items are generally considered when drafting resolutions for the declaration of corporate dividends:[19]

♦ Kind of dividend to be declared.
  — cash
  — stock
  — property
  — scrip
♦ Whether the dividend is being paid from an appropriate fund.
♦ Class or series of stock on which the dividend is being declared.
♦ Whether the dividend is regular or extraordinary.
♦ The cash amount or value of the dividend.
♦ Formal declaration of the dividend by the board of directors, which distinguishes the date the dividend is declared from the date the dividend is to be paid.
♦ Declaration of the dividend as payable to registered owners of stock, as listed on the corporate books, as of a specified date.

> ### EXAMPLE: Board of Director Resolution Declaring Dividend
>
> Whereas, the sum of _____ Dollars ($_____) constitutes surplus profits earned by this corporation in ____ [year].
>
> RESOLVED, the sum of _____ Dollars ($_____) is hereby set aside from the surplus profits to be distributed to the stockholders of this corporation by a declaration of a dividend in the sum of _____ Dollars ($_____) per share for each and every share of common stock owned by the shareholders and by the declaration of the dividend in the sum of _____ Dollars ($_____) per share for each and every share of preferred stock owned by the stockholders. The dividend is payable to the stockholders of record as of the close of business on _____ [date]; and the dividend is hereby declared and the secretary of this corporation is hereby instructed to distribute on _____ [date], the sum of _____ Dollars ($_____), in checks of this corporation, aggregating a dividend of _____ Dollars ($_____) per share on the common

stock and a dividend of _____ Dollars ($_____) per share on the preferred stock, for every share owned by its stockholders.[20]

Right to Receive Dividends

When a dividend is declared, the declaration includes a date on which all shareholders of record will be entitled to dividends. Once the declaration has been made, those individuals have a right to those dividends, as specified by contract and the declaration. Typically, if no date is declared to determine the shareholders of record entitled to a dividend, the record date is considered the date on which the declaration is made.

Directors are usually under no obligation to declare a dividend in the corporation and may often decide that it is in the company's best interest to reinvest the surplus and profits in the business. The corporation is not under an obligation to pay dividends unless a dividend is declared. Although the courts generally abide by the discretion of the board of directors regarding the declaration of dividends, when the rights of minority shareholders or preferred shareholders are being infringed upon, the courts may intervene. The courts have held many times that the "rights of holders of preferred stock to dividends will be enforced in equity against the corporation in accordance with the terms of the contract."[21]

In addition, if the evidence shows that the board of directors is wrongfully withholding dividends from the profits of the corporation from minority shareholders, a court of equity may order the board of directors to declare a dividend out of surplus profits.

Figure 8-4 illustrates the payment of corporate dividends.

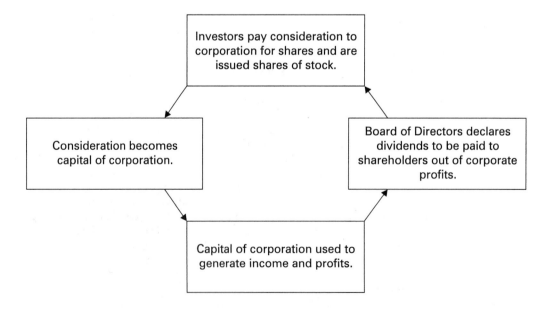

FIGURE 8-4   Payment of Corporate Dividends

§ 8.8 STOCK SPLITS

Although **stock splits** increase the issued number of shares, they are not considered stock dividends. Stock splits are used to lower the price of a corporation's stock. Stock splits are especially frequent among publicly held corporations with stock that has appreciated significantly, to the point where the price per share may appear prohibitive to the small investor. The effect of a stock split is to "split" the value of each share of stock into smaller denominations. For example, if a corporation's stock appreciates to the point where it is valued at the price of $100 per share, the board of directors may declare a two-for-one split and issue two $50 shares for each outstanding $100 share.

It is important to recognize the difference between a stock split and a stock dividend. Although stock splits increase the number of outstanding shares of a corporation that represent its capital, the actual amount of capital and surplus remain unchanged. A stock dividend, on the other hand, represents a transfer of earnings or profits to the capital of the corporation, together with a distribution of additional shares, which represents the addition of the earnings or profits to the corporation's capital.

EXAMPLE: *Board of Directors Resolution Approving Stock Split*

Whereas, the _____ [articles or certificate] of incorporation of _____ [corporation] _____ [authorize or authorizes] the issuance of _____ [number, description, and value of authorized shares to be affected by stock split] shares of which _____ [number] shares are now issued and outstanding; and

Whereas, it is deemed to be in the best interest of the corporation and its stockholders to split the outstanding shares of _____ [class] stock into _____ [number] shares of the same class;

RESOLVED, that subject to the approval of the stockholders, the _____ [articles or certificate] of incorporation of the corporation be amended by increasing the total number of shares of all classes that the corporation is authorized to issue from _____ [number] to _____ [number], and by decreasing the par value of _____ [class] stock from _____ Dollars ($_____) per share to _____ Dollars ($_____) per share with a concomitant increase in the authorized number of such shares from _____ shares to _____ shares;

FURTHER RESOLVED, that on the effective date of the amendment, each share of _____ [class] stock of the par value of _____ Dollars ($_____) per share outstanding before the amendment shall be divided and changed into _____ [number] fully paid and nonassessable shares of _____ [class] stock of the par value of _____ Dollars ($_____) per share; and that after the effective date of the amendment, each holder of record of one or more certificates representing shares of the old _____ [class] stock shall be entitled to receive one or more certificates

stock split A dividing of a company's stock into a greater number of shares without changing each stockholder's proportional ownership.

representing the proportionate number of shares of the new _____ [class] stock on surrender of the stockholder's old certificate or certificates for cancellation;

FURTHER RESOLVED, that a proposed amendment reflecting the proposed change be submitted to a vote of all the stockholders entitled to vote thereon at a special meeting of the stockholders to be held on _____ [date], at _____ [time], at the principal office of the corporation at _____ [address], _____ [city], _____ County, _____ [state], and that the secretary give notice of such meeting and such proposal in the manner and form required by _____ [cite statute] and the bylaws of this corporation.[22]

§ 8.9   DEBT FINANCING

Debt financing refers to obtaining capital through loans to the corporation, which must be repaid with interest upon the terms agreed to by contract between the corporation and lender or the holder of the debt securities. Debt financing refers to anything from a simple loan, represented by a promissory note, to the issuance of debt securities in the form of **bonds**. Short-term capital can often be acquired by bank loans, either secured or unsecured. Intermediate and long-term debt capital is often acquired through the issuance of debt securities, including bonds and **debentures**.

Because of the significant tax (and nontax) advantages of raising capital through the issuance of bonds or other debt obligations, the board of directors often decides to maximize the use of debt financing. The interest paid to bondholders is generally deductible as a corporate expense, whereas dividends paid on shares of stock of the corporation are not deductible.

See Figure 8-5 for a comparison of equity financing and debt financing.

In this section, we look at the authority required to obtain debt financing on behalf of a corporation. We then focus on the two most common types of debt financing: bank loans and bonds.

Authority for Debt Financing

The board of directors usually decides what type of debt capital must be acquired to suit the corporation's needs. This capital can be raised in the form of short-term, intermediate-term, or long-term financing, or any combination of the foregoing.

The board of directors generally has the power to obtain debt financing on behalf of the corporation, although in some instances this power may be granted to

---

bond   A document that states a debt owed by a company or a government. The company, government, or government agency promises to pay the owner of the bond a specific amount of interest for a set period of time and to repay the debt on a certain date. A bond, unlike a stock, gives the holder no ownership rights in the company.

debenture   A corporation's obligation to pay money (usually in the form of a note or bond) often unsecured (not backed up) by any specific property. Usually refers only to long-term bonds.

Equity	*Debt*
◆ Represents an ownership in the company.	◆ Represents a loan of capital to the company that must be repaid.
◆ Payment of dividends to shareholders is usually optional.	◆ Periodic payment of fixed interest to debt holders is usually mandatory.
◆ Dividends paid on shares of stock are not tax deductible.	◆ Interest paid on debt financing is tax deductible.
◆ Issuance of stock maintains a lower debt/equity ratio for the corporation.	◆ Too high a debt/equity ratio in a corporation increases the likelihood of insolvency.
◆ Issuance of equity securities may dilute the current shareholder's control over the corporation.	◆ Incurring debt financing usually does not affect the current shareholders' control over the corporation.
◆ Shareholders are entitled to dividends only from the profits of the corporation (if any).	◆ Interest on debt is an expense that must be paid before profits can be calculated or dividends paid.

FIGURE 8-5   Equity Financing vs. Debt Financing

the shareholders of the corporation in the articles of incorporation or state statutes. The amount of indebtedness that a corporation can incur may be limited under the corporation's articles of incorporation.

Bank Loans

The terms of corporate bank loans are established in the loan agreements between the bank and the corporation. The loan can be for a specific term, or it can be in the form of a line of credit, on which the corporation can draw from time to time when additional cash is required. Depending on the corporation's credit rating, it may be able to obtain unsecured bank loans, but most corporate bank loans are secured, with the corporation pledging collateral to the bank, which will be executed or foreclosed on by the bank in the event of default.

Bonds

Bonds can be issued so as to grant the bondholder a wide variety of rights. The rights of bondholders are defined by the terms of the bond contract between the corporation and the bondholder. However, the status of the bondholder differs from that of the stockholder, in that the relationship of the bondholder to the corporation is more that of a creditor than an owner. Bondholders have no voting rights. Bonds are usually long-term secured debt instruments payable to the bearer, with interest, upon the terms indicated on the bond. Many bonds are *coupon bonds* that have detachable coupons, which may be presented to the corporation at prescribed intervals for interest payments.

Bonds that represent an unsecured loan to the corporation are referred to as *debentures* or *simple debentures.*

Bonds, or the contracts representing the agreement between the corporation and the bondholder, typically include the face value of the bond, the date when the principal repayment is due (the *maturity date*), and the terms for payment of interest, usually a fixed rate payable in periodic installments until the bond matures. Bonds may be issued for face value, or at a discount or premium.

Discounted Bonds   A debt obligation that bears no interest or interest at a lower-than-current-market rate is usually issued at less than its face amount—that is, at a discount. If bonds are issued at a discount, the difference between the issue price and the face value is deductible by the corporation over the life of the bonds. The discount is considered a form of interest for use of the funds received.

Premium Bonds   If the current market rate is higher than the interest rate on the debt security, the bonds may be issued at a premium. Any amount received for the bond which is over the face value on the bond is considered a premium.

Bonds are typically issued with accompanying bond contracts and indenture agreements setting forth the entire agreement between the corporation and the bondholder. The bond contract sets forth the terms for payment of interest on the bond, the maturity date of the bond, and any applicable conversion or redemption rights.

Conversion Rights   Bonds are often issued with *conversion rights*—the right of the bondholder to convert the bond to stock of the corporation at a set price at some time in the future. Investors who want initially to enjoy a higher income, with the potential to participate in appreciation, may find it desirable to purchase bonds with conversion rights. Basic conversion terms are typically set forth on the face of the bond, with further information in the accompanying bond contract. Bonds often have limitations within which the bondholder must exercise conversion rights, if they are to be exercised at all.

Redemption   Debt securities are often issued with a redemption right granted to the corporation. The right of redemption allows the corporation to buy back its securities on terms specified by the bond agreement. The corporation is usually required to notify the bondholder of its decision to exercise its right of redemption, and there is often a specified time after notice within which the conversion rights must be exercised.

§ 8.10 THE PARALEGAL'S ROLE IN CORPORATE FINANCIAL MATTERS

Paralegals are involved in corporate financial matters in several significant ways. It is important for all corporate paralegals to understand the basics of corporate financial matters and the relevant terminology.

Corporate paralegals may be involved in researching questions concerning the requirements for debt and equity financing, and for drafting several different types of documents relating to the corporate financial structure, including:

1. Provisions in the articles of incorporation concerning the authorized stock of the corporation, including the par value and the rights and preferences associated with each class of stock issued.
2. Stock subscription agreements.
3. Resolutions of the board of directors approving the issuance of stock.
4. Resolutions of the board of directors approving the payment of dividends on shares of issued stock.
5. Resolutions of the board of directors concerning the redemption of stock.
6. Resolutions of the board of directors approving stock dividends and stock splits.
7. Resolutions of the board of directors approving bank loans and other types of debt financing.

Corporate Paralegal Profile
Paula L. Peterson

I find the most interesting clients are the start-up companies. I get to play a role in developing and providing the financial backing they require whether it be through venture capital funding private placements or a possible initial public offering. It is most gratifying to see these clients realize their ideas and business plans and to know that I was a part of that success.

Name Paula L. Peterson

Location Minneapolis, Minnesota

Title Senior Paralegal

Specialty Corporate Transactional

Education Bachelor of Arts from the University of Minnesota; Graduate of Minnesota Paralegal Institute

Experience 7 years

Paula Peterson is a paralegal with Robins, Kaplan, Miller & Ciresi, L.L.P., a national law firm that employs over 200 attorneys and 65 paralegals. Paula works in the firm's Minneapolis office where she specializes in corporate transactional matters. Her work has a heavy emphasis on corporate financing and financial issues.

Paula relies heavily on Internet research and her skills in working with spreadsheets and databases to assist her with corporate formations, drafting organizational documents, maintaining corporate stock records, and performing due diligence research. She is also responsible for drafting merger and acquisition documents and all types of financing agreements, including loan agreements, promissory notes, and security and guaranty agreements.

Paula's favorite aspects of her position are the ability to work unassisted and the substantial interaction she has with clients. Because she works with numerous attorneys in the law firm's business department, which includes several offices, Paula receives a wide variety of substantive assignments that can cover the gamut of venture capital funding private placements, initial public offerings, mergers and acquisitions, financing, and trademark/service mark work.

Paula works with the attorneys of Robins, Kaplan, Miller & Ciresi to assist with their work for corporations of all sizes—both publicly held and private. But the work she enjoys the most is her work with start-up companies. Paula gets to play a role in developing and providing the financial backing these companies require, whether it be through venture capital funding private placement or a possible initial public stock offering. Paula reports that working with the start-up companies is most gratifying because she can see the clients realize their ideas and business plans and know that she has been a part of that success.

Paula admits that multiple assignments and pending due dates can often create stressful days and she needs to rely heavily on her prioritization and organizational skills. Most days, Paula will be responsible for billing her time on as many as 12 assignments and projects. Her billing records must report clearly and concisely to the client the work being done for them.

Paula is a member of the National Federation of Paralegal Associations and a voting member of the Minnesota Paralegal Association. She has volunteered her time by assisting nonprofit entities with their formation and organizational documents, as well as drafting federal and state applications for tax exempt status.

For more information on careers for corporate paralegals, log on to the companion Web page to this text at **www.westlegalstudies.com.**

Paralegals are often directly involved in assisting with the closing of large bank loans and debt financing projects. Transactions involving debt financing may be very document intensive, and the corporate paralegal is often responsible for assisting with the drafting of the documents and for assembling the documents for closing. Figure 8-6 lists some of the documents that may be required for closing a corporate loan transaction.

Loan Documents
Loan Agreement
Promissory Note

Security Documents
Security Agreement
Form UCC-1 Filings
Mortgage
Pledge Agreements
Personal Guaranties

Documents Concerning Corporate Existence and Good Standing
Certified Copy of the Corporation's Articles of Incorporation
Certificate of Good Standing from Secretary of State
Board of Directors Resolution Approving the Transaction

FIGURE 8-6 Documents That May Be Required for Closing a Corporate Loan Transaction

§ 8.11 RESOURCES

The most important resources for paralegals who are concerned with corporate financial matters will be the pertinent state statutes and forms and form books. Financial matters concerning the public offering of securities that are subject to securities laws will be discussed in Chapter 9.

State Statutes

The authorized stock and par value provisions of the corporation's articles of incorporation must comply with the statutes of the corporation's state of domicile. For that reason, state statutes are a very important resource for paralegals.

Forms and Form Books

Corporate financial transactions tend to be document intensive. Paralegals who are working with corporate financial transactions will rely heavily on forms available in the office and standard forms found in form books and CLE materials.

Internet Resources www.

Following is a list of some Web pages that may be useful when assisting with corporate financial matters:

For state statutes

American Law Source Online	**www.lawsource/also**
Findlaw.com	**www.findlaw.com/11stategov/**
Legal Information Institute	**www.law.cornell.edu/states/listing.html**

For forms for drafting documents for corporate financial transactions

All About Forms.com	**www.allaboutforms.com/**
Findlaw.com (Legal Forms)	**www.findlaw.com**
The 'Lectric Law Library's Business and General Forms	**www.lectlaw.com/formb.htm**

Web Page

For updates and links to several of the previously listed sites, log on to **www.westlegalstudies.com**, and click through to the book link for this text.

SUMMARY

- ◆ The corporation's directors and officers rely on equity and debt capital to operate the business of the corporation.
- ◆ Equity securities represent an ownership interest in the corporation.
- ◆ Common stock and preferred stock are equity securities.
- ◆ The corporation's articles or certificate of incorporation may provide for different classes of common and preferred stock, granting the holders different rights and preferences.

- If the corporation only issues one type of stock, it is common stock that grants the holders unlimited voting rights and the right to receive the assets of the corporation upon its dissolution.
- Debt securities represent a loan to the corporation that must be paid.
- Dividends are often paid to the holders of equity securities.
- Interest must be paid to the holders of debt securities.
- Preferred stock is stock that entitles the holders of shares to a priority over the holders of shares of common stock, usually with regard to dividends and distribution of the assets of the corporation in the event of dissolution or liquidation of the corporation.
- Preferred stock is often issued with conversion rights, allowing the preferred stockholders to convert their shares to shares of common stock under prescribed conditions.
- Par value is the nominal value assigned to shares of stock, which is imprinted upon the face of the stock certificate as a dollar value. The trend in corporate law is to allow stock without par value.
- Dividends may be paid in cash, stock, or any other property deemed appropriate by the board of directors.
- Debt financing may be in the form of bank loans, loans from shareholders, or bonds or other instruments issued by the corporation.
- Debt capital is an obligation that must be repaid by the corporation.

REVIEW QUESTIONS

1. The owners of A & S Marketing, Inc. need financing to expand their business. A & S has only three shareholders and few assets. However, they do have a marketing plan for substantial, sustained growth in revenue. What type of financing may be most beneficial to the owners of A & S Marketing, Inc.? Why?

2. What are some of the factors to be considered when deciding on the authorized stock of a corporation?

3. The articles of incorporation of the Jerry Corporation authorize "10,000 shares of stock, no par value." No further information is given in the articles. Are these shares of common stock or preferred stock?

4. What two widely accepted requirements must be granted to shareholders under the MBCA?

5. Are all common stockholders always granted voting rights?

6. What are redemption rights?

7. What are conversion rights?

8. What are some possible drawbacks to issuing stock with a par value?

9. What information is typically required to be included on stock certificates?

10. The authorized stock of Rob's Boatworks, Inc. is 10,000 shares of common stock, $1.00 par value. If Rob's Boatworks issues 1,000 shares to Bud Peterson for $800, what term is used to describe Mr. Peterson's shares? What are the possible consequences to Mr. Peterson?

PRACTICAL PROBLEMS

What are the statutory requirements for par value in your state? Find the pertinent statutes for your state to answer the following questions:

1. Must corporations in your state issue stock with a stated par value?

2. Does the number of shares or par value of authorized stock of new corporations in your state affect the filing fee for the corporation's articles of incorporation? If yes, how?

WORKPLACE SCENARIO

Assume that the directors of our fictional corporation, Cutting Edge Computer Repair, Inc., have decided that it is in the best interest of the corporation to lease a retail location for their business. They will need approximately $250,000 to make the necessary improvements to the location they have decided on. Because they do not want to involve another owner in the business, Bradley Harris and Cynthia Lund have agreed on debt financing.

Using the above information, the information in appendix D-3 to this text, and the information and

examples in this chapter, prepare a unanimous written consent of the board of directors of Cutting Edge Computer Repair, Inc., approving a $250,000 loan from the First Bank of Center City. The First Bank of Center City will provide the loan documents. The board of directors must authorize the appropriate officers to execute the loan agreement on behalf of the corporation.

END NOTES

1. 18A AM. JUR. 2d *Corporations* § 431 (1999).
2. *Radaszewski v. Telecom*, 981 F2d 305 (CA8 1982).
3. 18A AM. JUR. 2d *Corporations* § 438 (1999).
4. *Id*.
5. *Fletcher's Cyclopedia of the Law of Private Corporations* § 5080.40 (2000).
6. 18A AM. JUR. 2d *Corporations* § 452 (1985).
7. 6 AM. JUR. Legal Forms 2d *Corporations* § 74:682 (Rev. 1995). Reprinted with permission from *American Jurisprudence Legal Forms 2d*. © 2000 West Group.
8. Revised Model Business Corporation Act § 6.22.
9. 18A AM. JUR. 2d *Corporations* § 453 (1999).
10. Revised Model Business Corporation Act § 6.21(b).
11. *Id*. § 6.26.
12. *Id*. § 6.25(c).
13. *Id*. § 6.31.
14. 6A AM. JUR. Legal Forms 2d *Corporations* § 74:2044 (Rev. 1995). Reprinted with permission from *American Jurisprudence Legal Forms 2d*. © 2000 West Group.
15. 18A AM. JUR. 2d *Corporations* § 1185 (1999).
16. 18B AM. JUR. 2d *Corporations* § 1175 (1985).
17. *Id*. § 1185.
18. *Englander v. Osborne*, 261 Pa. 366, 104 A. 614, 6 ALR 800 (1918).
19. 18B AM. JUR. 2d *Corporations* § 1207 (1999).
20. 6B AM. JUR. Legal Forms 2d *Corporations* § 74:2455 (Rev 1995). Reprinted with permission from *American Jurisprudence Legal Forms 2d*. © 2000 West Group.
21. 18B AM. JUR. 2d *Corporations* § 1283 (1999).
22. 6A AM. JUR. Legal Forms 2d *Corporations* § 74:2111 (Rev 1995). Reprinted with permission from *American Jurisprudence Legal Forms 2d*. © 2000 West Group.

CHAPTER 9

Publicly Held Corporations and Securities Regulations

CHAPTER OUTLINE

§ 9.1   The Publicly Held Corporation

§ 9.2   Securities and Securities Markets

§ 9.3   The Securities and Exchange Commission

§ 9.4   Federal Regulation of Securities Offerings Under the Securities Act of 1933

§ 9.5   Exemptions from the Registration Requirements of the Securities Act of 1933

§ 9.6   Antifraud Provisions of the Securities Act

§ 9.7   Federal Regulations Imposed on Publicly Held Corporations Under the Securities Exchange Act of 1934

§ 9.8   State Securities Regulation—Blue Sky Laws

§ 9.9   State Regulation of Stock Offerings

§ 9.10 State Securities Regulation—Antifraud Provisions

§ 9.11 The Paralegal's Role

§ 9.12 Resources

INTRODUCTION

Securities regulation of **publicly held corporations** is a very complex topic that is often treated separately from the law of corporations. However, because many corporate paralegals spend a significant portion of their time working with matters related to securities, and because this topic is generally not addressed in separate

---

publicly held corporation   A corporation with stock sold to a large number of persons.

paralegal texts, this chapter gives a brief overview of the effect of securities regulation on publicly held corporations. It discusses certain aspects of the publicly held corporation, including the distinction between publicly held and closely held corporations, and then examines the markets in which securities are traded, the Securities Exchange Commission, the federal regulations imposed by the Securities Act of 1933 and the Securities Exchange Act of 1934, and state securities regulations or "blue sky laws." This chapter concludes with a look at the paralegal's role in working with securities matters and discusses the resources available in this area.

§ 9.1 THE PUBLICLY HELD CORPORATION

Although publicly held corporations represent only a small percentage of all corporations in the United States, their enormous economic impact in this country is immeasurable. During 1999, an average of more than 800 million shares of stock of publicly held corporations was traded on the New York Stock Exchange on a daily basis.[1] The market value of shares of publicly held corporations traded on the stock exchanges and over the counter exceeded $21 trillion during 1999.[2]

In contrast to the closely held corporation, the publicly held corporation has a public market for its shares, regardless of the size of the corporation. During 1998, 48 percent of the families in the United States had direct or indirect stock holdings.[3] Indirect ownership of stock may mean that the stock is held in an individual's pension or profit sharing plan. Also, unlike the securities of closely held corporations, securities that are offered and traded publicly are subject to federal securities regulations. Any securities offered, sold, or delivered through any means of interstate commerce (including the United States Postal Service) are considered to be part of a **public offering**, and must first be registered in accordance with the Securities Act of 1933 and any applicable state securities law. When a corporation decides to sell its securities to the public, it is often referred to as *going public*, and the first offering of a corporation's securities to the public is often referred to as the **initial public offering**.

Initial public offerings were very popular during the 1990s, led by a boom in high tech and Internet company stocks. Record numbers of corporations went public during the late 1990s. Overall, initial public offerings are much more common when stock market values and investor optimism are high. In times when market values and market confidence are lower, the number of initial public offerings tends to decline. Figure 9-1 on page 334 shows a graph of the total new securities issued by corporations from 1994 through 1999.

The decision to go public with a corporation is typically made by its directors and principal shareholders, with the advice of their attorneys and accountants. Going public with a corporation has significant ramifications for the company's future as well as the future stake of its shareholders.

---

public offering Offering of securities for sale to the public by means of interstate commerce.

initial public offering The first offering of a corporation's securities to the public.

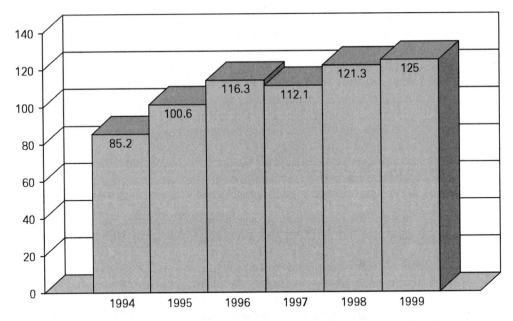

Total New Securities Issued by Corporations—Common and Preferred Stock in Billions of Dollars. (Includes the issue of new securities by corporations that have previously issued public stock).

FIGURE 9-1 New Securities Issued. From *The Statistical Abstract of the United States (2000)* § 828.

The most obvious advantage to going public is the increased availability of capital, which can be acquired through the sale of stock, and the potential increase in the availability of future capital because of the corporation's ability to offer investors a security that is liquid and has an ascertainable market value. Publicly held corporations also may have an advantage over closely held corporations when it comes to hiring and retaining qualified personnel. In addition, the corporation that goes public often has the advantage of gaining national exposure for itself and its products or services.

When making the decision to go public, there are considerable disadvantages that must be weighed, including the fact that the current shareholders of the corporation will experience a certain loss of control, especially in matters requiring shareholder approval. The cost of going public and complying with the federal and state securities regulations that are imposed on publicly held corporations can be significant. Also, the federal and state reporting regulations to which publicly held corporations are subject may require public disclosure of information that corporate management would prefer to keep private. Federal securities regulations can impose a significant burden on a corporation, both financially and on the time of the corporation's management.

After the decision to go public is made, an agreement is entered into between the issuer of the securities and the underwriter for the initial public offering. The *issuer* of securities is any person who issues or proposes to issue securities, including one who promotes the sale of a corporation not yet in existence.[4] The **underwriter** is any person or organization that purchases securities from an issuer, with a view to distribution of those securities, or any person who offers or sells, or participates in the offer or sale for an issuer, of any security.[5] Large financial institutions and brokers typically serve as underwriters, who purchase the securities from the issuer and in turn sell those securities to dealers for resale.

The issuers and underwriters agree to the terms and details of their relationship in an underwriting agreement. The issuer may enter into underwriting agreements with more than one underwriter. The underwriters agree to sell the securities on a "firm commitment" or "best-efforts" basis. If the underwriters give a firm commitment, they commit to purchasing an agreed-upon amount of securities of the corporation at an agreed-upon price; the resale of those securities becomes the responsibility of the underwriters. Unlike the firm commitment, whereby the underwriter assumes the risk for the sale of the securities, underwriters selling on a best-efforts basis are obligated to use their best efforts to sell the securities of the issuer, but are required to take and pay for only those securities that they may sell to the public. When a best-efforts arrangement is made, the proceeds paid to the issuers will depend on the amount of securities sold by the underwriters.

§ 9.2 SECURITIES AND SECURITIES MARKETS

When a corporation goes public, it is offering shares of the corporation to the public in the form of securities. Those securities are then traded on a market.

Definition of Securities

The securities offered when a corporation goes public are usually in the form of stocks, bonds, or debentures. However, securities can take on many different forms. In *SEC v. W. J. Howey Co.*, 328 U.S. 293 (1946), the Supreme Court found that the sale of individual rows of orange trees in conjunction with a service contract for maintenance of the trees and the marketing of their crop involved a "security." The test used by the Supreme Court to detect a security was whether "the person invests his money in a common enterprise and is led to expect profits solely from the efforts of the promoter or a third party." Several types of instruments are generally recognized as securities under federal regulations, including

> any note, stock, treasury stock, bond, debenture, evidence of indebtedness, certificate of interest or participation in any profit-sharing agreement, collateral-trust certificate, preorganization certificate or subscription, transferable share, investment contract, voting-trust certificate, certificate of deposit for a security, fractional undivided interest in oil, gas, or other mineral rights, or, in general, any interest or instrument commonly known as a "security," or

---

underwriter With regard to securities offerings, any person or organization that purchases securities from an issuer with a view to distributing them, or any person who offers or sells or participates in the offer or sale for an issuer of any security.

any certificate of interest or participation in, temporary or interim certificate for, receipt for, guarantee of, or warrant or right to subscribe to or purchase, any of the foregoing.[6]

Markets

After a decision is made to take a corporation public, the decision must be made as to the best means to trade the corporation's securities. The securities of a publicly held corporation may be traded at a stock **exchange** or **over the counter**. Trading on either of these types of markets is not confined to stock, but may also include bonds and many other types of securities, both corporate and governmental.

Both stock exchanges and over-the-counter markets are subject to significant federal regulation, and the type of market chosen for trading will depend upon the circumstances surrounding the securities offering.

Generally, over-the-counter trading has been subject to less stringent regulation than trading on exchanges. However, the regulation of the Securities Exchange Act of 1934 applies to over-the-counter trading, and the Securities and Exchange Commission (SEC) has authority over both types of trading.

In addition to the regulations imposed directly by the Securities and Exchange Commission, both the exchanges and the over-the-counter markets are self-regulating to a certain extent. The exchanges, such as the New York Stock Exchange (NYSE), have regulated themselves since before the formation of the SEC, and continue to do so by imposing rules relating to the transactions on their exchanges as well as rules relating to the members of the exchanges. The Securities Exchange Act of 1934 provides for the formation of self-regulating "national securities associations" of over-the-counter markets, such as the National Association of Securities Dealers (the NASD).

Exchanges An exchange is considered to be ...

> any organization, association, or group of persons, whether incorporated or unincorporated, which constitutes, maintains, or provides a market place or facilities for bringing together purchasers and sellers of securities or for otherwise performing with respect to securities the functions commonly performed by a stock exchange as that term is generally understood, and includes the market place and the market facilities maintained by such exchange.[7]

Registered stock exchanges in the United States include two national stock exchanges: the New York Stock Exchange (NYSE) and the American Stock Exchange (AMEX). In addition, there are several regional stock exchanges, including the Chicago Stock Exchange, the Chicago Board Options Exchange, the Pacific Stock Exchange, and the Philadelphia Stock Exchange.

The stock exchanges vary in their prestige and listing requirements. The NYSE is generally considered to be the most prestigious exchange. It sets listing standards

---

exchange An organization set up to buy and sell securities such as stocks.

over the counter Describes securities, such as stocks and bonds, sold directly from broker to broker or broker to customer rather than through an exchange.

Dividends ◆

The Paralegal as an "Insider"

Suppose that one of your first duties in your new paralegal position is to organize the file of the XYZ Corporation, a publicly held corporation, and to assemble information to be discussed at an upcoming board of directors' meeting. On review of the XYZ Corporation's preliminary financial statements, you notice that the XYZ Corporation has had a surprisingly good year. The financial forecast for the upcoming year also looks very good. With this in mind, you decide that it might be fun to buy some stock in the XYZ Corporation, just 100 shares or so.

Is this a smart move? Should you be congratulated, or sent to prison? According to the Securities and Exchange Commission, you may be guilty of *insider trading,* a criminal offense punishable by fine or imprisonment. Individuals who are in a position to obtain information on a corporation that is not generally available to the public and who use that information to their unfair advantage are considered to be guilty of insider trading.

In recent years, the SEC has spent considerable time and effort on detecting and prosecuting violators of the insider trading rules. Although most of this time and attention has been focused on the "big guys" on Wall Street, the SEC has also expanded its efforts to include lawyers and law firm personnel. Lawyers found to be in violation of the rules under the Securities Exchange Act are subject to sanctions under state bar association disciplinary rules, in addition to possible criminal prosecution

and civil lawsuits brought by shareholders. The Model Code of Professional Responsibility Disciplinary Rule 4-101, which has been adopted by many states, requires that an attorney shall not knowingly reveal a client's confidences or secrets or use such information to his or her advantage. Further, Disciplinary Rule 4-101 provides that an attorney must use such care as is necessary to prevent his or her employees from disclosing confidential information concerning a client, or from acting on that confidential information to their advantage.

Because the penalties for insider trading can be imposed on members of a law firm's staff, most law firms that represent publicly held corporations have written policies that must be adhered to by all office personnel. Effective law firm policies regarding trading in the securities of corporations represented by the firm serve to educate the firm's personnel about the potential risks involved in such trading. Such policies often place restrictions on trading in the securities of a corporation that the law firm represents by all individuals who may even appear to have access to inside information.

The best policy for you, as a paralegal who may be in doubt as to whether you are at risk of violating insider trading rules, is to cease any trading in the securities of corporations represented by the law firm, at least until you have had a chance to talk with a securities attorney within the firm who can advise you of your potential risks.

---

that include a minimum shareholder distribution, minimum number of shares traded, and minimum assets and revenue. Corporations listed on the NYSE must have a minimum of $40 million in net tangible assets.

The NYSE is also the largest stock exchange in the United States. The market value of the sales and exchanges on the NYSE in 1999 exceeded $9 trillion.[8] Figure 9-2 on page 338 shows a graph of the 1998 sales of stocks and options on the registered exchanges.

Securities traded on an exchange are traded on the floor of an exchange by members of the exchange. When trading securities on a stock exchange, only a registered firm acting as a specialist for a particular stock may act as a dealer for that stock on the floor of the exchange. Any other stockbroker wishing to buy or sell that particular security must act through the designated specialist for that security.

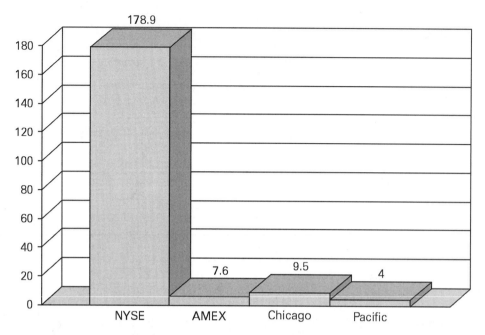

FIGURE 9-2 1998 Sales of Stocks and Options on Registered Exchanges (billions of dollars). From *The Statistical Abstract of the United States* (*2000*) § 834.

Corporations may trade their stock on more than one exchange. It is not uncommon for larger corporations to trade their stock on both a national and a regional stock exchange.

Over-the-Counter Markets Over-the-counter markets differ from exchanges in that they are not represented by actual physical locations. Over-the-counter transactions take place through a series of computer networks, among broker-dealers. Unlike securities traded on an exchange, more than one firm may act as a broker-dealer for any particular security.

The National Association of Securities Dealers Automated Quotation System (NASDAQ), which was created in 1971, is an electronic automated quotation system for selected over-the-counter securities which has gained in popularity in recent years. With NASDAQ, dealers can insert, and instantaneously update, bid and asked quotations for certain securities that are traded over the counter. In 1998 more than 5,000 companies were listed on NASDAQ,[9] which has become a favorite with the issuers of the high-tech stocks. Since 1995, the NASDAQ has consistently surpassed the NYSE in the number of shares sold annually. See Figure 9-3.

Initially, newer, start-up companies would commonly list their stock with the NASDAQ until they could meet the financial requirements of the NYSE, then they would transfer their stock to the more prestigious exchange. In 1997, more than 100 companies left the NASDAQ to go to the NYSE.[10] In recent years, however, the NYSE and NASDAQ often compete for the same corporations, and some of

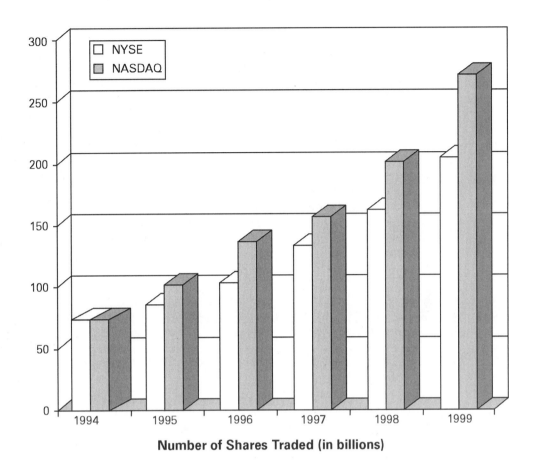

Number of Shares Traded (in billions)

FIGURE 9-3   Number of Shares Traded on the NASDAQ and NYSE. From *The Statistical Abstract of the United States (2000)* §§ 833, 835.

the corporations formerly listed on the NYSE have transferred their stock to the NASDAQ.

Some analysts feel that advances in technology and the Internet may make both systems obsolete in the not too distant future. In March 2000, a group of Wall Street's largest firms began lobbying Congress to create a single stock market that would effectively replace both the NYSE and the NASDAQ. The firms believe that "technology has advanced so much that the new market would enable them to buy and sell stocks faster and cheaper and would speed the conversion of the stock markets to 24-hour trading."[11]

§ 9.3 THE SECURITIES AND EXCHANGE COMMISSION

Prior to enactment of the Securities Exchange Act of 1934, the only federal regulation of securities was under the jurisdiction of the Federal Trade Commission. The enactment of the Securities Exchange Act of 1934 created the **Securities and Exchange Commission** (SEC). The primary mission of the SEC is to protect investors and to maintain the integrity of the securities markets. The SEC is headed by five presidential appointees, each appointed for five years. Not more than three of the members of the SEC may be of the same political party.

The SEC does not have the authority to rule upon what securities may be issued. However, it does have the authority to impose disclosure requirements upon corporations that are offering securities to the public. The SEC has the power to enforce the Securities Act of 1933, which relates to the initial registration and issuance of securities through means of interstate commerce, and the Securities Exchange Act of 1934, which relates to ongoing public disclosures by publicly held corporations and requires registration of all over-the-counter brokers and dealers of securities and stock exchanges. Each year the SEC brings between 400 and 500 civil enforcement actions against individuals and corporations for violations of securities laws.

§ 9.4   FEDERAL REGULATION OF SECURITIES OFFERINGS UNDER THE SECURITIES ACT OF 1933

Underlying the attempt to regulate securities is the generally accepted belief that "absent some type of governmental control in the area of the issuance of and transactions in securities, some opportunistic and often unscrupulous issuers and dealers in securities will defraud naïve or unsophisticated purchasers."[12] Initial attempts to protect investors were at the state level, with the enactment of state statutes to regulate securities offered within each state. The **Securities Act of 1933** (the Securities Act) was the first significant federal legislation to be passed. It was intended to protect the investor through the imposition of disclosure and antifraud requirements on corporations issuing securities through means of interstate commerce.

The SEC may prevent the distribution of securities if the disclosure requirements of the Securities Act are not complied with. Further, material misstatements in the disclosure documents or noncompliance with the anti-fraud provisions of the Securities Act may subject the issuer of the securities to civil liabilities or even criminal sanctions. The most significant provisions of the Securities Act for the corporation that is going public are the requirements for registering the securities to be offered to the public and for using prospectuses for the sale of all registered securities.

◆ ───

Securities and Exchange Commission A federal agency that administers the federal securities acts, primarily by regulating the sale and trading of stocks and other securities.

Securities Act of 1933 Federal securities act which requires the registration of securities that are to be sold to the public and the disclosure of complete information to potential buyers.

The SEC makes the registration statement and other disclosure documents of public corporations available to the public through the **EDGAR** database, a database containing required disclosure documents of all public companies. This database can be accessed by the public through the SEC's Web page at **www.sec.gov.**

Securities Registration

The application of the Securities Act of 1933 extends beyond stocks and bonds traded in the stock exchange and over-the-counter markets. Any "securities" as that term is defined in the Securities Act[13] must be registered under the Securities Act or offered and sold pursuant to an exemption from registration under that Act, Generally, prior to the issuance of any securities through interstate commerce, the issuer must file a registration statement with the SEC. The intended purpose of the registration statement is to disclose the information necessary to allow investors to make an informed decision.

Section 5 of the Securities Act contains the major provisions regarding the registration of securities. Section 5(a) prohibits the sale and delivery of unregistered securities.

Section 5. (a) Unless a registration statement is in effect as to a security, it shall be unlawful for any person, directly or indirectly—

(1) to make use of any means or instruments of transportation or communication in interstate commerce or of the mails to sell such security through the use or medium of any prospectus or otherwise; or

(2) to carry or cause to be carried through the mails or in interstate commerce, by any means or instruments of transportation, any such security for the purpose of sale or for delivery after sale.

The registration statement is filed electronically via EDGAR in the form prescribed by the SEC. Form S-1 (see Figure 9-4 on page 342) is commonly used. However, several other forms are prescribed for certain types of registrations.

The registration statement consists of two parts. Part I is the prospectus, which must be furnished to all purchasers of the corporation's securities. Part II consists of additional information required by the SEC, including information with respect to the securities being offered for sale, the corporation, the issuer, and the underwriters. The information required by the registration statement is set forth in Schedule A of the Securities Act (see Figure 9-5 on page 343).

The registration statement is filed with the SEC and must be accompanied by a filing fee that is based on the maximum aggregate price at which the securities are to be offered. The registration statement is considered to be filed, but not effective, on the date it is received by the SEC with the proper fee.

♦ ———————————————————————————————————

EDGAR Electronic Data Gathering, Analysis, and Retrieval system established by the Securities and Exchange Commission to collect, validate, index, and provide to the public, documents that are required to be filed with the Securities and Exchange Commission.

SECURITIES AND EXCHANGE COMMISSION
FORM S-1
REGISTRATION STATEMENT UNDER THE SECURITIES ACT OF 1933

_____
(Exact name of registrant as specified in charter)

_____
(State or other jurisdiction of incorporation or organization)

_____
(Primary Standard Industrial Classification Code Number)

_____
(I.R.S. Employer Identification Number)

_____
(Address, including zip code, and telephone number,
including area code, of registrant's principal executive offices)

_____
(Name, address, including zip code, and telephone number,
including area code, of agent for service)

_____
(Approximate date of commencement of proposed sale to public)

If any of the securities being registered on this Form are to be offered on a delayed or continuous basis pursuant to Rule 415 under the Securities Act of 1933 check the following box. ☐

If this Form is filed to register additional securities for an offering pursuant to Rule 462(b) under the Securities Act, please check the following box and list the Securities Act registration statement number of the earlier effective registration statement for the same offering. ☐ _____

If this Form is a post-effective amendment filed pursuant to Rule 462(c) under the Securities Act, check the following box and list the Securities Act registrations statement number of the earlier effective registration statement for the same offering. ☐ _____

If this Form is a post-effective amendment filed pursuant to Rule 462(d) under the Securities Act, check the following box and list the Securities Act registration statement number of the earlier effective registration statement for the same offering. ☐ _____

If delivery of the prospectus is expected to be made pursuant to Rule 434, please check the following box. ☐

Calculation of Registration Fee

Title of each class of securities to be registered	Amount to be registered	Proposed maximum offering price per unit	Proposed maximum aggregate offering price	Amount of registration fee

FIGURE 9-4 Form S-1

SCHEDULE A

1. The name under which the issuer is doing or intends to do business;

2. the name of the State or other sovereign power under which the issuer is organized;

3. the location of the issuer's principal business office, and if the issuer is a foreign or territorial person, the name and address of its agent in the United States authorized to receive notice;

4. the names and addresses of the directors or persons performing similar functions, and the chief executive, financial and accounting officers, chosen or to be chosen if the issuer be a corporation, association, trust, or other entity; of all partners, if the issuer be a partnership; and of the issuer, if the issuer be an individual; and of the promoters in the case of a business to be formed, or formed within two years prior to the filing of the registration statement;

5. the names and addresses of the underwriters;

6. the names and addresses of all persons, if any, owning of record or beneficially, if known, more than 10 per centum of any class of stock of the issuer, or more than 10 per centum in the aggregate of the outstanding stock of the issuer as of a date within twenty days prior to the filing of the registration statement;

7. the amount of securities of the issuer held by any person specified in paragraphs (4), (5), and (6) of this schedule, as of a date within twenty days prior to the filing of the registration statement, and, if possible, as of one year prior thereto, and the amount of the securities, for which the registration statement is filed, to which such persons have indicated their intention to subscribe;

8. the general character of the business actually transacted or to be transacted by the issuer;

9. a statement of the capitalization of the issuer, including the authorized and outstanding amounts of its capital stock and the proportion thereof paid up, the number and classes of shares in which such capital stock is divided, par value thereof, or if it has no par value, the stated or assigned value thereof, a description of the respective voting rights, preferences, conversion and exchange rights, rights to dividends, profits, or capital of each class, with respect to each other class, including the retirement and liquidation rights or values thereof;

10. a statement of the securities, if any, covered by options outstanding or to be created in connection with the security to be offered, together with the names and addresses of all persons, if any, to be allotted more than 10 per centum in the aggregate of such options;

11. the amount of capital stock of each class issued or included in the shares of stock to be offered;

12. the amount of the funded debt outstanding and to be created by the security to be offered, with a brief description of the date, maturity, and character of such debt, rate of interest, character of amortization provisions, and the security, if any, therefor. If substitution of any security is permissible, a summarized statement

FIGURE 9-5 Securities Act of 1933, Schedule A

of the conditions under which such substitution is permitted. If substitution is permissible without notice, a specific statement to that effect;

13. the specific purposes in detail and the approximate amounts to be devoted to such purposes, so far as determinable, for which the security to be offered is to supply funds, and if the funds are to be raised in part from other sources, the amounts thereof and the sources thereof, shall be stated;

14. the remuneration, paid or estimated to be paid, by the issuer or its predecessor, directly or indirectly, during the past year and ensuing year to (a) the directors or persons performing similar functions, and (b) its officers and other persons, naming them wherever such remuneration exceeded $25,000 during any such year;

15. the estimated net proceeds to be derived from the security to be offered;

16. the price at which it is proposed that the security shall be offered to the public or the method by which such price is computed and any variation therefrom at which any portion of such security is proposed to be offered to any persons or classes of persons, other than the underwriters, naming them or specifying the class. A variation in price may be proposed prior to the date of the public offering of the security, but the Commission shall immediately be notified of such variation;

17. all commissions or discounts paid or to be paid, directly or indirectly, by the issuer to the underwriters in respect of the sale of the security to be offered. Commissions shall include all cash, securities, contracts, or anything else of value, paid, to be set aside, disposed of, or understandings with or for the benefit of any other persons in which any underwriter is interested, made, in connection with the sale of such security. A commission paid or to be paid in connection with the sale of such security by a person in which the issuer has an interest or which is controlled or directed by, or under common control with, the issuer shall be deemed to have been paid by the issuer. Where any such commission is paid the amount of such commission paid to each underwriter shall be stated;

18. the amount or estimated amounts, itemized in reasonable detail, of expenses, other than commissions specified in paragraph (17) of this schedule, incurred or borne by or for the account of the issuer in connection with the sale of the security to be offered or properly chargeable thereto, including legal, engineering, certification, authentication, and other charges;

19. the net proceeds derived from any security sold by the issuer during the two years preceding the filing of the registration statement, the price at which such security was offered to the public, and the names of the principal underwriters of such security;

20. any amount paid within two years preceding the filing of the registration statement or intended to be paid to any promoter and the consideration for any such payment;

21. the names and addresses of the vendors and the purchase price of any property, or good will, acquired or to be acquired, not in the ordinary course of business, which is to be defrayed in whole or in part from the proceeds of the security to be offered, the amount of any commission payable to any person in

FIGURE 9-5 (*continued*)

connection with such acquisition, and the name or names of such person or persons, together with any expense incurred or to be incurred in connection with such acquisition, including the cost of borrowing money to finance such acquisition;

22. full particulars of the nature and extent of the interest, if any, of every director, principal executive officer, and of every stockholder holding more than 10 per centum of any class of stock or more than 10 per centum in the aggregate of the stock of the issuer, in any property acquired, not in the ordinary course of business of the issuer, within two years preceding the filing of the registration statement or proposed to be acquired at such date;

23. the names and addresses of counsel who have passed on the legality of the issue;

24. dates of and parties to, and the general effect concisely stated of every material contract made, not in the ordinary course of business, which contract is to be executed in whole or in part at or after the filing of the registration statement or which contract has been made not more than two years before such filing. Any management contract or contract providing for special bonuses or profit-sharing arrangements, and every material patent or contract for a material patent right, and every contract by or with a public utility company or an affiliate thereof, providing for the giving or receiving of technical or financial advice or service (if such contract may involve a charge to any party thereto at a rate in excess of $2,500 per year in cash or securities or anything else of value), shall be deemed a material contract;

25. a balance sheet as of a date not more than ninety days prior to the date of the filing of the registration statement showing all of the assets of the issuer, the nature and cost thereof, whenever determinable, in such detail and in such form as the Commission shall prescribe (with intangible items segregated), including any loan in excess of $20,000 to any officer, director, stockholder or person directly or indirectly controlling or controlled by the issuer, or person under direct or indirect common control with the issuer. All the liabilities of the issuer in such detail and such form as the Commission shall prescribe, including surplus of the issuer showing how and from what sources such surplus was created, all as of a date not more than ninety days prior to the filing of the registration statement. If such statement be not certified by an independent public or certified accountant, in addition to the balance sheet required to be submitted under this schedule, a similar detailed balance sheet of the assets and liabilities of the issuer, certified by an independent public or certified accountant, of a date not more than one year prior to the filing of the registration statement, shall be submitted;

26. a profit and loss statement of the issuer showing earnings and income, the nature and source thereof, and the expenses and fixed charges in such detail and such form as the Commission shall prescribe for the latest fiscal year for which such statement is available and for the two preceding fiscal years, year by year, or, if such issuer has been in actual business for less than three years, then for such time as the issuer has been in actual business, year by year. If the date of the filing of the registration statement is more than six months after the close of the last fiscal year, a statement from such closing date to the latest practicable date. Such statement shall show what the practice of the issuer has been during the three years or lesser

FIGURE 9-5 *(continued)*

period as to the character of the charges, dividends or other distributions made against its various surplus accounts, and as to depreciation, depletion, and maintenance charges, in such detail and form as the Commission shall prescribe, and if stock dividends or avails from the sale of rights have been credited to income, they shall be shown separately with a statement of the basis upon which the credit is computed. Such statement shall also differentiate between any recurring and nonrecurring income and between any investment and operating income. Such statement shall be certified by an independent public or certified accountant;

27. if the proceeds, or any part of the proceeds, of the security to be issued is to be applied directly or indirectly to the purchase of any business, a profit and loss statement of such business certified by an independent public or certified accountant, meeting the requirements of paragraph (26) of this schedule, for the three preceding fiscal years, together with a balance sheet, similarly certified, of such business, meeting the requirements of paragraph (25) of this schedule of a date not more than ninety days prior to the filing of the registration statement or at the date such business was acquired by the issuer if the business was acquired by the issuer more than ninety days prior to the filing of the registration statement;

28. a copy of any agreement or agreements (or, if identical agreements are used, the forms thereof) made with any underwriter, including all contracts and agreements referred to in paragraph (17) of this schedule;

29. a copy of the opinion or opinions of counsel in respect to the legality of the issue, with a translation of such opinion, when necessary, into the English language;

30. a copy of all material contracts referred to in paragraph (24) of this schedule, but no disclosure shall be required of any portion of any such contract if the Commission determines that disclosure of such portion would impair the value of the contract and would not be necessary for the protection of the investors;

31. unless previously filed and registered under the provisions of this title, and brought up to date, (a) a copy of its articles of incorporation, with all amendments thereof and of its existing bylaws or instruments corresponding thereto, whatever the name, if the issuer be a corporation; (b) copy of all instruments by which the trust is created or declared, if the issuer is a trust; (c) a copy of its articles of partnership or association and all other papers pertaining to its organization, if the issuer is a partnership, unincorporated association, joint-stock company, or any other form of organization; and

32. a copy of the underlying agreements or indentures affecting any stock, bonds, or debentures offered or to be offered.

In case of certificates of deposit, voting trust certificates, collateral trust certificates, certificates of interest or shares in unincorporated investment trusts, equipment trust certificates, interim or other receipts for certificates, and like securities, the Commission shall establish rules and regulations requiring the submission of information of a like character applicable to such cases, together with such other information as it may deem appropriate and necessary regarding the character, financial or otherwise, of the actual issuer of the securities and/or the person performing the acts and assuming the duties of depositor or manager.

FIGURE 9-5 (*continued*)

The registration statement is effective twenty days from the date of filing with the SEC, unless an accelerated date is requested by the issuer and granted by the SEC. If any amendment to the registration statement is filed prior to its effective date, the date of filing is deemed to be the date on which the amendment was filed, unless the amendment was ordered or approved by the SEC. The SEC has the power to accelerate the effective date and generally will do so, provided that the issuer has submitted all necessary information and acts quickly to furnish the SEC with any different or additional information requested. The SEC also has the power to delay the effective date of any registration statement that is "on its face incomplete or inaccurate in any material respect,"[14] by refusing to permit the registration statement to become effective until after it has been amended in accordance with a notice served upon the issuer not later than ten days after the filing of the registration statement. If, after the effective date of the registration statement, it appears to the SEC that the registration statement includes any untrue statements of material fact, or omits to state any material fact required to be stated therein, the SEC may issue a *stop order* suspending the effectiveness of the registration statement until such time as the registration statement has been amended in accordance with the stop order.

After the registration statement has been filed, a waiting period begins and lasts until the registration statement is effective. During this waiting period, securities may be offered for sale, but they may not actually be sold until the registration statement becomes effective. During the waiting period, preliminary prospectuses may be used to offer for sale securities that will be sold after the effective date of the registration statement. After the registration statement becomes effective, the securities may be sold through use of a prospectus.

Prospectus Requirements

The **prospectus**, which constitutes part I of the registration statement, contains disclosures required by the SEC, including information regarding the corporation, its assets, its officers and directors, and other information material to the business of the corporation. It must be furnished to the purchaser of the securities after the securities have been registered with the SEC.

Section 5(b) of the Securities Act prohibits the use of any prospectus to sell securities, unless the prospectus meets the requirements of the Securities Act, and it prohibits the sale of securities without a prospectus.

> (b) It shall be unlawful for any person, directly or indirectly—
>> (1) to make use of any means or instruments of transportation or communication in interstate commerce or of the mails to carry

---

prospectus 1. A document put out to describe a corporation and to interest persons in buying its stock. When new stock is sold to the public, the SEC requires a prospectus that contains such things as a statement of income, a balance sheet, an auditor's report, etc. 2. Any offer (written, by radio or television, etc.) to interest persons in buying any securities, such as stock. 3. A document put out to interest persons in any financial deal (such as the offer to sell a building or the offer of shares in a limited partnership).

or transmit any prospectus relating to any security with respect to which a registration statement has been filed under this title, unless such prospectus meets the requirements of section 10 of this title; or

(2) to carry or cause to be carried through the mails or in interstate commerce any such security for the purpose of sale or for delivery after sale, unless accompanied or preceded by a prospectus that meets the requirements of subsection (a) of section 10 of this title.

The Securities Act of 1933 also permits the use of a **summary prospectus** to sell securities of a registered corporation. A summary prospectus includes a summary of much of the information in the registration statement, pursuant to the rules of the SEC Regulation C, 17 CFR § 230.431. Corporations may use summary prospectuses as long as the summary prospectus contains the information required by Regulation C, the summary prospectus does not include any false or misleading statements, and as long as a statement to the following effect shall be prominently set forth in conspicuous print at the beginning or at the end of every summary prospectus:

"Copies of a more complete prospectus may be obtained from (Insert name(s), address(es) and telephone number(s)). Copies of a summary prospectus filed with the Commission pursuant to paragraph (g) of this section may omit the names of persons from whom the complete prospectus may be obtained."[15]

A preliminary prospectus without the offering price and related information may be used by the issuer of securities during the waiting period to inform prospective buyers of the nature of the securities to be sold. A prospectus used before the effective date of a registration statement is often called a **red herring prospectus** because, pursuant to Regulation § 229.501(c)(8), it is required to contain the following legend on the outside front cover in red ink:

Information contained herein is subject to completion or amendment. A registration statement relating to these securities has been filed with the Securities and Exchange Commission. These securities may not be sold nor may offers to buy be accepted prior to the time the registration statement becomes effective. This prospectus shall not constitute an offer to sell or the solicitation of an offer to buy nor shall there be any sale of these securities in any State in which such offer, solicitation or sale would be unlawful prior to registration or qualification under the securities laws of any such state.

---

summary prospectus   A shortened version of the prospectus required by the SEC that includes a summary of much of the information in the registration statement and is prepared pursuant to the pertinent rules of the SEC.

red herring prospectus   A preliminary prospectus, used during the "waiting period" between filing a registration statement with the SEC and approval of the statement. It has a red "for information only" statement on the front and states that the securities described may not be offered for sale until SEC approval. The red herring must be filed with the SEC before use.

Also commonly used during the waiting period, to announce a securities offering and to disseminate certain information regarding the offering, are **tombstone ads**. Tombstone advertisements are not considered to be prospectuses and are not subject to the requirements set forth for prospectuses in the Rules to the Securities Act. However, they must follow certain guidelines and contain certain legends prescribed by the rules. Tombstone ads are frequently found in the business section of major newspapers and are surrounded by a thick black border, which accounts for their name. Figure 9-6 shows a tombstone ad.

FIGURE 9-6   Tombstone Advertisement

tombstone ad   A stock (or other securities) or land sales notice that clearly states that it is informational only and not itself an offer to buy or sell. It has a black border that resembles one on a death notice.

EDGAR

Form S-1 and most disclosure documents filed with the Securities Exchange Commission are filed via the SEC's Electronic Data Gathering, Analysis and Retrieval system (EDGAR). Since May 1996, all publicly held companies have been required to submit certain documents to the SEC in electronic form for inclusion in the EDGAR database.

Registration statements, annual reports, quarterly reports, and other disclosure documents of all publicly held corporations may be accessed through the EDGAR database by company name, keyword, or by the EDGAR Central Index Key (CIK) lookup. The CIK is a unique identifier assigned by the SEC to all companies and people who file disclosure documents with the SEC.

Although EDGAR offers many benefits, both to filers and those seeking information about publicly held corporations, many users complain that EDGAR is not very user friendly. Documents to be filed via the EDGAR system must be prepared with required formatting, tagging, headers, and footers. Exhibits and tables must be prepared to specification. Specific instructions for filing via the EDGAR system can be found in the SEC's Regulation S-T, and the EDGAR Filing Manual, both available at the SEC Web page. Regulations concerning EDGAR filings and the EDGAR Filing Manual are continually being updated as the system is improved.

§ 9.5   EXEMPTIONS FROM THE REGISTRATION REQUIREMENTS OF THE SECURITIES ACT OF 1933

Not all securities and transactions involving securities are subject to the registration requirements of the Securities Act. An issue of securities may be exempt from registration because of either the type or class of the securities, or the specific transaction involving the securities. Securities that are scrutinized by other governmental agencies, such as the banking or insurance commissions, or securities that are sold to a specific group of informed investors often fall under the category of exempted securities. Exemption from the registration requirements of the Securities Act does not guarantee exemption from the other provisions of the Securities Act or related securities regulations, especially the antifraud provisions. In addition, the issuer of securities that qualify under one of the exemptions may not be required to *register* the securities, but may be required to file other disclosure documentation with the SEC.

Exempted Securities

Section 3 of the Securities Act specifies certain classes of securities that are exempted from the registration provisions of the Act. Some of the securities exempted by this section include:

1. Certain securities issued or guaranteed by the United States or state or local governments.
2. Certain securities issued or guaranteed by banks.

3. Short-term commercial paper, including certain notes, drafts, or bills of exchange.

4. Securities of nonprofit issuers.

5. Securities issued by certain savings and loan associations, building and loan associations, cooperative banks, homestead associations, or similar institutions.

6. Interests in railroad equipment trusts.

7. Certificates issued by receivers, trustees, or debtors in possession in a case under Title 11 of the United States Code (the Bankruptcy Code), with the approval of the court.

8. Insurance or endowment policies, annuity contracts, and optional annuity contracts that are subject to the supervision of the insurance commissioner, bank commissioner, or any similar agency or officer.

9. Certain securities issued in exchange for one or more bona fide outstanding securities, claims or property interests where the terms and conditions of such issuance and exchange are approved by any court, or by any official or agency of the United States, including any state or territorial banking or insurance commission.

10. Certain securities exchanged by the issuer when no commission or other remuneration is paid or given for soliciting such exchange.

11. Securities that are sold only to residents of a single state or territory if the issuer is both a resident of and doing business within that state or territory.

In addition, Section 3(b) of the Securities Act gives the SEC authority to exempt other classes of securities from its rules and regulations, provided that the aggregate amount of the issue does not exceed $5 million. Section 3(c) gives the SEC that same authority with regard to securities issued by a small business investment company under the Small Business Investment Act of 1958.

Exemptions for Limited Offerings and Offerings of Limited Dollar Amounts

Section 3(b) of the Securities Act of 1933 provides the SEC with the authority to exempt certain offerings from the registration requirements of the Act when the securities to be offered involve a relatively small dollar amount ($5,000,000). Regulations A and D adopted by the SEC set forth the various conditions that must be met to qualify for the exemption authorized under Section 3(b).

Regulation A   Issuers of stock with a value of less than $5 million may find they are eligible for exemptions under Regulation A, which are available to issuers who qualify under Rule 251 for offerings that do not exceed $5,000,000. Issuers who claim an exemption under Regulation A are required to comply with the provisions of Rule 251, which require the use and filing with the SEC of an offering statement and circular, among other things. The simplified registration procedure provided by Regulation A allows that the financial statements required for filing with the SEC may be in a simplified format and unaudited. In addition, issuers that have registered under Regulation A need not file periodic reports with the SEC unless the issuers have more than $5 million in assets and more than 500 shareholders.

Regulation D   Regulation D provides rules governing the limited offer and sale of securities without registration under the Securities Act of 1933. It exempts qualifying issuers of securities from the registration requirements of the Securities Act, but specifically states that "such transactions are not exempt from the antifraud, civil liability, or other provisions of the federal securities laws."

Rule 504 under Regulation D provides for exemptions for limited offerings. This rule provides exemption from registration pursuant to the following conditions:

1. The sale of securities must not exceed $1 million in a twelve-month period.
2. There are no restrictions on the number of the purchasers of the securities under this exemption.
3. Securities exempted pursuant to Regulation D may not be offered through any form of general solicitation or general advertising.
4. A Form D notice must be filed with the SEC headquarters within fifteen days after the first sale of securities under this rule.

Rule 505 under Regulation D offers exemption from registration pursuant to the following conditions:

1. The issuer may not sell securities totaling more than $5 million in any twelve-month period.
2. The issuer must file financial statements as specifically required by Rule 505.
3. The offering may not be made by means of a general solicitation or general advertising.
4. There is no restriction on the number of accredited investors to which the issuer may sell its securities.
5. The issuer may sell securities to no more than thirty-five nonaccredited investors.
6. The issuer must make an effort to ensure that the purchase of its securities are for investment purposes only (not for resale).
7. Fifteen days after the first sale in the offering, the issuer must file a notice of sales on Form D.

An *accredited investor,* as defined in the Securities Act, includes:

1. Certain banks and savings and loan associations.
2. Certain private business development companies.

3. Certain nonprofit organizations described in § 501(c)(3) of the Internal Revenue Code.

4. Directors, executive officers, or general partners of the issuer of the securities being offered or sold, or any director, executive officer, or general partner of a general partner of that issuer.

5. Individuals with a net worth, or joint net worth with that person's spouse, that at the time of the purchase exceeds $1 million.

6. Individuals who have an income in excess of $200,000 in each of the two most recent years, or joint income with that person's spouse in excess of $300,000 in each of those years, and has a reasonable expectation of reaching the same income level in the current year.

7. Certain trusts with total assets in excess of $5 million.

8. Entities in which all of the equity owners are accredited investors.

Rule 506 establishes certain conditions for a private offering under Section 4(2) of the Securities Act. Section 4(2) of the Securities Act provides an exemption from the registration requirements of the Act for the issuance of securities, by the issuer, that do not involve any "public offering." Under Rule 506, an offering is not a public offering if it meets with all the conditions of Rules 501 and 502 of Regulation D, and if there are no more than 35 purchasers of the securities. Rules 501 and 502 provide several conditions for the offering, including requirements for certain types of information that must be made available to purchasers of the securities. The purchasers must all be accredited investors, or they must have sufficient knowledge and experience in financial and business matters to allow them to evaluate the merits and risks of the investment.

To qualify for this exemption, the offering may not be made by public solicitation or general advertising, and the sale of the securities must generally be to individuals who have sufficient knowledge of the corporation to make an informed decision or are able to bear the risk. The purchasers must have access to the type of information normally provided in a prospectus and must agree not to resell or distribute the securities. Another consideration of this exemption is the sophistication of the purchasers of the securities.

Most private placements under this rule involve the sale of large blocks of securities to institutional investors such as insurance companies or pension funds. In such private placements, the investor is in a position to insist on receiving adequate information from the issuer of securities—possibly even more than would be required by the SEC in a registration statement. The purchaser is not placed at a disadvantage because of the issuer's lack of public disclosure with the SEC. Sales to employees and those who have access to information about the corporation generally are also not considered to be public offerings. The SEC has reported that "[w]hether a transaction is one not involving any public offering is essentially a question of fact and necessitates a consideration of all surrounding circumstances, including such factors as the relationship between the offerees and the issuer, the nature, scope, size, type and manner of the offering."[16]

Intrastate Offering Exemptions

Section 3(a)(11) of the Securities Act offers an exemption, commonly referred to as the *intrastate offering exemption,* for corporations that issue securities only within the state in which they are located and doing business. To qualify for the intrastate offering exemption, the issuer must meet the following conditions:

1. The issuer must be a corporation incorporated in the state in which it is making the offering.
2. The issuer must carry out a significant amount of its business in that state.
3. The issuer must make offerings and sales only to residents of that state.

The issuer has an obligation to ensure that each investor who purchases shares of the corporation is a resident of the state of the offering. If the corporation sells shares to investors who are not residents, or if residents resell their shares to nonresidents within nine months of the date the offering is completed, the issuer may lose the right to use the exemption. For this reason, the intrastate offering exemption is often used for relatively small offerings to a limited number of investors.

Transactions by Persons Other Than Issuers, Underwriters, and Dealers   This exemption ordinarily permits investors to make casual sales of their securities holdings without registration. Transactions that are a part of the scheme of distribution do not qualify under this exemption, which is available only for routine trading transactions.

§ 9.6   ANTIFRAUD PROVISIONS OF THE SECURITIES ACT

Antifraud provisions are found mainly in Sections 11, 12, and 17 of the Securities Act. These antifraud provisions are intended to protect the investors who rely on the disclosures mandated by the Securities Act of 1933. Section 11 of the Securities Act concerns the truthfulness of statements made in the registration statement of a registered corporation. Section 12 concerns the truthfulness of statements made in the prospectus and other statements made to sell the registered securities, and Section 17 covers all fraudulent conduct with regard to the offer, sale, or any other type of transaction regarding securities. The prohibited acts or practices addressed in those provisions are not limited to the common law concept of fraud, but also include acts and practices that tend to be fraudulent in nature, such as the publication of misstatements or half-truths, devices directed toward market manipulation, and improper touting of securities being offered for sale.[17] These provisions, for jurisdictional reasons, apply to acts involving use of facilities of interstate commerce, the mails, or facilities of the registered National Securities Exchange.[18] The antifraud provisions of the Securities Act are of specific concern to the issuer and all other parties signing or otherwise responsible for the information contained in the registration statement.

Section 11

Every person who signs or contributes information to the registration statement has a duty to provide complete and accurate information. Failure to do so may provide the purchaser of securities with a cause of action under § 11 of the Securities Act for any damages stemming from the purchase of securities for which an inaccurate or misleading registration statement was filed. Section 11 places a relatively minimal burden on a plaintiff, requiring simply that the plaintiff allege that he purchased the security and that the registration statement contains false or misleading statements concerning a material fact.[19] Section 11(a) of the Securities Act specifies when a purchaser may sue and who may be sued in conjunction with a registration statement containing untrue or misleading information:

> Section 11. (a) In case any part of the registration statement, when such part became effective, contained an untrue statement of a material fact or omitted to state a material fact required to be stated therein or necessary to make the statements therein not misleading, any person acquiring such security (unless it is proved that at the time of such acquisition he knew of such untruth or omission) may, either at law or in equity, in any court of competent jurisdiction, sue—
>
> (1) every person who signed the registration statement;
> (2) every person who was a director of (or person performing similar functions) or partner in, the issuer at the time of the filing of the part of the registration statement with respect to which his liability is asserted;
> (3) every person who, with his consent, is named in the registration statement as being or about to become a director, person performing similar functions, or partner;
> (4) every accountant, engineer, or appraiser, or any person whose profession gives authority to a statement made by him, who has with his consent been named as having prepared or certified any part of the registration statement, or as having prepared or certified any report or valuation which is used in connection with the registration statement, with respect to the statement in such registration statement, report, or valuation, which purports to have been prepared or certified by him;
> (5) every underwriter with respect to such security.

Obviously, it is not possible for every individual named in § 11(a) to be personally knowledgeable about the truth and validity of every statement in the registration statement. For that reason, the Securities Act provides several defenses to the liabilities in § 11. Section 11(b) provides that no persons, other than the issuer, shall be liable as provided therein if they can prove that: (1) they had resigned from the positions causing their relationships with the issuer; (2) if the registration statement became effective without their knowledge, they advised the SEC upon becoming aware of such fact, and they gave reasonable public notice that the registration statement became effective without their knowledge; or (3) they had, after reasonable investigation, reasonable ground to believe and did believe, the information to be true and accurate. This is referred to as the **due diligence** defense. Corporate directors and others who participate in preparing and filing registration statements and prospectuses relating to domestic securities are required to have made a reasonable investigation of all material facts before they may avail themselves of the statutory defense of due diligence. Attorneys and paralegals often assist with gathering and verifying information to be included in the registration statement.

Section 12

Section 12 of the Securities Act is designed to protect investors from purchasing securities based on false or misleading prospectuses or sales pitches. Section 12 provides that offers of sale of securities, including prospectuses and oral statements, must not include any false or misleading statements of a material fact. The purchaser may not recover if he or she knew about the misstatement, but made the purchase anyway.

Section 12 also protects purchasers of securities that are unregistered in violation of Section 5 of the Securities Act.

Section 12. (a) In general, any person who—
(1) offers or sells a security in violation of section 77e of this title, or
(2) offers or sells a security (whether or not exempted by the provisions of section 77c of this title, other than paragraph (2) of subsection (a) of said section), by the use of any means or instruments of transportation or communication in interstate commerce or of the mails, by means of a prospectus or oral communication, which includes an untrue statement of a material fact or omits to state a material fact necessary in order to make the statements, in the light of the circumstances under which they were made, not misleading (the purchaser not knowing of such untruth or omission), and who shall not sustain the burden of proof that he did not know, and in the exercise of reasonable care could not have known, of such untruth or omission, shall be liable, subject to subsection (b) of this section, to the person purchasing such security from him, who may sue either at law or in equity in any court of competent jurisdiction, to recover the consideration paid for such security with interest thereon, less the amount of any income received thereon, upon the tender of such security, or for damages if he no longer owns the security.

Section 17

Section 17 of the Securities Act is much broader in its scope than Sections 11 and 12. It prohibits fraudulent conduct with respect to securities transactions, and pertains to the sale of, or an offer to sell, securities, not to their purchase.

---

due diligence Enough care, enough timeliness, or enough investigation to meet legal requirements, to fulfill a duty, or to evaluate the risks of a course of action. Due diligence often refers to a professional investigation of the financial risks of a merger or a securities purchase, or the legal obligation to do the investigation. Due diligence is also used as a synonym for due care.

Section 17. (a) It shall be unlawful for any person in the offer or sale of any securities by the use of any means or instruments of transportation or communication in interstate commerce or by the use of the mails, directly or indirectly—

(1) to employ any device, scheme, or artifice to defraud, or

(2) to obtain money or property by means of any untrue statement of a material fact or any omission to state a material fact necessary in order to make the statements made, in the light of the circumstances under which they were made, not misleading, or

(3) to engage in any transaction, practice, or course of business which operates or would operate as a fraud or deceit upon the purchaser.

(b) It shall be unlawful for any person, by the use of any means or instruments of transportation or communication in interstate commerce or by the use of the mails, to publish, give publicity to, or circulate any notice, circular, advertisement, newspaper, article, letter, investment service, or communication which, though not purporting to offer a security for sale, describes such security for a consideration received or to be received, directly or indirectly, from an issuer, underwriter, or dealer, without fully disclosing the receipt, whether past or prospective, of such consideration and the amount thereof.

(c) The exemptions provided in section 3 shall not apply to the provisions of this section.

§ 9.7 FEDERAL REGULATIONS IMPOSED ON PUBLICLY HELD CORPORATIONS UNDER THE SECURITIES EXCHANGE ACT OF 1934

Whereas the Securities Act of 1933 deals primarily with the registration of initial issues of securities, the **Securities Exchange Act of 1934** (Exchange Act) pertains to dealings in securities subsequent to their initial issue and to ongoing reporting requirements. The aim of the Exchange Act is to protect securities investors and the general public by regulating securities exchanges and markets, by providing information regarding the issuance of securities to persons who buy and sell securities, by preventing fraud in securities trading and manipulation of the markets, and by protecting the national credit by controlling the amount of such credit that may be used in the securities market.[20]

With regard to publicly traded corporations, the Exchange Act contains provisions requiring registration with the exchange on which the securities are traded. In addition, the Exchange Act contains provisions requiring periodic reporting to the exchanges and the SEC, and provisions regulating the use of proxies. The Exchange Act also contains several antifraud provisions that affect the public corporation and its officers, directors, and principal shareholders. Securities exchanges and brokers and dealers are also regulated under the Exchange Act.

◆────────────────────────────────

Securities Exchange Act of 1934   Federal securities act which regulates stock exchanges and over-the-counter stock sales.

Figure 9-7 lists the purposes of the Securities Exchange Act of 1934.

[From AM. JUR. 2d *Securities Regulation* § 301 (1993)]

PURPOSES OF THE SECURITIES EXCHANGE ACT OF 1934

♦ To regulate transactions by officers, directors and principal security holders.

♦ To outlaw the use of insider information for the financial gain of privileged insiders to the detriment of uninformed security holders.

♦ To require appropriate reports.

♦ To make information available to persons trading in securities on the markets.

♦ To remove impediments to and perfect the mechanisms of a national market system for securities transactions.

♦ To safeguard funds and securities related to a national market system.

♦ To protect interstate commerce, the national credit and the federal taxing power.

♦ To protect and make more effective the national banking and Federal Reserve system.

♦ Insure, through regulation and self regulation, the maintenance of fair and honest markets in transactions conducted on securities exchanges and on the over-the-counter markets.

♦ To prevent fraud and manipulation in the securities markets by substituting a philosophy of full disclosure for the philosophy of caveat emptor.

♦ To prevent those whose business is dealing in securities and who are experienced and knowledgeable in the practical process of securities and the property and potential backing of such issues from imposing upon the public by reason of such background knowledge.

FIGURE 9-7   Purposes of the Securities Exchange Act of 1934.

Registration Under the Exchange Act

In addition to the registration requirements of the Securities Act, § 12(a) of the Exchange Act requires that every nonexempt security that is traded on a national securities exchange must be registered with that exchange. All exchanges in the United States must be registered with the SEC as a national securities exchange unless exempt from the registration requirements by the SEC because of a limited volume of trading. Section 12(a) of the Exchange Act provides:

Section 12. (a) It shall be unlawful for any member, broker, or dealer to effect any transaction in any security (other than an exempted security) on a national securities exchange unless a registration is effective as to such security for such exchange in accordance with the provisions of this title and the rules and regulations thereunder.

A security is registered by filing an application with the appropriate exchange, with duplicate originals submitted to the SEC as required. The application contains information regarding the issuer, the corporation, and the securities to be traded. In addition, copies of corporate documents, including articles of incorporation and certain material contracts, may be required to supplement the application. The registration of the security on the exchange is generally effective thirty days after the filing of the application with the exchange and the SEC.

In addition to the issuers of securities actively traded on a national exchange, § 12(g)(1) requires registration with the SEC by every issuer that is engaged in interstate commerce, or in a business affecting interstate commerce, or whose securities are traded by use of the mails or any means or instrumentality of interstate commerce, if the corporation has total assets exceeding $1 million and a class of securities held by 750 or more persons.

Periodic Reporting Requirements

Every issuer of securities that have been registered pursuant to § 12 of the Exchange Act is subject to the periodic reporting requirements of § 13 of the Act. Issuers who are not nominally subject to the registration requirements of the Exchange Act, but have filed a registration statement with the SEC pursuant to the Securities Act, also become subject to the reporting requirements of the Exchange Act. Corporations that do not have an active registration statement filed with the SEC, but are otherwise subject to the reporting requirements of the Exchange Act, may be required to file a special registration statement to activate those reporting requirements.

Section 13 of the Exchange Act requires issuers to make periodic disclosures electronically, on forms prescribed by the SEC, in accordance with the Act. The issuer of securities that are registered on a national securities exchange is required to file duplicate originals of such disclosure forms with the exchange.

Failure to comply with the disclosure requirements of the Exchange Act can leave the publicly held corporation liable for damages to injured parties in some instances. False reporting may subject the issuers to criminal liability.

The periodic reports required of publicly held corporations are the 10-K, the 10-Q, and the 8-K.

The 10-K Report   Annual **10-K reports** must be filed with the SEC by every issuer subject to the reporting requirements of the Exchange Act. The Form 10-K must be filed electronically via EDGAR with the SEC within ninety days after the end of the corporation's fiscal year. The information that must be included in the 10-K report is similar to that required for the initial registration statement filed by the corporation, and includes detailed information as to the nature of the registrant's

---

10-K report   The annual report required by the SEC of publicly held corporations that sell stock.

business and significant changes therein during the previous fiscal year, as well as a summary of its operation for the last five fiscal years, or for the life of the registrant if less than five years, and for any additional fiscal years necessary to keep the summary from being misleading.[21] The annual 10-K report also includes identification of principal securities holders of the corporation and any transactions involving the transfer of significant percentages of the securities of the corporation. Parts I and II of the 10-K report consist of information that is typically included in the annual report to shareholders, and much of the information required by the 10-K report is often provided by reference to that information in the annual report to shareholders, which is submitted for filing with the 10-K.

The Form 10-K must be completed to the exact specifications of the SEC as set forth in the instructions to the Form 10-K, and the pertinent rules and regulations of the SEC. Figure 9-8 illustrates the type of information required by the Form 10-K. The Form 10-K and instructions, as well as thousands of filed Form 10-K's, can be found on the SEC Web page at **www.sec.gov.**

PARTS OF THE FORM 10-K

Part I

Item 1.   Business.

Item 2.   Properties.

Item 3.   Legal Proceedings.

Item 4.   Submission of Matters to a Vote of Security Holders.

Part II

Item 5.   Market for Registrant's Common Equity and Related Stockholder Matters.

Item 6.   Selected Financial Data.

Item 7.   Management's Discussion and Analysis of Financial Condition and Results of Operation.

Item 7A.   Quantitative and Qualitative Disclosures About Market Risk.

Item 8.   Financial Statements and Supplementary Data.

Item 9.   Changes in and Disagreements With Accountants on Accounting and Financial Disclosure.

Part III

Item 10.   Directors and Executive Officers of the Registrant.

Item 11.   Executive Compensation.

Item 12.   Security Ownership of Certain Beneficial Owners and Management.

Item 13.   Certain Relationships and Related Transactions.

Part IV

Item 14.   Exhibits, Financial Statement Schedules, and Reports on Form 8-K.

SIGNATURES

FIGURE 9-8   Parts of the Form 10-K

The 10-Q Report Registrants that are required to file 10-K (annual) reports must also file **10-Q quarterly reports**. The 10-Q contains financial information regarding the registrant, the registrant's capitalization and stockholders' equity, and the registrant's sale of unregistered securities during the reporting period. Quarterly reports must be filed for the first three quarters of a corporation's fiscal year, with information concerning the fourth quarter being included in the corporation's annual report. The Form 10-Q must be filed with the SEC within forty-five days of the close of the quarter.

Much of the information required on the 10-Q reports is identical to the information included in the corporation's quarterly reports to shareholders. Hence, it is often incorporated in the 10-Q reports by reference.

Form 8-K Form 8-K must be completed and filed electronically by the issuer of registered securities when certain information contained in the registration statement of the issuer changes. Generally, within ten days after the close of the month in which any of the events requiring reporting occur, a Form 8-K must be filed. Typical of the events that require filing of a Form 8-K are changes in control of the registrant, acquisition or disposition of a significant amount of assets (other than in the normal course of business), nonroutine legal proceedings, changes in securities of the registrant or modification of the rights of holders of securities, any material default with respect to senior securities, any increase or decrease in outstanding securities of the registrant, and any grants or extensions of options with respect to the purchase of securities of the registrant or of its subsidiaries, if such options relate to an amount of securities exceeding 5 percent of the outstanding securities of the class to which they belong. The Form 8-K, which may be found on the SEC's Web page at **www.sec.gov**, gives detailed instructions as to which items require the filing of the form. See Figure 9-9.

- ◆ Changes in control of registrant.
- ◆ Acquisition or disposition of assets of registrant.
- ◆ Bankruptcy or receivership of registrant.
- ◆ Changes in registrant's certifying accountant.
- ◆ Resignations of registrant's directors.

FIGURE 9-9 Activities Requiring the Filing of a Form 8-K

10-Q quarterly report Quarterly report that must be filed with the SEC by all corporations that are required to file 10-K reports.

Form 8-K Form that must be filed with the SEC by the issuer of registered securities when certain pertinent information contained in the registration statement of the issuer changes.

Liability for Short-Swing Profits

Because of their advantageous position and the availability of inside information to a corporation's officers, directors, and principal shareholders, the Exchange Act imposes specific reporting requirements for shareholders falling into these categories. Section 16 of the Exchange Act provides that any profits realized from the purchase and sale (or sale and purchase) of the equity securities of a corporation by its officers, directors, or 10 percent or more shareholders in any period of less than six months normally shall inure to and be recoverable by the issuer. Profits made by an insider on the purchase and sale of securities within a six-month period are often referred to as **short-swing profits**.

Section 16(a) of the Exchange Act specifically provides that a statement setting forth the beneficial ownership of the securities must be filed by "every person who is directly or indirectly the beneficial owner of more than 10 percentum of any class of any equity security (other than an exempted security) which is registered pursuant to section 12 of this title, or who is a director or an officer of the issuer of such security." The statement must be filed with the SEC and the exchange on which the securities are registered, on the effective date of the registration statement or at the time of registration of the securities on the exchange. Additional reports are required within ten days after the close of each calendar month if there has been a change in such ownership during the month.

Section 16(b) specifically prohibits short-swing profits as follows:

> (b) For the purpose of preventing the unfair use of information which may have been obtained by such beneficial owner, director, or officer by reason of his relationship to the issuer, any profit realized by him from any purchase and sale, or any sale and purchase, of any equity security of such issuer (other than an exempted security) within any period of less than six months, unless such security was acquired in good faith in connection with a debt previously contracted, shall inure to and be recoverable by the issuer ... .

Although the stated purpose of this requirement is to prevent the unfair use of inside information, it is not necessary to prove actual use of inside information to impose short-swing liability.

The rule against short-swing profits does not apply to all employees of a corporation or even all employees who hold a title generally given to an officer. The individual's access to confidential inside information, regardless of his or her title, is more determinative as to whom the short-swing profits rules apply. In *Merrill Lynch v. Livingston,* the case which follows in this chapter, the court determined that although the defendant held the title of vice president, he did not have access to "that kind of confidential information about the company's affairs that would help the particular employee to make decisions affecting his market transactions in his employer's securities."

---

short-swing profits Profits made by a company insider on the short-term sale of company stock.

CASE

United States Court of Appeals,
Ninth Circuit.

MERRILL LYNCH, PIERCE, FENNER & SMITH, INC., Plaintiff-Appellee,

v.

William G. LIVINGSTON, Defendant-Appellant.

No. 75-3779.

Jan. 4, 1978.

HUFSTEDLER, Circuit Judge:

Merrill Lynch, Pierce, Fenner & Smith, Inc. ("Merrill Lynch") obtained judgment against its employee Livingston requiring him to pay Merrill Lynch $14,836.37 which was the profit that he made on short-swing transactions in the securities of his employer in alleged violation of Section 16(b) of the Securities Exchange Act of 1934 (15 U.S.C. § 78p (1971)). We reverse because Livingston was not an officer with access to inside information within the purview of Section 16(b) of the Securities Exchange Act of 1934.

From 1951 to 1972, Livingston was employed by Merrill Lynch as a securities salesman with the title of "Account Executive." In January, 1972, Merrill Lynch began an "Account Executive Recognition Program" for its career Account Executives to reward outstanding sales records. As part of the program, Merrill Lynch awarded Livingston and 47 other Account Executives the title "Vice President." Livingston had exactly the same duties after he was awarded the title as he did before the recognition. Livingston never attended, nor was he invited or permitted to attend, meetings of the Board of Directors or the Executive Committee. He acquired no executive or policy making duties. Executive and managerial functions were performed by approximately 350 "Executive Vice Presidents."

Livingston received the same kind of information about the company as an Account Executive both before and after he acquired his honorary title. As an Account Executive, he did obtain some information that was not generally available to the investing public, such as the growth production rankings on the various Merrill Lynch retail offices. Information of this kind was regularly distributed to other salesmen for Merrill Lynch. Livingston's supervisor, a branch office manager, testified that he gave Livingston the same kind of information that he gave other salesmen about the company, none of which was useful for purposes of stock trading.

In November and December, 1972, Livingston sold a total of 1,000 shares of Merrill Lynch stock. He repurchased 1,000 shares of Merrill Lynch stock in March, 1973, realizing the profit in question.

The district court held that Livingston was an officer with access to inside information within the meaning of Section 16(b) of the Securities Exchange Act of 1934. The predicate for the district court's decision was that Section 16(b) imposes strict liability on any person who holds the title of "officer" and who has access to information about his company that is not generally available to the members of the investing public.

The district court used an incorrect legal standard in applying Section 16(b). Liability under Section 16(b) is not based simply upon a person's title within his corporation; rather, liability follows from the existence of a relationship with the corporation that makes it more probable than not that the individual has access to insider information. Insider information, to which Section 16(b) is addressed, does not mean all information about the company that is not public knowledge. Insider information within the meaning of Section 16(b) encompasses that kind of confidential information about the company's affairs that would help the particular employee to make decisions affecting his market transactions in his employer's securities.

Strict liability to the issuer is imposed upon any "beneficial owner, director, or officer" for entering into such a short-swing transaction "(f)or the purpose of preventing the unfair use of information which may have been obtained by such ... officer by reason of his relationship to the issuer." "The purpose of the statute was to take 'the profits out of a class of transactions in which the possibility of abuse was believed to be intolerably great' and to prevent the use by 'insiders' of confidential information, accessible because of one's corporate position or status, in speculative trading in the securities of one's corporation for personal profit." ...

To achieve the beneficial purposes of the statute, the court must look behind the title of the purchaser or seller to ascertain that person's real duties. Thus, a person who does not have the title of an officer, may, in fact, have a relationship to the company which gives him the very access to insider information that the statute was designed to reach. ...

The title "Vice President" does no more than raise an inference that the person who holds the title has the executive duties and the opportunities for confidential information that the title implies. The inference can be overcome by proof that the title was merely honorary and did not carry with it any of the executive responsibilities that might otherwise be assumed. The record in this case convincingly demonstrates that Livingston was simply a securities salesman who had none of the powers of an executive officer of Merrill Lynch.

Livingston did not have the job in fact which would have given him presumptive access to insider information. Information that is freely circulated among non-management employees is not insider information within the meaning of Section 16(b), even if the general public does not have the same information. Employees of corporations know all kinds of things about the companies they work for and about the personnel of their concerns that are not within the public domain. Rather, insider information to which Section 16(b) refers is the kind of information that is commonly reserved for company management and is thus the type of information that would "aid (one) if he engaged in personal market transactions." ...

Livingston did not receive insider information within the meaning of Section 16(b). The only information that he received was that generally available to all Merrill Lynch salesmen. It was not information reserved for company management, nor was it in any way useful to give him any kind of advantage in his security transactions over any other salesmen for Merrill Lynch.

REVERSED.

Proxy Regulations

The Exchange Act also regulates the content and use of **proxies** and **proxy statements** by public corporations. As discussed in Chapter 7, proxies may be used to register the vote of a shareholder not in attendance at a shareholder meeting. The proxy statement contains the information required by the SEC to be given to stockholders in conjunction with the solicitation of a proxy. The purpose of the proxy statement is to give the shareholder adequate information to make a decision regarding the use of the proxy.

Generally, any corporation that is subject to the registration requirements of the Securities Act or the Exchange Act is subject to proxy requirements of the Exchange Act. Section 14(a) of the Exchange Act specifically provides that it is unlawful to solicit proxies "in contravention of such rules and regulations as the Commission

proxy A person who acts for another person (usually to vote in place of the other person in a meeting the other cannot attend). A document giving that right.

proxy statement The document sent or given to stockholders when their voting proxies are requested for a corporate decision. The SEC has rules for when the statements must be given out and what must be in them.

may prescribe as necessary or appropriate in the public interest or for the protection of investors." The proxy statement must disclose certain material facts concerning the matters on which shareholders are being asked to vote. Rules 14a-1 through 14b-1 under the Exchange Act set forth the specific requirements for soliciting proxies, including the filing of proxy statements with the SEC.

Rule 14a-3 provides, among other things, that no solicitations shall be made unless those solicitations are accompanied by a proxy statement containing the information required by the SEC. Rule 14a-3 further provides that proxy solicitation by management relating to an annual meeting at which directors are to be elected must be accompanied by an annual report disclosing certain information regarding the company, including annual financial statements for the latest fiscal year. All required reports must be set forth in the manner prescribed by the rules.

Rule 14a-4 sets forth, among other things, the exact format to be followed for the proxy form.

Rule 14a-5 sets forth the exact manner for the presentation of information in a proxy statement.

Rule 14a-6 provides for the filing of the proxy statement with the SEC. Generally, statements filed under § 14 must be filed electronically via EDGAR. However, certain preliminary proxy materials and information statements for which confidential treatment has been requested must be submitted in paper format. The preliminary proxy statement, proxy form, and all other pertinent materials must be filed with the SEC at least ten days prior to the mailing of the proxies. Rule 14a-6 further provides that definitive proxy statements must be filed with the SEC as of the date those proxy statements are furnished to the security holders.

Pursuant to Rule 14a-8 of the Exchange Act, eligible shareholders that follow specified procedures may notify the corporation's management of the shareholder's intent to present a proposal for action at an upcoming meeting of the shareholders, to be put to a vote. In that event, the corporation must set forth the proposal in its proxy statement. Also pursuant to Rule 14a-8, the corporate management must allow the shareholder to include in the proxy statement a statement of no more than 500 words supporting his or her proposal. By following the procedures under Rule 14a-8, disgruntled shareholders have a chance to present and support a proposal for a shareholder vote, even if the management is in opposition.

Antifraud Provisions Under the Exchange Act

Section 10(b) of the Exchange Act, regarding the prohibition of manipulative and deceptive devices, is the Act's principal antifraud provision. It is very broad and applies to both the sale and purchase of securities. Section 10(b) deems it unlawful for any person to use or employ any "manipulative or deceptive device or contrivance in contravention of such rules and regulations as the Commission may prescribe as necessary or appropriate in the public interest or for the protection of investors." The primary fraud-control rule adopted under § 10(b) of the Exchange Act is Securities Exchange Act Rule 10b-5:

RULE 10b-5. EMPLOYMENT OF MANIPULATIVE AND DECEPTIVE DEVICES

It shall be unlawful for any person, directly or indirectly, by the use of any means or instrumentality of interstate commerce, or the mails, or of any facility of any national securities exchange,

(1) to employ any device, scheme, or artifice to defraud,

(2) to make any untrue statement of a material fact or to omit to state a material fact necessary in order to make the statements made, in light of the circumstances under which they were made, not misleading, or

(3) to engage in any act, practice, or course of business which operates or would operate as a fraud or deceit upon any person,

in connection with the purchase or sale of any security.

The general nature of Rule 10b-5 allows its imposition on several types of securities cases, including market manipulation, insider trading, corporate misstatements, and corporate mismanagement.

One of the most infamous applications of Rule 10b-5 has been in deciding **insider trading** cases. Publicly held corporations must release to the public, in a timely manner, all information concerning their earnings, potential mergers or acquisitions, and other information that may affect the price of their stock. Disclosures of nonpublic information must be made broadly by filing the information with the SEC or by other nonexclusive means, such as a press release.[22] This rule is intended to give all investors, regardless of the size of their holdings, the same information to base their investment decisions on. Insider trading occurs when *insiders* have information that has not been released to the public, and they act on that information by buying or selling stock in the corporation, taking unfair advantage of the uninformed investor.

Insiders are generally considered to be individuals who have access to information intended to be available only for a corporate purpose and not for the personal benefit of anyone. Courts have found that the "Exchange Act and the Rule impose upon an insider the duty to speak and to make full disclosure in those circumstances in which silence would constitute fraud."[23] It has been found that Rule 10b-5 makes it unlawful for an insider to purchase the stock of a minority stockholder without disclosing material facts affecting the value of the stock, when such facts are known to the insider by virtue of his or her inside position.[24] When material information concerning the corporation is released, insiders must wait until the news can be widely disseminated before the insider buys or sells shares of equity securities of the corporation based on that information.

In October 2000, the SEC, for the first time, adopted a Rule to define insider trading. Previously, the law of insider trading was defined by judicial opinions. Rule 10b5-1 reads, in part, as follows:

10b5-1 Trading "on the basis of" material nonpublic information in insider trading cases.

---

insider trading   The purchase or sale of securities by corporate insiders based on nonpublic information.

(a) General. The "manipulative and deceptive devices" prohibited by Section 10(b) of the Act (15 U.S.C. 78j) and § 240.10b-5 thereunder include, among other things, the purchase or sale of a security of any issuer, on the basis of material nonpublic information about that security or issuer, in breach of a duty of trust or confidence that is owed directly, indirectly, or derivatively, to the issuer of that security or the shareholders of that issuer, or to any other person who is the source of the material nonpublic information.

(b) Definition of "on the basis of." Subject to the affirmative defenses in paragraph (c) of this section, a purchase or sale of a security of an issuer is "on the basis of" material nonpublic information about that security or issuer if the person making the purchase or sale was aware of the material nonpublic information when the person made the purchase or sale.

Insider trading made the headlines in the 1980s when high-level insiders Michael Milken and Ivan Boesky were accused of insider trading. Michael Milken pled guilty to six felony counts and paid $600 million in fines and **disgorgement**. Ivan Boesky was sentenced to 3½ years in prison and fined $100 million.

Although insider trading cases have not been making the headlines regularly since the 1980s, the Securities and Exchange Commission is still investigating and prosecuting such charges with fervor. The Enforcement Division of the SEC regularly seeks injunctions, disgorgement, and significant fines against insiders who trade illegally. In addition, the SEC commonly refers the matter for federal criminal prosecution. Each of the Securities Exchanges and the NASDAQ have investigators who review trading activity for suspected insider trading and report to the SEC.

In *Carpenter v. United States,* a reporter for a financial newspaper and a stockbroker were convicted of conspiring in an insider trading case, when the reporter passed information to his stockbroker who made trades based on that information before it appeared in the newspaper.

CASE

Supreme Court of the United States

David CARPENTER, Kenneth P. Felis, and R. Foster Winans, Petitioners

v.

UNITED STATES.

No. 86-422.
Argued Oct. 7, 1987.
Decided Nov. 16, 1987.

Justice WHITE delivered the opinion of the Court.

Petitioners Kenneth Felis and R. Foster Winans were convicted of violating § 10(b) of the Securities Exchange Act of 1934, 48 Stat. 891, 15 U.S.C. § 78j(b), and Rule 10b-5, 17 CFR § 240.10b-5 (1987). ... They were also found guilty of violating the federal mail and wire fraud statutes, 18 U.S.C. §§ 1341, 1343, and were convicted for conspiracy under 18 U.S.C. § 371. Petitioner David Carpenter, Winans' roommate, was convicted for aiding and abetting. With a minor exception, the Court of Appeals for the Second Circuit affirmed, 791 F.2d

disgorgement To give up something (usually illegal profits) on demand or by court order.

1024 (1986); we granted certiorari, 479 U.S. 1016, 107 S.Ct. 666, 93 L.Ed.2d 718 (1986).

In 1981, Winans became a reporter for the Wall Street Journal (the Journal) and in the summer of 1982 became one of the two writers of a daily column, "Heard on the Street." That column discussed selected stocks or groups of stocks, giving positive and negative information about those stocks and taking "a point of view with respect to investment in the stocks that it reviews." ... Winans regularly interviewed corporate executives to put together interesting perspectives on the stocks that would be highlighted in upcoming columns, but, at least for the columns at issue here, none contained corporate inside information or any "hold for release" information... . Because of the "Heard" column's perceived quality and integrity, it had the potential of affecting the price of the stocks which it examined. The District Court concluded on the basis of testimony presented at trial that the "Heard" column "does have an impact on the market, difficult though it may be to quantify in any particular case." ...

The official policy and practice at the Journal was that prior to publication, the contents of the column were the Journal's confidential information. Despite the rule, with which Winans was familiar, he entered into a scheme in October 1983 with Peter Brant and petitioner Felis, both connected with the Kidder Peabody brokerage firm in New York City, to give them advance information as to the timing and contents of the "Heard" column. This permitted Brant and Felis and another conspirator, David Clark, a client of Brant, to buy or sell based on the probable impact of the column on the market. Profits were to be shared.

The conspirators agreed that the scheme would not affect the journalistic purity of the "Heard" column, and the District Court did not find that the contents of any of the articles were altered to further the profit potential of petitioners' stock-trading scheme ... . Over a 4-month period, the brokers made prepublication trades on the basis of information given them by Winans about the contents of some 27 "Heard" columns. The net profits from these trades were about $690,000.

In November 1983, correlations between the "Heard" articles and trading in the Clark and Felis accounts were noted at Kidder Peabody and inquiries began. Brant and Felis denied knowing anyone at the Journal and took steps to conceal the trades. Later, the Securities and Exchange Commission began an investigation. Questions were met by denials both by the brokers at Kidder Peabody and by Winans at the Journal. As the investigation progressed, the conspirators quarreled, and on March 29, 1984, Winans and Carpenter went to the SEC and revealed the entire scheme. This indictment and a bench trial followed. Brant, who had pleaded guilty under a plea agreement, was a witness for the Government.

The District Court found, and the Court of Appeals agreed, that Winans had knowingly breached a duty of confidentiality by misappropriating prepublication information regarding the timing and contents of the "Heard" column, information that had been gained in the course of his employment under the understanding that it would not be revealed in advance of publication and that if it were, he would report it to his employer. It was this appropriation of confidential information that underlay both the securities laws and mail and wire fraud counts. With respect to the § 10(b) charges, the courts below held that the deliberate breach of Winans' duty of confidentiality and concealment of the scheme was a fraud and deceit on the Journal. Although the victim of the fraud, the Journal, was not a buyer or seller of the stocks traded in or otherwise a market participant, the fraud was nevertheless considered to be "in connection with" a purchase or sale of securities within the meaning of the statute and the rule. The courts reasoned that the scheme's sole purpose was to buy and sell securities at a profit based on advance information of the column's contents. ...

Petitioners' arguments that they did not interfere with the Journal's use of the information or did not publicize it and deprive the Journal of the first public use of it, ... miss the point. The confidential information was generated from the business, and the business had a right to decide how to use it prior to disclosing it to the public. ...

We cannot accept petitioners' further argument that Winans' conduct in revealing prepublication information was no more than a violation of workplace rules and did not amount to fraudulent activity that is proscribed by the mail fraud statute. Sections 1341 and 1343 reach any scheme to deprive another of money or property by means of false or fraudulent pretenses, representations, or promises. ...

We have little trouble in holding that the conspiracy here to trade on the Journal's confidential information is not outside the reach of the mail and wire fraud statutes, provided the other elements of the offenses are satisfied. The Journal's business information that it intended to be kept confidential was its property; the declaration to that effect in the employee manual merely removed any doubts on that score and made the finding of specific intent to defraud that much easier. Winans continued in the employ of the Journal, appropriating its confidential business information for his own use, all the while pretending to perform his duty of safeguarding it. ... Furthermore, the District Court's

conclusion that each of the petitioners acted with the required specific intent to defraud is strongly supported by the evidence. ...

Lastly, we reject the submission that using the wires and the mail to print and send the Journal to its customers did not satisfy the requirement that those mediums be used to execute the scheme at issue. The courts below were quite right in observing that circulation of the "Heard" column was not only anticipated but an essential part of the scheme. Had the column not been made available to Journal customers, there would have been no effect on stock prices and no likelihood of profiting from the information leaked by Winans.

The judgment below is Affirmed.

Figure 9-10 provides a detailed comparison of the major provisions of the federal Securities Acts.

Securities Act of 1933	Securities Exchange Act of 1934
Section 2: *Definition of Securities.* "... any note, stock, treasury stock, bond, debenture, evidence of indebtedness, certificate of interest or participation in any profit-sharing agreement, collateral-trust certificate, preorganization certificate or subscription, transferable share, investment contract, voting-trust certificate, certificate of deposit for a security, fractional undivided interest in oil, gas, or other mineral rights, any put, call, straddle, option, or privilege on any security, certificate of deposit, or group or index of securities (including any interest therein or based on the value thereof), or any put, call, straddle, option, or privilege entered into on a national securities exchange relating to foreign currency, or, in general, any interest or instrument commonly known as a "security", or any certificate of interest or participation in, temporary or interim certificate for, receipt for, guarantee of, or warrant or right to subscribe to or purchase, any of the foregoing."	**Section 10:** *It is unlawful to use or employ any manipulative or deceptive device or contrivance in connection with the purchase or sale of any registered security.* It is unlawful to effect a short sale or use or employ any stop-loss order in connection with the purchase or sale of any registered security in contravention of the rules and regulations of the Securities Exchange Commission. Insider trading is prohibited under this Section.

FIGURE 9-10 Major Provisions of the Federal Securities Act

Securities Act of 1933	Securities Exchange Act of 1934
Section 3: *The following classes of securities are exempted from the registration provisions of the Securities Act.* (See Section 3 of the Securities Act for a more detailed description of these securities.) • Certain securities issued or guaranteed by the United States or state or local governments. • Certain securities issued or guaranteed by banks. • Short-term commercial paper, including certain notes, drafts, or bills of exchange. • Securities of nonprofit issuers. • Securities issued by certain savings and loan associations, building and loan associations, cooperative banks, homestead associations, or similar institutions. • Interests in railroad equipment trusts. • Certificates issued by receivers, trustees, or debtors in possession in a case under Title 11 of the United States Code (the Bankruptcy Code), with the approval of the court. • Insurance or endowment policies, annuity contracts and optional annuity contracts that are subject to the supervision of the insurance commissioner, bank commissioner, or any similar agency or officer. • Certain securities exchanged by the issuer when no commission or other remuneration is paid or given for soliciting such exchange. • Certain securities issued in exchange for one or more bona fide outstanding securities, claims or property interests where the terms and conditions of such issuance and exchange are approved by any court, or by any official or agency of the United States, including any state or territorial banking or insurance commission. • Securities that are sold only to residents of a single state or territory if the issuer is both a resident of and doing business within that state or territory.	**Section 12(a):** *Every nonexempt security traded on a national securities exchange must be registered with that exchange.* In addition to securities actively traded on a national exchange, every issuer that is engaged in interstate commerce, or in a business affecting interstate commerce, or whose securities are traded by use the mails or through interstate commerce, must register with the Securities Exchange Commission if it has total assets exceeding $1 million and a class of securities held by 750 or more persons.

FIGURE 9-10 (*continued*)

Securities Act of 1933	*Securities Exchange Act of 1934*
Section 4: *The following types of transactions are exempted from the registration provisions of the Securities Act of 1933* (see Section 4 of the Securities Act of 1933 for a more detailed description), including: ♦ Transactions by any person other than an issuer, underwriter or dealer of the securities. ♦ Transactions not involving any public offering. ♦ Certain transactions by dealers subsequent to the offering of the securities to the public. ♦ Brokers' transactions executed upon customers' orders on any exchange or in the over-the-counter market but not the solicitation of such orders. ♦ Transactions involving offers or sales by an issuer solely to accredited advisors.	**Section 13:** *Every issuer of registered securities must file annual and quarterly reports,* and such other information as deemed necessary, as required by the Rules and Regulations of the Securities Exchange Commission as appropriate for the proper protection of investors and to insure fair dealing in the security. These required reports include the Form 10-K, 10-Q, and 8-K. The beneficial owner of more than 5 percent of a class of a registered security must file required reports with the issuer and with the Securities Exchange Commission.
Section 5(a): *The issuers of securities that are not considered exempt must file a registration statement with the Securities Exchange Commission.* It is unlawful to sell or transfer securities by any means or instruments of transportation or communication in interstate commerce or the mail unless a registration statement is in effect with the Securities Exchange Commission.	**Section 14:** *Any solicitation of proxies with regard to the voting of registered securities must comply with the Rules and Regulations of the Securities Exchange Commission regarding Proxies.*
Section 5(b): *It is unlawful to use a prospectus to sell securities that have been registered pursuant to the Registration Act, unless the prospectus meets the requirements of Section 10(a) of the Securities Act.*	**Section 16:** *Short-swing profits are prohibited.* To prevent the unfair use of information which may have been obtained by a beneficial owner, director, or officer of the issuer, by reason of his or her relationship to the issuer, any profit realized from any purchase and sale or any sale and purchase of an equity security of such issuer within a period of less than six months, shall inure to and be recoverable by the issuer, irrespective of any intention on the part of the beneficial owner, director, or officer in entering into such transaction.

FIGURE 9-10 (*continued*)

Securities Act of 1933	Securities Exchange Act of 1934
Section 10: *The prospectus must contain certain information contained in the registration statement of the Corporation.* The information in the prospectus must not be more than 16 months old (for corporations that have had their registration statement effective for more than nine months). Summarized prospectuses may be used to the extent permitted by the Rules and Regulations of the Securities Exchange Commission.	
Section 11: *Every person who signs or contributes information to the registration statement has a duty to provide complete and accurate information.* Any person acquiring securities for which there has been filed a registration statement containing false or misleading information concerning a material fact required to be stated therein may sue: • Every person who signed the registration statement. • Every person who is a director or partner of the issuer or is named in the registration as being or about to become a director or partner of the issuer. • Every accountant, engineer, or other expert who has prepared or certified a part of the registration statement. • Every underwriter of the securities.	
Section 12: *Individuals who sell unregistered securities or who use false or misleading means to sell securities may be liable to the purchaser.* Any person who sells securities that are not registered in compliance with Section 5 of the Securities Act is liable to the purchaser of the securities for the consideration paid for the securities, plus interest. Every person who sells securities by means of a prospectus that contains false or misleading information, or by means of an untrue or misleading oral	

FIGURE 9-10 (*continued*)

Securities Act of 1933	*Securities Exchange Act of 1934*
statement, is liable to the purchaser of the securities for the consideration paid for the securities, plus interest.	
Section 17: *It is unlawful for any person to offer or sell securities through interstate commerce through fraudulent or deceitful means,* or to obtain money or property by means of untrue statements or omissions concerning material facts. It is unlawful to engage in any transaction, practice, or course of business which operates as fraud or deceit.	

FIGURE 9-10 (*continued*)

§ 9.8 STATE SECURITIES REGULATION—BLUE SKY LAWS

Decades before the adoption of the federal Securities Act and Exchange Act, there was an attempt to regulate securities at the state level. These state statutes regulating securities were an attempt to "stop the sale of stock in fly-by-night concerns, visionary oil wells, distant gold mines, and other like, fraudulent exploitations."[25] The term **blue sky laws**, which is commonly used to refer to state statutes regulating securities, was derived from an early Supreme Court case, in which the Court found that the legislative purpose of the acts were aimed at "speculative schemes which have no more basis than so many feet of blue sky."[26]

Blue sky laws act in concert with the federal securities acts and are considered to be valid so long as they do not conflict with the pertinent federal acts.

Most blue sky laws require the registration of securities and of brokers or dealers dealing in securities. They regulate the sale and purchase of securities within the state of domicile through antifraud provisions relating to securities transactions.

It is clear that blue sky laws apply to intrastate sales of securities of a domestic corporation, but several other common circumstances raise the question of jurisdiction. Clearly, blue sky laws do not apply to transactions that occur entirely outside the state, even if residents of the state are purchasers of the securities. However, blue sky laws do apply to securities sold by foreign corporations within the state. Courts have generally found that "if a blue sky law requires registration of a security before it may be offered for sale in the state, or before solicitation with respect to such security lawfully may be made in the state, there must be compliance with such

---

blue sky law Any state law regulating sales of stock or other investment activities to protect the public from fly-by-night or fraudulent stock deals, or to ensure that an investor gets enough information to make a reasoned purchase of stock or other security.

requirements even though the issuance of the stock and transfer of the title thereto is to take place entirely in a foreign state."[27]

Blue sky laws vary from state to state, and the laws of any state where a contract for the sale of securities is entered into or executed must be consulted. Most states have adopted, at least to a significant extent, the Uniform Securities Act, approved by the Conference of Commissioners on Uniform State Laws and the American Bar Association in 1956 and amended in 1988. As of July 1, 1990, six states had adopted the most recent version of the Uniform Act—the Uniform Securities Act (1985) with 1988 amendments.[28]

§ 9.9   STATE REGULATION OF STOCK OFFERINGS

Blue sky laws typically require the registration of securities of public corporations at the state level (in addition to the federal requirements). Under the Uniform Securities Act, the issuer is required to register the securities by one of three means, depending on the "demonstrated degree of stability of the registrant and the information available to prospective investors by reason of a registration statement having been filed with the Securities and Exchange Commission under the Securities Act of 1933."[29]

Registration by Filing

Registration by filing is a procedure available to issuers that have filed a registration statement under the Securities Act and have been actively engaged in business operations in the United States for at least three years prior to that filing. The issuer desiring to register by filing must also meet several other criteria set forth by state statute. Registration by filing is accomplished by submitting the following to the state securities authority with the appropriate filing fee:

1. A statement demonstrating eligibility for registration by filing.
2. The name, address, and form of organization of the issuer.
3. With respect to a person on whose behalf a part of the offering is to be made in a nonissuer distribution: name and address; the amount of securities of the issuer held by the person as of the date of the filing of the registration statement; and a statement of the reasons for making the offering.
4. A description of the security being registered.
5. A copy of the latest prospectus filed with the registration statement under and satisfying the requirements of § 10 of the Securities Act of 1933.

Registration by Coordination

The procedures for registration by coordination may be followed in most states for any securities for which a registration statement has been filed under the Securities Act. The procedures for registration by coordination are similar to those of registration by filing. Because issuers registering by coordination need not be established corporations that have been transacting business in the United States for several years, slightly more information is required to be filed with this type of registration.

Registration by Qualification

Registration by qualification is available to the issuer of any securities. Registration by qualification is the type of registration that must be completed by corporations that are not required to file a registration statement under the Securities Act, but are required to register at the state level. This is the most complex type of registration, and it requires the most information to be filed at the state level, because there is no available copy of a prospectus filed with the SEC.

Exemptions

As with federal registration requirements, there are many exemptions from state registration requirements. The exemptions for each individual state are found in that state's statutes. Often, the securities may be exempt from registration because of either the type or class of the securities, or the specific transaction involving the securities. Exemption from the registration requirements of the state securities regulations does not guarantee exemption from the other provisions of the regulations.

§ 9.10 STATE SECURITIES REGULATION—ANTIFRAUD PROVISIONS

State statutes prohibit fraudulent activities connected with the offer, sale, and purchase of securities, as do the similar antifraud provisions found in the Securities Act and the Exchange Act. The antifraud provisions of the Uniform Securities Act are found in §§ 501 through 505. Section 505, which parallels Rule 10b-5 of the Securities Act, reads as follows:

§ 501. OFFER, SALE, AND PURCHASE.

In connection with an offer to sell, sale, offer to purchase, or purchase, of a security, a person may not, directly or indirectly:
  (1) employ a device, scheme, or artifice to defraud;
  (2) make an untrue statement of a material fact or omit to state a material fact necessary in order to make the statements made not misleading, in light of the circumstances under which they are made; or
  (3) engage in an act, practice, or course of business that operates or would operate as a fraud or deceit upon a person.

The Uniform Securities Act also contains provisions prohibiting market manipulation; regulating the transactions of investment advisors; and prohibiting misleading filings and unlawful representation concerning licensing, registration, or exemption.

§ 9.11 THE PARALEGAL'S ROLE

Paralegals are often involved in all aspects of the public securities offering and in complying with the ongoing reporting requirements for publicly held corporations.

Initial Public Offerings

Once a decision to go public has been made, a date for filing the registration statement is usually agreed upon by the corporation's directors, its attorneys, and the underwriters. All plans for the public offering depend on that target date, and it is usually crucial that the registration statement be filed on time. For that reason, work on securities offerings often must be completed within very tight time constraints.

The following is a sample timeline for a public stock offering. This timeline is by no means all-inclusive; rather, it is intended to demonstrate the ordinary sequence of the main events leading to a public stock offering.

Week 1 Organizational meeting attended by corporate management, corporate counsel, underwriters, underwriters' counsel, and corporation's accountants. Schedule is decided on, as well as format for registration statement.
Preliminary agreement with underwriters.

Week 2 Circulate first draft of registration statement and underwriting agreement for comments and revisions.
Begin corporate "housekeeping" to make sure financial and corporate records are in order.

Week 3 Due diligence work; drafting and revision of registration statement and underwriting agreement.

Week 4 Continue work on drafting and revision of registration statement and underwriting agreement.

Week 5 Registration statement and underwriting agreement sent to printer.

Week 6 Review proofs of registration statement and underwriting agreement from printer.

Week 7 Meeting of the board of directors to discuss and approve registration statement and other matters related to public offering.

Week 8 Finalize and file registration statement.
Submit press release regarding offering to appropriate papers.
File appropriate documents with NASD.
Begin work to comply with blue sky requirements.

Weeks 8–10 Review comments from SEC.
Prepare amendments to registration statement, if necessary.
Negotiations on price of stock to be offered.
Registration statement becomes effective.
Commence offering.

File copies of prospectuses with SEC, including price.

Closing with corporation and underwriters after price of stock has been set and offering has commenced.

Week 11   Continue work on blue sky requirements.

Set schedule to comply with periodic reporting requirements.

Paralegal's may be assigned the task of collecting the necessary information and drafting certain sections of the registration statement and prospectus. Collecting all

---

Corporate Paralegal Profile
LAURIE R. MANSELL, RP

I enjoy the level of substantive and sophisticated work in my position. Recently I assisted with the successful closing of a $1.5 billion bond offering—the largest in our company's history.

Name Laurie R. Mansell, RP

Location Pittsburgh, Pennsylvania

Title Senior Paralegal

Specialty Securities/Finance

Education Corporate Paralegal Certificate; General Paralegal Certificate; Graduate Certificate in Archival, Museum and Editing Studies; B.A. and M.A. in History

Experience 14 years

Laurie Mansell specializes in corporate finance and securities law at Equitable Resources, Inc., an integrated energy company. Equitable employs eight attorneys; Laurie is the only paralegal. In addition to corporate subsidiary work, such as incorporation, qualifications, dissolutions, and mergers, she has rewritten the proxy statement in plain English and reviewed the Form 10-K for accuracy of disclosure. She also is leading a team of corporate personnel to identify and implement a company-wide records management and retention system.

Prior to accepting a position with Equitable Resources in 2001, Laurie was a paralegal at Alcoa Inc. for nine years, where she assisted with all finance and securities closings and offerings and prepared New York Stock Exchange listing applications. Laurie drafted sections of the 10-Qs, 10-Ks, and proxy statements required by the SEC. In addition, she completed all EDGAR filings for Alcoa.

Laurie enjoys the level of substantive and sophisticated work she is given, but acknowledges that there is always that distinction between the attorneys and the paralegals, even in the corporate legal department setting. As a result, she feels that recognition and advancement are often difficult for corporate paralegals.

Laurie is a PACE Registered Paralegal and a past president of the Pittsburgh Paralegal Association. She is currently the Pittsburgh Paralegal Association's Primary Representative with the NFPA. Laurie was one of the first paralegals in the country to pass the PACE exam and achieve the RP designation after her name. Currently she is pursuing a second Master's Degree in Nonfiction Writing at Chatham College in Pittsburgh, PA.

Laurie has been a dedicated volunteer at the Allegheny County Protection From Abuse program and the Neighborhood Legal Services Association Hill House Family Law Clinic. She is the NFPA's pro bono coordinator and the co-chair of the Pittsburgh Paralegal Association Pro Bono Committee.

On January 1, 2001, Laurie was appointed the NFPA liaison to the American Bar Association Standing Committee on Pro Bono and Public Service. Laurie was the first paralegal ever to hold such a position. She has also received several awards for her pro bono work.

Laurie's advice to new paralegals?

Select a specialty area and learn as much as possible about that area. Aggressively seek out assignments of a substantive nature.

For more information on careers for corporate paralegals, log on to the companion Web page to this text at **www.westlegalstudies.com**.

of the necessary information to complete the registration statement under the Securities Act of 1933 can be a monumental task. The information gathered to prepare the registration statement required under the Securities Act can also be used to complete the necessary documentation under the Exchange Act and the pertinent blue sky laws.

Periodic Reporting Requirements

Paralegals often assist with drafting and filing the periodic reports required by the Exchange Act. It is important for the paralegal or other assigned individual to keep track of the required filing dates for periodic reporting requirements, to assure that all 10-K, 10-Q, and 8-K reports are filed in a timely manner.

Another area in which the legal assistant often participates is in researching the blue sky laws of the pertinent states, to determine the procedures that must be followed in each of the applicable states. Complying with blue sky laws often involves thorough research into the statutes of several states.

ETHICAL CONSIDERATION

Keeping a client's confidentiality is very important in every aspect of a paralegal's work, but it is absolutely crucial when dealing with publicly held corporations. Leaks from a law firm that might appear to be harmless can actually lead to serious consequences, including fluctuation in the price of the corporation's stock. In some cases, it may not only be unethical for a paralegal to divulge information about a corporate client to the press or other outsiders, but it may also be in violation of federal statutes.

Law firms typically have strict policies with regard to divulging information regarding any corporate clients to the press or any outsider. Typically, all requests for information regarding a client should be directed to an attorney who is responsible for the client's affairs, and no one else will be permitted to pass on any information regarding a client without permission, even information that may seem quite inconsequential.

---

§ 9.12 RESOURCES

As discussed in this chapter, the primary sources of law regarding securities regulations are the Securities Act of 1933, 15 U.S.C. § 77a *et seq.*, the Securities Exchange Act of 1934, 15 U.S.C. § 78a *et seq.*, and the rules and regulations that accompany these acts. State statutes must also be consulted for the pertinent blue sky laws.

Federal Law

The federal securities acts are a part of the United States Code and may be found anywhere federal statutes are found. The Securities Act of 1933 is located at

15 U.S.C. §§ 77a *et seq.,* and the Securities Exchange Act of 1934 is located at 15 U.S.C. § 78a *et seq.*

The federal rules and regulations are found in the Code of Federal Regulation. The rules and regulations for filing under the Securities Act of 1933 are found at 17 C.F.R. § 230.100 *et seq.,* and the rules and regulations under the Securities Exchange Act of 1934 are located at 17 C.F.R. § 240.0-1 *et seq.*

The CCH Federal Securities Law Reporter is a comprehensive resource that may be found on-line or in loose-leaf volumes. Many lawyers who practice securities law subscribe to this service, which contains the federal laws, rules, and regulations. In addition, the service provides up-to-date court decisions concerning securities laws and SEC releases.

In addition to the hardbound volumes of the United States Code, the federal securities acts and the accompanying rules and regulations may be found at several locations on-line.

Federal Securities Forms and Information

The securities forms required for filing under the federal securities acts are available through the Securities Exchange Commission. Most of the forms may be downloaded from the SEC's Web page at **www.sec.gov.**

Blue Sky Laws

Blue sky laws are found within the state securities acts of the state statutes of each state.

Web Page

For updates and links to several of the previously listed sites, log on to **www. westlegalstudies.com,** and click through to the book link for this text.

Internet Resources

Following is a list of some Web pages that may be useful when assisting with corporate financial matters:

For the securities acts and rules and regulations

The Securities and Exchange Commission	**www.sec.gov**
The Securities Lawyer Deskbook	**www.law.uc.edu/CCL/sldtoc.html**

For state and federal statutes

Findlaw.com	**www.findlaw.com**
Legal Information Institute	**www.law.cornell.edu/topics/securities.html**

For a list of several Web pages concerning securities laws, including state securities laws, the stock exchanges, and several other helpful Web pages relating to securities law, see appendix B to this text.

SUMMARY

- ◆ Publicly held corporations are corporations with stock held by a large number of persons.

- ◆ Securities that are offered and traded publicly are subject to federal securities regulations.

- ◆ Any securities offered, sold, or delivered through interstate commerce, including the United States Postal Service, are considered to be part of a public offering and must first be registered in accordance with the Securities Act of 1933.

- ◆ When a corporation first offers its securities for sale to the public, it is considered an initial public offering.

- ◆ Securities of publicly held corporations are traded on a stock exchange, such as the New York Stock Exchange, or they are listed over-the-counter on NASDAQ.

- ◆ The Securities and Exchange Commission was created by the Securities Exchange Act of 1934. It is headed by five presidential appointees and its mission is to protect investors and maintain the integrity of the securities markets.

- ◆ Section 5 of the Securities Act of 1933 makes it illegal to sell securities through interstate commerce or the mail unless a registration statement has been filed with the SEC for those securities.

- ◆ Regulations A and D provide for several exemptions to the registration requirements of the Securities Act of 1933 for smaller offerings and offerings that are made to a limited group of individuals.

- ◆ Section 11 of the Securities Act provides that everyone who signs or contributes material information to the registration statement has a duty to provide complete and accurate information.

- ◆ Section 17 prohibits fraudulent conduct with respect to the sale or offer to sell securities.

- ◆ The Securities Exchange Act of 1934 protects securities investors and the general public by regulating securities exchanges and markets, by requiring periodic reporting of information by the issuers of securities, and by prohibiting fraud and manipulation in the trading of securities.

- ◆ All securities traded on a securities exchange must be registered with that exchange.

- ◆ Every issuer subject to the reporting requirements of the Exchange Act must file Form 10-K annual reports and Form 10-Q quarterly reports in the form provided by the Securities and Exchange Commission.

- ◆ A Form 8-K must be filed with the Securities and Exchange commission when certain information contained in the registration statement of the issuer changes.

- Profits made by an insider on the purchase and sale of securities within a six-month period are referred to as short-swing profits and are prohibited under Section 16 of the Securities Exchange Act of 1934.

- The Securities Exchange Act of 1934 provides certain requirements for the use of proxies and proxy statements.

- Section 10(b) of the Securities Exchange Act of 1934 prohibits any misleading or fraudulent means in connection with the purchase or sale of any security.

- Insider trading, which is prosecuted in Section 10(b) of the Securities Exchange Act, makes it unlawful for insiders who have information that has not been released to the public to act on that information by buying or selling stock in the corporation, taking unfair advantage of the uninformed investor.

- Documents are filed electronically with the Securities and Exchange Commission via EDGAR, the Electronic Data Gathering, Analysis and Retrieval system. Most documents filed via EDGAR are available to the public via the Internet.

- Blue sky laws are state laws concerning the sale of securities.

- In addition to filing at the federal level, blue sky laws may require the issuers of securities to file at the state level.

REVIEW QUESTIONS

1. What are some of the advantages and disadvantages of taking a privately held corporation public?

2. Describe the differences between a firm commitment underwriting agreement and a best-efforts underwriting agreement.

3. What are the two general requirements of § 5 of the Securities Act of 1933 with regard to securities that are offered or sold through any means of interstate commerce?

4. What is a "red herring" prospectus?

5. May accountants and attorneys and others who contribute information and sign a registration statement be found liable for damages due to misstatements made therein?

6. What is the due diligence defense? To whom is the due diligence defense available?

7. What is the purpose of Form 8-K?

8. What are short-swing profits?

9. What is the definition and the origin of the term "blue sky laws"?

10. As a 20 percent shareholder in a publicly owned corporation, Jane has decided to sell her shares. What special requirements must she comply with because she owns such a large stake in the company?

PRACTICAL PROBLEMS

Locate the securities act within the statutes of your state to answer the following questions:

1. What is the cite of your state's securities act?

2. What statute section requires the registration of securities in your state?

3. Where are securities registration documents filed in your state?

4. How can securities be registered in your state? List the cites of any statutes in your state permitting the following:
   a. Registration by filing.
   b. Registration by coordination.
   c. Registration by qualification.

WORKPLACE SCENARIO

Assume that our fictional clients, Bradley Harris and Cynthia Lund, have just finished meeting with your supervising attorney, Belinda Benson. Ms. Benson has informed you that Mr. Harris and Ms. Lund have been approached by a large electronics retailer in your hometown. The electronics retailer would like to purchase Cutting Edge Computer Repair, Inc., and hire Mr. Harris and Ms. Lund. They are considering the offer, but would like more information about the retailer.

Pick a publicly held electronics company that you are somewhat familiar with. Using the above facts and the resources discussed in this chapter, locate the most current Form 10-K for the retailer to answer the following questions:

1. When was the Form 10-K Report filed?
2. What is the Central Index Key?
3. What is the Company's Standard Industrial Classification?
4. What is the Company's IRS Number?
5. What is the Company's state of incorporation?
6. What is the Company's fiscal year end?

END NOTES

1. U.S. Census Bureau, *The Statistical Abstract of the United States (2000)* § 835.
2. *Id.* at §§ 833, 835.
3. Infoplease.com, Stock Ownership by Age and Income, 1989–1998, **www.infoplease.com** (November 1, 2000).
4. Securities Act of 1933 § 2(4), 15 U.S.C. § 77b(4).
5. *Id.* § 2(11), 15 U.S.C. § 77b(11).
6. *Id.* § 2(1), 15 U.S.C. § 77b(1).
7. Securities Exchange Act of 1934 § 3(a)(1), 15 U.S.C. § 78c(a)(1).
8. United States Bureau of the Census, *The Statistical Abstract of the United States (2000)* § 855.
9. United States Bureau of the Census, *The Statistical Abstract of the United States (2000)* § 853.
10. Kelly, Bruce, Changing Times: NYSE Formulating Plans to Stay Competitive in an Electronic Era, *Pensions & Investments,* July 10, 2000, p. 55.
11. Vogelstein, Fred, Are Nasdaq and the NYSE Fossils?, *U.S. News & World Report,* March 13, 2000, p. 40.
12. 69 Am. Jur. 2d (Rev.) *Securities Regulation—Federal* § 1 (1993).
13. Section 2(a) of the Securities Act of 1933 defines the term *security* as "any note, stock, treasury stock, bond, debenture, evidence of indebtedness, certificate of interest or participation in any profit-sharing agreement, collateral-trust certificate, preorganization certificate or subscription, transferable share, investment contract, voting-trust certificate, certificate of deposit for a security, fractional undivided interest in oil, gas, or other mineral rights, any put, call, straddle, option, or privilege on any security, certificate of deposit, or group or index of securities (including any interest therein or based on the value thereof), or any put, call, straddle, option, or privilege entered into on a national securities exchange relating to foreign currency, or, in general, any interest or instrument commonly known as a "security", or any certificate of interest or participation in, temporary or interim certificate for, receipt for, guarantee of, or warrant or right to subscribe to or purchase, any of the foregoing."
14. Securities Act of 1933 § 8(b), 15 U.S.C. § 77.
15. Reg. 17 CFR § 230.431.
16. United States Securities and Exchange Commission Release No. 4552 (Nov. 6, 1962).
17. 69 Am. Jur. 2d (Rev.) *Securities Regulation—Federal* § 1 (1993).
18. *Id.* § 5.
19. *Herman & MacLean v. Huddleston,* 459 U.S. 375, 381–82 (1983).
20. *Id.* § 301.

21. *Id.* § 617.

22. Securities Exchange Commission Regulation FD (2000).

23. *Connelly v. Balkwill,* 174 F. Supp. 49 (N.D. Ohio 1959), *aff'd.* 279 F.2d 685.

24. 69 AM. JUR. 2d *Securities Regulation—Federal* § 1528 (1993).

25. *Hall v. Geiger-Jones Co.,* 242 U.S. 539 (1917).

26. *Id.*

27. 69 AM. JUR. 2d *Securities Regulation—State* § 1 (1993).

28. Maine, Nevada, New Mexico, Rhode Island, South Dakota, and Vermont have adopted the Uniform Securities Act with the 1988 amendments.

29. 69 AM. JUR. 2d *Securities Regulation—State* § 25 (1985).

CHAPTER 10

Mergers, Acquisitions, and Other Changes to the Corporate Structure

CHAPTER OUTLINE

§ 10.1   Statutory Mergers and Share Exchanges

§ 10.2   Statutory Merger and Share Exchange Procedures

§ 10.3   Asset and Stock Acquisitions

§ 10.4   Asset and Stock Acquisition Procedures

§ 10.5   Amendments to Articles of Incorporation

§ 10.6   Reorganizations

§ 10.7   The Paralegal's Role in Mergers and Acquisitions

§ 10.8   Resources

INTRODUCTION

Mergers and acquisitions have been a hot topic since the late 1980s, when news about megamergers, leveraged buyouts, and hostile takeovers made the headlines almost daily and the number of completed mergers and acquisitions reached all-time highs. The year 1989 set a record with 3,752 mergers and acquisitions in the United States that were valued at over $5 million. The total value of those transactions was $316.8 billion.[1] Surprisingly, the activity did not slow down in the 1990s as many had predicted. Record numbers of mergers and acquisitions continued throughout the 1990s. In 1999, nearly 9,600 merger and acquisition transactions valued at over $5 million were reported, with a total value exceeding $3.4 trillion.[2] See Figures 10-1 and 10-2 on page 386. While much of the volume accounting for these incredible numbers stems from megamergers (mergers in excess of $1 billion), mergers and acquisitions also take place daily between smaller corporations—including those that are closely held.

This chapter looks at some of the different types of corporate **amalgamations** that are specifically provided for by statute and discusses the procedures for approving and effecting those types of transactions. It also discusses the acquisition of

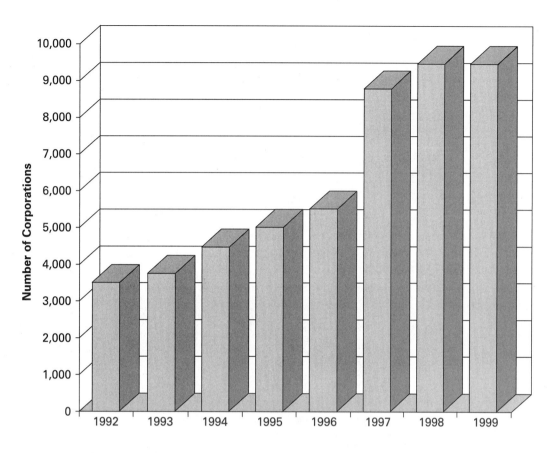

FIGURE 10-1 Number of Mergers and Acquisitions in the United States over $5 Million in Value. Based on statistics from *The Statistical Abstract of the United States (2000)* at 882.

corporate assets and stock and the procedures for approving and completing acquisition transactions. We then examine the procedures and requirements for amending a corporation's articles of incorporation. After a brief look at the definitions of *reorganization* and certain types of reorganizations, the focus turns to the paralegal's role in merger and acquisition work.

§ 10.1 STATUTORY MERGERS AND SHARE EXCHANGES

State statutes generally set forth requirements for certain types of corporate amalgamations, including mergers, share exchanges, and consolidations. Unions that are

---

amalgamation A complete joining or blending together of two or more things into one; for example, a consolidation or merger of two or more corporations to create a single company.

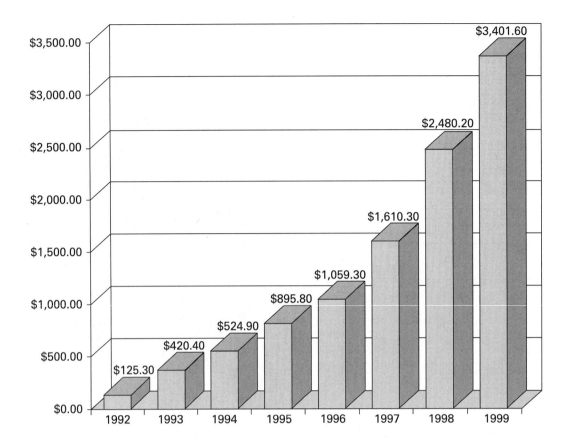

FIGURE 10-2 Total Value of Mergers in the United States over $5 Million (in billions of dollars). Based on statistics from *The Statistical Abstract of the United States (2000)* at 882.

provided for by statute are typically referred to as **statutory mergers**. Statutory mergers and share exchanges may be between domestic corporations, or domestic and foreign corporations, provided that the transaction is permitted by the statutes of the state of domicile of each corporation.

Under the statutes of states following the Model Business Corporation Act (MBCA), two types of transactions involving the combination of corporations are addressed: the merger and the share exchange. This section focuses on the flexible mergers and share exchanges provided for in the MBCA. We then briefly discuss *consolidations,* another type of corporate amalgamation provided for by the statutes of some states. We also review the state and federal laws affecting statutory mergers and share exchanges.

statutory merger A type of merger that is specifically provided for by state statute.

Mergers

A **merger** is a combination of two or more corporations whereby one of the corporations survives (the surviving corporation) and absorbs one or more other corporations (the merging corporations), which cease to exist. Mergers have the effect of transferring all assets, liabilities, and obligations of the merging corporation to the surviving corporation alone.

Section 11.06(a) of the MBCA sets forth the effect of a merger:

§ 11.06 EFFECT OF MERGER OR SHARE EXCHANGE

(a) When a merger takes effect:

   (1) every other corporation party to the merger merges into the surviving corporation and the separate existence of every corporation except the surviving corporation ceases;

   (2) the title to all real estate and other property owned by each corporation party to the merger is vested in the surviving corporation without reversion or impairment;

   (3) the surviving corporation has all liabilities of each corporation party to the merger;

   (4) a proceeding pending against any corporation party to the merger may be continued as if the merger did not occur or the surviving corporation may be substituted in the proceeding for the corporation whose existence ceased;

   (5) the articles of incorporation of the surviving corporation are amended to the extent provided in the plan of merger; and

   (6) the shares of each corporation party to the merger that are to be converted into shares, obligations, or other securities of the surviving or any other corporation or into cash or other property are converted, and the former holders of the shares are entitled only to the rights provided in the articles of merger or to their rights under chapter 13.

Chapter 13 of the MBCA concerns dissenter's rights, which is discussed in more detail in § 10.2 of this chapter.

There are numerous reasons for merging two or more corporations. A statutory merger is one means often employed to achieve the acquisition of one corporation by another.

When management decides that it is in the best interests of the corporation to expand into a new geographical area, or to acquire new competencies or products, this change is often accomplished by acquiring a corporation that already exists in that market, or that already has the desired expertise.

Corporate management may have a strategy that includes continued growth and expansion through acquisition and merger. Some large corporations routinely acquire and merge several corporations into the parent corporation each year. For

---

merger The union of two or more corporations, with one corporation ceasing to exist and becoming a part of the other.

example, in 2000, General Electric Co. entered into 33 acquisition agreements, and AT&T Corp. agreed to acquire 23 other companies.[3]

Corporations with common shareholders, and parent and subsidiary corporations are also often merged to decrease the paperwork, taxes, and other expenses associated with maintaining two separate corporate entities.

Although megamergers involving the merger of huge conglomerates will naturally be much more complex than the merger of a closely held parent corporation with its subsidiary, the same state statutes and basic procedures apply. In addition, larger merger transactions must comply with federal antitrust statutes and require the approval of the Federal Trade Commission and the Department of Justice.

The shareholders of the merging corporation generally receive shares of the surviving corporation in exchange for their shares and become shareholders of the surviving corporation. However, § 11.01 of the MBCA and the statutes of most states specifically permit the shares of the merging corporation to be converted into "shares, obligations, or other securities of the surviving or any other corporation or into cash or other property in whole or part." This provision allows the surviving corporation to pay cash as all or part of the consideration given to the merging corporation, so long as the terms are agreed to in the plan of merger.

In some instances the majority shareholders of a corporation may seek to eliminate the interests of the minority shareholders by entering into a merger in which the minority shareholders are forced either to take cash in consideration for their shares, or to dissent and seek appraisal. This type of transaction is sometimes called a *freeze-out* or *take-out,* and may be found invalid in certain jurisdictions, especially if the merger has no clear business purpose other than elimination of the minority shareholders. The management and majority shareholders owe a duty to the corporation and to the minority shareholders to enter into transactions only to promote the best interests of the corporation and all its shareholders, including the minority shareholders.

There are many variations from the simple statutory merger whereby one unrelated corporation merges into another. Some of the more common deviations from that design are upstream mergers, downstream mergers, triangle mergers, and reverse triangle mergers.

Mergers Between Subsidiaries and Parents   Mergers may take place between a parent and a subsidiary corporation. When the subsidiary corporation merges into its parent corporation, it is referred to as an **upstream merger**. Upstream mergers may be eligible for a short-form merger under statute, whereby the statutory merger requirements are simplified because of the relationship between the two corporations. Shareholder approval of the subsidiary corporation is not required when the parent corporation owns at least 90 percent of the outstanding stock of the subsidiary, as the minority shareholders do not have sufficient voting power to block the merger.

---

upstream merger   Merger whereby a subsidiary corporation merges into its parent.

Dividends ── ◆

The Mega Merger

In mergers and acquisitions, there are deals, and then there are megadeals. There has been a huge wave of megamergers (those transactions valued at over $1 billion) in recent years. The year 1991 set a record with 13 reported megadeals. But by 1999, the new record was set at 194 deals valued at over $1 billion. In 1998 alone, there were seven deals worth over $50 billion.*

In 1995 it was the Disney and Capital Cities/ABC, Inc. merger, valued at $19 billion. In 1998, it was the Exxon and Mobil merger valued at $86 billion. But then, in 2000, America Online Inc. and Time Warner broke all records with their mega-megamerger, valued at approximately $176 billion. Prior to the merger, these two corporations employed more than 79,600 employees and had annual sales totaling $31.6 billion.

The union of America Online, the world's top Internet company, and Time Warner, the world's largest media and cable conglomerate, has been billed as a merger of the past and the future. Time Warner brings media content to the merger, while America Online brings the new technology to deliver. The new corporation will own AOL, CompuServe, Netscape, and several other computer services; CNN, Warner Bros., and various movie studios; and *Time, Sports Illustrated, Fortune* and several other magazines.

Fierce competition, globalization, and improving technology are fueling the wave of megamergers in the United States and throughout the world. Consolidation appears to be the key strategy for success and survival in many key industries, such as communication, computer supplies and software, and technology, as corporations strive to compete in the global marketplace and keep pace with the latest technological advances. Corporations acquire other corporations for their presence in foreign markets and for their advanced technology. Deregulation has permitted mergers in sectors where it was previously prohibited.

No one can know the full implications of the current waive of megamergers or where it might lead, but most experts agree that as long as the economy remains strong and ample sources of funds are available for acquisitions, the wave has yet to peak.

───────────

* Colvin, Geoffrey, The Year of the Mega Merger, *Fortune*, January 11, 1999.

──

When the parent corporation is merged into a subsidiary it is referred to as a **downstream merger**.

Triangle Mergers The **triangle merger** involves three corporations: a parent corporation, a subsidiary of the parent corporation, and a target corporation. In a triangle merger, the parent corporation forms a subsidiary and funds it with sufficient cash or shares of stock to perform a merger with the target corporation, which is merged into the subsidiary corporation. Both the parent and the subsidiary are surviving corporations in a triangle merger. See Figure 10-3 on page 390.

◆ ──

downstream merger Merger whereby a parent corporation is merged into a subsidiary.

triangle merger Merger involving three corporations, whereby a corporation forms a subsidiary corporation and funds it with sufficient cash or shares of stock to perform a merger with the target corporation, which is merged into the subsidiary. The parent corporation and the subsidiary corporation both survive a triangle merger.

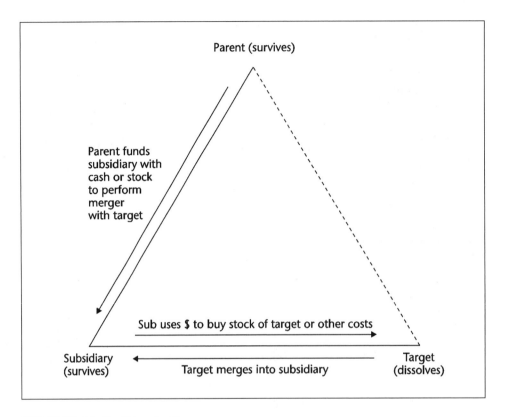

FIGURE 10-3 Triangle Mergers

Reverse Triangle Mergers A **reverse triangle merger** is also a three-way merger. Its distinction from the triangle merger is that in the reverse triangle merger the subsidiary is merged into the target corporation. The end result is the survival of the parent corporation and the target corporation, which will become a new subsidiary (see Figure 10-4). The survival of the target corporation may be important when it is a special type of corporation that is difficult to form, or when the target corporation being acquired is a party to non-assignable contracts.

The same result achieved by a reverse triangle merger may be achieved by a share exchange of the type permitted by § 11.02 of the MBCA. Unlike the merger, the end result of a share exchange is the survival of both corporations, one that becomes a parent and the other a subsidiary.

reverse triangle merger Three-way merger whereby a subsidiary corporation is merged into the target corporation. The end result is the survival of the parent corporation and the target corporation, which becomes a new subsidiary.

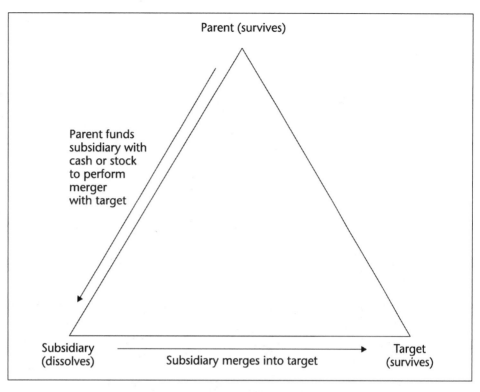

FIGURE 10-4 Reverse Triangle Mergers

Share Exchanges

A **share exchange** is a transaction whereby one corporation (the acquiring corporation) acquires all of the outstanding shares of one or more classes or series of another corporation (the target corporation) by an exchange that is compulsory on the shareholders of the target corporation. The shareholders of the target corporation may receive shares of stock in the acquiring corporation, shares of stock in a third corporation, or cash in consideration for their shares. In this type of transaction, both the acquiring and the target corporation survive, with the target corporation becoming a subsidiary of the acquiring corporation. Section 11.06(b) of the MBCA sets forth the effect of a share exchange:

> (b) When a share exchange takes effect, the shares of each acquired corporation are exchanged as provided in the plan, and the former holders of the shares are entitled only to the exchange rights provided in the articles of share exchange or to their rights under chapter 13.

share exchange Transaction whereby one corporation acquires all of the outstanding shares of one or more classes or series of another corporation by an exchange that is compulsory on the shareholders of the target corporation.

Consolidations

A **consolidation** involves the merger of two or more corporations into a newly formed corporation and the subsequent disappearance of the merging corporations. Although the statutes of many states still allow such consolidations, the MBCA no longer provides for a statutory consolidation, because it is almost always advantageous for one of the merging corporations to survive. The same result obtained in a consolidation may be obtained by a statutory merger involving the merger of two corporations into a corporation formed for the purpose of acting as the surviving corporation of the transaction.

Celotex Corporation v. Pickett, demonstrates the importance of the type of transaction used to combine businesses. It is pointed out that in a merger transaction all debts, liabilities, and duties of the merging corporation are transferred to the surviving corporation.

CASE

CELOTEX CORPORATION
v.
PICKETT

Supreme Court of Florida
490 So. 2d 35 (Fla. 1986)
May 8, 1986
Ehrlich, Justice

We have for our review a decision of the First District Court of Appeal reported as *Celotex Corp. v. Pickett,* 459 So. 2d 375 ... .

The facts relevant for our review here are that the respondent husband (Pickett) was employed in a Jacksonville shipyard from 1965 through June 1968, where as part of his employment as an insulator of ships, he extensively used Philip Carey asbestos cement. Pickett developed severe lung problems, due to the devastating effects on the human body which result from exposure to asbestos. The Picketts sued, on the grounds of negligence and strict liability, several defendants including the petitioner (Celotex) in its capacity as the corporate successor to Philip Carey. Finding that Philip Carey was negligent in placing "defective" asbestos-containing insulating products on the market which caused Pickett's injuries, the jury awarded compensatory damages of $500,000 to

Pickett and $15,000 to his wife. The jury also determined that Philip Carey had acted so as to warrant punitive damages in the amount of $100,000 against Celotex. Celotex's appeal of the imposition of punitive damages formed the basis for the First District's opinion below which affirmed the award.

The threshold question involved here is the legal status of Celotex as the successor to Philip Carey. The district court opinion set forth the following background:

The Philip Carey Corporation was begun in 1888 and subsequently merged with Glen Alden Corporation in 1967. Thereafter, Philip Carey merged with another Glen Alden subsidiary, Briggs Manufacturing Company, and became known as Panacon Corporation. Celotex purchased Glen Alden's controlling interest in 1972 and later purchased the remaining shares of Panacon and merged it into Celotex.

The effect of this merger, as correctly recognized by the First District, is controlled by [Fla. Stat. §] 607.231(3) ... (1983), which reads:

(c) Such surviving or new corporation shall have all the rights, privileges, immunities and powers, and shall be subject to all of

---

consolidation Two corporations joining together to form a third, new one.

the duties and liabilities, of a corporation organized under this chapter.

Celotex has admitted that it is liable, because of the merger, for the compensatory damages awarded to the Picketts. The sole and narrow issue before us here is whether punitive damages were properly assessed against petitioner, the surviving corporation in a statutory merger.

Celotex, however, maintains that the trial court and the district court below misapplied our prior decisions by holding Celotex liable for punitive damages, when Philip Carey, not Celotex, as the "real wrongdoer." Celotex also claims that imposition of punitive damages against Celotex, simply because it is the statutory successor of Philip Carey, contravenes the purpose of such damages in Florida, We disagree with both contentions. ...

Celotex seeks here to characterize its liability as "vicarious," ... since, according to it, Philip Carey/Panacon is the "real wrongdoer" and there is no evidence of fault by Celotex. We disagree with this characterization. Because of its merger agreement with Panacon, whereby "all debts, liabilities and duties" of Panacon are enforceable against Celotex, and because of the effect of Section 607.231(3), the liability imposed upon Celotex is direct, not vicarious. Liability for the reckless misconduct of Philip Carey/Panacon legally continues to exist within, and under the name of, Celotex. ...

Further, corporations are in a very real sense, "molders of their own destinies" in acquisition transactions, with the full panoply of corporation transformations at their disposal. When a corporation, such as Celotex here, voluntarily chooses a formal merger, it will take the "bad will" along with the "good will." ... We will not allow such an acquiring corporation to "jettison inchoate liabilities into a never-never land of transcorporate limbo." *Wall v. Owens-Corning Fiberglass Corp.*, 602 F. Supp. 252, 255 (N.D. Tex. 1985). ...

We approve the decision of the First District Court of Appeal.

It is so ordered.

State and Federal Laws Affecting Statutory Mergers and Share Exchanges

Research must be conducted throughout the merger or share exchange transaction to assure that all state and federal laws are being complied with. All parties to a merger or share exchange are typically subject to the statutes of their state of domicile. State statutes typically prescribe the following:

1. Requirements for the plan of merger or plan of exchange.
2. The method for adopting a plan of merger or plan of exchange.
3. Requirements for articles of merger or articles of share exchange.
4. Requirements for filing the articles of merger or articles of share exchange.
5. Provisions regarding the effect of the merger or share exchange.
6. Provisions for short-form mergers.
7. Provisions for dissenting shareholder rights.

A foreign corporation that is being merged into a domestic corporation may also be subject to the laws of the state of domicile of the surviving corporation. Corporations whose shares are being acquired subject to a share exchange typically must be domestic corporations.

In addition to the applicable state statutes regarding statutory mergers and share exchanges, compliance must be made with any federal securities regulations and blue sky laws applicable to mergers and share exchanges, as well as the Internal Revenue Code and pertinent provisions of the federal and state **antitrust laws**. Both the Federal Trade Commission and the Department of Justice have responsibility for overseeing the enforcement of federal antitrust statutes.

The primary federal statutes affecting mergers and acquisitions are the **Clayton Act** (15 U.S.C. § 18), the **Sherman Act** (15 U.S.C. § 1), the Federal Trade Commission Act (15 U.S.C. § 45), and the **Hart-Scott-Rodino Act** (15 U.S.C. § 18a). Section 7 of the Clayton Act prohibits certain acquisitions that may lessen competition or create a monopoly. Sections 1 and 2 of the Sherman Act proscribe unreasonable restraints of trade and monopolization and attempted monopolization. Section 5 of the Federal Trade Commission Act permits the Federal Trade Commission to declare unlawful "unfair methods of competition." Finally, the Hart-Scott-Rodino Act provides that notice of certain contemplated mergers and acquisitions must be filed with the Federal Trade Commission before they are completed. Currently, the premerger notification applies only to mergers and acquisitions valued at more than $50 million. Further guidance for compliance under the Hart-Scott-Rodino Act can be found at **www.ftc.gov.**

Significant Federal Antitrust Law Provisions Affecting Mergers and Acquisitions

Section 7 of the Clayton Act (15 U.S.C. § 18)

Prohibits certain acquisitions that will lessen competition or create a monopoly.

"No person engaged in commerce or in any activity affecting commerce shall acquire, directly or indirectly, the whole or any part of the stock or other share capital and no person subject to the jurisdiction of the Federal Trade Commission shall acquire the whole or any part of the assets of another person engaged also in commerce or in any activity affecting commerce, where in any line of commerce or in any activity affecting commerce in any section of the country, the effect of such acquisition may be substantially to lessen competition, or to tend to create a monopoly. ..."

◆————————————————————————————————————

antitrust laws Federal and state laws to protect trade from monopoly control and from price fixing and other restraints of trade. The main federal antitrust laws are the Sherman, Clayton, Federal Trade Commission and Robinson-Patman Acts.

Clayton Act (15 U.S.C. 12) A 1914 federal law that extended the Sherman Act's prohibition against monopolies and price discrimination.

Sherman Act (15 U.S.C. 1) The first antitrust (antimonopoly) law, passed by the federal government in 1890 to break up combinations in restraint of trade.

Hart-Scott-Rodino Act (15 U.S.C. § 18a) A federal law passed in 1976 that strengthens the enforcement powers of the Justice Department. The Act requires entities to give notice to the Federal Trade Commission and the Justice Department prior to mergers and acquisitions when the size of the transaction is valued at $50 million or more.

Sections 1 and 2 of the Sherman Act (15 U.S.C. §§ 1, 2)

Prohibits restraint of trade and makes it a felony. Declares unfair methods of competition and unfair and deceptive acts or practices affecting commerce unlawful. Grants the Federal Trade Commission the power to prevent unfair methods of competition.

"§ 1. Trusts, etc., in restraint of trade illegal; penalty

Every contract, combination in the form of trust or otherwise, or conspiracy, in restraint of trade or commerce among the several States, or with foreign nations, is hereby declared to be illegal. Every person who shall make any contract or engage in any combination or conspiracy hereby declared to be illegal shall be deemed guilty of a felony, and, on conviction thereof, shall be punished by fine not exceeding $10,000,000 if a corporation, or, if any other person, $350,000, or by imprisonment not exceeding three years, or by both said punishments, in the discretion of the court."

Sections 5 of the Federal Trade Commission Act (15 U.S.C. § 45)

Declares unfair methods of competition and unfair and deceptive acts or practices affecting commerce unlawful. Grants the Federal Trade Commission the power to prevent unfair methods of competition.

"... § 45. Unfair methods of competition unlawful; prevention by Commission

(a) Declaration of unlawfulness; power to prohibit unfair practices; inapplicability to foreign trade

(1) Unfair methods of competition in or affecting commerce, and unfair or deceptive acts or practices in or affecting commerce, are hereby declared unlawful.

(2) The Commission is hereby empowered and directed to prevent persons, partnerships, or corporations, except banks, savings and loan institutions described in section 57a(f)(3) of this title, Federal credit unions described in section 57a(f)(4) of this title, common carriers subject to the Acts to regulate commerce, air carriers and foreign air carriers subject to part A of subtitle VII of Title 49, and persons, partnerships, or corporations insofar as they are subject to the Packers and Stockyards Act, 1921, as amended [§ 7 U.S.C.A. 181 *et seq.*], except as provided in section 406(b) of said Act [§ 7 U.S.C.A. 227(b)], from using unfair methods of competition in or affecting commerce and unfair or deceptive acts or practices in or affecting commerce. ..."

Hart-Scott-Rodino Antitrust Improvements Act of 1976 (15 U.S.C. § 18a)

Requires notification to the Federal Trade Commission prior to certain mergers and acquisitions.

... § 18a. Premerger notification and waiting period

(a) Filing

Except as exempted pursuant to subsection (c) of this section, no person shall acquire, directly or indirectly, any voting securities or assets of any other person, unless both persons (or in the case of a tender offer, the acquiring person) file notification pursuant to rules under subsection (d)(1) of this section and the waiting period described in subsection (b)(1) of this section has expired, if—

(1) the acquiring person, or the person whose voting securities or assets are being acquired, is engaged in commerce or in any activity affecting commerce; ...

§ 10.2   STATUTORY MERGER AND SHARE EXCHANGE PROCEDURES

The procedures followed for completing statutory mergers and share exchanges will depend on the type of transaction and the parties involved. Obviously, mergers between related parties will involve less negotiation and due diligence than those between unrelated parties. Likewise, mergers or share exchanges involving publicly owned corporations can be much more complex than those involving smaller, closely held corporations.

This section begins with an investigation of some of the procedures common to all types of mergers and share exchanges, including negotiations and the letter of intent. Next it focuses on details necessary to perform a statutory merger, such as the plan of merger and the articles of merger. After examining the documents necessary to the exchange of shares, the section concludes with discussions of due diligence work, closings, and postclosing matters.

Negotiations and Letter of Intent

The first step in the merger or share exchange process of two unrelated parties generally involves meetings and preliminary negotiations between the parties. The parties involved must agree on the general terms and conditions of the transaction and all significant issues involving the proposed merger or share exchange.

If successful, negotiations often lead to a letter of intent. The **letter of intent** is a short document, often just a few pages in length, entered into between the proposed parties to a transaction to set forth their preliminary understandings and intent with regard to the transaction. The letter of intent may contain several contingencies, including a specific date by which a formal agreement must be entered into. It may contain the parties' agreement concerning the due diligence process that will take place by both parties prior to closing and a statement concerning the confidentiality of the information exchanged during negotiations and the due diligence process. The letter of intent demonstrates the seriousness of the parties to go to the next step in the process, which involves entering into a plan of merger or plan of exchange.

◆ ———

letter of intent   A preliminary written agreement setting forth the intention of the parties to enter into a contract.

Plan of Merger

A **plan of merger**, which is required by statute, sets forth the terms of the agreement between the parties in detail. Specific requirements for the plan of merger, which is sometimes referred to as an "agreement and plan of merger," are contained in the statutes of most states. Following is § 11.01(b) of the MBCA, which sets forth the requirements for the plan of merger:

> (b) The plan of merger must set forth:
>
> > (1) the name of each corporation planning to merge and the name of the surviving corporation into which each other corporation plans to merge;
> >
> > (2) the terms and conditions of the merger; and
> >
> > (3) the manner and basis of converting the shares of each corporation into shares, obligations, or other securities of the surviving or any other corporation or into cash or other property in whole or in part.

Section 11.01 further states that the plan of merger may contain an amendment to the articles of incorporation of the surviving corporation, and any other provisions relating to the merger.

The terms and conditions of a merger transaction between unrelated parties may be complex and detailed, and may concern many issues in addition to those required by state statutes for the plan of merger. In states where the plan of merger is filed for public record with the secretary of state or other state authority, additional provisions concerning the agreement between the parties may be set forth in a separate agreement.

Figure 10-5 on page 398 is a sample agreement and plan of merger for a downstream merger.

Following is a list of items often included in the plan of merger or a separate agreement.

- Date of agreement.
- Name and authorized capitalization of each original corporation.
- Name, purpose, location of the principal office, number of directors, and capital stock of the surviving corporation.
- Method and rate of exchange for converting shares of the merging corporation into shares of the surviving corporation.
- Provisions acknowledging the transfer of the rights, property, and liabilities of the merging corporation to the surviving corporation.
- Recital that each board of directors believes it to be in the best interest of its respective corporation that the merger take place.
- Provisions for submitting the plan of merger to the shareholders of each corporation for approval, as necessary.

---

plan of merger   Document required by state statute that sets forth the terms of the agreement between the two merging parties in detail.

AGREEMENT AND PLAN OF MERGER

This Agreement is made February 12, 2002, between Quality Home Repair, Inc., a corporation organized and existing under the laws of State of Minnesota, having its principal office at 3492 Oak Street, St. Paul, Ramsey County, Minnesota, and Dependable Restorations Corp., a corporation organized and existing under the laws of Minnesota, having its principal office and place of business at 2834 Main Street, Stillwater, Washington County, Minnesota.

I. SURVIVING CORPORATION

1. Dependable Restorations Corp. shall be the subsidiary corporation, and all references in this plan of merger to "subsidiary corporation" shall be to Dependable Restorations Corp.

2. Quality Home Repair, Inc. shall be the surviving corporation which owns all of the issued and outstanding stock of the above-named subsidiary corporation, and all references in this plan of merger to "surviving corporation" shall be to Quality Home Repair, Inc.

II. MANAGEMENT

1. The articles of incorporation of Quality Home Repair, Inc. shall continue to be its articles of incorporation following the effective date of the merger, until the same shall be altered or amended.

2. The bylaws of Quality Home Repair, Inc. shall be and remain the bylaws of the surviving corporation until altered, amended, or repealed.

3. The officers and directors of Quality Home Repair, Inc. in office on the effective date of the merger shall continue in office and shall constitute the directors and officers of Quality Home Repair, Inc. for the term elected until their respective successors shall be elected or appointed and qualified.

III. RIGHTS AND PRIVILEGES

On the effective date of the merger, Quality Home Repair, Inc. shall possess all the rights, privileges, immunities, powers, and franchises of a public and private nature, and shall be subject to all of the restrictions, disabilities, and duties of the subsidiary corporation. All of the property, real, personal, and mixed, and all debts due on whatever account, and all other choices in action, and all and every other interest of or belonging to or due to the subsidiary corporation shall be deemed to be transferred to and vested in Quality Home Repair, Inc. without further act or deed, and the title to any property or any interest therein, vested in the subsidiary corporation shall not revert or be in any way impaired by reason of the merger.

IV. LIABILITIES, DEBTS, AND OBLIGATIONS

On the effective date of the merger, Quality Home Repair, Inc. shall be deemed responsible and liable for all the liabilities and obligations of the subsidiary corporation; and any claims existing by or against the subsidiary corporation may be prosecuted to judgment as if the merger had not taken place, or Quality Home Repair, Inc. may be substituted in place of the subsidiary corporation. The rights of

FIGURE 10-5 Sample Agreement and Plan of Merger for Downstream Merger

the creditors shall not be impaired by this merger. Quality Home Repair, Inc. shall execute and deliver any and all documents which may be required for it to assume or otherwise comply with the outstanding obligations of the subsidiary corporation.

V. SURRENDER OF SHARES

Quality Home Repair, Inc. at present owns all of the outstanding shares of stock of the subsidiary corporation. On the effective date of the merger, all the outstanding shares of stock of the subsidiary corporation shall be surrendered and canceled. The shares of common stock of Quality Home Repair, Inc., whether authorized or issued on the effective date of the merger, shall not be converted, exchanged, or otherwise affected as a result of the merger, and no new shares of stock shall be issued by reason of this merger.

VI. SUBSEQUENT ACTS

If at any time Quality Home Repair, Inc. shall consider or be advised that any further assignment or assurances in law are necessary or desirable to vest or to perfect or confirm of record in Quality Home Repair, Inc. the title to any property or rights of the subsidiary corporation or to otherwise carry out the provisions hereof, the proper officers and directors of the subsidiary corporation as of the effective date of the merger shall execute and deliver any and all proper assignments and assurances in law, and do all things necessary or proper to vest, perfect, or confirm title to such property or rights in Quality Home Repair, Inc. and to otherwise carry out the provisions hereof.

IN WITNESS WHEREOF, the directors, or a majority thereof, of Quality Home Repair, Inc., the surviving corporation, and the directors, or a majority thereof, of Dependable Restorations Corp., the nonsurviving corporation, have executed this plan of merger under their respective corporate seals on the day and year first above written.

_____

_____

FIGURE 10-5 (*continued*)

◆ Amendments to the articles of incorporation of the surviving corporation.

◆ Provisions for amending the bylaws of the surviving corporation.

◆ Provisions for dissolving the merging corporation.

◆ Names and addresses of the directors of the surviving corporation.

◆ Treatment of outstanding stock options, if any.

◆ Restrictions on transactions outside the normal course of business by either corporation prior to the effective date of the merger.

◆ Provisions for corporate distributions during the period prior to the effective date of the merger.

◆ Provisions for possible abandonment of the merger prior to the completion thereof by the directors of either corporation.

- Provisions for filing the articles of merger or share exchange with the appropriate state office, as required by statute.
- Closing and effective date of the merger.

In addition, the agreement between the merging corporations includes specific information (usually in the form of schedules or exhibits) regarding the business status of each corporation involved, including the corporation's financial status, assets, pending litigation, employees, and all matters that might affect the business or earning potential of the corporation.

Director and Shareholder Approval of the Plan of Merger   With the possible exception of upstream mergers, the plan of merger must be approved by the board of directors and shareholders of each corporation that will be a party to the merger, pursuant to state statutes. Class voting and special voting requirements unique to the plan of merger are often required. Under the MBCA, when shareholder approval is required for a plan of merger, the following procedures must be used:

1. The board of directors must recommend the plan to the shareholders, unless the board determines that it should make no recommendation and communicates the basis for its determination to the shareholders with the plan. Reasons for not rendering a recommendation may include a conflict of interest or other special circumstances.[4] The board may condition its submission of the proposed plan on any basis.[5]

2. Each shareholder, whether or not entitled to vote, must be notified of the shareholder meeting pursuant to statute. The notice must state that the purpose of the meeting is to consider the plan of merger, and it must contain or be accompanied by a summary of the plan.[6]

3. Unless otherwise provided by state statutes, the articles of incorporation, or the board of directors, the plan must be approved by each voting group entitled to vote separately on the plan. Approval of each voting group is given by the majority vote of all votes within each voting group.[7] A **voting group**, as defined by § 1.40 of the MBCA, is:

> all shares of one or more classes or series that under the articles of incorporation or this Act are entitled to vote and be counted together collectively on a matter at a meeting of shareholders. All shares entitled by the articles of incorporation or this Act to vote generally on the matter are for that purpose a single voting group.

4. Separate voting by voting groups is required if the plan contains a provision that, if contained in a proposed amendment to the articles of incorporation, would require action by one or more separate voting groups on the proposed amendment pursuant to statute.[8]

---

voting group   All shares of one or more classes that are entitled to vote and be counted together collectively on a certain matter under the corporation's articles of incorporation or the pertinent state statute.

Under the MBCA, as in most states, approval of the shareholders of the surviving corporation is not required under certain circumstances when the position and rights of the shareholders of the surviving corporation are not significantly affected by the merger. This allows the board of directors acting on behalf of large, publicly held corporations to acquire several corporations or merge several corporations into the corporation, without the formality of a shareholder meeting to approve each merger. The following paragraphs are examples of board of director and shareholder resolutions approving plans of merger.

EXAMPLE: Resolution of Directors Authorizing Merger into Another Corporation

RESOLVED, that the plan of merger this day proposed to the board, pursuant to which this corporation will transfer to _____ [other corporation], a corporation organized and existing under the laws of the State of _____, all of the assets, tangible and intangible, of this corporation as they exist on _____, 20___, subject to the liabilities of this corporation, in the manner and to the extent set forth in the draft agreement heretofore presented and read to this meeting, be and the same hereby is declared to be in the best interests of this corporation and is hereby ratified, approved, and adopted.[9]

EXAMPLE: Stockholders' Resolution Adopting Merger Agreement

Whereas, the board of directors of this corporation has approved an agreement of merger at a meeting of the directors duly held at the corporation's _____ [principal executive office] at _____ [address], _____ [city], _____ County, _____ [state], on _____ [date], and ordered that the agreement be submitted to the shareholders for approval at this meeting as provided by law;

RESOLVED, that the shareholders of this corporation hereby ratify, adopt, and approve the agreement of merger dated _____, between the corporation and _____ [name of other corporation(s)], and direct the secretary of the corporation to insert a copy of such agreement in the minute book of the corporation immediately following the minutes of this meeting.

FURTHER RESOLVED, that the officers of this corporation are hereby authorized and directed to execute all documents and to take such further action as may be deemed necessary or advisable to implement this resolution.[10]

Dissenting Shareholders Shareholders entitled to vote on a plan of merger may be granted the right to dissent under the statutes of the corporation's state of domicile. A shareholder's *right to dissent* refers to the right to object to certain extraordinary actions being taken by the corporation and to obtain payment of the fair value of the shares held by the dissenting shareholder from the corporation. Under the MBCA, any shareholder who is entitled to vote on a plan of merger, or shareholders of subsidiaries that are merged with the parent in an upstream merger, have the right to dissent. Other events, including consummation of a plan of exchange and amendment of the articles of incorporation, that materially and adversely affect the rights of shareholders will also entitle shareholders to the right to dissent. Certain statutory formalities, including the submission of a written notice of intent to demand payment, must be followed by the dissenting shareholder in order to exercise their right to payment.

When the dissenting shareholder challenges the fair value placed on his or her shares by the corporation, an appraisal proceeding may be commenced. An appraisal proceeding involves judicial appraisal of the fair value of the stock of the dissenting shareholders. Figure 10-6 is an example of a notice that may be given to the corporation by a dissenting shareholder to demand the fair market value of his or her shares upon merger.

State statutes concerning shareholder dissent usually include very specific requirements that must be met by dissenting shareholders, including deadlines for presenting demand for the fair market value of the shareholder's shares. The dissenting shareholder must comply exactly with the provisions of state statutes to exercise his or her rights under these statutes.

Articles of Merger   After the plan of merger has been adopted pursuant to statute, **articles of merger** must be filed with the secretary of state or other appropriate state authority. (See appendix A for a secretary of state directory.) Under § 11.05 of the MBCA, the articles of merger must set forth:

1. The plan of merger.
2. A statement that shareholder approval of the plan was not required, if that is the case.
3. A statement regarding the approval of the plan of merger by the shareholders, including the number of votes voted for and against the merger in each voting group, if shareholder approval was necessary.

Figure 10-7 on page 404 shows an example of articles of merger between two domestic corporations in the state of Missouri.

Plan of Exchange

Procedures for a **plan of exchange** are set forth in the MBCA and the statutes of several states that have followed the Model Act closely. Section 11.02(b) of the MBCA, which follows, sets forth the requirements for a plan of exchange:

> (b) The plan of exchange must set forth:
>   (1) the name of the corporation whose shares will be acquired and the name of the acquiring corporation;
>   (2) the terms and conditions of the exchange;
>   (3) the manner and basis of exchanging the shares to be acquired for shares, obligations, or other securities of the acquiring or any other corporation or for cash or other property in whole or part.

◆ ───

articles of merger   Documents filed with the secretary of state or other appropriate authority to effect a merger.

plan of exchange   Document required by statute that sets forth the terms of the agreement between the parties to a statutory share exchange.

**DEMAND BY DISSENTING STOCKHOLDER FOR
FAIR MARKET VALUE OF SHARES ON
MERGER OF CORPORATION**

**STATEMENT OF FAIR MARKET VALUE
OF SHARES**

To: _____ [corporation]

_____ [address]

The shareholders of this corporation, at a _____ [special] meeting held on _____, _____, at its principal executive office at _____ [address], purported to approve an agreement providing for the merger of the corporation with _____ [constituent corporation], a _____ [state] corporation.

Notice of the purported approval by the shareholders was mailed to the undersigned on _____, _____, and _____ [30] days have not yet expired since the date of mailing of the notice, and the undersigned has not approved such proposed merger.

The undersigned is the holder of record of _____ [number] shares of _____ [common] stock of _____ [corporation], evidenced by Certificate No. _____. These shares were voted against the merger.

The undersigned hereby makes written demand for the payment to him of the fair market value of such shares as of _____, _____, being the date prior to the first announcement of the terms of the proposed merger.

The undersigned hereby states that _____ dollars ($_____) per share is the fair market value of such shares as of the date prior to the first announcement of the terms of the proposed merger.

The undersigned hereby submits to the corporation at its principal executive office the certificate for such shares with respect to which the undersigned makes this demand, in order that the certificate may be stamped or endorsed with the statement that such shares are dissenting shares and thereupon returned to him at the address stated below.

Dated _____, _____.[11]

[Signature and address]

FIGURE 10-6 Demand by Dissenting Stockholder for Fair Market Value of Shares on Merger of Corporation. Reprinted with permission from *American Jurisprudence Legal Forms 2d.* © 2000 West Group.

As with a plan of merger, the plan of exchange may also contain any other provisions relating to the transaction.

Following is a list of items often included in a plan of exchange:

♦ Date of agreement.

♦ Name and authorized capitalization of each original corporation.

State of Missouri
Matt Blunt, Secretary of State

Corporations Division
P.O. Box 778, Jefferson City, MO 65102

James C. Kirkpatrick State Information Center
600 W. Main Street, Rm 322, Jefferson City, MO 65101

Articles of Merger
(Submit in duplicate with filing fee of $30)

Pursuant to the provisions of The General and Business Corporation Law of Missouri, the undersigned corporations certify the following:

1. That _____ of _____

(Name of Corporation)   (Parent State)

    _____ of _____

(Name of Corporation)   (Parent State)

    and _____ of _____

(Name of Corporation)   (Parent State)

    are hereby merged and that the above named _____

is the surviving corporation.   (Name of Corporation)

2. That the Board of Directors of each of the above-named corporations met, and by resolution adopted by a majority vote of the members of such boards approved the Plan of Merger set forth in these Articles.

3. The Plan of Merger thereafter was submitted to a vote at a meeting of the shareholders of each of the above-named corporations, and at such meeting the following votes were recorded:

Corporation	Number of Shares Outstanding	Number voting for plan	Number voting against plan

4. If the above-named surviving corporation is to be governed by the laws of any state other than Missouri, the surviving corporation agrees that it will promptly pay to the dissenting shareholders of any Missouri Corporation which is a party to this merger the amount, if any, to which they shall be entitled under provisions of Missouri law with respect to the rights of dissenting shareholders. It also agrees that it may be served with process in this state, and irrevocably appoints the Missouri Secretary of State as its agent to accept service of process in any proceeding based upon any cause of action against any such Missouri corporation arising in this state prior to the issuance of the certificate of merger, and in any proceeding for the enforcement of the rights of a dissenting shareholder of any such Missouri corporation against the surviving corporation. The address to which the service of process in any such proceeding shall be mailed is:

    _____

5. PLAN OF MERGER

    1. _____ of _____

is the survivor.

    2. All of the property, rights, privileges, leases and patents of the _____

    _____Corporation and

    _____ Corporation

Corp. #51 (11/00)

FIGURE 10-7   Articles of Merger for Corporation in the State of Missouri

are to be transferred to and become the property of _____

_____ the survivor. The officers and board of directors of the above named corporations are authorized to execute all deeds, assignments, and documents of every nature which may be needed to effectuate a full and complete transfer of ownership.

3. The officers and board of directors of _____
shall continue in office until their successors are duly elected and qualified under the provisions of the bylaws of the surviving corporation.

4. The outstanding shares of _____

shall be exchanged for shares of _____
on the following basis:

5. The outstanding shares of _____

shall be exchanged for shares of _____
on the following basis:

6. The articles of Incorporation of the survivor are/are not amended as follows:

     IN WITNESS WHEREOF, these Articles of Merger have been executed in duplicate by the aforementioned corporations as of the day and year hereafter acknowledged.

CORPORATE SEAL

            _____
                          Name of Corporation

            By_____
                       President or Vice President

ATTEST:

                          Printed Name   Date
_____
        Secretary or Assistant Secretary

CORPORATE SEAL

            _____
                          Name of Corporation

            By_____
                       President or Vice President

ATTEST:

                          Printed Name   Date
_____
        Secretary or Assistant Secretary
Corp. #51 (Page 2)

FIGURE 10-7 (*continued*)

CORPORATE SEAL

_____
Name of Corporation

By_____
President or Vice President

ATTEST:

_____
Printed Name   Date

_____
Secretary or Assistant Secretary

State of _____

County of _____ } ss

    I, _____, a Notary Public,

do hereby certify that on _____ personally appeared before me

_____ who being by me first duly sworn, declared

that he/she is the _____

of _____

that he/she signed the foregoing documents as _____ of the corporation, and

that the statements therein contained are true.

(Notarial Seal or Stamp)

_____
Notary Public

My commission expires _____

My County of Commission _____

Corp. #51 (Page 3)

FIGURE 10-7 (_continued_)

State of _____ } ss
County of _____

    I, _____, a Notary Public,

do hereby certify that on _____ personally appeared before me

_____ who being by me first duly sworn, declared

that he/she is the _____

of _____

that he/she signed the foregoing documents as _____ of the corporation, and

that the statements therein contained are true.

        (Notarial Seal or Stamp)

                                _____
                                          Notary Public

                                  My commission expires _____

                                  My County of Commission _____

State of _____ } ss
County of _____

    I, _____, a Notary Public,

do hereby certify that on _____ personally appeared before me

_____ who being by me first duly sworn, declared

that he/she is the _____

of _____

that he/she signed the foregoing documents as _____ of the corporation, and

that the statements therein contained are true.

        (Notarial Seal or Stamp)

                                _____
                                          Notary Public

                                  My commission expires _____

                                  My County of Commission _____

Corp. #51 (Page 4)

FIGURE 10-7 (*continued*)

◆ Recital that each board of directors believes it to be in the best interest of its respective corporation that the share exchange take place.

◆ Provisions for the method of exchanging the shares of the target corporation for shares of the acquiring corporation and for continuing the target corporation as a subsidiary of the acquiring corporation.

◆ Name, purposes, location of the principal offices, number of directors, and capital stock of the acquiring corporation and the subsidiary corporation after the exchange.

◆ Amendments to the articles of incorporation of each corporation, reflecting the share exchange.

◆ Provisions for amending the bylaws of each corporation, as necessary.

◆ Treatment of outstanding stock options, if any.

◆ Restrictions on transactions outside the normal course of business by either corporation prior to the effective date of the share exchange.

◆ Provisions for corporate distributions during the period prior to the effective date of the share exchange, if desired.

◆ Provisions for submitting the plan of exchange to the shareholders of each corporation for approval, as necessary.

◆ Agreement regarding the inspection of books, records, and other property of each corporation.

◆ Provisions for possible abandonment of the plan of exchange prior to the completion thereof by the directors of either corporation.

◆ Provisions for filing the articles of share exchange with the appropriate state office, as required by statute.

◆ Closing and effective date of the share exchange.

In addition, the plan of exchange may include schedules and exhibits setting forth the specific assets and liabilities of each corporation, and any other information relevant to the business of each corporation, including pending or threatened litigation.

Director and Shareholder Approval of the Plan of Exchange The statutory requirements for approving a plan of exchange are substantially the same as those for approving a plan of merger. State statutes generally require that the plan be recommended by the board of directors and approved by the shareholders of the corporation. In addition, the MBCA provides that "separate voting by voting groups is required on a plan of share exchange by each class or series of shares included in the exchange, with each class or series constituting a separate voting group."[12]

Dissenting Shareholders The share exchange, if properly approved by a majority of the shareholders pursuant to statute, is binding on all shareholders. However, shareholders who dissent from the share exchange may have the right to obtain payment for their shares and withdraw from the corporation. Shareholders entitled to vote on a plan of exchange are granted the same right to dissent that is prescribed for shareholders entitled to vote on a plan of merger.

Articles of Share Exchange   After the plan of exchange has been adopted pursuant to statute, the **articles of share exchange** must be filed with the secretary of state or other appropriate state authority, generally in the same manner prescribed for articles of merger (discussed above). The statutes of the state of domicile will dictate the contents of the articles of share exchange. Under the MBCA, the articles of share exchange must set forth:

1. The plan of share exchange.
2. A statement regarding the approval of the plan of exchange by the shareholders, including the number of votes voted for and against the exchange in each voting group.[13]

The share exchange generally becomes effective as the effective date of the articles.

As with the articles of merger, forms for the articles of plan exchange are often available through the office of the secretary of state where the articles must be filed. Figure 10-8 on page 410 is a sample of a form that may be filed in the State of Oregon.

Due Diligence and Preclosing Matters

Although the plan of merger or plan of exchange sets forth specific information regarding the business and financial condition of each corporation, the parties to a merger or share exchange and their professional representatives must use due diligence to ascertain the validity of the statements in the plan. *Due diligence* refers to the standard of care that must be exercised by each responsible party, and *due diligence work* refers to the investigation done to ascertain the validity of statements made in an agreement prior to closing.

In a statutory merger or share exchange transaction, due diligence work often involves a thorough review of the documentation supporting the information in the plan of merger or plan of exchange, as well as possible on-site investigations to see and inspect the real estate, buildings, assets, and inventory involved in the transaction, and also to inspect corporate books and records that are too cumbersome to photocopy or remove from the corporate offices. Due diligence work can be very time-consuming, and it often involves the paralegals working on the transaction, who work on producing the documentation requested by the other party or parties to the transaction and on collecting and reviewing the documentation requested on behalf of the corporate client.

Usually, the plan of merger or share exchange is used to produce a checklist of documentation that must be produced by each party prior to closing. In addition to the corporate clients involved in a merger, accountants and other parties may also

---

articles of share exchange   Document filed with the secretary of state or other appropriate state authority to effect a share exchange.

Phone: (503) 986-2200
Fax: (503) 378-4381

Secretary of State
Corporation Division
255 Capitol St. NE, Suite 151
Salem, OR 97310-1327

Articles of Share Exchange

For office use only

Registry Number: _____

Attach Additional Sheet if Necessary
Please Type or Print Legibly in **Black** Ink

1) **NAME OF CORPORATIONS PROPOSING TO EXCHANGE SHARES**

A. NAME OF THE CORPORATION WHOSE SHARES ARE BEING ACQUIRED

B. NAME OF THE CORPORATION ACQUIRING THE SHARES OF CORPORATION A ABOVE

2) ☐ A copy of the plan of exchange is attached.

3) **VOTE OF THE SHAREHOLDERS OF CORPORATION A WHOSE SHARES ARE BEING ACQUIRED**

Class or series of shares	Number of shares outstanding	Number of votes entitled to be cast	Number of votes cast FOR	Number of votes cast AGAINST

4) **EXECUTION FOR CORPORATION A**

Printed Name   Signature   Title

4) **EXECUTION FOR CORPORATION B**

Printed Name   Signature   Title

6) **CONTACT NAME**   **DAYTIME PHONE NUMBER – INCLUDING AREA CODE**

FEES

Make check for $10 payable to "Corporation Division."

NOTE: Filing fees may be paid with VISA or MasterCard. The card number and expiration date should be submitted on a separate sheet for your protection.

CR118 (Rev. 12/99)

FIGURE 10-8 Articles of Share Exchange for Corporations in the State of Oregon

be responsible for producing documents. Figure 10-9 is an excerpt from a sample checklist used to assure that all documents are prepared, exchanged, reviewed, and approved before the closing of the merger or share exchange.

AGREEMENT OF MERGER BETWEEN
CORPORATION A AND CORPORATION B

PROPOSED CLOSING DATE JUNE 20, 2004

Document/Page Reference	Resp. Party	Received or Prepared	Approved or Submitted
Corporation A Articles of Incorporation/ Page 3, Para. 2	Corp. A		
Corporation A Corporate Bylaws (Certified) Page 3, Para. 3	Corp. A		
Corporation A Corporate Minutes 1990 through Present Date/Page 3, Para. 4	Corp. A		
Corporation B Articles of Incorporation/ Page 3, Para. 2	Corp. B		
Corporation B Corporate Bylaws (Certified) Page 3, Para. 3	Corp. B		
Corporation B Corporate Minutes 1990 through Present Date/ Page 3, Para. 4	Corp. B		
Lease to 2348 Elm Street Exhibit A	Corp. B		
Lease to 3484 Maple Street Exhibit A	Corp. B		
Title to 390 Main Street Exhibit A	Corp. A		
Agreement with ABC Mfg. Exhibit B	Corp. A		
Agreement with Acme Plastics/Exhibit B	Corp. A		

FIGURE 10-9 Excerpt from Sample Closing Checklist

The list of documents that must be exchanged and reviewed prior to closing can be very extensive, and may include the following:

- Proof of corporate existence and good standing of each corporation.
- Copies of all documents typically included in corporate minute books, including articles of incorporation and any amendments thereto, bylaws, and minutes of the board of directors and shareholder meetings.
- Copies of stock ledgers and stock certificates.
- Financial statements for each corporation.
- Tax returns for each corporation and results of any tax audits.
- Leases and/or titles to all real property that is owned and/or leased by each corporation.
- Lists of all equipment and personal property at each location occupied by each corporation.
- All paperwork concerning any patents, trademarks, and copyrights pending or owned by each corporation.
- Copies of all employment and noncompetition agreements to which each corporation is a party.
- Descriptions of all employee benefits, including the names of all employees entitled thereto.
- Certified Uniform Commercial Code searches for each corporation.
- Copies of any loan agreements to which each corporation is a party.
- Lists of accounts payable for each corporation.
- Lists of accounts receivable for each corporation.
- Copies of all material contracts to which each corporation is a party.
- Customer lists.
- Vendor lists.
- Copies of pleadings in any pending litigation.

The documents that must be produced and reviewed will vary depending on the type of transaction and the relationship of the parties. If the transaction being contemplated is a merger between parent and subsidiary corporations, much of the information required for the transaction will be available to the parties in the normal course of business, and many of the documents in the preceding list will be irrelevant.

Due diligence work also involves ascertaining whether any outside parties may be required to give consent to any part of the transaction. All agreements to which the merging or target corporation is a party must be reviewed to determine whether consent of the other party to the agreement must be obtained before assigning the contract to the surviving or acquiring corporation. For example, if a merging corporation is a tenant under a lease, the landlord's consent will probably be required to transfer the lease to the acquiring corporation. If consent must be obtained, it should be requested promptly to ensure that it is received before closing.

Closing the Statutory Merger or Share Exchange Transaction

The agreement and plan of merger or share exchange typically set forth a date and time for closing the transaction. At the closing, the shares of stock will change hands, assignments and transfers of contracts and real and personal property will be made, and any cash, or contractual obligations to pay out cash at a future date, will be paid out. The key officers from each corporation, the legal team for each corporation, and any other individuals who may be required to sign closing documents usually attend the closing.

The closing is typically conducted by executing and exchanging all documents referred to in the agreement and plan of merger or share exchange, as well as any supplemental documents necessary to effect the transfers referred to therein. A closing agenda is typically prepared from the plan of merger or plan of exchange and the checklist used in accumulating and reviewing the documents. Each party is responsible for preparing or producing certain documents required for the closing, as specified in the agenda. Paralegals who have been instrumental in getting the transaction to the closing table are often involved in the actual closing, and are usually responsible for seeing that each document is properly executed and that the proper parties are given copies. This may be no small task in complex transactions that could literally involve several boxes of documents.

Merger Closings Following is a list of some of the types of documents typically required for closing a merger transaction:

1. Articles of merger, including any necessary articles of amendment to the articles of incorporation.
2. Instruments assigning and transferring the appropriate shares of stock of each corporation.
3. New stock certificates representing stock ownership pursuant to the plan of merger.
4. Deeds or other instruments assigning or transferring any real property.
5. Bills of sale or other instruments assigning or transferring any equipment, motor vehicles, or other personal property.
6. Assignments or other instruments assigning or transferring any patents, trademarks, or copyrights.
7. Instruments assigning or transferring bank accounts.
8. Legal opinions of transfer agents.
9. Legal opinions of attorneys for each party.
10. Notices or filings required by the Securities and Exchange Commission (SEC).
11. Officers' certificates.
12. Certified copies of board of director and shareholder resolutions approving the transaction.
13. Announcements to shareholders and/or employees, if necessary.

Share Exchange Closings   Closings of share exchange transactions are very similar to merger closings, with more emphasis placed on documents transferring the ownership of the target corporation. Following is a list of some of the items that may be required for closing a share exchange transaction:

1. Articles of share exchange, including amendments to the articles of the target corporation and the acquiring corporation, as needed.
2. Instruments transferring the appropriate shares of stock of each corporation.
3. New stock certificates representing the ownership of the acquiring corporation and the target corporation, which will become a subsidiary.
4. Any necessary assignments.
5. Legal opinions of attorneys for each party.
6. Any notices required by the SEC or blue sky laws.
7. Officers' certificates.
8. Certified copies of board of director and shareholder resolutions approving the transaction.

Postclosing Matters

After the closing, there are typically several tasks that need to be completed to finalize the transaction. Most of these tasks involve notification of interested parties of the merger or share exchange and filings at the county or state level, or with the SEC. Some of the steps that may be required after the closing of a statutory merger or statutory share exchange include the following:

1. Filing the articles of merger or share exchange (if not done prior to closing) and any amendments to the articles of incorporation required by the transaction.
2. Organizing new corporate minute books and stock ledgers.
3. Filing any deeds transferring real estate.
4. Changing title on motor vehicles, as necessary.
5. Sending copies of any lease assignments to the proper landlords or tenants.
6. Filing any Uniform Commercial Code documents.
7. Completing any filings required by the SEC or blue sky laws.

§ 10.3 ASSET AND STOCK ACQUISITIONS

In addition to statutory mergers and share exchanges, there are several other means of combining or acquiring corporations. This section discusses nonstatutory transactions involving the acquisition of corporate assets and stock.

The discussion in this section concerns nonstatutory corporate acquisitions that are completed through the purchase of all or substantially all of the assets or outstanding shares of stock of a corporation. Although asset acquisitions and stock acquisitions have an economic effect that is very similar to that of statutory mergers and acquisitions, there are significant differences. Courts have held that "the mere purchase by, and transfer to, one corporation of the property and franchises of another corporation, or the purchase by one corporation of the stock of another corporation, is not a consolidation of the two corporations."[14]

This section focuses on asset acquisition and stock acquisition of closely held corporations and the advantages and disadvantages of each type of transaction. It also examines the state and federal laws affecting asset and stock acquisitions.

Asset Acquisitions

One means of acquiring the business of a corporation is to purchase all, or substantially all, of its assets. In *asset acquisitions*, the acquiring corporation purchases all of the assets of the target corporation, leaving the target corporation a mere corporate shell to be dissolved. This type of transaction has the advantage of permitting the buyers to know exactly what they are getting. The fact that the acquiring corporation will generally not be held liable for any future liabilities and obligations of the target corporation may also be a very important advantage. However, the necessity of identifying each specific asset being acquired can make an asset acquisition much more cumbersome than a stock acquisition.

Stock Acquisitions

A *stock acquisition transaction* involves the purchase of all or substantially all of the outstanding stock of a corporation, either by an individual, a group of individuals, or, more commonly, another corporation. The target corporation generally becomes a subsidiary of the acquiring corporation, or it is merged into the acquiring corporation.

One advantage of this type of purchase is the simplification in transferring the corporation from one individual or group of individuals to another. Instead of transferring each asset owned by the corporation, the ownership of the corporation itself is transferred to the new owner or owners. Disadvantages include the fact that the acquiring corporation will be responsible for all debts and liabilities of the corporation being acquired, even those that have an unknown or undisclosed value at the time of closing. Another disadvantage is that the acquiring corporation may have to deal with several individual shareholders.

Barring any share transfer restrictions on shares of stock, shareholders of closely held or publicly held corporations may sell their shares of stock at will. However, most stock acquisitions involving the purchase of substantially all of the stock of a corporation must have a consensus of the shareholders. Obviously, the shares of a corporation may not be purchased unless the holders of those shares all agree to sell their stock.

Hostile Takeovers

When one corporation attempts to purchase or *take over* another corporation against the wishes of the management and board of directors of the target corporation, the transaction is referred to as a hostile takeover.

Most hostile takeovers are completed by tender offers. This means that the acquirer makes a public offer to purchase, usually at a premium, enough shares of the target corporation to control it. In most instances, if the acquirer purchases a simple majority of the shares of the target corporation, the acquirer will have the power to replace the board of directors of the target corporation, and effectively, to control the corporation. Tender offers and hostile takeovers are legal as long as they comply with state statutes and federal securities laws which control publicly held corporations.

Hostile takeovers became popular during the 1980s and consistently made the headlines. Legislators in many states countered by drafting anti-takeover legislation—laws that allowed corporations to take measures to defeat hostile takeovers.

Defensive measures adopted by a corporation to deflect hostile takeovers are referred to as *shark repellants*. Some of these defensive measures include amending the corporation's articles to establish staggered terms for directors and to require the approval of a super majority of its shareholders to approve a merger.

Corporations may also employ tactics to make themselves less attractive as takeover targets, such as authorizing additional classes of stock to give superiority to existing shareholders in the event of a takeover. Tactics that make the corporation less attractive as a takeover target are often referred to as *poison pills*.

The board of directors has a responsibility to the corporation and the corporation's shareholders. If the directors determine that the takeover is not in the best interests of the shareholders, the board of directors can take steps to try to prevent it. If, however, the board determines that the takeover is in the best interests of the corporation and its shareholders, they must help to facilitate the purchase.

De Facto Mergers

Under some circumstances, the courts may consider a transaction between two or more corporations to be a merger, even if the parties have intended the transaction to be merely an asset purchase.

The de facto merger doctrine allows courts to view a transaction as a merger if it has the characteristics of a merger, even when it is called something else by the parties. The de facto merger is used to avoid injustices to third parties when one corporation transfers all of its assets to another corporation and disappears, making it impossible for creditors of the first corporation to collect debts owed to them.

For example, assume Corporation A sells all of its assets to Corporation B. Corporation B assumes all of the previous business of Corporation A, which then discontinues doing business. Any unpaid creditors of Corporation A are then unable to collect because Corporation A no longer has any assets. The Courts may determine that a de facto merger exists and that Corporation B is liable to Corporation

A's creditors, even if the transaction between the two corporations was an asset purchase.

The following factors may be considered to determine if a de facto merger has taken place:

1. Continuation of previous business activity and corporate personnel.
2. Continuity of shareholders resulting from the sale of assets in exchange for stock.
3. Immediate or rapid dissolution of predecessor corporation.
4. Assumption by purchasing corporation of all liabilities and obligations ordinarily necessary to continue predecessor's business operations.

State and Federal Laws Affecting Asset and Stock Acquisitions

Although the procedures for asset and stock purchases are not set forth in state statutes, certain aspects of these transactions, such as shareholder approval of the sale of a corporation's assets, are subject to state law. The statutes of the state of domicile of each party to the transaction must be consulted to be sure that all statutory requirements are complied with. In addition, certain asset or stock acquisition transactions may trigger SEC or blue sky law reporting requirements and the antitrust provisions found in the Hart-Scott-Rodino Act.

§ 10.4 ASSET AND STOCK ACQUISITION PROCEDURES

Unlike statutory mergers and share exchanges, there are no specific statutory procedures to be followed for asset and stock acquisitions. The procedures to be followed for each of these types of transactions will depend on the type of transaction and the parties involved. Procedures for acquiring the assets of a corporation focus much more on the identification and transfer of the assets; stock acquisitions focus more on the entire corporate entity represented by the shares of stock.

Often, the decision as to whether a transaction should involve the purchase of a corporation's stock or the corporation's assets is made only after a preliminary agreement has been made by the corporations for one to buy out the other. The decision is made based upon the implications of tax laws to all parties involved.

This section looks at the procedures for completing transactions involving asset and stock acquisitions of closely held corporations. First it considers the negotiations involved in those types of transactions. Next it examines the asset purchase agreement and its approval by the shareholders of the target corporation. It then focuses on requirements for an agreement for the purchase and sale of all, or substantially all, of the outstanding stock of a corporation. This section concludes with a discussion of the due diligence and preclosing work involved in asset and stock acquisitions and the closing and postclosing matters concerning acquisitions.

Negotiations and Letter of Intent

The first step in the asset purchase or stock purchase procedures is often very similar to that involved with mergers or share exchanges. Preliminary negotiations, which involve meetings between the two parties and their legal counsel, generally commence with the aim of entering into a preliminary agreement and signing a letter of intent. Price, terms, and the format of the acquisition of the corporation all must be agreed upon before an agreement can be entered into.

Asset Purchase Agreement

An asset purchase agreement specifically sets forth the agreement between the parties with regard to the purchase of all or substantially all of the assets of one corporation by another, based on the letter of intent or preliminary agreement entered into between the parties. The asset purchase agreement must set forth very specifically all the assets that are to be purchased by the acquiring corporation, as well as the terms for the disposition of any debts or liens related to those assets. Following is a list of items often included in an asset purchase agreement:

- Names and other identification of the parties.
- Description of the property and assets subject to the agreement.
- The nature and amount of the consideration to be paid for the assets.
- Terms for assuming any debts and liabilities.
- Acts required of the seller, including the delivery of the instruments of transfer.
- Agreement regarding the inspection of books, records, and property of the selling corporation.
- Warranties of the seller, including the authority to enter into the agreement, the accuracy and completeness of the books and records, title to the property and assets being acquired, and the care and preservation of the property and assets.
- Indemnification of the buyer.
- Buyer's right to use seller's name.
- Remedies in the event of a default by either party.
- Governing law.
- Date of the agreement.
- Signature of all parties involved.
- The date, time, and place of closing.

The sale of all or substantially all of the assets of a corporation requires shareholder approval of the selling corporation. The MBCA provides for the sale of assets, other than in the regular course of business, as follows:

> (a) A corporation may sell, lease, exchange, or otherwise dispose of all, or substantially all, of its property (with or without the good will), otherwise than in the usual and regular course of business, on the terms and conditions and

for the consideration determined by the corporation's board of directors, if the board of directors proposes and its shareholders approve the proposed transaction.[15]

The statutory procedures for obtaining shareholder approval for the sale of all, or substantially all, of the assets of a corporation are usually very similar to those prescribed for the approval of statutory mergers and share exchanges because, in effect, the business of the corporation as it has existed will terminate upon the sale of its assets. The statutes of the selling corporation's state of domicile should always be consulted to be sure that the exact procedures for obtaining shareholder approval are followed. Shareholders of the selling corporation almost always have the right to dissent. Figure 10-10 is an example of a stockholders' written consent approving the sale of all or substantially all assets of the corporation.

STOCKHOLDERS' WRITTEN CONSENT
APPROVING SALE OF ALL OR SUBSTANTIALLY ALL ASSETS

Whereas, at a _____ [regular or special] meeting of the board of directors of _____ [corporation] held on _____ [date], the board duly passed the following resolution authorizing the sale, conveyance, exchange, and transfer of all or substantially all of the property and assets of the corporation to _____ [name of purchasing corporation]: _____ [set forth board's resolution].

[If principal terms of transaction and nature and amount of consideration are not specified in board's resolution, add the following: Whereas, the principal terms of the transaction and the nature and amount of the consideration of the sale, conveyance, exchange, and transfer authorized by the board at such meeting are as follows: _____];

RESOLVED, that the undersigned shareholders, and each of them, hereby approve and consent to the principal terms of the transaction and the nature and amount of the consideration, and the resolutions of the board as set forth above.

In witness whereof, each of the undersigned has signed his or her name and the date of signing and the number of shares of the corporation entitled to vote held by him or her _____ [of record] on such date.

Name	Signature	Date of Execution	Number of Shares
_____	_____	_____	_____
_____	_____	_____	_____
_____	_____	_____	_____ [16]

FIGURE 10-10   Stockholders' Written Consent Approving Sale of All or Substantially All Assets. Reprinted with permission from *American Jurisprudence Legal Forms 2d.* © 2000 West Group.

Stock Purchase Agreement

In a stock purchase agreement, the purchaser accepts all of the rights and obligations incident to ownership of the stock of the target corporation. It is not necessary to specify the exact assets and liabilities of the selling corporation. Each selling shareholder must be in agreement with the terms of the purchase of the stock and enter into the stock purchase agreement. Special warranties regarding the corporation and its financial and legal status are typically given by the officers of the corporation. Common provisions in a stock purchase agreement include the following:

- Names and other identification of the parties.
- Price for purchase of stock.
- Method of payment.
- Seller's representations regarding the authority to sell the stock being purchased.
- Seller's warranty that all securities laws have been and will be complied with to the date of the contemplated transaction.
- Disclosure of any pending litigation against the selling corporation.
- Seller's warranties as to the good standing of the corporation, its authorized, issued, and outstanding stock, and its financial condition.
- Buyer's representations with regard to its ability to finance the purchase of the stock.
- The agreement between the acquiring and selling corporations with regard to the payment of any tax liability of the selling corporation or any tax liability to be incurred as a result of the sale of the stock.
- Covenants not to compete of certain officers and key employees of the corporation.
- A general release of the seller from any future liability incurred by the selling corporation.
- The date, location, and method of closing.
- Execution of all parties.

Due Diligence and Preclosing Matters

The due diligence and preclosing procedures for asset and stock purchases are very similar to those for statutory mergers and share exchanges. The asset purchase transaction focuses more on the specific assets being purchased, whereas the stock purchase transaction involves all aspects of the corporation whose shares are being purchased, with specific attention to any potential future liability of the target corporation. The majority of the due diligence work in an asset or share acquisition transaction is done by the acquiring corporation's representatives and legal counsel. The purchase agreement is used to produce a checklist of documents to be prepared, accumulated, and reviewed in much the same way as the checklist for mergers and share exchange documents is prepared.

Closing the Asset or Stock Acquisition Transaction

The procedures for closing an acquisition transaction are usually very similar to those discussed for mergers and share exchanges. The parties in attendance and the documents executed and exchanged will vary depending on the type of transaction.

In an asset purchase transaction, the purchasers and representatives of the selling corporation with authority to sign on behalf of the corporation must be present. In a share purchase, any shareholders selling their stock, who have not presigned the necessary documents, must be in attendance.

Asset Acquisition Closing   Following is a list of some of the documents that might be included in a closing agenda for an asset acquisition:

1. Certified checks, wire transfer documentation, and/or promissory notes representing the consideration being given for the assets.
2. Certified copies of the resolutions of the board of directors and shareholders of the selling corporation approving the transaction.
3. Deeds or other instruments assigning or transferring any real property.
4. Bills of sale or other instruments assigning or transferring any equipment, motor vehicles, or other personal property, including inventory.
5. Assignments or other instruments transferring any patents, trademarks, or copyrights.
6. Assignments or other instruments assigning any loans on the real or personal property being purchased.
7. Documents assigning the name of the corporation, if applicable.
8. Instruments assigning or transferring bank accounts.
9. Legal opinions of attorneys for each party.
10. Notices or filings required by the SEC.
11. Officers' certificates.
12. Assignments of accounts receivable and payable.

Stock Acquisition Closing   Following is a list of some of the types of documents that may be included in the closing agenda for a stock acquisition transaction:

1. Instruments assigning and transferring the appropriate shares of stock of each corporation.
2. New stock certificates representing stock ownership pursuant to the agreement for purchase of shares.
3. Legal opinions of transfer agents.
4. Legal opinions of attorneys for each party.
5. Any required consents or approvals.
6. Notices or filings required by the SEC.
7. Officers' certificates.

The transfer of real and personal property, as well as loans, contracts, and other agreements entered into by the corporation, will depend on the circumstances. In the event of a stock purchase transaction, when the corporation whose shares are being sold will retain its name, it may not be necessary to prepare and execute assignments for all real and personal property, because the *corporation* is the owner and will remain the owner after the sale; only the shareholders have changed. However, the sale of all or substantially all of the stock of a corporation will probably require an assignment of certain assets and liabilities. Bank loans, for instance, may require an assignment, and usually permission, because the ownership of the corporation that has entered into the loan agreement is changing. In any event, the terms of all agreements to which the selling corporation is a party should be reviewed to be sure that all such transfers and assignments are ready for execution prior to closing.

Postclosing Matters

As with the statutory merger or share exchange, there are always several items that require attention after the closing of an asset or stock acquisition transaction. Following is a list of some of the tasks that may need to be completed after the closing of an asset acquisition:

1. Deeds or other instruments assigning or transferring any real property must be filed at the proper county office.
2. Copies of any loan assignments must be sent to any interested third party.
3. If the name of any corporation involved in the transaction must be changed, the proper articles of amendment must be filed.
4. Copies of instruments assigning or transferring bank accounts must be sent to interested third parties.
5. Any reporting requirements of the SEC or state securities authorities must be complied with.

Following is a list of some of the types of documents and tasks that may require attention after the closing of a stock acquisition transaction:

1. New stock certificates must be prepared (if not done at closing).
2. Any reporting requirements of the SEC or state securities authorities must be complied with.
3. Notification to insurance companies of any insurance policies that have been assigned must be completed.

§ 10.5 AMENDMENTS TO ARTICLES OF INCORPORATION

Many of the transactions discussed previously in this chapter require amendments to the articles of incorporation of one or more corporations. Under the MBCA, "A corporation may amend its articles of incorporation at any time to add or change a provision that is required or permitted in the articles of incorporation or to delete a provision not required in the articles of incorporation."[17] Generally, whenever any information contained in a corporation's articles of incorporation changes, the articles must be amended in accordance with the statutes of the corporation's state of domicile.

Approval of the Articles of Amendment

The statutes of the corporation's state of domicile provide the necessary procedures for approving and filing amendments to the articles of incorporation. In general, any amendments that affect the rights or position of the shareholders in any way must be approved by the shareholders.

Amendments Not Requiring Shareholder Approval Although shareholder approval is generally required to amend a corporation's articles of incorporation, the incorporators or board of directors have the authority to amend the articles under certain circumstances. The incorporators or the board of directors of the corporation are usually authorized to amend the articles of incorporation prior to the issuance of shares of stock of the corporation. Under the MBCA, "If a corporation has not yet issued shares, its incorporators or board of directors may adopt one or more amendments to the corporation's articles of incorporation."[18]

The statutes of the state of a corporation's domicile may also expressly provide certain circumstances under which the board of directors may amend the articles of incorporation *after* issuance of the corporation's shares. The type of amendments typically permitted in this manner are routine amendments that will not affect the rights of the shareholders, or amendments required by law, such as the termination of statutory close corporation status if such status is terminated by operation of law.

Amendments Requiring Shareholder Approval For amendments that require shareholder approval, the method of obtaining approval is often very similar to that required for approving a statutory merger or plan of exchange. Under the MBCA, when shareholder approval is required for an amendment to the articles of incorporation, these procedures must be followed:

1. The board of directors must recommend the amendment to the shareholders, unless the board determines that it should make no recommendation and communicates the basis for its determination to the shareholders with the amendment.[19] Reasons for not rendering a recommendation may include a conflict of interest or other special circumstances.[20] The board may condition its submission of the proposed amendment on any basis.[21]

2. Each shareholder, whether or not entitled to vote, must be notified of the shareholder meeting pursuant to statute. The notice must state that the purpose of the meeting is to consider the proposed amendment, and it must contain or be accompanied by a copy or summary of the amendment.[22]

3. Unless the articles of incorporation or the board of directors require a greater vote or a vote by voting groups, the amendment to be adopted must be approved by a majority of the votes entitled to be cast on the amendment by any voting group with respect to which the amendment would create dissenters' rights,

and the votes generally required by statute with regard to every other voting group entitled to vote on the amendment.[23]

The MBCA further sets forth the conditions under which voting on amendments by voting groups is required. Generally, the holders of the outstanding shares of a class are entitled to vote as a separate voting group on a proposed amendment if the rights of that class of shareholder would be affected by the proposed amendment.

Right to Dissent   A shareholder may be entitled to dissent, and obtain payment of the fair value of his or her shares due to, the amendment of the corporation's articles of incorporation. A shareholder is generally entitled to dissent and be paid the fair value of his or her shares if the amendment of the articles of incorporation adversely affects the shareholder's position in the corporation.

Articles of Amendment

The document amending the articles of incorporation is typically called the **articles of amendment** or the *certificate of amendment*. The requirements for the articles of amendment are set by state statute. In general, the amendment must include the information required by statute, and it must be filed in the office where the original articles of incorporation are filed. (See appendix A for a secretary of state directory.) Any state requirements for county filing and publishing articles of incorporation generally apply to amendments of the articles of incorporation as well. Section 10.06 of the MBCA sets forth the requirements for the contents of the articles of amendment:

§ 10.06. ARTICLES OF AMENDMENT

A corporation amending its articles of incorporation shall deliver to the secretary of state for filing articles of amendment setting forth:

  (1) the name of the corporation;
  (2) the text of each amendment adopted;
  (3) if an amendment provides for an exchange, reclassification, or cancellation of issued shares, provisions for implementing the amendment if not contained in the amendment itself;
  (4) the date of each amendment's adoption;
  (5) if an amendment was adopted by the incorporators or board of directors without shareholder action, a statement to that effect and that shareholder action was not required;
  (6) if an amendment was approved by the shareholders;
     (i) the designation, number of outstanding shares, number of votes entitled to be cast by each voting group entitled to vote separately on the amendment, and number of votes of each voting group indisputably represented at the meeting;

◆──

articles of amendment   Document filed with the secretary of state or other appropriate state authority to amend a corporation's articles of incorporation.

(ii) either the total number of votes cast for and against the amendment by each voting group entitled to vote separately on the amendment or the total number of undisputed votes cast for the amendment by each voting group and a statement that the number cast for the amendment by each voting group was sufficient for approval by that voting group.

The secretary of state's office or other appropriate state office should always be contacted to be sure that the proper rules are followed for amending the articles of incorporation. Forms for amending the articles of incorporation are available from the secretary of state's office in most states. Figure 10-11 is an example of a form that may be filed to amend the articles of incorporation in the State of Florida.

**ARTICLES OF AMENDMENT
TO
ARTICLES OF INCORPORATION
OF**

_____

_____
(present name)

Pursuant to the provisions of section 607.1006, Florida Statutes, this Florida profit corporation adopts the following articles of amendment to its articles of incorporation:

FIRST: Amendment(s) adopted: *(indicate article number(s) being amended, added or deleted)*

SECOND: If an amendment provides for an exchange, reclassification or cancellation of issued shares, provisions for implementing the amendment if not contained in the amendment itself, are as follows:

THIRD: The date of each amendment's adoption: _____.

FIGURE 10-11   Articles of Amendment to Articles of Incorporation Form for Florida Corporations

FOURTH: Adoption of Amendment(s) **(Check One)**

☐ The amendment(s) was/were approved by the shareholders. The number of votes cast for the amendment(s) was/were sufficient for approval.

☐ The amendment(s) was/were approved by the shareholders through voting groups. *The following statement must be separately provided for each voting group entitled to vote separately on the amendment(s):*

"The number of votes cast for the amendment(s) was/were sufficient for approval by _____."
                                                    voting group

☐ The amendment(s) was/were adopted by the board of directors without shareholder action and shareholder action was not required.

☐ The amendment(s) was/were adopted by the incorporators without shareholder action and shareholder action was not required.

Signed this _____ day of _____, _____.

Signature   _____
              (By the Chairman or Vice Chairman of the Board of Directors,
              President or other officer if adopted by the shareholders)

OR
(By a director if adopted by the directors)

OR
(By an incorporator if adopted by the incorporators)

_____
Typed or printed name

_____
Title

FIGURE 10-11 (*continued*)

Restated Articles of Incorporation

Most state statutes grant corporations the right to restate their articles of incorporation at any time. If the restated articles contain no amendments that require shareholder approval, shareholder approval is generally not required merely to restate the articles. If any amendments in the restated articles of incorporation do require shareholder approval, the restated articles must be approved by the shareholders in the manner prescribed by law. Restated articles are generally filed in the same manner as articles of amendment.

§ 10.6 REORGANIZATIONS

The term *reorganization* is often used to describe any types of change to the corporate structure, including mergers and acquisitions. Reorganizations often involve financially distressed corporations, as demonstrated by the following commonly used court definition of the term:

> It is not ordinarily the combination of several existing corporations, but is simply the carrying out by proper agreements and legal proceedings of a business plan or scheme for winding up the affairs of, or foreclosing a mortgage or mortgages upon, the property of insolvent corporations, and the organization of a new corporation to take over the property and business of the distressed corporation.[24]

The Internal Revenue Service (IRS) has its own definitions of corporate reorganizations, including statutory mergers and share exchanges, to determine whether a particular reorganization is tax-free.

Type A Transactions

A statutory merger or consolidation is considered by the IRS to be a Type A transaction.

Type B Transactions

The exchange of voting shares between two corporations is considered by the IRS to be a Type B transaction.

Type C Transactions

A Type C reorganization is the acquisition of substantially all of the properties of another corporation in exchange solely for shares of the acquiring corporation.

Type D Transactions

A Type D transaction is a transaction whereby one corporation transfers all or part of its assets to another corporation which it controls.

Type E Transactions

Type E transactions are changes to the capital structure of the corporation that involve amendments to the articles of incorporation. These types of transactions are referred to as *recapitalizations*.

Type F Transactions

Mere change in identity, form, or place of organization of one corporation, however effected, is considered a Type F transaction.

Type G Transactions

A Type G transaction is one in which a transfer is made by a corporation of all or part of its assets to another corporation in a Title 11 (federal Bankruptcy Act) or similar case. This type of transaction only applies if, in pursuance of the plan, stock or securities of the corporation to which the assets are transferred are distributed in a transaction that qualifies under 26 U.S.C. §§ 354, 355, or 356.

§ 10.7 THE PARALEGAL'S ROLE IN MERGERS AND ACQUISITIONS

Paralegals are essential members of most merger and acquisition teams. While the attorneys may be negotiating the details of the merger or acquisition agreement—often until the final documents are signed at the closing table—the paralegals are often responsible for preparing the necessary supplementary documents on behalf of the client, collecting and reviewing the necessary documents from other parties, and preparing for the closing. The paralegal is often instrumental in organizing and conducting the closing of the transaction and in completing the follow-up work after closing. If the paralegal is working on the legal team that represents the seller of assets or shares of stock in a transaction, he or she may directly assist the corporate client at their offices to assemble information required by the buyers.

Paralegals who perform tasks associated with mergers and acquisitions may be asked to:

- Assist in preparation of the letter of intent.
- Assist in preparation of the agreement for merger, share exchange, stock purchase or asset purchase.
- Assist in complying with federal antitrust laws.
- Review the agreement and prepare the closing checklist.
- Assist with the preparation of supplementary documents.
- Collect documents from the client for review by opposing counsel.
- Review documents supplied by the other party.
- Prepare the plan of merger and articles of merger or plan of exchange and articles of exchange.
- Prepare necessary corporate resolutions.
- Prepare articles of amendment to articles of incorporation.
- Prepare consents to assignment of leases and other contracts.
- Prepare new stock certificates.
- Prepare documents transferring assets.
- Assemble all documents for closing.
- Attend the closing.
- Assist with post-closing filings.

Corporate Paralegal Profile
Brian Haberly

I like the excitement of working in a leading-edge technology company with preeminent businesses in four of the hottest areas of the "new economy" (Internet infrastructure, ebusiness, wireless and broadband markets).

Name Brian Haberly

Location Bellevue, Washington

Title Corporate Paralegal and Assistant Corporate Secretary

Specialty Corporate and Securities Law

Education Bachelor of Arts in Earth Science from California State University, Northridge; Paralegal Certificate (Corporate Specialization), magna cum laude, from the University of West Los Angeles

Experience 11 years

Brian Haberly is one of just two paralegals at InfoSpace, a leading global Internet infrastructure services company in Bellevue, Washington. InfoSpace provides commerce, information, and communication infrastructure services to wireless devices, merchants, and more than 3,200 Web pages. Brian reports to the General Counsel of Info-Space, who is also the corporate secretary and senior vice president.

Brian's position often puts him in the middle of merger acquisition activity. InfoSpace is a frequent participant in mergers and acquisitions and may be involved in as many as ten mergers or acquisitions in one year. In 2000, Brian assisted with the $3 billion acquisition of a publicly traded corporation.

In addition to mergers and acquisitions, Brian has numerous responsibilities within the corporate legal department, including corporate formation and maintenance; preparation of board meeting minutes and consent resolutions; foreign qualifications; annual shareholder meeting organization; and compliance with securities laws and regulations including Section 16 filings.

Brian enjoys a lot of responsibility and independence in his position. He has the ability to make a noticeable difference in how the corporation functions by making recommendations and taking action based on experience gained from prior in-house and law firm positions. He also enjoys the chance to work with senior management on a first name basis and the respect he receives from co-workers who appreciate timely responses to requests for information and assistance.

The level of Brian's responsibility and independence also means a certain amount of stress. The short deadlines associated with an Internet company, as well as the constant frenetic pace of ongoing merger and acquisition activity, mean that he is often working long hours.

Brian is also involved in the paralegal profession outside of the office. He is an active member of the Washington State Paralegal Association (WSPA), and co-founder of the East King County Chapter of WSPA. He has served as the East King County Chapter's Steering Committee Chairman and Programs Chairman for three years, and moderated the NFPA Intellectual Property ListServe for two years. He has also served as "mentor" to paralegals in a community college paralegal program on the east coast, via email, for the past two years.

Brian's advice to new paralegals?

If you are still in school, talk to as many practicing paralegals as you can early on to help shape your course of study. Join a local professional association affiliated with NFPA or NALA and attend programs in your area to network and to keep up on trends. Decide if you are more interested in a particular specialty area because it interests you, or are instead seeking the highest paying position, even if that means stretching yourself a bit to get there by a harder or longer path.

Remove the terms "but" and "if only" from your vocabulary. At the end of the day and of your career, don't have any regrets for what you should have/would have/could have done differently. Persevere!

For more information on careers for corporate paralegals, log on to the companion Web page to this text at **www.westlegalstudies.com**.

Letter of Intent

Paralegals may be asked to assist with drafting the letter of intent establishing the parameters of the agreement between the parties, using samples from form books and transactions previously done in the office.

Agreement

Paralegals may assist with preparing the main agreement between the parties. This often involves several drafts of the agreement which may be passed back and forth between counsel and amended several times before signing.

Paralegals are often responsible for reviewing the agreement once it has been signed by the parties, or even reviewing the drafts as they are prepared, to determine what further documents will be required to close the transaction. A thorough review of the agreement should be made and every action that must be taken and every document that must be prepared or produced should be included in a closing checklist. The closing checklist should include all the documents that will be drafted or reviewed prior to or at the closing, along with a reference as to who is responsible for preparing or producing the document. It should also include any actions that must be taken by any party to the agreement prior to closing. Once this checklist has been prepared, copies should be circulated to all parties involved in the transaction or to all parties who are in any way responsible for producing documents or materials prior to or at closing.

Federal Antitrust Law Compliance

Experienced paralegals are often responsible for seeing that the transaction complies with federal antitrust laws. Often, this includes researching the appropriate requirements and filing Hart-Scott-Rodino notification with the Federal Trade Commission.

Supplementary Documents

It is not unusual for a merger or acquisition agreement to require several certifications and warranties by all parties involved. These supplementary documents, which are often drafted by paralegals for attorney approval, may include certifications by the secretaries or other officers of the corporations, and the attorneys for all parties involved. These documents may certify certain facts concerning the corporate existence of the parties, and other warranties and representations. The agreement between the parties may establish exactly what must be included in each supplementary document.

Review and Production of Documents

Between the time of the initial agreement between the parties and the closing of the transaction, numerous documents typically trade hands for review by the other party. Using the closing checklist, paralegals may be responsible for assisting the client to produce the required documents and for obtaining the documents required of the other party. The paralegal is often responsible for ensuring that the documents arrive in time to be reviewed prior to closing, and possibly for summarizing longer documents to save the time of the attorney and client, who will undoubtedly be busy with other aspects of the transaction. Each document that leaves the office should be copied, tracked on the appropriate checklist, and approved by the responsible attorney. Each document that is received in the office should be reviewed, noted on the appropriate checklist, and filed for quick retrieval.

Plan and Articles of Merger or Share Exchange

When the transaction involves a statutory merger or share exchange, the appropriate documents must be drafted for filing with the secretary of state or other appropriate state authority. If the plan of merger or share exchange includes an amendment to the articles of incorporation, that document must be prepared for filing as well. Often, the secretary of state's office supplies forms that may be completed and filed. The paralegal should check with the appropriate state authority to determine the availability of forms, the appropriate filing fee, and filing procedures.

Corporate Resolutions

Paralegals often assist with preparing the corporate resolutions approving the transaction. If a meeting of the shareholders is required, the paralegal may assist with all formalities associated with calling a meeting of the shareholders pursuant to state statute.

Stock and Asset Transfer Documents

If the transaction is to be an asset transfer, separate documents must be prepared transferring all affected assets. Paralegals may assist by preparing bills of sale for all personal property and deeds for all real estate included in the agreement between the parties. Extra documentation may be required to transfer motor vehicles and intangible property.

New stock certificates must be prepared for stock purchase transactions and share exchanges.

Assignments of Contracts

Depending on how the transaction is structured, assignments may be required for all contracts that the acquiring party is assuming. The paralegal may be responsible for drafting such assignments pursuant to the acquisition agreement and the provisions of each contract. The individual contracts must be reviewed to determine if it is necessary to obtain permission or consent for the assignment from other parties to the contract.

Closing

By the closing date, the responsible paralegal should have a closing checklist indicating that all tasks have been completed. All documents should be assembled so that they are readily available. With the multitude of documents often required to close mergers and acquisitions, organization is crucial. Often, documents are arranged by responsible party, or in groups, such as real estate assets, equipment and machinery, etc. Other times, they may be assembled in the order of their reference in the agreement between the parties, so that the agreement can be reviewed and each document executed in order at the closing table. Whatever order is chosen, sufficient copies should be made for each party involved, usually with one or two extra sets. These documents are usually placed in labeled file folders, numbered, and indexed as they are drafted or received at the office. This system also allows for good organization at the closing, when the paralegal may be responsible for seeing that each document is signed by the proper individual or individuals and witnessed and notarized (if necessary), and that each copy is delivered to the appropriate person.

The paralegal may also be responsible for arranging for the physical location of the closing and wire transfers of funds. The paralegal should also take notes at the closing of any tasks that will need to be handled after the closing.

Post Closing

After the closing, the paralegal may be responsible for any loose ends. Typically, documents will need to be filed at state and local levels. The paralegal may also assist with the compilation of copies of all merger and acquisition documents in a bound *closing book*.

Many corporate paralegals work in the mergers and acquisitions area and find it very exciting work. It is also very demanding work that requires exceptional organizational skills, attention to detail, and the ability to work under a certain amount of stress.

§ 10.8 RESOURCES

Resources that paralegals may find particularly useful in the mergers and acquisitions area include state statutes, federal statutes, the office of the secretary of state or other pertinent state office, and forms and form books.

State Statutes

Statutes concerning statutory mergers and acquisitions are typically found within the business corporation act of each state. State statutes of most states include requirements for the plan of merger or plan of share exchange, the articles of merger or articles of share exchange, and obtaining shareholder approval for the transactions. State statutes may also have special provisions for mergers between related corporations, such as the merger of a subsidiary into a parent corporation.

Federal Antitrust Law

Larger transactions will require research of the pertinent federal antitrust laws, especially the provisions of the Hart-Scott-Rodino Act. Following is a list of the primary federal statutes affecting mergers and acquisitions:

> The Clayton Act, 15 U.S.C. § 18.
> The Sherman Act, 15 U.S.C. § 1.
> The Federal Trade Commission Act, 15 U.S.C. § 45.
> The Hart-Scott-Rodino Act, 15 U.S.C. § 18a.

Secretary of State

Most merger and acquisition transactions involve filings at the secretary of state's office or the office of another appropriate state official. The appropriate office should be contacted to ensure that all rules for filing are complied with, and to obtain any forms that are needed. Appendix A to this text is a directory of secretary of state offices.

Forms and Form Books

Mergers and acquisitions tend to be document centered, and forms and form books can be a valuable resource for preparing those documents. State CLE materials may be one good source of forms for state-specific merger and acquisition documents. Other resources include the forms files in your office, and form books such as:

> *American Jurisprudence Legal Forms 2d.*
> *Fletcher Corporation Forms Annotated.*
> *Nichol's Cyclopedia of Legal Forms.*
> *West's Legal Forms.*

Internet Resources

There are an abundance of Web pages that paralegals will find useful when working on mergers and acquisitions. These Web pages include general information on mergers and acquisitions, state and federal laws, forms, and antitrust information.

For state and federal law

American Law Source Online   **www.lawsource.com/also/**

For state statutes

Findlaw.com   **www.findlaw.com/11stategov/**

Legal Information Institute   **www.law.cornell.edu/states/listing.html**

Further information concerning the required filings under the Hart-Scott-Rodino Act and antitrust laws

Federal Trade Commission   **www.ftc.gov**

FindLaw Antitrust and Trade Regulation Web page	www.findlaw.com/01topics/ 01antitrust/index.html
Forms	
FindLaw	forms.lp.findlaw.com/
Find Forms	findforms.com/
Law Guru	www.lawguru.com/lawlinks/Legal_Forms/
For links to the secretary of state offices	
Corporate Housekeeper	www.danvi.vi/link2.html
National Association of Secretaries of State	www.nass.org

An alphabetical list of Internet Resources for the Corporate Paralegal is included as appendix B to this text.

Web Page

For updates and links to several of the previously listed sites, log on to **www. westlegalstudies.com**, and click through to the book link for this text.

SUMMARY

- ◆ The state business corporation act of most states includes provisions for statutory mergers and share exchanges between corporations.

- ◆ A merger is a combination of two or more corporations whereby one of the corporations survives (the surviving corporation), and the other merges into it and ceases to exist (the merging corporation).

- ◆ A triangle merger is a type of merger that uses a subsidiary corporation to acquire a target corporation. The parent corporation funds a subsidiary corporation with cash or shares of stock. The target corporation is then merged into the subsidiary corporation. The parent and subsidiary corporation are both surviving corporations.

- ◆ In a reverse triangle merger, the subsidiary is merged into the target corporation (which then becomes a subsidiary of the parent corporation). The target corporation and parent corporation both survive.

- ◆ In a statutory share exchange, all of the stock of the target corporation is acquired by another corporation, which becomes its parent corporation. The shareholders of the target corporation may receive cash or shares of stock in exchange for their shares.

- ◆ Larger mergers and acquisitions may be subject to federal antitrust laws, including reporting requirements under the Hart-Scott-Rodino Act.

- A plan of merger and articles of merger are executed and filed with the secretary of state or other appropriate state authority to effect a statutory merger.

- A plan of share exchange and articles of share exchange are executed and filed with the secretary of state or other appropriate state authority to effect a statutory share exchange.

- Statutory mergers and statutory share exchanges, as well as the sale of assets or all of the stock of a corporation, require the approval of at least the majority of the shareholders of the corporation.

- Shareholders who object to a corporate merger or acquisition may be eligible to dissent and obtain payment of the fair value of their shares.

- The investigation and examination of documents prior to the closing of a merger or acquisition transaction is referred to as the due diligence process.

- If a corporation is acquired by the purchase of all its outstanding stock, the acquiring corporation typically assumes the obligations and liabilities of the target corporation.

- If a corporation is acquired by the purchase of all of its assets, the acquiring corporation typically does not assume the obligations and liabilities of the target corporation.

- The de facto merger doctrine allows courts to consider a certain transaction with characteristics of a merger to be a merger, regardless of what it is called, to prevent an injustice to third parties.

- When the information that must be included in the corporation's articles of incorporation changes, articles of amendment must usually be filed with the secretary of state or other appropriate state official.

- Under most circumstances, amendments to the articles of incorporation require the consent of shareholders.

REVIEW QUESTIONS

1. What is the difference between a consolidation and a merger?

2. What is the final relationship between two corporations who were parties to a share exchange?

3. What is a "surviving" corporation in a merger transaction?

4. What type of mergers might not require shareholder approval of both parties under certain circumstances?

5. If the sole shareholder of Diane's Auto Parts, Inc., which holds the stock of 95 percent of the D.G. Auto Parts Corporation, decides to merge the two corporations together, with Diane's Auto Parts, Inc. being the surviving corporation, what type of merger would it be? Why are the requirements for shareholder approval different for this type of merger? Why are approval requirements different for upstream mergers?

6. What is a letter of intent?

7. Are there statutory requirements for the contents of an agreement for asset acquisition?

8. What constitutes due diligence work?

9. Suppose that the shareholders of Kate's Household Products, Inc. are interested in acquiring one of their biggest suppliers, Nixon Chemical Corporation, but they are concerned about

past problems that Nixon Chemical has had with toxic waste disposal. What type of acquisition might be the most beneficial to Kate's Household Products, Inc.?

10. What are some possible disadvantages of acquiring an auto dealer, or a corporation that owns several pieces of real estate, through an asset acquisition rather than a stock acquisition transaction?

PRACTICAL PROBLEMS

1. Locate the statute sections in your state that deal with mergers and share exchanges to answer the following questions:
   a. What is the cite for the statute section dealing with corporate mergers in your state?
   b. Do the statutes of your state provide for both statutory mergers and share exchanges? If yes, what is the cite for the statute section dealing with share exchanges in your state?
   c. What information is required for articles of merger (or similarly-named document) in your state?

WORKPLACE SCENARIO

Assume that our fictional clients, Bradley Harris and Cynthia Lund, have decided to merge their business with a competing computer repair business by the name of Kohler's Computer Repair, Inc. Your supervising attorney has asked you to prepare drafts of the merger documents, including a plan of merger and articles of merger. Sandra and Scott Kohler, the shareholders of Kohler's Computer Repair, Inc., will surrender all the shares they hold in Kohler's Computer Repair, Inc. and they will be issued an identical number of shares of Cutting Edge Computer Repair, Inc. Cutting Edge Computer Repair, Inc. will be the surviving corporation. Kohler's Computer Repair, Inc. will be dissolved. Bradley Harris and Cynthia Lund will retain their current offices in Cutting Edge Computer Repair, Inc. Sandra and Scott Kohler will both become vice presidents and directors of the surviving corporation. Using the above information and the information found in appendices D-3 and D-4 to this text, prepare a plan of merger and articles of merger for filing in your home state. Also prepare a cover letter filing the required documents with the appropriate state authority, and enclosing the required filing fee.

END NOTES

1. The Reference Press, *The American Almanac Statistical Abstract of the United States: 1994–1995,* 114th ed. at 855 (Austin, Texas 1994).
2. U.S. Census Bureau, *The Statistical Abstract of the United States (2000)* at 882.
3. Two Tales Can Be Told About the M&A Market in 2000, *Mergerstat Press Release,* **www.mergerstat.com** (December 28, 2000).
4. 1984 Revised Model Business Corporation Act § 11.03(b).
5. *Id.* § 11.03(c).
6. *Id.* § 11.03(d).
7. *Id.* § 11.03(e).
8. *Id.* § 11.03(f)(1).
9. 6B AM. JUR. *Legal Forms* 2d § 74:2692 (1995). Reprinted with permission from *American Jurisprudence Legal Forms 2d.* © 2000 West Group.
10. *Id.* § 74:2796. Reprinted with permission from *American Jurisprudence Legal Forms 2d.* © 2000 West Group.

11. *Id.* § 74:2800. Reprinted with permission from *American Jurisprudence Legal Forms 2d.* © 2000 West Group.

12. 1984 Revised Model Business Corporation Act § 11.03(f)(2).

13. *Id.* § 11.05.

14. 19 AM. JUR. 2d *Corporations* § 2512 (1985).

15. 1984 Revised Model Business Corporation Act § 12.02.

16. 6B AM. JUR. *Legal Forms* 2d (Rev.) § 74:2886 (2000).

17. 1984 Revised Model Business Corporation Act § 10.01.

18. *Id.* § 10.05.

19. *Id.* § 10.03(b)(1).

20. *Id.* § 10.03(b)(1).

21. *Id.* § 10.03(c).

22. *Id.* § 10.03(d).

23. *Id.* § 10.03(e).

24. 19 AM. JUR. 2d *Corporations* § 2514 (1985).

CHAPTER 11

Qualification of a Foreign Corporation

CHAPTER OUTLINE

§ 11.1 Determining When Foreign Corporation Qualification Is Necessary

§ 11.2 Rights, Privileges, and Responsibilities of a Foreign Corporation

§ 11.3 Qualification Requirements

§ 11.4 Amending the Certificate of Authority

§ 11.5 Maintaining the Good Standing of the Foreign Corporation

§ 11.6 Withdrawing from Doing Business as a Foreign Corporation

§ 11.7 Registration of a Corporate Name

§ 11.8 The Paralegal's Role

§ 11.9 Resources

INTRODUCTION

The state or jurisdiction of the corporation's charter or incorporation is considered to be the corporation's state of domicile, regardless of where the company is physically located or transacts the majority of its business. A corporation is considered to be a **foreign corporation** in every state or jurisdiction other than its state of domicile. Foreign corporations must be qualified in every state in which they are considered to be doing business. Corporations are qualified to transact business in a particular state by obtaining permission from the appropriate authority of the foreign state.

This chapter examines the factors to be considered when deciding whether foreign corporation qualification is necessary. Next, it examines the qualification requirements typically imposed by state statutes, followed by a discussion of what is

---

foreign corporation A corporation incorporated in a state or country other than the state referred to. A corporation is considered a foreign corporation in every state other than its state of incorporation.

required to maintain the good standing of a foreign corporation and to withdraw it from doing business in a foreign state. After a brief discussion regarding foreign corporation name registration, this chapter concludes with a look at the paralegal's role in qualifying foreign corporations and the resources available to assist in that area.

§ 11.1 DETERMINING WHEN FOREIGN CORPORATION QUALIFICATION IS NECESSARY

A corporation does not legally exist beyond the boundaries of its state of domicile and must therefore be granted permission, or *qualify*, to do business with the proper authorities of any state, other than its state of domicile, in which it transacts business. When a corporation is formed or when an existing corporation expands, a decision must be made as to where the corporation must qualify to do business as a foreign corporation. An examination of the corporation's business must be made and research must be done on any state in which there is potential for business to be transacted. The following factors must be considered when deciding whether it is necessary to qualify a corporation to do business in a particular foreign state:

1. The extent, duration, and nature of the corporation's involvement in the foreign state.
2. The foreign state's statutory interpretation of what does, or does not, constitute transacting business in that state.
3. The cost of qualification and the penalties for transacting business in the foreign state without authority.

State Long-Arm Statutes and Jurisdiction over Foreign Corporations

Whenever a corporation transacts business in a state other than its state of domicile, it subjects itself to the jurisdiction of the courts of that other state for any causes of action arising from the corporation's activities in that state. State **long-arm statutes** give the courts of each state personal jurisdiction over corporations that voluntarily go into that state for the purpose of transacting business. The defendant corporation need not be physically present in a foreign state for the courts of that state to render a binding judgment against it, but it must have minimum contacts within the state. In many instances courts have required that "to subject a defendant to a judgment in personam, if he be not present within the territory of the forum,

◆―――――――――――――――――――――――――――――――――――――――

long-arm statute A state law that allows the courts of that state to claim jurisdiction over (decide cases directly involving) persons outside the state who have allegedly committed torts or other wrongs inside the state. Even with a long-arm statute, the court will not have jurisdiction unless the person sued has certain minimum contacts with the state.

Dividends ◆

Corporate Service Companies to the Rescue

Even the experienced corporate paralegal can feel lost when dealing with foreign states and countries. Even if you have mastered all the ins and outs of the state requirements for incorporating or qualifying foreign corporations in your state and a few neighboring states, it is virtually impossible to keep track of appropriate fees, forms, and technicalities in every jurisdiction.

Don't give up hope; there's help. Corporate service companies—which can be found throughout the United States—may offer the expertise or service you need for dealing with corporations in foreign states. Many of these are centered in Delaware, although some of the bigger service companies have offices in nearly every state. So, if you work in Texas and need a same-day filing in the Oregon secretary of state's office, a corporate service company may be able to help.

Corporate service companies offer numerous services. Their two major functions are performing corporate filings at the office of the secretary of state and similar offices and acting as registered agent for foreign corporations. For example, if you are in Missouri and have a client who wishes to incorporate in Delaware, the corporate service company can assist you in preparing the required documentation, filing the documentation, and then acting as the registered agent for service of process in the state of Delaware.

Other services offered by corporate service companies include:

- ◆ Preparing and filing incorporation documents.
- ◆ Preparing and filing foreign corporation qualification documents.
- ◆ Filing miscellaneous corporate documents at state and county levels.
- ◆ Performing UCC filings and searches.
- ◆ Searching court records.
- ◆ Performing motor vehicle searches.
- ◆ Performing various real estate searches and filings.

Corporate service companies cannot provide the services listed above without the assistance of corporate paralegals or those who hire them to perform the tasks. If you hire a corporate service company to perform an incorporation in a foreign state, you will still need to provide them with all of the information required for incorporating in that state. What the service company can do for you is to let you know what information is required, to put it into the proper format, and then to file it for you.

You can locate a corporate service company by looking in your telephone directory, scanning advertising in various legal publications, searching the Internet, or by contacting the secretary of state and requesting a list of companies in the area.

---

he have certain minimum contacts with it such that the maintenance of the suit does not offend 'traditional notions of fair play and substantial justice.'"[1] Because corporations are subject to the jurisdiction of the courts in any state in which they transact business, in addition to qualifying or registering to do business as a foreign corporation, they must provide an agent to receive service of process in the foreign state in accordance with the laws of that state.

Statutory Requirements for Qualification of Foreign Corporations

Exactly what does, or does not, constitute transacting business in each state is defined by the state's code or statutes. Typically, the state statutes list a number of activities that do not constitute transacting business, but remain silent on exactly what does constitute transacting business. Most states have adopted a modified version of § 15.01 of the Model Business Corporation Act (MBCA), which reads:

(a) A foreign corporation may not transact business in this state until it obtains a certificate of authority from the secretary of state.

(b) The following activities, among others, do not constitute transacting business within the meaning of subsection (a):

(1) maintaining, defending, or settling any proceeding;

(2) holding meetings of the board of directors or shareholders or carrying on other activities concerning internal corporate affairs;

(3) maintaining bank accounts;

(4) maintaining offices or agencies for the transfer, exchange, and registration of the corporation's own securities or maintaining trustees or depositories with respect to those securities;

(5) selling through independent contractors;

(6) soliciting or obtaining orders, whether by mail or through employees or agents or otherwise, if the orders require acceptance outside this state before they become contracts;

(7) creating or acquiring indebtedness, mortgages, and security interests in real or personal property;

(8) securing or collecting debts or enforcing mortgages and security interests in property securing the debts;

(9) owning, without more, real or personal property;

(10) conducting an isolated transaction that is completed within 30 days and that is not one in the course of repeated transactions of a like nature;

(11) transacting business in interstate commerce.

(c) The list of activities in subsection (b) is not exhaustive.

Although the list set forth in this statute section is helpful, determining whether qualification as a foreign corporation is necessary still is usually a judgment call. One test that may be applied when making the determination is whether the corporation is engaging in regular and continuous business in the foreign state in question.

Consequences of Not Qualifying as a Foreign Corporation

When making a determination as to whether to qualify to do business in a particular state, the consequences of not qualifying must be considered. Penalties for transacting business in a foreign state without first qualifying vary from state to state. One of the most severe consequences is that the corporation usually is prohibited from commencing legal action to enforce contracts in the foreign state in question. This penalty is enforced under state **door-closing statutes**, which provide that a

---

door-closing statute   State statute providing that a corporation doing business in the state without the necessary authority is precluded from maintaining an action in that state.

corporation doing business in the state without the necessary authority is precluded from maintaining an action in that state.

In the two cases that follow in this chapter, both from the state of Michigan, the defendants claimed that the plaintiffs did not have the right to bring suit against them in the state of Michigan because the plaintiffs were foreign corporations conducting business in that state, but not qualified pursuant to state statute.

In *Republic Acceptance Corporation v. Bennett,* the court found that the plaintiff was transacting business in Michigan and was not qualified to do business. The lower court's directed verdict for the defendants was affirmed. In contrast, in *Electric Railway Securities Co. v. Hendricks,* on page 444, the court determined that the plaintiff's presence in that state did not constitute the transaction of business. The Supreme Court of Michigan upheld a decree in favor of the plaintiff.

Foreign corporations that transact business without the proper authority also may be subject to substantial fines. Although it is often unclear whether a corporation is considered to be transacting business in a particular state, when in doubt it is usually in the best interests of the corporation to qualify.

C A S E

Supreme Court of Michigan.

REPUBLIC ACCEPTANCE CORPORATION
v.
BENNETT et al.

No. 28.
Oct. 2, 1922.
220 Mich. 249, 189 N.W. 901

SHARPE, J.

The plaintiff, a foreign corporation, with its home office at Pittsburgh, Pa., as successor to the Republic Mortgage Company, brings this suit to recover on three contracts of guaranty of certain securities executed by defendants. The defense raised was that the failure of the mortgage company, hereafter spoken of as the plaintiff, to comply with the statutes of this state requiring such corporations to take out a state license, pay a franchise fee, etc., barred its recovery. The trial judge so found, and directed a verdict for defendants.

There is little dispute about the facts. The business conducted by plaintiff at Pittsburgh was that of purchasing or discounting securities obtained on the sale of motor vehicles. It desired to enter the Detroit field. It was apparent that in order to

secure any considerable amount of business it must have a local representative. It sent one William Lininger to Detroit to investigate.

On his reporting that 'there was an excellent field in Detroit to do business' it instructed him by long distance telephone to make arrangements for the rental of offices. He secured rooms in the Free Press Building, and forwarded a lease of same to the Pittsburgh office for approval. It was approved. Plaintiff forwarded the office furniture, and caused its name to be lettered on the door with the name of Mr. Lininger as manager below it. It paid at least a part of the office expenses. The contract of employment with Lininger was in the form of a proposal to him by letter accepted in writing by him. The first paragraph reads:

'It is hereby agreed and understood that you are to come into the Republic Mortgage organization as manager of the Detroit office....'

He prepared circular letters, which he sent to the trade, and advertisements for insertion in the city papers, which were approved by plaintiff. Bulletins sent from Pittsburgh were transcribed by him and mailed to local dealers. ...

The negotiations with defendants and others from whom securities were purchased were conducted by Lininger as agent or manager for plaintiff. A representative of the company from Pittsburgh rendered him some assistance. The blank forms of conditional sales agreements, assignments, and guaranties were prepared by plaintiff and sent to Lininger for distribution among the dealers. When filled out and executed they were delivered to Lininger, who recorded them with the city clerk and sent them to the office at Pittsburgh for approval. On approval, checks were mailed to him for delivery to the persons from whom the securities were purchased. ...

Act 310 of the Public Acts of 1907 (2 Comp. Laws 1915, §§ 9063–9072) requires foreign corporations engaging in business in this state to comply with the provisions thereof. The pertinent sections of the act follow:

'(9063) Section 1. It shall be unlawful for any corporation organized under the laws of any state of the United States, except the state of Michigan, or of any foreign country, to carry on its business in this state, until it shall have procured from the secretary of state of this state a certificate of authority for that purpose. * * *

'(9067) Sec. 5. * * * Every corporation subject to the provisions of this act, which shall neglect or fail to comply with its requirements, shall be subject to a penalty of not less than one hundred dollars nor more than one thousand dollars for every month that it continues to transact business in Michigan, without complying with the requirements of this act. * * *

'(9068) Sec. 6. No foreign corporation, subject to the provisions of this act, shall be capable of making a valid contract in this state until it shall have fully complied with the requirements of this act, and at the time holds an unrevoked certificate to that effect from the secretary of state.'

Section 7 (9069) prescribes a penalty for any one acting as agent for a foreign corporation not authorized to do business under the act.

The errors assigned present the following questions: (1) Was plaintiff carrying on its business in this state? (2) Was the transaction one of interstate commerce? (3) Is the statute applicable to the contract sued on?

1. Under any reasonable interpretation of the language of the statute plaintiff was carrying on its business in this state. It established and maintained a branch office in Detroit; employed a manager to take charge thereof; through him and others sent to assist him solicited and obtained a large amount of business; furnished the blanks on which securities and assignments were written; secured investigation of the financial standing of customers; recorded the securities purchased; made payments of the consideration—in fact, transacted all the business with the persons from whom it purchased securities in such branch office.

In 14a C. J. 1270, it is said:

'The general rule is that when a foreign corporation transacts some substantial part of its ordinary business in a state, it is doing, transacting, carrying on or engaging in business therein, within the meaning of the statutes under consideration.'

The following from *Vaughn Machine Co. v. Lighthouse*, 64 App. Div. 142, 71 N.Y. Supp. 801, was quoted approvingly in *Neyens, v. Worthington*, 150 Mich. 580, 588, 114 N. W. 404, 18 L. R. A. (N. S.) 142:

'The crucial test in doing business within the meaning of this statute is not an isolated transaction within the state or the transshipment of goods from the home office, pursuant to orders taken by drummers within the state, but it is the establishment of an agency or branch office within our state limits.' ...

2. We do not think the transaction was one in interstate commerce. The purpose of the plaintiff was to establish a branch office in Detroit in which its Michigan business should be transacted. The defendants and other Michigan customers had nothing to do with the officials of the home office. Their dealings were with the Detroit manager. ...

3. Counsel for plaintiff contend that the contract sued upon was not made in Michigan, and therefore not subject to the provision of section 9068, which applies only to contracts 'made in this state.' As before stated, all the negotiations leading up to the purchase of the securities by the plaintiff

were conducted in Detroit. The assignments and guaranties were executed there, and delivered to plaintiff's manager. He sent them to Pittsburgh for approval, and after such approval the transaction, which theretofore had been but a proposal on the part of the defendants, became a binding contract by the delivery of plaintiff's check to the defendants at Detroit in payment of the consideration therefor. The contract clearly was one made in this state and subject to the applicable provisions of the statute.

The views we have expressed render it unnecessary to consider the other interesting questions discussed by counsel.

The judgment is affirmed.

CASE

Supreme Court of Michigan.

ELECTRIC RAILWAY SECURITIES CO.
v.
HENDRICKS et al.

No. 37.
Oct. 3, 1930.
251 Mich. 602, 232 N.W. 367

WIEST, C. J.

The bill herein was filed, in the Kent circuit, in January, 1928, to foreclose a purchase-money mortgage of $165,000, upon property in the city of Grand Rapids. The mortgagors appeared, raised no issue of amount due, but interposed the defense that plaintiff, a foreign corporation, not admitted to carry on business in this state, was carrying on business here in holding title to real property and in selling and conveying the same to defendants and taking the mortgage in suit, and therefore could not bring suit and have decree of foreclosure. From time to time the hearing was postponed, but finally set for a day certain. Plaintiff subpoenaed the defendant Augustin Hendricks, and he was in court on the day set. The attorneys for defendants did not appear when the case was taken up, neither did they send any excuse nor ask for delay. The court heard the testimony offered by plaintiff, asked Mr. Hendricks if he wished to examine the one witness called and was informed by him, 'I have nothing to examine.' Within a few minutes after the decree was granted one of the attorneys for defendants appeared, claimed he had been delayed by attendance upon the probate court, and that his partner had been called out of the city, and later defendants' attorneys opposed signing of the decree, then moved for a rehearing, and, upon denial thereof, defendants appealed.

Upon the argument of the case in this court counsel were asked to point out the claimed acts of business carried on by plaintiff and were requested to brief the legal question involved. If the claimed defense, as presented to the circuit judge, has no merit, there should be no rehearing or further delay. Have defendants shown a defense calling for a rehearing?

The General Corporation Act, 1922 Supp. Comp. Laws 1915, § 9053(164), provides:

'It shall be unlawful for any corporation organized under the laws of any state, district or territory of the United States, except the state of Michigan, or of any foreign country, to carry on its business in this state, until it shall have procured from the Secretary of State of this state a certificate of authority for that purpose.'

Plaintiff acquired title to the property here involved and to a parcel of real estate in another county.

The language of our statute is not to be construed as prohibitive of transacting any business in the state, but only in its true restrictive sense of forbidding the carrying on of the business of the corporation in this state. The record, so far as competent for our consideration in review of the action of the circuit judge, fails to show transactions of a character indicative of a purpose by plaintiff to carry on its business in this state. It is true that a single transaction may disclose the purpose of a corporation to carry on its business in the state, but such a transaction must be something more than an independent or isolated transaction, not necessarily of a character to indicate a purpose to engage in the carrying on of the corporate business in the state. ...

In order for defendants to have a rehearing it was necessary for them to show affirmatively that, in acquiring, managing as owner, conveying, and taking a purchase-money mortgage, plaintiff was carrying on its business in this state. This defendants failed to do, for the showing made falls short of any degree of certitude, and a rehearing would but afford defendants an opportunity to make proof, if they can, bringing plaintiff within the statute.

We do not agree with counsel for defendants that 'what this court will determine now is whether there is a fair probability, when all of the testimony is in, that it will support an adjudication by the courts that the plaintiff was doing business within the state of Michigan.'

We cannot grant a rehearing until satisfied that defendants have a defense upon the merits.

Defendants alleged in their answer to the bill that plaintiff is a corporation, organized under the laws of the state of Maine, with authority to purchase and convey real estate, if not prohibited by law. There is no statute prohibiting a foreign corporation from merely acquiring, holding, and disposing of real property in this state and exercising the ordinary incidents of ownership. Some states, by statute, prohibit such acquisition of real property without admission to the state. In the absence of a statute prohibiting a foreign corporation from acquiring, holding, or disposing of real property in this state, without admission, such a corporation may acquire, hold, and dispose of real property in this state under the rule of comity. ...The true test is not whether a foreign corporation has acquired real property in this state,

for such has been permitted since *Thompson v. Waters*, 25 Mich. 214, 12 Am. ... but the test is whether in so doing the corporation was carrying on its business in this state.

As stated in Thompson on Corporations (3d Ed.) § 6640:

'Express statutory provision is not necessary to give a foreign corporation the right to acquire and hold real estate. The law of comity gives a foreign corporation the power to purchase or otherwise acquire and hold real property in states other than that of its creation, provided its charter and the laws of the state of its domicile give it such right, and there is no statute prohibiting it from so doing, and this, though it has failed to comply with statutory provisions required by the state as a condition precedent to doing business therein.'

In *Penn Colleries Co. v. McKeever*, 183 N. Y. 98, 75 N. E. 935, it was said (syllabus):

'The phrase 'doing business in this state,' contained in section 15 of the General Corporation Law (L. 1892, ch. 687, as amd.), which requires a foreign corporation to procure a certificate of authority to transact business in this state from the secretary of state, implies corporate continuity of conduct in that respect; such as might be evidenced by the investment of capital here, with the maintenance of an office for the transaction of its business and those incidental circumstances which attest the corporate intent to avail itself of the privilege of carrying on business.'...

Beyond the usual incidents of ordinary ownership of real property we have but the fact that plaintiff is a foreign corporation, privileged to acquire and dispose of real property in this state, but not to carry on its business here.

The decree in the circuit court is affirmed, with costs to plaintiff.

BUTZEL, CLARK, McCONALD, POTTER, NORTH, and FEAD, JJ., concur.

Following is Minnesota Statutes Ann. § 303.20, which provides the consequences of transacting business in the state of Minnesota without a certificate of authority. Many states have similar statutes.

§ 303.20 FOREIGN CORPORATION MAY NOT MAINTAIN ACTION UNLESS LICENSED

No foreign corporation transacting business in this state without a certificate of authority shall be permitted to maintain an action in any court in this state until such corporation shall have obtained a certificate of authority; nor shall an action be maintained in any court by any successor or assignee of such corporation on any right, claim, or demand arising out of the transaction of business by such corporation in this state until a certificate of authority to transact business in this state shall have been obtained by such corporation or by a corporation which has acquired all, or substantially all, of its assets. If such assignee shall be a purchaser without actual notice of such violation by the corporation, recovery may be had to an amount not greater than the purchase price. This section shall not be construed to alter the rules applicable to a holder in due course of a negotiable instrument.

The failure of a foreign corporation to obtain a certificate of authority to transact business in this state does not impair the validity of any contract or act of such corporation, and shall not prevent such corporation from defending any action in any court of this state.

Any foreign corporation which transacts business in this state without a certificate of authority shall forfeit and pay to this state a penalty, not exceeding $1,000, and an additional penalty, not exceeding $100, for each month or fraction thereof during which it shall continue to transact business in this state without a certificate of authority therefor. Such penalties may be recovered in the district court of any county in which such foreign corporation has done business or has property or has a place of business, by an action, in the name of the state, brought by the attorney general.

§ 11.2 RIGHTS, PRIVILEGES, AND RESPONSIBILITIES OF A FOREIGN CORPORATION

Except where otherwise specified by state statute, qualified foreign corporations have the same, but no greater, rights and privileges as domestic corporations. As a general rule, a qualified foreign corporation may transact all of the business conferred by its own charter and the laws of its state of domicile, unless those laws are in conflict with the laws of the foreign state. The foreign corporation also is subject to many of the same duties and restrictions applicable to domestic corporations in the foreign state. However, most state statutes provide that the laws of the state of domicile shall govern over all matters concerning the internal affairs of the corporation.

§ 11.3 QUALIFICATION REQUIREMENTS

Although the requirements for qualifying to do business vary from state to state, in general, the corporation must obtain a **certificate of authority** or similar document from the proper state authority before it begins transacting business in that state. For ease of explanation, we refer to the certificate of authority and all similar documents, whatever they are called, as the "certificate of authority" throughout the rest of this chapter. Usually the secretary of state's corporate division has jurisdiction over all foreign corporations doing business in the state. However, in some states the agency with jurisdiction is the Corporation Commission or a similar agency. For ease in explanation, we refer to the state agency with jurisdiction over foreign corporations as the "secretary of state" throughout the rest of this chapter.

Qualification requirements are usually the same for all types of corporations, including not-for-profit corporations and professional corporations. However, some of the fees and forms required by the secretary of state may vary for these different types of corporations. The foreign state's statutes and the appropriate secretary of state must be consulted to make sure that all requirements are met for these special types of corporations. The statutes of many states also provide qualification requirements for limited liability companies, limited partnerships, and other types of business organizations.

Application for Certificate of Authority

The certificate of authority is obtained by filing an application, along with any other required documents, with the secretary of state in the foreign state. Many states require that the application be made on a form prescribed by their offices. It is important to consult the secretary of state of the foreign state and the foreign state's statutes or code to be sure that all application requirements have been complied with. Most states have adopted a version of § 15.03 of the MBCA, which sets forth the requirements for the application for certificate of authority:

§ 15.03. APPLICATION FOR CERTIFICATE OF AUTHORITY

(a) A foreign corporation may apply for a certificate of authority to transact business in this state by delivering an application to the secretary of state for filing. The application must set forth:

 (1) The name of the foreign corporation or, if its name is unavailable for use in this state, a corporate name that satisfies the requirements of section 15.06;

 (2) the name of the state or country under whose law it is incorporated;

 (3) its date of incorporation and period of duration;

 (4) the street address of its principal office;

---

certificate of authority   Certificate issued by secretary of state or similar state authority granting a foreign corporation the right to transact business in that state.

(5) the address of its registered office in this state and the name of its registered agent at that office; and

(6) the name and usual business addresses of its current directors and officers.

(b) The foreign corporation shall deliver with the completed application a certificate of existence (or a document of similar import) duly authenticated by the secretary of state or other official having custody of corporate records in the state or country under whose law it is incorporated.

Figure 11-1 is a sample of an application for certificate of authority form that may be used in states following the MBCA.

The application often must be accompanied by a *certificate of existence* or **certificate of good standing** from the state of domicile and a filing fee. Some states require that the application be recorded at the county level in the foreign state, and some states require publication of the application or a notice of the application in a legal newspaper in the county where the registered office is located within the foreign state.

A thorough review of the pertinent state statutes, as well as any information available from the secretary of state, must be made to ensure that all application procedures are properly followed.

Foreign Name Requirements

Each state has its own requirements that must be met with respect to the names of foreign corporations. These name requirements can be found in the state statutes, or they may be obtained by contacting the secretary of state of the foreign state. In general, most states require that the corporate name be available and that the corporate name meet the same requirements set for the names of domestic corporations in that state.

Mandatory Inclusions   Corporate names must clearly indicate that the corporation is a corporate entity, not an individual or partnership. State statutes typically require that the names of foreign corporations include one of the following words or abbreviations:

Corporation	Corp.
Limited	Ltd.
Incorporated	Inc.
Company	Co.

If the name of the corporation does not include a word or abbreviation that is required by the foreign state's statutes, the secretary of state will usually allow the

---

certificate of good standing   Sometimes referred to as a certificate of existence. Certificate issued by the secretary of state or other appropriate state authority proving the incorporation and good standing of the corporation in that state.

APPLICATION FOR CERTIFICATE OF
AUTHORITY OF

_____

The undersigned corporation hereby makes application for a Certificate of Authority to Transact Business in the State of _____, pursuant to the provisions of § _____ of the _____ Business Corporation Act.

1. The name of the corporation is: _____.

2. The name that the corporation desires to use in your state, if its name is unavailable for use in this state, is _____.

3. This corporation is incorporated under the laws of the state of _____, and is currently in good standing, as evidenced by the attached Certificate of Good Standing.

4. The corporation was incorporated on _____, _____, and its period of duration is _____.

5. The street address of the corporation's principal office is _____.

6. The address of the corporation's registered office in this state and the name of its registered agent at that office are _____.

7. The names and usual business addresses of the corporation's current directors and officers are as follows:

Name	Title	Address
_____	_____	_____
_____	_____	_____
_____	_____	_____
_____	_____	_____

Dated this _____ day of _____, _____.

By _____

Its _____

FIGURE 11-1 Sample Application for Certificate of Authority

corporation to add one of the required words or abbreviations to its name for use in the foreign state in order to comply with this requirement.

Name Availability   Each state requires that the name of the foreign corporation be available for use in the foreign state. For example, if AB Johnson Corporation, a Minnesota corporation, decides to do business in Wisconsin, it must first make sure that its name is not already in use in Wisconsin and that no deceptively similar name is in use. If there is already a Wisconsin corporation by the name of AB Johnson Corporation, or even AB Johnson Company, there is a conflict.

Several different ways are prescribed by law to get around this problem. Many states allow the addition of a distinguishing word or words to the name of the foreign corporation for use in the foreign state. Following the preceding example, AB Johnson Corporation, the Minnesota corporation, might be able to qualify to do business in Wisconsin under the name of "AB Johnson of Minnesota, Inc." or a similar name. In such an event, the foreign corporation must use this full name designation for all of its transactions within the foreign state.

Another common solution to the problem of an unavailable name is to obtain permission to use the name from the corporation or entity with a similar name. Most states that allow this option also require that the established corporation or entity change its name to a distinguishable name. This is sometimes possible if the existing corporation with the conflicting name is dormant or if the holders of the name wish to sell their right to use the name.

Finally, many states allow foreign corporations to adopt an available fictitious name for use in their state if the company's name is unavailable. A fictitious name is simply a different name that the foreign corporation uses for all its business transactions within the foreign state. Often, it is a name similar to its own name, but distinguishable from the conflicting name of the established corporation or entity.

The state's statutes or code should be consulted for further details of the options available in each foreign state. Most states provide a service that allows you to check name availability over the telephone or via the Internet. This is a preliminary check and does not guarantee that the name will be available when the application for certificate of authority is filed. (See appendix A for a secretary of state directory.)

Corporate Name Reservation Often, the only way to assure that a name will be available before submitting an application for certificate of authority is to reserve the name with the secretary of state of the foreign state. Most state statutes provide that an available name may be reserved for a period of up to 120 days, at a minimal cost. This is usually done by submitting the appropriate name reservation form to the secretary of state with the correct filing fee. Some states will accept a letter requesting the reservation, and a few will reserve an available name over the telephone or via the Internet.

Registered Agent and Registered Office

Foreign corporations must appoint and maintain a registered agent and registered office in each state in which they are qualified to do business. The registered office must be an actual physical location in the foreign state where service of process may be made personally on an individual who is authorized to accept service on behalf of the corporation. In most states, the registered agent must be a resident of the foreign state, a domestic corporation, or qualified foreign corporation. The registered agent must be appointed by the foreign corporation to receive service of process on behalf of the corporation. In many instances the state statutes provide that if no registered agent is appointed and serving, the secretary of state of the foreign state is authorized to accept service on behalf of the foreign corporation. Thus, a foreign corporation often has an officer or employee in each foreign state who acts as the registered agent for that state. Other times, a professional registered agent is appointed. There are corporation service companies that will act as a registered agent for foreign corporations in each foreign state. These services can be appointed, for a fee, to provide a registered office address and an agent to accept service for corporations in each state.

§ 11.4 AMENDING THE CERTIFICATE OF AUTHORITY

Although each state's statutes define when it is necessary to amend the certificate of authority, typically whenever any significant information that was included in the original certificate changes, an application for amended certificate of authority must be completed and filed. The same filing requirements that cover the application for certificate of authority in each state are generally applied to any amendments. The MBCA provides that whenever the authorized foreign corporation changes its corporate name, the period of its duration, or the state or country of its incorporation, an application for amended certificate of authority must be filed.[2]

Whenever any change in information concerning service of the foreign corporation in the foreign state occurs, such as a change in the registered agent or office in the state, the secretary of state must be notified immediately, either by an amended application for certificate of authority, or by other means prescribed by the foreign state's statutes. Again, a thorough review of the state statutes or code of the foreign state must be made to be sure that all requirements are met.

Figure 11-2 on page 452 is a sample of a form that may be used to amend the certificate of authority for a foreign corporation in the state of Missouri.

§ 11.5 MAINTAINING THE GOOD STANDING OF THE FOREIGN CORPORATION

A corporation may continue to transact business as a foreign corporation as long as it continues to meet the requirements of the foreign state, including timely filing of any required reports and the payment of all required fees and taxes. Most states require annual reports from every domestic and qualified foreign corporation. This is usually done on forms generated by the office of the secretary of state and sent to the principal office or registered office of the corporation, to be completed and returned within a prescribed time period. Many states require that the reports be filed with an annual fee, either a flat fee or a fee based upon the amount of business transacted within the foreign state.

Although these forms are generated by the secretary of state, it is the responsibility of the corporation to be aware of the annual reporting requirements in each state in which it transacts business and to see that the reports are filed in a timely manner. The secretary of state must be contacted immediately if the corporation does not receive an annual report form to be completed when prescribed by law.

State of Missouri
Matt Blunt, Secretary of State

Corporations Division
P.O. Box 778, Jefferson City, MO 65102

James C. Kirkpatrick State Information Center
600 W. Main Street, Rm 322, Jefferson City, MO 65101

Application for an Amended Certificate of
Authority for a Foreign Corporation
(Submit in duplicate with filing fee of $25.00)

The below corporation, relating to amending its certificate of authority of Foreign Corporation, does hereby state:

(1)   Its name is: _____

and is incorporated in the State of: _____; and it

was qualified in the State of Missouri on _____.
(month/day/year)

(2)   By appropriate corporate action on: _____, the corporation:
(month/day/year)

    (1)   Changed its corporate name to: _____

        Name it will use in Missouri if new name not available: _____

    (2)   Changed its period of duration to: _____

    (3)   Changed the state or country of its incorporation to: _____

(3)   There is attached hereto a Certificate of the Secretary of State of the State of_____
relating to the amendment(s), set forth in item 2 above and showing that the Corporation is in existence and in
good standing in said State.

(4)   The effective date of this document is the date it is filed by the Secretary of State of Missouri, unless you indicate

a future date, as follows: _____
(Date may not be more than 90 days after the filing date in this office)

In affirmation thereof, the facts stated above are true.

_____   _____   _____   _____
(Authorized Signature)   (Printed Name)   (Title)   (month/day/year)

Attached is an original current certificate attesting to the change, duly authenticated by the secretary of state or
other official having custody of corporate records in the state or country of incorporation.

Corp. #43 (11/00)

FIGURE 11-2   Application for an Amended Certificate of Authority for a Foreign Corporation
from the State of Missouri

Failure to file an annual report may have severe consequences, such as an additional fee or a fine, and even loss of good standing in the state.

Often, any state taxes that are payable by the qualified foreign corporation are included in the fee paid to the secretary of state. In some instances, however, a separate tax report may be required by a separate tax authority within the foreign state. Again, it is the responsibility of the corporation to see that all necessary tax reporting is completed in a timely manner.

§ 11.6 WITHDRAWING FROM DOING BUSINESS AS A FOREIGN CORPORATION

When a corporation dissolves or ceases to do business in any state in which it is qualified, and there are no plans to recommence business in that state in the near future, it is beneficial for the corporation to withdraw from doing business so that the corporation no longer will be subject to annual reporting, registered office, registered agent, and taxation requirements in the foreign state. The procedures for withdrawing from doing business as a foreign corporation are set by state statute and generally involve obtaining a certificate of withdrawal from the secretary of state of the foreign state. Under the MBCA, the qualified foreign corporation may not withdraw from the foreign state until it obtains a certificate of withdrawal from that secretary of state.

The certificate of withdrawal is obtained by filing an application for withdrawal with the secretary of state. MBCA § 15.20(b) sets forth the requirements for the application for withdrawal:

> (b) A foreign corporation authorized to transact business in this state may apply for a certificate of withdrawal by delivering an application to the secretary of state for filing. The application must set forth:
> (1) the name of the foreign corporation and the name of the state or country under whose law it is incorporated;
> (2) that it is not transacting business in this state and that it surrenders its authority to transact business in this state;
> (3) that it revokes the authority of its registered agent to accept service on its behalf and appoints the secretary of state as its agent for service of process in any proceeding based on a cause of action arising during the time it was authorized to transact business in this state;
> (4) a mailing address to which the secretary of state may mail a copy of any process served on him under subdivision (3); and
> (5) a commitment to notify the secretary of state in the future of any change in its mailing address.

Most states provide a form to be completed and filed with the secretary of state. Others prescribe instructions in the state statutes that must be followed. It is important to familiarize yourself with the state statutes on withdrawing from doing business in the state you are concerned with and to be certain all requirements, such as county recording and publication, are complied with.

Figure 11-3 is a sample of a form that may be used in the state of Michigan to apply for a certificate of withdrawal.

BCS/CD-561 (Rev. 07/01)

MICHIGAN DEPARTMENT OF CONSUMER & INDUSTRY SERVICES
BUREAU OF COMMERCIAL SERVICES

Date Received	(FOR BUREAU USE ONLY)
	This document is effective on the date filed, unless a subsequent effective date within 90 days after received date is stated in the document.

Name

Address

City   State   Zip Code

EFFECTIVE DATE:

↞ **Document will be returned to the name and address you enter above.** ↠
If left blank document will be mailed to the registered office.

APPLICATION FOR CERTIFICATE OF WITHDRAWAL
For use by Foreign Corporations
(Please read information and instructions on reverse side)

Pursuant to the provisions of Act 284, Public Acts of 1972 (profit corporations), or Act 162, Public Acts of 1982 (nonprofit corporations), the undersigned corporation executes the following Application:

1. The name of the corporation is:

   _____

2. The identification number assigned by the Bureau is: [   ]

3. It is incorporated under the laws of_____

4. The corporation is not transacting business or conducting affairs in Michigan.

5. The corporation hereby surrenders its authority to transact business or conduct affairs in Michigan.

Signed this _____ day of _____ , _____

By_____
              (Signature of authorized officer or agent)

_____
              (Type or Print Name)

FIGURE 11-3 Application for Certificate of Withdrawal for Use by Foreign Corporations for the State of Michigan

§ 11.7 REGISTRATION OF A CORPORATE NAME

Several states provide that a foreign corporation that is not doing business in the state may register its name with the state, in lieu of qualifying to do business. This is very useful to corporations that may commence doing business in a particular state at some time in the future, and would like to reserve their names for an extended period of time. It is also useful to corporations that want to use their names in a state but are not considered to be transacting business in that state under the statutes of that state.

The name to be registered must be available for use in that foreign state and, in most instances, must comply with the requirements for names of foreign corporations who are applying for a certificate of authority. The name of the foreign corporation typically is registered for renewable one-year periods.

§ 11.8 THE PARALEGAL'S ROLE

The role of the paralegal in working with foreign corporations must be defined by the paralegal, the responsible attorney, and the client. In general, with the exception of providing the client with legal advice, the paralegal can perform almost all the services required to qualify a foreign corporation, see that it remains in good standing, or withdraw the foreign corporation from doing business in the foreign state. In some instances, the paralegal will work closely with the corporate secretary to assist in complying with the necessary requirements imposed on foreign corporations. In other instances, the corporate secretary may not be so closely involved, and the paralegal and responsible attorney will see to these matters, while keeping the corporate client informed.

Corporate Paralegal Profile
Edward Galante

I enjoy the flexibility of working for the legal department of a company rather than a law firm. I can work on more advanced projects as long as I can complete them timely and accurately.

Name Edward Galante

Location Brighton, Massachusetts

Title Corporate Paralegal

Specialty International Corporate Transactions

Education Bachelor of Arts Degree in Political Science from Framingham State College; Masters of Public Administration, Suffolk University Sawyer School of Management; Second year law

student in the evening division of Suffolk University School of Law

Experience 7 years

Ed Galante is one of four paralegals who work in the legal department of Thermo Electron Corporation, a large, multinational Fortune 500 company based in Waltham, Massachusetts. Thermo Electron is a global technology company that provides scientific instruments and related components and systems. Ed reports to the deputy general counsel of Thermo Electron, one of twelve attorneys employed by the company.

Ed's work involves a lot of variety. He is responsible for filing foreign corporation qualifications and researching state and foreign country statutes. He also handles routine maintenance of the companies' corporate records and has responsibility for forming, dissolving, and merging corporations and other legal entities.

In addition, Ed is often involved in several aspects of major sales and acquisition transactions, including due diligence on the companies involved. Ed assists in reviewing and drafting complex agreements; researching domestic and international statutes, including antitrust regulations which could effect the transaction; and he acts as a liaison between the attorneys in the legal department and their foreign counsel on international transactions.

Ed enjoys the flexibility of working for the legal department of a company rather than a law firm. It allows him to work on more advanced projects as long as they are completed timely and accurately. He also appreciates that he has no billable requirements to meet and no direct accountability to clients. This allows him to spend more time concentrating on his work, without the worries of billing too much or too little toward the assignments.

Ed notes that one of the drawbacks of a corporate legal department is the level of office support and the amount of administrative responsibilities that are routinely assigned to the paralegals. The paralegals in his legal department don't have the benefit of office assistants to help with the organization of files, preparation of closing binders, and other administrative tasks. They also don't have an evening secretarial staff to handle the overflow of the day's administrative work. As a result, he has to incorporate additional time into his daily agenda to handle more administrative issues than he would if working for a law firm.

In addition to his responsibilities during the day, Ed attends classes in the evening. He is in his second year of law school at Suffolk University School of Law. He is also co-chairperson of the Corporate Law Practice of the Massachusetts Paralegal Association, Inc. and a member of the National Federation of Paralegal Associations, Inc. In 1999, Ed was a panelist at the Massachusetts Continuing Legal Education, Inc. seminar "Corporate Due Diligence—for Paralegals", and in 2000, he was chair and panelist on the Massachusetts Continuing Legal Education, Inc. seminar "Perfecting a Security Interest in Collateral—for Paralegals".

Ed's advice to new paralegals?

The best advice I can give to paralegal students is to build up experience within the field. Accept a position as a temporary paralegal or a legal intern, put in additional time and attempt to become familiar with the work. Paralegals become more marketable if they can show that they have actually performed the work and been involved in transactions. In addition, it's a great way to network with attorneys and senior paralegals who have connections with other firms and companies, and who will be willing to write recommendations on your behalf. From my experience, after gaining a few years of experience in the field, you will become extremely marketable and have more flexibility when choosing the type of professional setting in which you work (such as a law firm, company, or governmental agency.)

For more information on careers for corporate paralegals, log on to the companion Web page to this text at **www.westlegalstudies.com.**

More specifically, in the qualification process, the paralegal can locate the pertinent state statutes and any other available information to help the attorney and client make a decision on the necessity of qualifying as a foreign corporation. From there, the paralegal can obtain the necessary paperwork from the secretary of state and assist the client with the completing and filing of these documents. The paralegal should also check to see that any county recording, publishing, and other detail requirements are complied with. Following is a checklist to assist the paralegals with the foreign corporation qualification process.

FOREIGN CORPORATION QUALIFICATION CHECKLIST

☐ Locate and review copy of pertinent state statutes relating to the necessity of qualifying as a foreign corporation to determine if qualification is required.

☐ Review statutes relevant to qualification requirements in foreign state, including any publication requirements, county recording requirements, or other requirements unique to that foreign state.

☐ Contact secretary of state of foreign state to check name availability in foreign state and request all forms necessary for qualifying as a foreign corporation, including application for corporate name reservation, when appropriate, and application for certificate of authority. Also request up-to-date fee schedule and any printed information and instructions for qualifying as a foreign corporation in that state.

☐ Contact tax authority of foreign state, if separate from secretary of state, to request information on taxation of foreign corporations.

☐ Resolve any name conflicts, if applicable.

☐ Decide on registered agent and registered office and contact corporation service company, if necessary.

☐ When information and forms are received from secretary of state of foreign state, complete necessary forms and send to client for review and signature.

☐ Obtain certificate of good standing or certificate of existence and certified copy of articles or certificate of incorporation, when necessary, from secretary of state of state of domicile.

☐ Submit application for certificate of authority to proper state authority, along with any of the following that may be required:

— Any additional copies of the certificate of authority that may be required.

— A current certificate of existence or certificate of good standing from the state of domicile.

— A certified copy of the corporation's articles or certificate of incorporation.

— The appropriate filing fee.

— Separate documents appointing registered agent.

— Any other documents required by the state statutes or secretary of state of the foreign state.

☐ Make sure any publication requirements are complied with.

☐ Make sure any county recording requirements are complied with.

☐ Re-check statutes of foreign state to make sure that all qualification requirements have been met and to see when first annual report will be due, if applicable.

The paralegal will often perform similar tasks involved in amending the certificate of authority and in withdrawing the foreign corporation from each state when necessary. Another important task that the paralegal can perform is to keep track of all necessary annual reporting requirements and see that the annual report of each foreign corporation is completed and filed in a timely manner.

§ 11.9 RESOURCES

The primary resources for paralegals working with foreign corporations are the state statutes and secretaries of state of the foreign states. In certain circumstances, corporation service companies can be most helpful and efficient.

State Statutes

It is important that the Business Corporation Act or similar act for each foreign state be carefully reviewed for every state in which the corporate client may be considered a foreign corporation. A list of the pertinent state statutes is included in Figure 5-5 in this text.

Secretaries of State

Many secretary of state offices provide information on their Web pages in addition to printed pamphlets or other forms of information regarding foreign corporations. Most of this information is free of charge and may be obtained by writing to or calling the secretary of state of the appropriate state. (See appendix A for a secretary of state directory.)

Corporation Service Companies

Corporation service companies will assist you with almost all aspects of services for foreign corporations. These services can help you complete all the necessary paperwork to qualify a foreign corporation and see that it is filed correctly. In addition, the services can act as a registered agent for a foreign corporation in any foreign state in the country. Using these services involves paying a third party to perform work on behalf of the corporate client. However, they are usually quick and convenient. Information concerning specific corporation service companies can be found in your telephone directory, by searching the Internet, or by contacting the secretary of state's office to request a list.

 Internet Resources   WWW.

There are several on-line resources to assist paralegals with the foreign corporation qualification process. Some of these resources include state statutes, secretary of state Web pages, and Web pages of corporate service companies.

Following is a list of some Web pages that may be useful to paralegals who are assisting with the foreign corporation qualification process:

For state statutes

Findlaw.com	**www.findlaw.com/11stategov/**
Legal Information Institute	**www.law.cornell.edu/states/listing.html**

For links to state foreign corporation qualification forms

Findlaw.com State Corporation and Business Forms	**www.findlaw.com/11stategov/indexcorp.html**

For links to the secretary of state offices

Corporate Housekeeper	**www.danvi.vi/link2.html**
National Association of Secretaries of State	**www.nass.org**

An alphabetical list of Internet Resources for the Corporate Paralegal is included as appendix B to this text.

Web Page

For updates and links to several of the previously listed sites, as well as down-loadable state foreign corporation qualification forms, log on to **www.westlegalstudies. com**, and click through to the book link for this text.

SUMMARY

- The state of the corporation's charter or incorporation is the corporation's state of domicile, regardless of where the corporation transacts its business.
- A corporation is considered a foreign corporation in every state or jurisdiction other than its state of domicile.
- If a corporation is to transact business as a foreign corporation, it must first obtain a certificate of authority from the proper state official of the foreign state.
- State long-arm statutes give the courts of each state personal jurisdiction over corporations that voluntarily go into that state for the purpose of transacting business.
- Although guidance can be found in the statutes of the foreign state, determining exactly when a corporation is considered to be transacting business in a particular state, and is subject to foreign corporation qualification requirements, is usually a judgment call.
- State door-closing statutes provide that corporations that do business in a state without the necessary authority are precluded from maintaining an action in that state.

◆ Qualified foreign corporations are subject to the statutes of the foreign states in which they are qualified. However, the internal affairs of the corporation are usually governed by the laws of the corporation's state of domicile.

◆ An application for a certificate of authority is usually filed with the appropriate state authority, along with any other required documents, to qualify a corporation to do business in a foreign state.

◆ Corporations may register their names in most states, giving them the exclusive right to use that name in the state of registration.

REVIEW QUESTIONS

1. Assume that Quality Liquor Company has its main office in your home state, where it transacts the majority of its wholesale liquor business. Recently, Quality Liquor has been taking orders from a neighboring state. It has begun sending its sales people into the state in an attempt to increase its business. Assuming that the neighboring state follows the Model Business Corporation Act, does Quality Liquor need to qualify as a foreign corporation in that state? What if Quality Liquor were to set up a branch office in the neighboring state?

2. What are "door-closing" statutes as they relate to foreign corporations?

3. Explain why a foreign corporation that is qualified in a foreign state may not be able to transact all of the same business in the foreign state that it is authorized to transact in its state of domicile.

4. Assume that it is your responsibility to qualify your corporate client, Alex Enterprises, in a foreign state that has adopted the Model Business

Corporation Act. Will there be a problem getting a certificate of authority issued under the name "Alex Enterprises"? What are the possible solutions to this problem?

5. What is a fictitious name, and why is it used?

6. What is the purpose of a registered agent in a foreign state?

7. Why do many states require that the registered office address used in their state not be a post office box?

8. Assume that you represent a foreign corporation that is qualified in a state that has adopted the Model Business Corporation Act. What steps must be taken when the corporation amends its articles of incorporation to change its authorized shares of stock? What steps must be taken when the corporation amends its articles of incorporation to change its corporate name?

9. Under what circumstances might it be beneficial for a corporation to register its name in a foreign state?

PRACTICAL PROBLEMS

1. Locate the pertinent provisions for foreign corporations in your state's business corporation code and contact the secretary of state's office, if necessary, to answer the following questions:

   a. What is the cite for the statute that requires foreign corporations to qualify to do business in your state?

   b. What guidance is given by your state's statutes to foreign corporations trying to determine whether or not they are "doing business" in your state and need to qualify?

   c. What are the procedures for qualifying to do business as a foreign corporation in your state?

WORKPLACE SCENARIO

Assume that our fictional corporation, Cutting Edge Computer Repair, Inc., has decided to hire an employee to set up a shop in a neighboring state. Bradley Harris and Cynthia Lund have discussed the details with your supervising attorney, Belinda Benson. Ms. Benson has advised the clients to qualify Cutting Edge Computer Repair, Inc., as a foreign corporation in the neighboring state, and she has asked you to prepare the necessary paperwork.

Using the above information and the information in appendix D-3, prepare the necessary paperwork to qualify Cutting Edge Computer Repair, Inc., to do business as a foreign corporation in a neighboring state of your choice. Is the name available in the state you have chosen? For purposes of this assignment, you may disregard the merger performed between Cutting Edge Computer Repair, Inc. and Kohler's Computers, Inc. in Chapter 10.

END NOTES

1. *International Shoe Co. v. Washington,* 326 U.S. 310, 66 S. Ct. 154, 90 L. Ed 95 (1945).

2. 1984 Revised Model Business Corporation Act § 15.04.

CHAPTER 12

Corporate Dissolution

CHAPTER OUTLINE

§ 12.1   Voluntary Dissolution

§ 12.2   Involuntary Dissolution

§ 12.3   The Paralegal's Role in Dissolving Corporations

§ 12.4   Resources

INTRODUCTION

Corporations are given life by the statutes of their state of domicile, and that life must be terminated in accordance with those statutes. Although articles of incorporation can generally provide for a date or an event upon the happening of which the corporation will be dissolved, most corporations exist perpetually and must be dissolved when there is no further reason for their existence. The *dissolution* of a corporation generally refers to the termination of the legal existence of the corporation. However, as discussed in § 12.1, the corporate existence continues after dissolution for certain purposes.

Corporations are dissolved for many reasons, including bankruptcy or insolvency, the cessation of the business of the corporation, the sale of all or substantially all of the assets of the corporation, or the death of key shareholders, directors, or officers. Extensive planning involving the corporation's management, board of directors, attorneys, and accountants is usually necessary to execute the dissolution, winding up, and liquidation of the corporation in the manner most beneficial to the shareholders of the corporation.

In addition to dissolving in accordance with the statutes of its state of domicile, the corporation is required to surrender its certificate of authority to transact business in any state in which it is qualified to transact business, and to file the appropriate forms and returns with the Internal Revenue Service. The statutes regarding corporate dissolution vary considerably from state to state. Every state requires, at a minimum, that one document be filed with the secretary of state, or other appropriate state authority, notifying the state of the dissolution. Other common statutory provisions include requirements for obtaining and filing good-standing certificates from all state tax authorities, publishing notice in a legal newspaper of the corporation's intent to dissolve, and a second and final filing with the state after all corporate debts have been paid and all assets distributed. There are also significant differences in state statutes for obtaining director and shareholder approval of the corporate dissolution.

This chapter examines the procedures under the Model Business Corporation Act (MBCA) to effect the most common type of dissolution, the voluntary dissolution. It also investigates administrative dissolution and involuntary dissolution by the state of domicile, the shareholders of the corporation, and the creditors of the corporation. The chapter concludes with a brief discussion of the role of the paralegal in dissolving a corporation.

§ 12.1 VOLUNTARY DISSOLUTION

The most common type of corporate dissolution is the **voluntary dissolution**, which is approved by the directors and shareholders of the corporation. The procedures followed for voluntarily dissolving a corporation depend on the statutes of the state of domicile, but generally involve obtaining the appropriate approval from the directors and shareholders, filing articles of dissolution or another appropriate document with the proper state authority, and winding up the affairs of the corporation by liquidating its assets, paying the creditors' claims, and distributing the balance to the shareholders.

Board of Director and Shareholder Approval of Dissolution

The voluntary dissolution of a corporation must be approved by at least a majority of the corporation's shareholders in most instances. Under certain circumstances, the incorporators or initial board of directors of the corporation may act to dissolve a corporation.

Dividends ◆

Bankruptcies for Business

Corporations dissolve for numerous reasons. Corporate dissolutions are not necessarily due to failure or bankruptcy of the corporation. Likewise, corporate bankruptcies do not necessarily result in dissolution of the corporation. However, the two often go hand in hand. In 1999, nearly 40,000 businesses filed bankruptcy petitions in the United States.*

Paralegals who assist with corporate dissolutions may find themselves working with corporations that are involved in the bankruptcy process. For that reason, it is important to have a basic knowledge of corporate bankruptcy procedures in the United States.

Bankruptcy is a procedure provided for under the Federal Bankruptcy Act (11 U.S.C. 101). Federal bankruptcy courts have jurisdiction over all bankruptcy proceedings. Filing a bankruptcy petition suspends the normal relationship between the debtor and the creditor. Bankruptcy allows debtors to eliminate their debts or repay them under the protection of the bankruptcy court. A corporation filing for bankruptcy protection may petition for a liquidation bankruptcy, or it may seek a reorganization.

If the directors of a corporation feel that their business is so far in debt that there is no hope of becoming profitable again, they may seek a liquidation bankruptcy under Chapter 7 of the Bankruptcy Code. Under Chapter 7, the corporation ceases all operation and goes completely out of business. A

◆ ————————————————————

voluntary dissolution   Dissolution that is approved by the directors and shareholders of the corporation.

trustee is appointed to liquidate the corporation's assets and use the money to pay off as much of the debt as possible to the corporation's creditors and investors as provided by bankruptcy law.

Chapter 11 of the Bankruptcy Code allows companies that are in serious financial trouble to *reorganize* their business without liquidating. Chapter 11 provides a rehabilitative procedure for corporations to retain their assets, restructure their debt, and repay obligations over an extended period of time. Under Chapter 11, the debtor company works with committees appointed to represent the interests of creditors and stockholders to create a proposed plan of reorganization to help the company get out of debt. The reorganization plan usually includes provisions for paying off at least a portion of the debt owed by the corporation. The plan must be accepted by creditors and stockholders, and it must be confirmed by the Bankruptcy Court. Corporations may complete their plan of reorganization and emerge from a Chapter 11 bankruptcy to continue their business—sometimes more successfully than ever.

_____

* U.S. Census Bureau, *The Statistical Abstract of the United States (2000)* § 879.

Dissolution Prior to Commencement of Business If a decision is made to dissolve a corporation before it commences doing business or before it issues stock, a streamlined method for dissolution is generally provided by statute. The dissolution of a corporation that has not issued stock may be approved by the incorporators or the initial board of directors, if one was named in the articles of incorporation. The MBCA provides the method for dissolving a corporation by the incorporators or board of directors in § 14.01:

§ 14.01. DISSOLUTION BY INCORPORATORS OR INITIAL DIRECTORS

A majority of the incorporators or initial directors of a corporation that has not issued shares or has not commenced business may dissolve the corporation by delivering to the secretary of state for filing articles of dissolution that set forth:

(1) the name of the corporation;

(2) the date of its incorporation;

(3) either (i) that none of the corporation's shares has been issued or (ii) that the corporation has not commenced business;

(4) that no debt of the corporation remains unpaid;

(5) that the net assets of the corporation remaining after winding up have been distributed to the shareholders, if shares were issued; and

(6) that a majority of the incorporators or initial directors authorized the dissolution.

When a corporation has not commenced business, it will typically have no debts to satisfy and no assets to distribute. Unless there are other statutory requirements in the state of domicile, the dissolution process can be satisfied merely by filing the articles of dissolution as prescribed by statute. Articles of dissolution are discussed further in this section.

Dissolution Subsequent to Commencement of Business After the corporation has commenced business or after shares of the corporation's stock have been issued, its dissolution must be approved by the shareholders of the corporation pursuant to statute. The statutes of the state of domicile may set forth special requirements for obtaining shareholder approval. Those requirements are often similar to the requirements for approving a merger or share exchange (discussed in Chapter 10). Shareholders are generally not granted the right to dissent in the event of a dissolution. However, courts may prohibit dissolutions that are aimed at freezing out the minority shareholders of the corporation if the board of directors and majority shareholders are not acting in good faith. It has been held that "majority stockholders cannot vote to discontinue the business of the corporation for the purpose of turning it over to another corporation and excluding minority stockholders from participating therein."[1] The MBCA sets forth the requirements for approving a voluntary corporate dissolution in § 14.02:

§ 14.02. DISSOLUTION BY BOARD OF DIRECTORS AND SHAREHOLDERS

(a) A corporation's board of directors may propose dissolution for submission to the shareholders.

(b) For a proposal to dissolve to be adopted:
   (1) the board of directors must recommend dissolution to the shareholders unless the board of directors determines that because of conflict of interest or other special circumstances it should make no recommendation and communicates the basis for its determination to the shareholders; and
   (2) the shareholders entitled to vote must approve the proposal to dissolve as provided in subsection (e).

(c) The board of directors may condition its submission of the proposal for dissolution on any basis.

(d) The corporation shall notify each shareholder, whether or not entitled to vote, of the proposed shareholders' meeting in accordance with § 7.05. The notice must also state that the purpose, or one of the purposes, of the meeting is to consider dissolving the corporation.

(e) Unless the articles of incorporation or the board of directors (acting pursuant to subsection (c)) require a greater vote or a vote by voting groups, the proposal to dissolve to be adopted must be approved by a majority of all the votes entitled to be cast on that proposal.

Following are sample resolutions that might be passed by the board of directors and by the shareholders of a corporation, respectively, to approve the dissolution of the corporation.

EXAMPLE: *Directors' Resolution to Dissolve Corporation—Submission of Proposition to Stockholders*[2]

Resolution of the board of directors of _____ [name of corporation], adopted on _____ [date].

Whereas, this corporation has entirely ceased to do the business for which it was formed and organized; and whereas, all indebtedness has been paid, and it appears to be to the best interests of the stockholders that it should be dissolved, its business terminated, and its remaining assets distributed among the stockholders, or otherwise disposed of according to law;

Resolved, that in the opinion of this board of directors it is advisable to dissolve this corporation forthwith, and that a meeting of the stockholders be held on _____ [date], at _____ [time], at the corporation's office at _____ [address], _____ [city], _____ [county], _____ [state], for the purpose of voting upon the proposition that the corporation be forthwith dissolved.

Further resolved, that unless notice of such meeting be waived by all the stockholders, the secretary shall cause notice of such meeting to be both published and served as prescribed by law.

Further resolved, that the president or vice president and secretary execute a certificate showing the adoption of these resolutions and setting forth the proceedings of the meeting of stockholders, and that they also attest the written consent of the stockholders that the corporation be dissolved, and execute and verify all statements required by law to dissolve the corporation.

Further resolved, that the president or vice president and the secretary cause such certificate and consent to be filed in the office of the Secretary of State of the State of _____, together with a duly verified statement of the names and residences of the members of the existing board of directors and of the names and residences of the officers of the corporation, and all certificates and waivers of all notices required by law, and that the officers and board of directors of the corporation take such further action as may be required to effectuate the dissolution of the corporation and wind up its business affairs.

EXAMPLE: Stockholders' Resolution—Election to Dissolve Corporation— Approval and Adoption of Directors' Resolution[3]

Whereas, a special meeting of the stockholders of _____ [name of corporation] was held _____ [date] at the principal office of the corporation at _____ [address], _____ [city], _____ [county], _____ [state], and

Whereas, the secretary of the corporation reported that _____ shares of the outstanding capital stock of the corporation were represented in person or by proxy, being _____ percent (_____%) of the total stock outstanding; and

Whereas, the secretary presented the resolution that had been adopted at a meeting of the board of directors held on _____ [date], which resolution provided that the corporation go into liquidation, dispose of its assets, wind up its affairs, be dissolved, and the charter thereof be surrendered and canceled;

After full consideration of the directors' resolution and on motion duly made and seconded, the stockholders have:

Resolved, that _____ [name of corporation], a corporation chartered by the State of _____, be completely liquidated at the earliest practicable date, that all debts of the corporation be paid and the remaining cash together with securities owned, or the cash realized from the sale thereof, be distributed pro rata to its stockholders prior to _____ [date], and that all other assets of the corporation be disposed of as soon as practicable and the proceeds therefrom, after payment of any remaining liabilities, be distributed pro rata to the stockholders upon surrender by the stockholders to the corporation of all the outstanding stock thereof.

Resolved further, that the officers of the corporation be authorized and directed to take immediate steps to complete the liquidation of the corporation so that its assets or the proceeds therefrom can be distributed to its stockholders prior to _____ [date], and that promptly thereafter steps be taken to surrender the charter and franchise of the corporation to the State of _____ and to dissolve the corporation.

Resolved further, that the corporation cease the transaction of all business as of this date, except such as may be necessary or incidental to the complete liquidation thereof and the winding up of its affairs, including the payment of any obligations of the corporation now outstanding and any expenses incident to the liquidation thereof.

Articles of Dissolution and Notice of Intent to Dissolve

In states following the MBCA, the first and only filing required with the secretary of state, or other appropriate state authority, is the **articles of dissolution**. (See Figure 12-1 on page 468 for individual state requirements.) After the articles of dissolution are filed, the corporate existence continues, but the corporation is considered to be a "dissolved corporation" and may continue its business only for the purpose of winding up its affairs. The MBCA sets forth the requirements for articles of dissolution in § 14.03:

§ 14.03. ARTICLES OF DISSOLUTION

(a) At any time after dissolution is authorized, the corporation may dissolve by delivering to the secretary of state for filing articles of dissolution setting forth:
  (1) the name of the corporation;
  (2) the date dissolution was authorized;
  (3) if dissolution was approved by the shareholders:
    (i) the number of votes entitled to be cast on the proposal to dissolve; and
    (ii) either the total number of votes cast for and against dissolution or the total number of undisputed votes cast for dissolution and a statement that the number cast for dissolution was sufficient for approval.
  (4) If voting by voting groups was required, the information required by subparagraph (3) must be separately provided for each voting group entitled to vote separately on the plan to dissolve.
(b) A corporation is dissolved upon the effective date of its articles of dissolution.

---

articles of dissolution Document filed with the secretary of state or other appropriate state authority to dissolve the corporation.

State	Corporate Dissolution Statute	Document(s) Filed at State Level to Dissolve Corporation
Alabama	Ala. Code § 10-2B–14.01 *et seq.*	Articles of Dissolution[4]
Alaska	Alaska Stat. § 10.06.605 *et seq.*	Certificate of Election to Dissolve and Articles of Dissolution
Arizona	Ariz. Rev. Stat. Ann. § 10-1401 *et seq.*	Articles of Dissolution
Arkansas	Ark. Stat. Ann. § 4-27-1401	Articles of Dissolution
California	Cal. Corp. Code § 1900 *et seq.*	Certificate of Election to Wind Up and Dissolve and Certificate of Dissolution
Colorado	Colo. Bus. Corp. Act § 7-114-101	Articles of Dissolution
Connecticut	Conn. Gen. Stat. § 1170 *et seq.*	Certificate of Dissolution
Delaware	Del. Code Ann. tit. 8 § 275	Certificate of Dissolution
District of Columbia	D.C. Code Ann. § 29-378(4) *et seq.*	Statement of Intent to Dissolve and Articles of Dissolution[5]
Florida	Fla. Stat. § 607.1401	Articles of Dissolution
Georgia	Ga. Code Ann. § 14-2-1401 *et seq.*	Notice of Intent to Dissolve and Articles of Dissolution[6]
Hawaii	Haw. Rev. Stat. § 414-381 *et seq.*	Articles of Dissolution
Idaho	Idaho Code § 30-1-1401 *et seq.*	Articles of Dissolution
Illinois	805 ILCS § 105/112.05 *et seq.*	Articles of Dissolution
Indiana	Ind. Code § 23-1-45-1 *et seq.*	Articles of Dissolution
Iowa	Iowa Code § 490.1401 *et seq.*	Articles of Dissolution
Kansas	Kan. Stat. Ann. § 17-6803 *et seq.*	Certificate of Dissolution
Kentucky	Ky. Rev. Stat. Ann. § 271B.14-010 *et seq.*	Articles of Dissolution
Louisiana	La. Rev. Stat. Ann. § 12:141	Certificate of Dissolution[7]
Maine	Me. Rev. Stat. Ann. tit. 13-A § 1101 *et seq.*	Statement of Intent to Dissolve and Articles of Dissolution
Maryland	Md. Corps. & Ass'ns Code Ann. § 3-401 *et seq.*	Articles of Dissolution
Massachusetts	Mass. Gen. Laws Ann. ch. 56B, § 100 *et seq.*	Articles of Dissolution
Michigan	Mich. Comp. Laws § 450.180 *et seq.*	Certificate of Dissolution
Minnesota	Minn. Stat. 302A.701 *et seq.*	Notice of Intent to Dissolve and Articles of Dissolution
Mississippi	Miss. Code Ann. § 79-4-14.01 *et seq.*	Articles of Dissolution

FIGURE 12-1 State Corporate Dissolution Statutes

State	Corporate Dissolution Statute	Document(s) Filed at State Level to Dissolve Corporation
Missouri	Mo. Rev. Stat. § 351.462 *et seq.*	Articles of Dissolution
Montana	Mont. Code Ann. § 35-1-931 *et seq.*	Articles of Dissolution
Nebraska	Neb. Rev. Stat. § 21-20.151 *et seq.*	Articles of Dissolution
Nevada	Nev. Rev. Stat. § 78.580 *et seq.*	Certified copy of Resolution to Dissolve
New Hampshire	N.H. Rev. Stat. Ann. § 293-A:14.01 *et seq.*	Articles of Dissolution
New Jersey	N.J. Rev. Stat. § 14A:12-1 *et seq.*	Certificate of Dissolution
New Mexico	N.M. Stat. Ann. § 53-16-1 *et seq.*	Statement of Intent to Dissolve and Articles of Dissolution
New York	N.Y. Bus. Corp. Law § 1001 *et seq.*	Certificate of Dissolution
North Carolina	N.C. Gen. Stat. § 55-14-01 *et seq.*	Articles of Dissolution
North Dakota	N.D. Cent. Code § 10-19.1-105 *et seq.*	Notice of Intent to Dissolve and Articles of Dissolution
Ohio	Ohio Rev. Code Ann. § 1701.8 *et seq.*	Articles of Dissolution
Oklahoma	Okla. Stat. tit. 18 § 1096 *et seq.*	Certificate of Dissolution
Oregon	Or. Rev. Stat. § 60.621 *et seq.*	Articles of Dissolution
Pennsylvania	Pa. Cons. Stat. tit. 15 § 1971 *et seq.*	Articles of Dissolution
Rhode Island	R.I. Gen. Laws § 7-1.1-75 *et seq.*	Statement of Intent to Dissolve and Articles of Dissolution
South Carolina	S.C. Code Ann. § 33-14-101 *et seq.*	Articles of Dissolution
South Dakota	S.D. Codified Laws Ann. § 47-7-1 *et seq.*	Articles of Dissolution
Tennessee	Tenn. Code Ann. § 48-24-101 *et seq.*	Articles of Dissolution
Texas	Tex. Bus. Corp. Act arts. 6.01 *et seq.*	Articles of Dissolution
Utah	Utah Code Ann. § 16-10a-1401 *et seq.*	Articles of Dissolution
Vermont	Vt. Stat. Ann. tit. 11A § 14-01 *et seq.*	Articles of Dissolution
Virginia	Va. Code § 13.1-742 *et seq.*	Articles of Dissolution
Washington	Wash. Rev. Code Ann. § 23B.14.010 *et seq.*	Articles of Dissolution
West Virginia	W. Va. Code § 31-1-124 *et seq.*	Statement of Intent to Dissolve and Articles of Dissolution
Wisconsin	Wis. Stat. § 180.1401 *et seq.*	Articles of Dissolution
Wyoming	Wyo. Stat. § 17-16-1401 *et seq.*	Articles of Dissolution

FIGURE 12-1 (*continued*)

The articles of dissolution must be submitted with the appropriate filing fee in accordance with state statute. Figure 12-2 shows sample articles of dissolution that may be appropriate in states following the MBCA. Figure 12-3 is a sample certificate of dissolution form for dissolving Connecticut corporations.

ARTICLES OF DISSOLUTION
OF

_____

Pursuant to _____ [statute], as amended, the undersigned, does hereby state the following as the Articles of Dissolution of said Corporation.

I.

The name of the corporation is _____.

II.

The authorized stock of the corporation consists of 10,000 shares of Class A Common Stock, without par value, 5,000 of which are issued and outstanding. At a meeting of the shareholders held on _____, _____, at the registered office of the corporation, a resolution to dissolve the corporation effective _____, _____, was passed by unanimous vote of all 5,000 issued and outstanding shares of the corporation.

Dated: _____, _____.

_____

By _____

Subscribed and sworn to before me
this _____ day of _____, _____.

_____
Notary Public

FIGURE 12-2 Sample Articles of Dissolution

In several jurisdictions that deviate from the MBCA in this regard, a notice of intent to dissolve must be filed with the secretary of state or other appropriate state authority prior to the winding-up process. This document may also be referred to as a statement of intent to dissolve. The articles of dissolution are generally filed in these jurisdictions only after all the corporation's debts have been paid, including any tax liabilities, and all the corporation's assets have been distributed. Figure 12-4 on page 472 is a sample notice of intent to dissolve. Figure 12-5 on page 473 is a sample statement of intent to dissolve from the state of Maine. In addition to requiring that the notice of intent to dissolve be filed with the secretary of state, state statutes often require that the notice be published in a legal newspaper in the county in which the registered office of the corporation is located.

CERTIFICATE OF DISSOLUTION
STOCK CORPORATION
Office of the Secretary of the State
30 Trinity Street / P.O. Box 150470 / Hartford, CT 06115-0470 /Rev 12/1999

Please see reverse for instruction.

Space For Office Use Only

1. NAME OF CORPORATION:

2. DATE ON WHICH DISSOLUTION WAS AUTHORIZED: _____/_____/_____

3. Complete Block (A) if Dissolution was authorized by incorporators or initial directors <u>or</u> block (B)
    if Dissolution was authorized by directors and shareholders.

(A)   Place a check mark next to either 1 <u>or</u> 2 as appropriate:

_____ 1. None of the corporation's shares have been issued   _____ 2. The corporation has not commenced business

The undersigned makes the following assertions in connection with the selection made under section (A) of this form: that no debt of the corporation remains unpaid; that if shares were issued, the net assets of the corporation remaining after winding up have been distributed to the shareholders; and that a majority of the incorporators or initial directors authorized the dissolution.

(B)   The dissolution was approved by resolution of the board of directors and authorized by
       shareholders as follows:

Number of votes entitled to be cast	Number of votes cast in favor of dissolution	Number of votes cast against dissolution

(Note: If voting by voting groups was required, please provide the above voting information for each group)

CHECK THE FOLLOWING STATEMENT IF APPLICABLE

_____The number of shareholder votes cast in favor of dissolution was sufficient for approval.

4. EXECUTION
Dated this_____day of _____, 20_____.

Print or type name of signatory	Capacity of signatory	Signature

<u>**NOTE: A corporation may only revoke its dissolution within 120 days following the effective date of such dissolution.**</u>

FIGURE 12-3 Sample Form for a Certificate of Dissolution for Dissolving a Connecticut Corporation

NOTICE OF INTENT TO DISSOLVE

_____

   Pursuant to _____ [statute], the undersigned hereby provides the following notice of intent to dissolve _____ to the Secretary of State.

I.

   The name of the corporation is _____.

II.

   On _____, _____, a meeting of the shareholders of the corporation was held at the principal office of the corporation. At that meeting a resolution was unanimously adopted by all of the shareholders to begin a voluntary dissolution of the Corporation, effective _____, _____.

III.

   The board of directors of the corporation is hereby authorized to take any and all actions necessary to wind up the business of the corporation, and distribute the corporation's assets in accordance with statute.

Dated: _____.

                                           _____
                                           By _____
                                           Its _____

Subscribed and Sworn to before me
this _____ day of _____, _____.

_____
   Notary Public

FIGURE 12-4 Sample Notice of Intent to Dissolve

Winding Up and Liquidation

After the dissolved corporation has filed its articles or notice of dissolution, it will begin the process of winding up its affairs and liquidating. The statutes of virtually every state provide for the complete and orderly winding up of the affairs of dissolved corporations and for the protection of the creditors and shareholders of liquidating corporations.[8] In § 14.05, the MBCA lists the following activities that may be appropriate to wind up the affairs of a corporation and liquidate its business:

1. Collection of assets.
2. Disposition of properties that will not be distributed in kind to shareholders.
3. Discharge or making provision for discharge of liabilities of the corporation.

Filing Fee $20.00

**DOMESTIC
BUSINESS CORPORATION**

STATE OF MAINE

STATEMENT OF INTENT TO DISSOLVE

(Written Consent of All Shareholders)

_____
Deputy Secretary of State

A True Copy When Attested By Signature

_____
Deputy Secretary of State

_____
(Name of Corporation)

Pursuant to 13-A MRSA §1102, the undersigned corporation intends to dissolve the corporation.

FIRST: The names and respective addresses of its officers and directors are:

<u>Title</u>	<u>Name</u>	<u>Address</u>
President	_____	_____
Treasurer	_____	_____
Secretary	_____	_____
Clerk	_____	_____
Directors:	_____	_____
	_____	_____
	_____	_____

SECOND: Exhibit A attached hereto is a copy of the written consent signed by all shareholders of the corporation, or signed in their names by their duly authorized attorneys.

THIRD: All required Annual Reports have been filed with the Secretary of State. (Note: If the dissolution process is completed on or before June 1st, then the Annual Report covering the previous calendar year is not required.)

FOURTH: The undersigned corporation understands that the filing of this document **DOES NOT** complete the dissolution process. You must **ALSO FILE** Articles of Dissolution.

FIFTH: The address of the registered office of the corporation in the State of Maine is _____

_____
(street, city, state and zip code)

FIGURE 12-5   Sample Statement of Intent to Dissolve from the State of Maine

DATED _____

*By _____
                (signature)

_____
(type or print name and capacity)

**MUST BE COMPLETED FOR VOTE
OF SHAREHOLDERS**

I certify that I have custody of the minutes showing
the above action by the shareholders.

_____
(signature of clerk, secretary or asst. secretary)

---

*By _____
                (signature)

_____
(type or print name and capacity)

Notice of the filing of this statement shall be mailed to each known creditor of the corporation and to the State Tax Assessor pursuant to 13-A MRSA §1106.2.

---

*This document **MUST** be signed by
    (1) the <u>Clerk</u> OR
    (2) the <u>President</u> or a vice-pres. **together with** the <u>Secretary</u> or an ass't. sec., or a 2nd certifying officer OR
    (3) if no such officers, then a majority of the <u>Directors</u> OR
    (4) if no such directors, then the <u>Holders of a majority of all outstanding shares</u> OR
    (5) the <u>Holders of all of the outstanding shares</u>.

SUBMIT COMPLETED FORMS TO: CORPORATE EXAMINING SECTION, SECRETARY OF STATE,
101 STATE HOUSE STATION, AUGUSTA, ME 04333-0101

FORM NO. MBCA-11 Rev. 4/16/2001

TEL. (207) 624-7740

FIGURE 12-5 (*continued*)

4. Distribution of remaining property among shareholders according to their interests.

5. Every other act necessary to wind up and liquidate the business and affairs of the corporation.

The **liquidation** of a corporation refers to the "winding up of the affairs of the corporation by reducing its assets, paying its debts, and apportioning the profit or loss."[9] Depending on the provisions of the pertinent state statutes, corporations may be liquidated either before or after they are dissolved. Figure 12-6 is a sample plan of liquidation that might be adopted by the board of directors and shareholders of a dissolving corporation.

PLAN OF LIQUIDATION

WHEREAS, the Board of Directors and Shareholders have approved the dissolution, winding up, and liquidation of the corporation pursuant to _____ [statute]; and

WHEREAS, it is the desire of the directors and shareholders to adopt a plan of liquidation to provide for the liquidation and winding up of the corporation.

NOW, THEREFORE, the following plan is hereby adopted:

1. The officers of the corporation are hereby authorized and directed to wind up the affairs of the corporation, collect its assets, and pay or provide for the payment of the corporation's debts and liabilities.

2. As soon as may be reasonably practicable, the officers of the corporation shall transfer all its remaining property (subject to all its remaining liabilities) to the corporation stockholders, in proportion to their stock ownership, in cancellation of their shares.

3. As soon as may be reasonably practicable, the officers of the corporation shall cause it to be dissolved.

Dated this _____ day of _____, _____.

By: _____

Its: _____

FIGURE 12-6 Sample Plan of Liquidation

Voluntary dissolutions in jurisdictions that follow the MBCA are typically nonjudicial dissolutions. This means that it is not necessary for the courts to supervise or approve either the liquidation or the dissolution process. Under certain circumstances, the court may supervise the liquidation of a corporation that is voluntarily dissolving, if

---

liquidation Winding up the affairs of a business by identifying assets, converting them into cash, and paying off liabilities (liquidate the company).

requested to do so by a shareholder or creditor. The statutes of some jurisdictions may require judicial liquidation or offer incentives to corporations to choose judicial liquidations.

Notice to Creditors   As a part of the winding up and liquidation process, state statutes may require that the creditors of the corporation be given notice and that they must be allowed to submit claims to the corporation for payment of any debt owed by the corporation. Often notification must be sent to each individual creditor, and notice must be given to the public.

Notice to Known Claimants   Corporations domiciled in states following the MBCA are given guidelines to follow for notifying creditors of known claims, and for notifying the public in the event there are any unknown claims against the corporation. Section 14.06 of the MBCA provides procedures for disposing of known claims against a dissolved corporation. Corporations following the procedures of this section must notify known creditors in writing of the dissolution at any time after the effective date of the dissolution and allow creditors sufficient time to make claim on the corporation's assets. The notice must include the following:

1. A description of the information that must be included in a claim.
2. A mailing address to which the claim may be sent.
3. The deadline, which may not be fewer than 120 days from the effective date of the written notice, by which the dissolved corporation must receive the claim.
4. A statement that the claim will be barred if not received by the deadline.

Figure 12-7 shows a sample notice to creditors that might be used in compliance with state statutes modeled after the MBCA.

Claims against corporations that follow this procedure for disposing of their known claims are barred if the claimant received proper notice and did not deliver a claim to the corporation by the stated deadline. Claims are also barred if they are rejected by the corporation and the claimant does not commence a proceeding to enforce the claim within 90 days of the rejection.

In *Mo. ex rel. National Supermarkets v. Sweeny,* the case on page 478, the court found that a suit brought by an individual who slipped and fell in a grocery store owned by a corporation that later dissolved was not a valid claim. The dissolving corporation notified the claimant of its dissolution under state statute, but the plaintiff failed to present her claim within the permitted time period under state statute.

Notice to Unknown Claimants   The MBCA, and the statutes of several states also provide procedures for disposing of unknown claims—claims against the corporation of which the corporation's principals are unaware of at the time of dissolution. Corporations following this procedure publish notice of their dissolution and request that any persons with claims against the corporation present them in accordance with the notice.

When corporations follow this procedure, all claims against the corporation will be barred unless a proceeding to enforce a claim is commenced within five years after the date of publication.

NOTICE TO THE CREDITORS OF

_____

    The directors and shareholders of the above corporation have adopted a resolution to voluntarily dissolve the corporation pursuant to _____ [statute].

    1. Any claims against the assets of the corporation must be made in writing and include the amount of the claim, the basis of the claim, and the date on which the claim originated.

    2. The claim must be sent, by U.S. Mail, to the registered office address of the corporation at _____.

    3. The deadline for submitting claims to this corporation is _____, ____ [no sooner than 120 days from the effective date of this notice].

    4. Any claims not received by the corporation on or prior to the above deadline will be barred.

    Dated this ____ day of _____, ____.

                                        _____

                                        Secretary

FIGURE 12-7 Sample Notice to Creditors

Requirements for notifying claimants of a corporation's dissolution vary greatly among the states. It is very important that the appropriate procedures set forth in state statutes are reviewed and followed carefully.

Distributions to Shareholders As a part of the winding-up and liquidation process, the assets remaining after the debts of the corporation have been paid must be distributed to the shareholders of the dissolved corporation. The assets may be reduced to cash prior to distribution, or they may be distributed in kind. The shareholders will receive a pro rata portion of the assets of the corporation, based on the number of shares owned by them and the rights of each particular class of shares. Preferred shareholders may have a priority right to the distribution of assets upon the dissolution of a corporation.

Postdissolution Claims The dissolution of a corporation does not invalidate claims against the corporation which have not been paid or provided for in the liquidation proceedings. Dissolution does not relieve a corporation of liability to creditors, including tort claimants. State statutes vary in their treatment of postdissolution claims. Several states set a specific number of years after a corporation is dissolved in which a claimant must commence an action. As discussed in the previous section, even if a dissolving corporation publishes notice of its dissolution as provided under the MBCA, certain claimants have up to five years to commence an action against the dissolved corporation. In the _Hunter v. Fort Worth Capital Corporation_ case on page 480, the court found that the defendant corporation was not liable to the petitioner for injuries sustained as the result of a defective product

CASE

Missouri Court of Appeals,
Eastern District,
Writ Division One.

STATE of Missouri, ex rel. NATIONAL
SUPER MARKETS, INC., Relator,
v.
The Honorable Phillip J. SWEENEY, Judge,
Circuit Court of St. Louis County,
Missouri, Respondent.

No. 72687.

Aug. 5, 1997.

GARY M. GAERTNER, Presiding Judge.

Relator, National Super Markets, Inc. ("National"), filed a **writ of prohibition** to prevent respondent from taking further action in the underlying suit filed by Portia Scott (hereinafter "plaintiff") for damages sustained by plaintiff when she slipped and fell on National's premises. Respondent filed suggestions in opposition. In the interest of justice, as permitted by Rule 84.24, we dispense with a preliminary order, answer, further briefing and oral argument, and now issue a **peremptory** writ of prohibition and direct respondent to enter an order of dismissal as provided herein. ...

National, a dissolved Michigan corporation, operated a chain of food stores and was licensed to transact business in Missouri.

Plaintiff was a patron of one of the National stores on October 26, 1994, when she slipped on a substance on the floor of an aisle and fell, thereby sustaining injuries requiring chiropractic care.

On September 25, 1995, National dissolved in accordance with the Michigan Business Corporations Act. Pursuant to Michigan law, National sent notices to all of its known claimants informing them of the corporation's dissolution and the procedure they must follow in order to lodge a claim with the company. National sent such notice to plaintiff in a letter dated September 29, 1995. This letter informed plaintiff she must file her claim with National no later than March 29, 1996, or her claim would be barred.

Plaintiff appropriately responded to the notice in a letter dated October 18, 1995. National then rejected plaintiff's claim in a letter dated November 8, 1995, the relevant text being:

National Super Markets, Inc., is in receipt of your letter in which you express an interest in pursuing a claim against the dissolved corporation. After careful consideration, National has decided to reject your claim. Please be advised that, pursuant to applicable laws, you have ninety (90) days within which to commence a proceeding to enforce the claim against National, or the claim will be barred. This letter is not intended to be a recognition that you have a valid claim against National.

Neither party took further action in the matter until March 25, 1996, when plaintiff sent a letter to National reasserting her claim and offering a settlement. National responded that, because plaintiff had failed to commence a proceeding to enforce her claim within ninety days, her claim was barred. Plaintiff then filed the underlying lawsuit on March 28, 1996. National filed a motion to dismiss the action, which the trial court denied. This request for a writ of prohibition followed.

National argues plaintiff's claim is barred under Michigan law. National claims it was incorporated under the laws of Michigan, and the same governed its dissolution. Moreover, National asserts that,

---

relator A person in whose name a state brings a legal action (the person who "relates" the facts on which the action is based). The name of the case might be State ex rel ("on the relation of") *Smith v. Jones.* [pronounce: re-*late*-or]

writ of prohibition Order prohibiting specific action.

peremptory Absolute; conclusive; final; or arbitrary. Not requiring any explanation or cause to be shown.

even should Missouri law apply, plaintiff's claim is nonetheless barred. Plaintiff disagrees, however, arguing Missouri law, specifically RSMo section 516.120(4) governing personal injury actions, controls the instant proceeding. We hold plaintiff's claim is barred under both Michigan and Missouri law. We therefore refrain from deciding the choice of law issue raised by the parties, but rather analyze plaintiff's claim under each state's statutory scheme.

Generally, the dissolution of a corporation is governed by the laws of the state in which it is domiciled. ... The Michigan Business Corporations Act contains a statute providing a procedure whereby a dissolved corporation may wind up its affairs, including claims against it. Section 450.1841a M.C.L.A. (Supp.1995) sets forth a two-part procedure for the filing of claims against a dissolved corporation. Specifically, the provision states:

> Sec. 841a. (1) The dissolved corporation may notify its existing claimants in writing of the dissolution at any time after the effective date of the dissolution. The written notice shall include all of the following:
>
> (a) A description of the information that must be included in the claim. ...
>
> (b) A mailing address where a claim may be sent.
>
> (c) The deadline, which may not be less than 6 months from the effective date of the written notice, by which the dissolved corporation must receive the claim.
>
> (d) A statement that the claim will be barred if not received by the deadline.
>
> * * *
>
> (3) A claim against the dissolved corporation is barred if either of the following applies:
>
> (a) If a claimant who was given written notice under subsection (1) does not deliver the claim to the dissolved corporation by the deadline.
>
> (b) If a claimant whose claim was rejected by a written notice of rejection by the dissolved corporation does not commence a proceeding to enforce the claim within 90 days from the effective date of the written notice of rejection.

The parties do not dispute National's compliance with the statute's notification requirements. Rather, plaintiff argues her suit was filed within the March 29, 1996, deadline set forth in National's first notice. However, plaintiff's position misconstrues the statute's requirements and ignores the second step of the procedure: plaintiff filed her claim with the company in her letter dated October 18, 1995. It was only with respect to this initial claim that plaintiff was given until March 29, 1996, to file. The rejection of this claim by National on November 8, 1995, triggered plaintiff's duty to commence a proceeding to enforce her claim within ninety days. This plaintiff failed to do, as she delayed filing her petition until March 28, 1996, 141 days after the date National sent its written notice of rejection. Therefore, plaintiff's claim is barred under Michigan law. ...

Prohibition is an appropriate remedy to " 'forbear patently unwarranted and expensive litigation, inconvenience and waste of time and talent.' ... Where the issue before the trial court and this court is solely a matter of law, a writ of prohibition is proper to prevent needless litigation." *State ex rel. Conway v. Dowd,* 922 S.W.2d 461, 463 (Mo.App. E.D.1996). ...

In the instant case, plaintiff failed to timely commence a proceeding to enforce her claim against National, and, therefore, her action is barred under both Michigan and Missouri law. Accordingly, we issue a peremptory writ of prohibition directing respondent to take no further action in the instant proceeding except to enter an order dismissing plaintiff's claim with prejudice.

CRANDALL and RHODES RUSSELL, JJ., concur.

CASE

HUNTER
v.
FORT WORTH CAPITAL CORPORATION

Supreme Court of Texas
620 S.W.2d 547, 20 A.L.R.4th 399 (Tex. 1981)
July 15, 1981

The question is whether Theodore Moeller can recover damages against the former shareholders of Hunter-Hayes Elevator Company (Hunter-Hayes) for post-dissolution injuries resulting from the negligence of the company. The trial court rendered summary judgment for the shareholders. The court of civil appeals reversed the judgment and remanded the cause for trial. 608 S.W.2d 352. We reverse the judgment of the court of civil appeals and affirm the judgment of the trial court.

In 1960, Hunter-Hayes installed an elevator in a building under construction in Fort Worth, Texas. The company inspected and serviced the elevator until February 1, 1964, when it transferred its assets to Dover Corporation for 25,000 shares of Dover preferred stock. Hunter-Hayes then changed its name to H.H. Hunter Corporation and distributed the shares of Dover stock among its shareholders. On March 11, 1964, H.H. Hunter Corporation (formerly Hunter-Hayes) was issued a certificate of dissolution by the Secretary of State.

Approximately eleven years later, on May 13, 1975, Theodore Moeller was permanently injured when the elevator fell on him. At the time of the accident, Moeller was working in the elevator pit, which is located in the bottom of the elevator shaft, at the direction of his employer, Dover Elevator Company. The elevator fell when a valve in the elevator pit allegedly came apart, allowing its hydraulic system to lose fluid.

Theodore Moeller sued the former shareholders of Hunter-Hayes and others to recover damages for his personal injuries. He alleged causes of action based on negligence and strict liability. The other defendants filed cross-actions against the shareholders, seeking contribution and indemnity. In his suit against the shareholders, Moeller alleged his injuries were proximately caused by the negligent installation, inspection, and maintenance of the elevator by Hunter-Hayes. He also alleged the shareholders were personally liable to him, to the extent of the assets they received on dissolution, under the "trust fund theory."

In response, the shareholders moved for a summary judgment. They alleged Moeller's action and the cross-actions against them were barred because they were not brought within three years after the company dissolved as required by Article 7.12 of the Texas Business Corporation Act. The trial court granted the motion and severed all causes of action against the shareholders so that it could render a final and appealable judgment. ... The court of civil appeals reversed the judgment and remanded the cause for trial. The court of civil appeals held that Article 7.12 was vitiated in this cause by the "trust fund theory."

Article 7.12, which is derived from Section 105 of the Model Business Corporation Act, provides:

Survival of Remedy
After Dissolution

A. The dissolution of a corporation ... shall not take away or impair any remedy available to or against such corporation, its officers, directors, or shareholders, for any right or claim existing, or any liability incurred, prior to such dissolution ... .

Article 7.12 provides statutory remedies for pre-dissolution claims only and thus is in the nature of a survival statute. Moeller's cause of action did not accrue until he was injured more than eleven years after the company dissolved. ... Consequently, Moeller cannot recover against the shareholders for his post-dissolution claim against the corporation, unless his suit is authorized by some other statute or legal theory. ...

At common law, dissolution terminated the legal existence of a corporation. Once dissolved, the corporation could neither sue nor be sued, and all legal proceedings in which it was a party abated. ...

To alleviate the harsh effects of the common law on creditors, an equitable doctrine evolved. This doctrine provided that when the assets of a dissolved corporation are distributed among its shareholders, a creditor of the dissolved corporation may pursue the assets on the theory that in equity they are burdened with a lien in his favor.... This doctrine is often referred to as the "trust fund theory." Actually, the equitable doctrine has a much broader application. The trust fund theory applies whenever the assets of a dissolved corporation are held by any third party, including corporate officers and directors, so long as the assets are traceable and have not been acquired by a bona fide purchaser. ...

We agree with defendant that extension of the trust fund theory to cover plaintiff's claim would mean that the corporation could never completely dissolve but would live on indefinitely through its shareholders. We do not believe that this result would be in accordance with the spirit of the laws governing the dissolution of corporations. ...

We reverse the judgment of the court of civil appeals and affirm the judgment of the trial court.

that was manufactured by the defendant, a corporation which had dissolved seven years prior to the injury.

Valid claims may be enforced against the undistributed assets of a dissolved corporation, or against a shareholder of the dissolved corporation to the extent of the shareholder's share of the distribution upon the corporation's liquidation. Shareholders may not be held liable in excess of their distribution received upon dissolution of the corporation.

Tax Considerations

The dissolving corporation's attorneys often work closely with its in-house accountants or with an independent certified public accountant to dissolve the corporation in the manner that is the most advantageous, with regard to taxes, to its shareholders. The dissolving corporation must notify the Internal Revenue Service by filing a Form 966 (see Figure 12-8 on page 482) together with a certified copy of the resolution or plan of liquidation within thirty days of adoption of the liquidation plan. In addition, the distributions of the liquidating corporation must be reported on Forms 1096 and 1099.

Revocation of Dissolution

Because the dissolution of a corporation is such a final step, the statutes of most states provide for the revocation of dissolution proceedings. The revocation of a dissolution typically must be approved by the directors and shareholders of a corporation in the same manner in which the dissolution was approved. The MBCA provides that a corporation may revoke its dissolution within 120 days after its effective date.[10]

Articles of revocation of dissolution or some other, similar document typically must be filed with the secretary of state to revoke the dissolution of a corporation. Section 14.04(c) of the MBCA sets forth the requirements for the articles of revocation of dissolution:

> (c) After the revocation of dissolution is authorized, the corporation may revoke the dissolution by delivering to the secretary of state for filing

---

Form 966

(Rev. August 1998)
Department of the Treasury
Internal Revenue Service

Corporate Dissolution or Liquidation

(Required under section 6043(a) of the Internal Revenue Code)

OMB No. 1545-0041

Please type or print

Name of corporation	Employer identification number

Number, street, and room or suite no. (If a P.O. box number, see instructions below.)

City or town, state, and ZIP code

Check type of return

☐ 1120   ☐ 1120-L
☐ 1120-IC-DISC   ☐ 1120S
☐ Other ▶

1 Date incorporated	**2** Place incorporated	**3** Type of liquidation ☐ Complete ☐ Partial	**4** Date resolution or plan of complete or partial liquidation was adopted
5 Service Center where corporation filed its immediately preceding tax return	**6** Last month, day, and year of immediately preceding tax year	**7a** Last month, day, and year of final tax year	**7b** Was corporation's final tax return filed as part of a consolidated income tax return? If "Yes," complete 7c, 7d, and 7e. ☐ Yes ☐ No
7c Name of common parent		**7d** Employer identification number of common parent	**7e** Service Center where consolidated return was filed

	Common	Preferred
8 Total number of shares outstanding at time of adoption of plan of liquidation		

9 Date(s) of any amendments to plan of dissolution . . . .

10 Section of the Code under which the corporation is to be dissolved or liquidated . . .

11 If this return concerns an amendment or supplement to a resolution or plan, enter the date the previous Form 966 was filed . . . .

Attach a certified copy of the resolution or plan and all amendments or supplements not previously filed.

Under penalties of perjury, I declare that I have examined this return, including accompanying schedules and statements, and to the best of my knowledge and belief, it is true, correct, and complete.

▶ _____ | _____ | _____
   Signature of officer   Title   Date

Instructions

Who must file. A corporation must file Form 966 if it adopts a resolution or plan to dissolve the corporation or liquidate any of its stock. Exempt organizations are not required to file Form 966. These organizations should see the Instructions for Form 990 or 990-PF.

When and where to file. File Form 966 within 30 days after the resolution or plan is adopted to dissolve the corporation or liquidate any of its stock. If the resolution or plan is amended or supplemented after Form 966 is filed, file another Form 966 within 30 days after the amendment or supplement is adopted. The additional form will be sufficient if the date the earlier form was filed is entered on line 11 and a certified copy of the amendment or supplement is attached. Include all information required by Form 966 that was not given in the earlier form.

File Form 966 with the Internal Revenue Service Center where the corporation is required to file its income tax return.

Distribution of property. A corporation must recognize gain or loss on the distribution of its assets in the complete liquidation of its stock. For purposes of determining gain or loss, the distributed assets are valued at fair market value. Exceptions to this rule apply to liquidation of a subsidiary and to a distribution that is made pursuant to a plan of reorganization.

Address. Include the suite, room, or other unit number after the street address. If mail is not delivered to the street address and the corporation has a P.O. box, enter the box number instead of the street address.

Signature. The return must be signed and dated by the president, vice president, treasurer, assistant treasurer, chief accounting officer, or any other corporate officer (such as tax officer) authorized to sign. A receiver, trustee, or assignee must sign and date any return required to be filed on behalf of a corporation.

Paperwork Reduction Act Notice. We ask for the information on this form to carry out the Internal Revenue laws of the United States. You are required to give us the information. We need it to ensure that you are complying with these laws and to allow us to figure and collect the right amount of tax.

You are not required to provide the information requested by a form or its instructions that is subject to the Paperwork Reduction Act unless the form displays a valid OMB control number. Books and records relating to a form or its instructions must be retained as long as their content may become material in the administration of any Internal Revenue law. Generally, tax returns and return information are confidential, as required by section 6103.

The time needed to complete and file this form will vary depending on individual circumstances. The estimated average time is:

Recordkeeping . . . . 5 hr., 1 min.
Learning about the law or the form . . . . 6 min.
Preparing and sending the form to the IRS . . . . . 11 min.

If you have comments concerning the accuracy of these time estimates or suggestions for making this form simpler, we would be happy to hear from you. You can write to the Tax Forms Committee, Western Area Distribution Center, Rancho Cordova, CA 95743-0001. **DO NOT** send the tax form to this office. Instead, see **When and where to file** on this page.

Cat. No. 17053B   Form **966** (Rev. 8-98)

FIGURE 12-8 IRS Form 966—Corporate Dissolution or Liquidation

articles of revocation of dissolution, together with a copy of its articles of dissolution, that set forth:

(1) the name of the corporation;

(2) the effective date of the dissolution that was revoked;

(3) the date that the revocation of dissolution was authorized;

(4) if the corporation's board of directors (or incorporators) revoked the dissolution, a statement to that effect;

(5) if the corporation's board of directors revoked a dissolution authorized by the shareholders, a statement that revocation was permitted by action by the board of directors alone pursuant to that authorization; and

(6) if shareholder action was required to revoke the dissolution, the information required by section 14.03(a)(3) or (4).

The MBCA further provides that the revocation of dissolution is effective upon the effective date of the articles of revocation of dissolution, and that it relates back to the effective date of the dissolution as if the dissolution had never occurred.

§ 12.2 INVOLUNTARY DISSOLUTION

Whereas most corporate dissolutions are voluntary, under certain circumstances a corporation may be forced into dissolving by the state in which it is domiciled, by shareholders of the corporation, or by unsatisfied creditors of the corporation. State statutes generally require that **involuntary dissolutions** be accomplished through judicial proceedings. However, the statutes of several states that have adopted the provisions of the MBCA in this regard provide for an administrative dissolution by the secretary of state or other appropriate state official, without the necessity of a judicial proceeding.

Administrative Dissolution

A corporation's life is granted to it by the state and that life may be taken away by the state. It has been held that "[c]orporate privileges may be withdrawn by a state if they are abused or misemployed."[11] In an **administrative dissolution**, the state of the corporation's domicile dissolves the corporation. The corporation forfeits its right to exist, usually by failing to pay income taxes, failing to file annual reports, or failing to provide a registered agent or office in compliance with state statutes.

Although state statutes provide several different grounds for dissolution of a corporation by its state of domicile, the corporation is generally given several opportunities to rectify the situation that creates the grounds for involuntary dissolution. Section 14.20 of the MBCA sets forth the grounds for administrative dissolution in states patterned on the Model Act:

---

involuntary dissolution Dissolution that is not approved by the board of directors or shareholders of a corporation, often initiated by creditors of an insolvent corporation.

administrative dissolution Dissolution of a corporation by the state of the corporation's domicile, usually for failing to pay income taxes or file annual reports.

§ 14.20. GROUNDS FOR ADMINISTRATIVE DISSOLUTION

The secretary of state may commence a proceeding under section 14.21 to administratively dissolve a corporation if:

(1) the corporation does not pay within 60 days after they are due any franchise taxes or penalties imposed by this Act or other law;

(2) the corporation does not deliver its annual report to the secretary of state within 60 days after it is due;

(3) the corporation is without a registered agent or registered office in this state for 60 days or more;

(4) the corporation does not notify the secretary of state within 60 days that its registered agent or registered office has been changed, that its registered agent has resigned, or that its registered office has been discontinued; or

(5) the corporation's period of duration stated in its articles of incorporation expires.

The fact that one or more of the grounds for involuntary dissolution exists does not automatically dissolve the corporation. Specific statutory procedures must be followed for involuntary dissolution of a corporation. Typically, notice must be given to the corporation, and the corporation will have a prescribed time period within which to rectify the offending situation. Under the MBCA, the secretary of state must serve the corporation with written notice and the corporation must be given sixty days after service of the notice to correct the grounds for dissolution to the reasonable satisfaction of the secretary of state. If the grounds for dissolution are not corrected within that sixty-day period, the secretary of state may administratively dissolve the corporation by signing and filing a certificate of dissolution. Any corporation that has been administratively dissolved may continue its existence only for the purpose of winding up and liquidating its business and affairs.

Even after the corporation has been administratively dissolved, statutes typically provide a time period within which the corporation may be reinstated. However, once a corporation is dissolved, it may lose the right to use its name in the state, and that name may be taken by another corporation. In order for a corporation to be reinstated, its corporate name must be available, or it must use a different name. Section 14.22(a) of the MBCA provides for the reinstatement of a corporation following an administrative dissolution:

(a) A corporation administratively dissolved under section 14.21 may apply to the secretary of state for reinstatement within two years after the effective date of dissolution. The application must:

(1) recite the name of the corporation and the effective date of the administrative dissolution;

(2) state that the ground or grounds for dissolution either did not exist or have been eliminated;

(3) state that the corporation's name satisfies the requirements of section 4.01; and

(4) contain a certificate from the [taxing authority] reciting that all taxes owed by the corporation have been paid.

If the reinstatement is determined by the secretary of state to be effective, it relates back to the effective date of the administrative dissolution, and the corporation resumes its business as if the administrative dissolution had never occurred.

Judicial Dissolutions

Judicial dissolutions are supervised by the proper court. Although in some instances the shareholders and directors of a dissolving corporation will request judicial supervision over a voluntary dissolution, judicial dissolutions are usually involuntary. Judicial proceedings for dissolutions are usually initiated by a petition of the state attorney general, by minority shareholders, or by an unsatisfied creditor. After it is determined that grounds for a judicial dissolution exist, the court may enter a decree dissolving the corporation and directing the commencement of the winding up of the corporation's affairs and the liquidation of its assets.

The court in which the judicial proceedings are brought often appoints a receiver to manage the business and affairs of the corporation during the winding up process. This court-appointed receiver typically has all the rights and powers assigned by the court to sell and dispose of the assets of the corporation and to distribute the remaining assets of the corporation to the shareholders as directed by the court.

Judicial Proceedings by State Authority State statutes usually provide for involuntary dissolution of corporations by judicial proceedings at the behest of the attorney general or other appropriate state authority. Under the MBCA, the court may dissolve a corporation in a proceeding by the attorney general if it is found that the corporation obtained its articles of incorporation through fraud or the corporation has continued to exceed or abuse the authority conferred upon it by law.[12]

Judicial Proceedings by Shareholders Although statutes generally require the consensus of a majority of the shareholders to dissolve a corporation, a corporation may be dissolved by judicial proceedings brought by minority shareholders under certain circumstances. Some of the grounds set forth in state statutes for the judicial dissolution of a corporation by minority shareholders include insolvency of the corporation, corporate mismanagement or deadlock, and oppressive conduct by the controlling shareholders. It has been held that "even if there is no explicit statutory authority for dissolution of a corporation upon the petition of a minority stockholder, such relief is available as a matter of judicial sponsorship."[13] Section 14.30(2) of the MBCA sets forth the grounds for shareholder-initiated judicial dissolution in states following the Model Act:

> The [name or describe court or courts] may dissolve a corporation: ...
> (2) in a proceeding by a shareholder if it is established that:
>   (i) the directors are deadlocked in the management of the corporate affairs, the shareholders are unable to break the deadlock, and irreparable injury to the corporation is threatened or being suffered, or the business and affairs of the corporation can no longer be conducted to the advantage of the shareholders generally, because of the deadlock;

      (ii) the directors or those in control of the corporation have acted,
          are acting, or will act in a manner that is illegal, oppressive, or
          fraudulent;

      (iii) the shareholders are deadlocked in voting power and have failed,
          for a period that includes at least two consecutive annual meeting
          dates, to elect successors to directors whose terms have expired; or

      (iv) the corporate assets are being misapplied or wasted.

Judicial Proceedings by Creditor At times, corporations that are in severe financial trouble may continue to transact business despite having several judgments filed against them. Creditors may be unable to collect on their judgments if the corporation has insufficient liquid assets. For this reason, the statutes of most states provide for the involuntary dissolution of a corporation in a proceeding initiated by the corporation's creditors. The MBCA provides that the court may dissolve a corporation in a proceeding initiated by a creditor if the creditor's claim has been reduced to judgment, the execution on the judgment is returned unsatisfied, and the corporation is insolvent; or if the corporation has admitted in writing that the creditor's claim is due and owing and the corporation is insolvent.[14]

Buyouts and Other Alternatives to Involuntary Dissolutions The MBCA further provides that, under certain circumstances, when a shareholder has brought a petition for judicial dissolution, for any of the reasons given under § 14.30(2), the corporation or one or more of the other shareholders may elect to purchase all of the shares of the petitioning shareholder for their fair value. Election to purchase the shares of the petitioning shareholders in lieu of corporate dissolution under the MBCA is subject to many restrictions and conditions designed to protect the interests of the petitioning shareholders. The statutes of several states contain provisions similar to those of the MBCA, which recognize the fact that restructuring a corporation or buying out disgruntled shareholders is often a better alternative than the dissolution of a deadlocked corporation or a corporation that is otherwise unable to operate as presently structured.

§ 12.3 THE PARALEGAL'S ROLE IN DISSOLVING CORPORATIONS

Corporate dissolution and liquidation often involve the corporation's attorney, an assisting paralegal, and an accountant. The attorney and paralegal work with the client to see that all statutory formalities are complied with, while the accountant advises the client regarding the income tax aspects of dissolving and liquidating a corporation and the necessary tax filings.

    The paralegal can assist with all aspects of the dissolution process, including drafting the plans of dissolution and liquidation and the resolutions of the board of directors and shareholders approving the plan. The paralegal may also be responsible for drafting the articles of dissolution or other documents required for filing in the state of domicile, as well as drafting and publishing notices to the creditors of the dissolving corporation. The corporate paralegal often works directly with the client to obtain necessary information regarding the corporation's assets, liabilities, and creditors. The paralegal also may assist the corporate client with the distribution of assets by drafting deeds, assignments, and other instruments of transfer.

Following is a checklist of tasks that are typically undertaken in connection with a corporate dissolution:

- ☐ A plan of dissolution is agreed upon. This will usually take some planning involving the attorney, the corporate client and the corporation's accountants.
- ☐ A board of director resolution is prepared approving the dissolution and recommending the dissolution to the shareholders. This may be in the form of a unanimous writing, or the directors may hold an actual meeting.
- ☐ Notice of shareholders' meeting to approve the dissolution is prepared.
- ☐ A shareholder resolution approving the dissolution is prepared and adopted. Again, this may be in the form of a unanimous writing, or the resolution may be passed at a meeting of the shareholders.
- ☐ A statement of intent to dissolve is filed in states requiring the filing of such a document.
- ☐ Proper notice is given to all known creditors.
- ☐ In some cases, notice of the dissolution is published.
- ☐ Form 966 is prepared and filed with the IRS.
- ☐ The corporation's assets are liquidated and distributed.
- ☐ Final tax payments are made on behalf of the corporation.
- ☐ Articles of dissolution are filed.

Corporate Paralegal Profile
Angela C. Rhode

We outsource a lot of cases to other attorneys, which is helpful to me. However, we still have to keep track of those cases and the status of each case.

Name Angela C. Rhode

Location Columbia, South Carolina

Title Senior Paralegal

Education Associate Degree in Public Service; major in Paralegal Studies

Experience 7 years

Angela Rhode is a paralegal for Collins Entertainment, Inc., in Columbia, South Carolina. Collins Entertainment is an amusement and gaming machine operating company. The company provides gaming and amusement equipment to its customers, including video and arcade games, jukeboxes, and pool tables.

She is the only paralegal at the corporation's offices in Columbia, where she reports to a vice president of the corporation who is also chief counsel. In addition, Angela is responsible for coordinating the outsourcing of numerous cases to outside counsel, and tracking the status of each case.

Angela's responsibilities mainly concern the litigation Collins Entertainment becomes involved in. Although she specializes in litigation and not *corporate* work, Angela works for a corporation that is involved in lawsuits with other corporations. It is very important for her to be familiar with the law of corporations.

Her duties include preparing contracts, maintaining civil cases from beginning to end, collections, receiving payments, and maintaining legal status reports, judgment reports, and recovery reports. Angela also has several administrative duties.

Angela is a member of the Palmetto Paralegal Association and the National Federation of Paralegal Associations. She is attending Columbia College to earn a Bachelor's Degree in Public Affairs, with a major in Political Science.

Angela's advice to new paralegals?

Try to find a job that fits your personality. Whether it be a large law firm or sole practitioner, do not limit yourself. Find a working

environment that encourages you to advance. Respect yourself and look forward to going to work everyday. Get involved in paralegal associations. (You meet a lot of interesting people at the meetings.)

For more information on careers for corporate paralegals, log on to the companion Web page to this text at **www.westlegalstudies.com.**

§ 12.4 RESOURCES

The most valuable resources for information regarding corporate dissolutions, and assistance in filing corporate dissolution documents, are the state statutes, forms and form books, the appropriate secretary of state office, and corporation service companies.

State Statutes

Provisions for corporate dissolutions are typically found in the Business Corporation Act or similar act adopted by the state of domicile. See Figure 12-1 of this chapter for a list of state corporation dissolution statutes.

Legal Form Books

A corporate dissolution can be a very document-intensive procedure. Legal form books, such as *Am. Jur. Forms 2d, Nichols Cyclopedia of Legal Forms Annotated, Rabkin & Johnson Current Legal Forms,* and *West's Legal Forms (second edition),* can be good sources for forms for the corporate resolutions approving the dissolution, notices of dissolution, statements of intent to dissolve, and articles of dissolution. Some secretary of state offices may provide forms or even require the use of their forms for certain dissolution purposes. Any forms used for the corporate dissolution process must be tailored to meet the specific requirements of the state of dissolution.

Secretary of State or Other Appropriate State Authority

The secretary of state or other appropriate state authority must be contacted to determine what the specific filing requirements are for corporate dissolution documents. The on-line services of these offices often include forms and general information on dissolution procedures. See appendix A to this text for a secretary of state directory.

Corporation Service Companies

When a corporation dissolves, it must withdraw from every state where it is qualified to do business as a foreign corporation. Some states require the filing of a certificate of termination from the corporation's state of domicile. For corporations that are qualified in several states, this can be quite an undertaking. Corporation service companies can assist you with this process. They can provide the necessary forms for each state and take care of filing them for you. For the names of services in your location, you can consult your telephone directory, search the Internet, or ask for referrals from attorneys and other paralegals.

Local and Federal Tax Offices

The Internal Revenue Service provides information concerning the filing of the forms required for filing by dissolving corporations on its Web page at **www.irs.gov**. In addition, state and sometimes local taxing authorities should be contacted to determine the state and local requirements.

 Internet Resources www.

There are several on-line resources to assist paralegals with the dissolution process. Some of these resources include general information on the dissolution process, state statutes, the Internal Revenue Service, and secretary of state Web pages.

Following is a list of some Web pages that may be useful to paralegals who are assisting with the corporate dissolution process:

For links to state dissolution forms

Findlaw.com State Corporation   www.findlaw.com/11stategov/indexcorp.html
  and Business Forms

For links to the secretary of state offices

Corporate Housekeeper   www.danvi.vi/link2.html

National Association of   www.nass.org
  Secretaries of State

For federal tax information concerning the dissolution of a corporation

Internal Revenue Service   www.irs.gov

An alphabetical list of Internet Resources for the Corporate Paralegal is included as appendix B to this text.

Web Page

For updates and links to several of the previously listed sites, as well as downloadable state dissolution forms, log on to **www.westlegalstudies.com,** and click through to the book link for this text.

SUMMARY

- Corporations are given their life by state statute and they must be dissolved according to state statute.
- A dissolving corporation must surrender its certificate of authority in every state in which it is qualified to do business as a foreign corporation.

- ◆ A dissolving corporation must file a Form 966, Corporate Dissolution or Liquidation, with the IRS, and it must file a final income tax return.
- ◆ Voluntary dissolutions are approved by the directors and shareholders of the corporation.
- ◆ In some states the corporation is dissolved by filing articles of dissolution or a certificate of dissolution with the secretary of state.
- ◆ In some states the corporation first files a notice (or statement) of intent to dissolve with the secretary of state, and then files articles of dissolution at a later date.
- ◆ All state statutes provide procedures for notifying a corporation's creditors of its dissolution.
- ◆ After a dissolving corporation has filed either its notice of dissolution (in states that require such a document), or its articles of dissolution, with the secretary of state, it begins the process of winding up its affairs and liquidating its assets.
- ◆ Shareholders may be liable for valid claims made after the dissolution of a corporation, but only to the extent of the distribution they received when the corporation dissolved.
- ◆ Corporations may be dissolved involuntarily by a court action brought by creditors.
- ◆ In an administrative dissolution, the corporation is dissolved by its state of domicile, usually for failure to pay taxes or file annual reports.

REVIEW QUESTIONS

1. Suppose that Ann, Bob, and Christie are all incorporators of the ABC Corporation. Dennis and Elaine are elected directors, and all five are to become shareholders of the new corporation. Before shares of stock are actually issued, the five investors decide to form a limited liability company instead. Bob has taken on responsibility for dissolving the corporation. Who must approve the dissolution? What if shares of stock had been issued?

2. What are the duties of the individual or individuals who are responsible for winding up the affairs of a dissolving corporation?

3. In states following the MCBA, what documentation must be filed with the secretary of state?

4. Does the corporate existence dissolve upon the filing of the articles of dissolution in states following the MCBA? If not, for what purpose(s) is the corporate existence extended?

5. Under the MBCA, what notice of liquidation must be given to the creditors of a corporation?

6. What possible recourse does a minority shareholder have when the corporate management is deadlocked?

7. To what extent may the shareholders of a dissolved corporation be held liable for the debts of the corporation incurred prior to dissolution?

8. Suppose that the ABC Corporation is administratively dissolved on January 1, 1992, for failure to file annual reports in compliance with the statutes of its state of domicile. On June 30, the ABC Corporation eliminates the grounds for its dissolution to the satisfaction of the secretary of state and becomes reinstated. Could the shareholders of the ABC Corporation be held personally liable for obligations incurred on behalf of the corporation on

March 15, on the grounds that the corporation did not legally exist?

9. In a state following the MCBA, can a creditor of a dissolved corporation who has received proper notice collect on that claim six months after the notice was received?

PRACTICAL PROBLEMS

1. Find the pertinent corporate dissolution statute in your state to answer the following questions:
   a. What document(s) must be filed in your state to dissolve a corporation?
   b. What information is required in the document(s) that needs to be filed to dissolve a corporation?
2. What provisions are made in your state for notifying the creditors of a dissolving corporation?
   a. Briefly describe the notice that must be given to known creditors of a dissolving corporation.
   b. If your state provides for publishing a notice of dissolution, how long do claimants have to commence proceedings to collect a claim after notice of a corporation's dissolution has been published?

WORKPLACE SCENARIO

Assume that our fictional clients, Bradley Harris and Cynthia Lund, have decided to go their separate ways, and they want to dissolve their corporation. Your supervising attorney has asked you to draft the necessary paperwork for her review.

Using the information in appendix D-3, prepare the documents required for filing with the appropriate state authority in your state to dissolve Cutting Edge Computer Repair, Inc. Also prepare a cover letter with accompanying filing fee. Again, disregard the merger performed in Chapter 10.

END NOTES

1. 19 Am. Jur. 2d *Corporations* § 2752 (1985).
2. 6B Am. Jur. 2d *Legal Forms* 2d § 74:3001 (1995). Reprinted with permission from *American Jurisprudence Legal Forms 2d.* © 2000 West Group.
3. *Id.* § 3025. Reprinted with permission from *American Jurisprudence Legal Forms 2d.* © 2000 West Group.
4. Articles of Dissolution are filed with probate judge.
5. Articles of Dissolution are filed with mayor.
6. Notice of Intent to Dissolve must be published.
7. Certificates are required from the Department of Revenue and Taxation and the Department of Labor certifying that all fees, charges, taxes, etc., have been paid.
8. 19 Am. Jur. 2d *Corporations* § 2828 (1985).
9. *Id.* § 2733 (1985).
10. *Id.* § 14.04(a).
11. 19 Am. Jur. 2d *Corporations* § 2788 (1985).
12. 1984 Revised Model Business Corporation Act § 14.30(1).
13. 19A Am. Jur. 2d *Corporations* § 2758 (1985).
14. 1984 Revised Model Business Corporation Act § 14.30(3).

CHAPTER 13

Employee Benefit Plans

CHAPTER OUTLINE

§ 13.1   Qualified Plans

§ 13.2   Laws Governing Qualified Plans

§ 13.3   Elements of a Qualified Plan

§ 13.4   ERISA and IRC Requirements Common to All Types of Qualified Plans

§ 13.5   Qualified Pension Plans

§ 13.6   Nonqualified Pension Plans

§ 13.7   Employee Welfare Benefit Plans

§ 13.8   Qualified Plan Adoption and IRS Approval

§ 13.9   Annual Reporting Requirements and Disclosure Requirements

§ 13.10   The Paralegal's Role in Working with Qualified Plans

§ 13.11   Resources

INTRODUCTION

The salary paid to employees by a corporation accounts for only a portion of their total compensation. Employers also compensate their employees with a mixture of other benefits, some of which are mandated by law, such as Social Security and workers' compensation, and some of which the employer may elect to offer to compensate its current employees and entice new employees. There are a wide variety of employee benefit plans that employers may elect to adopt, including pension plans and welfare benefit plans.

Plans that meet with certain requirements of the Internal Revenue Code (IRC) and qualify for special tax treatment are referred to as **qualified plans**. Because of the frequent passage of legislation that favors qualified plans, the number and value

---

qualified plan   Pension plan that meets I.R.S. requirements for the payments to be deducted by the employer and initially tax-free to the employee.

of qualified plans have been increasing significantly in recent years. As of the end of 1996, nearly 92 million people in this country were participants in private pension plans, and nearly $170 billion in annual contributions were made to those plans.[1]

§ 13.1 QUALIFIED PLANS

In addition to compensating valuable employees and enticing new employees, qualified plans offer several unique benefits to both the employer and the employee.

Qualified pension plans offer tax incentives to employers by allowing a tax deduction for the employers' contributions to qualified plans. In addition, investment income earned on contributions is tax-free until it is distributed to plan participants.

Tax benefits to the qualified pension plan participant include deferred income tax payments: No income tax is payable on the contribution to the plan, only on the benefit received from it in the future. Under certain circumstances, income tax payable on the benefits received from a qualified plan may also be deferred.

Qualified welfare benefit plans allow the employer a tax deduction for certain health and welfare benefits they offer to their employees. In addition, employees may be allowed to pay for their portion of welfare benefits with pre-tax dollars.

§ 13.2 LAWS GOVERNING QUALIFIED PLANS

Qualified plans are subject to the restrictions and requirements set forth in the IRC §§ 401–418E, and the **Employee Retirement Income Security Act of 1974 (ERISA),** which is the main act regulating qualified plans.

Employee Retirement Income Security Act of 1974 (ERISA)

ERISA was adopted in 1974 to protect the participants and beneficiaries of employee benefit plans—a growing population of individuals in the United States—in response to congressional findings that "employee benefit plans substantially affect interstate commerce, federal tax revenues, and the national public interest, as well as the continued well-being and security of millions of employees and their beneficiaries."[2]

The provisions of ERISA govern most pension and welfare benefit plans, including those that are not *qualified* plans under the Internal Revenue Code. This means that even certain plans that are not allowed special income tax treatment may be subject to the provisions of ERISA, which establish:

♦ Reporting and disclosure requirements.

♦ Minimum participation requirements.

Employee Retirement Income Security Act (ERISA) (29 U.S.C. 1000) A federal law that established a program to protect employees' pension plans. The law set up a fund to pay pensions when plans go broke and regulates pension plans as to *vesting* (when a person's pension rights become permanent), nondiversion of benefits to anyone other than those entitled, nondiscrimination against lower-paid employees, etc.

- ◆ Minimum vesting requirements.
- ◆ Minimum funding requirements for certain pension plans.

In addition, ERISA imposes fiduciary duties on fiduciaries of employee benefit plans, and it gives employees the ability to enforce their rights in federal court.

Internal Revenue Code

For a plan to receive special income taxation treatment, it must be qualified under the IRC. The IRC protects employees covered by employee benefit plans by providing tax incentives for corporations that comply with IRC provisions that establish rules for participation, coverage, vesting, and other matters concerning the funding and administration of employee benefit plans.

Dividends ————————————————————————◆

An ESOP Fable

Once upon a time, corporate management decided to do something nice for corporate employees. Management wanted to reward its employees for their hard work and to give their employees incentive to produce more. So management gave their employees stock in the corporation through an employee stock ownership plan (ESOP).

This made corporate employees very happy, and they worked harder and harder. They knew that the harder they worked, the more profitable their corporation would become, and the more valuable their stock would be. Workers also enjoyed their ability to have a say in the management of the corporation through the voting of their stock. Although they were usually not able to effect any major changes in the corporation, they felt that they had an outlet to express their opinions.

Corporate management soon found that not only did ESOPs make corporate employees happy, but it made the IRS happy too. Corporate management found that they gained a significant income tax savings through use of the ESOP. In addition to other income tax benefits, they were able to deduct dividends paid on all shares of stock owned by the ESOP.

Corporate management also discovered that the ESOP was a good vehicle for raising capital for the corporation. ESOPs can be used to borrow money from a lending institution to purchase stock from the corporation, which qualifies for a tax break on interest paid on the loan. Thus, the corporation receives cash from the ESOP, the ESOP receives stock from the corporation, and the money is borrowed from the bank at a low interest rate. This also made corporate management happy.

Retiring corporate management of closely held corporations were also happy, because now they had a market for their stock when they decided to retire. The ESOP became a market for the stock of retiring employees. Finally, corporate management found that the ESOP was good protection from hostile corporate takeovers. By putting a substantial amount of the stock of the corporation in the hands of the friendly corporate employees, corporate raiders could not obtain the requisite amount of stock to take over the corporation. Delaware state law provides that hostile bidders must buy 85 percent of the stock of a corporation. Therefore, if 15 percent or more of the stock of a Delaware corporation is in the hands of an ESOP, a hostile takeover cannot be completed.

All of these things made corporate management very happy.

The moral of this story is: "Be nice to your employees, and your employees (and the IRS) will be nice to you."

§ 13.3 ELEMENTS OF A QUALIFIED PLAN

The terms and conditions of a qualified plan will depend on the type of plan and the specific plan provisions. However, generally all types of qualified plans have some common elements. Qualified plans usually are adopted by an employer who acts as the sponsor of the plan. Qualified plans are administered by a plan administrator for the benefit of the plan participants or their beneficiaries.

The Sponsor

The **sponsor** of a qualified plan is typically a corporate employer. However, a partnership or even a self-employed individual may act as a plan sponsor. In addition, under certain circumstances, unions, associations, or similar groups may act as plan sponsors. A sponsor must adopt a qualified plan for the exclusive benefit of the sponsor's employees or their beneficiaries.

The Plan

The plan that is adopted by the sponsor must be a written document that includes the minimum provisions required for qualified plans by law. The plan or its significant provisions must be communicated to the sponsor's employees. The plan must be communicated to employees through use of a summary plan description. This is a document that is furnished to participants and beneficiaries and written in a manner that can be understood by the average plan participant. This simplified version of the plan provisions that affect the plan participants is often distributed to employees in booklet form. The requirements for a summary plan description under ERISA § 102 are listed in Figure 13-1 on page 496.

The Plan Administrator

Qualified plans may be administered and managed by one or more individuals who are considered to be fiduciaries of the plan. The plan sponsor or trustee may act as the administrator, or the administrator may be a professional plan administrator or investment manager. **Plan administrators** are generally responsible for calculating and processing all contributions to and distributions from the plan, and for all other aspects of plan administration. The specific duties assigned to the plan administrator are typically set forth in the plan document or in a supplement thereto.

---

sponsor   In ERISA terms, an employer who adopts a qualified plan for the exclusive benefit of the sponsor's employees and/or their beneficiaries.

plan administrator   Individual or entity responsible for calculating and processing all contributions to and distributions from a qualified plan, and for all other aspects of plan administration.

The Summary Plan Description must contain the following information:

- Name of the Plan
- Type of Administration
- Name and Address of Person Designated as Agent for Service of Legal Process
- Name and Address of Plan Administrator
- Names, Titles, and Addresses of any Trustees
- Description of Relevant Provisions of any Applicable Collective Bargaining Agreement
- Eligibility Requirements for Plan Participation
- Eligibility Requirements for Receiving Plan Benefits
- Description of Provisions Providing for Nonforfeitable Pension Benefits
- Circumstances which May Result in Disqualification, Ineligibility, or Denial or Loss of Benefits
- Source of Financing of the Plan
- Identity of any Organization through which Benefits Are Provided
- Date of End of Plan Year; and Whether Records are Kept on Plan or Calendar Year
- Claims Procedures
- Remedies Available for Redress of Denied Claims
- If the Plan is a Group Health Plan, a Statement as to whether a Health Insurance Issuer is Responsible for the Financing or Administration (including payment of claims) of the Plan and (if so) the Name and Address of Such Issuer

FIGURE 13-1   Requirements for Summary Plan Description Under ERISA § 102

The Plan Participants

The terms of the plan document determine who may participate in the plan. **Plan participants** are generally any employees of the sponsor who meet certain minimum requirements set forth in the plan in compliance with ERISA.

§ 13.4 ERISA AND IRC REQUIREMENTS COMMON TO ALL TYPES OF QUALIFIED PLANS

The plan requirements under ERISA and the IRC are numerous, and depend on the type of qualified plan and, in some instances, the plan sponsor. This section discusses some of the fundamental requirements that typically apply to all types of qualified plans. In general, ERISA provides that the qualified plan must be permanent, must be in writing, and must be for the exclusive benefit of the sponsor's

plan participant Employees who meet with certain minimum requirements to participate in a qualified plan.

employees. In addition, ERISA sets forth minimum coverage requirements that apply to most plans.

Plan Must Be Established for the Exclusive Benefit of Employees

Qualified plans must be established for the exclusive benefit of employees or their beneficiaries. The plan participants usually may choose their beneficiaries freely. However, if the provisions of the plan so specify, the choice of beneficiaries may be limited. For a plan to be qualified under IRC § 401(a), it must be "impossible, at any time prior to the satisfaction of all liabilities with respect to employees and their beneficiaries under the trust, for any part of the corpus or income to be … diverted to purposes other than for the exclusive benefit of his employees or their beneficiaries." Plan sponsors are prohibited from removing funds from a qualified plan trust for their own use.

Minimum Coverage and Participation Requirements

Qualified plans must meet certain minimum participation and minimum coverage standards set forth in the IRC and ERISA, or the plan will lose its qualified status. Minimum participation and minimum coverage rules are established to ensure that the qualified plans do not discriminate in favor of the corporation's owners or its most highly compensated employees.

The current minimum participation rules established under IRC § 401(a)(26) state that the plan must, for each day of the plan year, benefit the lesser of (1) fifty employees of the employer, or (2) the greater of (a) 40 percent or more of all employees of the employer or (b) two employees (or if there is only one employee, such employee). This means that for a 100-employee corporation to pass the test, it must benefit at least forty employees (40 percent) every day of each year that the plan is in effect. A 1,000-employee corporation must benefit at least 50 employees to pass this test.

Under IRC § 410(a)(3), a qualified plan cannot require, as a condition of plan participation, that an employee complete a period of service extending beyond the later of (1) the date the employee reaches age 21, or (2) the day the employee completes one year of service.

The minimum coverage rules provide that qualified plans must not benefit too high of a percentage of highly compensated employees. IRC § 410(b)(1) requires that for any determination year:

1. The plan must benefit at least 70 percent of employees who are not highly compensated employees (the "percentage test"); or

2. The plan must benefit a percentage of nonhighly compensated employees, which is at least 70 percent of the percentage of highly compensated employees benefiting under the plan (the "ratio test"); or

3. The plan must meet the "average benefit percentage test." The plan will qualify under the *average benefit percentage test* if (1) the plan benefits employees

qualifying under a classification set up by the employer which does not discriminate in favor of highly compensated employees, and (2) the average benefit percentage for nonhighly compensated employees is at least 70 percent of the average benefit percentage for highly compensated employees.

A *highly compensated employee* is any employee who:

1. Was a five percent owner at any time during the year or the preceding year; or
2. For the preceding year, received compensation from the employer in excess of $80,000 (as adjusted for cost-of-living increases), and, if the employer elects, was in the top paid group of employees for the preceding year. The employer can make the election annually, without the consent of IRS.

Certain employees, such as those who have not met minimum age and service requirements established by the plan, nonresident aliens, and employees who are covered by a collective bargaining agreement may be disregarded for purposes of the calculations for complying with the minimum participation and minimum coverage tests.

Exemptions from the Provisions of ERISA

Not all plans are subject to the provisions of ERISA. Government plans, certain plans of nonprofit corporations, workers' compensation, unemployment and certain disability plans, and unfunded excess benefit plans are among those that are exempt.[3]

§ 13.5 QUALIFIED PENSION PLANS

Qualified pension plans are qualified plans that are designed to provide retirement income to participants. Benefits may be paid in a lump sum or in the form of an **annuity**. Disbursements from qualified pension plans are typically not made until the participant retires, reaches retirement age, becomes disabled, or terminates employment with the sponsoring employer.

Contributions made to the qualified pension plan are held in a trust where the funds are managed until they are fully distributed.

Qualified pension plans generally fall into one of two broad categories: the defined benefit plan or the defined contribution plan. At times, an employer may adopt both a defined benefit plan and a defined contribution plan and design them to complement each other.

---

annuity A fixed sum of money, usually paid to a person at fixed times for a fixed time period or for life. If for life, or for some other uncertain period of time, it is called a contingent annuity. A retirement annuity is a right to receive payments starting at some future date, usually retirement, but sometimes a fixed date. There are many ways a retirement annuity can be paid. For example, *life* (equal monthly payments for the retiree's life); *lump sum* (one payment); *certain and continuous* (like *life,* but if the person dies within a set time period, benefits continue for the rest of that period); and *joint and survivor* (benefits continue for the life of either the retiree or the spouse).

Contributions

Qualified plan contributions are made to the plan by the plan sponsor, the plan participant, or both. The amount of the contribution is established in accordance with the provisions of the plan, but is limited by provisions of IRC § 415. Contributions to qualified plans are subject to several different limitations imposed by law, including limitations based on the total amount of the contribution per employee, and the total amount of compensation of each employee which may be considered when calculating the contribution. In addition, contributions to qualified plans must be made in accordance with special rules that prohibit discrimination in favor of highly compensated employees. Contributions are deductible if made to qualified plans so long as they are reasonable compensation for services actually rendered to the contributing employer, and so long as the contribution does not exceed statutory limits.

If contributions are made in excess of the IRC § 415 limits, the plan may become disqualified, which can have severe consequences for plan sponsors and participants. If a plan is deemed to be disqualified, contributions made to the plan become taxable, as well as the income earned by the trust holding the assets.

The Trust

The contributions made to the plan are generally held in a **qualified plan trust** that is managed by trustees, who are appointed by the plan sponsors in the plan document or a supplement thereto. The contributions will be invested by the trustees or others who are designated to manage the trust assets. As long as the pension plan remains "qualified," the trust will pay no income tax on the income of its assets.

Benefits

In addition to meeting certain requirements concerning the pension plan participation by employees, pension plans must be designed to provide certain minimum benefits to employees. Qualified pension plan benefits must not exceed certain limitations and discriminate in favor of highly compensated employees, and all pension plans must meet certain accrued benefit rules and minimum vesting standards for all employees.

Accrued Benefit Rules   Qualified pension plans generally must meet the **accrued benefit** rules in the IRC and ERISA. The term *accrued benefits* refers to the amount of benefit each participant has accumulated or has been allocated in his or her name as of a particular point in time. With a few exceptions, a participant's

---

qualified plan contributions Contributions made to a qualified plan by the sponsor, participants, or third parties. Limitations on the amount of contributions are set forth in the Internal Revenue Code.

qualified plan trust Trust managed by trustees who are appointed by the qualified plan sponsors to manage the assets of the qualified plan.

accrued benefit The amount of benefit a participant has accumulated or that has been allocated to him or her as of a particular point in time.

accrued benefits under a qualified plan may not be reduced or eliminated by plan amendment.

Vesting   Qualified plans must provide that participants become **vested** in their benefits in accordance with certain requirements set forth in ERISA § 203. *Vesting* refers to the participant's nonforfeitable right to receive the benefit. To comply with ERISA's minimum vesting standards, qualified plans must:

1. Provide that the employee's right to the normal retirement benefit is nonforfeitable upon the attainment of normal retirement age.

2. Provide that the employee's right in the accrued benefit derived from the employee's own contributions is nonforfeitable.

3. Comply with the minimum vesting provisions set forth in ERISA § 203(a)(2).

ERISA § 203(a)(2) provides that any employee who has at least five years of service with the employer has a nonforfeitable right to 100 percent of the employee's accrued benefit derived from employer contributions. In the alternative, a plan may provide for vesting on the following schedule:

Years of Service	Nonforfeitable Percentage
3	20%
4	40%
5	60%
6	80%
7 or more	100%

Top-Heavy Plans   If a plan primarily favors officers, directors, stockholders, partners, or other key employees, it is considered to be "top-heavy." Top-heavy plans must comply with certain vesting, benefits, and contribution rules for nonkey employees that are prescribed in ERISA specifically for top-heavy plans. Defined benefit plans are considered to be top-heavy if more than 60 percent of the accrued benefits are for the key employees. Defined contribution plans are considered to be top-heavy when more than 60 percent of the aggregate of the account balances is for key employees.

Distributions

Distributions are made from the plan to the plan participants or their beneficiaries in accordance with the terms and provisions of the plan. **Qualified plan distributions** are usually made at the time of the participant's retirement, death, or

vested   Absolute, accrued, complete, not subject to any conditions that could take it away; not contingent on anything. For example, if a person sells you a house and gives you a deed, you have a vested interest in the property; and a pension is vested if you get it at retirement age even if you leave the company before that. There are several types of pension plan vesting. For example, "cliff" vesting (until you work a certain number of years, you get nothing; after that, you get all your accrued benefits); "graded" vesting (additional percentages of your accrued benefits are added the longer you work).

termination from the plan sponsor's employment. ERISA § 206 provides that plan provisions of qualified pension plans must provide that benefit payments will begin in the year following the latest of the following events (unless the plan participant elects otherwise):

1. The date the participant reaches the age of 65 (or the normal retirement age set forth in the plan).
2. The date the participant reaches the tenth anniversary of plan participation.
3. The date of the participant's termination of service.

For example, suppose an individual becomes a participant in a plan when she is 45 years old, then leaves her position 10 years later. The plan must provide that she will be entitled to begin receiving benefit payments the year following the year in which she turns 65 (or the normal retirement age set forth in the plan). If that same individual were to work until her 71st birthday, she would be entitled to begin receiving benefits the year following her termination.

Distributions from qualified plans are usually taxable when they are paid out. Distributions made prior to retirement age may be subject to additional excise tax. Plan participants may be allowed to roll over distributions from one qualified pension plan to another. For example, an employee who receives a distribution from a qualified pension plan may be able to roll over that distribution by investing it in an individual retirement account or another qualified plan within 60 days, and defer the income tax owing on the distribution until it is withdrawn from the new plan.

Defined Benefit Plans

As the name implies, **defined benefit plans** are those in which the benefit payable to the participant or the participant's beneficiaries is definitely determinable from a benefit formula set forth in the plan. Contributions to defined benefit plans are based on the amount that will eventually be paid out to the participant, not on the income or profits of the corporation. Benefits are generally calculated by a formula that takes into consideration the employees' years of service and their salaries.

Benefits payable from qualified defined benefit plans are limited by the provisions of IRC § 415(b)(1), which states in part that benefits exceed the limitations allowed under that section if they are greater than the lesser of (a) $130,000, or (b) 100 percent of the participant's average compensation for his or her high three years. For example, to meet the requirements of IRC § 415(b)(1), an employee who made an average of $150,000 per year for the last three years of employment could not receive over $130,000 (80 percent of his or her average salary). The benefit payable to an employee who averaged $50,000 per year for the last three

---

qualified plan distributions Distributions made to qualified plan participants or their beneficiaries from a qualified retirement plan trust, usually on the retirement, death, or termination of employment of the plan participant.

defined benefit plans Retirement plans in which the benefit payable to the participant is definitely determinable from a benefit formula set forth in the plan.

years of employment could not exceed $50,000 (100 percent of his or her average salary). The $130,000 limit is subject to indexing for inflation. $130,000 is the correct figure for 1999.

Most defined benefit pension plans provide for the payment of benefits to employees over a period of years, usually for life, after retirement.[4] Pension plan contributions may be made by employers, employees, and third parties. The actual contribution to be made to the plan is typically calculated by an **actuary** or by use of actuarial tables. The basis for contributions to qualified pension plans must be established in the plan, and the contributions must meet the funding requirements of ERISA, which are designed to insure that funds in the pension plan trust will be adequate to meet the plan's obligation to pay benefits as defined in the pension plan.

The amount of investment income generated by the pension trust's assets will not affect the benefit payable to the participant of a defined benefit pension plan. The amount of investment income (or loss) may, however, affect the amount of the contribution required each year to maintain adequate assets in the pension trust.

The pension plan's provisions determine when a participant's benefits commence. A qualified pension plan must provide *retirement* benefits to its participants, but the plan determines when payment of those retirement benefits will commence, within certain limitations set forth in ERISA § 206(a). Distributions from a qualified pension plan may be either in a lump sum or by distribution of an **annuity policy**.

The benefits payable under the pension plan must be calculated in a reasonable manner. The most common formulas for providing benefits for qualified pension plans include the fixed benefit formula, the unit benefit formula, and the variable benefit formula:[5]

> The **fixed benefit formula** provides participants with a definite percentage of their income. For example, benefits could be 35 percent of the employee's average compensation during the last five years of employment.
>
> The **unit benefit formula** provides participants with a unit of pension for each year of credited service. The unit may be either a percentage of compensation or a stated dollar amount.
>
> The **variable benefit formula** provides participants with benefits that are related to the market value of the trust assets or are tied to a recognized cost of living index.

---

actuary A person skilled in mathematical calculations to determine insurance risks, premiums, etc. A statistician.

annuity policy An insurance policy that may be purchased to provide an annuity.

fixed benefit formula Formula for calculating pension plan benefits that provides participant with a definite percentage of their income.

unit benefit formula Formula for calculating the benefits payable under a pension plan that provides participants with a unit of pension for each year of credited service.

variable benefit formula A formula used to calculate benefits payable under a pension plan that provides participants with benefits that are related to the market value of the trust assets or are tied to a recognized cost of living index.

Annuity Plans An **annuity plan** is a type of defined benefit pension plan with no trust. When annuity plans are used, contributions to the pension plan are used to purchase retirement annuities directly from an insurance company. Although annuity contracts are not "trusts," annuity contracts held by an insurance company are treated as qualified trusts, and the person holding the contract is treated as the trustee.[6]

Defined Contribution Plans

Defined contribution plans establish an individual account for each participant and provide benefits based solely on the amount contributed to the participant's account. They are often designed to allow the plan participants, and beneficiaries of the participants, to share in the profits of the corporation.

Contributions to participants' accounts, which may be made by the employer, the employee, or a third party, are determined by a formula prescribed in the plan, which may be based on any or all of the following: the corporation's profits, the salary of the participant, and/or the contributions made to the plan by the participant. Each participant's account is credited with the participant's share of the contribution pursuant to the terms of the plan.

Contributions to qualified defined contribution plans are limited by the provisions of IRC § 415(c)(1), which states in part that annual contributions to qualified defined contribution plans exceed the limits allowed under that section if the annual contribution is greater than the lesser of: (1) $30,000 (or, if greater, one-quarter of the dollar limitations in effect under subsection (b)(1)(A), or (2) 25 percent of the participant's compensation. The dollar amount referred to under subsection (b)(1)(A) is the dollar amount limit placed on the benefits receivable under defined benefit plans, which is currently $130,000. Following is an example of a calculation to determine the maximum amount that can be contributed to the account of a defined contribution participant who has an annual salary of $100,000.

Pursuant to IRC § 415(c)(1), the contribution may be no greater than the *lesser* of the following:

(A) $30,000 (or, if greater, one-quarter of the dollar limitations in effect under subsection (b)(1)(A) which is currently $130,000 (in 1995)).
   ¼ of $130,000 = $32,500.
   Because ¼ of the subsection (b)(1)(A) figure is greater than the $30,000 limit, $32,500 is the figure to use for subsection (A) of this section.

---

annuity plan Type of qualified plan that does not involve a qualified plan trust. Contributions to an annuity plan are used to buy annuity policies directly from an insurance company.

defined contribution plan Retirement plan that establishes individual accounts for each plan participant and provides benefits based solely on the amount contributed to the participants' accounts.

(B) 25 percent of the participant's compensation.

   25% of $100,000 = $25,000.

The lesser of the figures calculated from (A) and (B) is $25,000, so the annual contribution to the defined contribution plan in this instance may not exceed $25,000.

Plan contributions are retained in a qualified plan trust and income earned through investment of the plan assets is credited to each account, generally in the same proportion as plan contributions. The benefit payable to the participant or the participant's beneficiaries is calculated based upon contributions to the participant's account and any income, expenses, gains, losses, and forfeitures attributable to the participant's account.

Contributions made by the employer to the plan will be vested pursuant to a schedule set forth in the plan, which must comply with the minimum vesting standards of ERISA. Contributions made by employees are 100 percent vested as of the date of the contribution.

Distributions are made from the defined contribution plan pursuant to plan provisions and the provisions of ERISA § 206(a).

Profit-Sharing Plans   The **profit-sharing** plan is the most common type of qualified defined contribution plan. The profit-sharing plan is a type of deferred compensation plan whereby contributions are typically made to the account of the individual participants based on the profits of the corporation for the previous fiscal year. Employer contributions are often calculated as a percentage of the corporation's profits. However, the plan may provide that the board of directors has the discretion to set the annual contribution. The employer's contribution is generally credited to the account of each profit-sharing plan participant based on a formula that takes into consideration each participant's income as a fraction of the total income of all participants.

A profit-sharing plan offers the employer the flexibility to reduce or omit contributions to the plan during years of adversity. At the same time, it can increase employee motivation by giving employees an added benefit when the corporation does well.

401(k) Provisions and Plans   IRC § 401(k) provides for qualified cash or deferred arrangements whereby employees may elect to defer a certain percentage of their compensation each year to provide for their own retirement benefits. Salary deferrals are considered to be employer contributions and are not taxable to employees until distributed. 401(k) provisions are often found within profit sharing plans that provide for matching contributions by the employer (as permitted by IRC § 401(m)) and discretionary profit sharing contributions (also by the employer). Participants are always 100 percent vested in their plan benefits to the extent

---

profit-sharing   Describes a plan set up by an employer to distribute part of the firm's profits to some or all of its employees. A *qualified plan* (one that meets requirements for tax benefits) must have specific criteria and formulas for who gets what, how, and when.

that those benefits are attributed to salary deferrals. Plans that contain only 401(k) provisions are sometimes referred to as **401(k) plans**. To receive favorable tax treatment 401(k) plans must not discriminate in favor of highly compensated individuals with regard either to eligibility to participate in the plan or to the actual deferrals made.

Money Purchase Pension Plans The **money purchase pension plan** is a defined contribution pension plan whereby the employer contributes a fixed amount based on a formula, set forth in the plan, that is based on the employee's salary. The money purchase pension plan is a defined contribution plan, because the employer's contribution is allocated to individual accounts on behalf of the employees and because the benefit received depends on the amount contributed to each account. However, it also resembles a defined benefit plan, because the employer is obligated to contribute to the plan each year and the amount of the contribution is not discretionary, and because the amount of the contributions to the plan each year is not dependent on any profits made by the corporation.

Benefit payments under a money purchase pension plan generally commence with the employee's retirement, as defined in the plan, or at age 70½ .

Target Benefit Plan Similar to the money purchase pension plan, the **target benefit plan** is a defined contribution plan that has many features in common with the defined benefit plan. Like a defined benefit plan, contributions to the target benefit plan are based on the amount of the fixed retirement benefit for each participant. However, like most defined contribution plans, the actual amount distributed to the participant of a target benefit plan depends on the value of the assets of the participant's account at the time of retirement.

Stock Bonus Plans The **stock bonus plan** is similar to the profit-sharing plan in design. As with the profit-sharing plan, the employer has the discretion to set the amount of the plan contribution each year. However, unlike the profit-sharing plan, the main investment of the stock bonus plan is in the employer's stock. Contributions to the plan may be in the form of cash or the corporation's stock, and distributions to the retiring or terminating employee are in the form of the corporation's

---

401(k) plan Type of savings plan, established for the benefit of employees, which allows employees to elect to defer a certain percentage of their compensation to provide for their retirement benefits.

money purchase pension plan Defined contribution pension plan whereby the employer contributes a fixed amount based on a formula set forth in the plan that is based on the employee's salary.

target benefit plan Type of qualified plan that has many characteristics of both a defined benefit plan and a defined contribution plan. Contributions are based on the amount of the fixed retirement for each participant. However, the amount distributed to plan participants will depend on the value of the assets in the participant's account at the time of retirement.

stock bonus plan Type of defined contribution plan, similar to the profit-sharing plan, in which the main investment is in the employer's stock.

stock. If the stock being distributed is not publicly traded, the plan participant is granted the option of receiving cash instead of shares of stock, at a fair price according to a formula established in the plan. Stock bonus plans allow plan participants to own equity in the corporation without committing the corporation to a large cash outlay each year for plan contributions.

Employee Stock Ownership Plans An **employee stock ownership plan (ESOP)** is designed to give partial ownership of the corporation to the employees of the corporation. ESOPs are generally established by completing the following steps (see Figure 13-2):

1. A contribution is made to the employee stock ownership trust (ESOT). This contribution may be either profits from the corporation, or it may be in the form of a loan. Lenders and borrowers involved in loan transactions may enjoy beneficial tax treatment.

2. The money in the ESOT is used to purchase stock of the corporation. This stock may be newly issued shares of the corporation, or it may be the shares of major stockholders of the corporation who wish to sell some of those shares to the company's employees.

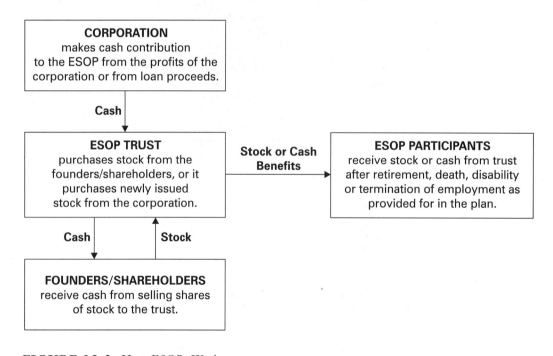

FIGURE 13-2 How ESOPs Work

Employee Stock Ownership Plan (ESOP) Qualified plan designed to give partial ownership of the corporation to the employees.

3. Stock (or the cash equivalent of the shares of stock held in the name of each employee) is distributed to the employees upon their termination, retirement, or other event specified in the plan.

ESOPs offer many unique advantages to both the employer and the plan participant. Instead of being a drain on the cash reserves of the corporation, the ESOP can actually aid the employer in raising cash. This occurs when a corporate employer establishes an ESOP and then borrows money from a bank or other financial institution to fund the ESOT. The borrowed cash can then be loaned to the ESOT, and the ESOT in turn invests the cash in newly issued stock of the corporation. The result to the corporation is that it has more issued and outstanding stock and more cash on hand. The result to the plan participants is that they own an equity interest in the corporation that employs them. ESOPs have also been used to thwart hostile takeover attempts by distributing stock to employees of the corporation in an amount sufficient to prevent the aggressor from obtaining a controlling interest. As with the stock bonus plan, plan participants may receive distributions in the form of stock of the corporation, or they may opt to have the corporation purchase their stock for a fair price.

Integrated Plans

Both defined benefit and defined contribution plans may be integrated with Social Security. **Integrated plans** consider the employer's contribution to Social Security on behalf of a participant or the participant's Social Security benefit, when calculating the amount of contribution or the amount of benefit to be received by the participant from the plan.

Qualified plans that are integrated with Social Security benefits may provide benefits favoring highly compensated employees so long as the plan complies with the rules that limit the disparity above and below the integration level and provide for minimum benefits for all employees.[7]

Self-Employed Plans

In general, any employer may adopt a qualified employee benefit plan, including partnerships and self-employed persons, who often adopt qualified **Keogh plans**. Contributions are made to the plan by the employer, the employee, or both. Self-employed plans, or *Keogh plans* as they are often referred to, are a type of qualified plan available to self-employed individuals. For purposes of the Keogh plan, the self-employed person is considered to be an employer. Self-employed persons and partnerships are usually allowed to adopt the same type of qualified plans available to corporations. However, Keogh plans are subject to special rules regarding coverage, vesting, distribution, limitations on contributions and deductions, and taxation of retirement payouts.

◆ ──

integrated plan Type of retirement plan that is integrated with the employer's contribution to Social Security on behalf of the participant.

Keogh plan A tax-free retirement account for persons with self-employment income.

Individual Retirement Accounts

Individual retirement accounts, or *IRAs* as they are commonly called, are a special type of retirement account that offers tax benefits to self-employed individuals and to employees who are not active participants in a retirement plan maintained by their employer. Currently, individuals may contribute the lesser of $2,000 or an amount equal to the compensation included in the individual's gross income for a taxable year. That amount is increased to $2,250 for individuals who are married if their spouses have no compensation. The amount contributed to an IRA is treated as an income tax deduction for federal income tax purposes.

Distributions from an IRA cannot begin before the participant attains the age of 59½, or the tax benefits of the IRA will be lost and the participant will be subject to a tax penalty upon withdrawal of funds from the IRA.

§ 13.6 NONQUALIFIED PENSION PLANS

Qualified plans are not the only type of pension or profit-sharing plans available. Plan sponsors may determine that their needs would be better met by an unqualified plan—that is, a plan that is not required to comply with all of the rules established for qualified plans. Nonqualified plans often take the form of an agreement between the employer and the employer's executives or otherwise highly compensated individual employees. Nonqualified plans are subject to much less regulation than qualified plans; however, they do not enjoy the same tax benefits as qualified plans.

Plan sponsors who wish to discriminate in favor of highly compensated employees often choose to adopt a nonqualified plan because nonqualified plans are not subject to the nondiscrimination, funding, participation, and vesting requirements of qualified plans. In addition, there are no benefit limits for nonqualified plans and there are fewer reporting requirements. Although nonqualified plans are not subject to the extensive regulation imposed upon qualified plans, they are governed by a number of IRC provisions that apply to both qualified and nonqualified plans, including certain portions of §§ 83 and 451 of the IRC.

Simplified employee pension plans, or *SEPs,* are an alternative to qualified plans and are often used by small businesses and self-employed individuals. The SEP is an individual retirement account or annuity that must satisfy certain requirements under the IRC. Specifically, the plan must satisfy certain participation requirements; it must not discriminate in favor of key employees; it must permit withdrawals; and

---

individual retirement account (IRA) A bank or investment account into which some persons may set aside a certain amount of their earnings each year and have their interest taxed only later when withdrawn. (Some spouses without income may have IRAs, and some persons who have tax deferred pension or profit-sharing plans have limited or no use of IRAs, depending on their income.)

simplified employee pension plan (SEP) An employer's contribution to an employee's IRA (Individual Retirement Account) that meets certain federal requirements. Self-employed persons often use a SEP.

contributions must be made pursuant to a written allocation formula. SEPs have the advantage of offering simplified administration and certain tax breaks. Employer contributions to a SEP are deductible to the employer. The employee must include the contribution on his or her income tax return, but may deduct up to the lesser of $22,500 or 15 percent of his or her compensation.

§ 13.7 EMPLOYEE WELFARE BENEFIT PLANS

An **employee welfare benefit plan** is defined as "any plan, fund, or program ... maintained for the purpose of providing for its participants or their beneficiaries, through the purchase of insurance or otherwise, (A) medical, surgical, or hospital care or benefits, or benefits in the event of sickness, accident, disability, death or unemployment, or vacation benefits, apprenticeship or other training programs, or day care centers, scholarship funds, or prepaid legal services. ... "[8] Most welfare benefit plans are plans offered to employees that include benefits such as medical, life, and dental insurance. A single welfare benefit plan may include one or several types of benefits.

Welfare benefit plans are subject to most of the same requirements that apply to qualified pension plans under ERISA and the IRC, including coverage requirements and nondiscrimination requirements.

Welfare Benefits

The most popular welfare benefit is health insurance. In addition, welfare plans may offer such benefits as dental insurance, long- and short-term disability benefits, and life insurance.

Section 125 Cafeteria Plans Cafeteria plans are a special type of welfare benefit plan that offer participants a choice of benefits. This type of plan is designed to cut costs to the employer and offer only the desired benefits to the participant. Benefits offered under cafeteria plans usually include health insurance (possibly more than one option), as well as dependent care reimbursement accounts and medical expense reimbursement accounts.

Funding

The simplest form of welfare benefit plan is the plan that consists only of insurance that is paid directly by the employer for the benefit of the employee, often with contributions made by the employee through salary reduction agreements. These welfare benefit plans are fully insured and typically no trust is involved. Unlike qualified pension plans, certain qualified welfare plans may be funded through the employer's general account.

---

employee welfare benefit plan An employee benefit plan that provides participants with welfare benefits such as medical, disability, life insurance, dental, and death benefits. A welfare benefit plan may provide benefits either entirely or partially through insurance coverage.

Voluntary Employee Benefit Association (VEBA)

A Voluntary Employees Benefit Association (VEBA) is a special type of tax exempt welfare benefit plan trust that provides for the payment of life, sick, accident, or other benefits to the members of such association, their dependents, or their beneficiaries under IRC § 501(c)(9). This type of trust receives contributions from the employer and holds the contribution until welfare benefits are purchased for or on behalf of the employee.

§ 13.8 QUALIFIED PLAN ADOPTION AND IRS APPROVAL

When employers adopt qualified plans, they want to be assured that the plans will be considered "qualified" and that the tax benefits associated with qualified plans will be available. The employer can attain that assurance by submitting the qualified plan to the Internal Revenue Service to obtain a favorable **determination letter**, which states that the plan has been reviewed by the Internal Revenue Service and that it complies with the requirements for a qualified plan.

Each employee considered to be an interested party must be notified that an application for a favorable determination letter is to be made. After notice has been given, the employer must file a Form 5300 (see Figure 13-3) or other applicable form with the IRS. The Form 5300 is used to request determination letters for the qualification of defined benefit and defined contribution plans.

In addition to the Form 5300, the following must be submitted to the IRS to complete the application:

1. A User Fee for Employee Plan Determination Letter Request (Form 8717) and the appropriate user fee.
2. A copy of the plan.
3. Any other information requested on the Form 5300 or by the IRS.

Employers may cut down on the time required to receive a favorable determination by adopting a master or prototype plan. A *master* or *prototype plan* is designed for the purpose of being adopted by several employers. These plans may have special preapproval status that will expedite the IRS's review.

§ 13.9 ANNUAL REPORTING REQUIREMENTS AND DISCLOSURE REQUIREMENTS

Although qualified plans are typically not subject to taxation, they must file annual reports with the Internal Revenue Service. These annual reports provide the

---

determination letter A letter issued by the Internal Revenue Service in response to an inquiry as to the tax implications of a given situation or transaction. The Internal Revenue Service may issue a determination letter with regard to the *qualified* status of an employee benefit plan based upon the information in the plan's Application for Determination for Employee Benefit Plan (Form 5300).

< 5300 >
<Rev 7/98>
Department of the Treasury
Internal Revenue Service

**Application for
Determination for Employee Benefit Plan**
(Under sections 401(a) and 501(a) of the Internal Revenue Code)
Attach user fee and Schedule Q to this application. (See What To File.)

OMB No. 1545-0197
For IRS Use Only
File folder number ▶
Case number ▶

You must file the pink copy of page 1 and the duplicate page 1 of this application. The pink copy of page 1 is read by the computer and all the information filled in must be typed in either 10 pitch type, Elite type, Courier 12 type, or Titan 12 type. If you wish to computer generate this form, contact your key district office for more information.
Review the list of Procedural Requirements on page 3 before submitting this application.

1a Name of plan sponsor (employer if single-employer plan)
<   >
Number, street, and room or suite no. (If a P.O. box, see instructions.)
<   >
City   State   ZIP code
<   > <   > <   >

1b Employer identification number
<   >
1c Employer's tax year ends-Enter N/A or (MM)
1d Telephone number
(   )

2 Person to be contacted if more information is needed. (See instructions.) (If the same as line 1a, leave blank.) (Complete even if a Power of Attorney is attached):
Name
<   >
Number, street, and room or suite no. (If a P.O. box, see instructions.)
<   >
City   State   ZIP code   Telephone number
<   > <   > <   > (   )

3a Determination requested for (enter applicable number(s) at left and fill in required information). (See instructions.)
<   >   Enter 1 for Initial Qualification—Date plan signed . . . . _____
<   >   Enter 2 for a request after initial qualification—Is complete plan attached? (See instructions.) . . . . Yes <   > No <   >
Date amendment signed _____ Date amendment effective _____
<   >   Enter 3 for Affiliated Service Group status (section 414(m))—Date effective _____
<   >   Enter 4 for Leased Employee Status
<   >   Enter 5 for Partial termination—Date effective _____
b Has the plan received a determination letter? If "Yes," submit a copy of the latest letter .. Yes <   > No <   >
c Have interested parties been given the required notification of this application? (See instructions) . . . . Yes <   > No <   >
d Does the plan have a cash or deferred arrangement, or employee or matching contributions (section 401(k) or (m))? . . . . Yes <   > No <   >
Name of Plan:

4a <   >
<   >   **b** Enter plan number (3 digits) _____   **d** Enter year plan originally effective
<   >   **c** Enter date plan year ends (MMDD) _____ <   > **e** Enter number of participants in plan
5a If this is a defined benefit plan, enter the appropriate number in box at left.
<   >   Enter 1 for unit benefit   Enter 3 for flat benefit
                Enter 2 for fixed benefit   Enter 4 for other (specify) _____
b If this is a defined contribution plan, enter the appropriate number in box at left.
<   >   Enter 1 for profit sharing   Enter 4 for target benefit
                Enter 2 for stock bonus   Enter 5 for ESOP
                Enter 3 for money purchase   Enter 6 for other (Specify)
6a Is the employer a member of an affiliated service group?
<   >   Enter 1 if "Yes"   Enter 2 if "No"   Enter 3 if "Not Certain"
b Is the employer a member of a controlled group of corporations or a group of trades or businesses under common control?
<   >   Enter 1 if "Yes"   Enter 2 if "No"
7 Enter type of plan:
<   >   Enter 1 if governmental plan   Enter 4 if section 412(i) plan
                Enter 2 if nonelecting church plan (i.e. an election   Enter 5 if other
                under section 410(d) has not been made)
                Enter 3 if multiple employer plan (described in section 413(c)). Enter number of participating employers ▶

Under penalties of perjury, I declare that I have examined this application, including accompanying statements, and to the best of my knowledge and belief, it is true, correct, and complete. **Both copies of this page must be signed.**

Signature ▶   Title ▶   Date ▶

For Paperwork Reduction Act Notice, see page 1 of separate instructions.   Cat. No. 11740X   Form **5300** (Rev. 7-98)

FIGURE 13-3 Sample Form 5300—Application for Determination for Employee Benefit Plan

Internal Revenue Service with information concerning the plan, the plan benefits, plan participants, and coverage. In addition, qualified plans are required to provide plan participants with a summary of the annual reports.

Form 5500

All qualified employee benefit plans are required to file a Form 5500 annually. See Figure 13-4. Smaller plans may file an abbreviated Form 5500R. Form 5500R filers must file a Form 5500C (which requires more information than a Form 5500R) at least every third year. Single participant plans may file a simplified, one-page Form 5500-EZ. Form 5500s must be filed with the Internal Revenue Service within seven months after the close of the plan year. Substantial penalties may be assessed for plans that do not file or file delinquently.

The reporting requirements for larger pension plans may be quite extensive, and include a full audit of the plan by an independent auditor.

Summary Annual Reports

Plans that are required to file a Form 5500 or 5500C must provide plan participants with a summary of the annual report that has been filed. Filers of the Form 5500R need only make a copy of the form available to participants.

§ 13.10 THE PARALEGAL'S ROLE IN WORKING WITH QUALIFIED PLANS

Paralegals are often involved in drafting qualified plans and supplementary documents, and in submitting the application for a determination letter to the IRS. Pension plans and other employee benefit plans can be very lengthy documents; many are between 50 and 100 pages long. For that reason, many law firms purchase prepared employee benefit plans from services that prepare them commercially. In that event, the attorney or paralegal completes a detailed form containing the pertinent information regarding the desired qualified plan, and the service prepares the documents as specified. Even though these documents are not prepared within the law firm, the law firm will be responsible for their content, and they must be read carefully. In some instances, plans that have been prepared by commercial services may qualify for a special submission status to the IRS that will expedite the determination letter. Other law firms, with more extensive word processing capabilities, may choose to prepare the required plan documents internally.

Once the qualified plan and related documents have been prepared, the paralegal often attends to the notice that must be given to employees and to submitting the application for a determination letter to the Internal Revenue Service. The paralegal may also be requested to draft the corporate client's board of director resolutions approving and adopting the employee benefit plan.

With the new legislation that continues to be introduced regarding qualified plan requirements, there has been extensive work in this area for paralegals in recent years. Much of this work involves adopting new qualified plans and terminating or amending existing qualified plans to comply with new requirements.

Form **5500**

Department of the Treasury
Internal Revenue Service
Department of Labor
Pension and Welfare Benefits Administration
Pension Benefit Guaranty Corporation

Annual Return/Report of Employee Benefit Plan

This form is required to be filed under sections 104 and 4065 of the Employee Retirement Income Security Act of 1974 (ERISA) and sections 6039D, 6047(e), 6057(b), and 6058(a) of the Internal Revenue Code (the Code).

▶ Type or print all entries in accordance with the instructions to the Form 5500.

Official Use Only
OMB Nos. 1210-0110 / 1210-0089

2000

This Form is Open to Public Inspection.

Part I   Annual Report Identification Information

For the calendar plan year 2000 or fiscal plan year beginning   MM / DD / YYYY   and ending   MM / DD / YYYY

A   This return/report is for: **(1)** ☐ a multiemployer plan;   **(3)** ☐ a multiple-employer plan; or

(2) ☐ a single-employer plan (other than a multiple-employer plan);   **(4)** ☐ a DFE (specify) .... ☐

B   This return/report is: **(1)** ☐ the first return/report filed for the plan;   **(3)** ☐ the final return/report filed for the plan;

(2) ☐ an amended return/report;   **(4)** ☐ a short plan year return/report (less than 12 months).

C   If the plan is a collectively-bargained plan, check here .... ▶ ☐

D   If you filed for an extension of time to file, check the box and attach a copy of the extension application .... ▶ ☐

Part II   Basic Plan Information -- enter all requested information.

1a   Name of plan

1b   Three-digit plan number (PN) ▶ ☐☐☐   **1c**   Effective date of plan   MM / DD / YYYY

Caution: *A penalty for the late or incomplete filing of this return/report will be assessed unless reasonable cause is established.*

Under penalties of perjury and other penalties set forth in the instructions, I declare that I have examined this return/report, including accompanying schedules, statements, and attachments, and to the best of my knowledge and belief, it is true, correct, and complete.

Signature of plan administrator ▶ _____   Date   MM / DD / YYYY

Typed or printed name of individual signing as plan administrator

a

Signature of employer/ plan sponsor/DFE ▶ _____   Date   MM / DD / YYYY

Typed or printed name of individual signing as employer, plan sponsor or DFE as applicable

b

For Paperwork Reduction Act Notice and OMB Control Numbers, see the instructions for Form 5500.   Cat. No. 13500F   Form **5500** (2000)

0 1 0 0 0 0 0 1 0 2

v3.2

FIGURE 13-4   Sample Form 5500—Annual Return/Report of Employee Benefit Plan

Corporate Paralegal Profile
Annette R. Brown, CLA

I am active as a leader and proponent of the legal assistant profession in Montana. ... What I like most about the position is the opportunity to work with dedicated professionals toward a defined goal.

Name Annette R. Brown

Location Missoula, Montana

Title Legal Assistant

Specialty Real Estate, Intellectual Property, and Gaming Compliance

Education Associates of Applied Science in Legal Assisting; Certified Legal Assistant designation through the National Association of Legal Assistants.

Experience 5 years

Annette Brown is the only legal assistant in the legal department of the Rocky Mountain Elk Foundation, Inc. at its national headquarters in Missoula, Montana. The Rocky Mountain Elk Foundation is an international, nonprofit conservation organization whose mission is to ensure the future of elk, other wildlife, and their habitat. It was founded in 1984, and now has 130,000 members who have helped generate the funds to conserve and enhance three million acres of wildlife habitat across North America.

The Legal Department at the Elk Foundation currently consists of three attorneys and two staff positions. Annette reports directly to the Foundation's general counsel, who also serves as vice president–legal, and secretary of the organization. Her primary duties are in the areas of real estate, intellectual property, and gaming compliance. Annette also works with many other areas of the law, such as employment law, contracts, litigation, charitable giving, collections, and nonprofit tax law. She is responsible for factual and legal research, drafting, editing, and proofing multiple documents such as deeds, option and purchase agreements, conservation easements, contracts, correspondence, trademark applications, and pleadings. This entails contacts with both the client and numerous outside sources such as agency personnel, Elk Foundation partners, and volunteers. She is also on the Intellectual Property Committee and works closely with the attorney in protecting the Elk Foundation's multiple trademarks. In addition, Annette provides assistance to the interns participating in the Elk Foundation's UM Law Clinic program, and she works in a supervisory position with interns through the UM College of Technology Legal Assisting program.

Annette's favorite aspect of her position is the opportunity to work with dedicated professionals toward a defined goal. She is very proud to work with the Elk Foundation, which has an outstanding reputation in the conservation community throughout the nation. Her work with the Elk Foundation has given her experience with many elements of the law on federal, state, and international levels.

Annette is an active leader and proponent of the legal assistant profession in Montana. She is a member of the National Association of Legal Assistants, a recipient of the NALA 2000 Affiliates Award, and has been a member of the Montana Association of Legal Assistants since 1994. She has held many officer and committee positions, including service on the Paralegal Study Committee of the State Bar of Montana in 1998. Annette currently serves on the governing council of the Paralegal Section of the State Bar of Montana.

Annette's advice to new paralegals?

Develop a career goal and then pursue that goal, but be willing to adjust the goal to your circumstances. Be willing to think "outside the box" when considering positions. Keep yourself open to opportunities, and be flexible and creative. This may include developing network opportunities in diverse forums. Above all, be professional, and seek involvement with your profession through local, state, or national organizations. I believe that you will be both personally and professionally rewarded.

For more information on careers for corporate paralegals, log on to the companion Web page to this text at **www.westlegalstudies.com.**

§ 13.11 RESOURCES

Paralegals working in the qualified plan area will frequently need to reference the pertinent Internal Revenue Code sections and ERISA. There are several secondary sources that include further explanation of these codes. In addition, federal agencies that deal with pension plans can be very helpful.

Federal Law

Internal Revenue Code provisions dealing with pension plans can be found at: 26 U.S.C. § 401 *et seq.* ERISA is located within the United States Code at 29 U.S.C. § 1001 *et seq.*

Secondary Materials

Secondary materials that provide explanation of the pertinent federal law, as well as forms and practice tips, can be very useful to paralegals who work with qualified plans. Some of the more popular secondary materials include: *Pension Coordinator,* by RIA; *Pension & Profit Sharing,* by Prentice Hall; *Pension Plan Guide,* by CCH and *Pension Reporter,* by BNA. These resources also include several references to form books that may be used in conjunction with these materials.

Federal Agencies

The federal agencies that offer the most assistance with qualified plans, are generally those that regulate them, including:

> The Internal Revenue Service, **www.irs.gov**
> Pension Benefit Guaranty Corporation, **www.pbgc.gov/**
> The Pension and Welfare Benefits Administration, **www.dol.gov/dol/pwba**
> United States Department of Labor, **www.dol.gov**

For a list of several Web pages concerning employee benefits laws, see appendix B to this text.

 Internet Resources www.

Following is a list of some Web pages that may be useful when assisting with employee benefit plan matters:

For the Internal Revenue Code and ERISA

Findlaw.com	**www.findlaw.com/casecode/uscodes/**
Legal Information Institute	**www.law.cornell.edu**

For general employee benefit plan information

Benefit News	**www.benefitnews.com/**

Benefits Link	**www.benefitslink.com/index**
Employee Benefits Research Institute	**www.ebri.org/**
FreeErisa	**www.freeerisa.com**

For information on employee stock ownership plans

National Center for Employee Ownership	**www.nceo.org/**

For federal agencies that regulate employee benefit plans, see above.

Web Page

For updates and links to several of the previously listed sites, log on to **www. westlegalstudies.com**, and click through to the book link for this text.

SUMMARY

- Plans that meet certain requirements of the Internal Revenue Code and qualify for special tax treatment are referred to as qualified plans.
- Employers are allowed a tax deduction for their contributions to qualified plans.
- Investment income earned on contributions to qualified plans is generally tax free until distributed to plan participants.
- Participants of qualified plans can defer their income tax liability on the amount of their contributions until they receive the benefit from the plan in the future, when their income will generally be less.
- Qualified plans are subject to provisions of the Internal Revenue Code and the Employee Retirement Income Security Act of 1974 (ERISA).
- Qualified plans must meet minimum participation rules set forth in the Internal Revenue Code.
- Minimum participation and coverage rules and standards are established to ensure that qualified plans do not discriminate in favor of the corporation's owners or highly compensated employees.
- Qualified plans must meet certain vesting requirements set forth in ERISA.
- Employees are always 100 percent vested in any contribution they make to the qualified plans unless an alternative seven year incremental vesting plan has been adopted.
- ERISA provides that any employee who has at least five years of service with an employer must have a nonforfeitable right to 100 percent of his or her accrued benefits under qualified plans unless an alternative seven-year incremental vesting plan has been adopted.

◆ Employee stock ownership plans (ESOPs) are a type of qualified plan that give partial ownership of the corporation to the corporation's employees. Distributions may be made to participants in the form of stock or cash.

◆ Keoghs are a type of qualified plan available to self-employed individuals.

◆ Employee welfare benefit plans are plans designed to provide participants and their beneficiaries with medical, dental, disability, life insurance, and similar benefits.

◆ Sponsors of employee benefit plans may request favorable determination letters from the Internal Revenue Service to ensure that their plans will be considered *qualified* plans by the IRS.

◆ Qualified employee benefit plans must file a Form 5500 Annual Report with the Internal Revenue Service each year.

REVIEW QUESTIONS

1. How can an employer be certain that an employee benefit plan will be considered a qualified plan by the IRS?

2. Under the current minimum participation rules, what is the minimum number of employees that must benefit from a qualified plan if the plan sponsor (employer) has 500 employees?

3. When is an employee's contribution to a plan considered to be fully vested?

4. Under the provisions of ERISA, could a qualified plan participant ever be ineligible to receive benefits until after his or her 65th birthday? If so, under what circumstances?

5. What are integrated plans?

6. In what ways do target benefit plans resemble typical defined benefit plans? In what way do they resemble typical defined contribution plans?

7. What unique benefit does an ESOP offer to the employer?

8. If Andrews Electronics wants to adopt an employee benefit plan that will pay its employees a specific amount upon their retirement, what type of plan would the company most likely want to adopt?

9. Suppose the management of Gregory Tool & Die Company decides that they would like to offer an employee benefit plan that would allow their employees to share in the corporation's profits and pay a benefit to the employees upon retirement or termination from the corporation. Management is uncertain about the future of the corporation, but they would like to base the contributions upon its earnings and profits. What type of plan might Gregory Tool & Die elect to adopt?

10. The owners of Gabrielle Foods, Inc. would like to adopt an employee benefit plan that would encourage their employees to save money for retirement. They are willing to pay up to a certain amount per employee, per year, provided that the employee invests an equal amount of his or her pretax income. What type of plan might the owners of Gabrielle Foods, Inc. adopt?

PRACTICAL PROBLEMS

Locate a copy of ERISA to answer the following questions:

1. What is the full cite for this Act?

2. Under § 1021(a), who must receive copies of the summary plan description?

3. Under § 1102(b), what are the requisite features of a plan?

4. Under § 1052(a)(1)(A), may a plan require, as a condition of participation, that participants have at least three years of service and attain the age of 25?

WORKPLACE SCENARIO

Suppose that your supervising attorney, Belinda Benson, has just met with Bradley Harris, CEO of Cutting Edge Computer Repair, Inc., our fictional corporation. Cutting Edge Computer Repair now has 20 employees, and Bradley Harris and Cynthia Lund have decided to adopt a defined contribution profit sharing plan with 401(k) provisions for their employees. Mr. Harris is working with a financial planner and accountant to establish the plan. He would like your law firm to submit the plan to the Internal Revenue Service for a favorable determination letter. Using the following information, and the form and instructions for Form 5300, which may be downloaded from the Internal Revenue Service Web page at **www.irs.gov**, prepare a draft of Form 5300 for submission to the Internal Revenue Service. Assume that Mr. Harris will provide the Schedule Q that must be filed with Form 5300. Also, prepare a cover letter submitting the application and all required supporting documents indicated in the Form 5300 instructions.

Employer identification number 41-1234567

Employer's tax year ends December

Contact person Bradley Harris

Telephone number 651-555-1212

Name of plan Cutting Edge Computer Repair, Inc. 401(k) Plan

Plan number 001

Plan year ends December 31

Number of plan participants 10

Other plans maintained by employer None

General eligibility All employees

Vesting Full vesting after 2 years

Benefits and requirements for benefits Profit sharing plan with a definite formula

Miscellaneous Trust earnings and losses are allocated on the basis of account balances.

END NOTES

1. U.S. Census Bureau, *The Statistical Abstract of the United States (2000)* § 613.

2. 60A AM. JUR. 2d *Pensions and Retirement Funds* § 1 (1998).

3. ERISA § 4(b).

4. 60A AM. JUR. 2d *Pensions and Retirement Funds* § 16.

5. AM. JUR. *Legal Forms Federal Tax Guide* § 133-E-25.

6. IRC § 401(f).

7. IRC § 401(e).

8. ERISA § 3.

CHAPTER 14

Employment Agreements

CHAPTER OUTLINE

§ 14.1   Special Considerations for the Employer
§ 14.2   Special Considerations for the Employee
§ 14.3   Drafting the Employment Agreement
§ 14.4   Sample Employment Agreement
§ 14.5   The Paralegal's Role in Drafting Employment Agreements
§ 14.6   Resources

INTRODUCTION

Most individuals employed in the United States are employees at will. That is, they are hired by an employer for agreed-upon compensation, and they can be dismissed at the employer's discretion, with or without cause. However, many corporations in the United States require at least some of their employees to enter into employment agreements. An **employment agreement** sets forth the rights and obligations of both the employer and employee with regard to the employee's employment. Corporations frequently enter into employment agreements with their top executives, but they may also enter into employment agreements with other key employees, especially in the sales and technical areas. Often corporations require entire classes of employees to enter into employment agreements as a condition of employment. Corporations may have simple employment agreements that they require their employees to enter into before commencing work, or the terms may be negotiated with potential key employees prior to hiring. The employment agreement is typically drafted by the attorneys for the employer, often with the assistance of a paralegal.

◆ ——————————————————————————————————————

employment agreement   Agreement entered into between an employer and an employee to set forth the rights and obligations of each party with regard to the employee's employment.

This chapter investigates special considerations for both the employer and the employee when entering into an employment agreement. It then focuses on the drafting of the employment agreement, first with a discussion of some general considerations, then with an examination of specific provisions that are often included in employment agreements, and a sample employment agreement. This chapter concludes with a look at the paralegal's role in drafting employment agreements and resources to aid in that drafting.

§ 14.1 SPECIAL CONSIDERATIONS FOR THE EMPLOYER

Some of the benefits to the employer who is a party to an employment agreement are apparent. An employer who enters into an employment agreement with an individual is reasonably assured of hiring and retaining the services of that individual as an employee for a specific period of time. Although the employer cannot compel employees to continue their employment against their will, employees who have entered into employment agreements for a specified time period will probably be more reluctant than others to terminate their employment before the expiration of the agreement's term.

The continued employment of an employee means that the employer will not be forced to search for another individual to fill the position for the duration of the agreement—a task that can be both time-consuming and costly. Also, the person being hired will not be working for the competition. This can be a particular benefit to the employer when hiring individuals with unique experience or knowledge in a very competitive business. Although complete certainty can never exist when the human element is involved, employment agreements offer decidedly more certainty than employment at will.

Another benefit to the employer entering into an employment agreement is that the employee's actions, both during the term of employment and after, may be restricted to protect the employer's confidentiality, trade secrets, and work products. Employment agreements may include provisions restricting the future employment and actions of the employee and protecting the trade secrets, patents, and work product of the employer.

The contractual nature of the employment agreement may also result in drawbacks to the employer. For instance, it may be difficult to dismiss an employee who has an employment agreement. Even if the employee does not work out as well as planned, because of lack of performance, personality conflicts, or some other reason. The employer may be considered to be in breach of contract if the employee is terminated before the expiration of the agreement's term. The terms of an employment agreement frequently provide that the employee's employment may be terminated before expiration of the contract only "with cause," and cause for dismissing an employee may be difficult to prove.

Even if the employee performs as expected, the compensation provided for in the employment agreement may result in a hardship to the employer if the employer's business or profits do not meet projections. An employment agreement may require the employer to compensate the employee at a certain level even when the employer's business is performing poorly or losing money.

§ 14.2 SPECIAL CONSIDERATIONS FOR THE EMPLOYEE

Although an employment agreement may initially seem to be for the primary benefit of the employer, it also offers several potential benefits to the employee. Most importantly, it usually assures the employee of continued employment for a definite period of time for definite compensation. This may be a significant benefit when unemployment is high, either in general or in the specific field of the employee's expertise. The employee with an employment agreement that sets a definite term and definite compensation can also usually be assured of receiving that compensation, regardless of the employer's profitability. The employment agreement may also formalize certain benefits, incentives, or rewards that will become a future obligation of the employer to be awarded to the employee upon completion of certain deadlines or the attainment of specific goals.

Disadvantages to the employee include the facts that the employee must typically commit to a position that may not live up to the employee's expectations, and that the employee's obligations may extend beyond the term of the employment. The employee may be required to restrict his or her future employment or actions pursuant to the employment agreement. However, restrictions on future activities must be "reasonable" to be enforceable.

§ 14.3 DRAFTING THE EMPLOYMENT AGREEMENT

An employment agreement is considered to be a binding contract between the employee and the employer, and it must contain all of the elements of a valid contract, including an offer and acceptance, a meeting of minds, and the exchange of consideration. The discussion of employment agreements in this chapter is limited to written employment agreements. This section first discusses the items that must be agreed upon and included in employment agreements. It then examines more closely some of the most important provisions that are commonly included in employment agreements.

A corporation that routinely hires several new employees per year may have a standard employment agreement that each new employee is requested to sign before commencing employment. In that event, the attorney for the corporation typically drafts a "master" agreement, and the corporation tailors it as necessary to suit the particular circumstances surrounding the employment of each new employee. A smaller corporation may find it necessary to draft unique employment agreements for its executives and for key personnel.

In any event, certain key elements must be agreed to by both parties and must be included in each employment agreement for the agreement to be enforceable and for it to attain the desired results. The following checklist sets out some of the items that should be agreed to and included in any employment agreement.[1]

- ☐ Identification of parties.
  - — Employer.
  - — Employee.
- ☐ Term of agreement.

- ☐ Place where agreement is to be performed.
- ☐ Duties of employee.
  - — Hours of employment.
  - — Best efforts to be devoted to employment.
  - — Maintaining outside job or interest.
- ☐ Working facilities.
- ☐ Maintaining trade secrets.
- ☐ Inventions and patents.
  - — Discovery in course of employment.
  - — Use of employer's facilities.
  - — Relation of discovery to employer's business.
- ☐ Compensation.
  - — Wages, salary, or commission.
  - — Overtime work or night differential.
  - — Pay while unable to work because of illness.
  - — Effect of termination or noncompletion of employment.
- ☐ Special compensation plans.
  - — Deferred compensation.
  - — Percentage of sales or profits.
  - — Incentive bonus.
  - — Profit sharing.
  - — Stock options.
  - — Pension and retirement plans.
- ☐ Expense account.
  - — Travel.
  - — Meals.
  - — Lodging.
- ☐ Covenant not to compete after leaving employment.
  - — Length of time.
  - — Geographical limitations.
  - — Irreparable harm suffered by employer.
  - — Hardship not greater than necessary on employee.
  - — Agreement not injurious to public interest.
- ☐ Employee benefits.
  - — Life and disability insurance.
  - — Medical insurance.
  - — Dental insurance.
  - — Worker's compensation.
- ☐ Termination of employment.
- ☐ Right of either party to terminate on proper notice.
- ☐ Discharge of employee for cause.

☐ Remedies for breach.
  — Liquidated damages.
☐ Arbitration of disputes.
☐ Vacations and holidays.
☐ Assignability of contract by employer or employee.
☐ Modification, renewal, or extension of agreement.
☐ Complete agreement in written contract.
☐ Law to govern interpretation of agreement.
☐ Effective date of agreement.
☐ Signatures.
☐ Date(s) of signing.

Term of the Agreement

The term of the agreement should be specifically set forth in the agreement. Often a specific time period, such as one year, is set forth, and the agreement is made renewable with the mutual consent of both parties. If the employment agreement does not specify a definite term of employment, the employer may have the discretion to terminate the employee at will. Likewise, the employee may have the option of terminating the agreement at any time.

EXAMPLE: Term of Employment

The term of this agreement shall be a period of ＿＿＿ years, commencing ＿＿＿＿＿ [date], and terminating ＿＿＿＿ [date], subject, however, to prior termination as provided in this agreement. At the expiration date of ＿＿＿＿＿ [date], this agreement shall be considered renewed for regular periods of one year, provided neither party submits a notice of termination.[2]

Description of Duties

The duties and obligations of the employee should be set forth with a certain degree of specificity. Although it would be impossible to set forth every duty and obligation that might possibly be expected of the employee during the term of the employment agreement, the position should be defined well enough to give both the employer and employee a reasonable understanding of the work the employee will be expected to perform and the authority the employee will be granted in accordance with the position. In addition to a description of specific duties, this section of the agreement should include the agreed-upon hours of employment, and a statement that the employee will devote his or her best efforts to the satisfactory performance of the position's duties.

EXAMPLE: Duties of Employee

Employee will serve employer faithfully and to the best of ＿＿＿ [his or her] ability under the direction of the board of directors of employer. Employee will devote all of ＿＿＿ [his or her] time, energy, and skill during regular business hours to such employment. Employee shall perform such services and act in such executive capacity as the board of directors of employer shall direct.[3]

EXAMPLE: Best Efforts

Employee agrees that [he or she] will at all times faithfully, industriously, and to best of [his or her] ability, experience, and talents, perform all of the duties that may be required of and from employee pursuant to the express and implicit terms of this agreement, to the reasonable satisfaction of corporation.[4]

Covenant Not to Compete

Covenants not to compete, which restrict the future employment and actions of the employee, are commonly found in employment agreements. The purpose behind these covenants is to prevent the employee from leaving one employer, from which he or she has gained significant experience and knowledge, and taking that experience and knowledge to the employer's competition.

Because covenants not to compete restrict the free actions and future employment of the employee, there are limitations on their enforcement. Under the common law of England, covenants not to compete were considered agreements in restraint of a man's right to exercise his trade or calling, and thus were considered void as against public policy.[5] However, the modern view of noncompetition clauses is that an "anticompetitive covenant supported by consideration and ancillary to a lawful contract is enforceable if reasonable and consistent with public interest."[6]

The test of reasonableness depends on the facts of the case. Generally, an agreement not to compete is considered reasonable if it is restricted to a specific time period and a specific geographical location. For instance, an agreement not to work for the competition for the rest of the employee's life anywhere in the United States would not be enforceable. Although exactly what is considered reasonable will depend on the circumstances of the particular case, the following characteristics are often assigned to anticompetition covenants that are considered to be reasonable and enforceable:

1. The covenant is legal in the state in which it is to be executed. (Covenants not to compete may be subject to state statutes that deal specifically with anticompetition covenants.)
2. The covenant is supported by sufficient consideration.
3. The restriction is reasonably necessary to protect some legitimate interest of the employer.
4. The restriction is not contrary to public interests.
5. The covenant applies to only a limited geographical location.
6. The covenant is applicable for only a limited time period.

---

covenant not to compete A part of an employee contract, partnership agreement, or agreement to sell a business in which a person promises not to engage in the same business for a certain amount of time after the relationship ends.

Dividends ━━━ ◆

How Much Does a CEO Make?

Unless you are a professional baseball player or a superstar, it is hard not to be impressed by the salaries earned by chief executive officers in this country. According to a 2000 *BusinessWeek* survey,* the 1999 salaries and bonuses of the top twenty-paid CEOs ranged from $654,000 to $13,325,000. Taking long-term compensation (usually in the form of stock options) into consideration, their total compensation packages for 1999 ranged from $49,252,000 to $655,424,000! Charles Wang, Chief Executive Officer of Computer Associates International made the top of the list with his 1999 salary and bonus, plus long-term compensation of $655,424,000. According to one survey, average earnings of the CEOs of 50 of the nation's largest companies averaged $10.9 million.†

It is not just the CEOs of the nation's most successful corporations that are bringing home these impressive salaries. With the weaker stock market at the end of 2000, shareholders of several of the largest companies saw the value in their holdings drop, while the compensation of the companies' CEOs soared. Steven Case, CEO of America Online, earned over $300 million for the three-year period beginning in 1996, while the average return on equity of AOL shares for that same period decreased 119 percent.

Shareholder outrage in the 1990s led to several attempts to rein in CEO salaries. SEC proxy rules now give shareholders more information with regard to executive pay and more power to act. In 1993, President Clinton and Congress passed a new law placing a $1,000,000 cap on the corporate income tax deduction that may be taken for an executive's pay. The Internal Revenue Service has implemented rules restricting the appointment of corporate *insiders* to the corporation's compensation committee.

Another effect of shareholder concern regarding increasing CEO salaries in relation to their pay has been to link performance more closely to pay. The compensation packages of most of the CEOs of the larger corporations include stock bonuses and stock options. The average CEO has a vested interest in increasing the value of the corporation's stock. The effect of performance-based stock bonuses and stock options in the 1990s, when the stock market was reaching new highs daily, was to increase the compensation of many CEOs to levels they had never dreamed of. On the other hand, when the stock market has been weaker, and stock of the corporation is not doing well, CEOs have seen their compensation levels fall.

While the compensation of most CEOs will be tied to the corporation's stock performance in the future, overall CEO compensation levels are likely to stay high regardless of stock market performance. Expectations among corporations and CEOs have been established, and talented, successful CEOs will most certainly command compensation in the eight-figure range.

─────────

* Executive Pay, *BusinessWeek*, April 17, 2000, 100.

† $10 Million: Par for the Course, *BusinessWeek*, February 26, 2001, 40.

───

Another consideration with regard to covenants not to compete is that they are considered unethical, or even illegal in some instances, for certain professionals such as doctors or lawyers. The following example would generally be found to be a reasonable covenant not to compete.

EXAMPLE: *Noncompetition with Former Employer*

Employee agrees that for a period of _____ [one year] after termination of ____ [his or her] employment with employer in any manner, whether with or without cause, employee will not, within the state of _____, directly or indirectly engage in the business of _____ [employer's business] or in any business competitive with employer for a period of _____ [one year] from such termination of employment. Directly or indirectly engaging in the business of _____ [employer's business] or in any competitive business shall include, but not be limited to, engaging in business as owner, partner, or agent, or as employee of any person, firm, corporation, or other entity engaged in such business, or in being interested directly or indirectly in any such business conducted by any person, firm, corporation, or other entity.[7]

In the *Beckman v. Cox Broadcasting Corporation* case, involving a noncompetition clause in a television weatherman's employment agreement, the agreement was found valid primarily because it was for only a limited time period and a limited geographical location.

CASE

BECKMAN
v.
COX BROADCASTING CORPORATION

Supreme Court of Georgia
250 Ga. 127, 296 S.E.2d 566 (1982)
October 27, 1982

From 1962 until June 3, 1982, appellant Beckman was employed by Cox Broadcasting Corporation (Cox) as a meteorologist and "television personality," appearing primarily on Cox's affiliate, WSB-TV. In April, 1981, Beckman entered into a five-year contractual agreement with WXIA-TV, a competitor of Cox, to commence working for WXIA as a meteorologist and "television personality" when his contract with Cox expired on July 1, 1982. Cox was made aware of Beckman's plans and in July, 1981, Cox filed a petition for declaratory judgment, [Ga.] Code Ann. § 110-1101, seeking a determination that the restriction against competition in its employment agreement with Beckman was valid. This restriction provides: "Employee shall not, for a period of one hundred-eighty (180) days after the end of the Term of Employment, allow his/her voice or image to be broadcast 'on air' by any commercial television station whose broadcast transmission tower is located within a radius of thirty-five (35) miles from Company's offices at 1601 West Peachtree Street, N.E., Atlanta, Georgia, unless such broadcast is part of a nationally broadcast program." Following a hearing the trial court dismissed the action finding there was no evidence to conclude either that WXIA-TV would require Beckman to violate the restrictive covenant

or that Beckman would violate the covenant. Therefore, the trial court determined, Cox had not presented a justifiable controversy.

On June 16, 1982, Beckman formally demanded to be released from the restrictive covenant in his contract. When Cox refused Beckman filed this declaratory judgment action to ascertain the validity of the restrictive covenant under Georgia law.

The trial court found that the employment contract with WXIA-TV does not require Beckman to appear "on-air" during the first six months of his employment; that Beckman, under the terms of this agreement, is rendering "substantial duties and services to WXIA-TV" for which he is being compensated; that during the term of Beckman's employment with Cox, WSB-TV spent in excess of a million dollars promoting "Beckman's name, voice and image as an individual television personality and as part of WSB-TV's Action News Team," that Beckman is one of the most recognized "television personalities" in the Atlanta area; that television viewers select a local newscast, to a certain degree, based on their "appreciation of the personalities appearing on the newscast"; and that local television personalities "are strongly identified in the minds of television viewers with the stations upon which they appear." The trial court also found that in March, 1982, WSB-TV instituted a "transition plan" to reduce the impact Beckman's departure would have on the station's image. As part of this transition plan Beckman was removed from one of the two nightly WSB-TV news programs. Additionally, WSB-TV undertook an extensive promotional campaign, featuring both Beckman and his replacement as members of the "Action News Team." This transition plan contemplated the gradual phasing out of Beckman from the "Action News Team." The station projected that Beckman would then be "off the air" in the Atlanta market for six months, permitting WSB-TV to diminish its association with Beckman in the public's mind and providing the viewing public an opportunity to adjust to Beckman's replacement.

The trial court concluded that to permit Beckman to appear "on air" in the Atlanta area during the first six months of his contract with WXIA-TV would "disrupt the plans and ability of WSB-TV to adjust successfully to the loss of a well-known personality that it has heavily promoted before it must begin competing with that personality in the same marketplace." The trial court also determined that WSB-TV would be injured by allowing a competitor to take advantage of the popularity of a television personality which WSB-TV had expended great sums to promote before WSB-TV had time to compensate for the loss of that personality. The trial court further found that WSB-TV has a legitimate and protectable interest in the image which it projects to the viewing public.

While the trial court concluded the damage to WSB-TV would be great if Beckman were permitted to compete against it within the proscribed six months, the court reasoned that Beckman would suffer little harm if the covenant was enforced against him. The trial court found that Beckman is currently employed, without loss of remuneration, and that, based on the testimony of expert witnesses at trial, "Beckman will not suffer substantial damage or loss of recognition and popularity solely as a result of being off the air during the first 180 days of his five year contract with WXIA-TV."

The trial court ruled that the restrictive covenant is valid under Georgia law as it is reasonable and definite with regard to time and territory and is otherwise reasonable considering the interest of Cox to be protected and the impact on Beckman.

Beckman appeals this decision in Case No. 39176. ...

(1) Case No. 39176. Beckman concedes the covenant not to compete is reasonable with regard to the time and territorial restrictions, but urges that it is otherwise unreasonable in that it is broader than is necessary for Cox's protection. ...

A covenant not to compete, being in partial restraint of trade, is not favored in the law, and will be upheld only when strictly limited in time, territorial effect, the capacity in which the employee is prohibited from competing and when it is otherwise reasonable. ... In determining whether a covenant is reasonably limited with regard to these factors, the court must balance the interest the employer seeks to protect against the impact the covenant will have on the employee, factoring in the effect of the covenant on the public's interest in promoting competition and the freedom of individuals to contract. ... The evidence supports the trial court's finding that WSB-TV has a significant interest in the image of its television station which it has created, in large measure, by promoting those individuals who appear on behalf of the station, whether as newscasters ... or "television personalities." This interest is entitled to protection. We further agree with the trial court that WSB-TV would be greatly harmed by Beckman's appearance on a competing station prior to the completion of WSB-TV's transition plan.

Beckman argues, however, that the detrimental impact of the restrictive covenant on him outweighs the need to protect the interests of WSB-TV. ... While the evidence is not without conflict, the trial court's finding that a six month absence from the air will not substantially damage Beckman's popularity or recognition among the public is well-supported by the record.

... [W]e conclude that for a limited time and in a narrowly restricted area, WSB-TV is entitled to prevent Beckman from using the popularity and recognition he gained as a result of WSB-TV's investment in the creation of his image so that WSB-TV may protect its interest in its own image by implementing its transition plan. We find that the restrictive covenant in this case is reasonably tailored to that end. ... We agree with the trial court that the restrictive covenant in this case is valid. ...

Judgment affirmed.

Inventions and Patents

Often an employment agreement between an employer and its research or technical staff includes a provision that assigns any inventions of the employee, and subsequent patents on those inventions, to the employer. Unless inventions are assigned to the employer by the employee, or some special circumstances exist, the employer generally has no right to the employee's inventions. Any assignment of inventions must include provisions that define exactly which inventions are covered under the assignment. The assignment may specifically exclude any inventions by the employee during his or her own time that are unrelated to the employee's work for the employer. The employee may also specifically exempt from this assignment prior inventions that he or she brings to the employer.

EXAMPLE: *Employer to Have Ownership of Employee's Inventions*

All ideas, inventions, and other developments or improvements conceived or reduced to practice by employee, alone or with others, during the term of this employment agreement, whether or not during working hours, that are within the scope of employer's business operations or that relate to any of employer's work or projects, shall be the exclusive property of employer. Employee agrees to assist employer, at its expense, to obtain patents on any such patentable ideas, inventions, and other developments, and agrees to execute all documents necessary to obtain such patents in the name of employer.[8]

In the *Cubic Corporation v. Marty* case, involving a device to train airplane pilots, the court found that an assignment of inventions between the employee and the employer was valid and binding and that the employer was entitled to the patent on the employee's invention.

Trade Secrets

Another common type of restrictive covenant found in employment agreements restricts the divulgence of an employer's trade secrets. A *trade secret* has been defined as "any formula, pattern, device or compilation of information which is used in one's business and which gives him an opportunity to obtain an advantage over competitors who do not know it or use it."[9] This covenant may extend for a period of time beyond the term of the employment agreement, but it must be reasonable to be enforceable, and it generally loses any effect once the covered trade secrets have become common knowledge. The employment agreement usually also covers confidentiality in a general way, preventing the employee from divulging information to the press, the public, or the competition without permission.

EXAMPLE: *Trade Secrets*

Employee shall not at any time or in any manner, either directly or indirectly, divulge, disclose or communicate to any person, firm, corporation, or other entity in any manner whatsoever any information concerning any matters affecting or relating to the business of employer, including without limitation, any of its customers, the prices it obtains or has obtained from the sale of, or at which it sells or has sold, its products, or any other information concerning the business

CASE

CUBIC CORPORATION
v.
MARTY

185 Cal. App. 3d 438,
229 Cal. Rptr. 828 (1996)
August 27, 1986
Staniforth, Associate Judge

William B. Marty, Jr., appeals a judgment awarding Cubic Corporation $34,102 for Marty's breach of an invention agreement signed when he began his employment with Cubic, awarding the patent to the invention to Cubic and enjoining Marty from exploiting any rights under the patent or using or disclosing Cubic's confidential information to others.

FACTS

When Marty became a Cubic employee in December 1976, he signed an invention and secrecy agreement (hereafter the Agreement) which provided in pertinent part that the employee agreed:

"To promptly disclose to Company all ideas, processes, inventions, improvements, developments and discoveries coming within the scope of Company's business or related to Company's products or to any research, design, experimental or production work carried on by Company, or to any problems specifically assigned to Employee, conceived alone or with others during this employment, and whether or not conceived during regular working hours. All such ideas, processes, trademarks, inventions, improvements, developments and discoveries shall be the sole and exclusive property of Company, and Employee assigns and hereby agrees to assign his entire right, title and interest in and to the same to Company."

The agreement also provided the employee would cooperate in obtaining a patent on any such inventions and would not disclose any of Cubic's records, files, drawings, documents or equipment from Cubic without prior written consent. Under the agreement, Cubic promised to pay all expenses in connection with obtaining a patent, pay the employee a $75 cash bonus upon the employee's execution of the patent application and an additional $75 if a patent was obtained.

In mid-May 1977, Marty came up with an idea for an electronic warfare simulator (EWS), a device for training pilots in electronic warfare. Marty's invention had advantages over current training methods which involved the use of very expensive, security-risky, mimic radars. He developed a block diagram in May 1977 and in June 1977 a manuscript describing his invention.

He showed both the diagram and manuscript to Minton Kronkhite of Cubic, representing it might be a new product which Cubic could add to its product for training pilots, the ACMR (air combat maneuvering range). ... Kronkhite thought Marty's invention was a good idea and passed along the manuscript to Hubert Kohnen, another Cubic employee involved with the ACMR. Kohnen also thought the idea was good. He assumed it was another product for the ACMR since Marty had suggested his invention responded to some of the things Kohnen had been talking about. Kohnen made some technical comments on the manuscript. ...

Cubic funded an internal project to study Marty's invention. Marty used a Cubic computer programmer to help design necessary circuitry. Marty's background in microprocessors was weak.

Based on the developed invention, Cubic submitted a proposal to the Navy for Marty's invention under Kohnen's name. Kohnen told Marty if they got a program from the Navy, Marty would be made the program manager. Cubic did get a government program to study Marty's invention and Marty was made program manager. Marty was also given a more than average raise.

In June 1978, Marty, without telling Cubic, applied for a patent on his invention. The patent was issued in December 1979. Marty's patent attorney forwarded a copy of the patent to Cubic and offered to discuss giving Cubic a license under the patent. Cubic took the position the patent belonged to them under the Agreement Marty had signed. Cubic offered to reimburse Marty's expenses in obtaining the patent if he assigned the patent to Cubic. Marty refused. Cubic told Marty his continued employment at Cubic was contingent on his assigning the patent. Marty continued to refuse and was terminated from his employment at Cubic in early 1980.

Cubic filed a complaint against Marty seeking declaratory relief as to ownership of the patent and alleging breach of contract, confidential relationship and trust, interference with prospective economic advantage and specific enforcement of the secrecy and invention agreement. Marty cross-complained for wrongful discharge, breach of contract, fraudulent misrepresentation, breach of confidential disclosure, copyright infringement, defamation and injunction.

The trial court awarded the patent to Cubic and $34,102 in damages resulting from a government withhold on a Cubic contract (subject to a credit to Marty if and when the amount was recovered from the government). The court also enjoined Marty from exploiting any rights under the patent and from using or disclosing to others confidential information owned by Cubic in specific documents. ...

Marty contends the Agreement was not specifically enforceable because there was inadequate consideration to support a promise to convey the invention to Cubic.

Civil Code section 3391 provides in pertinent part:

> Specific performance cannot be enforced against a party to a contract in any of the following cases:
> "1. If he has not received an adequate consideration for the contract;

"2. If it is not, as to him, just and reasonable ..."

The adequacy of consideration is to be determined in light of the conditions existing at the time a contract is made.

Marty argues the only consideration for the Agreement was a "token" bonus of $150. He argues his employment could not have been the consideration for the Agreement because Cubic hired him before he signed the Agreement.

The evidence shows that on the Monday mornings when new employees were scheduled to begin working at Cubic, they attended an orientation session at which employee benefits were explained. The new hires completed insurance and medical forms as well as the secrecy and invention agreement. Cubic required all new employees to sign the secrecy and invention agreement.

The evidence also shows during the course of his employment, in part because of his invention, Marty was given a substantial raise in salary and made a program manager.

This evidence supports the trial court's conclusion the Agreement was a condition of employment and that the employment was adequate consideration for the Agreement. ...

Marty also contends the court erred in awarding damages of $34,102 which represents a government withhold on a Cubic design contract. ...

Marty's wrongful assertion of ownership caused the government withhold and therefore he was liable for that sum unless and until the government paid it to Cubic.

The judgment is affirmed.

◆

of employer, its manner of operation, its plans, processes, or other data without regard to whether all of the above-stated matters will be deemed confidential, material, or important, employer and employee specifically and expressly stipulating that as between them, such matters are important, material, and confidential and gravely affect the effective and successful conduct of the business of employer, and employer's good will, and that any breach of the terms of this section shall be a material breach of this agreement.[10]

EXAMPLE: Trade Secrets After Termination of Employment

All of the terms of [section with regard to maintaining employer's trade secrets] of this agreement shall remain in full force and effect for the period of

_____ years after the termination of employee's employment for any reason, and during such _____-year period, employee shall not make or permit the making of any public announcement or statement of any kind that _____ [he or she] was formerly employed by or connected with employer.[11]

Compensation

Provisions regarding compensation should address the areas of wages, salary, or commission, special incentives, overtime work or night differential, and sick pay.

EXAMPLE: Compensation of Employee

Employer shall pay employee, and employee shall accept from employer, in full payment for employee's services under this agreement, compensation at the rate of _____ dollars ($_____) per ____ [year], payable twice a month on the ____ [number] and ____ [number] days of each month while this agreement shall be in force.

Employer shall reimburse employee for all necessary expenses incurred by employee while traveling pursuant to employer's directions.[12]

Employee Benefits

Provision should be made in the employment agreement to describe the benefits to which the employee is entitled. This may be done either by describing each benefit in detail, or merely by stating that the employee will be entitled to any employee benefits which the employer maintains for workers in similar positions.

EXAMPLE: Participation in Other Employer Benefits

Employee shall be entitled to and shall receive all other benefits and conditions of employment available generally to other employees of employer employed at the same level and responsibility of employee pursuant to employer plans and programs, including by way of illustration, but not by way of limitation, group health insurance benefits, life insurance benefits, profit-sharing benefits, and pension and retirement benefits.[13]

Termination of Employment

Termination of the employee's employment prior to expiration of the term of the employment agreement may be grounds for a breach-of-contract action, either on behalf of the employer or the employee, if the agreement is so structured. An employment agreement often includes provisions allowing for the employee's termination upon notice given by either party, with or without cause. Although this type of loosely structured agreement affords maximum flexibility to both parties, it provides little certainty of continued employment.

Another commonly used employment agreement provision allows the employee to terminate the contract prior to its expiration upon certain specified conditions. This type of agreement generally allows the employer to terminate the employee only "with cause." Special care must be given to define the cause for which the employee may be terminated.

EXAMPLE: Termination

A. This agreement may be terminated by either party on _____ days' written notice to the other. If employer shall so terminate this agreement, employee shall be entitled to compensation for _____ days.

B. In the event of any violation by employee of any of the terms of this agreement, employer may terminate employment without notice and with compensation to employee only to the date of such termination.

C. It is further agreed that any breach or evasion of any of the terms of this agreement by either party will result in immediate and irreparable injury to the other party and will authorize recourse to injunction and/or specific performance, as well as to all other legal or equitable remedies to which such injured party may be entitled under this agreement.[14]

Arbitration of Disputes

Because even the most carefully drafted employment agreement is subject to interpretation, litigation often results when problems arise between the employee and employer. To curb potential legal fees and to resolve disputes expeditiously, both parties to an employment agreement often agree in advance to submit any disputes to binding arbitration.

EXAMPLE: Arbitration

Any differences, claims, or matters in dispute arising between employer and employee out of or connected with this agreement shall be submitted by them to arbitration by the American Arbitration Association or its successor and the determination of the American Arbitration Association or its successor shall be final and absolute. The arbitrator shall be governed by the duly promulgated rules and regulations of the American Arbitration Association or its successor, and the pertinent provisions of the laws of the state of _____, relating to arbitration. The decision of the arbitrator may be entered as a judgment in any court in the state of _____ or elsewhere.[15]

Vacations

The employment agreement should include language defining the employer's policy as it pertains to the employee with regard to vacations.

EXAMPLE: Vacations

During the term of this agreement, the employee shall be entitled to _____ days of paid vacation per year. Employer and employee shall mutually agree upon the time for such vacation.

Assignability of Contract

An employment agreement is typically not an assignable contract, especially on the part of the employee. However, the contract may be assignable by the employer under certain circumstances that involve a merger or acquisition.

EXAMPLE: Assumption and Assignability of Agreement— Employer's Merger, Consolidation, etc.

The rights and duties of employer and employee under this agreement shall not be assignable by either party except that this agreement and all rights under this agreement may be assigned by employer to any corporation or other business entity that succeeds to all or substantially all of the business of employer through merger, consolidation, corporate reorganization, or by acquisition of all or substantially all of the assets of employer and which assumes employer's obligations under this agreement.[16]

Amendment or Renewal of Agreement

The employment agreement should contain the agreed-upon provisions for amending and renewing the agreement.

EXAMPLE: Modification of Agreement

Any modification of this agreement or additional obligation assumed by either party in connection with this agreement shall be binding only if evidenced in writing signed by each party or an authorized representative of each party.[17]

Date and Signatures

The employment agreement should be dated and signed by both the employee and an authorized representative of the employer prior to the commencement of the employee's employment. Certain employment agreements may require the approval of the employer's board of directors or designated officers.

§ 14.4 SAMPLE EMPLOYMENT AGREEMENT

The sample agreement in Figure 14-1 on page 534 incorporates many of the clauses previously discussed in this chapter. Of course, any actual agreement must be drafted with the needs of the particular situation and client in mind.

§ 14.5 THE PARALEGAL'S ROLE IN DRAFTING EMPLOYMENT AGREEMENTS

Although they may not give legal advice with regard to the employment agreement and other employment matters, paralegals are often involved in every aspect of collecting the information necessary to draft an employment agreement, drafting the agreement, obtaining the signatures, and obtaining approval from the corporation's board of directors when necessary.

When a corporate client requests an attorney to prepare an employment agreement on its behalf, the first step is to collect the pertinent information from the client. The use of an employment agreement worksheet, such as the one shown

From 7B AM. JUR. *Legal Forms 2d Employment Contracts*
§ 99:11 (Rev. 1998)]

EMPLOYMENT OF EXECUTIVE—SALARY PLUS
CASH EQUIVALENT TO STOCK DIVIDENDS—
RETIREMENT BENEFITS

Agreement made, effective as of _____ [date], by and between _____, a corporation duly organized and existing under the laws of the State of _____, with a place of business at _____ [address], City of _____, County of _____, State of _____, hereinafter referred to as employer, and _____ of _____ [address], City of _____, County of _____, State of _____, hereinafter referred to as employee.

RECITALS

The parties recite and declare:

A. Employer desires to hire employee because of employee's vast business experience and expertise in _____ [specify business of employer].

B. Employee desires to be employed by employer in the executive capacity described below.

For the reasons set forth above, and in consideration of the mutual covenants and promises of the parties set forth in this agreement, employer and employee agree as follows:

SECTION ONE
EMPLOYMENT

Employer employs employee on the terms and conditions stated in this agreement to perform _____ [designate generally services employee is to perform], and employee agrees to perform such services for employer on the terms and conditions stated in this agreement.

SECTION TWO
TERM OF EMPLOYMENT

The term of employee's employment shall be _____ years commencing _____ [date]. Continued employment of employee by employer after _____ [date] shall be for the term and on the conditions agreed to by the parties prior to the expiration of this agreement.

SECTION THREE
COMPENSATION

A. Employer shall pay employee an annual salary of _____ dollars ($_____), payable monthly, on the _____ [number] day of each month, commencing _____ [date].

B. In addition to the compensation stated in Paragraph A of this section, employer shall pay employee on _____ [date], and annually thereafter, for the term of this agreement, a sum equal to dividends payable on _____ [number]

FIGURE 14-1   Sample Employment Agreement. Reprinted with permission from *American Jurisprudence Legal Forms 2d.* © 2000 West Group.

shares of the present authorized _____ [class] stock of employer to the extent that dividends are declared for that year. If employer declares a stock, rather than a cash dividend, employee shall receive in cash an amount equal to the fair market value of the stock dividend payable on ____ [number] shares. The fair market value of the stock dividends shall be _____ [if stock traded on exchange, the closing market price on the date of the stock dividend; or, if stock not openly traded, determined by mutual agreement of the parties; or, if that fails, by arbitration as provided for in Section Eight of this agreement]. If there is a stock split, the number of shares on which employee shall receive dividends shall increase on a basis proportionate with the stock split.

SECTION FOUR
RETIREMENT BENEFITS

If employee remains in the employ of employer until employee reaches the age of ____ years, employer shall pay employee or ____ [his or her] heirs or designated beneficiary _____ dollars ($_____) per month for ____ [number] years certain. Employer shall also pay employee, but not a designated beneficiary or employee's heirs or legatees, _____ dollars ($_____) after the term certain for so long as employee shall live.

SECTION FIVE
DEATH BENEFITS

If employee remains in the employ of employer continuously until employee's death, employer will pay to employee's designated beneficiary, or in lieu of a designated beneficiary, employee's heirs, a monthly income of _____ dollars ($_____) for ____ years.

SECTION SIX
EMPLOYER'S OBLIGATION ON ITS
TERMINATING EMPLOYEE'S EMPLOYMENT

If, during the term of this agreement, employer terminates this agreement for any reason, employer shall nevertheless continue the payments provided for in this agreement for the above-stated term so long as employee does not engage in gainful employment for another employer or enter into self-employment. If employee engages in gainful employment for another employer or enters into self-employment during the remaining term of this employment agreement, employer will pay employee [one-half] of the monthly payments designated in this agreement.

SECTION SEVEN
EMPLOYER'S OBLIGATION ON TERMINATION OF
EMPLOYMENT BY EMPLOYEE

If, during the term of this agreement, employee should fail or refuse to perform the services contemplated by this agreement, or should be unable to perform such services, or should engage in gainful employment with another employer, employer's obligation to make the payments provided in this agreement shall cease, but employer shall pay the additional compensation based on dividends declared on employer's stock to employee under Section Three of this agreement on a pro-rata basis for the number of months employee has been in the employ of employer for which no payment equal to such dividends has been paid.

FIGURE 14-1 (*continued*)

SECTION EIGHT
ARBITRATION

Any differences, claims, or matters in dispute arising between employer and employee out of or connected with this agreement shall be submitted by them to arbitration by the American Arbitration Association or its successor and the determination of the American Arbitration Association or its successor shall be final and absolute. The arbitrator shall be governed by the duly promulgated rules and regulations of the American Arbitration Association or its successor, and the pertinent provisions of the laws of the State of _____, relating to arbitration. The decision of the arbitrator may be entered as a judgment in any court of the State of _____ or elsewhere.

SECTION NINE
ATTORNEY'S FEES

In the event that any action is filed in relation to this agreement, the unsuccessful party in the action shall pay to the successful party, in addition to all the sums that either party may be called on to pay, a reasonable sum for the successful party's attorney's fees.

SECTION TEN
GOVERNING LAW

It is agreed that this agreement shall be governed by, construed, and enforced in accordance with the laws of the State of _____.

SECTION ELEVEN
ENTIRE AGREEMENT

This agreement shall constitute the entire agreement between the parties and any prior understanding or representation of any kind preceding the date of this agreement shall not be binding upon either party except to the extent incorporated in this agreement.

SECTION TWELVE
MODIFICATION OF AGREEMENT

Any modification of this agreement or additional obligation assumed by either party in connection with this agreement shall be binding only if evidenced in writing signed by each party or an authorized representative of each party.

SECTION THIRTEEN
NOTICES

Any notice provided for or concerning this agreement shall be in writing and be deemed sufficiently given when sent by certified or registered mail if sent to the respective address of each party as set forth at the beginning of this agreement.

SECTION FOURTEEN
PARAGRAPH HEADINGS

The titles to the paragraphs of this agreement are solely for the convenience of the parties and shall not be used to explain, modify, simplify, or aid in the interpretation of the provisions of this agreement.

FIGURE 14-1   (*continued*)

In witness whereof, each party to this agreement has caused it to be executed
at _____ [place of execution] on the date indicated below.

[Signatures and date(s) of signing]

[Title of person representing corporation]

FIGURE 14-1 (*continued*)

in Figure 14-2, to gather all pertinent information can be very effective. This
worksheet illustrates the types of information that must be gathered from the corporate client before drafting an employment agreement. After gathering the pertinent information from the client, the paralegal can draft the employment
agreement, under the supervision of an attorney, and see to its proper execution.

EMPLOYMENT AGREEMENT WORKSHEET

Identification of parties

Employer _____

Address _____

_____

Employee _____

Address _____

_____

Term of agreement

Number of years _____

Automatically renewable _____

Position

Title _____

Supervisor _____

Duties of employee

_____

_____

_____

_____

_____

Hours of employment _____

Compensation

Salary or commission _____

Rate of pay _____

FIGURE 14-2 Employment Agreement Worksheet

Scheduled pay periods _____

Overtime compensation _____

Sick pay _____

Vacations and holidays

_____

Employee benefits

Benefits that the employee is entitled to

_____

_____

_____

_____

_____

_____

Date on which employee becomes entitled to benefits

_____

Expense account

_____

_____

Covenant not to compete after leaving employment

Length of time _____

Geographical location _____

_____

Termination of employment

Right of either party to terminate after giving notice

_____

_____

Right of employee to terminate agreement _____

Conditions _____

_____

Right of employer to terminate agreement _____

Conditions _____

_____

FIGURE 14-2 (*continued*)

Typically, employment agreements entered into with officers or executives of a corporation are approved by a simple resolution of the board of directors, either by a unanimous written consent or at a regular board meeting. The paralegal can also see to it that the employment agreement is properly approved.

Corporate Paralegal Profile
Vicki Kunz, CLAS

I love customer service and providing our clients (the corporation and its subsidiaries) with services for which they would otherwise have to pay an outside law firm.

Name Vicki J. Kunz

Location Bismarck, North Dakota

Title Paralegal/Risk Management Specialist

Specialty Civil Litigation

Education College classes; Continuing Legal Education classes

Experience 22 years

Vicki Kunz is a paralegal with MDU Resources Group, Inc. MDU is a natural resources company based in North Dakota, with more than 60 subsidiaries located throughout the United States. MDU employs five attorneys and four paralegals. Vicki works with two of the attorneys in the legal department and she reports to the Risk Manager.

Vicki's has worked for MDU in several different positions. She started out in the legal department for the company as a Legal Assistant I. Her responsibilities included copyright, oil and gas law, and employment law. Less than two years later she was promoted to Legal Assistant II, with responsibilities in mergers and acquisitions, intellectual property, Hart-Scott-Rodino filings, and restricted stock management. After gaining extensive knowledge of MDU's corporate structure and financial background, Vicki was promoted to the position of Risk Management Specialist.

Vicki's main job function is to assist in minimizing or eliminating all risks to MDU. Her responsibilities as a risk management specialist include securing and maintaining various insurance coverages for MDU. She maintains and monitors all claims files and those that have moved into litigation. She is also responsible for contract review and risk management due diligence for new acquisitions.

There are several aspects of her position that Vicki enjoys. She especially enjoys the variety. Vicki

likes the fact that she is not doing the same thing ever day. Her frequent contact with *clients* at MDU and its many subsidiaries by phone, e-mail and fax keeps her position interesting.

On the down side, Vicki has found that corporations have considerably more rules and policies than any of the law firms she has worked for. Sometimes the decision-making process can be very cumbersome. She also misses the level of secretarial support that she has enjoyed in law firms. In her current position, there is one secretary for every 8 to 15 people. She has found that she has many more clerical and administrative responsibilities working for a corporation than for a law firm. The good still outweighs the downside, as she has found there are more opportunities for paralegals in the corporate setting than what she experienced in the law firm. After 19 years in one of the top North Dakota firms, she had reached her peak—not only in salary, but in legal assignments. She states that MDU has been challenging her for more than three years and it still has other opportunities for her.

Vicki is a Certified Legal Assistant. She has met the National Association of Legal Assistant's requirements for both the Certified Legal Assistant designation, and the Certified Legal Assistant Specialist designation. Vicki was the founding member of the Western Dakota Association of Legal Assistants, and she has served in various officer positions, including NALA liaison and president. In addition, she has served in officer positions of NALA, including treasurer, secretary, and vice president.

Vicki's advice for new paralegals?

Continue your education. Read, read, read, and don't settle to do just what you are told. Learn to look further into your assignment and take that extra step. Watch and learn! You'll be the top in your profession before you know it.

For more information on careers for corporate paralegals, log on to the companion Web page to this text at **www.westlegalstudies.com**.

§ 14.6 RESOURCES

Numerous form books are available to aid in drafting employment agreements, including Am. Jur. *Forms* 2d, *Nichols Cyclopedia of Legal Forms Annotated, Rabkin & Johnson Current Legal Forms,* and *West's Legal Forms, (second edition)*. In addition, state statutes should be consulted with regard to any covenants not to compete included in the employment agreement. Statutes of certain states include provisions that specifically restrict the use of such covenants.

Internet Resources www.

For employment agreement forms

All About Forms.Com	www.allaboutforms.com/
AllLaw.com	www.alllaw.com/forms/employment/ employment_agreement/
Findlaw.com (Legal Forms)	www.findlaw.com
Internet Legal Resource Guide	www.ilrg.com/forms/employmt.html
The 'Lectric Law Library's Business and General Forms	www.lectlaw.com/formb.htm

An alphabetical list of Internet Resources for the Corporate Paralegal is included as appendix B to this text.

Web Page

For updates and links to several of the previously listed sites, log on to **www. westlegalstudies.com,** and click through to the book link for this text.

SUMMARY

- An employment agreement sets forth the rights and obligations of the employer and employee.
- An employment agreement is considered a binding contract on both the employer and employee, and it must include all the elements of a contract.
- A covenant not to compete restricts the future employment and actions of the employee. Covenants not to compete are only enforceable if they are considered reasonable.
- Employees at will are hired by an employer for agreed-upon compensation and they can quit at any time or be dismissed at the employer's discretion, without cause.

REVIEW QUESTIONS

1. What is employment "at will"?
2. May the employee's actions be restricted even after termination of employment?
3. What possible recourse might an employee have if he or she is unfairly demoted?
4. Why were covenants not to compete void under the common law of England? What is the modern view toward covenants not to compete?
5. Suppose that Alex is hired as a salesperson for the Miles Medical Supply Corporation, a regional medical supplies corporation that sells directly to hospitals in the Midwest. Before Alex commences employment, he is required to sign an employment agreement that specifically provides that he will not sell medical supplies for any competing business within the United States for a period of 10 years after leaving his employment. Five years after termination of Alex's employment with Miles Medical Supply, he is unable to find work in the Midwest, so he relocates to Florida, where he takes a management position with a national medical supply company. Could Miles Medical Supply prevail in a suit against Alex for damages due to his breach of contract? Why or why not?
6. If an employment agreement remains silent on the issue, is the employer necessarily entitled to all inventions of the employee while the employee is working for the employer?
7. Are the rights and obligations of either the employee or employer under an employment agreement ever assignable? If so, under what conditions?

PRACTICAL PROBLEMS

Has the reasonableness of covenants not to compete been defined by the courts of your state? Research the case law in your state to locate a case that discusses the reasonableness of covenants not to compete in employment agreements, and write a brief summary of what the court in that case found to be reasonable (or not reasonable). If you are unable to locate such a case in the courts of your state, locate such a case in a neighboring state.

WORKPLACE SCENARIO

Assume that our fictional clients, the owners of Cutting Edge Computer Repair, Inc., have decided to expand their business by hiring a computer technician. This individual will be a salaried, full-time employee. He will not be an officer or director of the corporation.

Using the following information, and the information in this chapter, prepare a draft of an employment agreement between Cutting Edge Computer Repair, Inc., and its new employee.

Employee's Name Brian Anderson, 3856 Main Street, Oakdale, (your home state)

Term of Agreement Indefinite, to terminate on 60 days notice of either party

Position Computer Repair Technician

Duties Those typical of a computer repair technician

Hours of Employment 9:00 A.M. to 5:00 P.M., Monday through Friday

Compensation $30,000 annual salary; Paid on the 1st and 15th of each month

Vacations 2 weeks for the first 5 years of service; 3 weeks for 5 to 10 years of service; 4 weeks after 10 years of service

Employee Benefits 5 days sick pay per year; Health insurance policy adopted by corporation

Covenant Not to Compete Brian is not to establish his own computer repair business within a 25-mile radius of Cutting Edge Computer Repair, Inc., for a period of three years after terminating his employment.

END NOTES

1. 7B AM. JUR. *Legal Forms* 2d *Employment Contracts* § 99:5 (1998). Reprinted with permission from *American Jurisprudence Legal Forms 2d.* © 2000 West Group.

2. *Id.* § 99:7. Reprinted with permission from *American Jurisprudence Legal Forms 2d.* © 2000 West Group.

3. *Id.* § 99:12. Reprinted with permission from *American Jurisprudence Legal Forms 2d.* © 2000 West Group.

4. *Id.* § 99:15. Reprinted with permission from *American Jurisprudence Legal Forms 2d.* © 2000 West Group.

5. Annotation, *Anticompetitive Covenants,* 60 A.L.R.4th 965 (1986).

6. *Id.*

7. 7B AM. JUR. *Legal Forms* 2d *Employment Contracts* § 99:198 (Rev. 1988). Reprinted with permission from *American Jurisprudence Legal Forms 2d.* © 2000 West Group.

8. *Id.* § 99:202. Reprinted with permission from *American Jurisprudence Legal Forms 2d.* © 2000 West Group.

9. *Restatement of Torts* § 757, comment (1985).

10. 7B AM. JUR. *Legal Forms* 2d *Employment Contracts* § 99:7 (Rev. 1998). Reprinted with permission from *American Jurisprudence Legal Forms 2d.* © 2000 West Group.

11. *Id.* Reprinted with permission from *American Jurisprudence Legal Forms 2d.* © 2000 West Group.

12. *Id.* Reprinted with permission from *American Jurisprudence Legal Forms 2d.* © 2000 West Group.

13. *Id.* § 99:176. Reprinted with permission from *American Jurisprudence Legal Forms 2d.* © 2000 West Group.

14. *Id.* § 99:7. Reprinted with permission from *American Jurisprudence Legal Forms 2d.* © 2000 West Group.

15. *Id.* § 99:11. Reprinted with permission from *American Jurisprudence Legal Forms 2d.* © 2000 West Group.

16. *Id.* § 99:205. Reprinted with permission from *American Jurisprudence Legal Forms 2d.* © 2000 West Group.

17. *Id.* § 99:7. Reprinted with permission from *American Jurisprudence Legal Forms 2d.* © 2000 West Group.

APPENDIX A

Secretary of State Directory

Alabama Secretary of State
Corporation Division
P.O. Box 5616
Montgomery, AL
36103-5616
(334) 242-5324
www.sos.state.al.us/

Alaska Dept. of Commerce and Economic Development
Corporations Section
Floor 9, Alaska State Office Building
Juneau, AK 99811
(907) 465-2530
www.gov.state.ak.us/ltgov/

Arizona Corporation Commission
300 West Washington
Phoenix, AZ 85007
(602) 542-3026
www.sosaz.com/

Arkansas Secretary of State
Corporations Division
Aegon Building, #310
Little Rock, AR 72201
(501) 682-3409
www.sosweb.state.ar.us

California Secretary of State
Corporation Filing Division
1500 11th Street
Sacramento, CA 95814
(916) 653-2121
www.ss.ca.gov/

Colorado Secretary of State
1560 Broadway, Suite 200
Denver, CO 80202
(303) 894-2200
www.sos.state.co.us/

Connecticut Secretary of State
Division of Corporations
30 Trinity Street
Hartford, CT 06106
(860) 509-6000
www.sots.state.ct.us/

Delaware Secretary of State
Division of Corporations
P.O. Box 898
Dover, DE 19903
(302) 739-3073
www.state.de.us/corp/index.htm

District of Columbia
Department of Consumer and Regulatory
Affairs
441 Fourth Street
Washington, DC 20001
(202) 727-1000
www.dcra.org/main.shtm

Florida Department of State
Division of Corporations
P.O. Box 6327
Tallahassee, FL 32314
(904) 488-9000
www.dos.state.fl.us/

Georgia Secretary of State
Business Services and Regulation
2 Martin Luther King, Jr. Dr.
Atlanta, GA 30334
(404) 656-2817
www.sos.state.ga.us/

Hawaii Department of Commerce and Consumer Affairs
Business Registration Division
P.O. Box 40
Honolulu, HI 96810
(808) 586-2727
www.state.hi.us

Idaho Secretary of State
700 W. Jefferson, Room 203
Boise, ID 83720
(208) 334-2300
www.idsos.state.id.us/

Illinois Secretary of State
Dept. of Business Services
213 State Capitol Building
Springfield, IL 62706
(217) 782-2201
www.sos.state.il.us/

Indiana Secretary of State
Corporations Division
302 West Washington Street, Room E018
Indianapolis, IN 46204
(317) 232-6576
www.ai.org/sos/index.html

Iowa Secretary of State
Division of Corporations
Hoover State Office Building
1305 E. Walnut, 2nd Floor
Des Moines, IA 50319
(515) 281-5204
www.sos.state.ia.us/

Kansas Secretary of State
120 SW 10th Ave., Room 100
Topeka, KS 66612
(913) 296-4564
www.kssos.org/

Kentucky Secretary of State
Corporations Department
700 Capital Avenue Suite 152, State Capitol
Frankfort, KY 40601
(502) 564-3490
www.sos.state.ky.us/

Louisiana Secretary of State
Corporate Division
P.O. Box 94125
Baton Rouge, LA 70804-9125
(504) 925-4704
www.sec.state.la.us/

Maine Secretary of State
Bureau of Corporations, Elections and
Commissions
State House Station 101
Augusta, ME 04333-0101
(207) 624-7740
www.state.me.us/sos/

**Maryland State Department of Assessments
and Taxation**
301 West Preston Street
Baltimore, MD 21201
(410) 767-1184
www.dat.state.md.us/sdatweb/charter.html

Massachusetts Secretary of State
Corporations Division
One Ashburton Place
Boston, MA 02108
(617) 727-9640
www.state.ma.us/sec/indexf.htm

Michigan Department of Commerce
Corporation and Securities Corporation
Department Division
6546 Mercantile Way
Lansing, MI 48911
(517) 241-6470
www.cis.state.mi.us/bcs/corp/

Minnesota Secretary of State
Business Services Division
180 State Office Building
St. Paul, MN 55155
(612) 296-2803
www.sos.state.mn.us/

Mississippi Secretary of State
Corporate Division
P.O. Box 136
Jackson, MS 39205
(601) 359-1333
www.sos.state.ms.us/

Missouri Secretary of State
Corporation Division
Truman Building
P.O. Box 778
Jefferson City, MO 65102
(573) 751-4153
mosl.sos.state.mo.us/

Montana Corporation Bureau
Secretary of State's Office
State Capitol
Helena, MT 59620
(406) 444-2034
www.state.mt.us/isd/index.htm

Nebraska Secretary of State
State Capitol Building
Lincoln, NE 68509
(402) 471-4079
www.state.ne.us

Nevada Secretary of State
Corporate Division
Capitol Complex
Carson City, NV 89710
(775) 684-5708
www.sos.state.nv.us/

**New Hampshire Secretary of
State/Corporations**
204 State House
107 North Main Street
Concord, NH 03301
(603) 271-3246
www.state.nh.us/sos/corporate/index.htm

New Jersey Secretary of State
Division of Commercial Recordings
225 West State Street, CN 300
Trenton, NJ 08608
(609) 530-6400
www.state.nj.us/state/

New Mexico State Corporation Commission
Corporation Department
State Capitol North Annex, #300
Santa Fe, NM 87503
(505) 827-3600
www.sos.state.nm.us/

New York Department of State
41 State Street
Albany, NY 12231
(518) 473-2492
www.dos.state.ny.us/

North Carolina Secretary of State
Corporations Division
P.O. Box 29622
Raleigh, NC 27626
(919) 807-2225
www.secstate.state.nc.us/

North Dakota Secretary of State
State Capitol Building
600 East Boulevard Avenue
Bismarck, ND 58505-0500
(701) 328-4284
www.state.nd.us/sec/

Ohio Secretary of State
Division of Corporations
30 East Broad Street, 14th Floor
Columbus, OH 43266-0418
(614) 466-3910
www.state.oh.us/

Oklahoma Secretary of State
101 State Capitol
Oklahoma City, OK 73105
(405) 521-3911
www.sos.state.ok.us/

Oregon Secretary of State
Corporation Division
255 Capitol Street NE
Salem, OR 97310
(503) 986-2200
www.sos.state.or.us/

Pennsylvania Department of State
Corporation Bureau
308 North Office Building
Harrisburg, PA 17120
(717) 787-1057
www.dos.state.pa.us/

Rhode Island Secretary of State
Corporations Division
100 North Main Street
Providence, RI 02903
(401) 222-3040
www.state.ri.us/

South Carolina Secretary of State
Corporate Division
P.O. Box 11350
Columbia, SC 29211
(803) 734-2158
www.scsos.com/

South Dakota Secretary of State
Corporate Department
500 East Capitol Street
Pierre, SD 57501
(605) 773-4845
www.state.sd.us/sos/sos.htm

Tennessee Secretary of State
James K. Polk Building, 18th Floor
Nashville, TN 37243
(615) 741-2286
www.state.tn.us/sos/

Texas Secretary of State
Statutory Filings Division Corporations Section
P.O. Box 13967
Austin, TX 78711-3697
(512) 463-5555
www.sos.state.tx.us/

Utah Corporations and Commercial Code Division
160 E. 300 Street
Salt Lake City, UT 84145
(801) 530-4849
www.commerce.state.ut.us/

Vermont Secretary of State Corporations
81 River Street, Drawer 09
Montpelier, VT 05609
(802) 828-2386
www.sec.state.vt.us/

Virginia State Corporation Commission
P.O. Box 1197
Richmond, VA 23218
(804) 371-9967
www.state.va.us/scc/index.html

Washington Secretary of State
Corporations Division
505 East Union (MS-PM 21)
Olympia, WA 98504
(360) 753-7115
www.secstate.wa.gov/

West Virginia Secretary of State
Corporate Division
Bldg. 1, Suite 157-K
Charleston, WV 25305
(304) 558-8000
www.state.wv.us/sos/

Wisconsin Secretary of State
Corporation Division
P.O. Box 7846
Madison, WI 53707
(608) 266-3590
www.wdfi.org/

Wyoming Secretary of State
State Capitol Building
Cheyenne, WY 82002
(307) 777-7311
soswy.state.wy.us/

APPENDIX B

On-line Resources for the Corporate Paralegal

Corporate Law Information

Law.com
www.law.com/professionals/corplaw.html

The 'Lectric Law Library's Business Lounge
www.lectlaw.com/bus.html

Legal Information Institute
www.law.cornell.edu/topics/corporations.html

Corporation Information
(information about specific corporations)

Business.com—Pure Business Information
www.business.com/

Corporate Information
www.corporateinformation.com/

Hoover's Online—The Business Network
www.hoovers.com

Employee Benefit Plan Information

Benefit News
www.benefitnews.com

Benefits Link
www.benefitslink.com/index.shtml

Employee Benefits Research Institute
www.ebri.org

FreeERISA
www.freeerisa.com

National Center for Employee Ownership
www.nceo.org

Federal Government

Antitrust Division—Department of Justice
www.usdoj.gov/atr

Bureau of Labor Statistics
www.stats.bls.gov

FedWorld
www.FedWorld.gov

FirstGov—Links to sites of the U.S. Government
www.firstgov.org/

Internal Revenue Service
www.irs.gov

Securities and Exchange Commission
www.sec.gov

U.S. Patent and Trademark Office
www.ustpo.gov

Federal Statutes

American Law Source Online
www.lawsource.com/also/

Forms

All About Forms.Com
www.allaboutforms.com/

Findlaw.com (Legal Forms)
www.findlaw.com

The 'Lectric Law Library's Business and General Forms
www.lectlaw.com/formb.htm

Intellectual Property

United States Patent and Trademark Office
www.uspto.gov

Legal Ethics Information

Legal Information Institute (links to state codes of
ethics)
www.law.cornell.edu/ethics/

Legalethics.com
www.legalethics.com

Legal Research
(General Comprehensive Sites)

All Law
www.aallnet.org/research/

American Law Sources Online
www.lawsource.com/also/

Cornell University School of Law's Legal
Information Institute
www.law.cornell.edu/

FindLaw
www.findlaw.com/

Hieros Gamos
www.hg.org/

Internet Legal Resource Guide
www.ilrg.com/

Jurist
www.jurist.law.pitt.edu/

Katsuey Kat's Legal Links
www.katsuey.com/

Law.Com
www.law.com

Law Guru
www.lawguru.com/

The 'Lectric Law Library's Paralegal's Reading
Room
www.lectlaw.com/ppara.htm

Limited Liability Company Information

LLCC-USA.COM
www.llc-usa.com/

Limited Partnership Information
Mergers and Acquisitions

Merger Network.com
www.mergernetwork.com/

Paralegal Associations

American Association for Paralegal Education
www.aafpe.org

American Bar Association
www.abanet.org

Association of Legal Administrators
www.alanet.org

Legal Assistant Management Association
www.lamanet.org

National Association of Legal Assistants
www.nala.org

National Federation of Paralegal Associations
www.paralegals.org

Partnership Information

Legal Information Institute
www.law.cornell.edu/topics/partnership.html

Paralegal Publications

Legal Assistant Today
www.legalassistanttoday.com

National Paralegal Reporter
www.paralegals.org/Reporter/home.html

Secretary of State Offices

Corporate Housekeeper
www.danvi.vi/link2.html

National Association of Secretaries of State
www.nass.org

Securities Information

The Securities and Exchange Commission
www.sec.gov

The Securities Lawyer's Deskbook
Provided by The Center for Corporate Law
University of Cincinnati College of Law
www.law.uc.edu/CCL/intro.html

Small Business Information

Business Plans
www.bplans.com

Business Resource Center
www.morebusiness.com/

Small Business Administration
www.sbaonline.sba.gov/

State and Local Government Links

Piper Resources
www.piperinfo.com/state/index.cfm

State Government Forms

Findlaw.com State Corporation and Business
Forms
www.findlaw.com/11stategov/indexcorp.html

State Statutes

American Law Source Online
www.lawsource.com/also/

Findlaw.com
www.findlaw.com/11stategov/

Legal Information Institute
www.law.cornell.edu/states/listing.html

Tax Information

Internal Revenue Service
www.irs.gov

Uniform Acts

National Conference of Commissioners on
Uniform State Law
www.law.upenn.edu/bll/ulc/ulc_frame.htm

APPENDIX C

Ethics for Corporate Paralegals

C-1
On-line Resources for Researching Legal Ethics

American Bar Association
www.abanet.org/

Hieros Gamos
www.hg.org/

Katsuey Kat's Legal Links
www.katsuey.com/

The 'Lectric Law Library's Paralegal's Reading Room
www.lectlaw.com/ppara.htm

Legal Information Institute (links to state codes of ethics)
www.law.cornell.edu/ethics/

Legalethics.com: The Internet Ethics Site
www.legalethics.com/

National Association of Legal Assistants
www.nala.org/

National Federation of Paralegal Associations
www.paralegals.org/

C-2
Code of Ethics and Professional Responsibility of the National Association of Legal Assistants

Reprinted with permission of the
National Association of Legal Assistants,
1516 S. Boston, Tulsa, OK,
918-587-6828,
www.nala.org

Canon 1

A legal assistant must not perform any of the duties that attorneys only may perform nor take any actions that attorneys may not take.

Canon 2

A legal assistant may perform any task which is properly delegated and supervised by an attorney, as long as the attorney is ultimately responsible to the client, maintains a direct relationship with the client, and assumes professional responsibility for the work product.

Canon 3

A legal assistant must not (a) engage in, encourage, or contribute to any act which could constitute the unauthorized practice of law; and (b) establish attorney-client relationships, set fees, give legal opinions or advice or represent a client before a court or agency unless so authorized by that court or agency; or (c) engage in conduct or take any action which would assist or involve the attorney in a violation of professional ethics or give the appearance of professional impropriety.

Canon 4

A legal assistant must use discretion and professional judgment commensurate with knowledge and experience but must not render independent legal judgment in place of an attorney. The services of an attorney are essential in the public interest whenever such legal judgment is required.

Canon 5

A legal assistant must disclose his or her status as a legal assistant at the outset of any professional relationship with a client, attorney, a court or administrative agency or personnel thereof, or a member of the general public. A legal assistant must act prudently in determining the extent to which a client may be assisted without the presence of an attorney.

Canon 6

A legal assistant must strive to maintain integrity and a high degree of competency through education and training with respect to professional responsibility, local rules and practice, and through continuing education in substantive areas of law to better assist the legal profession in fulfilling its duty to provide legal service.

Canon 7

A legal assistant must protect the confidences of a client and must not violate any rule or statute now in effect or hereafter to be enacted controlling privileged communications.

Canon 8

A legal assistant must do all other things incidental, necessary, or expedient for the attainment of the ethics and responsibilities as defined by statute or rule of court.

Canon 9

A legal assistant's conduct is guided by bar associations' codes of professional responsibility and rules of professional conduct.

C-3
National Federation of Paralegal Associations, Inc. Model Code of Ethics and Professional Responsibility and Guidelines for Enforcement

Reprinted with permission of the National Federation of Paralegal Associations, Inc., (NFPA), P.O. Box 33108, Kansas City, MO 64114-0108, **www.paralegals.org.**

Preamble

The National Federation of Paralegal Associations, Inc. ("NFPA") is a professional organization comprised of paralegal associations and individual paralegals throughout the United States and Canada. Members of NFPA have varying backgrounds, experiences, education and job responsibilities that reflect the diversity of the paralegal profession. NFPA promotes the growth, development and recognition of the paralegal profession as an integral partner in the delivery of legal services.

In May 1993 NFPA adopted its Model Code of Ethics and Professional Responsibility ("Model Code") to delineate the principles for ethics and conduct to which every paralegal should aspire.

Many paralegal associations throughout the United States have endorsed the concept and content of NFPA's Model Code through the adoption of their own ethical codes. In doing so, paralegals have confirmed the profession's commitment to increase the quality and efficiency of legal services, as well as recognized its responsibilities to the public, the legal community, and colleagues.

Paralegals have recognized, and will continue to recognize, that the profession must continue to evolve to enhance their roles in the delivery of legal services. With increased levels of responsibility comes the need to define and enforce mandatory rules of professional conduct. Enforcement of codes of paralegal conduct is a logical and necessary step to enhance and ensure the confidence of the legal community and the public in the integrity and professional responsibility of paralegals.

In April 1997 NFPA adopted the Model Disciplinary Rules ("Model Rules") to make possible the enforcement of the Canons and Ethical Considerations contained in the NFPA Model Code. A concurrent determination was made that the Model Code of Ethics and Professional Responsibility, formerly aspirational in nature, should be recognized as setting forth the enforceable obligations of all paralegals.

The Model Code and Model Rules offer a framework for professional discipline, either voluntarily or through formal regulatory programs.

§ 1. NFPA Model Disciplinary Rules and Ethical Considerations

1.1 A paralegal shall achieve and maintain a high level of competence.

Ethical Considerations

EC-1.1(a) A paralegal shall achieve competency through education, training, and work experience.

EC-1.1(b) A paralegal shall participate in continuing education in order to keep informed of current legal, technical and general developments.

EC-1.1(c) A paralegal shall perform all assignments promptly and efficiently.

1.2   A paralegal shall maintain a high level of personal and professional integrity.

Ethical Considerations

EC-1.2(a)   A paralegal shall not engage in any ex parte communications involving the courts or any other adjudicatory body in an attempt to exert undue influence or to obtain advantage or the benefit of only one party.

EC-1.2(b)   A paralegal shall not communicate, or cause another to communicate, with a party the paralegal knows to be represented by a lawyer in a pending matter without the prior consent of the lawyer representing such other party.

EC-1.2(c)   A paralegal shall ensure that all time-keeping and billing records prepared by the paralegal are thorough, accurate, honest, and complete.

EC-1.2(d)   A paralegal shall not knowingly engage in fraudulent billing practices. Such practices may include, but are not limited to: inflation of hours billed to a client or employer; misrepresentation of the nature of tasks performed; and/or submission of fraudulent expense and disbursement documentation.

EC-1.2(e)   A paralegal shall be scrupulous, thorough and honest in the identification and maintenance of all funds, securities, and other assets of a client and shall provide accurate accounting as appropriate.

EC-1.2(f)   A paralegal shall advise the proper authority of non-confidential knowledge of any dishonest or fraudulent acts by any person pertaining to the handling of the funds, securities or other assets of a client. The authority to whom the report is made shall depend on the nature and circumstances of the possible misconduct, (e.g., ethics committees of law firms, corporations and/or paralegal associations, local or state bar associations, local prosecutors, administrative agencies, etc.). Failure to report such knowledge is in itself misconduct and shall be treated as such under these rules.

1.3   A paralegal shall maintain a high standard of professional conduct.

Ethical Considerations

EC-1.3(a)   A paralegal shall refrain from engaging in any conduct that offends the dignity and decorum of proceedings before a court or other adjudicatory body and shall be respectful of all rules and procedures.

EC-1.3(b)   A paralegal shall avoid impropriety and the appearance of impropriety and shall not engage in any conduct that would adversely affect his/her fitness to practice. Such conduct may include, but is not limited to: violence, dishonesty, interference with the administration of justice, and/or abuse of a professional position or public office.

EC-1.3(c)   Should a paralegal's fitness to practice be compromised by physical or mental illness, causing that paralegal to commit an act that is in direct violation of the Model Code/Model Rules and/or the rules and/or laws governing the jurisdiction in which the paralegal practices, that paralegal may be protected from sanction upon review of the nature and circumstances of that illness.

EC-1.3(d)   A paralegal shall advise the proper authority of non-confidential knowledge of any action of another legal professional that clearly demonstrates fraud, deceit, dishonesty, or misrepresentation. The authority to whom the report is made shall depend on the nature and circumstances of the possible misconduct, (e.g., ethics committees of law firms, corporations and/or paralegal associations, local or state bar associations, local prosecutors, administrative agencies, etc.). Failure to report such knowledge is in itself misconduct and shall be treated as such under these rules.

EC-1.3(e) A paralegal shall not knowingly assist any individual with the commission of an act that is in direct violation of the Model Code/Model Rules and/or the rules and/or laws governing the jurisdiction in which the paralegal practices.

EC-1.3(f) If a paralegal possesses knowledge of future criminal activity, that knowledge must be reported to the appropriate authority immediately.

1.4 A paralegal shall serve the public interest by contributing to the delivery of quality legal services and the improvement of the legal system.

Ethical Considerations

EC-1.4(a) A paralegal shall be sensitive to the legal needs of the public and shall promote the development and implementation of programs that address those needs.

EC-1.4(b) A paralegal shall support bona fide efforts to meet the need for legal services by those unable to pay reasonable or customary fees for example, participation in pro bono projects and volunteer work.

EC-1.4(c) A paralegal shall support efforts to improve the legal system and access thereto and shall assist in making changes.

1.5 A paralegal shall preserve all confidential information provided by the client or acquired from other sources before, during, and after the course of the professional relationship.

Ethical Considerations

EC-1.5(a) A paralegal shall be aware of and abide by all legal authority governing confidential information in the jurisdiction in which the paralegal practices.

EC-1.5(b) A paralegal shall not use confidential information to the disadvantage of the client.

EC-1.5(c) A paralegal shall not use confidential information to the advantage of the paralegal or of a third person.

EC-1.5(d) A paralegal may reveal confidential information only after full disclosure and with the client's written consent; or, when required by law or court order; or, when necessary to prevent the client from committing an act that could result in death or serious bodily harm.

EC-1.5(e) A paralegal shall keep those individuals responsible for the legal representation of a client fully informed of any confidential information the paralegal may have pertaining to that client.

EC-1.5(f) A paralegal shall not engage in any indiscreet communications concerning clients.

1.6 A paralegal shall avoid conflicts of interest and shall disclose any possible conflict to the employer or client, as well as to the prospective employers or clients.

Ethical Considerations

EC-1.6(a) A paralegal shall act within the bounds of the law, solely for the benefit of the client, and shall be free of compromising influences and loyalties. Neither the paralegal's personal or business interest, nor those of other clients or third persons, should compromise the paralegal's professional judgment and loyalty to the client.

EC-1.6(b) A paralegal shall avoid conflicts of interest that may arise from previous assignments, whether for a present or past employer or client.

EC-1.6(c) A paralegal shall avoid conflicts of interest that may arise from family relationships and from personal and business interests.

EC-1.6(d) In order to be able to determine whether an actual or potential conflict of interest exists a paralegal shall create and maintain an effective record-keeping system that identifies clients, matters, and parties with which the paralegal has worked.

EC-1.6(e) A paralegal shall reveal sufficient non-confidential information about a client or former client to reasonably ascertain if an actual or potential conflict of interest exists.

EC-1.6(f) A paralegal shall not participate in or conduct work on any matter where a conflict of interest has been identified.

EC-1.6(g) In matters where a conflict of interest has been identified and the client consents to continued representation, a paralegal shall comply fully with the implementation and maintenance of an Ethical Wall.

1.7 A paralegal's title shall be fully disclosed.

Ethical Considerations

EC-1.7(a) A paralegal's title shall clearly indicate the individual's status and shall be disclosed in all business and professional communications to avoid misunderstandings and misconceptions about the paralegal's role and responsibilities.

EC-1.7(b) A paralegal's title shall be included if the paralegal's name appears on business cards, letterhead, brochures, directories, and advertisements.

EC-1.7(c) A paralegal shall not use letterhead, business cards or other promotional materials to create a fraudulent impression of his/her status or ability to practice in the jurisdiction in which the paralegal practices.

EC-1.7(d) A paralegal shall not practice under color of any record, diploma, or certificate that has been illegally or fraudulently obtained or issued or which is misrepresentative in any way.

EC-1.7(e) A paralegal shall not participate in the creation, issuance, or dissemination of fraudulent records, diplomas, or certificates.

1.8 A paralegal shall not engage in the unauthorized practice of law.

Ethical Considerations

EC-1.8(a) A paralegal shall comply with the applicable legal authority governing the unauthorized practice of law in the jurisdiction in which the paralegal practices.

§ 2. NFPA Guidelines for the Enforcement of the Model Code of Ethics and Professional Responsibility

2.1 Basis for Discipline

2.1(a) Disciplinary investigations and proceedings brought under authority of the Rules shall be conducted in accord with obligations imposed on the paralegal professional by the Model Code of Ethics and Professional Responsibility.

2.2 Structure of Disciplinary Committee

2.2(a) The Disciplinary Committee ("Committee") shall be made up of nine (9) members including the Chair.

2.2(b) Each member of the Committee, including any temporary replacement members, shall have demonstrated working knowledge of ethics/professional responsibility-related issues and activities.

2.2(c) The Committee shall represent a cross-section of practice areas and work experience. The following recommendations are made regarding the members of the Committee.

1) At least one paralegal with one to three years of law-related work experience.

2) At least one paralegal with five to seven years of law related work experience.

3) At least one paralegal with over ten years of law related work experience.

4) One paralegal educator with five to seven years of work experience; preferably in the area of ethics/professional responsibility.

5) One paralegal manager.

6) One lawyer with five to seven years of law-related work experience.

7) One lay member.

2.2(d)   The Chair of the Committee shall be appointed within thirty (30) days of its members' induction. The Chair shall have no fewer than ten (10) years of law-related work experience.

2.2(e)   The terms of all members of the Committee shall be staggered. Of those members initially appointed, a simple majority plus one shall be appointed to a term of one year, and the remaining members shall be appointed to a term of two years. Thereafter, all members of the Committee shall be appointed to terms of two years.

2.2(f)   If for any reason the terms of a majority of the Committee will expire at the same time, members may be appointed to terms of one year to maintain continuity of the Committee.

2.2(g)   The Committee shall organize from its members a three-tiered structure to investigate, prosecute and/or adjudicate charges of misconduct. The members shall be rotated among the tiers.

2.3   Operation of Committee

2.3(a)   The Committee shall meet on an as-needed basis to discuss, investigate, and/or adjudicate alleged violations of the Model Code/Model Rules.

2.3(b)   A majority of the members of the Committee present at a meeting shall constitute a quorum.

2.3(c)   A Recording Secretary shall be designated to maintain complete and accurate minutes of all Committee meetings. All such minutes shall be kept confidential until a decision has been made that the matter will be set for hearing as set forth in Section 6.1 below.

2.3(d)   If any member of the Committee has a conflict of interest with the Charging Party, the Responding Party, or the allegations of misconduct, that member shall not take part in any hearing or deliberations concerning those allegations. If the absence of that member creates a lack of a quorum for the Committee, then a temporary replacement for the member shall be appointed.

2.3(e)   Either the Charging Party or the Responding Party may request that, for good cause shown, any member of the Committee not participate in a hearing or deliberation. All such requests shall be honored. If the absence of a Committee member under those circumstances creates a lack of a quorum for the Committee, then a temporary replacement for that member shall be appointed.

2.3(f)   All discussions and correspondence of the Committee shall be kept confidential until a decision has been made that the matter will be set for hearing as set forth in Section 6.1 below.

2.3(g)   All correspondence from the Committee to the Responding Party regarding any charge of misconduct and any decisions made regarding the charge shall be mailed certified mail, return receipt requested, to the Responding Party's last known address and shall be clearly marked with a "Confidential" designation.

2.4   Procedure for the Reporting of Alleged Violations of the Model Code/ Disciplinary Rules

2.4(a)   An individual or entity in possession of non-confidential knowledge or information concerning possible instances of misconduct shall make a confidential written report to the Committee within thirty (30) days of obtaining same. This report shall include all details of the alleged misconduct.

2.4(b)   The Committee so notified shall inform the Responding Party of the allegation(s) of misconduct no later than ten (10) business days after receiving the confidential written report from the Charging Party.

2.4(c)   Notification to the Responding Party shall include the identity of the Charging Party, unless, for good cause shown, the Charging Party requests anonymity.

2.4(d)   The Responding Party shall reply to the allegations within ten (10) business days of notification.

2.5   Procedure for the Investigation of a Charge of Misconduct

2.5(a)   Upon receipt of a Charge of Misconduct ("Charge"), or on its own initiative, the Committee shall initiate an investigation.

2.5(b)   If, upon initial or preliminary review, the Committee makes a determination that the charges are either without basis in fact or, if proven, would not constitute professional misconduct, the Committee shall dismiss the allegations of misconduct. If such determination of dismissal cannot be made, a formal investigation shall be initiated.

2.5(c)   Upon the decision to conduct a formal investigation, the Committee shall:

1) mail to the Charging and Responding Parties within three (3) business days of that decision notice of the commencement of a formal investigation. That notification shall be in writing and shall contain a complete explanation of all Charge(s), as well as the reasons for a formal investigation and shall cite the applicable codes and rules;

2) allow the Responding Party thirty (30) days to prepare and submit a confidential response to the Committee, which response shall address each charge specifically and shall be in writing; and

3) upon receipt of the response to the notification, have thirty (30) days to investigate the Charge(s). If an extension of time is deemed necessary, that extension shall not exceed ninety (90) days.

2.5(d)   Upon conclusion of the investigation, the Committee may:

1) dismiss the Charge upon the finding that it has no basis in fact;

2) dismiss the Charge upon the finding that, if proven, the Charge would not constitute Misconduct;

3) refer the matter for hearing by the Tribunal; or

4) in the case of criminal activity, refer the Charge(s) and all investigation results to the appropriate authority.

2.6   Procedure for a Misconduct Hearing Before a Tribunal

2.6(a)   Upon the decision by the Committee that a matter should be heard, all parties shall be notified and a hearing date shall be set. The hearing shall take place no more than thirty (30) days from the conclusion of the formal investigation.

2.6(b)   The Responding Party shall have the right to counsel. The parties and the Tribunal shall have the right to call any witnesses and introduce any documentation that they believe will lead to the fair and reasonable resolution of the matter.

2.6(c)   Upon completion of the hearing, the Tribunal shall deliberate and present a written decision to the parties in accordance with procedures as set forth by the Tribunal.

2.6(d)   Notice of the decision of the Tribunal shall be appropriately published.

2.7   Sanctions

2.7(a)   Upon a finding of the Tribunal that misconduct has occurred, any of the following sanctions, or others as may be deemed appropriate, may be imposed upon the Responding Party, either singularly or in combination:

1) letter of reprimand to the Responding Party; counseling;

2) attendance at an ethics course approved by the Tribunal; probation;

3) suspension of license/authority to practice; revocation of license/authority to practice;

4) imposition of a fine; assessment of costs; or

5) in the instance of criminal activity, referral to the appropriate authority.

2.7(b)   Upon the expiration of any period of probation, suspension, or revocation, the Responding Party may make application for reinstatement. With the application for reinstatement, the Responding Party must show proof of having complied with all aspects of the sanctions imposed by the Tribunal.

2.8   Appellate Procedures

2.8(a)   The parties shall have the right to appeal the decision of the Tribunal in accordance with the procedure as set forth by the Tribunal.

Definitions

Appellate Body means a body established to adjudicate an appeal to any decision made by a Tribunal or other decision-making body with respect to formally-heard Charges of Misconduct.

Charge of Misconduct means a written submission by any individual or entity to an ethics committee, paralegal association, bar association, law enforcement agency, judicial body, government agency, or other appropriate body or entity, that sets forth non-confidential information regarding any instance of alleged misconduct by an individual paralegal or paralegal entity.

Charging Party means any individual or entity who submits a Charge of Misconduct against an individual paralegal or paralegal entity.

Competency means the demonstration of: diligence, education, skill, and mental, emotional, and physical fitness reasonably necessary for the performance of paralegal services.

Confidential Information means information relating to a client, whatever its source, that is not public knowledge nor available to the public. ("Non-Confidential Information" would generally include the name of the client and the identity of the matter for which the paralegal provided services.)

Disciplinary Hearing means the confidential proceeding conducted by a committee or other designated body or entity concerning any instance of alleged misconduct by an individual paralegal or paralegal entity.

Disciplinary Committee means any committee that has been established by an entity such as a paralegal association, bar association, judicial body, or government agency to: (a) identify, define and investigate general ethical considerations and concerns with respect to paralegal practice; (b) administer and enforce the Model Code and Model Rules and; (c) discipline any individual paralegal or paralegal entity found to be in violation of same.

Disclose means communication of information reasonably sufficient to permit identification of the significance of the matter in question.

Ethical Wall means the screening method implemented in order to protect a client from a conflict of interest. An Ethical Wall generally includes, but is not limited to, the following elements: (1) prohibit the paralegal from having any connection with the matter; (2) ban discussions with or the transfer of documents to or from the paralegal; (3) restrict access to files; and (4) educate all members of the firm, corporation, or entity as to the separation of the paralegal (both organizationally and physically) from the pending matter. For more information regarding the Ethical Wall, see the NFPA publication entitled "The Ethical Wall—Its Application to Paralegals."

Ex parte means actions or communications conducted at the instance and for the benefit of one party only, and without notice to, or contestation by, any person adversely interested.

Investigation means the investigation of any charge(s) of misconduct filed against an individual paralegal or paralegal entity by a Committee.

Letter of Reprimand means a written notice of formal censure or severe reproof administered to an individual paralegal or paralegal entity for unethical or improper conduct.

Misconduct means the knowing or unknowing commission of an act that is in direct violation of those Canons and Ethical Considerations of any and all applicable codes and/or rules of conduct.

Paralegal is synonymous with "Legal Assistant" and is defined as a person qualified through education, training, or work experience to perform substantive legal work that requires knowledge of legal concepts and is customarily, but not exclusively performed by a lawyer. This person may be retained or employed by a lawyer, law office, governmental agency, or other entity or may be authorized by administrative, statutory, or court authority to perform this work.

Proper Authority means the local paralegal association, the local or state bar association, Committee(s) of the local paralegal or bar association(s), local prosecutor, administrative agency, or other tribunal empowered to investigate or act upon an instance of alleged misconduct.

Responding Party means an individual paralegal or paralegal entity against whom a Charge of Misconduct has been submitted.

Revocation means the recision of the license, certificate or other authority to practice of an individual paralegal or paralegal entity found in violation of those Canons and Ethical Considerations of any and all applicable codes and/or rules of conduct.

Suspension means the suspension of the license, certificate or other authority to practice of an individual paralegal or paralegal entity found in violation of those Canons and Ethical Considerations of any and all applicable codes and/or rules of conduct.

Tribunal means the body designated to adjudicate allegations of misconduct.

APPENDIX D

Workplace Scenario Data

Workplace Information

Supervising Attorney: Belinda Benson

Law Firm Employer Name and Address:
  Abrahams & Benson, PLLC
  4759 Main Street
  Pine City, [Home State] 33221

Law Firm Phone Number: 612-555-2468

D-1
Client Information Sheet

Client Name: Bradley Steven Harris

Home Address: 1753 Oakland Drive
Pine City, [Home State] 33221

Telephone: 612-555-1234

County: [Home County]

Business Address: [Home Address]

Social Security Number: 472-84-5544

D-2
Client Information Sheet

Client Name: Cynthia Ann Lund

Home Address: 4827 Willow Drive
Kenwood, [Home State] 33221

Telephone: 612-555-5678

County: [Home County]

Business Address: [Home Address]

Social Security Number: 421-94-9576

D-3
Corporate Information Sheet

Corporate Name: Cutting Edge Computer Repair, Inc.

State of Domicile: [Home State]

Corporate Purpose: Computer Repair Business

Corporate Duration: Perpetual

Authorized Shares: 10,000, No Par Value Common Stock

Preemptive Rights: No Preemptive Rights

Cumulative Voting: Not Allowed

Number of Initial Directors: Two

Names and Addresses of Initial Directors:
  Bradley Steven Harris,
  1753 Oakland Drive,
  Pine City, [Home State] 33221

  Cynthia Lund,
  4827 Willow Drive,
  Kenwood, [Home State] 33221

Registered Agent: Bradley Steven Harris

Registered Office Address:
  1753 Oakland Drive,
  Pine City, [Home State] 33221

Officers:
  Chief Executive Officer: Bradley Steven Harris
  Chief Financial Officer: Cynthia Lund
  Secretary: Cynthia Lund

Shareholders:
  Bradley Steven Harris 2,000 Shares
  Cynthia Ann Lund 2,000 Shares

Consideration for Shares: $10.00 per share

D-4
Corporate Information Sheet

Corporate Name: Kohler's Computers, Inc.

State of Domicile: [Home State]

Corporate Purpose: Computer Repair Business

Corporate Duration: Perpetual

Authorized Shares: 10,000, No Par Value Common Stock

Preemptive Rights: No Preemptive Rights

Cumulative Voting: Not Allowed

Number of Initial Directors: Two

Names and Addresses of Initial Directors:
    Sandra Kohler,
    455 Kent Street,
    Pine City, [Home State] 33221

    Scott Kohler,
    455 Kent Street,
    Pine City, [Home State] 33221

Registered Agent: Bradley Steven Harris

Registered Office Address:
    455 Kent Street,
    Pine City, [Home State] 33221

Officers:
    Chief Executive Officer: Sandra Kohler
    Chief Financial Officer: Scott Kohler
    Secretary: Sandra Kohler

Shareholders:
    Sandra Kohler 2,000 Shares
    Scott Kohler 2,000 Shares

Consideration for Shares: $10.00 per share

APPENDIX E

Uniform Partnership Act

UNIFORM PARTNERSHIP ACT

drafted by the

NATIONAL CONFERENCE OF COMMISSIONERS ON UNIFORM STATE LAWS

and by it

Approved and Recommended for Enactment in All the States

at its

Conference at Washington, D.C. October 14, 1914

And Approved by the American Bar Association August 18, 1915

(Edition of 1934)

Prefatory Notes

I
The Commissioners on Uniform State Laws

The National Conference of Commissioners on Uniform State Laws was organized in 1892. It is composed of Commissioners deriving their authority from appointment by the Governors of their respective States. The District of Columbia, Alaska, Puerto Rico, Hawaii, and the Philippine Islands also appoint Commissioners. With these added to the 48 States there are 53 jurisdictions represented.

The Commissioners are members of the legal profession and all serve without compensation, but the legislatures of many of the States provide for defraying traveling expenses of their Commissioners in attending meetings.

The Commissioners meet annually in a conference of six days at which most of the States, the District of Columbia, and some of the other jurisdictions mentioned above are represented. At these Conferences the Acts drafted by Committees, assisted in many cases by experts, and under the instructions from the Conference, are carefully considered and discussed section by section by the entire body. Acts are not approved until they have been considered in this manner by at least two, and generally more, annual Conferences. When finally approved and recommended to the several States for adoption, the Acts are also reported to the American Bar Association for its approval before being presented to the States for enactment.

There are now about 53 of the Uniform Laws approved and recommended by the Conference of Commissioners.

The Uniform Negotiable Instruments Law has been adopted in 48 States and the other 5 jurisdictions, making 53 in all. The Bills of Lading Act has been adopted in 29 jurisdictions, the Declaratory Judgments Act in 18, the Fiduciaries Act in 16, the Fraudulent Conveyance Act in 16, the Limited Partnership Act in 20, the Partnership Act in 19, the Proof of Statutes Act in 23, the Reciprocal Transfer Tax Act in 16, the Sales Act in 33, the Stock Transfer Act in 23, the Act Regulating Traffic on Highways in 18, the Veterans Guardianship Act in 32, and the Warehouse Receipts Act in 48.

Many of the States have adopted 20 or more of the Uniform Acts.

II
The Uniform Partnership Act

The Uniform Partnership Act is the result of ten years' consideration by the Conference of Commissioners on Uniform State Laws. The Committee which prepared the Act was assisted at first by Dean James Barr Ames of the Law School of Harvard University as draftsman, and after his death by Dean

William Draper Lewis of the Law School of the University of Pennsylvania.

In the fall of 1910 the Committee invited to a Conference, held in Philadelphia, all the teachers of, and writers on, partnerships, besides several other lawyers known to have made a special study of the subject. There was a large attendance. For two days the members of the Committee and their guests discussed the theory on which the proposed act should be drawn. At the conclusion of the discussion the experts recommended that the act be drawn on the aggregate or common law theory, with the modification that the partners be treated as owners of partnership property holding by a special tenancy which should be called tenancy in partnership. (See Section 2 of the Act recommended.) Accordingly, at the meeting of the Conference in the summer of 1911, the Committee reported that, after hearing the discussion of experts, it had voted that Dean Lewis be requested to prepare a draft of a partnership act on the so-called common law theory.

At the National Conferences of the Commissioners in 1912 and 1913 several sessions were devoted to the consideration of the Act, and at the Conference of 1914 the final draft prepared by Dean Lewis was approved and recommended for enactment by the States. The approval of the American Bar Association was given at its meeting on August 18, 1915. The nineteen States which have adopted the Act up to the present time (1934) are the following:

Alaska, California, Colorado, Idaho, Illinois, Maryland, Massachusetts, Michigan, Minnesota, Nevada, New Jersey, New York, Pennsylvania, South Dakota, Tennessee, Utah, Virginia, Wisconsin, Wyoming.

As to the importance of this Act, the following paragraphs are quoted from the Explanatory Note preceding the pamphlet copy issued in 1915. This note was written by Mr. Walter George Smith of Philadelphia, the Chairman of the Committee which prepared the Act.

Uniformity of the law of partnerships is constantly becoming more important as the number of firms increases which not only carry on business in more than one state, but have among the members residents of different states.

It is, however, proper here to emphasize the fact that there are other reasons, in addition to the advantages which will result from uniformity, for the adoption of the act now issued by the Commissioners. There is probably no other subject connected with our business law in which a greater number of instances can be found where, in matters of almost daily occurrence, the law is uncertain. This uncertainty is due, not only to conflict between the decisions of different states, but more to the general lack of consistency in legal theory. In several of the sections, but especially in those which relate to the rights of the partner and his separate creditors in partnership property, and to the rights of firm creditors where the personnel of the partnership has been changed without liquidation of partnership affairs, there exists an almost hopeless confusion of theory and practice, making the actual administration of the law difficult and often inequitable.

Another difficulty of the present partnership law is the scarcity of authority on matters of considerable importance in the daily conduct and in the winding up of partnership affairs. In any one state it is often impossible to find an authority on a matter of comparatively frequent occurrence, while not infrequently an exhaustive research of the reports of the decisions of all the states and the federal courts fails to reveal a single authority throwing light on the question. The existence of a statute stating in detail the rights of the partners inter se during the carrying on of the partnership business, and on the winding up of partnership affairs, will be a real practical advantage of moment to the business world.

John Hinkley, *Chairman,*
Section on Uniform Commercial Acts.
August 1, 1934.

UNIFORM PARTNERSHIP ACT CONTENTS

Part I. Preliminary Provisions

§ 1   Name of Act.
§ 2   Definition of Terms.
§ 3   Interpretation of Knowledge and Notice.
§ 4   Rules of Construction.

§ 5   Rules for Cases Not Provided for in This Act.

Part II. Nature of Partnership

§ 6   Partnership Defined.

§ 7   Rules for Determining the Existence of a Partnership.

§ 8   Partnership Property.

Part III. Relations of Partners to Persons Dealing with the Partnership

§ 9   Partner Agent of Partnership as to Partnership Business.

§ 10   Conveyance of Real Property of the Partnership.

§ 11   Partnership Bound by Admission of Partner.

§ 12   Partnership Charged with Knowledge of or Notice to Partner.

§ 13   Partnership Bound by Partner's Wrongful Act.

§ 14   Partnership Bound by Partner's Breach of Trust.

§ 15   Nature of Partner's Liability.

§ 16   Partner by Estoppel.

§ 17   Liability of Incoming Partner.

Part IV. Relations of Partners to One Another

§ 18   Rules Determining Rights and Duties of Partners.

§ 19   Partnership Books.

§ 20   Duty of Partners to Render Information.

§ 21   Partner Accountable as a Fiduciary.

§ 22   Right to an Account.

§ 23   Continuation of Partnership Beyond Fixed Term.

Part V. Property Rights of a Partner

§ 24   Extent of Property Rights of a Partner.

§ 25   Nature of a Partner's Right in Specific Partnership Property.

§ 26   Nature of Partner's Interest in the Partnership.

§ 27   Assignment of Partner's Interest.

§ 28   Partner's Interest Subject to Charging Order.

Part VI. Dissolution and Winding Up

§ 29   Dissolution Defined.

§ 30   Partnership Not Terminated by Dissolution.

§ 31   Causes of Dissolution.

§ 32   Dissolution by Decree of Court.

§ 33   General Effect of Dissolution on Authority of Partner.

§ 34   Right of Partner to Contribution from Co-partners After Dissolution.

§ 35   Power of Partner to Bind Partnership to Third Persons After Dissolution.

§ 36   Effect of Dissolution on Partner's Existing Liability.

§ 37   Right to Wind Up.

§ 38   Rights of Partners to Application of Partnership Property.

§ 39   Rights Where Partnership is Dissolved for Fraud or Misrepresentation.

§ 40   Rules for Distribution.

§ 41   Liability of Persons Continuing the Business in Certain Cases.

§ 42   Rights of Retiring or Estate of Deceased Partner When the Business is Continued.

§ 43   Accrual of Actions.

Part VII. Miscellaneous Provisions

§ 44   When Act Takes Effect.

§ 45   Legislation Repealed.

AN ACT TO MAKE UNIFORM THE LAW OF PARTNERSHIPS

(Be it enacted...)

Part I
Preliminary Provisions

1. *Name of Act.* This act may be cited as Uniform Partnership Act.

2. *Definition of Terms.* In this act, "Court" includes every court and judge having jurisdiction in the case.

"Business" includes every trade, occupation, or profession.

"Person" includes individuals, partnerships, corporations, and other associations.

"Bankrupt" includes bankrupt under the Federal Bankruptcy Act or insolvent under any state insolvent act.

"Conveyance" includes every assignment, lease, mortgage, or encumbrance.

"Real property" includes land and any interest or estate in land.

3. *Interpretation of Knowledge and Notice.* (1) A person has "knowledge" of a fact within the meaning of this act not only when he has actual knowledge thereof, but also when he has knowledge of such other facts as in the circumstances shows bad faith.

(2) A person has "notice" of a fact within the meaning of this act when the person who claims the benefit of the notice:

(a) States the fact to such person, or

(b) Delivers through the mail, or by other means of communication, a written statement of the fact to such person or to a proper person at his place of business or residence.

4. *Rules of Construction.* (1) The rule that statutes in derogation of the common law are to be strictly construed shall have no application to this act.

(2) The law of estoppel shall apply under this act.

(3) The law of agency shall apply under this act.

(4) This act shall be so interpreted and construed as to effect its general purpose to make uniform the law of those states which enact it.

(5) This act shall not be construed so as to impair the obligations of any contract existing when the act goes into effect, nor to affect any action or proceedings begun or right accrued before this act takes effect.

5. *Rules for Cases Not Provided for in This Act.* In any case not provided for in this act the rules of law and equity, including the law merchant, shall govern.

Part II
Nature of Partnership

6. *Partnership Defined.* (1) A partnership is an association of two or more persons to carry on as co-owners a business for profit.

(2) But any association formed under any other statute of this state, or any statute adopted by authority, other than the authority of this state, s not a partnership under this act, unless such association would have been a partnership in this state prior to the adoption of this act; but this act shall apply to limited partnerships except in so far as the statutes relating to such partnerships are inconsistent herewith.

7. *Rules for Determining the Existence of a Partnership.* In determining whether a partnership exists, these rules shall apply:

(1) Except as provided by section 16 persons who are not partners as to each other are not partners as to third persons.

(2) Joint tenancy, tenancy in common, tenancy by the entireties, joint property, common property, or part ownership does not of itself establish a partnership, whether such co-owners do or do not share any profits made by the use of the property.

(3) The sharing of gross returns does not of itself establish a partnership, whether or not the persons sharing them have a joint or common right or interest in any property from which the returns are derived.

(4) The receipt by a person of a share of the profits of a business is *prima facie* evidence that he is a partner in the business, but no such inference shall be drawn if such profits were received in payment:

(a) As a debt by installments or otherwise,

(b) As wages of an employee or rent to a landlord,

(c) As an annuity to a widow or representative of a deceased partner,

(d) As interest on a loan, though the amount of payment vary with the profits of the business,

(e) As the consideration for the sale of a good-will of a business or other property by installments or otherwise.

8. *Partnership Property.* (1) All property originally brought into the partnership stock or subsequently acquired by purchase or otherwise, on account of the partnership, is partnership property.

(2) Unless the contrary intention appears, property acquired with partnership funds is partnership property.

(3) Any estate in real property may be acquired in the partnership name. Title so acquired can be conveyed only in the partnership name.

(4) A conveyance to a partnership in the partnership name, though without words of inheritance, passes the entire estate of the grantor unless a contrary intent appears.

Part III
Relations of Partners to Persons Dealing with the Partnership

9. *Partner Agent of Partnership as to Partnership Business.* (1) Every partner is an agent of the partnership for the purpose of its business, and the act of every partner, including the execution in the partnership name of any instrument, for apparently carrying on in the usual way the business of the partnership of which he is a member binds the partnership, unless the partner so acting has in fact no authority to act for the partnership in the particular matter, and the person with whom he is dealing has knowledge of the fact that he has no such authority.

(2) An act of a partner which is not apparently for the carrying on of the business of the partnership in the usual way does not bind the partnership unless authorized by the other partners.

(3) Unless authorized by the other partners or unless they have abandoned the business, one or more but less than all the partners have no authority to:

(a) Assign the partnership property in trust for creditors or on the assignee's promise to pay the debts of the partnership,

(b) Dispose of the good-will of the business,

(c) Do any other act which would make it impossible to carry on the ordinary business of a partnership,

(d) Confess a judgment,

(e) Submit a partnership claim or liability to arbitration or reference.

(4) No act of a partner in contravention of a restriction on authority shall bind the partnership to persons having knowledge of the restriction.

10. *Conveyance of Real Property of the Partnership.*

(1) Where title to real property is in the partnership name, any partner may convey title to such property by a conveyance executed in the partnership name; but the partnership may recover such property unless the partner's act binds the partnership under the provisions of paragraph (1) of section 9, or unless such property has been conveyed by the grantee or a person claiming through such grantee to a holder for value without knowledge that the partner, in making the conveyance, has exceeded his authority.

(2) Where title to real property is in the name of the partnership, a conveyance executed by a partner, in his own name, passes the equitable interest of the partnership, provided the act is one within the authority of the partner under the provisions of paragraph (1) of section 9.

(3) Where title to real property is in the name of one or more but not all the partners, and the record does not disclose the right of the partnership, the partners in whose name the title stands may convey title to such property, but the partnership may recover such property if the partners' act does not bind the partnership under the provisions of paragraph (1) of section 9, unless the purchaser or his assignee, is a holder for value, without knowledge.

(4) Where the title to real property is in the name of one or more or all the partners, or in a third person in trust for the partnership, a conveyance executed by a partner in the partnership name, or in his own name, passes the equitable interest of the partnership, provided the act is one within the authority of the partner under the provisions of paragraph (1) of section 9.

(5) Where the title to real property is in the names of all the partners a conveyance executed by all the partners passes all their rights in such property.

11. *Partnership Bound by Admission of Partner.* An admission or representation made by any partner concerning partnership affairs within the scope of his authority as conferred by this act is evidence against the partnership.

12. *Partnership Charged with Knowledge of or Notice to Partner.* Notice to any partner of any matter relating to partnership affairs, and the knowledge of the partner acting in the particular matter, acquired while a partner or then present to his mind, and the knowledge of any other partner who reasonably could and should have communicated it to the acting partner, operate as notice to or knowledge of the partnership, except in the case of a fraud on the partnership committed by or with the consent of that partner.

13. *Partnership Bound by Partner's Wrongful Act.* Where, by any wrongful act or omission of any partner acting in the ordinary course of the business of the partnership or with the authority of his co-partners, loss or injury is caused to any person, not being a partner in the partnership, or any penalty is incurred, the partnership is liable therefore to the same extent as the partner so acting or omitting to act.

14. *Partnership Bound by Partner's Breach of Trust.* The partnership is bound to make good the loss:

(a) Where one partner acting within the scope of his apparent authority receives money or property of a third person and misapplies it; and

(b) Where the partnership in the course of its business receives money or property of a third person and the money or property so received is misapplied by any partner while it is in the custody of the partnership.

15. *Nature of Partner's Liability.* All partners are liable

(a) Jointly and severally for everything chargeable to the partnership under sections 13 and 14.

(b) Jointly for all other debts and obligations of the partnership; but any partner may enter into a separate obligation to perform a partnership contract.

16. *Partner by Estoppel.* (1) When a person, by words spoken or written or by conduct, represents himself, or consents to another representing him to any one, as a partner in an existing partnership or with one or more persons not actual partners, he is liable to any such person to whom such representation has been made, who has, on the faith of such representation, given credit to the actual or apparent partnership, and if he has made such representation or consented to its being made in a public manner he is liable to such person, whether the representation has or has not been made or communicated to such person so giving credit by or with the knowledge of the apparent partner making the representation or consenting to its being made.

(a) When a partnership liability results, he is liable as though he were an actual member of the partnership.

(b) When no partnership liability results, he is liable jointly with the other persons, if any, so consenting to the contract or representation as to incur liability, otherwise separately.

(2) When a person has been thus represented to be a partner in an existing partnership, or with one or more persons not actual partners, he is an agent of the persons consenting to such representation to bind them to the same extent and in the same manner as though he were a partner in fact, with respect to persons who rely upon the representation. Where all the members of the existing partnership consent to the representation, a partnership act or obligation results; but in all other cases it is the joint act or obligation of the person acting and the persons consenting to the representation.

17. *Liability of Incoming Partner.* A person admitted as a partner into an existing partnership is liable for all the obligations of the partnership arising before his admission as though he had been a partner when such obligations were incurred, except that this liability shall be satisfied only out of partnership property.

Part IV
Relations of Partners to One Another

18. *Rules Determining Rights and Duties of Partners.* The rights and duties of the partners in relation to the partnership shall be determined, subject to any agreement between them, by the following rules:

(a) Each partner shall be repaid his contributions, whether by way of capital or advances to the partnership property and share equally in the profits and surplus remaining after all liabilities, including those to partners, are satisfied; and must contribute toward the losses, whether of capital or otherwise, sustained by the partnership according to his share in the profits.

(b) The partnership must indemnify every partner in respect of payments made and personal liabilities reasonably incurred by him in the ordinary and proper conduct of its business, or for the preservation of its business or property.

(c) A partner, who in aid of the partnership makes any payment or advance beyond the amount of capital which he agreed to contribute, shall be paid interest from the date of the payment or advance.

(d) A partner shall receive interest on the capital contributed by him only from the date when repayment should be made.

(e) All partners have equal rights in the management and conduct of the partnership business.

(f) No partner is entitled to remuneration for acting in the partnership business, except that a surviving partner is entitled to reasonable compensation for his services in winding up the partnership affairs.

(g) No person can become a member of a partnership without the consent of all the partners.

(h) Any difference arising as to ordinary matters connected with the partnership business may be decided by a majority of the partners; but no act in contravention of any agreement between the partners may be done rightfully without the consent of all the partners.

19. *Partnership Books.* The partnership books shall be kept, subject to any agreement between the partners, at the principal place of business of the partnership, and every partner shall at all times have access to and may inspect and copy any of them.

20. *Duty of Partners to Render Information.* Partners shall render on demand true and full information of all things affecting the partnership to any partner or the legal representative of any deceased partner or partner under legal disability.

21. *Partner Accountable as a Fiduciary.* (1) Every partner must account to the partnership for any benefit, and hold as trustee for it any profits derived by him without the consent of the other partners from any transaction connected with the formation, conduct, or liquidation of the partnership or from any use by him of its property.

(2) This section applies also to the representatives of a deceased partner engaged in the liquidation of the affairs of the partnership as the personal representatives of the last surviving partner.

22. *Right to an Account.* Any partner shall have the right to a formal account as to partnership affairs:

(a) If he is wrongfully excluded from the partnership business or possession of its property by his co-partners,

(b) If the right exists under the terms of any agreement,

(c) As provided by section 21,

(d) Whenever other circumstances render it just and reasonable.

23. *Continuation of Partnership Beyond Fixed Term.* (1) When a partnership for a fixed term or particular undertaking is continued after the termination of such term or particular undertaking without any express agreement, the rights and duties of the partners remain the same as they were at such termination, so far as is consistent with a partnership at will.

(2) A continuation of the business by the partners or such of them as habitually acted therein during the term, without any settlement or liquidation of the partnership affairs, is *prima facie* evidence of a continuation of the partnership.

Part V
Property Rights of a Partner

24. *Extent of Property Rights of a Partner.* The property rights of a partner are (1) his rights in specific partnership property, (2) his interest in the partnership, and (3) his right to participate in the management.

25. *Nature of a Partner's Right in Specific Partnership Property.* (1) A partner is co-owner with his partners of specific partnership property holding as a tenant in partnership.

(2) The incidents of this tenancy are such that:

(a) A partner, subject to the provisions of this act and to any agreement between the partners, has an equal right with his partners to possess specific partnership property for partnership purposes; but he has no right to possess such property for any other purpose without the consent of his partners.

(b) A partner's right in specific partnership property is not assignable except in connection with the assignment of rights of all the partners in the same property.

(c) A partner's right in specific partnership property is not subject to attachment or execution, except on a claim against the partnership. When partnership property is attached for a partnership debt the partners, or any of them, or the representatives of a deceased partner, cannot claim any right under the homestead or exemption laws.

(d) On the death of a partner his right in specific partnership property vests in the surviving partner or partners, except where the deceased was the last surviving partner, when his right in such property vests in his legal representative. Such surviving partner or partners, or the legal representative of the last surviving partner, has no right to possess the partnership property for any but a partnership purpose.

(e) A partner's right in specific partnership property is not subject to dower, curtesy, or allowances to widows, heirs, or next of kin.

26. *Nature of Partner's Interest in the Partnership.* A partner's interest in the partnership is his share of the profits and surplus, and the same is personal property.

27. *Assignment of Partner's Interest.* (1) A conveyance by a partner of his interest in the partnership does not of itself dissolve the partnership, nor, as against the other partners in the absence of agreement, entitle the assignee, during the continuance of the partnership, to interfere in the management or administration of the partnership business or affairs, or to require any information or account of partnership transactions, or to inspect the partnership books; but it merely entitles the assignee to receive in accordance with his contract the profits to which the assigning partner would otherwise be entitled.

(2) In case of a dissolution of the partnership, the assignee is entitled to receive his assignor's interest and may require an account from the date only of the last account agreed to by all the partners.

28. *Partner's Interest Subject to Charging Order.* (1) On due application to a competent court by any judgment creditor of a partner, the court which entered the judgment, order, or decree, or any other court, may charge the interest of the debtor partner with payment of the unsatisfied amount of such judgment debt with interest thereon; and may then or later appoint a receiver of his share of the profits, and of any other money due or to fall due to him in respect of the partnership, and make all other orders, directions, accounts and inquiries which the debtor partner might have made, or which the circumstances of the case may require.

(2) The interest charged may be redeemed at any time before foreclosure, or in case of a sale being directed by the court may be purchased without thereby causing a dissolution:

(a) With separate property, by any one or more of the partners, or

(b) With partnership property, by any one or more of the partners with the consent of all the partners whose interests are not so charged or sold.

(3) Nothing in this act shall be held to deprive a partner of his right, if any, under the exemption laws, as regards his interest in the partnership.

Part VI
Dissolution and Winding Up

29. *Dissolution Defined.* The dissolution of a partnership is the change in the relation of the partners caused by any partner ceasing to be associated in the carrying on as distinguished from the winding up of the business.

30. *Partnership Not Terminated by Dissolution.* On dissolution the partnership is not terminated, but continues until the winding up of partnership affairs is completed.

31. *Causes of Dissolution.* Dissolution is caused:

(1) Without violation of the agreement between the partners,

(a) By the termination of the definite term or particular undertaking specified in the agreement,

(b) By the express will of any partner when no definite term or particular undertaking is specified,

(c) By the express will of all the partners who have not assigned their interests or suffered them to be charged for their separate debts, either before or after the termination of any specified term or particular undertaking,

(d) By the expulsion of any partner from the business *bona fide* in accordance with such a power conferred by the agreement between the partners;

(2) In contravention of the agreement between the partners, where the circumstances do not permit a dissolution under any other provision of this section, by the express will of any partner at any time;

(3) By any event which makes it unlawful for the business of the partnership to be carried on or for the members to carry it on in partnership;

(4) By the death of any partner;

(5) By the bankruptcy of any partner or the partnership;

(6) By decree of court under section 32.

32. *Dissolution by Decree of Court.* (1) On application by or for a partner the court shall decree a dissolution whenever:

(a) A partner has been declared a lunatic in any judicial proceeding or is shown to be of unsound mind,

(b) A partner becomes in any other way incapable of performing his part of the partnership contract,

(c) A partner has been guilty of such conduct as tends to affect prejudicially the carrying on of the business,

(d) A partner wilfully or persistently commits a breach of the partnership agreement, or otherwise so conducts himself in matters relating to the partnership business that it is not reasonably practicable to carry on the business in partnership with him,

(e) The business of the partnership can only be carried on at a loss,

(f) Other circumstances render a dissolution equitable.

(2) On the application of the purchaser of a partner's interest under sections 27 and 28:

(a) After the termination of the specified term or particular undertaking,

(b) At any time if the partnership was a partnership at will when the interest was assigned or when the charging order was issued.

33. *General Effect of Dissolution on Authority of Partner.* Except so far as may be necessary to wind up partnership affairs or to complete transactions begun but not then finished, dissolution terminates all authority of any partner to act for the partnership,

(1) With respect to the partners,

(a) When the dissolution is not by the act, bankruptcy or death of a partner; or

(b) When the dissolution is by such act, bankruptcy or death of a partner, in cases where section 34 so requires.

(2) With respect to persons not partners, as declared in section 35.

34. *Right of Partner to Contribution From Co-partners After Dissolution.* Where the dissolution is caused by the act, death or bankruptcy of a partner, each partner is liable to his co-partners for his share of any liability created by any partner acting for the partnership as if the partnership had not been dissolved unless

(a) The dissolution being by act of any partner, the partner acting for the partnership had knowledge of the dissolution, or

(b) The dissolution being by the death or bankruptcy of a partner, the partner acting for the partnership had knowledge or notice of the death or bankruptcy.

35. *Power of Partner to Bind Partnership to Third Persons After Dissolution.* (1) After dissolution a partner can bind the partnership except as provided in Paragraph (3).

(a) By any act appropriate for winding up partnership affairs or completing transactions unfinished at dissolution;

(b) By any transaction which would bind the partnership if dissolution had not taken place, provided the other party to the transaction

(I) Had extended credit to the partnership prior to dissolution and had no knowledge or notice of the dissolution; or

(II) Though he had not so extended credit, had nevertheless known of the partnership prior to dissolution, and, having no knowledge or notice of dissolution, the fact of dissolution had not been advertised in a newspaper of general circulation in the place (or in each place if more than one) at which the partnership business was regularly carried on.

(2) The liability of a partner under Paragraph (1b) shall be satisfied out of partnership assets alone when such partner had been prior to dissolution

(a) Unknown as a partner to the person with whom the contract is made; and

(b) So far unknown and inactive in partnership affairs that the business reputation of the partnership could not be said to have been in any degree due to his connection with it.

(3) The partnership is in no case bound by any act of a partner after dissolution

(a) Where the partnership is dissolved because it is unlawful to carry on the business, unless the act is appropriate for winding up partnership affairs; or

(b) Where the partner has become bankrupt; or

(c) Where the partner has no authority to wind up partnership affairs; except by a transaction with one who

(I) Had an extended credit to the partnership prior to dissolution and had no knowledge or notice of his want of authority; or

(II) Had not extended credit to the partnership prior to dissolution, and, having no knowledge or notice of his want of authority, the fact of his want of authority has not been advertised in the manner provided for advertising the fact of dissolution in Paragraph (1bII).

(4) Nothing in this section shall affect the liability under Section 16 of any person who after dissolution represents himself or consents to another representing him as a partner in a partnership engaged in carrying on business.

36. *Effect of Dissolution on Partner's Existing Liability.* (1) The dissolution of the partnership does not of itself discharge the existing liability of any partner.

(2) A partner is discharged from any existing liability upon dissolution of the partnership by an agreement to that effect between himself, the partnership creditor and the person or partnership continuing the business; and such agreement may be inferred from the course of dealing between the creditor having knowledge of the dissolution and the person or partnership continuing the business.

(3) Where a person agrees to assume the existing obligations of a dissolved partnership, the partners whose obligations have been assumed shall be discharged from any liability to any creditor of the partnership who, knowing of the agreement, consents to a material alteration in the nature or time of payment of such obligations.

(4) The individual property of a deceased partner shall be liable for all obligations of the partnership incurred while he was a partner but subject to the prior payment of his separate debts.

37. *Right to Wind Up.* Unless otherwise agreed the partners who have not wrongfully dissolved the partnership or the legal representative of the last surviving partner, not bankrupt, has the right to wind up the partnership affairs; provided, however, that any partner, his legal representative or his assignee, upon cause shown, may obtain winding up by the court.

38. *Rights of Partners to Application of Partnership Property.* (1) When dissolution is caused in any way, except in contravention of the partnership agreement, each partner, as against his co-partners and all persons claiming through them in respect of their interests in the partnership, unless otherwise agreed, may have the partnership property applied to discharge its liabilities, and the surplus applied to pay in cash the net amount owing to the respective partners. But if dissolution is caused by expulsion of a partner, *bona fide* under the partnership agreement and if the expelled partner is discharged from all partnership liabilities, either by payment or agreement under section 36 (2), he shall receive in cash only the net amount due him from the partnership.

(2) When dissolution is caused in contravention of the partnership agreement the rights of the partners shall be as follows:

(a) Each partner who has not caused dissolution wrongfully shall have,

(I) All the rights specified in paragraph (1) of this section, and

(II) The right, as against each partner who has caused the dissolution wrongfully, to damages for breach of the agreement.

(b) The partners who have not caused the dissolution wrongfully, if they all desire to continue the business in the same name, either by themselves or jointly with others, may do so, during the agreed term for the partnership and for that purpose may possess the partnership property, provided they secure the payment by bond approved by the court, or pay to any partner who has caused the dissolution wrongfully, the value of his interest in the partnership at the dissolution, less any damages recoverable under clause (2aII) of this section, and in like manner indemnify him against all present or future partnership liabilities.

(c) A partner who has caused the dissolution wrongfully shall have:

(I) If the business is not continued under the provisions of paragraph (2b) all the rights of a partner under paragraph (1), subject to clause (2aII), of this section,

(II) If the business is continued under paragraph (2b) of this section the right as against this co-partners and all claiming through them in respect of their interests in the partnership, to have the value of his interest in the partnership, less any damages caused to his co-partners by the dissolution, ascertained and paid to him in cash, or the payment secured by bond approved by the court, and to be released from all existing liabilities of the partnership; but in ascertaining the value of the partner's interest the value of the good-will of the business shall not be considered.

39. *Rights Where Partnership is Dissolved for Fraud or Misrepresentation.* Where a partnership contract is rescinded on the ground of the fraud or misrepresentation of one of the parties thereto, the party entitled to rescind is, without prejudice to any other right, entitled,

(a) To a lien on, or a right of retention of, the surplus of the partnership property after satisfying the partnership liabilities to third persons for any sum of money paid by him for the purchase of an interest in the partnership and for any capital or advances contributed by him; and

(b) To stand, after all liabilities to third persons have been satisfied, in the place of the creditors of the partnership for any payments made by him in respect of the partnership liabilities; and

(c) To be indemnified by the person guilty of the fraud or making the representation against all debts and liabilities of the partnership.

40. *Rules for Distribution.* In settling accounts between the partners after dissolution, the following rules shall be observed, subject to any agreement to the contrary:

(a) The assets of the partnership are;

(I) The partnership property,

(II) The contributions of the partners necessary for the payment of all the liabilities specified in clause (b) of this paragraph.

(b) The liabilities of the partnership shall rank in order of payment, as follows:

(I) Those owing to creditors other than partners,

(II) Those owing to partners other than for capital and profits,

(III) Those owing to partners in respect of capital,

(IV) Those owing to partners in respect of profits.

(c) The assets shall be applied in the order of their declaration in clause (a) of this paragraph to the satisfaction of the liabilities.

(d) The partners shall contribute, as provided by section 18 (a) the amount necessary to satisfy the liabilities; but if any, but not all, of the partners are insolvent, or, not being subject to process, refuse to contribute, the other partners shall contribute their share of the liabilities, and, in the relative proportions in which they share the profits, the additional amount necessary to pay the liabilities.

(e) An assignee for the benefit of creditors or any person appointed by the court shall have the right to enforce the contributions specified in clause (d) of this paragraph.

(f) Any partner or his legal representative shall have the right to enforce the contributions specified in clause (d) of this paragraph, to the extent of the amount which he has paid in excess of his share of the liability.

(g) The individual property of a deceased partner shall be liable for the contributions specified in clause (d) of this paragraph.

(h) When partnership property and the individual properties of the partners are in possession of a court for distribution, partnership creditors shall have priority on partnership property and separate creditors on individual property, saving the rights of lien or secured creditors as heretofore.

(i) Where a partner has become bankrupt or his estate is insolvent the claims against his separate property shall rank in the following order:

(I) Those owing to separate creditors,

(II) Those owing to partnership creditors,

(III) Those owing to partners by way of contribution.

41. *Liability of Persons Continuing the Business in Certain Cases.* (1) When any new partner is admitted into an existing partnership, or when any partner retires and assigns (or the representative of the deceased partner assigns) his rights in partnership property to two or more of the partners, or to one or more of the partners and one or more third persons, if the business is continued without liquidation of the partnership affairs, creditors of the first or dissolved partnership are also creditors of the partnership so continuing the business.

(2) When all but one partner retire and assign (or the representative of a deceased partner assigns) their rights in partnership property to the remaining partner, who continues the business without liquidation of partnership affairs, either alone or with others, creditors of the dissolved partnership are also creditors of the person or partnership continuing the business.

(3) When any partner retires or dies and the business of the dissolved partnership is continued as set forth in paragraphs (1) and (2) of this section, with the consent of the retired partners or the representative of the deceased partner, but without any assignment of his right in partnership property, rights of creditors of the dissolved partnership and of the creditors of the person or partnership continuing the business shall be as if such assignment had been made.

(4) When all the partners or their representative assign their rights in partnership property to one or more third persons who promise to pay the debts and who continue the business of the dissolved partnership, creditors of the dissolved partnership are also creditors of the person or partnership continuing the business.

(5) When any partner wrongfully causes a dissolution and the remaining partners continue the business under the provisions of section 38 (2b), either alone or with others, and without liquidation of the partnership affairs, creditors of the dissolved partnership are also creditors of the person or partnership continuing the business.

(6) When a partner is expelled and the remaining partners continue the business either alone or with others, without liquidation of the partnership affairs, creditors of the dissolved partnership are also creditors of the person or partnership continuing the business.

(7) The liability of a third person becoming a partner in the partnership continuing the business, under this section, to the creditors of the dissolved partnership shall be satisfied out of partnership property only.

(8) When the business of a partnership after dissolution is continued under any conditions set forth in this section the creditors of the dissolved partnership, as against the separate creditors of the retiring or deceased partner or the representative of the deceased partner, have a prior right to any claim of the retired partner or the representative of the deceased partner against the person or partnership continuing the business, on account of the retired or deceased partner's interest in the dissolved partnership or on account of any consideration promised for such interest or for his right in partnership property.

(9) Nothing in this section shall be held to modify any right of creditors to set aside any assignment on the ground of fraud.

(10) The use by the person or partnership continuing the business of the partnership name, or the name of a deceased partner as part thereof, shall not of itself make the individual property of the deceased partner liable for any debts contracted by such person or partnership.

42. *Rights of Retiring or Estate of Deceased Partner When the Business is Continued.* When any partner retires or dies, and the business is continued under any of the conditions set forth in section 41 (1, 2, 3, 5, 6), or section 38 (2b), without any settlement of accounts as between him or his estate and the person or partnership continuing the business, unless otherwise agreed, he or his legal representative as against such persons or partnership may have the value of his interest at the date of dissolution ascertained, and shall receive as an ordinary creditor an amount equal to the value of his interest in the dissolved partnership with interest, or, at his option or at the option of his legal representative, in lieu of interest, the profits attributable to the use of his right in the property of the dissolved partnership; provided that the creditors of the dissolved partnership as against the separate creditors, or the representative of the retired or sdeceased partner, shall have priority on any claim arising under this section, as provided by section 41 (8) of this act.

43. *Accrual of Actions.* The right to an account of his interest shall accrue to any partner, or his legal representative, as against the winding up partners or the surviving partners or the person or partnership continuing the business, at the date of dissolution, in the absence of any agreement to the contrary.

Part VII
Miscellaneous Provisions

44. *When Act Takes Effect.* This act shall take effect on the _____ day of _____ one thousand nine hundred and _____.

45. *Legislation Repealed.* All acts or parts of acts inconsistent with this act are hereby repealed.

APPENDIX F

Uniform Partnership Act (1997)

Reprinted with permission of the National Conference of Commissioners on Uniform State Laws
211 East Ontario Street, Suite 1300
Chicago, IL 60611
www.nccusl.org.

[ARTICLE] 1
GENERAL PROVISIONS

SECTION 101. *Definitions.* In this [Act]:

(1) "Business" includes every trade, occupation, and profession.

(2) "Debtor in bankruptcy" means a person who is the subject of:

(i) an order for relief under Title 11 of the United States Code or a comparable order under a successor statute of general application; or

(ii) a comparable order under federal, state, or foreign law governing insolvency.

(3) "Distribution" means a transfer of money or other property from a partnership to a partner in the partner's capacity as a partner or to the partner's transferee.

(4) "Foreign limited liability partnership" means a partnership that:

(i) is formed under laws other than the laws of this State; and

(ii) has the status of a limited liability partnership under those laws.

(5) "Limited liability partnership" means a partnership that has filed a statement of qualification under Section 1001 and does not have a similar statement in effect in any other jurisdiction.

(6) "Partnership" means an association of two or more persons to carry on as co-owners a business for profit formed under Section 202, predecessor law, or comparable law of another jurisdiction.

(7) "Partnership agreement" means the agreement, whether written, oral, or implied, among the partners concerning the partnership, including amendments to the partnership agreement.

(8) "Partnership at will" means a partnership in which the partners have not agreed to remain partners until the expiration of a definite term or the completion of a particular undertaking.

(9) "Partnership interest" or "partner's interest in the partnership" means all of a partner's interests in the partnership, including the partner's transferable interest and all management and other rights.

(10) "Person" means an individual, corporation, business trust, estate, trust, partnership, association, joint venture, government, governmental subdivision, agency, or instrumentality, or any other legal or commercial entity.

(11) "Property" means all property, real, personal, or mixed, tangible or intangible, or any interest therein.

(12) "State" means a State of the United States, the District of Columbia, the Commonwealth of Puerto Rico, or any territory or insular possession subject to the jurisdiction of the United States.

(13) "Statement" means a statement of partnership authority under Section 303, a statement of denial under Section 304, a statement of dissociation under Section 704, a statement of dissolution under Section 805, a statement of merger under Section 907, a statement of qualification under Section 1001, a statement of foreign qualification under Section 1102, or an amendment or cancellation of any of the foregoing.

(14) "Transfer" includes an assignment, conveyance, lease, mortgage, deed, and encumbrance.

SECTION 102. *Knowledge and Notice.*

(a) A person knows a fact if the person has actual knowledge of it.

(b) A person has notice of a fact if the person:

(1) knows of it;

(2) has received a notification of it; or

(3) has reason to know it exists from all of the facts known to the person at the time in question.

(c) A person notifies or gives a notification to another by taking steps reasonably required to inform the other person in ordinary course, whether or not the other person learns of it.

(d) A person receives a notification when the notification:

(1) comes to the person's attention; or

(2) is duly delivered at the person's place of business or at any other place held out by the person as a place for receiving communications.

(e) Except as otherwise provided in subsection (f), a person other than an individual knows, has notice, or receives a notification of a fact for purposes of a particular transaction when the individual conducting the transaction knows, has notice, or receives a notification of the fact, or in any event when the fact would have been brought to the individual's attention if the person had exercised reasonable diligence. The person exercises reasonable diligence if it maintains reasonable routines for communicating significant information to the individual conducting the transaction and there is reasonable compliance with the routines. Reasonable diligence does not require an individual acting for the person to communicate information unless the communication is part of the individual's regular duties or the individual has reason to know of the transaction and that the transaction would be materially affected by the information.

(f) A partner's knowledge, notice, or receipt of a notification of a fact relating to the partnership is effective immediately as knowledge by, notice to, or receipt of a notification by the partnership, except in the case of a fraud on the partnership committed by or with the consent of that partner.

SECTION 103. Effect of Partnership Agreement; Nonwaivable Provisions.

(a) Except as otherwise provided in subsection (b), relations among the partners and between the partners and the partnership are governed by the partnership agreement. To the extent the partnership agreement does not otherwise provide, this [Act] governs relations among the partners and between the partners and the partnership.

(b) The partnership agreement may not:

(1) vary the rights and duties under Section 105 except to eliminate the duty to provide copies of statements to all of the partners;

(2) unreasonably restrict the right of access to books and records under Section 403(b);

(3) eliminate the duty of loyalty under Section 404(b) or 603(b)(3), but:

(i) the partnership agreement may identify specific types or categories of activities that do not violate the duty of loyalty, if not manifestly unreasonable; or

(ii) all of the partners or a number or percentage specified in the partnership agreement may authorize or ratify, after full disclosure of all material facts, a specific act or transaction that otherwise would violate the duty of loyalty;

(4) unreasonably reduce the duty of care under Section 404(c) or 603(b)(3);

(5) eliminate the obligation of good faith and fair dealing under Section 404(d), but the partnership agreement may prescribe the standards by which the performance of the obligation is to be measured, if the standards are not manifestly unreasonable;

(6) vary the power to dissociate as a partner under Section 602(a), except to require the notice under Section 601(1) to be in writing;

(7) vary the right of a court to expel a partner in the events specified in Section 601(5);

(8) vary the requirement to wind up the partnership business in cases specified in Section 801(4), (5), or (6);

(9) vary the law applicable to a limited liability partnership under Section 106(b); or

(10) restrict rights of third parties under this [Act].

SECTION 104. Supplemental Principles of Law.

(a) Unless displaced by particular provisions of this [Act], the principles of law and equity supplement this [Act].

(b) If an obligation to pay interest arises under this [Act] and the rate is not specified, the rate is that specified in [applicable statute].

SECTION 105. Execution, Filing, and Recording of Statements.

(a) A statement may be filed in the office of [the Secretary of State]. A certified copy of a statement that is filed in an office in another State may be filed in the office of [the Secretary of State]. Either filing has the effect provided in this [Act] with respect to partnership property located in or transactions that occur in this State.

(b) A certified copy of a statement that has been filed in the office of the [Secretary of State] and recorded in the office for recording transfers of real property has the effect provided for recorded statements in this [Act]. A recorded statement that is not a certified copy of a statement filed in the office of the [Secretary of State] does not have the effect provided for recorded statements in this [Act].

(c) A statement filed by a partnership must be executed by at least two partners. Other statements must be executed by a partner or other person authorized by this [Act]. An individual who executes a statement as, or on behalf of, a partner or other person named as a partner in a statement shall personally declare under penalty of perjury that the contents of the statement are accurate.

(d) A person authorized by this [Act] to file a statement may amend or cancel the statement by filing an amendment or cancellation that names the partnership, identifies the statement, and states the substance of the amendment or cancellation.

(e) A person who files a statement pursuant to this section shall promptly send a copy of the statement to every nonfiling partner and to any other person named as a partner in the statement. Failure to send a copy of a statement to a partner or other person does not limit the effectiveness of the statement as to a person not a partner.

(f) The [Secretary of State] may collect a fee for filing or providing a certified copy of a statement. The [officer responsible for recording transfers of real property] may collect a fee for recording a statement.

SECTION 106. *Governing Law.*

(a) Except as otherwise provided in subsection (b), the law of the jurisdiction in which a partnership has its chief executive office governs relations among the partners and between the partners and the partnership.

(b) The law of this State governs relations among the partners and between the partners and the partnership and the liability of partners for an obligation of a limited liability partnership.

SECTION 107. *Partnership Subject to Amendment or Repeal of [Act].* A partnership governed by this [Act] is subject to any amendment to or repeal of this [Act].

[ARTICLE] 2
NATURE OF PARTNERSHIP

SECTION 201. *Partnership as Entity.*

(a) A partnership is an entity distinct from its partners.

(b) A limited liability partnership continues to be the same entity that existed before the filing of a statement of qualification under Section 1001.

SECTION 202. *Formation of Partnership.*

(a) Except as otherwise provided in subsection (b), the association of two or more persons to carry on as co-owners a business for profit forms a partnership, whether or not the persons intend to form a partnership.

(b) An association formed under a statute other than this [Act], a predecessor statute, or a comparable statute of another jurisdiction is not a partnership under this [Act].

(c) In determining whether a partnership is formed, the following rules apply:

(1) Joint tenancy, tenancy in common, tenancy by the entireties, joint property, common property, or part ownership does not by itself establish a partnership, even if the co-owners share profits made by the use of the property.

(2) The sharing of gross returns does not by itself establish a partnership, even if the persons sharing them have a joint or common right or interest in property from which the returns are derived.

(3) A person who receives a share of the profits of a business is presumed to be a partner in the business, unless the profits were received in payment:

(i) of a debt by installments or otherwise;

(ii) for services as an independent contractor or of wages or other compensation to an employee;

(iii) of rent;

(iv) of an annuity or other retirement or health benefit to a beneficiary, representative, or designee of a deceased or retired partner;

(v) of interest or other charge on a loan, even if the amount of payment varies with the profits of the business, including a direct or indirect present or future ownership of the collateral, or rights to income, proceeds, or increase in value derived from the collateral; or

(vi) for the sale of the goodwill of a business or other property by installments or otherwise.

SECTION 203. *Partnership Property.* Property acquired by a partnership is property of the partnership and not of the partners individually.

SECTION 204. *When Property is Partnership Property.*

(a) Property is partnership property if acquired in the name of:

(1) the partnership; or

(2) one or more partners with an indication in the instrument transferring title to the property of the person's capacity as a partner or of the existence of a partnership but without an indication of the name of the partnership.

(b) Property is acquired in the name of the partnership by a transfer to:

(1) the partnership in its name; or

(2) one or more partners in their capacity as partners in the partnership, if the name of the partnership is indicated in the instrument transferring title to the property.

(c) Property is presumed to be partnership property if purchased with partnership assets, even if not acquired in the name of the partnership or of one or more partners with an indication in the instrument transferring title to the property of the person's capacity as a partner or of the existence of a partnership.

(d) Property acquired in the name of one or more of the partners, without an indication in the instrument transferring title to the property of the person's capacity as a partner or of the existence of a partnership and without use of partnership assets, is presumed to be separate property, even if used for partnership purposes.

[ARTICLE] 3
RELATIONS OF PARTNERS TO PERSONS DEALING WITH PARTNERSHIP

SECTION 301. *Partner Agent of Partnership.* Subject to the effect of a statement of partnership authority under Section 303:

(1) Each partner is an agent of the partnership for the purpose of its business. An act of a partner, including the execution of an instrument in the partnership name, for apparently carrying on in the ordinary course the partnership business or business of the kind carried on by the partnership binds the partnership, unless the partner had no authority to act for the partnership in the particular matter and the person with whom the partner was dealing knew or had received a notification that the partner lacked authority.

(2) An act of a partner which is not apparently for carrying on in the ordinary course the partnership business or business of the kind carried on by the partnership binds the partnership only if the act was authorized by the other partners.

SECTION 302. *Transfer of Partnership Property.*

(a) Partnership property may be transferred as follows:

(1) Subject to the effect of a statement of partnership authority under Section 303, partnership property held in the name of the partnership may be transferred by an instrument of transfer executed by a partner in the partnership name.

(2) Partnership property held in the name of one or more partners with an indication in the instrument transferring the property to them of their capacity as partners or of the existence of a partnership, but without an indication of the name of the partnership, may be transferred by an instrument of transfer executed by the persons in whose name the property is held.

(3) Partnership property held in the name of one or more persons other than the partnership, without an indication in the instrument transferring the property to them of their capacity as partners or of the existence of a partnership, may be transferred by an instrument of transfer executed by the persons in whose name the property is held.

(b) A partnership may recover partnership property from a transferee only if it proves that execution of the instrument of initial transfer did not bind the partnership under Section 301 and:

(1) as to a subsequent transferee who gave value for property transferred under subsection (a)(1) and (2), proves that the subsequent transferee knew or had received a notification that

the person who executed the instrument of initial transfer lacked authority to bind the partnership; or

(2) as to a transferee who gave value for property transferred under subsection (a)(3), proves that the transferee knew or had received a notification that the property was partnership property and that the person who executed the instrument of initial transfer lacked authority to bind the partnership.

(c) A partnership may not recover partnership property from a subsequent transferee if the partnership would not have been entitled to recover the property, under subsection (b), from any earlier transferee of the property.

(d) If a person holds all of the partners' interests in the partnership, all of the partnership property vests in that person. The person may execute a document in the name of the partnership to evidence vesting of the property in that person and may file or record the document.

SECTION 303. *Statement of Partnership Authority.*

(a) A partnership may file a statement of partnership authority, which:

(1) must include:

(i) the name of the partnership;

(ii) the street address of its chief executive office and of one office in this State, if there is one;

(iii) the names and mailing addresses of all of the partners or of an agent appointed and maintained by the partnership for the purpose of subsection (b); and

(iv) the names of the partners authorized to execute an instrument transferring real property held in the name of the partnership; and

(2) may state the authority, or limitations on the authority, of some or all of the partners to enter into other transactions on behalf of the partnership and any other matter.

(b) If a statement of partnership authority names an agent, the agent shall maintain a list of the names and mailing addresses of all of the partners and make it available to any person on request for good cause shown.

(c) If a filed statement of partnership authority is executed pursuant to Section 105(c) and states

the name of the partnership but does not contain all of the other information required by subsection (a), the statement nevertheless operates with respect to a person not a partner as provided in subsections (d) and (e).

(d) Except as otherwise provided in subsection (g), a filed statement of partnership authority supplements the authority of a partner to enter into transactions on behalf of the partnership as follows:

(1) Except for transfers of real property, a grant of authority contained in a filed statement of partnership authority is conclusive in favor of a person who gives value without knowledge to the contrary, so long as and to the extent that a limitation on that authority is not then contained in another filed statement. A filed cancellation of a limitation on authority revives the previous grant of authority.

(2) A grant of authority to transfer real property held in the name of the partnership contained in a certified copy of a filed statement of partnership authority recorded in the office for recording transfers of that real property is conclusive in favor of a person who gives value without knowledge to the contrary, so long as and to the extent that a certified copy of a filed statement containing a limitation on that authority is not then of record in the office for recording transfers of that real property. The recording in the office for recording transfers of that real property of a certified copy of a filed cancellation of a limitation on authority revives the previous grant of authority.

(e) A person not a partner is deemed to know of a limitation on the authority of a partner to transfer real property held in the name of the partnership if a certified copy of the filed statement containing the limitation on authority is of record in the office for recording transfers of that real property.

(f) Except as otherwise provided in subsections (d) and (e) and Sections 704 and 805, a person not a partner is not deemed to know of a limitation on the authority of a partner merely because the limitation is contained in a filed statement.

(g) Unless earlier canceled, a filed statement of partnership authority is canceled by operation of law five years after the date on which the statement, or the most recent amendment, was filed with the [Secretary of State].

SECTION 304. Statement of Denial. A partner or other person named as a partner in a filed statement of partnership authority or in a list maintained by an agent pursuant to Section 303(b) may file a statement of denial stating the name of the partnership and the fact that is being denied, which may include denial of a person's authority or status as a partner. A statement of denial is a limitation on authority as provided in Section 303(d) and (e).

SECTION 305. Partnership Liable for Partner's Actionable Conduct.

(a) A partnership is liable for loss or injury caused to a person, or for a penalty incurred, as a result of a wrongful act or omission, or other actionable conduct, of a partner acting in the ordinary course of business of the partnership or with authority of the partnership.

(b) If, in the course of the partnership's business or while acting with authority of the partnership, a partner receives or causes the partnership to receive money or property of a person not a partner, and the money or property is misapplied by a partner, the partnership is liable for the loss.

SECTION 306. Partner's Liability.

(a) Except as otherwise provided in subsections (b) and (c), all partners are liable jointly and severally for all obligations of the partnership unless otherwise agreed by the claimant or provided by law.

(b) A person admitted as a partner into an existing partnership is not personally liable for any partnership obligation incurred before the person's admission as a partner.

(c) An obligation of a partnership incurred while the partnership is a limited liability partnership, whether arising in contract, tort, or otherwise, is solely the obligation of the partnership. A partner is not personally liable, directly or indirectly, by way of contribution or otherwise, for such an obligation solely by reason of being or so acting as a partner. This subsection applies notwithstanding anything inconsistent in the partnership agreement that existed immediately before the vote required to become a limited liability partnership under Section 1001(b).

SECTION 307. Actions by and Against Partnership and Partners.

(a) A partnership may sue and be sued in the name of the partnership.

(b) An action may be brought against the partnership and, to the extent not inconsistent with Section 306, any or all of the partners in the same action or in separate actions.

(c) A judgment against a partnership is not by itself a judgment against a partner. A judgment against a partnership may not be satisfied from a partner's assets unless there is also a judgment against the partner.

(d) A judgment creditor of a partner may not levy execution against the assets of the partner to satisfy a judgment based on a claim against the partnership unless the partner is personally liable for the claim under Section 306 and:

(1) a judgment based on the same claim has been obtained against the partnership and a writ of execution on the judgment has been returned unsatisfied in whole or in part;

(2) the partnership is a debtor in bankruptcy;

(3) the partner has agreed that the creditor need not exhaust partnership assets;

(4) a court grants permission to the judgment creditor to levy execution against the assets of a partner based on a finding that partnership assets subject to execution are clearly insufficient to satisfy the judgment, that exhaustion of partnership assets is excessively burdensome, or that the grant of permission is an appropriate exercise of the court's equitable powers; or

(5) liability is imposed on the partner by law or contract independent of the existence of the partnership.

(e) This section applies to any partnership liability or obligation resulting from a representation by a partner or purported partner under Section 308.

SECTION 308. Liability of Purported Partner.

(a) If a person, by words or conduct, purports to be a partner, or consents to being represented by another as a partner, in a partnership or with one or more persons not partners, the purported partner is liable to a person to whom the representation is made, if that person, relying on the representation, enters into a transaction with the actual or purported partnership. If the representation, either by the purported partner or by a person with the purported partner's consent, is made in a public manner, the purported partner is liable to a person who relies upon the purported partnership even if the purported partner is not aware of being held out as a partner to the claimant. If partnership liability results, the purported partner is liable with respect to that liability as if the purported partner were a partner. If no partnership liability results, the purported partner is liable with respect to that liability jointly and severally with any other person consenting to the representation.

(b) If a person is thus represented to be a partner in an existing partnership, or with one or more persons not partners, the purported partner is an agent of persons consenting to the representation to bind them to the same extent and in the same manner as if the purported partner were a partner, with respect to persons who enter into transactions in reliance upon the representation. If all of the partners of the existing partnership consent to the representation, a partnership act or obligation results. If fewer than all of the partners of the existing partnership consent to the representation, the person acting and the partners consenting to the representation are jointly and severally liable.

(c) A person is not liable as a partner merely because the person is named by another in a statement of partnership authority.

(d) A person does not continue to be liable as a partner merely because of a failure to file a statement of dissociation or to amend a statement of partnership authority to indicate the partner's dissociation from the partnership.

(e) Except as otherwise provided in subsections (a) and (b), persons who are not partners as to each other are not liable as partners to other persons.

[ARTICLE] 4
RELATIONS OF PARTNERS TO EACH OTHER
AND TO PARTNERSHIP

SECTION 401. *Partner's Rights and Duties.*

(a) Each partner is deemed to have an account that is:

(1) credited with an amount equal to the money plus the value of any other property, net of the amount of any liabilities, the partner contributes to the partnership and the partner's share of the partnership profits; and

(2) charged with an amount equal to the money plus the value of any other property, net of the amount of any liabilities, distributed by the partnership to the partner and the partner's share of the partnership losses.

(b) Each partner is entitled to an equal share of the partnership profits and is chargeable with a share of the partnership losses in proportion to the partner's share of the profits.

(c) A partnership shall reimburse a partner for payments made and indemnify a partner for liabilities incurred by the partner in the ordinary course of the business of the partnership or for the preservation of its business or property.

(d) A partnership shall reimburse a partner for an advance to the partnership beyond the amount of capital the partner agreed to contribute.

(e) A payment or advance made by a partner which gives rise to a partnership obligation under subsection (c) or (d) constitutes a loan to the partnership which accrues interest from the date of the payment or advance.

(f) Each partner has equal rights in the management and conduct of the partnership business.

(g) A partner may use or possess partnership property only on behalf of the partnership.

(h) A partner is not entitled to remuneration for services performed for the partnership, except for reasonable compensation for services rendered in winding up the business of the partnership.

(i) A person may become a partner only with the consent of all of the partners.

(j) A difference arising as to a matter in the ordinary course of business of a partnership may be decided by a majority of the partners. An act outside the ordinary course of business of a partnership and an amendment to the partnership agreement may be undertaken only with the consent of all of the partners.

(k) This section does not affect the obligations of a partnership to other persons under Section 301.

SECTION 402. *Distributions in Kind.* A partner has no right to receive, and may not be required to accept, a distribution in kind.

SECTION 403. Partner's Rights and Duties with Respect to Information.

(a) A partnership shall keep its books and records, if any, at its chief executive office.

(b) A partnership shall provide partners and their agents and attorneys access to its books and records. It shall provide former partners and their agents and attorneys access to books and records pertaining to the period during which they were partners. The right of access provides the opportunity to inspect and copy books and records during ordinary business hours. A partnership may impose a reasonable charge, covering the costs of labor and material, for copies of documents furnished.

(c) Each partner and the partnership shall furnish to a partner, and to the legal representative of a deceased partner or partner under legal disability:

(1) without demand, any information concerning the partnership's business and affairs reasonably required for the proper exercise of the partner's rights and duties under the partnership agreement or this [Act]; and

(2) on demand, any other information concerning the partnership's business and affairs, except to the extent the demand or the information demanded is unreasonable or otherwise improper under the circumstances.

SECTION 404. General Standards of Partner's Conduct.

(a) The only fiduciary duties a partner owes to the partnership and the other partners are the duty of loyalty and the duty of care set forth in subsections (b) and (c).

(b) A partner's duty of loyalty to the partnership and the other partners is limited to the following:

(1) to account to the partnership and hold as trustee for it any property, profit, or benefit derived by the partner in the conduct and winding up of the partnership business or derived from a use by the partner of partnership property, including the appropriation of a partnership opportunity;

(2) to refrain from dealing with the partnership in the conduct or winding up of the partnership business as or on behalf of a party having an interest adverse to the partnership; and

(3) to refrain from competing with the partnership in the conduct of the partnership business before the dissolution of the partnership.

(c) A partner's duty of care to the partnership and the other partners in the conduct and winding up of the partnership business is limited to refraining from engaging in grossly negligent or reckless conduct, intentional misconduct, or a knowing violation of law.

(d) A partner shall discharge the duties to the partnership and the other partners under this [Act] or under the partnership agreement and exercise any rights consistently with the obligation of good faith and fair dealing.

(e) A partner does not violate a duty or obligation under this [Act] or under the partnership agreement merely because the partner's conduct furthers the partner's own interest.

(f) A partner may lend money to and transact other business with the partnership, and as to each loan or transaction the rights and obligations of the partner are the same as those of a person who is not a partner, subject to other applicable law.

(g) This section applies to a person winding up the partnership business as the personal or legal representative of the last surviving partner as if the person were a partner.

SECTION 405. Actions By Partnership And Partners.

(a) A partnership may maintain an action against a partner for a breach of the partnership agreement, or for the violation of a duty to the partnership, causing harm to the partnership.

(b) A partner may maintain an action against the partnership or another partner for legal or equitable relief, with or without an accounting as to partnership business, to:

(1) enforce the partner's rights under the partnership agreement;

(2) enforce the partner's rights under this [Act], including:

(i) the partner's rights under Sections 401, 403, or 404;

(ii) the partner's right on dissociation to have the partner's interest in the partnership purchased pursuant to Section 701 or enforce any other right under [Article] 6 or 7; or

(iii) the partner's right to compel a dissolution and winding up of the partnership business under or enforce any other right under [Article] 8; or

(3) enforce the rights and otherwise protect the interests of the partner, including rights and interests arising independently of the partnership relationship.

(c) The accrual of, and any time limitation on, a right of action for a remedy under this section is governed by other law. A right to an accounting upon a dissolution and winding up does not revive a claim barred by law.

SECTION 406. *Continuation of Partnership Beyond Definite Term or Particular Undertaking.*

(a) If a partnership for a definite term or particular undertaking is continued, without an express agreement, after the expiration of the term or completion of the undertaking, the rights and duties of the partners remain the same as they were at the expiration or completion, so far as is consistent with a partnership at will.

(b) If the partners, or those of them who habitually acted in the business during the term or undertaking, continue the business without any settlement or liquidation of the partnership, they are presumed to have agreed that the partnership will continue.

[ARTICLE] 5
TRANSFEREES AND CREDITORS OF PARTNER

SECTION 501. *Partner Not Co-owner of Partnership Property.* A partner is not a co-owner of partnership property and has no interest in partnership property which can be transferred, either voluntarily or involuntarily.

SECTION 502. *Partner's Transferable Interest in Partnership.* The only transferable interest of a partner in the partnership is the partner's share of the profits and losses of the partnership and the partner's right to receive distributions. The interest is personal property.

SECTION 503. *Transfer of Partner's Transferable Interest.*

(a) A transfer, in whole or in part, of a partner's transferable interest in the partnership:

(1) is permissible;

(2) does not by itself cause the partner's dissociation or a dissolution and winding up of the partnership business; and

(3) does not, as against the other partners or the partnership, entitle the transferee, during the continuance of the partnership, to participate in the management or conduct of the partnership business, to require access to information concerning partnership transactions, or to inspect or copy the partnership books or records.

(b) A transferee of a partner's transferable interest in the partnership has a right:

(1) to receive, in accordance with the transfer, distributions to which the transferor would otherwise be entitled;

(2) to receive upon the dissolution and winding up of the partnership business, in accordance with the transfer, the net amount otherwise distributable to the transferor; and

(3) to seek under (6) a judicial determination that it is equitable to wind up the partnership business.

(c) In a dissolution and winding up, a transferee is entitled to an account of partnership transactions only from the date of the latest account agreed to by all of the partners.

(d) Upon transfer, the transferor retains the rights and duties of a partner other than the interest in distributions transferred.

(e) A partnership need not give effect to a transferee's rights under this section until it has notice of the transfer.

(f) A transfer of a partner's transferable interest in the partnership in violation of a restriction on transfer contained in the partnership agreement is ineffective as to a person having notice of the restriction at the time of transfer.

SECTION 504. *Partner's Transferable Interest Subject to Charging Order.*

(a) On application by a judgment creditor of a partner or of a partner's transferee, a court having jurisdiction may charge the transferable interest of the judgment debtor to satisfy the judgment. The court may appoint a receiver of the share of the distributions due or to become due to the judgment debtor in respect of the partnership and make all other orders, directions, accounts, and inquiries the judgment debtor might have made or which the circumstances of the case may require.

(b) A charging order constitutes a lien on the judgment debtor's transferable interest in the partnership. The court may order a foreclosure of the interest subject to the charging order at any time. The purchaser at the foreclosure sale has the rights of a transferee.

(c) At any time before foreclosure, an interest charged may be redeemed:

(1) by the judgment debtor;

(2) with property other than partnership property, by one or more of the other partners; or

(3) with partnership property, by one or more of the other partners with the consent of all of the partners whose interests are not so charged.

(d) This [Act] does not deprive a partner of a right under exemption laws with respect to the partner's interest in the partnership.

(e) This section provides the exclusive remedy by which a judgment creditor of a partner or partner's transferee may satisfy a judgment out of the judgment debtor's transferable interest in the partnership.

[ARTICLE] 6
PARTNER'S DISSOCIATION

SECTION 601. *Events Causing Partner's Dissociation.* A partner is dissociated from a partnership upon the occurrence of any of the following events:

(1) the partnership's having notice of the partner's express will to withdraw as a partner or on a later date specified by the partner;

(2) an event agreed to in the partnership agreement as causing the partner's dissociation;

(3) the partner's expulsion pursuant to the partnership agreement;

(4) the partner's expulsion by the unanimous vote of the other partners if:

(i) it is unlawful to carry on the partnership business with that partner;

(ii) there has been a transfer of all or substantially all of that partner's transferable interest in the partnership, other than a transfer for security purposes, or a court order charging the partner's interest, which has not been foreclosed;

(iii) within 90 days after the partnership notifies a corporate partner that it will be expelled because it has filed a certificate of dissolution or the equivalent, its charter has been revoked, or its right to conduct business has been suspended by the jurisdiction of its incorporation, there is no revocation of the certificate of dissolution or no reinstatement of its charter or its right to conduct business; or

(iv) a partnership that is a partner has been dissolved and its business is being wound up;

(5) on application by the partnership or another partner, the partner's expulsion by judicial determination because:

(i) the partner engaged in wrongful conduct that adversely and materially affected the partnership business;

(ii) the partner willfully or persistently committed a material breach of the partnership agreement or of a duty owed to the partnership or the other partners under Section 404; or

(iii) the partner engaged in conduct relating to the partnership business which makes it not reasonably practicable to carry on the business in partnership with the partner;

(6) the partner's:

(i) becoming a debtor in bankruptcy;

(ii) executing an assignment for the benefit of creditors;

(iii) seeking, consenting to, or acquiescing in the appointment of a trustee, receiver, or liquidator of that partner or of all or substantially all of that partner's property; or

(iv) failing, within 90 days after the appointment, to have vacated or stayed the appointment of a trustee, receiver, or liquidator of the partner or of all or substantially all of the partner's property obtained without the partner's consent or acquiescence, or failing within 90 days after the expiration of a stay to have the appointment vacated;

(7) in the case of a partner who is an individual:

(i) the partner's death;

(ii) the appointment of a guardian or general conservator for the partner; or

(iii) a judicial determination that the partner has otherwise become incapable of performing the partner's duties under the partnership agreement;

(8) in the case of a partner that is a trust or is acting as a partner by virtue of being a trustee of a trust, distribution of the trust's entire transferable interest in the partnership, but not merely by reason of the substitution of a successor trustee;

(9) in the case of a partner that is an estate or is acting as a partner by virtue of being a personal representative of an estate, distribution of the estate's entire transferable interest in the partnership, but not merely by reason of the substitution of a successor personal representative; or

(10) termination of a partner who is not an individual, partnership, corporation, trust, or estate.

SECTION 602. *Partner's Power to Dissociate; Wrongful Dissociation.*

(a) A partner has the power to dissociate at any time, rightfully or wrongfully, by express will pursuant to Section 601(1).

(b) A partner's dissociation is wrongful only if:

(1) it is in breach of an express provision of the partnership agreement; or

(2) in the case of a partnership for a definite term or particular undertaking, before the expiration of the term or the completion of the undertaking:

(i) the partner withdraws by express will, unless the withdrawal follows within 90 days after another partner's dissociation by death or otherwise under Section 601(6) through (10) or wrongful dissociation under this subsection;

(ii) the partner is expelled by judicial determination under Section 601(5);

(iii) the partner is dissociated by becoming a debtor in bankruptcy; or

(iv) in the case of a partner who is not an individual, trust other than a business trust, or estate, the partner is expelled or otherwise dissociated because it willfully dissolved or terminated.

(c) A partner who wrongfully dissociates is liable to the partnership and to the other partners for damages caused by the dissociation. The liability is in addition to any other obligation of the partner to the partnership or to the other partners.

SECTION 603. *Effect of Partner's Dissociation.*

(a) If a partner's dissociation results in a dissolution and winding up of the partnership business, [Article] 8 applies; otherwise, [Article] 7 applies.

(b) Upon a partner's dissociation:

(1) the partner's right to participate in the management and conduct of the partnership business terminates, except as otherwise provided in Section 803;

(2) the partner's duty of loyalty under Section 404(b)(3) terminates; and

(3) the partner's duty of loyalty under Section 404(b)(1) and (2) and duty of care under Section 404(c) continue only with regard to matters arising and events occurring before the partner's dissociation, unless the partner participates in winding up the partnership's business pursuant to Section 803.

[ARTICLE] 7
PARTNER'S DISSOCIATION WHEN BUSINESS NOT WOUND UP

SECTION 701. *Purchase of Dissociated Partner's Interest.*

(a) If a partner is dissociated from a partnership without resulting in a dissolution and winding up of the partnership business under Section 801, the partnership shall cause the dissociated partner's interest in the partnership to be purchased for a buyout price determined pursuant to subsection (b).

(b) The buyout price of a dissociated partner's interest is the amount that would have been distributable to the dissociating partner under Section 807(b) if, on the date of dissociation, the assets of the partnership were sold at a price equal to the greater of the liquidation value or the value based on a sale of the entire business as a going concern without the dissociated partner and the partnership were wound up as of that date. Interest must be paid from the date of dissociation to the date of payment.

(c) Damages for wrongful dissociation under Section 602(b), and all other amounts owing, whether or not presently due, from the dissociated partner to the partnership, must be offset against the buyout price. Interest must be paid from the date the amount owed becomes due to the date of payment.

(d) A partnership shall indemnify a dissociated partner whose interest is being purchased against all partnership liabilities, whether incurred before or after the dissociation, except liabilities incurred by an act of the dissociated partner under Section 702.

(e) If no agreement for the purchase of a dissociated partner's interest is reached within 120 days after a written demand for payment, the partnership shall pay, or cause to be paid, in cash to the dissociated partner the amount the partnership estimates to be the buyout price and accrued interest, reduced by any offsets and accrued interest under subsection (c).

(f) If a deferred payment is authorized under subsection (h), the partnership may tender a written offer to pay the amount it estimates to be the buyout price and accrued interest, reduced by any offsets under subsection (c), stating the time of payment, the amount and type of security for payment, and the other terms and conditions of the obligation.

(g) The payment or tender required by subsection (e) or (f) must be accompanied by the following:

(1) a statement of partnership assets and liabilities as of the date of dissociation;

(2) the latest available partnership balance sheet and income statement, if any;

(3) an explanation of how the estimated amount of the payment was calculated; and

(4) written notice that the payment is in full satisfaction of the obligation to purchase unless, within 120 days after the written notice, the dissociated partner commences an action to determine the buyout price, any offsets under subsection (c), or other terms of the obligation to purchase.

(h) A partner who wrongfully dissociates before the expiration of a definite term or the completion of a particular undertaking is not entitled to payment of any portion of the buyout price until the expiration of the term or completion of the undertaking, unless the partner establishes to the satisfaction of the court that earlier payment will not cause undue hardship to the business of the partnership. A deferred payment must be adequately secured and bear interest.

(i) A dissociated partner may maintain an action against the partnership, pursuant to Section 405(b)(2)(ii), to determine the buyout price of that partner's interest, any offsets under subsection (c), or other terms of the obligation to purchase. The action must be commenced within 120 days after the partnership has tendered payment or an offer to pay or within one year after written demand for payment if no payment or offer to pay is tendered. The court shall determine the buyout price of the dissociated partner's interest, any offset due under subsection (c), and accrued interest, and enter judgment for any additional payment or refund. If deferred payment is authorized under subsection (h), the court shall also determine the security for payment and other terms of the obligation to purchase. The court may assess reasonable attorney's fees and the fees and expenses of appraisers or other experts for a party to the action, in amounts the court finds equitable, against a party that the court finds acted arbitrarily, vexatiously, or not in good faith. The finding may be based on the partnership's failure to tender payment or an offer to pay or to comply with subsection (g).

SECTION 702. *Dissociated Partner's Power to Bind and Liability to Partnership.*

(a) For two years after a partner dissociates without resulting in a dissolution and winding up of the partnership business, the partnership, including a surviving partnership under [Article] 9, is bound by an act of the dissociated partner which would have bound the partnership under Section 301 before dissociation only if at the time of entering into the transaction the other party:

(1) reasonably believed that the dissociated partner was then a partner;

(2) did not have notice of the partner's dissociation; and

(3) is not deemed to have had knowledge under Section 303(e) or notice under Section 704(c).

(b) A dissociated partner is liable to the partnership for any damage caused to the partnership arising from an obligation incurred by the dissociated partner after dissociation for which the partnership is liable under subsection (a).

SECTION 703. *Dissociated Partner's Liability to Other Persons.*

(a) A partner's dissociation does not of itself discharge the partner's liability for a partnership obligation incurred before dissociation. A dissociated partner is not liable for a partnership obligation incurred after dissociation, except as otherwise provided in subsection (b).

(b) A partner who dissociates without resulting in a dissolution and winding up of the partnership business is liable as a partner to the other party in a transaction entered into by the partnership, or a surviving partnership under [Article] 9, within two years after the partner's dissociation, only if the partner is liable for the obligation under Section 306 and at the time of entering into the transaction the other party:

(1) reasonably believed that the dissociated partner was then a partner;

(2) did not have notice of the partner's dissociation; and

(3) is not deemed to have had knowledge under Section 303(e) or notice under Section 704(c).

(c) By agreement with the partnership creditor and the partners continuing the business, a dissociated partner may be released from liability for a partnership obligation.

(d) A dissociated partner is released from liability for a partnership obligation if a partnership creditor, with notice of the partner's dissociation but without the partner's consent, agrees to a material alteration in the nature or time of payment of a partnership obligation.

SECTION 704. Statement of Dissociation.

(a) A dissociated partner or the partnership may file a statement of dissociation stating the name of the partnership and that the partner is dissociated from the partnership.

(b) A statement of dissociation is a limitation on the authority of a dissociated partner for the purposes of Section 303(d) and (e).

(c) For the purposes of Sections 702(a)(3) and 703(b)(3), a person not a partner is deemed to have notice of the dissociation 90 days after the statement of dissociation is filed.

SECTION 705. Continued Use of Partnership Name. Continued use of a partnership name, or a dissociated partner's name as part thereof, by partners continuing the business does not of itself make the dissociated partner liable for an obligation of the partners or the partnership continuing the business.

[ARTICLE] 8
WINDING UP PARTNERSHIP BUSINESS

SECTION 801. Events Causing Dissolution and Winding Up of Partnership Business. A partnership is dissolved, and its business must be wound up, only upon the occurrence of any of the following events:

(1) in a partnership at will, the partnership's having notice from a partner, other than a partner who is dissociated under Section 601(2) through (10), of that partner's express will to withdraw as a partner, or on a later date specified by the partner;

(2) in a partnership for a definite term or particular undertaking:

(i) within 90 days after a partner's dissociation by death or otherwise under Section 601(6) through (10) or wrongful dissociation under Section 602(b), the express will of at least half of the remaining partners to wind up the partnership business, for which purpose a partner's rightful dissociation pursuant to Section 602(b)(2)(i) constitutes the expression of that partner's will to wind up the partnership business;

(ii) the express will of all of the partners to wind up the partnership business; or

(iii) the expiration of the term or the completion of the undertaking;

(3) an event agreed to in the partnership agreement resulting in the winding up of the partnership business;

(4) an event that makes it unlawful for all or substantially all of the business of the partnership to be continued, but a cure of illegality within 90 days after notice to the partnership of the event is effective retroactively to the date of the event for purposes of this section;

(5) on application by a partner, a judicial determination that:

(i) the economic purpose of the partnership is likely to be unreasonably frustrated;

(ii) another partner has engaged in conduct relating to the partnership business which makes it not reasonably practicable to carry on the business in partnership with that partner; or

(iii) it is not otherwise reasonably practicable to carry on the partnership business in conformity with the partnership agreement; or

(6) on application by a transferee of a partner's transferable interest, a judicial determination that it is equitable to wind up the partnership business:

(i) after the expiration of the term or completion of the undertaking, if the partnership was for a definite term or particular undertaking at the time of the transfer or entry of the charging order that gave rise to the transfer; or

(ii) at any time, if the partnership was a partnership at will at the time of the transfer or entry of the charging order that gave rise to the transfer.

SECTION 802. Partnership Continues After Dissolution.

(a) Subject to subsection (b), a partnership continues after dissolution only for the purpose of winding up its business. The partnership is terminated when the winding up of its business is completed.

(b) At any time after the dissolution of a partnership and before the winding up of its business is completed, all of the partners, including any dissociating partner other than a wrongfully dissociating partner, may waive the right to have the partnership's business wound up and the partnership terminated. In that event:

(1) the partnership resumes carrying on its business as if dissolution had never occurred, and any liability incurred by the partnership or a partner after the dissolution and before the waiver is determined as if dissolution had never occurred; and

(2) the rights of a third party accruing under Section 804(1) or arising out of conduct in reliance on the dissolution before the third party knew or received a notification of the waiver may not be adversely affected.

SECTION 803. Right to Wind Up Partnership Business.

(a) After dissolution, a partner who has not wrongfully dissociated may participate in winding up the partnership's business, but on application of any partner, partner's legal representative, or transferee, the [designate the appropriate court], for good cause shown, may order judicial supervision of the winding up.

(b) The legal representative of the last surviving partner may wind up a partnership's business.

(c) A person winding up a partnership's business may preserve the partnership business or property as a going concern for a reasonable time, prosecute and defend actions and proceedings, whether civil, criminal, or administrative, settle and close the partnership's business, dispose of and transfer the partnership's property, discharge the partnership's liabilities, distribute the assets of the partnership pursuant to Section 807, settle disputes by mediation or arbitration, and perform other necessary acts.

SECTION 804. Partner's Power to Bind Partnership After Dissolution.

Subject to Section 805, a partnership is bound by a partner's act after dissolution that:

(1) is appropriate for winding up the partnership business; or

(2) would have bound the partnership under Section 301 before dissolution, if the other party to the transaction did not have notice of the dissolution.

SECTION 805. Statement of Dissolution.

(a) After dissolution, a partner who has not wrongfully dissociated may file a statement of dissolution stating the name of the partnership and that the partnership has dissolved and is winding up its business.

(b) A statement of dissolution cancels a filed statement of partnership authority for the purposes of Section 303(d) and is a limitation on authority for the purposes of Section 303(e).

(c) For the purposes of Sections 301 and 804, a person not a partner is deemed to have notice of the dissolution and the limitation on the partners' authority as a result of the statement of dissolution 90 days after it is filed.

(d) After filing and, if appropriate, recording a statement of dissolution, a dissolved partnership may file and, if appropriate, record a statement of partnership authority which will operate with respect to a person not a partner as provided in Section 303(d) and (e) in any transaction, whether or not the transaction is appropriate for winding up the partnership business.

SECTION 806. Partner's Liability to Other Partners After Dissolution.

(a) Except as otherwise provided in subsection (b) and Section 306, after dissolution a partner is liable to the other partners for the partner's share of any partnership liability incurred under Section 804.

(b) A partner who, with knowledge of the dissolution, incurs a partnership liability under Section 804(2) by an act that is not appropriate for winding up the partnership business is liable to the partnership for any damage caused to the partnership arising from the liability.

SECTION 807. Settlement of Accounts and Contributions Among Partners.

(a) In winding up a partnership's business, the assets of the partnership, including the contributions of the partners required by this section, must be applied to discharge its obligations to creditors, including, to the extent permitted by law, partners who are creditors. Any surplus must be applied to pay in cash the net amount distributable to partners in accordance with their right to distributions under subsection (b).

(b) Each partner is entitled to a settlement of all partnership accounts upon winding up the partnership business. In settling accounts among the partners, profits and losses that result from the liquidation of the partnership assets must be credited and charged to the partners' accounts. The partnership shall make a distribution to a partner in an amount equal to any excess of the credits over the charges in the partner's account. A partner shall contribute to the partnership an amount equal to any excess of the charges over the credits in the partner's account but excluding from the calculation charges attributable to an obligation for which the partner is not personally liable under Section 306.

(c) If a partner fails to contribute the full amount required under subsection (b), all of the other partners shall contribute, in the proportions in which those partners share partnership losses, the additional amount necessary to satisfy the partnership obligations for which they are personally liable under Section 306. A partner or partner's legal representative may recover from the other partners any contributions the partner makes to the extent the amount contributed exceeds that partner's share of the partnership obligations for which the partner is personally liable under Section 306.

(d) After the settlement of accounts, each partner shall contribute, in the proportion in which the partner shares partnership losses, the amount necessary to satisfy partnership obligations that were not known at the time of the settlement and for which the partner is personally liable under Section 306.

(e) The estate of a deceased partner is liable for the partner's obligation to contribute to the partnership.

(f) An assignee for the benefit of creditors of a partnership or a partner, or a person appointed by a court to represent creditors of a partnership or a partner, may enforce a partner's obligation to contribute to the partnership.

[ARTICLE] 9
CONVERSIONS AND MERGERS

SECTION 901. Definitions. In this [article]:

(1) "General partner" means a partner in a partnership and a general partner in a limited partnership.

(2) "Limited partner" means a limited partner in a limited partnership.

(3) "Limited partnership" means a limited partnership created under the [State Limited Partnership Act], predecessor law, or comparable law of another jurisdiction.

(4) "Partner" includes both a general partner and a limited partner.

SECTION 902. Conversion of Partnership to Limited Partnership.

(a) A partnership may be converted to a limited partnership pursuant to this section.

(b) The terms and conditions of a conversion of a partnership to a limited partnership must be approved by all of the partners or by a number or percentage specified for conversion in the partnership agreement.

(c) After the conversion is approved by the partners, the partnership shall file a certificate of limited partnership in the jurisdiction in which the limited partnership is to be formed. The certificate must include:

(1) a statement that the partnership was converted to a limited partnership from a partnership;

(2) its former name; and

(3) a statement of the number of votes cast by the partners for and against the conversion and, if the vote is less than unanimous, the

number or percentage required to approve the conversion under the partnership agreement.

(d)   The conversion takes effect when the certificate of limited partnership is filed or at any later date specified in the certificate.

(e)   A general partner who becomes a limited partner as a result of the conversion remains liable as a general partner for an obligation incurred by the partnership before the conversion takes effect. If the other party to a transaction with the limited partnership reasonably believes when entering the transaction that the limited partner is a general partner, the limited partner is liable for an obligation incurred by the limited partnership within 90 days after the conversion takes effect. The limited partner's liability for all other obligations of the limited partnership incurred after the conversion takes effect is that of a limited partner as provided in the [State Limited Partnership Act].

SECTION 903. *Conversion of Limited Partnership to Partnership.*

(a)   A limited partnership may be converted to a partnership pursuant to this section.

(b)   Notwithstanding a provision to the contrary in a limited partnership agreement, the terms and conditions of a conversion of a limited partnership to a partnership must be approved by all of the partners.

(c)   After the conversion is approved by the partners, the limited partnership shall cancel its certificate of limited partnership.

(d)   The conversion takes effect when the certificate of limited partnership is canceled.

(e)   A limited partner who becomes a general partner as a result of the conversion remains liable only as a limited partner for an obligation incurred by the limited partnership before the conversion takes effect. Except as otherwise provided in Section 306, the partner is liable as a general partner for an obligation of the partnership incurred after the conversion takes effect.

SECTION 904. *Effect of Conversion; Entity Unchanged.*

(a)   A partnership or limited partnership that has been converted pursuant to this [article] is for all purposes the same entity that existed before the conversion.

(b)   When a conversion takes effect:

(1)   all property owned by the converting partnership or limited partnership remains vested in the converted entity;

(2)   all obligations of the converting partnership or limited partnership continue as obligations of the converted entity; and

(3)   an action or proceeding pending against the converting partnership or limited partnership may be continued as if the conversion had not occurred.

SECTION 905. *Merger of Partnerships.*

(a)   Pursuant to a plan of merger approved as provided in subsection (c), a partnership may be merged with one or more partnerships or limited partnerships.

(b)   The plan of merger must set forth:

(1)   the name of each partnership or limited partnership that is a party to the merger;

(2)   the name of the surviving entity into which the other partnerships or limited partnerships will merge;

(3)   whether the surviving entity is a partnership or a limited partnership and the status of each partner;

(4)   the terms and conditions of the merger;

(5)   the manner and basis of converting the interests of each party to the merger into interests or obligations of the surviving entity, or into money or other property in whole or part; and

(6)   the street address of the surviving entity's chief executive office.

(c)   The plan of merger must be approved:

(1)   in the case of a partnership that is a party to the merger, by all of the partners, or a number or percentage specified for merger in the partnership agreement; and

(2)   in the case of a limited partnership that is a party to the merger, by the vote required for approval of a merger by the law of the State or foreign jurisdiction in which the limited partnership is organized and, in the absence of such a specifically applicable law, by all of the partners, notwithstanding a provision to the contrary in the partnership agreement.

(d)   After a plan of merger is approved and before the merger takes effect, the plan may be amended or abandoned as provided in the plan.

(e) The merger takes effect on the later of:

(1) the approval of the plan of merger by all parties to the merger, as provided in subsection (c);

(2) the filing of all documents required by law to be filed as a condition to the effectiveness of the merger; or

(3) any effective date specified in the plan of merger.

SECTION 906. *Effect of Merger.*

(a) When a merger takes effect:

(1) the separate existence of every partnership or limited partnership that is a party to the merger, other than the surviving entity, ceases;

(2) all property owned by each of the merged partnerships or limited partnerships vests in the surviving entity;

(3) all obligations of every partnership or limited partnership that is a party to the merger become the obligations of the surviving entity; and

(4) an action or proceeding pending against a partnership or limited partnership that is a party to the merger may be continued as if the merger had not occurred, or the surviving entity may be substituted as a party to the action or proceeding.

(b) The [Secretary of State] of this State is the agent for service of process in an action or proceeding against a surviving foreign partnership or limited partnership to enforce an obligation of a domestic partnership or limited partnership that is a party to a merger. The surviving entity shall promptly notify the [Secretary of State] of the mailing address of its chief executive office and of any change of address. Upon receipt of process, the [Secretary of State] shall mail a copy of the process to the surviving foreign partnership or limited partnership.

(c) A partner of the surviving partnership or limited partnership is liable for:

(1) all obligations of a party to the merger for which the partner was personally liable before the merger;

(2) all other obligations of the surviving entity incurred before the merger by a party to the merger, but those obligations may be satisfied only out of property of the entity; and

(3) except as otherwise provided in Section 306, all obligations of the surviving entity incurred after the merger takes effect, but those obligations may be satisfied only out of property of the entity if the partner is a limited partner.

(d) If the obligations incurred before the merger by a party to the merger are not satisfied out of the property of the surviving partnership or limited partnership, the general partners of that party immediately before the effective date of the merger shall contribute the amount necessary to satisfy that party's obligations to the surviving entity, in the manner provided in Section 807 or in the [Limited Partnership Act] of the jurisdiction in which the party was formed, as the case may be, as if the merged party were dissolved.

(e) A partner of a party to a merger who does not become a partner of the surviving partnership or limited partnership is dissociated from the entity, of which that partner was a partner, as of the date the merger takes effect. The surviving entity shall cause the partner's interest in the entity to be purchased under Section 701 or another statute specifically applicable to that partner's interest with respect to a merger. The surviving entity is bound under Section 702 by an act of a general partner dissociated under this subsection, and the partner is liable under Section 703 for transactions entered into by the surviving entity after the merger takes effect.

SECTION 907. *Statement of Merger.*

(a) After a merger, the surviving partnership or limited partnership may file a statement that one or more partnerships or limited partnerships have merged into the surviving entity.

(b) A statement of merger must contain:

(1) the name of each partnership or limited partnership that is a party to the merger;

(2) the name of the surviving entity into which the other partnerships or limited partnership were merged;

(3) the street address of the surviving entity's chief executive office and of an office in this State, if any; and

(4) whether the surviving entity is a partnership or a limited partnership.

(c) Except as otherwise provided in subsection (d), for the purposes of Section 302, property of the surviving partnership or limited partnership which before the merger was held in the name of another party to the merger is property held in the name of the surviving entity upon filing a statement of merger.

(d) For the purposes of Section 302, real property of the surviving partnership or limited partnership which before the merger was held in the name of another party to the merger is property held in the name of the surviving entity upon recording a certified copy of the statement of merger in the office for recording transfers of that real property.

(e) A filed and, if appropriate, recorded statement of merger, executed and declared to be accurate pursuant to Section 105(c), stating the name of a partnership or limited partnership that is a party to the merger in whose name property was held before the merger and the name of the surviving entity, but not containing all of the other information required by subsection (b), operates with respect to the partnerships or limited partnerships named to the extent provided in subsections (c) and (d).

SECTION 908. *Nonexclusive.* This [article] is not exclusive. Partnerships or limited partnerships may be converted or merged in any other manner provided by law.

[ARTICLE] 10
LIMITED LIABILITY PARTNERSHIP

SECTION 1001. *Statement of Qualification.*

(a) A partnership may become a limited liability partnership pursuant to this section.

(b) The terms and conditions on which a partnership becomes a limited liability partnership must be approved by the vote necessary to amend the partnership agreement except, in the case of a partnership agreement that expressly considers obligations to contribute to the partnership, the vote necessary to amend those provisions.

(c) After the approval required by subsection (b), a partnership may become a limited liability partnership by filing a statement of qualification. The statement must contain:

(1) the name of the partnership;

(2) the street address of the partnership's chief executive office and, if different, the street address of an office in this State, if any;

(3) if the partnership does not have an office in this State, the name and street address of the partnership's agent for service of process;

(4) a statement that the partnership elects to be a limited liability partnership; and

(5) a deferred effective date, if any.

(d) The agent of a limited liability partnership for service of process must be an individual who is a resident of this State or other person authorized to do business in this State.

(e) The status of a partnership as a limited-liability partnership is effective on the later of the filing of the statement or a date specified in the statement. The status remains effective, regardless of changes in the partnership, until it is canceled pursuant to Section 105(d) or revoked pursuant to Section 1003.

(f) The status of a partnership as a limited liability partnership and the liability of its partners is not affected by errors or later changes in the information required to be contained in the statement of qualification under subsection (c).

(g) The filing of a statement of qualification establishes that a partnership has satisfied all conditions precedent to the qualification of the partnership as a limited liability partnership.

(h) An amendment or cancellation of a statement of qualification is effective when it is filed or on a deferred effective date specified in the amendment or cancellation.

SECTION 1002. *Name.* The name of a limited liability partnership must end with "Registered Limited Liability Partnership", "Limited Liability Partnership", "R.L.L.P.", "L.L.P.", "RLLP," or "LLP".

SECTION 1003. *Annual Report.*

(a) A limited liability partnership, and a foreign limited liability partnership authorized to transact business in this State, shall file an annual report in the office of the [Secretary of State] which contains:

(1) the name of the limited liability partnership and the State or other jurisdiction under whose laws the foreign limited liability partnership is formed;

(2) the street address of the partnership's chief executive office and, if different, the street address of an office of the partnership in this State, if any; and

(3) if the partnership does not have an office in this State, the name and street address of the partnership's current agent for service of process.

(b) An annual report must be filed between [January 1 and April 1] of each year following the calendar year in which a partnership files a statement of qualification or a foreign partnership becomes authorized to transact business in this State.

(c) The [Secretary of State] may revoke the statement of qualification of a partnership that fails to file an annual report when due or pay the required filing fee. To do so, the [Secretary of State] shall provide the partnership at least 60 days' written notice of intent to revoke the statement. The notice must be mailed to the partnership at its chief executive office set forth in the last filed statement of qualification or annual report. The notice must specify the annual report that has not been filed, the fee that has not been paid, and the effective date of the revocation. The revocation is not effective if the annual report is filed and the fee is paid before the effective date of the revocation.

(d) A revocation under subsection (c) only affects a partnership's status as a limited liability partnership and is not an event of dissolution of the partnership.

(e) A partnership whose statement of qualification has been revoked may apply to the [Secretary of State] for reinstatement within two years after the effective date of the revocation. The application must state:

(1) the name of the partnership and the effective date of the revocation; and

(2) that the ground for revocation either did not exist or has been corrected.

(f) A reinstatement under subsection (e) relates back to and takes effect as of the effective date of the revocation, and the partnership's status as a limited liability partnership continues as if the revocation had never occurred.

[ARTICLE] 11
FOREIGN LIMITED LIABILITY PARTNERSHIP

SECTION 1101. *Law Governing Foreign Limited Liability Partnership.*

(a) The law under which a foreign limited liability partnership is formed governs relations among the partners and between the partners and the partnership and the liability of partners for obligations of the partnership.

(b) A foreign limited liability partnership may not be denied a statement of foreign qualification by reason of any difference between the law under which the partnership was formed and the law of this State.

(c) A statement of foreign qualification does not authorize a foreign limited liability partnership to engage in any business or exercise any power that a partnership may not engage in or exercise in this State as a limited liability partnership.

SECTION 1102. *Statement of Foreign Qualification.*

(a) Before transacting business in this State, a foreign limited liability partnership must file a statement of foreign qualification. The statement must contain:

(1) the name of the foreign limited liability partnership which satisfies the requirements of the State or other jurisdiction under whose law it is formed and ends with "Registered Limited Liability Partnership", "Limited Liability Partnership", "R.L.L.P.", "L.L.P.", "RLLP," or "LLP";

(2) the street address of the partnership's chief executive office and, if different, the street address of an office of the partnership in this State, if any;

(3) if there is no office of the partnership in this State, the name and street address of the partnership's agent for service of process; and

(4) a deferred effective date, if any.

(b) The agent of a foreign limited liability company for service of process must be an individual who is a resident of this State or other person authorized to do business in this State.

(c) The status of a partnership as a foreign limited liability partnership is effective on the later of the filing of the statement of foreign qualification or a date specified in the statement. The status remains effective, regardless of changes in the partnership, until it is canceled pursuant to Section 105(d) or revoked pursuant to Section 1003.

(d) An amendment or cancellation of a statement of foreign qualification is effective when it is filed or on a deferred effective date specified in the amendment or cancellation.

SECTION 1103. *Effect of Failure to Qualify.*

(a) A foreign limited liability partnership transacting business in this State may not maintain an action or proceeding in this State unless it has in effect a statement of foreign qualification.

(b) The failure of a foreign limited liability partnership to have in effect a statement of foreign qualification does not impair the validity of a contract or act of the foreign limited liability partnership or preclude it from defending an action or proceeding in this State.

(c) A limitation on personal liability of a partner is not waived solely by transacting business in this State without a statement of foreign qualification.

(d) If a foreign limited liability partnership transacts business in this State without a statement of foreign qualification, the [Secretary of State] is its agent for service of process with respect to a right of action arising out of the transaction of business in this State.

SECTION 1104. *Activities Not Constituting Transacting Business.*

(a) Activities of a foreign limited liability partnership which do not constitute transacting business for the purpose of this [article] include:

(1) maintaining, defending, or settling an action or proceeding;

(2) holding meetings of its partners or carrying on any other activity concerning its internal affairs;

(3) maintaining bank accounts;

(4) maintaining offices or agencies for the transfer, exchange, and registration of the partnership's own securities or maintaining trustees or depositories with respect to those securities;

(5) selling through independent contractors;

(6) soliciting or obtaining orders, whether by mail or through employees or agents or otherwise, if the orders require acceptance outside this State before they become contracts;

(7) creating or acquiring indebtedness, with or without a mortgage, or other security interest in property;

(8) collecting debts or foreclosing mortgages or other security interests in property securing the debts, and holding, protecting, and maintaining property so acquired;

(9) conducting an isolated transaction that is completed within 30 days and is not one in the course of similar transactions; and

(10) transacting business in interstate commerce.

(b) For purposes of this [article], the ownership in this State of income-producing real property or tangible personal property, other than property excluded under subsection (a), constitutes transacting business in this State.

(c) This section does not apply in determining the contacts or activities that may subject a foreign limited liability partnership to service of process, taxation, or regulation under any other law of this State.

SECTION 1105. *Action by [Attorney General].*
The [Attorney General] may maintain an action to restrain a foreign limited liability partnership from transacting business in this State in violation of this [article].

[ARTICLE] 12
MISCELLANEOUS PROVISIONS

SECTION 1201. *Uniformity of Application and Construction.* This [Act] shall be applied and construed to effectuate its general purpose to make uniform the law with respect to the subject of this [Act] among States enacting it.

SECTION 1202. *Short Title.* This [Act] may be cited as the Uniform Partnership Act (1997).

SECTION 1203. *Severability Clause.* If any provision of this [Act] or its application to any person or circumstance is held invalid, the invalidity does not affect other provisions or applications of this [Act] which can be given effect without the invalid provision or application, and to this end the provisions of this [Act] are severable.

SECTION 1204. *Effective Date.* This [Act] takes effect _____.

SECTION 1205. *Repeals.* Effective January 1, 199___, the following acts and parts of acts are repealed: [the State Partnership Act as amended and in effect immediately before the effective date of this [Act]].

SECTION 1206. *Applicability.*

(a) Before January 1, 199___, this [Act] governs only a partnership formed:

(1) after the effective date of this [Act], except a partnership that is continuing the business of a dissolved partnership under [Section 41 of the superseded Uniform Partnership Act]; and

(2) before the effective date of this [Act], that elects, as provided by subsection (c), to be governed by this [Act].

(b) On and after January 1, 199___, this [Act] governs all partnerships.

(c) Before January 1, 199___, a partnership voluntarily may elect, in the manner provided in its partnership agreement or by law for amending the partnership agreement, to be governed by this [Act]. The provisions of this [Act] relating to the liability of the partnership's partners to third parties apply to limit those partners' liability to a third party who had done business with the partnership within one year before the partnership's election to be governed by this [Act] only if the third party knows or has received a notification of the partnership's election to be governed by this [Act].

SECTION 1207. *Savings Clause.* This [Act] does not affect an action or proceeding commenced or right accrued before this [Act] takes effect.

SECTION 1208. *Effective Date.* These [Amendments] take effect _____.

SECTION 1209. *Repeals.* Effective January 1, 199___, the following acts and parts of acts are repealed: [the Limited Liability Partnership amendments to the State Partnership Act as amended and in effect immediately before the effective date of these [Amendments]].

SECTION 1210. *Applicability.*

(a) Before January 1, 199___, these [Amendments] govern only a limited liability partnership formed:

(1) on or after the effective date of these [Amendments], unless that partnership is continuing the business of a dissolved limited liability partnership; and

(2) before the effective date of these [Amendments], that elects, as provided by subsection (c), to be governed by these [Amendments].

(b) On and after January 1, 199___, these [Amendments] govern all partnerships.

(c) Before January 1, 199___, a partnership voluntarily may elect, in the manner provided in its partnership agreement or by law for amending the partnership agreement, to be governed by these [Amendments]. The provisions of these [Amendments] relating to the liability of the partnership's partners to third parties apply to limit those partners' liability to a third party who had done business with the partnership within one year before the partnership's election to be governed by these [Amendments], only if the third party knows or has received a notification of the partnership's election to be governed by these [Amendments].

(d) The existing provisions for execution and filing a statement of qualification of a limited liability partnership continue until either the limited liability partnership elects to have this [Act] apply or January 1, 199___.

SECTION 1211. *Savings Clause.* These [Amendments] do not affect an action or proceeding commenced or right accrued before these [Amendments] take effect.

APPENDIX G

Uniform Limited Partnership Act (1976) With 1985 Amendments

The Uniform Limited Partnership Act has been reprinted through the permission of the National Conference of Commissioners on Uniform State Laws, 211 East Ontario Street, Suite 1300, Chicago, IL 60611; **www.nccusl.org**

ARTICLE 1
General Provisions

§ 101. Definitions.
§ 102. Name.
§ 103. Reservation of Name.
§ 104. Specified Office and Agent.
§ 105. Records to be Kept.
§ 106. Nature of Business.
§ 107. Business Transactions of Partner with Partnership.

ARTICLE 2
Formation; Certificate of Limited Partnership

§ 201. Certificate of Limited Partnership.
§ 202. Amendment to Certificate.
§ 203. Cancellation of Certificate.
§ 204. Execution of Certificates.
§ 205. Execution by Judicial Act.
§ 206. Filing in Office of Secretary of State.
§ 207. Liability for False Statement in Certificate.
§ 208. Scope of Notice.
§ 209. Delivery of Certificates to Limited Partners.

ARTICLE 3
Limited Partners

§ 301. Admission of Limited Partners.
§ 302. Voting.
§ 303. Liability to Third Parties.
§ 304. Person Erroneously Believing Himself [or Herself] Limited Partner.
§ 305. Information.

ARTICLE 4
General Partners

§ 401. Admission of Additional General Partners.
§ 402. Events of Withdrawal.
§ 403. General Powers and Liabilities.
§ 404. Contributions by General Partner.
§ 405. Voting.

ARTICLE 5
Finance

§ 501. Form of Contribution.
§ 502. Liability for Contribution.
§ 503. Sharing of Profits and Losses.
§ 504. Sharing of Distributions.

ARTICLE 6
Distributions and Withdrawal

§ 601. Interim Distributions.
§ 602. Withdrawal of General Partner.
§ 603. Withdrawal of Limited Partner.
§ 604. Distribution Upon Withdrawal.
§ 605. Distribution in Kind.
§ 606. Right to Distribution.
§ 607. Limitations on Distribution.
§ 608. Liability Upon Return of Contribution.

ARTICLE 7
Assignment of Partnership Interests

§ 701. Nature of Partnership Interest.
§ 702. Assignment of Partnership Interest.

§ 703. Rights of Creditor.

§ 704. Right of Assignee to Become Limited Partner.

§ 705. Power of Estate of Deceased or Incompetent Partner.

ARTICLE 8
Dissolution

§ 801. Nonjudicial Dissolution.

§ 802. Judicial Dissolution.

§ 803. Winding Up.

§ 804. Distribution of Assets.

ARTICLE 9
Foreign Limited Partnerships

§ 901. Law Governing.

§ 902. Registration.

§ 903. Issuance of Registration.

§ 904. Name.

§ 905. Changes and Amendments.

§ 906. Cancellation of Registration.

§ 907. Transaction of Business Without Registration.

§ 908. Action by [Appropriate Official].

ARTICLE 10
Derivative Actions

§ 1001. Right of Action.

§ 1002. Proper Plaintiff.

§ 1003. Pleading.

§ 1004. Expenses.

ARTICLE 11
Miscellaneous

§ 1101. Construction and Application.

§ 1102. Short Title.

§ 1103. Severability.

§ 1104. Effective Date, Extended Effective Date and Repeal.

§ 1105. Rules for Cases Not Provided for in This [Act].

§ 1106. Savings Clause.

ARTICLE 1
GENERAL PROVISIONS

§ 101. Definitions

As used in this [Act], unless the context otherwise requires:

(1) "Certificate of limited partnership" means the certificate referred to in Section 201, and the certificate as amended or restated.

(2) "Contribution" means any cash, property, services rendered, or a promissory note or other binding obligation to contribute cash or property or to perform services, which a partner contributes to a limited partnership in his capacity as a partner.

(3) "Event of withdrawal of a general partner" means an event that causes a person to cease to be a general partner as provided in Section 402.

(4) "Foreign limited partnership" means a partnership formed under the laws of any state other than this State and having as partners one or more general partners and one or more limited partners.

(5) "General partner" means a person who has been admitted to a limited partnership as a general partner in accordance with the partnership agreement and named in the certificate of limited partnership as a general partner.

(6) "Limited partner" means a person who has been admitted to a limited partnership as a limited partner in accordance with the partnership agreement.

(7) "Limited partnership" and "domestic limited partnership" mean a partnership formed by two or more persons under the laws of this State and having one or more general partners and one or more limited partners.

(8) "Partner" means a limited or general partner.

(9) "Partnership agreement" means any valid agreement, written or oral, of the partners as to the affairs of a limited partnership and the conduct of its business.

(10) "Partnership interest" means a partner's share of the profits and losses of a limited partnership and the right to receive distributions of partnership assets.

(11) "Person" means a natural person, partnership, limited partnership (domestic or foreign), trust, estate, association, or corporation.

(12) "State" means a state, territory, or possession of the United States, the District of Columbia, or the Commonwealth of Puerto Rico.

Comment The definitions in this section clarify a number of uncertainties in the law existing prior to the 1976 Act, and also make certain changes in such prior law. The 1985 Act makes very few additional changes in Section 101.

Contribution: this definition makes it clear that a present contribution of services and a promise to make a future payment of cash, contribution of property or performance of services are permissible forms for a contribution. Section 502 of the 1985 Act provides that a limited partner's promise to make a contribution is enforceable only when set out in a writing signed by the limited partner. (This result is not dissimilar from that under the 1976 Act, which required all promises of future contributions to be described in the certificate of limited partnership, which was to be signed by, among others, the partners making such promises.) The property or services contributed presently or promised to be contributed in the future must be accorded a value in the partnership agreement or the partnership records required to be kept pursuant to Section 105, and, in the case of a promise, that value may determine the liability of a partner who fails to honor his agreement (Section 502). Section 3 of the 1916 Act did not permit a limited partner's contribution to be in the form of services, although that inhibition did not apply to general partners.

Foreign limited partnership: the Act only deals with foreign limited partnerships formed under the laws of another "state" of the United States (see subdivision 12 of Section 101), and any adopting state that desires to deal by statute with the status of entities formed under the laws of foreign countries must make appropriate changes throughout the Act. The exclusion of such entities from the Act was not intended to suggest that their "limited partners" should not be accorded limited liability by the courts of a state adopting the Act. That question would be resolved by the choice-of-law rules of the forum state.

General partner: this definition recognizes the separate functions of the partnership agreement and the certificate of limited partnership. The partnership agreement establishes the basic grant of management power to the persons named as general partners; but because of the passive role played by the limited partners, the separate, formal step of memorializing that grant of power in the certificate of limited partnership has been preserved to emphasize its importance and to provide notice of the identity of the partnership's general partners to persons dealing with the partnership.

Limited partner: unlike the definition of general partners, this definition provides for admission of limited partners through the partnership agreement alone and does not require identification of any limited partner in the certificate of limited partnership (Section 201). Under the 1916 and the 1976 Acts, being named as a limited partner in the certificate of limited partnership was a statutory requirement and, in most if not all cases, probably also a prerequisite to limited partner status. By eliminating the requirement that the certificate of limited partnership contain the name, address, and capital contribution of each limited partner, the 1985 Act all but eliminates any risk that a person intended to be a limited partner may be exposed to liability as a general partner as a result of the inadvertent omission of any of that information from the certificate of limited partnership, and also dispenses with the need to amend the certificate of limited partnership upon the admission or withdrawal of, transfer of an interest by, or change in the address or capital contribution of, any limited partner.

Partnership agreement: the 1916 Act did not refer to the partnership agreement, assuming that all important matters affecting limited partners would be set forth in the certificate of limited partnership. Under modern practice, however, it has been common for the partners to enter into a comprehensive partnership agreement, only part of which was required to be included or summarized in the certificate of limited partnership. As reflected in Section 201 of the 1985 Act, the certificate of limited partnership is confined principally to matters respecting the partnership itself and the identity of general partners, and other important issues are left to the partnership agreement. Most of the information formerly provided by, but no longer required to be included in, the certificate of limited partnership is now required to be kept in the partnership records (Section 105).

Partnership interest: this definition first appeared in the 1976 Act and is intended to define what it is that is transferred when a partnership interest is assigned.

§ 102. Name

The name of each limited partnership as set forth in its certificate of limited partnership:

(1) shall contain without abbreviation the words "limited partnership";

(2) may not contain the name of a limited partner unless (i) it is also the name of a general partner or the corporate name of a corporate general partner, or (ii) the business of the limited partnership had been carried on under that name before the admission of that limited partner;

(3) may not be the same as, or deceptively similar to, the name of any corporation or limited partnership organized under the laws of this State or licensed or registered as a foreign corporation or limited partnership in this State; and

(4) may not contain the following words [here insert prohibited words].

Comment Subdivision (2) of Section 102 has been carried over from Section 5 of the 1916 Act with certain editorial changes. The remainder of Section 102 first appeared in the 1976 Act and primarily reflects the intention to integrate the registration of limited partnership names with that of corporate names. Accordingly, Section 201 provides for central, state-wide filing of certificates of limited partnership, and subdivisions (3) and (4) of Section 102 contain standards to be applied by the filing officer in determining whether the certificate should be filed. Subdivision (1) requires that the proper name of a limited partnership contain the words "limited partnership" in full. Subdivision (3) of the 1976 Act has been deleted, to reflect the deletion from Section 201 of any requirement that the certificate of limited partnership describe the partnership's purposes or the character of its business.

§ 103. Reservation of Name

(a) The exclusive right to the use of a name may be reserved by:

(1) any person intending to organize a limited partnership under this [Act] and to adopt that name;

(2) any domestic limited partnership or any foreign limited partnership registered in this State which, in either case, intends to adopt that name;

(3) any foreign limited partnership intending to register in this State and adopt that name; and

(4) any person intending to organize a foreign limited partnership and intending to have it register in this State and adopt that name.

(b) The reservation shall be made by filing with the Secretary of State an application, executed by the applicant, to reserve a specified name. If the Secretary of State finds that the name is available for use by a domestic or foreign limited partnership, he [or she] shall reserve the name for the exclusive use of the applicant for a period of 120 days. Once having so reserved a name, the same applicant may not again reserve the same name until more than 60 days after the expiration of the last 120-day period for which that applicant reserved that name. The right to the exclusive use of a reserved name may be transferred to any other person by filing in the office of the Secretary of State a notice of the transfer, executed by the applicant for whom the name was reserved and specifying the name and address of the transferee.

Comment Section 103 first appeared in the 1976 Act. The 1916 Act did not provide for registration of names.

§ 104. Specified Office and Agent

Each limited partnership shall continuously maintain in this State:

(1) an office, which may but need not be a place of its business in this State, at which shall be kept the records required by Section 105 to be maintained; and

(2) an agent for service of process on the limited partnership, which agent must be an individual resident of this State, a domestic corporation, or a foreign corporation authorized to do business in this State.

Comment Section 104 first appeared in the 1976 Act. It requires that a limited partnership have certain minimum contacts with its State of organization, i.e., an office at which the constitutive documents and basic financial information is kept and an agent for service of process.

§ 105. Records to be Kept

(a)   Each limited partnership shall keep at the office referred to in Section 104(1) the following:

(1)   a current list of the full name and last known business address of each partner, separately identifying the general partners (in alphabetical order) and the limited partners (in alphabetical order);

(2)   a copy of the certificate of limited partnership and all certificates of amendment thereto, together with executed copies of any powers of attorney pursuant to which any certificate has been executed;

(3)   copies of the limited partnership's federal, state and local income tax returns and reports, if any, for the three most recent years;

(4)   copies of any then effective written partnership agreements and of any financial statements of the limited partnership for the three most recent years; and

(5)   unless contained in a written partnership agreement, a writing setting out:

(i)   the amount of cash and a description and statement of the agreed value of the other property or services contributed by each partner and which each partner has agreed to contribute;

(ii)   the times at which or events on the happening of which any additional contributions agreed to be made by each partner are to be made;

(iii)   any right of a partner to receive, or of a general partner to make, distributions to a partner which include a return of all or any part of the partner's contribution; and

(iv)   any events upon the happening of which the limited partnership is to be dissolved and its affairs wound up.

(b)   Records kept under this section are subject to inspection and copying at the reasonable request and at the expense of any partner during ordinary business hours.

Comment Section 105 first appeared in the 1976 Act. In view of the passive nature of the limited partner's position, it has been widely felt that limited partners are entitled to access to certain basic documents and information, including the certificate of limited partnership, any partnership agreement and a writing setting out certain important matters which, under the 1916 and 1976 Acts, were required to be set out in the certificate of limited partnership. In view of the great diversity among limited partnerships, it was thought inappropriate to require a standard form of financial report, and Section 105 does no more than require retention of tax returns and any other financial statements that are prepared. The names and addresses of the general partners are made available to the general public in the certificate of limited partnership.

§ 106. Nature of Business

A limited partnership may carry on any business that a partnership without limited partners may carry on except [here designate prohibited activities].

Comment Section 106 is identical to Section 3 of the 1916 Act. Many states require that certain regulated industries, such as banking, may be carried on only by entities organized pursuant to special statutes, and it is contemplated that the prohibited activities would be confined to the matters covered by those statutes.

§ 107. Business Transactions of Partner with Partnership

Except as provided in the partnership agreement, a partner may lend money to and transact other business with the limited partnership and, subject to other applicable law, has the same rights and obligations with respect thereto as a person who is not a partner.

Comment Section 107 makes a number of important changes in Section 13 of the 1916 Act. Section 13, in effect, created a special fraudulent conveyance provision applicable to the making of secured loans by limited partners and the repayment by limited partnerships of loans from limited partners. Section 107 leaves that question to a state's general fraudulent conveyance statute. In addition, Section 107 eliminates the prohibition in Section 13 against a general partner's sharing pro rata with general creditors in the case of an unsecured loan. Of course, other doctrines developed under bankruptcy and insolvency laws may require the subordination of loans by partners under appropriate circumstances.

ARTICLE 2
FORMATION; CERTIFICATE OF
LIMITED PARTNERSHIP

§ 201. Certificate of Limited Partnership

(a)   In order to form a limited partnership, a certificate of limited partnership must be executed and filed in the office of the Secretary of State. The certificate shall set forth:

(1)   the name of the limited partnership;

(2)   the address of the office and the name and address of the agent for service of process required to be maintained by Section 104;

(3)   the name and the business address of each general partner;

(4)   the latest date upon which the limited partnership is to dissolve; and

(5)   any other matters the general partners determine to include therein.

(b)   A limited partnership is formed at the time of the filing of the certificate of limited partnership in the office of the Secretary of State or at any later time specified in the certificate of limited partnership if, in either case, there has been substantial compliance with the requirements of this section.

Comment The 1985 Act requires far fewer matters to be set forth in the certificate of limited partnership than did Section 2 of the 1916 Act and Section 201 of the 1976 Act. This is in recognition of the fact that the partnership agreement, not the certificate of limited partnership, has become the authoritative and comprehensive document for most limited partnerships, and that creditors and potential creditors of the partnership do and should refer to the partnership agreement and to other information furnished to them directly by the partnership and by others, not to the certificate of limited partnership, to obtain facts concerning the capital and finances of the partnership and other matters of concern. Subparagraph (b), which is based upon the 1916 Act, has been retained to make it clear that existence of the limited partnership depends only upon compliance with this section. Its continued existence is not dependent upon compliance with other provisions of this Act.

§ 202. Amendment to Certificate

(a)   A certificate of limited partnership is amended by filing a certificate of amendment thereto in the office of the Secretary of State. The certificate shall set forth:

(1)   the name of the limited partnership;

(2)   the date of filing the certificate; and

(3)   the amendment to the certificate.

(b)   Within 30 days after the happening of any of the following events, an amendment to a certificate of limited partnership reflecting the occurrence of the event or events shall be filed:

(1)   the admission of a new general partner;

(2)   the withdrawal of a general partner; or

(3)   the continuation of the business under Section 801 after an event of withdrawal of a general partner.

(c)   A general partner who becomes aware that any statement in a certificate of limited partnership was false when made or that any arrangements or other facts described have changed, making the certificate inaccurate in any respect, shall promptly amend the certificate.

(d)   A certificate of limited partnership may be amended at any time for any other proper purpose the general partners determine.

(e)   No person has any liability because an amendment to a certificate of limited partnership has not been filed to reflect the occurrence of any event referred to in subsection (b) of this section if the amendment is filed within the 30-day period specified in subsection (b).

(f)   A restated certificate of limited partnership may be executed and filed in the same manner as a certificate of amendment.

Comment Section 202 of the 1976 Act made substantial changes in Section 24 of the 1916 Act. Further changes in this section are made by the 1985 Act. Paragraph (b) lists the basic events—the addition or withdrawal of a general partner—that are so central to the function of the certificate of limited partnership that they require prompt amendment. With the elimination of the requirement that the certificate of limited partnership include the names of all limited partners and the amount and character of all capital contributions, the requirement of the 1916 and 1976 Acts that the certificate be amended upon the admission or withdrawal of limited partners or on any change in the partnership capital must also be eliminated. This change should greatly reduce the frequency and complexity of amendments to the certificate of limited partnership. Paragraph (c) makes it clear, as it was not clear under Section 24(2)(g) of the 1916 Act, that the certificate of limited partnership is intended to be an accurate description of the facts to which it relates at all times and does not speak merely as of the date it is executed.

Paragraph (e) provides a "safe harbor" against claims of creditors or others who assert that they have been misled by the failure to amend the certificate of limited partnership to reflect changes in any of the important facts referred to in paragraph (b); if the certificate of limited partnership is amended within 30 days of the occurrence of the event, no creditor or other person can recover for damages sustained during the interim. Additional protection is afforded by the provisions of Section 304. The elimination of the requirement that the certificate of limited partnership identify all limited partners and their respective capital contributions may have rendered paragraph (e) an obsolete and unnecessary vestige. The principal, if not the sole, purpose of the paragraph (e) in the 1976 Act was to protect limited partners newly admitted to a partnership from being held liable as general partners when an amendment to the certificate identifying them as limited partners and describing their contributions was not filed contemporaneously with their admission to the partnership. Such liability cannot arise under the 1985 Act because such information is not required to be stated in the certificate. Nevertheless, the 1985 Act retains paragraph (e) because it is protective of partners, shielding them from liability to the extent its provisions apply, and does not create or impose any liability.

Paragraph (f) is added in the 1985 Act to provide explicit statutory recognition of the common practice of restating an amended certificate of limited partnership. While a limited partnership seeking to amend its certificate of limited partnership may do so by recording a restated certificate which incorporates the amendment, that is by no means the only purpose or function of a restated certificate, which may be filed for the sole purpose of restating in a single integrated instrument all the provisions of a limited partnership's certificate of limited partnership which are then in effect.

§ 203. Cancellation of Certificate

A certificate of limited partnership shall be cancelled upon the dissolution and the commencement of winding up of the partnership or at any other time there are no limited partners. A certificate of cancellation shall be filed in the office of the Secretary of State and set forth:

(1)   the name of the limited partnership;

(2)   the date of filing of its certificate of limited partnership;

(3)   the reason for filing the certificate of cancellation;

(4)   the effective date (which shall be a date certain) of cancellation if it is not to be effective upon the filing of the certificate; and

(5)   any other information the general partners filing the certificate determine.

Comment Section 203 changes Section 24 of the 1916 Act by making it clear that the certificate of cancellation should be filed upon the commencement of winding up of the limited partnership. Section 24 provided for cancellation "when the partnership is dissolved."

§ 204. Execution of Certificates

(a)   Each certificate required by this Article to be filed in the office of the Secretary of State shall be executed in the following manner:

(1)   an original certificate of limited partnership must be signed by all general partners;

(2)   a certificate of amendment must be signed by at least one general partner and by each other general partner designated in the certificate as a new general partner; and

(3)   a certificate of cancellation must be signed by all general partners.

(b)   Any person may sign a certificate by an attorney-in-fact, but a power of attorney to sign a certificate relating to the admission of a general partner must specifically describe the admission.

(c)   The execution of a certificate by a general partner constitutes an affirmation under the penalties of perjury that the facts stated therein are true.

Comment Section 204 collects in one place the formal requirements for the execution of certificates which were set forth in Section 2 and 25 of the 1916 Act. Those sections required that each certificate be signed by all partners, and there developed an unnecessarily cumbersome practice of having each limited partner sign powers of attorney to authorize the general partners to execute certificates of amendment on their behalf. The 1976 Act, while simplifying the execution requirements, nevertheless required that an original certificate of limited partnership be signed by all partners and a certificate of amendment by all new partners being admitted to the limited partnership. However the certificate of limited partnership is no longer required to include the name or capital contribution of any limited partner. Therefore, while the 1985 Act still requires all general partners to sign the original certificate of limited partnership, no limited partner is required to sign any certificate. Certificates of amendment are required to be signed by only one general partner, and all general partners must sign certificates of cancellation. The requirement in the 1916 Act that all certificates be sworn was deleted in the 1976 and 1985 Acts as potentially an unfair trap for the unwary (see, e.g., Wisniewski v. Johnson, 223 Va. 141, 286 S.E.2d 223 [1982]); in its place, paragraph (c) now provides, as a matter of law, that the execution of a certificate by a general partner subjects him to the penalties of perjury for inaccuracies in the certificate.

§ 205. Execution by Judicial Act

If a person required by Section 204 to execute any certificate fails or refuses to do so, any other person who is adversely affected by the failure or refusal may petition the [designate the appropriate court] to direct the execution of the certificate. If the court finds that it is proper for the certificate to be executed and that any person so designated has failed or refused to execute the certificate, it shall order the Secretary of State to record an appropriate certificate.

Comment Section 205 of the 1976 Act changed subdivisions (3) and (4) of Section 25 of the 1916 Act by confining the persons who have standing to seek judicial intervention to partners and to those assignees who were adversely affected by the failure or refusal of the appropriate persons to file a certificate of amendment or cancellation. Section 205 of the 1985 Act reverses that restriction, and provides that any person adversely affected by a failure or refusal to file any certificate (not only a certificate of cancellation or amendment) has standing to seek judicial intervention.

§ 206. Filing in Office of Secretary of State

(a) Two signed copies of the certificate of limited partnership and of any certificates of amendment or cancellation (or of any judicial decree of amendment or cancellation) shall be delivered to the Secretary of State. A person who executes a certificate as an agent or fiduciary need not exhibit evidence of his [or her] authority as a prerequisite to filing. Unless the Secretary of State finds that any certificate does not conform to law, upon receipt of all filing fees required by law he [or she] shall:

(1) endorse on each duplicate original the word "Filed" and the day, month, and year of the filing thereof;

(2) file one duplicate original in his [or her] office; and

(3) return the other duplicate original to the person who filed it or his [or her] representative.

(b) Upon the filing of a certificate of amendment (or judicial decree of amendment) in the office of the Secretary of State, the certificate of limited partnership shall be amended as set forth therein, and upon the effective date of a certificate of cancellation (or a judicial decree thereof), the certificate of limited partnership is cancelled.

Comment Section 206 first appeared in the 1976 Act. In addition to providing mechanics for the central filing system, the second sentence of this section does away with the requirement, formerly imposed by some local filing officers, that persons who have executed certificates under a power of attorney exhibit executed copies of the power of attorney itself. Paragraph (b) changes subdivision (5) of Section 25 of the 1916 Act by providing that certificates of cancellation are effective upon their effective date under Section 203.

§ 207. Liability for False Statement in Certificate

If any certificate of limited partnership or certificate of amendment or cancellation contains a false statement, one who suffers loss by reliance on the statement may recover damages for the loss from:

(1) any person who executes the certificate, or causes another to execute it on his behalf, and knew, and any general partner who knew or should have known, the statement to be false at the time the certificate was executed; and

(2) any general partner who thereafter knows or should have known that any arrangement or other fact described in the certificate has changed, making the statement inaccurate in any respect

within a sufficient time before the statement was relied upon reasonably to have enabled that general partner to cancel or amend the certificate, or to file a petition for its cancellation or amendment under Section 205.

Comment Section 207 changes Section 6 of the 1916 Act by providing explicitly for the liability of persons who sign a certificate as agent under a power of attorney and by confining the obligation to amend a certificate of limited partnership in light of future events to general partners.

§ 208. Scope of Notice

The fact that a certificate of limited partnership is on file in the office of the Secretary of State is notice that the partnership is a limited partnership and the persons designated therein as general partners are general partners, but it is not notice of any other fact.

Comment Section 208 first appeared in the 1976 Act, and referred to the certificate's providing constructive notice of the status as limited partners of those so identified therein. The 1985 Act's deletion of any requirement that the certificate name limited partners requires that Section 208 be modified accordingly.

By stating that the filing of a certificate of limited partnership only results in notice of the general liability of the general partners, Section 208 obviates the concern that third parties may be held to have notice of special provisions set forth in the certificate. While this section is designed to preserve by implication the limited liability of limited partners, the implicit protection provided is not intended to change any liability of a limited partner which may be created by his action or inaction under the law of estoppel, agency, fraud or the like.

§ 209. Delivery of Certificates to Limited Partners

Upon the return by the Secretary of State pursuant to Section 206 of a certificate marked "Filed," the general partners shall promptly deliver or mail a copy of the certificate of limited partnership and each certificate of amendment or cancellation to each limited partner unless the partnership agreement provides otherwise.

Comment This section first appeared in the 1976 Act.

ARTICLE 3
LIMITED PARTNERS

§ 301. Admission of Limited Partners

(a) A person becomes a limited partner:

(1) at the time the limited partnership is formed; or

(2) at any later time specified in the records of the limited partnership for becoming a limited partner.

(b) After the filing of a limited partnership's original certificate of limited partnership, a person may be admitted as an additional limited partner:

(1) in the case of a person acquiring a partnership interest directly from the limited partnership, upon compliance with the partnership agreement or, if the partnership agreement does not so provide, upon the written consent of all partners; and

(2) in the case of an assignee of a partnership interest of a partner who has the power, as provided in Section 704, to grant the assignee the right to become a limited partner, upon the exercise of that power and compliance with any conditions limiting the grant or exercise of the power.

Comment Section 301(a) is new; no counterpart was found in the 1916 or 1976 Acts. This section imposes on the partnership an obligation to maintain in its records the date each limited partner becomes a limited partner. Under the 1976 Act, one could not become a limited partner until an appropriate certificate reflecting his status as such was filed with the Secretary of State. Because the 1985 Act eliminates the need to name limited partners in the certificate of limited partnership, an alternative mechanism had to be established to evidence the fact and date of a limited partner's admission. The partnership records required to be maintained under Section 105 now serve that function, subject to the limitation that no person may become a limited partner before the partnership is formed (Section 201(b)).

Subdivision (1) of Section 301(b) adds to Section 8 of the 1916 Act an explicit recognition of the fact that unanimous consent of all partners is required for admission of new limited partners unless the partnership agreement provides otherwise. Subdivision (2) is derived from Section 19 of the 1916

Act but abandons the former terminology of "substituted limited partner."

§ 302. Voting

Subject to Section 303, the partnership agreement may grant to all or a specified group of the limited partners the right to vote (on a per capita or other basis) upon any matter.

Comment Section 302 first appeared in the 1976 Act, and must be read together with subdivision (b)(6) of Section 303. Although the 1916 Act did not speak specifically of the voting powers of limited partners, it was not uncommon for partnership agreements to grant such powers to limited partners. Section 302 is designed only to make it clear that the partnership agreement may grant such power to limited partners. If such powers are granted to limited partners beyond the "safe harbor" of subdivision (6) or (8) of Section 303(b), a court may (but of course need not) hold that, under the circumstances, the limited partners have participated in "control of the business" within the meaning of Section 303(a). Section 303(c) makes clear that the exercise of powers beyond the ambit of Section 303(b) is not ipso facto to be taken as taking part in the control of the business.

§ 303. Liability to Third Parties

(a)   Except as provided in subsection (d), a limited partner is not liable for the obligations of a limited partnership unless he [or she] is also a general partner or, in addition to the exercise of his [or her] rights and powers as a limited partner, he [or she] participates in the control of the business. However, if the limited partner participates in the control of the business, he [or she] is liable only to persons who transact business with the limited partnership reasonably believing, based upon the limited partner's conduct, that the limited partner is a general partner.

(b)   A limited partner does not participate in the control of the business within the meaning of subsection (a) solely by doing one or more of the following:

(1) being a contractor for or an agent or employee of the limited partnership or of a general partner or being an officer, director, or shareholder of a general partner that is a corporation;

(2)   consulting with and advising a general partner with respect to the business of the limited partnership;

(3)   acting as surety for the limited partnership or guaranteeing or assuming one or more specific obligations of the limited partnership;

(4)   taking any action required or permitted by law to bring or pursue a derivative action in the right of the limited partnership;

(5)   requesting or attending a meeting of partners;

(6)   proposing, approving, or disapproving, by voting or otherwise, one of more of the following matters:

(i) the dissolution and winding up of the limited partnership;

(ii) the sale, exchange, lease, mortgage, pledge, or other transfer of all or substantially all of the assets of the limited partnership;

(iii) the incurrence of indebtedness by the limited partnership other than in the ordinary course of its business;

(iv) a change in the nature of the business;

(v) the admission or removal of a general partner;

(vi) the admission or removal of a limited partner;

(vii) a transaction involving an actual or potential conflict of interest between a general partner and the limited partnership or the limited partners;

(viii) an amendment to the partnership agreement or certificate of limited partnership; or

(ix) matters related to the business of the limited partnership not otherwise enumerated in this subsection (b), which the partnership agreement states in writing may be subject to the approval or disapproval of limited partners;

(7)   winding up the limited partnership pursuant to Section 803; or

(8)   exercising any right or power permitted to limited partners under this [Act] and not specifically enumerated in this subsection (b).

(c)   The enumeration in subsection (b) does not mean that the possession or exercise of any other powers by a limited partner constitutes participation by him [or her] in the business of the limited partnership.

(d)   A limited partner who knowingly permits his [or her] name to be used in the name of the limited partnership, except under circumstances permitted by Section 102(2), is liable to creditors who extend credit to the limited partnership without actual knowledge that the limited partner is not a general partner.

Comment   Section 303 makes several important changes in Section 7 of the 1916 Act. The first sentence of Section 303(a) differs from the text of Section 7 of the 1916 Act in that it speaks of participating (rather than taking part) in the control of the business; this was done for the sake of consistency with the second sentence of Section 303(a), not to change the meaning of the text. It is intended that judicial decisions interpreting the phrase "takes part in the control of the business" under the prior uniform law will remain applicable to the extent that a different result is not called for by other provisions of Section 303 and other provisions of the Act. The second sentence of Section 303(a) reflects a wholly new concept in the 1976 Act that has been further modified in the 1985 Act. It was adopted partly because of the difficulty of determining when the "control" line has been overstepped, but also (and more importantly) because of a determination that it is not sound public policy to hold a limited partner who is not also a general partner liable for the obligations of the partnership except to persons who have done business with the limited partnership reasonably believing, based on the limited partner's conduct, that he is a general partner. Paragraph (b) is intended to provide a "safe harbor" by enumerating certain activities which a limited partner may carry on for the partnership without being deemed to have taken part in control of the business. This "safe harbor" list has been expanded beyond that set out in the 1976 Act to reflect case law and statutory developments and more clearly to assure that limited partners are not subjected to general liability where such liability is inappropriate. Paragraph (d) is derived from Section 5 of the 1916 Act, but adds a condition to the limited partner's liability the requirement that a limited partner must have knowingly permitted his name to be used in the name of the limited partnership.

§ 304.   Person Erroneously Believing Himself [or Herself] Limited Partner

(a)   Except as provided in subsection (b), a person who makes a contribution to a business enterprise and erroneously but in good faith believes that he [or she] has become a limited partner in the enterprise is not a general partner in the enterprise and is not bound by its obligations by reason of making the contribution, receiving distributions from the enterprise, or exercising any rights of a limited partner, if, on ascertaining the mistake, he [or she]:

(1)   causes an appropriate certificate of limited partnership or a certificate of amendment to be executed and filed; or

(2)   withdraws from future equity participation in the enterprise by executing and filing in the office of the Secretary of State a certificate declaring withdrawal under this section.

(b)   A person who makes a contribution of the kind described in subsection (a) is liable as a general partner to any third party who transacts business with the enterprise (i) before the person withdraws and an appropriate certificate is filed to show withdrawal, or (ii) before an appropriate certificate is filed to show that he [or she] is not a general partner, but in either case only if the third party actually believed in good faith that the person was a general partner at the time of the transaction.

Comment   Section 304 is derived from Section 11 of the 1916 Act. The "good faith" requirement has been added in the first sentence of Section 304(a). The provisions of subdivision (2) of Section 304(a) are intended to clarify an ambiguity in the prior law by providing that a person who chooses to withdraw from the enterprise in order to protect himself from liability is not required to renounce any of his then current interest in the enterprise so long as he has no further participation as an equity participant. Paragraph (b) preserves the liability of the equity participant prior to withdrawal by such person from the limited partnership or amendment to the certificate demonstrating that such person is not a general partner to any third party who has transacted business with the person believing in good faith that he was a general partner.

Evidence strongly suggests that Section 11 of the 1916 Act and Section 304 of the 1976 Act were rarely used, and one might expect that Section

304 of the 1985 Act may never have to be used. Section 11 of the 1916 Act and Section 304 of the 1976 Act could have been used by a person who invested in a limited partnership believing he would be a limited partner but who was not identified as a limited partner in the certificate of limited partnership. However, because the 1985 Act does not require limited partners to be named in the certificate, the only situation to which Section 304 would now appear to be applicable is one in which a person intending to be a limited partner was erroneously identified as a general partner in the certificate.

§ 305. Information

Each limited partner has the right to:

(1) inspect and copy any of the partnership records required to be maintained by Section 105; and

(2) obtain from the general partners from time to time upon reasonable demand (i) true and full information regarding the state of the business and financial condition of the limited partnership, (ii) promptly after becoming available, a copy of the limited partnership's federal, state, and local income tax returns for each year, and (iii) other information regarding the affairs of the limited partnership as is just and reasonable.

Comment Section 305 changes and restates the rights of limited partners to information about the partnership formerly provided by Section 10 of the 1916 Act. Its importance has increased as a result of the 1985 Act's substituting the records of the partnership for the certificate of limited partnership as the place where certain categories of information are to be kept.

Section 305, which should be read together with Section 105(b), provides a mechanism for limited partners to obtain information about the partnership useful to them in making decisions concerning the partnership and their investments in it. Its purpose is not to provide a mechanism for competitors of the partnership or others having interests or agendas adverse to the partnership's to subvert the partnership's business. It is assumed that courts will protect limited partnerships from abuses and attempts to misuse Section 305 for improper purposes.

ARTICLE 4
GENERAL PARTNERS

§ 401. Admission of Additional General Partners

After the filing of a limited partnership's original certificate of limited partnership, additional general partners may be admitted as provided in writing in the partnership agreement or, if the partnership agreement does not provide in writing for the admission of additional general partners, with the written consent of all partners.

Comment Section 401 is derived from, but represents a significant departure from, Section 9(1)(e) of the 1916 Act and Section 401 of the 1976 Act, which required, as a condition to the admission of an additional general partner, that all limited partners consent and that such consent specifically identify the general partner involved. Section 401 of the 1985 Act provides that the written partnership agreement determines the procedure for authorizing the admission of additional general partners, and that the written consent of all partners is required only when the partnership agreement fails to address the question.

§ 402. Events of Withdrawal

Except as approved by the specific written consent of all partners at the time, a person ceases to be a general partner of a limited partnership upon the happening of any of the following events:

(1) the general partner withdraws from the limited partnership as provided in Section 602;

(2) the general partner ceases to be a member of the limited partnership as provided in Section 702;

(3) the general partner is removed as a general partner in accordance with the partnership agreement;

(4) unless otherwise provided in writing in the partnership agreement, the general partner: (i) makes an assignment for the benefit of creditors; (ii) files a voluntary petition in bankruptcy; (iii) is adjudicated a bankrupt or insolvent; (iv) files a petition or answer seeking for himself [or herself] any reorganization, arrangement, composition, readjustment, liquidation, dissolution, or similar relief under any statute, law, or regulation; (v) files an answer or other pleading admitting or failing to

contest the material allegations of a petition filed against him [or her] in any proceeding of this nature; or (vi) seeks, consents to, or acquiesces in the appointment of a trustee, receiver, or liquidator of the general partner or of all or any substantial part of his [or her] properties;

(5)   unless otherwise provided in writing in the partnership agreement, [120] days after the commencement of any proceeding against the general partner seeking reorganization, arrangement, composition, readjustment, liquidation, dissolution, or similar relief under any statute, law, or regulation, the proceeding has not been dismissed, or if within [90] days after the appointment without his [or her] consent or acquiescence of a trustee, receiver, or liquidator of the general partner or of all or any substantial part of his [or her] properties, the appointment is not vacated or stayed or within [90] days after the expiration of any such stay, the appointment is not vacated;

(6)   in the case of a general partner who is a natural person,

(i)   his [or her] death; or

(ii)   the entry of an order by a court of competent jurisdiction adjudicating him [or her] incompetent to manage his [or her] person or his [or her] estate;

(7)   in the case of a general partner who is acting as a general partner by virtue of being a trustee of a trust, the termination of the trust (but not merely the substitution of a new trustee);

(8)   in the case of a general partner that is a separate partnership, the dissolution and commencement of winding up of the separate partnership;

(9)   in the case of a general partner that is a corporation, the filing of a certificate of dissolution, or its equivalent, for the corporation or the revocation of its charter; or

(10)   in the case of an estate, the distribution by the fiduciary of the estate's entire interest in the partnership.

Comment   Section 402 expands considerably the provisions of Section 20 of the 1916 Act, which provided for dissolution in the event of the retirement, death or insanity of a general partner. Subdivisions (1), (2) and (3) recognize that the general partner's agency relationship is terminable at will, although it may result in a breach of the partnership agreement giving rise to an action for damages.

Subdivisions (4) and (5) reflect a judgment that, unless the limited partners agree otherwise, they ought to have the power to rid themselves of a general partner who is in such dire financial straits that he is the subject of proceedings under the National Bankruptcy Code or a similar provision of law. Subdivisions (6) through (10) simply elaborate on the notion of death in the case of a general partner who is not a natural person. Subdivisions (4) and (5) differ from their counterparts in the 1976 Act, reflecting the policy underlying the 1985 revision of Section 201, that the partnership agreement, not the certificate of limited partnership, is the appropriate document for setting out most provisions relating to the respective powers, rights and obligations of the partners inter se. Although the partnership agreement need not be written, the 1985 Act provides that, to protect the partners from fraud, these and certain other particularly significant provisions must be set out in a written partnership agreement to be effective for the purposes described in the Act.

§ 403. General Powers and Liabilities

(a)   Except as provided in this [Act] or in the partnership agreement, a general partner of a limited partnership has the rights and powers and is subject to the restrictions of a partner in a partnership without limited partners.

(b)   Except as provided in this [Act], a general partner of a limited partnership has the liabilities of a partner in a partnership without limited partners to persons other than the partnership and the other partners. Except as provided in this [Act] or in the partnership agreement, a general partner of a limited partnership has the liabilities of a partner in a partnership without limited partners to the partnership and to the other partners.

Comment   Section 403 is derived form Section 9(1) of the 1916 Act.

§ 404. Contributions by General Partner

A general partner of a limited partnership may make contributions to the partnership and share in the profits and losses of, and in distributions from, the limited partnership as a general partner. A general partner also may make contributions to and share in profits, losses, and distributions as a limited partner. A person who is both a general partner and a limited partner has the rights and powers, and is subject to the restrictions and liabilities, of a general partner and, except as provided in the partnership agreement, also has the powers, and is subject to the restrictions, of a limited partner to the extent of his [or her] participation in the partnership as a limited partner.

Comment Section 404 is derived from Section 12 of the 1916 Act and makes clear that the partnership agreement may provide that a general partner who is also a limited partner may exercise all of the powers of a limited partner.

§ 405. Voting

The partnership agreement may grant to all or certain identified general partners the right to vote (on a per capita or any other basis), separately or with all or any class of the limited partners, on any matter.

Comment Section 405 first appeared in the 1976 Act and is intended to make it clear that the Act does not require that the limited partners have any right to vote on matters as a separate class.

ARTICLE 5
FINANCE

§ 501. Form of Contribution

The contribution of a partner may be in cash, property, or services rendered, or a promissory note or other obligation to contribute cash or property or to perform services.

Comment As noted in the comment to Section 101, the explicit permission to make contributions of services expands Section 4 of the 1916 Act.

§ 502. Liability for Contribution

(a) A promise by a limited partner to contribute to the limited partnership is not enforceable unless set out in a writing signed by the limited partner.

(b) Except as provided in the partnership agreement, a partner is obligated to the limited partnership to perform any enforceable promise to contribute cash or property or to perform services, even if he [or she] is unable to perform because of death, disability, or any other reason. If a partner does not make the required contribution of property or services, he [or she] is obligated at the option of the limited partnership to contribute cash equal to that portion of the value, as stated in the partnership records required to be kept pursuant to

Section 105, of the stated contribution which has not been made.

(c) Unless otherwise provided in the partnership agreement, the obligation of a partner to make a contribution or return money or other property paid or distributed in violation of this [Act] may be compromised only by consent of all partners. Notwithstanding the compromise, a creditor of a limited partnership who extends credit or otherwise acts in reliance on that obligation after the partner signs a writing which reflects the obligation and before the amendment or cancellation thereof to reflect the compromise, may enforce the original obligation.

Comment Section 502(a) is new; it has no counterpart in the 1916 or 1976 Act. Because, unlike the prior uniform acts, the 1985 Act does not require that promises to contribute cash, property, or services be described in the limited partnership certificate, to protect against fraud it requires instead that such important promises be in a signed writing.

Although Section 17(1) of the 1916 Act required a partner to fulfill his promise to make contributions, the addition of contributions in the form of a promise to render services means that a partner who is unable to perform those services because of death or disability as well as because of an intentional default is required to pay the cash value of the services unless the partnership agreement provides otherwise.

Subdivision (c) is derived from, but expands upon, Section 17(3) of the 1916 Act.

§ 503. Sharing of Profits and Losses

The profits and losses of a limited partnership shall be allocated among the partners, and among classes of partners, in the manner provided in writing in the partnership agreement. If the partnership agreement does not so provide in writing, profits and losses shall be allocated on the basis of the value, as stated in the partnership records required to be kept pursuant to Section 105, of the contributions made by each partner to the extent they have been received by the partnership and have not been returned.

Comment Section 503 first appeared in the 1976 Act. The 1916 Act did not provide the basis on which partners would share profits and losses in the absence of agreement. The 1985 Act differs from its counterpart in the 1976 Act by requiring that, to be effective, the partnership agreement provisions concerning allocation of profits and losses be in writing, and by its reference to records required to be kept pursuant to Section 105, the latter reflecting the 1985 changes in Section 201.

§ 504. Sharing of Distributions

Distributions of cash or other assets of a limited partnership shall be allocated among the partners and among classes of partners in the manner provided in writing in the partnership agreement. If the partnership agreement does not so provide in writing, distributions shall be made on the basis of the value, as stated in the partnership records required to be kept pursuant to Section 105, of the contributions made by each partner to the extent they have been received by the partnership and have not been returned.

Comment   Section 504 first appeared in the 1976 Act. The 1916 Act did not provide the basis on which partners would share distributions in the absence of agreement. Section 504 also differs from its counterpart in the 1976 Act by requiring that, to be effective, the partnership agreement provisions concerning allocation of distributions be in writing, and in its reference to records required to be kept pursuant to Section 105, the latter reflecting the 1985 changes in Section 201. This section also recognizes that partners may choose to share in distributions on a basis different from that on which they share in profits and losses.

ARTICLE 6
DISTRIBUTIONS AND WITHDRAWAL

§ 601. Interim Distributions

Except as provided in this Article, a partner is entitled to receive distributions from a limited partnership before his [or her] withdrawal from the limited partnership and before the dissolution and winding up thereof to the extent and at the times or upon the happening of the events specified in the partnership agreement.

Comment   Section 601 first appeared in the 1976 Act. The 1976 Act provisions have been modified to reflect the 1985 changes made in Section 201.

§ 602. Withdrawal of General Partner

A general partner may withdraw from a limited partnership at any time by giving written notice to the other partners, but if the withdrawal violates the partnership agreement, the limited partnership may recover from the withdrawing general partner damages for breach of the partnership agreement and offset the damages against the amount otherwise distributable to him [or her].

Comment   Section 602 first appeared in the 1976 Act, but is generally derived from Section 38 of the Uniform Partnership Act.

§ 603. Withdrawal of Limited Partner

A limited partner may withdraw from a limited partnership at the time or upon the happening of events specified in writing in the partnership agreement. If the agreement does not specify in writing the time or the events upon the happening of which a limited partner may withdraw or a definite time for the dissolution and winding up of the limited partnership, a limited partner may withdraw upon not less than six months' prior written notice to each general partner at his [other] address on the books of the limited partnership at its office in this State.

Comment   Section 603 is derived from Section 16 of the 1916 Act. The 1976 Act provision has been modified to reflect the 1985 changes made in Section 201. This section additionally reflects the policy determination, also embodied in certain other sections of the 1985 Act, that to avoid fraud, agreements concerning certain matters of substantial importance to the partners will be enforceable only if in writing. If the partnership agreement does provide, in writing, whether a limited partner may withdraw and, if he may, when and on what terms and conditions, those provisions will control.

§ 604. Distribution Upon Withdrawal

Except as provided in this Article, upon withdrawal any withdrawing partner is entitled to receive any distribution to which he [or she] is entitled under the partnership agreement and, if not otherwise provided in the agreement, he [or she] is entitled to receive, within a reasonable time after withdrawal, the fair value of his [or her] interest in the limited partnership as of the date of withdrawal based upon his [or her] right to share in distributions from the limited partnership.

Comment   Section 604 first appeared in the 1976 Act. It fixes the distributive share of a withdrawing partner in the absence of an agreement among the partners.

§ 605. Distribution in Kind

Except as provided in writing in the partnership agreement, a partner, regardless of the nature of his [or her] contribution, has no right to demand and receive any distribution from a limited partnership in any form other than cash. Except as provided in writing in the partnership agreement, a partner may not be compelled to accept a distribution of any asset in kind from a limited partnership to the extent that the percentage of the asset distributed to him [or her] exceeds a percentage of that asset which is equal to the percentage in which he [or she] shares in distributions from the limited partnership.

Comment The first sentence of Section 605 is derived from Section 16(3) of the 1916 Act; it also differs from its counterpart in the 1976 Act, reflecting the 1985 changes made in Section 201. The second sentence first appeared in the 1976 Act, and is intended to protect a limited partner (and the remaining partners) against a distribution in kind of more than his share of particular assets.

§ 606. Right to Distribution

At the time a partner becomes entitled to receive a distribution, he [or she] has the status of, and is entitled to all remedies available to, a creditor of the limited partnership with respect to the distribution.

Comment Section 606 first appeared in the 1976 Act, and is intended to make it clear that the right of a partner to receive a distribution, as between the partners, is not subject to the equity risks of the enterprise. On the other hand, since partners entitled to distributions have creditor status, there did not seem to be a need for the extraordinary remedy of Section 16(4)(a) of the 1916 Act, which granted a limited partner the right to seek dissolution of the partnership if he was unsuccessful in demanding the return of his contribution. It is more appropriate for the partner to simply sue as an ordinary creditor and obtain a judgment.

§ 607. Limitations on Distribution

A partner may not receive a distribution from a limited partnership to the extent that, after giving effect to the distribution, all liabilities of the limited partnership, other than liabilities to partners on account of their partnership interests, exceed the fair value of the partnership assets.

Comment Section 607 is derived from Section 16(1)(a) of the 1916 Act.

§ 608. Liability Upon Return of Contribution

(a) If a partner has received the return of any part of his [or her] contribution without violation of the partnership agreement or this [Act], he [or she] is liable to the limited partnership for a period of one year thereafter for the amount of the returned contribution, but only to the extent necessary to discharge the limited partnership's liabilities to creditors who extended credit to the limited partnership during the period the contribution was held by the partnership.

(b) If a partner has received the return of any part of his [or her] contribution in violation of the partnership agreement or this [Act], he [or she] is liable to the limited partnership for a period of six years thereafter for the amount of the contribution wrongfully returned.

(c) A partner receives a return of his [or her] contribution to the extent that a distribution to him [or her] reduces his [or her] share of the fair value of the net assets of the limited partnership below the value, as set forth in the partnership records required to be kept pursuant to Section 105, of his contribution which has not been distributed to him [or her].

Comment Paragraph (a) is derived from Section 17(4) of the 1916 Act, but the one year statute of limitations has been added. Paragraph (b) is derived from Section 17(2)(b) of the 1916 Act but, again, a statute of limitations has been added.

Paragraph (c) first appeared in the 1976 Act. The provisions of former Section 17(2) that referred to the partner holding as "trustee" any money or specific property wrongfully returned to him have been eliminated. Paragraph (c) in the 1985 Act also differs from its counterpart in the 1976 Act to reflect the 1985 changes made in Sections 105 and 201.

ARTICLE 7
ASSIGNMENT OF
PARTNERSHIP INTERESTS

§ 701. Nature of Partnership Interest

A partnership interest is personal property.

Comment This section is derived from Section 18 of the 1916 Act.

§ 702. Assignment of Partnership Interest

Except as provided in the partnership agreement, a partnership interest is assignable in whole or in part. An assignment of a partnership interest does not dissolve a limited partnership or entitle the assignee to become or to exercise any rights of a partner. An assignment entitles the assignee to receive, to the extent assigned, only the distribution to which the assignor would be entitled. Except as provided in the partnership agreement, a partner ceases to be a partner upon assignment of all his [or her] partnership interest.

Comment Section 19(1) of the 1916 Act provided simply that "a limited partner's interest is assignable," raising a question whether any limitations on the right of assignment were permitted. While the first sentence of Section 702 recognizes that the power to assign may be restricted in the partnership agreement, there was no intention to affect in any way the usual rules regarding restraints on alienation of personal property. The second and third sentences of Section 702 are derived from Section 19(3) of the 1916 Act. The last sentence first appeared in the 1976 Act.

§ 703. Rights of Creditor

On application to a court of competent jurisdiction by any judgment creditor of a partner, the court may charge the partnership interest of the partner with payment of the unsatisfied amount of the judgment with interest. To the extent so charged, the judgment creditor has only the rights of an assignee of the partnership interest. This [Act] does not deprive any partner of the benefit of any exemption laws applicable to his [or her] partnership interest.

Comment Section 703 is derived from Section 22 of the 1916 Act but has not carried over some provisions that were thought to be superfluous. For example, references in Section 22(1) to specific remedies have been omitted, as has a prohibition in Section 22(2) against discharge of the lien with partnership property. Ordinary rules governing the remedies available to a creditor and the fiduciary obligations of general partners will determine those matters.

§ 704. Right of Assignee to Become Limited Partner

(a) An assignee of a partnership interest, including an assignee of a general partner, may become a limited partner if and to the extent that (i) the assignor gives the assignee that right in accordance with authority described in the partnership agreement, or (ii) all other partners consent.

(b) An assignee who has become a limited partner has, to the extent assigned, the rights and powers, and is subject to the restrictions and liabilities, of a limited partner under the partnership agreement and this [Act]. An assignee who becomes a limited partner also is liable for the obligations of his [or her] assignor to make and return contributions as provided in Articles 5 and 6. However, the assignee is not obligated for liabilities unknown to the assignee at the time he [or she] became a limited partner.

(c) If an assignee of a partnership interest becomes a limited partner, the assignor is not released from his [or her] liability to the limited partnership under Sections 207 and 502.

Comment Section 704 is derived from Section 19 of the 1916 Act, but paragraph (b) defines more narrowly than Section 19 the obligations of the assignor that are automatically assumed by the assignee. Section 704 of the 1985 Act also differs from the 1976 Act to reflect the 1985 changes made in Section 201.

§ 705. Power of Estate of Deceased or Incompetent Partner

If a partner who is an individual dies or a court of competent jurisdiction adjudges him [or her] to be incompetent to manage his [or her] person or his [or her] property, the partner's executor, administrator, guardian, conservator, or other legal representative may exercise all of the partner's rights for the purpose of settling his [or her] estate or administering his [or her] property, including any power the partner had to give an assignee the right to become a limited partner. If a partner is a corporation, trust, or other entity and is dissolved or terminated, the powers of that partner may be exercised by its legal representative or successor.

Comment Section 705 is derived from Section 21(1) of the 1916 Act. Former Section 21(2), making a deceased limited partner's estate liable for his liabilities as a limited partner was deleted as superfluous, with no intention of changing the liability of the estate.

ARTICLE 8
DISSOLUTION

§ 801. Nonjudicial Dissolution

A limited partnership is dissolved and its affairs shall be wound up upon the happening of the first to occur of the following:

(1) at the time specified in the certificate of limited partnership;

(2) upon the happening of events specified in writing in the partnership agreement;

(3) written consent of all partners;

(4) an event of withdrawal of a general partner unless at the time there is at least one other general partner and the written provisions of the partnership agreement permit the business of the limited partnership to be carried on by the remaining general partner and that partner does so, but the limited partnership is not dissolved and is not required to be wound up by reason of any event of withdrawal if, within 90 days after the withdrawal, all partners agree in writing to continue the business of the limited partnership and to the appointment of one or more additional general partners if necessary or desired; or

(5) entry of a decree of judicial dissolution under Section 802.

Comment Section 801 merely collects in one place all of the events causing dissolution. Paragraph (3) is derived from Sections 9(1)(g) and 20 of the 1916 Act, but adds the 90-day grace period. Section 801 also differs from its counterpart in the 1976 Act to reflect the 1985 changes made in Section 201.

§ 802. Judicial Dissolution

On application by or for a partner the [designate the appropriate court] court may decree dissolution of a limited partnership whenever it is not reasonably practicable to carry on the business in conformity with the partnership agreement.

Comment Section 802 first appeared in the 1976 Act.

§ 803. Winding Up

Except as provided in the partnership agreement, the general partners who have not wrongfully dissolved a limited partnership or, if none, the limited partners, may wind up the limited partnership's affairs; but the [designate the appropriate court] court may wind up the limited partnership's affairs upon application of any partner, his [or her] legal representative, or assignee.

Comment Section 803 first appeared in the 1976 Act, and is derived in part from Section 37 of the Uniform Partnership Act.

§ 804. Distribution of Assets

Upon the winding up of a limited partnership, the assets shall be distributed as follows:

(1) to creditors, including partners who are creditors, to the extent permitted by law in satisfaction of liabilities of the limited partnership other than liabilities for distributions to partners under Section 601 or 604;

(2) except as provided in the partnership agreement, to partners and former partners in satisfaction of liabilities for distributions under Section 601 or 604; and

(3) except as provided in the partnership agreement, to partners first for the return of their contributions and secondly respecting their partnership interests, in the proportions in which the partners share in distributions.

Comment Section 804 revises Section 23 of the 1916 Act by providing that (1) to the extent partners are also creditors, other than in respect of their interests in the partnership, they share with other creditors, (2) once the partnership's obligation to make a distribution accrues, it must be paid before any other distributions of an "equity" nature are made, and (3) general and limited partners rank on the same level except as otherwise provided in the partnership agreement.

ARTICLE 9
FOREIGN LIMITED PARTNERSHIPS

§ 901. Law Governing

Subject to the Constitution of this State, (i) the laws of the state under which a foreign limited partnership is organized govern its organization and internal affairs and the liability of its limited partners, and (ii) a foreign limited partnership may not be denied registration by reason of any difference between those laws and the laws of this State.

Comment Section 901 first appeared in the 1976 Act.

§ 902. Registration

Before transacting business in this State, a foreign limited partnership shall register with the Secretary of State. In order to register, a foreign limited partnership shall submit to the Secretary of State, in duplicate, an application for registration as a foreign limited partnership, signed and sworn to by a general partner and setting forth:

(1) the name of the foreign limited partnership and, if different, the name under which it proposes to register and transact business in this State;

(2) the State and date of its formation;

(3) the name and address of any agent for service of process on the foreign limited partnership whom the foreign limited partnership elects to appoint; the agent must be an individual resident of this State, a domestic corporation, or a foreign corporation having a place of business in, and authorized to do business in, this State;

(4) a statement that the Secretary of State is appointed the agent of the foreign limited partnership for service of process if no agent has been appointed under paragraph (3) or, if appointed, the agent's authority has been revoked or if the agent cannot be found or served with the exercise of reasonable diligence;

(5) the address of the office required to be maintained in the state of its organization by the laws of that state or, if not so required, of the principal office of the foreign limited partnership;

(6) the name and business address of each general partner; and

(7) the address of the office at which is kept a list of the names and addresses of the limited partners and their capital contributions, together with an undertaking by the foreign limited partnership to keep those records until the foreign limited partnership's registration in this State is cancelled or withdrawn.

Comment Section 902 first appeared in the 1976 Act. It was thought that requiring a full copy of the certificate of limited partnership and all amendments thereto to be filed in each state in which the partnership does business would impose an unreasonable burden on interstate limited partnerships and that the information Section 902 required to be filed would be sufficient to tell interested persons where they could write to obtain copies of those basic documents. Subdivision (3) of the 1976 Act has been omitted, and subdivisions (6) and (7) differ from their counterparts in the 1976 Act, to conform these provisions relating to the registration of foreign limited partnerships to the corresponding changes made by the Act in the provisions relating to domestic limited partnerships. The requirement that an application for registration be sworn to by a general partner is simply intended to produce the same result as is provided for in Section 204(c) with respect to certificates of domestic limited partnerships; the acceptance and endorsement by the Secretary of State (or equivalent authority) of an application which was not sworn by a general partner should be deemed a mere technical and insubstantial shortcoming, and should not result in the limited partners' being subjected to general liability for the obligations of the foreign limited partnership (See Section 907(c)).

§ 903. Issuance of Registration

(a) If the Secretary of State finds that an application for registration conforms to law and all requisite fees have been paid, he [or she] shall:

(1) endorse on the application the word "Filed", and the month, day, and year of the filing thereof;

(2) file in his [or her] office a duplicate original of the application; and

(3) issue a certificate of registration to transact business in this State.

(b) The certificate of registration, together with a duplicate original of the application, shall be returned to the person who filed the application or his [or her] representative.

Comment Section 903 first appeared in the 1976 Act.

§ 904. Name

A foreign limited partnership may register with the Secretary of State under any name, whether or not it is the name under which it is registered in its state of organization, that includes without abbreviation the words "limited partnership" and that could be registered by a domestic limited partnership.

Comment Section 904 first appeared in the 1976 Act.

§ 905. Changes and Amendments

If any statement in the application for registration of a foreign limited partnership was false when made or any arrangements or other facts described have changed, making the application inaccurate in any respect, the foreign limited partnership shall promptly file in the office of the Secretary of State a certificate, signed and sworn to by a general partner, correcting such statement.

Comment Section 905 first appeared in the 1976 Act. It corresponds to the provisions of Section 202(c) relating to domestic limited partnerships.

§ 906. Cancellation of Registration

A foreign limited partnership may cancel its registration by filing with the Secretary of State a certificate of cancellation signed and sworn to by a general partner. A cancellation does not terminate the authority of the Secretary of State to accept service of process on the foreign limited partnership with respect to [claims for relief] [causes of action] arising out of the transactions of business in this State.

Comment Section 906 first appeared in the 1976 Act.

§ 907. Transaction of Business Without Registration

(a) A foreign limited partnership transacting business in this State may not maintain any action, suit, or proceeding in any court of this State until it has registered in this State.

(b) The failure of a foreign limited partnership to register in this State does not impair the validity of any contract or act of the foreign limited partnership or prevent the foreign limited partnership from defending any action, suit, or proceeding in any court of this State.

(c) A limited partner of a foreign limited partnership is not liable as a general partner of the foreign limited partnership solely by reason of having transacted business in this State without registration.

(d) A foreign limited partnership, by transacting business in this State without registration, appoints the Secretary of State as its agent for service of process with respect to [claims for relief] [causes of action] arising out of the transaction of business in this State.

Comment Section 907 first appeared in the 1976 Act.

§ 908. Action by [Appropriate Official]

The [designate the appropriate official] may bring an action to restrain a foreign limited

partnership from transacting business in this State in violation of this Article.

Comment Section 908 first appeared in the 1976 Act.

ARTICLE 10
DERIVATIVE ACTIONS

§ 1001. Right of Action

A limited partner may bring an action in the right of a limited partnership to recover a judgment in favor if general partners with authority to do so have refused to bring the action or if an effort to cause those general partners to bring the action is not likely to succeed.

Comment Section 1001 first appeared in the 1976 Act.

§ 1002. Proper Plaintiff

In a derivative action, the plaintiff must be a partner at the time of bringing the action and (i) must have been a partner at the time of the transaction of which he [or she] complains or (ii) his [or her] status as a partner must have devolved upon him [or her] by operation of law or pursuant to the terms of the partnership agreement from a person who was a partner at the time of the transaction.

Comment Section 1002 first appeared in the 1976 Act.

§ 1003. Pleading

In a derivative action, the complaint shall set forth with particularity the effort of the plaintiff to secure initiation of the action by a general partner or the reasons for not making the effort.

Comment Section 1003 first appeared in the 1976 Act.

§ 1004. Expenses

If a derivative action is successful, in whole or in part, or if anything is received by the plaintiff as a result of a judgment, compromise, or settlement of an action or claim, the court may award the plaintiff reasonable expenses, including reasonable attorney's fees, and shall direct him [or her] to remit to the limited partnership the remainder of those proceeds received by him [or her].

Comment Section 1004 first appeared in the 1976 Act.

ARTICLE 11
MISCELLANEOUS

§ 1101. Construction and Application

This [Act] shall be so applied and construed to effectuate its general purpose to make uniform the law with respect to the subject of this [Act] among states enacting it.

Comment Because the principles set out in Sections 28(1) and 29 of the 1916 Act have become so universally established, it was felt that the 1976 and 1985 Acts need not contain express provisions to the same effect. However, it is intended that the principles enunciated in those provisions of the 1916 Act also apply to this Act.

§ 1102. Short Title

This [Act] may be cited as the Uniform Limited Partnership Act.

§ 1103. Severability

If any provision of this [Act] or its application to any person or circumstance is held invalid, the invalidity does not affect other provisions or applications of the [Act] which can be given effect without the invalid provision or application, and to this end the provisions of this [Act] are severable.

§ 1104. Effective Date, Extended Effective Date and Repeal

Except as set forth below, the effective date of this [Act] is _____ and the following acts [list existing limited partnership acts] are hereby repealed:

(1) The existing provisions for execution and filing of certificates of limited partnerships and amendments thereunder and cancellations thereof continue in effect until [specify time required to create central filing system], the extended effective date, and Sections 102, 103, 104, 105, 201, 202, 203, 204 and 206 are not effective until the extended effective date.

(2) Section 402, specifying the conditions under which a general partner ceases to be a member of a limited partnership, is not effective until the extended effective date, and the applicable provisions of existing law continue to govern until the extended effective date.

(3) Sections 501, 502 and 608 apply only to contributions and distributions made after the effective date of this [Act].

(4) Section 704 applies only to assignments made after the effective date of this [Act].

(5) Article 9, dealing with registration of foreign limited partnerships, is not effective until the extended effective date.

(6) Unless otherwise agreed by the partners, the applicable provisions of existing law governing allocation of profits and losses (rather than the provisions of Section 503), distributions to a withdrawing partner (rather than the provisions of Section 604), and distributions of assets upon the winding up of a limited partnership (rather than the provisions of Section 804) govern limited partnerships formed before the effective date of this [Act].

Comment Subdivisions (6) and (7) did not appear in Section 1104 of the 1976 Act. They are included in the 1985 Act to ensure that the application of the Act to limited partnerships formed and existing before the Act becomes effective would not violate constitutional prohibitions against the impairment of contracts.

§ 1105. Rules for Cases Not Provided for in This [Act]

In any case not provided for in this [Act] the provisions of the Uniform Partnership Act govern.

Comment The result provided for in Section 1105 would obtain even in its absence in a jurisdiction which had adopted the Uniform Partnership Act, by operation of Section 6 of that act.

§ 1106. Savings Clause

The repeal of any statutory provision by this [Act] does not impair, or otherwise affect, the organization or the continued existence of a limited partnership existing at the effective date of this [Act], nor does the repeal of any existing statutory provision by this [Act] impair any contract or affect any right accrued before the effective date of this [Act].

Comment Section 1106 did not appear in the 1976 Act. It is included in the 1985 Act to ensure that the application of the Act to limited partnerships formed and existing before the Act becomes effective would not violate constitutional prohibitions against the impairment of contracts.

APPENDIX H

Uniform Limited Liability Company Act

Reprinted with permission of the National Conference of Commissioners on Uniform State Laws, 211 East Ontario Street, Suite 1300, Chicago, IL 60611
www.nccusl.org

[ARTICLE] 1
GENERAL PROVISIONS

Section 101. Definitions.

Section 102. Knowledge and Notice.

Section 103. Effect of Operating Agreement; Nonwaivable Provisions.

Section 104. Supplemental Principles of Law.

Section 105. Name.

Section 106. Reserved Name.

Section 107. Registered Name.

Section 108. Designated Office and Agent for Service of Process.

Section 109. Change of Designated Office or Agent for Service of Process.

Section 110. Resignation of Agent for Service of Process.

Section 111. Service of Process.

Section 112. Nature of Business and Powers.

SECTION 101. Definitions.

In this [Act]:

(1) "Articles of organization" means initial, amended, and restated articles of organization and articles of merger. In the case of a foreign limited liability company, the term includes all records serving a similar function required to be filed in the office of the [Secretary of State] or comparable office of the company's jurisdiction of organization.

(2) "Business" includes every trade, occupation, profession, and other lawful purpose, whether or not carried on for profit.

(3) "Debtor in bankruptcy" means a person who is the subject of an order for relief under Title 11 of the United States Code or a comparable order under a successor statute of general application or a comparable order under federal, state, or foreign law governing insolvency.

(4) "Distribution" means a transfer of money, property, or other benefit from a limited liability company to a member in the member's capacity as a member or to a transferee of the member's distributional interest.

(5) "Distributional interest" means all of a member's interest in distributions by the limited liability company.

(6) "Entity" means a person other than an individual.

(7) "Foreign limited liability company" means an unincorporated entity organized under laws other than the laws of this State which afford limited liability to its owners comparable to the liability under Section 303 and is not required to obtain a certificate of authority to transact business under any law of this State other than this [Act].

(8) "Limited liability company" means a limited liability company organized under this [Act].

(9) "Manager" means a person, whether or not a member of a manager-managed limited liability company, who is vested with authority under Section 301.

(10) "Manager-managed limited liability company" means a limited liability company which is so designated in its articles of organization.

(11) "Member-managed limited liability company" means a limited liability company other than a manager-managed company.

(12) "Operating agreement" means the agreement under Section 103 concerning the relations among the members, managers, and limited liability company. The term includes amendments to the agreement.

(13) "Person" means an individual, corporation, business trust, estate, trust, partnership, limited liability company, association, joint venture, government, governmental subdivision, agency, or instrumentality, or any other legal or commercial entity.

(14) "Principal office" means the office, whether or not in this State, where the principal executive office of a domestic or foreign limited liability company is located.

(15) "Record" means information that is inscribed on a tangible medium or that is stored in an electronic or other medium and is retrievable in perceivable form.

(16) "Signed" includes any symbol executed or adopted by a person with the present intention to authenticate a record.

(17) "State" means a State of the United States, the District of Columbia, the Commonwealth of Puerto Rico, or any territory or insular possession subject to the jurisdiction of the United States.

(18) "Transfer" includes an assignment, conveyance, deed, bill of sale, lease, mortgage, security interest, encumbrance, and gift.

SECTION 102. *Knowledge and Notice.*

(a) A person knows a fact if the person has actual knowledge of it.

(b) A person has notice of a fact if the person:

(1) knows the fact;

(2) has received a notification of the fact; or

(3) has reason to know the fact exists from all of the facts known to the person at the time in question.

(c) A person notifies or gives a notification of a fact to another by taking steps reasonably required to inform the other person in ordinary course, whether or not the other person knows the fact.

(d) A person receives a notification when the notification:

(1) comes to the person's attention; or

(2) is duly delivered at the person's place of business or at any other place held out by the person as a place for receiving communications.

(e) An entity knows, has notice, or receives a notification of a fact for purposes of a particular transaction when the individual conducting the transaction for the entity knows, has notice, or receives a notification of the fact, or in any event when the fact would have been brought to the individual's attention had the entity exercised reasonable diligence. An entity exercises reasonable diligence if it maintains reasonable routines for communicating significant information to the individual conducting the transaction for the entity and

there is reasonable compliance with the routines. Reasonable diligence does not require an individual acting for the entity to communicate information unless the communication is part of the individual's regular duties or the individual has reason to know of the transaction and that the transaction would be materially affected by the information.

SECTION 103. *Effect of Operating Agreement Nonwaivable Provisions.*

(a) Except as otherwise provided in subsection (b), all members of a limited liability company may enter into an operating agreement, which need not be in writing, to regulate the affairs of the company and the conduct of its business, and to govern relations among the members, managers, and company. To the extent the operating agreement does not otherwise provide, this [Act] governs relations among the members, managers, and company.

(b) The operating agreement may not:

(1) unreasonably restrict a right to information or access to records under Section 408;

(2) eliminate the duty of loyalty under Section 409(b) or 603(b)(3), but the agreement may:

(i) identify specific types or categories of activities that do not violate the duty of loyalty, if not manifestly unreasonable; and

(ii) specify the number or percentage of members or disinterested managers that may authorize or ratify, after full disclosure of all material facts, a specific act or transaction that otherwise would violate the duty of loyalty;

(3) unreasonably reduce the duty of care under Section 409(c) or 603(b)(3);

(4) eliminate the obligation of good faith and fair dealing under Section 409(d), but the operating agreement may determine the standards by which the performance of the obligation is to be measured, if the standards are not manifestly unreasonable;

(5) vary the right to expel a member in an event specified in Section 601(5);

(6) vary the requirement to wind up the limited liability company's business in a case specified in Section 801(4) or (5); or

(7) restrict rights of third parties under this [Act], other than managers, members, or their transferees.

SECTION 104. *Supplemental Principles of Law.*

(a) Unless displaced by particular provisions of this [Act], the principles of law and equity supplement this [Act].

(b) If an obligation to pay interest arises under this [Act] and the rate is not specified, the rate is that specified in [applicable statute].

SECTION 105. *Name.*

(a) The name of a limited liability company must contain "limited liability company" or "limited company" or the abbreviation "L.L.C.," "LLC," "L.C.," or "LC." "Limited" may be abbreviated as "Ltd.," and "company" may be abbreviated as "Co.".

(b) Except as authorized by subsections (c) and (d), the name of a limited liability company must be distinguishable upon the records of the [Secretary of State] from:

(1) the name of any corporation, limited partnership, or company incorporated, organized or authorized to transact business, in this State;

(2) a company name reserved or registered under Section 106 or 107;

(3) a fictitious name approved under Section 1005 for a foreign company authorized to transact business in this State because its real name is unavailable.

(c) A limited liability company may apply to the [Secretary of State] for authorization to use a name that is not distinguishable upon the records of the [Secretary of State] from one or more of the names described in subsection (b). The [Secretary of State] shall authorize use of the name applied for if:

(1) the present user, registrant, or owner of a reserved name consents to the use in a record and submits an undertaking in form satisfactory to the [Secretary of State] to change the name to a name that is distinguishable upon the records of the [Secretary of State] from the name applied for; or

(2) the applicant delivers to the [Secretary of State] a certified copy of the final judgment of a court of competent jurisdiction establishing the applicant's right to use the name applied for in this State.

(d) A limited liability company may use the name, including a fictitious name, of another domestic or foreign company which is used in this State if the other company is organized or authorized to transact business in this State and the company proposing to use the name has:

(1) merged with the other company;

(2) been formed by reorganization with the other company; or

(3) acquired substantially all of the assets, including the company name, of the other company.

SECTION 106. *Reserved Name.*

(a) A person may reserve the exclusive use of the name of a limited liability company, including a fictitious name for a foreign company whose company name is not available, by delivering an application to the [Secretary of State] for filing. The application must set forth the name and address of the applicant and the name proposed to be reserved. If the [Secretary of State] finds that the name applied for is available, it must be reserved for the applicant's exclusive use for a nonrenewable 120-day period.

(b) The owner of a name reserved for a limited liability company may transfer the reservation to another person by delivering to the [Secretary of State] a signed notice of the transfer which states the name and address of the transferee.

SECTION 107. *Registered Name.*

(a) A foreign limited liability company may register its company name subject to the requirements of Section 1005, if the name is distinguishable upon the records of the [Secretary of State] from company names that are not available under Section 105(b).

(b) A foreign limited liability company registers its company name, or its company name with any addition required by Section 1005, by delivering to the [Secretary of State] for filing an application:

(1) setting forth its company name, or its company name with any addition required by Section 1005, the State or country and date of its organization, and a brief description of the nature of the business in which it is engaged; and

(2) accompanied by a certificate of existence, or a record of similar import, from the State or country of organization.

(c)   A foreign limited liability company whose registration is effective may renew it for successive years by delivering for filing in the office of the [Secretary of State] a renewal application complying with subsection (b) between October 1 and December 31 of the preceding year. The renewal application renews the registration for the following calendar year.

(d)   A foreign limited liability company whose registration is effective may qualify as a foreign company under its company name or consent in writing to the use of its name by a limited liability company later organized under this [Act] or by another foreign company later authorized to transact business in this State. The registered name terminates when the limited liability company is organized or the foreign company qualifies or consents to the qualification of another foreign company under the registered name.

SECTION 108. Designated Office and Agent for Service of Process.

(a)   A limited liability company and a foreign limited liability company authorized to do business in this State shall designate and continuously maintain in this State:

(1)   an office, which need not be a place of its business in this State; and

(2)   an agent and street address of the agent for service of process on the company.

(b)   An agent must be an individual resident of this State, a domestic corporation, another limited liability company, or a foreign corporation or foreign company authorized to do business in this State.

SECTION 109. Change of Designated Office or Agent for Service of Process.

A limited liability company may change its designated office or agent for service of process by delivering to the [Secretary of State] for filing a statement of change which sets forth:

(1)   the name of the company;

(2)   the street address of its current designated office;

(3)   if the current designated office is to be changed, the street address of the new designated office;

(4)   the name and address of its current agent for service of process; and

(5)   if the current agent for service of process or street address of that agent is to be changed, the new address or the name and street address of the new agent for service of process.

SECTION 110. Resignation of Agent for Service of Process.

(a)   An agent for service of process of a limited liability company may resign by delivering to the [Secretary of State] for filing a record of the statement of resignation.

(b)   After filing a statement of resignation, the [Secretary of State] shall mail a copy to the designated office and another copy to the limited liability company at its principal office.

(c)   An agency is terminated on the 31st day after the statement is filed in the office of the [Secretary of State].

SECTION 111. Service of Process.

(a)   An agent for service of process appointed by a limited liability company or a foreign limited liability company is an agent of the company for service of any process, notice, or demand required or permitted by law to be served upon the company.

(b)   If a limited liability company or foreign limited liability company fails to appoint or maintain an agent for service of process in this State or the agent for service of process cannot with reasonable diligence be found at the agent's address, the [Secretary of State] is an agent of the company upon whom process, notice, or demand may be served.

(c)   Service of any process, notice, or demand on the [Secretary of State] may be made by delivering to and leaving with the [Secretary of State], the [Assistant Secretary of State], or clerk having charge of the limited liability company department of the [Secretary of State's] office duplicate copies of the process, notice, or demand. If the process, notice, or demand is served on the [Secretary of State], the [Secretary of State] shall forward one of the copies by registered or certified mail, return receipt requested, to the company at its designated office. Service is effected under this subsection at the earliest of:

(1)   the date the company receives the process, notice, or demand;

(2)   the date shown on the return receipt, if signed on behalf of the company; or

(3) five days after its deposit in the mail, if mailed postpaid and correctly addressed.

(d) The [Secretary of State] shall keep a record of all processes, notices, and demands served pursuant to this section and record the time of and the action taken regarding the service.

(e) This section does not affect the right to serve process, notice, or demand in any manner otherwise provided by law.

SECTION 112. *Nature of Business and Powers.*

(a) A limited liability company may be organized under this [Act] for any lawful purpose, subject to any law of this State governing or regulating business.

(b) Unless its articles of organization provide otherwise, a limited liability company has the same powers as an individual to do all things necessary or convenient to carry on its business or affairs, including power to:

(1) sue and be sued, and defend in its company name;

(2) purchase, receive, lease, or otherwise acquire, and own, hold, improve, use, and otherwise deal with real or personal property, or any legal or equitable interest in property, wherever located;

(3) sell, convey, mortgage, grant a security interest in, lease, exchange, and otherwise encumber or dispose of all or any part of its property;

(4) purchase, receive, subscribe for, or otherwise acquire, own, hold, vote, use, sell, mortgage, lend, grant a security interest in, or otherwise dispose of and deal in and with, shares or other interests in or obligations of any other entity;

(5) make contracts and guarantees, incur liabilities, borrow money, issue its notes, bonds, and other obligations, which may be convertible into or include the option to purchase other securities of the limited liability company, and secure any of its obligations by a mortgage on or a security interest in any of its property, franchises, or income;

(6) lend money, invest and reinvest its funds, and receive and hold real and personal property as security for repayment;

(7) be a promoter, partner, member, associate, or manager of any partnership, joint venture, trust, or other entity;

(8) conduct its business, locate offices, and exercise the powers granted by this [Act] within or without this State;

(9) elect managers and appoint officers, employees, and agents of the limited liability company, define their duties, fix their compensation, and lend them money and credit;

(10) pay pensions and establish pension plans, pension trusts, profit sharing plans, share bonus plans, share option plans, and benefit or incentive plans for any or all of its current or former members, managers, officers, employees, and agents;

(11) make donations for the public welfare or for charitable, scientific, or educational purposes; and

(12) make payments or donations, or do any other act, not inconsistent with law, that furthers the business of the limited liability company.

[ARTICLE] 2
ORGANIZATION

Section 201. Limited Liability Company as Legal Entity.

Section 202. Organization.

Section 203. Articles of Organization.

Section 204. Amendment or Restatement of Articles of Organization.

Section 205. Signing of Records.

Section 206. Filing in Office of [Secretary of State].

Section 207. Correcting Filed Record.

Section 208. Certificate of Existence or Authorization.

Section 209. Liability for False Statement in Filed Record.

Section 210. Filing By Judicial Act.

Section 211. Annual Report for [Secretary of State].

SECTION 201. *Limited Liability Company As Legal Entity.*

A limited liability company is a legal entity distinct from its members.

SECTION 202. *Organization.*

(a)   One or more persons may organize a limited liability company, consisting of one or more members, by delivering articles of organization to the office of the [Secretary of State] for filing.

(b)   Unless a delayed effective date is specified, the existence of a limited liability company begins when the articles of organization are filed.

(c)   The filing of the articles of organization by the [Secretary of State] is conclusive proof that the organizers satisfied all conditions precedent to the creation of the organization.

SECTION 203. *Articles of Organization.*

(a)   Articles of organization of a limited liability company must set forth:

(1)   the name of the company;

(2)   the address of the initial designated office;

(3)   the name and street address of the initial agent for service of process;

(4)   the name and address of each organizer;

(5)   whether the duration of the company is for a specified term and, if so, the period specified;

(6)   whether the company is to be manager-managed, and, if so, the name and address of each initial manager; and

(7)   whether the members of the company are to be liable for its debts and obligations under Section 303(c).

(b)   Articles of organization of a limited liability company may set forth:

(1)   provisions permitted to be set forth in an operating agreement; or

(2)   other matters not inconsistent with law.

(c)   Articles of organization of a limited liability company may not vary the nonwaivable provisions of Section 103(b). As to all other matters, if any provision of an operating agreement is inconsistent with the articles of organization:

(1)   the operating agreement controls as to managers, members, and members' transferees; and

(2)   the articles of organization control as to persons other than managers, members, and their transferees who rely on the articles to their detriment.

(d)   The duration of a limited liability company is at-will unless a term for its duration is specified in its articles of organization.

SECTION 204. *Amendment or Restatement of Articles of Organization.*

(a)   Articles of organization of a limited liability company may be amended at any time by delivering articles of amendment to the [Secretary of State] for filing. The articles of amendment must set forth the:

(1)   name of the limited liability company;

(2)   date of filing of the articles of organization; and

(3)   amendment to the articles.

(b)   A limited liability company may restate its articles of organization at any time. Restated articles of organization must be signed and filed in the same manner as articles of amendment. Restated articles of organization must be designated as such in the heading and state in the heading or in an introductory paragraph the limited liability company's present name and, if it has been changed, all of its former names and the date of the filing of its initial articles of organization.

SECTION 205. *Signing of Records.*

(a)   Except as otherwise provided in this [Act], a record to be filed by or on behalf of a limited liability company in the office of the [Secretary of State] must be signed in the name of the company by a:

(1)   manager of a manager-managed company;

(2)   member of a member-managed company;

(3)   person organizing the company, if the company has not been formed; or

(4)   fiduciary, if the company is in the hands of a receiver, trustee, or other court-appointed fiduciary.

(b)   A record signed under subsection (a) must state adjacent to the signature the name and capacity of the signer.

(c)   A person signing a record to be filed under subsection (a) may do so as an attorney-in-fact without any formality. An authorization, including a power of attorney, to sign a record need not be in writing, sworn to, verified, or acknowledged or filed in the office of the [Secretary of State].

SECTION 206. Filing in Office of [Secretary of State].

(a)   Articles of organization or any other record authorized to be filed under this [Act] must be in a medium permitted by the [Secretary of State] and must be delivered to the office of the [Secretary of State]. Unless the [Secretary of State] determines that a record fails to comply as to form with the filing requirements of this [Act], and if all filing fees have been paid, the [Secretary of State] shall file the record and send a receipt for the record and the fees to the limited liability company or its representative.

(b)   Upon request and payment of a fee, the [Secretary of State] shall send to the requester a certified copy of the requested record.

(c)   A record accepted for filing by the [Secretary of State] is effective:

(1)   on the date it is filed, as evidenced by the [Secretary of State] maintaining a record of the date and time of the filing;

(2)   at the time specified in the record as its effective time; or

(3)   on the date and at the time specified in the record if the record specifies a delayed effective date and time.

(d)   If a delayed effective date for a record is specified but no time is specified, the record is effective at 12:01 A.M. on that date. A delayed effective date that is later than the 90th day after the record is filed makes the record effective as of the 90th day.

SECTION 207. Correcting Filed Record.

(a)   A limited liability company or foreign limited liability company may correct a record filed by the [Secretary of State] if the record contains a false or erroneous statement or was defectively signed.

(b)   A record is corrected:

(1)   by preparing articles of correction that:

(i)   describe the record, including its filing date, or attach a copy of it to the articles of correction;

(ii)   specify the incorrect statement and the reason it is incorrect or the manner in which the signing was defective; and

(iii)   correct the incorrect statement or defective signing; and

(2)   by delivering the corrected record to the [Secretary of State] for filing.

(c)   Articles of correction are effective retroactively to the effective date of the record they correct. However, a person who has relied on the uncorrected record and was adversely affected by the correction is not bound by the correction until the articles are filed.

SECTION 208. Certificate of Existence or Authorization.

(a)   A person may request the [Secretary of State] to furnish a certificate of existence for a limited liability company or a certificate of authorization for a foreign limited liability company.

(b)   A certificate of existence for a limited liability company must set forth:

(1)   the company's name;

(2)   that it is duly organized under the laws of this State, the date of organization, whether its duration is at-will or for a specified term, and, if the latter, the period specified;

(3)   if payment is reflected in the records of the [Secretary of State] and nonpayment affects the existence of the company, that all fees, taxes, and penalties owed to this State have been paid;

(4)   whether its most recent annual report required by Section 211 has been filed with the [Secretary of State];

(5)   that articles of termination have not been filed; and

(6)   other facts of record in the office of the [Secretary of State] which may be requested by the applicant.

(c)   A certificate of authorization for a foreign limited liability company must set forth:

(1)   the company's name used in this State;

(2)   that it is authorized to transact business in this State;

(3)   if payment is reflected in the records of the [Secretary of State] and nonpayment affects the authorization of the company, that all fees, taxes, and penalties owed to this State have been paid;

(4)   whether its most recent annual report required by Section 211 has been filed with the [Secretary of State];

(5)   that a certificate of cancellation has not been filed; and

(6)   other facts of record in the office of the [Secretary of State] which may be requested by the applicant.

(d)   Subject to any qualification stated in the certificate, a certificate of existence or authorization issued by the [Secretary of State] may be relied upon as conclusive evidence that the domestic or foreign limited liability company is in existence or is authorized to transact business in this State.

SECTION 209. *Liability for False Statement in Filed Record.*

If a record authorized or required to be filed under this [Act] contains a false statement, one who suffers loss by reliance on the statement may recover damages for the loss from a person who signed the record or caused another to sign it on the person's behalf and knew the statement to be false at the time the record was signed.

SECTION 210. *Filing by Judicial Act.*

If a person required by Section 205 to sign any record fails or refuses to do so, any other person who is adversely affected by the failure or refusal may petition the [designate the appropriate court] to direct the signing of the record. If the court finds that it is proper for the record to be signed and that a person so designated has failed or refused to sign the record, it shall order the [Secretary of State] to sign and file an appropriate record.

SECTION 211. *Annual Report for [Secretary of State].*

(a)   A limited liability company, and a foreign limited liability company authorized to transact business in this State, shall deliver to the [Secretary of State] for filing an annual report that sets forth:

(1)   the name of the company and the State or country under whose law it is organized;

(2)   the address of its designated office and the name and address of its agent for service of process in this State;

(3)   the address of its principal office; and

(4)   the names and business addresses of any managers.

(b)   Information in an annual report must be current as of the date the annual report is signed on behalf of the limited liability company.

(c)   The first annual report must be delivered to the [Secretary of State] between [January 1 and April 1] of the year following the calendar year in which a limited liability company was organized or a foreign company was authorized to transact business. Subsequent annual reports must be delivered to the [Secretary of State] between [January 1 and April 1] of the following calendar years.

(d)   If an annual report does not contain the information required in subsection (a), the [Secretary of State] shall promptly notify the reporting limited liability company or foreign limited liability company and return the report to it for correction. If the report is corrected to contain the information required in subsection (a) and delivered to the [Secretary of State] within 30 days after the effective date of the notice, it is timely filed.

[ARTICLE] 3
RELATIONS OF MEMBERS AND MANAGERS TO PERSONS DEALING WITH LIMITED LIABILITY COMPANY

Section 301.   Agency of Members and Managers.

Section 302.   Limited Liability Company Liable for Member's or Manager's Actionable Conduct.

Section 303.   Liability of Members and Managers.

SECTION 301. *Agency of Members and Managers.*

(a)   Subject to subsections (b) and (c):

(1)   each member is an agent of the limited liability company for the purpose of its business;

(2)   an act of a member, including the signing of an instrument in the company name, for apparently carrying on in the ordinary course the company's business or business of the kind carried on by the company binds the company, unless the member had no authority to act for the company in the particular matter and the person with whom the member was dealing knew or had notice that the member lacked authority; and

(3)   an act of a member which is not apparently for carrying on in the ordinary course the company's business or business of the kind carried on by the company binds the company only if the act was authorized by the other members.

(b)   Subject to subsection (c), in a manager-managed limited liability company:

(1)   a member is not an agent of the company for the purpose of its business solely by reason of being a member;

(2)   each manager is an agent of the company for the purpose of its business;

(3) an act of a manager, including the signing of an instrument in the company name, for apparently carrying on in the ordinary course the company's business or business of the kind carried on by the company binds the company, unless the manager had no authority to act for the company in the particular matter and the person with whom the manager was dealing knew or had notice that the manager lacked authority; and

(4) an act of a manager which is not apparently for carrying on in the ordinary course the company's business or business of the kind carried on by the company binds the company only if the act was authorized under Section 404(b)(2).

(c) Unless the articles of organization limit their authority, any member of a member-managed limited liability company, or any manager of a manager-managed company, may sign and deliver any instrument transferring or affecting the company's interest in real property. The instrument is conclusive in favor of a person who gives value without knowledge of the lack of the authority of the person signing and delivering the instrument.

SECTION 302. Limited Liability Company Liable for Member's or Manager's Actionable Conduct.

A limited liability company is liable for loss or injury caused to a person, or for a penalty incurred, as a result of a wrongful act or omission, or other actionable conduct, of a member or manager acting in the ordinary course of business of the company or with authority of the company.

SECTION 303. Liability of Members and Managers.

(a) Except as otherwise provided in subsection (c), the debts, obligations, and liabilities of a limited liability company, whether arising in contract, tort, or otherwise, are solely the debts, obligations, and liabilities of the company. A member or manager is not personally liable for a debt, obligation, or liability of the company solely by reason of being or acting as a member or manager.

(b) The failure of a limited liability company to observe the usual company formalities or requirements relating to the exercise of its company powers or management of its business is not a ground

for imposing personal liability on the members or managers for liabilities of the company.

(c) All or specified members of a limited liability company are liable in their capacity as members for all or specified debts, obligations, or liabilities of the company if:

(1) a provision to that effect is contained in the articles of organization; and

(2) a member so liable has consented in writing to the adoption of the provision or to be bound by the provision.

[ARTICLE] 4
RELATIONS OF MEMBERS TO ACH OTHER AND TO LIMITED LIABILITY COMPANY

Section 401. Form of Contribution.
Section 402. Member's Liability for Contributions.
Section 403. Member's and Manger's Rights to Payments and Reimbursement.
Section 404. Management of Limited Liability Company.
Section 405. Sharing of and Right to Distributions.
Section 406. Limitations on Distributions.
Section 407. Liability for Unlawful Distributions.
Section 408. Member's Right to Information.
Section 409. General Standards of Member's and Manager's Conduct.
Section 410. Actions by Members.
Section 411. Continuation of Limited Liability Company After Expiration of Specified Term.

SECTION 401. Form of Contribution.

A contribution of a member of a limited liability company may consist of tangible or intangible property or other benefit to the company, including money, promissory notes, services performed, or other obligations to contribute cash or property, or contracts for services to be performed.

SECTION 402. Member's Liability for Contributions.

(a) A member's obligation to contribute money, property, or other benefit to, or to perform

services for, a limited liability company is not ex-
cused by the member's death, disability, or other inability to perform personally. If a member does not
make the required contribution of property or services, the member is obligated at the option of the
company to contribute money equal to that portion
of the value of the stated contribution which has
not been made.

(b)   A creditor of a limited liability company
who extends credit or otherwise acts in reliance on
an obligation described in subsection (a), and without notice of any compromise under Section
404(c)(5), may enforce the original obligation.

SECTION 403. Member's and Manager's Rights to Payments and Reimbursement.

(a)   A limited liability company shall reimburse
a member or manager for payments made and indemnify a member or manager for liabilities incurred by the member or manager in the ordinary
course of the business of the company or for the
preservation of its business or property.

(b)   A limited liability company shall reimburse
a member for an advance to the company beyond
the amount of contribution the member agreed to
make.

(c)   A payment or advance made by a member
which gives rise to an obligation of a limited liability company under subsection (a) or (b) constitutes
a loan to the company upon which interest accrues
from the date of the payment or advance.

(d)   A member is not entitled to remuneration
for services performed for a limited liability company, except for reasonable compensation for services rendered in winding up the business of the
company.

SECTION 404. Management of Limited Liability Company.

(a)   In a member-managed limited liability
company:

(1)   each member has equal rights in the
management and conduct of the company's
business; and

(2)   except as otherwise provided in subsection (c) or in Section 801(3)(i), any matter
relating to the business of the company may be
decided by a majority of the members.

(b)   In a manager-managed limited liability
company:

(1)   the managers have the exclusive authority to manage and conduct the company's
business;

(2)   except as specified in subsection (c) or
in Section 801(3)(i), any matter relating to the
business of the company may be exclusively decided by the manager or, if there is more than
one manager, by a majority of the managers; and

(3)   a manager:

(i)   must be designated, appointed,
elected, removed, or replaced by a vote,
approval, or consent of a majority of the
members; and

(ii)   holds office until a successor has
been elected and qualified, unless sooner
resigns or is removed.

(c)   The only matters of a limited liability company's business requiring the consent of all of the
members are:

(1)   the amendment of the operating
agreement under Section 103;

(2)   the authorization or ratification of acts
or transactions under Section 103(b)(2)(ii)
which would otherwise violate the duty of
loyalty;

(3)   an amendment to the articles of organization under Section 204;

(4)   the compromise of an obligation to
make a contribution under Section 402(b);

(5)   the compromise, as among members,
of an obligation of a member to make a contribution or return money or other property paid
or distributed in violation of this [Act];

(6)   the making of interim distributions
under Section 405(a);

(7)   the admission of a new member;

(8)   the use of the company's property to
redeem an interest subject to a charging order;

(9)   the consent to dissolve the company
under Section 801(2);

(10) a waiver of the right to have the company's business wound up and the company
terminated under Section 802(b);

(11) the consent of members to merge with
another entity under Section 904(c)(l); and

(12) the sale, lease, exchange, or other disposal of all, or substantially all, of the company's
property with or without goodwill.

(d)   Action requiring the consent of members
or managers under this [Act] may be taken with or

without a meeting. In the event a meeting is otherwise required and a written action in lieu thereof is not prohibited, the written action must be evidenced by one or more consents reflected in a record describing the action taken and signed by all of the members or managers entitled to vote on the action.

(e)   A member or manager may appoint a proxy to vote or otherwise act for the member or manager by signing an appointment instrument, either personally or by the member's or manager's attorney-in-fact. An appointment of a proxy is valid for 11 months unless a different time is specified in the appointment instrument. An appointment is revocable by the member or manager unless the appointment form conspicuously states that it is irrevocable and the appointment is coupled with an interest, in which case the appointment is revoked when the interest is extinguished.

SECTION 405. *Sharing of and Right to Distributions.*

(a)   Any distributions made by a limited liability company before its dissolution and winding up must be in equal shares.

(b)   A member has no right to receive, and may not be required to accept, a distribution in kind.

(c)   If a member becomes entitled to receive a distribution, the member has the status of, and is entitled to all remedies available to, a creditor of the limited liability company with respect to the distribution.

SECTION 406. *Limitations on Distributions.*

(a)   A distribution may not be made if:

(1)   the limited liability company would not be able to pay its debts as they become due in the ordinary course of business; or

(2)   the company's total assets would be less than the sum of its total liabilities plus the amount that would be needed, if the company were to be dissolved, wound up, and terminated at the time of the distribution, to satisfy the preferential rights upon dissolution, winding up, and termination of members whose preferential rights are superior to those receiving the distribution.

(b)   A limited liability company may base a determination that a distribution is not prohibited under subsection (a) on financial statements prepared on the basis of accounting practices and principles that are reasonable in the circumstances or on a fair valuation or other method that is reasonable in the circumstances.

(c)   Except as otherwise provided in subsection (e), the effect of a distribution under subsection (a) is measured:

(1)   in the case of distribution by purchase, redemption, or other acquisition of a distributional interest in a limited liability company, as of the date money or other property is transferred or debt incurred by the company; and

(2)   in all other cases, as of the date the:

(i)   distribution is authorized if the payment occurs within 120 days after the date of authorization; or

(ii)   payment is made if it occurs more than 120 days after the date of authorization.

(d)   A limited liability company's indebtedness to a member incurred by reason of a distribution made in accordance with this section is at parity with the company's indebtedness to its general, unsecured creditors.

(e)   Indebtedness of a limited liability company, including indebtedness issued in connection with or as part of a distribution, is not considered a liability for purposes of determinations under subsection (a) if its terms provide that payment of principal and interest are made only if and to the extent that payment of a distribution to members could then be made under this section. If the indebtedness is issued as a distribution, each payment of principal or interest on the indebtedness is treated as a distribution, the effect of which is measured on the date the payment is made.

SECTION 407. *Liability for Unlawful Distributions.*

(a)   A member of a member-managed limited liability company or a member or manager of a manager-managed company who votes for or assents to a distribution made in violation of Section 406, the articles of organization, a written operating agreement, or a signed record is personally liable to the company for the amount of the distribution which exceeds the amount that could have been distributed without violating Section 406, the articles of organization, a written operating agreement, or a signed record if it is established that the member or manager did not perform the member's or manager's duties in compliance with Section 409.

(b)   A member of a manager-managed limited liability company who knew a distribution was made in violation of Section 406 is personally liable to the limited liability company, but only to the extent that the distribution received by the member exceeded the amount that could properly have been paid under Section 406.

(c)   A member or manager against whom an action is brought under this section may implead in the action all:

(1)   other members or managers who voted for or assented to the distribution in violation of subsection (a) and may compel contribution from them; and

(2)   members who received a distribution in violation of subsection (b) and may compel contribution from the member in the amount received in violation of subsection (b).

(d)   A proceeding under this section is barred unless it is commenced within two years after the distribution.

SECTION 408. *Members Right to Information.*

(a)   A limited liability company shall provide members and their agents and attorneys access to any of its records at reasonable locations specified in the operating agreement. The company shall provide former members and their agents and attorneys access for proper purposes to records pertaining to the period during which they were members. The right of access provides the opportunity to inspect and copy records during ordinary business hours. The company may impose a reasonable charge, limited to the costs of labor and material, for copies of records furnished.

(b)   A limited liability company shall furnish to a member, and to the legal representative of a deceased member or member under legal disability:

(1)   without demand, information concerning the company's business or affairs reasonably required for the proper exercise of the member's rights and performance of the member's duties under the operating agreement or this [Act]; and

(2)   on demand, other information concerning the company's business or affairs, except to the extent the demand or the information demanded is unreasonable or otherwise improper under the circumstances.

(c)   A member has the right upon a signed record given to the limited liability company to obtain at the company's expense a copy of any operating agreement in record form.

SECTION 409. *General Standards of Member's and Manager's Conduct.*

(a)   The only fiduciary duties a member owes to a member-managed limited liability company and its other members are the duty of loyalty and the duty of care imposed by subsections (b) and (c).

(b)   A member's duty of loyalty to a member-managed limited liability company and its other members is limited to the following:

(1)   to account to the company and to hold as trustee for it any property, profit, or benefit derived by the member in the conduct or winding up of the company's business or derived from a use by the member of the company's property, including the appropriation of a company's opportunity;

(2)   to refrain from dealing with the company in the conduct or winding up of the company's business as or on behalf of a party having an interest adverse to the company; and

(3)   to refrain from competing with the company in the conduct of the company's business before the dissolution of the company.

(c)   A member's duty of care to a member-managed limited liability company and its other members in the conduct of and winding up of the company's business is limited to refraining from engaging in grossly negligent or reckless conduct, intentional misconduct, or a knowing violation of law.

(d)   A member shall discharge the duties to a member-managed limited liability company and its other members under this [Act] or under the operating agreement and exercise any rights consistently with the obligation of good faith and fair dealing.

(e)   A member of a member-managed limited liability company does not violate a duty or obligation under this [Act] or under the operating agreement merely because the member's conduct furthers the member's own interest.

(f)   A member of a member-managed limited liability company may lend money to and transact other business with the company. As to each loan or transaction, the rights and obligations of the member are the same as those of a person who is not a member, subject to other applicable law.

(g)   This section applies to a person winding up the limited liability company's business as the personal or legal representative of the last surviving member as if the person were a member.

(h)   In a manager-managed limited liability company:

(1)   a member who is not also a manager owes no duties to the company or to the other members solely by reason of being a member;

(2)   a manager is held to the same standards of conduct prescribed for members in subsections (b) through (f);

(3)   a member who pursuant to the operating agreement exercises some or all of the rights of a manager in the management and conduct of the company's business is held to the standards of conduct in subsections (b) through (f) to the extent that the member exercises the managerial authority vested in a manager by this [Act]; and

(4)   a manager is relieved of liability imposed by law for violation of the standards prescribed by subsections (b) through (f) to the extent of the managerial authority delegated to the members by the operating agreement.

SECTION 410. *Actions by Members.*

(a)   A member may maintain an action against a limited liability company or another member for legal or equitable relief, with or without an accounting as to the company's business, to enforce:

(1)   the member's rights under the operating agreement;

(2)   the member's rights under this [Act]; and

(3)   the rights and otherwise protect the interests of the member, including rights and interests arising independently of the member's relationship to the company.

(b)   The accrual, and any time limited for the assertion, of a right of action for a remedy under this section is governed by other law. A right to an accounting upon a dissolution and winding up does not revive a claim barred by law.

SECTION 411. *Continuation of Limited Liability Company After Expiration of Specified Term.*

(a)   If a limited liability company having a specified term is continued after the expiration of the term, the rights and duties of the members and managers remain the same as they were at the expiration of the term except to the extent inconsistent with rights and duties of members and managers of an at-will company.

(b)   If the members in a member-managed limited liability company or the managers in a manager-managed company continue the business without any winding up of the business of the company, it continues as an at-will company.

[ARTICLE] 5
TRANSFEREES AND CREDITORS OF MEMBER

Section 501.   Member's Distributional Interest.
Section 502.   Transfer of Distributional Interest.
Section 503.   Rights of Transferee.
Section 504.   Rights of Creditor.

SECTION 501. *Member's Distributional Interest.*

(a)   A member is not a co-owner of, and has no transferable interest in, property of a limited liability company.

(b)   A distributional interest in a limited liability company is personal property and, subject to Sections 502 and 503, may be transferred in whole or in part.

(c)   An operating agreement may provide that a distributional interest may be evidenced by a certificate of the interest issued by the limited liability company and, subject to Section 503, may also provide for the transfer of any interest represented by the certificate.

SECTION 502. *Transfer of Distributional Interest.*

A transfer of a distributional interest does not entitle the transferee to become or to exercise any rights of a member. A transfer entitles the transferee to receive, to the extent transferred, only the distributions to which the transferor would be entitled. A member ceases to be a member upon transfer of all of the member's distributional interest, other than a transfer for security purposes, or a court order charging the member's distributional interest, which has not been foreclosed.

SECTION 503. *Rights of Transferee.*

(a)   A transferee of a distributional interest may become a member of a limited liability company if and to the extent that the transferor gives the transferee the right in accordance with authority described in the operating agreement or all other members consent.

(b)   A transferee who has become a member, to the extent transferred, has the rights and powers, and is subject to the restrictions and liabilities, of a member under the operating agreement of a limited liability company and this [Act]. A transferee who becomes a member also is liable for the transferor member's obligations to make contributions under Section 402 and for obligations under Section 407 to return unlawful distributions, but the transferee is not obligated for the transferor member's liabilities unknown to the transferee at the time the transferee becomes a member and is not personally liable for any obligation of the company incurred before the transferee's admission as a member.

(c)   Whether or not a transferee of a distributional interest becomes a member under subsection (a), the transferor is not released from liability to the limited liability company under the operating agreement or this [Act].

(d)   A transferee who does not become a member is not entitled to participate in the management or conduct of the limited liability company's business, require access to information concerning the company's transactions, or inspect or copy any of the company's records.

(e)   A transferee who does not become a member is entitled to:

(1)   receive, in accordance with the transfer, distributions to which the transferor would otherwise be entitled;

(2)   receive, upon dissolution and winding up of the limited liability company's business:

(i)   in accordance with the transfer, the net amount otherwise distributable to the transferor;

(ii)   a statement of account only from the date of the latest statement of account agreed to by all the members;

(3)   seek under Section 801(6) a judicial determination that it is equitable to dissolve and wind up the company's business.

(f)   A limited liability company need not give effect to a transfer until it has notice of the transfer.

SECTION 504. *Rights of Creditor.*

(a)   On application by a judgment creditor of a member of a limited liability company or of a member's transferee, a court having jurisdiction may charge the distributional interest of the judgment debtor to satisfy the judgment. The court may appoint a receiver of the share of the distributions due or to become due to the judgment debtor and make all other orders, directions, accounts, and inquiries the judgment debtor might have made or which the circumstances may require to give effect to the charging order.

(b)   A charging order constitutes a lien on the judgment debtor's distributional interest. The court may order a foreclosure of a lien on a distributional interest subject to the charging order at any time. A purchaser at the foreclosure sale has the rights of a transferee.

(c)   At any time before foreclosure, a distributional interest in a limited liability company which is charged may be redeemed:

(1)   by the judgment debtor;

(2)   with property other than the company's property, by one or more of the other members; or

(3)   with the company's property, but only if permitted by the operating agreement.

(d)   This [Act] does not affect a member's right under exemption laws with respect to the member's distributional interest in a limited liability company.

(e)   This section provides the exclusive remedy by which a judgment creditor of a member or a transferee may satisfy a judgment out of the judgment debtor's distributional interest in a limited liability company.

[ARTICLE] 6
MEMBER'S DISSOCIATION

Section 601.   Events Causing Member's Dissociation.

Section 602.   Member's Power to Dissociate; Wrongful Dissociation.

Section 603.   Effect of Member's Dissociation.

SECTION 601. *Events Causing Member's Dissociation.*

A member is dissociated from a limited liability company upon the occurrence of any of the following events:

(1) the company's having notice of the member's express will to withdraw upon the date of notice or on a later date specified by the member;

(2) an event agreed to in the operating agreement as causing the member's dissociation;

(3) the member's expulsion pursuant to the operating agreement;

(4) the member's expulsion by unanimous vote of the other members if:

(i) it is unlawful to carry on the company's business with the member;

(ii) there has been a transfer of substantially all of the member's distributional interest, other than a transfer for security purposes, or a court order charging the member's distributional interest, which has not been foreclosed;

(iii) within 90 days after the company notifies a corporate member that it will be expelled because it has filed a certificate of dissolution or the equivalent, its charter has been revoked, or its right to conduct business has been suspended by the jurisdiction of its incorporation, the member fails to obtain a revocation of the certificate of dissolution or a reinstatement of its charter or its right to conduct business; or

(iv) a partnership or a limited liability company that is a member has been dissolved and its business is being wound up;

(5) on application by the company or another member, the member's expulsion by judicial determination because the member:

(i) engaged in wrongful conduct that adversely and materially affected the company's business;

(ii) willfully or persistently committed a material breach of the operating agreement or of a duty owed to the company or the other members under Section 409; or

(iii) engaged in conduct relating to the company's business which makes it not reasonably practicable to carry on the business with the member;

(6) the member's:

(i) becoming a debtor in bankruptcy;

(ii) executing an assignment for the benefit of creditors;

(iii) seeking, consenting to, or acquiescing in the appointment of a trustee, receiver, or liquidator of the member or of all or substantially all of the member's property; or

(iv) failing, within 90 days after the appointment, to have vacated or stayed the appointment of a trustee, receiver, or liquidator of the member or of all or substantially all of the member's property obtained without the member's consent or acquiescence, or failing within 90 days after the expiration of a stay to have the appointment vacated;

(7) in the case of a member who is an individual:

(i) the member's death;

(ii) the appointment of a guardian or general conservator for the member; or

(iii) a judicial determination that the member has otherwise become incapable of performing the member's duties under the operating agreement;

(8) in the case of a member that is a trust or is acting as a member by virtue of being a trustee of a trust, distribution of the trust's entire rights to receive distributions from the company, but not merely by reason of the substitution of a successor trustee;

(9) in the case of a member that is an estate or is acting as a member by virtue of being a personal representative of an estate, distribution of the estate's entire rights to receive distributions from the company, but not merely the substitution of a successor personal representative;

(10) termination of the existence of a member if the member is not an individual, estate, or trust other than a business trust; or

(11) a termination of a member's continued membership in a limited liability company for any other reason.

SECTION 602. *Member's Power to Dissociate; Wrongful Dissociation.*

(a) A member has the power to dissociate from a limited liability company at any time, rightfully or wrongfully, by express will pursuant to Section 601(1).

(b) A member's dissociation from a limited liability company is wrongful only if:

(1) it is in breach of an express provision of the operating agreement; or

(2) before the expiration of the term of a company having a specified term:

    (i) the member withdraws by express will;

    (ii) the member is expelled by judicial determination under Section 601(5);

    (iii) the member is dissociated by becoming a debtor in bankruptcy; or

    (iv) in the case of a member who is not an individual, trust other than a business-trust, or estate, the member is expelled or otherwise dissociated because it willfully dissolved or terminated its existence.

(c) A member who wrongfully dissociates from a limited liability company is liable to the company and to the other members for damages caused by the dissociation. The liability is in addition to any other obligation of the member to the company or to the other members.

(d) If a limited liability company does not dissolve and wind up its business as a result of a member's wrongful dissociation under subsection (b), damages sustained by the company for the wrongful dissociation must be offset against distributions otherwise due the member after the dissociation.

SECTION 603. Effect of Member's Dissociation.

(a) If under Section 801 a member's dissociation from a limited liability company results in a dissolution and winding up of the company's business, [Article] 8 applies. If a member's dissociation from the company does not result in a dissolution and winding up of the company's business under Section 801:

(1) in an at-will company, the company must cause the dissociated member's distributional interest to be purchased under [Article] 7; and

(2) in a company having a specified term:

    (i) if the company dissolves and winds up its business on or before the expiration of its specified term, [Article] 8 applies to determine the dissociated member's rights to distributions; and

    (ii) if the company does not dissolve and wind up its business on or before the

expiration of its specified term, the company must cause the dissociated member's distributional interest to be purchased under [Article] 7 on the date of the expiration of the term specified at the time of the member's dissociation.

(b) Upon a member's dissociation from a limited liability company:

(1) the member's right to participate in the management and conduct of the company's business terminates, except as otherwise provided in Section 803, and the member ceases to be a member and is treated the same as a transferee of a member;

(2) the member's duty of loyalty under Section 409(b)(3) terminates, and

(3) the member's duty of loyalty under Section 409(b)(l) and (2) and duty of care under Section 409(c) continue only with regard to matters arising and events occurring before the member's dissociation, unless the member participates in winding up the company's business pursuant to Section 803.

[ARTICLE] 7
MEMBER'S DISSOCIATION WHEN BUSINESS NOT WOUND UP

Section 701. Company Purchase of Distributional Interest.

Section 702. Court Action to Determine Fair Value of Distributional Interest.

Section 703. Dissociated Member's Power to Bind Limited Liability Company.

Section 704. Statement of Dissociation.

SECTION 701. Company Purchase of Distributional Interest.

(a) A limited liability company shall purchase a distributional interest of a:

(1) member of an at-will limited liability company for its fair value determined as of the date of the member's dissociation if the member's dissociation does not result in a dissolution and winding up of the company's business under Section 801; or

(2) member of a company having a specified term for its fair value determined as of the date of the expiration of the specified term

that existed on the member's dissociation if the expiration of the specified term does not result in a dissolution and winding up of the company's business under Section 801.

(b)   A limited liability company must deliver a purchase offer to the dissociated member whose distributional interest is entitled to be purchased not later than 30 days after the date determined under subsection (a). The purchase offer must be accompanied by:

(1)   a statement of the company's assets and liabilities as of the date determined under subsection (a);

(2)   the latest available balance sheet and income statement, if any; and

(3)   an explanation of how the estimated amount of the payment was calculated.

(c)   If the price and other terms of a purchase of a distributional interest are fixed or are to be determined by the operating agreement, the price and terms so fixed or determined govern the purchase unless the purchaser defaults. In that case the dissociated member is entitled to commence a proceeding to have the company dissolved under Section 801(5)(iv).

(d)   If an agreement to purchase the distributional interest is not made within 120 days after the date determined under subsection (a), the dissociated member, within another 120 days, may commence a proceeding against the limited liability company to enforce the purchase. The company at its expense shall notify in writing all of the remaining members, and any other person the court directs, of the commencement of the proceeding. The jurisdiction of the court in which the proceeding is commenced under this subsection is plenary and exclusive.

(e)   The court shall determine the fair value of the distributional interest in accordance with the standards set forth in Section 702 together with the terms for the purchase. Upon making these determinations, the court shall order the limited liability company to purchase or cause the purchase of the interest.

(f)   Damages for wrongful dissociation under Section 602(b), and all other amounts owing, whether or not currently due, from the dissociated member to a limited liability company, must be offset against the purchase price.

SECTION 702.   *Court Action to Determine Fair Value of Distributional Interest.*

(a)   In an action brought to determine the fair value of a distributional interest in a limited liability company, the court shall:

(1)   determine the fair value of the interest, considering among other relevant evidence the going concern value of the company, any agreement among some or all of the members fixing the price or specifying a formula for determining value of distributional interests for any purpose, the recommendations of any appraiser appointed by the court, and any legal constraints on the company's ability to purchase the interest;

(2)   specify the terms of the purchase, including, if appropriate, terms for installment payments, subordination of the purchase obligation to the rights of the company's other creditors, security for a deferred purchase price, and a covenant not to compete or other restriction on a dissociated member; and

(3)   require the dissociated member to deliver an assignment of the interest to the purchaser upon receipt of the purchase price or the first installment of the purchase price.

(b)   After an order to purchase is entered, a party may petition the court to modify the terms of the purchase and the court may do so if it finds that changes in the financial or legal ability of the limited liability company or other purchaser to complete the purchase justify a modification.

(c)   After the dissociated member delivers the assignment, the dissociated member has no further claim against the company, its members, officers, or managers, if any, other than a claim to any unpaid balance of the purchase price and a claim under any agreement with the company or the remaining members that is not terminated by the court.

(d)   If the purchase is not completed in accordance with the specified terms, the company is to be dissolved upon application under Section 801(5)(iv). If a limited liability company is so dissolved, the dissociated member has the same rights and priorities in the company's assets as if the sale had not been ordered.

(e)   If the court finds that a party to the proceeding acted arbitrarily, vexatiously, or not in good faith, it may award one or more other parties their reasonable expenses, including attorney's fees and the expenses of appraisers or other experts, incurred in the proceeding. The finding may be based on the company's failure to make an offer to pay or to comply with Section 70l(b).

(f) Interest must be paid on the amount awarded from the determined under Section 70l(a) to the date of payment.

SECTION 703. Dissociated Member's Power to Bind Limited Liability Company.

For two years after a member dissociates without the dissociation resulting in a dissolution and winding up of a limited liability company's business, the company, including a surviving company under [Article] 9, is bound by an act of the dissociated member which would have bound the company under Section 301 before dissociation only if at the time of entering into the transaction the other party.

(1) reasonably believed that the dissociated member was then a member;

(2) did not have notice of the member's dissociation; and

(3) is not deemed to have had notice under Section 704.

SECTION 704. Statement of Dissociation.

(a) A dissociated member or a limited liability company may file in the office of the [Secretary of State] a statement of dissociation stating the name of the company and that the member is dissociated from the company.

(b) For the purposes of Sections 301 and 703, a person not a member is deemed to have notice of the dissociation 90 days after the statement of dissociation is filed.

[ARTICLE] 8
WINDING UP COMPANY'S BUSINESS

Section 801. Events Causing Dissolution and Winding Up of Company's Business.

Section 802. Limited Liability Company Continues After Dissolution.

Section 803. Right to Wind Up Limited Liability Company's Business.

Section 804. Member's or Manager's Power and Liability as Agent After Dissolution.

Section 805. Articles of Termination.

Section 806. Distribution of Assets in Winding Up Limited Liability Company's Business.

Section 807. Known Claims Against Dissolved Limited Liability Company.

Section 808. Other Claims Against Dissolved Limited Liability Company.

Section 809. Grounds for Administrative Dissolution.

Section 810. Procedure for and Effect of Administrative Dissolution.

Section 811. Reinstatement Following Administrative Dissolution.

Section 812. Appeal from Denial of Reinstatement.

SECTION 801. Events Causing Dissolution and Winding Up of Company's Business.

A limited liability company is dissolved, and its business must be wound up, upon the occurrence of any of the following events:

(1) an event specified in the operating agreement;

(2) consent of the number or percentage of members specified in the operating agreement;

(3) dissociation of a member of an at-will company, and dissociation of a member of a company having a specified term but only if the dissociation was for a reason provided in Section 601(6) through (10) and occurred before the expiration of the specified term, but the company is not dissolved and required to be wound up by reason of the dissociation:

(i) if, within 90 days after the dissociation, a majority in interest of the remaining members agree to continue the business of the company; or

(ii) the business of the company is continued under a right to continue stated in the operating agreement;

(4) an event that makes it unlawful for all or substantially all of the business of the company to be continued, but any cure of illegality within 90 days after notice to the company of the event is effective retroactively to the date of the event for purposes of this section;

(5) on application by a member or a dissociated member, upon entry of a judicial decree that:

(i) the economic purpose of the company is likely to be unreasonably frustrated;

(ii) another member has engaged in conduct relating to the company's business that makes it not reasonably practicable to carry on the company's business with that member;

(iii) it is not otherwise reasonably practicable to carry on the company's business in conformity with the articles of organization and the operating agreement;

(iv) the company failed to purchase the petitioner's distributional interest as required by Section 701; or

(v) the managers or members in control of the company have acted, are acting, or will act in a manner that is illegal, oppressive, fraudulent, or unfairly prejudicial to the petitioner;

(6) on application by a transferee of a member's interest, a judicial determination that it is equitable to wind up the company's business:

(i) after the expiration of the specified term, if the company was for a specified term at the time the applicant became a transferee by member dissociation, transfer, or entry of a charging order that gave rise to the transfer; or

(ii) at any time, if the company was at will at the time the applicant became a transferee by member dissociation, transfer, or entry of a charging order that gave rise to the transfer; or

(7) the expiration of a specified term.

SECTION 802. Limited Liability Company Continues After Dissolution.

(a) Subject to subsection (b), a limited liability company continues after dissolution only for the purpose of winding up its business.

(b) At any time after the dissolution of a limited liability company and before the winding up of its business is completed, the members, including a dissociated member whose dissociation caused the dissolution, may unanimously waive the right to have the company's business wound up and the company terminated. In that case:

(1) the limited liability company resumes carrying on its business as if dissolution had never occurred and any liability incurred by the company or a member after the dissolution and before the waiver is determined as if the dissolution had never occurred; and

(2) the rights of a third party accruing under Section 804(a) or arising out of conduct in reliance on the dissolution before the third party knew or received a notification of the waiver are not adversely affected.

SECTION 803. Right to Wind Up Limited Liability Company's Business.

(a) After dissolution, a member who has not wrongfully dissociated may participate in winding up a limited liability company's business, but on application of any member, member's legal representative, or transferee, the [designate the appropriate court], for good cause shown, may order judicial supervision of the winding up.

(b) A legal representative of the last surviving member may wind up a limited liability company's business.

(c) A person winding up a limited liability company's business may preserve the company's business or property as a going concern for a reasonable time, prosecute and defend actions and proceedings, whether civil, criminal, or administrative, settle and close the company's business, dispose of and transfer the company's property, discharge the company's liabilities, distribute the assets of the company pursuant to Section 806, settle disputes by mediation or arbitration, and perform other necessary acts.

SECTION 804. Member's or Manager's Power and Liability As Agent After Dissolution.

(a) A limited liability company is bound by a member's or manager's act after dissolution that:

(1) is appropriate for winding up the company's business; or

(2) would have bound the company under Section 301 before dissolution, if the other party to the transaction did not have notice of the dissolution.

(b) A member or manager who, with knowledge of the dissolution, subjects a limited liability company to liability by an act that is not appropriate for winding up the company's business is liable to the company for any damage caused to the company arising from the liability.

SECTION 805. Articles of Termination.

(a) At any time after dissolution and winding up, a limited liability company may terminate its existence by filing with the [Secretary of State] articles of termination stating:

    (1) the name of the company;

    (2) the date of the dissolution; and

    (3) that the company's business has been wound up and the legal existence of the company has been terminated.

(b) The existence of a limited liability company is terminated upon the filing of the articles of termination, or upon a later effective date, if specified in the articles of termination.

SECTION 806. Distribution of Assets in Winding Up Limited Liability Company's Business.

(a) In winding up a limited liability company's business, the assets of the company must be applied to discharge its obligations to creditors, including members who are creditors. Any surplus must be applied to pay in money the net amount distributable to members in accordance with their right to distributions under subsection (b).

(b) Each member is entitled to a distribution upon the winding up of the limited liability company's business consisting of a return of all contributions which have not previously been returned and a distribution of any remainder in equal shares.

SECTION 807. Known Claims Against Dissolved Limited Liability Company.

(a) A dissolved limited liability company may dispose of the known claims against it by following the procedure described in this section.

(b) A dissolved limited liability company shall notify its known claimants in writing of the dissolution. The notice must:

    (1) specify the information required to be included in a claim;

    (2) provide a mailing address where the claim is to be sent;

    (3) state the deadline for receipt of the claim, which may not be less than 120 days after the date the written notice is received by the claimant; and

    (4) state that the claim will be barred if not received by the deadline.

(c) A claim against a dissolved limited liability company is barred if the requirements of subsection (b) are met, and:

    (1) the claim is not received by the specified deadline; or

    (2) in the case of a claim that is timely received but rejected by the dissolved company, the claimant does not commence a proceeding to enforce the claim within 90 days after the receipt of the notice of the rejection.

(d) For purposes of this section, "claim" does not include a contingent liability or a claim based on an event occurring after the effective date of dissolution.

SECTION 808. Other Claims Against Dissolved Limited Liability Company.

(a) A dissolved limited liability company may publish notice of its dissolution and request persons having claims against the company to present them in accordance with the notice.

(b) The notice must:

    (1) be published at least once in a newspaper of general circulation in the [county] in which the dissolved limited liability company's principal office is located or, if none in this State, in which its designated office is or was last located;

    (2) describe the information required to be contained in a claim and provide a mailing address where the claim is to be sent; and

    (3) state that a claim against the limited liability company is barred unless a proceeding to enforce the claim is commenced within five years after publication of the notice.

(c) If a dissolved limited liability company publishes a notice in accordance with subsection (b), the claim of each of the following claimants is barred unless the claimant commences a proceeding to enforce the claim against the dissolved company within five years after the publication date of the notice:

    (1) a claimant who did not receive written notice under Section 807;

    (2) a claimant whose claim was timely sent to the dissolved company but not acted on; and

    (3) a claimant whose claim is contingent or based on an event occuring after the effective date of dissolution.

(d) A claim not barred under this section may be enforced:

(1) against the dissolved limited liability company, to the extent of its undistributed assets; or

(2) if the assets have been distributed in liquidation, against a member of the dissolved company to the extent of the member's proportionate share of the claim or the company's assets distributed to the member in liquidation, whichever is less, but a member's total liability for all claims under this section may not exceed the total amount of assets distributed to the member.

SECTION 809. Grounds for Administrative Dissolution.

The [Secretary of State] may commence a proceeding to dissolve a limited liability company administratively if the company does not:

(1) pay any franchise taxes or penalties imposed by this [Act] or other law within 60 days after they are due;

(2) deliver its annual report to the [Secretary of State] within 60 days after it is due, or

(3) file articles of termination under Section 805 following the expiration of the specified term designated in its articles of organization.

SECTION 810. Procedure for and Effect of Administrative Dissolution.

(a) If the [Secretary of State] determines that a ground exists for administratively dissolving a limited liability company, the [Secretary of State] shall enter a record of the determination and serve the company with a copy of the record.

(b) If the company does not correct each ground for dissolution or demonstrate to the reasonable satisfaction of the [Secretary of State] that each ground determined by the [Secretary of State] does not exist within 60 days after service of the notice, the [Secretary of State] shall administratively dissolve the company by signing a certification of the dissolution that recites the ground for dissolution and its effective date. The [Secretary of State] shall file the original of the certificate and serve the company with a copy of the certificate.

(c) A company administratively dissolved continues its existence but may carry on only business necessary to wind up and liquidate its business and

affairs under Section 802 and to notify claimants under Sections 807 and 808.

(d) The administrative dissolution of a company does not terminate the authority of its agent for service of process.

SECTION 811. Reinstatement Following Administrative Dissolution.

(a) A limited liability company administratively dissolved may apply to the [Secretary of State] for reinstatement within two years after the effective date of dissolution. The application must:

(1) recite the name of the company and the effective date of its administrative dissolution;

(2) state that the grounds for dissolution either did not exist or have been eliminated;

(3) state that the company's name satisfies the requirements of Section 105; and

(4) contain a certificate from the [taxing authority] reciting that all taxes owed by the company have been paid.

(b) If the [Secretary of State] determines that the application contains the information required by subsection (a) and that the information is correct, the [Secretary of State] shall cancel the certificate of dissolution and prepare a certificate of reinstatement that recites this determination and the effective date of reinstatement, file the original of the certificate, and serve the company with a copy of the certificate.

(c) When reinstatement is effective, it relates back to and takes effect as of the effective date of the administrative dissolution and the company may resume its business as if the administrative dissolution had never occurred.

SECTION 812. Appeal from Denial of Reinstatement.

(a) If the [Secretary of State] denies a limited liability company's application for reinstatement following administrative dissolution, the [Secretary of State] shall serve the company with a record that explains the reason or reasons for denial.

(b) The company may appeal the denial of reinstatement to the [name appropriate] court within 30 days after service of the notice of denial is perfected. The company appeals by petitioning the court to set aside the dissolution and attaching to the petition copies of the [Secretary of State's] certificate of dissolution, the company's application for reinstatement, and the [Secretary of State's] notice of denial.

(c)   The court may summarily order the [Secretary of State] to reinstate the dissolved company or may take other action the court considers appropriate.

(d)   The court's final decision may be appealed as in other civil proceedings.

[ARTICLE] 9
CONVERSIONS AND MERGERS

Section 901.   Definitions.

Section 902.   Conversion of Partnership or Limited Partnership To Limited Liability Company.

Section 903.   Effect of Conversion; Entity Unchanged.

Section 904.   Merger of Entities.

Section 905.   Articles of Merger.

Section 906.   Effect of Merger.

Section 907.   [Article] Not Exclusive.

SECTION 901. *Definitions.*

In this [article]:

(1)   "Corporation" means a corporation under [the State Corporation Act], a predecessor law, or comparable law of another jurisdiction.

(2)   "General partner" means a partner in a partnership and a general partner in a limited partnership.

(3)   "Limited partner" means a limited partner in a limited partnership.

(4)   "Limited partnership" means a limited partnership created under [the State Limited Partnership Act], a predecessor law, or comparable law of another jurisdiction.

(5)   "Partner" includes a general partner and a limited partner.

(6)   "Partnership" means a general partnership under [the State Partnership Act], a predecessor law, or comparable law of another jurisdiction.

(7)   "Partnership agreement" means an agreement among the partners concerning the partnership or limited partnership.

(8)   "Shareholder" means a shareholder in a corporation.

SECTION 902. *Conversion of Partnership or Limited Partnership to Limited Liability Company.*

(a)   A partnership or limited partnership may be converted to a limited liability company pursuant to this section.

(b)   The terms and conditions of a conversion of a partnership or limited partnership to a limited liability company must be approved by all of the partners or by a number or percentage of the partners required for conversion in the partnership agreement.

(c)   An agreement of conversion must set forth the terms and conditions of the conversion of the interests of partners of a partnership or of a limited partnership, as the case may be, into interests in the converted limited liability company or the cash or other consideration to be paid or delivered as a result of the conversion of the interests of the partners, or a combination thereof.

(d)   After a conversion is approved under subsection (b), the partnership or limited partnership shall file articles of organization in the office of the [Secretary of State] which satisfy the requirements of Section 203 and contain:

(1)   a statement that the partnership or limited partnership was converted to a limited liability company from a partnership or limited partnership, as the case may be;

(2)   its former name;

(3)   a statement of the number of votes cast by the partners entitled to vote for and against the conversion and, if the vote is less than unanimous, the number or percentage required to approve the conversion under subsection (b); and

(4)   in the case of a limited partnership, a statement that the certificate of limited partnership is to be canceled as of the date the conversion took effect.

(e)   In the case of a limited partnership, the filing of articles of organization under subsection (d) cancels its certificate of limited partnership as of the date the conversion took effect.

(f)   A conversion takes effect when the articles of organization are filed in the office of the [Secretary of State] or at any later date specified in the articles of organization.

(g)   A general partner who becomes a member of a limited liability company as a result of a conversion remains liable as a partner for an obligation incurred by the partnership or limited partnership before the conversion takes effect.

(h)   A general partner's liability for all obligations of the limited liability company incurred after the conversion takes effect is that of a member of the company. A limited partner who becomes a member as a result of a conversion remains liable only to the extent the limited partner was liable for an obligation incurred by the limited partnership before the conversion takes effect.

SECTION 903. *Effect of Conversion;Entity Unchanged.*

(a)   A partnership or limited partnership that has been converted pursuant to this [article] is for all purposes the same entity that existed before the conversion.

(b)   When a conversion takes effect:

(1)   all property owned by the converting partnership or limited partnership is vested in the limited liability company;

(2)   all debts, liabilities, and other obligations of the converting partnership or limited partnership continue as obligations of the limited liability company;

(3)   an action or proceeding pending by or against the converting partnership or limited partnership may be continued as if the conversion had not occurred;

(4)   except as prohibited by other law, all of the rights, privileges, immunities, powers, and purposes of the converting partnership or limited partnership are vested in the limited liability company; and

(5)   except as otherwise provided in the agreement of conversion under Section 902(c), all of the partners of the converting partnership continue as members of the limited liability company.

SECTION 904. *Merger of Entities.*

(a)   Pursuant to a plan of merger approved under subsection (c), a limited liability company may be merged with or into one or more limited liability companies, foreign limited liability companies, corporations, foreign corporations, partnerships, foreign partnerships, limited partnerships, foreign limited partnerships, or other domestic or foreign entities.

(b)   A plan of merger must set forth:

(1)   the name of each entity that is a party to the merger;

(2)   the name of the surviving entity into which the other entities will merge;

(3)   the type of organization of the surviving entity;

(4)   the terms and conditions of the merger;

(5)   the manner and basis for converting the interests of each party to the merger into interests or obligations of the surviving entity, or into money or other property in whole or in part; and

(6)   the street address of the surviving entity's principal place of business.

(c)   A plan of merger must be approved:

(1)   in the case of a limited liability company that is a party to the merger, by the members representing the percentage of ownership specified in the operating agreement, but not fewer than the members holding a majority of the ownership or, if provision is not made in the operating agreement, by all the members;

(2)   in the case of a foreign limited liability company that is a party to the merger, by the vote required for approval of a merger by the law of the State or foreign jurisdiction in which the foreign limited liability company is organized;

(3)   in the case of a partnership or domestic limited partnership that is a party to the merger, by the vote required for approval of a conversion under Section 902(b); and

(4)   in the case of any other entities that are parties to the merger, by the vote required for approval of a merger by the law of this State or of the state or foreign jurisdiction in which the entity is organized and, in the absence of such a requirement, by all the owners of interests in the entity.

(d)   After a plan of merger is approved and before the merger takes effect, the plan may be amended or abandoned as provided in the plan.

(e)   The merger is effective upon the filing of the articles of merger with the [Secretary of State], or at such later date as the articles may provide.

SECTION 905. *Articles of Merger.*

(a)   After approval of the plan of merger under Section 904(c), unless the merger is abandoned under Section 904(d), articles of merger must be signed on behalf of each limited liability company and other entity that is a party to the merger and delivered to the [Secretary of State] for filing. The articles must set forth:

(1)   the name and jurisdiction of formation or organization of each of the limited liability companies and other entities that are parties to the merger;

(2)   for each limited liability company that is to merge, the date its articles of organization were filed with the [Secretary of State];

(3)   that a plan of merger has been approved and signed by each limited liability company and other entity that is to merge;

(4)   the name and address of the surviving limited liability company or other surviving entity;

(5)   the effective date of the merger;

(6)   if a limited liability company is the surviving entity, such changes in its articles of organization as are necessary by reason of the merger;

(7)   if a party to a merger is a foreign limited liability company, the jurisdiction and date of filing of its initial articles of organization and the date when its application for authority was filed by the [Secretary of State] or, if an application has not been filed, a statement to that effect; and

(8)   if the surviving entity is not a limited liability company, an agreement that the surviving entity may be served with process in this State in any action or proceeding for the enforcement of any liability or obligation of any limited liability company previously subject to suit in this State which is to merge, and for the enforcement, as provided in this [Act], of the right of members of any limited liability company to receive payment for their interest against the surviving entity.

(b)   If a foreign limited liability company is the surviving entity of a merger, it may not do business in this State until an application for that authority is filed with the [Secretary of State].

(c)   The surviving limited liability company or other entity shall furnish a copy of the plan of merger, on request and without cost, to any member of any limited liability company or any person holding an interest in any other entity that is to merge.

(d)   Articles of merger operate as an amendment to the limited liability company's articles of organization.

SECTION 906. *Effect of Merger.*

(a)   When a merger takes effect:

(1)   the separate existence of each limited liability company and other entity that is a party to the merger, other than the surviving entity, terminates;

(2)   all property owned by each of the limited liability companies and other entities that are party to the merger vests in the surviving entity;

(3)   all debts, liabilities, and other obligations of each limited liability company and other entity that is party to the merger become the obligations of the surviving entity;

(4)   an action or proceeding pending by or against a limited liability company or other party to a merger may be continued as if the merger had not occurred or the surviving entity may be substituted as a party to the action or proceeding; and

(5)   except as prohibited by other law, all the rights, privileges, immunities, powers, and purposes of every limited liability company and other entity that is a party to a merger become vested in the surviving entity.

(b)   The [Secretary of State] is an agent for service of process in an action or proceeding against the surviving foreign entity to enforce an obligation of any party to a merger if the surviving foreign entity fails to appoint or maintain an agent designated for service of process in this State or the agent for service of process cannot with reasonable diligence be found at the designated office. Upon receipt of process, the [Secretary of State] shall send a copy of the process by registered or certified mail, return receipt requested, to the surviving entity at the address set forth in the articles of merger. Service is effected under this subsection at the earliest of:

(1)   the date the company receives the process, notice, or demand;

(2)   the date shown on the return receipt, if signed on behalf of the company; or

(3)   five days after its deposit in the mail, if mailed postpaid and correctly addressed.

(c)   A member of the surviving limited liability company is liable for all obligations of a party to the merger for which the member was personally liable before the merger.

(d)   Unless otherwise agreed, a merger of a limited liability company that is not the surviving entity in the merger does not require the limited liability company to wind up its business under this [Act] or pay its liabilities and distribute its assets pursuant to this [Act].

(e)   Articles of merger serve as articles of dissolution for a limited liability company that is not the surviving entity in the merger.

SECTION 907. *[Article] Not Exclusive.*

This [article] does not preclude an entity from being converted or merged under other law.

[ARTICLE] 10
FOREIGN LIMITED
LIABILITY COMPANIES

Section 1001.   Law Governing Foreign Limited Liability Companies.

Section 1002.   Application for Certificate of Authority.

Section 1003.   Activities Not Constituting Transacting Business.

Section 1004.   Issuance of Certificate of Authority.

Section 1005.   Name of Foreign Limited Liability Company.

Section 1006.   Revocation of Certificate of Authority.

Section 1007.   Cancellation of Authority.

Section 1008.   Effect of Failure to Obtain Certificate of Authority.

Section 1009.   Action by [Attorney General].

SECTION 1001. *Law Governing Foreign Limited Liability Companies.*

(a)   The laws of the State or other jurisdiction under which a foreign limited liability company is organized govern its organization and internal affairs and the liability of its managers, members, and their transferees.

(b)   A foreign limited liability company may not be denied a certificate of authority by reason of any difference between the laws of another jurisdiction under which the foreign company is organized and the laws of this State.

(c)   A certificate of authority does not authorize a foreign limited liability company to engage in any business or exercise any power that a limited liability company may not engage in or exercise in this State.

SECTION 1002. *Application for Certificate of Authority.*

(a)   A foreign limited liability company may apply for a certificate of authority to transact business in this State by delivering an application to the [Secretary of State] for filing. The application must set forth:

(1)   the name of the foreign company or, if its name is unavailable for use in this State, a name that satisfies the requirements of Section 1005;

(2)   the name of the State or country under whose law it is organized;

(3)   the street address of its principal office;

(4)   the address of its initial designated office in this State;

(5)   the name and street address of its initial agent for service of process in this State;

(6)   whether the duration of the company is for a specified term and, if so, the period specified;

(7)   whether the company is manager-managed, and, if so, the name and address of each initial manager; and

(8)   whether the members of the company are to be liable for its debts and obligations under a provision similar to Section 303(c).

(b)   A foreign limited liability company shall deliver with the completed application a certificate of existence or a record of similar import authenticated by the [Secretary of State] or other official having custody of company records in the State or country under whose law it is organized.

SECTION 1003. *Activities Not Constituting Transacting Business.*

(a)   Activities of a foreign limited liability company that do not constitute transacting business within the meaning of this [article] include:

(1)   maintaining, defending, or settling an action or proceeding;

(2)   holding meetings of its members or managers or carrying on any other activity concerning its internal affairs;

(3) maintaining bank accounts;

(4) maintaining offices or agencies for the transfer, exchange, and registration of the foreign company's own securities or maintaining trustees or depositories with respect to those securities;

(5) selling through independent contractors;

(6) soliciting or obtaining orders, whether by mail or through employees or agents or otherwise, if the orders require acceptance outside this State before they become contracts;

(7) creating or acquiring indebtedness, mortgages, or security interests in real or personal property;

(8) securing or collecting debts or enforcing mortgages or other security interests in property securing the debts, and holding, protecting, and maintaining property so acquired;

(9) conducting an isolated transaction that is completed within 30 days and is not one in the course of similar transactions of a like manner; and

(10) transacting business in interstate commerce.

(b) For purposes of this [article], the ownership in this State of income-producing real property or tangible personal property, other than property excluded under subsection (a), constitutes transacting business in this State.

(c) This section does not apply in determining the contacts or activities that may subject a foreign limited liability company to service of process, taxation, or regulation under any other law of this State.

SECTION 1004. *Issuance of Certificate of Authority.*

Unless the [Secretary of State] determines that an application for a certificate of authority fails to comply as to form with the filing requirements of this [Act], the [Secretary of State], upon payment of all filing fees, shall file the application and send a receipt for it and the fees to the limited liability company or its representative.

SECTION 1005. *Name of Foreign Limited Liability Company.*

(a) If the name of a foreign limited liability company does not satisfy the requirements of Section 105, the company, to obtain or maintain a certificate of authority to transact business in this State, must use a fictitious name to transact business in this State if its real name is unavailable and it delivers to the [Secretary of State] for filing a copy of the resolution of its managers, in the case of a manager-managed company, or of its members, in the case of a member-managed company, adopting the fictitious name.

(b) Except as authorized by subsections (c) and (d), the name, including a fictitious name, of a foreign limited liability company must be distinguishable upon the records of the [Secretary of State] from:

(1) the name of any corporation, limited partnership, or company incorporated, organized, or authorized to transact business in this State;

(2) a company name reserved or registered under Section 106 or 107; and

(3) the fictitious name of another foreign limited liability company authorized to transact business in this State.

(c) A foreign limited liability company may apply to the [Secretary of State] for authority to use in this State a name that is not distinguishable upon the records of the [Secretary of State] from a name described in subsection (b). The [Secretary of State] shall authorize use of the name applied for if:

(1) the present user, registrant, or owner of a reserved name consents to the use in a record and submits an undertaking in form satisfactory to the [Secretary of State] to change its name to a name that is distinguishable upon the records of the [Secretary of State] from the name of the foreign applying limited liability company; or

(2) the applicant delivers to the [Secretary of State] a certified copy of a final judgment of a court establishing the applicant's right to use the name applied for in this State.

(d) A foreign limited liability company may use in this State the name, including the fictitious name, of another domestic or foreign entity that is used in this State if the other entity is incorporated, organized, or authorized to transact business in this State and the foreign limited liability company:

(1) has merged with the other entity;

(2) has been formed by reorganization of the other entity; or

(3) has acquired all or substantially all of the assets, including the name, of the other entity.

(e) If a foreign limited liability company authorized to transact business in this State changes its name to one that does not satisfy the requirements of Section 105, it may not transact business in this State under the name as changed until it adopts a name satisfying the requirements of Section 105 and obtains an amended certificate of authority.

SECTION 1006. *Revocation of Certificate of Authority.*

(a) A certificate of authority of a foreign limited liability company to transact business in this State may be revoked by the [Secretary of State] in the manner provided in subsection (b) if:

    (1) the company fails to:

        (i) pay any fees prescribed by law;

        (ii) appoint and maintain an agent for service of process as required by this [article]; or

        (iii) file a statement of a change in the name or business address of the agent as required by this [article]; or

    (2) a misrepresentation has been made of any material matter in any application, report, affidavit, or other record submitted by the company pursuant to this [article].

(b) The [Secretary of State] may not revoke a certificate of authority of a foreign limited liability company unless the [Secretary of State] sends the company notice of the revocation, at least 60 days before its effective date, by a record addressed to its agent for service of process in this State, or if the company fails to appoint and maintain a proper agent in this State, addressed to the office required to be maintained by Section 108. The notice must identify the cause for the revocation of the certificate of authority. The authority of the company to transact business in this State ceases on the effective date of the revocation unless the foreign limited liability company cures the failure before that date.

SECTION 1007. *Cancellation of Authority.*

A foreign limited liability company may cancel its authority to transact business in this State by filing in the office of the [Secretary of State] a certificate of cancellation. Cancellation does not terminate the authority of the [Secretary of State] to accept service of process on the company for [claims for relief] arising out of the transactions of business in this State.

SECTION 1008. *Effect of Failure to Obtain Certificate of Authority.*

(a) A foreign limited liability company transacting business in this State may not maintain an action or proceeding in this State unless it has a certificate of authority to transact business in this State.

(b) The failure of a foreign limited liability company to have a certificate of authority to transact business in this State does not impair the validity of a contract or act of the company or prevent the foreign limited liability company from defending an action or proceeding in this State.

(c) Limitations on personal liability of managers, members, and their transferees are not waived solely by transacting business in this State without a certificate of authority.

(d) If a foreign limited liability company transacts business in this State without a certificate of authority, it appoints the [Secretary of State] as its agent for service of process for [claims for relief] arising out of the transaction of business in this State.

SECTION 1009. *Action by [Attorney General].*

The [Attorney General] may maintain an action to restrain a foreign limited liability company from transacting business in this State in violation of this [article].

[ARTICLE] 11
DERIVATIVE ACTIONS

Section 1101. Right of Action.
Section 1102. Proper Plaintiff.
Section 1103. Pleading.
Section 1104. Expenses.

SECTION 1101. *Right of Action.*

A member of a limited liability company may maintain an action in the right of the company if the members or managers having authority to do so have refused to commence the action or an effort to cause those members or managers to commence the action is not likely to succeed.

SECTION 1102. *Proper Plaintiff.*

In a derivative action for a limited liability company, the plaintiff must be a member of the company when the action is commenced; and:

(1)   must have been a member at the time of the transaction of which the plaintiff complains; or

(2)   the plaintiff's status as a member must have devolved upon the plaintiff by operation of law or pursuant to the terms of the operating agreement from a person who was a member at the time of the transaction.

SECTION 1103. *Pleading.*

In a derivative action for a limited liability company, the complaint must set forth with particularity the effort of the plaintiff to secure initiation of the action by a member or manager or the reasons for not making the effort.

SECTION 1104. *Expenses.*

If a derivative action for a limited liability company is successful, in whole or in part, or if anything is received by the plaintiff as a result of a judgment, compromise, or settlement of an action or claim, the court may award the plaintiff reasonable expenses, including reasonable attorney's fees, and shall direct the plaintiff to remit to the limited liability company the remainder of the proceeds received.

[ARTICLE] 12
MISCELLANEOUS PROVISIONS

Section 1201. Uniformity of Application and
             Construction.
Section 1202. Short Title.
Section 1203. Severability Clause.
Section 1204. Effective Date.
Section 1205. Transitional Provisions.
Section 1206. Savings Clause.

SECTION 1201. *Uniformity of Application and Construction.*

This [Act] shall be applied and construed to effectuate its general purpose to make uniform the law with respect to the subject of this [Act] among States enacting it.

SECTION 1202. *Short Title.*

This [Act] may be cited as the Uniform Limited Liability Company Act.

SECTION 1203. *Severability Clause.*

If any provision of this [Act] or its application to any person or circumstance is held invalid, the invalidity does not affect other provisions or applications of this [Act] which can be given effect without the invalid provision or application, and to this end the provisions of this [Act] are severable.

SECTION 1204. *Effective Date.*

This [Act] takes effect [_____].

SECTION 1205. *Transitional Provisions.*

(a)   Before January 1, 199___, this [Act] governs only a limited liability company organized:

(1)   after the effective date of this [Act], unless the company is continuing the business of a dissolved limited liability company under [Section of the existing Limited Liability Company Act]; and

(2)   before the effective date of this [Act], which elects, as provided by subsection (c), to be governed by this [Act].

(b)   On and after January 1, 199___, this [Act] governs all limited liability companies.

(c)   Before January 1, 199___, a limited liability company voluntarily may elect, in the manner provided in its operating agreement or by law for amending the operating agreement, to be governed by this [Act].

SECTION 1206. *Savings Clause.*

This [Act] does not affect an action or proceeding commenced or right accrued before the effective date of this [Act].

APPENDIX I

Excerpts from the Model Business Corporation Act

[Chapter 1 omitted]

CHAPTER 2
Incorporation

§ 2.01.   Incorporators
§ 2.02.   Articles of incorporation
§ 2.03.   Incorporation
§ 2.04.   Liability for preincorporation transactions
§ 2.05.   Organization of corporation
§ 2.06.   Bylaws
§ 2.07.   Emergency bylaws

CHAPTER 3
Purposes and Powers

§ 3.01.   Purposes
§ 3.02.   General powers
§ 3.03.   Emergency powers
§ 3.04.   Ultra vires

CHAPTER 4
Name

§ 4.01.   Corporate name
§ 4.02.   Reserved name
§ 4.03.   Registered name

CHAPTER 5
Office and Agent

§ 5.01.   Registered office and registered agent
§ 5.02.   Change of registered office or registered agent
§ 5.03.   Resignation of registered agent
§ 5.04.   Service on corporation

CHAPTER 6
Shares and Distributions

Subchapter A
Shares

§ 6.01.   Authorized shares

§ 6.02.   Terms of class or series determined by board of directors
§ 6.03.   Issued and outstanding shares
§ 6.04.   Fractional shares

Subchapter B
Issuance of Shares

§ 6.20.   Subscription for shares before incorporation
§ 6.21.   Issuance of shares
§ 6.22.   Liability of shareholders
§ 6.23.   Share dividends
§ 6.24.   Share options
§ 6.25.   Form and content of certificates
§ 6.26.   Shares without certificates
§ 6.27.   Restriction on transfer of shares and other securities
§ 6.28.   Expense of issue

Subchapter C
Subsequent Acquisition of Shares by Shareholders and Corporation

§ 6.30.   Shareholders' preemptive rights
§ 6.31.   Corporation's acquisition of its own shares

Subchapter D
Distributions

§ 6.40.   Distributions to shareholders

CHAPTER 7
Shareholders

Subchapter A
Meetings

§ 7.01.   Annual meeting
§ 7.02.   Special meeting
§ 7.03.   Court-ordered meeting
§ 7.04.   Action without meeting
§ 7.05.   Notice of meeting
§ 7.06.   Waiver of notice

§ 7.07.   Record date

§ 7.08.   Conduct of the meeting

Subchapter B
Voting

§ 7.20.   Shareholders' list for meeting

§ 7.21.   Voting entitlement of shares

§ 7.22.   Proxies

§ 7.23.   Shares held by nominees

§ 7.24.   Corporation's acceptance of votes

§ 7.25.   Quorum and voting requirements for voting groups

§ 7.26.   Action by single and multiple voting groups

§ 7.27.   Greater quorum or voting requirements

§ 7.28.   Voting for directors; cumulative voting

§ 7.29.   Inspectors of election

Subchapter C
Voting Trusts and Agreements

§ 7.30.   Voting trusts

§ 7.31.   Voting agreements

§ 7.32.   Shareholder agreements

Subchapter D
Derivative Proceedings

§ 7.40.   Subchapter definitions

§ 7.41.   Standing

§ 7.42.   Demand

§ 7.43.   Stay of proceedings

§ 7.44.   Dismissal

§ 7.45.   Discontinuance or settlement

§ 7.46.   Payment of expenses

§ 7.47.   Applicability to foreign corporations

CHAPTER 8
Directors and Officers

Subchapter A
Board of Directors

§ 8.01.   Requirement for and duties of board of directors

§ 8.02.   Qualifications of directors

§ 8.03.   Number and election of directors

§ 8.04.   Election of directors by certain classes of shareholders

§ 8.05.   Terms of directors generally

§ 8.06.   Staggered terms for directors

§ 8.07.   Resignation of directors

§ 8.08.   Removal of directors by shareholders

§ 8.09.   Removal of directors by judicial proceeding

§ 8.10.   Vacancy on board

§ 8.11.   Compensation of directors

Subchapter B
Meetings and Action of the Board

§ 8.20.   Meetings

§ 8.21.   Action without meeting

§ 8.22.   Notice of meeting

§ 8.23.   Waiver of notice

§ 8.24.   Quorum and voting

§ 8.25.   Committees

Subchapter C
Standards of Conduct

§ 8.30.   General standards for directors

§ 8.31.   Liability for Directors

§ 8.32.   [Reserved]

§ 8.33.   Liability for unlawful distributions

Subchapter D
Officers

§ 8.40.   Required officers

§ 8.41.   Duties of officers

§ 8.42.   Standards of conduct for officers

§ 8.43.   Resignation and removal of officers

§ 8.44.   Contract rights of officers

Subchapter E
Indemnification

§ 8.50.   Subchapter definitions

§ 8.51.   Permissible indemnification

§ 8.52.   Mandatory indemnification

§ 8.53.   Advance for expenses

§ 8.54.   Court-ordered indemnification and advance for expenses

§ 8.55.   Determination and authorization of indemnification

§ 8.56.   Officers

§ 8.57.   Insurance

§ 8.58.   Application of subchapter

§ 8.59.   Exclusivity of subchapter

Subchapter F
Directors' Conflicting Interest Transactions

§ 8.60.   Subchapter definitions
§ 8.61.   Judicial action
§ 8.62.   Directors' action
§ 8.63.   Shareholders' action

CHAPTER 9
[Reserved]

[Chapter 10 omitted]

CHAPTER 11
Merger and Share Exchange

§ 11.01.   Merger
§ 11.02.   Share exchange
§ 11.03.   Action on plan
§ 11.04.   Merger of subsidiary
§ 11.05.   Articles of merger or share exchange
§ 11.06.   Effect of merger or share exchange
§ 11.07.   Merger or share exchange with foreign corporation

CHAPTER 12
Sale of Assets

§ 12.01.   Sale of assets in regular course of business and mortgage of assets
§ 12.02.   Sale of assets other than in regular course of business

CHAPTER 13
Dissenters' Rights

Subchapter A
Right to Appraisal And Payment for Shares

§ 13.01.   Definitions
§ 13.02.   Right to appraisal
§ 13.03.   Assertion of rights by nominees and beneficial owners

Subchapter B
Procedure for Exercise of Appraisal Rights

§ 13.20.   Notice of appraisal rights
§ 13.21.   Notice of intent to demand payment
§ 13.22.   Appraisal notice and form
§ 13.23.   Perfection of rights; Right to withdraw
§ 13.24.   Payment
§ 13.25.   After-acquired shares

§ 13.26.   Procedure if shareholder dissatisfied with payment or offer

Subchapter C
Judicial Appraisal of Shares

§ 13.30.   Court Action
§ 13.31.   Court costs and counsel fees

CHAPTER 14
Dissolution

Subchapter A
Voluntary Dissolution

§ 14.01.   Dissolution by incorporators or initial directors
§ 14.02.   Dissolution by board of directors and shareholders
§ 14.03.   Articles of dissolution
§ 14.04.   Revocation of dissolution
§ 14.05.   Effect of dissolution
§ 14.06.   Known claims against dissolved corporation
§ 14.07.   Unknown claims against dissolved corporation

Subchapter B
Administrative Dissolution

§ 14.20.   Grounds for administrative dissolution
§ 14.21.   Procedure for and effect of administrative dissolution
§ 14.22.   Reinstatement following administrative dissolution
§ 14.23.   Appeal from denial of reinstatement

Subchapter C
Judicial Dissolution

§ 14.30.   Grounds for judicial dissolution
§ 14.31.   Procedure for judicial dissolution
§ 14.32.   Receivership or custodianship
§ 14.33.   Decree of dissolution
§ 14.34.   Election to purchase in lieu of dissolution

[Subchapter D omitted]

CHAPTER 15
Foreign Corporations

Subchapter A
Certificate of Authority

§ 15.01.   Authority to transact business required

§ 15.02. Consequences of transacting business without authority

§ 15.03. Application for certificate of authority

§ 15.04. Amended certificate of authority

§ 15.05. Effect of certificate of authority

§ 15.06. Corporate name of foreign corporation

§ 15.07. Registered office and registered agent of foreign corporation

§ 15.08. Change of registered office or registered agent of foreign corporation

§ 15.09. Resignation of registered agent of foreign corporation

§ 15.10. Service on foreign corporation

Subchapter B
Withdrawal

§ 15.20. Withdrawal of foreign corporation

[Subchapter C omitted]

[Chapters 16 and 17 omitted]

[Chapter 1, General Provisions, omitted]

CHAPTER 2
INCORPORATION

§ 2.01. Incorporators

One or more persons may act as the incorporator or incorporators of a corporation by delivering articles of incorporation to the secretary of state for filing.

§ 2.02. Articles of Incorporation

(a) The articles of incorporation must set forth:

(1) a corporate name for the corporation that satisfies the requirements of section 4.01;

(2) the number of shares the corporation is authorized to issue;

(3) the street address of the corporation's initial registered office and the name of its initial registered agent at that office; and

(4) the name and address of each incorporator.

(b) The articles of incorporation may set forth:

(1) the names and addresses of the individuals who are to serve as the initial directors;

(2) provisions not inconsistent with law regarding:

(i) the purpose or purposes for which the corporation is organized;

(ii) managing the business and regulating the affairs of the corporation;

(iii) defining, limiting, and regulating the powers of the corporation, its board of directors, and shareholders;

(iv) a par value for authorized shares or classes of shares;

(v) the imposition of personal liability on shareholders for the debts of the corporation to a specified extent and upon specified conditions;

(3) any provision that under this Act is required or permitted to be set forth in the bylaws;

(4) a provision eliminating or limiting the liability of a director to the corporation or its shareholders for money damages for any action taken, or any failure to take any action, as a director, except liability for (A) the amount of a financial benefit received by a director to which he is not entitled; (B) an intentional infliction of harm on the corporation or the shareholders; (C) a violation of section 8.33; or (D) an intentional violation of criminal law; and

(5) a provision permitting or making obligatory indemnification of a director for liability (as defined in section 8.50(5)) to any person for any action taken, or any failure to take any action, as a director, except liability for (A) receipt of a financial benefit to which he is not entitled, (B) an intentional infliction of harm on the corporation or its shareholders, (C) a violation of section 8.33, or (D) an intentional violation of criminal law.

(c) The articles of incorporation need not set forth any of the corporate powers enumerated in this Act.

§ 2.03. Incorporation

(a) Unless a delayed effective date is specified, the corporate existence begins when the articles of incorporation are filed.

(b) The secretary of state's filing of the articles of incorporation is conclusive proof that the incorporators satisfied all conditions precedent to incorporation except in a proceeding by the state to cancel or revoke the incorporation or involuntarily dissolve the corporation.

§ 2.04. *Liability for Preincorporation Transactions*

All persons purporting to act as or on behalf of a corporation, knowing there was no incorporation under this Act, are jointly and severally liable for all liabilities created while so acting.

§ 2.05. *Organization of Corporation*

(a)   After incorporation:

(1)   if initial directors are named in the articles of incorporation, the initial directors shall hold an organizational meeting, at the call of a majority of the directors, to complete the organization of the corporation by appointing officers, adopting bylaws, and carrying on any other business brought before the meeting;

(2)   if initial directors are not named in the articles, the incorporator or incorporators shall hold an organizational meeting at the call of a majority of the incorporators:

(i)   to elect directors and complete the organization of the corporation; or

(ii)   to elect a board of directors who shall complete the organization of the corporation.

(b)   Action required or permitted by this Act to be taken by incorporators at an organizational meeting may be taken without a meeting if the action taken is evidenced by one or more written consents describing the action taken and signed by each incorporator.

(c)   An organizational meeting may be held in or out of this state.

§ 2.06. *Bylaws*

(a)   The incorporators or board of directors of a corporation shall adopt initial bylaws for the corporation.

(b)   The bylaws of a corporation may contain any provision for managing the business and regulating the affairs of the corporation that is not inconsistent with law or the articles of incorporation.

§ 2.07. *Emergency Bylaws*

(a)   Unless the articles of incorporation provide otherwise, the board of directors of a corporation may adopt bylaws to be effective only in an emergency defined in subsection (d). The emergency bylaws, which are subject to amendment or repeal by the shareholders, may make all provisions necessary for managing the corporation during the emergency, including:

(1)   procedures for calling a meeting of the board of directors;

(2)   quorum requirements for the meeting; and

(3)   designation of additional or substitute directors.

(b)   All provisions of the regular bylaws consistent with the emergency bylaws remain effective during the emergency. The emergency bylaws are not effective after the emergency ends.

(c)   Corporate action taken in good faith in accordance with the emergency bylaws:

(1)   binds the corporation; and

(2)   may not be used to impose liability on a corporate director, officer, employee, or agent.

(d)   An emergency exists for purposes of this section if a quorum of the corporation's directors cannot readily be assembled because of some catastrophic event.

CHAPTER 3
PURPOSES AND POWERS

§ 3.01. *Purposes*

(a)   Every corporation incorporated under this Act has the purpose of engaging in any lawful business unless a more limited purpose is set forth in the articles of incorporation.

(b)   A corporation engaging in a business that is subject to regulation under another statute of this state may incorporate under this Act only if permitted by, and subject to all limitations of, the other statute.

§ 3.02. *General Powers*

Unless its articles of incorporation provide otherwise, every corporation has perpetual duration and succession in its corporate name and has the same powers as an individual to do all things necessary or convenient to carry out its business and affairs, including without limitation power:

(1)   to sue and be sued, complain and defend in its corporate name;

(2)   to have a corporate seal, which may be altered at will, and to use it, or a facsimile of it, by impressing or affixing it or in any other manner reproducing it;

(3) to make and amend bylaws, not inconsistent with its articles of incorporation or with the laws of this state, for managing the business and regulating the affairs of the corporation;

(4) to purchase, receive, lease, or otherwise acquire, and own, hold, improve, use, and otherwise deal with, real or personal property, or any legal or equitable interest in property, wherever located;

(5) to sell, convey, mortgage, pledge, lease, exchange, and otherwise dispose of all or any part of its property;

(6) to purchase, receive, subscribe for, or otherwise acquire; own, hold, vote, use, sell, mortgage, lend, pledge, or otherwise dispose of; and deal in and with shares or other interests in, or obligations of, any other entity;

(7) to make contracts and guarantees, incur liabilities, borrow money, issue its notes, bonds, and other obligations (which may be convertible into or include the option to purchase other securities of the corporation), and secure any of its obligations by mortgage or pledge of any of its property, franchises, or income;

(8) to lend money, invest and reinvest its funds, and receive and hold real and personal property as security for repayment;

(9) to be a promoter, partner, member, associate, or manager of any partnership, joint venture, trust, or other entity;

(10) to conduct its business, locate offices, and exercise the powers granted by this Act within or without this state;

(11) to elect directors and appoint officers, employees, and agents of the corporation, define their duties, fix their compensation, and lend them money and credit;

(12) to pay pensions and establish pension plans, pension trusts, profit sharing plans, share bonus plans, share option plans, and benefit or incentive plans for any or all of its current or former directors, officers, employees, and agents;

(13) to make donations for the public welfare or for charitable, scientific, or educational purposes;

(14) to transact any lawful business that will aid governmental policy;

(15) to make payments or donations, or do any other act, not inconsistent with law, that furthers the business and affairs of the corporation.

§ 3.03. *Emergency Powers*

(a) In anticipation of or during an emergency defined in subsection (d), the board of directors of a corporation may:

(1) modify lines of succession to accommodate the incapacity of any director, officer, employee, or agent; and

(2) relocate the principal office, designate alternative principal offices or regional offices, or authorize the officers to do so.

(b) During an emergency defined in subsection (d), unless emergency bylaws provide otherwise:

(1) notice of a meeting of the board of directors need be given only to those directors whom it is practicable to reach and may be given in any practicable manner, including by publication and radio; and

(2) one or more officers of the corporation present at a meeting of the board of directors may be deemed to be directors for the meeting, in order of rank and within the same rank in order of seniority, as necessary to achieve a quorum.

(c) Corporate action taken in good faith during an emergency under this section to further the ordinary business affairs of the corporation:

(1) binds the corporation; and

(2) may not be used to impose liability on a corporate director, officer, employee, or agent.

(d) An emergency exists for purposes of this section if a quorum of the corporation's directors cannot readily be assembled because of some catastrophic event.

§ 3.04. *Ultra Vires*

(a) Except as provided in subsection (b), the validity of corporate action may not be challenged on the ground that the corporation lacks or lacked power to act.

(b) A corporation's power to act may be challenged:

(1) in a proceeding by a shareholder against the corporation to enjoin the act;

(2) in a proceeding by the corporation, directly, derivatively, or through a receiver, trustee, or other legal representative, against an incumbent or former director, officer, employee, or agent of the corporation; or

(3) in a proceeding by the Attorney General under section 14.30.

(c) In a shareholder's proceeding under subsection (b)(l) to enjoin an unauthorized corporate act, the court may enjoin or set aside the act, if equitable and if all affected persons are parties to the proceeding, and may award damages for loss (other than anticipated profits) suffered by the corporation or another party because of enjoining the unauthorized act.

CHAPTER 4
NAME

§ 4.01. Corporate Name

(a) A corporate name:

(1) must contain the word "corporation," "incorporated," "company," or "limited," or the abbreviation "corp.," "inc.," "co.," or "ltd.," or words or abbreviations of like import in another language; and

(2) may not contain language stating or implying that the corporation is organized for a purpose other than that permitted by section 3.01 and its articles of incorporation.

(b) Except as authorized by subsections (c) and (d), a corporate name must be distinguishable upon the records of the secretary of state from:

(1) the corporate name of a corporation incorporated or authorized to transact business in this state;

(2) a corporate name reserved or registered under section 4.02 or 4.03;

(3) the fictitious name adopted by a foreign corporation authorized to transact business in this state because its real name is unavailable; and

(4) the corporate name of a not-for-profit corporation incorporated or authorized to transact business in this state.

(c) A corporation may apply to the secretary of state for authorization to use a name that is not distinguishable upon his records from one or more of the names described in subsection (b). The secretary of state shall authorize use of the name applied for if:

(1) the other corporation consents to the use in writing and submits an undertaking in form satisfactory to the secretary of state to change its name to a name that is distinguishable

upon the records of the secretary of state from the name of the applying corporation; or

(2) the applicant delivers to the secretary of state a certified copy of the final judgment of a court of competent jurisdiction establishing the applicant's right to use the name applied for in this state.

(d) A corporation may use the name (including the fictitious name) of another domestic or foreign corporation that is used in this state if the other corporation is incorporated or authorized to transact business in this state and the proposed user corporation:

(1) has merged with the other corporation;

(2) has been formed by reorganization of the other corporation; or

(3) has acquired all or substantially all of the assets, including the corporate name, of the other corporation.

(e) This Act does not control the use of fictitious names.

§ 4.02. Reserved Name

(a) A person may reserve the exclusive use of a corporate name, including a fictitious name for a foreign corporation whose corporate name is not available, by delivering an application to the secretary of state for filing. The application must set forth the name and address of the applicant and the name proposed to be reserved. If the secretary of state finds that the corporate name applied for is available, he shall reserve the name for the applicant's exclusive use for a nonrenewable 120-day period.

(b) The owner of a reserved corporate name may transfer the reservation to another person by delivering to the secretary of state a signed notice of the transfer that states the name and address of the transferee.

§ 4.03. Registered Name

(a) A foreign corporation may register its corporate name, or its corporate name with any addition required by section 15.06, if the name is distinguishable upon the records of the secretary of state from the corporate names that are not available under section 4.01(b)(3).

(b) A foreign corporation registers its corporate name, or its corporate name with any addition required by section 15.06, by delivering to the secretary of state for filing an application:

(1)   setting forth its corporate name, or its corporate name with any addition required by section 15.06, the state or country and date of its incorporation, and a brief description of the nature of the business in which it is engaged; and

(2)   accompanied by a certificate of existence (or a document of similar import) from the state or country of incorporation.

(c)   The name is registered for the applicant's exclusive use upon the effective date of the application.

(d)   A foreign corporation whose registration is effective may renew it for successive years by delivering to the secretary of state for filing a renewal application, which complies with the requirements of subsection (b), between October 1 and December 31 of the preceding year. The renewal application when filed renews the registration for the following calendar year.

(e)   A foreign corporation whose registration is effective may thereafter qualify as a foreign corporation under the registered name or consent in writing to the use of that name by a corporation thereafter incorporated under this Act or by another foreign corporation thereafter authorized to transact business in this state. The registration terminates when the domestic corporation is incorporated or the foreign corporation qualifies or consents to the qualification of another foreign corporation under the registered name.

CHAPTER 5
OFFICE AND AGENT

§ 5.01. *Registered Office and Registered Agent*

Each corporation must continuously maintain in this state:

(1)   a registered office that may be the same as any of its places of business; and

(2)   a registered agent, who may be:

(i)   an individual who resides in this state and whose business office is identical with the registered office;

(ii)   a domestic corporation or not-for-profit domestic corporation whose business office is identical with the registered office; or

(iii)   a foreign corporation or not-for-profit foreign corporation authorized to transact business in this state whose business office is identical with the registered office.

§ 5.02. *Change of Registered Office or Registered Agent*

(a)   A corporation may change its registered office or registered agent by delivering to the secretary of state for filing a statement of change that sets forth:

(1)   the name of the corporation;

(2)   the street address of its current registered office;

(3)   if the current registered office is to be changed, the street address of the new registered office;

(4)   the name of its current registered agent;

(5)   if the current registered agent is to be changed, the name of the new registered agent and the new agent's written consent (either on the statement or attached to it) to the appointment; and

(6)   that after the change or changes are made, the street addresses of its registered office and the business office of its registered agent will be identical.

(b)   If a registered agent changes the street address of his business office, he may change the street address of the registered office of any corporation for which he is the registered agent by notifying the corporation in writing of the change and signing (either manually or in facsimile) and delivering to the secretary of state for filing a statement that complies with the requirements of subsection (a) and recites that the corporation has been notified of the change.

§ 5.03. *Resignation of Registered Agent*

(a)   A registered agent may resign his agency appointment by signing and delivering to the secretary of state for filing the signed original and two exact or conformed copies of a statement of resignation. The statement may include a statement that the registered office is also discontinued.

(b)   After filing the statement the secretary of state shall mail one copy to the registered office (if not discontinued) and the other copy to the corporation at its principal office.

(c)   The agency appointment is terminated, and the registered office discontinued if so provided, on the 31st day after the day on which the statement was filed.

§ 5.04. *Service on Corporation*

(a) A corporation's registered agent is the corporation's agent for service of process, notice, or demand required or permitted by law to be served on the corporation.

(b) If a corporation has no registered agent, or the agent cannot with reasonable diligence be served, the corporation may be served by registered or certified mail, return receipt requested, addressed to the secretary of the corporation at its principal office. Service is perfected under this subsection at the earliest of:

(1) the date the corporation receives the mail;

(2) the date shown on the return receipt, if signed on behalf of the corporation; or

(3) five days after its deposit in the United States Mail, as evidenced by the postmark, if mailed postpaid and correctly addressed.

(c) This section does not prescribe the only means, or necessarily the required means, of serving a corporation.

CHAPTER 6
SHARES AND DISTRIBUTIONS
SUBCHAPTER A.
SHARES

§ 6.01. *Authorized Shares*

(a) The articles of incorporation must prescribe the classes of shares and the number of shares of each class that the corporation is authorized to issue. If more than one class of shares is authorized, the articles of incorporation must prescribe a distinguishing designation for each class, and, prior to the issuance of shares of a class, the preferences, limitations, and relative rights of that class must be described in the articles of incorporation. All shares of a class must have preferences, limitations, and relative rights identical with those of other shares of the same class except to the extent otherwise permitted by section 6.02.

(b) The articles of incorporation must authorize (1) one or more classes of shares that together have unlimited voting rights, and (2) one or more classes of shares (which may be the same class or classes as those with voting rights) that together are

entitled to receive the net assets of the corporation upon dissolution.

(c) The articles of incorporation may authorize one or more classes of shares that:

(1) have special, conditional, or limited voting rights, or no right to vote, except to the extent prohibited by this Act;

(2) are redeemable or convertible as specified in the articles of incorporation (i) at the option of the corporation, the shareholder, or another person or upon the occurrence of a designated event; (ii) for cash, indebtedness, securities, or other property; (iii) in a designated amount or in an amount determined in accordance with a designated formula or by reference to extrinsic data or events;

(3) entitle the holders to distributions calculated in any manner, including dividends that may be cumulative, noncumulative, or partially cumulative;

(4) have preference over any other class of shares with respect to distributions, including dividends and distributions upon the dissolution of the corporation.

(d) The description of the designations, preferences, limitations, and relative rights of share classes in subsection (c) is not exhaustive.

§ 6.02. *Terms of Class or Series Determined by Board of Directors*

(a) If the articles of incorporation so provide, the board of directors may determine, in whole or part, the preferences, limitations, and relative rights (within the limits set forth in section 6.01) of (1) any class of shares before the issuance of any shares of that class or (2) one or more series within a class before the issuance of any shares of that series.

(b) Each series of a class must be given a distinguishing designation.

(c) All shares of a series must have preferences, limitations, and relative rights identical with those of other shares of the same series and, except to the extent otherwise provided in the description of the series, with those of other series of the same class.

(d) Before issuing any shares of a class or series created under this section, the corporation must deliver to the secretary of state for filing articles of amendment, which are effective without shareholder action, that set forth:

(1) the name of the corporation;

(2) the text of the amendment determining the terms of the class or series of shares;

(3) the date it was adopted; and

(4) a statement that the amendment was duly adopted by the board of directors.

§ 6.03. Issued and Outstanding Shares

(a) A corporation may issue the number of shares of each class or series authorized by the articles of incorporation. Shares that are issued are outstanding shares until they are reacquired, redeemed, converted, or cancelled.

(b) The reacquisition, redemption, or conversion of outstanding shares is subject to the limitations of subsection (c) of this section and to section 6.40.

(c) At all times that shares of the corporation are outstanding, one or more shares that together have unlimited voting rights and one or more shares that together are entitled to receive the net assets of the corporation upon dissolution must be outstanding.

§ 6.04. Fractional Shares

(a) A corporation may:

(1) issue fractions of a share or pay in money the value of fractions of a share;

(2) arrange for disposition of fractional shares by the shareholders;

(3) issue scrip in registered or bearer form entitling the holder to receive a full share upon surrendering enough scrip to equal a full share.

(b) Each certificate representing scrip must be conspicuously labeled "scrip" and must contain the information required by section 6.25(b).

(c) The holder of a fractional share is entitled to exercise the rights of a shareholder, including the right to vote, to receive dividends, and to participate in the assets of the corporation upon liquidation. The holder of scrip is not entitled to any of these rights unless the scrip provides for them.

(d) The board of directors may authorize the issuance of scrip subject to any condition considered desirable, including:

(1) that the scrip will become void if not exchanged for full shares before a specified date; and

(2) that the shares for which the scrip is exchangeable may be sold and the proceeds paid to the scripholders.

SUBCHAPTER B.
ISSUANCE OF SHARES

§ 6.20. Subscription for Shares
Before Incorporation

(a) A subscription for shares entered into before incorporation is irrevocable for six months unless the subscription agreement provides a longer or shorter period or all the subscribers agree to revocation.

(b) The board of directors may determine the payment terms of subscriptions for shares that were entered into before incorporation, unless the subscription agreement specifies them. A call for payment by the board of directors must be uniform so far as practicable as to all shares of the same class or series, unless the subscription agreement specifies otherwise.

(c) Shares issued pursuant to subscriptions entered into before incorporation are fully paid and nonassessable when the corporation receives the consideration specified in the subscription agreement.

(d) If a subscriber defaults in payment of money or property under a subscription agreement entered into before incorporation, the corporation may collect the amount owed as any other debt. Alternatively, unless the subscription agreement provides otherwise, the corporation may rescind the agreement and may sell the shares if the debt remains unpaid more than 20 days after the corporation sends written demand for payment to the subscriber.

(e) A subscription agreement entered into after incorporation is a contract between the subscriber and the corporation subject to section 6.21.

§ 6.21. Issuance of Shares

(a) The powers granted in this section to the board of directors may be reserved to the shareholders by the articles of incorporation.

(b) The board of directors may authorize shares to be issued for consideration consisting of any tangible or intangible property or benefit to the corporation, including cash, promissory notes, services performed, contracts for services to be performed, or other securities of the corporation.

(c) Before the corporation issues shares, the board of directors must determine that the consideration received or to be received for shares to be issued is adequate. That determination by the board of directors is conclusive insofar as the adequacy of consideration for the issuance of shares relates to whether the shares are validly issued, fully paid, and nonassessable.

(d)　When the corporation receives the consideration for which the board of directors authorized the issuance of shares, the shares issued therefor are fully paid and nonassessable.

(e)　The corporation may place in escrow shares issued for a contract for future services or benefits or a promissory note, or make other arrangements to restrict the transfer of the shares, and may credit distributions in respect of the shares against their purchase price, until the services are performed, the note is paid, or the benefits received. If the services are not performed, the note is not paid, or the benefits are not received, the shares escrowed or restricted and the distributions credited may be cancelled in whole or part.

§ 6.22.　Liability of Shareholders

(a)　A purchaser from a corporation of its own shares is not liable to the corporation or its creditors with respect to the shares except to pay the consideration for which the shares were authorized to be issued (section 6.21) or specified in the subscription agreement (section 6.20).

(b)　Unless otherwise provided in the articles of incorporation, a shareholder of a corporation is not personally liable for the acts or debts of the corporation except that he may become personally liable by reason of his own acts or conduct.

§ 6.23.　Share Dividends

(a)　Unless the articles of incorporation provide otherwise, shares may be issued pro rata and without consideration to the corporation's shareholders or to the shareholders of one or more classes or series. An issuance of shares under this subsection is a share dividend.

(b)　Shares of one class or series may not be issued as a share dividend in respect of shares of another class or series unless (1) the articles of incorporation so authorize, (2) a majority of the votes entitled to be cast by the class or series to be issued approve the issue, or (3) there are no outstanding shares of the class or series to be issued.

(c)　If the board of directors does not fix the record date for determining shareholders entitled to a share dividend, it is the date the board of directors authorizes the share dividend.

§ 6.24.　Share Options

A corporation may issue rights, options, or warrants for the purchase of shares of the corporation. The board of directors shall determine the terms upon which the rights, options, or warrants are issued, their form and content, and the consideration for which the shares are to be issued.

§ 6.25.　Form and Content of Certificates

(a)　Shares may but need not be represented by certificates. Unless this Act or another statute expressly provides otherwise, the rights and obligations of shareholders are identical whether or not their shares are represented by certificates.

(b)　At a minimum each share certificate must state on its face:

(1)　the name of the issuing corporation and that it is organized under the law of this state;

(2)　the name of the person to whom issued; and

(3)　the number and class of shares and the designation of the series, if any, the certificate represents.

(c)　If the issuing corporation is authorized to issue different classes of shares or different series within a class, the designations, relative rights, preferences, and limitations applicable to each class and the variations in rights, preferences, and limitations determined for each series (and the authority of the board of directors to determine variations for future series) must be summarized on the front or back of each certificate. Alternatively, each certificate may state conspicuously on its front or back that the corporation will furnish the shareholder this information on request in writing and without charge.

(d)　Each share certificate (1) must be signed (either manually or in facsimile) by two officers designated in the bylaws or by the board of directors and (2) may bear the corporate seal or its facsimile.

(e)　If the person who signed (either manually or in facsimile) a share certificate no longer holds office when the certificate is issued, the certificate is nevertheless valid.

§ 6.26.　Shares Without Certificates

(a)　Unless the articles of incorporation or bylaws provide otherwise, the board of directors of a corporation may authorize the issue of some or all of the shares of any or all of its classes or series without certificates. The authorization does not affect shares already represented by certificates until they are surrendered to the corporation.

(b)   Within a reasonable time after the issue or transfer of shares without certificates, the corporation shall send the shareholder a written statement of the information required on certificates by section C.25(b) and (c), and, if applicable, section 6.27.

§ 6.27.   Restriction on Transfer of Shares and Other Securities

(a)   The articles of incorporation, bylaws, an agreement among shareholders, or an agreement between shareholders and the corporation may impose restrictions on the transfer or registration of transfer of shares of the corporation. A restriction does not affect shares issued before the restriction was adopted unless the holders of the shares are parties to the restriction agreement or voted in favor of the restriction.

(b)   A restriction on the transfer or registration of transfer of shares is valid and enforceable against the holder or a transferee of the holder if the restriction is authorized by this section and its existence is noted conspicuously on the front or back of the certificate or is contained in the information statement required by section 6.26(b). Unless so noted, a restriction is not enforceable against a person without knowledge of the restriction.

(c)   A restriction on the transfer or registration of transfer of shares is authorized:

(1)   to maintain the corporation's status when it is dependent on the number or identity of its shareholders;

(2)   to preserve exemptions under federal or state securities law;

(3)   for any other reasonable purpose.

(d)   A restriction on the transfer or registration of transfer of shares may:

(1)   obligate the shareholder first to offer the corporation or other persons (separately, consecutively, or simultaneously) an opportunity to acquire the restricted shares;

(2)   obligate the corporation or other persons (separately, consecutively, or simultaneously) to acquire the restricted shares;

(3)   require the corporation, the holders of any class of its shares, or another person to approve the transfer of the restricted shares, if the requirement is not manifestly unreasonable;

(4)   prohibit the transfer of the restricted shares to designated persons or classes of persons, if the prohibition is not manifestly unreasonable.

(e)   For purposes of this section, "shares" includes a security convertible into or carrying a right to subscribe for or acquire shares.

§ 6.28.   Expense of Issue

A corporation may pay the expenses of selling or underwriting its shares, and of organizing or reorganizing the corporation, from the consideration received for shares.

SUBCHAPTER C.
SUBSEQUENT ACQUISITION OF SHARES BY SHAREHOLDERS AND CORPORATION

§ 6.30.   Shareholders' Preemptive Rights

(a)   The shareholders of a corporation do not have a preemptive right to acquire the corporation's unissued shares except to the extent the articles of incorporation so provide.

(b)   A statement included in the articles of incorporation that "the corporation elects to have preemptive rights" (or words of similar import) means that the following principles apply except to the extent the articles of incorporation expressly provide otherwise:

(1)   The shareholders of the corporation have a preemptive right, granted on uniform terms and conditions prescribed by the board of directors to provide a fair and reasonable opportunity to exercise the right, to acquire proportional amounts of the corporation's unissued shares upon the decision of the board of directors to issue them.

(2)   A shareholder may waive his preemptive right. A waiver evidenced by a writing is irrevocable even though it is not supported by consideration.

(3)   There is no preemptive right with respect to:

(i)   shares issued as compensation to directors, officers, agents, or employees of the corporation, its subsidiaries or affiliates;

(ii)   shares issued to satisfy conversion or option rights created to provide compensation to directors, officers, agents, or employees of the corporation, its subsidiaries or affiliates;

(iii) shares authorized in articles of incorporation that are issued within six months from the effective date of incorporation;

(iv) shares sold otherwise than for money.

(4) Holders of shares of any class without general voting rights but with preferential rights to distributions or assets have no preemptive rights with respect to shares of any class.

(5) Holders of shares of any class with general voting rights but without preferential rights to distributions or assets have no preemptive rights with respect to shares of any class with preferential rights to distributions or assets unless the shares with preferential rights are convertible into or carry a right to subscribe for or acquire shares without preferential rights.

(6) Shares subject to preemptive rights that are not acquired by shareholders may be issued to any person for a period of one year after being offered to shareholders at a consideration set by the board of directors that is not lower than the consideration set for the exercise of preemptive rights. An offer at a lower consideration or after the expiration of one year is subject to the shareholders' preemptive rights.

(c) For purposes of this section, "shares" includes a security convertible into or carrying a right to subscribe for or acquire shares.

§ 6.31. Corporation's Acquisition of Its Own Shares

(a) A corporation may acquire its own shares and shares so acquired constitute authorized but unissued shares.

(b) If the articles of incorporation prohibit the reissue of acquired shares, the number of authorized shares is reduced by the number of shares acquired, effective upon amendment of the articles of incorporation.

(c) The board of directors may adopt articles of amendment under this section without shareholder action and deliver them to the secretary of state for filing. The articles must set forth:

(1) the name of the corporation;

(2) the reduction in the number of authorized shares, itemized by class and series; and

(3) the total number of authorized shares, itemized by class and series, remaining after reduction of the shares.

SUBCHAPTER D. DISTRIBUTIONS

§ 6.40 Distributions to Shareholders

(a) A board of directors may authorize and the corporation may make distributions to its shareholders subject to restriction by the articles of incorporation and the limitation in subsection (c).

(b) If the board of directors does not fix the record date for determining shareholders entitled to a distribution (other than one involving a purchase, redemption, or other acquisition of the corporation's shares), it is the date the board of directors authorizes the distribution.

(c) No distribution may be made if, after giving it effect:

(1) the corporation would not be able to pay it debts as they become due in the usual course of business; or

(2) the corporation's total assets would be less than the sum of its total liabilities plus (unless the articles of incorporation permit otherwise) the amount that would be needed, if the corporation were to be dissolved at the time of the distribution, to satisfy the preferential rights upon dissolution of shareholders whose preferential rights are superior to those receiving the distribution.

(d) The board of directors may base a determination that a distribution is not prohibited under subsection (c) either on financial statements prepared on the basis of accounting practices and principles that are reasonable in the circumstances or on a fair valuation or other method that is reasonable in the circumstances.

(e) Except as provided in subsection (g), the effect of a distribution under subsection (c) is measured:

(1) in the case of distribution by purchase, redemption, or other acquisition of the corporation's shares, as of the earlier of (i) the date money or other property is transferred or debt incurred by the corporation or (ii) the date the shareholder ceases to be a shareholder with respect to the acquired shares;

(2) in the case of any other distribution of indebtedness, as of the date the indebtedness is distributed; and

(3) in all other cases, as of (i) the date the distribution is authorized if the payment occurs within 120 days after the date of authorization

or (ii) the date the payment is made if it occurs more than 120 days after the date of authorization.

(f) A corporation's indebtedness to a shareholder incurred by reason of a distribution made in accordance with this section is at parity with the corporation's indebtedness to its general, unsecured creditors except to the extent subordinated by agreement.

(g) Indebtedness of a corporation, including indebtedness issued as a distribution, is not considered a liability for purposes of determinations under subsection (c) if its terms provide that payment of principal and interest are made only if and to the extent that payment of a distribution to shareholders could then be made under this section. If the indebtedness is issued as a distribution, each payment of principal or interest is treated as a distribution, the effect of which is measured on the date the payment is actually made.

CHAPTER 7
SHAREHOLDERS
SUBCHAPTER A.
MEETINGS

§ 7.01. *Annual Meeting*

(a) A corporation shall hold a meeting of shareholders annually at a time stated in or fixed in accordance with the bylaws.

(b) Annual shareholders' meetings may be held in or out of this state at the place stated in or fixed in accordance with the bylaws. If no place is stated in or fixed in accordance with the bylaws, annual meetings shall be held at the corporation's principal office.

(c) The failure to hold an annual meeting at the time stated in or fixed in accordance with a corporation's bylaws does not affect the validity of any corporate action.

§ 7.02. *Special Meeting*

(a) A corporation shall hold a special meeting of shareholders:

(1) on call of its board of directors or the person or persons authorized to do so by the articles of incorporation or bylaws; or

(2) if the holders of at least 10 percent of all the votes entitled to be cast on any issue proposed to be considered at the proposed special meeting sign, date, and deliver to the

corporation's secretary one or more written demands for the meeting describing the purpose or purposes for which it is to be held, provided that the articles of incorporation may fix a lower percentage or a higher percentage not exceeding 25 percent of all the votes entitled to be cast on any issue proposed to be considered. Unless otherwise provided in the articles of incorporation, a written demand for a special meeting may be revoked by a writing to that effect received by the corporation prior to the receipt by the corporation of demands sufficient in number to require the holding of a special meeting.

(b) If not otherwise fixed under section 7.03 or 7.07, the record date for determining shareholders entitled to demand a special meeting is the date the first shareholder signs the demand.

(c) Special shareholders' meetings may be held in or out of this state at the place stated in or fixed in accordance with the bylaws. If no place is stated or fixed in accordance with the bylaws, special meetings shall be held at the corporation's principal office.

(d) Only business within the purpose or purposes described in the meeting notice required by section 7.05(c) may be conducted at a special shareholders' meeting.

§ 7.03. *Court-ordered Meeting*

(a) The [name or describe] court of the county where a corporation's principal office (or, if none in this state, its registered office) is located may summarily order a meeting to be held:

(1) on application of any shareholder of the corporation entitled to participate in an annual meeting if an annual meeting was not held within the earlier of 6 months after the end of the corporation's fiscal year or 15 months after its last annual meeting; or

(2) on application of a shareholder who signed a demand for a special meeting valid under section 7.02, if:

(i) notice of the special meeting was not given within 30 days after the date the demand was delivered to the corporation's secretary; or

(ii) the special meeting was not held in accordance with the notice.

(b) The court may fix the time and place of the meeting, determine the shares entitled to participate in the meeting, specify a record date for determining shareholders entitled to notice of and to vote at the meeting, prescribe the form and content of the meeting notice, fix the quorum required for specific matters to be considered at the meeting (or direct that the votes represented at the meeting constitute a quorum for action on those matters), and enter other orders necessary to accomplish the purpose or purposes of the meeting.

§ 7.04. *Action Without Meeting*

(a)   Action required or permitted by this Act to be taken at a shareholders' meeting may be taken without a meeting if the action is taken by all the shareholders entitled to vote on the action. The action must be evidenced by one or more written consents bearing the date of signature and describing the action taken, signed by all the shareholders entitled to vote on the action, and delivered to the corporation for inclusion in the minutes or filing with the corporate records.

(b)   If not otherwise fixed under section 7.03 or 7.07, the record date for determining shareholders entitled to take action without a meeting is the date the first shareholder signs the consent under subsection (a). No written consent shall be effective to take the corporate action referred to therein unless, within 60 days of the earliest date appearing on a consent delivered to the corporation in the manner required by this section, written consents signed by all shareholders entitled to vote on the action are received by the corporation. A written consent may be revoked by a writing to that effect received by the corporation prior to the receipt by the corporation of unrevoked written consents sufficient in number to take corporate action.

(c)   A consent signed under this section has the effect of a meeting vote and may be described as such in any document.

(d)   If this Act requires that notice of proposed action be given to nonvoting shareholders and the action is to be taken by unanimous consent of the voting shareholders, the corporation must give its nonvoting shareholders written notice of the proposed action at least 10 days before the action is taken. The notice must contain or be accompanied by the same material that, under this Act, would have been required to be sent to nonvoting shareholders in a notice of meeting at which the proposed action would have been submitted to the shareholders for action.

§ 7.05. *Notice of Meeting*

(a)   A corporation shall notify shareholders of the date, time, and place of each annual and special shareholders' meeting no fewer than 10 nor more than 60 days before the meeting date. Unless this Act or the articles of incorporation require otherwise, the corporation is required to give notice only to shareholders entitled to vote at the meeting.

(b)   Unless this Act or the articles of incorporation require otherwise, notice of an annual meeting need not include a description of the purpose or purposes for which the meeting is called.

(c)   Notice of a special meeting must include a description of the purpose or purposes for which the meeting is called.

(d)   If not otherwise fixed under section 7.03 or 7.07, the record date for determining shareholders entitled to notice of and to vote at an annual or special shareholders' meeting is the day before the first notice is delivered to shareholders.

(e)   Unless the bylaws require otherwise, if an annual or special shareholders' meeting is adjourned to a different date, time, or place, notice need not be given of the new date, time, or place if the new date, time, or place is announced at the meeting before adjournment. If a new record date for the adjourned meeting is or must be fixed under section 7.07, however, notice of the adjourned meeting must be given under this section to persons who are shareholders as of the new record date.

§ 7.06. *Waiver of Notice*

(a)   A shareholder may waive any notice required by this Act, the articles of incorporation, or bylaws before or after the date and time stated in the notice. The waiver must be in writing, be signed by the shareholder entitled to the notice, and be delivered to the corporation for inclusion in the minutes or filing with the corporate records.

(b)   A shareholder's attendance at a meeting:

(1)   waives objection to lack of notice or defective notice of the meeting, unless the shareholder at the beginning of the meeting objects to holding the meeting or transacting business at the meeting;

(2)   waives objection to consideration of a particular matter at the meeting that is not within the purpose or purposes described in the meeting notice, unless the shareholder objects to considering the matter when it is presented.

§ 7.07. Record Date

(a)   The bylaws may fix or provide the manner of fixing the record date for one or more voting groups in order to determine the shareholders entitled to notice of a shareholders' meeting, to demand a special meeting, to vote, or to take any other action. If the bylaws do not fix or provide for fixing a record date, the board of directors of the corporation may fix a future date as the record date.

(b)   A record date fixed under this section may not be more than 70 days before the meeting or action requiring a determination of shareholders.

(c)   A determination of shareholders entitled to notice of or to vote at a shareholders' meeting is effective for any adjournment of the meeting unless the board of directors fixes a new record date, which it must do if the meeting is adjourned to a date more than 120 days after the date fixed for the original meeting.

(d)   If a court orders a meeting adjourned to a date more than 120 days after the date fixed for the original meeting, it may provide that the original record date continues in effect or it may fix a new record date.

§ 7.08 Conduct of the Meeting

(a)   At each meeting of shareholders, a chair shall preside. The chair shall be appointed as provided in the bylaws or, in the absence of such provision, by the board.

(b)   The chair, unless the articles of incorporation or bylaws provide otherwise, shall have the authority to determine the order of business and shall establish rules for the conduct of the meeting.

(c)   Any rules adopted for, and the conduct of, the meeting shall be fair to shareholders.

(d)   The chair of the meeting shall announce at the meeting when the polls close for each matter voted upon. If no announcement is made, the polls shall be deemed to have closed upon the final adjournment of the meeting. After the polls close, no ballots, proxies or votes nor any revocations or changes thereto may be accepted.

SUBCHAPTER B.
VOTING

§ 7.20. Shareholders' List for Meeting

(a)   After fixing a record date for a meeting, a corporation shall prepare an alphabetical list of the names of all its shareholders who are entitled to notice of a shareholders' meeting. The list must be arranged by voting group (and within each voting group by class or series of shares) and show the address of and number of shares held by each shareholder.

(b)   The shareholders' list must be available for inspection by any shareholder, beginning two business days after notice of the meeting is given for which the list was prepared and continuing through the meeting, at the corporation's principal office or at a place identified in the meeting notice in the city where the meeting will be held. A shareholder, his agent, or attorney is entitled on written demand to inspect and, subject to the requirements of section 16.02(c), to copy the list, during regular business hours and at his expense, during the period it is available for inspection.

(c)   The corporation shall make the shareholders' list available at the meeting, and any shareholder, his agent, or attorney is entitled to inspect the list at any time during the meeting or any adjournment.

(d)   If the corporation refuses to allow a shareholder, his agent, or attorney to inspect the shareholders' list before or at the meeting (or copy the list as permitted by subsection (b)), the [name or describe] court of the county where a corporation's principal office (or, if none in this state, its registered office) is located, on application of the shareholder, may summarily order the inspection or copying at the corporation's expense and may postpone the meeting for which the list was prepared until the inspection or copying is complete.

(e)   Refusal or failure to prepare or make available the shareholders' list does not affect the validity of action taken at the meeting.

§ 7.21. Voting Entitlement of Shares

(a)   Except as provided in subsections (b) and (c) or unless the articles of incorporation provide otherwise, each outstanding share, regardless of class, is entitled to one vote on each matter voted on at a shareholders' meeting. Only shares are entitled to vote.

(b)   Absent special circumstances, the shares of a corporation are not entitled to vote if they are owned, directly or indirectly, by a second corporation, domestic or foreign, and the first corporation owns, directly or indirectly, a majority of the shares entitled to vote for directors of the second corporation.

(c)   Subsection (b) does not limit the power of a corporation to vote any shares, including its own shares, held by it in a fiduciary capacity.

(d)   Redeemable shares are not entitled to vote after notice of redemption is mailed to the holders and a sum sufficient to redeem the shares has been deposited with a bank, trust company, or other financial institution under an irrevocable obligation to pay the holders the redemption price on surrender of the shares.

§ 7.22. *Proxies*

(a)   A shareholder may vote his shares in person or by proxy.

(b)   A shareholder or his agent or attorney-in-fact may appoint a proxy to vote or otherwise act for the shareholder by signing an appointment form, or by an electronic transmission. An electronic transmission must contain or be accompanied by information from which one can determine that the shareholder, the shareholder's agent, or the shareholder's attorney-in-fact authorized the electronic transmission.

(c)   An appointment of a proxy is effective when a signed appointment form or an electronic transmission of the appointment is received by the inspector of election or the officer or agent of the corporation authorized to tabulate votes. An appointment is valid for 11 months unless a longer period is expressly provided in the appointment.

(d)   An appointment of a proxy is revocable by the shareholder unless the appointment form conspicuously states that it is irrevocable and the appointment is coupled with an interest. Appointments coupled with an interest include the appointment of:

(1)   a pledgee;

(2)   a person who purchased or agreed to purchase the shares;

(3)   a creditor of the corporation who extended it credit under terms requiring the appointment;

(4)   an employee of the corporation whose employment contract requires the appointment; or

(5)   a party to a voting agreement created under section 7.31.

(e)   The death or incapacity of the shareholder appointing a proxy does not affect the right of the corporation to accept the proxy's authority unless notice of the death or incapacity is received by the secretary or other officer or agent authorized to tabulate votes before the proxy exercises his authority under the appointment.

(f)   An appointment made irrevocable under subsection (d) is revoked when the interest with which it is coupled is extinguished.

(g)   A transferee for value of shares subject to an irrevocable appointment may revoke the appointment if he did not know of its existence when he acquired the shares and the existence of the irrevocable appointment was not noted conspicuously on the certificate representing the shares or on the information statement for shares without certificates.

(h)   Subject to section 7.24 and to any express limitation on the proxy's authority appearing on the face of the appointment form, a corporation is entitled to accept the proxy's vote or other action as that of the shareholder making the appointment.

§ 7.23. *Shares Held by Nominees*

(a)   A corporation may establish a procedure by which the beneficial owner of shares that are registered in the name of a nominee is recognized by the corporation as the shareholder. The extent of this recognition may be determined in the procedure.

(b)   The procedure may set forth:

(1)   the types of nominees to which it applies;

(2)   the rights or privileges that the corporation recognizes in a beneficial owner;

(3)   the manner in which the procedure is selected by the nominee;

(4)   the information that must be provided when the procedure is selected;

(5)   the period for which selection of the procedure is effective; and

(6)   other aspects of the rights and duties created.

§ 7.24. *Corporation's Acceptance of Votes*

(a)   If the name signed on a vote, consent, waiver, or proxy appointment corresponds to the name of a shareholder, the corporation if acting in good faith is entitled to accept the vote, consent, waiver, or proxy appointment and give it effect as the act of the shareholder.

(b)   If the name signed on a vote, consent, waiver, or proxy appointment does not correspond to the name of its shareholder, the corporation if acting in good faith is nevertheless entitled to accept the vote, consent, waiver, or proxy appointment and give it effect as the act of the shareholder if:

(1) the shareholder is an entity and the name signed purports to be that of an officer or agent of the entity;

(2) the name signed purports to be that of an administrator, executor, guardian, or conservator representing the shareholder and, if the corporation requests, evidence of fiduciary status acceptable to the corporation has been presented with respect to the vote, consent, waiver, or proxy appointment;

(3) the name signed purports to be that of a receiver or trustee in bankruptcy of the shareholder and, if the corporation requests, evidence of this status acceptable to the corporation has been presented with respect to the vote, consent, waiver, or proxy appointment;

(4) the name signed purports to be that of a pledgee, beneficial owner, or attorney-in-fact of the shareholder and, if the corporation requests, evidence acceptable to the corporation of the signatory's authority to sign for the shareholder has been presented with respect to the vote, consent, waiver, or proxy appointment;

(5) two or more persons are the shareholder as cotenants or fiduciaries and the name signed purports to be the name of at least one of the coowners and the person signing appears to be acting on behalf of all the coowners.

(c) The corporation is entitled to reject a vote, consent, waiver, or proxy appointment if the secretary or other officer or agent authorized to tabulate votes, acting in good faith, has reasonable basis for doubt about the validity of the signature on it or about the signatory's authority to sign for the shareholder.

(d) The corporation and its officer or agent who accepts or rejects a vote, consent, waiver, or proxy appointment in good faith and in accordance with the standards of this section or section 7.22(b) are not liable in damages to the shareholder for the consequences of the acceptance or rejection.

(e) Corporate action based on the acceptance or rejection of a vote, consent, waiver, or proxy appointment under this section or section 7.22(b) is valid unless a court of competent jurisdiction determines otherwise.

§ 7.25. Quorum and Voting Requirements for Voting Groups

(a) Shares entitled to vote as a separate voting group may take action on a matter at a meeting only if a quorum of those shares exists with respect to that matter. Unless the articles of incorporation or this Act provide otherwise, a majority of the votes entitled to be cast on the matter by the voting group constitutes a quorum of that voting group for action on that matter.

(b) Once a share is represented for any purpose at a meeting, it is deemed present for quorum purposes for the remainder of the meeting and for any adjournment of that meeting unless a new record date is or must be set for that adjourned meeting.

(c) If a quorum exists, action on a matter (other than the election of directors) by a voting group is approved if the votes cast within the voting group favoring the action exceed the votes cast opposing the action, unless the articles of incorporation or this Act require a greater number of affirmative votes.

(d) An amendment of articles of incorporation adding, changing, or deleting a quorum or voting requirement for a voting group greater than specified in subsection (a) or (c) is governed by section 7.27.

(e) The election of directors is governed by section 7.28.

§ 7.26. Action by Single and Multiple Voting Groups

(a) If the articles of incorporation or this Act provide for voting by a single voting group on a matter, action on that matter is taken when voted upon by that voting group as provided in section 7.25.

(b) If the articles of incorporation or this Act provide for voting by two or more voting groups on a matter, action on that matter is taken only when voted upon by each of those voting groups counted separately as provided in section 7.25. Action may be taken by one voting group on a matter even though no action is taken by another voting group entitled to vote on the matter.

§ 7.27. *Greater Quorum or Voting Requirements*

(a)   The articles of incorporation may provide for a greater quorum or voting requirement for shareholders (or voting groups of shareholders) than is provided for by this Act.

(b)   An amendment to the articles of incorporation that adds, changes, or deletes a greater quorum or voting requirement must meet the same quorum requirement and be adopted by the same vote and voting groups required to take action under the quorum and voting requirements then in effect or proposed to be adopted, whichever is greater.

§ 7.28. *Voting for Directors; Cumulative Voting*

(a)   Unless otherwise provided in the articles of incorporation, directors are elected by a plurality of the votes cast by the shares entitled to vote in the election at a meeting at which a quorum is present.

(b)   Shareholders do not have a right to cumulate their votes for directors unless the articles of incorporation so provide.

(c)   A statement included in the articles of incorporation that "[all] [a designated voting group of] shareholders are entitled to cumulate their votes for directors" (or words of similar import) means that the shareholders designated are entitled to multiply the number of votes they are entitled to cast by the number of directors for whom they are entitled to vote and cast the product for a single candidate or distribute the product among two or more candidates.

(d)   Shares otherwise entitled to vote cumulatively may not be voted cumulatively at a particular meeting unless:

(1)   the meeting notice or proxy statement accompanying the notice states conspicuously that cumulative voting is authorized; or

(2)   a shareholder who has the right to cumulate his votes gives notice to the corporation not less than 48 hours before the time set for the meeting of his intent to cumulate his votes during the meeting, and if one shareholder gives this notice all other shareholders in the same voting group participating in the election are entitled to cumulate their votes without giving further notice.

§ 7.29 *Inspectors of Election*

(a)   A corporation having any shares listed on a national securities exchange or regularly traded in a market maintained by one or more members of a national or affiliated securities association shall, and any other corporation may, appoint one or more inspectors to act at a meeting of shareholders and make a written report of the inspectors' determinations. Each inspector shall take and sign an oath faithfully to execute the duties of inspector with strict impartiality and according to the best of the inspector's ability.

(b)   The inspectors shall

(1)   ascertain the number of shares outstanding and the voting power of each;

(2)   determine the shares represented at a meeting;

(3)   determine the validity of proxies and ballots;

(4)   count all the votes; and

(5)   determine the result.

(c)   An inspector may be an officer or employee of the corporation.

SUBCHAPTER C.
VOTING TRUSTS AND AGREEMENTS

§ 7.30. *Voting Trusts*

(a)   One or more shareholders may create a voting trust, conferring on a trustee the right to vote or otherwise act for them, by signing an agreement setting out the provisions of the trust (which may include anything consistent with its purpose) and transferring their shares to the trustee. When a voting trust agreement is signed, the trustee shall prepare a list of the names and addresses of all owners of beneficial interests in the trust, together with the number and class of shares each transferred to the trust, and deliver copies of the list and agreement to the corporation's principal office.

(b)   A voting trust becomes effective on the date the first shares subject to the trust are registered in the trustee's name. A voting trust is valid for not more than 10 years after its effective date unless extended under subsection (c).

(c)   All or some of the parties to a voting trust may extend it for additional terms of not more than 10 years each by signing an extension agreement and obtaining the voting trustee's written consent to the extension. An extension is valid for 10 years from the date the first shareholder signs the extension agreement. The voting trustee must deliver copies of the extension agreement and list of beneficial owners to the corporation's principal office.

An extension agreement binds only those parties signing it.

§ 7.31. *Voting Agreements*

(a)   Two or more shareholders may provide for the manner in which they will vote their shares by signing an agreement for that purpose. A voting agreement created under this section is not subject to the provisions of section 7.30.

(b)   A voting agreement created under this section is specifically enforceable.

§ 7.32. *Shareholder Agreements*

(a)   An agreement among the shareholders of a corporation that complies with this section is effective among the shareholders and the corporation even though it is inconsistent with one or more other provisions of this Act in that it:

(1)   eliminates the board of directors or restricts the discretion or powers of the board of directors;

(2)   governs the authorization or making of distributions whether or not in proportion to ownership of shares, subject to the limitations in section 6.40;

(3)   establishes who shall be directors or officers of the corporation, or their terms of office or manner of selection or removal;

(4)   governs, in general or in regard to specific matters, the exercise or division of voting power by or between the shareholders and directors or by or among any of them, including use of weighted voting rights or director proxies;

(5)   establishes the terms and conditions of any agreement for the transfer or use of property or the provision of services between the corporation and any shareholder, director, officer or employee of the corporation or among any of them;

(6)   transfers to one or more shareholders or other persons all or part of the authority to exercise the corporate powers or to manage the business and affairs of the corporation, including the resolution of any issue about which there exists a deadlock among directors or shareholders;

(7)   requires dissolution of the corporation at the request of one or more of the shareholders or upon the occurrence of a specified event or contingency; or

(8)   otherwise governs the exercise of the corporate powers or the management of the business and affairs of the corporation or the relationship among the shareholders, the directors and the corporation, or among any of them, and is not contrary to public policy.

(b)   An agreement authorized by this section shall be:

(1)   set forth (A) in the articles of incorporation or bylaws and approved by all persons who are shareholders at the time of the agreement or (B) in a written agreement that is signed by all persons who are shareholders at the time of the agreement and is made known to the corporation;

(2)   subject to amendment only by all persons who are shareholders at the time of the amendment, unless the agreement provides otherwise; and

(3)   valid for 10 years, unless the agreement provides otherwise.

(c)   The existence of an agreement authorized by this section shall be noted conspicuously on the front or back of each certificate for outstanding shares or on the information statement required by section 6.26(b). If at the time of the agreement the corporation has shares outstanding represented by certificates, the corporation shall recall the outstanding certificates and issue substitute certificates that comply with this subsection. The failure to note the existence of the agreement on the certificate or information statement shall not affect the validity of the agreement or any action taken pursuant to it. Any purchaser of shares who, at the time of purchase, did not have knowledge of the existence of the agreement shall be entitled to rescission of the purchase. A purchaser shall be deemed to have knowledge of the existence of the agreement if its existence is noted on the certificate or information statement for the shares in compliance with this subsection and, if the shares are not represented by a certificate, the information statement is delivered to the purchaser at or prior to the time of purchase of the shares. An action to enforce the right of rescission authorized by this subsection must be commenced within the earlier of 90 days after discovery of the existence of the agreement or two years after the time of purchase of the shares.

(d)   An agreement authorized by this section shall cease to be effective when shares of the corporation are listed on a national securities exchange or regularly traded in a market maintained by one or more members of a national or affiliated securities association. If the agreement ceases to be effective for any reason, the board of directors may, if the agreement is contained or referred to in the corporation's articles of incorporation or bylaws, adopt an amendment to the articles of incorporation or bylaws, without shareholder action, to delete the agreement and any references to it.

(e) An agreement authorized by this section that limits the discretion or powers of the board of directors shall relieve the directors of, and impose upon the person or persons in whom such discretion or powers are vested, liability for acts or omissions imposed by law on directors to the extent that the discretion or powers of the directors are limited by the agreement.

(f) The existence or performance of an agreement authorized by this section shall not be a ground for imposing personal liability on any shareholder for the acts or debts of the corporation even if the agreement or its performance treats the corporation as if it were a partnership or results in failure to observe the corporate formalities otherwise applicable to the matters governed by the agreement.

(g) Incorporators or subscribers for shares may act as shareholders with respect to an agreement authorized by this section if no shares have been issued when the agreement is made.

SUBCHAPTER D.
DERIVATIVE PROCEEDINGS

§ 7.40. Subchapter Definitions

In this subchapter:

(1) "Derivative proceeding" means a civil suit in the right of a domestic corporation or, to the extent provided in section 7.47, in the right of a foreign corporation.

(2) "Shareholder" includes a beneficial owner whose shares are held in a voting trust or held by a nominee on the beneficial owner's behalf.

§ 7.41. Standing

A shareholder may not commence or maintain a derivative proceeding unless the shareholder:

(1) was a shareholder of the corporation at the time of the act or omission complained of or became a shareholder through transfer by operation of law from one who was a shareholder at that time; and

(2) fairly and adequately represents the interests of the corporation in enforcing the right of the corporation.

§ 7.42. Demand

No shareholder may commence a derivative proceeding until:

(1) a written demand has been made upon the corporation to take suitable action; and

(2) 90 days have expired from the date the demand was made unless the shareholder has earlier been notified that the demand has been rejected by the corporation or unless irreparable injury to the corporation would result by waiting for the expiration of the 90 day period.

§ 7.43. Stay of Proceedings

If the corporation commences an inquiry into the allegations made in the demand or complaint, the court may stay any derivative proceeding for such period as the court deems appropriate.

§ 7.44. Dismissal

(a) A derivative proceeding shall be dismissed by the court on motion by the corporation if one of the groups specified in subsections (b) or (f) has determined in good faith after conducting a reasonable inquiry upon which its conclusions are based that the maintenance of the derivative proceeding is not in the best interests of the corporation.

(b) Unless a panel is appointed pursuant to subsection (f), the determination in subsection (a) shall be made by:

(1) a majority vote of independent directors present at a meeting of the board of directors if the independent directors constitute a quorum; or

(2) a majority vote of a committee consisting of two or more independent directors appointed by majority vote of independent directors present at a meeting of the board of directors, whether or not such independent directors constituted a quorum.

(c) None of the following shall by itself cause a director to be considered not independent for purposes of this section:

(1) the nomination or election of the director by persons who are defendants in the derivative proceeding or against whom action is demanded;

(2) the naming of the director as a defendant in the derivative proceeding or as a person against whom action is demanded; or

(3) the approval by the director of the act being challenged in the derivative proceeding or demand if the act resulted in no personal benefit to the director.

(d) If a derivative proceeding is commenced after a determination has been made rejecting a demand by a shareholder, the complaint shall allege with particularity facts establishing either (1) that a majority of the board of directors did not consist of independent directors at the time the determination was made or (2) that the requirements of subsection (a) have not been met.

(e) If a majority of the board of directors does not consist of independent directors at the time the determination is made, the corporation shall have the burden of proving that the requirements of subsection (a) have been met. If a majority of the board of directors consists of independent directors at the time the determination is made, the plaintiff shall have the burden of proving that the requirements of subsection (a) have not been met.

(f) The court may appoint a panel of one or more independent persons upon motion by the corporation to make a determination whether the maintenance of the derivative proceeding is in the best interests of the corporation. In such case, the plaintiff shall have the burden of proving that the requirements of subsection (a) have not been met.

§ 7.45. Discontinuance or Settlement

A derivative proceeding may not be discontinued or settled without the court's approval. If the court determines that a proposed discontinuance or settlement will substantially affect the interests of the corporation's shareholders or a class of shareholders, the court shall direct that notice be given to the shareholders affected.

§ 7.46. Payment of Expenses

On termination of the derivative proceeding the court may:

(1) order the corporation to pay the plaintiff's reasonable expenses (including counsel fees) incurred in the proceeding if it finds that the proceeding has resulted in a substantial benefit to the corporation;

(2) order the plaintiff to pay any defendant's reasonable expenses (including counsel fees) incurred in defending the proceeding if it finds that the proceeding was commenced or maintained without reasonable cause or for an improper purpose; or

(3) order a party to pay an opposing party's reasonable expenses (including counsel fees) incurred because of the filing of a pleading, motion or other paper, if it finds that the pleading, motion or other paper was not well grounded in fact, after reasonable inquiry, or warranted by existing law or a good faith argument for the extension, modification or reversal of existing law and was interposed for an improper purpose, such as to harass or to cause unnecessary delay or needless increase in the cost of litigation.

§ 7.47. Applicability to Foreign Corporations

In any derivative proceeding in the right of a foreign corporation, the matters covered by this subchapter shall be governed by the laws of the jurisdiction of incorporation of the foreign corporation except for sections 7.43, 7.45 and 7.46.

CHAPTER 8
DIRECTORS AND OFFICERS
SUBCHAPTER A.
BOARD OF DIRECTORS

§ 8.01. Requirements for and Duties of Board of Directors

(a) Except as provided is [*sic*] section 7.32, each corporation must have a board of directors.

(b) All corporate powers shall be exercised by or under the authority of, and the business and affairs of the corporation managed under the direction of, its board of directors, subject to any limitation set forth in the articles of incorporation or in an agreement authorized under section 7.32.

§ 8.02. Qualifications of Directors

The articles of incorporation or bylaws may prescribe qualifications for directors. A director need not be a resident of this state or a shareholder of the corporation unless the articles of incorporation or bylaws so prescribe.

§ 8.03. Number and Election of Directors

(a) A board of directors must consist of one or more individuals, with the number specified in or fixed in accordance with the articles of incorporation or bylaws.

(b)   If a board of directors has power to fix or change the number of directors, the board may increase or decrease by 30 percent or less the number of directors last approved by the shareholders, but only the shareholders may increase or decrease by more than 30 percent the number of directors last approved by the shareholders.

(c)   The articles of incorporation or bylaws may establish a variable range for the size of the board of directors by fixing a minimum and maximum number of directors. If a variable range is established, the number of directors may be fixed or changed from time to time, within the minimum and maximum, by the shareholders or the board of directors. After shares are issued, only the shareholders may change the range for the size of the board or change from a fixed to a variable-range size board or vice versa.

(d)   Directors are elected at the first annual shareholders' meeting and at each annual meeting thereafter unless their terms are staggered under section 8.06.

§ 8.04.   Election of Directors by Certain Classes of Shareholders

If the articles of incorporation authorize dividing the shares into classes, the articles may also authorize the election of all or a specified number of directors by the holders of one or more authorized classes of shares. A class (or classes) of shares entitled to elect one or more directors is a separate voting group for purposes of the election of directors.

§ 8.05.   Terms of Directors Generally

(a)   The terms of the initial directors of a corporation expire at the first shareholders' meeting at which directors are elected.

(b)   The terms of all other directors expire at the next annual shareholders' meeting following their election unless their terms are staggered under section 8.06.

(c)   A decrease in the number of directors does not shorten an incumbent director's term.

(d)   The term of a director elected to fill a vacancy expires at the next shareholders' meeting at which directors are elected.

(e)   Despite the expiration of a director's term, he continues to serve until his successor is elected and qualifies or until there is a decrease in the number of directors.

§ 8.06.   Staggered Terms for Directors

If there are nine or more directors, the articles of incorporation may provide for staggering their terms by dividing the total number of directors into two or three groups, with each group containing one half or one-third of the total, as near as may be. In that event, the terms of directors in the first group expire at the first annual shareholders' meeting after their election, the terms of the second group expire at the second annual shareholders' meeting after their election, and the terms of the third group, if any, expire at the third annual shareholders' meeting after their election. At each annual shareholders' meeting held thereafter, directors shall be chosen for a term of two years or three years, as the case may be, to succeed those whose terms expire.

§ 8.07.   Resignation of Directors

(a)   A director may resign at any time by delivering written notice to the board of directors, its chairman, or to the corporation.

(b)   A resignation is effective when the notice is delivered unless the notice specifies a later effective date.

§ 8.08.   Removal of Directors by Shareholders

(a)   The shareholders may remove one or more directors with or without cause unless the articles of incorporation provide that directors may be removed only for cause.

(b)   If a director is elected by a voting group of shareholders, only the shareholders of that voting group may participate in the vote to remove him.

(c)   If cumulative voting is authorized, a director may not be removed if the number of votes sufficient to elect him under cumulative voting is voted against his removal. If cumulative voting is not authorized, a director may be removed only if the number of votes cast to remove him exceeds the number of votes cast not to remove him.

(d)   A director may be removed by the shareholders only at a meeting called for the purpose of removing him and the meeting notice must state that the purpose, or one of the purposes, of the meeting is removal of the director.

§ 8.09. *Removal of Directors by Judicial Proceeding*

(a)   The [name or describe] court of the county where a corporation's principal office (or, if none in this state, its registered office) is located may remove a director of the corporation from office in a proceeding commenced either by the corporation or by its shareholders holding at least 10 percent of the outstanding shares of any class if the court finds that (1) the director engaged in fraudulent or dishonest conduct, or gross abuse of authority or discretion, with respect to the corporation and (2) removal is in the best interest of the corporation.

(b)   The court that removes a director may bar the director from reelection for a period prescribed by the court.

(c)   If shareholders commence a proceeding under subsection (a), they shall make the corporation a party defendant.

§ 8.10. *Vacancy on Board*

(a)   Unless the articles of incorporation provide otherwise, if a vacancy occurs on a board of directors, including a vacancy resulting from an increase in the number of directors:

(1)   the shareholders may fill the vacancy;

(2)   the board of directors may fill the vacancy; or

(3)   if the directors remaining in office constitute fewer than a quorum of the board, they may fill the vacancy by the affirmative vote of a majority of all the directors remaining in office.

(b)   If the vacant office was held by a director elected by a voting group of shareholders, only the holders of shares of that voting group are entitled to vote to fill the vacancy if it is filled by the shareholders.

(c)   A vacancy that will occur at a specific later date (by reason of a resignation effective at a later date under section 8.07(b) or otherwise) may be filled before the vacancy occurs but the new director may not take office until the vacancy occurs.

§ 8.11. *Compensation of Directors*

Unless the articles of incorporation or bylaws provide otherwise, the board of directors may fix the compensation of directors.

SUBCHAPTER B.
MEETINGS AND ACTION OF THE BOARD

§ 8.20. *Meetings*

(a)   The board of directors may hold regular or special meetings in or out of this state.

(b)   Unless the articles of incorporation or bylaws provide otherwise, the board of directors may permit any or all directors to participate in a regular or special meeting by, or conduct the meeting through the use of, any means of communication by which all directors participating may simultaneously hear each other during the meeting. A director participating in a meeting by this means is deemed to be present in person at the meeting.

§ 8.21. *Action Without Meeting*

(a)   Unless the articles of incorporation or bylaws provide otherwise, action required or permitted by this Act to be taken at a board of directors' meeting may be taken without a meeting if the action is taken by all members of the board. The action must be evidenced by one or more written consents describing the action taken, signed by each director, and included in the minutes or filed with the corporate records reflecting the action taken.

(b)   Action taken under this section is effective when the last director signs the consent, unless the consent specifies a different effective date.

(c)   A consent signed under this section has the effect of a meeting vote and may be described as such in any document.

§ 8.22. *Notice of Meeting*

(a)   Unless the articles of incorporation or bylaws provide otherwise, regular meetings of the board of directors may be held without notice of the date, time, place, or purpose of the meeting.

(b)   Unless the articles of incorporation or bylaws provide for a longer or shorter period, special meetings of the board of directors must be preceded by at least two days' notice of the date, time, and place of the meeting. The notice need not describe the purpose of the special meeting unless required by the articles of incorporation or bylaws.

§ 8.23. *Waiver of Notice*

(a)   A director may waive any notice required by this Act, the articles of incorporation, or bylaws before or after the date and time stated in the notice. Except as provided by subsection (b), the waiver must be in writing, signed by the director entitled to the notice, and filed with the minutes or corporate records.

(b)   A director's attendance at or participation in a meeting waives any required notice to him of the meeting unless the director at the beginning of the meeting (or promptly upon his arrival) objects to holding the meeting or transacting business at the meeting and does not thereafter vote for or assent to action taken at the meeting.

§ 8.24. *Quorum and Voting*

(a)   Unless the articles of incorporation or by-laws require a greater number, a quorum of a board of directors consists of:

(1)   a majority of the fixed number of directors if the corporation has a fixed board size; or

(2)   a majority of the number of directors prescribed, or if no number is prescribed the number in office immediately before the meeting begins, if the corporation has a variable-range size board.

(b)   The articles of incorporation or bylaws may authorize a quorum of a board of directors to consist of no fewer than one-third of the fixed or prescribed number of directors determined under subsection (a).

(c)   If a quorum is present when a vote is taken, the affirmative vote of a majority of directors present is the act of the board of directors unless the articles of incorporation or bylaws require the vote of a greater number of directors.

(d)   A director who is present at a meeting of the board of directors or a committee of the board of directors when corporate action is taken is deemed to have assented to the action taken unless: (1) he objects at the beginning of the meeting (or promptly upon his arrival) to holding it or transacting business at the meeting; (2) his dissent or abstention from the action taken is entered in the minutes of the meeting; or (3) he delivers written notice of his dissent or abstention to the presiding officer of the meeting before its adjournment or to the corporation immediately after adjournment of the meeting. The right of dissent or abstention is not available to a director who votes in favor of the action taken.

§ 8.25. *Committees*

(a)   Unless the articles of incorporation or bylaws provide otherwise, a board of directors may create one or more committees and appoint members of the board of directors to serve on them. Each committee must have two or more members, who serve at the pleasure of the board of directors.

(b)   The creation of a committee and appointment of members to it must be approved by the greater of (1) a majority of all the directors in office when the action is taken or (2) the number of directors required by the articles of incorporation or bylaws to take action under section 8.24.

(c)   Sections 8.20 through 8.24, which govern meetings, action without meetings, notice and waiver of notice, and quorum and voting requirements of the board of directors, apply to committees and their members as well.

(d)   To the extent specified by the board of directors or in the articles of incorporation or bylaws, each committee may exercise the authority of the board of directors under section 8.01.

(e)   A committee may not, however:

(1)   authorize distributions;

(2)   approve or propose to shareholders action that this Act requires be approved by shareholders;

(3)   fill vacancies on the board of directors or on any of its committees;

(4)   amend articles of incorporation pursuant to section 10.02;

(5)   adopt, amend, or repeal bylaws;

(6)   approve a plan of merger not requiring shareholder approval;

(7)   authorize or approve reacquisition of shares, except according to a formula or method prescribed by the board of directors; or

(8)   authorize or approve the issuance or sale or contract for sale of shares, or determine the designation and relative rights, preferences, and limitations of a class or series of shares, except that the board of directors may authorize a committee (or a senior executive officer of the corporation) to do so within limits specifically prescribed by the board of directors.

(f)   The creation of, delegation of authority to, or action by a committee does not alone constitute compliance by a director with the standards of conduct described in section 8.30.

SUBCHAPTER C.
STANDARDS OF CONDUCT

§ 8.30. *Standards of Conduct for Directors*

(a)   Each member of the board of directors, when discharging the duties of a director, shall act: (1) in good faith, and (2) in a manner the director reasonably believes to be in the best interests of the corporation.

(b)   The members of the board of directors or a committee of the board, when becoming informed in connection with their decision-making function or devoting attention to their oversight function, shall discharge their duties with the care that a person in a like position would reasonably believe appropriate under similar circumstances.

(c)   In discharging board or committee duties a director, who does not have knowledge that makes reliance unwarranted, is entitled to rely on the performance by any of the persons specified in sub-section (e)(1) or subsection (e)(3) to whom the board may have delegated, formally or informally by course of conduct, the authority or duty to perform one or more of the board's functions that are delegable under applicable law.

(d)   In discharging board or committee duties a director, who does not have knowledge that makes reliance unwarranted, is entitled to rely on information, opinions, reports or statements, including financial statements and other financial data, prepared or presented by any of the persons specified in subsection (e).

(e)   A director is entitled to rely, in accordance with sub-section (c) or (d), on:

(1)   one or more officers or employees of the corporation whom the director reasonably believes to be reliable and competent in the functions performed or the information, opinions, reports or statements provided;

(2)   legal counsel, public accountants, or other persons retained by the corporation as to matters involving skills or expertise the director reasonably believes are matters (i) within the particular person's professional or expert competence or (ii) as to which the particular person merits confidence; or

(3)   a committee of the board of directors of which the director is not a member if the director reasonably believes the committee merits confidence.

§ 8.31. *Standards of Liability for Directors*

(a)   A director shall not be liable to the corporation or its shareholders for any decision to take or not to take action, or any failure to take any action, as a director, unless the party asserting liability in a proceeding establishes that:

(1)   any provision in the articles of incorporation authorized by section 2.02(b)(4) or the protection afforded by section 8.61 for action taken in compliance with section 8.62 or 8.63, if interposed as a bar to the proceeding by the director, does not preclude liability; and

(2)   the challenged conduct consisted or was the result of:

(i)   action not in good faith; or

(ii)   a decision

(A)   which the director did not reasonably believe to be in the best interests of the corporation, or

(B)   as to which the director was not informed to an extent the director reasonably believed appropriate in the circumstances; or

(iii)   a lack of objectivity due to the director's familial, financial or business relationship with, or lack of independence due to the director's domination or control by, another person having a material interest in the challenged conduct

(A)   which relationship or which domination or control could reasonably be expected to have affected the director's judgment respecting the challenged conduct in a manner adverse to the corporation, and

(B)   after a reasonable expectation to such effect has been established, the director shall not have established that the challenged conduct was reasonably believed by the director to be in the best interests of the corporation; or

(iv)   a sustained failure of the director to devote attention to ongoing oversight of the business and affairs of the corporation, or a failure to devote timely attention, by making (or causing to be made) appropriate inquiry, when particular facts and circumstances of significant concern materialize that would alert a reasonably attentive director to the need therefor; or

(v) receipt of a financial benefit to which the director was not entitled or other breach of the director's duties to deal fairly with the corporation and its shareholders that is actionable under applicable law.

(b) The party seeking to hold the director liable:

(1) for money damages, shall also have the burden of establishing that:

(i) harm to the corporation or its shareholders has been suffered, and

(ii) the harm suffered was proximately caused by the director's challenged conduct; or

(2) for other money payment under a legal remedy, such as compensation for the unauthorized use of corporate assets, shall also have whatever persuasion burden may be called for to establish that the payment sought is appropriate in the circumstances; or

(3) for other money payment under an equitable remedy, such as profit recovery by or disgorgement to the corporation, shall also have whatever persuasion burden may be called for to establish that the equitable remedy sought is appropriate in the circumstances.

(c) Nothing contained in this section shall (1) in any instance where fairness is at issue, such consideration of the fairness of a transaction to the corporation under section 8.61(b)(3), alter the burden of proving the fact or lack of fairness otherwise applicable, (2) alter the fact or lack of liability of a director under another section of this Act, such as the provisions governing the consequences of an unlawful distribution under section 8.33 or a transactional interest under section 8.61, or (3) affect any rights to which the corporation or a shareholder may be entitled under another statute of this state or the United States.

§ 8.32 [Reserved]

§ 8.33 Directors' Liability for Unlawful Distributions

(a) A director who votes for or assents to a distribution in excess of what may be authorized and made pursuant to section 6.40(a) is personally liable to the corporation for the amount of the distribution that exceeds what could have been distributed without violating section 6.40(a) if the party assert-

ing liability establishes that when taking the action the director did not comply with section 8.30.

(b) A director held liable under subsection (a) for an unlawful distribution is entitled to:

(1) contribution from every other director who could be held liable under subsection (a) for the unlawful distribution; and

(2) recoupment from each shareholder of the pro-rata portion of the amount of the unlawful distribution the shareholder accepted, knowing the distribution was made in violation of section 6.40(a).

(c) A proceeding to enforce:

(1) The liability of a director under subsection (a) is barred unless it is commenced within two years after the date on which the effect of the distribution was measured under section 6.40(e) or (g) or as of which the violation of section 6.40(a) occurred as the consequence of disregard of a restriction in the articles of incorporation; or

(2) Contribution or recoupment under subsection (b) is barred unless it is commenced within one year after the liability of the claimant has been finally adjudicated under subsection (a).

SUBCHAPTER D.
OFFICERS

§ 8.40. Required Officers

(a) A corporation has the officers described in its bylaws or appointed by the board of directors in accordance with the bylaws.

(b) A duly appointed officer may appoint one or more officers or assistant officers if authorized by the bylaws or the board of directors.

(c) The bylaws or the board of directors shall delegate to one of the officers responsibility for preparing minutes of the directors' and shareholders' meetings and for authenticating records of the corporation.

(d) The same individual may simultaneously hold more than one office in a corporation.

§ 8.41. Duties of Officers

Each officer has the authority and shall perform the duties set forth in the bylaws or, to the extent consistent with the bylaws, the duties prescribed by the board of directors or by direction of an officer authorized by the board of directors to prescribe the duties of other officers.

§ 8.42. *Standards of Conduct for Officers*

(a)   An officer with discretionary authority shall discharge his duties under that authority:

(1)   in good faith;

(2)   with the care an ordinarily prudent person in a like position would exercise under similar circumstances; and

(3)   in a manner he reasonably believes to be in the best interests of the corporation.

(b)   In discharging those duties an officer, who does not have knowledge that makes reliance unwarranted, is entitled to rely on:

(1)   the performance of properly delegated responsibilities by one or more employees of the corporation whom the officer reasonably believes to be reliable and competent in performing the responsibilities delegated; or

(2)   information, opinions, reports or statements, including financial statements and other financial data, prepared or presented by one or more employees of the corporation whom the officer reasonably believes to be reliable and competent in the matters presented or by legal counsel, public accountants, or other persons retained by the corporation as to matters involving skills or expertise the officer reasonably believes are matters (i) within the particular person's professional or expert competence or (ii) as to which the particular person merits confidence.

(c)   An officer shall not be liable to the corporation or its shareholders for any decision to take or not to take action, or any failure to take any action, as an officer, if the duties of the office are performed in compliance with this section. Whether an officer who does not comply with this section shall have liability will depend in such instance on applicable law, including those principles of § 8.31 that have relevance.

§ 8.43. *Resignation and Removal of Officers*

(a)   An officer may resign at any time by delivering notice to the corporation. A resignation is effective when the notice is delivered unless the notice specifies a later effective date. If a resignation is made effective at a later date and the corporation accepts the future effective date, its board of directors may fill the pending vacancy before the effective date if the board of directors provides that the successor does not take office until the effective date.

(b)   A board of directors may remove any officer at any time with or without cause.

§ 8.44. *Contract Rights of Officers*

(a)   The appointment of an officer does not itself create contract rights.

(b)   An officer's removal does not affect the officer's contract rights, if any, with the corporation. An officer's resignation does not affect the corporation's contract rights, if any, with the officer.

SUBCHAPTER E.
INDEMNIFICATION

§ 8.50. *Subchapter Definitions*

In this subchapter:

(1)   "Corporation" includes any domestic or foreign predecessor entity of a corporation in a merger.

(2)   "Director" or "officer" means an individual who is or was a director or officer, respectively, of a corporation or who, while a director or officer of the corporation, is or was serving at the corporation's request as a director, officer, partner, trustee, employee, or agent of another domestic or foreign corporation, partnership, joint venture, trust, employee benefit plan, or other entity. A director or officer is considered to be serving an employee benefit plan at the corporation's request if his duties to the corporation also impose duties on, or otherwise involve services by, him to the plan or to participants in or beneficiaries of the plan. "Director" or "officer" includes, unless the context requires otherwise, the estate or personal representative of a director or officer.

(3)   "Disinterested director" means a director who, at the time of a vote referred to in section 8.53(c) or a vote or selection referred to in section 8.55(b) or (c), is not (i) a party to the proceeding, or (ii) an individual having a familial, financial, professional or employment relationship with the director whose indemnification or advance for expenses is the subject of the decision being made, which relationship would, in the circumstances, reasonably be expected to exert an influence on the director's judgment when voting on the decision being made.

(4)   "Expenses" includes counsel fees.

(5)   "Liability" means the obligation to pay a judgment, settlement, penalty, fine (including an excise tax assessed with respect to an employee

benefit plan), or reasonable expenses incurred with respect to a proceeding.

(6) "Official capacity" means: (i) when used with respect to a director, the office of director in a corporation; and (ii) when used with respect to an office, as contemplated in section 8.56, the office in a corporation held by the officer. "Official capacity" does not include service for any other foreign or domestic corporation or any partnership, joint venture, trust, employee benefit plan, or other enterprise.

(7) "Party" means an individual who was, is, or is threatened to be made, a named defendant or respondent in a proceeding.

(8) "Proceeding" means any threatened, pending, or completed action, suit, or proceeding, whether civil, criminal, administrative, arbitrative, or investigative and whether formal or informal.

§ 8.51. Permissible Indemnification

(a) Except as otherwise provided in this section, a corporation may indemnify an individual who is a party to a proceeding because he is a director against liability incurred in the proceeding if:

(1) (i) he conducted himself in good faith; and

(ii) he reasonably believed:

(A) in the case of conduct in his official capacity, that his conduct was in the best interests of the corporation; and

(B) in all other cases, that his conduct was at least not opposed to the best interests of the corporation; and

(iii) in the case of any criminal proceeding, he had no reasonable cause to believe his conduct was unlawful.

(2) he engaged in conduct for which broader indemnification has been made permissible or obligatory under a provision of the articles of incorporation (as authorized by section 2.02(b)(5)).

(b) A director's conduct with respect to an employee benefit plan for a purpose he reasonably believed to be in the interests of the participants in, and beneficiaries of, the plan is conduct that satisfies the requirement of subsection (a)(1)(ii)(B).

(c) The termination of a proceeding by judgment, order, settlement, or conviction, or upon a plea of nolo contendere or its equivalent, is not, of itself, determinative that the director did not meet the relevant standard of conduct described in this section.

(d) Unless ordered by a court under section 8.54(a)(3), a corporation may not indemnify a director:

(1) in connection with a proceeding by or in the right of the corporation, except for reasonable expenses incurred in connection with the proceeding if it is determined that the director has met the relevant standard of conduct under subsection (a); or

(2) in connection with any proceeding with respect to conduct for which he was adjudged liable on the basis that he received a financial benefit to which he was not entitled, whether or not involving action in his official capacity.

§ 8.52. Mandatory Indemnification

A corporation shall indemnify a director who was wholly successful, on the merits or otherwise, in the defense of any proceeding to which he was a party because he was a director of the corporation against reasonable expenses incurred by him in connection with the proceeding.

§ 8.53. Advance for Expenses

(a) A corporation may, before final disposition of a proceeding, advance funds to pay for or reimburse the reasonable expenses incurred by a director who is a party to a proceeding because he is a director if he delivers to the corporation:

(1) a written affirmation of his good faith belief that he has met the relevant standard of conduct described in section 8.51 or that the proceeding involves conduct for which liability has been eliminatd under a provision of the articles of incorporation as authorized by section 2.02(b)(4); and

(2) his written undertaking to repay any funds advanced if he is not entitled to mandatory indemnification under section 8.52 and it is ultimately determined under section 8.54 or section 8.55 that he has not met the relevant standard of conduct described in section 8.51.

(b) The undertaking required by subsection (a)(2) must be an unlimited general obligation of the director but need not be secured and may be accepted without reference to the financial ability of the director to make repayment.

(c)   Authorizations under this section shall be made:

(1)   by the board of directors:

(i)   If there are two or more disinterested directors, by a majority vote of all the disinterested directors (a majority of whom shall for such purpose constitute a quorum) or by a majority of the members of a committee of two or more disinterested directors appointed by such a vote; or

(ii)   if there are fewer than two disinterested directors, by the vote necessary for action by the board in accordance with section 8.24(c), in which authorization directors who do not qualify as disinterested directors may participate; or

(2)   by the shareholders, but shares owned by or voted under the control of a director who at the time does not qualify as a disinterested director may not be voted on the authorization.

§ 8.54.   Court-ordered Indemnification and Advance for Expenses

(a)   A director who is a party to a proceeding because he is a director may apply for indemnification or an advance for expenses to the court conducting the proceeding or to another court of competent jurisdiction. After receipt of an application and after giving any notice it considers necessary, the court shall:

(1)   order indemnification if the court determines that the director is entitled to mandatory indemnification under section 8.52;

(2)   order indemnification or advance for expenses if the court determines that the director is entitled to indemnification or advance for expenses pursuant to a provision authorized by section 8.58(a); or

(3)   order indemnification or advance for expenses if the court determines, in view of all the relevant circumstances, that it is fair and reasonable

(i)   to indemnify the director, or

(ii)   to advance expenses to the director, even if he has not met the relevant standard of conduct set forth in section 8.51(a), failed to comply with section 8.53 or was adjudged liable in a proceeding referred to in subsection 8.51(d)(1) or (d)(2), but if he was adjudged so liable his indemnification shall be limited to reasonable expenses incurred in connection with the proceeding.

(b)   If the court determines that the director is entitled to indemnification under subsection (a)(1) or to indemnification or advance for expenses under subsection (a)(2), it shall also order the corporation to pay the director's reasonable expenses incurred in connection with obtaining court-ordered indemnification or advance for expenses. If the court determines that the director is entitled to indemnification or advance for expenses under subsection (a)(3), it may also order the corporation to pay the director's reasonable expenses to obtain court-ordered indemnification or advance for expenses.

§ 8.55.   Determination and Authorization of Indemnification

(a)   A corporation may not indemnify a director under section 8.51 unless authorized for a specific proceeding after a determination has been made that indemnification of the director is permissible because he has met the standard of conduct set forth in section 8.51.

(b)   The determination shall be made:

(1)   if there are two or more disinterested directors, by the board of directors by a majority vote of all the disinterested directors (a majority of whom shall for such purpose constitute a quorum), or by a majority of the members of a committee of two or more disinterested directors appointed by such a vote;

(2)   by special legal counsel:

(i)   selected in the manner prescribed in subdivision (1); or

(ii)   if there are fewer than two disinterested directors, selected by the board of directors (in which selection directors who do not qualify as disinterested directors may participate); or

(3)   by the shareholders, but shares owned by or voted under the control of a director who at the time does not qualify as a disinterested director may not be voted on the determination.

(c)   Authorization of indemnification shall be made in the same manner as the determination that indemnification is permissible, except that if there are fewer than two disinterested directors or if the determination is made by special legal counsel, authorization of indemnification shall be made by those entitled under subsection (b)(2)(ii) to select special legal counsel.

§ 8.56. Officers

(a)   A corporation may indemnify and advance expenses under this subchapter to an officer of the corporation who is a party to a proceeding because he is an officer of the corporation

(1)   to the same extent as a director; and

(2)   if he is an officer but not a director, to such further extent as may be provided by the articles of incorporation, the bylaws, a resolution of the board of directors, or contract except for (A) liability in connection with a proceeding by or in the right of the corporation other than for reasonable expenses incurred in connection with the proceeding or (B) liability arising out of conduct that constitutes (i) receipt by him of a financial benefit to which he is not entitled, (ii) an intentional infliction of harm on the corporation or the shareholders, or (iii) an intentional violation of criminal law.

(b)   The provisions of subsection (a)(2) shall apply to an officer who is also a director if the basis on which he is made a party to the proceeding is an act or omission solely as an officer.

(c)   An officer of a corporation who is not a director is entitled to mandatory indemnification under section 8.52, and may apply to a court under section 8.54 for indemnification or an advance for expenses, in each case to the same extent to which a director may be entitled to indemnification or advance for expenses under those provisions.

§ 8.57. Insurance

A corporation may purchase and maintain insurance on behalf of an individual who is a director or officer of the corporation, or who, while a director or officer of the corporation, serves at the corporation's request as a director, officer, partner, trustee, employee, or agent of another domestic or foreign corporation, partnership, joint venture, trust, employee benefit plan, or other entity, against liability asserted against or incurred by him in that capacity or arising from his status as a director or officer, whether or not the corporation would have power

to indemnify or advance expenses to him against the same liability under this subchapter.

§ 8.58. Variation by Corporate Action; Application of Subchapter

(a)   A corporation may, by a provision in its articles of incorporation or bylaws or in a resolution adopted or a contract approved by its board of directors or shareholders, obligate itself in advance of the act or omission giving rise to a proceeding to provide indemnification in accordance with section 8.51 or advance funds to pay for or reimburse expenses in accordance with section 8.53. Any such obligatory provision shall be deemed to satisfy the requirements for authorization referred to in section 8.53(c) and in section 8.55(c). Any such provision that obligates the corporation to provide indemnification to the fullest extent permitted by law shall be deemed to obligate the corporation to advance funds to pay for or reimburse expenses in accordance with section 8.53 to the fullest extent permitted by law, unless the provision specifically provides otherwise.

(b)   Any provision pursuant to subsection (a) shall not obligate the corporation to indemnify or advance expenses to a director of a predecessor of the corporation, pertaining to conduct with respect to the predecessor, unless otherwise specifically provided. Any provision for indemnification or advance for expenses in the articles of incorporation, bylaws, or a resolution of the board of directors or shareholders of a predecessor of the corporation in a merger or in a contract to which the predecessor is a party, existing at the time the merger takes effect, shall be governed by section 11.06(a)(3).

(c)   A corporation may, by a provision in its articles of incorporation, limit any of the rights to indemnification or advance for expenses created by or pursuant to this subchapter.

(d)   This subchapter does not limit a corporation's power to pay or reimburse expenses incurred by a director or an officer in connection with his appearance as a witness in a proceeding at a time when he is not a party.

(e)   This subchapter does not limit a corporation's power to indemnify, advance expenses to or provide or maintain insurance on behalf of an employee or agent.

§ 8.59. *Exclusivity of Subchapter*

A corporation may provide indemnification or advance expenses to a director or an officer only as permitted by this subchapter.

SUBCHAPTER F.
DIRECTORS' CONFLICTING INTEREST TRANSACTIONS

§ 8.60. *Subchapter Definitions*

In this subchapter:

(1) "Conflicting interest" with respect to a corporation means the interest a director of the corporation has respecting a transaction effected or proposed to be effected by the corporation (or by a subsidiary of the corporation or any other entity in which the corporation has a controlling interest) if:

(i) whether or not the transaction is brought before the board of directors of the corporation for action, the director knows at the time of commitment that he or a related person is a party to the transaction or has a beneficial financial interest in or so closely linked to the transaction and of such financial significance to the director or a related person that the interest would reasonably be expected to exert an influence on the director's judgment if he were called upon to vote on the transaction; or

(ii) the transaction is brought (or is of such character and significance to the corporation that it would in the normal course be brought) before the board of directors of the corporation for action, and the director knows at the time of commitment that any of the following persons is either a party to the transaction or has a beneficial financial interest in or so closely linked to the transaction and of such financial significance to the person that the interest would reasonably be expected to exert an influence on the director's judgment if he were called upon to vote on the transaction: (A) an entity (other than the corporation) of which the director is a director, general partner, agent, or employee; (B) a person that controls one or more of the entities specified in subclause (A) or an entity that is controlled by, or is under common control with, one or more of the entities specified in subclause (A); or (C) an individual who is a general partner, principal, or employer of the director.

(2) "Director's conflicting interest transaction" with respect to a corporation means a transaction effected or proposed to be effected by the corporation (or by a subsidiary of the corporation or any other entity in which the corporation has a controlling interest) respecting which a director of the corporation has a conflicting interest.

(3) "Related person" of a director means (i) the spouse (or a parent or sibling thereof) of the director, or a child, grandchild, sibling, parent (or spouse of any thereof) of the director, or an individual having the same home as the director, or a trust or estate of which an individual specified in this clause (i) is a substantial beneficiary; or (ii) a trust, estate, incompetent, conservatee, or minor of which the director is a fiduciary.

(4) "Required disclosure" means disclosure by the director who has a conflicting interest of (i) the existence and nature of his conflicting interest, and (ii) all facts known to him respecting the subject matter of the transaction that an ordinarily prudent person would reasonably believe to be material to a judgment about whether or not to proceed with the transaction.

(5) "Time of commitment" respecting a transaction means the time when the transaction is consummated or, if made pursuant to contract, the time when the corporation (or its subsidiary or the entity in which it has a controlling interest) becomes contractually obligated so that its unilateral withdrawal from the transaction would entail significant loss, liability, or other damage.

§ 8.61. *Judicial Action*

(a) A transaction effected or proposed to be effected by a corporation (or by a subsidiary of the corporation or any other entity in which the corporation has a controlling interest) that is not a director's conflicting interest transaction may not be enjoined, set aside, or give rise to an award of damages or other sanctions, in a proceeding by shareholder or by or in the right of the corporation, because a director of the corporation, or any person with whom or which he has a personal, economic, or other association, has an interest in the transaction.

(b) A director's conflicting interest transaction may not be enjoined, set aside, or give rise to an award of damages or other sanctions, in a proceeding by a shareholder or by or in the right of the corporation, because the director, or any person with whom or which he has a personal, economic, or other association, has an interest in the transaction, if:

(1) directors' action respecting the transaction was at any time taken in compliance with section 8.62;

(2) shareholders' action respecting the transaction was at any time taken in compliance with section 8.63;

(3) the transaction, judged according to the circumstances at the time of commitment, is established to have been fair to the corporation.

§ 8.62. *Directors' Action*

(a) Directors' action respecting a transaction is effective for purposes of section 8.61(b)(1) if the transaction received the affirmative vote of a majority (but no fewer than two) of those qualified directors on the board of directors or on a duly empowered committee of the board who voted on the transaction after either required disclosure to them (to the extent the information was not known by them) or compliance with subsection (b); provided that action by a committee is so effective only if (1) all its members are qualified directors, and (2) its members are either all the qualified directors on the board or are appointed by the affirmative vote of a majority of the qualified directors on the board.

(b) If a director has a conflicting interest respecting a transaction, but neither he nor a related person of the director specified in section 8.60(3)(i) is a party to the transaction, and if the director has a duty under law or professional canon, or a duty of confidentiality to another person, respecting information relating to the transaction such that the director may not make the disclosure described in section 8.60(4)(ii), then disclosure is sufficient for purposes of subsection (a) if the director (I) discloses to the directors voting on the transaction the existence and nature of his conflicting interest and informs them of the character and limitations imposed by that duty before their vote on the transaction, and (2) plays no part, directly or indirectly, in their deliberations or vote.

(c) A majority (but no fewer than two) of all the qualified directors on the board of directors, or on the committee, constitutes a quorum for purposes of action that complies with this section. Directors' action that otherwise complies with this

section is not affected by the presence or vote of a director who is not a qualified director.

(d) For purposes of this section, "qualified director" means, with respect to a director's conflicting interest transaction, any director who does not have either (1) a conflicting interest respecting the transaction, or (2) a familial, financial, professional, or employment relationship with a second director who does have a conflicting interest respecting the transaction, which relationship would, in the circumstances, reasonably be expected to exert an influence on the first director's judgment when voting on the transaction.

§ 8.63. *Shareholders' Action*

(a) Shareholders' action respecting a transaction is effective for purposes of section 8.61(b)(2) if a majority of the votes entitled to be cast by the holders of all qualified shares were cast in favor of the transaction after (1) notice to shareholders describing the director's conflicting interest transaction, (2) provision of the information referred to in subsection (d), and (3) required disclosure to the shareholders who voted on the transaction (to the extent the information was not known by them).

(b) For purposes of this section, "qualified shares" means any shares entitled to vote with respect to the director's conflicting interest transaction except shares that, to the knowledge, before the vote, of the secretary (or other officer or agent of the corporation authorized to tabulate votes), are beneficially owned (or the voting of which is controlled) by a director who has a conflicting interest respecting the transaction or by a related person of the director, or both.

(c) A majority of the votes entitled to be cast by the holders of all qualified shares constitutes a quorum for purposes of action that complies with this section. Subject to the provisions of subsections (d) and (e), shareholders' action that otherwise complies with this section is not affected by the presence of holders, or the voting, of shares that are not qualified shares.

(d) For purposes of compliance with subsection (a), a director who has a conflicting interest respecting the transaction shall, before the shareholders' vote, inform the secretary (or other officer or agent of the corporation authorized to tabulate votes) of the number, and the identity of persons holding or controlling the vote, of all shares that the director knows are beneficially owned (or the voting of which is controlled) by the director or by a related person of the director, or both.

(e)   If a shareholders' vote does not comply with subsection (a) solely because of a failure of a director to comply with subsection (d), and if the director establishes that his failure did not determine and was not intended by him to influence the outcome of the vote, the court may, with or without further proceedings respecting section 8.61(b)(3), take such action respecting the transaction and the director, and give such effect, if any, to the shareholders' vote, as it considers appropriate in the circumstances.

Chapter 9 [Reserved]

[Chapter 10, Amendment of Articles of Incorporation and Bylaws, Omitted]

CHAPTER 11
MERGER AND SHARE EXCHANGE

§ 11.01. *Merger*

(a)   One or more corporations may merge into another corporation if the board of directors of each corporation adopts and its shareholders (if required by section 11.03) approve a plan of merger.

(b)   The plan of merger must set forth:

(1)   the name of each corporation planning to merge and the name of the surviving corporation into which each other corporation plans to merge;

(2)   the terms and conditions of the merger; and

(3)   the manner and basis of converting the shares of each corporation into shares, obligations, or other securities of the surviving or any other corporation or into cash or other property in whole or part.

(c)   The plan of merger may set forth:

(1)   amendments to the articles of incorporation of the surviving corporation; and

(2)   other provisions relating to the merger.

§ 11.02. *Share Exchange*

(a)   A corporation may acquire all of the outstanding shares of one or more classes or series of another corporation if the board of directors of each corporation adopts and its shareholders (if required by section 11.03) approve the exchange.

(b)   The plan of exchange must set forth:

(1)   the name of the corporation whose shares will be acquired and the name of the acquiring corporation;

(2)   the terms and conditions of the exchange;

(3)   the manner and basis of exchanging the shares to be acquired for shares, obligations, or other securities of the acquiring or any other corporation or for cash or other property in whole or part.

(c)   The plan of exchange may set forth other provisions relating to the exchange.

(d)   This section does not limit the power of a corporation to acquire all or part of the shares of one or more classes or series of another corporation through a voluntary exchange or otherwise.

§ 11.03. *Action on Plan*

(a)   After adopting a plan of merger or share exchange, the board of directors of each corporation party to the merger, and the board of directors of the corporation whose shares will be acquired in the share exchange, shall submit the plan of merger (except as provided in subsection (g)) or share exchange for approval by its shareholders.

(b)   For a plan of merger or share exchange to be approved:

(1)   the board of directors must recommend the plan of merger or share exchange to the shareholders, unless the board of directors determines that because of conflict of interest or other special circumstances it should make no recommendation and communicates the basis for its determination to the shareholders with the plan; and

(2)   the shareholders entitled to vote must approve the plan.

(c)   The board of directors may condition its submission of the proposed merger or share exchange on any basis.

(d)   The corporation shall notify each shareholder, whether or not entitled to vote, of the proposed shareholders' meeting in accordance with section 7.05. The notice must also state that the purpose, or one of the purposes, of the meeting is to consider the plan of merger or share exchange and contain or be accompanied by a copy or summary of the plan.

(e)   Unless this Act, the articles of incorporation, or the board of directors (acting pursuant to subsection (c)) require a greater vote or a vote by voting groups, the plan of merger or share exchange to be authorized must be approved by each voting group entitled to vote separately on the plan by a majority of all the votes entitled to be cast on the plan by that voting group.

(f)   Separate voting by voting groups is required:

(1)   on a plan of merger if the plan contains a provision that, if contained in a proposed amendment to articles of incorporation, would require action by one or more separate voting groups on the proposed amendment under section 10.04;

(2)   on a plan of share exchange by each class or series of shares included in the exchange, with each class or series constituting a separate voting group.

(g)   Action by the shareholders of the surviving corporation on a plan of merger is not required if:

(1)   the articles of incorporation of the surviving corporation will not differ (except for amendments enumerated in section 10.02) from its articles before the merger;

(2)   each shareholder of the surviving corporation whose shares were outstanding immediately before the effective date of the merger will hold the same number of shares, with identical designations, preferences, limitations, and relative rights, immediately after;

(3)   the number of voting shares outstanding immediately after the merger, plus the number of voting shares issuable as a result of the merger (either by the conversion of securities issued pursuant to the merger or the exercise of rights and warrants issued pursuant to the merger), will not exceed by more than 20 percent the total number of voting shares of the surviving corporation outstanding immediately before the merger; and

(4)   the number of participating shares outstanding immediately after the merger, plus the number of participating shares issuable as a result of the merger (either by the conversion of securities issued pursuant to the merger or the exercise of rights and warrants issued pursuant to the merger), will not exceed by more than 20 percent the total number of participating shares outstanding immediately before the merger.

(h)   As used in subsection (g):

(1)   "Participating shares" means shares that entitle their holders to participate without limitation in distributions.

(2)   "Voting shares" means shares that entitle their holders to vote unconditionally in elections of directors.

(i)   After a merger or share exchange is authorized, and at any time before articles of merger or share exchange are filed, the planned merger or share exchange may be abandoned (subject to any contractual rights), without further shareholder action, in accordance with the procedure set forth in the plan of merger or share exchange or, if none is set forth, in the manner determined by the board of directors.

§ 11.04. Merger of Subsidiary

(a)   A parent corporation owning at least 90 percent of the outstanding shares of each class of a subsidiary corporation may merge the subsidiary into itself without approval of the shareholders of the parent or subsidiary.

(b)   The board of directors of the parent shall adopt a plan of merger that sets forth:

(1)   the names of the parent and subsidiary; and

(2)   the manner and basis of converting the shares of the subsidiary into shares, obligations, or other securities of the parent or any other corporation or into cash or other property in whole or part.

(c)   The parent shall mail a copy or summary of the plan of merger to each shareholder of the subsidiary who does not waive the mailing requirement in writing.

(d)   The parent may not deliver articles of merger to the secretary of state for filing until at least 30 days after the date it mailed a copy of the plan of merger to each shareholder of the subsidiary who did not waive the mailing requirement.

(e)   Articles of merger under this section may not contain amendments to the articles of incorporation of the parent corporation (except for amendments enumerated in section 10.02).

§ 11.05. Articles of Merger or Share Exchange

(a)   After a plan of merger or share exchange is approved by the shareholders, or adopted by the board of directors if shareholder approval is not required, the surviving or acquiring corporation shall deliver to the secretary of state for filing articles of merger or share exchange setting forth:

(1)   the plan of merger or share exchange;

(2)   if shareholder approval was not required, a statement to that effect;

(3)   if approval of the shareholders of one or more corporations party to the merger or share exchange was required:

(i)   the designation, number of outstanding shares, and number of votes entitled to be cast by each voting group entitled to vote separately on the plan as to each corporation; and

(ii)   either the total number of votes cast for and against the plan by each voting group entitled to vote separately on the plan or the total number of undisputed votes cast for the plan separately by each voting group and a statement that the number cast for the plan by each voting group was sufficient for approval by that voting group.

(b)   A merger or share exchange takes effect upon the effective date of the articles of merger or share exchange.

§ 11.06. *Effect of Merger or Share Exchange*

(a)   When a merger takes effect:

(1)   every other corporation party to the merger merges into the surviving corporation and the separate existence of every corporation except the surviving corporation ceases;

(2)   the title to all real estate and other property owned by each corporation party to the merger is vested in the surviving corporation without reversion or impairment;

(3)   the surviving corporation has all liabilities of each corporation party to the merger;

(4)   a proceeding pending against any corporation party to the merger may be continued as if the merger did not occur or the surviving corporation may be substituted in the proceeding for the corporation whose existence ceased;

(5)   the articles of incorporation of the surviving corporation are amended to the extent provided in the plan of merger; and

(6)   the shares of each corporation party to the merger that are to be converted into shares, obligations, or other securities of the surviving or any other corporation or into cash or other property are converted, and the former holders of the shares are entitled only to the rights provided in the articles of merger or to their rights under chapter 13.

(b)   When a share exchange takes effect, the shares of each acquired corporation are exchanged as provided in the plan, and the former holders of the shares are entitled only to the exchange rights provided in the articles of share exchange or to their rights under chapter 13.

§ 11.07. *Merger or Share Exchange with Foreign Corporation*

(a)   One or more foreign corporations may merge or enter into a share exchange with one or more domestic corporations if:

(1)   in a merger, the merger is permitted by the law of the state or country under whose law each foreign corporation is incorporated and each foreign corporation complies with that law in effecting the merger;

(2)   in a share exchange, the corporation whose shares will be acquired is a domestic corporation, whether or not a share exchange is permitted by the law of the state or country under whose law the acquiring corporation is incorporated;

(3)   the foreign corporation complies with section 11.05 if it is the surviving corporation of the merger or acquiring corporation of the share exchange; and

(4)   each domestic corporation complies with the applicable provisions of sections 11.01 through 11.04 and, if it is the surviving corporation of the merger or acquiring corporation of the share exchange, with section 11.05.

(b)   Upon the merger or share exchange taking effect, the surviving foreign corporation of a merger and the acquiring foreign corporation of a share exchange is deemed:

(1)   to appoint the secretary of state as its agent for service of process in a proceeding to enforce any obligation or the rights of dissenting shareholders of each domestic corporation party to the merger or share exchange; and

(2)   to agree that it will promptly pay to the dissenting shareholders of each domestic corporation party to the merger or share exchange the amount, if any, to which they are entitled under chapter 13.

(c)   This section does not limit the power of a foreign corporation to acquire all or part of the shares of one or more classes or series of a domestic corporation through a voluntary exchange or otherwise.

CHAPTER 12
SALE OF ASSETS

§ 12.01. Sale of Assets in Regular Course of Business and Mortgage of Assets

(a)   A corporation may, on the terms and conditions and for the consideration determined by the board of directors:

(1)   sell, lease, exchange, or otherwise dispose of all, or substantially all, of its property in the usual and regular course of business;

(2)   mortgage, pledge, dedicate to the repayment of indebtedness (whether with or without recourse), or otherwise encumber any or all of its property whether or not in the usual and regular course of business; or

(3)   transfer any or all of its property to a corporation all the shares of which are owned by the corporation.

(b)   Unless the articles of incorporation require it, approval by the shareholders of a transaction described in subsection (a) is not required.

§ 12.02. Sale of Assets Other Than in Regular Course of Business

(a)   A corporation may sell, lease, exchange, or otherwise dispose of all, or substantially all, of its property (with or without the good will), otherwise than in the usual and regular course of business, on the terms and conditions and for the consideration determined by the corporation's board of directors, if the board of directors proposes and its shareholders approve the proposed transaction.

(b)   For a transaction to be authorized:

(1)   the board of directors must recommend the proposed transaction to the shareholders unless the board of directors determines that because of conflict of interest or other special circumstances it should make no recommendation and communicates the basis for its determination to the shareholders with the submission of the proposed transaction; and

(2)   the shareholders entitled to vote must approve the transaction.

(c)   The board of directors may condition its submission of the proposed transaction on any basis.

(d)   The corporation shall notify each shareholder, whether or not entitled to vote, of the proposed shareholders' meeting in accordance with section 7.05. The notice must also state that the purpose, or one of the purposes, of the meeting is to consider the sale, lease, exchange, or other disposition of all, or substantially all, the property of the corporation and contain or be accompanied by a description of the transaction.

(e)   Unless the articles of incorporation or the board of directors (acting pursuant to subsection (c)) require a greater vote or a vote by voting groups, the transaction to be authorized must be approved by a majority of all the votes entitled to be cast on the transaction.

(f)   After a sale, lease, exchange, or other disposition of property is authorized, the transaction may be abandoned (subject to any contractual rights) without further shareholder action.

(g)   A transaction that constitutes a distribution is governed by section 6.40 and not by this section.

CHAPTER 13
DISSENTERS' RIGHTS
SUBCHAPTER A.

§ 13.01. Definitions

In this chapter:

(1)   "Affiliate" means a person that directly or indirectly through one or more intermediaries controls, is controlled by, or is under common control with another person or is a senior executive thereof. For purposes of section 13.02(b)(4), a person is deemed to be an affiliate of its senior executives.

(2)   "Beneficial shareholder" means a person who is the beneficial owner of shares held in a voting trust or by a nominee on the beneficial owner's behalf.

(3)   "Corporation" means the issuer of the shares held by a shareholder demanding appraisal and, for matters covered in sections 13.22–13.31, includes the surviving entity in a merger.

(4)   "Fair value" means the value of the corporation's shares determined:

(i)   immediately before the effectuation of the corporate action to which the shareholder objects;

(ii)   using customary and current valuation concepts and techniques generally employed for similar businesses in the context of the transaction requiring appraisal; and

(iii)   without discounting for lack of marketability or minority status except, if appropriate, for amendments to the articles pursuant to section 13.02(a)(5).

(5)   "Interest" means interest from the effective date of the corporate action until the date of payment, at the rate of interest on judgments in this state on the effective date of the corporate action.

(6)   "Preferred shares" means a class or series of shares whose holders have preferences over any other class or series with respect to distributions.

(7)   "Record shareholder" means the person in whose name shares are registered in the records of the corporation or the beneficial owner of shares to the extent of the rights granted by a nominee certificate on file with the corporation.

(8)   "Senior executive" means the chief executive officer, chief operating officer, chief financial officer, and anyone in charge of a principal business unit or function.

(9)   "Shareholder" means both a record shareholder and a beneficial shareholder.

§ 13.02.   *Right to Appraisal*

(a)   A shareholder is entitled to appraisal rights, and to obtain payment of the fair value of that shareholder's shares, in the event of any of the following corporate actions:

(1)   consummation of a merger to which the corporation is a party (i) if shareholder approval is required for the merger by section 11.04 and the shareholder is entitled to vote on the merger, except that appraisal rights shall not be available to any shareholder of the corporation with respect to shares of any class or series that remain outstanding after consummation of the merger, or (ii) if the corporation is a subsidiary and the merger is governed by section 11.05;

(2)   consummation of a share exchange to which the corporation is a party as the corporation whose shares will be acquired if the shareholder is entitled to vote on the exchange, except that appraisal rights shall not be available to any shareholder of the corporation with respect to any class or series of shares of the corporation that is not exchanged;

(3)   consummation of a disposition of assets pursuant to section 12.02 if the shareholder is entitled to vote on the disposition;

(4)   an amendment of the articles of incorporation with respect to a class or series of shares that reduces the number of shares of a class or series owned by the shareholder to a fraction of a share if the corporation has the obligation or right to repurchase the fractional share so created; or

(5)   any other amendment to the articles of incorporation, merger, share exchange or disposition of assets to the extent provided by the articles of incorporation, bylaws or a resolution of the board of directors.

(b)   Notwithstanding subsection (a), the availability of appraisal rights under subsections (a)(1), (2), (3) and (4) shall be limited in accordance with the following provisions:

(1)   Appraisal rights shall not be available for the holders of shares of any class or series of shares which is:

(i)   listed on the New York Stock Exchange or the American Stock Exchange or designated as a national market system security on an interdealer quotation system by the National Association of Securities Dealers, Inc.; or

(ii)   not so listed or designated, but has at least 2,000 shareholders and the outstanding shares of such class or series has a market value of at least $20 million (exclusive of the value of such shares held by its subsidiaries, senior executives, directors and beneficial shareholders owning more that 10 percent of such shares).

(2)   The applicability of subsection (b)(1) shall be determined as of:

(i)   the record date fixed to determine the shareholders entitled to receive notice of, and to vote at, the meeting of shareholders to act upon the corporate action requiring appraisal rights; or

(ii)   the day before the effective date of such corporate action if there is no meeting of shareholders.

(3)   Subsection (b)(1) shall not be applicable and appraisal rights shall be available

pursuant to subsection (a) for the holders of any class or series of shares who are required by the terms of the corporate action requiring appraisal rights to accept for such shares anything other than cash or shares of any class or any series of shares of any corporation, or any other proprietary interest of any other entity, that satisfies the standards set forth in subsection (b)(1) at the time the corporate action becomes effective.

(4) Subsection (b)(1) shall not be applicable and appraisal rights shall be available pursuant to subsection (a) for the holders of any class or series of shares where:

(i) any of the shares or assets of the corporation are being acquired or converted, whether by merger, share exchange or otherwise, pursuant to the corporate action by a person, or by an affiliate of a person, who:

(A) is, or at any time in the one-year period immediately preceding approval by the board of directors of the corporate action requiring appraisal rights was, the beneficial owner of 20 percent or more of the voting power of the corporation, excluding any shares acquired pursuant to an offer for all shares having voting power if such offer was made within one year prior to the corporate action requiring appraisal rights for consideration of the same kind and of a value equal to or less than that paid in connection with the corporate action; or

(B) directly or indirectly has, or at any time in the one-year period immediately preceding approval by the board of directors of the corporation of the corporate action requiring appraisal rights had, the power, contractually or otherwise, to cause the appointment or election of 25 percent or more of the directors to the board of directors of the corporation; or

(ii) any of the shares or assets of the corporation are being acquired or converted, whether by merger, share exchange or otherwise, pursuant to such corporate action by a person, or by an affiliate of

a person, who is, or at any time in the one-year period immediately preceding approval by the board of directors of the corporate action requiring appraisal rights was, a senior executive or director of the corporation or a senior executive of any affiliate thereof, and that senior executive or director will receive, as a result of the corporate action, a financial benefit not generally available to other shareholders as such, other than:

(A) employment, consulting, retirement or similar benefits established separately and not as part of or in contemplation of the corporate action; or

(B) employment, consulting, retirement or similar benefits established in contemplation of, or as part of, the corporate action that are not more favorable than those existing before the corporate action or, if more favorable, that have been approved on behalf of the corporation in the same manner as is provided in section 8.62; or

(C) in the case of a director of the corporation who will, in the corporate action, become a director of the acquiring entity in the corporate action or one of its affiliates, rights and benefits as a director that are provided on the same basis as those afforded by the acquiring entity generally to other directors of such entity or such affiliate.

(5) For the purposes of paragraph (4) only, the term "beneficial owner" means any person who, directly or indirectly, through any contract, arrangement, or understanding, other than a revocable proxy, has or shares the power to vote, or to direct the voting of, shares, provided that a member of a national securities exchange shall not be deemed to be a beneficial owner of securities held directly or indirectly by it on behalf of another person solely because such member is the record holder of such securities if the member is precluded by the rules of such exchange from voting without instruction on contested matters or matters that may affect substantially the rights or privileges of the holders of the securities to be voted. When two or more persons agree to act together for the purpose of voting

their shares of the corporation, each member of the group formed thereby shall be deemed to have acquired beneficial ownership, as of the date of such agreement, of all voting shares of the corporation beneficially owned by any member of the group.

(c) Notwithstanding any other provision of section 13.02, the articles of incorporation as originally filed or any amendment thereto may limit or eliminate appraisal rights for any class or series of preferred shares, but, any such limitation or elimination contained in an amendment to the articles of incorporation that limits or eliminates appraisal rights for any of such shares that are outstanding immediately prior to the effective date of such amendment or that the corporation is or may be required to issue or sell thereafter pursuant to any conversion, exchange or other right existing immediately before the effective date of such amendment shall not apply to any corporate action that becomes effective within one year of that date if such action would otherwise afford appraisal rights.

(d) A shareholder entitled to appraisal rights under this chapter may not challenge a completed corporate action for which appraisal rights are available unless such corporation action:

(i) was not effectuated in accordance with the applicable provisions of chapters 10, 11 or 12 or the corporation's articles of incorporation, bylaws or board of directors' resolution authorizing the corporate action; or

(ii) was procured as a result of fraud or material misrepresentation.

§ 13.03. *Assertion of Rights by Nominees and Beneficial Owners*

(a) A record shareholder may assert appraisal rights as to fewer than all the shares registered in the record shareholder's name but owned by a beneficial shareholder only if the record shareholder object with respect to all shares of the class or series owned by the beneficial shareholder and notifies the corporation in writing of the name and address of each beneficial shareholder on whose behalf appraisal rights are being asserted. The rights of a record shareholder who asserts appraisal rights for only part of the shares held of record in the record shareholder's name under this subsection shall be determined as if the shares as to which the

record shareholder objects and the record shareholder's other shares were registered in the names of different record shareholders.

(b) A beneficial shareholder may assert appraisal rights as to shares of any class or series held on behalf of the shareholder only if such shareholder:

(1) submits to the corporation the record shareholder's written consent to the assertion of such rights no later than the date referred to in section 13.22(b)(2)(ii); and

(2) does so with respect to all shares of the class or series that are beneficially owned by the beneficial shareholder.

SUBCHAPTER B. PROCEDURE FOR EXERCISE OF APPRAISAL RIGHTS

§ 13.20. *Notice of Appraisal Rights*

(a) If proposed corporate action described in section 13.02(a) is to be submitted to a vote at a shareholders' meeting, the meeting notice must state that the corporation has concluded that shareholders are, are not or may be entitled to assert appraisal rights under this chapter. If the corporation concludes that appraisal rights are or may be available, a copy of this chapter must accompany the meeting notice sent to those record shareholders entitled to exercise appraisal rights.

(b) In a merger pursuant to section 11.05, the parent corporation must notify in writing all record shareholders of the subsidiary who are entitled to assert appraisal rights that the corporate action became effective. Such notice must be sent within ten days after the corporate action became effective and include the materials described in section 13.22.

§ 13.21. *Notice of Intent to Demand Payment*

(a) If proposed corporate action requiring appraisal rights under section 13.02 is submitted to a vote at a shareholders' meeting, a shareholder who wishes to assert appraisal rights with respect to any class or series of shares:

(1) must deliver to the corporation before the vote is taken written notice of the shareholder's intent to demand payment if the proposed action is effectuated; and

(2) must not vote, or cause or permit to be voted, any shares of such class or series in favor of the proposed action.

(b) A shareholder who does not satisfy the requirements of subsection (a) is not entitled to payment under this chapter.

§ 13.22. *Appraisal Notice and Form*

(a) If proposed corporate action requiring appraisal rights under section 13.02(a) becomes effective, the corporation must deliver a written appraisal notice and form required by subsection (b)(1) to all shareholders who satisfied the requirements of section 13.21. In the case of a merger under section 11.05, the parent must deliver a written appraisal notice and form to all record shareholders who may be entitled to assert appraisal rights.

(b) The appraisal notice must be sent no earlier than the date the corporate action became effective and no later than ten days after such date and must:

(1) supply a form that specifies the date of the first announcement to shareholders of the principal terms of the proposed corporate action and requires the shareholder asserting appraisal rights to certify (i) whether or not beneficial ownership of those shares for which appraisal rights are asserted was acquired before that date and (ii) that the shareholder did not vote for the transaction;

(2) state:

(i) where the form must be sent and where certificates for certificated shares must be deposited and the date by which those certificates must be deposited, which date may not be earlier than the date for receiving the required form under subsection (2)(ii);

(ii) a date by which the corporation must receive the form which date may not be fewer than 40 nor more than 60 days after the date the subsection (a) appraisal notice and form are sent, and state that the shareholder shall have waived the right to demand appraisal with respect to the shares unless the form is received by the corporation by such specified date;

(iii) the corporation's estimate of the fair value of the shares;

(iv) that, if requested in writing, the corporation will provide, to the shareholder so requesting, within ten days after the date specified in subsection (2)(ii) the number of shareholders who return the forms by the specified date and the total number of shares owned by them; and

(v) the date by which the notice to withdraw under section 13.23 must be received, which date must be within 20 days after the date specified in subsection (2)(ii); and

(3) be accompanied by a copy of this chapter.

§ 13.23. *Perfection of Rights;*
Right to Withdraw

(a) A shareholder who receives notice pursuant to section 13.22 and who wishes to exercise appraisal rights must certify on the form sent by the corporation whether the beneficial owner of such shares acquired beneficial ownership of the shares before the date required to be set forth in the notice pursuant to section 13.22(b)(1). If a shareholder fails to make this certification, the corporation may elect to treat the shareholder's shares as after-acquired shares under section 13.25. In addition, a shareholder who wishes to exercise appraisal rights must execute and return the form and, in the case of certificated shares, deposit the shareholder's certificates in accordance with the terms of the notice by the date referred to in the notice pursuant to section 13.22(b)(2)(ii). Once a shareholder deposits that shareholder's certificates or, in the case of uncertificated shares, returns the executed forms, that shareholder loses all rights as a shareholder, unless the shareholder withdraws pursuant to sub-section (b).

(b) A shareholder who has complied with subsection (a) may nevertheless decline to exercise appraisal rights and withdraw from the appraisal process by so notifying the corporation in writing by the date set forth in the appraisal notice pursuant to section 13.22(b)(2)(v). A shareholder who fails to so withdraw from the appraisal process may not thereafter withdraw without the corporation's written consent.

(c) A shareholder who does not execute and return the form and, in the case of certificated shares, deposit that shareholder's share certificates where required, each by the date set forth in the notice described in section 13.22(b), shall not be entitled to payment under this chapter.

§ 13.24. Payment

(a) Except as provided in section 13.25, within 30 days after the form required by section 13.22(b)(2)(ii) is due, the corporation shall pay in cash to those shareholders who complied with section 13.23(a) the amount the corporation estimates to be the fair value of the shares, plus interest.

(b) The payment to each shareholder pursuant to subsection (a) must be accompanied by:

(1) financial statements of the corporation that issued the shares to be appraised, consisting of a balance sheet as of the end of a fiscal year ending not more than 16 months before the date of payment, an income statement for that year, a statement of changes in shareholders' equity for that year, and the latest available interim financial statements, if any;

(2) a statement of the corporation's estimate of the fair value of the shares, which estimate must equal or exceed the corporation's estimate given pursuant to section 13.22(b)(2)(iii);

(3) a statement that shareholders described in subsection (a) have the right to demand further payment under section 13.26 and that if any such shareholder does not do so within the time period specified therein, such shareholder shall be deemed to have accepted such payment in full satisfaction of the corporation's obligations under this chapter.

§ 13.25. After-Acquired Shares

(a) A corporation may elect to withhold payment required by section 13.24 from any shareholder who did not certify that beneficial ownership of all of the shareholder's shares for which appraisal rights are asserted was acquired before the date set forth in the appraisal notice sent pursuant to section 13.22(b)(1).

(b) If the corporation elected to withhold payment under subsection (a), it must, within 30 days after the form required by section 13.22(b)(2)(ii) is due, notify all shareholders who are described in subsection (a):

(1) of the information required by section 13.24(b)(1);

(2) of the corporation's estimate of fair value pursuant to section 13.24(b)(2);

(3) that they may accept the corporation's estimate of fair value, plus interest, in full satisfaction of their demands or demand appraisal under section 13.26;

(4) that those shareholders who wish to accept such offer must so notify the corporation of their acceptance of the corporation's offer within 30 days after receiving the offer; and

(5) that those shareholders who do not satisfy the requirements for demanding appraisal under section 13.26 shall be deemed to have accepted the corporation's offer.

(c) Within ten days after receiving the shareholder's acceptance pursuant to subsection (b), the corporation must pay in cash the amount it offered under subsection (b)(2) to each shareholder who agreed to accept the corporation's offer in full satisfaction of the shareholder's demand.

(d) Within 40 days after sending the notice described in subsection (b), the corporation must pay in cash the amount it offered to pay under subsection (b)(2) to each shareholder described in subsection (b)(5).

§ 13.26. Procedure if Shareholder Dissatisfied With Payment or Offer

(a) A shareholder paid pursuant to section 13.24 who is dissatisfied with the amount of the payment must notify the corporation in writing of that shareholder's estimate of the fair value of the shares and demand payment of that estimate plus interest (less any payment under section 13.24). A shareholder offered payment under section 13.25 who is dissatisfied with that offer must reject the offer and demand payment of the shareholder's stated estimate of the fair value of the shares plus interest.

(b) A shareholder who fails to notify the corporation in writing of that shareholder's demand to be paid the shareholder's stated estimate of the fair value plus interest under subsection (a) within 30 days after receiving the corporation's payment or offer of payment under section 13.24 or section 13.25, respectively, waives the right to demand payment under this section and shall be entitled only to the payment made or offered pursuant to those respective sections.

SUBCHAPTER C.
JUDICIAL APPRAISAL OF SHARES

§ 13.30. Court Action

(a) If a shareholder makes demand for payment under section 13.26 which remains unsettled, the corporation shall commence a proceeding within 60 days after receiving the payment demand and petition the court to determine the fair value of the shares and accrued interest. If the corporation does not commence the proceeding within the 60-day period, it shall pay in cash to each shareholder the amount the shareholder demanded pursuant to section 13.26 plus interest.

(b)   The corporation shall commence the proceeding in the appropriate court of the county where the corporation's principal office (or, if none, its registered office) in this state is located. If the corporation is a foreign corporation without a registered office in this state, it shall commence the proceeding in the county in this state where the principal office or registered office of the domestic corporation merged with the foreign corporation was located at the time of the transaction.

(c)   The corporation shall make all shareholders (whether or not residents of this state) whose demands remain unsettled parties to the proceeding as in an action against their shares, and all parties must be served with a copy of the petition. Nonresidents may be served by registered or certified mail or by publication as provided by law.

(d)   The jurisdiction of the court in which the proceeding is commenced under subsection (b) is plenary and exclusive. The court may appoint one or more persons as appraisers to receive evidence and recommend a decision on the question of fair value. The appraisers shall have the powers described in the order appointing them, or in any amendment to it. The shareholders demanding appraisal rights are entitled to the same discovery rights as parties in other civil proceedings. There shall be no right to a jury trial.

(e)   Each shareholder made a party to the proceeding is entitled to judgment (i) for the amount, if any, by which the court finds the fair value of the shareholder's shares, plus interest, exceeds the amount paid by the corporation to the shareholder for such shares or (ii) for the fair value, plus interest, of the shareholder's shares for which the corporation elected to withhold payment under section 13.25.

§ 13.31. *Court Costs and Counsel Fees*

(a) The court in an appraisal proceeding commenced under section 13.30 shall determine all costs of the proceeding, including the reasonable com-

pensation and expenses of appraisers appointed by the court. The court shall assess the costs against the corporation, except that the court may assess costs against all or some of the shareholders demanding appraisal, in amounts the court finds equitable, to the extent the court finds such shareholders acted arbitrarily vexatiously, or not in good faith with respect to the rights provided by this chapter.

(b)   The court in an appraisal proceeding may also assess the fees and expenses of counsel and experts for the respective parties, in amounts the court finds equitable:

(1)   against the corporation and in favor of any or all shareholders demanding appraisal if the court finds the corporation did not substantially comply with the requirements of sections 13.20, 13.22, 13.24 or 13.25; or

(2)   against either the corporation or a shareholder demanding appraisal, in favor of any other party, if the court finds that the party against whom the fees and expenses are assessed acted arbitrarily vexatiously, or not in good faith with respect to the rights provided by this chapter.

(c)   If the court in an appraisal proceeding finds that the services of counsel for any shareholder were of substantial benefit to other shareholders similarly situated, and that the fees for those services should not be assessed against the corporation, the court may award to such counsel reasonable fees to be paid out of the amounts awarded the shareholders who were benefited.

(d)   To the extent the corporation fails to make a required payment pursuant to sections 13.24, 13.25, or 13.26, the shareholder may sue directly for the amount owed and, to the extent successful, shall be entitled to recover from the corporation all costs and expenses of the suit, including counsel fees.

CHAPTER 14
DISSOLUTION
SUBCHAPTER A.
VOLUNTARY DISSOLUTION

§ 14.01. *Dissolution by Incorporators or*
Initial Directors

A majority of the incorporators or initial directors of a corporation that has not issued shares or has not commenced business may dissolve the corporation by delivering to the secretary of state for filing articles of dissolution that set forth:

(1) the name of the corporation;

(2) the date of its incorporation;

(3) either (i) that none of the corporation's shares has been issued or (ii) that the corporation has not commenced business;

(4) that no debt of the corporation remains unpaid;

(5) that the net assets of the corporation remaining after winding up have been distributed to the shareholders, if shares were issued; and

(6) that a majority of the incorporators or initial directors authorized the dissolution.

§ 14.02. Dissolution by Board of Directors and Shareholders

(a) A corporation's board of directors may propose dissolution for submission to the shareholders.

(b) For a proposal to dissolve to be adopted:

(1) the board of directors must recommend dissolution to the shareholders unless the board of directors determines that because of conflict of interest or other special circumstances it should make no recommendation and communicates the basis for its determination to the shareholders; and

(2) the shareholders entitled to vote must approve the proposal to dissolve as provided in subsection (e).

(c) The board of directors may condition its submission of the proposal for dissolution on any basis.

(d) The corporation shall notify each shareholder, whether or not entitled to vote, of the proposed shareholders' meeting in accordance with section 7.05. The notice must also state that the purpose, or one of the purposes, of the meeting is to consider dissolving the corporation.

(e) Unless the articles of incorporation or the board of directors (acting pursuant to subsection (c)) require a greater vote or a vote by voting groups, the proposal to dissolve to be adopted must be approved by a majority of all the votes entitled to be cast on that proposal.

§ 14.03. Articles of Dissolution

(a) At any time after dissolution is authorized, the corporation may dissolve by delivering to the

secretary of state for filing articles of dissolution setting forth:

(1) the name of the corporation;

(2) the date dissolution was authorized;

(3) if dissolution was approved by the shareholders:

(i) the number of votes entitled to be cast on the proposal to dissolve; and

(ii) either the total number of votes cast for and against dissolution or the total number of undisputed votes cast for dissolution and a statement that the number cast for dissolution was sufficient for approval.

(4) If voting by voting groups was required, the information required by subparagraph (3) must be separately provided for each voting group entitled to vote separately on the plan to dissolve.

(b) A corporation is dissolved upon the effective date of its articles of dissolution.

§ 14.04. Revocation of Dissolution

(a) A corporation may revoke its dissolution within 120 days of its effective date.

(b) Revocation of dissolution must be authorized in the same manner as the dissolution was authorized unless that authorization permitted revocation by action of the board of directors alone, in which event the board of directors may revoke the dissolution without shareholder action.

(c) After the revocation of dissolution is authorized, the corporation may revoke the dissolution by delivering to the secretary of state for filing articles of revocation of dissolution, together with a copy of its articles of dissolution, that set forth:

(1) the name of the corporation;

(2) the effective date of the dissolution that was revoked;

(3) the date that the revocation of dissolution was authorized;

(4) if the corporation's board of directors (or incorporators) revoked the dissolution, a statement to that effect;

(5) if the corporation's board of directors revoked a dissolution authorized by the shareholders, a statement that revocation was permitted by action by the board of directors alone pursuant to that authorization; and

(6) if shareholder action was required to revoke the dissolution, the information required by section 14.03(a)(3) or (4).

(d) Revocation of dissolution is effective upon the effective date of the articles of revocation of dissolution.

(e) When the revocation of dissolution is effective, it relates back to and takes effect as of the effective date of the dissolution and the corporation resumes carrying on its business as if dissolution had never occurred.

§ 14.05. Effect of Dissolution

(a) A dissolved corporation continues its corporate existence but may not carry on any business except that appropriate to wind up and liquidate its business and affairs, including:

(1) collecting its assets;

(2) disposing of its properties that will not be distributed in kind to its shareholders;

(3) discharging or making provision for discharging its liabilities;

(4) distributing its remaining property among its shareholders according to their interests; and

(5) doing every other act necessary to wind up and liquidate its business and affairs.

(b) Dissolution of a corporation does not:

(1) transfer title to the corporation's property;

(2) prevent transfer of its shares or securities, although the authorization to dissolve may provide for closing the corporation's share transfer records;

(3) subject its directors or officers to standards of conduct different from those prescribed in chapter 8;

(4) change quorum or voting requirements for its board of directors or shareholders; change provisions for selection, resignation, or removal of its directors or officers or both; or change provisions for amending its bylaws;

(5) prevent commencement of a proceeding by or against the corporation in its corporate name;

(6) abate or suspend a proceeding pending by or against the corporation on the effective date of dissolution; or

(7) terminate the authority of the registered agent of the corporation.

§ 14.06. Known Claims Against Dissolved Corporation

(a) A dissolved corporation may dispose of the known claims against it by following the procedure described in this section.

(b) The dissolved corporation shall notify its known claimants in writing of the dissolution at any time after its effective date. The written notice must:

(1) describe information that must be included in a claim;

(2) provide a mailing address where a claim may be sent;

(3) state the deadline, which may not be fewer than 120 days from the effective date of the written notice, by which the dissolved corporation must receive the claim; and

(4) state that the claim will be barred if not received by the deadline.

(c) A claim against the dissolved corporation is barred:

(1) if a claimant who was given written notice under subsection (b) does not deliver the claim to the dissolved corporation by the deadline;

(2) if a claimant whose claim was rejected by the dissolved corporation does not commence a proceeding to enforce the claim within 90 days from the effective date of the rejection notice.

(d) For purposes of this section, "claim" does not include a contingent liability or a claim based on an event occurring after the effective date of dissolution.

§ 14.07. Unknown Claims Against Dissolved Corporation

(a) A dissolved corporation may also publish notice of its dissolution and request that persons with claims against the corporation present them in accordance with the notice.

(b) The notice must:

(1) be published one time in a newspaper of general circulation in the county where the dissolved corporation's principal office (or, if none in this state, its registered office) is or was last located;

(2)   describe the information that must be included in a claim and provide a mailing address where the claim may be sent; and

(3)   state that a claim against the corporation will be barred unless a proceeding to enforce the claim is commenced within five years after the publication of the notice.

(c)   If the dissolved corporation publishes a newspaper notice in accordance with subsection (b), the claim of each of the following claimants is barred unless the claimant commences a proceeding to enforce the claim against the dissolved corporation within five years after the publication date of the newspaper notice:

(1)   a claimant who did not receive written notice under section 14.06;

(2)   a claimant whose claim was timely sent to the dissolved corporation but not acted on;

(3)   a claimant whose claim is contingent or based on an event occurring after the effective date of dissolution.

(d)   A claim may be enforced under this section:

(1)   against the dissolved corporation, to the extent of its undistributed assets; or

(2)   if the assets have been distributed in liquidation, against a shareholder of the dissolved corporation to the extent of his pro rata share of the claim or the corporate assets distributed to him in liquidation, whichever is less, but a shareholder's total liability for all claims under this section may not exceed the total amount of assets distributed to him.

SUBCHAPTER B.
ADMINISTRATIVE DISSOLUTION

§ 14.20. *Grounds for Administrative Dissolution*

The secretary of state may commence a proceeding under section 14.21 to administratively dissolve a corporation if:

(1)   the corporation does not pay within 60 days after they are due any franchise taxes or penalties imposed by this Act or other law;

(2)   the corporation does not deliver its annual report to the secretary of state within 60 days after it is due;

(3)   the corporation is without a registered agent or registered office in this state for 60 days or more;

(4)   the corporation does not notify the secretary of state within 60 days that its registered agent

or registered office has been changed, that its registered agent has resigned, or that its registered office has been discontinued; or

(5)   the corporation's period of duration stated in its articles of incorporation expires.

§ 14.21. *Procedure for and Effect of Administrative Dissolution*

(a)   If the secretary of state determines that one or more grounds exist under section 14.20 for dissolving a corporation, he shall serve the corporation with written notice of his determination under section 5.04.

(b)   If the corporation does not correct each ground for dissolution or demonstrate to the reasonable satisfaction of the secretary of state that each ground determined by the secretary of state does not exist within 60 days after service of the notice is perfected under section 5.04, the secretary of state shall administratively dissolve the corporation by signing a certificate of dissolution that recites the ground or grounds for dissolution and its effective date. The secretary of state shall file the original of the certificate and serve a copy on the corporation under section 5.04.

(c)   A corporation administratively dissolved continues its corporate existence but may not carry on any business except that necessary to wind up and liquidate its business and affairs under section 14.05 and notify claimants under sections 14.06 and 14.07.

(d)   The administrative dissolution of a corporation does not terminate the authority of its registered agent.

§ 14.22. *Reinstatement Following Administrative Dissolution*

(a)   A corporation administratively dissolved under section 14.21 may apply to the secretary of state for reinstatement within two years after the effective date of dissolution. The application must:

(1)   recite the name of the corporation and the effective date of its administrative dissolution;

(2)   state that the ground or grounds for dissolution either did not exist or have been eliminated;

(3)   state that the corporation's name satisfies the requirements of section 4.01; and

(4) contain a certificate from the [taxing authority] reciting that all taxes owed by the corporation have been paid.

(b) If the secretary of state determines that the application contains the information required by subsection (a) and that the information is correct, he shall cancel the certificate of dissolution and prepare a certificate of reinstatement that recites his determination and the effective date of reinstatement, file the original of the certificate, and serve a copy on the corporation under section 5.04.

(c) When the reinstatement is effective, it relates back to and takes effect as of the effective date of the administrative dissolution and the corporation resumes carrying on its business as if the administrative dissolution had never occurred.

§ 14.23. Appeal From Denial of Reinstatement

(a) If the secretary of state denies a corporation's application for reinstatement following administrative dissolution, he shall serve the corporation under section 5.04 with a written notice that explains the reason or reasons for denial.

(b) The corporation may appeal the denial of reinstatement to the [name or describe] court within 30 days after service of the notice of denial is perfected. The corporation appeals by petitioning the court to set aside the dissolution and attaching to the petition copies of the secretary of state's certificate of dissolution, the corporation's application for reinstatement, and the secretary of state's notice of denial.

(c) The court may summarily order the secretary of state to reinstate the dissolved corporation or may take other action the court considers appropriate.

(d) The court's final decision may be appealed as in other civil proceedings.

SUBCHAPTER C. JUDICIAL DISSOLUTION

§ 14.30. Grounds for Judicial Dissolution

The [name or describe court or courts] may dissolve a corporation:

(1) in a proceeding by the attorney general if it is established that:

　(i) the corporation obtained its articles of incorporation through fraud; or

　(ii) the corporation has continued to exceed or abuse the authority conferred upon it by law;

(2) in a proceeding by a shareholder if it is established that:

　(i) the directors are deadlocked in the management of the corporate affairs, the shareholders are unable to break the deadlock, and irreparable injury to the corporation is threatened or being suffered, or the business and affairs of the corporation can no longer be conducted to the advantage of the shareholders generally, because of the deadlock;

　(ii) the directors or those in control of the corporation have acted, are acting, or will act in a manner that is illegal, oppressive, or fraudulent;

　(iii) the shareholders are deadlocked in voting power and have failed, for a period that includes at least two consecutive annual meeting dates, to elect successors to directors whose terms have expired; or

　(iv) the corporate assets are being misapplied or wasted;

(3) in a proceeding by a creditor if it is established that:

　(i) the creditor's claim has been reduced to judgment, the execution on the judgment returned unsatisfied, and the corporation is insolvent; or

　(ii) the corporation has admitted in writing that the creditor's claim is due and owing and the corporation is insolvent; or

(4) in a proceeding by the corporation to have its voluntary dissolution continued under court supervision.

§ 14.31. Procedure for Judicial Dissolution

(a) Venue for a proceeding by the attorney general to dissolve a corporation lies in [name the county or counties]. Venue for a proceeding brought by any other party named in section 14.30 lies in the county where a corporation's principal office (or, if none in this state, its registered office) is or was last located.

(b) It is not necessary to make shareholders parties to a proceeding to dissolve a corporation unless relief is sought against them individually.

(c) A court in a proceeding brought to dissolve a corporation may issue injunctions, appoint a receiver or custodian pendente lite with all powers and duties the court directs, take other action required to preserve the corporate assets wherever located, and carry on the business of the corporation until a full hearing can be held.

(d) Within 10 days of the commencement of a proceeding under section 14.30(2) to dissolve a corporation that has no shares listed on a national securities exchange or regularly traded in a market maintained by one or more members of a national securities exchange, the corporation must send to all shareholders, other than the petitioner, a notice stating that the shareholders are entitled to avoid the dissolution of the corporation by electing to purchase the petitioner's shares under section 14.34 and accompanied by a copy of section 14.34.

§ 14.32. *Receivership or Custodianship*

(a) A court in a judicial proceeding brought to dissolve a corporation may appoint one or more receivers to wind up and liquidate, or one or more custodians to manage, the business and affairs of the corporation. The court shall hold a hearing, after notifying all parties to the proceeding and any interested persons designated by the court, before appointing a receiver or custodian. The court appointing a receiver or custodian has exclusive jurisdiction over the corporation and all of its property wherever located.

(b) The court may appoint an individual or a domestic or foreign corporation (authorized to transact business in this state) as a receiver or custodian. The court may require the receiver or custodian to post bond, with or without sureties, in an amount the court directs.

(c) The court shall describe the powers and duties of the receiver or custodian in its appointing order, which may be amended from time to time. Among other powers:

(1) the receiver (i) may dispose of all or any part of the assets of the corporation wherever located, at a public or private sale, if authorized by the court; and (ii) may sue and defend in his own name as receiver of the corporation in all courts of this state;

(2) the custodian may exercise all of the powers of the corporation, through or in place of its board of directors or officers, to the extent necessary to manage the affairs of the corporation in the best interests of its shareholders and creditors.

(d) The court during a receivership may redesignate the receiver a custodian, and during a custodianship may redesignate the custodian a receiver, if doing so is in the best interests of the corporation, its shareholders, and creditors.

(e) The court from time to time during the receivership or custodianship may order compensation paid and expense disbursements or reimbursements made to the receiver or custodian and his counsel from the assets of the corporation or proceeds from the sale of the assets.

§ 14.33. *Decree of Dissolution*

(a) If after a hearing the court determines that one or more grounds for judicial dissolution described in section 14.30 exist, it may enter a decree dissolving the corporation and specifying the effective date of the dissolution, and the clerk of the court shall deliver a certified copy of the decree to the secretary of state, who shall file it.

(b) After entering the decree of dissolution, the court shall direct the winding up and liquidation of the corporation's business and affairs in accordance with section 14.05 and the notification of claimants in accordance with sections 14.06 and 14.07.

§ 14.34. *Election to Purchase in Lieu of Dissolution*

(a) In a proceeding under section 14.30(2) to dissolve a corporation that has no shares listed on a national securities exchange or regularly traded in a market maintained by one or more members of a national or affiliated securities association, the corporation may elect or, if it fails to elect, one or more shareholders may elect to purchase all shares owned by the petitioning shareholder at the fair value of the shares. An election pursuant to this section shall be irrevocable unless the court determines that it is equitable to set aside or modify the election.

(b) An election to purchase pursuant to this section may be filed with the court at any time within 90 days after the filing of the petition under section 14.30(2) or at such later time as the court in its discretion may allow. If the election to purchase is filed by one or more shareholders, the corporation shall, within 10 days thereafter, give written notice to all shareholders, other than the petitioner. The notice must state the name and number of shares owned by the petitioner and the name and number of shares owned by each electing shareholder and must advise the recipients of their right to join in the election to purchase shares in accordance with this section. Shareholders who wish to participate must file notice of their intention to join in the purchase no later than 30 days after the effective date of the notice to them. All shareholders who have filed an election or notice of their intention to participate in the election to purchase thereby become parties to ownership of shares as of the date the first election was filed, unless they otherwise agree or the court otherwise directs. After an election has been filed by the corporation or one or more shareholders, the proceeding under section 14.30(2) may not be discontinued or settled, nor may the petitioning shareholder sell or otherwise dispose of his shares, unless the court determines that it would be equitable to the corporation and the shareholders, other than the petitioner, to permit such discontinuance, settlement, sale, or other disposition.

(c)   If, within 60 days of the filing of the first election, the parties reach agreement as to the fair value and terms of purchase of the petitioner's shares, the court shall enter an order directing the purchase of petitioner's shares upon the terms and conditions agreed to by the parties.

(d)   If the parties are unable to reach an agreement as provided for in subsection (c), the court, upon application of any party, shall stay the section 14.30(2) proceedings and determine the fair value of the petitioner's shares as of the day before the date on which the petition under section 14.30(2) was filed or as of such other date as the court deems appropriate under the circumstances.

(e)   Upon determining the fair value of the shares, the court shall enter an order directing the purchase upon such terms and conditions as the court deems appropriate, which may include payment of the purchase price in installments, where necessary in the interests of equity, provision for security to assure payment of the purchase price and any additional costs, fees, and expenses as may have been awarded, and, if the shares are to be purchased by shareholders, the allocation of shares among them. In allocating petitioner's shares among holders of different classes of shares, the court should attempt to preserve the existing distribution of voting rights among holders of different classes insofar as practicable and may direct that holders of a specific class or classes shall not participate in the purchase. Interest may be allowed at the rate and from the date determined by the court to be equitable, but if the court finds that the refusal of the petitioning shareholder to accept an offer of payment was arbitrary or otherwise not in good faith, no interest shall be allowed. If the court finds that the petitioning shareholder had probable grounds for relief under paragraphs (ii) or (iv) of section 14.30(2), it may award to the petitioning shareholder reasonable fees and expenses of counsel and of any experts employed by him.

(f)   Upon entry of an order under subsections (c) or (e), the court shall dismiss the petition to dissolve the corporation under section 14.30, and the petitioning shareholder shall no longer have any rights or status as a shareholder of the corporation, except the right to receive the amounts awarded to him by the order of the court which shall be enforceable in the same manner as any other judgment.

(g)   The purchase ordered pursuant to subsection (e), shall be made within 10 days after the date the order becomes final unless before that time the corporation files with the court a notice of its intention to adopt articles of dissolution pursuant to sections 14.02 and 14.03, which articles must then be adopted and filed within 50 days thereafter. Upon filing of such articles of dissolution, the corporation shall be dissolved in accordance with the provisions of sections 14.05 through 07, and the order entered pursuant to subsection (e) shall no longer be of any force or effect, except that the court may award petitioning shareholder reasonable fees and expenses in accordance with the provisions of the last sentence of subsection (e) and the petitioner may continue to pursue any claims previously asserted on behalf of the corporation.

(h)   Any payment by the corporation pursuant to an order under subsections (c) or (e), other than an award of fees and expenses pursuant to subsection (e), is subject to the provisions of section 6.40.

[Subchapter D omitted]

CHAPTER 15
FOREIGN CORPORATIONS
SUBCHAPTER A.
CERTIFICATE OF AUTHORITY

§ 15.01. *Authority to Transact Business Required*

(a)   A foreign corporation may not transact business in this state until it obtains a certificate of authority from the secretary of state.

(b)   The following activities, among others, do not constitute transacting business within the meaning of subsection (a):

   (1)   maintaining, defending, or settling any proceeding;

   (2)   holding meetings of the board of directors or shareholders or carrying on other activities concerning internal corporate affairs;

   (3)   maintaining bank accounts;

   (4)   maintaining offices or agencies for the transfer, exchange, and registration of the corporation's own securities or maintaining trustees or depositaries with respect to those securities;

   (5)   selling through independent contractors;

   (6)   soliciting or obtaining orders, whether by mail or through employees or agents or otherwise, if the orders require acceptance outside this state before they become contracts;

   (7)   creating or acquiring indebtedness, mortgages, and security interests in real or personal property;

   (8)   securing or collecting debts or enforcing mortgages and security interests in property securing the debts;

   (9)   owning, without more, real or personal property;

   (10) conducting an isolated transaction that is completed within 30 days and that is not one in the course of repeated transactions of a like nature;

   (11) transacting business in interstate commerce.

(c)   The list of activities in subsection (b) is not exhaustive.

§ 15.02. *Consequences of Transacting Business Without Authority*

(a)   A foreign corporation transacting business in this state without a certificate of authority may not maintain a proceeding in any court in this state until it obtains a certificate of authority.

(b)   The successor to a foreign corporation that transacted business in this state without a certificate of authority and the assignee of a cause of action arising out of that business may not maintain a proceeding based on that cause of action in any court in this state until the foreign corporation or its successor obtains a certificate of authority.

(c)   A court may stay a proceeding commenced by a foreign corporation, its successor, or assignee until it determines whether the foreign corporation or its successor requires a certificate of authority. If it so determines, the court may further stay the proceeding until the foreign corporation or its successor obtains the certificate.

(d)   A foreign corporation is liable for a civil penalty of $____ for each day, but not to exceed a total of $____ for each year, it transacts business in this state without a certificate of authority. The attorney general may collect all penalties due under this subsection.

(e)   Notwithstanding subsections (a) and (b), the failure of a foreign corporation to obtain a certificate of authority does not impair the validity of its corporate acts or prevent it from defending any proceeding in this state.

§ 15.03. *Application for Certificate of Authority*

(a)   A foreign corporation may apply for a certificate of authority to transact business in this state by delivering an application to the secretary of state for filing. The application must set forth:

   (1)   the name of the foreign corporation or, if its name is unavailable for use in this state, a corporate name that satisfies the requirements of section 15.06;

   (2)   the name of the state or country under whose law it is incorporated;

   (3)   its date of incorporation and period of duration;

   (4)   the street address of its principal office;

   (5)   the address of its registered office in this state and the name of its registered agent at that office; and

   (6)   the names and usual business addresses of its current directors and officers.

(b)   The foreign corporation shall deliver with the completed application a certificate of existence (or a document of similar import) duly authenticated by the secretary of state or other official having custody of corporate records in the state or country under whose law it is incorporated.

§ 15.04. *Amended Certificate of Authority*

(a)   A foreign corporation authorized to transact business in this state must obtain an amended certificate of authority from the secretary of state if it changes:

(1)   its corporate name;

(2)   the period of its duration; or

(3)   the state or country of its incorporation.

(b)   The requirements of section 15.03 for obtaining an original certificate of authority apply to obtaining an amended certificate under this section.

§ 15.05.   Effect of Certificate of Authority

(a)   A certificate of authority authorizes the foreign corporation to which it is issued to transact business in this state subject, however, to the right of the state to revoke the certificate as provided in this Act.

(b)   A foreign corporation with a valid certificate of authority has the same but no greater rights and has the same but no greater privileges as, and except as otherwise provided by this Act is subject to the same duties, restrictions, penalties, and liabilities now or later imposed on, a domestic corporation of like character.

(c)   This Act does not authorize this state to regulate the organization or internal affairs of a foreign corporation authorized to transact business in this state.

§ 15.06.   Corporate Name of Foreign Corporation

(a)   If the corporate name of a foreign corporation does not satisfy the requirements of section 4.01, the foreign corporation to obtain or maintain a certificate of authority to transact business in this state:

(1)   may add the word "corporation," "incorporated," "company," or "limited," or the abbreviation "corp.," "inc.," "co.," or "ltd.," to its corporate name for use in this state; or

(2)   may use a fictitious name to transact business in this state if its real name is unavailable and it delivers to the secretary of state for filing a copy of the resolution of its board of directors, certified by its secretary, adopting the fictitious name.

(b)   Except as authorized by subsections (c) and (d), the corporate name (including a fictitious name) of a foreign corporation must be distinguishable upon the records of the secretary of state from:

(1)   the corporate name of a corporation incorporated or authorized to transact business in this state;

(2)   a corporate name reserved or registered under section 4.02 or 4.03;

(3)   the fictitious name of another foreign corporation authorized to transact business in this state; and

(4)   the corporate name of a not-for-profit corporation incorporated or authorized to transact business in this state.

(c)   A foreign corporation may apply to the secretary of state for authorization to use in this state the name of another corporation (incorporated or authorized to transact business in this state) that is not distinguishable upon his records from the name applied for. The secretary of state shall authorize use of the name applied for if:

(1)   the other corporation consents to the use in writing and submits an undertaking in form satisfactory to the secretary of state to change its name to a name that is distinguishable upon the records of the secretary of state from the name of the applying corporation; or

(2)   the applicant delivers to the secretary of state a certified copy of a final judgment of a court of competent jurisdiction establishing the applicant's right to use the name applied for in this state.

(d)   A foreign corporation may use in this state the name (including the fictitious name) of another domestic or foreign corporation that is used in this state if the other corporation is incorporated or authorized to transact business in this state and the foreign corporation:

(1)   has merged with the other corporation;

(2)   has been formed by reorganization of the other corporation; or

(3)   has acquired all or substantially all of the assets, including the corporate name, of the other corporation.

(e)   If a foreign corporation authorized to transact business in this state changes its corporate name to one that does not satisfy the requirements of section 4.01, it may not transact business in this state under the changed name until it adopts a name satisfying the requirements of section 4.01 and obtains an amended certificate of authority under section 15.04.

§ 15.07. *Registered Office and Registered Agent of Foreign Corporation*

Each foreign corporation authorized to transact business in this state must continuously maintain in this state:

(1) a registered office that may be the same as any of its places of business; and

(2) a registered agent, who may be:

(i) an individual who resides in this state and whose business office is identical with the registered office;

(ii) a domestic corporation or not-for-profit domestic corporation whose business office is identical with the registered office; or

(iii) a foreign corporation or foreign not-for-profit corporation authorized to transact business in this state whose business office is identical with the registered office.

§ 15.08. *Change of Registered Office or Registered Agent of Foreign Corporation*

(a) A foreign corporation authorized to transact business in this state may change its registered office or registered agent by delivering to the secretary of state for filing a statement of change that sets forth:

(1) its name;

(2) the street address of its current registered office;

(3) if the current registered office is to be changed, the street address of its new registered office;

(4) the name of its current registered agent;

(5) if the current registered agent is to be changed, the name of its new registered agent and the new agent's written consent (either on the statement or attached to it) to the appointment; and

(6) that after the change or changes are made, the street addresses of its registered office and the business office of its registered agent will be identical.

(b) If a registered agent changes the street address of his business office, he may change the street address of the registered office of any foreign corporation for which he is the registered agent by notifying the corporation in writing of the change and signing (either manually or in facsimile) and delivering to the secretary of state for filing a statement

of change that complies with the requirements of subsection (a) and recites that the corporation has been notified of the change.

§ 15.09. *Resignation of Registered Agent of Foreign Corporation*

(a) The registered agent of a foreign corporation may resign his agency appointment by signing and delivering to the secretary of state for filing the original and two exact or conformed copies of a statement of resignation. The statement of resignation may include a statement that the registered office is also discontinued.

(b) After filing the statement, the secretary of state shall attach the filing receipt to one copy and mail the copy and receipt to the registered office if not discontinued. The secretary of state shall mail the other copy to the foreign corporation at its principal office address shown in its most recent annual report.

(c) The agency appointment is terminated, and the registered office discontinued if so provided, on the 31st day after the date on which the statement was filed.

§ 15.10. *Service on Foreign Corporation*

(a) The registered agent of a foreign corporation authorized to transact business in this state is the corporation's agent for service of process, notice, or demand required or permitted by law to be served on the foreign corporation.

(b) A foreign corporation may be served by registered or certified mail, return receipt requested, addressed to the secretary of the foreign corporation at its principal office shown in its application for a certificate of authority or in its most recent annual report if the foreign corporation:

(1) has no registered agent or its registered agent cannot with reasonable diligence be served;

(2) has withdrawn from transacting business in this state under section 15.20; or

(3) has had its certificate of authority revoked under section 15.31.

(c) Service is perfected under subsection (b) at the earliest of:

(1) the date the foreign corporation receives the mail;

(2) the date shown on the return receipt, if signed on behalf of the foreign corporation; or

(3) five days after its deposit in the United States Mail, as evidenced by the postmark, if mailed postpaid and correctly addressed.

(d) This section does not prescribe the only means, or necessarily the required means, of serving a foreign corporation.

SUBCHAPTER B.
WITHDRAWAL

§ 15.20. *Withdrawal of Foreign Corporation*

(a) A foreign corporation authorized to transact business in this state may not withdraw from this state until it obtains a certificate of withdrawal from the secretary of state.

(b) A foreign corporation authorized to transact business in this state may apply for a certificate of withdrawal by delivering an application to the secretary of state for filing. The application must set forth:

(1) the name of the foreign corporation and the name of the state or country under whose law it is incorporated;

(2) that it is not transacting business in this state and that it surrenders its authority to transact business in this state;

(3) that it revokes the authority of its registered agent to accept service on its behalf and appoints the secretary of state as its agent for service of process in any proceeding based on a cause of action arising during the time it was authorized to transact business in this state;

(4) a mailing address to which the secretary of state may mail a copy of any process served on him under subdivision (3); and

(5) a commitment to notify the secretary of state in the future of any change in its mailing address.

(c) After the withdrawal of the corporation is effective, service of process on the secretary of state under this section is service on the foreign corporation. Upon receipt of process, the secretary of state shall mail a copy of the process to the foreign corporation at the mailing address set forth under subsection (b).

[Subchapter C omitted]

[Chapter 16, Records and Reports, omitted]

[Chapter 17, omitted]

APPENDIX J

Forms

Reprinted with permission from *American Jurisprudence Legal Forms 2d.* © 2000 West Group.

J-1
PARTNERSHIP AGREEMENT

[14 AM. JUR. *Legal Forms* 2d *Partnership* § 194:18 (Rev 2000)]

Partnership agreement made on _____ [date], between _____ [A.B.], of _____ [address], _____ [city], _____ County, _____ [state], and _____ [C.D.], of _____ [address], _____ [city], _____ County, _____ [state] ("partners").

RECITALS

A. Partners desire to join together for the pursuit of common business goals.

B. Partners have considered various forms of joint business enterprises for their business activities.

C. Partners desire to enter into a partnership agreement as the most advantageous business form for their mutual purposes.

In consideration of the mutual promises contained in this agreement, partners agree as follows:

ARTICLE ONE
NAME, PURPOSE, AND DOMICILE

The name of the partnership shall be _____. The partnership shall be conducted for the purposes of _____. The principal place of business shall be at _____ [address], _____ [city], _____ County, _____ [state], unless relocated by majority consent of the partners.

ARTICLE TWO
DURATION OF AGREEMENT

The term of this agreement shall be for _____ years, commencing on _____ [date], and terminating on _____ [date], unless sooner terminated by mutual consent of the parties or by operation of the provisions of this agreement.

ARTICLE THREE
CLASSIFICATION AND PERFORMANCE
BY PARTNERS

A. Partners shall be classified as active partners, advisory partners, or estate partners.

An active partner may voluntarily become an advisory partner, may be required to become one irrespective of age, and shall automatically become one after attaining the age of ____ years, and in each case shall continue as such for ____ years unless the partner sooner withdraws or dies.

If an active partner dies, the partner's estate will become an estate partner for ____ years. If an advisory partner dies within ____ years of having become an advisory partner, the partner will become an estate partner for the balance of the ____-year period.

Only active partners shall have any vote in any partnership matter.

At the time of the taking effect of this partnership agreement, all the partners shall be active partners except _____ and _____, who shall be advisory partners.

B. An active partner, after attaining the age of ____ years, or prior to that age if the _____ [executive committee or as the case may be] with the approval of _____ [two-thirds or as the case may be] of all the other active partners determines that the reason for the change in status is bad health, may become an advisory partner at the end of any calendar month on giving ____ [number] calendar months' prior notice in writing of the partner's intention to do so. The notice shall be deemed to be sufficient if sent by registered mail addressed to the partnership at its principal office at _____ [address], _____ [city], _____ County, _____ [state] not less than ____ [number] calendar months prior to the date when the change is to become effective.

C. Any active partner may at any age be required to become an advisory partner at any time if the _____ [executive committee or as the case may be] with the approval of _____ [two-thirds or as the case may be] of the other active partners shall decide that the change is for any reason in the best interests of the partnership, provided notice of the decision shall be given in writing to the partner. The notice shall be signed by the _____ [chairman or as the case may be] of the _____ [executive committee or as the case may be] or, in the event of his or her being unable to sign at the time, by another member of the _____ [executive committee or as the case may be]. The notice shall be served personally on the partner required to change his or her status, or mailed by registered mail to the partner's last known address. Change of the partner's status shall become effective as of the date specified in the notice.

D. Every active partner shall automatically and without further act become an advisory partner at the end of the fiscal year in which the partner's _____ birthday occurs.

E. In the event that an active partner becomes an advisory partner or dies, the partner or the partner's estate shall be entitled to the following payments at the following times: _____ [describe].

Each active partner shall apply all of the partner's experience, training, and ability in discharging the partner's assigned functions in the partnership and in the performance of all work that may be necessary or advantageous to further the business interests of the partnership.

ARTICLE FOUR
CONTRIBUTION

Each partner shall contribute $_____ on or before _____ [date] to be used by the partnership to establish its capital position. Any additional contribution required of partners shall only be determined and established in accordance with Article Nineteen.

ARTICLE FIVE
BUSINESS EXPENSES

The rent of the buildings where the partnership business shall be carried on, and the cost of repairs and alterations, all rates, taxes, payments for insurance, and other expenses in respect to the buildings used by the partnership, and the wages for all persons employed by the partnership are all to become payable on the account of the partnership. All losses incurred shall be paid out of the capital of the partnership or the profits arising from the partnership business, or, if both shall be deficient, by the

partners on a pro rata basis, in proportion to their original contributions, as provided in Article Nineteen.

ARTICLE SIX
AUTHORITY

No partner shall buy any goods or articles or enter into any contract exceeding the value of $_____ without the prior consent in writing of the other partners. If any partner exceeds this authority, the other partners shall have the option to take the goods or accept the contract on account of the partnership or to let the goods remain the sole property of the partner who shall have obligated himself or herself.

ARTICLE SEVEN
SEPARATE DEBTS

No partner shall enter into any bond, or become surety or cosigner, or provide security for any person, partnership, or corporation, or knowingly condone anything by which the partnership property may be attached or taken in execution, without the prior written consent of the other partners.

Each partner shall punctually pay the partner's separate debts and indemnify the other partners and the capital and property of the partnership against the partner's separate debts and all expenses relating to such separate debts.

ARTICLE EIGHT
BOOKS AND RECORDS

Books of account shall be maintained by the partners, and proper entries made in the books of all sales, purchases, receipts, payments, transactions, and property of the partnership. The books of account and all records of the partnership shall be retained at the principal place of business as specified in Article One. Each partner shall have free access at all times to all books and records maintained relative to the partnership business.

ARTICLE NINE
ACCOUNTING

The fiscal year of the partnership shall be from _____ [month and day] to _____ [month and day] of each year. On the _____ day of _____ [month], commencing in ____ [year], and on the ____ day of _____ [month] in each succeeding year, a general accounting shall be made and taken by the partners of all sales, purchases, receipts, payments, and transactions of the partnership during the preceding fiscal year, and of all the capital property and current liabilities of the partnership. The general accounting shall be written in the partnership account books and signed in each book by each partner immediately after it is completed. After the signature of each partner is entered, each partner shall keep one of the books and shall be bound by every account, except that if any manifest error is found in an account book by any partner and shown to the other partners within ____ months after the error shall have been noted by all of them, the error shall be rectified.

ARTICLE TEN
DIVISION OF PROFITS AND LOSSES

Each partner shall be entitled to ____% of the net profits of the business, and all losses occurring in the course of the business shall be borne in the same proportion, unless the losses are occasioned by the willful neglect or default, and not the mere mistake or error, of any of the partners, in which case the loss so incurred shall be made good by the partner through whose neglect or default the losses shall arise. Distribution of profits shall be made on the ____ day of _____ [month] each year.

ARTICLE ELEVEN
ADVANCE DRAWS

Each partner shall be at liberty to draw out of the business in anticipation of the expected profits any sums that may be mutually agreed on, and the sums are to be drawn only after there has been entered in the books of the partnership the terms of agreement, giving the date, the amount to be drawn by the respective partners, the time at which the sums shall be drawn, and any other conditions or matters mutually agreed on. The signatures of each partner shall be affixed on the books of the partnership.

The total sum of the advanced draw for each partner shall be deducted from the sum that partner is entitled to under the distribution of profits as provided for in Article Ten.

ARTICLE TWELVE
SALARY

No partner shall receive any salary from the partnership, and the only compensation to be paid shall be as provided in Articles Ten and Eleven.

ARTICLE THIRTEEN
RETIREMENT

In the event any partner shall desire to retire from the partnership, the partner shall give ____ months' notice in writing to the other partners. The continuing partners shall pay to the retiring partner at the termination of the ____ months' notice the value of the interest of the retiring partner in the partnership. The value shall be determined by a closing of the books and a rendition of the appropriate profit and loss, trial balance, and balance sheet statements. All disputes arising from such determination shall be resolved as provided in Article Twenty.

ARTICLE FOURTEEN
RIGHTS OF CONTINUING PARTNERS

On the retirement of any partner, the continuing partners shall be at liberty, if they so desire, to retain all trade names designating the firm name used. Each of the partners shall sign and execute any assignments, instruments, or papers that shall be reasonably required for effectuating an amicable retirement.

ARTICLE FIFTEEN
DEATH OF PARTNER

In the event of the death of one partner, the legal representative of the deceased partner shall remain as a partner in the firm, except that the exercise of this right on the part of the representative of the deceased partner shall not continue for a period in excess of ____ months, even though under the terms of this agreement a greater period of time is provided before the termination of this agreement. The original rights of the partners shall accrue to their heirs, executors, or assigns.

ARTICLE SIXTEEN
EMPLOYEE MANAGEMENT

No partner shall hire or dismiss any person in the employment of the partnership without the consent of the other partners, except in cases of gross misconduct by the employee.

ARTICLE SEVENTEEN
RELEASE OF DEBTS

No partner shall compound, release, or discharge any debt that shall be due or owing to the partnership, without receiving the full amount of the debt, unless that partner obtains the prior written consent of the other partners to the discharge of the indebtedness.

ARTICLE EIGHTEEN
COVENANT AGAINST REVEALING
TRADE SECRETS

No partner shall, during the continuance of the partnership or for _____ years after its termination by any means, divulge to any person not a member of the firm any trade secret or special information employed in or conducive to the partnership business and which may come to the partner's knowledge in the course of this partnership, without the consent in writing of the other partners, or of the other partners' heirs, administrators, or assigns.

ARTICLE NINETEEN
ADDITIONAL CONTRIBUTIONS

The partners shall not have to contribute any additional capital to the partnership to that required under Article Four, except as follows: (1) each partner shall be required to contribute a proportionate share in additional contributions if the fiscal year closes with an insufficiency in the capital account or profits of the partnership to meet current expenses; or (2) the capital account falls below $_____ for a period of _____ months.

ARTICLE TWENTY
ARBITRATION

If any differences shall arise between or among the partners as to their rights or liabilities under this agreement, or under any instrument made in furtherance of the partnership business, the difference shall be determined and the instrument shall be settled by _____ [name of arbitrator], acting as arbitrator, and the decision shall be final as to the contents and interpretations of the instrument and as to the proper mode of carrying the provision into effect.

ARTICLE TWENTY-ONE
ADDITIONS, ALTERATIONS,
OR MODIFICATIONS

Where it shall appear to the partners that this agreement, or any terms and conditions contained in this agreement, are in any way ineffective or deficient, or not expressed as originally intended, and any alteration or addition shall be deemed necessary, the partners will enter into, execute, and perform all further deeds and instruments as their

counsel shall advise. Any addition, alteration, or modification shall be in writing, and no oral agreement shall be effective.

The parties have executed this agreement at _____ [designate place of execution] the day and year first above written.

[Signatures]

J-2
LIMITED PARTNERSHIP AGREEMENT

[14A Am. Jur. *Legal Forms* 2d *Partnership* § 194:664 (Rev 2000)]

Agreement of limited partnership made on _____ [date], between _____ [A.B.], of _____ [address], _____ [city], _____ County, _____ [state], _____ ("general partner"), and _____ [C.D.], of _____ [address], _____ [city], _____ County, _____ [state], and _____ [E.F.], of _____ [address], _____ [city], _____ County, _____ [state] ("limited partners").

RECITALS

A. General and limited partners desire to enter into the business of _____.

B. General partner desires to manage and operate the business.

C. Limited partners desire to invest in the business and limit their liabilities.

In consideration of the matters described above, and of the mutual benefits and obligations set forth in this agreement, the parties agree as follows:

ARTICLE ONE
GENERAL PROVISIONS

The limited partnership is organized pursuant to the provisions of _____ [cite statute] of _____ [state], and the rights and liabilities of the general and limited partners shall be as provided in that statute, except as otherwise stated in this agreement.

ARTICLE TWO
NAME OF PARTNERSHIP

The name of the partnership shall be _____ (the "partnership").

ARTICLE THREE
BUSINESS OF PARTNERSHIP

The purpose of the partnership is to engage in the business of _____.

ARTICLE FOUR
PRINCIPAL PLACE OF BUSINESS

The principal place of business of the partnership shall be at _____ [address], _____ [city], _____ County, _____ [state]. The partnership shall also have other places of business as from time to time shall be determined by general partner.

ARTICLE FIVE
CAPITAL CONTRIBUTION OF
GENERAL PARTNER

General partner shall contribute $_____ to the original capital of the partnership. The contribution of general partner shall be made on or before _____ [date]. If general partner does not make _____ [his or her] entire contribution to the capital of the partnership on or before that date, this agreement shall be void. Any contributions to the capital of the partnership made at that time shall be returned to the partners who have made the contributions.

ARTICLE SIX
CAPITAL CONTRIBUTIONS OF
LIMITED PARTNERS

The capital contributions of limited partners shall be as follows:

Name	Amount
_____	$_____
_____	$_____

Receipt of the capital contribution from each limited partner as specified above is acknowledged by the partnership. No limited partner has agreed to contribute any additional cash or property as capital for use of the partnership.

ARTICLE SEVEN
DUTIES AND RIGHTS OF PARTNERS

General partner shall diligently and exclusively apply _____ [himself or herself] in and about the business of the partnership to the utmost of _____ [his or her] skill and on a full-time basis.

General partner shall not engage directly or indirectly in any business similar to the business of the partnership at any time during the term of this agreement without obtaining the written approval of all other partners.

General partner shall be entitled to _____ days' vacation and _____ days' sick leave in each calendar year, commencing with the calendar year _____. If general partner uses sick leave or vacation days in a calendar year in excess of the number specified above, the effect on _____ [his or her] capital interest and share of the profits and losses of the partnership for that year shall be determined by a majority vote of limited partners.

No limited partner shall have any right to be active in the conduct of the partnership's business, nor have power to bind the partnership in any contract, agreement, promise, or undertaking.

ARTICLE EIGHT
SALARY OF GENERAL PARTNER

General partner shall be entitled to a monthly salary of $_____ for the services rendered by general partner. The salary shall commence on _____ [date], and be payable on the _____ day of each subsequent month. The salary shall be treated as an expense of the operation of the partnership business and shall be payable whether or not the partnership shall operate at a profit.

ARTICLE NINE
LIMITATIONS ON DISTRIBUTION
OF PROFITS

General partner shall have the right, except as provided below, to determine whether from time to time partnership profits shall be distributed in cash or shall be left in the business, in which event the capital account of all partners shall be increased.

In no event shall any profits be payable for a period of _____ months until _____% of those profits have been deducted to accumulate a reserve fund of $_____ over and above the normal monthly requirements of working capital. This accumulation is to enable the partnership to maintain a sound financial operation.

ARTICLE TEN
PROFITS AND LOSSES FOR
LIMITED PARTNERS

Limited partners shall be entitled to receive a share of the annual net profits equivalent to their share in the capitalization of the partnership.

Limited partners shall each bear a share of the losses of the partnership equal to the share of profits to which each limited partner is entitled.

The share of losses of each limited partner shall be charged against the limited partner's capital contribution.

Limited partners shall at no time become liable for any obligations or losses of the partnership beyond the amounts of their respective capital contributions.

ARTICLE ELEVEN
PROFITS AND LOSSES FOR
GENERAL PARTNER

After provisions have been made for the shares of profits of limited partners, all remaining profits of the partnership shall be paid to general partner. After giving effect to the share of losses chargeable against the capital contributions of limited partners, the remaining partnership losses shall be borne by general partner.

ARTICLE TWELVE
BOOKS OF ACCOUNT

There shall be maintained during the continuance of this partnership an accurate set of books of account of all transactions, assets, and liabilities of the partnership. The books shall be balanced and closed at the end of each year, and at any other time on reasonable request of the general partner. The books are to be kept at the principal place of business of the partnership and are to be open for inspection by any partner at all reasonable times. The profits and losses of the partnership and its books of account shall be maintained on a fiscal year basis, terminating annually on _____ [month and day], unless otherwise determined by general partner.

ARTICLE THIRTEEN
SUBSTITUTIONS, ASSIGNMENTS, AND
ADMISSION OF ADDITIONAL PARTNERS

General partner shall not substitute a partner in _____ [his or her] place, or sell or assign all or any part of general partner's interest in the partnership business without the written consent of limited partners.

Additional limited partners may be admitted to this partnership on terms that may be agreed on in writing between general partner and the new limited partners. The terms so stipulated shall constitute an amendment to this partnership agreement.

No limited partner may substitute an assignee as a limited partner in _____ [his or her] place; but the person or persons entitled by rule or by intestate laws, as the case may be, shall succeed to all the rights of limited partner as a substituted limited partner.

ARTICLE FOURTEEN
TERMINATION OF INTEREST
OF LIMITED PARTNER; RETURN
OF CAPITAL CONTRIBUTION

The interest of any limited partner may be terminated by (1) dissolution of the partnership for any reason provided in this agreement; (2) the agreement of all partners; or (3) the consent of the personal representative of a deceased limited partner and the partnership.

On the termination of the interest of a limited partner there shall be payable to that limited partner, or the limited partner's estate, as the case may be, a sum to be determined by all partners, which sum shall not be less than _____ times the capital account of the limited partner as shown on the books at the time of the termination, including profits or losses from the last closing of the books of the partnership to the date of the termination, when the interest in profits and losses terminated. The amount payable shall be an obligation payable only out of partnership assets, and at the option of the partnership, may be paid within _____ years after the termination of the interest, provided that interest at the rate of _____% shall be paid on the unpaid balance.

ARTICLE FIFTEEN
BORROWING BY PARTNER

In case of necessity as determined by a majority vote of all partners, a partner may borrow up to $_____ from the partnership. Any such loan shall be repayable at _____ [describe terms of repayment], together with interest at the rate of _____% per year.

ARTICLE SIXTEEN
TERM OF PARTNERSHIP
AND DISSOLUTION

The partnership term commences on _____ [date], and shall end on (1) the dissolution of the partnership by operation of law; (2) the dissolution of the partnership at any time designated by general partner; or (3) the dissolution of the partnership at the close of the month following the qualification and appointment of the personal representative of deceased general partner.

ARTICLE SEVENTEEN
PAYMENT FOR INTEREST OF DECEASED GENERAL PARTNER

In the event of the death of general partner there shall be paid out of the partnership's assets to decedent's personal representative for decedent's interest in the partnership a sum equal to the capital account of decedent as shown on the books at the time of the decedent's death, adjusted to reflect profits or losses from the last closing of the books of the partnership to the day of the decedent's death.

ARTICLE EIGHTEEN
AMENDMENTS

This agreement, except with respect to vested rights of partners, may be amended at any time by a majority vote as measured by the interest and the sharing of profits and losses.

ARTICLE NINETEEN
BINDING EFFECT OF AGREEMENT

This agreement shall be binding on the parties to the agreement and their respective heirs, executors, administrators, successors, and assigns.

The parties have executed this agreement at _____ [designate place of execution] the day and year first above written.

[Signatures]

J-3
OPERATING AGREEMENT OF
_____ _____, LLC

[12 Am. Jur. *Legal Forms* 2d *Limited Liability Companies* § 167A:9 (Rev 1999)]

This Operating Agreement (this "Agreement") of _____ [Limited Liability Company or L.L.C. or LLC], a _____ [state] limited liability company (the "Company"), is adopted and entered into on _____ [date], by and among _____ and _____, as members (the "Members," which term includes any other persons who may become members of the Company in accordance with the terms of this Agreement and the Act) and the Company pursuant to and in accordance with the Limited Liability Company Law of the State of _____, as amended from time to time (the "Act"). Terms used in this Agreement which are not otherwise de-

fined shall have the respective meanings given those terms in the Act.

In consideration of the matters described above, and of the mutual benefits and obligations set forth in this agreement, the parties agree as follows:

ARTICLE ONE
NAME

The name of the limited liability company under which it was formed is _____ [Limited Liability Company or L.L.C. or LLC].

ARTICLE TWO
TERM

_____ [The Company shall dissolve on _____ (date) unless dissolved before such date in accordance with the Act.] or

[The Company shall continue until dissolved in accordance with the Act.]

ARTICLE THREE
MANAGEMENT

Management of the Company is vested in its Members, who will manage the Company in accordance with the Act. Any Member exercising management powers or responsibilities will be deemed to be a manager for purposes of applying the provisions of the Act, unless the context otherwise requires, and that Member will have and be subject to all of the duties and liabilities of a manager provided in the Act. The Members will have the power to do any and all acts necessary or convenient to or for the furtherance of the purposes of the Company set forth in this Agreement, including all powers of Members under the Act.

ARTICLE FOUR
PURPOSE

The purpose of the Company is to engage in any lawful act or activity for which limited liability companies may be formed under the Act and to engage in any and all activities necessary or incidental to these acts.

ARTICLE FIVE
MEMBERS

The names and the business, residence or mailing address of the members are as follows:

Name	Address
_____	_____
_____	_____
_____	_____

ARTICLE SIX
CAPITAL CONTRIBUTIONS

The Members have contributed to the Company the following amounts, in the form of cash, property or services rendered, or a promissory note or other obligation to contribute cash or property or to render services:

Member	Amount of Capital Contribution
_____	$_____
_____	$_____
_____	$_____

ARTICLE SEVEN
ADDITIONAL CONTRIBUTIONS

No member is required to make any additional capital contribution to the Company.

ARTICLE EIGHT
ALLOCATION OF PROFITS AND LOSSES

The Company's profits and losses will be allocated in proportion to the value of the capital contributions of the Members.

ARTICLE NINE
DISTRIBUTIONS

Distributions shall be made to the Members at the times and in the aggregate amounts determined by the Members. Such distributions shall be allocated among the Members in the same proportion as their then capital account balances.

ARTICLE TEN
WITHDRAWAL OF MEMBER

A Member may withdraw from the Company in accordance with the Act.

ARTICLE ELEVEN
ASSIGNMENTS

A Member may assign in whole or part his or her membership interest in the Company; provided, however, an assignee of a membership interest may not become a Member without the vote or written consent of at least a majority in interest of the Members, other than the Member who assigns or proposes to assign his or her membership interest.

ARTICLE TWELVE
ADMISSION OF ADDITIONAL MEMBERS

One or more additional Members of the Company may be admitted to the Company with the vote or written consent of a majority in interest of the Members (as defined in the Act).

ARTICLE THIRTEEN
LIABILITY OF MEMBERS

The members do not have any liability for the obligations or liabilities of the Company, except to the extent provided in the Act.

ARTICLE FOURTEEN
EXCULPATION OF MEMBER-MANAGERS

A Member exercising management powers or responsibilities for or on behalf of the Company will not have personal liability to the Company or its members for damages for any breach of duty in that capacity, provided that nothing in this Article shall eliminate or limit: (i) the liability of any Member-Manager if a judgment or other final adjudication adverse to him or her establishes that his or her acts or omissions were in bad faith or involved intentional misconduct or a knowing violation of law, or that he or she personally gained in fact a financial profit or other advantage to which he or she was not legally entitled, or that, with respect to a distribution to Members, his or her acts were not performed in accordance with Section _____ of the Act; or (ii) the liability of any Member-Manager for any act or omission prior to the date of first inclusion of this paragraph in this Agreement.

ARTICLE FIFTEEN
GOVERNING LAW

This Agreement shall be governed by, and construed in accordance with, the laws of the State of _____, all rights and remedies being governed by those laws.

ARTICLE SIXTEEN
INDEMNIFICATION

To the fullest extent permitted by law, the Company shall indemnify and hold harmless, and may advance expenses to, any Member, manager or other person, or any testator or intestate of such Member, manager or other person (collectively, the "Indemnitees"), from and against any and all claims and demands whatsoever; provided, however, that no indemnification may be made to or on behalf of any Indemnitee if a judgment or other final adjudication adverse to such Indemnitee establishes: (i) that his or her acts were committed in bad faith or were the result of active and deliberate dishonesty and were material to the cause of action so adjudicated; or (ii) that he or she personally gained in fact a financial profit or other advantage to which he or she was not legally entitled. The provisions of this section shall continue to afford protection to each Indemnitee regardless of whether he or she remains a Member, manager, employee or agent of the Company.

ARTICLE SEVENTEEN
TAX MATTERS

The Members of the Company and the Company intend that the Company be treated as a partnership for all income tax purposes, and will file all necessary and appropriate forms in furtherance of that position.

In witness, the parties have executed this agreement the day and year first above written.

[Signatures]

[Attach exhibits]

J-4
BYLAWS

[6 AM. JUR. *Legal Forms* 2d *Corporations* § 74:991 (Rev 1995)]

ARTICLE ONE
OFFICES

The principal office of the corporation shall be located at _____ [address], _____ [city], _____ County, _____ [state]. The board of directors shall have the power and authority to establish and maintain branch or subordinate offices at any other locations _____ [within the same city or within the same state or as the case may be].

ARTICLE TWO
STOCKHOLDERS

Section 1. Annual Meeting. The annual meeting of the stockholders shall be held on the ____ [ordinal number] day in the month of _____ in each year, beginning with the year ____, at ____ [time], for the purpose of electing directors and for the transaction of such other business as may come before the meeting. If the day fixed for the annual meeting shall be a legal holiday in the State of _____, such meeting shall be held on the next succeeding business day. If the election of directors is not held on the day designated herein for any annual meeting of the shareholders, or at any adjournment thereof, the board of directors shall cause the election to be held at a special meeting of the stockholders as soon thereafter as is convenient.

Section 2. Special Meetings. Special meetings of the stockholders, for any purpose or purposes, unless otherwise prescribed by statute, may be called by the president or by the board of directors, and shall be called by the president at the request of the holders of not less than ____ [number] of all the outstanding shares of the corporation entitled to vote at the meeting.

Section 3. Place of Meeting. The board of directors may designate any place within _____ [if desired, add: or without] the State of _____, as the place of meeting for any annual meeting or for any special meeting called by the board of directors. A waiver of notice signed by all stockholders entitled to vote at a meeting may designate any place, either within or without the State of _____, as the place for the holding of such meeting. If no designation is made, or if a special meeting is otherwise called, the place of meeting shall be the principal office of the corporation in the City of _____, _____ [state].

Section 4. Notice of Meeting. Written or printed notice stating the place, day, and hour of the meeting and, in case of a special meeting, the purpose or purposes for which the meeting is called, shall be delivered not less than ____ nor more than ____ days before the date of the meeting, either personally or by mail, by or at the direction of the president, or the secretary, or the officer or persons calling the meeting, to each shareholder of record entitled to vote at such meeting. If mailed, such notice shall be deemed to be delivered when deposited in the United States mail, addressed to the shareholder at his address as it appears on the stock transfer books of the corporation, with postage thereon prepaid. _____ [If appropriate, add: Notice of each meeting shall also be mailed to holders of stock not entitled to vote, as herein provided, but lack of such notice shall not affect the legality of any meeting otherwise properly called and noticed.]

Section 5. Closing Transfer Books or Fixing Record Date. For the purpose of determining stockholders entitled to notice of, or to vote at, any meeting of stockholders or any adjournment thereof, or stockholders entitled to receive payment of any dividend, or to make a determination of shareholders for any other proper purpose, the board of directors of the corporation may provide that the stock transfer books shall be closed for a stated period, but not to exceed ____ days. If the stock transfer books shall be closed for the purpose of determining stockholders entitled to notice of, or to vote at, a meeting of stockholders, such books shall be closed for at least ____ days immediately preceding such meeting. In lieu of closing the stock transfer books, the board of directors may fix in advance a date as the record date for any such determination of stockholders, such date in any event to be not more than ____ days, and in case of a meeting of stockholders, not less than ____ days prior to the date on which the particular action requiring such determination of stockholders is to be taken.

If the stock transfer books are not closed and no record date is fixed for the determination of stockholders entitled to notice of, or to vote at, a meeting of stockholders, or of stockholders entitled to receive payment of a dividend, the date that notice of the meeting is mailed or the date on which the resolution of the board of directors declaring such dividend is adopted, as the case may be, shall be the record date for such determination of stockholders. When a determination of stockholders entitled to vote at any meeting of stockholders has been made as provided in this section, such Determination shall apply to any adjournment thereof except where the determination has been made through the closing of the stock transfer books and the stated period of closing has expired.

Section 6. Quorum. A majority of the outstanding shares of the corporation entitled to vote, represented in person or by proxy, shall constitute a quorum at a meeting of stockholders. If less than a majority of such outstanding shares are represented at a meeting, a majority of the shares so represented may adjourn the meeting from time to time without further notice. At such adjourned meeting at which a quorum is present or represented, any business may be transacted that might have been transacted at the meeting as originally notified. The stockholders present at a duly organized meeting may continue to transact business until adjournment, notwithstanding the withdrawal of enough stockholders to leave less than a quorum.

Section 7. Proxies. At all meetings of stockholders, a stockholder may vote by proxy executed in writing by the stockholder or by his duly authorized attorney in fact. Such proxy shall be filed with the secretary of the corporation before or at the time of the meeting. No proxy shall be valid after ____ months from the date of its execution unless otherwise provided in the proxy.

Section 8. Voting of Shares. Subject to the provisions of any applicable law _____ [if desired, add: or any provision of the _____ (articles or certificate) of incorporation or of these bylaws concerning cumulative voting], each outstanding share entitled to vote shall be entitled to one vote on each matter submitted to a vote at a meeting of stockholders.

ARTICLE THREE
BOARD OF DIRECTORS

Section 1. General Powers. The business and affairs of the corporation shall be managed by its board of directors.

Section 2. Number, Tenure, and Qualifications. The number of directors of the corporation shall be ____. Directors shall be elected at the annual meeting of stockholders, and the term of office of each director shall be until the next annual meeting of stockholders and the election and qualification of his or her successor. Directors need not be residents of the State of _____, _____ [but shall be stockholders of the corporation or and need not be stockholders of the corporation].

Section 3. Regular Meetings. A regular meeting of the board of directors shall be held without notice other than this bylaw immediately after and at the same place as the annual meeting of stockholders. The board of directors may provide, by resolution, the time and place for holding additional regular meetings without other notice than such resolution. Additional regular meetings shall be held at the principal office of the corporation in the absence of any designation in the resolution.

Section 4. Special Meetings. Special meetings of the board of directors may be called by or at the request of the president or any _____ [two] directors, and shall be held at the principal office of the corporation or at such other place as the directors may determine.

Section 5. Notice. Notice of any special meeting shall be given at least _____ [48 hours or as the case may be] before the time fixed for the meeting, by written notice delivered personally or mailed to each director at his or her business address, or by telegram. If mailed, such notice shall be deemed to be delivered when deposited in the United States mail so addressed, with postage thereon prepaid, not less than _____ days prior to the commencement of the above-stated notice period. If notice is given by telegram, such notice shall be deemed to be delivered when the telegram is delivered to the telegraph company. Any director may waive notice of any meeting. The attendance of a director at a meeting shall constitute a waiver of notice of such meeting, except where a director attends a meeting for the express purpose of objecting to the transaction of any business because the meeting is not lawfully called or convened. Neither the business to be transacted at, nor the purpose of, any regular or special meeting of the board of directors need be specified in the notice or waiver of notice of such meeting.

Section 6. *Quorum.* A majority of the number of directors fixed by these bylaws shall constitute a quorum for the transaction of business at any meeting of the board of directors, but if less than such majority is present at a meeting, a majority of the directors present may adjourn the meeting from time to time without further notice.

Section 7. *Board Decisions.* The act of the majority of the directors present at a meeting at which a quorum is present shall be the act of the board of directors _____ [except that vote of not less than _____ (fraction) of all the members of the board shall be required for the amendment of or addition to these bylaws or as the case may be].

Section 8. *Vacancies.* Any vacancy occurring in the board of directors may be filled by the affirmative vote of a majority of the remaining directors though less than a quorum of the board of directors. A director elected to fill a vacancy shall be elected for the unexpired term of his or her predecessor in office. Any directorship to be filled by reason of an increase in the number of directors shall be filled by election at an annual meeting or at a special meeting of stockholders called for that purpose.

Section 9. *Compensation.* By resolution of the board of directors, the directors may be paid their expenses, if any, of attendance at each meeting of the board of directors, and may be paid a fixed sum for attendance at each meeting of the board of directors or a stated salary as director. No such

payment shall preclude any director from serving the corporation in any other capacity and receiving compensation therefor.

Section 10. *Presumption of Assent.* A director of the corporation who is present at a meeting of the board of directors at which action on any corporate matter is taken shall be presumed to have assented to the action taken unless his or her dissent shall be entered in the minutes of the meeting or unless he or she shall file his or her written dissent to such action with the person acting as the secretary of the meeting before the adjournment thereof or shall forward such dissent by registered mail to the secretary of the corporation immediately after the adjournment of the meeting. Such right to dissent shall not apply to a director who voted in favor of such action.

ARTICLE FOUR
OFFICERS

Section 1. *Number.* The officers of the corporation shall be a president, one or more vice-presidents (the number thereof to be determined by the board of directors), a secretary, and a treasurer, each of whom shall be elected by the board of directors. Such other officers and assistant officers as may be deemed necessary may be elected or appointed by the board of directors. Any two or more offices may be held by the same person, except the offices of _____ [president and secretary or as the case may be].

Section 2. *Election and Term of Office.* The officers of the corporation to be elected by the board of directors shall be elected annually at the first meeting of the board of directors held after each annual meeting of the stockholders. If the election of officers is not held at such meeting, such election shall be held as soon thereafter as is convenient. Each officer shall hold office until his or her successor has been duly elected and qualifies or until his or her death or until he or she resigns or is removed in the manner hereinafter provided.

Section 3. *Removal.* Any officer or agent elected or appointed by the board of directors may be removed by the board of directors whenever in its judgment the best interests of the corporation would be served thereby, but such removal shall be without prejudice to the contract rights, if any, of the person so removed.

Section 4. Vacancies. A vacancy in any office because of death, resignation, removal, disqualification or otherwise, may be filled by the board of directors for the unexpired portion of the term.

Section 5. Powers and Duties. The powers and duties of the several officers shall be as provided from time to time by resolution or other directive of the board of directors. In the absence of such provisions, the respective officers shall have the powers and shall discharge the duties customarily and usually held and performed by like officers of corporations similar in organization and business purposes to this corporation.

Section 6. Salaries. The salaries of the officers shall be fixed from time to time by the board of directors, and no officer shall be prevented from receiving such salary by reason of the fact that he or she is also a director of the corporation.

ARTICLE FIVE
CONTRACTS, LOANS, CHECKS, AND DEPOSITS

Section 1. Contracts. The board of directors may authorize any officer or officers, agent or agents, to enter into any contract or execute and deliver any instrument in the name of and on behalf of the corporation, and such authority may be general or confined to specific instances.

Section 2. Loans. No loans shall be contracted on behalf of the corporation and no evidences of indebtedness shall be issued in its name unless authorized by a resolution of the board of directors. Such authority may be general or confined to specific instances.

Section 3. Checks, Drafts, or Orders. All checks, drafts, or other orders for the payment of money, notes, or other evidences of indebtedness issued in the name of the corporation shall be signed by such officer or officers, agent or agents of the corporation and in such manner as shall from time to time be determined by resolution of the board of directors.

Section 4. Deposits. All funds of the corporation not otherwise employed shall be deposited from time to time to the credit of the corporation in such banks, trust companies, or other depositaries as the board of directors may select.

ARTICLE SIX
CERTIFICATES FOR SHARES; TRANSFERS

Section 1. Certificates for Shares. Certificates representing shares of the corporation shall be in such form as shall be determined by the board of directors. Such certificates shall be signed by the president or a vice-president and by the secretary or an assistant secretary. All certificates for shares shall be consecutively numbered or otherwise identified. The name and address of the person to whom the shares represented thereby are issued, with the number of shares and date of issue, shall be entered on the stock transfer books of the corporation. All certificates surrendered to the corporation for transfer shall be canceled and no new certificate shall be issued until the former certificate for a like number of shares shall have been surrendered and canceled, except that in case of a lost, destroyed, or mutilated certificate a new one may be issued therefor on such terms and indemnity to the corporation as the board of directors may prescribe.

Section 2. Transfer of Shares. Transfer of shares of the corporation shall be made in the manner specified in the _____ [Uniform Commercial Code or as the case may be]. The corporation shall maintain stock transfer books, and any transfer shall be registered thereon only on request and surrender of the stock certificate representing the transferred shares, duly endorsed. The corporation shall have the absolute right to recognize as the owner of any shares of stock issued by it, the person or persons in whose name the certificate representing such shares stands according to the books of the corporation for all proper corporate purposes, including the voting of the shares represented by the certificate at a regular or special meeting of stockholders, and the issuance and payment of dividends on such shares.

ARTICLE SEVEN
FISCAL YEAR

The fiscal year of the corporation shall _____ [be the calendar year or begin on the _____ (ordinal number) day of _____ (month) of each year and end at Midnight on the _____ (ordinal number) day of _____ (month) of the following year or as the case may be].

ARTICLE EIGHT
DIVIDENDS

The board of directors may from time to time declare, and the corporation may pay, dividends on its outstanding shares in the manner and on the terms and conditions provided by law and its _____ [articles or certificate] of incorporation.

ARTICLE NINE
SEAL

The board of directors shall provide a corporate seal, which shall be circular in form and shall have inscribed thereon the name of the corporation and the state of incorporation and the words "Corporate Seal." The seal shall be stamped or affixed to such documents as may be prescribed by law or custom or by the board of directors.

ARTICLE TEN
WAIVER OF NOTICE

Whenever any notice is required to be given to any stockholder or director of the corporation under the provisions of these bylaws or under the provisions of the _____ [articles or certificate] of incorporation or under the provisions of law, a waiver thereof in writing, signed by the person or persons entitled to such notice, whether before or after the time stated therein, shall be deemed equivalent to the giving of such notice.

ARTICLE ELEVEN
AMENDMENTS

These bylaws may be altered, amended, or repealed and new bylaws may be adopted by the board of directors at any regular or special meeting of the board; provided, however, that the number of directors shall not be increased or decreased nor shall the provisions of Article Two, concerning the stockholders, be substantially altered _____ [add other limitations as desired], without the prior approval of the stockholders at a regular or special meeting of the stockholders, or by written consent. _____ [If appropriate, add: Changes in and additions to the bylaws by the board of directors shall be reported to the stockholders at their next regular meeting and shall be subject to the approval or disapproval of the stockholders at such meeting. If no action is then taken by the stockholders on a change in or addition to the bylaws, such change or addition shall be deemed to be fully approved and ratified by the stockholders.]

GLOSSARY

abrogate To abolish, annul, or repeal a former law, rule, or custom.

accrued benefit The amount of benefit a participant has accumulated or that has been allocated to him or her as of a particular point in time.

actual authority In the law of agency, the right and power to act that a principal (often an employer) intentionally gives to an agent (often an employee) or at least allows the agent to believe has been given. This includes both express and implied authority.

actuary A person skilled in mathematical calculations to determine insurance risks, premiums, etc. A statistician.

administrative dissolution Dissolution of a corporation by the state of the corporation's domicile, usually for failing to pay income taxes or file annual reports.

affiliate A person or company with an inside business connection to another company. Under bankruptcy, securities, and other laws, if one company owns more than a certain amount of another company's voting stock, or if the companies are under common control, they are affiliates.

aggregate theory Theory regarding partnerships suggesting that a partnership is the totality of the partners rather than a separate entity.

amalgamation A complete joining or blending together of two or more things into one; for example, a consolidation or merger of two or more corporations to create a single company.

annuity A fixed sum of money, usually paid to a person at fixed times for a fixed time period or for life. If for life, or for some other uncertain period of time, it is called a contingent annuity. A retirement annuity is a right to receive payments starting at some future date, usually retirement, but sometimes a fixed date. There are many ways a retirement annuity can be paid. For example, *life* (equal monthly payments for the retiree's life); *lump sum* (one payment); *certain and continuous* (like *life,* but if the person dies within a set time period, benefits continue for the rest of that period); and *joint and survivor* (benefits continue for the life of either the retiree or the spouse).

annuity plan Type of qualified plan that does not involve a qualified plan trust. Contributions to an annuity plan are used to buy annuity policies directly from an insurance company.

annuity policy An insurance policy that may be purchased to provide an annuity.

antitrust laws Federal and state laws to protect trade from monopoly control and from price fixing and other restraints of trade. The main federal antitrust laws are the Sherman, Clayton, Federal Trade Commission and Robinson-Patman Acts.

apparent authority Authority an agent appears to have, judged by the words or actions of the person who gave the authority or by the agent's own words or actions. You may be liable for the actions of a person who has apparent authority to act for you.

articles of amendment Document filed with the secretary of state or other appropriate state authority to amend a corporation's articles of incorporation.

articles of dissolution Document filed with the secretary of state or other appropriate state authority to dissolve the corporation.

articles of incorporation The document used to set up a corporation. Articles of incorporation contain the most basic rules of the corporation and control other corporate rules such as the bylaws.

articles of merger Documents filed with the secretary of state or other appropriate authority to effect a merger.

articles of organization Document required to be filed with the proper state authority to form a limited liability company.

articles of share exchange Document filed with the secretary of state or other appropriate state authority to effect a share exchange.

articles of termination Document filed with proper state authority to dissolve a limited liability company. Same as articles of dissolution.

assignment of error Alleged errors of the trial court specified by an appellant in seeking a reversal, vacation, or modification of the trial court's judgment.

assumed name Alias that may be used to transact business. Usually requires filing or notification at the state or local level. Same as fictitious name.

authorized shares Total number of shares, provided for in the articles or certificate of incorporation, that the corporation is authorized to issue.

blue sky law Any state law regulating sales of stock or other investment activities to protect the public from fly-by-night or fraudulent stock deals, or to ensure that an investor gets enough information to make a reasoned purchase of stock or other security.

board of managers Group of individuals elected by the members of a limited liability company to manage the limited liability company. Similar to a corporation's board of directors.

bond A document that states a debt owed by a company or a government. The company,

government, or government agency promises to pay the owner of the bond a specific amount of interest for a set period of time and to repay the debt on a certain date. A bond, unlike a stock, gives the holder no ownership rights in the company.

business judgment rule The principle that if persons running a corporation make honest, careful decisions within their corporate powers, no court will interfere with these decisions even if the results are bad.

buy-sell agreement An agreement among partners or owners of a company that if one dies or withdraws from the business, his or her share will be bought by the others or disposed of according to a pre-arranged plan.

bylaws Rules or regulations adopted by an organization such as a corporation, club, or town.

capital surplus Property paid into a corporation by the shareholders in excess of capital stock liability.

certificate of assumed name, trade name, or fictitious name A certificate issued by the proper state authority to an individual or an entity that grants the right to use an assumed or fictitious name for the transaction of business in that state.

certificate of authority Certificate issued by secretary of state or similar state authority granting a foreign corporation the right to transact business in that state.

certificate of authority to transact business as a foreign limited liability company Certificate issued by the secretary of state, or other appropriate state official, to a foreign limited liability company to allow it to transact business in that state.

certificate of good standing Sometimes referred to as a certificate of existence. Certificate issued by the secretary of state or other appropriate state authority proving the incorporation and good standing of the corporation in that state.

charter An organization's basic starting document (for example, a corporation's articles of incorporation).

civil law 1. Law that originated from ancient Rome rather than from the common law or from canon law. 2. The law governing private rights and remedies as opposed to criminal law, military law, international law, natural law, etc.

Clayton Act (15 U.S.C. 12) A 1914 federal law that extended the Sherman Act's prohibition against monopolies and price discrimination.

close corporation A corporation with total ownership in a few hands.

closely held corporation Refers to stock or a company that is owned by a family or another company.

commission on uniform state laws An organization that, along with the American Law Institute, proposes various Model Acts and Uniform Acts for adoption by the states.

common law 1. Judge-made law (based on ancient customs, mores, usages, and principles handed down through the ages) in the absence of controlling statutory or other enacted law. 2. All the statutory and case law of England and the American colonies before the American Revolution.

common stock Shares in a corporation that depend for their value on the value of the company. These shares usually have voting rights (which other types of company stock may lack). Usually, they earn a dividend (profit) only after all other types of the company's obligations and stocks have been paid.

consolidation Two corporations joining together to form a third, new one.

conversion Any act that deprives an owner of property without that owner's permission and without just cause. For example, it is conversion to refuse to return a borrowed book.

conversion rights Rights, often granted to preferred shareholders with the issuance of preferred stock, that allow the preferred shareholders to convert their shares of preferred stock into common stock at some specific point in time, usually at the shareholder's option.

copyright The right to control the copying, distributing, performing, displaying, and adapting of works (including paintings, music, books and movies). The right belongs to the creator, or to persons employing the creator, or to persons who buy the right from the creator. The right is created, regulated, and limited by the federal Copyright Act of 1976 and by the Constitution. The symbol for copyright is ©. The legal life (*duration*) of a copyright is the author's life plus 50 years, or 75 years from publication date, or 100 years from creation, depending on the circumstances.

covenant not to compete A part of an employee contract, partnership agreement, or agreement to sell a business in which a person promises not to engage in the same business for a certain amount of time after the relationship ends.

cumulative voting The type of voting in which each person (or each share of stock, in the case of a corporation) has as many votes as there are positions to be filled. Votes can be either concentrated on one or on a few candidates or spread around.

debenture A corporation's obligation to pay money (usually in the form of a note or bond) often unsecured (not backed up) by any specific property. Usually refers only to long-term bonds.

debt securities Securities that represent loans to the corporation, or other interests that must be repaid.

deed of trust A document, similar to a mortgage, by which a person transfers the legal ownership of land to independent trustees to be held until a debt on the land is paid off.

defined benefit plans   Retirement plans in which the benefit payable to the participant is definitely determinable from a benefit formula set forth in the plan.

defined contribution plan   Retirement plan that establishes individual accounts for each plan participant and provides benefits based solely on the amount contributed to the participants' accounts.

demurrer   A legal pleading that says, in effect, "even if, for the sake of argument, the facts presented by the other side are correct, those facts do not give the other side a legal argument that can possibly stand up in court." The demurrer has been replaced in many courts by a motion to dismiss.

deposition   The process of taking a witness's sworn out-of-court testimony. The questioning is usually done by a lawyer, with the lawyer from the other side given a chance to attend and participate.

derivative action   A lawsuit by a stockholder of a corporation against another person (usually an officer of the company) to enforce claims the stockholder thinks the corporation has against that person.

determination letter   A letter issued by the Internal Revenue Service in response to an inquiry as to the tax implications of a given situation or transaction. The Internal Revenue Service may issue a determination letter with regard to the *qualified* status of an employee benefit plan based upon the information in the plan's Application for Determination for Employee Benefit Plan (Form 5300).

direct action   A lawsuit by a stockholder to enforce his or her own rights against a corporation or its officers rather than to enforce the corporation's rights in a derivative action.

disgorgement   To give up something (usually illegal profits) on demand or by court order.

dissociation   The event that occurs when a partner withdraws or otherwise ceases to be associated in the carrying on of the partnership business.

dissolution   The termination of a corporation, partnership or other business entity's existence.

dividend   A share of profits or property; usually a payment per share of a corporation's stock.

domicile   A person's permanent home, legal home, or main residence. The words "abode," "citizenship," "habitancy," and "residence" sometimes mean the same as *domicile* and sometimes not. A *corporate domicile* is the corporation's legal home (usually where its headquarters is located); an elected domicile is the place the persons who make a contract specify as their legal homes in the contract.

door-closing statute   State statute providing that a corporation doing business in the state without the necessary authority is precluded from maintaining an action in that state.

downstream merger   Merger whereby a parent corporation is merged into a subsidiary.

due diligence   Enough care, enough timeliness, or enough investigation to meet legal requirements, to fulfill a duty, or to evaluate the risks of a course of action. Due diligence often refers to a professional investigation of the financial risks of a merger or a securities purchase, or the legal obligation to do the investigation. Due diligence is also used as a synonym for due care.

EDGAR   Electronic Data Gathering, Analysis, and Retrieval system established by the Securities and Exchange Commission to collect, validate, index, and provide to the public, documents that are required to be filed with the Securities and Exchange Commission.

Employee Retirement Income Security Act (ERISA)   (29 U.S.C. 1000) A federal law that established a program to protect employees' pension plans. The law set up a fund to pay pensions when plans go broke and regulates pension plans as to *vesting* (when a person's pension rights become permanent), nondiversion of benefits to anyone other than those entitled, nondiscrimination against lower-paid employees, etc.

Employee Stock Ownership Plan (ESOP) Qualified plan designed to give partial ownership of the corporation to the employees.

employee welfare benefit plan An employee benefit plan that provides participants with welfare benefits such as medical, disability, life insurance, dental, and death benefits. A welfare benefit plan may provide benefits either entirely or partially through insurance coverage.

employment agreement Agreement entered into between an employer and an employee to set forth the rights and obligations of each party with regard to the employee's employment.

entity at will Entity that may be dissolved at the wish of one or more members or owners.

entity theory Theory that suggests that a partnership is an entity separate from its partners, much like a corporation.

equity securities Securities that represent an ownership interest in the corporation.

exchange An organization set up to buy and sell securities such as stocks.

express authority Authority delegated to an agent by words that expressly, plainly, and directly authorize him or her to perform a delegated act.

fictitious name Alias that may be used to transact business. Usually requires filing or notification at the state or local level. Same as assumed name.

fiduciary 1. A person who manages money or property for another person and in whom that other person has a right to place great trust. 2. A relationship like that in definition (no. 1).

3. Any relationship between persons in which one person acts for another in a position of trust; for example, lawyer and client or parent and child.

fixed benefit formula Formula for calculating pension plan benefits that provides participant with a definite percentage of their income.

foreign corporation A corporation incorporated in a state or country other than the state referred to. A corporation is considered a foreign corporation in every state other than its state of incorporation.

foreign limited liability company A limited liability company that is transacting business in any state other than the state of its organization.

Form 8-K Form that must be filed with the SEC by the issuer of registered securities when certain pertinent information contained in the registration statement of the issuer changes.

401(k) plan Type of savings plan, established for the benefit of employees, which allows employees to elect to defer a certain percentage of their compensation to provide for their retirement benefits.

general partner 1. Synonymous with *partner*. A partner in a general partnership, or limited partnership, who typically has unlimited personal liability for the debts and liabilities of the partnership. 2. A member of a general or limited partnership who shares in the profits and losses of the partnership and may participate fully in the management of the partnership. General partners are usually personally liable for the debts and obligations of the partnership.

general partnership A typical partnership in which all partners are general partners.

goodwill The reputation and patronage of a company. The monetary worth of a company's *goodwill* is roughly what a company would sell for over the value of its physical property, money owed to it, and other assets.

Hart-Scott-Rodino Act (15 U.S.C. § 18a) A federal law passed in 1976 that strengthens the enforcement powers of the Justice Department. The Act requires entities to give notice to the Federal Trade Commission and the Justice Department prior to mergers and acquisitions when the size of the transaction is valued at $50 million or more.

heir A person who inherits property; a person who has a right to inherit property; or a person who has a right to inherit property only if another person dies without leaving a valid, complete will. [pronounce: air]

implied authority Actual power given by a principal to his or her agent, which necessarily follows from the express authority that is given; authority that is necessary, usual, and proper to accomplish the main authority that is expressly conferred.

in personam Against the person. In personam jurisdiction is the power that a court has over the defendant himself or herself as distinguished from the more limited power a court has over his or her interest in property (quasi in rem) or over the property itself (in rem).

indemnification The act of compensating or promising to compensate a person who has suffered a loss or may suffer a future loss.

individual retirement account (IRA) A bank or investment account into which some persons may set aside a certain amount of their earnings each year and have their interest taxed only later when withdrawn. (Some spouses without income may have IRAs, and some persons who have tax deferred pension or profit-sharing plans have limited or no use of IRAs, depending on their income.)

initial public offering The first offering of a corporation's securities to the public.

insider trading The purchase or sale of securities by corporate insiders based on nonpublic information.

inspectors of election Impartial individuals who are often appointed to oversee the election of directors at the shareholder meetings of large corporations.

integrated plan Type of retirement plan that is integrated with the employer's contribution to Social Security on behalf of the participant.

intellectual property 1. A copyright, patent trademark, trade secret, or similar intangible right in an original tangible or perceivable work. 2. The works themselves in (no. 1). 3. The right to obtain a copyright, patent, etc., for the works in no. 1.

investment contract Under federal law, any agreement that involves an investment of money pooled with others' money to gain profits solely from the efforts of others.

involuntary dissolution Dissolution that is not approved by the board of directors or shareholders of a corporation, often initiated by creditors of an insolvent corporation.

issued and outstanding shares The total shares of stock of a corporation that have been authorized by the corporation's articles or certificate of incorporation and issued to shareholders.

joint and several Both together and individually. For example, a liability or debt is joint and several if the creditor may sue the debtors either together as a group (with the result that the debtors would have to split the loss) or individually (with the result that one debtor might have to pay the whole thing).

joint venture Sometimes referred to as a joint adventure; the relationship created when two or more persons combine jointly in a business enterprise with the understanding that they will share in the profits or losses and that each will have a voice in its management. Although a joint venture is a form of partnership, it customarily involves a single business project rather than an ongoing business relationship.

Keogh plan A tax-free retirement account for persons with self-employment income.

letter of intent A preliminary written agreement setting forth the intention of the parties to enter into a contract.

limited liability company A cross between a partnership and a corporation owned by members who may manage the company directly or delegate to officers or managers who are similar to a corporation's directors. Governing documents are usually publicly-filed articles of organization and a private operating agreement. Members are not usually liable for company debts, and company income and losses are usually divided among and taxed to the members individually according to share.

limited liability limited partnership A type of limited partnership permissible in some states in which the general partners have less than full liability for the actions of other general partners.

limited liability partnership A partnership in which the partners have less than full liability for the actions of other partners, but full liability for their own actions.

limited partner A partner who invests in a limited partnership, but does not assume personal liability for the debts and obligations of the partnership. Limited partners may not participate in the management of the limited partnership.

limited partnership A partnership formed by general partners (who run the business and have liability for all partnership debts) and limited partners (who partly or fully finance the business, take no part in running it, and have no liability for partnership debts beyond the money they put in or promise to put in).

limited partnership certificate Document required for filing at the state level to form a limited partnership.

liquidation Winding up the affairs of a business by identifying assets, converting them into cash, and paying off liabilities (liquidate the company).

long-arm statute A state law that allows the courts of that state to claim jurisdiction over (decide cases directly involving) persons outside the state who have allegedly committed torts or other wrongs inside the state. Even with a long-arm statute, the court will not have jurisdiction unless the person sued has certain minimum contacts with the state.

manager-managed limited liability company A limited liability company in which the members have agreed to have the company's affairs managed by one or more managers.

member An owner of a limited liability company.

member-managed limited liability company A limited liability company in which the members have elected to share the managing of the company's affairs.

merger The union of two or more corporations, with one corporation ceasing to exist and becoming a part of the other.

money purchase pension plan Defined contribution pension plan whereby the employer contributes a fixed amount based on a formula set forth in the plan that is based on the employee's salary.

nomenclature Designation, title, or name of something.

novation The substitution by agreement of a new contract for an old one, with all the rights under the old one ended. The new contract is often the same as the old one, except that one or more of the parties is different.

operating agreement Document that governs the limited liability company. Similar to a corporation's bylaws.

over the counter Describes securities, such as stocks and bonds, sold directly from broker to broker or broker to customer rather than through an exchange.

par value The nominal value assigned to shares of stock, which is imprinted upon the face of the stock certificate as a dollar value. Most state statutes do not require corporations to assign a par value to their shares of stock.

parent corporation A corporation that fully controls or owns another company.

partnership An association of two or more persons to carry on as co-owners a business for profit.

partnership at will Partnership formed for an indefinite period of time, without a designated date for termination.

patent An exclusive right granted by the federal government to a person for a limited number of years (usually 20) for the manufacture and sale of something that person has discovered or invented.

peremptory Absolute; conclusive; final; or arbitrary. Not requiring any explanation or cause to be shown.

plan administrator Individual or entity responsible for calculating and processing all contributions to and distributions from a qualified plan, and for all other aspects of plan administration.

plan of exchange Document required by statute that sets forth the terms of the agreement between the parties to a statutory share exchange.

plan of merger Document required by state statute that sets forth the terms of the agreement between the two merging parties in detail.

plan participant Employees who meet with certain minimum requirements to participate in a qualified plan.

preemptive right The right of some stockholders to have the first opportunity to buy any new stock the company issues.

preferred stock A type of stock that is entitled to certain rights and privileges over other outstanding stock of the corporation.

preincorporation agreement Agreement entered into between parties setting forth their intentions with regard to the formation of a corporation.

preincorporation transaction Actions taken by promoters or incorporators prior to the actual formation of the corporation.

profit-sharing Describes a plan set up by an employer to distribute part of the firm's profits to some or all of its employees. A *qualified plan* (one that meets requirements for tax benefits) must have specific criteria and formulas for who gets what, how, and when.

promoter A person who forms a corporation.

prospectus 1. A document put out to describe a corporation and to interest persons in buying its stock. When new stock is sold to the public, the SEC requires a prospectus that contains such things as a statement of income, a balance sheet, an auditor's report, etc. 2. Any offer (written, by radio or television, etc.) to interest persons in buying any securities, such as stock. 3. A document put out to interest persons in any financial deal (such as the offer to sell a building or the offer of shares in a limited partnership).

proxy A person who acts for another person (usually to vote in place of the other person in a meeting the other cannot attend). A document giving that right.

proxy statement The document sent or given to stockholders when their voting proxies are requested for a corporate decision. The SEC has rules for when the statements must be given out and what must be in them.

public offering Offering of securities for sale to the public by means of interstate commerce.

publicly held corporation A corporation with stock sold to a large number of persons.

punitive damages Extra money given to punish the defendant and to help keep a particular bad act from happening again.

qualified plan Pension plan that meets I.R.S. requirements for the payments to be deducted by the employer and initially tax-free to the employee.

qualified plan contributions Contributions made to a qualified plan by the sponsor, participants, or third parties. Limitations on the amount of contributions are set forth in the Internal Revenue Code.

qualified plan distributions Distributions made to qualified plan participants or their beneficiaries from a qualified retirement plan trust, usually on the retirement, death, or termination of employment of the plan participant.

qualified plan trust Trust managed by trustees who are appointed by the qualified plan sponsors to manage the assets of the qualified plan.

quorum The number of persons who must be present to make the votes and other actions of a group (such as a board) valid. This number is often a majority (over half) of the whole group, but is sometimes much less or much more.

red herring prospectus A preliminary prospectus, used during the "waiting period" between filing a registration statement with the SEC and approval of the statement. It has a red "for information only" statement on the front and states that the securities described may not be offered for sale until SEC approval. The red herring must be filed with the SEC before use.

registered agent Individual appointed by a corporation to receive service of process on behalf of the corporation and perform such other duties as may be necessary. Registered agents may be required in the corporation's state of domicile and in each state in which the corporation is qualified to transact business.

registered office Office designated by the corporation as the office where process may be served. The secretary of state or other appropriate state authority must be informed as to the location of the registered office. Corporations are generally required to maintain a registered office in each state in which the corporation is qualified to transact business.

relator A person in whose name a state brings a legal action (the person who "relates" the facts on which the action is based). The name of the case might be State ex rel ("on the relation of") *Smith v. Jones.* [pronounce: re-*late*-or]

representative action A lawsuit brought by one stockholder in a corporation to claim rights or to fix wrongs done to many or all stockholders in the company.

reverse triangle merger Three-way merger whereby a subsidiary corporation is merged into the target corporation. The end result is the survival of the parent corporation and the target corporation, which becomes a new subsidiary.

scrip A piece of paper that is a temporary indication of a right to something valuable. Scrip includes paper money issued for temporary use; partial shares of stock after a stock split; certificates of a deferred stock dividend that can be cashed in later, etc.

Securities Act of 1933 Federal securities act which requires the registration of securities that are to be sold to the public and the disclosure of complete information to potential buyers.

Securities and Exchange Commission A federal agency that administers the federal securities acts, primarily by regulating the sale and trading of stocks and other securities.

Securities Exchange Act of 1934 Federal securities act which regulates stock exchanges and over-the-counter stock sales.

security A share of stock, a bond, a note, or one of many different kinds of documents showing a share in a company or a debt owed by a company or a government. ... The U.S. Supreme Court has defined a security as any investment in a common enterprise from which the investor is "led to expect profits solely from the efforts of a promoter or a third party."

share exchange Transaction whereby one corporation acquires all of the outstanding shares of one or more classes or series of another corporation by an exchange that is compulsory on the shareholders of the target corporation.

Sherman Act (15 U.S.C. 1) The first antitrust (antimonopoly) law, passed by the federal government in 1890 to break up combinations in restraint of trade.

short-swing profits Profits made by a company insider on the short-term sale of company stock.

simplified employee pension plan (SEP) An employer's contribution to an employee's IRA (Individual Retirement Account) that meets certain federal requirements. Self-employed persons often use a SEP.

sister corporations Two (or more) companies with the same or mostly the same owners.

sole proprietor The owner of a sole proprietorship.

sole proprietorship An unincorporated business owned by one person.

special interrogatories Written questions asked by a judge to a jury to see if the jury's answers conflict with the jury's verdict.

sponsor In ERISA terms, an employer who adopts a qualified plan for the exclusive benefit of the sponsor's employees and/or their beneficiaries.

stated capital The amount of capital contributed by stockholders. The capital or equity of a corporation as it appears in the balance sheet.

statement of authority A statement filed for public record by the partners of a partnership to expand or limit the agency authority of a partner, to deny the authority or status of a partner or to give notice of certain events such as the dissociation of a partner or the dissolution of the partnership.

statement of denial A statement filed for public record by a partner or other interested party to contradict the information included in a statement of authority.

statute of frauds Any of various state laws, modeled after an old English law, that require many types of contracts (such as contracts for the sale of real estate or of goods over a certain dollar amount, contracts to guarantee another's debt, and certain long-term contracts) to be signed and in writing to be enforceable in court.

statutory close corporation A closely held corporation having no more than 50 shareholders that has elected to be treated as a statutory close corporation under the relevant statutes of its state of domicile.

statutory merger A type of merger that is specifically provided for by state statute.

stock bonus plan Type of defined contribution plan, similar to the profit-sharing plan, in which the main investment is in the employer's stock.

stock dividend Profits of stock ownership (dividends) paid out by a corporation in more stock rather than in money. This additional stock reflects the increased worth of the company.

stock split A dividing of a company's stock into a greater number of shares without changing each stockholder's proportional ownership.

stock subscription agreement Agreement to purchase a specific number of shares of a corporation.

subsidiary corporation A corporation that is owned by another corporation (the parent corporation).

summary prospectus A shortened version of the prospectus required by the SEC that includes a summary of much of the information in the registration statement and is prepared pursuant to the pertinent rules of the SEC.

target benefit plan Type of qualified plan that has many characteristics of both a defined benefit plan and a defined contribution plan. Contributions are based on the amount of the fixed retirement for each participant. However, the amount distributed to plan participants will depend on the value of the assets in the participant's account at the time of retirement.

10-K report The annual report required by the SEC of publicly held corporations that sell stock.

10-Q quarterly report Quarterly report that must be filed with the SEC by all corporations that are required to file 10-K reports.

tenancy in partnership Form of ownership provided for under the Uniform Partnership Act whereby all partners are co-owners with the other partners. Each partner has an equal right to possess the property for partnership purposes, but has no right to possess the property for any other purpose without the consent of the other partners.

tombstone ad A stock (or other securities) or land sales notice that clearly states that it is informational only and not itself an offer to buy or sell. It has a black border that resembles one on a death notice.

tortious Wrongful. A civil (as opposed to a criminal) wrong [tort], other than a breach of contract. For an act to be a tort, there must be: a legal duty owed by one person to another, a breach (breaking) of that duty and harm done as a direct result of the action. Examples of torts are negligence, battery, and libel.

trade name The name of a business. It will usually be legally protected in the area where the company operates and for the types of products in which it deals.

trademark A distinctive mark, brand name, motto, or symbol used by a company to identify or advertise the products it makes or sells. *Trademarks* (and *service marks*) can be federally registered and protected against use by other companies if the marks meet certain criteria. A federally registered mark bears the symbol ®.

transfer agent A person (or an institution such as a bank) who keeps track of who owns a company's stocks and bonds. Also called a registrar. A transfer agent sometimes also arranges dividend and interest payments.

treasury shares Shares of stock that have been rebought by the corporation that issued them.

triangle merger Merger involving three corporations, whereby a corporation forms a subsidiary corporation and funds it with sufficient cash or shares of stock to perform a merger with the target corporation, which is merged into the subsidiary. The parent corporation and the subsidiary corporation both survive a triangle merger.

unauthorized practice of law Nonlawyers doing things that only lawyers are permitted to do. Who and what fits into this definition is constantly changing and the subject of dispute. If, however, a clear case comes up (for example, a nonlawyer pretending to be a lawyer and setting up a law office), the practice may be prohibited and the person punished under the state's criminal laws.

underwriter With regard to securities offerings, any person or organization that purchases securities from an issuer with a view to distributing them, or any person who offers or sells or participates in the offer or sale for an issuer of any security.

Uniform Limited Liability Company Act   Uniform Act adopted by the National Conference of the Commissions of Uniform State Laws in 1994 and amended in 1995 to give states guidance when drafting limited liability company statutes.

unit benefit formula   Formula for calculating the benefits payable under a pension plan that provides participants with a unit of pension for each year of credited service.

upstream merger   Merger whereby a subsidiary corporation merges into its parent.

variable benefit formula   A formula used to calculate benefits payable under a pension plan that provides participants with benefits that are related to the market value of the trust assets or are tied to a recognized cost of living index.

vested   Absolute, accrued, complete, not subject to any conditions that could take it away; not contingent on anything. For example, if a person sells you a house and gives you a deed, you have a vested interest in the property; and a pension is vested if you get it at retirement age even if you leave the company before that. There are several types of pension plan vesting. For example, "cliff" vesting (until you work a certain number of years, you get nothing; after that, you get all your accrued benefits); "graded" vesting (additional percentages of your accrued benefits are added the longer you work).

voluntary dissolution   Dissolution that is approved by the directors and shareholders of the corporation.

voting group   All shares of one or more classes that are entitled to vote and be counted together collectively on a certain matter under the corporation's articles of incorporation or the pertinent state statute.

watered stock   A stock issue that is sold as if fully paid for, but that is not (often because some or all of the shares were given out for less than full price).

wind up   Finish current business, settle accounts and turn property into cash in order to end a corporation or a partnership and split up the assets.

writ of mandamus   Court order that directs a public official or government department to do something. It may be sent to the executive branch, the legislative branch, or a lower court.

writ of prohibition   Order prohibiting specific action.

INDEX

A

Abrogation, 85
Access, partner rights to, 38
Accounting. *See also* Finance
  partnership, 53, 59
  for par value stock, 313
Accounting methods
  approval of, 224
  in limited partnerships, 101
Accredited investors, 352
Accrued benefits, 499–500
Acquisitions, 384. *See also* Asset
    acquisitions; Corporate
    structure changes; Mergers
  antitrust laws affecting, 394–396
  on-line resources for, A6
  paralegal's role in, 428–432
  resources for, 432–434
  state statutes
    concerning, 432–434
Actual authority, 26
Actuary, 502
Addy v. Myers, 142–144
Administrative dissolution,
    483–485. *See also* Dissolution
  under the Model Business
    Corporation Act (MBCA),
    A146–A147
  under the Uniform Limited
    Liability Company Act, A93
Affiliates, 183
Agency organizations, 25
Agent authority, 26
Agents, 25. *See also* Transfer agent
  duties of, 26
  liability for acts of, 26
  members as, 128
  partners as, 29
  registered, 207, 450–451
Aggregate theory, 27, 28
Agreement and plan of
    merger, 397
  sample, 398–399
Agreement of merger, 401
  sample, 411
Agreements
  employment, 521–533
  paralegal preparation of, 430
Alabama Secretary of State, A1

Alaska Department of Commerce
    and Economic
    Development, A1
Amalgamation, 385
Amended certificate of authority,
    452, A150–A151
American Stock Exchange
    (AMEX), 336
Annual reports, 57. *See also*
    Reporting
  for limited liability
    companies, 136–137
  in limited liability partnerships,
    A48–A49
  summary, 512
Annual shareholder meetings,
    requirements for, 277
Annuities, 498
Annuity plans, 503
Annuity policy, 502
Antitrust laws, 388, 394, 433
  compliance with, 430
AOL/Time Warner merger, 389
Apparent authority, 26
Application for Determination
    for Employee Benefit
    Plan, 510–511
Appraisal notice, A141
Appraisal proceedings, 402
Appraisal rights, A138–A140
  exercise of, A140–A142
Arbitration
  in employment agreements, 532
  in general partnerships, 56
Arizona Corporation
    Commission, A1
Arkansas Secretary of State, A1
Articles of amendment, 424–426.
    See also Documentation
  approval of, 423–424
  sample, 425–426
Articles of dissolution, 141,
    467–470
  under the Model Business
    Corporation Act
    (MBCA), A144
  sample, 470
Articles of incorporation, 170,
    205–216

  amendment of, 213, 422–426
  approval and acceptance of, 222
  effective time and date of, 215
  executing and filing, 214,
    238–239
  under the Model Business
    Corporation Act
    (MBCA), A104
  preparing, 238
  provisions of, 209–213
  restated, 426
  sample, 208–209, 235–236
Articles of merger, 402
  sample, 404–407
  under the Model Business
    Corporation Act (MBCA),
    A135–A136
  under the Uniform Limited
    Liability Company Act,
    A95–A96
Articles of organization, 118
  checklist for drafting, 152
  for limited liability companies,
    129–133
  sample, 132–133
  under the Uniform Limited
    Liability Company Act, A78
Articles of share exchange, 409
  sample, 410
Articles of termination
  for limited liability
    companies, 140
  under the Uniform Limited
    Liability Company Act,
    A91–A92
Asset acquisitions, 414–415
  due diligence and preclosing
    matters for, 420
  laws affecting, 417
  procedures for, 417–422
Asset acquisition transactions
  closing, 421
  postclosing matters for, 422
Asset distribution
  for limited liability
    companies, 140
  in limited partnerships, 107–108
  under the Uniform Limited
    Liability Company Act, A92

Asset purchase agreement,
    418–419
Assets
    of limited partnerships, 98
    partnership, 35–36, 50
Asset sales
    under the Model Business
        Corporation Act
        (MBCA), A137
    stockholder consent for, 419
Asset transfer documents, paralegal
    preparation of, 431
Assignment of contracts, 431,
    532–533
Assignment of error, 215, 216
Assistant secretary, 272
Assumed names
    certificates of, 3
    in sole proprietorships, 8–9
    state statutes concerning, 15–16
Authorized shares, 309, A109
Authorized stock, 207, 305–308
    statutory requirements for,
        307–308
Average benefit percentage
    test, 497

B

Balance sheet, corporate, 314
Banking resolutions, 224–225
Bank loans, 325
Bankruptcies, corporate, 463–464
Bankruptcy Code, 463–464
*Beckman v. Cox Broadcasting
    Corporation,* 526–527
Beneficial owners, rights of, A140
Benefit formulas, 502
Benefit plans. *See also* Employee
    benefit plans
    corporate, 173
    defined, 501–503
    target, 505
Benefits
    accrued, 499–500
    employee, 531
    for limited partners, 100
*Biondi v. Beekman Hill House
    Apartment Corporation,*
    257–259
Blue sky laws, 373–374, 379, 417
Board meetings, 230–231,
    262–269
    under the Model Business
        Corporation Act (MBCA),
        A124–A125
Board of directors. *See also*
    Directors

approval of dissolution by,
    463–467
approval of plan of merger by,
    400–401
bylaws concerning, A163–A164
corporate, 211
dissolution by, A144
electing, 218
meetings of, 230–231, 262–269,
    A124–A125
liability of, 212–213
under the Model Business
    Corporation Act (MBCA),
    A122–A134
non-meeting actions of,
    265–269
resolutions of, 218–225,
    262–269
vacancies on, 262
Board of managers, 119
Boesky, Ivan, 367
Bonds, 324, 325–326
Bonus plans, stock, 505–506
Brown, Annette R., 514
Bryant, Sherryl D., 184
*BT-I v. Equitable Life Assurance
    Society,* 84–86
Business, transacting as a foreign
    limited liability company,
    146–151
Business bankruptcies, 463–464
Business continuity
    corporations and, 174
    in general partnerships, 45
    under limited partnerships, 89
    in sole proprietorships, 5–6
Business control
    under general partnerships,
        52–53
    under limited partnerships, 90
Business Corporation Acts,
    182–183
    state, 187–189
Business corporations, 176
Business entities, choosing
    among, 119
Business judgment rule, 253–254
Business organizations, 25
    characteristics of, 120–121
Business policies, review of,
    100–101
Business receipts, 2
Buyouts, 486
Buy-sell agreements, 288
    purchase price in, 290
Bylaws, 228–233
    adoption of, 218, 223–224
    amending, 233, A166

approval of, 226
corporate, 212, 295
under the Model Business
    Corporation Act
    (MBCA), A105
signing, 233
Bylaws form, A162–A166

C

Cafeteria plans, 509
California Revised Limited
    Partnership Act, 86
California Secretary of State, A1
Callable shares, 318
Capital. *See also* Finance
    ability to raise, 45
    corporate, 174, 303–304
    equity and debt, 303
    in limited liability
        companies, 142
    partnership, 57–59
    raising in sole proprietorships, 7
    stated, 313
Capital contributions
    in a limited liability company
        operating agreement, A161
    in limited partnerships, 103
Capital resources
    in general partnerships, 43
    under limited partnerships,
        89–90
Capital surplus, 313
Carpenter v. United States,
    367–369
Case law, corporations and,
    169–170
Cash dividends, 320
CCH Federal Securities Law
    Reporter, 379
Celotex Corporation v. Pickett,
    392–393
CEO salaries, 525
Certain and continuous annuity
    payments, 498
Certificate of amendment,
    424–426
Certificate of assumed name, trade
    name, or fictitious name, 3
Certificate of authority. *See also*
    Amended certificate of
    authority
    amending, 451
    for foreign corporations, 446,
        447–448, A149–A153
    for foreign limited liability
        companies, A97, A98, A99
    for limited liability companies,
        150–151

sample application for, 449
Certificate of authority to transact
    business as a foreign limited
    liability company, 146,
    148–149
Certificate of Cancellation, 108
Certificate of Dissolution,
    sample, 471
Certificate of existence (good
    standing), 448, A79–A80
Certificate of incorporation, 205
Certificate of limited partnership,
    A57–A60
Certificate of withdrawal, 453
    sample, 454
Certificates for shares, bylaws
    concerning, A165
Chairman of the Board, 271
Charter, 205
Checklists
    closing, 432
    corporate dissolution, 487
    for drafting articles of
        organization, 152
    employment agreement,
        521–523
    Foreign Corporation
        Qualification, 457
    incorporation, 239
    Limited Partnership
        Agreement, 109
    Operating Agreement, 135–136
    Partnership Agreement, 67–69
    for starting sole
        proprietorships, 13
Checks, bylaws concerning, A165
Check the Box regulations, 123
Chief executive officer (CEO),
    271. See also CEO salaries
Chief financial officer, 271
Civil law, 24
Claimants, notices to, 476–477
Claims
    against dissolved corporations,
        A145–A146
    postdissolution, 477–481
Clayton Act, 394, 433
Client confidentiality, 378
Client information sheet, A17
Client meetings, 238
"Cliff" vesting, 500
Close (closely held) corporations,
    182–183
Close Corporation Supplement,
    181–183, 289
Closing book, 432
Closing checklist, 432
Codes of ethics. See also Ethics

National Association of Legal
    Assistants, A8–A9
National Federation of Paralegal
    Associations, Inc., A9–A16
Colorado Secretary of State, A1
Commission on Uniform State
    Laws, 24–27
Committees, delegation of
    authority to, 246–247
Common law, 24
    corporations and, 169–170
Common stock, 207, 308–309
Commonwealth of Pennsylvania,
    Department of Revenue for the
    Bureau of Accounts Settlement
    v. McKelvey, 87–88
Compensation
    CEO, 525
    of directors, 256, A124
    in employment agreements, 531
    for limited partners, 100
Competition, unfair methods
    of, 394
Conduct
    under the Model Business
        Corporation Act (MBCA),
        A126–A127
    under the Uniform Limited
        Liability Company Act,
        A84–A85
Confidential information,
    preserving, A11
Conflicts of interest
    avoiding, A11–A12
    under the Model Business
        Corporation Act (MBCA),
        A132–A134
Connecticut Secretary of State, A1
Consideration
    for par value stock, 312–313
    for shares of stock, 313–315
Consolidations, 392
Continuity of life, 119, 122
Contracts
    assignment of, 431
    bylaws concerning, A165
Contribution plans, 503–507
Control, of general partnerships, 47
Conversion rights, 310–311, 326
Conversions, 8
    of partnerships, A45–A48
    under the Uniform Limited
        Liability Company Act,
        A94–A97
Copyrights, 12
Corporate balance sheet, 314
Corporate bankruptcies, 463–464
Corporate bylaws, 212

Corporate dissolution, 462–489.
    See also Dissolution
    by incorporators, 464
    involuntary, 483–486
    under Model Business
        Corporation Act (MBCA),
        A143–A149
    paralegal's role in, 486–488
    resources for, 488–489
    revocation of, 481–483
    voluntary, 463–483
Corporate dissolution
    checklist, 487
Corporate dividends, payment
    of, 322
Corporate domicile, 165
Corporate financial matters. See
    also Capital; Finance
    paralegal's role in, 326–328
    resources for, 328–329
Corporate financial structure,
    302–329
    corporate capitalization,
        303–304
    debt financing, 324–326
    dividends, 319–322
    equity financing, 304–311
    issuance of stock, 315–317
    par value stocks and, 311–313
Corporate information sheet,
    A17–A18
Corporate law, 315. See also Law
    on-line resources for, A5
    paralegal's role in, 183–187
Corporate laws, liberal, 196
Corporate legal departments, pro
    bono work in, 164
Corporate minute books, 269
Corporate name, 205–206
    of foreign corporation,
        455, A151
    reservation of, 238, 450
    under the Model Business
        Corporation Act (MBCA),
        A107–A108
Corporate officers, 269–272
    election of, 223, 231–232
Corporate organization, 244–297
    board of directors meetings and
        resolutions, 262–269
    corporate officers, 269–272
    director authority and duties,
        245–253
    director compensation and
        indemnification, 255–259
    election and term of directors,
        259–262
    ethical considerations in, 296

paralegal's role in, 293–297
personal liability of directors, 253–255
resources for, 297
shareholder actions in, 291–293
shareholder meetings, 276–286
shareholder rights and responsibilities, 272–276
Corporate paralegal profiles
Angela C. Rhode, 487–488
Annette R. Brown, 514
Beckie K. Mills, 237–238
Brian Haberly, 429
Donna G. Frye, 13–14
Edward Galante, 455–456
Gail M. Pell, 68
Laurie R. Mansell, 377
Linda M. Racette, 153
Mary Beth Riley-Wallis, 294
Patricia E. Rodgers, 110
Paula L. Peterson, 327–328
Sherryl D. Bryant, 184
Vicki Kunz, 539
Corporate paralegals. *See also* Paralegals
ethics for, A8–A16
on-line resources for, A5–A7
Corporate records, shareholder inspection of, 274
Corporate resolutions, paralegal preparation of, 431
Corporate seal, 224, 233
Corporate service companies, 440, 458, 488–489
Corporate stock, restrictions on transfer of, 286–291
Corporate structure, decisions about, 195. *See also* Corporate structure changes
Corporate structure changes, 384–434
amendments to articles of incorporation, 422–426
asset and stock acquisition procedures, 417–422
asset and stock acquisitions, 414–417, 414–417
merger and share exchange procedures, 396–414
mergers and share exchanges, 385–396
paralegal's role in, 428–432
reorganizations, 427–428
resources for, 432–434
Corporation formation, 194–241
articles of incorporation, 205–216
bylaws, 228–233

incorporators, 204–205
organizational meetings, 216–227
paralegal's role in, 234–239
preincorporation matters, 194–204
purpose of, 211–212
resources for, 239–241
of special types of corporations, 233–234
stock splits, 323–324
Corporations, 162–191. *See also* Corporate dissolution; Corporation formation; Foreign corporations; Publicly held corporations
advantages of, 172–175
classifications of, 176–183
disadvantages of, 175–176
ethical considerations for, 185
laws governing, 165–170
on-line resources for, A5
resources for, 187–191
rights and powers of, 170–172
as separate legal entities, 163
wind up and liquidation of, 472–481
Coupon bonds, 325–326
Covenants not to compete, 524–526
Creditor rights
under the Uniform Limited Partnership Act (ULPA), A68
under the Uniform Limited Liability Company Act, A86
Creditors. *See also* Creditor rights
judicial proceedings by, 486
notice to, 476
of partners, A39–A40
under the Uniform Limited Liability Company Act, A85–A86
Cubic Corporation v. Marty, 529–530
Cumulative dividends, 321
Cumulative voting, 285
Custodianship, under the Model Business Corporation Act (MBCA), A148

D

Debentures, 324, 326
Debt, in partnership agreements, A156–A157
Debt capital, 303. *See also* Capital
Debt financing, 324–326
Debt securities, 303
redemption of, 326

Deception, in securities cases, 366
Decree of dissolution, A148
Deed of trust, 85
De facto mergers, 416–417
Defined benefit plans, 501–503
Defined contribution plans, 503–507
Delaware
certificate of incorporation for, 210
incorporation in, 196
Secretary of State in, A1
Demurrer, 8
Deposition, 275
Deposits, bylaws concerning, A165
Derivative actions, 105–106, 292–293
Derivative proceedings, under the Model Business Corporation Act (MBCA), A121–A122
Determination letter, 510
Digital economy, sole proprietorships in, 4–5
Direct action, 291
Director liability, under the Model Business Corporation Act (MBCA), A126–A127
Directors. *See also* Board of directors
approval of plan of exchange by, 408
approval of plan of merger by, 400–401
authority and duties of, 245–253
compensation and indemnification of, 231, 255–259
conflicting interest transactions of, A132–A134
election and term of, 225, 259–262, 285
indemnification of, 213
liability of, 231
merger authorization by, 401
under the Model Business Corporation Act (MBCA), A122–A134
number and term of, 229–230
personal liability of, 253–255
qualifications of, 260
removal and resignation of, 231, 261–262
unauthorized acts of, 254
Directors' Resolution to Dissolve Corporation, 465–466
Director voting, under the Model Business Corporation Act (MBCA), A119

Disbursements, in limited partnerships, 104
Discounted bonds, 326
Disgorgement, 367
Dispute arbitration, in employment agreements, 532
Dissenters' rights, 424
 under the Model Business Corporation Act (MBCA), A137–A143
Dissenting shareholders, 401–402, 408–409
Dissociated member interest, purchasing, 139
Dissociation. *See also* Dissolution; Wind up
 effects of, 62
 partnership, 60, A40–A43
 statement of, A43
 wrongful, 61, 138–139
Dissolution, 60. *See also* Articles of dissolution; Corporate dissolution; Partnership dissolution
 administrative, 483–485
 in a limited partnership agreement, A159–A160
 judicial, 485–486
 of limited liability companies, 138–140
 of limited partnerships, 102, 106–108
 priority rights to assets upon, 311
 revocation of, 481–483, A144–A145
 statement of, A44
 under the Uniform Partnership Act, A26–A30
 under the Uniform Limited Liability Company Act, A90–A91
 under Uniform Limited Partnership Act (ULPA), A69
Dissolution agreement, 64–65
Dissolution statutes, state, 468–469
Distributional interest, under the Uniform Limited Liability Company Act, A88–A90
Distributional interest transfers, under the Uniform Limited Liability Company Act, A85–A86
Distributions. *See also* Qualified plan distributions
 in a limited liability company operating agreement, A161

under the Model Business Corporation Act (MBCA), A109–A114
to shareholders, 477
Subchapter D, A113–A114
under the Uniform Limited Partnership Act (ULPA), A66–A67
under the Uniform Limited Liability Company Act, A83–A84
under Uniform Partnership Act (1997), A37–A38
District of Columbia Department of Consumer and Regulatory Affairs, A1
Dividend preferences, 320
Dividends, 233, 303, 319–322. *See also* Shares; Stock
 authority to declare, 321–322
 bylaws concerning, A165–A166
 declaration of, 320–322
 priority rights to, 311
 right to receive, 322
 types of, 319–320
Documentation. *See also* "Articles" entries
 for asset acquisition transactions, 421
 for closing merger transactions, 413
 limited liability, 152
 for mergers and share exchanges, 412
 review and production of, 430–431
 for share exchange transactions, 414
 for stock acquisition transactions, 421–422
 stock and asset transfer, 431
 supplementary, 430
Domicile, 165
 choosing, 195–197
Door-closing statutes, 441–442
Double taxation, 176
DOVE program, 153
Downstream mergers, 389
Dreyfuss v. Dreyfuss and Brickell Earth Station, Inc., 22–23
Due diligence, 356, 409–412
 for asset and stock purchases, 420
Duty of care, 41, 251–252
 breach of, 254
Duty of loyalty, 41, 252
 breach of, 254
Duval v. Midwest Auto City, Inc., 9

E
EDGAR Central Index Key (CIK), 350
Electric Railway Securities Co. v. Hendricks, 442, 444–445
Electronic Data Gathering, Analysis, and Retrieval (EDGAR) database, 341, 350. *See also* EDGAR Central Index Key (CIK)
Employee benefit plans, 225, 492–516
 elements of qualified plans, 495–496
 ERISA and IRC requirements for, 496–498
 laws governing qualified plans, 493–494
 nonqualified pension plans, 508–509
 on-line resources for, A5
 paralegal's role in, 512–514
 qualified pension plans, 498–508
 qualified plan adoption and IRS approval, 510
 qualified plan reporting and disclosure requirements, 510–512
 qualified plans, 492–493
 resources for, 515–516
 welfare benefit plans, 509–510
Employee benefits, in employment agreements, 531
Employee duties, description of, 523–524
Employee management, in partnership agreements, A156
Employee Retirement Income Security Act of 1974 (ERISA), 493–494
 exemptions from, 498
 qualified plan requirements under, 496–498
 Section 206 of, 502
 vesting standards under, 500
Employees
 highly compensated, 498
 in sole proprietorships, 9–11
Employee stock ownership plans (ESOPs), 304, 494, 506–507
Employee stock ownership trust (ESOT), 506–507
Employee vacations, 532
Employer identification number (EIN), 9–11
Employment agreement checklist, 521–523

Employment agreements, 519–540
 amendment or renewal of, 533
 considerations for
  employees, 521
 considerations for
  employers, 520
 drafting, 521–533
 paralegal's role in drafting,
  533–538
 resources for, 540
 sample, 534–537
 terms of, 523
Employment Agreement
 Worksheet, 537–538
Employment termination, 520
 in employment agreements,
  531–532
 trade secrets after, 528–531
English common law, 524
Entity at will, 119
Entity theory, 27
Equity capital, 303
Equity financing, 304–311, 325
Equity securities, 303
Equity shares, redemption of,
 317–318
Ethics. *See also* Codes of ethics
 client confidentiality and, 378
 corporations and, 185, 296
 on-line resources for, A8
 partnerships and, 69–70
 sole proprietorships and, 16–17
Event of withdrawal, 106
Exchange, plan of, 402–409
Exchanges, 336–338
Executives, white-collar crime
 by, 248
Express authority, 25

F

Family limited partnerships, 80–81
Federal agencies, as resources for
 employee benefit plans, 515
Federal antitrust laws, 433
 compliance with, 430
Federal Bankruptcy Act, 165, 463
Federal government, on-line
 resources for, A5
Federal laws. *See also* Federal
 statutes
 affecting asset and stock
  acquisitions, 417
 affecting statutory mergers and
  share exchanges, 393–394
 concerning pension plans, 515
Federal Securities Acts, 378–379
 major provisions of, 369–373
Federal securities forms, 379

Federal statutes. *See also* Federal
 laws; Law
 corporate, 170, 189
 on-line resources for, A5
Federal tax offices, as resources for
 corporate dissolution, 489
Federal Trade Commission, 394
Federal Trade Commission
 Act, 433
 Section 5 of, 395
Fictitious name
 certificate of, 3
 in sole proprietorships, 8–9
 state statutes concerning, 15–16
Fiduciary, 28
Fiduciary duties, 247–250
 breach of, 254
 in partnerships, 41
Finance, under the Uniform
 Limited Partnership Act
 (ULPA), A65–A66. *See also*
 Accounting; Capital
Financial structure. *See also*
 Corporate financial structure
 of limited liability companies,
  137–138
 of limited partnerships, 103–105
 of partnerships, 57–60
Financing, equity, 304–311
*First National Bank and Trust
 Company of Williston v. Scherr,*
 31–32
Fiscal year, 233
 bylaws concerning, A165
Fixed benefit formula, 502
Florida Department of State, A1
Foreign corporation qualification,
 438–459
 amending certificates of
  authority, 451
 necessity of, 439–446
 paralegal's role in, 455–458
 registering of a corporate
  name, 455
 requirements for, 447–451
 resources for, 458–459
 statutory requirements for,
  440–441
Foreign Corporation Qualification
 Checklist, 457
Foreign corporations. *See also*
 Foreign corporation
 qualification
 defined, 438
 jurisdiction over, 439–440
 licensing of, 446
 maintaining the good standing
  of, 451–453

mergers or share exchanges with,
 393, A136–A137
under the Model Business
 Corporation Act (MBCA),
 A149–A153
name requirements for,
 448–450, A151
rights, privileges, and
 responsibilities of, 446
withdrawal from doing business
 as, 453–454
withdrawal of, A153
Foreign limited liability companies,
 146–151
 naming, A98–A99
 under the Uniform Limited
  Liability Company Act,
  A97–A99
Foreign limited liability
 partnerships, under Uniform
 Partnership Act (1997),
 A49–A50
Foreign limited partnerships, under
 Uniform Limited Partnership
 Act (ULPA), A69–A71
Foreign qualification, statement
 of, A49
Form 8-K, 361
Form 966 (Corporate Dissolution
 or Liquidation), 481, 482
Form 2553, 180
Form 5300 (Application for
 Determination for Employee
 Benefit Plan), 510–511
Form 5500, 512, 513
Form books. *See also* Legal form
 books
 for corporate financial
  matters, 329
 incorporation and, 240
 as a resource for mergers and
  acquisitions, 433
 for corporations, 189–190
Forms
 bylaws, A162–A166
 limited liability company
  operating agreement,
  A160–A162
 limited partnership agreement,
  A157–A160
 on-line resources for, A5
 partnership agreement,
  A154–A157
Form SS-4 (Application for
 Employer Identification
 Number), 10, 11
401(k) plans, 504–505
Fractional shares, 317, A110

Fraud
   by directors, 254
   securities, 354–357,
     365–373, 375
Freeze-outs, 388
Frye, Donna G., 13–14
ftc.gov, 394
Funding, of welfare benefit plans,
   509
Funds, availability for
   dividends, 319

G

Galante, Edward, 455–456
General partner duties, under
   limited partnerships, 99–100
General partners, 21, 79
   business management by, 100
   under the Uniform Limited
     Partnership Act (ULPA),
     A63–A65
General partnerships, 21
   advantages of, 41–43
   disadvantages of, 44–46
   organization and management
     of, 46–57
   versus limited partnerships, 82
General proxy, 282
Georgia Secretary of State, A1
Good standing
   certificate of, 448
   of foreign corporations,
     451–453
Goodwill, 7
Government, on-line resources
   for, A5
Government forms, on-line
   resources for, A7
Government links, A7
Government resources, 15, 72
Government tax offices, as limited
   partnership resources,
     112–113
"Graded" vesting, 500

H

Haberly, Brian, 429
Hart-Scott-Rodino Act, 394,
   395–396, 417, 430, 433
Hawaii Department of Commerce
   and Consumer Affairs, A1
Heir, defined, 5
Highly compensated
   employees, 498
Hiring, for sole
   proprietorships, 9–11
Hostile takeovers, 416

*Hunter v. Fort Worth Capital
   Corporation,* 477, 480–481

I

Idaho Secretary of State, A1
Illegal acts, by directors, 254
Illinois Secretary of State, A1
Implied authority, 26
Income, in limited
   partnerships, 104
Income taxation. *See also*
   Taxation
   in general partnerships, 43, 46
   under limited partnerships,
     88–89, 104
   of sole proprietorships, 4
Incorporation
   gathering client information for,
     203–204
   under the Model Business
     Corporation Act (MBCA),
     A104–A105
Incorporation checklist, 239
Incorporation documents, 295
Incorporations, by state, 198
Incorporation services,
   240–241
Incorporators, 204–205
   dissolution by, 464
   name and address of, 208
Incorporators' acts, ratification
   of, 223
Incorporators' resolutions, 218
Indemnification
   of directors, 213, 256–259
   in general partnerships, 51
   in a limited liability company
     operating agreement,
     A161–A162
   under limited partnerships, 99
   under the Model Business
     Corporation Act (MBCA),
     A128–A132
   prohibited, 257
Indiana Secretary of State, A2
Individual retirement accounts
   (IRAs), 508
Individual shareholders, damage
   suits by, 291
Information
   director reliance on,
     252–253
   for incorporation, 203–204
   partner duty to render, 41
Information rights, under the
   Uniform Limited Liability
   Company Act, A84

Initial public offerings, 333
   paralegal's role in, 376–378
In personam, 166
Insiders, 366
Insider trading, 337, 366
Inspectors of election, 284
Insurance funding, 290
   under the Model Business
     Corporation Act
     (MBCA), A131
Integrated plans, 507
Intellectual property, 12
   on-line resources for, A5
Interest on Lawyers Trust
   Accounts (IOLTA), 306
Internal Revenue Code (IRC),
   178, 394, 492, 494
   as a limited liability company
     resource, 157
   qualified plan requirements
     under, 496–498
   Section 401(k) of, 504–505
   Section 401 of, 497
   Section 415 of, 499,
     501, 503
Internal Revenue Service (IRS),
   124, 173, 427. *See also* IRS
   Web page
Internet resources
   for corporate dissolution, 489
   for corporate financial
     matters, 329
   for corporate organization, 297
   for corporations, 190–191
   for employee benefit plans,
     515–516
   for employment agreements, 540
   for foreign corporation
     qualification, 458–459
   for incorporation, 240–241
   for limited liability
     companies, 158
   for limited partnerships, 113
   for mergers and acquisitions,
     433–434
   for partnerships, 73
   for publicly held
     corporations, 379
   for sole proprietorships, 17–18
Intrastate offering exemption, 354
Inventions, employment
   agreements and, 528
Investment contracts, 125
Investors, accredited, 352
Involuntary corporate dissolution,
   483–486
   alternatives to, 486
Iowa Secretary of State, A2

IRS Web page, 10
Issued and outstanding shares, 305–308
Issuer of securities, 335

J

Jacobson v. Buffalo Rock Shooters Supply, 165, 167–169
Joint and several liability, 34
Joint and survivor annuity payments, 498
Joint ventures, 24
Judicial appraisal of shares, A142–A143
Judicial dissolution, 485–486
under the Model Business Corporation Act (MBCA), A147–A149

K

Kansas Secretary of State, A2
Kentucky Secretary of State, A2
Keogh plans, 507
Kunz, Vicki, 539

L

Lakota Girl Scout Council v. Havey Fund-Raising Management, 165, 166–167
Law. *See also* Federal laws
corporate, 165–170, 315
for limited liability companies, 125–126
for limited partnerships, 81
for partnerships, 24–27
unauthorized practice of, 185–187, A12
Law firms, pro bono work in, 164
Legal encyclopedias, 189
Legal entities, corporations as, 163
Legal ethics, on-line resources for, A6. *See also* Ethics
Legal expenses
of general partnerships, 45–46
of limited partnerships, 91–92
Legal form books, 70, 112. *See also* Form books
for corporate dissolution, 488
Legal research, on-line resources for, A6
Letter of intent, 396, 418, 430
Liability. *See also* Unlimited liability
for acts of agents, 26
of dissociated partners, A42–A43
joint and several, 34
limited, 118

in a limited liability company operating agreement, A161
under limited partnerships, 90, 98–99
under the Model Business Corporation Act (MBCA), A105, A111, A126–A127
of partners, A44–A45
partnership, 50
shareholder, 276
for short-swing profits, 362
of sole proprietorships, 5–6
under the Uniform Limited Partnership Act (ULPA), A61–A62
under the Uniform Limited Liability Company Act, A81–A83
under Uniform Partnership Act (1997), A36–A37
Licensing
of foreign corporations, 446
of sole proprietorships, 12
Limited liability
of corporations, 173
of limited liability company owners, 142
Limited liability companies (LLCs), 117–159. *See also* Foreign limited liability companies
advantages of, 140–144
characteristics of, 118–123
claims against, A92–A93
defined, 118
disadvantages of, 145–146
dissolution of, 138–140
financial structure of, 137–138
laws governing, 125–126
management of, 133–135, A82–A83
member power to bind, A90
member rights and responsibilities in, 127–128
naming, 139–130
on-line resources for, A6
organization and management of, 128–137
organizers of, 129
paralegals' role in, 152–154
professional, 123
relationships in, A80–A85
research on, 153–154
resources for, 154–159
rights and powers of, 126–127
statutory requirements for, 131–132
unrestrictive ownership of, 142

Limited Liability Company Operating Agreement form, A160–A162
Limited liability documentation, 152
Limited liability limited partnership (LLLP) election, 93–94
Limited liability limited partnerships (LLLPs), 79
Limited liability partnership election, 56–57
Limited liability partnerships (LLPs), 23–24, 34–35, 79
under Uniform Partnership Act (1997), A48–A49
Limited Liability Partnership Statement of Qualification form, 58
Limited offerings, exempted from registration provisions, 351–353
Limited partners, 79. *See also* Partners
changes in, 101
compensation and benefits for, 100
duties of, 100
liability of, 87–88
relationships with general partners, 84–86
rights of substitution of, 100
sale/purchase of interests of, 101
termination of interest of, A159
under Uniform Limited Partnership Act (ULPA), A60–A63
Limited Partnership Agreement Checklist, 109
Limited Partnership Agreement form, A157–A160
Limited partnership agreements, 96–102
duration of, 97
Limited partnership certificate, 90, 92–93
amending, 94
cancellation of, 107
Limited partnerships, 23, 78–114. *See also* Partnerships
advantages of, 86–90
changes in, 102–103
defined, 79
disadvantages of, 90–92
financial structure of, 103–105
laws governing, 81
naming, A55
on-line resources for, A6

organization and management
of, 92–102
paralegal's role in, 108–111
partner rights and
responsibilities in, 82–86
purpose of, 97
resources for, 111–114
as separate entities, 81
termination of, 101–102,
106–108
Limited proxy, 282. *See also*
Proxies
Liquidation. *See also* Dissolution;
Wind up
corporate, 472–481
sample plan of, 475
Liquidation rights, for holders of
common stock, 309
Loans. *See also* Capital; Finance
bank, 325
bylaws concerning, A165
from partners, 59
Local government resources, 15
Local tax offices, as resources for
corporate dissolution, 489
Long-arm statutes, 439–440
Louisiana Secretary of State, A2
Lump sum annuity payments, 498

M

Maine Secretary of State, A2
Majority vote, partner submission
to, 40
Management. *See also* Management
flexibility
corporate, 174, 212
of general partnerships, 46–57,
52–53
of limited liability companies,
118–119, 128–137, 133–135,
A82–A83
in a limited liability company
operating agreement, A160
of limited partnerships,
92–102, 100
partner participation in, 38
Management authority, in sole
proprietorships, 3
Management diversity, in sole
proprietorships, 7
Management flexibility
in limited liability
companies, 144
in partnerships, 41–42
Management structure, in general
partnerships, 44
Manager-managed limited liability
companies, 134

Managing partner, 47
Mandatory indemnification, 256
Mansell, Laurie R., 377
Market value of stock, 290
Maryland State Department of
Assessments and Taxation, A2
Massachusetts Secretary of
State, A2
Master agreement, 521
Master plan, 510
Maturity date of a bond, 326
Meetings. *See also* Organizational
meetings
board-of-director, 230–231,
262–269
shareholder, 228–229, 276–286
special, 278
telephonic, 269
Mega mergers, 389
Member consent, matters
requiring, 134–135
Member contributions, 137
Member dissociation, 138–139
under the Uniform Limited
Liability Company Act,
A86–A90
Member-managed limited liability
companies, 133–134
Member reimbursement, 137
Members, 118
as agents, 128
distributions to, 137–138
personal liability of, 131
rights and responsibilities of,
127–128
Members' rights, under the
Uniform Limited Liability
Company Act, A82
Merger, articles of, 402
Merger agreement, 401, 411
Mergers, 384. *See also* Corporate
structure changes
antitrust laws affecting,
394–396
de facto, 416–417
defined, 387
director resolution
authorizing, 401
downstream, 389
laws affecting, 393–394
mega, 389
under the Model Business
Corporation Act (MBCA),
A134–A137
on-line resources for, A6
paralegal's role in, 428–432
parent/subsidiary, 388–389
partnership, A45–A48

postclosing matters
concerning, 414
preclosing matters concerning,
409–412
resources for, 432–434
reverse triangle, 390
state statutes concerning,
432–434
statutory, 385–391
triangle, 389
under the Uniform Limited
Liability Company Act,
A94–A97
upstream, 388
Merger transactions, closing, 413
Merrill Lynch v. Livingston,
362–364
Michigan Department of
Commerce, A2
Milken, Michael, 367
Mills, Beckie K., 237–238
Minnesota Secretary of State, A2
Minute books, 269
Minutes, 219–222, 226, 265
corporate, 295
sample, 266–267
of shareholder meetings,
285–286, 287–288
Mississippi Secretary of State, A2
Missouri Secretary of State, A2
*Mo. ex rel. National Supermarkets
v. Sweeny*, 476, 478–479
Model Business Corporation Act
(MBCA), 169, 197, 204, 205,
208, 245, 246, 260, 306,
386, A101–A153
Close Corporation Supplement
to, 181–183, 289
corporate dissolution under,
A143–A149
corporate name under,
A107–A108
directors and officers under,
A122–A134
dissenters' rights under,
A137–A143
foreign corporations under,
A149–A153
incorporation under,
A104–A105
merger and share exchange
under, A134–A137
office and agent under,
A108–A109
purposes and powers of,
A105–A107
sale of assets under, A137
Section 14.01 of, 464

Section 14.02 of, 465
Section 14.03 of, 467
Section 14.04 of, 481
Section 14.05 of, 472
Section 14.22 of, 484
Section 14.30 of, 485
Section 15.01 of, 441
Section 15.03 of, 447–448
Section 15.20 of, 453
shareholders under, A114–A122
shares and distributions under,
   A109–A114
Model Nonprofit Corporation
   Act, 178
Model Professional Corporation
   Act, 177
Money purchase pension
   plans, 505
Moneywatch Companies v. Wilbers,
   197, 199–200
Montana Corporation Bureau, A2

N

Name registration, for foreign
   limited liability
   companies, 149
National Association of Legal
   Assistants, 187
   code of ethics of, A8–A9
National Association of Securities
   Dealers (NASD), 336
National Association of Securities
   Dealers Automated Quotation
   System (NASDAQ), 338
National Conference of
   Commissioners on Uniform
   State Laws, A19
National Federation of Paralegal
   Associations, 186
   code of ethics of, A9–A16
*National Surety Co. v. Oklahoma
   Presbyterian College for
   Girls,* 9
Nebraska Secretary of State, A2
Negligence, of directors, 254
Negotiations
   for asset and stock
      purchases, 418
   for mergers and share
      exchanges, 396
Nevada Secretary of State, A2
New Hampshire Secretary of
   State/Corporations, A2
New Jersey Secretary of State, A3
New Mexico State Corporation
   Commission, A3
New York Department of
   State, A3

New York Stock Exchange
   (NYSE), 336–337
Neyens v. Worthington, 443
Nomenclature, 9
Nominees' rights, A140
Noncompetition clauses, 524–526
Nonprofit corporations,
   177–178, 234
Nonqualified pension plans,
   508–509
North Carolina Secretary of
   State, A3
North Dakota Secretary of
   State, A3
Notice of Intent to Dissolve,
   467–470
   sample, 472
Notices to claimants, 476–477
Notice to creditors, 476
   sample, 477
Notice to third parties, 65
Novation, 199

O

Office of the corporation, 228
Officer conduct, under the Model
   Business Corporation Act
   (MBCA), A128
Officers, 231–232. *See also*
   Corporate officers
   authority of, 245–246
   bylaws concerning, A164–A165
   election and term of office of,
      223, 272
   indemnification of, A131
   under the Model Business
      Corporation Act (MBCA),
      A127–A134
   personal liability of, 272
Ohio Secretary of State, A3
Oklahoma Secretary of State, A3
On-line resources, for corporate
   paralegals, A5–A7. *See also*
   Internet resources
Operating Agreement Checklist,
   for limited liability companies,
   135–136
Operating Agreement form,
   A160–A162
Operating agreements, 119
   for limited liability companies,
   135–136
Optional indemnification, 256–257
Oral partnership agreements, 48
Ordinarily prudent person test,
   251–252
Oregon Secretary of State, A3
Organizational charter, 205

Organizational expenses
   in general partnerships, 43,
      45–46
   in limited partnerships, 91–92
   in sole proprietorships, 4
Organizational meetings, 216–227.
   See also Meetings
   minutes of, 219–222, 226,
      265–267
   purpose of, 218
Organizations, agency and
   business, 25
Outside directors, 259
Over-the-counter markets,
   338–339
Over-the-counter securities
   sales, 336
Ownership interest transfers, 122
Ownership transferability,
   of limited liability
   companies, 145
Ownership transfers, corporate,
   174–175

P

Paralegal associations, on-line
   resources for, A6
Paralegal profiles. *See* Corporate
   paralegal profiles
Paralegal publications, on-line
   resources for, A6
Paralegals
   client confidentiality and, 378
   as "insiders," 337
   misconduct by, A14
   on-line resources for, A5–A7
   role in corporate dissolution,
      486–488
   role in corporate financial
      matters, 326–328
   role in corporate law matters,
      183–187
   role in corporate organization,
      293–297
   role in corporation formation,
      234–239
   role in drafting employment
      agreements, 533–538
   role in employee benefit plans,
      512–514
   role in foreign corporation
      qualification, 455–458
   role in limited liability
      companies, 152–154
   role in limited partnerships,
      108–111
   role in mergers and acquisitions,
      428–432

role in partnerships, 66–70
role in publicly held corporations, 376–378
role in reporting, 378
role in sole proprietorships, 12–14
Paralegal title, disclosure of, A12
Parent corporations, 183
Parent/subsidiary mergers, 388–389
Partner compensations/benefits, 52
Partner conduct standards, A38
Partner contribution, 49–50
Partner death, 55
Partner duties, 40–41, 51–52
Partner powers, 52
Partner property rights, under the Uniform Partnership Act, A25–A26
Partner relationships, 29–41
    under the Uniform Partnership Act, A23–A25
    under Uniform Partnership Act (1997), A34–A39
Partner rights, 35–36
    to access books and records, 38
    to an equal share of profits, 38
    in a limited partnership agreement, A158
    to participate in management, 38
    in partnership agreements, A156
    to reimbursement, 38
    to a separate account, 37–38
    to wind up partnership business, 38–40, 56
Partners. See also Limited partners; Partnership
    as agents, 29
    changes in, 54–55
    dissociation of, A40–A43
    liability of, A36–A37, A44–A45
    loans and advances from, 59
    power of estate of, A68–A69
    rights and duties of, A37–A38
    transferees and creditors of, A39–A40
    unanimous consent requirements and, 29–33
Partnership accounting, 53, 59
Partnership Agreement Checklist, 67–69
Partnership Agreement form, A154–A157
Partnership agreements, A32
    oral, 48
    term of, 49

Partnership articles, components of, 48–56
Partnership assets, 50
    distribution of, 65–66
    partner rights in, 35–36
Partnership at will, 45
Partnership authority statement, 33–34, A35
Partnership dissolution, causes of, 62–64
Partnership expenses, 52
Partnership interests
    assignment of, A67–A69
    sale or purchase of, 55–56
Partnership interest transfers, 45
    under limited partnerships, 89
Partnership liability, 34
Partnership losses, 40
Partnership merger, statement of, A47–A48
Partnership property, 36–37
    transfer of, A34–A35
    under Uniform Partnership Act (1997), A34
Partnership Return (Form 1065), 43
Partnerships, 20–75. See also General partnerships; Limited liability partnerships (LLPs); Limited partnerships
    conversions and mergers of, A45–A48
    conversion to limited liability companies, A94–A95
    defined, 21–23
    ethical considerations for, 69–70
    financial structure of, 57–60
    law governing, 24–27
    on-line resources for, A6
    paralegal's role in, 66–70
    purpose of, 48–49
    resources for, 70–73
    as separate entities, 27–28
    termination of, 56, 60–66
    under the Uniform Partnership Act, A22
    under Uniform Partnership Act (1997), A33–A34
    wind up of, A26–A30
Par value, 212
Par value stock, 311–313
    accounting for, 313
Patent and Trademark Office, 17
Patents, 12
    employment agreements and, 528
Pell, Gail, 68
Penn Colleries Co. v. McKeever, 445

Pennsylvania Department of State, A3
Pension plans. See also Qualified pension plans
    federal law concerning, 515
    money purchase, 505
    nonqualified, 508–509
Peremptory writ, 478
Personal liability, in general partnerships, 43
Peterson, Paula L., 327–328
Plan administrators, 495
Planning, for mergers, 397–402
Plan of exchange, 402–409
    director and shareholder approval of, 408
    paralegal preparation of, 431
Plan of liquidation, sample, 475
Plan of merger, 397–402
    director and shareholder approval of, 400–401
    paralegal preparation of, 431
Plan participants, 496
Poison pills, 416
Post closing matters, 432
Postdissolution claims, 477–481
Powers of corporation, 212
Practice of law, 186
Preemptive rights, 273–274
Preferred dividends, 320
Preferred stocks, 304, 307, 309–311
    conversion of, 310–311
    issue decisions for, 311
    series of, 311
Preincorporation, 194–204
Preincorporation agreements, 200–201
Preincorporation transactions, 197
Premium bonds, 326
President, corporate, 271
Principals, duties of, 26
Priority rights, of holders of preferred stocks, 311
Pro bono legal work, 164
Professional conduct, for paralegals, A10–A11
Professional corporations, 177, 234
Profit/loss. See also Profits
    in a limited liability company operating agreement, A161
    in a limited partnership agreement, A158–A159
    in limited partnerships, 104
    partnership, 59–60

in partnership agreements, A156
under the Uniform Limited
    Partnership Act (ULPA),
    A65–A66
Profit/loss distribution
under general partnerships,
    50–51
under limited partnerships, 99
Profits. *See also* Profit/loss
partnership, 38
short-swing, 362
Profit-sharing plans, 504
Promoters, 197
Property. *See also* Assets
as dividends, 320
partnership, 36–37
Property rights, of partners,
    A25–A26
Proprietary interests, in sole
    proprietorships, 7
Prospectus, 347–349
Prototype plan, 510
Proxies, 282–283, 364
under the Model Business
    Corporation Act
    (MBCA), A117
Proxy regulations, under Securities
    Exchange Act of 1934,
    364–365
Proxy statement, 283, 283, 364
Prudent person test, 251–252
Publications
on-line resources for, A6
as resources for limited liability
    companies, 158–159
Public interest, serving, A11
Publicly held corporations,
    332–380. *See also* Securities
    Act of 1933
antifraud regulations
    and, 375
resources for, 378–380
role of paralegals in,
    376–378
Securities and Exchange
    Commission (SEC) and,
    339–340
securities and securities markets
    and, 335–339
Securities Exchange Act
    regulations and, 357–373
state securities regulation and,
    373–374
state stock offerings regulation
    and, 374–375
Public offerings, 333
Punitive damages, 257
Put, 318

Q

Qualified pension plans, 498–508
top-heavy, 500
Qualified plan contributions, 499
Qualified plan distributions,
    500–501
Qualified plans, 492–493, 504
adoption and IRS approval
    of, 510
coverage and participation
    requirements for, 497–498
elements of, 495–496
laws governing, 493–494
paralegal's role in, 512–514
reporting and disclosure
    requirements for, 510–512
Qualified plan trust, 499
Quorum, 246, 264–265, 283

R

Racette, Linda M., 153
Receivership, under the Model
    Business Corporation Act
    (MBCA), A148
Record date, 278, 279
Records
corporate, 233
for limited partnerships, 94–96
partner access to, 38
partnership, 59
in partnership agreements, A155
shareholder inspection of, 274
Redemption. *See also* Stock
of debt securities, 326
of equity shares, 317–318
Redemption rights, for holders of
    preferred stock, 310
Red herring prospectus, 348
Registered agent, 207, 450–451
for foreign corporations, A152
under the Model Business
    Corporation Act (MBCA),
    A108–A109
Registered office, 207, 450–451
for foreign corporations, A152
under the Model Business
    Corporation Act
    (MBCA), A108
Registration by coordination,
    374–375
Registration by filing, 374
Registration by qualification, 375
Regulation A (Securities Act of
    1933), 351–352
Regulation D (Securities Act of
    1933), 352
Regulatory requirements
for general partnerships, 42–43

for limited partnerships, 90–91
for sole proprietorships, 3–4
Reimbursement, partner rights
    to, 38
Reinstatement, of limited liability
    companies, A93–A94
Relator, 478
Reorganizations, 385, 427–428.
    See also Corporate structure
    changes
Reporting
paralegal's role in, 378
under the Securities Exchange
    Act of 1934, 359–361
Reporting requirements
corporate, 175–176
for general partnerships,
    42–43
for limited liability
    companies, 146
for limited partnerships, 90–91
for sole proprietorships, 3–4
Representative action, 291–292
*Republic Acceptance Corporation v.
    Bennett,* 442–444
Research, on limited liability
    companies, 153–154
Resources
for corporate dissolution,
    488–489
for corporate financial matters,
    328–329
for corporate organization, 297
for corporation formation,
    239–241
for corporations, 187–191
for employee benefit plans,
    515–516
for employment
    agreements, 540
for foreign corporation
    qualification, 458–459
for limited liability companies,
    154–159
for limited partnerships,
    111–114
for mergers and acquisitions,
    432–434
for publicly held corporations,
    378–380
Restated articles of
    incorporation, 426
Retirement, in partnership
    agreements, A156
Retirement benefits, 502
Reverse triangle mergers, 390
Revised Model Business
    Corporation Act, 169

Revised Uniform Limited Partnership Act (RULPA), 81, 83–84
Revised Uniform Partnership Act (RUPA), 27, 30, 35, 66
partner rights under, 39–40
partnership asset distribution under, 67
partnership dissociation under, 60
partnership dissolution under, 63
partnership property under, 37
Revocation of dissolution, 481–483
Rhode, Angela C., 487–488
Rhode Island Secretary of State, A3
Rights
of foreign corporations, 446
partner, 35–36
Rights of substitution, 100
Right to dissent, 401
Riley-Wallis, Mary Beth, 294
Rodgers, Patricia E., 110
Rule 504 (Securities Act of 1933), 352
Rule 506 (Securities Act of 1933), 353

S

Salaman v. National Media Corp., 257
Sales tax permits, 12
Schedule A, 343–346
Schedule K-1, 43, 104–105
S corporation election, 225, 226
S corporations, 173, 178–181
Scrip, 317
Secretaries of state
directory of, A1–A4
incorporation and, 240
as resources, 17
as resources for foreign corporation qualification, 458
as resources for mergers and acquisitions, 433
Secretary, 271
Secretary of state offices, on-line resources for, A6
Section 11 (Securities Act of 1933), 355–356
Section 12 (Securities Act of 1933), 356
Section 17 (Securities Act of 1933), 356–357

Section 125 cafeteria plans, 509
Section 505 (Uniform Securities Act), 375
Securities, 125–126, 335–336
equity and debt, 303
exempted from registration provisions, 350–351
federal regulation of, 339–340
issuer of, 335
on-line resources for, A6–A7
Securities Act of 1933, 170, 304, 333
antifraud provisions of, 354–357
exemptions from registration requirements of, 350–354
federal regulation under, 340–350
Regulation A of, 351–352
Regulation D of, 352
Section 11 of, 355–356
Section 12 of, 356
Section 17 of, 356–357
Securities acts
federal, 378–379
major provisions of, 369–373
Securities and Exchange Commission (SEC), 339–340
registration statement of, 342
Securities Exchange Act of 1934, 170, 304, 333, 336, 340
antifraud provisions under, 365–373
Enforcement Division of, 367
proxy regulations under, 364–365
publicly held corporation regulations under, 357–373
purposes of, 358
registration under, 358–359
reporting requirements under, 359–361
short-swing profits under, 362–364
Securities Exchange Act Rule 10b-5, 365–367
Securities filings, 224
Securities forms, federal, 379
Securities laws, 125–126
Securities markets, 336–339
over-the-counter, 338–339
Securities registration, 341–347
Securities regulation, state, 373–374
SEC v. W. J. Howey Co., 335
Self-employed plans, 507
Separate accounts, 37–38
Series of preferred stocks, 311

Share dividends, A111
Share exchanges, 386, 391. *See also* Shares; Stock
closing, 414
effects of, 387
laws affecting, 393–394
under the Model Business Corporation Act (MBCA), A134–A137
postclosing matters concerning, 414
preclosing matters concerning, 409–412
procedures for, 396–414
Shareholder agreements
drafting, 290
under the Model Business Corporation Act (MBCA), A120–A121
for restriction of stock transfers, 288–290
Shareholder liability
for corporations, 212
under the Model Business Corporation Act (MBCA), A111
Shareholder meetings, 228–229, 276–286
minutes of, 285–286, 287–288
notification of, 278–281
voting at, 283–284
Shareholder resolutions, 225–226
Shareholders. *See also* Stockholders
approval of, 285, 286
approval of articles of amendment by, 423–424
approval of dissolution by, 463–467
approval of plan of exchange by, 408
approval of plan of merger by, 400–401
consent of, 286
dissenting, 401–402, 408–409
dissolution by, A144
distributions to, 477
inspection of corporate records by, 274
judicial proceedings by, 485–486
under the Model Business Corporation Act (MBCA), A114–A122
personal liability of, 276
preemptive rights of, 273–274
rights and responsibilities of, 272–276
right to dissent of, 424

Shareholders' rights, under the
    Model Business Corporation
    Act (MBCA), A112–A113
Shares. *See also* Share exchanges
    judicial appraisal of, A142–A143
    under the Model Business
        Corporation Act (MBCA),
        A109–A114
    statement of fair market value
        of, 403
Share transfers
    bylaws concerning, A165
    under the Model Business
        Corporation Act
        (MBCA), A112
"Shark repellants," 416
Sherman Act, 394, 433
    sections 1 and 2 of, 395
Short-swing profits, liability
    for, 362
Simple debentures, 326
Simplified employee pension plans
    (SEPs), 508–509
Sister corporations, 183
Small Business Administration
    (SBA), 14–15
Small businesses, on-line resources
    for, A7
Sole proprietors, 1, 4
Sole proprietorships, 1–18
    advantages of, 3–5
    checklist for starting, 13
    in the digital economy, 4–5
    disadvantages of, 5–7
    ethical considerations for, 16–17
    forming and operating, 7–12
    paralegal's role in, 12–14
    resources for, 14–18
    in the United States, 2
South Carolina Secretary of
    State, A3
South Dakota Secretary of
    State, A3
Special interrogatories, 166
Special meetings, requirements
    for, 278
Sponsor, 495
State authorities, 70
    judicial proceedings by, 485
    as limited liability company
        resources, 157
    as limited partnership
        resources, 112
    as resources for corporate
        dissolution, 488
State corporation authorities,
    190–191
Stated capital, 313

"Stated capital account," 311
State dissolution statutes, 468–469
State ex rel. Conway v. Dowd, 479
*State ex rel. Pillsbury v. Honeywell,
    Inc.,* 274–276
State government resources, 15
State laws. *See also* State statutes
    affecting asset and stock
        acquisitions, 417
    affecting statutory mergers and
        share exchanges, 393–394
    lack of uniformity in, 145
State long-arm statutes, 439–440
Statement of authority, 33–34
Statement of denial, 34
Statement of dissociation, 62, A43
Statement of dissolution, A44
Statement of Fair Market Value of
    Shares, 403
Statement of Intent to Dissolve,
    sample, 473–474
Statement of partnership merger,
    A47–A48
Statement of qualification, 57
State of domicile, 195
State securities regulation,
    373–374
    antifraud provisions of, 375
State statutes, 15–16
    concerning corporate
        dissolution, 488
    concerning mergers and
        acquisitions, 432–434
    corporate, 165–169, 187–189
    corporate financial matters
        and, 329
    for foreign corporation
        qualification, 458
    for incorporation, 239
    for limited liability companies,
        154–157
    for limited partnerships,
        111–112
    on-line resources for, A7
    as partnership resources, 70–72
Statute of frauds, 48
Statutes, door-closing, 441–442.
    See also Federal statutes; State
    statutes
Statutory close corporations,
    182–183, 233–234
Statutory mergers, 385–391
    closing, 413
    laws affecting, 393–394
    procedures for, 396–414
Statutory requirements, for foreign
    corporation qualification,
    440–441

Stock, 207. *See also* Shareholders;
    Stock acquisitions
    agreements granting options to
        purchase, 289
    agreements mandating purchase
        of, 289–290
    authorized and issued, 305–308
    common, 308–309
    consideration for shares of,
        313–315
    issuance of, 315–317
    market value of, 290
    par value, 311–313
    preferred, 304, 309–311
    restrictions on transfer of,
        286–291
    value and classes of, 212
    watered, 312
Stock acquisitions, 414–415
    closing, 421–422
    due diligence and preclosing
        matters for, 420
    laws affecting, 417
    postclosing matters for, 422
    procedures for, 417–422
Stock bonus plans, 505–506
Stock certificate form, 224
Stock certificates, 232, 295–296,
    315–317
Stock dividends, 317, 320, 323
Stock exchanges, 336–338
Stockholders. *See also* Shareholders
    adoption of merger agreement
        by, 401
    approval of asset sales by, 419
    bylaws concerning, A162–A163
    demand for fair market value of
        shares by, 403
Stockholders' Resolution to
    Dissolve Corporation,
    466–467
Stock offerings regulation, state,
    374–375
Stock ownership plans, employee,
    506–507
Stock purchase agreement, 420
Stock splits, 323–324
Stock Subscription Agreement
    form, 202
Stock subscription agreements,
    201–202, 315
Stock subscriptions, 201–202
    acceptance of, 222–223
Stock transfer, restriction of,
    288–290
Stock transfer documents, paralegal
    preparation of, 431
Stop order, 347

Straight voting, 285
Subchapter A shares, A109–A110
Subchapter B shares, A110–A112
Subchapter C shares, A112–A113
Subchapter D distributions,
    A113–A114
Subsidiary corporations, 183
    merger of, A135
Summary annual reports, 512
Summary prospectus, 348

T

Take-outs, 388
Target benefit plans, 505
Taxation. *See also* Income taxation
    corporate, 176
    corporate dissolution and, 481
    in general partnerships, 46
    of limited liability companies,
        122–123, 142–144
    in a limited liability company
        operating agreement, A162
Tax identification numbers, 9–11
Tax information, on-line resources
    for, A7
Tax offices, as resources for
    corporate dissolution, 489
Tax returns, corporate, 171
Tax year, choice of, 173
Telephonic meetings, 269
Tenancy in partnership, 35
Tender offers, 416
10-K reports, 359–360
    components of, 360
Tennessee Secretary of State, A3
10-Q quarterly reports, 361
10-Q reports, 361
Texas Secretary of State, A3
*Thomas v. Colvin, and R. A. Coker,
    d/b/a Sherwood Motors,* 8–9
Tombstone ads, 349
Top-heavy pension plans, 500
Tortious, defined, 254
Trademarks, 12
Trade names
    certificates of, 3
    in sole proprietorships, 8–9
    state statutes concerning, 15–16
Trade secrets, 528–531
    in partnership agreements, A157
Transfer agent, 279
Treasurer, 271
Treasury shares, 318
Triangle mergers, 389
Type A transactions
    (reorganizations), 427
Type B transactions
    (reorganizations), 427

Type C transactions
    (reorganizations), 427
Type D transactions
    (reorganizations), 427
Type E transactions
    (reorganizations), 427
Type F transactions
    (reorganizations), 427
Type G transactions
    (reorganizations), 428

U

Unanimous writings, 226–227,
    267–269
Unauthorized practice of law,
    185–187, A12
Underwriter, 335
Unfair methods of competition,
    394
Uniform acts, on-line resources
    for, A7
Uniform Limited Liability
    Company Act, 125,
    A73–A100
    conversions and mergers under,
        A94–A97
    derivative actions under,
        A99–A100
    foreign limited liability
        companies under, A97–A99
    general provisions of, A73–A77
    member dissociation under,
        A86–A90
    member transferees and creditors
        under, A85–A86
    miscellaneous provisions under,
        A100
    organization of, A77–A80
Uniform Limited Partnership Act
    (ULPA), 81, A52–A72
    assignment of partnership
        interests under, A67–A69
    derivative actions under, A71
    dissolution under, A69
    distributions and withdrawal
        under, A66–A67
    finance under, A65–A66
    foreign limited partnerships
        under, A69–A71
    general partners under,
        A63–A65
    general provisions of, A53–A56
    limited partners under,
        A60–A63
    miscellaneous provisions of, A72
Uniform Partnership Act (1997),
    A31–A51
    general provisions of, A31–A33

miscellaneous provisions of,
    A50–A51
nature of partnership under,
    A33–A34
partner relationships under,
    A34–A39
Uniform Partnership Act (UPA),
    27, 30, 35, 66, A19–A30. *See
    also* Uniform Partnership Act
    (1997)
    contents of, A20–A21
    partner rights under, 39–40
    partnership asset distribution
        under, 67
    partnership dissolution
        under, 63
    partnership property
        under, 37
Uniform Securities Act, 374
    Section 505 of, 375
Unit benefit formula, 502
United States
    corporations in, 170
    limited liability companies
        in, 124
    limited partnerships in, 79–80
    mergers in, 386
    partnership law in, 28
    partnerships in, 24
    S corporations in, 179
    sole proprietorships in, 2
United States Small Business
    Administration (SBA), 14–15
Unlimited liability, in general
    partnerships, 44
Upstream mergers, 388
U.S. Patent and Trademark
    Office, 17
Utah Corporations and
    Commercial Code
    Division, A3

V

Vacations, employee, 532
Variable benefit formula, 502
Vaughn Machine Co. v. Lighthouse,
    443
Vermont Secretary of State
    Corporations, A3
Vesting, 493, 500
Vice president, 271
Virginia State Corporation
    Commission, A4
Voluntary corporate dissolution,
    463–483
Voluntary dissolution, under the
    Model Business Corporation
    Act (MBCA), A143–A146

Voluntary Employee Benefit
    Association (VEBA), 510
Voting
    under the Model Business
        Corporation Act (MBCA),
        A116–A119
    at shareholder meetings,
        283–284
    straight versus cumulative, 285
    under the Uniform Limited
        Partnership Act (ULPA), A61
Voting agreements, 284
    under the Model Business
        Corporation Act
        (MBCA), A120
Voting groups, 400
    under the Model Business
        Corporation Act
        (MBCA), A118
Voting rights
    for holders of common stock,
        308–309
    for holders of preferred
        stock, 310

Voting trusts, 284
    under the Model Business
        Corporation Act (MBCA),
        A119–A121

W

Waiver of notice, 280–281
Washington Secretary of State, A4
Watered stock, 312
*Weatherby v. Weatherby Lumber
    Company,* 250–251
Welch v. Fuhrman, 215–216
Welfare benefit plans, employee,
    509–510
westlegalstudies.com, 18
West Virginia Secretary of
    State, A4
White-collar criminals, 248–249
Wind up. *See also* Dissociation;
        Dissolution
    corporate, 472–481
    events causing, 62–64
    of limited liability
        companies, 140

of limited partnerships, 102,
    106–108
of partnership, A43–A45
of partnership business, 38–40,
    56, 60–66
under the Uniform Limited
    Liability Company Act,
    A90–A94
under the Uniform Partnership
    Act, A26–A30
Wisconsin Secretary of State, A4
Withdrawal rights, A141
Workplace scenario data,
    A17–A18
Writ of mandamus, 274
Writ of prohibition, 478
Written consent, 267–269. *See also*
        Unanimous writings
Wrongful dissociation, A41
    under the Uniform Limited
        Liability Company Act,
        A87–A88
Wyoming Secretary of State, A4